■ For Students

MyAccountingLab provides students with a personalized interactive learning environment, where they can learn at their own pace and measure their progress.

Interactive Tutorial Exercises

MyAccountingLab's homework and practice questions are correlated to the textbook, and "similar to" versions regenerate algorithmically to give students unlimited opportunity for practice and mastery. Questions offer helpful feedback when students enter incorrect answers, and they include "Help Me Solve This" guided solutions as well as other learning aids for extra help when students need it.

▼

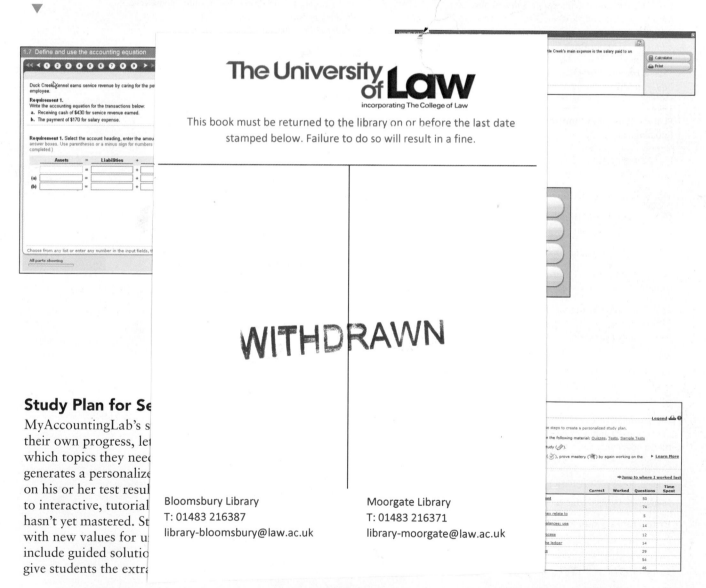

Study Plan for Se

MyAccountingLab's s
their own progress, le
which topics they nee
generates a personalize
on his or her test resul
to interactive, tutorial
hasn't yet mastered. St
with new values for u
include guided solutio
give students the extr

View a guided tour of MyAccountingLab at http://www.myaccountinglab.com/support/tours.

To Joan, Scott, Mary, Susie, Cathy, Liz, Garth,
Jens, Laura, Dawn, Jesse, and Duncan

VP/Editorial Director: Sally Yagan
AVP/Editor in Chief: Donna Battista
Acquisitions Editor: Julie Broich
Senior International Acquisitions Editor: Laura Dent
Director of Editorial Services: Ashley Santora
Senior Editorial Project Manager: Karen Kirincich
Editorial Assistant: Brian Reilly
International Editorial Assistant: Emily Jones
Exec. Director of Digital Development: Lisa Strite
Editorial Media Project Manager: Allison Longley

VP/Director of Marketing: Patrice Lumumba Jones
International Marketing Manager: Dean Erasmus
Marketing Assistant: Ian Gold
Sr. Managing Editor, Production: Cynthia Zonneveld
Production Manager: Carol O'Rourke
Sr. Operations Specialist: Diane Peirano
Sr. Art Director: Jon Boylan
Interior Design: Lisa Delgado
Cover Design: Jodi Notowitz
Art Studio: GEX Publishing Services

Pearson Education Limited
Edinburgh Gate
Harlow
Essex CM20 2JE
England

and Associated Companies throughout the world

Visit us on the World Wide Web at:
www.pearson.com/uk

© Pearson Education Limited 2012

The right of Charles T. Horngren, Gary L. Sundem, John A. Elliott, and Donna Philbrick to be identified as
authors of this work has been asserted by them in accordance with the Copyright, Designs and Patents Act 1988.

*Authorised adaptation from the United States edition, entitled Introduction to Financial Accounting, 10th Edition,
ISBN 978-0-13-612297-5 by Charles T. Horngren, Gary L. Sundem, John A. Elliott, and Donna Philbrick,
published by Pearson Education, publishing as Prentice Hall © 2012.*

ISBN: 978-0-273-77017-6

British Library Cataloguing-in-Publication Data
A catalogue record for this book is available from the British Library

10 9 8 7 6 5 4 3 2
15 14 13 12

Typeset in 10/12 Times Roman by GEX Publishing Services

Printed and bound by Courier Kendallville in the United States of America

The publisher's policy is to use paper manufactured from sustainable forests.

Introduction to FINANCIAL ACCOUNTING

Global Edition

Tenth Edition

Charles T. Horngren

Stanford University

Gary L. Sundem

University of Washington

John A. Elliott

City University of New York—Baruch College

Donna R. Philbrick

Portland State University

London
School of Business
& Finance

LIBRARY

PEARSON

Boston   Columbus   Indianapolis   New York   San Francisco   Upper Saddle River
Amsterdam   Cape Town   Dubai   London   Madrid   Milan   Munich   Paris   Montréal   Toronto
Delhi   Mexico City   São Paulo   Sydney   Hong Kong   Seoul   Singapore   Taipei   Tokyo

About the Authors

Charles T. Horngren is the Edmund W. Littlefield professor of accounting emeritus at Stanford University. A graduate of Marquette University, he received his MBA from Harvard University and his PhD from the University of Chicago. He is also the recipient of honorary doctorates from Marquette University and DePaul University.

A certified public accountant, Horngren served on the Accounting Principles Board for 6 years, the Financial Accounting Standards Board Advisory Council for 5 years, and the Council of the American Institute of Certified Public Accountants for 3 years. For 6 years, he served as a trustee of the Financial Accounting Foundation, which oversees the Financial Accounting Standards Board and the Government Accounting Standards Board.

Horngren is a member of the Accounting Hall of Fame.

A member of the American Accounting Association, Horngren has been its president and its director of research. He received the association's first annual Outstanding Accounting Educator Award. He also received its Lifetime Contribution to Management Accounting Award.

The California Certified Public Accountants Foundation gave Horngren its Faculty Excellence Award and its Distinguished Professor Award. He is the first person to have received both awards.

The American Institute of Certified Public Accountants presented its first Outstanding Educator Award to Horngren.

Horngren was named Accountant of the Year, Education, by the national professional accounting fraternity, Beta Alpha Psi.

Professor Horngren is also a member of the Institute of Management Accountants, where he has received its Distinguished Service Award. He was a member of the Institute's Board of Regents, which administers the Certified Management Accountant examinations.

Horngren is the author of other accounting books published by Prentice Hall: *Cost Accounting: A Managerial Emphasis, Introduction to Management Accounting, Accounting*, and *Financial Accounting*.

Horngren is the Consulting Editor for the Charles T. Horngren Series in Accounting.

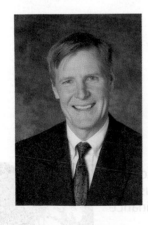

Gary L. Sundem is professor of accounting emeritus at the University of Washington, Seattle. He received his BA from Carleton College and his MBA and PhD from Stanford University.

Professor Sundem was the 1992–1993 president of the American Accounting Association. He was executive director of the Accounting Education Change Commission, 1989–1991, and served as editor of the *Accounting Review*, 1982–1986. He is currently vice president of education for the International Association for Accounting Education and Research.

Sundem is past president of the Seattle chapter of the Institute of Management Accountants. He has served on IMA's national board of directors and chaired its Academic Relations and Professional Development committees. He chaired the AACSB's Accounting Accreditation Committee, 1997–1999, and currently serves on the Board of Trustees of Rainier Mutual Funds and the Board of Trustees of Carleton College. He received the Carleton College Outstanding Alumni award in 2002.

Professor Sundem has numerous publications in accounting and finance journals including *Issues in Accounting Education*, the *Accounting Review*, *Journal of Accounting Research*, and *Journal of Finance*. He was selected as the Outstanding Accounting Educator by the American Accounting Association in 1998 and by the Washington Society of CPAs in 1987.

John A. Elliott is the dean of the Zickin School of Business at Baruch College and vice president of Baruch College, which is part of the City University of New York (CUNY). He is the Irwin and Arlene Ettinger professor of accountancy. He received his BS and MBA from the University of Maryland and his PhD from Cornell University. Prior to accepting the deanship at the Zicklin School, he spent 20 years on the faculty at Cornell University's Johnson Graduate School of Management, most recently as associate dean for academic affairs.

Dean Elliott is a certified public accountant with professional experience as an auditor and consultant for Arthur Andersen & Co. and in the controller's office of the Westinghouse Defense and Space Center. During his career he has taught at six different institutions. His responsibilities have included financial accounting, intermediate accounting, financial statement analysis, taxation, and extensive executive teaching. He is currently teaching introductory financial accounting in the Zicklin Masters of Science Program in Financial Statement Analysis.

In 2004 his paper on earnings management (with Nelson and Tarpley) received the award from the American Accounting Association for Notable Contributions to Accounting Literature. His research is concentrated on the role of accounting information in financial analysis and contracts.

He serves on two corporate boards, NFP and Liquidnet, and chairs their audit committees. He has previously served and chaired the boards for the Hangar Theatre, Cayuga Medical Center, and the Graduate Management Admissions Council.

Donna R. Philbrick is Professor of Accounting at Portland State University. She received her BS from the University of Oregon and her MBA and PhD from Cornell University.

Professor Philbrick is a certified public accountant (inactive) and worked in public accounting prior to returning for her graduate degrees. Before joining the faculty at Portland State, she taught at the University of Oregon and Duke University.

She currently teaches financial reporting and financial statement analysis. Professor Philbrick also teaches in the Oregon Executive MBA program and has experience teaching in numerous corporate programs.

Professor Philbrick's research has been published in accounting journals including the *Accounting Review*, *Journal of Accounting Research*, and *Journal of Accounting and Economics*. She served on the Advisory Board of *Accounting Horizons* from 1994 to 2000 and as associate editor of that journal from 2000 to 2003.

Brief Contents

Contents

Preface

"You have to know what something is before you know how to use it."

Introduction to Financial Accounting, 10/E, describes the most widely accepted accounting theory and practice with an emphasis on using and analyzing the information in financial statements. It compares U.S. generally accepted accounting principles to international financial reporting standards where appropriate.

IFA, 10/E, takes the view that business is an exciting process and that accounting is the perfect window through which to see how economic events affect businesses. Because we believe that accounting aids the understanding of economic events and that accounting builds on simple principles, this book introduces a number of concepts earlier than many other textbooks. We cover these early concepts at the most accessible level and illustrate them with carefully chosen examples from real companies. Our coverage addresses the choices that management makes when preparing financial statements and how these choices affect the way users interpret the information. We also discuss ethical issues throughout the book and in the assignment materials.

This is the tenth edition of this text, and that is a testimonial to its effectiveness. But it also is a testimonial to our former colleagues, students, and adopters who, in each prior edition, have shared their thoughts and suggestions and driven us to change and adapt it to better meet the needs of today's students and adopting faculty.

New to this edition:

- Totally updated text to include current examples from real companies.
- Updated problem material to include more recent examples from real companies.
- Increased number of both examples and problems that involve non-U.S. companies.
- Extensive revisions for clarity, including deletion of some less significant material.
- Updated and expanded use of real-company examples.
- Coverage of U.S. GAAP and IFRS requirements where they differ.
- Expanded use of international-company examples, especially to illustrate differences in U.S. GAAP and IFRS.
- Continued expansion and integration of ethics coverage.

Our Philosophy

Introduce the simple concepts early, revisit concepts at more complex levels as students gain understanding, and provide appropriate real-company examples at every stage—that's our philosophy. Our goal is for students to be able to read and interpret a real company's financial statements: balance sheet, income statement, statement of cash flows, and statement of changes in stockholders' equity.

We want students to view accounting as a tool that enhances their understanding of economic events. Students should be asking questions such as "After this transaction, are we better or worse off?" and "What do these statements tell us about the company's financial position and performance?"

Students cannot understand financial statements in isolation. Rather, they must look at all the financial statements within the context of the company's business environment. They need to understand the accrual basis of accounting that underlies the balance sheet and income statement, but they must also understand the importance of cash as presented in the statement of cash flows. We present the balance sheet, income statement, statement of changes in stockholders' equity, and statement of cash flows in the first five chapters. By presenting the statement of cash flows in Chapter 5, immediately after the presentation of the basics of accrual accounting, students learn the importance of all the statements and the unique information each statement presents before encountering details about financial reporting practices in the later chapters.

One of our former colleagues, Hal Bierman, often focuses on an economic event by asking, "Are you happy or are you sad?" We believe that accounting provides a way to understand what is happening and to answer that question. You might think of the basic financial statements as scorecards in the most fundamental economic contests. Each year the financial statements help you answer the most important questions: Are you happy or sad? Did you make or lose money? Are you prospering or just surviving? Will you have the cash you need for the next big step?

Who Should Use This Book?

Introduction to Financial Accounting, 10/E, presupposes no prior knowledge of accounting and is suitable for any undergraduate or MBA student enrolled in a financial accounting course. It is also appropriate for management education programs where the participants have little or no accounting background. It deals with important topics that all managers should know and all business students should study. We have aimed to present relevant subject matter and to present it clearly and accessibly.

This text is oriented to the user of financial statements but gives ample attention to the needs of potential accounting practitioners. *IFA*, 10/E, stresses underlying concepts yet makes them concrete with numerous illustrations, many taken from recent corporate annual reports. Moreover, accounting procedures such as transaction analysis, journalizing, and posting are given due consideration where appropriate. Managers and accountants can develop a better understanding of the economic consequences of a company's transactions by summarizing those transactions into journal entries and T-accounts. However, the ultimate objective is an understanding of financial position and prospects, which we achieve by a focus on the balance sheet equation.

Enhanced Coverage of IFRS

- Coverage of differences between U.S. generally accepted accounting principles (GAAP) and International Financial Reporting Standards (IFRS) without unnecessary details about the differences.
- Problem materials from companies reporting under IFRS as well as U.S. GAAP.

Emphasis on Understanding and Analyzing Financial Statements

- **Financial Statement Portfolio** provides a visual roadmap to financial statement analysis by highlighting key financial ratios and how to derive them from the financial statements. The Financial Statement Portfolio also refers students to appropriate chapters in the book for in-depth coverage of these ratios. The Portfolio can be found before the "Highlights to Remember" section of chapter 2, a green vertical bar provides easy access to give students reference to the Portfolio all semester long.
- **Interpreting Financial Statements** sections in each chapter permit students to pause and ponder how to use the information they are learning to better understand the financial position and prospects of a company.
- **Analyzing and Interpreting Financial Statements problems at the end of each chapter** include financial statement research, analyses of Starbucks financial statements, and analysis of other companies' financial statements using the Internet.
- **Focus on Starbucks' Annual Report** is used to illustrate various methods for analyzing financial statements. There is a problem based on Starbucks in each chapter, allowing students to get a more complete picture of many financial reporting issues relating to one particular company.

Other Enhanced Features

- Extensive treatment of ethics, with both text coverage and end-of-chapter problems focusing on this important topic in nearly every chapter.
- Critical Thinking Exercises in the assignment material of each chapter that ask students to consider conceptual issues that may have no right answer.

- Business First Boxes in each chapter, many new or completely revised. These boxes provide insights into operations at well-known domestic and international companies, accenting today's real-world issues.

Teaching and Learning Support: Because Resources Should Simplify, Not Overwhelm: A successful accounting course requires more than a well-written book. Today's classroom requires a dedicated teacher and a fully integrated teaching package. The following material supports this title.

Student Resources

MyAccountingLab®

www.myaccountinglab.com

MyAccountingLab is Web-based tutorial and assessment software for accounting that gives students more "I get it!" moments. MyAccountingLab provides students with a personalized interactive learning environment where they can complete their course assignments with immediate tutorial assistance, learn at their own pace, and measure their progress.

In addition to completing assignments and reviewing tutorial help, students have access to the following resources in MyAccountingLab:

- **Flash-based eText**
- **Study Guide**
- **Excel Templates**
- **PowerPoints**

Student Resource Website: www.pearsonglobaleditions.com/horngren

- **Excel Templates**

Instructor Resources

MyAccountingLab®

www.myaccountinglab.com

MyAccountingLab provides instructors the flexibility to make technology an integral part of their course. And, because practice makes perfect, MyAccountingLab offers exactly the same end-of-chapter material found in the text with algorithmic options that instructors can assign for homework. MyAccountingLab also replicates the text's exercises and problems with journal entries and financial statements so that students are familiar and comfortable working with the material.

Solutions Manual

The Solutions Manual, written by the text authors, is available electronically. It contains the fully worked-through and accuracy-checked solutions for every question, exercise, and problem in the text. Special thanks to Carolyn Streuly for reviewing this material.

Instructor Resources www.pearsonglobaleditions.com/horngren

For your convenience, many of our instructor supplements are available for download from the textbook's catalog page or your MyAccountingLab account. Available resources include the following:

- **Test Item File:** The Test Item File includes multiple choice, true/false, exercises, comprehensive problems, short answer problems, critical thinking essay questions, etc. Each test item is tied to the corresponding learning objective and has an assigned difficulty level.
- **TestGen:** This PC/MAC-compatible test generating software is powerful and easy to use. It is preloaded with all of the questions from the new Test Item File and allows users to manually or randomly view test bank questions and drag and drop them to create a test. Add or modify questions using the built-in Question Editor, print up to 25 variations of a single test, and create and export tests that are compatible with commonly used course management systems.

- **Instructor's Resource Manual:** This manual contains the following elements for each chapter of the text: chapter overviews, chapter outlines organized by objectives, teaching tips, chapter quiz.
- **PowerPoint Slides:** Designed to aid in presentation of key chapter concepts
- **Excel Templates and Solutions, Image Library**
- **Solutions Manual**

Technical support is available at http://247pearsoned.custhelp.com.

Acknowledgements

Our appreciation extends to our present and former mentors, colleagues, and students. This book and our enthusiasm for accounting grew out of their collective contributions to our knowledge and experience.

A special thanks to Norbert Tschakert, University of the Virgin Islands for his suggestions on IFRS for this edition. Thank you to the following people who provided valuable contributions on the supplements: LuAnn Bean, Florida Institute of Technology; Victoria Kaskey, Ashland University; Vic Stanton, University of California, Berkeley and Stanford University; William Wells, University of Washington.

We would also like to thank those who gave valuable feedback on previous editions: John E. Armstrong, Dominican College; Frances L. Ayers, University of Oklahoma; Roderick S. Barclay, University of Texas at Dallas; Ronald S. Barden, Georgia State University; Mary Barth, Stanford University; Paul E. Bayes, East Tennessee State University; Martin J. Birr, Indiana University; Marianne Bradford, The University of Tennesse; Nancy Cassidy, Texas A&M University; David T. Collins, Bellarmine College; Michele J. Daley, Rice University; Ray D. Dillon, Georgia State University; Patricia A. Doherty, Boston University; Philip D. Drake, Thunderbird, The American Graduate School of International Management; Allan R. Drebin, Northwestern University; Robert Dunn, Georgia Institute of Technology; Alan H. Falcon, Loyola Marymount University; Anita Feller, University of Illinois; Richard Frankel, University of Michigan; John D. Gould, Western Carolina University; D. Jacque Grinnell, University of Vermont; Leon J. Hanouille, Syracuse University; Al Hartgraves, Emory University; Suzanne Hartley, Franklin University; Peter Huey, Collin County Community College; Yuji Ijiri, Carnegie Mellon University; M. Zafar Iqbal, California Polytechnic State University–San Luis Obispo; Gregory D. Kane, University of Delaware; Sungsoo Kim, Rutgers University; April Klein, New York University; Joan Luft, Michigan State University; Maureen McNichols, Stanford University; Mark J. Myring, Ball State University; Brian M. Nagle, Duquesne University; John L. Norman Jr., Keller Graduate School of Management; Mohamed Onsi, Syracuse University; Elizabeth Plummer, Southern Methodist University; Renee A. Price, University of Nebraska; Patrick M. Premo, St. Bonaventure University; Leo A. Ruggle, Mankato State University; James A. Schweikart, Rhode Island College; Chandra Seethamraju, Washington University– St. Louis; Bill Shoemaker, University of Dallas; William Smith, Xavier University; Robert Swieringa, Cornell University; Katherene P. Terrell, University of Central Oklahoma; Michael G. Vasilou, DeVry Institute of Technology–Chicago; Deborah Welch, Tyler Junior College; Christine Wiedman, University of Western Ontario; Patrick T. Wirtz, University of Detroit Mercy; and Peter D. Woodlock, Youngstown State University.

Finally, we'd like to thank the following people at Prentice Hall: Julie Broich, Donna Battista, Sally Yagan, Ashley Santora, Karen Kirincich, Allison Longley, Carol O'Rourke, and Cynthia Zonneveld, and Kelly Morrison, GEX Publishing Services.

Charles T. Horngren
Gary L. Sundem
John A. Elliott
Donna R. Philbrick

Pearson gratefully acknowledges and thanks the following people for their work on the Global Edition:

International Contributors

Simon Lee, School of Hotel and Tourism Management, The Chinese University of Hong Kong, Hong Kong

Adele Maree, Department of Financial Management, University of Pretoria, South Africa

Professor Jeff Ng, School of Accountancy, The Chinese University of Hong Kong, Hong Kong

Gretha Steenkamp, Department of Accounting, Stellenbosch University, South Africa

Paul N. C. Tiong, Department of Accounting, Multimedia University, Malaysia

International Reviewers

Ng Huey Chyi, Taylor's Business School, Taylor's University, Malaysia

Petri Ferreira, Department of Accounting, University of Pretoria, South Africa

Dr. Allen Huang, Department of Accounting, Hong Kong University of Science and Technology, Hong Kong

Dr. Gagan Kukreja, College of Business & Finance, Ahlia University, Kingdom of Bahrain

Ms Debbie Ng, School of Business, Temasek Polytechnic, Singapore

Dr. Philip O'Regan, Department of Accounting and Finance, University of Limerick, Ireland

Charles T. Horngren Series in Accounting
Charles T. Horngren, Consulting Editor

Auditing and Assurance Services: An Integrated Approach, 13/E
Arens/Elder/Beasley

Governmental and Nonprofit Accounting: Theory & Practice, 9/E
Freeman/Shoulders/Allison/ Patton/Smith

Financial Accounting, 8/E
Harrison/Horngren/Thomas

Cost Accounting: A Managerial Emphasis, 13/E
Horngren/Foster/Datar/Rajan/Ittner

Accounting, 9/E
Horngren/Harrison/Oliver

Introduction to Financial Accounting, 10/E
Horngren/Sundem/Elliott/Philbrick

Introduction to Management Accounting, 15/E
Horngren/Sundem/Stratton/Burgstahler/Schatzberg

1

Accounting: The Language of Business

Accounting is the language of business. It is the method companies use to communicate financial information to their employees and to the public. Until recently, the accounting language, like spoken languages, differed country to country. Today only two main accounting languages have survived, one used in the United States and another used in Europe and most of the rest of the world. These are actually more like dialects of a single language because they are identical in most respects and are gradually converging into a single language. In this text we focus on the U.S. perspective but discuss the significant differences between the languages when they arise.

We also use numerous real companies to illustrate the language of accounting in practice. Consider Starbucks Corporation, a U.S.-based company that uses the accounting language employed by all U.S. companies. You have probably bought a latte in, or at least walked by, one of Starbucks' 9,000 coffee stores throughout the world. Did you know that you could also buy a share of Starbucks stock, making you a part owner of Starbucks? To buy a latte, you want to know how it tastes. To buy a share of stock, you want to know about the financial condition and prospects of Starbucks Corporation. You would want to own part of Starbucks only if you think it will be successful into the future. To learn this, you need to understand accounting. By the time you finish reading this book, you will be comfortable reading the financial reports of Starbucks and other companies and be able to use those reports to assess the financial health of these companies.

Starbucks was founded in 1985 and first issued shares of stock to the public in 1992. If you had bought shares at that time, as of the writing of

Starbucks has a prime location on this busy street in Seoul, Korea. Whether in Beijing, Tokyo, or Singapore, Starbucks is turning tea drinkers into coffee lovers. Starbucks reports its economic performance in its financial statements. As you read this text, you will learn how to read and analyze the financial statements of Starbucks and other companies, large and small, throughout the world.

this textbook your investment would be worth more than $20 for every $1 you invested. (Before the bear market of 2008–2009 it was worth almost $40.) Will Starbucks be a good investment in the future? No one can predict with certainty Starbucks' financial prospects. However, the company's financial statements, which are available on Starbucks' Web site, can give you clues. But you need to understand accounting to make sense of this financial information.

Starbucks has established a worldwide reputation in a short time. It was #6 on *Fortune* magazine's list of Most Admired Companies in 2008 and #24 among *Fortune*'s 100 Best Companies to Work For in 2009. It was named one of the Top 5 Global Brands of the Year by Brandchannel.com's Readers Choice survey in 2006 and ranked among CRO's 100 Best Corporate Citizens in 2008 for the 9th year in a row, one of only three companies to make the list all 9 years. Despite all these awards, potential investors want to know something about Starbucks' financial prospects. Let's look at a few financial facts. As you proceed through this book you will develop a better understanding of how to interpret these facts.

In 2009, Starbucks' total revenues—the amount the company received for all the items sold—were $9.8 billion, compared with only $700 million in 1996. Net income—the profit that Starbucks made—was $391 million, up from $42 million in 1996 but down from a high of $673 million in 2007. Total assets—the value of the items owned by Starbucks—grew from less than $900 million to almost $5.6 billion from 1996 to 2009. You can see that the amount of business done by Starbucks has grown quickly. However, there is much more to be learned from the details in Starbucks' financial statements. You will learn about revenues, income, assets, and other elements of accounting as you read this book. ●

As we embark on our journey into the world of financial accounting, we explore what it takes for a company such as Starbucks to manage its financial activities and how investors use this accounting information to better understand Starbucks. Keep this in mind: The same basic accounting framework that supported a small coffee company like Starbucks in 1985 supports the larger company today, and indeed it supports businesses (big and small, old and new) worldwide.

This book is an introduction to financial accounting. **Accounting** is a process of identifying, recording, and summarizing economic information and reporting it to decision makers. **Financial accounting** focuses on the specific needs of decision makers external to the organization, such as stockholders, suppliers, banks, and government agencies. You are correct if you expect to learn a set of rules and procedures about how to record and report financial information. You will see rules and procedures. However, understanding accounting reports goes beyond rules and procedures. To use your financial accounting education effectively, you must also understand the underlying business transactions that give rise to the economic information and why the information is helpful in making financial decisions.

We hope that you want to know how businesses work. When you understand that Starbucks' financial reports help its management make decisions about producing and selling products, as well as helping investors to assess the performance and prospects of Starbucks, you will see why being able to read and interpret these reports is important. Both outside investors and internal managers need this information.

Our goal is to help you understand business transactions—to know how accounting information describes such transactions and how decision makers both inside the company (managers) and outside the company (investors) use that information in deciding how, when, and what to buy or sell. In the process, you will learn about some of the world's premier companies. You may wonder about what it costs to open a new Starbucks store. Are new stores worth such a major investment? How many people visit each Starbucks store every year? Can Starbucks keep track of them all, and are there enough customers to make the stores profitable? If investors consider purchasing Starbucks stock, what do they need to know to decide whether the current price is a reasonable one? Accounting information cannot completely answer every such question, but it provides important insights into many of them. To illustrate how to use accounting information, we will often explore real issues in real companies.

accounting

The process of identifying, recording, and summarizing economic information and reporting it to decision makers.

financial accounting

The field of accounting that serves external decision makers, such as stockholders, suppliers, banks, and government agencies.

Company	Symbol	Year Added	Company	Symbol	Year Added
General Electric	GE	1907	Walt Disney	DIS	1991
ExxonMobil	XOM	1928	Hewlett-Packard	HPQ	1997
Procter & Gamble	PG	1932	Johnson & Johnson	JNJ	1997
DuPont	DD	1935	Wal-Mart	WMT	1997
United Technologies Corporation	UTX	1939	AT&T	T	1999
Alcoa	AA	1959	Home Depot	HD	1999
3M	MMM	1976	Intel	INTC	1999
IBM	IBM	1979	Microsoft	MSFT	1999
Merck	MRK	1979	Pfizer	PFE	2004
American Express	AXP	1982	Verizon Communications	VZ	2004
McDonald's	MCD	1985	Bank of America	BAC	2008
Boeing	BA	1987	Chevron Corporation	CVX	2008
Coca-Cola	KO	1987	Kraft Foods	KFT	2008
Caterpillar	CAT	1991	Cisco Systems	CSCO	2009
JPMorgan Chase	JPM	1991	The Travelers Companies	TRV	2009

EXHIBIT 1-1

Dow Industrials

Listed by Year Added to the Index

In pursuing actual business examples, we consider details about many of the 30 companies in the Dow Jones Industrial Average (the DJIA), the most commonly reported stock market index in the world. Well-known companies, such as Coca-Cola, Microsoft, and McDonald's, are among these 30 companies, along with many other large but less familiar companies, such as Alcoa and United Technologies Corporation. Exhibit 1-1 lists the 30 Dow companies together with their ticker symbol—the common shorthand used by stock brokers and investors to identify these companies. The Business First box on page 20 describes other stock exchanges around the world. We also consider younger and faster-growing companies, such as Starbucks, Amazon, Apple, and Timberland and international companies such as Toyota, Nokia, Nestlé, and Volkswagen to illustrate various accounting issues and practices. For now, we start with the basics, most of which are the same regardless of the accounting language a company uses.

The Nature of Accounting

Accounting organizes and summarizes economic information so decision makers can use it. Accountants present this information in reports called financial statements. To prepare these statements, accountants analyze, record, quantify, accumulate, summarize, classify, report, and interpret economic events and their financial effects on an organization.

A company's accounting system is the series of steps it uses to record financial data and convert them into informative financial statements. Accountants analyze the information needed by managers and other decision makers and create the accounting system that best meets those needs. Bookkeepers and computers then perform the routine tasks of collecting and compiling economic data. The real value of any accounting system lies in the information it provides to decision makers.

Consider the accounting system at a university. It collects information about tuition charges and payments and tracks the status of each student. The university must be able to bill individuals with unpaid balances. It must be able to schedule courses and hire faculty to meet the course demands of students. It must ensure that tuition and other cash inflows are sufficient to pay the faculty and keep the buildings warm (or cool) and well lit. In the past, students often became frustrated with university accounting systems. Perhaps there were too many waiting lines at registration or too many complicated procedures in filing for financial aid. However, modern systems allow electronic registration for courses and electronic payments of tuition. The right information system can streamline your life. Every business maintains an accounting system, from the store where you bought this book to the company that issued the credit card you used. MasterCard, Visa, and American Express maintain fast, complicated accounting systems. At any moment, thousands of credit card transactions occur around the globe, and accounting systems keep track of them all. When you use your charge card, a scanner reads it electronically and transmits the transaction amount to the card company's central computer. The computer verifies that your charges are within acceptable limits and approves or denies the transaction. At the same time, the computer also conducts security checks. For example, if stores in Chicago and London registered sales using your card within an hour of each other, the system might sense that something is wrong and require you to call a customer service representative before the credit card company approves the second charge. Without reliable accounting systems, credit cards simply could not exist.

Accounting as an Aid to Decision Making

Accounting information is useful to anyone making decisions that have economic consequences. Such decision makers include managers, owners, investors, and politicians. Consider the following examples:

OBJECTIVE 1

Explain how accounting information assists in making decisions.

- When the engineering department of Apple Computer developed the iPad, accountants developed reports on the potential profitability of the product, including estimated sales and estimated production and selling costs. Managers used the reports to help decide whether to produce and market the product.
- When QBC Information Services, a small consulting firm with five employees, decides who to promote (and possibly who to fire), the managing partner produces reports on the productivity of each employee and compares productivity to the salary and other costs associated with the employee's work for the year.

BUSINESS FIRST

STOCK EXCHANGES AND INDICES AROUND THE WORLD

Nearly all of the largest, multinational companies are publicly traded corporations. For example, Apple, Microsoft, HSBC, Toyota, and BP are all authorized to sell their shares on a particular stock exchange.

The New York Stock Exchange (NYSE) is the largest stock exchange in the world when measured by value of stocks listed on the exchange. The total market capitalization of stocks traded on the NYSE was $15.4 trillion in 2006 and the average monthly volume was almost $40 billion during 2010[1]. Besides the NYSE, there are dozens of other stock exchanges that operate around the world. A sample of these is shown below:

Country	City	Exchange Name	Website
USA	New York	New York Stock Exchange	www.nyse.com
Japan	Tokyo	Tokyo Stock Exchange	www.tse.or.jp/english
United Kingdom	London	London Stock Exchange	www.londonstockexchange.com
China	Shanghai	Shanghai Stock Exchange	www.sse.com.cn/sseportal/en
Hong Kong	Hong Kong	Hong Kong Stock Exchange	www.hkex.com.hk
India	Bombay	Bombay Stock Exchange	www.bseindia.com

Stock price indices track the value of a number of companies and there are indices all over the world. In fact, many indices cover stocks traded on a specific stock exchange such as those listed above. For example, the FTSE 100 covers the largest 100 stocks traded on the London Stock Exchange while the Hang Seng Stock Index covers 46 of the largest stocks traded on the Hong Kong Stock Exchange.

Stock price indices the value of many different stocks into a single measure, providing a quick way to assess the general trend of an economy.

Indices including a small number of companies are still useful. The 46 stocks in the Hang Seng Stock Index represent 58.3% of the value on the Hong Kong Stock Exchange even though there are over 1,300 total companies listed.

Stock indices have their limitations. They cover a small geographic area, focus on a particular sector or industry, and may ignore firm specific information that is useful to investors.

Index	Market	Number of Companies	Year first used
Dow Jones Industrial Average	United States (mainly NYSE, some NASDAQ)	30	1896
FTSE 100	London	100	1984
Hang Seng Stock Index	Hong Kong	46	1969
DAX	Germany	100	1988
MSCI All Country World Investable Market Index	45 different countries	9,000	1987

[1]Represents values traded on the New York Stock Exchange exclusive of affiliated international exchanges. Source: http://www.nyxdata.com.

- When portfolio managers at Vanguard Group consider buying stock in either Ford Motor Company or Volkswagen Group, they consult published accounting reports to compare the most recent financial results of the companies. They must be able to compare Ford's information reported in the accounting language of U.S. companies with that of Volkswagen reported in the accounting language of Europe. Understanding the information in the reports helps the managers decide which company would be the better investment choice.
- When President Barack Obama developed his economic stimulus plan, he needed to predict how the proposed plan would affect the country's budget. Accounting information helped predict how much the plan would cost and where the money would come from.

- When Bank of America considers a loan to a company that wants to expand, it examines the historical performance of the company and analyzes projections the company provides about how it will use the borrowed funds to produce new business.

Accounting helps decision making by showing where and when a company spends money and makes commitments, providing information for evaluating financial performance and illustrating the financial implications of choosing one plan instead of another. Accounting also helps predict the future effects of decisions, and it helps direct attention to current problems, imperfections, and inefficiencies, as well as opportunities.

Consider some basic relationships in the decision-making process:

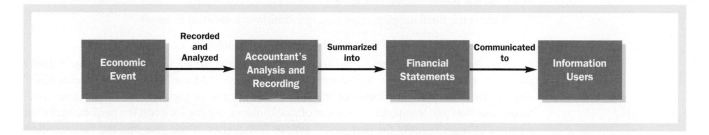

When economic events occur, accountants analyze and record the events. Periodically, accountants summarize the results of the events into financial statements. Users then rely on the financial statements to make decisions. Our focus includes all four boxes. All financial accounting courses cover the analysis and recording of information and preparing financial statements. We pay more attention to the underlying business processes creating the events and to the way in which the financial reports help decision makers to take action.

Financial and Management Accounting

The financial statements we discuss in this book are common to all areas of accounting. Accountants often distinguish "financial accounting" from "management accounting" based on who uses the information. Recall that financial accounting serves external decision makers, such as stockholders, suppliers, banks, and government agencies. In contrast, **management accounting** serves internal decision makers, such as top executives, department heads, college deans, hospital administrators, and people at other management levels within the organization.[1] The two fields of accounting share many of the same procedures for analyzing and recording the effects of individual transactions.

The most common source of financial information used by investors and others outside the company is the **annual report**. The annual report is a document prepared by management and distributed to current and potential investors to inform them about the company's past performance and future prospects. Firms distribute their annual reports to stockholders automatically. Potential investors may request the report by calling the investor relations department of the company or by visiting the company's Web site to access the report. In addition to the financial statements, annual reports usually include the following:

1. A letter from corporate management
2. A discussion and analysis by management of recent economic events
3. Footnotes that explain many elements of the financial statements in more detail
4. The report of the independent registered public accounting firm (auditors)
5. Statements by both management and auditors on the company's internal controls
6. Other corporate information

Some large companies also use their annual reports to promote the company, using pleasing photographs extensively to communicate their message.

Although all elements of the annual report are important, we concentrate on the principal financial statements and how accountants collect and report this information. You can also find

management accounting
The field of accounting that serves internal decision makers, such as top executives, department heads, college deans, hospital administrators, and people at other management levels within an organization.

annual report
A document prepared by management and distributed to current and potential investors to inform them about the company's past performance and future prospects.

---

[1]For a book-length presentation of the field, see C. Horngren, G. Sundem, W. Stratton, D. Burgstahler, and J. Schatzberg, *Introduction to Management Accounting*, 15th ed. (Upper Saddle River, NJ: Prentice-Hall, 2011), the companion volume to this textbook.

Form 10-K
A document that U.S. companies file annually with the Securities and Exchange Commission. It contains the companies' financial statements.

Securities and Exchange Commission (SEC)
The government agency responsible for regulating capital markets in the United States.

U.S. companies' financial statements in their **Form 10-K** filed annually with the **Securities and Exchange Commission (SEC)**, the government agency responsible for regulating capital markets in the United States. Companies with stock that is publicly traded in the U.S. must file 10-Ks and many other forms with the SEC. The 10-K contains more than the basic financial statements, including detailed financial information beyond that included in annual reports. A growing number of U.S. companies are eliminating their expensive and glossy annual reports and simply issuing the 10-K to investors and potential investors.

While decision makers are most interested in a company's future performance, the information in an annual report or 10-K is largely historical. However, past performance is an important input in predicting future success. Therefore, the annual report or 10-K enables decision makers to answer the following relevant questions:

What is the financial picture of the organization at a moment in time?

How well did the organization do during a period of time?

Accountants answer these questions with four major financial statements: the balance sheet, the income statement, the statement of cash flows, and the statement of stockholders' equity. The balance sheet focuses on the financial picture as of a given day. The income statement, cash flow statement, and statement of stockholders' equity focus on the performance over a period of time. Usually the period is a year or one quarter of the year and the balance sheet shows the company's status on the last day of the period. We discuss the balance sheet in this chapter, the income statement and statement of stockholders' equity in Chapter 2, and the statement of cash flows in Chapter 5. After introducing the balance sheet, this chapter also explores several topics that are important to understanding the environment in which a business operates. You can find financial statements for most companies on their Web sites, as described in the Business First box.

The Balance Sheet

OBJECTIVE 2

Describe the components of the balance sheet.

balance sheet (statement of financial position)
A financial statement that shows the financial status of a business entity at a particular instant in time.

balance sheet equation
Assets = Liabilities + Owners' equity

assets
Economic resources that a company expects to help generate future cash inflows or help reduce future cash outflows.

liabilities
Economic obligations of the organization to outsiders, or claims against its assets by outsiders.

notes payable
Promissory notes that are evidence of a debt and state the terms of payment.

owners' equity
The owners' claims on an organization's assets, or total assets less total liabilities.

The **balance sheet**, also called the **statement of financial position**, shows the financial status of a company at a particular instant in time. It is essentially a snapshot of the organization at a given date. It has two counterbalancing sections. One section lists the resources of the firm (everything the firm owns and controls—from cash to buildings, etc.). The other section lists the claims against the resources. The resources and claims form the **balance sheet equation**:

$$\text{Assets} = \text{Liabilities} + \text{Owners' equity}$$

Some accountants prefer the following (equivalent) form of the balance sheet equation:

$$\text{Assets} - \text{Liabilities} = \text{Owners' Equity}$$

We define the terms in this equation as follows:

Assets are economic resources that the company expects to help generate future cash inflows or reduce or prevent future cash outflows. Examples are cash, inventories, and equipment.
Liabilities are economic obligations of the organization to outsiders, or claims against its assets by outsiders. An example is a debt to a bank. When a company takes out a bank loan, it generally signs a promissory note that states the terms of repayment. Accountants use the term **notes payable** to describe the existence of promissory notes.
Owners' equity is the owners' claim on the organization's assets. Because debt holders have first claim on the assets, the owners' claim is equal to the assets less the liabilities.

To illustrate the balance sheet, suppose Hector Lopez, a salaried employee of a local bicycle company, quits his job and opens his own bicycle shop, Biwheels Company, on January 2, 20X2. Lopez has heard about the problems encountered by new businesses that lack money, so he invests plenty: $400,000. Then Lopez, acting for the business, borrows $100,000 from a local

BUSINESS FIRST

ANNUAL REPORTS AND THE INTERNET

Until the last decade, annual reports were generally glossy documents produced by companies about 3 months after year-end. In addition to being a primary source of financial information about the company, annual reports also contained much other information (some might call it propaganda) about the company. However, the Internet has changed and continues to change the way investors get information about a company. Today, more information is available more quickly on the Web than on paper.

Most publicly held companies, and certainly the large ones, include their annual reports on their Web site. You can usually find a company's annual report in a segment of its site called "Investors" or "Investor Relations." Often this comes under a heading "Corporate Information," "About the Company," or some such title included on the company's home page.

Most companies provide at least an indexed electronic version of their financial statement in PDF format. But many companies are providing files that are more flexible, mainly statements that users can download into Excel spreadsheets. This allows users to perform their own analyses of the data. Further, some companies provide information in a variety of languages. For example, Microsoft presents its shareholder letter and financial highlights in the currency and language of the United Kingdom, France, Germany, Japan, Australia, Canadian French, and Spanish.

There is even a competition for the best annual reports. The League of American Communications Professionals (LACP) rates annual reports based on how well they communicate their messages. The top 2007 annual reports by category, selected from more than 3,000 entries representing more than 20 countries, are as follows:

Category	Company	Country
Best Agency Report	Grupo Modelo	Mexico
Communicators' Choice	Goodwill Industries of Middle Tennessee	USA
Most Creative	D. Logistics AG	Germany
Most Engaging	Novartis	Switzerland
Most Improved	Anglo Platinum	South Africa
Best In-House Report	Heidelberger Druckmaschinen	Germany
Best Shareholder Letter	Wal-Mart Stores, Inc.	USA
Best Report Cover	Fresenius Medical Care AG & Co.	Germany
Best Report Financials	SAP AG	USA
Best Report Narrative	PT Antam Tbk	Indonesia

Some executives use their company's annual report to educate investors. Warren Buffett, chairman and CEO of Berkshire Hathaway, always includes a long letter explaining his philosophies as well as his company's performance. In 2009, his letter contained 19 pages of insightful comments. For example, in 2008 he commented on the housing and credit crisis as one where "borrowers who shouldn't have borrowed [were] being financed by lenders who shouldn't have lent." One year he even compared financial reporting to his golf game.

Annual reports are venerable documents that have been useful to investors for many years. They are not likely to go away. However, their content and format are changing. Use of the Internet opens up possibilities for presenting financial information (as well as other information) to investors that were previously impossible. This should lead to better information for those making investment decisions and therefore better functioning capital markets.

Sources: LACP 2007 Annual Report Competition Results, http://www.lacp.com/2007vision/competition.htm; Microsoft, 2009 Annual Report; Berkshire Hathaway, 2008 and 2009 Annual Reports.

---

bank. That gives Biwheels $500,000 in assets, all currently in the form of cash. The opening balance sheet of this new business enterprise follows:

Biwheels Company
Balance Sheet
January 2, 20X2

Assets		Liabilities and Owners' Equity	
Cash	$500,000	Liabilities (note payable)	$100,000
		Lopez, capital	400,000
Total assets	$500,000	Total liabilities and owners' equity	$500,000

Because the balance sheet shows the financial status at a particular point in time, it always includes a particular date. The elements in this balance sheet show the financial status of the Biwheels Company as of January 2, 20X2. The Biwheels balance sheet lists the company's assets at this point in time ($500,000) on the left. They are balanced on the right by an equal amount of liability and owners' equity ($100,000 liability owed to the bank plus $400,000 paid in by Lopez). The double underscores (double ruling) under the column totals denote final numbers. Note that we always keep the left and right sides in balance.

When someone first starts a business, the owners' equity is equal to the total amount invested by the owner or owners. As illustrated by "Lopez, capital" in the Biwheels Company example, accountants often use the term capital instead of owners' equity to designate an owner's investment in the business. We can emphasize the residual, or "leftover," nature of owners' equity by expressing the balance sheet equation as follows:

$$\text{Owners' equity} = \text{Assets} - \text{Liabilities}$$

This shows that the owners' claims are the amount left over after deducting the liabilities from the assets. Accountants also use the term **net assets** to refer to assets less liabilities.

Balance Sheet Transactions

net assets
Assets less liabilities.

OBJECTIVE 3

Analyze business transactions and relate them to changes in the balance sheet.

entity
An organization or a section of an organization that stands apart from other organizations and individuals as a separate economic unit.

transaction
Any event that affects the financial position of an entity and that an accountant can reliably record in money terms.

Accountants record every transaction entered into by an entity. An **entity** is an organization or a section of an organization that stands apart from other organizations and individuals as a separate economic unit. For most of our examples the entity is a company. A **transaction** is any event that affects the financial position of an entity and that an accountant can reliably record in monetary terms. Every transaction affects the balance sheet. When accountants record a transaction, they make at least two entries so the total assets always equal the total liabilities plus owners' equity. That is, they must maintain the equality of the balance sheet equation for every transaction. If a balance sheet balances before a transaction, adding or subtracting a single amount would necessarily leave the balance sheet out of balance. Because single entries cannot maintain the balance in the balance sheet, we often call the system that records transactions a *double-entry* accounting system, as we explain further in Chapter 3.

Let's take a look at some transactions of Biwheels Company to see how typical transactions affect the balance sheet.

TRANSACTION 1, INITIAL INVESTMENT The first Biwheels transaction was the investment by the owner on January 2, 20X2. Lopez deposited $400,000 in a business bank account entitled Biwheels Company. The transaction affects the balance sheet equation as follows:

	Assets	=	Liabilities	+	Owners' Equity
	Cash				Lopez, Capital
(1)	+400,000	=			+400,000
					(Owner investment)

This transaction increases both the assets, specifically Cash, and the owners' equity of the business, specifically Lopez, Capital. It does not affect liabilities. Why? Because Lopez's business has no obligation to an outside party because of this transaction. We use a parenthetical note, "Owner investment," to identify the reason for the transaction's effect on owners' equity. The total amounts on the left side of the equation are equal to the total amounts on the right side, as they should be.

TRANSACTION 2, LOAN FROM BANK On January 2, 20X2, Biwheels Company also borrows from a bank, signing a promissory note for $100,000. The $100,000 increases Biwheels' cash. The effect of this loan transaction on the balance sheet equation is as follows:

	Assets	=	Liabilities +	Owners' Equity
	Cash		Note Payable	Lopez, Capital
(1)	+400,000	=		+400,000
(2)	+100,000	=	+100,000	
Bal.	500,000	=	100,000	400,000
	500,000		500,000	

The loan increases the asset, Cash, and increases the liability, Note Payable, by the same amount, $100,000. After completing the transaction, Biwheels has assets of $500,000, liabilities of $100,000, and owners' equity of $400,000. As always, the sums of the individual account balances (abbreviated Bal.) on each side of the equation are equal.

TRANSACTION 3, ACQUIRE STORE EQUIPMENT FOR CASH   On January 3, 20X2, Biwheels acquires miscellaneous store equipment for $15,000 cash. Store equipment is an example of a **long-lived asset**—an asset that a company expects to use for more than 1 year.

long-lived asset
An asset that a company expects to use for more than 1 year.

	Assets		=	Liabilities + Owners' Equity	
	Cash	Store Equipment		Note Payable	Lopez, Capital
Bal.	500,000		=	100,000	400,000
(3)	−15,000	+15,000	=		
Bal.	485,000	15,000	=	100,000	400,000
	500,000			500,000	

This transaction increases one asset, Store Equipment, and decreases another asset, Cash, by the same amount. The form of the assets changes, but the total amount of assets remains the same. Moreover, the right-side items do not change.

Biwheels can prepare a balance sheet at any point in time. The balance sheet for January 3, after the first three transactions, would look like this:

Biwheels Company
Balance Sheet
January 3, 20X2

Assets		Liabilities and Owners' Equity	
Cash	$485,000	Liabilities (note payable)	$100,000
Store equipment	15,000	Lopez, capital	400,000
Total assets	$500,000	Total liabilities and owners' equity	$500,000

Transaction Analysis

Accountants record transactions in an organization's accounts. An **account** is a summary record of the changes in a particular asset, liability, or owners' equity, and the account balance is the total of all entries to the account to date. For example, Biwheels' cash account through January 3 shows increases of $400,000 and $100,000 and a decrease of $15,000, leaving an account balance of $485,000. The analysis of transactions is the heart of accounting. For each transaction, the accountant determines (1) which specific accounts the transaction affects, (2) whether it increases or decreases each account balance, and (3) the amount of the change in each account balance. After recording all the transactions for some period, the accountant will summarize these transactions into financial statements that managers, investors, and others use in their decision-making process.

account
A summary record of the changes in a particular asset, liability, or owners' equity.

Exhibit 1-2 shows how to analyze a series of transactions using the balance sheet equation. We number the transactions for easy reference. Examine the first three transactions in Exhibit 1-2, which summarize the transactions we have already discussed.

Next, consider how to analyze each of the following additional transactions:

4. January 4. Biwheels acquires bicycles from Trek for $120,000 cash.
5. January 5. Biwheels buys bicycle parts for $10,000 from Shimano. Biwheels will sell these parts in addition to the bicycles themselves. No cash changes hands on January 5. Rather, Shimano requires $4,000 by January 10 and the balance in 30 days.
6. January 6. Biwheels buys bicycles from Schwinn for $30,000. Schwinn requires a cash down payment of $10,000, and Biwheels must pay the remaining balance in 60 days.
7. January 7. Biwheels sells a store showcase to a business neighbor after Lopez decides he dislikes it. Its selling price, $1,000, happens to be exactly equal to its cost. The neighbor pays cash.
8. January 8. Biwheels returns four bicycles (which it had acquired for $800) to Schwinn for full credit (an $800 reduction of the amount that Biwheels owes Schwinn).

Description of Transactions	Assets			=	Liabilities + Owners' Equity		
	Cash +	Merchandise Inventory +	Store Equipment =		Note Payable +	Accounts Payable +	Lopez, Capital
(1) Initial investment	+400,000			=			+400,000
(2) Loan from bank	+100,000			=	+100,000		
(3) Acquire store equipment for cash	–15,000		+15,000	=			
(4) Acquire inventory for cash	–120,000	+120,000		=			
(5) Acquire inventory on credit		+10,000		=		+10,000	
(6) Acquire inventory for cash plus credit	–10,000	+30,000		=		+20,000	
(7) Sale of equipment	+1,000		–1,000	=			
(8) Return of inventory acquired on January 6		–800		=		–800	
(9) Payments to creditors	–4,000			=		–4,000	
Balance, January 12, 20X2	352,000 +	159,200 +	14,000	=	100,000 +	25,200 +	400,000
		525,200				525,200	

EXHIBIT 1-2

Biwheels Company

Analysis of Transactions for January 2 to January 12, 20X2

9. January 10. Biwheels pays $4,000 to Shimano.
10. January 12. Lopez remodels his home for $35,000, paying by check from his personal bank account.

Use the format in Exhibit 1-2 to analyze each transaction. Try to do your own analysis of each transaction before looking at the entries in the exhibit. For example, you could cover the numerical entries with a sheet of paper or a ruler and then proceed through each transaction, one by one.

INTERPRETING FINANCIAL STATEMENTS

Transaction 10 does not appear in Exhibit 1-2. Why not?

Answer

Transaction 10 is a personal transaction by Lopez and does not involve Biwheels as a business. Lopez would record it in his personal accounts, but it does not belong in Biwheels' business accounts. It is important for readers of financial statements to identify the entity accounted for in the financial statements—which in our case is Biwheels, a business.

inventory

Goods held by a company for the purpose of sale to customers.

TRANSACTION 4, PURCHASE INVENTORY FOR CASH **Inventory** refers to goods held by the company for the purpose of sale to customers. The bicycles are inventory, or Merchandise Inventory, to Biwheels. Inventory increases by the amount paid for the bicycles, and cash decreases by the same amount.

	Assets			=	Liabilities + Owners' Equity	
	Cash	Merchandise Inventory	Store Equipment		Note Payable	Lopez, Capital
Bal.	485,000		15,000	=	100,000	400,000
(4)	−120,000	+120,000		=		
Bal.	365,000	120,000	15,000	=	100,000	400,000
		500,000			500,000	

TRANSACTION 5, PURCHASE INVENTORY ON CREDIT   Companies throughout the world make most purchases on credit instead of for cash. An authorized signature of the buyer is usually good enough to ensure payment. We call this practice buying on **open account**. The buyer records the money owed on its balance sheet as an account payable. Thus, an **account payable** is a liability that results from a purchase of goods or services on open account. As Exhibit 1-2 shows for this transaction, the merchandise inventory (an asset account) of Biwheels increases and we add an account payable to Shimano (a liability account) in the amount of $10,000 to keep the equation in balance. Both total assets and total liabilities and owners' equity increase to $510,000.

open account
Buying or selling on credit, usually by just an "authorized signature" of the buyer.

account payable
A liability that results from a purchase of goods or services on open account.

	Assets			=	Liabilities + Owners' Equity		
	Cash	Merchandise Inventory	Store Equipment		Note Payable	Accounts Payable	Lopez, Capital
Bal.	365,000	120,000	15,000	=	100,000		400,000
(5)		+10,000		=		+10,000	
Bal.	365,000	130,000	15,000	=	100,000	10,000	400,000
		510,000				510,000	

TRANSACTION 6, PURCHASE INVENTORY FOR CASH PLUS CREDIT   This transaction illustrates a **compound entry** because it affects more than two balance sheet accounts (two asset accounts and one liability account, in this case). Merchandise inventory increases by the full amount of its cost regardless of whether Biwheels makes its payment in full now, in full later, or partially now and partially later. Therefore, Biwheels' Merchandise Inventory (an asset account) increases by $30,000, Cash (an asset account) decreases by $10,000, and Accounts Payable (a liability account) increases by the difference, $20,000.

compound entry
A transaction that affects more than two accounts.

	Assets			=	Liabilities + Owners' Equity		
	Cash	Merchandise Inventory	Store Equipment		Note Payable	Accounts Payable	Lopez, Capital
Bal.	365,000	130,000	15,000	=	100,000	10,000	400,000
(6)	−10,000	+30,000		=		+20,000	
Bal.	355,000	160,000	15,000	=	100,000	30,000	400,000
		530,000				530,000	

TRANSACTION 7, SALE OF ASSET FOR CASH   This transaction increases cash by $1,000 and decreases Store Equipment by $1,000. In this case, the transaction affects asset accounts only. One increases and one decreases, with no change in total assets. Liabilities and owners' equity do not change.

	Assets			=	Liabilities + Owners' Equity		
	Cash	Merchandise Inventory	Store Equipment		Note Payable	Accounts Payable	Lopez, Capital
Bal.	355,000	160,000	15,000	=	100,000	30,000	400,000
(7)	+1,000		−1,000	=			
Bal.	356,000	160,000	14,000	=	100,000	30,000	400,000
		530,000				530,000	

TRANSACTION 8, RETURN OF INVENTORY TO SUPPLIER   When a company returns merchandise to its suppliers for credit, the transaction reduces its merchandise inventory account and reduces its liabilities. In this instance, the amount of the decrease on each side of the equation is $800.

	Assets			=	Liabilities + Owners' Equity		
	Cash	Merchandise Inventory	Store Equipment		Note Payable	Accounts Payable	Lopez, Capital
Bal.	356,000	160,000	14,000	=	100,000	30,000	400,000
(8)		−800		=		−800	
Bal.	356,000	159,200	14,000	=	100,000	29,200	400,000
		529,200				529,200	

creditor

A person or entity to whom a company owes money.

TRANSACTION 9, PAYMENT TO CREDITOR   A **creditor** is one to whom the company owes money. For Biwheels, Shimano, who supplied the bicycle parts on credit, is a creditor. The payment to Shimano decreases both assets (Cash) and liabilities (Accounts Payable) by $4,000.

	Assets			=	Liabilities + Owners' Equity		
	Cash	Merchandise Inventory	Store Equipment		Note Payable	Accounts Payable	Lopez, Capital
Bal.	356,000	159,200	14,000	=	100,000	29,200	400,000
(9)	−4,000			=		−4,000	
Bal.	352,000	159,200	14,000	=	100,000	25,200	400,000
		525,200				525,200	

Preparing the Balance Sheet

OBJECTIVE 4

Prepare a balance sheet from transactions data.

To prepare a balance sheet, we can compute a cumulative total for each account in Exhibit 1-2 at any date. The following balance sheet uses the totals at the bottom of Exhibit 1-2. Observe once again that a balance sheet represents the financial impact of all transactions up to a specific point in time, here January 12, 20X2.

Biwheels Company
Balance Sheet
January 12, 20X2

Assets		Liabilities and Owner's Equity	
Cash	$352,000	Note payable	$100,000
Merchandise		Accounts payable	25,200
inventory	159,200	Total liabilities	$125,200
Store equipment	14,000	Lopez, capital	$400,000
Total	$525,200	Total	$525,200

Although Biwheels could prepare a new balance sheet after each transaction, companies usually produce balance sheets only when needed by managers and at the end of each quarter for reporting to the public.

	Starbucks	Jack in the Box
Assets		
Cash and cash equivalents	$ 269.8	$ 47.9
Inventories	692.8	45.2
Prepaid expenses	169.2	20.1
Property, plant, and equipment	2,956.4	943.1
Other assets	1,584.4	442.1
Total assets	$5,672.6	1,498.4
Liabilities and Owners' Equity		
Accounts payable	$ 324.9	$ 99.7
Long-term debt	549.6	516.2
Other liabilities	2,307.2	425.4
Total liabilities	3,181.7	1,041.3
Total owners' equity	2,490.9	457.1
Total liabilities and owners' equity	$5,672.6	$1,498.4

EXHIBIT 1-3

Comparative Consolidated Condensed Balance Sheets, September 28, 2008

($ in millions)

Examples of Actual Corporate Balance Sheets

To become more familiar with the balance sheet, consider the balance sheet information for Starbucks and Jack in the Box for 2008, shown in Exhibit 1-3. (We have omitted many details present in the actual balance sheets to simplify and condense the examples.) Both Starbucks and Jack in the Box provide food services, but their strategies are different. Starbucks focuses on coffee, has more than four times as many outlets, and has expanded internationally. Jack in the Box sells fast food and has outlets primarily in the western and southern United States.

From the companies' balance sheets, we learn that Starbucks has almost four times more total assets but only three times more property, plant, and equipment. Therefore, Jack in the Box has more invested in each outlet. Just think about the investment required by a drive-in restaurant compared with that in a coffee shop—the difference is logical. We also see that the two companies have close to the same amount of long-term debt, and Starbucks has more owners' equity. Notice that on the balance sheets of both companies the total assets are equal to the total liabilities and owners' equity. Every balance sheet maintains this equality. Details about various items in the balance sheet will gradually become more understandable as each chapter explains the nature of the various major financial statements and examines their components.

Summary Problems for Your Review

PROBLEM

Analyze the following additional transactions of Biwheels Company. Begin with the balances shown for January 12, 20X2, in Exhibit 1-2 on page 26. Prepare a balance sheet for Biwheels Company on January 16, after recording these additional transactions.

  i. Biwheels pays $10,000 on the bank loan (ignore interest).

  ii. Lopez buys furniture for his home for $5,000, using his family's charge account at Macy's.

  iii. Biwheels buys more bicycles for inventory from Cannondale for $50,000. Biwheels pays one-half the amount in cash and owes one-half on open account.

  iv. Biwheels pays another $4,000 to Shimano.

SOLUTION

See Exhibits 1-4 and 1-5. Note that we ignored transaction 2 because it is wholly personal. However, visualize how this transaction would affect Lopez's personal balance sheet. His assets, Home Furniture, would increase by $5,000, and his liabilities, Accounts Payable, would also increase by $5,000.

Description of Transaction	Cash	+	Merchandise Inventory	+	Store Equipment	=	Note Payable	+	Accounts Payable	+	Lopez, Capital
	Assets					**=**	**Liabilities + Owners' Equity**				
Balance, January 12, 20X2	352,000	+	159,200	+	14,000	=	100,000	+	25,200	+	400,000
(i) Payment on bank loan	–10,000					=	–10,000				
(ii) Personal; no effect											
(iii) Acquire inventory, half for cash, half on credit	–25,000		+50,000			=			+25,000		
(iv) Payment to suppliers	–4,000					=			–4,000		
Balance, January 16, 20X2	313,000	+	209,200	+	14,000	=	90,000	+	46,200	+	400,000
			$536,200			=			$536,200		

EXHIBIT 1-4

Biwheels Company

Analysis of Additional January Transactions

PROBLEM

Exhibit 1-6 contains Starbucks' condensed balance sheets for 2007 and 2008. Respond to the following questions:

1. As of what date were the 2007 and 2008 balance sheets prepared? Are these points in time or spans of time?
2. What are total assets for each of the 2 years shown in the balance sheets? What elements explain the difference in the asset levels for the 2 years?
3. Total assets increased by $328.7 million from September 30, 2007, to September 28, 2008. What was the change in total liabilities plus owners' equity over that same time period?
4. Of the following items on Starbucks' balance sheet, which are assets and which are liabilities: Property, Plant, and Equipment; Cash and Cash Equivalents; Long-Term Debt; Inventories; and Accounts Payable?

SOLUTION

1. Starbucks presents two balance sheets. The most recent is dated September 28, 2008, and the earlier one is dated September 30, 2007. These are both points in time; all balance sheets represent a single point in time.
2. Total assets increased by $328.7 million, from $5,343.9 million to $5,672.6 million. Most of the increase occurred in Property, Plant, and Equipment ($66.0 million) and Other Assets ($252.7 million).
3. Total Liabilities and Owners' Equity increased by the same amount as the increase in total assets: $328.7 million. The two increases must be the same to keep the balance sheet equation in balance.
4. Property, Plant, and Equipment, Cash and Cash Equivalents, and Inventories are assets. Long-term Debt and Accounts Payable are liabilities.

EXHIBIT 1-5

Biwheels Company

Balance Sheet
January 16, 20X2

Assets		Liabilities and Owner's Equity	
		Liabilities:	
Cash	$313,000	Note payable	$ 90,000
		Accounts payable	46,200
Merchandise inventory	209,200	Total liabilities	$136,200
Store equipment	14,000	Lopez, capital	400,000
Total	$536,200	Total	$536,200

Assets	September 28, 2008	September 30, 2007
Cash and cash equivalents	$ 269.8	$ 281.3
Inventories	692.8	691.7
Prepaid expenses	169.2	148.8
Property, plant, and equipment	2,956.4	2,890.4
Other assets	1,584.4	1,331.7
Total assets	$5,672.6	$5,343.9
Liabilities and Owners' Equity		
Accounts payable	$ 324.9	$ 390.8
Long-term debt	549.6	549.6
Other liabilities	2,307.2	2,119.4
Total liabilities	3,181.7	3,059.8
Total owners' equity	2,490.9	2,284.1
Total liabilities and owners' equity	$5,672.6	$5,343.9

EXHIBIT 1-6

Starbucks Corporation
Consolidated Balance Sheets ($ in millions)

Types of Ownership

Although most accounting processes are the same for all types of companies, a few differences arise because of the legal structure of the company, especially in accounting for owners' equity. We next look at the three basic forms of ownership structures for business entities: sole proprietorships, partnerships, and corporations.

OBJECTIVE 5

Compare the features of sole proprietorships, partnerships, and corporations.

Sole Proprietorships

A **sole proprietorship** is a business with a single owner. Most often, the owner is also the manager. Therefore, sole proprietorships tend to be small businesses such as local stores and restaurants and professionals such as dentists or attorneys who operate alone. Biwheels started out as a sole proprietorship owned and operated by Hector Lopez. From an accounting viewpoint, a sole proprietorship is a separate entity that is distinct from the proprietor. Thus, the cash in a dentist's business account is an asset of the dental practice, whereas the cash in the dentist's personal account is not. Similarly, Lopez's remodeling of his home (see transaction 10, p. 26) was a personal transaction, not a business transaction.

sole proprietorship
A business with a single owner.

Partnerships

A **partnership** is an organization that joins two or more individuals who act as co-owners. Many auto dealerships are partnerships, as are groups of physicians, attorneys, or accountants who group together to provide services. Partnerships can be gigantic. The largest international accounting firms have thousands of partners. Again, from an accounting viewpoint, each partnership is an individual entity that is separate from the personal activities of each partner.

partnership
A form of organization that joins two or more individuals together as co-owners.

Corporations

Most large businesses, including all 30 Dow companies listed in Exhibit 1-1 (p. 18), are corporations. **Corporations** are business organizations created under state laws in the United States. The owners of a corporation have **limited liability**, which means that corporate creditors (such as banks or suppliers) ordinarily have claims against the corporate assets only, not against the personal assets of the owners. In contrast, owners in sole proprietorships and partnerships are usually personally liable for any obligations of the business. (An exception is limited liability partnerships, which limit the liability of partners.) Another difference is that the owners of proprietorships and partnerships are typically active managers of the business, whereas large corporations generally hire professional managers.

Most large corporations are **publicly owned**. This means that the company sells shares in its ownership to the public. Purchasers of the shares become shareholders (or stockholders). Large

corporation
A business organization that is created by individual state laws.

limited liability
A feature of the corporate form of organization whereby corporate creditors (such as banks or suppliers) ordinarily have claims against the corporate assets only, not against the personal assets of the owners.

publicly owned
A corporation that sells shares in its ownership to the public.

privately owned

A corporation owned by a family, a small group of shareholders, or a single individual, in which shares of ownership are not publicly sold.

publicly owned corporations often have thousands of shareholders. In contrast, some corporations are **privately owned** by families, small groups of shareholders, or a single individual, with shares of ownership not sold to the public. Corporations in the United States often use one of the abbreviations Co., Corp., or Inc. in their names.

Internationally, organizational forms similar to corporations are common. In the United Kingdom, such companies frequently use the word "limited" (Ltd.) in their names. In Germany it is AG (for Aktiengesellschaft, which means a company with shares that are traded on a stock market) or GmbH (for Gesellschaft mit beschränkter Haftung, which translates as a company with limited liability). In Spain, corporations use the initials S.A., which refer to Spanish words that we translate as "society anonymous," meaning that multiple unidentified owners stand behind the company. Corporate laws vary in details across countries, but the basic characteristics of corporations are quite universal.

Advantages and Disadvantages of the Corporate Form

stock certificate

Formal evidence of ownership shares in a corporation.

The corporate form of organization has many advantages. We have already discussed limited liability. What are some other advantages? One is easy transfer of ownership. To sell shares in its ownership, the corporation usually issues **stock certificates** as formal evidence of ownership. Some shareholders may hold the physical certificates. However, the most common type of ownership is a brokerage account that electronically registers ownership shares. Owners of these shares, whether they hold them physically or electronically, can sell them to others. Numerous stock exchanges in the United States and worldwide facilitate buying and selling of shares. Investors buy and sell more than 2 billion shares on an average day on the New York Stock Exchange (NYSE), the largest exchange in the world. Another U.S. exchange, NASDAQ, lists the stock of more than 3,200 companies from 35 countries, primarily smaller, tech-oriented companies, but it also includes Microsoft, Intel, and a few other large companies among its listings. Other large exchanges include those in Tokyo, Hong Kong, Shanghai, Frankfurt, and London. Companies can be listed on more than one exchange. Many Japanese, German, and British firms have shares traded on the NYSE, and many U.S. companies list their shares abroad. The London Stock Exchange is one of the most international of the exchanges. Exhibit 1-7 displays just a few of the international companies listed on the London exchange.

Because owners can easily trade shares of stock, corporations have the advantage of raising ownership capital from hundreds or thousands of potential stockholders. For example, General Electric has millions of stockholders, owning a total of nearly 10 billion shares of stock. More than 20 million shares trade hands daily.

A corporation also has the advantage of continuity of existence. The life of a corporation is indefinite in the sense that it continues even if its ownership changes. In contrast, proprietorships and partnerships in the United States officially terminate on the death or complete withdrawal of an owner.

Finally, the tax laws may favor a corporation or a partnership or a proprietorship. This depends heavily on the personal tax situations of the owners and is beyond the scope of this book.

Although only 20% of U.S. businesses are corporations, they do almost 90% of the business. The 72% of businesses that are sole proprietorships generate only 5% of the business activity. Because of the economic importance of corporations, this book emphasizes the corporate form of ownership.

INTERPRETING FINANCIAL STATEMENTS

Biwheels is organized as a sole proprietorship. What would be the biggest advantage for Mr. Lopez in converting it to a corporation?

limited to the investment he has already made. There may also be tax advantages, and Mr. Lopez would find it easier to sell part of the business by issuing shares if it is a corporation.

Answer

As a sole proprietorship, Mr. Lopez is personally liable for all the liabilities of Biwheels. If it were a corporation, his liability would be

Company	Country	Company	Country
Platinum Australia Ltd.	Australia	Kazkommertsbank JCS	Kazakhstan
Arab Insurance Group	Bahrain	Press Corp.	Malawi
Beximco Pharmaceuticals	Bangladesh	Steppe Cement	Malaysia
Worldsec	Bermuda	Go PLC	Malta
Canadian Pacific Railways	Canada	Royal Dutch Shell	Netherlands
Integra Group	Cayman Islands	Norsk Hydro ASA	Norway
China Petroleum and Chemical Corp.	China	MCB Bank	Pakistan
Hvratske Telekomunikacije	Croatia	Telekomunikacja Polska	Poland
Komercni Banka	Czech Repubilc	Qatar Telecom	Qatar
Novo-Nordisk A/S	Denmark	Bank of Ireland	Republic of Ireland
Suez Cement Company	Egypt	Gazprom OAO	Russia
Powerflute OYJ	Finland	Harmony Gold Mining Co.	South Africa
Groupe Eurotunnel SA	France	Hyundai Motor Co.	South Korea
Bayer AG	Germany	Telefonica SA	Spain
National Bank of Greece	Greece	Electrolux AB	Sweden
Tisza Chemical Group	Hungary	IBC Financial Group	Switzerland
Amtek Auto	India	Sunplus Technology	Taiwan
Emblaze Systems	Israel	Boeing Co.	USA
Honda Motor Co.	Japan	Ford Motor Co.	USA
Sony Corp.	Japan	General Electric	USA

EXHIBIT 1-7

Sample of Companies Traded on the London Stock Exchange

Accounting Differences Between Proprietorships, Partnerships, and Corporations

All business entities account for assets and liabilities similarly. However, corporations account for owners' equity differently than do sole proprietorships and partnerships. The basic concepts that underlie the owners' equity section of the balance sheet are the same for all three forms of ownership. That is, owners' equity always equals total assets less total liabilities. However, we often label the owners' equities for proprietorships and partnerships with the word capital. In contrast, we call owners' equity for a corporation **stockholders' equity** or **shareholders' equity**. Examine the possibilities for the Biwheels Company in Exhibit 1-8.

The accounts for the proprietorship and the partnership show owners' equity as straightforward records of the capital invested by the owners. (In the partnership example, we assume that Lopez has two partners, each with a 10% stake in Biwheels.) For a corporation, though, we call the total capital investment by owners, both at and subsequent to the inception of the business, **paid-in capital**. We record it in two parts: common stock (or capital stock) at par value and paid-in capital in excess of par value. Let's next explore what par value means.

The Meaning of Par Value

Most states require stock certificates to have some dollar amount printed on them. We call this amount **par value** or **stated value**. Typically, a company sells stock at a price that is higher than its par value. The difference between the total amount the company receives for the stock and the par value is called **paid-in capital in excess of par value** or **additional paid-in capital**. This distinction is of little economic importance, and we introduce it here only because you will frequently encounter it in actual financial statements.

Let's take a closer look at par value by altering our Biwheels example. We now assume that Biwheels is a corporation and that Lopez received 10,000 shares of stock for his $400,000 investment. Thus, he paid $40 per share. The par value is $10 per share, and the paid-in capital in

OBJECTIVE 6

Identify how the owners' equity section in a corporate balance sheet differs from that in a sole proprietorship or a partnership.

stockholders' equity (shareholders' equity)
Owners' equity of a corporation. The excess of assets over liabilities of a corporation.

paid-in capital
The total capital investment in a corporation by its owners both at and subsequent to the inception of business.

par value (stated value)
The nominal dollar amount printed on stock certificates.

paid-in capital in excess of par value (additional paid-in capital)
When issuing stock, the difference between the total amount the company receives for the stock and the par value.

EXHIBIT 1-8

Owners' Equity for Different Organizations

OWNERS' EQUITY FOR A PROPRIETORSHIP (Assume Hector Lopez Is the Sole Owner)	
Hector Lopez, capital	$400,000
OWNERS' EQUITY FOR A PARTNERSHIP (Assume Lopez Has Two Partners)	
Hector Lopez, capital	$320,000
Alex Handl, capital	40,000
Susan Eastman, capital	40,000
Total partners' capital	$400,000
OWNERS' EQUITY FOR A CORPORATION (Assume Lopez Has Incorporated)	
Stockholders' equity:	
Paid-in capital:	
Capital stock, 10,000 shares issued at par value of $10 per share	$100,000
Paid-in capital in excess of par value	300,000
Total paid-in capital	$400,000

excess of par value is $30 per share. The total ownership claim of $400,000 arising from the investment is split between two equity claims, one for $100,000 capital stock at par value and one for $300,000 paid-in capital in excess of par value:

$$
\begin{array}{lcccc}
\text{Total Paid-in Capital} & = & \text{Capital Stock at Par} & + & \text{Paid-in Capital in} \\
& & & & \text{Excess of Par Value} \\
\$400{,}000 & = & \$100{,}000 & + & \$300{,}000 \\
\text{Average Issue Price per Share} & & \text{Par Value per Share} & & \text{(Average Issue Price per Share} - \\
\times \text{ Number of Shares Issued} & = & \times \text{ Number of Shares Issued} & + & \text{Par Value per Share)} \\
& & & & \times \text{ Number of Shares Issued} \\
\$40 \times 10{,}000 & = & \$10 \times 10{,}000 & + & (\$40 - \$10) \times 10{,}000
\end{array}
$$

common stock

Par value of the stock purchased by common shareholders of a corporation.

Exhibit 1-9 shows the paid-in capital for Starbucks. Notice that Starbucks separates the par value from the capital in excess of par value. It uses the label **common stock** to describe the par value of the stock purchased by the common shareholders. Starbucks uses "other additional paid-in capital" to describe the amount paid-in above the par value. Some companies, such as General Motors, use a less descriptive term, capital surplus, for this amount. Although it would be nice to stick to one phrase for each item in this textbook, the world is full of different words used for identical accounting items. One of our goals is to help you to prepare to read and understand actual financial statements and reports. Therefore, we use many of the synonyms you will encounter when reading financial statements.

The par value per share for Starbucks is only $0.001, much smaller than the amount investors paid Starbucks for the common shares. We know this because the capital in excess of par value is much larger than the common stock at par value. The extremely small amount of par

EXHIBIT 1-9

Paid-in Capital for Starbucks

(in millions except per share amounts)

Starbucks September 28, 2008	
Common stock ($0.001 par value)—authorized, 1,200.0 shares; issued and outstanding, 735.5 shares	$ 0.7
Other additional paid-in capital	39.4
Total paid-in capital	$40.1

value is common in practice and illustrates the insignificance of par value in today's business world. Some companies provide a single total for par value and additional paid-in capital on their balance sheets. This combined reporting is acceptable because readers of financial statements would learn little of significance from separating the two components. Just remember that the total of common stock at par value and additional paid-in capital is the amount that owners actively contributed to the firm. These **common stockholders** have a "residual" ownership in the corporation, that is, they have a claim on whatever is left over after all other claimants have been paid. This could be a large amount for a successful company or nothing for an unsuccessful one. Although these paid-in capital accounts identify the amount the stockholders contributed, this is not the amount they might receive now or in the future.

common stockholders
The owners who have a "residual" ownership in the corporation.

Common stockholders buy shares of stock as investments. Sometimes they purchase the stock from the company. In such a case, the company increases both its cash and its paid-in capital. However, the majority of stock transactions occur between stockholders. Often, a broker matches a buyer and seller using the services of one of the stock exchanges such as the NYSE or the NASDAQ. When Mary sells 100 shares of Starbucks stock to Carlos, the transaction does not affect Starbucks' balance sheet. Starbucks does not receive cash, and it issues no new shares. The only effect on Starbucks will be to replace Mary with Carlos on the corporate records as an owner of the 100 shares of stock.

Summary Problems for Your Review

PROBLEM

"If I purchase 100 shares of the outstanding stock of Google, I invest my money directly in that corporation. Google must record that event." Do you agree? Explain.

SOLUTION

Stockholders invest directly in a corporation only when the corporation originally issues the stock. For example, Google may issue 100,000 shares of stock at $30 per share, bringing in $3 million to the corporation. This is a transaction between the corporation and the stockholders. It affects the corporate financial position:

Cash $3,000,000   Stockholders' equity $3,000,000

Subsequently, an original stockholder (Kyung Sung) may sell 100 shares of that stock to another individual (Jane Soliman) for $50 per share. This is a private transaction. The corporation receives no cash. Of course, the corporation records the fact that Soliman now owns the 100 shares originally owned by Sung, but the corporate financial position is unchanged. Accounting focuses on the business entity. Private stock trades of the owners have no effect on the financial position of the entity.

PROBLEM

"One individual can be an owner, an employee, and a creditor of a corporation." Do you agree? Explain.

SOLUTION

The corporation enters contracts, hires employees, buys buildings, and conducts other business. The chairman of the board, the president, the other officers, and all the workers are employees of the corporation. Thus, Bill Gates could own some of the capital stock of Microsoft and also be an employee. Because money owed to employees for salaries is a liability, he could be an owner, an employee, and a creditor. Similarly, Carmen Smith could be an employee of a telephone company, a stockholder of the company, and also receive telephone services from the same company. Suppose she has earned wages that the company has not yet paid and she has not yet paid her current telephone bill. She is simultaneously an owner, employee, customer, creditor, and debtor of the company.

Stockholders and the Board of Directors

In sole proprietorships and partnerships, the owners are usually also managers. In contrast, corporate shareholders (that is, the owners) delegate responsibility for management of the company to professional managers. To oversee managers, the shareholders elect a **board of directors**, which is responsible for appointing and monitoring the managers, as shown in the following diagram:

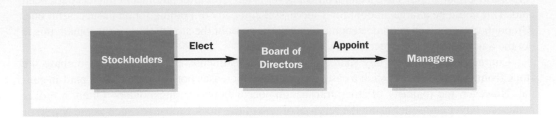

Why is the separation of ownership and management in a corporation desirable? With such separation, stockholders can invest resources but do not need to devote time to managing, and the company can select managers for their managerial skills, not their ability to invest large sums of money in the firm. The board of directors is the link between stockholders and managers. The board's duty is to ensure that managers act in the best interests of shareholders. In some of the business scandals of the last decade, shareholders have accused boards of not fulfilling this responsibility and thereby causing shareholders to lose billions of dollars.

When boards of directors do their duty in monitoring management, the corporate form of organization has proved to be very effective. When such monitoring fails, management may line its own pockets at the expense of shareholders. One problem that may cause such failure is when management has too much influence on the election of board members, generally by nominating a slate of candidates beholden to management. Additionally, in the United States it has been common for the top manager (**chief executive officer**, or **CEO**) to also serve as chairman of the board. It is difficult for the chairman of the board to monitor the CEO when they are the same person. In the UK and much of the rest of Europe it is common for the chairman of the board to be an independent director rather than a member of management, and this practice is becoming more common in the United States. Often, other top managers of the company, such as the president, financial vice president, and marketing vice president, are also members of the board of directors. However, it is increasingly common for these company officers to attend board meetings as needed but not to serve as directors.

Independent members of a board often include CEOs and presidents of other corporations, university presidents and professors, attorneys, and community representatives. For example, the nine-member board of Starbucks in 2009 included CEO and Board Chair Howard Schultz, three retired executives from companies other than Starbucks, the current CEO of a major company, an investment banker, a mutual fund president, a venture capitalist, and a foundation president. Although boards once often had 15–20 members, many companies are moving toward having smaller boards of directors that include fewer members of the company's management team.

Regulation of Financial Reporting

Financial statements are the result of a measurement process that rests on a set of principles. If every accountant used a different set of measurement rules, investors would find it difficult to use and compare financial statements. For example, consider the recording of an asset such as a machine on the balance sheet. If one accountant listed the purchase cost, another the amount for which the company could sell the used machine, and others listed various other amounts, the readers of financial statements would be confused. It would be as if each accountant were speaking a different language. Therefore, accountants have agreed to apply a common set of measurement principles—that is, a common language—to report information on financial statements.

Generally Accepted Accounting Principles

Generally accepted accounting principles (GAAP) is the term that applies to all the broad concepts and detailed practices to be followed in preparing and distributing financial statements. There are two primary sets of GAAP. Companies reporting in more than 100 countries around the world, including all European Union countries, use **International Financial Reporting Standards (IFRS)**. U.S. companies use **Financial Accounting Standards**, usually referred to as **U.S. GAAP**. Each set of standards contains conventions, rules, and procedures that determine acceptable accounting practices. The standards are identical on most significant issues. However, there are a few conceptual differences and more differences in specific measurement details. Authorities are working to eliminate (or at least minimize) the differences in standards between IFRS and U.S. GAAP statements, but many differences are likely to remain in the near future.

Until recently, all companies with stock traded on U.S. stock exchanges had to report using U.S. GAAP or to prepare a report detailing the differences between their statements and ones prepared under U.S. GAAP. However, as of 2010, regulators in the United States allow foreign companies listed on U.S. exchanges to use IFRS for their financial statements, but companies based in the United States must still use U.S. GAAP. Many accountants believe that U.S. regulators will allow all companies to use IFRS within a few years. Why? Because they believe that global capital markets will function more efficiently if all companies issue financial statements based on the same GAAP.

In this book we focus first on reporting regulations under U.S. GAAP, and then we point out differences between U.S. GAAP and IFRS requirements when they are significant. Where we do not specifically mention the standards, there are no significant differences between IFRS and U.S. GAAP requirements. Many of the differences in details are beyond the scope of this text, but when a difference affects issues being discussed, we will point out the differences. But before exploring the standards, let's look more closely at the bodies that set the standards.

Standard Setting Bodies

Until recently most accounting standards were set country by country. However, forces ranging from the creation of the European Union to the emergence of global financial markets have resulted in most companies adopting one of the two main competing sets of standards—U. S. GAAP or IFRS.

The **Financial Accounting Standards Board (FASB)** has been responsible for establishing U.S. GAAP since 1973. The FASB is an independent entity within the private sector consisting of five individuals who work full-time with a staff to support them. A mandatory fee to all public companies and sales of publications provide the FASB's annual budget of more than $33 million. Between 1973 and 2009 the FASB issued 168 Financial Accounting Standards, and in 2009 it compiled all standards and other elements of U.S. GAAP into a single searchable database, **FASB Financial Standards Codification**. The Codification classifies U.S. GAAP by topic to make it easy to research financial reporting issues.

The U.S. Congress has charged the Securities and Exchange Commission (SEC) with the ultimate responsibility for specifying GAAP for companies whose stock is held by the general investing public. However, the SEC has formally delegated much rule-making power to the FASB. This public sector–private sector authority relationship can be sketched as follows:

International Financial Reporting Standards (IFRS)
The set of GAAP that applies to companies reporting in more than 100 countries around the world.

Financial Accounting Standards (U.S. GAAP)
The set of GAAP that applies to financial reporting in the United States.

Financial Accounting Standards Board (FASB)
The private sector body that is responsible for establishing GAAP in the United States.

FASB Financial Standards Codification
A compilation of all standards and other elements of U.S. GAAP into a single searchable database that is organized by topic to make it easy to research financial reporting issues.

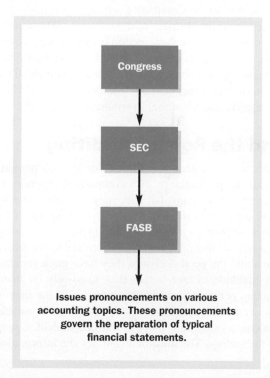

Issues pronouncements on various accounting topics. These pronouncements govern the preparation of typical financial statements.

Take a careful look at this three-tiered structure. Note that Congress can overrule both the SEC and the FASB, and the SEC can overrule the FASB. The FASB and the SEC work closely together and seldom have public disagreements. However, on occasion Congress has overruled FASB decisions. The accounting for stock options is an example of this political interplay. In the 1990s, Congress heeded the pleas of constituents and donors and threatened to overrule the FASB if it required companies to recognize stock options granted to managers as an expense of doing business. This caused the FASB to rescind such a proposed requirement and issue a standard that allowed companies flexibility in accounting for stock options. In 2001 and 2002, the FASB received much criticism for going along with the wishes of Congress. In 2004, after the financial turmoil of the early 2000s and with support from the SEC, the FASB was able to assert its original plan and require companies to record an expense for stock options. Although you may not understand the accounting for stock options at this point, you can see from the example that the setting of accounting principles in the United States (and, indeed, globally) is a complex political process involving heavy interactions among the affected parties: public regulators (Congress and the SEC), private regulators (FASB), companies, those in the public accounting profession, representatives of investors, and other interested groups and lobbyists. GAAP is not a set of arcane rules of interest only to accountants. GAAP can affect many people and companies, and it is an important part of a country's public policy.

A prime example of accounting's effect on public policy is the concern that mark-to-market accounting—listing some financial assets on the balance sheet at their market values rather than their cost—may have contributed to the failure or near failure of many banks in 2008 and 2009. Under much political pressure, the FASB in April of 2009 revised its rules for mark-to-market accounting, although it did not rescind the rule, as advocated by some lobbyists and politicians.

International Accounting
Standards Board (IASB)

An international body established to develop, in the public interest, a single set of high-quality, understandable, and enforceable global accounting standards.

The **International Accounting Standards Board (IASB)**, which was established in 2001 (as successor to the International Accounting Standards Committee) "to develop, in the public interest, a single set of high quality, understandable and enforceable global accounting standards," sets International Financial Reporting Standards (IFRS). The IASB has 16 members who represent a diversity of geographic and professional backgrounds. Originally compliance with international accounting standards was voluntary in most countries, but a growing number of countries are mandating the use of IFRS. A significant step for international accounting standards was the required use of IFRS by companies in the European Union for financial statements prepared after 2005. By 2009 nearly 40% of the 500 largest companies in the world used IFRS, and this will reach 60% by 2015 (and would be over 90% if the United States were to adopt IFRS).

The motivation for this conformity movement lies in the explosive growth of international commerce. Increasingly, investors commit their money worldwide either as individuals or through retirement accounts or mutual funds. Companies rely on international capital to finance their growth. In early 2009, the NYSE listed shares of more than 3,600 companies, including 415 non-U.S. companies from 45 countries. This phenomenon is even more pronounced in London where approximately two-thirds of the market value of traded firms on the London Stock Exchange are non-U.K. firms. Examples of major multinational firms that now publish their financial statements in conformity with international accounting standards are Allianz (Germany), Nestlé (Switzerland), Nokia (Finland), and Shanghai Petrochemical (China).

Credibility and the Role of Auditing

OBJECTIVE 8

Describe auditing and how it enhances the value of financial information.

auditor

A person who examines the information used by managers to prepare the financial statements and attests to the credibility of those statements.

The separation of owners and managers in a corporation creates potential problems in getting truthful information about the performance of a company. Corporate managers have the best access to information about the company, but they may also have incentives to make the company's performance look better than it really is. Perhaps doing so will make it easier to raise money to open new stores, or perhaps it would lead to increases in managers' compensation. In addition, managers often believe that company conditions are better than they really are because managers are optimistic about the good decisions they have made and the plans they are implementing. The problem shareholders face is that they must rely on managers to tell the truth, because shareholders cannot personally see what is going on in the firm.

One way to solve this credibility problem is to introduce an honorable, expert third party. In the area of financial statements this third party is an independent registered public accounting firm, commonly called the auditor. The **auditor** examines the information that managers use to prepare the financial statements and provides assurances about the credibility of those statements. On seeing the auditor's assurance that the financial statements fairly present a company's economic circumstances, shareholders and potential shareholders can feel more comfortable about using the information to guide their investing activity.

The Certified Public Accountant and the Auditor's Opinion

The desire for third-party assurance about the credibility of financial statements gave rise naturally to a profession dedicated to that purpose. Providing credibility requires individuals who have both the technical knowledge to assess financial statements and the integrity and independence to assure that they will honestly tell shareholders and other interested parties if management has not produced reliable financial statements. Such audit professionals are called certified public accountants (CPAs) in many countries, including the United States, and chartered accountants (CAs) in many others, including most British Commonwealth countries. They are part of a profession of **public accountants** who offer services to the general public on a fee basis.

In the United States, each state has a Board of Accountancy that sets standards of both knowledge and integrity that public accountants must meet to be licensed as a **certified public accountant (CPA)**. Only CPAs have the right to issue official opinions on financial statements in the United States. To assess management's financial disclosures, CPAs conduct an **audit**—an examination of a company's transactions and the resulting financial statements. The

public accountants
Accountants who offer services to the general public on a fee basis.

certified public accountant (CPA)
In the United States, a person earns this designation by meeting standards of both knowledge and integrity set by a State Board of Accountancy. Only CPAs can issue official opinions on financial statements in the United States.

audit
An examination of a company's transactions and the resulting financial statements.

EXHIBIT 1-10

Report of Independent Auditors

REPORT OF INDEPENDENT REGISTERED PUBLIC ACCOUNTING FIRM

To the Board of Directors and Shareholders of Starbucks Corporation
Seattle, Washington

We have audited the accompanying consolidated balance sheets of Starbucks Corporation and subsidiaries (the "Company") as of September 28, 2008 and September 30, 2007, and the related consolidated statements of earnings, shareholders' equity, and cash flows for each of the three years in the period ended September 28, 2008. These financial statements are the responsibility of the Company's management. Our responsibility is to express an opinion on these financial statements based on our audits.

We conducted our audits in accordance with the standards of the Public Company Accounting Oversight Board (United States). Those standards require that we plan and perform the audit to obtain reasonable assurance about whether the financial statements are free of material misstatement. An audit includes examining, on a test basis, evidence supporting the amounts and disclosures in the financial statements. An audit also includes assessing the accounting principles used and significant estimates made by management, as well as evaluating the overall financial statement presentation. We believe that our audits provide a reasonable basis for our opinion.

In our opinion, such consolidated financial statements present fairly, in all material respects, the financial position of Starbucks Corporation and subsidiaries as of September 28, 2008 and September 30, 2007, and the results of their operations and their cash flows for each of the three years in the period ended September 28, 2008, in conformity with accounting principles generally accepted in the United States of America.

As discussed in Note 1 to the consolidated financial statements, on October 1, 2006, the Company changed its method of accounting for conditional asset retirement obligations upon adoption of Financial Accounting Standards Board Interpretation No. 47, "Accounting for Conditional Asset Retirement Obligations - an interpretation of FASB Statement No. 143".

We have also audited, in accordance with the standards of the Public Company Accounting Oversight Board (United States), the Company's internal control over financial reporting as of September 28, 2008, based on criteria established in Internal Control—Integrated Framework issued by the Committee of Sponsoring Organizations of the Treadway Commission and our report dated November 24, 2008 expressed an unqualified opinion on the Company's internal control over financial reporting.

/s/ DELOITTE & TOUCHE LLP
Seattle, Washington
November 24, 2008

**auditor's opinion
(independent opinion)**
A report describing the scope and results of an audit. Companies include the opinion with the financial statements in their annual reports.

auditor's opinion (also called an **independent opinion**) describes the scope and results of the audit, and companies include the opinion with the financial statements in their annual reports and 10-K filings. Auditors use a standard phrasing for their opinions, as illustrated by the opinion rendered by a large CPA firm, Deloitte & Touche LLP, for Starbucks Corporation that appears in Exhibit 1-10. Some phrases in this opinion may be unfamiliar now, but they will become more clear as you read further. For now, reflect on the fact that auditors do not prepare a company's financial statements. Instead, the auditor's opinion is the public accountant's judgment about whether the financial statements prepared by management fairly present economic reality.

The Accounting Profession

To understand auditors and auditors' opinions, you need to know something about the accounting profession. There are many ways to classify accountants, but the easiest and most common way is to divide them into public and private accountants. We already learned that public accountants offer services to the general public for a fee. All other accountants would be **private accountants**. This category consists not only of those individuals who work for businesses, but also of those who work for government agencies, including the Internal Revenue Service (IRS), and other nonprofit organizations.

private accountants
Accountants who work for businesses, government agencies, and other nonprofit organizations.

Public Accounting Firms

Public accountants work for firms that vary in size and in the type of accounting services they perform. There are small sole proprietorships and partnerships that focus entirely on income tax reporting and bookkeeping services for clients who are not equipped to do their own accounting. Other small- to medium-sized firms provide some audit services, as well, and generally serve local, regional, or national clients. There are also a handful of large firms with more than 2,000 partners and offices located throughout the world. Such enormous firms are necessary because their clients also tend to be enormous. For instance, one large CPA firm reported that its annual audit of one client takes the equivalent of 72 accountants working a full year. Another client has 300 separate corporate entities in 40 countries that it must ultimately consolidate into one set of overall financial statements.

The four largest international public accounting firms are as follows:

- Deloitte Touche Tohmatsu
- Ernst & Young
- KPMG
- PricewaterhouseCoopers

These four firms audit more than 95% of the companies listed on the NYSE. They have annual billings in excess of a $1 billion each.

Audit Regulation

**American Institute of
Certified Public Accountants
(AICPA)**
The principal professional association in the private sector that regulates the quality of the public accounting profession.

Sarbanes-Oxley Act
The source of most government regulation of the accounting profession in the United States.

**Public Company Accounting
Oversight Board (PCAOB)**
An agency that regulates many aspects of public accounting and sets standards for audit procedures.

Until recently, the U.S. audit profession regulated itself through the **American Institute of Certified Public Accountants (AICPA)**, a professional association of CPAs. The AICPA has counterparts in other parts of the world, such as the Institute of Chartered Accountants in England and Wales (ICAEW) and the Association of Chartered Certified Accountants (ACCA). The International Auditing and Assurance Standards Board, established by the International Federation of Accountants, is working to standardize audit regulation around the globe, but regulation of auditing continues to differ significantly across countries. We will focus just on the situation in the United States.

Most government regulation of the accounting profession in the United States stems from the **Sarbanes-Oxley Act** passed in 2002. Among other things, the act (1) established the **Public Company Accounting Oversight Board (PCAOB)** with powers to regulate many aspects of public accounting and to set standards for audit procedures; (2) prohibited public accounting firms from providing to audit clients certain nonaudit services, such as financial information systems design and implementation and internal audit outsourcing services; and (3) required rotation every five years of the lead audit or coordinating partner and the reviewing partner on an audit. All accounting firms that audit companies with publicly-traded stock in the United States must register with the PCAOB. These **registered public accounting firms** numbered nearly 2,200 in October 2009. The act also regulated corporate governance by requiring boards of publicly held companies to appoint an audit committee composed only of "independent" directors, requiring CEOs and chief financial officers (CFOs) to personally sign a statement taking responsibility for their companies' financial statements, and increasing the criminal penalties for knowingly misreporting financial information.

Despite the government's growing role, the AICPA remains a force in accounting regulation. It regulates entry to the accounting profession by requiring new accountants to (1) have adequate technical knowledge and know how to apply it, and (2) adhere to standards of integrity and independence. To ensure that CPAs have the necessary technical knowledge, the AICPA administers and grades a national examination. The 14-hour, 4-part, computer-based CPA examination covers auditing and attestation, financial accounting and reporting, regulation, and business environment and concepts. Each section of the exam generally has a pass rate of less than 50%, and less than 20% of the candidates pass all four parts in their first attempt.

To ensure proper application of a CPA's technical knowledge, the Public Company Accounting Oversight Board issues generally accepted auditing standards (GAAS). These standards prescribe the minimum steps that an auditor must take in examining the transactions and financial statements and issuing an auditor's opinion. Following GAAS ensures a reasonable chance of discovering any errors or omissions, intentional or unintentional, in a company's financial statements. However, in several well-publicized cases in the last decade, auditors were accused of failure to discover some accounting irregularities in companies such as WorldCom, Tyco, Fannie Mae, Washington Mutual, and others.

Professional Ethics

Auditors have a professional obligation to truthfully report their findings to the public. This is why we call them *public* accountants. Meeting this obligation requires accountants to act with integrity and be independent of management's influence. To help achieve this, members of the AICPA (and many other such organizations globally) must abide by a code of professional conduct. Surveys of public attitudes toward CPAs have consistently ranked the accounting profession as having high ethical standards. However, the corporate scandals in the last decade have caused investors to question some auditors' integrity and independence, especially their independence. This led to additional government regulation of auditor independence and a revision of the AICPA's independence and integrity standards. Exhibit 1-11 presents the major requirements of those standards.

The emphasis on ethics extends beyond public accounting. Various professional accounting organizations and state regulatory bodies have procedures for reviewing behavior alleged to violate codes of professional conduct and imposing appropriate penalties. For example, the Institute of Management Accountants (IMA) and the Association of Government Accountants (AGA) each has a code of ethics that its members must meet to retain their membership.

Beyond codes of ethics or codes of conduct, a major influence on the ethical decisions of employees is the "tone at the top." Complete integrity and outspoken support for ethical standards by senior managers is a great motivator of ethical behavior in any organization. Ultimately, ensuring ethical behavior begins with hiring employees who value ethical issues when making decisions.

High ethical standards by accountants and business executives are also important for a healthy economy. Even if only a few let power and greed drive them to ethically dubious actions, it affects the trust people put in companies. The 2008–2009 recession exposed mortgage frauds, investment schemes, and excessive executive compensation. While most companies maintained high ethical standards, enough violated them to create a distrust that negatively affected the entire world economy.

Some managers and accountants justify ethical lapses with statements such as "Everyone else is doing it, why shouldn't I?" However, the vast majority of successful accountants and managers recognize the ethical dimensions of their decisions and act with absolute integrity. Those who do not may get most of the publicity, but there has also been acclaim for those responsible for revealing the problems, as indicated in the Business First box on page 43.

registered public accounting firm
An accounting firm that registers with the PCAOB and therefore is allowed to audit companies with publicly-traded stock in the United States.

OBJECTIVE 9
Evaluate the role of ethics in the accounting process.

EXHIBIT 1-11

AICPA Code of Professional Conduct, Independence, Integrity, and Objectivity Standards: Excerpted and Paraphrased*

I. INDEPENDENCE: The standards indicate that independence will be impaired if

- During the period of the professional engagement a covered member a) had or was committed to acquire any direct or material indirect financial interest in the client, b) was a trustee of any trust or executor or administrator of any estate if such trust or estate had or was committed to acquire any direct or material indirect financial interest in the client, c) had a joint, closely held investment that was material to the covered member, or d) except as specifically permitted, had any loan to or from the client, any officer or director of the client, or any individual owning 10% or more of the client's outstanding equity securities or other ownership interests.
- During the period of the professional engagement, a partner or professional employee of the firm, his or her immediate family, or any group of such persons acting together owned more than 5% of a client's outstanding equity securities or other ownership interests.
- During the period covered by the financial statements or during the period of the professional engagement, a partner or professional employee of the firm was simultaneously associated with the client as a a) director, officer, or employee, or in any capacity equivalent to that of a member of management; b) promoter, underwriter, or voting trustee; or c) trustee for any pension or profit-sharing trust of the client.

II. INTEGRITY AND OBJECTIVITY: The standards indicate that integrity will be impaired by

- *Knowing misrepresentations in the preparation of financial statements or records.* A member shall be considered to have knowingly misrepresented facts when he or she knowingly a) makes, or permits or directs another to make, materially false and misleading entries in an entity's financial statements or records; or b) fails to correct an entity's financial statements or records that are materially false and misleading when he or she has the authority to record an entry; or c) signs, or permits or directs another to sign, a document containing materially false and misleading information.
- *Conflicts of interest.* A conflict of interest may occur if a member performs a professional service for a client or employer and the member or his or her firm has a relationship with another person, entity, product, or service that could, in the member's professional judgment, be viewed by the client, employer, or other appropriate parties as impairing the member's objectivity.

*For more details see http://www.aicpa.org/about/code/index.html.

Career Opportunities for Accountants

Most of you who read this book will not become accountants. You are or will be intelligent consumers of accounting information in your business and personal lives. Because accounting cuts across all management functions, including purchasing, manufacturing, wholesaling, retailing, and a variety of marketing and transportation activities, it provides an excellent background for almost any manager.

Knowledge of accounting is especially important for finance professionals. After many of the problems in the economy, a *BusinessWeek* article indicated that "even professional money managers are scared that they don't know enough accounting." However, accounting's value is not restricted to financial managers. Managers who want to move up in the management structure of a company need to know accounting. Surveys have ranked accounting as the most important business school course for future managers. A major business periodical reported that "more CEOs started out in finance or accounting than in any other area." Accounting is the language of business, and it is hard to succeed without speaking the language.

Accounting is an especially good entry position in a company. Because accountants are responsible for collecting and interpreting financial information about the entire company, they develop detailed knowledge about various parts of a company and form close relationships with

BUSINESS FIRST

ETHICS, ACCOUNTING, AND WHISTLE BLOWERS

Companies often rely on accountants to safeguard the ethics of the company. Accountants have a special responsibility to ensure that managers act with integrity and that the information disclosed to customers, suppliers, regulators, and the public is accurate. If accountants do not take this responsibility seriously, or if the company ignores the accountants' reports, bad consequences can follow. Just ask WorldCom or Enron. In both companies, an accountant decided to be a "whistle blower," one who reports wrongdoings to his or her supervisor. The WorldCom and Enron whistle blowers became Persons of the Year in *Time* magazine.

Cynthia Cooper, Vice President of Internal Audit for WorldCom, told the company's board of directors that fraudulent accounting entries had turned a $662 million loss into a $2.4 billion profit. This disclosure led to additional discoveries totaling $9 billion in erroneous accounting entries—the largest accounting fraud in history. Cooper was proud of WorldCom and highly committed to its success. Nevertheless, when she and her internal audit team discovered the unethical actions of superiors she admired, she did not hesitate to do the right thing. She saw no joy when CEO Bernie Ebbers and CFO Scott Sullivan were placed in handcuffs and led away. She simply applied what she had learned when she sat in the middle of the front row of seats in her accounting classes at Mississippi State University. Accountants ask hard questions, find the answers, and act with integrity. Being a whistle blower has not been easy for Cooper. She is a hero to some, a villain to others. However, regardless of the reaction of others, Cooper knows that she just did what any good accountant should do—no matter how painful it is to tell the truth. To read more about Cooper and WorldCom, see her book *Extraordinary Circumstances: Journey of a Corporate Whistleblower*.

At Enron, Sherron Watkins had a similar experience. An accounting major at the University of Texas at Austin, she started her career at Arthur Andersen. Then she went to work for Enron, eventually working directly for CFO Andrew Fastow. In her job she discovered the off-the-books liabilities that now have become famous. She first wrote a memo to CEO Kenneth Lay and had a personal meeting with him, explaining to him "an elaborate accounting hoax." Later she discovered that, rather than the hoax being investigated, her report had generated a memo from Enron's legal counsel titled "Confidential Employee Matter" that included the following: ". . . how to manage the case with the employee who made the sensitive report . . . . Texas law does not currently protect corporate whistle-blowers . . . ." In addition, her boss confiscated her hard drive and demoted her. She now regrets that she did not take the matter to higher levels, but she believed that Mr. Lay would take her allegations seriously. In the end, Watkins proved to be right. Although many at Enron knew what was happening, they ignored it. Watkins' accounting background made her both able to spot the irregularities and compelled to report them. Another Enron employee, Lynn Brewer, said that "hundreds, perhaps thousands, of people inside the company knew what was going on, and chose to look the other way." Watkins made the ethical decision and did not simply look the other way. As a result, she is a popular speaker on corporate governance, and Matt Lauer told her story on national television.

Sources: Amanda Ripley, "Whistle-Blower Cynthia Cooper," *Time.com*, February 4, 2008; Jennifer Reingold, "The Women of Enron: The Best Revenge," *Fast Company*, December 19, 2007; "The Party Crasher," *Time*, Jan. 30, 2002 to Jan. 6, 2003, pp. 52–56; "The Night Detective," *Time*, Jan. 30, 2002 to Jan. 6, 2003, pp. 45–50; M. Flynn, "Enron Insider Shares Her Insights," *Puget Sound Business Journal*, March 7–13, 2003, p. 50; Cynthia Cooper, *Extraordinary Circumstances: Journey of a Corporate Whistleblower*, Wiley, 2009.

key decision makers. Senior accountants or controllers in a corporation often become production or marketing executives. Why? Because they have acquired management skills through their dealings with a variety of managers. Others continue in the finance function to become vice-presidents of finance or CFOs. Exhibit 1-12 shows various potential career paths for those hired into entry-level accounting positions. Some accountants join a public accounting firm and reach partner after a series of promotions. Others join a business corporation or government agency and proceed up the ladder of success. Many others start in public accounting, even if they do not intend to stay for their entire careers. After being promoted once or twice in pubic accounting, they shift to a controller or treasurer position in government or industry, or even to a CFO position.

Accounting provides exciting career opportunities. It is a great training ground for future managers and executives. Accountants in public accounting firms perform work for many clients and encounter many different work experiences. Accountants in private companies work with managers throughout the organization and gain a broad understanding of the various functional

EXHIBIT 1-12

Common Accounting Career Paths

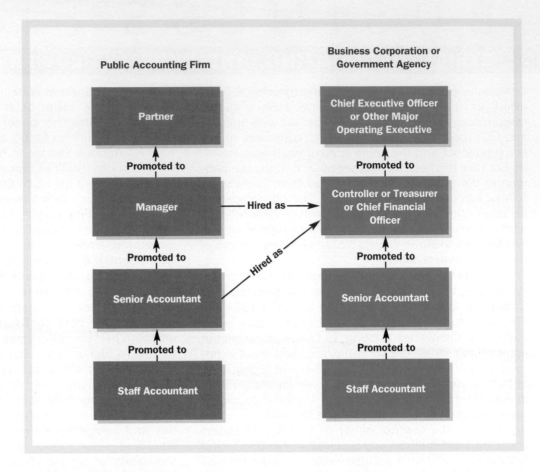

and product areas. In addition, accountants are well-rewarded. Beginning accountants in large public accounting firms earned about $50,000 a year in 2009—even more for those already holding a CPA. Top partners in the international accounting firms and CFOs at some of the largest corporations earn more than $1 million annually.

A Note on Nonprofit Organizations

The major focus of this book is on profit-seeking organizations, such as business firms. However, the fundamental accounting principles also apply to nonprofit organizations. Managers and accountants in hospitals, universities, government agencies, and other nonprofit organizations use financial statements. After all, such organizations must raise and spend money, prepare budgets, and judge financial performance. Some nonprofit organizations, such as the Red Cross or Girl Scouts, are as big as large corporations. Others, such as Bainbridge Island Land Trust or Northwest Harvest Food Bank, serve a specific local interest. There is a growing pressure on nonprofit organizations to disclose financial information to the public. In the United States, the Governmental Accounting Standards Board (GASB) regulates disclosures for governmental organizations, and the FASB regulates financial reporting for other nonprofit organizations.

Highlights to Remember

1 **Explain how accounting information assists in making decisions.** Financial statements provide information to help managers, creditors, and owners of all types of organizations make decisions. The balance sheet (or statement of financial position) provides a "snapshot" of the financial position of an organization at any instant. That is, it answers the basic question, "Where are we?"

2 **Describe the components of the balance sheet.** The balance sheet equation is Assets = Liabilities + Owners' Equity. This equation must always be in balance. The balance sheet presents the balances of the components of Assets, Liabilities, and Owners' Equity at a specific

point in time. Assets are things a company owns, liabilities are what it owes, and owners' equity is the owners' claims on assets less liabilities.

3 **Analyze business transactions and relate them to changes in the balance sheet.** Transaction analysis is the heart of accounting. A transaction is any event that both affects the financial position of an entity and can be reliably recorded in money terms. For each transaction, an accountant must determine what accounts the transaction affects and the amount to record.

4 **Prepare a balance sheet from transactions data.** Accountants can prepare a balance sheet at any time from the detailed transactions in the balance sheet equation. It is the sum of the beginning balance and the changes caused by the transactions for every balance sheet account. However, accountants generally prepare balance sheets only when needed by managers or at the end of each quarter for reporting to the public.

5 **Compare the features of sole proprietorships, partnerships, and corporations.** Sole proprietorships and partnerships usually have owners who also act as managers. In corporations, shareholders delegate management of the firm to professional managers. The shareholders elect a board of directors, which in turn appoints and monitors the managers. Owners of corporations have limited liability; their personal assets are not at risk. Corporations are the most important form of business ownership because corporations conduct a majority of the world's business.

6 **Identify how the owners' equity section in a corporate balance sheet differs from that in a sole proprietorship or a partnership.** The ownership equity of a corporation is usually called stockholders' equity. It initially takes the form of common stock at par value (or stated value) plus additional paid-in capital.

7 **Explain the regulation of financial reporting, including differences between U.S. GAAP and IFRS.** Financial statements throughout the world must adhere to generally accepted accounting principles (GAAP). There are two primary sets of GAAP. Companies in most countries follow the GAAP defined by International Financial Reporting Standards (IFRS), which are set by the International Accounting Standards Board (IASB). In contrast, companies in the United States follow U.S. GAAP. The SEC is responsible for setting U.S. GAAP, and it has delegated this responsibility to the Financial Accounting Standards Board (FASB). The AICPA administers the CPA exam that ensures that professional accountants meet minimum qualification standards. In addition, the Public Company Accounting Oversight Board regulates the accounting profession and sets auditing standards.

8 **Describe auditing and how it enhances the value of financial information.** Separation of ownership from management in corporations creates a demand for auditing, a third-party examination of the financial statements. Auditors evaluate the record-keeping system of the firm and test specific transactions and account balances to provide assurance that the balances fairly reflect the financial position and performance of the company.

9 **Evaluate the role of ethics in the accounting process.** Ethical behavior is critically important in professional activities such as accounting. In public accounting, the value of an audit is directly linked to the credibility of the auditor as an ethical, independent professional who is qualified to evaluate the financial statements of the firm and is also reliably committed to disclosing problems or concerns uncovered in the evaluation.

Accounting Vocabulary

account, p. 25
account payable, p. 27
accounting, p. 18
additional paid-in capital,
   p. 33
American Institute of Certified
   Public Accountants
   (AICPA), p. 40
annual report, p. 21
assets, p. 22
audit, p. 39

auditor, p. 38
auditor's opinion, p. 40
balance sheet, p. 22
balance sheet equation, p. 22
board of directors, p. 36
certified public accountant
   (CPA), p. 39
chief executive officer
   (CEO), p. 36
common stock, p. 34
common stockholders, p. 35

compound entry, p. 27
corporation, p. 31
creditor, p. 28
entity, p. 24
FASB Financial Standards
   Codification, p. 37
financial accounting, p. 18
Financial Accounting
   Standards (U.S.
   GAAP), p. 37

MyAccountingLab

Assignment Material

The assignment material for each chapter is divided into Questions, Critical Thinking Questions, Exercises, Problems, a Collaborative Learning Exercise, and three projects on Analyzing and Interpreting Financial Statements. One of these projects in each chapter involves analyzing Starbucks' financial statements, allowing students to develop more depth into the financial reporting of this one company. The assignment material contains problems based on fictitious companies and problems based on real-life situations. We hope our use of actual companies and news events enhances your interest in accounting.

We identify problems based on real companies by highlighting the name in blue. These problems underscore a major objective of this book: to increase your ability to read, understand, and use published financial reports and news articles. In later chapters, these problems provide the principal means of reviewing not only the immediate chapter but also the previous chapters.

Questions

1-1 Describe accounting.

1-2 "It's easier to learn accounting if you avoid real-world examples." Do you agree? Explain.

1-3 Give three examples of decisions where the decision maker is likely to use financial statements.

1-4 Give three examples of users of financial statements.

1-5 Briefly distinguish between financial accounting and management accounting.

1-6 Describe the balance sheet equation.

1-7 "The balance sheet may be out of balance after some transactions, but it is never out of balance at the end of an accounting period." Do you agree? Explain.

1-8 "When a company buys inventory for cash, total assets do not change. However, when it buys inventory on open account, total assets increase." Explain.

1-9 Explain the difference between a note payable and an account payable.

1-10 List three differences between a corporation and a sole proprietorship or a partnership.

1-11 Explain the meaning of limited liability.

1-12 Why does this book emphasize the corporation instead of the proprietorship or the partnership?

1-13 "International companies with Ltd. or S.A. after their name are essentially the same in organizational form as U.S. companies with Corp. after their name." Do you agree? Explain.

1-14 "The idea of par value is insignificant." Explain.

1-15 Explain the relationship between the board of directors and top management of a company.

1-16 How is GAAP set in the United States? How is it set internationally?

1-17 "All companies with stock traded on U.S. stock exchanges must issue financial statements that conform to U.S. GAAP." Do you agree? Explain.

1-18 What gives value to an audit?

1-19 What is a CPA, and how does someone become one? What is a CA?

1-20 What are the most important ethical standards for accountants?

1-21 "The accounting systems described in this book apply to corporations and are not appropriate for nonprofit organizations." Do you agree? Explain.

Critical Thinking Questions

1-22 Double-Entry Accounting
The accounting process in use today is typically called "double-entry" bookkeeping. Discuss the meaning and possible importance of this name.

1-23 Accountants as Historians
Critics sometimes refer to accountants as historians and do not mean it kindly. In what sense are accountants historians, and do you believe this is a compliment or a criticism?

1-24 The Corporation
Some historians were arguing over the most important innovation in the history of business. Most thought of things and processes such as the railroad, the automobile, the printing press, the telephone, television, or more recently, the computer chip, fiber-optic cable, or even the Internet. One person argued that the really important innovation was the corporation. How would this person argue for this idea? What role did accounting play in the rise of the corporation?

1-25 The Auditor's Opinion
In reviewing the annual report of a company in which you might invest, you noted that you did not recognize the name of the audit firm that signed the audit opinion. What questions would this raise in your mind, and how might you resolve them?

Exercises

1-26 The Balance Sheet Equation
El Paso Company reported total assets of $7 million and total liabilities of $3 million at the end of 20X0.

1. Construct the balance sheet equation for El Paso Company at the end of 20X0 and include the correct amount for owners' equity.
2. Suppose that during January 20X1 El Paso borrowed $1 million from Wells Fargo. How would this affect El Paso's assets, liabilities, and owners' equity?

1-27 Describing Underlying Transactions
Sokol's Furniture Company, which was recently formed, is engaging in some preliminary transactions before beginning full-scale operations for retailing household furnishings. The balances of each item in the company's accounting equation are given next for May 1 and for each of the next 9 business days.

	Cash	Furniture Inventory	Store Fixtures	Accounts Payable	Owners' Equity
May 1	$ 6,000	$18,000	$2,000	$ 4,000	$22,000
2	12,000	18,000	2,000	4,000	28,000
3	12,000	18,000	6,000	4,000	32,000
4	9,000	21,000	6,000	4,000	32,000
5	9,000	27,000	6,000	10,000	32,000
6	12,000	27,000	3,000	10,000	32,000
7	7,000	27,000	9,000	11,000	32,000
8	5,000	27,000	9,000	9,000	32,000
9	5,000	26,600	9,000	8,600	32,000
10	3,000	26,600	9,000	8,600	30,000

State briefly what you think took place on each of the 9 days beginning May 2, assuming that only one transaction occurred each day.

1-28 Describing Underlying Transactions
The balances of each item in Brisbane Company's accounting equation are given next for November 1 and for each of the next 7 business days.

	Cash	Computer Inventory	Store Fixtures	Accounts Payable	Owners' Equity
Nov. 1	$5,000	$ 9,000	$ 7,500	$5,500	$16,000
2	5,000	9,000	10,000	8,000	16,000
3	3,000	9,000	10,000	8,000	14,000
4	3,000	4,000	10,000	3,000	14,000
5	3,000	11,000	10,000	3,000	21,000
8	2,500	11,000	10,000	2,500	21,000
9	1,500	11,000	13,500	5,000	21,000
10	1,500	11,000	13,200	4,700	21,000

State briefly what you think took place on each of the 7 days beginning November 2, assuming that only one transaction occurred each day.

1-29 Prepare Balance Sheet

Atlanta Corporation's balance sheet at March 30, 20X1, contained only the following items (arranged here in random order):

Cash	$14,000	Accounts payable	$ 8,000
Notes payable	10,000	Furniture and fixtures	3,000
Merchandise inventory	40,000	Long-term debt payable	12,000
Paid-in capital	80,000	Building	24,000
Land	14,000	Machinery and equipment	15,000

On March 31, 20X1, these transactions and events took place:

1. Purchased merchandise on account, $4,000
2. Sold at cost for $1,000 cash some furniture that was not needed
3. Issued additional capital stock for machinery and equipment valued at $12,000
4. Purchased land for $25,000, of which $10,000 was paid in cash, the remaining being represented by a 5-year note (long-term debt)
5. The building was valued by professional appraisers at $43,000

Prepare in good form a balance sheet for March 31, 20X1, showing supporting computations for all new amounts.

1-30 Prepare Balance Sheet

Liverpool Company's balance sheet at November 29, 20X1, contained only the following items (arranged here in random order):

Paid-in capital	£200,000	Machinery and equipment	£ 20,000
Notes payable	21,000	Furniture and fixtures	8,000
Cash	22,000	Land	41,000
Accounts payable	16,000	Building	241,000
Merchandise inventory	29,000	Long-term debt payable	124,000

On the following day, November 30, these transactions and events occurred:

1. Purchased machinery and equipment for £13,000, paying £3,000 in cash and signing a 90-day note for the balance
2. Paid £7,000 on accounts payable

3. Sold some land that was not needed for cash of £6,000, which was the Liverpool Company's acquisition cost of the land
4. The remaining land was valued at £240,000 by professional appraisers
5. Issued capital stock as payment for £23,000 of the long-term debt, that is, debt due beyond 1 year

Prepare in good form a balance sheet for November 30, 20X1, showing supporting computations for all new amounts.

1-31 Balance Sheet

General Electric (GE) is one of the largest companies in the world with sales of more than $122 billion. The company's balance sheet on January 1, 2009, had total assets of $798 billion and stockholders' equity (called shareowners' equity by GE) of $105 billion.

1. Compute GE's total liabilities on January 1, 2009.
2. As of January 1, 2009, GE had issued 10,536,897,000 shares of common stock. Assume a par value of $.07 per share. Compute the balance in the account, Common Stock, Par Value on GE's balance sheet.

Problems

MyAccountingLab

1-32 Analysis of Transactions

Use the format of Exhibit 1-2 (p. 26) to analyze the following transactions for April of McLean Services, Inc. Then prepare a balance sheet as of April 30, 20X1. McLean Services was founded on April 1.

1. Issued 1,000 shares of common stock for cash, $50,000
2. Issued 500 shares of common stock for equipment, $20,000
3. Borrowed cash, signing a note payable for $35,000
4. Purchased equipment for cash, $33,000
5. Purchased office furniture on account, $10,000
6. Disbursed cash on account (to reduce the account payable), $4,000
7. Sold equipment for cash, $8,000, an amount equal to its cost
8. Discovered that the most prominent competitor in the area was bankrupt and was closing its doors on April 30

1-33 Analysis of Transactions

Consider the following January transactions:

1. On January 1, 20X1, three persons, Langdon, Metzel, and Nguen, formed LMN Corporation. LMN is a wholesale distributor of electronic equipment. The company issued 10,000 shares of common stock ($1 par value) to each of the three investors for $10 cash per share. Use two stockholders' equity accounts: Capital Stock (at par) and Additional Paid-in Capital.
2. LMN acquired merchandise inventory of $95,000 for cash.
3. LMN acquired merchandise inventory of $85,000 on open account.
4. LMN returned for full credit unsatisfactory merchandise that cost $11,000 in transaction 3.
5. LMN acquired equipment of $40,000 for a cash down payment of $10,000, plus a 3-month promissory note of $30,000.
6. As a favor, LMN sells equipment of $4,000 to a business neighbor for cash. The equipment had cost $4,000.
7. LMN pays $18,000 on the account described in transaction 3.
8. LMN buys merchandise inventory of $100,000. The company pays one-half of the amount in cash, and owes one-half on open account.
9. Nguen sells one-half of his common stock to Quigley for $13 per share.

Required

1. By using a format similar to Exhibit 1-2, prepare an analysis showing the effects of January transactions on the financial position of LMN Corporation.
2. Prepare a balance sheet as of January 31, 20X1.

1-34 Analysis of Transactions

You began a business as a wholesaler of auto parts in Madrid. The following events have occurred:

1. On March 1, 20X1, you invested €75,000 cash in your new sole proprietorship, which you call Autopartes Madrid.
2. You acquired €10,000 inventory for cash.
3. You acquired €8,000 inventory on open account.
4. You acquired equipment for €15,000 in exchange for a €5,000 cash down payment and a €10,000 promissory note.
5. A large retail store, which you had hoped would be a big customer, discontinued operations.
6. You take tires home for your family car. Autopartes Madrid's inventory carried the tires at €600. (Regard this as taking part of your capital out of Autopartes Madrid.)
7. Parts that cost €300 in transaction 2 were damaged in shipment. You returned them and obtained a full cash refund.
8. Parts that cost €800 in transaction 3 were the wrong size. You returned them and obtained parts of the correct size in exchange.
9. Parts that cost €500 in transaction 3 had an unacceptable quality. You returned them and obtained full credit on your account.
10. You paid €1,000 on the promissory note.
11. You use your personal cash savings of €5,000 to acquire some equipment for Autopartes Madrid. You consider this to be an additional investment in your business.
12. You paid €3,000 on open account.
13. Two transmission manufacturers who are suppliers for Autopartes Madrid announced a 7% rise in prices, effective in 60 days.
14. You use your personal cash savings of €1,000 to acquire a new TV set for your family.
15. You exchange equipment that cost €4,000 in transaction 4 with another wholesaler. However, the equipment received, which is almost new, is smaller and is worth only €1,500. Therefore, the other wholesaler also pays you €2,500 in cash. (You recognize no gain or loss on this transaction.)

Required

1. By using Exhibit 1-2 (p. 26) as a guide, prepare an analysis of Autopartes Madrid's transactions for March. Confine your analysis to the effects on the financial position of Autopartes Madrid.
2. Prepare a balance sheet for Autopartes Madrid as of March 31, 20X1.

1-35 Analysis of Transactions

Freida Cruz, a recent graduate of a law school, was penniless on December 25, 20X0.

1. On December 26, Cruz inherited an enormous sum of money.
2. On December 27, she placed $55,000 in a business checking account for her unincorporated law practice.
3. On December 28, she purchased a home for a down payment of $100,000 plus a home mortgage payable of $250,000.
4. On December 28, Cruz agreed to rent a law office. She provided a $1,000 cash damage deposit (from her business cash), which will be fully refundable when she vacates the premises. This deposit is a business asset. She will make rental payments in advance on the first business day of each month. (The first payment of $700 is not to be made until January 2, 20X1.)
5. On December 28, Cruz purchased a computer for her law practice for $2,000 cash, plus a $3,000 promissory note due in 90 days.
6. On December 28, she purchased legal supplies for $1,000 on open account.
7. On December 28, Cruz purchased office furniture for her practice for $4,000 cash.
8. On December 29, Cruz hired a legal assistant receptionist for $380 per week. She was to report to work on January 2.
9. On December 30, Cruz's law practice lent $2,000 of cash in return for a 1-year note from Gloria See, a local candy store owner. See had indicated that she would spread the news about the new lawyer.

Required

1. Use the format demonstrated in Exhibit 1-2 (p. 26) to analyze the transactions of Freida Cruz, lawyer. To avoid crowding, put your numbers in thousands of dollars. Do not restrict yourself to the account titles in Exhibit 1-2.
2. Prepare a balance sheet as of December 31, 20X0.

1-36 Analysis of Transactions

Walgreens Company is a well-known drugstore chain. A condensed balance sheet for May 31, 2009, follows ($ in millions):

Assets		Liabilities and Stockholders' Equity	
Cash	$ 2,300	Accounts payable	$ 4,599
Inventories	6,891	Other liabilities	6,357
Property and other assets	15,952	Stockholders' equity	14,187
Total	$25,143	Total	$25,143

Use a format similar to Exhibit 1-2 (p. 26) to analyze the following transactions for the first two days of June ($ amounts are in millions). Then prepare a balance sheet as of June 2.

1. Issued 1,000,000 shares of common stock to employees for cash, $30
2. Issued 1,500,000 shares of common stock for the acquisition of $42 of special equipment from a supplier
3. Borrowed cash, signing a note payable for $13
4. Purchased equipment for cash, $18
5. Purchased inventories on account, $94
6. Disbursed cash on account (to reduce the accounts payable), $35
7. Sold for $2 cash some display equipment at original cost of $2

1-37 Analysis of Transactions

Nike, Inc., had the following condensed balance sheet on May 31, 2009 ($ in millions):

Assets		Liabilities and Owners' Equity	
Cash	$ 2,291		
Inventories	2,357		
Property, plant, and equipment	1,958	Total liabilities	$ 4,557
Other assets	6,644	Owners' equity	8,693
Total assets	$13,250	Total liabilities and owners' equity	$13,250

Suppose the following transactions occurred during the first 3 days of June ($ in millions):

1. Nike acquired inventories for cash, $28.
2. Nike acquired inventories on open account, $19.
3. Nike returned for full credit, $4, some unsatisfactory shoes that it acquired on open account in May.
4. Nike acquired $14 of equipment for a cash down payment of $3, plus a 2-year promissory note of $11.
5. To encourage wider displays, Nike sold some special store equipment to New York area stores for $40 cash. The equipment had cost $40 in the preceding month.
6. Clint Eastwood produced, directed, and starred in a movie. As a favor to a Nike executive, he agreed to display Nike shoes in a basketball scene. Nike paid no fee.

7. Nike disbursed cash to reduce accounts payable, $16.
8. Nike borrowed cash from a bank, $50.
9. Nike sold additional common stock for cash to new investors, $90.
10. The president of the company sold 5,000 shares of his personal holdings of Nike stock through his stockbroker.

Required

1. By using a format similar to Exhibit 1-2 (p. 26), prepare an analysis showing the effects of the June transactions on the financial position of Nike.
2. Prepare a balance sheet as of June 3.

1-38 Prepare Balance Sheet

Rebecca Gurley is a realtor. She buys and sells properties on her own account, and she also earns commissions as a real estate agent for buyers and sellers. Her business was organized on November 24, 20X1, as a sole proprietorship. Gurley also owns her own personal residence. Consider the following on November 30, 20X1:

1. Gurley owes $95,000 on a mortgage on some undeveloped land, which her business acquired for a total price of $180,000.
2. Gurley had spent $18,000 cash for a Century 21 real estate franchise. Century 21 is a national affiliation of independent real estate brokers. This franchise is an asset.
3. Gurley owes $100,000 on a personal mortgage on her residence, which she acquired on November 20, 20X3, for a total price of $180,000.
4. Gurley owes $3,800 on a personal charge account with Nordstrom's Department Store.
5. On November 28, Gurley hired Benjamin Goldstein as her first employee. He was to begin work on December 1. Gurley was pleased because Goldstein was one of the best real estate salesmen in the area. On November 29, Goldstein was killed in an automobile accident.
6. Gurley acquired business furniture for $17,000 on November 25, for $6,000 on open account, plus $11,000 of business cash. On November 26, Gurley sold a $1,000 business chair for $1,000 to her next-door business neighbor for cash.
7. Gurley's balance at November 30 in her business checking account after all transactions was $6,000.

Prepare a balance sheet as of November 30, 20X1, for Rebecca Gurley, realtor.

1-39 Bank Balance Sheet

Consider the following simplified balance sheet accounts of Wells Fargo & Company as of June 30, 2009 (in billions of $):

Assets		Liabilities and Stockholders' Equity	
Cash	$ 21	Deposits	$ 814
Investment securities	309	Other liabilities	349
Loans receivable	799	Total liabilities	1,163
Other assets	155	Stockholders' equity	121
Total assets	$1,284	Total liabilities and stockholders' equity	$1,284

This balance sheet illustrates how Wells Fargo gathers and uses money. More than 86% of the total assets are in the form of investments and loans, and more than 63% of the total liabilities and stockholders' equity are in the form of deposits, a major liability. That is, financial institutions such as Wells Fargo are in the business of raising funds from depositors and, in turn, lending those funds to businesses, homeowners, and others. The stockholders' equity is usually tiny in comparison with the deposits (only about 9% of total liabilities and stockholders' equity in this case).

1. What Wells Fargo accounts would be affected if you deposited $1,000?
2. Why are deposits listed as liabilities?
3. What accounts would be affected if the bank loaned Jan Sigurdsen $75,000 for home renovations?
4. What accounts would be affected if Isabel Valdez withdrew $4,000 from her savings account?

1-40 Airline Balance Sheet

Air France-KLM S.A. is an international airline headquartered in France with stock traded in both Paris and Amsterdam. It has almost 650 aircraft and more than 106,000 employees. On June 30, 2009, Air France-KLM's noncash assets were €24,492 million. Total assets were €28,598 million, and total liabilities were €22,495 million. The symbol € represents the euro, the European currency.

1. Compute the following:
   a. Air France-KLM's cash on June 30, 2009.
   b. Air France-KLM's stockholders' equity on June 30, 2009.
2. Explain the easiest way to determine Air France-KLM's total liabilities and stockholders' equity from the information given in this problem.

1-41 Prepare Balance Sheet

United Technologies Corporation provides a broad range of high-technology products and support services to the building systems and aerospace industries. Those products include Pratt & Whitney aircraft engines, Carrier heating and air conditioning equipment, Otis elevators, and Sikorsky helicopters. United Technologies' June 30, 2009, balance sheet included the following items ($ in millions):

Fixed assets	$ 6,179
Accounts payable	4,599
Common stock	11,369
Cash	?
Total stockholders' equity	?
Long-term debt	8,721
Total assets	56,545
Inventories	8,539
Other assets	37,811
Other stockholders' equity	?
Other liabilities	24,819

Prepare a condensed balance sheet, including amounts for

1. Cash.
2. Total Stockholders' Equity.
3. Other Stockholders' Equity.

1-42 Prepare Balance Sheet

Macy's, Inc., headquartered in both Cincinnati and New York, operates more than 840 stores in 45 states under the Macy's and Bloomingdale's names. Its balance sheet on August 1, 2009, contained the following items ($ in millions):

Long-term debt	$ 8,632
Cash	(a)
Total liabilities	(b)
Shareholders' equity	(c)
Inventories	4,634
Merchandise accounts payable	1,683
Property, plant, and equipment	10,046
Other assets	5,589
Other liabilities	5,920
Total assets	20,784

Prepare a condensed balance sheet, including amounts for

a. Cash. What do you think of its relative size?
b. Total Liabilities.
c. Shareholders' Equity

1-43 Partnership and Corporation

Abboud Partners is a partnership started by two brothers, Adnan and Gamal Abboud. Each has an equal share of the total owners' equity of $60,000. There is only one asset, a rental house listed at $300,000, and one liability, a mortgage loan of $240,000. The date is June 15, 20X0. The Abboud brothers are considering changing their partnership to Abboud Corporation by issuing each brother 1,000 shares of common stock.

1. Prepare a balance sheet for the current partnership.
2. Prepare a balance sheet if the brothers form a corporation. The par value of each share of common stock is $1.

1-44 Presenting Paid-in Capital

Consider excerpts from two balance sheets (amounts in millions):

Citigroup

Common stock ($.01 par value; authorized shares: 15 billion), issued shares 5,671,743,807 at December 31, 2008	$ 57
Additional paid-in capital	19,165

IBM

Common stock, par value $.20 per share and additional paid-in capital	$39,129
Shares authorized: 4,687,500,000	
Shares issued: 2008, 2,096,981,860 shares	

1. How would the presentation of Citigroup stockholders' equity accounts be affected if the company issued 500 million more shares for $6 cash per share?
2. How would the presentation of IBM's stockholders' equity accounts be affected if the company issued 1 million more shares for $120 cash per share? Be specific.

1-45 Presenting Paid-in Capital

Chevron, the petroleum exploration, production, refining, and marketing company, presented the following in its June 30, 2009, balance sheet.

Common stock—$.75 par value, 2,442,676,580 shares issued	?
Additional paid-in capital	$14,359,000,000

What amount should be shown on the common stock line? What was the average price per share paid by the original investors for the Chevron common stock? How do your answers compare with the $66 market price of the stock on June 30, 2009? Comment briefly.

1-46 Presenting Paid-in Capital

Honda Motor Company is the largest producer of motorcycles in the world, as well as a major auto manufacturer. Honda included the following items in its 2009 balance sheet (in millions of Japanese Yen, ¥):

Common stock—authorized 7,086,000,000 shares; issued 1,834,828,430 shares	¥ 86,067
Capital surplus*	172,529

*Honda uses the term "capital surplus" instead of the better terms, additional paid-in capital or capital in excess of par value.

1. What is the par value of Honda's common stock?
2. What was the average price per share paid by the original investors for the Honda common stock?
3. How do your answers compare with the ¥2,150 market price of the stock at the end of fiscal 2009? Comment briefly.

1-47 Audit Opinion and IFRS Versus U.S. GAAP

Carrefour, the French supermarket company, included the following paragraph from its auditor in its 2008 annual report:

> In our opinion, the consolidated financial statements give a true and fair view of the assets and liabilities and of the financial position of the Group as of 31 December 2008 and of the results of its operations for the year then ended in accordance with the IFRS as adopted by the European Union.

Safeway the U.S. supermarket chain had a similar paragraph in its 2008 annual report:

> In our opinion, the consolidated financial statements referred to above present fairly, in all material respects, the financial position of Safeway Inc. and subsidiaries as of January 3, 2009, . . . and the results of their operations and their cash flows for [the year] ended January 3, 2009, in conformity with accounting principles generally accepted in the United States of America.

Explain what is meant by "in accordance with the IFRS as adopted by the European Union" and "in conformity with accounting principles generally accepted in the United States of America."

1-48 Board of Directors and Audit Committee

Examine the 2009 annual report of General Mills, maker of cereals such as Cheerios, Betty Crocker cake mixes, Progresso soups, and other foods (http://phx.corporate-ir.net/phoenix.zhtml?c=74271&p=irol-reportsannual). Turn to the listing of General Mills' Board of Directors on page 18 of the annual report.

1. How many board members does General Mills have? How many of them are General Mills executives?
2. How many of the nonexecutive directors are executives or retired executives of other companies? How many are academics? What other positions are represented on the board? How does the background of board members influence their ability to carry out the responsibilities of the board?
3. How many members of the General Mills' Board of Directors are on the audit committee? Are any audit committee members also General Mills executives? Why would investors want to know the composition of the audit committee?

1-49 Accounting and Ethics

A 2009 survey by Clemson University researchers examined the ethics concerns of chief executive officers of 300 large- and mid-sized corporations in the United States. Their number one concern was improper accounting practices. Recognizing the importance of ethics in accounting, professional associations for both internal accountants and external auditors place much emphasis on their standards of ethical conduct. Discuss why maintaining a reputation for ethical conduct is important for (1) accountants within an organization, and (2) external auditors. What can accountants do to foster a reputation for high ethical standards and conduct?

Collaborative Learning Exercise

1-50 Understanding Transactions

Form groups of three to five students each. Each group should choose one of the companies included in the Dow Jones Industrial Average (Exhibit 1-1), and find its most recent balance sheet. (You might try the company's homepage on the Internet or the SEC's Edgar database at www.sec.gov/edgar.shtml.) Ignore much of the detail on the balance sheet, focusing on the following accounts: Cash, Inventory, Equipment, Notes Payable, Accounts Payable, and Total Stockholders' Equity.

Divide the following six assumed transactions among the members of the group:

1. Sold 1 million shares of common stock for a total of $11 million cash (ignore par value)
2. Bought inventory for cash of $3 million
3. Borrowed $5 million from the bank, receiving the $5 million in cash
4. Bought inventory for $6 million on open account
5. Paid $4 million to suppliers for inventory bought on open account
6. Bought equipment for $9 million cash

Required

1. The student responsible for each transaction should explain to the group how the transaction would affect the company's balance sheet, using the accounts listed earlier.
2. By using the most recent published balance sheet as a starting point, prepare a balance sheet for the company, assuming the preceding six transactions are the only transactions since the date of the latest balance sheet.

Analyzing and Interpreting Financial Statements

1-51 Financial Statement Research

Select the financial statements of any company, and focus on the balance sheet.

1. Identify the amount of cash (including cash equivalents, if any) shown on the most recent balance sheet.
2. What were the total assets shown on the most recent balance sheet, and the total liabilities plus stockholders' equity? How do these two amounts compare?
3. Identify a) total liabilities and b) total stockholders' equity. (Assume that all items on the right side of the balance sheet that are not explicitly listed as stockholders' equity are liabilities.) Compare the size of the liabilities to stockholders' equity, and comment on the comparison. Write the company's accounting equation, as of the most recent balance sheet date, by filling in the dollar amounts.

1-52 Analyzing Starbucks' Financial Statements

This and similar problems in each succeeding chapter focus on the financial statements of Starbucks Corporation. Starbucks is a worldwide retailer of specialty coffees. As you solve each of these homework problems, you will gradually strengthen your understanding of Starbucks' complete financial statements. You can find these statements either on the investor relations page of Starbuck's Web site (http://investor.starbucks.com) or via the SEC's Edgar database (www.sec.gov/edgar.shtml).

Refer to Starbucks' balance sheet and answer the following questions:

1. How much cash did Starbucks have on September 27, 2009? (Include cash equivalent as part of cash.)
2. List the account titles and amounts from Starbucks' balance sheet that are accounts that were discussed in this chapter.
3. Write the company's accounting equation as of September 27, 2009, by filling in the dollar amounts: Assets = Liabilities + Stockholders' equity. Consider deferred income taxes to be a liability.

1-53 Analyzing Financial Statements Using the Internet: Cisco

Locate the Cisco annual report. Do this by searching for "Cisco Systems," clicking Investor Relations under About Cisco, and opening Annual Reports under the Financial Reporting tab. Then click Read Online Report in the box for the most recent annual report.

Answer the following questions concerning Cisco:

1. Select Letter to Shareholders from the menu. Is the message optimistic?
2. Select Corporate Information from the menu. When was the company founded? What was its initial focus?
3. Now find Cisco's balance sheet under Financial Information. What are Cisco's Total Assets, Total Liabilities, and Total Shareholders' Equity?
4. How much are Cisco's inventories? Have they increased or decreased in the last year? Do you think that change is good or bad?
5. Select the Report of Independent Public Accounting Firm under the Reports tab. Who is responsible for the preparation, integrity, and fair presentation of Cisco's financial statements? What is the auditor's responsibility?
6. Find Cisco's list of members of its board of directors under Shareholder Information under the Shareholder and Corporate Information tab. How many directors are there? How many are Cisco executives? How many are academics?

2

Measuring Income to Assess Performance

LEARNING OBJECTIVES

After studying this chapter, you should be able to:

1 Explain how accountants measure income.

2 Determine when a company should record revenue from a sale.

3 Use the concept of matching to record the expenses for a period.

4 Prepare an income statement and show how it is related to a balance sheet.

5 Account for cash dividends and prepare a statement of stockholders' equity.

6 Explain how the following concepts affect financial statements: entity, reliability, going concern, materiality, cost-benefit, and stable monetary unit.

7 Compute and explain earnings per share, price-earnings ratio, dividend-yield ratio, and dividend-payout ratio.

8 Explain how accounting regulators trade off relevance and faithful representation in setting accounting standards (Appendix 2).

Pick n Pay started as a family-controlled business. Four small stores were purchased in 1967 and the company was listed on the JSE Limited, the recognized stock exchange in South Africa, in 1968 as Pick n Pay Stores Limited. Today, the Group has more than 800 stores, employs over 38,000 people, and generates an annual turnover of R51.9 billion. The currency of South Africa is the Rand, denoted as R. Using an exchange rate of US$1 = R6.965, this is equal to US$7.45 billion.

Pick n Pay trades mostly in South Africa and their aim is to keep their customers happy by selling quality goods at competitive prices, and to provide courteous service in stores that are well-located and pleasant to shop in. Customers can buy groceries, clothes, meat, liquor, medication, and other goods at various stores ranging from large hypermarkets to smaller-sized express shops. These stores are conveniently situated throughout the country.

Pick n Pay Stores Ltd has grown dramatically over the last four decades and this suggests that its management has been successful. Although companies cannot measure success with any single measure, in this chapter we see one important measure of a company's success—its profitability. When owners and investors want to evaluate performance, they often use measures of profitability for the entire company, as well as measures related to segments of the company.

The most common measure of profitability for a company is its net income—its sales less its expenses—which is the topic of this chapter. In 2011, Pick n Pay had sales of more than R51.9 billion and expenses of about R50.6 billion, leaving a net income of approximately R1.3 billion or 2.5% of sales. This means that, on average, when you buy a product at Pick n Pay for R100, Pick n Pay ends up with R2.50 of

Most people in South Africa are familiar with **Pick n Pay**, a large and successful retailer that has been doing business since 1967. It consists of more than 800 hypermarkets, supermarkets, and family stores across the country which stock food, general merchandise, and clothing. Pick n Pay Stores' income statement, described in this chapter, is a summary of the profits the company makes.

income. It takes a lot of grocery trolleys to bring in sales worth R51.9 billion!

To generate this level of sales, Pick n Pay has to incur many expenditures, including payments to suppliers of the goods they sell, salaries and wages, advertising, and other promotional services—all of which add up to expenses worth R50.6 billion.

It takes skillful management to oversee such a large operation, and accounting reports are an important tool for management. It also takes large amounts of capital to support such operations, and Pick n Pay has raised part of that capital by selling more than 480 million shares. Shareholders will be interested in the financial reports on Pick n Pay's operations to help them evaluate their decision to invest in the firm. Current shareholders will not be the only group interested in Pick n Pay's profitability: future shareholders, employees, and government will also be interested.

Investors and other interested parties eagerly await reports about the company's annual income. Investors care about the price of their shares, and share prices generally reflect investors' expectations about income. Although the share price of a company is determined by supply and demand for the share, and share prices are influenced by both local and global economics, the income of a company still remains a very important factor in determining the share price.

If one were to look at the movement of Pick n Pay's share price over a period of time, one would see that the price fluctuates a lot. For the year ending 28 February 2011 (Pick n Pay's financial year end), the share price fluctuated between a low of 1.655 cents per share (100 cents equal R1), and a high of 2.115 cents per share. That is a fluctuation of 28%. The expected income of Pick n Pay, as confirmed in the yearly and half yearly results, is one of the reasons for the fluctuation in the share price. ●

Sources: http://www.picknpay-ir.co.za/financials/annual_reports/2011/report_chairman.html

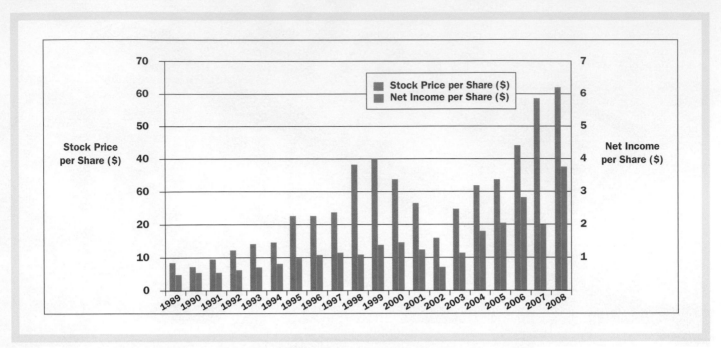

EXHIBIT 2-1

Relationship Between Stock Price and Net Income for McDonald's Corporation

Even rumors about earnings can have a major effect on stock prices. On February 29, 2009, headlines read "Earnings Rumors Pull Down CS [Credit Suisse]." The rumor that Credit Suisse would "report an annual loss of 8 billion Swiss francs," a larger than expected loss, contributed to a more than a 7% drop in CS's stock price even in the absence of any announcement by the company.

Although income and stock prices tend to move in the same direction, the relationship is not perfect. Look at Exhibit 2-1, which shows the income and stock price of McDonald's Corporation for the last 20 years. The left vertical axis and the brown bars represent the stock price in dollars per share, and the right vertical axis and green bars are the net income in dollars per share. As income increased, so did the stock price, and when income began to fall, the stock price also fell. However, you can see the stock price "bubbles" in 1998–2000 and in 2006–2008, when stock prices in the entire market generally rose faster than income. You can see that income—the topic of this chapter—is a key measure of performance and value.

Introduction to Income Measurement

OBJECTIVE 1

Explain how accountants measure income.

Measuring income is important to everyone, from individuals to businesses, because we all need to know how well we are doing economically. Income is like the number on the scoreboard that tells how well a team is performing. However, measuring income is not as easy as measuring the number of runs scored in a baseball game. Most people regard income as a measure of the increase in the "wealth" of an entity over a period of time. However, companies can measure wealth and income in various ways. To allow decision makers and investors to compare the performance of one company with that of another, generally accepted accounting principles specify certain measurement rules that all companies must follow in measuring net income. While measurement details differ slightly between the two sets of GAAP, IFRS and U.S. GAAP, the basic principles covered in this chapter apply to both. Let's take a look at how accountants measure income by first looking at the period over which they measure it.

Operating Cycle

The activities in most companies follow a repeating operating cycle. During the **operating cycle**, the company uses cash to acquire goods and services, which in turn it sells to customers. The customers in turn pay for their purchases with cash, which brings us back to the beginning of the cycle. Consider a retail company such as **Wal-Mart**:

operating cycle

The time span during which a company uses cash to acquire goods and services, which in turn it sells to customers, who in turn pay for their purchases with cash.

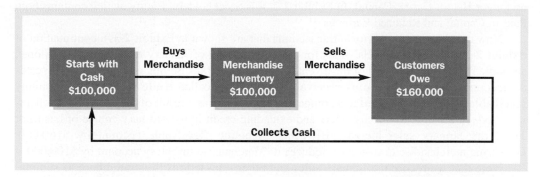

The box for the amounts owed to the entity by customers is larger than the other two boxes because the company's objective is to sell its goods at a price higher than it paid for them. The amount by which the selling price exceeds expenses is profit or income.

The Accounting Time Period

Because it is hard to accurately measure the success of an ongoing operation, the only way to be certain of a business's success is to close its doors, sell all its assets, pay all liabilities, and return any leftover cash to the owner. Actually, in the 1400s, Venetian merchant traders did exactly that for each and every voyage. Investors put up cash to buy merchandise and pay the crew, and after the voyage the traders paid the investors whatever profits they generated on the voyage. Because that system would not be feasible for companies today, we need to measure performance over time periods shorter than the life of the company.

The calendar year is the most popular time period for measuring income. However, about 40% of large companies use a **fiscal year** that differs from a calendar year. Established purely for accounting purposes, the fiscal year does not necessarily end on December 31. Instead, the fiscal year-end date is often the low point in annual business activity. For example, **Kmart** and **JCPenney** use a fiscal year ending on January 31 after completing holiday and post-holiday sales. **Pick n Pay** ends it fiscal year on February 28.

fiscal year

The year established for accounting purposes, which may differ from a calendar year.

Users of financial statements want information more than once a year. They want to know how well the business is doing at least each quarter. Therefore, companies also prepare financial statements for these **interim periods**—periods of less than a year. The SEC requires companies to officially file financial statements every quarter. However, in some countries, authorities require only annual statements.

interim periods

The time spans established for accounting purposes that are less than a year.

Revenues and Expenses

Now let's see how accountants measure income. Revenues and expenses are the key components. These terms apply to the inflows and outflows of assets that occur during a business's operating cycle. Companies obtain assets by selling products or services and use assets in producing and delivering those products or services. When they sell products or services, they record **revenue** (sometimes called **sales** or **sales revenue**), which is the increase in net assets resulting from selling products or services. Revenues increase owners' equity. In contrast , **expenses** are decreases in net assets as a result of consuming or giving up resources in the process of providing products or services to a customer. Expenses decrease the owners' equity. **Income** (also known as **profits** or **earnings**) is simply the excess of revenues over expenses. If expenses exceed revenues, we call it a loss.

revenue (sales, sales revenue)

The increase in net assets resulting from selling products or services. Revenues increase owners' equity.

expenses

Decreases in net assets as a result of consuming or giving up resources in the process of providing products or services to a customer. Expenses decrease the owners' equity.

Revenues arise when Pick n Pay sells goods (or groceries) to its customers. Expenses arise when Pick n Pay buys and pays for the goods from its suppliers. Pick n Pay earns income when

income (profits, earnings)

The excess of revenues over expenses.

retained earnings (retained income)

Total cumulative owners' equity generated by income or profits.

accounts receivable (trade receivables, receivables)

Amount owed to a company by customers as a result of the company's delivering goods or services and extending credit in the ordinary course of business.

revenues exceed the costs of selling the goods. The total cumulative owners' equity generated by income or profits is called **retained earnings** or **retained income**. You can learn the importance of income or earnings from the Business First box on page 64.

Consider again the Biwheels Company we examined in Chapter 1. Exhibit 2-2 is almost a direct reproduction of Exhibit 1-2, which summarized the nine transactions of Hector Lopez's business. However, the company has now been incorporated, and the owners' equity account is no longer Hector Lopez, Capital. In Exhibit 2-2, it is Stockholders' Equity, which contains both Paid-in Capital and Retained Earnings.

Now consider some additional transactions that are shown in Exhibit 2-3, a continuation of Exhibit 2-2. Suppose Biwheels' sales for the entire month of January total $160,000 on open account. The cost to Biwheels of the inventory sold is $100,000. Selling on open account creates an account receivable. **Accounts receivable** (sometimes called **trade receivables** or simply **receivables**) are amounts owed to a company by customers as a result of the company's delivering goods or services to the customers and extending credit in the ordinary course of business. Thus, the January sales increase Biwheels' Accounts Receivable account by $160,000. Delivering merchandise to customers reduces its Merchandise Inventory account by $100,000.

Note that we record the January sales and other transactions illustrated here as summarized transactions. The company's sales, purchases of inventory, collections from customers, or disbursements to suppliers do not take place all at once. Actual accounting systems record every sale at the time of sale using a cash register, a scanner, or some other data entry device, and then summarize the data over some period of time, such as the month of January for our example.

	Assets				=	Liabilities		+	Stockholders' Equity	
Description of Transactions	**Cash** +	**Merchandise Inventory** +	**Store Equipment** =			**Note Payable** +	**Accounts Payable** +		**Paid-in Capital** +	**Retained Earnings**
(1) Initial investment	+400,000			=					+400,000	
(2) Loan from bank	+100,000			=		+100,000				
(3) Acquire store equipment for cash	−15,000		+15,000	=						
(4) Acquire inventory for cash	−120,000	+120,000		=						
(5) Acquire inventory on credit		+10,000		=			+10,000			
(6) Acquire inventory for cash plus credit	−10,000	+30,000		=			+20,000			
(7) Sale of equipment	+1,000		−1,000	=						
(8) Return of inventory acquired on January 5		−800		=			−800			
(9) Payments to creditors	−4,000			=			−4,000			
Balance January 12, 20X2	352,000 +	159,200 +	14,000 =			100,000 +	25,200 +		400,000	
		525,200					525,200			

EXHIBIT 2-2

Biwheels Company

Analysis of Transactions for January 2, 20X2, to January 12, 20X2 (in $)

Assets = Liabilities + Stockholders' Equity

Description of Transactions	Cash	+	Accounts Receivable	+	Merchandise Inventory	+	Prepaid Rent	+	Store Equipment	=	Note Payable	+	Accounts Payable	+	Paid-in Capital	+	Retained Earnings
(1)–(9) See Exhibit 2-2 Balance, January 12, 20X2	352,000	+			159,200	+			14,000	=	100,000	+	25,200	+	400,000		
(10a) Sales on open account (inflow of assets)			+160,000							=							+160,000 (Sales Revenue)
(10b) Cost of merchandise inventory sold (outflow of assets)					−100,000					=							−100,000 (Cost of Goods Sold Expense)
(11) Collect accounts receivable	+5,000		−5,000							=							
(12) Pay rent in advance	−6,000						+6,000			=							
(13) Recognize expiration of rental services							−2,000			=							−2,000 (Rent Expense)
(14) Recognize expiration of equipment services									−100	=							−100 (Depreciation Expense)
Balance January 31, 20X2	351,000	+	155,000	+	59,200	+	4,000	+	13,900	=	100,000	+	25,200	+	400,000		57,900
					583,100										583,100		

EXHIBIT 2-3

Biwheels Company

Analysis of Transactions for January 20X2 (in $)

BUSINESS FIRST

EARNINGS AND EARNINGS EXPECTATIONS

Earnings are a critical measure of company performance, and investors watch earnings carefully. Almost every day the financial press reports on current and prospective earnings. A focus for both investors and the press is "consensus earnings forecasts." A major source of consensus forecasts is Thomson Reuters I/B/E/S (another source is Zacks Investment Research). A large number of Wall Street analysts follow the stocks of any major company, and I/B/E/S gathers these forecasts and publishes a continually updated average of the forecasts. These are important inputs to investors, even to sophisticated investors such as mutual fund managers. When a company announces its actual earnings, the press inevitably compares it to the consensus analysts' forecasts. Any difference between the forecast and actual is called an "earnings surprise." Companies try to keep their earnings surprises to a minimum by providing guidance to analysts about what to expect.

Consider Google's earnings announcements during 2008. The following table shows the I/B/E/S consensus forecast each quarter compared to the actual earnings:

Quarter	Reporting Date	Actual Earnings	Consensus Earnings	Earnings Surprise	Surprise %
1/2008	04/17/2008	$4.84	$4.52	$0.32	7.08
2/2008	07/17/2008	4.63	4.736	−0.106	−2.24
3/2008	10/16/2008	4.92	4.75	0.170	3.58
4/2008	01/22/2009	5.10	4.954	0.146	2.95

At each reporting date the number of Google shares traded was extraordinarily high, and significant movements in stock price occurred. The 7% positive market surprise in April contributed to a 20% price increase; the negative earnings surprise in July contributed to a 10% decline in price, and the positive surprises in October and January contributed to 5% and 6% increases in price, respectively.

You can see that meeting earnings expectations is important. Stocks of companies whose earnings exceed the consensus expectation generally do well, and vice versa. Even though Nordstrom's 2008 earnings of $1.83 per share fell 38% below 2007's earnings, they exceeded the consensus expectation of $1.80, and its stock price increased by about 20%. Microsoft had the opposite experience when its 2008 earnings fell short of expectations by just 1%. Its stock price dropped 7%, despite an earnings increase of nearly 30% over 2007. Investors derive information from earnings reports, and when the results surprise them, stock prices generally react—up for positive surprises and down for negative surprises.

Sources: E. Berte, "Nordstrom 4Q Earnings Fall Sharply, But Meet Expectations," Fox Business (February 23, 2009); BusinessWeek Web Site http://investing.businessweek.com/research/stocks/earnings/earnings.asp?symbol=MSFT.O; NASDAQ Web Site http://quotes.nasdaq.com/asp/MasterDataEntry.asp?page=analystsummary.

The accounting for the summarized sales transaction has two phases, a revenue phase (10a) and an expense phase (10b):

	Assets		=	Liabilities	+ Stockholders' Equity
	Accounts Receivable	Merchandise Inventory			Retained Earnings
(10a) Sales on open account	+160,000		=		
(10b) Cost of merchandise inventory sold		−100,000	=		−100,000 (Cost of Goods Sold Expense)

To understand this transaction, think of it as two steps occurring simultaneously in the balance sheet equation: an inflow of assets in the form of accounts receivable (10a) in exchange for an outflow of assets in the form of merchandise inventory (10b). This exchange of assets does not affect liabilities, so to keep the equation in balance, stockholders' equity must increase by $60,000 [that is, $160,000 (Sales Revenue) – $100,000 (Cost of Goods Sold expense)]. Note that

cost of goods sold expense (also called **cost of sales** or **cost of revenue**) is the original acquisition cost of the inventory that a company sells to customers during the reporting period.

As entries 10a and 10b show, we record revenue from sales as an increase in the asset Accounts Receivable and an increase in Retained Earnings. In contrast, we record the cost of goods sold expense as a decrease in the asset Merchandise Inventory and a decrease in Retained Earnings. You can thus see that revenues are positive entries to the Retained Earnings account in the stockholders' equity section of the balance sheet, and expenses are negative entries to Retained Earnings. We illustrate these relationships as follows, where the arrows show the components of the various accounts:

Assets = Liabilities + Stockholders' equity

Assets = Liabilities + Paid-in capital + Retained earnings

Accounts receivable +	Inventory	= Liabilities + Paid-in capital +	Revenues − Expenses
160,000	+ (−100,000) =	0 + 0	+ (+160,000) − (+100,000)

| Increase in assets | 60,000 | = Increase in retained earnings | 60,000 |

The ultimate purpose of sales is not to generate accounts receivable. Rather, Biwheels wants to eventually collect these receivables in cash. The company may receive some cash shortly after a credit sale, and some customers may delay payments for long periods. You have probably seen ads for furniture where the payments for the furniture are not due until 6 months or even a year after the sale. Suppose Biwheels collects $5,000 of its $160,000 of accounts receivable during January. This summary transaction, call it transaction 11, increases Cash and decreases Accounts Receivable. It does not affect Retained Earnings.

		Assets		=	Liabilities	+	Stockholders' Equity
	Cash	Accounts Receivable	Merchandise Inventory				Retained Earnings
(11) Collect accounts receivable	+5,000	−5,000		=			

We next consider how accountants decide when to record revenues in the books and how this affects measures of income.

Measuring Income

Accrual Basis and Cash Basis

There are two popular methods of measuring income, the accrual basis and the cash basis. Under the **accrual basis**, accountants record revenue as it is earned and record expenses as they are incurred, not necessarily when cash changes hands. In contrast, the **cash basis** recognizes revenue when a company receives cash and recognizes expenses when it pays cash.

For many years, accountants debated the merits of accrual-basis versus cash-basis accounting. Supporters of the accrual basis maintained that the cash basis ignores activities that increase or decrease assets other than cash. Supporters of the cash basis pointed out that a company, no matter how well it seems to be doing, can go bankrupt if it does not manage its cash properly. Who is correct? In the end, the debate has been declared a draw. Companies prepare their income statements on an accrual basis, and they also report a separate statement of cash flows (described in Chapter 5) in their annual reports. Although both cash and accrual bases have their merits, the accrual basis has the advantage of presenting a more complete summary of the entity's value-producing activities. It recognizes revenues as companies earn them and matches costs to revenues. We illustrated this accrual process in our analysis of the sale on open account in transaction 10. We recognized revenue although Biwheels received no cash, and we recorded an expense although Biwheels paid no cash. Let's now take a look at some of the specifics of the accrual basis.

cost of goods sold (cost of sales, cost of revenue)
The original acquisition cost of the inventory that a company sells to customers during the reporting period.

accrual basis
Accounting method in which accountants record revenue as a company earns it and expenses as the company incurs them—not necessarily when cash changes hands.

cash basis
Accounting method that recognizes revenue when a company receives cash and recognizes expenses when it pays cash.

Recognition of Revenues

OBJECTIVE 2

Determine when a company should record revenue from a sale.

revenue recognition

Criteria for determining whether to record revenue in the financial statements of a given period. To be recognized, revenues must be earned and realized or realizable.

When accountants measure income on an accrual basis, they use a set of **revenue recognition** criteria, which determine whether to record revenue in the financial statements of a given period. To be recognized, revenues must ordinarily meet two criteria:

1. *They must be earned.* A company earns revenues when it has completed all (or substantially all) that it has promised to a customer. Typically, this involves the delivery of goods or services to a customer.
2. *They must be realized or realizable.* Revenues are realized when a company receives cash or claims to cash in exchange for goods or services. A "claim to cash" usually means a customer's promise to pay. Revenues are realizable when the company receives assets that are readily convertible into known amounts of cash or claims to cash. To recognize revenue on the basis of a promise to pay, the company must be relatively certain that it will receive the cash.

Both U.S. GAAP and IFRS use these criteria, although they differ slightly in how they implement them.

Revenue recognition for most retail companies, such as Wal-Mart, Safeway, and McDonald's, is straightforward. Such companies earn and realize revenue at the point of sale—when a customer makes a full payment by cash, check, or credit card and takes possession of the goods. Other companies may earn and realize revenue at times other than the point of sale. However, even in such cases, they do not recognize revenue until both earning and realization are complete. Consider the following examples:

- *Newsweek* receives prepaid subscriptions. *Newsweek* realizes revenue when it receives the subscription, but it does not earn the revenue until delivery of each issue.
- A dealer in oriental rugs lets a potential customer take a rug home on a trial basis. The customer has possession of the goods, but the dealer records no revenue until the customer formally promises to accept the rug and pay for it.

INTERPRETING FINANCIAL STATEMENTS

Suppose you are examining the 2009 financial statements of a new theater company. The theater sells a subscription series that allows patrons to attend all nine of its productions that occur monthly from September through May. During August and September, the company sold 1,000 subscriptions for the 2009–2010 season at $180 each and collected the cash. How much revenue from these subscriptions did the theater recognize in its financial statements for the year ended December 31, 2009?

Answer

At December 31, 2009, the theater has produced only four out of nine productions, so the company has earned only four-ninths of the total or $80,000. Its total cash collections are $180,000. While the theater has realized all $180,000, it has earned only $80,000. Therefore, it recognizes and records only $80,000 of revenue in 2009.

Matching

OBJECTIVE 3

Use the concept of matching to record the expenses for a period.

product costs

Costs that are linked with revenues and are charged as expenses when the related revenue is recognized.

We have seen how to recognize revenues on the accrual basis. What about expenses? There are two types of expenses in every accounting period: (1) those linked to the revenues earned that period, and (2) those linked to the time period itself. Expenses that are naturally linked to revenues are **product costs**. Examples include cost of goods sold and sales commissions. If there are no revenues, there is no cost of goods sold or sales commissions. When do we recognize product costs? Accountants match such expenses to the revenues they help generate. We recognize and record expenses in the same period that we recognize the related revenues, a process called **matching**.

It is difficult to link some expenses directly to specific revenues. Rent and many administrative expenses are examples. These expenses support a company's operations for a given period, so we call them **period costs**. We record period costs as expenses in the period in which the company incurs them. For example, rent expense arises because of the passage of time, regardless of the sales level. Therefore, rent is an example of a period cost. Consider a Pick n Pay warehouse. The rent expense for May gives Pick n Pay the right to use the building for the month. Pick n Pay records the entire rent expense in May, regardless of whether May's sales are high or low.

To help us match expenses with revenues, we record purchases of some goods or services as assets because we want to match their costs with the revenues in future periods. For example, we might buy inventory that we will not sell until a future period. By recording this inventory first as an asset and then expensing it when we sell the item, we match the cost of the inventory with the revenue from the sale of the inventory. Another example is rent paid in advance. Suppose a firm pays annual rent of $12,000 on January 1 for the use of a building. We increase an asset account, Prepaid Rent, by $12,000 because we have not yet used the rental services. Each month we reduce the Prepaid Rent account by $1,000 and increase Rent Expense by $1,000, acknowledging that we use up the prepaid rent asset as we use the building.

Applying Matching

To focus on matching, assume that Biwheels Company has only two expenses other than the cost of goods sold: rent expense and depreciation expense. Rent is $2,000 per month, payable quarterly in advance. Biwheels makes a payment of $6,000 for store rent, covering January, February, and March of 20X2. (Assume that Biwheels made this initial payment on January 16, although rent is commonly paid at the start of the rental period.) This is transaction 12 in Exhibit 2-3.

The rent payment gives the company the right to use store facilities for the months of January, February, and March. The use of the facilities constitutes a future benefit, so Biwheels records the $6,000 in an asset account, Prepaid Rent. Transaction 12, the rent payment, has no effect on stockholders' equity in the balance sheet equation. Biwheels simply exchanges one asset, Cash, for another, Prepaid Rent:

	Assets		=	Liabilities	+	Stockholders' Equity
	Cash	Prepaid Rent				
(12) Pay rent in advance	−6,000	+6,000	=			

At the end of January, Biwheels records transaction 13. It recognizes that the company has used 1 month (one-third of the total) of the rental services. Therefore, Biwheels reduces Prepaid Rent by $2,000. It also reduces the Retained Earnings section of Stockholders' Equity by $2,000 as Rent Expense for January.

	Assets		=	Liabilities	+	Stockholders' Equity
	Cash	Prepaid Rent				
(13) Expiration of rental services		−2,000	=			−2,000 (Rent Expense)

This recognition of rent expense means that Biwheels has used $2,000 of the asset, Prepaid Rent, in the conduct of operations during January. That $2,000 worth of rent was a period cost for January, and Biwheels recognized it as an expense at the end of that period.

Prepaid rent of $4,000 remains an asset on January 31. Why? Suppose Biwheels had not prepaid the rent. It would then have to pay $2,000 in both February and March for rent. Therefore, the prepayment means that future cash outflows will be $4,000 less than they would have been without the prepayment.

The same matching concept that underlies the accounting for prepaid rent applies to **depreciation**, which is the systematic allocation of the acquisition cost of long-lived assets to the expense accounts of particular periods that benefit from the use of the assets. These are physical assets that a company owns, such as buildings, equipment, furniture, and fixtures. (Land is not subject to depreciation because it does not deteriorate over time.)

In both prepaid rent and depreciation, the business purchases an asset that gradually wears out or is used. As a company uses an asset, it transfers more and more of its original cost from

matching
The recording of expenses in the same time period that we recognize the related revenues.

period costs
Items supporting a company's operations for a given period. We record the expenses in the time period in which the company incurs them.

depreciation
The systematic allocation of the acquisition cost of long-lived assets to the expense accounts of particular periods that benefit from the use of the assets.

an asset account to an expense account. The main difference between depreciation and prepaid rent is the length of time taken before the asset loses its usefulness. Buildings, equipment, and furniture remain useful for many years; prepaid rent and other prepaid expenses usually expire within a year.

Transaction 14 in Exhibit 2-3 records the depreciation expense for the Biwheels equipment. A portion of the original cost of $14,000 becomes depreciation expense in each month of the equipment's useful life. Assume that Biwheels will use the equipment for 140 months. Under the matching concept, the depreciation expense for January is $14,000 ÷140 months, or $100 per month:

	Assets	=	Liabilities	+ Stockholders' Equity
	Store Equipment			**Retained Earnings**
(14) Recognize expiration of equipment services	−100	=		−100 (Depreciation Expense)

In this transaction, Biwheels decreases the asset account, Store Equipment, and also decreases the stockholders' equity account, Retained Earnings. Transactions 13 and 14 highlight the general concept of expense under the accrual basis. We can account for the purchase and use of goods and services—for example, inventories, rent, and equipment—in two basic steps: (1) the acquisition of the assets (transactions 3, 4, 5, and 6 in Exhibit 2-2 and transaction 12 in Exhibit 2-3), and (2) the expiration of the assets as expenses (transactions 10b, 13, and 14 in Exhibit 2-3). As these examples show, when a company uses prepaid expenses and long-lived assets, it decreases both total assets and stockholders' equity. Remember that expense accounts are deductions from stockholders' equity.

Recognition of Expired Assets

You can think of assets such as inventory, prepaid rent, and equipment as costs that a company stores and carries forward to future periods and records as expenses when it uses them. For inventory, we record the expense when the company sells the item and recognizes revenue from the sale. For rent, we recognize the expense in the period to which the rent applies. For equipment, we split the total cost of the long-lived asset into smaller pieces and recognize one piece of that total cost as an expense in each of the periods that benefits from the use of the equipment. In summary, inventory costs are *product costs* that accountants match to the revenue they produce. Rent is a *period cost* that accountants record in the period it benefits. Because equipment benefits many periods, accountants spread its cost over those periods as depreciation expense:

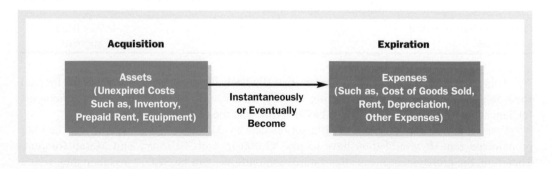

The analysis of the inventory, rent, and depreciation transactions in Exhibit 2-3 distinguishes between acquisition and expiration. Biwheels recorded inventory, rent, and equipment as assets when it acquired them. The unexpired costs of inventory, prepaid rent, and equipment then remain assets until used. When Biwheels uses them, they become expenses. What happens if Biwheels acquires assets and uses them right away? For example, companies often acquire services such as advertising and use them almost immediately. Conceptually, these costs are assets until the company uses them, at which time it recognizes them as expenses. For example, suppose Pick n Pay purchased newspaper advertising for $1,000 cash. To abide by the acquisition–expiration sequence, we could analyze the transaction in two phases as in alternative 1 that follows:

Transaction	Cash	+ Assets Other	+ Prepaid Advertising =	= Liabilities	Paid-in Capital +	Retained Earnings
Alternative 1: Two Phases						
Phase (a) Prepay for advertising	–1,000		+1,000 =			
Phase (b) Use advertising			–1,000 =			–1,000 (Advertising Expense)
Alternative 2: One Phase						
Phases (a) and (b) together	–1,000		=			–1,000 (Advertising Expense)

Assets = Liabilities + Stockholders' Equity

In practice, however, if a company uses prepaid advertising and other similar services in the same accounting period that it acquires them, accountants may not bother recording them as assets. Instead, accountants frequently use the recording shortcut shown in alternative 2. Although alternative 1 is technically correct, alternative 2 does not misstate the company's financial position as long as the advertising prepayment and the use of the advertising occur in the same accounting period.

Although this chapter focuses on the income statement, it is important to realize that the income statement is really just a way of explaining changes between one balance sheet and another. It shows how the performance of management moved the company from its beginning financial position to its end-of-the-period position. The balance sheet equation shows revenue and expense items as subparts of owners' equity. The income statement simply collects all these changes in owners' equity for the accounting period and combines them in one place.

(1) Assets (A) = Liabilities (L) + Stockholders' equity (SE)

(2) Assets (A) = Liabilities + Paid-in capital + Retained Earnings

(3) Assets (A) = Liabilities + Paid-in capital + Cumulative Revenues − Cumulative Expenses

Revenue and expense accounts are nothing more than subdivisions of stockholders' equity—temporary stockholders' equity accounts. Their purpose is to summarize the volume of sales and the various expenses so we can measure income.

The analysis of each transaction in Exhibits 2-2 and 2-3 illustrates the dual nature of the balance sheet equation, which always remains in balance. If the items affected are all on one side of the equation, the total amount added must equal the total amount subtracted on that side. If the items affected are on both sides, then equal amounts are simultaneously added or subtracted on each side.

The striking feature of the balance sheet equation is its universal applicability. No one has ever conceived a transaction, no matter how complex, that we cannot analyze via the equation. Business leaders and accountants employ the balance sheet equation constantly to be sure they understand the effects of business transactions they are planning.

INTERPRETING FINANCIAL STATEMENTS

You are examining the financial statements of a company that started in business on January 1, 2010, and rented an office for $4,000 per month. It paid 4 months of rent in advance for a total of $16,000. During January, the company earned no revenue. How much rent expense do you expect to see on the company's financial statements for January?

Answer

Rent expense is $4,000 for January. Companies charge rent expense in the period to which the rental applies. It is a period cost that becomes an expense when the company uses the space rented, regardless of the level of sales for that period.

The Income Statement

OBJECTIVE 4

Prepare an income statement and show how it is related to a balance sheet.

income statement (statement of earnings, statement of operations)
A report of all revenues and expenses pertaining to a specific time period.

net income (net earnings)
The remainder after deducting all expenses from revenues.

net loss
The difference between revenues and expenses when expenses exceed revenues.

You have now seen how companies record revenues and expenses and use them to measure income. We next consider how companies report revenues, expenses, and income in their financial statements. Chapter 1 introduced the balance sheet as a snapshot-in-time summary of a company's financial status. To report a company's performance as measured by income during the period, we need another basic financial statement, the income statement. An **income statement** (also called **statement of earnings** or **statement of operations**) is a report of all revenues and expenses pertaining to a specific time period. **Net income** (or **net earnings**) is the famous "bottom line" on an income statement—the remainder after deducting all expenses from revenues.

Look back at Exhibit 2-3 and notice that four of the accounting events (transactions 10a, 10b, 13, and 14) affect Biwheels Company's retained earnings account: sales revenue, cost of goods sold expense, rent expense, and depreciation expense. Exhibit 2-4 shows how an income statement arranges these transactions to arrive at a net income of $57,900.

Because the income statement measures performance over a period of time, whether it be a month, a quarter, or a year, it must always indicate the exact period covered. In Exhibit 2-4, the Biwheels income statement clearly shows it covers the month ended January 31, 20X2.

Public companies in most of the world publish income statements quarterly. In a few countries, companies publish only semiannual or annual statements. Worldwide, most companies prepare such statements monthly or weekly for internal management purposes. Some CEOs even ask for an income statement each morning that summarizes the income of the previous day.

Decision makers both inside and outside the company use income statements to assess the company's performance over a span of time. The income statement shows how the entity's operations for the period have increased net assets (that is, assets minus liabilities) through revenues and decreased net assets through expenses. Net income measures the amount by which the increase in net assets (revenues) exceeds the decrease in net assets (expenses). Of course, expenses could exceed revenues, in which case the company experiences a **net loss**. In essence, net income or net loss is one measure of the wealth an entity creates or loses from its operations during the accounting period. Tracking net income or loss from period to period and examining changes in its components helps investors and other decision makers evaluate the success of the period's operations.

EXHIBIT 2-4

Biwheels Company

Income Statement for the Month Ended January 31, 20X2

Sales revenue		$160,000
Deduct expenses		
Cost of goods sold	$100,000	
Rent	2,000	
Depreciation	100	
Total expenses		102,100
Net income		$ 57,900

For example, Pick n Pay reported 2011 net earnings of R1 417.7 million, 13% lower than in 2010. Management explained that the year had seen some of the toughest trading conditions in the Group's history, characterized by depressed consumer spending, costs rising ahead of internal sales inflation, and problematic industrial relations. Despite the disappointing figures, the chairman is still positive and reassures stakeholders that, "it was always inevitable that the significant investment we have made in the future of the business would impact on our bottom line. I am, however, in no doubt that this critical expenditure will greatly strengthen the foundations on which our business has been developed for the past 43 years."

Relationship Between the Income Statement and Balance Sheet

The income statement is the major link between two balance sheets:

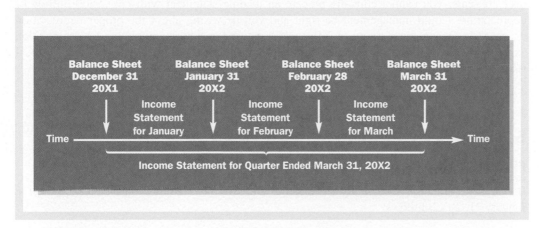

You can think of income statements as filling in the gaps between balance sheets. The balance sheets show the financial position of the company at discrete points in time, and the income statements explain the changes that have taken place between those points.

For example, the balance sheet for Biwheels Company on January 2, 20X2, showed assets of $500,000 and, to balance the equation, liabilities of $100,000 plus stockholders' equity of $400,000. There were no retained earnings. The January transactions analyzed in Exhibit 2-3 showed revenues of $160,000 and expenses of $102,100 recorded in the Retained Earnings account. The income statement in Exhibit 2-4 displays these revenues and expenses for the month of January, and shows the resulting net income of $57,900. On the balance sheet on January 31, 20X2, the stockholders' equity account, Retained Earnings, will be $57,900 greater than on January 2.

Ethics, Depreciation, and Net Income

Sometimes measuring net income can cause ethical dilemmas for accountants. In Chapter 1, we learned about the ethical standards of accountants. It is usually easy to avoid conduct that is clearly unethical. However, ethical standards and accounting standards often leave room for individual interpretation and judgment. The most difficult ethical situations arise when there is strong pressure to take an action in the gray area between ethical and unethical or when two ethical standards conflict. Because net income is so important in measuring managerial performance, occasionally managers put pressure on accountants to report higher revenues or lower expenses than is appropriate. In the two economic downturns in the last decade, authorities accused many companies of manipulating their income to make results look better than they actually were. For example, in 2002 authorities accused executives at **Enron** and **WorldCom** of manipulating net income, Enron by recognizing excess revenues and WorldCom by omitting required expenses. Later in the decade the SEC accused insurance giant **AIG** of "materially falsified financial statements . . . to paint a falsely rosy picture of [the company's] financial results to analysts and investors."

One area that requires judgment, and therefore leaves room for ethical conflicts, is depreciation. Suppose you are an accountant for an airline with $15 billion of new airplanes. Management wants to depreciate the airplanes over 30 years—leading to depreciation of $500 million per year. You discover that most airlines depreciate similar airplanes over 15 years, which would mean $1 billion of annual depreciation. Management argues that airplanes such as these will physically last at least 30 years, and there is no reason not to use them for the entire 30-year period. You believe that technological change is likely to make them obsolete in 15 years, but such technological improvements are not assured and may not occur. With depreciation of $500 million, before-tax income for the company would be $400 million, so increasing depreciation to $1 million will put the company in a loss position. If this happens, banks might ask for repayment of loans and force the company into bankruptcy. Should you prepare an income statement with $500 million of depreciation or insist on the larger $1 million depreciation expense?

There is no obviously right answer to this question. The important point is that you recognize the ethical dimensions of this problem and weigh them when forming your opinion. The company might be in dire straits if you refuse to prepare an income statement with the $500 million of depreciation. However, if you truly believe that it is not proper to depreciate the airplanes over 30 years, you cannot ethically prepare an income statement with only $500 million of depreciation. Could management be right and you be wrong about the proper depreciation expense? Is management trying to influence its net income by manipulating its depreciation expense? Accountants must assert their judgments in cases such as this. Recognizing the ethical issues involved is an important part of making those judgments.

Summary Problem for Your Review

PROBLEM

Biwheels' transactions for January were analyzed in Exhibits 2-2 and 2-3. The balance sheet at January 31, 20X2, follows:

Biwheels Company
Balance Sheet January 31, 20X2

Assets		Liabilities and Stockholders' Equity		
Cash	$351,000	Liabilities:		
Accounts receivable	155,000	Note payable		$100,000
Merchandise		Accounts payable		25,200
inventory	59,200	Total liabilities		$125,200
Prepaid rent	4,000	Stockholders' equity		
Store equipment	13,900	Paid-in capital	$400,000	
		Retained earnings	57,900	
		Total stockholders' equity		457,900
		Total liabilities and		
Total assets	$583,100	stockholders' equity		$583,100

The following series of transactions occurred during February:

15. Collections of accounts receivable, $130,000.
16. Payments of accounts payable, $15,000.
17. Acquisitions of inventory included $80,000 on open account and $10,000 acquired in exchange for cash.
18. Sales of merchandise for $176,000, of which $125,000 was on open account and $51,000 was for cash. The merchandise sold was carried in inventory at a cost of $110,000.
19. Recognition of rent expense for February.
20. Recognition of depreciation expense for February.
21. Borrowing of $10,000 from the bank, which Biwheels used to buy $10,000 of store equipment on February 28.

Required

1. Prepare an analysis of transactions, employing the balance sheet equation approach demonstrated in Exhibit 2-3.
2. Prepare a balance sheet as of February 28, 20X2, and an income statement for the month of February.

Assets = Liabilities + Stockholders' Equity

Description of Transactions	Cash	+	Accounts Receivable	+	Merchandise Inventory	+	Prepaid Rent	+	Store Equipment	=	Notes Payable	+	Accounts Payable	+	Paid-in Capital	+	Retained Earnings
Balance, January 31, 20X2	351,000	+	155,000	+	59,200	+	4,000	+	13,900	=	100,000	+	25,200	+	400,000	+	57,900
(15) Collect accounts receivable	+130,000		–130,000							=							
(16) Pay accounts payable	–15,000									=			–15,000				
(17) Acquire inventory on open account and for cash	–10,000				+90,000					=			+80,000				
(18a) Sales on open account and for cash	+51,000		+125,000							=							+176,000 (Sales Revenue)
(18b) Cost of inventory sold					–110,000					=							–110,000 (Cost of Goods Sold Expense)
(19) Recognize expiration of rental services							–2,000			=							–2,000 (Rent Expense)
(20) Recognize expiration of equipment services (depreciation)									–100	=							–100 (Depreciation Expense)
(21a) Borrow from bank	+10,000									=	+10,000						
(21b) Purchase store equipment	–10,000								+10,000	=							
Balance February 28, 20X2	507,000	+	150,000	+	39,200	+	2,000	+	23,800	=	110,000	+	90,200	+	400,000	+	121,800

722,000   722,000

EXHIBIT 2-5

Biwheels Company

Analysis of Transactions for February 20X2 (in $)

SOLUTION

1. The analysis of transactions is in Exhibit 2-5. All transactions are straightforward extensions or repetitions of the January transactions. Notice that some of these are summary transactions. For example, Biwheels made sales to many different customers; the $176,000 is the sum of all of these sales. Likewise, Biwheels acquired the $90,000 of inventory from several suppliers at different times during February.

2. Exhibit 2-6 contains the balance sheet and Exhibit 2-7 the income statement, which were both described earlier. Notice that the balance sheet lists the ending balances in all the accounts in Exhibit 2-5. The income statement summarizes the revenue and expense entries in the Retained Earnings account.

EXHIBIT 2-6

Biwheels Company

Balance Sheet February 28, 20X2 (before declaring dividends)

Assets		Liabilities and Stockholders' Equity		
Cash	$507,000	Liabilities		
Accounts receivable	150,000	Notes payable	$110,000	
Merchandise inventory	39,200	Accounts payable	90,200	$200,200
Prepaid rent	2,000	Stockholders' equity		
Store equipment	23,800	Paid-in capital	$400,000	
		Retained earnings	121,800	521,800
Total	$722,000	Total		$722,000

EXHIBIT 2-7

Biwheels Company

Income Statement for the Month Ended February 28, 20X2

Sales revenue		$176,000
Deduct expenses		
Cost of goods sold	$110,000	
Rent	2,000	
Depreciation	100	112,100
Net income		$ 63,900

Accounting for Dividends and Retained Earnings

Account for cash dividends and prepare a statement of stockholders' equity.

Recall that companies record revenues and expenses for a particular time period in Retained Earnings, a stockholders' equity account. Because net income is the excess of revenues over expenses, the Retained Earnings account increases by the amount of net income reported during the period. If expenses exceed revenues, the Retained Earnings account decreases by the amount of the period's net loss.

Cash Dividends

cash dividends

Distributions of cash to stockholders that reduce retained earnings.

Another decrease in Retained Earnings arises from **cash dividends**, distributions of cash to stockholders. Corporations pay out cash dividends to stockholders to provide a return on the stockholders' investment in the corporation. The ability to pay dividends is fundamentally a result of profitable operations. Retained earnings increase as profits accumulate, and they decrease as a company pays dividends.

Although cash dividends decrease retained earnings, they are not expenses like rent and depreciation. We do not deduct them from revenues because dividends are not directly linked to the generation of revenue or the cost of operating activities. They are voluntary distributions of cash to stockholders. Assume that on February 28, Biwheels declared and disbursed cash dividends of $50,000 to stockholders. We can analyze this transaction (22) as follows:

	Assets	=	Liabilities	+ Stockholders' Equity
	Cash			Retained Earnings
(22) Declaration and payment of cash dividends	–$50,000	=		–$50,000 (Dividends)

Cash dividends distribute some of the company's assets (cash) to shareholders, thus reducing the economic value of their remaining interest in Biwheels. Of course, companies must have sufficient cash on hand to pay cash dividends.

Transaction 22 presents the declaration and payment of a dividend as a single transaction. However, corporations usually approach dividend distributions in steps. The board of directors *declares*—announces its intention to pay—a dividend on one date (declaration date), payable to those *stockholders on record* as owning the stock on a second date (record date), and actually *pays* the dividend on a third date (payment date). The dividend amount becomes a liability on the declaration date. On the payment date, both the dividend liability and cash decrease.

Not all companies pay dividends. Starbucks has never paid dividends. Microsoft and McDonald's paid no dividends during their early, high-growth years, but today they pay regular dividends. As a successful company grows, the Retained Earnings account can grow rapidly if the company pays dividends that are significantly less than its income. Retained Earnings can easily be the largest stockholders' equity account. Its balance is the cumulative, lifetime earnings of the company less its cumulative, lifetime losses and dividends. For example, at the end of fiscal 2011, Pick n Pay had retained earnings of R1 977.5 million, whereas paid-in capital was only R6 million.

Retained Earnings and Cash

The existence of retained earnings and cash enable a board of directors to declare a cash dividend. However, Cash and Retained Earnings are two entirely separate accounts, sharing no necessary relationship. Consider the following illustration:

Step 1. Assume an opening balance sheet of

Cash	$100	Paid-in capital	$100

Step 2. Purchase inventory for $50 cash. The balance sheet now reads

Cash	$ 50	Paid-in capital	$100
Inventory	50		
Total assets	$100		

Step 3. Now sell the inventory for $80 cash. This results in a Retained Earnings balance of $30, $80 in Revenues minus $50 in Cost of Goods Sold.

Cash	$130	Paid-in capital	$100
		Retained earnings	30
		Total owners' equity	$130

At this stage, the balance in Retained Earnings seem to be directly linked to the cash increase of $30. It is, but do not think that retained earnings is a claim against the cash specifically. Remember, it is a claim against total assets. We can clarify this relationship by the transaction that follows:

Step 4. Purchase inventory and equipment, in the amounts of $60 and $50, respectively. Now, the balance sheet reads

Cash	$ 20	Paid-in capital	$100
Inventory	60	Retained earnings	30
Equipment	50		
Total assets	$130	Total owners' equity	$130

What claim does the $30 in Retained Earnings represent? Is it a claim on Cash? It cannot be because there is only $20 in Cash, and Retained Earnings is $30. The company reinvested part of the cash in inventory and equipment. This example helps to explain the nature of the Retained Earnings account. It is a residual claim, not a pot of gold. A residual claim means that if the company went out of business and sold its assets for cash, the owners would receive the amount left over after the company paid its liabilities. This amount might be either more or less than the current balance in the Cash account and more or less than the current balance in the Retained Earnings account.

Two examples highlight the lack of direct relationship between cash and retained earnings. At the beginning of 2009 Royal Dutch Shell had retained earnings more than eight times larger than its cash balance: Cash, $15,188 million, and Retained Earnings, $125,447 million. On the same date, Amgen, the largest biotech company in the world, had positive cash and negative retained earnings: Cash, $1,774 million, and Retained Earnings, $(5,258) million.

Statement of Stockholders' Equity

statement of stockholders' equity (statement of shareholders' equity)
A statement that shows all changes during the year in each stockholders' equity account.

Because owners are interested in tracing the sources of changes in stockholders' equity of a company, accountants have created a financial statement to do just that. The **statement of stockholders' equity** (or **statement of shareholders' equity**) shows all changes during the year in each stockholders' equity account. It lists the beginning balance in each account, followed by a listing of all changes that occurred during the period, followed by the ending balance.

Changes in stockholders' equity arise from three main sources:

1. Net income or net loss. A period's net income (net loss) increases (decreases) the balance in the retained earnings portion of stockholders' equity.
2. Transactions with shareholders. The most common transaction is the declaration of dividends, which reduces retained earnings. Other transactions include issuing or repurchasing shares, which we discuss in Chapter 10.

Other comprehensive income
Changes in stockholders' equity that do not result from net income (net loss) or transactions with shareholders.

3. **Other comprehensive income**. These are specific changes in stockholders' equity that do not result from net income or transactions with shareholders. Most items of other comprehensive income, except for one item discussed in Chapter 11, are beyond the scope of this text. Under IFRS, companies must prepare a separate statement of comprehensive income, but under U.S. GAAP it is sufficient to show these items only in the statement of stockholders' equity.

Exhibit 2-8 shows Biwheels' statement of stockholders' equity for February. So far we have introduced only two stockholders' equity accounts for Biwheels, Paid-in Capital (with possible sub-accounts for par value and additional paid-in capital) and Retained Earnings. We will focus

EXHIBIT 2-8

Biwheels Company

Statement of Stockholders' Equity for the Month Ended February 28, 20X2

	Paid-in Capital	Retained Earnings
Beginning balance, January 31, 20X2	$400,000	$57,900
Net income for February		63,900
Dividends declared		(50,000)
Ending balance, February 28, 20X2	$400,000	$71,800

here on Retained Earnings because it is the only Biwheels stockholders' equity account that had changes in February.

Most companies, like Biwheels, will have only two items that affect retained earnings: net income (or loss) and dividends. Other transactions, most having to do with repurchases of a company's own common stock, can affect retained earnings. However, these transactions are less frequent, so we ignore them at this point.

If Biwheels had a net loss (negative net income), we would *subtract* the amount from the beginning balance of retained earnings. If accumulated losses plus dividends exceed accumulated income, retained earnings would be negative. Many companies with negative retained earnings use the more descriptive term **accumulated deficit**.

Note how the income statement (Exhibit 2-7) and the changes in retained earnings (see Exhibit 2-8) are anchored to the balance sheet equation:

accumulated deficit
A more descriptive term for retained earnings when the accumulated losses plus dividends exceed accumulated income.

Assets = Liabilities + Paid-in capital + Retained earnings

$$\underbrace{[\text{Beginning balance} + \text{Revenues} - \text{Expenses} - \text{Dividends}]}$$
$$[57{,}900 \quad + 176{,}000 \quad - 112{,}100 \quad - \$50{,}000]$$

Ending retained earnings balance = \$71,800

INTERPRETING FINANCIAL STATEMENTS

A company's income statement reveals revenues of \$50,000 and expenses of \$40,000. Its balance sheet shows that retained earnings grew from \$15,000 at the beginning of the year to \$17,000 at the end of the year. What can you conclude about dividends declared?

Answer

Because net income = (revenues – expenses), net income is (\$50,000 – \$40,000) = \$10,000. Further, ending retained earnings = (beginning retained earnings + net income – dividends). This means that \$17,000 = (\$15,000 + \$10,000 – dividends). Retained earnings would have been (\$15,000 + \$10,000) = \$25,000 if the company had declared no dividends, but it was only \$17,000. Therefore, the company must have declared (\$25,000 – \$17,000) = \$8,000 in dividends.

Summary Problem for Your Review

PROBLEM

The following interpretations and remarks are common misinterpretations of financial statements. Explain fully the fallacy in each:

1. "Sales show the cash coming in from customers, and the various expenses show the cash going out for goods and services. The difference is net income."
2. Consider the following March 31, 2008, accounts of Sony Corporation, the large Japanese electronics company.

Sony Corporation
Stockholders' Equity (in billions of yen)

March 31	2008	2007
Stockholders' equity		
Common stock,		
Authorized shares: 2008 and 2007, 3,600		
Issued and outstanding shares: 2008, 1,004.4; 2007, 1,002.9	¥ 631	¥ 627
Additional paid-in capital	1,151	1,143
Retained earnings	2,059	1,720
Other	(376)	(119)
Total stockholders' equity	¥3,465	¥3,371

A Sony employee commented, "Why can't that big company pay higher wages and dividends, too? It can use its more than ¥2 trillion (more than $20 billion U.S. dollars) of retained earnings to do so."

3. "The total Sony stockholders' equity measures the amount that the shareholders would get today if the corporation ceased business, sold its assets, and paid off its liabilities."

SOLUTION

1. Cash receipts and disbursements are not the basis for the accrual accounting recognition of revenues and expenses. Sales could easily be credit sales for which the company has not yet received cash, and expenses could be those that the company has incurred but not yet paid out (or paid out in a previous accounting period). Depreciation is an example where the expense recognition does not coincide with the payment of cash. Depreciation recorded in today's income statement may result from the use of equipment that the company acquired for cash years ago. Therefore, under accrual accounting, sales and expenses are not equivalent to cash inflows and outflows. To determine net income under accrual accounting, we subtract expenses from revenues (expenses are linked to revenues via matching). This can be quite different from cash inflows minus cash outflows.

2. As the chapter indicated, retained earnings is not cash. It is a stockholders' equity account that represents the accumulated increase in ownership claims due to profitable operations. This claim may be lowered by declaring cash dividends, but a growing company will need to reinvest cash in receivables, inventories, plant, equipment, and other assets necessary for expansion. Paying higher wages may make it impossible to compete effectively and stay in business. Paying higher dividends may make it impossible to grow. The level of retained earnings does not lead to a specific wage or dividend policy for the firm.

3. Stockholders' equity is the excess of assets over liabilities. If a company carried its assets in the accounting records at their market value today and listed the liabilities at their market values, the remark would be true. However, many of the numbers on the balance sheet are historical numbers, not current numbers. Intervening changes in markets and general price levels in inflationary times may mean that some assets are woefully understated. Investors make a critical error if they think that balance sheets indicate current values for all assets.

Some Basic Concepts

<table>
<tr><td>**OBJECTIVE 6**

Explain how the following concepts affect financial statements: entity, reliability, going concern, materiality, cost-benefit, and stable monetary unit.</td></tr>
</table>

So far, we have looked at three of the four main financial statements. To develop your understanding of these statements we have implicitly relied on some basic concepts. Now it is time to make some of those concepts explicit. In this section, we discuss the entity, reliability, going concern, materiality, cost-benefit, and stable monetary unit concepts. We discuss some additional concepts that influence the regulation of accounting in Appendix 2.

THE ENTITY CONCEPT The first basic concept or principle in accounting is the entity concept. As you learned in Chapter 1, an accounting entity is an organization or a section of an organization that stands apart from other organizations and individuals as a separate economic unit. Accounting draws sharp boundaries around each entity to avoid confusing its affairs with those of other entities.

An example of an entity is **General Electric Corporation**, an enormous entity that encompasses many smaller entities such as GE Capital, a financial services company, and NBC Universal, an entertainment company. In turn, GE Capital encompasses many smaller entities such as GE Commercial Finance, GE Money, and GE Consumer Finance. Managers want accounting reports that are confined to their particular entities.

The entity concept helps the accountant relate events to a clearly defined area of accountability. For example, do not confuse business entities with personal entities. A purchase of groceries for merchandise inventory is an accounting transaction of a grocery store (the business entity), but the store owner's purchase of a DVD player with a personal check is a transaction of the owner (the personal entity).

THE RELIABILITY CONCEPT Users of financial statements want assurance that management did not fabricate the numbers. Consequently, accountants regard reliability as an essential characteristic of measurement. **Reliability** is a quality of information that assures decision makers that the information captures the conditions or events it purports to represent. Reliable data require convincing evidence that can be verified by independent auditors.

The accounting process focuses on reliable recording of events that affect an organization. Although many events may affect a company—including wars, elections, and general economic booms or depressions—accountants recognize only specified types of events as being reliably recorded as accounting transactions.

Suppose a top executive of **ExxonMobil** is killed in an airplane crash. The accountant would not record this event. Now suppose that ExxonMobil discovers that an employee has embezzled $1,000 in cash. The accountant would record this event. The death of the executive may have considerably more economic or financial significance for ExxonMobil than does the embezzlement, but the monetary effect is hard to measure in any reliable way.

GOING CONCERN CONVENTION The **going concern (continuity)** convention is the assumption that an entity will persist indefinitely. This notion implies that a company will use its existing resources, such as plant assets, to fulfill its general business needs rather than sell them in tomorrow's real estate or equipment markets. For a going concern, it is reasonable to use historical cost to record long-lived assets.

The opposite view of this going concern convention is an immediate liquidation assumption, whereby a company values all items on its balance sheet at the amounts appropriate if the entity were to be liquidated in piecemeal fashion within a few days or months. Companies use this liquidation approach to valuation only when the probability is high that the company will be liquidated.

MATERIALITY CONVENTION How does an accountant know what to include on the financial statements? There are a lot of rules and regulations about what must appear in those statements. However, some items are trivial enough that they need not be reported. The **materiality** convention asserts that an item should be included in a financial statement if its omission or misstatement would tend to mislead the reader of the financial statements under consideration.

Most large items, such as buildings and machinery, are clearly material. Smaller items, though, may not be so clear-cut. Many acquisitions that a company theoretically should record as assets are immediately expensed because of their insignificance. For example, coat hangers may last indefinitely but never appear in the balance sheet as assets. Many corporations require the immediate expensing of all outlays under a specified minimum, such as $1,000, regardless of the useful life of the asset acquired. The resulting $1,000 understatement of assets and stockholders' equity is considered too trivial to worry about. The FASB regularly includes the following statement in its standards: "The provisions of this statement need not be applied to immaterial items."

When is an item material? There will probably never be a universal, clear-cut answer. What is trivial to General Electric may be material to a local boutique. A working rule is that an item is material if its proper accounting is likely to affect the decision of an informed user of financial statements. In sum, materiality is an important convention, but it is difficult to use anything other than prudent judgment to tell whether an item is material.

COST-BENEFIT CRITERION Accounting systems vary in complexity—from the minimum crude records kept by a small business to satisfy government authorities, to the sophisticated budgeting and feedback schemes used to manage huge, multinational corporations. Of course, a system can start out small and grow as needs increase. When are changes to an accounting system necessary? The **cost-benefit** criterion states that an organization should change its system when the expected additional benefits of the change exceed its expected additional costs. Often the benefits are difficult to measure, but this criterion should always underlie the decisions about the design and change of accounting systems. In fact, the IASB and FASB use a cost-benefit criterion in judging new standards. The standard setting bodies safeguard the cost effectiveness of their standards by (1) ensuring a standard does not "impose costs on the many for the benefit of a few," and (2) seeking alternative ways of handling an issue that are "less costly and only slightly less efficient."

STABLE MONETARY UNIT The monetary unit (called the dollar in the United States, the yen in Japan, the euro in the European Union, and various names elsewhere) is the principal means for measuring assets and equities. It is the common denominator for quantifying the effects of a wide

reliability
A quality of information that assures decision makers that the information captures the conditions or events it purports to represent.

going concern (continuity)
A convention that assumes that an entity will persist indefinitely.

materiality
A convention that asserts that an item should be included in a financial statement if its omission or misstatement would tend to mislead the reader of the financial statements under consideration.

cost-benefit
A criterion that states that an organization should change its accounting system when the expected additional benefits of the change exceed its expected additional costs.

variety of transactions. Accountants record, classify, summarize, and report in terms of the monetary unit. The ability to use historical-cost accounting depends on a stable monetary unit. A stable monetary unit is simply one that is not expected to change in value significantly over time—that is, a 2010 dollar has about the same value as a 2000 dollar. Although this is not precisely correct, with low levels of inflation, the changes in the value of the monetary unit do not cause great problems.

Four Popular Financial Ratios

earnings per share (EPS)
Net income divided by weighted-average number of common shares outstanding during the period.

Now that you know the basics of balance sheets and income statements, you are ready to learn how investors use some of the information in these statements. Numbers are hard to understand out of context. Is $10 a lot to pay for a share of stock? Is $1 a good dividend? To show you how investors think about such questions, let's look at a few financial ratios that compare financial statement numbers in ways that help us to understand the economic meaning of the numbers.

We compute a financial ratio by dividing one number by another. For a set of complex financial statements, we can compute literally hundreds of ratios. Every analyst has a set of favorite ratios, but **earnings per share (EPS)** of common stock is among the most frequently used. EPS is net income divided by the weighted-average number of common shares outstanding during the period over which the net income is measured. It is the only financial ratio required in the body of the financial statements. Publicly held companies must report it on the face of their income statements under both IFRS and U.S. GAAP. Let us now examine EPS and three other popular ratios.

Earnings Per Share

EPS tells investors how much of a period's net income "belongs to" each share of common stock. When the owners' equity is relatively simple, computing EPS is straightforward. For example, consider Coca-Cola Company. It reported EPS of $2.16, $2.59, and $2.51 in 2006, 2007, and 2008, respectively. The calculation for 2008 follows:

$$\text{EPS} = \frac{\text{Net income}}{\text{Average number of common shares outstanding}}$$

$$\text{2008 EPS} = \frac{\$5,807,000,000}{2,315,000,000} = \$2.51$$

Most income statements show two EPS numbers, basic and diluted. At this point we focus only on basic EPS. (Diluted EPS shows the potential decline in EPS if persons who have a right to acquire common shares at less than full market value, mainly due to stock option grants and debt that is convertible into common stock, exercise that right.)

Investors interested in purchasing Coca-Cola stock might be concerned about the company's decrease in EPS in 2008. In its 10-K report, management explained that this drop in EPS was caused by one-time expenses of $.66 per share. Without these expenses, EPS would have been ($2.51 + $.66) = $3.17. Investors can weigh the reported EPS numbers and management's explanation when forming their predictions of future EPS and deciding whether to invest in the stock.

Price-Earnings Ratio

price-earnings (P-E) ratio
Market price per share of common stock divided by earnings per share of common stock.

Another popular ratio is the **price-earnings (P-E) ratio**:

$$\text{P-E ratio} = \frac{\text{Market price per share of common stock}}{\text{Earnings per share of common stock}}$$

The numerator is typically today's market price for a share of the company's stock. The denominator is the EPS for the most recent 12 months. Thus, the P-E ratio varies throughout a given year, depending on the fluctuations in the company's stock price. For example, Coca-Cola's P-E ratios on December 31, 2008, 2007, and 2006 were as follows:

$$2008 \text{ P-E} = \$45.27 \div \$2.51 = 18.0$$
$$2007 \text{ P-E} = \$61.37 \div \$2.59 = 23.7$$
$$2006 \text{ P-E} = \$48.25 \div \$2.16 = 22.3$$

Another name for the P-E ratio is the **earnings multiple**. It measures how much the investing public is willing to pay for a chance to share the company's potential earnings. Note especially that the marketplace determines the P-E ratio. Why? Because the market establishes the price of a company's shares. The P-E ratio may differ considerably for two companies within the same industry. It may also change for the same company through the years. Coca-Cola's P-E increased slightly between 2006 and 2007, but decreased in 2008 as the stock market plunged. The increase in 2007 may reflect investors' belief that Coca-Cola's EPS will continue to increase, but the drop in 2008 was due at least partly to an overall decline in the market. In general, the P-E ratio indicates investors' predictions about the company's future net income. Investors apparently were less optimistic about the growth rate for Coca-Cola's earnings at the end of 2008 than they were in 2007.

Consider Amazon.com's P-E of nearly 34 at the end of 2008 compared with Coca-Cola's 18. These ratios tell us that investors expect Amazon.com's earnings to grow more rapidly than Coca-Cola's. The Business First box on page 82 illustrates the P-E ratios of some of the largest companies in the world.

earnings multiple
Another name for the P-E ratio.

INTERPRETING FINANCIAL STATEMENTS

From Microsoft's financial statements, you can determine that its EPS grew from $1.21 in 2006 to $1.90 in 2008. At the same time, its stock price fell from about $30 per share to about $19 per share. What happened to Microsoft's P-E ratio between 2006 and 2008? What would its price have been in 2008 if it had maintained its 2006 P-E ratio?

Answer

Microsoft's P-E in 2006 was ($30 ÷ $1.21) = 25, and by 2008 it had fallen to ($19 ÷ $1.90) = 10. If the company had a P-E ratio of 25 in 2008, its price would have been (25 × $1.90) = $47.50, or 2.5 times higher than it was.

Dividend-Yield Ratio

Individual investors are usually interested in the profitability of their personal investments in common stock. That profitability takes two forms: cash dividends and increases in the market-price of the stock. Investors in common stock who seek regular cash returns on their investments pay particular attention to dividend ratios. One such ratio is the **dividend-yield ratio**, the common dividends per share divided by the current market price of the stock. Coca-Cola's recent dividend-yield ratios were as follows:

dividend-yield ratio
Common dividends per share divided by market price per share.

$$2008 \text{ Dividend-yield} = \$1.52 \div \$45.27 = 3.4\%$$
$$2007 \text{ Dividend-yield} = \$1.36 \div \$61.37 = 2.2\%$$
$$2006 \text{ Dividend-yield} = \$1.24 \div \$48.25 = 2.6\%$$

Investors who favor high current cash returns do not generally buy stock in growth companies. Growth companies have conservative dividend policies because they use most of their profit-generated resources to help finance expansion of their operations. Coca-Cola's dividend-yield is typical for a company with stable but not exceptional growth. The ratio increased in 2008 because the company maintained a record of increasing dividends even in a time of decreasing stock prices.

BUSINESS FIRST

MARKET VALUE, EARNINGS, AND P-E RATIOS

Forbes ranks the 500 largest global companies by a variety of criteria. Let's look at some statistics for the 10 largest companies on February 27, 2009, ranked by market value:

Company	Country	Market Value in Billions	EPS*	Stock Price*	P-E Ratio
ExxonMobil	U.S.	$335.54	$8.78	$67.90	7.7
PetroChina	China	270.56	.87	5.53	6.4
Wal-Mart	U.S.	193.95	3.40	49.24	14.5
ChinaMobile	China	175.85	4.65	68.00	14.6
CBC	China	170.83	N/A	3.49	N/A
Microsoft	U.S.	143.58	1.90	16.15	8.5
Procter & Gamble	U.S.	141.18	3.86	48.17	12.5
AT&T	U.S.	140.08	2.17	25.16	11.6
Johnson & Johnson	U.S.	138.29	4.62	50.00	10.8
Royal Dutch Shell	Netherlands	135.10	4.27	42.48	9.9

*Stock price is as of February 27, 2009, and EPS is for fiscal years ending December 31, 2008, or January 31, 2009. Amounts for Chinese companies are estimated from publicly available data where available.

First, consider what companies are among the 10 largest market cap companies. Just 4 years ago, 8 of the top 10 were U.S. companies and no company from China was in the top 25. In these 4 years, five companies (General Electric, Citigroup, BP, Pfizer, and Bank of America) fell off the list, replaced by three Chinese companies (PetroChina, ChinaMobile, and CBC), Procter & Gamble, and AT&T. Twenty-five years ago, only ExxonMobil among today's top 10 was in the top 10, together with companies such as IBM, General Motors, Sears Roebuck, Texaco, Xerox, and Gulf Oil. You can see that large companies do not always stay large and small companies do not always stay small.

Now look at the P-E ratios for these 10 companies. ChinaMobile and Wal-Mart have the largest P-E ratios, indicating that investors expect their earnings to grow the fastest. PetroChina, ExxonMobil, and Royal Dutch Shell have the lowest ratios, so apparently investors expect earnings of oil companies to grow more slowly. Nearly all of the companies have P-E ratios lower than they were for most of the first decade of the 2000s, reflecting investors' expectations that the recession will keep earnings for almost all companies from growing as fast as they have in the near past.

Sources: Forbes.com, "The Global 2000," April 8, 2009; Yahoo! Finance Web site; Web sites for ExxonMobil, Wal-Mart, Microsoft, Procter & Gamble, AT&T, Johnson & Johnson, and Royal Dutch Shell.

Dividend-Payout Ratio

dividend-payout ratio

Common dividends per share divided by earnings per share.

Analysts are also interested in what proportion of net income a company elects to pay in cash dividends to its shareholders. The formula for computing the **dividend-payout ratio** is given here, followed by Coca-Cola's recent ratios:

$$\text{Dividend-payout ratio} = \frac{\text{Common dividends per share}}{\text{Earnings per share}}$$

2008 Dividend-payout = $1.52 ÷ $2.51 = 60.6%

2007 Dividend-payout = $1.36 ÷ $2.59 = 52.5%

2006 Dividend-payout = $1.24 ÷ $2.16 = 57.4%

In 2008 Coca-Cola had a relatively high dividend-payout ratio. The company steadily increased its dividends from 2006 to 2008, while its EPS fluctuated. Many companies elect to continue a stable or increasing pattern of dividends, even if this creates variations in its dividend-payout ratio.

The Portfolio

The Portfolio is your key to understanding

a company's financial position and

prospects using the three major

financial statements—the balance sheet,

the statement of earnings, and the

statement of cash flows. It shows some of

the most important financial ratios used in

analyzing Starbucks' financial statements

—and the statements of other companies.

You can use this tool in financial

statement analysis throughout the course.

Current Ratio $= \dfrac{\$2{,}035.8}{\$1{,}581.0} = 1.29$

Starbucks has $1.29 in current assets for each $1 in current liabilities. *See Chapter 4.*

Consolidated Balance Sheets

In millions, except per share data

	Sept. 27, 2009	Sept. 28, 2008
ASSETS		
Current assets:		
Cash and cash equivalents	$ 599.8	$ 269.8
Short-term investments—available-for-sale securities	21.5	3.0
Short-term investments—trading securities	44.8	49.5
Accounts receivable, net	271.0	329.5
Inventories	664.9	692.8
Prepaid expenses and other current assets	147.2	169.2
Deferred income taxes, net	286.6	234.2
Total current assets	2,035.8	1,748.0
Long-term investments—available-for-sale securities	71.2	71.4
Equity and cost investments	352.3	302.6
Property, plant, and equipment, net	2,536.4	2,956.4
Other assets	253.8	261.1
Other intangible assets	68.2	66.6
Goodwill	259.1	266.5
TOTAL ASSETS	**$5,576.8**	**$5,672.6**

Debt-to-Total-Assets Ratio $= \dfrac{\$2{,}531.1}{\$5{,}576.8} = .45$

Starbucks' uses $.45 of debt financing for every $1 of total assets. *See Chapter 9.*

	Sept. 27, 2009	Sept. 28, 2008
LIABILITIES AND SHAREHOLDERS' EQUITY		
Current liabilities:		
Commercial paper and short-term borrowings	$ —	$ 713.0
Accounts payable	267.1	324.9
Accrued compensation and related costs	307.5	253.6
Accrued occupancy costs	188.1	136.1
Accrued taxes	127.8	76.1
Insurance reserves	154.3	152.5
Other accrued expenses	147.3	164.4
Deferred revenue	388.7	368.4
Current portion of long-term debt	.2	.7
Total current liabilities	1,581.0	2,189.7
Long-term debt	549.3	549.6
Other long-term liabilities	400.8	442.4
Total liabilities	2,531.1	3,181.7
Shareholders' equity:		
Common stock ($.001 par value) – authorized, 1,200.0 shares; issued and outstanding, 742.9 and 735.5 shares, respectively	.7	.7
Additional paid-in capital	147.0	—
Other additional paid-in capital	39.4	39.4
Retained earnings	2,793.2	2,402.4
Accumulated other comprehensive income	65.4	48.4
Total shareholders' equity	3,045.7	2,490.9
TOTAL LIABILITIES and SHAREHOLDERS' EQUITY	**$5,576.8**	**$5,672.6**

Book Value per Share $= \dfrac{(\$3{,}045.7 - 0)}{742.9} = \$4.10$

(The numerator is total stockholders' equity minus book value of preferred stock.)
The stockholders' equity associated with each share of Starbucks' common stock is $4.10. *See Chapter 10.*

Market-to-Book $= \dfrac{\$19.83}{\$4.10} = 4.84$

The price of one share of Starbucks on September 27, 2009, was $19.83. The $4.10 amount is the book value per share. Starbuck's' market value is 4.84 times its book value. *See Chapter 10.*

$$\text{Gross Profit Percentage} = \frac{(\$9,774.6 - \$4,324.9)}{\$9,774.6} = 56\%$$

Starbucks' gross margin above the cost of items sold (including occupancy costs) is $.56 out of every $1 of sales. *See Chapter 4*

Consolidated Statement of Earnings

In millions, except earnings per share

Fiscal year ended	Sept. 27, 2009
Net revenues	$9,774.6
Cost of sales including occupancy costs	4,324.9
Store operating expenses	3,425.1
Other operating expenses	264.4
Depreciation and amortization expenses	534.7
General and administrative expenses	453.0
Restructuring charges	332.4
Total operating expenses	9,334.5
Income from equity investees	121.9
Operating income	562.0
Interest and other income, net	36.3
Interest expense	(39.1)
Earnings before income taxes	559.2
Income taxes	168.4
Net earnings	$ 390.8
Net earnings per common share—basic	$ .53
Weighted average shares outstanding	738.7

$$\text{Return on Sales} = \frac{\$390.8}{\$9,774.6} = 4.0\%$$

For every $1 of sales Starbucks earns net income of $.04. *See Chapter 4.*

$$\text{Earnings Per Share} = \frac{\$390.8}{738.7} = \$.53$$

This tells shareholders how much of Starbucks' net earnings applies to each share of stock they own. *See Chapter 2.*

$$\text{Price-Earnings Ratio} = \frac{\$19.83}{\$.53} = 37.4$$

The price of one share of Starbucks' stock on September 27, 2009, was $19.83. This ratio reveals how much value the market places on each dollar of Starbucks' current earnings. *See Chapter 2.*

$$\text{Inventory Turnover} = \frac{\$4,324.9}{[1/2 \times (\$664.9 + \$692.8)]} = 6.4$$

Starbucks has cost of sales that is 5.6 times its average inventory level. This means it holds its inventory an average of (365 ÷ 6.4) = 57.0 days. *See Chapter 7.*

$$\text{Accounts Receivable Turnover} = \frac{\$9,774.6}{[1/2 \times (\$271.0 + \$329.5)]} = 32.6$$

Assuming that all Starbuck's sales are on credit, it has credit sales that are 32.6 times its average receivables. This means that it collects its receivables in an average of (365 ÷ 32.6) = 11.2 days. *See Chapter 6.*

Consolidated Balance Sheets

In millions, except per share data

	Sept. 27, 2009	Sept. 28, 2008
ASSETS		
Current assets:		
Cash and cash equivalents	$ 599.8	$ 269.8
Short-term investments—available-for-sale securities	21.5	3.0
Short-term investments—trading securities	44.8	49.5
Accounts receivable, net	271.0	329.5
Inventories	664.9	692.8
Prepaid expenses and other current assets	147.2	169.2
Deferred income taxes, net	286.6	234.2
Total current assets	2,035.8	1,748.0
Long-term investments—available-for-sale securities	71.2	71.4
Equity and cost investments	352.3	302.6
Property, plant, and equipment, net	2,536.4	2,956.4
Other assets	253.8	261.1
Other intangible assets	68.2	66.6
Goodwill	259.1	266.5
TOTAL ASSETS	$5,576.8	$5,672.6

$$\text{Return on Assets} = \frac{\$390.8}{[1/2 \times (\$5,576.8 + \$5,672.6)]} = 6.9\%$$

For each $1 of assets that Starbucks owns, it generates $.069 of net earnings. *See Chapter 4.*

LIABILITIES AND SHAREHOLDERS' EQUITY		
Current liabilities:		
Commercial paper and short-term borrowings	$ —	$ 713.0
Accounts payable	267.1	324.9
Accrued compensation and related costs	307.5	253.6
Accrued occupancy costs	188.1	136.1
Accrued taxes	127.8	76.1
Insurance reserves	154.3	152.5
Other accrued expenses	147.3	164.4
Deferred revenue	388.7	368.4
Current portion of long-term debt	.2	.7
Total current liabilities	1,581.0	2,189.7
Long-term debt	549.3	549.6
Other long-term liabilities	400.8	442.4
Total liabilities	2,531.1	3,181.7
Shareholders' equity:		
Common stock ($.001 par value) — authorized, 1,200.0 shares; issued and outstanding, 742.9 and 735.5 shares, respectively	.7	.7
Additional paid-in capital	147.0	—
Other additional paid-in capital	39.4	39.4
Retained earnings	2,793.2	2,402.4
Accumulated other comprehensive income	65.4	48.4
Total shareholders' equity	3,045.7	2,490.9
TOTAL LIABILITIES and SHAREHOLDERS' EQUITY	$5,576.8	$5,672.6

$$\text{Return on Common Stockholders' Equity} = \frac{\$390.8}{[1/2 \times (\$3,045.7 + \$2,490.9)]} = 14.1\%$$

For each $1 invested or reinvested by common stockholders, Starbucks generates $.141 of net earnings. *See Chapter 4.*

Consolidated Statement of Earnings

In millions, except share data

Fiscal year ended	Sept. 27, 2009
Net revenues	9,774.6
Cost of sales including occupancy costs	4,324.9
Store operating expenses	3,425.1
Other operating expenses	264.4
Depreciation and amortization expenses	534.7
General and administrative expenses	453.0
Restructuring charges	332.4
Total operating expenses	9,334.5
Income from equity investees	121.9
Operating income	562.0
Interest and other income, net	36.3
Interest expense	(39.1)
Earnings before income taxes	559.2
Income taxes	168.4
Net earnings	$ 390.8
Net earnings per common share—basic	$ .53
Weighted average shares outstanding	738.7

Consolidated Statements of Cash Flows

In millions

Fiscal year ended	Sept. 27, 2009
OPERATING ACTIVITIES:	
Net earnings	$ 390.8
Adjustments to reconcile net earnings to net cash provided by operating activities:	
Depreciation and amortization	563.3
Provision for impairments and asset disposals	224.4
Deferred income taxes	(69.6)
Equity in income of investees	(78.4)
Distributions of income from equity investees	53.0
Stock-based compensation	83.2
Tax benefit from exercise of stock options	2.0
Excess tax benefit from exercise of stock options	(15.9)
Other	5.4
Cash provided/(used) by changes in operating assets and liabilities:	
Inventories	28.5
Accounts payable	(53.0)
Accrued taxes	57.2
Deferred revenue	16.3
Other operating assets	120.5
Other operating liabilities	61.3
Net cash provided by operating activities	1,389.0
INVESTING ACTIVITIES:	
Purchase of available-for-sale securities	(129.2)
Maturity and calls of available-for-sale securities	111.0
Sales of available-for-sale securities	5.0
Net purchases of equity, other investments, and other assets	(4.8)
Additions to property, plant, and equipment	(445.6)
Proceeds from sale of property, plant, and equipment	42.5
Net cash used by investing activities	(421.1)
FINANCING ACTIVITIES:	
Proceeds from issuance of commercial paper	20,965.4
Repayments of commercial paper	(21,378.5)
Proceeds from short-term borrowings	1,338.0
Repayments of short-term borrowings	(1,638.0)
Proceeds from issuance of common stock	57.3
Excess tax benefit from exercise of stock options	15.9
Principal payments on long-term debt	(0.7)
Other	(1.6)
Net cash used by financing activities	(642.2)
Effect of exchange rate changes on cash and cash equivalents	4.3
Net increase in cash and cash equivalents	330.0
CASH AND CASH EQUIVALENTS:	
Beginning of period	269.8
End of period	$ 599.8

Free Cash Flow = ($1,389.0 − $445.6) = $943.4
Starbucks generated $943.4 more cash from its operations than it needed to invest in maintaining and expanding its property, plant, and equipment. See Chapter 5.

STOCK PRICE AND RATIO INFORMATION IN THE PRESS   The business section of many daily newspapers in the United States reports market prices for stocks listed on major stock exchanges, such as the NYSE, American Stock Exchange, or NASDAQ. The *Wall Street Journal* publishes end-of-day price quotes for the 1,000 largest stocks every day, and shows more details once a week on Saturday. Consider the following stock quotations for Coca-Cola in the Saturday, March 14, 2009, issue of the *Wall Street Journal*:

YTD % CHG	52 Weeks		Stock	SYM	YLD %	P-E	LAST	NET CHG
	High	Low						
−8.9	61.90	37.44	Coca-Cola	KO	4.0	17	41.22	0.38

These data represent trading on Friday, March 13. Notice that the fourth and fifth columns identify Coca-Cola and show that its ticker symbol is KO. All listed stocks have short ticker symbols that identify them. Stock exchanges created these symbols years ago to facilitate communication via ticker tape, but they remain effective for computer communication today.

Reading from left to right, Coca-Cola's stock price decreased by 8.9% between January 1 and March 13, 2009. The highest price at which Coca-Cola's common stock sold in the preceding 52 weeks was $61.90 per share; the lowest price was $37.44. The current annual dividend yield is 4.0% based on the day's closing price of the stock. The P-E ratio is 17, also based on the closing price. The closing price—that is, the price of the last trade for the day—was $41.22, which was $.38 higher than the last trade on Thursday, March 12. That means that the closing price on March 12 was ($41.22 − $.38) = $40.84, and shareholders gained $.38 on each share they held on March 13.

Keep in mind that transactions in publicly traded shares are between individual investors in the stock, not between the corporation and the individuals. Thus, a "typical trade" results in the selling of, for example, 100 shares of Coca-Cola stock held by Ms. Johnson in Minneapolis to Mr. Ruiz in Atlanta for $4,122 in cash. These parties would ordinarily transact the trade through their respective stockbrokers. The trade would not directly affect Coca-Cola, except that it would change its records of shareholders to show that Ruiz, not Johnson, holds the 100 shares.

Summary Problem for Your Review

PROBLEM

On January 31, 2010, The Home Depot stock sold for about $28.01 per share. The company had net income of $2,661 million for the fiscal year ending January 31, 2010, had an average of 1,683 million shares outstanding during the year, and paid dividends of $.90 per share. Calculate and interpret the following:

Earnings per share   Dividend-yield ratio
Price-earnings ratio   Dividend-payout ratio

SOLUTION

$$\text{Earnings per share} = \$2,661 \div 1,683 = \$1.58$$
$$\text{Price-earnings ratio} = \$28.01 \div \$1.58 = 17.7$$
$$\text{Dividend-yield ratio} = \$.90 \div \$28.01 = 3.2\%$$
$$\text{Dividend-payout ratio} = \$.90 \div \$1.58 = 57\%$$

The Home Depot had net income of $1.58 for each share of its common stock. Its market price was 17.7 times its earnings. This is relatively high for early 2010 and shows that investors expect continuing growth in The Home Depot's earnings. Home Depot pays out 57% of its income in dividends, and this results in a 3.2% return for investors as of January 31, 2010. Both the dividend-yield and dividend-payout ratios in fiscal 2010 are higher than the historical average for Home Depot (as they were also in fiscal 2009). Home Depot is apparently trying to maintain a record of increasing dividends despite falling earnings caused by the recession.

Highlights to Remember

1 **Explain how accountants measure income.** Accountants can measure income, the excess of revenues over expenses for a particular time period, on an accrual or cash basis. In accrual accounting, companies record revenue when they earn it and record expenses when they incur them. In cash accounting, companies record revenues and expenses only when cash changes hands. Accrual accounting is the standard basis for accounting today.

2 **Determine when a company should record revenue from a sale.** The concept of revenue recognition means that companies record revenues in the earliest period in which they are both earned and realized or realizable. Earning is typically tied to delivery of the product or service and realization requires a high probability that the company will receive the promised resources (usually cash). Recording revenues increases stockholders' equity.

3 **Use the concept of matching to record the expenses for a period.** Under matching, companies assign expenses to the period in which they use the pertinent goods and services to create revenues, or when assets have no future benefit. Recording expenses decreases stockholders' equity.

4 **Prepare an income statement and show how it is related to a balance sheet.** An income statement shows an entity's revenues and expenses for a particular period of time. The net income (loss) during the period increases (decreases) the amount of retained earnings on the balance sheet.

5 **Account for cash dividends and prepare a statement of stockholders' equity.** Cash dividends are not expenses. They are distributions of cash to stockholders that reduce retained earnings. Corporations are not obligated to pay dividends, but once the board of directors declares dividends they become a legal liability until paid in cash. The balance in retained earnings increases by the amount of net income and decreases by the amount of cash dividends. A statement of stockholders' equity shows how net income, transactions with shareholders, and other comprehensive income affect stockholders' equity accounts.

6 **Explain how the following concepts affect financial statements: entity, reliability, going concern, materiality, cost-benefit, and stable monetary unit.** Authorities achieve comparability of financial statements by adopting concepts and conventions that all companies must use. Such concepts and conventions include the following: (a) accounting statements apply to a specific entity, (b) all transactions must have reliable measures, (c) companies are assumed to be ongoing (not about to be liquidated), (d) items that are not large enough to be material need not follow normal rules, (e) information should be worth more than it costs, and (f) accountants use the monetary unit for measurement despite its changing purchasing power over time.

7 **Compute and explain EPS, P-E ratio, dividend-yield ratio, and dividend-payout ratio.** Ratios relate one element of a company's economic activity to another. EPS expresses overall earnings on a scale that individual investors can link to their own ownership level. The P-E ratio relates accounting earnings to market prices. The dividend-yield ratio relates dividends paid per share to market prices, and the dividend-payout ratio relates those same dividends to the earnings during the period.

Appendix 2: Cost-Benefit Criterion and Accounting Regulation

When the FASB or IASB sets standards for financial reporting, they must make many judgments. Consider the accounting for the expiration of prepaid expenses. In the case of prepaid rent, it is fairly easy to identify when the prepaid asset provides a benefit to the company. Rent becomes an expense in the period in which a company uses the rented facilities or equipment. However, some of the most difficult issues in accounting center on when a prepaid asset expires and becomes an expense. For example, some accountants believe that companies should first record research costs as an asset on the balance sheet and then gradually write them off to expense in some systematic manner over a period of years. After all, companies engage in research activities because they expect them to create future benefits. However, both the IASB and the FASB have ruled that such costs have vague future benefits that are difficult to measure reliably. Therefore, companies must treat research costs as expenses when incurred. They do not appear on the balance sheet as assets. In contrast, under IFRS (but not U.S. GAAP) development costs that meet very specific criteria are considered assets and appear on the balance sheet.

Other difficult questions faced by the FASB and IASB include the following: Should companies record an expense when they issue stock options to executives? How should companies measure and disclose the expense for retirement benefits? Should companies show assets and liabilities at historical cost or current market value? The list could go on and on.

Criteria for Accounting Regulation Decisions

How do the FASB and IASB decide that one level of disclosure or one measurement method is acceptable and another is not? They use the same main criterion that companies use when deciding whether to change their accounting system—cost-benefit. Accounting should improve decision making. This is a benefit. However, accounting information is an economic good that is costly to produce and use. The FASB or IASB must choose rules whose decision-making benefits exceed the information costs.

The cost of providing information to the investing public includes expenses incurred by both companies and investors. Companies incur expenses for data collecting and processing, auditing, and educating employees. In addition, disclosure of sensitive information can lead to lost competitive advantages or increased labor union pressures. Investors' expenses include the costs of education, analysis, and interpretation.

The benefits of accounting information are often harder to pinpoint than the costs. For example, countries with emerging market economies often need to create an infrastructure of financial markets and relevant information to guide their economic development. However, the specific benefits of any particular proposal are harder to articulate than the general benefits of an intelligent system of accounting rules and procedures.

To help identify benefits from various types of measurement and disclosure policies, the IASB and FASB are jointly developing a common conceptual framework to replace each board's separate framework. One part of this framework identifies characteristics of information that lead to increased benefits. As shown in Exhibit 2-9, the main objective of financial reporting is decision usefulness. If accounting information is not useful in making decisions, it provides no benefit. The rest of the characteristics are helpful in assessing decision usefulness.

OBJECTIVE 8

Explain how accounting regulators trade off relevance and faithful representation in setting accounting standards.

Aspects of Decision Usefulness

Relevance and faithful representation are the two main qualities that make accounting information useful for decision making. **Relevance** refers to whether the information makes a difference to the decision maker. If information has no impact on a decision, it is not relevant to that decision. The two things that can make information relevant are predictive value and confirmatory value. Information has **predictive value** if users of financial statements can use the information to help them form their expectations about the future. Information has **confirmatory value** if it can confirm or contradict existing expectations. Information that confirms expectations means that they become more likely to occur. Information that contradicts expectations will likely lead decision makers to change those expectations.

Users of financial statements want assurance that management has accurately and truthfully reported its financial results. Consequently, in addition to relevance, accountants want information to exhibit **faithful representation**—that is, information should truly capture the economic substance of the transactions, events, or circumstances it describes. Faithful representation requires information to be complete, neutral, and free from material errors. Information is complete if it contains all the information necessary to faithfully represent an economic phenomenon. It is neutral if it is free from bias—that is, the information is not slanted to influence behavior in a particular direction. Finally, information should be free from material errors. This does not mean complete absence of errors because much accounting information is based on estimates that are, by definition, imperfect. Being free from material errors simply means that estimates are based on appropriate inputs, which in turn are based on the best information available.

Accounting is filled with trade-offs between relevance and faithful representation. Consider the $4.2 billion balance sheet value of Weyerhaeuser Company's timberlands, which the company shows at historical cost. Some of the land was purchased more than 50 years ago. The balance sheet value faithfully represents the historical cost of the timberlands, but the cost of land

relevance
The capability of information to make a difference to the decision maker.

predictive value
A quality of information that allows it to help users form their expectations about the future.

confirmatory value
A quality of information that allows it to confirm or contradict existing expectations.

faithful representation
A quality of information that ensures that it captures the economic substance of the transactions, events, or circumstances it describes. It requires information to be complete, neutral, and free from material errors.

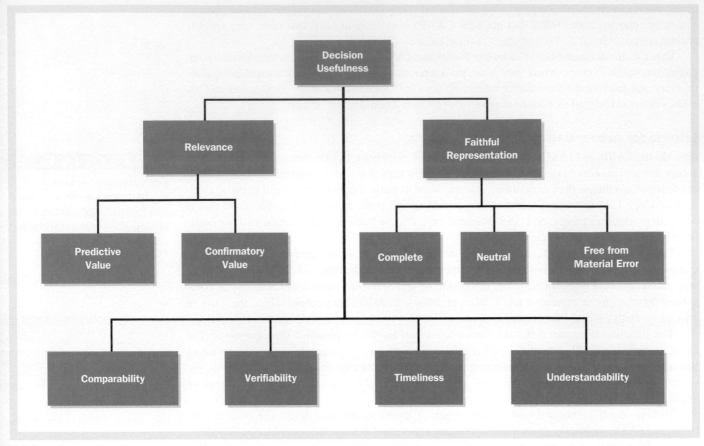

EXHIBIT 2-9

Qualities that Increase the Value of Information

50 years ago is not very relevant to today's decisions. In contrast, the current value of the land is more relevant, but estimates of this current value are subjective and would be more difficult to represent faithfully. Which quality is more important? That answer depends on the specific decision being made. However, the most desirable information has both qualities: It is relevant and faithfully represents the phenomenon of interest. The prevailing view in the United States is that many current market value estimates, especially for property, plant, and equipment, are not sufficiently reliable to be included in the accounting records, even though they are more relevant. However, under IFRS, companies can use current market values for such assets.

As you can see on the bottom of Exhibit 2-9, four characteristics can enhance both relevance and faithful representation. The first such characteristic is **comparability**—requiring all companies to use similar concepts and measurements and to use them consistently. It essentially requires accounting systems to treat like phenomena the same and unlike phenomena differently. Comparability helps decision makers identify similarities in and differences between the phenomena being represented. Note that comparability requires **consistency**, using the same accounting policies and procedures from period to period. Information is more useful if decision makers can compare it with similar information about other companies or with similar information for other reporting periods. For example, financial results of two companies are hard to compare if the companies used different methods of accounting for the value of their inventory. Further, we cannot make useful comparisons over time if a company constantly changes its accounting methods.

The second enhancing characteristic is **verifiability**, which means that information can be checked to ensure it is correct. That is, knowledgeable and independent observers would agree that the information presented has been appropriately measured. For example, the historical cost of an item is verifiable because we can check the records to verify that the amounts are correct. In contrast, some estimates and appraisals are not easily verifiable.

comparability

A characteristic of information produced when all companies use similar concepts and measurements and use them consistently.

consistency

Using the same accounting policies and procedures from period to period.

verifiability

A characteristic of information that can be checked to ensure it is correct.

Timeliness is obviously desirable. Information must reach decision makers while it can still influence their decisions. Information that is not available until after decision makers act is of little value.

Finally, information should be understandable. **Understandability** requires accountants to present information clearly and concisely. It does not require over-simplification of the data. That might fail to reveal important information. Complex phenomena sometimes require complex reporting. However, it is important to avoid unnecessary complexity.

timeliness
A characteristic of information that reaches decision makers while it can still influence their decisions.

understandability
A characteristic of information that is presented clearly and concisely.

Accounting Vocabulary

accounts receivable, p. 62
accrual basis, p. 65
accumulated deficit, p. 77
cash basis, p. 65
cash dividends, p. 74
comparability, p. 86
confirmatory value, p. 85
consistency, p. 86
continuity, p. 79
cost of goods sold, p. 65
cost of revenue, p. 65
cost of sales, p. 65
cost-benefit, p. 79
depreciation, p. 67
dividend-payout ratio, p. 82
dividend-yield ratio, p. 81
earnings, p. 61
earnings multiple, p. 81
earnings per share (EPS),
    p. 80
expenses, p. 61

faithful representation, p. 85
fiscal year, p. 61
going concern, p. 79
income, p. 61
income statement, p. 70
interim periods, p. 61
matching, p. 67
materiality, p. 79
net earnings, p. 70
net income, p. 70
net loss, p. 70
operating cycle, p. 61
other comprehensive income,
    p. 76
period costs, p. 67
predictive value, p. 85
price-earnings (P-E) ratio,
    p. 80
product costs, p. 66
profits, p. 61
receivables, p. 62

relevance, p. 85
reliability, p. 79
retained earnings, p. 62
retained income, p. 62
revenue recognition, p. 66
revenues, p. 61
sales, p. 61
sales revenue, p. 61
statement of earnings, p. 70
statement of operations, p. 70
statement of shareholders'
    equity, p. 76
statement of stockholders'
    equity, p. 76
timeliness, p. 87
trade receivables, p. 62
understandability, p. 87
verifiability, p. 86

Assignment Material

Questions

2-1 How long is a company's operating cycle?

2-2 What is the difference between a fiscal year and a calendar year? Why do companies use a fiscal year that differs from a calendar year?

2-3 "Expenses are negative stockholders' equity accounts." Explain.

2-4 What is the major defect of the cash basis of accounting?

2-5 What are the two tests for the recognition of revenue?

2-6 Give two examples where revenue is not recognized at the point of sale, one where recognition is delayed because the revenue is not yet earned, and one because it is not yet realized.

2-7 Distinguish product costs from period costs.

2-8 "Expenses are assets that have been used." Explain.

2-9 "Companies acquire goods and services, not expenses per se." Explain.

2-10 "The income statement is like a moving picture; in contrast, a balance sheet is like a snapshot." Explain.

2-11 Give two synonyms for income statement. Why is it important to learn synonyms that are used for various accounting terms?

2-12 Why might a manager put pressure on accountants to report higher revenues or lower expenses than accounting standards allow?

2-13 "Cash dividends are not expenses." Explain.

2-14 "Retained earnings is not a pot of gold." Explain.

2-15 What do users learn from the statement of stockholders' equity? What three types of changes are shown on the statement?

2-16 "An accounting entity is always a separate legal organization." Do you agree? Explain.

2-17 How do accountants judge whether an item is reliable enough for reporting in the financial statements?

2-18 The concepts of materiality and cost-benefit can limit the amount of detailed information included in the financial statements. Explain how an accountant might use each to exclude an item from the statements.

2-19 "Financial ratios are important tools for analyzing financial statements, but no ratios are shown on the statements." Do you agree? Explain.

2-20 "Fast-growing companies have high P-E ratios." Explain.

2-21 Give two ratios that provide information about a company's dividends, and explain what each means.

2-22 "Companies with a high dividend-payout ratio are good investments because stockholders get more of their share of earnings in cash." Do you agree? Explain.

2-23 Study Appendix 2. "Relevance and faithful representation are both desirable characteristics for accounting measurements, but often it is not possible to have both." Do you agree? Explain.

2-24 Study Appendix 2. What two characteristics of accounting measurements make them relevant? Explain each.

2-25 Study Appendix 2. Accounting numbers should be complete, neutral, and free from material errors. What characteristic of information do these criteria support?

Critical Thinking Questions

2-26 Quarterly Versus Annual Financial Statements

In the United States, it is common to provide abbreviated financial data quarterly with full financial statements provided annually. In some countries companies provide only annual data. Discuss the trade-offs.

2-27 Accrual or Cash Basis

Which would you rather have, a cash-basis income statement or an accrual-basis income statement? Why?

2-28 Dividends and Stock Prices

Suppose a company was going to pay out one-half of its total assets as a cash dividend. What would you expect to happen to the value of the company's stock as a result of the dividend?

2-29 Interpretation of the P-E Ratio

Would you rather own a company with a high P-E ratio or a low P-E ratio? Why?

Exercises

2-30 Synonyms and Antonyms

Consider the following terms: (1) sales, (2) net earnings, (3) accumulated deficit, (4) unexpired costs, (5) prepaid expenses, (6) accounts receivable, (7) statement of earnings, (8) used-up costs, (9) net profits, (10) net income, (11) revenues, (12) retained earnings, (13) expenses, (14) statement of financial condition, (15) statement of income, (16) statement of financial position, (17) operating statement, and (18) cost of goods sold.

Group the items into two major categories, those on the income statement and those on the balance sheet. Answer by indicating the numbered items that belong in each group. Specify items that are assets and items that are expenses.

2-31 Special Meanings of Terms

A news story described the disappointing sales of a new model car, the Jupiter. An auto dealer said, "Even if the Jupiter is a little slow to move out of dealerships, it is more of a plus than a minus....We're now selling 14 more cars per month at $20,000 per car. That's $280,000 more income."

Is the dealer confused about accounting terms? Explain.

2-32 Cash Versus Accrual Accounting

Yankton Company had sales of $240,000 during 20X0, all on account. Accounts receivable for the year grew from $60,000 on January 1 to $110,000 on December 31. Expenses for the year were $175,000, all paid in cash.

1. Compute Yankton's net income on the cash basis of accounting.
2. Compute Yankton's net income on the accrual basis of accounting.
3. Which basis gives a better measure of Yankton's performance for 20X0? Why?

2-33 Nature of Retained Earnings

This is an exercise on the relationships between assets, liabilities, and ownership equities. The numbers are small, but the underlying concepts are large.

1. Assume an opening balance sheet of

Cash	$1,000	Paid-in capital	$1,000

2. Purchase inventory for $600 cash. Prepare a balance sheet. A heading is unnecessary in this and subsequent requirements.
3. Sell the entire inventory for $750 cash. Prepare a balance sheet. What does retained earnings represent and how is it related to other balance sheet accounts? Explain in your own words.
4. Buy inventory for $300 cash and equipment for $800 cash. Prepare a balance sheet. What does retained earnings represent and how is it related to other balance sheet accounts? Explain in your own words.
5. Buy inventory for $500 on open account. Prepare a balance sheet. What do retained earnings and account payable represent and how are they related to other balance sheet accounts? Explain in your own words.

2-34 Asset Acquisition and Expiration

The Greenley Company had the following transactions in July:

a. Paid $18,000 cash for rent for the next 6 months on July 1.
b. Paid $2,000 cash for supplies on July 3.
c. Paid $4,000 cash for an advertisement in the next day's *New York Times* on July 10.
d. Paid $8,000 cash for a training program for employees on July 17. The training was completed in July.

Show the effects on the balance sheet equation in two phases—at acquisition and on expiration at the end of the month of acquisition. Show all amounts in thousands.

2-35 Find Unknowns

The following data pertain to Liverpool Auto, Ltd. Total assets at January 1, 20X1, were £110,000; at December 31, 20X1, they were £126,000. During 20X1, sales were £354,000, cash dividends declared were £5,000, and operating expenses (exclusive of cost of goods sold) were £200,000. Total liabilities at December 31, 20X1, were £55,000; at January 1, 20X1, they were £50,000. There was no additional capital paid in during 20X1.

Compute the following:

1. Stockholders' equity, January 1, 20X1, and December 31, 20X1
2. Net income for 20X1—ignore taxes
3. Cost of goods sold for 20X1

2-36 Recording Transactions

The Piedmont Company had the following transactions during June, 20X1:

a. Collections of accounts receivable, $75,000.
b. Payment of accounts payable, $45,000.

c. Acquisition of inventory, $18,000, on open account.
d. Sale of merchandise, $30,000 on open account and $23,000 for cash. The sold merchandise cost Piedmont Company $24,000.
e. Depreciation on equipment of $1,000 in June.
f. Declared and paid cash dividends of $13,000.

Use the balance sheet equation format to enter these transactions into the books of Piedmont Company. Suppose that Piedmont has a cash balance of $15,000 at the beginning of June. What was the cash balance on June 30?

2-37 Income Statement
A statement of an automobile dealer follows:

Freeway Volvo, Inc.
Statement of Profit and Loss December 31, 20X0

Revenues		
Sales	$1,050,000	
Increase in market value of land and building	$ 200,000	$1,250,000
Deduct expenses		
Advertising	$ 100,000	
Sales commissions	50,000	
Utilities	20,000	
Wages	170,000	
Dividends	100,000	
Cost of cars purchased	700,000	1,140,000
Net profit		$ 110,000

List and describe any shortcomings of this statement.

2-38 Income Statement and Retained Earnings
Borders Group, Inc., operates Borders Bookstores. In the year ended January 31, 2009, Borders had revenues of $3,275.4 million and total expenses of $3,462.1 million. Borders' retained earnings were $250.5 million at the beginning of the year and $63.8 million at the end of the year.

1. Compute Borders Group's net income (loss) for the year ended January 31, 2009.
2. Compute the amount of cash dividends declared by Borders Group during the year ended January 31, 2009.

2-39 Balance Sheet Equation
(Alternates are 2-40 and 2-55.) Each of the three following columns is an independent case. For each case, compute the amounts ($ in thousands) for the items indicated by letters and show your supporting computations:

	Case		
	1	**2**	**3**
Revenues	$165	$K	$280
Expenses	125	200	250
Dividends declared	—	7	Q
Additional investment by stockholders	—	40	35
Net income	E	20	P
Retained earnings			
Beginning of year	30	60	120
End of year	D	J	130
Paid-in capital			
Beginning of year	15	10	N
End of year	C	H	85
Total assets			
Beginning of year	80	F	L
End of year	95	280	M
Total liabilities			
Beginning of year	A	90	105
End of year	B	G	95

2-40 Balance Sheet Equation

(Alternates are 2-39 and 2-55.) Xcel Energy, provider of gas and electricity to customers in 12 Midwestern and Rocky Mountain states, has the following actual data ($ in millions) for the year 2008:

Total costs	$ B
Net income (loss)	646
Dividends	420
Assets, beginning of period	23,185
Assets, end of period	D
Liabilities, beginning of period	A
Liabilities, end of period	17,890
Shareholders' equity, beginning of period	6,406
Shareholders' equity, end of period	7,069
Retained earnings, beginning of period	962
Retained earnings, end of period	C
Total revenues	11,203

Find the unknowns ($ in millions), showing computations to support your answers.

2-41 Assessing Materiality

On June 30, 2009, ExxonMobil, the large petroleum company, reported total assets of $224,661 million and quarterly net income of $3,950 million. This net income is equivalent to nearly $16 billion annual income.

On the same date, Dayton Service Stations, Inc., operator of six stations in Dallas, reported total assets of $926,000 and quarterly net income of $56,000.

1. Suppose both companies made an investment of $250,000 in new equipment in July 2009. Would you expect the amount of detail about the investment that each company disclosed in its financial statements to differ? Why?
2. How would each company decide on its level of disclosure about the investment?

2-42 Nonprofit Operating Statement

Examine the accompanying statement of the Berlin University Faculty Club. Identify the Berlin U classifications and terms that would not be used by a profit-seeking hotel and restaurant in the United States. Suggest alternate terms. (€ is the European euro.)

Berlin U Faculty Club

Statement of Income and Expenses for Fiscal Year

Food Service			
Sales		€548,130	
Expenses			
Food	€287,088		
Labor	272,849		
Operating costs	30,537	590,474	
Deficit			€ (42,344)
Bar			
Sales		€ 90,549	
Expenses			
Cost of liquor	€ 29,302		
Labor	5,591		
Operating costs	6,125	41,018	
Surplus			49,531
Hotel			
Sales		€ 33,771	
Expenses		23,803	
Surplus			9,968
Total surplus from operations			€ 17,155
General income (members' dues, room fees, etc.)			95,546
General administration and operating expenses			(134,347)
Deficit before university subsidy			€ (21,646)
University subsidy			23,000
Net surplus after university subsidy			€ 1,354

2-43 Earnings and Dividend Ratios

Cadbury plc, the British candy company, reported 2008 earnings of £364 million under IFRS. Cash dividends were £295 million. The company had an average of 1,611 million common shares outstanding. No other type of stock was outstanding. The market price of the stock at the end of the year was approximately £6.000 per share.

Compute (1) EPS, (2) P-E ratio, (3) dividend-yield, and (4) dividend-payout ratio.

2-44 Earnings and Dividend Ratios

Chevron Corporation is one of the largest oil companies in the world. The company's revenue in 2008 was $273.005 billion. Net income was $23.931 billion. EPS was $11.74. The company's common stock is the only type of shares outstanding.

1. Compute the average number of common shares outstanding during the year.
2. The dividend-payout ratio was 21.55%. What was the amount of dividends per share? Compare this with EPS.
3. The market price of the stock at the end of the year was $76.50 per share. Compute (a) dividend-yield and (b) P-E ratio.

Problems

2-45 Fundamental Revenue and Expense

R. J. Sen Corporation was formed on June 1, 20X0, when some stockholders invested $100,000 in cash in the company. During the first week of June, the company spent $85,000 cash for merchandise inventory (sportswear). During the remainder of the month, total sales reached $115,000, of which $70,000 was on open account. The cost of the inventory sold was $60,000. For simplicity, assume that no other transactions occurred except that on June 28, R. J. Sen Corporation acquired $34,000 additional inventory on open account.

1. By using the balance sheet equation approach demonstrated in Exhibit 2-3 (p. 63), analyze all transactions for June. Show all amounts in thousands.
2. Prepare a balance sheet for June 30, 20X0.
3. Prepare two statements for June, side by side. The first should use the accrual basis of accounting to compute net income, and the second, the cash basis to compute the difference between cash inflows and cash outflows. Which basis provides a more informative measure of economic performance? Why?

2-46 Revenue Recognition

Footnote 1 to Microsoft's 2009 annual report contained the following:

Revenue Recognition

Revenue is recognized when persuasive evidence of an arrangement exists, delivery has occurred, the fee is fixed or determinable, and collectibility is probable. . . . Revenue for retail packaged products, products licensed to original equipment manufacturers (OEMs) . . . is recognized as products are shipped. . . . Revenue from multi-year licensing arrangements are accounted for as subscriptions, with billings recorded as unearned revenue and recognized as revenue ratably over the billing coverage period. . . . Revenue related to our Xbox 360 game console, games published by us, and other hardware components is generally recognized when ownership is transferred to the retailers. Revenue related to games published by third parties for use on the Xbox 360 platform is recognized when games are manufactured by the game publishers. Display advertising revenue is recognized as advertisements are displayed. Search advertising revenue is recognized when the ad appears in the search results or when the action necessary to earn the revenue has been completed. Consulting services revenue is recognized as services are rendered, generally based on the negotiated hourly rate in the consulting arrangement and the number of hours worked during the period.

1. Explain how Microsoft's revenue recognition policy meets the criteria of being earned and realized.
2. Discuss the accounting for multi-year licensing arrangements.
3. Discuss the accounting for revenue related to games published by third parties.

2-47 Analysis of Transactions, Preparation of Statements

(Alternates are 2-48, 2-50, 2-52, and 2-54.) The Montero Company, a wholesale distributor of furnace and air conditioning equipment, began business on July 1, 20X2. The following summarized transactions occurred during July:

1. Montero's stockholders contributed $300,000 in cash in exchange for their common stock.
2. On July 1, Montero signed a 1-year lease on a warehouse, paying $60,000 cash in advance for occupancy of 12 months.
3. On July 1, Montero acquired warehouse equipment for $100,000. A cash down payment of $40,000 was made, and a note payable was signed for the balance.
4. On July 1, Montero paid $24,000 cash for a 2-year insurance policy covering fire, casualty, and related risks.

5. Montero acquired assorted merchandise for $35,000 cash.
6. Montero acquired assorted merchandise for $190,000 on open account.
7. Total sales were $205,000, of which $30,000 were for cash.
8. Cost of inventory sold was $160,000.
9. Rent expense was recognized for the month of July.
10. Depreciation expense of $2,000 was recognized for the month.
11. Insurance expense was recognized for the month.
12. Collected $35,000 from credit customers.
13. Disbursed $80,000 to trade creditors.

For simplicity, ignore all other possible expenses.

Required

1. By using the balance sheet equation format demonstrated in Exhibit 2-3 (p. 63), prepare an analysis of each transaction. Show all amounts in thousands. What do transactions 8–11 illustrate about the theory of assets and expenses? (Use a Prepaid Insurance account, which is not illustrated in Exhibit 2-3.)
2. Prepare an income statement for July on the accrual basis. Ignore income taxes.
3. Prepare a balance sheet for July 31, 20X2.

2-48 Analysis of Transactions, Preparation of Statements

(Alternates are 2-47, 2-50, 2-52, and 2-54.) The Bekele Company was incorporated on April 1, 20X0. Bekele had 10 holders of common stock. Rosa Bekele, who was the president and chief executive officer, held 51% of the shares. The company rented space in chain discount stores and specialized in selling ladies' accessories. Bekele's first location was in a store that was part of The Old Market in Omaha.

The following events occurred during April:

1. The company was incorporated. Common stockholders invested $200,000 cash.
2. Purchased merchandise inventory for cash, $45,000.
3. Purchased merchandise inventory on open account, $35,000.
4. Merchandise carried in inventory at a cost of $37,000 was sold for cash for $25,000 and on open account for $75,000, for a grand total of $100,000. Bekele (not The Old Market) carries and collects these accounts receivable.
5. Collection of accounts receivable, $18,000. See transaction 4.
6. Payments of accounts payable $30,000. See transaction 3.
7. Special display equipment and fixtures were acquired on April 1 for $36,000. Their expected useful life was 36 months. This equipment was removable. Bekele paid $12,000 as a down payment and signed a promissory note for $24,000. Also see transaction 11.
8. On April 1, Bekele signed a rental agreement with The Old Market. The agreement called for a flat $2,000 per month, payable quarterly in advance. Therefore, Bekele paid $6,000 cash on April 1.
9. The rental agreement also called for a payment of 10% of all sales. This payment was in addition to the flat $2,000 per month. In this way, The Old Market would share in any success of the venture and be compensated for general services such as cleaning and utilities. This payment was to be made in cash on the last day of each month as soon as the sales for the month had been tabulated. Therefore, Bekele made the payment on April 30.
10. Employee wages and sales commissions were all paid for in cash. The amount was $34,000.
11. Depreciation expense of $1,000 was recognized ($36,000/36 months). See transaction 7.
12. The expiration of an appropriate amount of prepaid rental services was recognized. See transaction 8.

Required

1. Prepare an analysis of Bekele Company's transactions, employing the balance-sheet-equation approach demonstrated in Exhibit 2-3 (p. 63). Show all amounts in thousands.
2. Prepare a balance sheet as of April 30, 20X0, and an income statement for the month of April. Ignore income taxes.
3. Given these sparse facts, analyze Bekele's performance for April and its financial position as of April 30, 20X0.

2-49 Accrual Versus Cash-Based Revenues

(Alternate is 2-51.) Refer to the preceding problem. Suppose Bekele measured performance on the cash basis instead of on the accrual basis. Compute the cash receipts, cash disbursements, and net cash inflows (outflows) for April. Which measure, accrual-based net income or net cash inflows (outflows), provides a better measure of accomplishment? Why?

2-50 Analysis of Transactions, Preparation of Statements

(Alternates are 2-47, 2-48, 2-52, and 2-54.) H.J. Heinz Company's actual condensed balance sheet data for July 31, 2009, follow ($ in millions):

Cash	$ 551	Accounts payable	$ 1,084
Receivables	1,052	Other liabilities	7,363
Inventories	1,334		
Other assets	5,143	Shareholders' equity	1,702
Property, plant, and equipment	2,069		
Total	$10,149	Total	$10,149

The following summarizes a few transactions during August 2009 ($ in millions):

1. Ketchup carried in inventory at a cost of $4 was sold for cash of $3 and on open account of $8, for a grand total of $11.
2. Acquired inventory on account, $6.
3. Collected receivables, $5.
4. On August 2, used $12 cash to prepay some rent and insurance for 12 months. Heinz classifies prepaid expenses as Other Assets.
5. Payments on accounts payable (for inventories), $4.
6. Paid selling and administrative expenses in cash, $1.
7. Prepaid expenses of $1 for rent and insurance expired in August.
8. Depreciation expense of $1 was recognized for August.

Required

1. Prepare an analysis of Heinz's transactions, employing the balance-sheet-equation approach demonstrated in Exhibit 2-3 (p. 63). Show all amounts in millions.
2. Prepare a statement of earnings for the month ended August 31 and a balance sheet as of August 31. Ignore income taxes.

2-51 Accrual Versus Cash-Based Revenue

(Alternate is 2-49.) Refer to the preceding problem. Suppose Heinz measured performance on the cash basis instead of the accrual basis. Compute the cash receipts, cash disbursements, and net cash inflows (outflows) during August. Which measure, net income or net cash inflows (outflows), provides a better measure of overall performance? Why?

2-52 Analysis of Transactions, Preparation of Statements

(Alternates are 2-47, 2-48, 2-50, and 2-54.) Nestlé S.A. is a Swiss company that calls itself the world's leading nutrition, health, and wellness company. It produces many food products including Nestlé Milk Chocolate and Nescafé. Nestlé's actual condensed balance sheet data for January 1, 2009, reported under IFRS, follow (in millions of Swiss francs, CHF):

Cash	CHF 5,835	Accounts payable	CHF 12,608
Receivables	13,442	Income taxes payable	824
Inventories	9,342	Other liabilities	37,867
Property, plant, and equipment	21,097	Owners' equity	54,916
Other assets	56,499		
Total	CHF106,215	Total	CHF106,215

The following summarizes a few transactions during January 2009 (CHF in millions):

1. Products carried in inventory at a cost of CHF500 were sold for cash of CHF350 and on open account of CHF400, for a grand total of CHF750.

2. Collection of receivables, CHF420.
3. Depreciation expense of CHF30 was recognized.
4. Selling and administrative expenses of CHF240 were paid in cash.
5. Prepaid expenses of CHF50 expired in January. These included fire insurance premiums paid in the previous year that applied to future months. The expiration increases selling and administrative expenses and reduces other assets.
6. The January 1 liability for income taxes was paid in cash on January 25.

Required

1. Prepare an analysis of Nestlé's transactions, employing the balance-sheet-equation approach demonstrated in Exhibit 2-3 (p. 63). Show all amounts in millions.
2. Prepare a statement of earnings before taxes. Also prepare a balance sheet as of January 31.

2-53 Prepare Financial Statements

The Ludmilla Corporation does not use the services of a professional accountant. At the end of its second year of operations, 20X2, the company's office manager prepared its financial statements. Listed next in random order are the items appearing in these statements:

Accounts receivable	$ 31,400	Office supplies inventory	$ 2,000
Paid-in capital	100,000	Notes payable	7,000
Trucks	33,700	Merchandise inventory	61,000
Cost of goods sold	157,000	Accounts payable	14,000
Salary expense	86,000	Notes receivable	2,500
Unexpired insurance	1,800	Utilities expenses	5,000
Rent expense	19,500	Net income	8,200
Sales	285,000	Retained earnings	
Advertising expense	9,300	January 1, 20X2	18,000
Cash	14,800	December 31, 20X2	26,200

You are satisfied that the statements in which these items appear are correct, except for several matters that the office manager overlooked. The following information should have been entered on the books and reflected in the financial statements:

a. The amount shown for rent expense includes $1,500 that is actually prepaid for the first month in 20X3.
b. Of the amount shown for unexpired insurance, only $800 is prepaid for periods after 20X2.
c. Depreciation of trucks for 20X2 is $5,000.
d. About $1,200 of the office supplies in the inventory shown earlier was actually issued and used during 20X2 operations.
e. Cash dividends of $4,000 were declared in December 20X2 by the board of directors. The company will distribute these dividends in February 20X3.

Prepare in good form the following corrected financial statements, ignoring income taxes:

1. Income statement for 20X2
2. Statement of retained earnings for 20X2
3. Balance sheet at December 31, 20X2

It is not necessary to prepare a columnar analysis to show the transaction effects on each element of the accounting equation.

2-54 Transaction Analysis and Financial Statements, Including Dividends

(Alternates are 2-47, 2-48, 2-50, and 2-52.) Consider the following balance sheet of a wholesaler of children's toys:

Gecko Toy Company
Balance Sheet, December 31, 20X0

Assets		Liabilities and Stockholders' Equity		
		Liabilities		
Cash	400,000	Accounts payable		$ 800,000
Accounts receivable	400,000	Stockholders' equity		
Merchandise inventory	860,000	Paid-in capital	$360,000	
Prepaid rent	40,000	Retained earnings	640,000	
Equipment	100,000	Total stockholders' equity		1,000,000
Total	$1,800,000	Total		$1,800,000

The following is a summary of transactions that occurred during 20X1:

a. Acquisitions of inventory on open account, $1 million.
b. Sales on open account, $1.5 million; and for cash, $200,000. Therefore, total sales were $1.7 million.
c. Merchandise carried in inventory at a cost of $1.30 million was sold as described in b.
d. The warehouse 12-month lease expired on September 1, 20X1. However, the company immediately renewed the lease at a rate of $84,000 for the next 12-month period. The entire rent was paid in cash in advance.
e. Depreciation expense for 20X1 for the warehouse equipment was $20,000.
f. Collections on accounts receivable, $1.25 million.
g. Wages for 20X1 were paid in full in cash, $200,000.
h. Miscellaneous expenses for 20X1 were paid in full in cash, $70,000.
i. Payments on accounts payable, $900,000.
j. Cash dividends for 20X1 were declared and paid in full in December, $100,000.

Required
1. Prepare an analysis of transactions, employing the balance-sheet-equation approach demonstrated in Exhibit 2-3 (p. 63). Show the amounts in thousands of dollars.
2. Prepare an ending balance sheet, a statement of income, and the retained earnings column of the statement of stockholders' equity for 20X1.
3. Reconsider transaction j. Suppose the dividends were declared on December 15, 20X1, payable on January 31, 20X2, to shareholders of record on January 20. Indicate which accounts and financial statements in requirement 2 would be changed and by how much. Be complete and specific.

2-55 Balance Sheet Equation
(Alternates are 2-39 and 2-40.) Nordstrom, Inc., the fashion retailer, had the following actual data for fiscal year ended January 31, 2009 ($ in millions):

Assets, beginning of period	$5,600
Assets, end of period	5,661
Liabilities, beginning of period	A
Liabilities, end of period	D
Other shareholders' equity, beginning of period	914
Other shareholders' equity, end of period	987
Retained earnings, beginning of period	201
Retained earnings, end of period	C
Total revenues	8,573
Cost of sales and all other expenses	8,172
Net earnings	B
Dividends and other decreases in retained earnings	379

Find the unknowns ($ in millions), showing computations to support your answers.

2-56 Two Sides of a Transaction

For each of the following transactions, show the effects on the entities involved. As was illustrated in the chapter, use the A = L + OE equation to demonstrate the effects. Using the accounts in the illustration below, show the dollar amounts and indicate whether the effects are increases or decreases.

ILLUSTRATION

The Nebraska State Hospital collects $1,000 from the Blue Cross Health Care Plan.

		A		=	L + OE
Entity	Cash	Other Assets	Trucks		Liabilities
Hospital	+1,000	−1,000		=	
Blue Cross	−1,000			=	−1,000

1. Borrowing of $150,000 on a home mortgage from Fidelity Savings by David Stratton.
2. Payment of $10,000 principal on the preceding mortgage. Ignore interest.
3. Purchase of a 2-year subscription to *Newsweek* magazine for $90 cash by Cindy Silverton.
4. Purchase of used trucks by the U.S. Postal Service for $10 million cash from **FedEx**. The trucks were carried in the accounts at $10 million (original cost minus accumulated depreciation) by FedEx.
5. Purchase of U.S. government bonds for $100,000 cash by **Lockheed Corporation**.
6. Cash deposits of $18 on the returnable bottles sold by **Safeway Stores** to a retail customer, Philomena Simon.
7. Collections on open account of $100 by an **Office Depot** store from a retail customer, Gerald Arrow.
8. Purchase of traveler's checks of $1,000 from **American Express Company** by William Spence.
9. Cash deposit of $600 in a checking account in **Bank of America** by Jeffrey Hoskins.
10. Purchase of a **United Airlines** "supersaver" airline ticket for $400 cash by Peter Tanlu on June 15. The trip will be taken on September 10.

2-57 Net Income and Retained Earnings

McDonald's Corporation is a well-known fast-food restaurant company. The following data are from its 2008 annual report ($ in millions):

McDonald's Corporation

Retained earnings, beginning of year	$26,461	Dividends declared	$ 1,821
Revenues	23,522	Selling, general, and administrative expenses	2,356
Interest and other nonoperating expenses	285	Franchise restaurants— occupancy expenses	1,230
Provision for income taxes	1,845	Retained earnings, end of year	28,953
Food and paper expense	5,586		
Payroll and employee benefits	4,300	Occupancy and other operating expenses	3,607

1. Prepare the following for the year:
   a. Income statement. Label the final three lines of the income statement as follows: income before provision for income taxes, provision for income taxes, and net income.
   b. The retained earnings column of the statement of stockholders' equity.
2. Comment briefly on the relative size of the cash dividend.

2-58 Earnings Statement, Retained Earnings

Dell Inc. is a computer company with headquarters in Austin, Texas. The following amounts were in the financial statements contained in its annual report for the year ended January 30, 2009 ($ in millions):

Total revenues	$61,101	Retained earnings at beginning	
Cash	8,352	of year (February 1, 2008)	$18,199
Provision for income taxes	846	Cost of revenue	50,144
Accounts payable	58,309	Dividends declared	0
Total assets	26,500	Other expenses	7,633

Choose the relevant data and prepare (1) the income statement for the year and (2) the retained earnings column of the statement of stockholders' equity for the year. Label the final three lines of the income statement as follows: income before income taxes, provision for income taxes, and net income.

2-59 Continuity Convention and Liquidation

The following news report appeared in the financial press:

> The Bulgarian national airline Balkan is to be placed in liquidation after its creditors today rejected a reorganization plan, legal administrators for the carrier said. With debts of €92 million to 2,200 creditors, Balkan began bankruptcy procedures in March. Creditors today rejected a restructuring for the airline and insisted on the sale of its assets to pay off its debts.

Explain how the measurements used in the financial statements of Balkan would differ from those used in a similar airline that had not been placed in liquidation.

2-60 Financial Ratios

(Alternate is 2-61.) Following is a list of three well-known package delivery companies (UPS and FedEx from the United States and Deutsche Post World Net, owner of DHL, in Germany) and selected financial data of the sort typically included in letters sent by stock brokerage firms to clients. Note that € is the symbol for the euro, the European currency.

Company	Per Share Data			Ratios and Percentages		
	Price	Earnings	Dividends	P-E	Dividend-Yield	Dividend-Payout
FedEx	—	$3.64	—	5.5	—	8.2%
UPS	$56.11	—	—	19.0	3.2%	—
Deutsche Post	€23.51	€1.15	—	—	—	78%

The missing figures for this schedule can be computed from the data given.

1. Compute the missing figures and identify the company with the following:
   a. The highest dividend-yield
   b. The highest dividend-payout percentage
   c. The lowest market price relative to earnings
2. Assume you know nothing about any of these companies other than the data given and the computations you have made from the data. Which company would you choose as
   a. the most attractive investment? Why?
   b. the least attractive investment? Why?

2-61 Financial Ratios

(Alternate is 2-60.) Following is a list of three well-known petroleum companies and selected financial data of the sort typically included in letters sent by stock brokerage firms to clients.

Company	Per Share Data			Ratios and Percentages		
	Price	Earnings	Dividends	P-E	Dividend-Yield	Dividend-Payout
Royal Dutch Shell	$18.75	$4.27	$1.56	—	—	—
ExxonMobil	$79.83	—	—	9.10	2.1%	—
Chevron	—	$2.45	—	31.0	—	26.5%

The missing figures for this schedule can be computed from the data given.

1. Compute the missing figures and identify the company with the following:
   a. The highest dividend-yield
   b. The highest dividend-payout percentage
   c. The lowest market price relative to earnings
2. Assume that you know nothing about any of these companies other than the data given and the computations you have made from the data. Which company would you choose as
   a. the most attractive investment? Why?
   b. the least attractive investment? Why?

2-62 Classic Case of Revenue Recognition and Ethics

Kendall Square Research Corporation (KSR), located in Waltham, Massachusetts, produced high-speed computers and competed against companies such as **Cray Research** and **Sun Microsystems**.

In August 1993, the common stock of KSR reached an all-time high of $25.75 a share; by mid-December, it had plummeted to $5.25. Its financial policies were called into question in an article in *Financial Shenanigan Busters*. The main charge was that the company was recording revenues before it was appropriate.

KSR sold expensive computers to universities and other research institutions. Often, the customers took delivery before they knew how they might pay for the computers. Sometimes they anticipated receiving grants that would pay for the computers, but other times they had no prospective funding. KSR also recorded revenue when it shipped computers to distributors who did not yet have customers to buy them and when it sold computers contingent on future upgrades.

Comment on the ethical implications of KSR's revenue recognition practices.

2-63 Relevance and Faithful Representation

Study Appendix 2. **Plum Creek Timber Company, Inc.**, is a Washington State forest products company. Its largest asset is Timber and Timberlands carried on its balance sheet at $3,565 million on June 30, 2009. This represents 78% of Plum Creek's total assets. A footnote indicates that "timber and timberlands . . . are stated at cost." This means that the book value of the land and timber is the cost Plum Creek paid for it whenever it purchased the property. Also on Plum Creek's books are cash of $347 million and inventories of $53 million.

1. Does the timber and timberlands book value better meet the criterion of relevance or the criterion of faithful representation? Explain.
2. Plum Creek's total assets are the sum of the book value of timber and timberlands, cash, inventories, and several other relatively small assets. What problem do you see with adding these amounts together when measuring total assets?
3. Is there an alternative measure of the timber and timberlands that might be more relevant than the original cost? If so, what is it? Would your measure meet the criterion of faithful representation as well as the original cost does?

Collaborative Learning Exercise

2-64 Financial Ratios

Form groups of four to six persons each. Each member of the group should pick a different company and find the most recent annual report for that company. (If you do not have printed annual reports, try searching the Internet for one.)

1. Members should compute the following ratios for their company:
   a. EPS
   b. P-E ratio
   c. Dividend-yield ratio
   d. Dividend-payout ratio
2. As a group, list two possible reasons that each ratio differs across the selected companies. Focus on comparing the companies with the highest and lowest values for each ratio, and explain how the nature of the company might be the reason for the differences in ratios.

Analyzing and Interpreting Financial Statements

2-65 Financial Statement Research
Select the financial statements of any company.

1. What was the amount of sales (or total revenues), and the net income for the most recent year?
2. What was the total amount of cash dividends for the most recent year?
3. What was the ending balance in retained earnings in the most recent year? What were the two most significant items during the year that affected the retained earnings balance?

2-66 Analyzing Starbucks' Financial Statements
Find the Starbucks financial statements for 2009 either on Starbucks' Web site or on the SEC's Edgar Web site and answer the following questions:

1. What was the amount of net revenues (total sales) and net earnings for the year ended September 27, 2009?
2. How did Starbucks' net income and dividends affect its retained earnings?
3. What is Starbucks' EPS for the year ended September 27, 2009? Compute the P-E ratio, assuming the market price for Starbucks' stock was $19.83 at the time.
4. Suppose the average P-E ratio for companies at that time was 15. Do investors expect Starbucks' EPS to grow faster or slower than average? Explain.

2-67 Analyzing Financial Statements Using the Internet: Time Warner
Go to the Web site for Time Warner (www.timewarner.com). Click on Investor Relations, and then Reports & SEC Filings. Find and open the most recent annual report.
Answer the following questions:

1. Locate Time Warner's revenue recognition policy for publishing in the Notes to Consolidated Financial Statements. When does Time Warner recognize revenue from magazines? How does it account for subscriptions paid for in advance?
2. How much is Time Warner's "unearned revenue"? What does it represent and where is it found in the financial statements?
3. Refer to Time Warner's Statement of Income. What items comprise its total revenues? What is the total revenue? What are the total expenses (including income tax expense)?
4. Does Time Warner prepare its income statement using the cash or accrual basis? What items on the balance sheet are clues to answering this question?
5. Do you think Time Warner is a profit-seeking organization? What clues on the financial statements help you answer this?

3

Recording Transactions

LEARNING OBJECTIVES

After studying this chapter, you should be able to:

1 Use double-entry accounting.

2 Describe the five steps in the recording process.

3 Analyze and journalize transactions and post journal entries to the ledgers.

4 Prepare and use a trial balance.

5 Close revenue and expense accounts and update retained earnings.

6 Correct erroneous journal entries and describe how errors affect accounts.

7 Explain how computers have transformed the processing of accounting data.

Have you ever bought a shirt, a pair of jeans, or anything else from a Gap store? If so, your purchase was just one of hundreds of thousands of transactions that Gap Inc. had to record that day. With so many transactions happening, you might think that yours could get lost in the shuffle. Yet, you can read a report on your transaction combined with millions of others in any major newspaper in articles based on press releases such as this one issued by Gap on February 26, 2009, which can be found on the company's Web site:

> *Delivering solid financial results, Gap Inc. today reported [that] net earnings for fiscal 2008 increased to $967 million, or $1.34 per share . . . Net earnings increased by 16 percent over fiscal year 2007, while earnings per share increased 28 percent over the prior year . . . Net sales for the 52 weeks ended January 31, 2009 [fiscal 2008] were $14.5 billion compared with $15.8 billion for the 52 weeks ended February 2, 2008. The company's fiscal year 2008 comparable store sales decreased 12 percent compared with a decrease of 4 percent for the prior year. The company's online sales for the fiscal year increased 14 percent to $1.03 billion, compared with $903 million in the prior year.*

Are you not seeing that shirt you bought? The information contained in this news article comes directly from Gap's corporate headquarters and informs investors, stockholders, and other interested parties about the financial performance of the organization. Gap's corporate headquarters gets this information from the company's accounting records. Of course, these records contain every single Gap transaction, including your shirt purchase.

Gap Inc.'s transactions can take many forms—for example, merchandise sales for cash or credit or purchases of inventory for its stores. At the end of the month, quarter, or year, accountants compute the totals for each account

and use them to prepare the reports that tell the financial story for that period. As you can see from Gap's press release, net sales totaled $14.5 billion for fiscal 2008. After deducting expenses and other items, net earnings came to $967 million, or 6.7% of net sales ($967 ÷ $14,500). That is, on average Gap earns 6.7¢ on each dollar of sales.

Retailers such as Gap provide monthly information on sales levels. Fiscal 2008 sales were down more than 8% from the level a year earlier. When looking only at stores open for both years, sales decreased by 12%. One bright spot was the 14% increase in online sales. Thus, the February press release confirmed that Gap's earnings increased 16% despite a decrease in sales. Gap management reported that it achieved this by "our ability to drive healthy margins and achieve significant cost savings."

Information in press releases often leads to price changes in a company's stock. Gap's share price decreased by 6.6% during the week ending February 27, 2009, to close at $10.79. The earnings release contained significant information and caused investors to change their valuation of shares of Gap. The investors did not view the press release as good news, despite the positive spin put on it by management. Apparently the decrease in sales worried investors more than the good news about earnings.

Methods of processing accounting data have changed dramatically over time because computerized systems have replaced manual ones. However, the steps in recording, storing, and processing accounting data have not changed. Switching from pencil-and-paper accounting records to computerized ones is a little like switching from a car with a stick shift to one with an automatic transmission. You spend less time worrying about routine tasks, but you still need to understand how to use the vehicle. Whether a company enters data into the system by pencil, keyboard, or optical scanner, it must enter, summarize, and report the same basic data, and users must interpret the same basic financial statements.

To intelligently use the financial statements you learned about in the last two chapters, decision makers need to understand the methods accountants use to record and analyze the data in those reports. This chapter focuses on those methods. In particular, this chapter explains the double-entry accounting system that all companies use to record and process information about their transactions. As you will find, a working knowledge of this system is essential for anyone engaged in business. Ultimately, accounting practices constitute a language that managers in all organizations use to understand the economic progress of their organizations. ●

The Double-Entry Accounting System

OBJECTIVE 1

Use double-entry accounting.

double-entry system
The method usually followed for recording transactions, whereby every transaction affects at least two accounts.

In large businesses such as Gap, McDonald's, and Verizon, hundreds or thousands of transactions occur hourly. With so much activity, it might seem easy to lose track of one or two transactions. Even one lost transaction could wreak havoc on a company's accounting (just think of what happens when you miss one transaction in your checking account record). Such errors may lead to serious consequences. As a result, accountants must record these transactions in a systematic manner. Worldwide, the dominant recording process is a **double-entry system**, in which every transaction affects at least two accounts. Accountants analyze each transaction to determine which accounts it affects, whether to increase or decrease the account balances, and how much each balance will change. Accountants have used such a system for more than 500 years, as described in the Business First box.

Recall the first three transactions of the Biwheels Company introduced in Chapter 1:

	A		=	L	+	SE
	Cash	**Store Equipment**		**Note Payable**		**Paid-in Capital**
(1) Initial investment by owner	+400,000		=			+400,000
(2) Loan from bank	+100,000		=	+100,000		
(3) Acquire store equipment for cash	–15,000	+15,000	=			

This balance sheet equation format illustrates the basic concepts of the double-entry system by showing two entries for each transaction. It also emphasizes that the equation Assets = Liabilities + Stockholders' Equity must always remain in balance. Unfortunately, this format is too unwieldy for recording each and every transaction that occurs. In practice, accountants record the individual transactions as they occur and then organize the elements of the transaction into accounts that group similar items together. For example, the Cash account collects all elements that affect cash.

The remainder of this chapter describes the elements of a double-entry system, focusing on how accountants use general journals and general ledgers to record, summarize, and report financial information. The **general journal** is a chronological listing of an organization's transactions and how each transaction affects the balances in particular accounts. The **general ledger** is a collection of all ledger accounts that support the organization's financial statements, where a **ledger account** is a listing of all the increases and decreases in a particular account. Let's begin with the general ledger.

general journal
A complete chronological record of an organization's transactions and how each affects the balances in particular accounts.

general ledger
The collection of all ledger accounts that support an organization's financial statements.

ledger account
A listing of all the increases and decreases in a particular account.

The General Ledger

The general ledger traditionally was a bound or loose-leaf book of ledger accounts, but today it is more likely to be a set of records in an electronic file. However, for simplicity's sake, you can think of the general ledger as a book with one page for each account. When you hear about "keeping the books" or "auditing the books," the word *books* refers to the general ledger, even if it is an electronic file. Accountants always keep the ledger accounts current in a systematic manner.

We use ledger accounts that are simplified versions of those used in practice. We call them **T-accounts** because they take the form of the capital letter T. They capture the essence of the accounting process. The vertical line in the T divides the account into left and right sides for recording increases and decreases in the account. The account title is on the horizontal line of the T.

T-account
Simplified version of ledger accounts that takes the form of the capital letter T.

BUSINESS FIRST

DOUBLE-ENTRY ACCOUNTING: FIVE CENTURIES OF PROGRESS

Double-entry accounting is more than 500 years old. In the same decade that Columbus set sail for America, Luca Pacioli, an Italian friar and mathematician, published *Summa de Arithmetica, Geometria, Proportioni, et Proportionalita* ("Everything About Arithmetic, Geometry, and Proportions"), the first book that described a double-entry accounting system. Pacioli did not invent accounting. He simply described the system used by Venetian merchants. His system included journals and ledgers, with accounts for assets (including receivables and inventories), liabilities, equity, income, and expenses. His process included closing the books and preparing a trial balance. All these terms and concepts are still in use today, as described in this chapter. Pacioli also warned that "a person should not go to sleep at night until the debits equaled the credits," a good warning for accountants today.

The last five decades have seen more changes in accounting than did the preceding five centuries. First, automated data processing started replacing manual accounting systems. This, combined with the growth of complex business transactions, made accounting transactions more difficult and less transparent to financial statement users. Then a knowledge-based economy called into question an accounting system that focused mainly on physical assets.

The accounting scandals of the early twenty-first century put double-entry accounting at a crossroads. First, problems at Enron, WorldCom, Global Crossing, Tyco, Adelphia, and others caused critics to question the relevance of accounting in the modern business world. How could companies that had been reporting healthy financial results suddenly plunge into financial distress? Then some pundits blamed the financial crisis of 2008–2009 and the failure of companies such as AIG, Bear Stearns, and Merrill Lynch on financial reporting rules, especially the accounting for financial instruments. Now, a few years after the criticisms of accounting peaked, it is clear that reliable accounting systems are more important than ever. The discipline of a double-entry system cannot prevent managers and accountants from making bad decisions or entering fraudulent transactions in a company's books, but it does provide a framework for reporting economic results that is essential for disclosing information about a company to investors and potential investors.

In the 1920s, Werner Sombart, a German accountant, made the case that double-entry accounting played a major role in the development of capitalistic, market-based economies. The events of the last decade prove its importance to the smooth functioning of worldwide capital markets. From Pacioli's time until today, double-entry accounting systems have kept confirming their value. To understand a market economy, one must understand the basics of double-entry accounting.

Sources: L. Pacioli, *Summa de Arithmetica, Geometria, Proportioni, et Proportionalita*, 1494; W. Sombart, *Der Moderne Kapitalismus*, 1924.

Consider the format of the Cash account:

Cash	
Left side	Right side
Increases in cash	Decreases in cash

We place increases in asset accounts (such as Cash) on the left side of the T-account and decreases on the right side. We reverse this process for liabilities and owners' equity accounts—increases go on the right and decreases on the left. A **balance** is the difference between the total left-side and right-side amounts in an account at any particular time. Asset accounts have left-side balances, and liability and owners' equity accounts have right-side balances.

The T-accounts for the first three Biwheels Company transactions are as follows:

balance
The difference between the total left-side and right-side amounts in an account at any particular time.

Assets		=	Liabilities + Stockholders' Equity	
Cash			**Note Payable**	
Increases	Decreases		Decreases	Increases
(1) 400,000	(3) 15,000			(2) 100,000
(2) 100,000				

Store Equipment			**Paid-in Capital**	
Increases	Decreases		Decreases	Increases
(3) 15,000				(1) 400,000

Note that each numbered transaction affects two accounts. Remember that, under the double-entry system, each transaction will affect at least two accounts so that the balance sheet is always in balance. In practice, we create accounts as we need them. We call the process of creating a new T-account in preparation for recording a transaction "opening the account." For transaction 1, we opened Cash and Paid-in Capital. For transaction 2, we opened Note Payable, and for transaction 3, we opened Store Equipment. We know that we need a new account when a transaction requires an entry to an account that we have not yet opened.

Each T-account summarizes the changes—increases and decreases—in a particular asset, liability, or owners' equity account. Because T-accounts show only amounts and not transaction descriptions, we key each transaction in some way, such as by the numbering used in this illustration, by the date, or by both. This keying helps us to identify the transaction that caused each entry to the ledger.

Take a look at the analysis of the entries for each Biwheels transaction. Notice that each transaction generates a left-side entry in one T-account and a right-side entry of the same amount in another T-account. When you analyze a transaction, it is helpful to initially pinpoint the effects (if any) on cash. Did cash increase or decrease? Then think of the effects on other accounts. Usually, it is much easier to identify the effects of a transaction on cash than it is to identify the effects on other accounts.

Initial investment by owners, $400,000 cash.
Analysis: The asset **Cash** increases.
The stockholders' equity **Paid-in Capital** increases.

Cash		Paid-in Capital	
(1) 400,000			(1) 400,000

Loan from bank, $100,000.
Analysis: The asset **Cash** increases.
The liability **Note Payable** increases.

Cash		Note Payable	
(1) 400,000			(2) 100,000
(2) 100,000			

Acquired store equipment for cash, $15,000.
Analysis: The asset **Cash** decreases.
The asset **Store Equipment** increases.

Cash		Store Equipment	
(1) 400,000	(3) 15,000	(3) 15,000	
(2) 100,000			

Ledger accounts contain a record of all the changes in specific assets, liabilities, and owners' equities. Accountants can prepare financial statements at any point in time if the account balances are up-to-date. The ledger accounts provide the information needed for the financial statements. For example, Biwheels' balance sheet after its first three transactions would contain the following account balances:

Assets		Liabilities + Stockholders' Equity	
Cash	$485,000	Liabilities	
Store equipment	15,000	Note payable	$100,000
		Stockholders' equity	
		Paid-in capital	400,000
Total	$500,000	Total	$500,000

Three of the four accounts have only one transaction, so the transaction amount becomes the account balance. For Cash, the balance of $485,000 is the difference between the total increases on the left side of ($400,000 + $100,000) = $500,000 and the total decreases of $15,000 on the right side.

Debits and Credits

You have just seen that the double-entry system features entries on left sides and right sides of various accounts. Accountants use the term **debit** (abbreviated dr.) to denote an entry or balance on the left side of any account and the term **credit** (abbreviated cr.) to denote an entry or balance on the right side. Popular usage ascribes other meanings to debit and credit, but in accounting they mean simply left-side entry and right-side entry. Some accountants use the word **charge** instead of debit, but there is no such synonym for credit. Just remember that debit refers to left and credit refers to right, and you will be fine.

Accountants use debit and credit as verbs, adjectives, and nouns. "Debit $1,000 to Cash" and "credit $1,000 to Accounts Receivable" are examples using debit and credit as verbs, meaning that you should place $1,000 on the left side of the Cash account and on the right side of the Accounts Receivable account. In "make a debit to Cash," debit is a noun, and in "Cash has a debit balance of $12,000" it is an adjective describing the balance. From this point on you will see the terms debit and credit again and again. Be sure you understand their uses completely before moving on.

debit
An entry or balance on the left side of an account.

credit
An entry or balance on the right side of an account.

charge
A word often used instead of debit.

Summary Problem for Your Review

PROBLEM

Suppose Biwheels' accountant asked you to do the following: "Debit Note Payable for $5,000 and credit Cash for $5,000."

1. Describe the transaction the accountant is asking you to record.
2. What are the balances in Cash and Note Payable after you record this transaction?
3. After you correctly make the entries, the accountant tells you "I give you credit for correctly carrying out my instructions. If you had failed, it would be a debit on your record." What does she mean by "credit" and "debit" in this situation?

SOLUTION

1. Debiting the Note Payable account means to place an entry for $5,000 on the left side of the T-account. This decreases the Note Payable balance by $5,000 because Note Payable is a liability account. Crediting Cash for $5,000 means a right-hand entry to the Cash account, decreasing the balance in that asset account. Therefore, Cash and Note Payable both decrease by $5,000, so the transaction represents a repayment of $5,000 of the note payable.
2. The Cash account will decrease by $5,000 to ($485,000 − $5,000) = $480,000. The Note Payable account will also decrease by $5,000 to ($100,000 − $5,000) = $95,000.
3. These are popular uses of the terms credit and debit—credit meaning praise or recognition and debit meaning blame. These definitions have nothing to do with the accounting uses of the terms. Remember, in accounting debit means left side and credit means right side, nothing more.

<table>
<tr><td>**OBJECTIVE** 2</td></tr>
</table>

Describe the five steps in the recording process.

The Recording Process

In the preceding section, we entered Biwheels' transactions 1, 2, and 3 directly in the ledger accounts. In actual practice, accountants first record transactions in the general journal. The sequence of five steps in recording and reporting transactions is as follows:

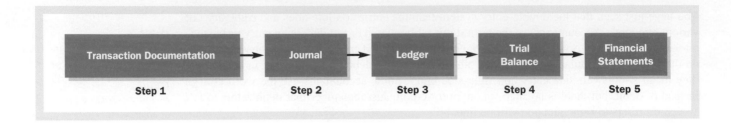

Transaction Documentation	Journal	Ledger	Trial Balance	Financial Statements
Step 1	Step 2	Step 3	Step 4	Step 5

source documents
The original records supporting any transaction.

Step 1: The recording process begins with **source documents**. These are the original records supporting any transaction. Examples of source documents include sales slips or invoices, check stubs, purchase orders, receiving reports, cash receipt slips, and minutes of the board of directors. Most transactions generate a source document. For example, when a company sells a product to a customer, it makes a receipt for the sale. Companies keep source documents on file so they can use them to verify the details of a transaction and the accuracy of subsequent records, if necessary.

book of original entry
Another name for the general journal.

Step 2: In the second step of the recording process, we place an analysis of the transaction, based on the source documents, in the general journal, also called the **book of original entry**. Recall that the general journal is a chronological listing of transactions. It is basically a diary of all events (transactions) in an entity's life.

Step 3: The third step is to enter transactions into the ledger accounts. As we have seen, we enter each component into the left side or the right side of the appropriate accounts.

trial balance
A list of all accounts in the general ledger with their balances.

Step 4: The fourth step is the preparation of the **trial balance**, which is a listing of the accounts in the general ledger together with their balances. This listing aids in verifying clerical accuracy and in preparing financial statements. Thus, we prepare it as needed, perhaps each month or each quarter as the firm prepares its financial statements. The timing of the first four steps varies. Transactions occur constantly so companies prepare source documents continuously. Depending on the size and nature of the organization, transaction summaries may occur continuously, weekly, or monthly. Basically, the timing of the steps in the recording process must conform to the needs of the users of the data.

Step 5: The final step, closing the books and preparing financial statements, occurs at least once a quarter, every 3 months, for publicly traded companies in the United States and at least annually for those reporting under IFRS. However, most companies prepare financial statements more frequently for management's benefit. For example, Springfield ReManufacturing Corporation, an employee-owned company in southern Missouri with more than 1,200 employees and sales of more than $400 million, prepares monthly financial statements. Springfield is a leader in "open book management," in which the company opens its accounting results to everyone in the firm. Management and all employees meet monthly to examine the results in detail. The company provides extensive training to employees on how the accounting process works and what the numbers mean. This management process has focused the attention of every employee and increased efficiency and profitability at Springfield.

Chart of Accounts

chart of accounts
A numbered or coded list of all account titles.

To ensure consistency in recording transactions, organizations specify a **chart of accounts**, which is a numbered or coded list of all account titles. This list specifies the accounts that the organization uses in recording its activities and is usually arranged in the order in which accounts appear in the financial statements. Accountants often use these account numbers as a shorthand way to identify the accounts. The following is the chart of accounts for Biwheels:

Account Number	Account Title	Account Number	Account Title
100	Cash	202	Note payable
120	Accounts receivable	203	Accounts payable
130	Merchandise inventory	300	Paid-in capital
140	Prepaid rent	400	Retained earnings
170	Store equipment	500	Sales revenue
170A	Accumulated	600	Cost of goods sold
	depreciation,	601	Rent expense
	store equipment	602	Depreciation expense
	(explained later)		

There is no universally agreed upon chart of accounts. The chart varies across companies as a function of the size, nature, and complexity of the organization. Large companies may have thousands of account numbers. Accountants often become so familiar with the various codes used in their company that they think, talk, and write in terms of account numbers instead of account names. Thus, they might journalize Biwheels' entry 3, the acquisition of Store Equipment (Account 170) for Cash (Account 100), as follows:

		dr.	cr.
20X2			
Jan. 3 170		15,000	
100			15,000

This journal entry employs the accountant's shorthand, which uses codes without account names. Its brevity and lack of explanation would hamper any outsider's understanding of the transaction, but the entry's meaning would be clear to any accountant within the organization.

Journalizing Transactions

Let's examine more closely step 2 in the recording process. We call this step **journalizing**—the process of entering transactions into the general journal. A **journal entry** is an analysis of the effects of a single transaction on the various accounts, usually accompanied by an explanation. For each transaction, this analysis identifies the accounts to be debited and credited. The top of Exhibit 3-1 shows how to journalize the opening three transactions for Biwheels.

We will use the following conventions for recording in the general journal:

1. The date and identification number of the entry make up the first two columns.
2. The next column, Accounts and Explanation, shows the accounts affected. At the left margin we place the title of the account or accounts to be debited. We indent the title of the account or accounts to be credited. Following the journal entry itself is the narrative explanation of the transaction. The length of the explanation depends on the complexity of the transaction and whether management wants the journal itself to contain all relevant information. Most often, explanations are brief because details are available in the file of supporting documents.
3. The Post Ref. (posting reference) column contains an identifying number that we assign to each account and use for cross-referencing to the ledger accounts.
4. The debit and credit columns show the amounts that we debit (left-entry) or credit (right-entry) to each account. It is customary not to use currency symbols (for example, dollar signs or yen or euro symbols) in either the journal or the ledger. Negative numbers never appear in the journal or the ledger. Instead, the side on which the number appears tells you whether to add or subtract the number in computing an account balance. Debits and credits tell the whole story in the recording process, so be sure you understand them fully.

Posting Transactions to the General Ledger

We call step 3, the transferring of amounts from the general journal to the appropriate accounts in the general ledger, **posting**. To see how this works, consider transaction 3 for Biwheels (see p. 106). The red arrows in Exhibit 3-1 show how we post the credit to Cash using the information and values from the journal entry. Note that the format of the sample general ledger in Exhibit 3-1 provides space for transferring all the information in the journal entry, not just the summary information

OBJECTIVE 3

Analyze and journalize transactions and post journal entries to the ledgers.

journalizing
The process of entering transactions into the general journal.

journal entry
An analysis of the effects of a transaction on the various accounts, usually accompanied by an explanation.

posting
The transferring of amounts from the general journal to the appropriate accounts in the general ledger.

EXHIBIT 3-1

Journal Entries—Recorded in the General Journal and Posted to the General Ledger Accounts

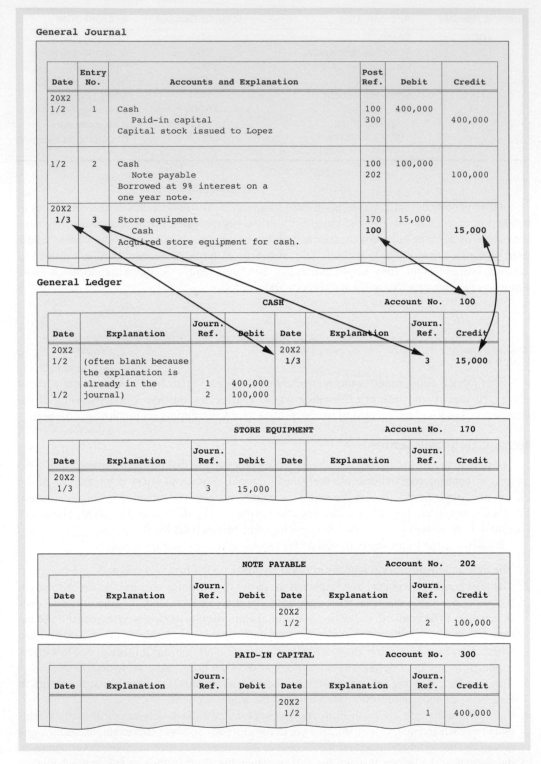

General Journal

Date	Entry No.	Accounts and Explanation	Post Ref.	Debit	Credit
20X2 1/2	1	Cash	100	400,000	
		Paid-in capital	300		400,000
		Capital stock issued to Lopez			
1/2	2	Cash	100	100,000	
		Note payable	202		100,000
		Borrowed at 9% interest on a one year note.			
20X2 1/3	3	Store equipment	170	15,000	
		Cash	100		15,000
		Acquired store equipment for cash.			

General Ledger

CASH   Account No. 100

Date	Explanation	Journ. Ref.	Debit	Date	Explanation	Journ. Ref.	Credit
20X2 1/2	(often blank because the explanation is already in the journal)	1	400,000	20X2 1/3		3	15,000
1/2		2	100,000				

STORE EQUIPMENT   Account No. 170

Date	Explanation	Journ. Ref.	Debit	Date	Explanation	Journ. Ref.	Credit
20X2 1/3		3	15,000				

NOTE PAYABLE   Account No. 202

Date	Explanation	Journ. Ref.	Debit	Date	Explanation	Journ. Ref.	Credit
				20X2 1/2		2	100,000

PAID-IN CAPITAL   Account No. 300

Date	Explanation	Journ. Ref.	Debit	Date	Explanation	Journ. Ref.	Credit
				20X2 1/2		1	400,000

cross-referencing

The process of numbering, dating, and/or some form of identification to relate each general ledger posting to the appropriate journal entry.

allowed in the simplified T-account format. There are columns for dates, explanations, journal references, and amounts. The structure is repeated for debits on the left side of the page and for credits on the right side.

Because posting is strictly a mechanical process of moving numbers from the general journal to the general ledger, it is most efficiently done by a computer. The accountant journalizes a transaction in an electronic general journal, and the computer automatically transfers the information to an electronic version of the general ledger. There is also cross-referencing between the general journal and the general ledger. **Cross-referencing** is the process of using numbering, dating, and/or some other form of identification to relate each general ledger posting to the appropriate journal entry. A single transaction from the general journal might be posted to several different

EXHIBIT 3-2

Ledger Account with Running Balance Column

	Cash		Account No.	100		
Date	Explanation	Journ. Ref.	Debit	Credit	Balance	
20X2						
1/2	(often blank because the explanation is	1	400,000		400,000	
1/2	already in the journal)	2	100,000		500,000	
1/3		3		15,000	485,000	

ledger accounts. Cross-referencing allows users to find all the components of the transactions in the general ledger no matter where they start. It also helps auditors to find and correct errors and reduces the frequency of errors.

General ledger entries do not always take the form of Exhibit 3-1. Exhibit 3-2 shows another popular general ledger format, one that has only one date column and one explanation column and adds an additional column to the presentation to provide a running balance of the account holdings. This format is very similar to the format found in a checkbook. The running balance feature is a useful addition because it provides a status report for an account at a glance. Although most accounting systems are now fully computerized, the reports generated by computers often look much like the paper-based general ledgers and general journals they replaced. After hundreds of years of use, these formats have become traditional and familiar.

Analyzing, Journalizing, and Posting the Biwheels Transactions

We have seen that accountants review source documents about a transaction, mentally analyze the transaction, record that analysis in a journal entry in the general journal, and then post the results to the general ledger. We can now apply this process to additional transactions from the Biwheels Company. We will omit explanations for the journal entries because we already presented them in the statement of the transaction. We indicate the posting of the elements of the transaction to the T-accounts by encircling the new number.

Acquired merchandise inventory for cash, $120,000.

Analysis: The asset **Merchandise Inventory** increases.
The asset **Cash** decreases.

Journal Entry: Merchandise inventory. 120,000
       Cash 120,000

Posting:

	Cash				Merchandise Inventory	
(1)	400,000	(3)	15,000	(4)	(120,000)	
(2)	100,000	(4)	(120,000)			

Acquired merchandise inventory on credit, $10,000.

Analysis: The asset **Merchandise Inventory** increases.
The liability **Accounts Payable** increases.

Journal Entry: Merchandise inventory. 10,000
       Accounts payable 10,000

Posting:

	Merchandise Inventory			Accounts Payable	
(4)	120,000			(5)	(10,000)
(5)	(10,000)				

simple entry
An entry for a transaction that affects only two accounts.

Transaction 5, like transactions 1, 2, 3, and 4, is a **simple entry** because the transaction affects only two accounts. Note that the balance sheet equation remains in balance with each new transaction.

Acquired merchandise inventory for $10,000 cash plus $20,000 trade credit.

Analysis: The asset **Cash** decreases.
The asset **Merchandise Inventory** increases.
The liability **Accounts Payable** increases.

Journal Entry: Merchandise inventory.   30,000
     Cash   10,000
     Accounts payable   20,000

Posting:

	Cash					Accounts Payable	
(1)	400,000	(3)	15,000			(5)	10,000
(2)	100,000	(4)	120,000			(6)	(20,000)
		(6)	(10,000)				

	Merchandise Inventory	
(4)	120,000	
(5)	10,000	
(6)	(30,000)	

compound entry
An entry for a transaction that affects more than two accounts.

Transaction 6 is a **compound entry**, which means that a single transaction affects more than two accounts. Whether transactions are simple (like transactions 1 through 5) or compound, the total of all left-side entries always equals the total of all right-side entries. The net effect is always to keep the accounting equation in balance:

$$\text{Assets} = \text{Liabilities} + \text{Stockholders' equity}$$
$$+30{,}000 - 10{,}000 = +20{,}000$$

7.
Transaction: Sold unneeded showcase to neighbor for $1,000 cash. The cost of the showcase was $1,000.
Analysis: The asset **Cash** increases.
The asset **Store Equipment** decreases.
Journal Entry: Cash   1,000
     Store equipment.   1,000
Posting:

	Cash					Store Equipment	
(1)	400,000	(3)	15,000	(3)	15,000	(7)	(1,000)
(2)	100,000	(4)	120,000				
(7)	(1,000)	(6)	10,000				

In transaction 7, one asset increases, and another asset decreases. The transaction affects only one side of the accounting equation because there is no entry to a liability or owners' equity account.

Returned merchandise inventory to supplier for full credit, $800.

Analysis: The asset **Merchandise Inventory** decreases.
The liability **Accounts Payable** decreases.

Journal Entry: Accounts payable   800
     Merchandise inventory   800

Posting:

	Merchandise Inventory					Accounts Payable	
(4)	120,000	(8)	(800)	(8)	(800)	(5)	10,000
(5)	10,000					(6)	20,000
(6)	30,000						

Paid cash to creditor, $4,000.

Analysis: The asset **Cash** decreases.
The liability **Accounts Payable** decreases.

Journal Entry: Accounts payable   4,000
Cash   4,000

Posting:

	Cash					Accounts Payable			
(1)	400,000	(3)	15,000		(8)	800	(5)	10,000
(2)	100,000	(4)	120,000		(9)	(4,000)	(6)	20,000
(7)	1,000	(6)	10,000					
		(9)	(4,000)					

Transactions 7, 8, and 9 are all simple entries. In transactions 8 and 9, an asset and a liability both decrease an equal amount, retaining the equality of the balance sheet equation.

INTERPRETING FINANCIAL STATEMENTS

Accountants are precise in their use of debit and credit. However, managers sometimes are not as careful. Critique the following statements by a manager.

1. We need to charge that account, so make a credit to it.
2. Debit and credit seem to mean different things to different companies. One company's debit is often another company's credit.

Answer

1. This statement is internally inconsistent. Charge, debit, and left side are synonyms. You cannot both charge and credit an account.
2. This statement can be true in certain situations. The clearest example is probably the sale of merchandise on open account. The buyer's Account Payable would have a credit (right) balance, and the seller's Account Receivable would have a debit (left) balance.

Revenue and Expense Transactions

Revenue and expense transactions deserve special attention because their relationship with the balance sheet equation is less obvious. Recall that the stockholders' equity section of the balance sheet equation includes both Paid-in Capital and Retained Earnings:

$$\text{Assets} = \text{Liabilities} + \text{Stockholders' equity}$$

$$\text{Assets} = \text{Liabilities} + (\text{Paid-in capital} + \text{Retained earnings})$$

Recall from Chapter 2 that, if we ignore dividends, retained earnings is merely accumulated revenue less accumulated expenses. Therefore, we can group the T-accounts as follows:

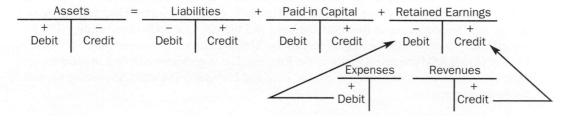

Why don't we simply increase or decrease the Retained Earnings account directly? To do so would make it harder to prepare an income statement because revenue and expense items would be mixed together in the Retained Earnings account. By accumulating information separately for categories of revenue and expense, we can more easily prepare an income statement.

Revenue and expense accounts are part of retained earnings. You can think of them as separate compartments within the larger Retained Earnings account.

A revenue account collects items that increase retained earnings. Any credit to revenue is effectively a credit to retained earnings. Therefore, when we record Sales Revenue, we increase both revenues and retained earnings. Similarly, the expense account collects items that decrease retained earnings. A debit to expense is effectively a debit to retained earnings. Although a debit entry increases expenses, it results in a decrease in retained earnings. Thus, when we record Wage Expense, we increase expenses but decrease Retained Eearnings. Revenue and expense accounts are fundamentally a part of owners' equity.

We can now examine a few transactions involving revenues and expenses. Consider Biwheels' transactions 10a and 10b:

10a. Transaction:	Sales on credit, $160,000.
Analysis:	The asset **Accounts Receivable** increases.
	The stockholders' equity **Sales Revenue** increases.
Journal Entry:	Accounts receivable. 160,000
	Sales revenue 160,000
Posting:	

Accounts Receivable		Sales Revenue	
(10a) (160,000)			(10a) (160,000)

A credit, or right-side, entry in transaction 10a increases the Sales Revenue account, increasing the stockholders' equity account, Retained Earnings. In transaction 10b, a debit, or left-side, entry increases the expense account, Cost of Goods Sold. The effect is to decrease the stockholders' equity account, Retained Earnings.

	Cost of merchandise inventory sold, $100,000.
Analysis:	The asset **Merchandise Inventory** decreases.
	The stockholders' equity decreases because an expense account, **Cost of Goods Sold**, increases.
Journal Entry:	Cost of goods sold 100,000
	Merchandise inventory 100,000
Posting:	

Merchandise Inventory			Cost of Goods Sold	
(4)	120,000	(8) 800	(10b) (100,000)	
(5)	10,000	(10b) (100,000)		
(6)	30,000			

Before we go on, let's look for a minute at the logic illustrated by transactions 10a and 10b. These transactions illustrate the relationship of revenue and expense to retained earnings. Revenues increase Retained Earnings, a stockholders' equity account, because the revenue accounts and the stockholders' equity accounts are right-side balance accounts. Expenses decrease Retained Earnings because expenses are left-side balance accounts. They reduce the normal right-side balance of stockholders' equity accounts. Therefore, increases in expenses are decreases in Retained Earnings and thereby in stockholders' equity. The following analysis shows that we could record the $160,000 in Sales Revenue and $100,000 in Cost of Goods Sold expense directly to the Retained Earnings account or first in separate revenue and expense accounts that are part of Retained Earnings. The latter alternative captures the most information.

	Paid-in Capital		Retained Earnings	
If direct to Retained Earnings:	Decreases	Increases		Increases
			100,000	160,000

	Expenses		Revenues	
If we create revenue and expense accounts that we will eventually summarize into a single net effect on retained earnings:	Increases 100,000			Increases 160,000

Exhibit 3-3 presents the rules of debit and credit and the normal balances of the accounts discussed in this section. It demonstrates the basic principles of the balance sheet equation and the double-entry accounting system:

$$\text{Left side} = \text{Right side}$$
$$\text{Debit} = \text{Credit}$$

The exhibit also emphasizes that revenues increase stockholders' equity. Therefore, we record them as credits. In contrast, expenses decrease stockholders' equity, and we record them as debits. Keeping separate accounts for revenues and expenses makes it easier to prepare an income statement. Revenues and expenses comprise the data used to calculate net income (or net loss) on the income statement, thereby providing a detailed explanation of how the period's transactions caused the balance sheet account, Retained Earnings, to change during the period.

Transaction 11 is the collection of some of the accounts receivable created by transaction 10a:

	Collected cash from debtors, $5,000.		
Analysis:	The asset **Cash** increases.		
	The asset **Accounts Receivable** decreases.		
Journal Entry:	Cash	5,000	
	Accounts receivable		5,000
Posting:			

Cash					Accounts Receivable			
(1)	400,000	(3)	15,000	(10a)	160,000	(11)	(5,000)
(2)	100,000	(4)	120,000				
(7)	1,000	(6)	10,000				
(11)	(5,000)	(9)	4,000				

Rules of Debit and Credit

Assets		=	Liabilities		+	Stockholders' Equity					
Assets		=	Liabilities		+	Paid-in Capital		+	Retained Earnings		
+	−	=	−	+	+	−	+	+	−	+	
Increase	Decrease		Decrease	Increase		Decrease	Increase		Decrease	Increase	
Debit	Credit		Debit	Credit		Debit	Credit		Debit	Credit	
Left	Right		Left	Right		Left	Right		Left	Right	
Normal Bal.				Normal Bal.			Normal Bal.			Normal Bal.	

	Expenses		Revenues	
	+*	−	−	+
	Increase	Decrease	Decrease	Increase
	Debit	Credit	Debit	Credit
	Left	Right	Left	Right
	Normal Bal.			Normal Bal.

*Remember that increases in expenses decrease retained earnings.

Normal Balances

Assets	Debit
Liabilities	Credit
Stockholders' equity (overall)	Credit
Paid-in capital	Credit
Revenues	Credit
Expenses	Debit

EXHIBIT 3-3

Rules of Debit and Credit and Normal Balances of Accounts

Prepaid Expenses and Depreciation Transactions

Recall from Chapter 2 that prepaid expenses, such as prepaid rent and depreciation expense, relate to assets having a useful life that will expire in the future. Biwheels' transactions 12, 13, and 14 demonstrate the journalizing and posting of prepaid rent expenses and depreciation of store equipment.

12. Transaction: Paid rent for 3 months in advance, $6,000.

Analysis: The asset **Cash** decreases.
The asset **Prepaid Rent** increases.

Journal Entry: Prepaid rent   6,000
Cash   6,000

Posting:

Cash				Prepaid Rent	
(1)	400,000	(3)	15,000	(12)	⊙6,000
(2)	100,000	(4)	120,000		
(7)	1,000	(6)	10,000		
(11)	5,000	(9)	4,000		
		(12)	⊙6,000		

Transaction 12 represents the prepayment of rent as the acquisition of an asset. It affects only asset accounts—Cash decreases (a credit) and Prepaid Rent increases (a debit). Transaction 13 represents the subsequent expiration of one-third of the asset as an expense.

Recognized expiration of rental services, $2,000.

Analysis: The asset **Prepaid Rent** decreases.
Rent Expense increases, decreasing stockholders' equity.

Journal Entry: Rent expense   2,000
Prepaid rent   2,000

Posting:

Prepaid Rent				Rent Expense	
(12)	6,000	(13)	⊙2,000	(13)	⊙2,000

Remember that, in this transaction, the effect of the $2,000 increase in Rent Expense is a decrease in stockholders' equity on the balance sheet.

Recognized depreciation, $100.

Analysis: The asset-reduction account **Accumulated Depreciation, Store Equipment** increases.
Depreciation Expense increases, decreasing stockholders' equity.

Journal Entry: Depreciation expense   100
Accumulated depreciation,
store equipment   100

Posting:

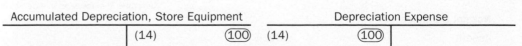

Accumulated Depreciation, Store Equipment			Depreciation Expense	
	(14)	⊙100	(14)	⊙100

accumulated depreciation (allowance for depreciation)
The cumulative sum of all depreciation recognized since the date of acquisition of an asset.

contra account
A separate but related account that offsets or is a deduction from a companion account. An example is accumulated depreciation.

In transaction 14, we open a new account, Accumulated Depreciation. As the name implies, **accumulated depreciation** (sometimes called **allowance for depreciation**) is the cumulative sum of all depreciation recognized since the date of acquisition of an asset. It is a **contra account**—a separate but related account that offsets or is a deduction from a companion account. A contra account has two distinguishing features: (1) It always has a companion account and (2) it has a balance on the opposite side from the companion account. In our illustration, accumulated depreciation is a **contra asset** account because we deduct it from an asset account. Although the normal balance of the asset account is a debit, the normal balance of accumulated depreciation is a credit. The asset and contra asset accounts on January 31, 20X2, are as follows:

Asset:	Store equipment	$14,000
Contra asset:	Accumulated depreciation, store equipment	100
Net asset:	Book value	$13,900

contra asset
A contra account that offsets an asset.

The **book value**, also called **net book value**, **carrying amount**, or **carrying value**, is the balance of an account minus the balance of any contra accounts. In our example, the book value of Store Equipment is $13,900, the original acquisition cost ($14,000) less the contra account for accumulated depreciation ($100).

book value (net book value, carrying amount, carrying value)
The balance of an account shown on the books, minus the value of any contra accounts. For example, the book value of equipment is its acquisition cost minus accumulated depreciation.

A Note on Accumulated Depreciation

Why do published balance sheets routinely report both the original cost of assets and the accumulated depreciation? Why do we not reduce Store Equipment directly by $100? Conceptually, we could. However, accountants have traditionally preserved the asset's original cost in the asset account throughout its useful life. They can then readily refer to that account to learn the asset's initial cost. Reports to management, government regulators, and tax authorities sometimes require such information. Moreover, the original $14,000 cost is the height of accuracy—it is a reliable, objective number. In contrast, the Accumulated Depreciation is an estimate, the result of a calculation, the accuracy of which depends heavily on the accountant's less reliable prediction of an asset's useful life. Recall that we calculated the monthly depreciation of $100 by dividing the $14,000 cost by an assumed useful life of 140 months. We do not *know* how long an asset will be useful. In calculating depreciation, we make estimates that are imperfect, but there is no better way to allocate the cost of the equipment over the periods that it benefits.

Investors also find it useful to know the assets' original costs. They can estimate the average age of the assets by dividing the balance in Accumulated Depreciation by the original cost of the assets. For example, recently **Gap Inc.** had accumulated depreciation of $4,312 million on property and equipment of $7,245 million, making it 60% depreciated. Five years ago Gap's assets were only 37% depreciated, so Gap is depreciating assets faster that it is replacing them. We can compare this with the French retailer **Carrefour**, which has accumulated depreciation of €14,688 million on an original cost of €29,439 million (€ stands for euro, the European currency). Therefore, its assets are (€14,688 ÷ €29,439) = 50% depreciated.

Summary Problem for Your Review

PROBLEM

An annual report of **Kobe Steel, Ltd.**, one of the world's largest producers of iron and steel, showed the following (Japanese yen in billions):

Plant and equipment, at cost	¥2,902
Accumulated depreciation	1,875

1. Open T-accounts for (a) Plant and Equipment, (b) Accumulated Depreciation, and (c) Depreciation Expense. Enter the balances in the Plant and Equipment and Accumulated Depreciation T-accounts.
2. Assume that during the ensuing year Kobe Steel purchased additional plant and equipment for cash of ¥63 billion and incurred depreciation expense of ¥107 billion. Prepare the journal entries, and post to the T-accounts opened in question 1.
3. Show how Kobe Steel would present its plant and equipment accounts in its balance sheet after the journal entries in requirement 2.

SOLUTION

1 & 2. Amounts are in billions of Japanese yen.

Plant and Equipment, at Cost

Bal.	2,902	
(a)	63	
Bal.	2,965	

Accumulated Depreciation

		Bal.	1,875
		(b)	107
		Bal.	1,982

Depreciation Expense

(b)	107	

a. Plant and equipment, at cost	63	
Cash		63
b. Depreciation expense	107	
Accumulated depreciation		107

3. The plant and equipment section would appear as follows:

Plant and equipment, at cost	¥2,965
Accumulated depreciation	1,982
Plant and equipment, net	¥ 983

Biwheels' Transactions in the Journal and Ledger

Exhibit 3-4 shows the journal entries for Biwheels' transactions 4–14 as analyzed in the previous section. The posting reference (Post Ref.) column uses the account numbers from the Biwheels chart of accounts on page 109. These account numbers also appear on each account in the Biwheels general ledger. Exhibit 3-5 shows the Biwheels general ledger in T-account form.

Pause and trace each of the following journal entries to its posting in the ledger in Exhibit 3-5. Recall that the first three journal entries are in Exhibit 3-1 on page 110; the rest of them are in Exhibit 3-4.

1. Initial investment
2. Loan from bank
3. Acquired store equipment for cash
4. Acquired merchandise inventory for cash
5. Acquired merchandise inventory for credit
6. Acquired merchandise inventory for cash plus credit
7. Sold store equipment for cash
8. Returned merchandise inventory for credit
9. Paid cash to creditor
10a. Sales on credit
10b. Cost of merchandise inventory sold
11. Collected cash from debtors
12. Paid rent in advance
13. Recognized expiration of rental services
14. Recognized depreciation

EXHIBIT 3-4
Biwheels Company
General Journal

Date	Entry No.	Accounts and Explanation	Post Ref.	Debit	Credit
20X2	4	Merchandise inventory Cash Acquired inventory for cash	130 100	120,000	 120,000
	5	Merchandise inventory Accounts payable Acquired inventory on credit	130 203	10,000	 10,000
	6	Merchandise inventory Cash Accounts payable Acquired merchandise inventory for cash plus credit (This is an example of a *compound journal entry* whereby more than two accounts are affected by the same transaction)	130 100 203	30,000	 10,000 20,000
	7	Cash Store equipment Sold store equipment to business neighbor	100 170	1,000	 1,000
	8	Accounts payable Merchandise inventory Returned some inventory to supplier	203 130	800	 800
	9	Accounts payable Cash Payments to creditors	203 100	4,000	 4,000
	10a	Accounts receivable Sales revenue Sales to customers on credit	120 500	160,000	 160,000
	10b	Cost of goods sold Merchandise inventory To record the cost of inventory sold	600 130	100,000	 100,000
	11	Cash Accounts receivable Collections from debtors	100 120	5,000	 5,000
	12	Prepaid rent Cash Payment of rent in advance	140 100	6,000	 6,000
	13	Rent expense Prepaid rent Recognize expiration of rental service	601 140	2,000	 2,000
	14	Depreciation expense Accumulated depreciation, store equipment Recognize depreciation for January	602 170A	100	 100

As you trace these items, ask yourself why they appear on the left or right side of each account. You might find it useful to state the relationships explicitly as follows: "The initial investment was a debit to Cash and a credit to Paid-in-Capital. The posting shows an entry on the left-hand side of the Cash account, which increases the balance in this asset account. It also shows a right-hand side entry to the Paid-in-Capital account, which increases the balance in this owners' equity account."

Accountants may update the ledger account balances from time to time as desired. We will use double horizontal lines, as in Exhibit 3-5, to signify that we have updated these accounts. A single number labeled "balance" (or Bal.) immediately below the double lines summarizes all postings above the double lines. We use this balance as a starting point for computing the next updated balance.

The accounts in Exhibit 3-5 that contain only one number do not have a double line. Why? If there is only one number in a given account, this number automatically serves as the ending balance. For example, the Note Payable entry of $100,000 also serves as the ending balance for the account.

Liabilities and Stockholders' Equity

=

(Increases on left, decreases on right)   **(Decreases on left, increases on right)**

Assets

Cash   Account No. 100

(1)	400,000	(3)	15,000
(2)	100,000	(4)	120,000
(7)	1,000	(6)	10,000
(11)	5,000	(9)	4,000
		(12)	6,000
1/31 Bal.	351,000		

Accounts Receivable   120

| (10a) | 160,000 | (11) | 5,000 |
| 1/31 Bal. | 155,000 | | |

Merchandise Inventory   130

(4)	120,000	(8)	800
(5)	10,000	(10b)	100,000
(6)	30,000		
1/31 Bal.	59,200		

Prepaid Rent   140

| (12) | 6,000 | (13) | 2,000 |
| 1/31 Bal. | 4,000 | | |

Store Equipment   170

| (3) | 15,000 | (7) | 1,000 |
| 1/31 Bal. | 14,000 | | |

Accumulated Depreciation, Store Equipment   170A

| | | (14) | 100 |

Note Payable   202

| | | (2) | 100,000 |

Accounts Payable   203

(8)	800	(5)	10,000
(9)	4,000	(6)	20,000
		1/31 Bal.	25,200

Paid-in Capital   300

| | | (1) | 400,000 |

Retained Earnings   400

| | | 1/31 Bal. | 57,900* |

Sales Revenues   500

| | | (10a) | 160,000 |

Expense and Revenue Accounts

Cost of Goods Sold   600

| (10b) | 100,000 | | |

Rent Expense   601

| (13) | 2,000 | | |

Depreciation Expense   602

| (14) | 100 | | |

Note: An ending balance is shown on the side of the account with the larger total.

*The details of the revenue and expense accounts appear in the income statement. Their net effect is then transferred to a single account, Retained Earnings, in the balance sheet. In this case, $160,000 − $100,000 − $2,000 − $100 = $57,900.

EXHIBIT 3-5
Biwheels Company
General Ledger

Preparing the Trial Balance

After posting journal entries to the ledger, accountants can prepare a trial balance (see step 4 on p. 108). Recall that a trial balance is a list of all accounts with their balances. Accountants prepare it as a test or check—a trial, as the name says—before proceeding further. Thus, the purpose of the trial balance is twofold: (1) to help check on the accuracy of postings by proving whether the total debits equal the total credits, and (2) to establish a convenient summary of the balances in all accounts for the preparation of financial statements.

We can prepare a trial balance at any time the accounts are up-to-date. For example, we might prepare a trial balance for Biwheels on January 3, 20X2, after the company's first three transactions:

OBJECTIVE 4

Prepare and use a trial balance.

Biwheels Company
Trial Balance, January 3, 20X2, for the Period January 1–3, 20X2

Account Number	Account Title	Balance Debit	Balance Credit
100	Cash	$485,000	
170	Store equipment	15,000	
202	Note payable		$100,000
300	Paid-in capital		400,000
	Total	$500,000	$500,000

The more accounts a company has, the more detailed the trial balance becomes and the more essential it is for checking the clerical accuracy of the ledger postings. Although the trial balance assures the accountant that the debits and credits are equal, errors can still exist. For example, an accountant may misread a $10,000 cash receipt on account as a $1,000 receipt and record the erroneous amount in both the Cash and Accounts Receivable accounts. Then both Cash and Accounts Receivable would be in error by offsetting amounts of $9,000. Or the accountant might record a $10,000 cash receipt on account as a credit to Sales Revenue instead of a credit reducing Accounts Receivable. Sales Revenue and Accounts Receivable would both be overstated by $10,000. Nevertheless, the trial balance would still show total debits equal to total credits.

Exhibit 3-6 shows the trial balance based on the general ledger shown in Exhibit 3-5. Accountants normally prepare the trial balance with the balance sheet accounts listed first, assets, then liabilities, and then stockholders' equity, followed by the income statement accounts,

	Debits	Credits
Cash	351,000	
Accounts receivable	155,000	
Merchandise inventory	59,200	
Prepaid rent	4,000	
Store equipment	14,000	
Accumulated depreciation, store equipment		$ 100
Note payable		100,000
Accounts payable		25,200
Paid-in capital		400,000
Retained earnings		0*
Sales revenue		160,000
Cost of goods sold	100,000	
Rent expense	2,000	
Depreciation expense	100	
Total	$685,300	$685,300

*If a Retained Earnings balance existed at the start of the accounting period, it would appear here. However, in our example, Retained Earnings was zero at the start of the period.

EXHIBIT 3-6

Biwheels Company

Trial Balance, January 31, 20X2, for the Period January 1 to January 31, 20X2

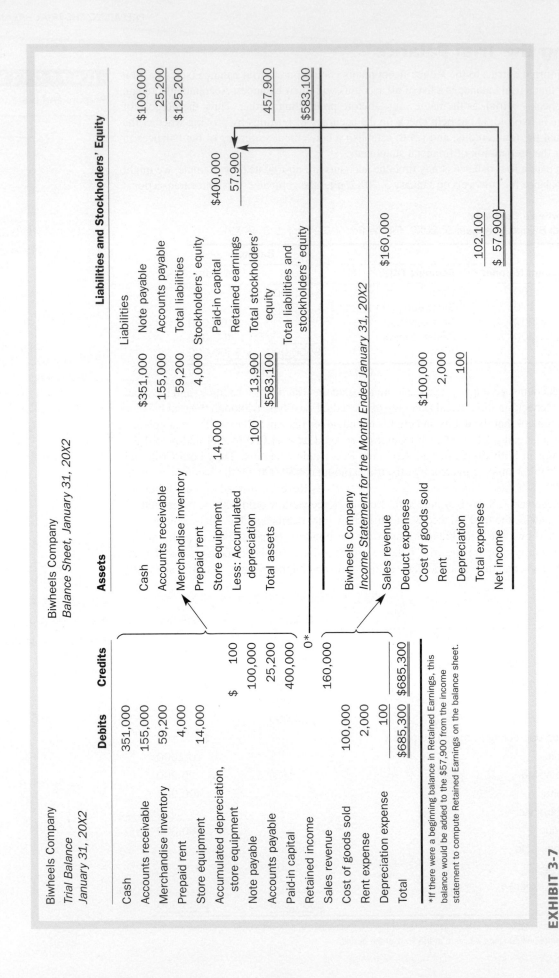

Biwheels Company
Trial Balance
January 31, 20X2

	Debits	Credits
Cash	351,000	
Accounts receivable	155,000	
Merchandise inventory	59,200	
Prepaid rent	4,000	
Store equipment	14,000	
Accumulated depreciation, store equipment		$ 100
Note payable		100,000
Accounts payable		25,200
Paid-in capital		400,000
Retained income		0*
Sales revenue		160,000
Cost of goods sold	100,000	
Rent expense	2,000	
Depreciation expense	100	
Total	$685,300	$685,300

*If there were a beginning balance in Retained Earnings, this balance would be added to the $57,900 from the income statement to compute Retained Earnings on the balance sheet.

Biwheels Company
Balance Sheet, January 31, 20X2

Assets

Cash		$351,000
Accounts receivable		155,000
Merchandise inventory		59,200
Prepaid rent		4,000
Store equipment	14,000	
Less: Accumulated depreciation	100	13,900
Total assets		$583,100

Liabilities and Stockholders' Equity

Liabilities		
Note payable	$351,000	$100,000
Accounts payable	155,000	25,200
Total liabilities	59,200	$125,200
Stockholders' equity	4,000	
Paid-in capital	$400,000	
Retained earnings	57,900	
Total stockholders' equity		457,900
Total liabilities and stockholders' equity		$583,100

Biwheels Company
Income Statement for the Month Ended January 31, 20X2

Sales revenue		$160,000
Deduct expenses		
Cost of goods sold	$100,000	
Rent	2,000	
Depreciation	100	
Total expenses		102,100
Net income		$ 57,900

EXHIBIT 3-7

Biwheels Company

Trial Balance, Balance Sheet, and Income Statement

revenues and expenses. Note that the last stockholders' equity account listed in Exhibit 3-6, Retained Earnings, has no balance because it was zero at the start of the period in our example. All balance sheet accounts except Retained Earnings show their balances as of the date the trial balance is prepared. Retained Earnings shows the balance at the *beginning* of the period. Why? Because we have recorded the changes in Retained Earnings for the current period in revenue and expense accounts rather than directly into Retained Earnings, so Retained Earnings remains at its beginning balance. When accountants prepare formal balance sheets, they reduce the revenue and expense accounts to zero and add their net effect to the beginning balance in the Retained Earnings account to get the ending balance in Retained Earnings.

Closing the Books and Deriving Financial Statements from the Trial Balance

The trial balance is the springboard for the last step of the process, closing the books and preparing the balance sheet and the income statement, as shown in Exhibit 3-7. To **close the books** we transfer the balances in all revenue and expense accounts to Retained Earnings, which resets the revenue and expense accounts to zero so that they are ready to record the next period's transactions. Note that the retained earnings amount in the balance sheet in Exhibit 3-7 is $57,900, although the amount of retained earnings in the trial balance is $0. Why? Because, after closing the books, the January 31 balance sheet shows the ending balance in Retained Earnings—the beginning balance of zero plus net income during the period. In future periods when we prepare a trial balance, the beginning balance will be the ending balance of the previous period. The beginning balance for February will be $57,900.

Let's examine the process of closing the books. Accountants make closing entries to transfer balances in the "temporary" stockholders' equity accounts (revenue and expense accounts) to the "permanent" stockholders' equity account, Retained Earnings. They usually do this in two steps. First they transfer the amounts in each revenue and expense account to an Income Summary account, which becomes the basis for preparing the income statement. Then they transfer the amount in the Income Summary account to the permanent Retained Earnings account.

We illustrate the closing process for Biwheels in Exhibit 3-8. The process closes the revenue accounts in entry C1 and closes the expense accounts in entry C2, transferring the amounts in revenue and expense accounts to the Income Summary account. Then, as a final step, entry C3 transfers the total net income for the period from Income Summary to Retained Earnings. Notice that we opened a new temporary account called Income Summary. We use it only momentarily to keep track of the process. We transfer the revenue and expense amounts into Income Summary and then immediately transfer the balance to Retained Earnings. Slight variations on this process occur in different companies, but the end result is always the same—revenue and expense account balances are reset to zero and the net income generated during the period increases retained earnings.

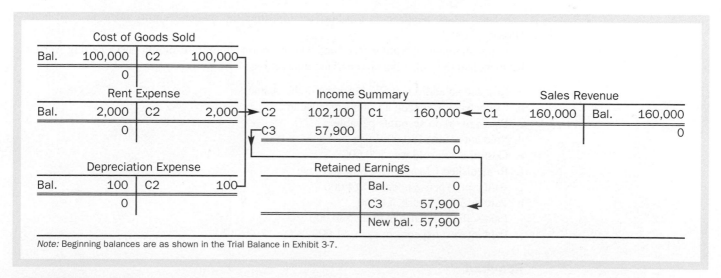

Note: Beginning balances are as shown in the Trial Balance in Exhibit 3-7.

EXHIBIT 3-8

Closing the Accounts

Data are from Exhibit 3-7

The following analysis gives the journal entries for the closing entries shown in Exhibit 3-8:

C1. Transaction:	Clerical procedure of transferring the ending balances of revenue accounts to the Income Summary account.	
Analysis:	The stockholders' equity account **Sales Revenue** decreases to zero. The stockholders' equity account **Income Summary** increases.	
Journal Entry:	Sales revenue. 160,000	
	Income summary	160,000
C2. Transaction:	Clerical procedure of transferring the ending balances of expense accounts to the Income Summary account.	
Analysis:	The negative stockholders' equity (expense) accounts **Cost of Goods Sold**, **Rent Expense** and **Depreciation Expense** decrease to zero. The stockholders' equity account **Income Summary** decreases.	
Journal Entry:	Income summary 102,100	
	Cost of goods sold	100,000
	Rent expense.	2,000
	Depreciation expense	100
C3. Transaction:	Clerical procedure of transferring the ending balance of Income Summary account to the Retained Earnings account.	
Analysis:	The stockholders' equity account **Income Summary** decreases to zero. The stockholders' equity account **Retained Earnings** increases.	
Journal Entry:	Income summary 57,900	
	Retained earnings.	57,900

Summary Problem for Your Review

PROBLEM

The balance sheet of Hassan Used Auto Company, on March 31, 20X1, follows:

Assets		Liabilities + Owners' Equity	
Cash	$ 10,000	Accounts payable	$ 3,000
Accounts receivable	20,000	Notes payable	70,000
Automobile inventory	100,000	Hassan, capital	57,000
Total assets	$130,000	Total liabilities and	
		owners' equity	$130,000

The Hassan business is a proprietorship, thus the owners' equity account used here is Hassan, Capital.

Hassan rented operating space and equipment on a month-to-month basis. During April, the business had the following summarized transactions:

a. Invested an additional $20,000 cash in the business
b. Collected $10,000 on accounts receivable
c. Paid $2,000 on accounts payable
d. Sold autos for $120,000 cash
e. Cost of autos sold was $70,000
f. Replenished inventory for $60,000 cash
g. Paid rent expense in cash, $14,000
h. Paid utilities in cash, $1,000
i. Paid selling expense in cash, $30,000
j. Paid interest expense in cash, $1,000

Required

1. Open the following T-accounts in the general ledger: Cash; Accounts Receivable; Automobile Inventory; Accounts Payable; Notes Payable; Hassan, Capital; Sales; Cost of Goods Sold;

Rent Expense; Utilities Expense; Selling Expense; and Interest Expense. Enter the March 31 balances in the appropriate accounts.

2. Journalize transactions a through j and post the entries to the ledger. Key entries by transaction letter.
3. Prepare the trial balance at April 30, 20X1.
4. Prepare an income statement for April. Ignore income taxes.
5. Give the closing entries.

SOLUTION

The solutions to requirements 1–5 are in Exhibits 3-9 through 3-12. Exhibit 3-9 shows the journal entries. Exhibit 3-10 includes the appropriate opening balances and shows the posting of all transactions to the general ledger. Exhibit 3-11 presents the trial balance and the income statement. The closing entries appear in Exhibit 3-12.

EXHIBIT 3-9

Hassan Used Auto Company

General Journal

ENTRY	ACCOUNTS AND EXPLANATION	POST REF.*	DEBIT	CREDIT
a.	Cash	✓	20,000	
	Hassan, capital	✓		20,000
	Investment in business by Hassan			
b.	Cash	✓	10,000	
	Accounts receivable	✓		10,000
	Collected cash on accounts			
c.	Accounts payable	✓	2,000	
	Cash	✓		2,000
	Disbursed cash on accounts owed to others			
d.	Cash	✓	120,000	
	Sales Revenue	✓		120,000
	Sales for cash			
e.	Cost of goods sold	✓	70,000	
	Automobile inventory	✓		70,000
	Cost of inventory that was sold to customers			
f.	Automobile inventory	✓	60,000	
	Cash	✓		60,000
	Replenished inventory			
g.	Rent expense	✓	14,000	
	Cash	✓		14,000
	Paid April rent			
h.	Utilities expense	✓	1,000	
	Cash	✓		1,000
	Paid April utilities			
i.	Selling expense	✓	30,000	
	Cash	✓		30,000
	Paid April selling expenses			
j.	Interest expense	✓	1,000	
	Cash	✓		1,000
	Paid April interest expense			

*Ordinarily, account numbers are used to denote specific posting references. Otherwise, check marks are used to indicate that the entry has been posted to the general ledger.

Cash

Bal.*	10,000	(c)	2,000
(a)	20,000	(f)	60,000
(b)	10,000	(g)	14,000
(d)	120,000	(h)	1,000
	160,000	(i)	30,000
		(j)	1,000
			108,000†
Bal.	52,000		

Accounts Receivable

Bal.*	20,000	(b)	10,000
Bal.	10,000		

Automobile Inventory

Bal.*	100,000	(e)	70,000
(f)	60,000		
Bal.	90,000		

Accounts Payable

(c)	2,000	Bal.*	3,000
		Bal.	1,000

Notes Payable

		Bal.*	70,000

Cost of Goods Sold

(e)	70,000

Selling Expense

(i)	30,000

Utilities Expense

(h)	1,000

Hassan, Capital

		Bal.*	57,000
		(a)	20,000
		Bal.	77,000

Sales Revenue

		(d)	120,000

Rent Expense

(g)	14,000

Interest Expense

(j)	1,000

*Balances denoted with an asterisk are as of March 31; balances without asterisks are as of April 30. A lone number in any account also serves as an ending balance.
†Subtotals are included in the Cash account. They are not an essential part of T-accounts. However, when an account contains many postings, subtotals ease the checking of arithmetic.

EXHIBIT 3-10
Hassan Used Auto Company
General Ledger

Account Title	Balance		Hassan Used Auto Company
	Debit	**Credit**	Income Statement for the Month Ended April 30, 20X1

Account Title	Debit	Credit
Cash	$ 52,000	
Accounts receivable	10,000	
Automobile inventory	90,000	
Accounts payable		$ 1,000
Notes payable		70,000
Hassan, capital		77,000*
Sales Revenue		120,000
Cost of goods sold	70,000	
Rent expense	14,000	
Utilities expense	1,000	
Selling expense	30,000	
Interest expense	1,000	
Total	$268,000	$268,000

Hassan Used Auto Company
Income Statement for the Month Ended April 30, 20X1

Sales		$120,000
Deduct expenses		
Cost of goods sold	$70,000	
Rent expense	14,000	
Utilities expense	1,000	
Selling expense	30,000	
Interest expense	1,000	116,000
Net income		$ 4,000

*Beginning balance ($57,000) plus additional investment ($20,000).

EXHIBIT 3-11

Hassan Used Auto Company

Trial Balance and Income Statement, for the Month Ended April 30, 20X1

C1.	Sales Revenue	120,000	
	Income summary		120,000
C2.	Income summary	116,000	
	Cost of goods sold		70,000
	Selling expense		30,000
	Utilities expense		1,000
	Rent expense		14,000
	Interest expense		1,000
C3.	Income summary	4,000	
	Retained earnings		4,000

EXHIBIT 3-12

Hassan Used Auto Company

Closing Entries

Effects of Errors

Now that we have completed all steps of the recording process, let's consider what happens when journal entries have errors. Suppose a journal entry contains an error. How do we correct it? If we discover the error immediately, we can rewrite the entry or reenter the correct data. However, if we detect the error after posting to ledger accounts, we must make a **correcting entry**. Correcting entries cancel a previous erroneous entry and add the correct amounts to the correct accounts. We record the correcting entry in the general journal and post it to the general ledger exactly as we would a regular entry. However, the end result is that we have corrected the balances in the accounts to what they should have been originally. Because we use the balances to prepare the financial statements, they must be correct.

OBJECTIVE 6

Correct erroneous journal entries and describe how errors affect accounts.

correcting entry

A journal entry that cancels a previous erroneous entry and adds the correct amounts to the correct accounts.

Consider the following examples:

1. A company erroneously debited a repair expense to Equipment on December 27. We discover the error on December 31:

CORRECT ENTRY	12/27	Repair expense.................	500	
		Cash......................		500
ERRONEOUS ENTRY	12/27	Equipment	500	
		Cash......................		500
CORRECTING ENTRY	12/31	Repair expense.................	500	
		Equipment		500

The correcting entry shows a credit to Equipment to cancel or offset the erroneous debit to Equipment. It also debits Repair Expense, recognizing the amount that should have been recorded on 12/27. Notice that the credit to Cash was correct, and therefore we did not change it.

2. A collection on account was erroneously credited to Sales on November 2. We discover the error on November 28:

CORRECT ENTRY	11/2	Cash	3,000	
		Accounts receivable		3,000
ERRONEOUS ENTRY	11/2	Cash	3,000	
		Sales revenue		3,000
CORRECTING ENTRY	11/28	Sales revenue.................	3,000	
		Accounts receivable		3,000

The debit to Sales Revenue in the correcting entry offsets the incorrect credit to Sales Revenue. The credit to Accounts Receivable in the correcting entry places the collected amount where it belongs, as a decrease in Accounts Receivable. Essentially, the correcting entry moves the $3,000 credit from the Sales Revenue account to the Accounts Receivable account. The debit to Cash in the original entry is correct, and thus we do not change it.

INTERPRETING FINANCIAL STATEMENTS

Suppose that on May 27, 20X0, a manager reported to the accounting department a purchase of equipment for $10,000 cash. The accountant recorded this transaction in the company's books. After the company had prepared its May financial statements, the manager indicated that he had been in error and that the $10,000 was for supplies that his department used up during May. Prepare a correcting entry. Would this situation raise any potential ethical issues? Explain.

Answer

CORRECTING ENTRY	Supplies expense	10,000	
	Equipment		10,000

The "error" kept the $10,000 expense from reducing May's income. This overstatement of income for May might have had a benefit for the manager, perhaps helping him meet a profit target needed for a bonus. The accountant would have an ethical obligation to investigate this transaction to make sure it was truly an error and not an attempt to manipulate May's income.

Temporary Errors

Undetected errors can affect a variety of accounts, including revenues and expenses for a given period. Some errors are automatically corrected in the ordinary bookkeeping process in the next period. Such errors misstate net income in both periods, which could mislead users of the financial statements. However, by the end of the second period the errors cancel each other out, and they affect the balance sheet of only the first period, not the second.

Consider a payment of $1,000 in December 20X1 for rent. Suppose this was for January 20X2's rent. Instead of recording it as Prepaid Rent, the accountant listed the payment as Rent Expense:

INCORRECT ENTRY	12/X1	Rent expense	1,000	
		Cash.		1,000
		One month's rent.		
CORRECT ENTRY	12/X1	Prepaid rent	1,000	
		Cash.		1,000
		Payment for January 20X2's rent.		
	1/X2	Rent expense	1,000	
		Prepaid rent.		1,000
		Expiration of January 20X2's rent.		

The effects of this recording error are (1) to overstate 20X1's rent expense (which understates pretax income and retained earnings) by $1,000 and understate year-end assets by $1,000 (because the prepayment would not be listed as an asset) and (2) to understate 20X2's rent expense (which overstates pretax income) by $1,000. These errors have no effect on 20X2's ending assets or retained earnings balances. Why? Because the same total assets exist whether the accountant records rent as used in January 20X2 or December 20X1. The total of the pretax incomes for the 2 years is the same with or without the error. The first year's understatement of pretax income by $1,000 offsets the second year's overstatement of $1,000. The retained earnings balance at the end of the second year is thus correct on a pretax basis.

Errors that Persist

Errors that do not automatically correct themselves will keep subsequent balance sheets in error until an accountant makes specific correcting entries. For example, overlooking a depreciation expense of $2,000 in 20X0 would (1) overstate pretax income, assets, and retained earnings by $2,000 in 20X0, and (2) continue to overstate assets and retained earnings on successive balance sheets for the life of the fixed asset. However, observe that the error would not affect pretax income for subsequent years unless accountants commit the same error again.

Incomplete Records

A company's accounting records are not always perfect. Someone may steal, lose, or destroy records, forcing accountants to make journal and ledger entries and create financial statements with incomplete information. Luckily, T-accounts can help accountants to discover unknown amounts. For example, suppose the proprietor of a local sports shop asks your help in calculating her sales for 20X1. She provides the following accurate but incomplete information:

List of customers who owe money	
December 31, 20X0	$ 4,000
December 31, 20X1	6,000
Cash receipts from customers during 20X1	
appropriately credited to customer's accounts	280,000

She further tells you that all sales were on credit, not cash. How can you use T-accounts to solve for the missing credit sales figure? There are two basic steps to follow:

Step 1: Enter all known items into the key T-account. In this case, we are looking for credit sales, which accountants debit to Accounts Receivable. By substituting S for the unknown credit sales, we get the following T-account values:

Accounts Receivable			
Bal. 12/31/X0	4,000	Collections	280,000
Credit sales	S		
Total debits	(4,000+S)	Total credits	280,000
Bal. 12/31/X1	6,000		

Step 2: Solve for the unknown. Finding this solution is a simple algebraic exercise. We can use the debit and credit relationships we have just learned to solve our problem:

$$\text{Total debits} - \text{Total credits} = \text{Balance}$$
$$(4{,}000 + S) - 280{,}000 = 6{,}000$$
$$S = 6{,}000 + 280{,}000 - 4{,}000$$
$$S = 282{,}000$$

The analyses of missing data become more complicated if there are more entries in a particular account or if there is more than one unknown value. Nevertheless, the key idea is to fill in the account with all known debits, credits, and balances, and then solve for the unknown.

Data Processing and Accounting Systems

OBJECTIVE 7

Explain how computers have transformed the processing of accounting data.

---

data processing
The procedures used to record, analyze, store, and report on chosen activities.

Data processing is a general term referring to the procedures used to record, analyze, store, and report on chosen activities. An accounting system is a data processing system. Today most accounting systems are computerized. Software packages are available in many sizes and types. Small companies might use QuickBooks, Peachtree, NetSuite, or Microsoft Small Business Manager. Many large companies build their accounting systems around larger enterprise resource planning (ERP) systems. The largest ERP companies are the large German company SAP and its American rival Oracle. These systems are based on the structure of journal entries and ledger accounts used in this book. They take the drudgery out of bookkeeping, but they have not fundamentally changed the way companies keep their accounting records. Whether you enter transactions data into a book or into a computer, the transactions data in general ledgers and general journals remain the same. The main advantage of a computerized accounting program is that the computer can automatically carry out steps such as general-ledger postings and financial statement preparation.

Computers affect more than the processing of data and preparation of reports. When you check out at a Walgreens drugstore or The Limited clothing store, the cash register often does more than just record a sale. It may be linked to a computer that also records a decrease in inventory. It may activate an order to a supplier if the inventory level is low. If a sale is on credit, the computer may check your credit limit, update the company's accounts receivable, and eventually prepare your monthly billing statement. Most important, the computer can automatically enter every transaction into the journal as it occurs, thereby reducing the amount of source-document paperwork and potential data-entry errors.

Automation has consistently decreased the cost of data processing. Consider American Express, a financial services company that has more than 92 million credit card holders. American Express would receive millions of separate sales slips daily if its system were manual. However, computers record most credit sales by reading the magnetic strips on credit cards. Grocery stores and other retail establishments get most payments by swiping a customer's credit card through a scanner. Most gas stations have the card-reading equipment built into the gasoline pumps, even eliminating the need for sales clerks. Information about each credit sale is electronically submitted to a central computer, which prepares all billing documents and financial statements. Companies automatically record millions of transactions into their general journals without any paperwork or keyboard entry, producing huge savings in time and money while increasing accuracy.

Computers also reduce the time it takes to close the books and prepare financial statements. IBM announced its financial results for the year ended December 31, 2009, in a Webcast at 4:30 PM ET on January 19, 2010. It took less than 3 weeks for a company with nearly $100 billion in sales to finalize its results. Computer-based systems have also allowed the SEC to require large companies to file 10-K reports within 60 days after year-end rather than the 90 days required until this decade. The most recent advance in data processing for financial reporting is the use of **XBRL** (extensible business reporting language), an XML-based computer language that allows easy comparisons across companies. We describe this in the Business First box.

XBRL
Extensible business reporting language, an XML-based computer language that allows easy comparisons across companies.

BUSINESS FIRST

DATA PROCESSING USING XBRL

The Internet has created new opportunities for companies to report and exchange financial information. The first step was putting financial statements on the Web in PDF format. This conveyed the information quickly and easily, but it did not allow analysis of the data. Some companies then made the statements available in Excel format. This allowed analysis between years and between different statements for the same company, but it did not allow intercompany analyses. To address this issue, an original group of 12 organizations (including the AICPA, Deloitte & Touche LLP, Ernst & Young LLP, Great Plains Software, KPMG LLP, Microsoft Corporation, and PricewaterhouseCoopers LLP) formed XBRL International in August 1999 to create a common XML-based language for the reporting of business information. Today, a consortium of more than 550 companies and agencies supports the efforts. In just over 10 years XBRL has become widely used throughout the world. You can view the current status of XBRL on the Web at www.xbrl.org. XBRL (extensible business reporting language) provides "an XML-based framework that the global business information supply chain will use to create, exchange, and analyze financial reporting information including, but not limited to, regulatory filings such as annual and quarterly financial statements, general ledger information, and audit schedules." XBRL will make it easier to share information within companies and to compare information across companies.

One reason for the growth in usage of XBRL is the growing number of regulators, lenders, and other consumers of financial information demanding information in this format. A major step forward for XBRL came in January 2009 when the SEC in the United States issued a rule requiring companies to submit their financial statements in XBRL format—large companies for fiscal periods ending after June 15, 2009, and all companies for fiscal periods ending after June 15, 2011. To facilitate international application of XBRL, the IASB and XBRL International have developed an XBRL taxonomy that models the primary financial statements that a commercial and industrial entity may use to report under International Financial Reporting Standards.

Companies can also improve their internal reporting with XBRL. For example, using XBRL they can quickly, efficiently, and cheaply assemble and integrate data from divisions that use different accounting systems. They can create a variety of reports with minimal effort. And they can use XBRL for tax and other regulatory filings.

Proponents of XBRL also claim that it can improve the quality of financial reporting by making monitoring of reporting easier. Today, the SEC reviews only 14% of the 14,000 filings made by publicly traded companies. If companies submitted financial statements in XBRL format, the SEC could use analytic software to electronically screen nearly all filings. Intra-industry and cross-industry analyses might reveal anomalies that would lead to further investigation of the financial reports. Can this eliminate fraudulent reporting? No, but it might more quickly and easily identify problems, making accountants and executives think twice before deciding to manipulate their financial numbers.

Sources: XBRL International Web site (www.xbrl.org); Securities and Exchange Commission, *Interactive Data to Improve Financial Reporting: Final Rule* (January 30, 2009) on SEC Web site (www.sec.gov/rules/final/2009/33-9002.pdf); "IASC Foundation and XBRL PFS Taxonomy Release," International Accounting Standards Board Press Release, 27 November 2002; N. Hannon, "Accounting Scandals: Can XBRL Help?" *Strategic Finance*, August 2002, pp. 61–62.

Highlights to Remember

1 **Use double-entry accounting.** Double-entry accounting refers to the fact that every transaction affects at least two accounts. For example, we not only keep track of an increase in cash, but we also keep track of whether that increase arose from making a sale or borrowing money.

2 **Describe the five steps in the recording process.** There are 5 steps in the process that leads to the preparation of financial statements: 1) create source documents, 2) record transactions in a general journal, 3) post transactions to the general ledger, 4) prepare a trial balance, and 5) close the books and prepare financial statements.

3 **Analyze and journalize transactions and post journal entries to the ledgers.** The general journal provides a chronological record of transactions. For each transaction it includes the date and an identification number for the transaction, the accounts affected, the amounts of the debits and credits, the identifying number used to post each account to the general ledger, and an explanation of the transaction. After we initially record transactions as journal entries in the

general journal, we post the elements of each transaction to the proper accounts in the general ledger. The general ledger accounts accumulate all the transactions affecting the account over time. We determine the balance in a specific general ledger account by adding all debits and all credits and subtracting the totals. We use a simplified version of general ledger accounts called T-accounts. Accountants at all levels use T-accounts to help think through complex transactions. Accountants use the terms debit and credit repeatedly. Remember that debit means "left side" and credit means "right side."

4 **Prepare and use a trial balance.** Trial balances are internal reports that list each account in the general ledger together with the balance in that account as of the trial balance date. Accountants use them for detecting errors in the accounts and in preparing financial statements. Trial balances that fail to balance are the result of errors in journalizing or posting. The good news is that the out-of-balance condition lets you know that an error has been made.

5 **Close revenue and expense accounts and update retained earnings.** At the end of each accounting period, accountants "close" the temporary revenue and expense accounts. This involves resetting them to zero by transferring their balances for the period into an Income Summary account, which we in turn transfer to the Retained Earnings account.

6 **Correct erroneous journal entries and describe how errors affect accounts.** Despite precautions, errors sometimes occur in accounting entries. Accountants correct such errors when discovered by making correcting entries that reverse the errors and adjust account balances so they equal the amounts that would have existed if the correct entries had been made.

7 **Explain how computers have transformed the processing of accounting data.** Computers are fast and efficient and enable the performance of repetitive tasks with complete accuracy, reducing human effort and errors. Many software packages are available to aid in the processing of accounting transactions. Computers perform tasks from initial recording of a sale, to journalizing and posting, to creation of trial balances and financial statements, and finally to sending financial information to interested parties over the Web.

Accounting Vocabulary

accumulated depreciation, p. 116
allowance for depreciation, p. 116
balance, p. 105
book of original entry, p. 108
book value, p. 117
carrying amount, p. 117
carrying value, p. 117
charge, p. 107
chart of accounts, p. 108

close the books, p. 123
compound entry, p. 112
contra account, p. 116
contra asset, p. 117
correcting entry, p. 127
credit, p. 107
cross-referencing, p. 110
data processing, p. 130
debit, p. 107
double-entry system, p. 104
general journal, p. 104

general ledger, p. 104
journal entry, p. 109
journalizing, p. 109
ledger account, p. 104
net book value, p. 117
posting, p. 109
simple entry, p. 112
source documents, p. 108
T-account, p. 104
trial balance, p. 108
XBRL, p. 130

MyAccountingLab

Assignment Material

Questions

3-1 "Double entry means that amounts are shown in the journal and ledger." Do you agree? Explain.

3-2 "Increases in cash and stockholders' equity are shown on the right side of their respective accounts." Do you agree? Explain.

3-3 "Debit and credit are used as verbs, adjectives, or nouns." Give examples of how debit may be used in these three meanings.

3-4 Name three source documents for transactions.

3-5 "The ledger is the major book of original entry because it is more essential than the journal." Do you agree? Explain.

3-6 "Revenue and expense accounts are really little stockholders' equity accounts." Explain.

3-7 Give two synonyms for book value.

3-8 "Accumulated depreciation is the total depreciation expense for the year." Do you agree? Explain.

3-9 "A trial balance assumes that the amounts in the financial statements are correct." Do you agree? Explain.

3-10 "If debits equal credits in a trial balance, you can be assured that no errors were made." Do you agree? Explain.

3-11 What is the role of the Income Summary account when closing the books?

3-12 "In double-entry accounting, errors are not a problem because they are self-correcting." Do you agree? Explain.

3-13 Are all data processing systems for accounting computerized? Explain.

Critical Thinking Questions

3-14 The Chart of Accounts

You have just joined the accounting staff of a fast-food company. You are surprised that this company has a chart of accounts with twice as many accounts as the fast-food company you previously worked for, even though the current client's sales are one-half as large. You are tempted to write a very critical memo to your manager about this issue. You have asked a more experienced friend for advice. What might this friend ask about these clients?

3-15 The Relation of Expense and Retained Earnings Accounts

A fellow student asked you the following: "I understand that a debit increases an expense account. I also understand that a debit decreases retained earnings. But if an expense account is a part of retained earnings (a 'little' stockholders' equity account), how can a debit entry have a different effect on retained earnings than it does on an expense account?" Provide an explanation to the student.

3-16 Reconstructing Transactions

Your supervisor in the accounting department has asked you to trace transactions from the general journal to the general ledger. You are part way into the task when you find at the top of one page in the general journal that a coffee spill has obliterated part of a transaction. You can see that the debit portion of the transaction was for $1,000 to rent expense, but the credit portion is illegible. How might you go about re-creating what happened?

3-17 Manual Versus Computerized Accounting Systems

As a new auditor, you have just been assigned to the audit of a company with a highly computerized accounting system. How would you expect an audit of such a system to differ from the audit of a small company whose records were maintained manually?

Exercises

3-18 Debits and Credits

For each of the following accounts, indicate whether it normally possesses a debit or a credit balance. Use dr. or cr.:

1. Sales
2. Supplies Expense
3. Accounts Receivable
4. Accounts Payable
5. Supplies Inventory
6. Retained Earnings
7. Dividends Payable
8. Depreciation Expense
9. Paid-in Capital
10. Subscription Revenue

3-19 Debits and Credits

Indicate for each of the following transactions whether an accountant will debit or credit the account named in parentheses:

1. Sold merchandise (Merchandise Inventory), $1,500
2. Bought merchandise on account (Merchandise Inventory), $4,000
3. Paid Napoli Associates $3,000 owed them (Accounts Payable)
4. Received cash from customers on accounts due (Accounts Receivable), $2,000
5. Bought merchandise on open account (Accounts Payable), $5,000
6. Borrowed money from a bank (Notes Payable), $10,000

3-20 Debits and Credits

For the following transactions, indicate whether the accountant for Jacksonville Company should debit or credit the accounts in parentheses. Use dr. or cr.:

1. Jacksonville sold merchandise on credit (Accounts Receivable).
2. Jacksonville received interest on an investment (Interest Revenue).
3. Jacksonville declared dividends and paid them in cash (Retained Earnings).
4. Jacksonville paid wages to employees (Wages Expense).
5. Jacksonville sold merchandise for cash (Sales Revenue).
6. Jacksonville acquired a 4-year fire insurance policy (Prepaid Expenses).

3-21 True or False

Use T or F to indicate whether each of the following statements is true or false:

1. Repayments of bank loans should be charged to Notes Payable and credited to Cash.
2. Cash payments of accounts payable should be recorded by a debit to Cash and a credit to Accounts Payable.
3. Inventory purchases on account should be credited to Accounts Payable and debited to an expense account.
4. In general, all debit entries are recorded on the left side of accounts and represent decreases in the account balances.
5. Cash collections of accounts receivable should be recorded as debits to Cash and credits to Accounts Receivable.
6. Credit purchases of equipment should be debited to Equipment and charged to Accounts Payable.
7. In general, entries on the right side of asset accounts represent decreases in the account balances.
8. Increases in liability and revenue accounts should be recorded on the left side of the accounts.
9. Decreases in retained earnings are recorded as debits.
10. Both increases in assets and decreases in liabilities are recorded on the debit sides of accounts.
11. Asset debits should be on the right and liability debits should be on the left.
12. In some cases, increases in account balances are recorded on the right sides of accounts.

3-22 5-Step Recording Process

Suppose you buy a $150 pair of shoes for cash from Timberland on November 12, 20X0. The shoes cost Timberland $90. Follow the recording of your purchase through the five steps that lead from recording your purchase to its inclusion in Timberland's financial statements. List each step and what happens to the record of your purchase in the step.

3-23 Matching Transaction Accounts

Listed here are a series of accounts that are numbered for identification. Accompanying this problem are columns in which you are to write the identification numbers of the accounts affected by the transactions described. You may use the same account in several answers. For each transaction, indicate which account or accounts are to be debited and which are to be credited. The first transaction is completed for you.

1. Cash
2. Accounts Receivable
3. Inventory
4. Equipment
5. Accumulated Depreciation, Equipment
6. Prepaid Insurance

7. Accounts Payable
8. Notes Payable
9. Paid-in Capital
10. Retained Earnings
11. Sales Revenue
12. Costs of Goods Sold
13. Operating Expense

		Debit	Credit
(a)	Purchased new equipment for cash plus a short-term note	4	1, 8
(b)	Paid some old trade bills with cash		
(c)	Made sales on credit: Inventory is accounted for as each sale is made		
(d)	Paid cash for salaries and wages for work done during the current fiscal period		
(e)	Collected cash from customers on account		
(f)	Bought regular merchandise on credit		
(g)	Purchased 3-year insurance policy on credit		
(h)	Paid cash for inventory that arrived today		
(i)	Paid off note owed to bank		
(j)	To secure additional funds, 400 new shares of common stock were sold for cash		
(k)	Recorded the entry for depreciation on equipment for the current fiscal period		
(l)	Paid cash for ad in today's *Chicago Tribune*		
(m)	Some insurance premiums have expired		

3-24 Prepaid Expenses

Continental AG is a large German supplier of auto parts. Continental had €54.3 million of prepaid expenses on January 1, 2009. (€ stands for euro, the European currency.) This item mainly consists of prepayments of rent, leasing fees, interest, and insurance premiums. Assume all these prepayments were for services that Continental used during 2009 and that Continental spent €155 million in cash during 2009 for rent, leasing, and interest, of which €38 million was a prepayment of expenses for 2010.

1. Prepare a journal entry recognizing the use of the €54.3 million of prepaid expenses during 2009.
2. Prepare a compound journal entry for the cash payment of €155 million for rent, leasing fees, interest, and insurance premiums during 2009, with the proper amounts going to expense and prepaid expenses.

3-25 Journalizing and Posting

(Alternate is 3-26.) Prepare journal entries and post to T-accounts the following transactions of Montréal Building Supplies:

a. Cash sales, $9,000; items sold cost $4,000
b. Collections on accounts, $7,000
c. Paid cash for wages, $3,500
d. Acquired inventory on open account, $5,000
e. Paid cash for janitorial services, $600

3-26 Journalizing and Posting

(Alternate is 3-25.) Prepare journal entries and post to T-accounts the following transactions of Lincoln Real Estate Company:

a. Acquired office supplies of $800 on open account. Use a Supplies Inventory account.
b. Sold a house and collected an $8,000 commission on the sale. Use a Commissions Revenue account.

c. Paid cash of $700 to a local newspaper for current advertisements.
d. Paid $500 for a previous credit purchase of office supplies.
e. Recorded office supplies used of $300.

3-27 Reconstruct Journal Entries
(Alternate is 3-28.) Reconstruct the journal entries (with explanations) that resulted in the postings to the following T-accounts of Dorst Heating Contractors:

Cash			
(a)	55,000	(b)	1,000
		(c)	5,000

Equipment	
(c)	15,000

Revenue from Fees	
(d)	87,000

Accounts Receivable	
(d)	87,000

Note Payable	
(c)	10,000

Supplies Inventory		
(b)	1,000	(e) 300

Paid-in Capital	
(a)	55,000

Supplies Expense	
(e)	300

3-28 Reconstruct Journal Entries
(Alternate is 3-27.) Reconstruct the journal entries (omit explanations) that resulted in the postings to the following T-accounts of a small fruit wholesaler:

Cash			
(a)	50,000	(e)	18,000

Accounts Payable			
(e)	18,000	(b)	90,000

Paid-in Capital	
(a)	50,000

Accounts Receivable	
(c)	100,000

Inventory			
(b)	90,000	(d)	57,000

Cost of Goods Sold	
(d)	57,000

Sales	
(c)	100,000

3-29 Trial Balance
Lambda Company had total assets (cash and inventories) of $50,000, total liabilities of $30,000, and stockholders' equity of $20,000 at the beginning of 20X0. During the year Lambda purchased inventory for $60,000 cash and sold it for $90,000 cash. Total expenses other than cost of goods sold were $18,000, all paid in cash.

1. Enter the beginning balances into three T-accounts: Total Assets, Total Liabilities, and Stockholders' Equity.
2. Prepare journal entries for the transactions in 20X0. Post the inventory purchases, sales revenue, and expenses to T-accounts, opening the accounts as needed.
3. Prepare a trial balance at the end of 20X0.

3-30 Closing accounts
Use the information for Lambda Company in exercise 3-29. Prepare closing entries to transfer all temporary accounts to an Income Summary account, and then close the Income Summary account to Stockholders' Equity. Note that Stockholders' Equity includes both paid-in capital and retained earnings; there is no way to separate the two with the information given.

3-31 Closing Accounts and Preparing Financial Statements
Bellina Company imports art and artifacts from Italy and Spain and sells them in its Bellina Gallery in London. At the end of 20X2 Bellina had the following trial balance:

Cash	£ 45,000	
Accounts receivable	23,000	
Inventories	78,000	
Fixed assets, net	121,000	
Accounts payable		£ 35,000
Paid-in capital		100,000
Retained earnings, Jan. 1, 20X2		97,000
Revenue		340,000
Cost of sales	170,000	
Operating expenses	135,000	
Totals	£572,000	£572,000

1. Prepare closing journal entries for Bellina Company.
2. Prepare an income statement for 20X2 and a balance sheet for December 31, 20X2.

3-32 Effects of Errors

The bookkeeper of Southeast Legal Services included the cost of a new computer, purchased on December 30 for $11,000 and to be paid for in cash in January, as an operating expense instead of an addition to the proper asset account. What was the effect of this error ("no effect," "overstated," or "understated"—use symbols N, O, or U, respectively) on the following?

1. Total assets as of December 31
2. Total liabilities as of December 31
3. Operating expenses for the year ended December 31
4. Profit from operations for the year
5. Retained earnings as of December 31 after the books are closed

3-33 Effects of Errors

Analyze the effect of the following errors on the net profit figures of Yokahama Trading Company (YTC) for 20X0 and 20X1. Choose one of three answers: understated (U), overstated (O), or no effect (N). Problem (a) has been answered as an illustration.

a. Example: Failure to adjust at end of 20X0 for prepaid rent that had expired during December 20X0. YTC charged the remaining prepaid rent in 20X1. 20X0: O; 20X1: U. (Explanation: In 20X0, expenses would be understated and profits overstated. This error would carry forward so expenses in 20X1 would be overstated and profits understated.)
b. YTC omitted recording depreciation on Office Machines in 20X0 only. Correct depreciation was taken in 20X1.
c. During 20X1, YTC purchased ¥40,000 of office supplies and debited Office Supplies, an asset account. At the end of 20X1, ¥10,000 worth of office supplies were left. No entry had recognized the use of ¥30,000 of office supplies during 20X1.
d. Machinery, cost price ¥500,000, bought in 20X0, was not entered in the books until paid for in 20X1. Ignore depreciation; answer in terms of the specific error described.
e. YTC debited 3 months' rent, paid in advance in December 20X0, for the first quarter of 20X1, directly to Rent Expense in 20X0. No prepaid rent was on the books at the end of 20X1.

Problems

3-34 Account Numbers, Journal, Ledger, and Trial Balance

Journalize and post the entries required by the following transactions for Stiglitz Furniture Repair Company. Prepare a trial balance as of April 30, 20X0, for the period April 1 to April 30, 20X0. Ignore interest. Use dates, posting references, and the following account numbers:

Cash	100	Note payable	130
Accounts receivable	101	Paid-in capital	140
Equipment	111	Retained earnings	150
Accumulated depreciation, equipment	111A	Revenues	200
		Expenses	300, 301, etc.
Accounts payable	120		

- April 1, 20X0. The Stiglitz Furniture Repair Company was formed with $75,000 cash on the issuance of common stock.
- April 2. Stiglitz acquired equipment for $70,000. Stiglitz made a cash down payment of $20,000. In addition, Stiglitz signed a note for $50,000.
- April 3. Sales on credit to repair furniture at a local hotel, $2,200.
- April 3. Supplies acquired (and used) on open account, $200.
- April 3. Wages paid in cash, $700.
- April 30. Depreciation expense for April, $2,000.

3-35 Account Numbers, T-Accounts, and Transaction Analysis
Consider the following ($ in thousands):

Winnipeg Computing
Trial Balance, December 31, 20X0

		Balance	
Account Number	Account Titles	Debit	Credit
10	Cash	$ 60	
20	Accounts receivable	115	
21	Note receivable	100	
30	Inventory	130	
40	Prepaid insurance	12	
70	Equipment	120	
70A	Accumulated depreciation, equipment		$ 30
80	Accounts payable		140
100	Paid-in capital		65
110	Retained earnings		182
130	Sales		950
150	Cost of goods sold	550	
160	Wages expense	200	
170	Miscellaneous expense	80	
		$1,367	$1,367

The following information had not been considered before preparing the trial balance:

a. The note receivable was signed by a major customer. It is a 3-month note dated November 1, 20X0. Interest earned during November and December was collected in cash at 4 PM on December 31. The interest rate is 12% per year.
b. The Prepaid Insurance account reflects a 1-year fire insurance policy acquired for $12,000 cash on August 1, 20X0.
c. Depreciation for 20X0 was $18,000.
d. Winnipeg Computing paid wages of $12,000 in cash at 5 PM on December 31.

Required

1. Enter the December 31 balances in T-accounts in a general ledger. Number the accounts. Allow room for additional T-accounts.
2. Prepare the journal entries prompted by the additional information. Show amounts in thousands.
3. Post the journal entries to the ledger. Key your postings. Create logical new account numbers as necessary.
4. Prepare a new trial balance, December 31, 20X0.

3-36 Trial Balance Errors

Consider the following trial balance ($ in thousands):

Valdez Paint Store
Trial Balance, Year Ended December 31, 20X0

Cash	$ 22	
Equipment	33	
	15	
Accounts payable	42	
Accounts receivable	14	
Prepaid insurance	1	
Prepaid rent		$ 3
Inventory	129	
Paid-in capital		17
Retained earnings		10
Cost of goods sold	500	
Wages expense	100	
Miscellaneous expenses	80	
Advertising expense		30
Sales		788
Note payable	40	
	$976	$848

List and describe all the errors in the preceding trial balance. Be specific. On the basis of the available data, prepare a corrected trial balance.

3-37 Journal, Ledger, and Trial Balance

(Alternates are 3-39 through 3-44.) The balance sheet accounts of Indianapolis Machinery, Inc., had the following balances on October 31, 20X0:

Cash	$ 41,000	
Accounts receivable	90,000	
Inventory	70,000	
Prepaid rent	2,000	
Accounts payable		$ 27,000
Paid-in capital		160,000
Retained earnings		16,000
	$203,000	$203,000

Following is a summary of the transactions that occurred during November:

a. Collections of accounts receivable, $79,000.
b. Payments of accounts payable, $19,000.

c. Acquisitions of inventory on open account, $80,000.

d. Merchandise carried in inventory at a cost of $70,000 was sold on open account for $91,000.

e. Recognition of rent expense for November, $1,000.

f. Wages paid in cash for November, $8,000.

g. Cash dividends declared and disbursed to stockholders on November 29, $10,000.

Required

1. Prepare journal entries.
2. Enter beginning balances in T-accounts. Post the journal entries to T-accounts. Use the transaction letters to key your postings.
3. Prepare a trial balance for the month ending November 30, 20X0.
4. Explain why accounts payable increased by so much during November.

3-38 Financial Statements

Refer to problem 3-37. Prepare a balance sheet as of November 30, 20X0, and an income statement for the month of November. Prepare the retained earnings column of a statement of stockholders' equity. Prepare the income statement first.

3-39 Journal, Ledger, and Trial Balance

(Alternates are 3-37 and 3-40 through 3-44.) The balance sheet accounts of Red Lake Appliance Company had the following balances on December 31, 20X1:

Account Title	Balance	
	Debit	Credit
Cash	$ 41,000	
Accounts receivable	29,000	
Merchandise inventory	120,000	
Accounts payable		$ 35,000
Notes payable		81,000
Paid-in capital		43,000
Retained earnings		31,000
Total	$190,000	$190,000

Operating space and equipment are rented on a month-to-month basis. A summary of January 20X2 transactions follows:

a. Collected $24,000 on accounts receivable.

b. Sold appliances for $60,000 cash and $45,000 on open account.

c. Cost of appliances sold was $50,000.

d. Paid $19,000 on accounts payable.

e. Replenished inventory for $64,000 on open account.

f. Paid selling expense in cash, $33,000.

g. Paid rent expense in cash, $7,000.

h. Paid interest expense in cash, $1,000.

Required

1. Open the appropriate T-accounts in the general ledger. In addition to the seven accounts listed in the trial balance of December 31, open accounts for Sales, Cost of Goods Sold, Selling Expense, Rent Expense, and Interest Expense. Enter the December 31 balances in the accounts.
2. Journalize transactions a through h. Post the entries to the ledger, keying by transaction letter.
3. Prepare a trial balance for the month ended January 31, 20X2.

3-40 Journal, Ledger, and Trial Balance

(Alternates are 3-37, 3-39, and 3-41 through 3-44.) Heraldo Ruiz owned and managed a franchise of Ithaca Espresso, Incorporated. The company's balance sheet accounts had the following balances on September 1, 20X0, the beginning of a fiscal year:

Ithaca Espresso
Balance Sheet Accounts, September 1, 20X0

Cash	$ 3,000	
Accounts receivable	25,200	
Merchandise inventory	77,800	
Prepaid rent	4,000	
Store equipment	21,000	
Accumulated depreciation, store equipment		6,150
Accounts payable		45,000
Paid-in capital		30,000
Retained earnings		49,850
	$131,000	$131,000

Summarized transactions for September were as follows:

a. Acquisitions of merchandise inventory on account, $51,000.
b. Sales for cash, $36,250.
c. Payments to creditors, $29,000.
d. Sales on account, $41,000.
e. Advertising in newspapers, paid in cash, $3,000.
f. Cost of goods sold, $40,000.
g. Collections on account, $33,150.
h. Miscellaneous expenses paid in cash, $8,000.
i. Wages paid in cash, $9,000.
j. Entry for rent expense. (Rent was paid quarterly in advance, $6,000 per quarter. Payments were due on February 1, May 1, August 1, and November 1.)
k. Depreciation of store equipment, $250.

Required

1. Enter the September 1 balances in T-accounts in a general ledger.
2. Prepare journal entries for each transaction.
3. Post the journal entries to the ledger. Key your postings by transaction letter.
4. Prepare an income statement for September and a balance sheet as of September 30, 20X0.

3-41 Journalizing, Posting, and Trial Balance
(Alternates are 3-37, 3-39, 3-40, and 3-42 through 3-44.) Harui Nursery, a retailer of garden plants and supplies, had the accompanying balance sheet accounts on December 31, 20X0:

Assets			Liabilities and Stockholders' Equity	
Cash		$ 24,000	Accounts payable*	$116,000
Accounts receivable		40,000	Paid-in capital	40,000
Inventory		131,000	Retained earnings	79,000
Prepaid rent		4,000		
Store equipment	$60,000			
Less: Accumulated depreciation	24,000	36,000		
Total		$235,000	Total	$235,000

*For merchandise only.

Following is a summary of transactions that occurred during 20X1:

a. Purchases of merchandise inventory on open account, $550,000.
b. Sales, all on credit, $810,000.
c. Cost of merchandise sold to customers, $445,000.

d. On June 1, 20X1, borrowed $80,000 from a supplier. The note is payable in 4 years. Interest is payable yearly on December 31 at a rate of 15% per annum.

e. Disbursed $25,000 for the rent of the store. Add to Prepaid Rent.

f. Disbursed $165,000 for wages through November.

g. Disbursed $75,000 for miscellaneous expenses such as utilities, advertising, and legal help. (Debit Miscellaneous Expenses.)

h. On July 1, 20X1, lent $20,000 to the office manager. He signed a note that will mature on July 1, 20X2, together with interest at 10% per annum. Interest for 20X1 is due on December 31, 20X1.

i. Collections on accounts receivable, $692,000.

j. Payments on accounts payable $472,000.

The following entries were made on December 31, 20X1:

k. Recognized rent expense for 20X1: $3,000 of prepaid rent is applicable to 20X2; the remainder expired in 20X1.

l. Depreciation for 20X1 was $6,000.

m. Wages earned by employees during December were paid on December 31, $6,000.

n. Interest on the loan from the supplier was disbursed. See transaction d.

o. Interest on the loan made to the office manager was received. See transaction h.

Required

1. Prepare journal entries in thousands of dollars.
2. Post the entries to T-accounts in the ledger, keying your postings by transaction letter.
3. Prepare a trial balance for the year ending December 31, 20X1.

3-42 Transaction Analysis, Trial Balance, and Closing Entries

(Alternates are 3-37, 3-39 through 3-41, 3-43, and 3-44.) Husker Auto Glass, Inc., had the accompanying balance sheet values on January 1, 20X0:

Husker Auto Glass, Inc.
Balance Sheet Accounts, January 1, 20X0

Cash	$ 8,000	
Accounts receivable	3,000	
Parts inventory	2,000	
Prepaid rent	2,000	
Trucks	36,000	
Equipment	8,000	
Accumulated depreciation, trucks		$15,000
Accumulated depreciation, equipment		5,000
Accounts payable		1,900
Paid-in capital		20,000
Retained earnings		17,100
Total	$59,000	$59,000

During January, the following summarized transactions occurred:

January 2 Collected accounts receivable, $2,500.

3 Rendered services to customers for cash, $4,200 ($700 collected for parts, $3,500 for labor). Use two accounts, Parts Revenue and Labor Revenue.

3 Cost of parts used for services rendered, $300.

7 Paid legal expenses, $500 cash.

9 Acquired parts on open account, $900.

11 Paid cash for wages, $1,000.

13 Paid cash for truck repairs, $500.

19 Billed customer for services, $3,600 ($800 for parts and $2,800 for labor).
19 Cost of parts used for services rendered, $500.
24 Paid cash for wages, $1,400.
27 Paid cash on accounts payable, $1,500.
31 Rent expense for January, $1,000 (reduce Prepaid Rent).
31 Depreciation for January: trucks, $600; equipment, $200.
31 Paid cash to local gas station for gasoline for trucks for January, $300.
31 Paid cash for wages, $800.

Required

1. Enter the January 1 balances in T-accounts. Leave room for additional accounts.
2. Record the transactions in the journal.
3. Post the journal entries to the T-accounts. Key your entries by date. (Note how keying by date is not as precise as by transaction number or letter. Why? There is usually more than one transaction on any given date.)
4. Prepare a trial balance for the month ended January 31, 20X0.
5. Prepare closing entries.

3-43 Transaction Analysis, Trial Balance

(Alternates are 3-37, 3-39 through 3-42, and 3-44.) **McDonald's Corporation** is a well-known fast-food restaurant company. Examine the accompanying balance sheet values, which are based on McDonald's annual report and actual terminology:

McDonald's Corporation
Balance Sheet Values, June 30, 2009 ($ in millions)

Cash	$ 2,161	
Accounts and notes receivable	930	
Inventories	103	
Prepaid expenses	403	
Property and equipment, at cost	32,210	
Other assets	4,856	
Accumulated depreciation		$11,456
Notes and accounts payable		540
Other liabilities		15,423
Paid-in capital		4,714
Retained earnings		29,927
Other stockholders' equity*	21,397	
Total	$62,060	$62,060

*These negative stockholders' equity items will be explained in later chapters.

Consider the following assumed partial summary of transactions for July 2009 ($ in millions):

a. Revenues in cash, company-owned restaurants, $1,500.
b. Revenues, on open account from franchised restaurants, $500. Open a separate revenue account for these sales.
c. Inventories acquired on open account, $827.
d. Cost of the inventories sold, $820.
e. Depreciation, $226. (Debit Depreciation Expense.)
f. Paid rent and insurance premiums in cash in advance, $42. (Debit Prepaid Expenses.)
g. Prepaid expenses expired, $37. (Debit Operating Expenses.)
h. Paid other liabilities, $148.
i. Cash collections on receivables, $590.

j. Cash disbursements on notes and accounts payable, $747.
k. Paid interest expense in cash, $100.
l. Paid other expenses in cash, mostly payroll and advertising, $1,010. (Debit Operating Expenses.)

Required
1. Record the transactions in the journal.
2. Enter beginning balances in T-accounts. Post the journal entries to the T-accounts. Key your entries with the transaction letters used here.
3. Prepare a trial balance for the month ended July 31, 2009.

3-44 Transaction Analysis, Trial Balance

(Alternates are 3-37 and 3-39 through 3-43.) Kellogg Company's major product line is ready-to-eat breakfast cereals. Examine the following balance sheet values, which are slightly revised from Kellogg's annual report:

Kellogg Company Balance Sheet Values
July 4, 2009 ($ in millions)

Cash	$ 424	
Accounts receivable	1,191	
Inventories	833	
Property and equipment, net	2,977	
Other assets	5,837	
Accounts payable		1,052
Other liabilities		8,238
Paid-in capital		546
Retained earnings		1,426
Total	$11,262	$11,262

Consider the following assumed partial summary of transactions for the last six months of 2009 ($ in millions):

a. Acquired inventories for $1,800 on open account.
b. Sold inventories that cost $1,600 for $2,500 on open account.
c. Collected $2,550 on open account.
d. Disbursed $1,650 on open accounts payable.
e. Paid cash of $300 for advertising expenses. (Use an Operating Expenses account.)
f. Paid rent and insurance premiums in cash in advance, $20. (Use a Prepaid Expenses account.)
g. Prepaid expenses expired, $18. (Use an Operating Expenses account.)
h. Other liabilities paid in cash, $110.
i. Interest expense of $8 was paid in cash. (Use an Interest Expense account.)
j. Depreciation of $50 was recognized. [Use an Operating Expenses account; instead of creating an Accumulated Depreciation account, reduce the Property and Equipment (net) account directly.]
k. Additional shares were sold for $10 in cash. (Record as an increase to paid-in capital.)

Required
1. Record the transactions in the journal.
2. Enter beginning balances in T-accounts. Post the journal entries to the T-accounts. Key your entries with the transaction letters used here.
3. Prepare a trial balance for the six months ended December 31, 2009.
4. Explain why cash more than doubled during 2009.

3-45 Preparation of Financial Statements from Trial Balance

PepsiCo produces snack foods such as Fritos and Lay's potato chips, as well as beverages such as Pepsi and Mug Root Beer. The company had the following trial balance as of June 13, 2009, for the six months ended June 13, 2009 ($ in millions):

PepsiCo Trial Balance

	Debits	Credits
Current assets	$11,630	
Property and equipment, net	11,848	
Intangible assets, net	7,223	
Other assets	6,349	
Current liabilities		$ 8,619
Long-term debt and other liabilities		14,022
Stockholders' equity*		12,968
Net revenue		18,855
Cost of sales	8,625	
Selling, general, and administrative expenses	6,428	
Other expenses	993	
Cash dividends declared	1,368	
Total	$54,464	$54,464

*Includes beginning retained earnings.

1. Prepare PepsiCo's income statement for the six months ended June 13, 2009.
2. Prepare PepsiCo's balance sheet as of June 13, 2009.

3-46 Accumulated Depreciation

Johnson Matthey, the British specialty chemical company, had the following balances on its March 31, 2009, balance sheet [£ (British pound) in millions]:

Tangible fixed assets, at cost	£1,609.4
Accumulated depreciation	684.7
Net tangible fixed assets	£ 924.7

Suppose that Johnson Matthey depreciates most of its tangible fixed assets over 15 years.

1. What is the approximate average age of Johnson Matthey's tangible fixed assets?
2. Johnson Matthey invested £209.3 million in tangible fixed assets during the prior year. Using this information and your answer to part 1, explain whether Johnson Matthey is growing or depleting its supply of fixed assets.

3-47 Effects of Errors

Toyota Motor Corporation, the world's largest automaker, employs more than 315,000 people worldwide. The company reported pretax profit of ¥2,437 billion in fiscal 2008 and a pretax loss of ¥560 billion in fiscal 2009. Assume that there are no income taxes so that these amounts are also after-tax amounts. Consider the following two independent scenarios.

1. Suppose Toyota built a new factory that began production at the beginning of fiscal 2008. Cost of the factory was ¥1,000 billion, and its life was estimated to be 20 years. If Toyota neglected to take depreciation on the factory in fiscal 2008 but correctly charged one year's depreciation in fiscal 2009, what misstatements would exist on Toyota's 2008 financial statements? On its 2009 financial statements?
2. Suppose in fiscal 2008 Toyota incorrectly recorded ¥1,000 billion of sales for orders of automobiles that were not delivered, and thus the revenue was not earned, until fiscal 2009. What errors would there be in the fiscal 2008 financial statements? In the fiscal 2009 financial statements? Assume that cost of goods sold averages 60% of sales.

3-48 Journal Entries, Posting

Sony Corporation is a leading international supplier of audio and video equipment. The Sony annual report at the end of the 2009 fiscal year included the following balance sheet items (Japanese yen in billions):

Cash	¥1,086
Receivables	1,184
Prepaid expenses	794
Land	158
Accounts payable, trade	897

Consider the following assumed transactions that occurred immediately subsequent to the balance sheet date (Japanese yen in billions):

a. Collections from customers	¥795
b. Purchase of land for cash	20
c. Purchase of 2-year insurance policy for cash	12
d. Disbursements to trade creditors	590

1. Enter the five account balances in T-accounts.
2. Journalize each transaction.
3. Post the journal entries to T-accounts. Key each posting by transaction letter.

3-49 Reconstructing Journal Entries, Posting

(Alternate is 3-50.) Procter & Gamble has brands such as Tide, Pampers, and Gillette. A partial income statement from its annual report for the fiscal year ending in June 30, 2009, showed the following actual numbers and nomenclature ($ in millions):

Net sales	$79,029
Costs and expenses	
Cost of products sold	38,898
Selling, general, and administrative expense	24,008
Interest expense	1,358
Other income, net	(560)
Income taxes	4,032
Total expenses	67,736
Net earnings	$11,293

1. Prepare six summary journal entries for the given data. Label your entries a through f. Omit explanations. For simplicity, assume that all transactions (except for cost of products sold) were for cash.
2. Post to T-accounts in a ledger for all affected accounts. Key your postings by transaction letter.

3-50 Reconstructing Journal Entries, Posting

(Alternate is 3-49.) Lowe's Companies, Inc., operates more than 1,700 home improvement retail stores in 50 states and Canada. It opened 62 new stores in 2009. A partial income statement from its annual report for the fiscal year ending January 30, 2009, showed the following actual numbers and nomenclature ($ in millions):

Net sales		$48,230
Expenses		
Cost of sales	$31,729	
Selling, general, and administrative expenses	11,074	
Other expenses	1,921	
Total costs and expenses		44,724
Pretax earnings		$ 3,506

1. Prepare four summary journal entries for the given data. Label your entries a through d. Omit explanations. For simplicity, assume that all transactions except for cost of sales were for cash.
2. Post to T-accounts in a ledger for all affected accounts. Key your postings by transaction letter.

3-51 Plant Assets and Accumulated Depreciation
Norsk Hydro, the Norwegian-based global supplier of aluminum and aluminum products, had the following in its January 1, 2009, balance sheet (in millions of Norwegian Kroner, NOK):

Total property, plant, and equipment, at cost	NOK66,777
Accumulated depreciation	37,439
Property, plant, and equipment, net	NOK29,338

1. Open T-accounts for (a) Property, Plant, and Equipment; (b) Accumulated Depreciation, Property, Plant, and Equipment; and (c) Depreciation Expense. Enter the balance sheet amounts into the T-accounts.
2. Assume that in 2009 Norsk Hydro purchased or sold no assets and that depreciation expense for 2009 was NOK3,200 million. Depreciation was the only item affecting the Property, Plant, and Equipment account in 2009. Prepare the journal entry, and post to the T-accounts.
3. Prepare the property, plant, and equipment section of Norsk Hydro's balance sheet at the end of 2009.
4. Land comprises $1,170 million of Norsk Hydro's property, plant, and equipment, and land is not depreciated. Comment on the age of the company's depreciable assets—that is, all property, plant, and equipment except land—at the January 1, 2009 balance sheet date.

3-52 Management Incentives, Financial Statements, and Ethics
Alicia Perez was controller of the vascular products division of a major medical instruments company. On December 30, 2009, Perez prepared a preliminary income statement and compared it with the 2009 budget:

Vascular Products Division
Income Statement for the Year Ended December 31, 2009
($ in thousands)

	Budget	Preliminary Actual
Sales revenue	$ 1,200	$ 1,600
Cost of goods sold	600	800
Gross margin	600	800
Other operating expenses	450	500
Operating income	$ 150	$ 300

The top managers of each division had a bonus plan that paid each a 10% bonus if operating income exceeded budgeted income by more than 20%. It was obvious to Perez that the vascular products division had easily exceeded the $180,000 of operating income needed for a bonus. In fact, she wondered if it would not be desirable to reduce operating income this year—after all, the higher the income this year, the higher top management is likely to set the budget next year. Besides, if some of December's sales could just be held back and recorded in January, the division would have a running start on next year.

Perez had always been a team player, and she saw holding back sales as the best strategy for her team of managers. Therefore, she recorded only $1,500,000 of sales in 2009—the other $100,000 was recorded as January 2010 sales. Operating income for 2009 then became $250,000 and there was a head start of $50,000 on 20010's operating income.

Comment on the ethical implications of Perez's decision.

Collaborative Learning Exercise

3-53 Income Statement and Balance Sheet Accounts
Form teams of two persons each. Each person should make a list of 10 account names, with approximately one-half being income statement accounts and one-half being balance sheet accounts. Give the list to the other member of the team, who is to write beside each account name the financial statement (I for income statement or B for balance sheet) on which it belongs. If there are errors or disagreements in classification, discuss the account and come to an agreement about which financial statement it belongs to.

Analyzing and Interpreting Financial Statements

3-54 Financial Statement Research
Select the financial statements of any company.

1. Prepare an income statement in the following format:
   Total sales (or revenue)
   Cost of goods sold
   Gross margin
   Other expenses
   Income before income taxes
   Be sure to include all revenue in the first line and all expenses (except income taxes) in either cost of goods sold or other expenses.
2. Prepare three summary journal entries for the income statement data you prepared. Use the given account titles and label your entries a, b, and c. Omit explanations. For simplicity, assume that all "other expenses" were paid in cash and all sales are on credit.
3. Post to T-accounts in a ledger for all affected accounts. Key your postings by transaction letter.

3-55 Analyzing Starbucks' Financial Statements
Using either the SEC Edgar Web site or **Starbucks'** Web site, find Starbucks' 2009 financial statements. Note the following summarized items (rounded to the nearest million) from the income statement for the year ended September 27, 2009:

Net revenues		9,775
Cost of sales including occupancy costs	$4,325	
Store and other operating expenses	5,010	
Non-operating income	(158)	
Interest expense	39	9,216
Pretax income		559
Income taxes		168
Net earnings		$ 391

1. Prepare six summary journal entries for the given data. Use Starbucks' account titles and label your entries a through f. Omit explanations. For simplicity, assume all transactions (except for cost of sales) were for cash. Assume cost of sales is 70% of the "cost of sales including occupancy costs," whereas occupancy costs are 30%.
2. Starbucks' balance sheet shows $2,536 million of Property, Plant, and Equipment, net. Explain what the term "net" means and find both gross and net amounts for Property, Plant, and Equipment.

3-56 Analyzing Financial Statements Using the Internet: Gap

Go to www.gapinc.com. Locate **Gap**'s Annual Reports under Investors and then Financials. Select the most recent annual report.

Answer the following questions about Gap Inc.:

1. Locate Gap's entry for accumulated depreciation under its property and equipment footnote. Does this represent an expense for Gap? Why does Gap keep track of accumulated depreciation?

2. Gap Inc. does not include a line for depreciation on its Consolidated Statements of Income. Where do you suppose depreciation expenses are included among Gap's expenses?

3. Locate Cash and Cash Equivalents at the end of the year on the Consolidated Balance Sheet. How much did cash and cash equivalents increase or decrease during the past year?

4. Locate Shareholders' Equity on the Consolidated Balance Sheets. Consider two amounts: Common Stock at par value and Additional Paid-in Capital. How did these amounts arise?

5. Suppose Gap overstated its merchandise inventory amount in its balance sheet at the end of this year. What is the effect on cost of goods sold, on net earnings, and on ending shareholders' equity? If no other errors are made, what will be the effect on these reported amounts next year?

4

Accrual Accounting and Financial Statements

LEARNING OBJECTIVES

After studying this chapter, you should be able to:

1 Understand the role of adjustments in accrual accounting.

2 Make adjustments for the expiration or consumption of assets.

3 Make adjustments for the earning of unearned revenues.

4 Make adjustments for the accrual of unrecorded expenses.

5 Make adjustments for the accrual of unrecorded revenues.

6 Describe the sequence of steps in the recording process and relate cash flows to adjusting entries.

7 Prepare a classified balance sheet and use it to assess short-term liquidity.

8 Prepare single- and multiple-step income statements.

9 Use ratios to assess profitability.

South Africa is a country that is rich in minerals and precious metals. Not surprisingly, some of the largest listed South African companies are in the mining industry. One of the (maybe lesser known) precious metals found in South Africa is platinum. Currently, platinum is more expensive than gold or silver. A large percentage of the world's platinum is produced by **Anglo Platinum Limited**, the largest platinum producer in the world. Anglo Platinum Limited is also one of the major players on the Johannesburg Stock Exchange (JSE) in South Africa.

As working in a mine can be unsafe, one of the key indicators of performance used by Anglo Platinum is their safety rating. However, investors and managers also want to know whether the company is performing well, making money, and economically stable. One of the most important ways used to assess this is by looking at the company's annual financial statements which are published on December 31

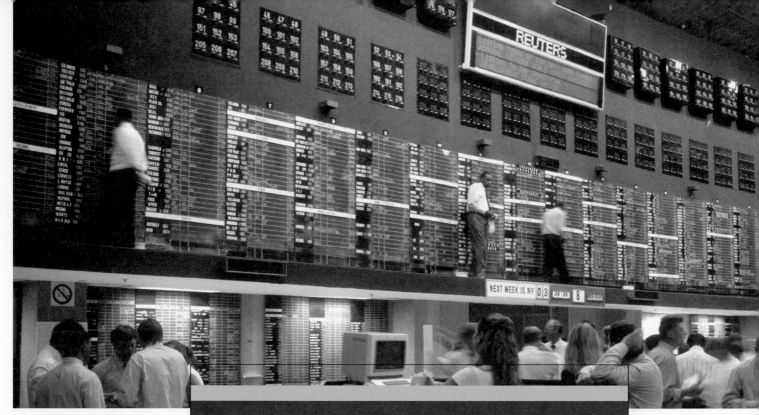

One of the primary usages of platinum is as a catalyst in chemical processes. It is also used in the making of laboratory equipment, vehicle emissions control devices, electrical contacts and electrodes, thermometers, dentistry equipment, anticancer drugs, and jewelry. It is a scarce material and therefore very valuable.

every year. These financial statements include reports detailing both the financial performance (income, expenses, and net profit) for the specific year and financial position at year-end (assets, equity, and liabilities).

A South African company is required by legislation to prepare annual financial statements using a specified accounting framework. Listed companies, such as Anglo Platinum, should use International Financial Reporting Standards (IFRS). The aim of IFRS is to produce accounting information which users including investors, employees, and suppliers find useful in decision-making. IFRS determines that financial statements should be prepared using accrual accounting: meaning that a company accounts for transactions in the financial year to which they pertain rather than when cash flow occurs. It is important that you understand this principle to be able to use and interpret financial statements. ●

Adjustments to the Accounts

Understand the role of adjustments in accrual accounting.

explicit transactions

Observable events such as cash receipts and disbursements, credit purchases, and credit sales that trigger the majority of day-to-day routine journal entries.

implicit transactions

Events (such as the passage of time) that do not generate source documents or any visible evidence that the event actually occurred. We do not recognize such events in the accounting records until the end of an accounting period.

adjustments (adjusting entries)

End-of-period entries that assign the financial effects of implicit transactions to the appropriate time periods.

accrue

To accumulate a receivable (asset) or payable (liability) during a given period, even though no explicit transaction occurs, and to record a corresponding revenue or expense.

Accountants record the majority of a company's transactions in journals and ledgers as the events occur. However, no observable event triggers transactions such as those discussed in Chapter 3 for depreciation and the expiration of prepaid rent. The difference between these transactions and the majority of the transactions we have recorded to date stems from how obvious or explicit they are.

Explicit transactions are observable events, such as cash receipts and disbursements, credit purchases, and credit sales that trigger the majority of day-to-day routine journal entries. Every explicit transaction is prompted by an economic event that has occurred, and we know that the accountant must make an entry to record the event. Entries for these transactions are supported by source documents, for example, sales slips, purchase invoices, employee payroll checks, or other tangible evidence. Note that not all explicit transactions require an actual exchange of goods and services between the company and another party. For instance, the loss of assets from fire or theft are explicit transactions, even though no market exchange occurs. In all cases, though, a specific observable event triggers the need to record a journal entry.

Implicit transactions are events, such as the passage of time, that do not generate source documents or any visible evidence that the event actually occurred. Because there is no specific notification to record such events, accountants do not formally recognize them in the accounting records until the end of an accounting period. For example, accountants prepare entries for depreciation expense or the expiration of prepaid rent from special schedules or memorandums at the end of an accounting period. An explicit event did not trigger such entries. Accountants recorded the related explicit transaction at the time the company purchased the depreciable asset or made the initial rent payment. We call the end-of-period entries that record these implicit events adjustments. **Adjustments** (also called **adjusting entries**) assign the financial effects of implicit transactions to the appropriate time periods. Thus, adjustments occur at periodic intervals, usually at the end of the accounting cycle when accountants are about to prepare the financial statements. They make adjustments by recording journal entries in the general journal and then posting them to the general ledger. After recognizing these adjustments for implicit transactions, they update the balances in the general ledger accounts through the end of the period and use these balances for preparing financial statements.

Adjusting entries are at the heart of accrual accounting. **Accrue** means to accumulate a receivable (asset) or payable (liability) during a given period, even though no explicit transaction occurs. The receivables or payables increase as time passes, even though no physical assets change hands. In order to maintain the equality of the balance sheet equation, as we accumulate the receivable or payable on the balance sheet, we must also recognize a revenue or expense on the income statement.

What routine business transactions require accruals? Examples are the wages earned by employees but not yet paid and the interest owed on borrowed money before the interest payment date. First, consider wages. Usually we recognize wage expense when a company pays its employees. However, suppose a company pays wages on Friday, and its accounting period ends on the following Wednesday. Employees have earned 3 days' wages, but no explicit event has prompted the company to record an entry. The company must make an adjustment to recognize the wages for Monday, Tuesday, and Wednesday as an increase in both Wages Payable and Wage Expense. Because accruals are not based on explicit transactions, we do not record them on a day-to-day basis. Rather, we make adjusting entries at the end of each accounting period to recognize unrecorded but relevant accruals.

You will see that each adjustment affects both an income statement account and a balance sheet account. Adjusting entries never affect cash, as any entry with a cash impact is the result of an explicit transaction. The goal of adjusting entries is to ensure that all the company's assets, liabilities, and stockholders' equity accounts are properly reflected in the financial statements. In the adjusting process, we consider whether the passage of time or other events has led to the creation of assets, the consumption of assets, or the creation or discharge of liabilities.

Adjustments help match revenues and expenses to a particular period and ensure the balance sheet correctly states assets and liabilities. For example, consider a $20 million annual contract for a baseball star, such as Albert Pujols, for the 2010 season. If the team pays all $20 million in cash in 2010, there is an explicit transaction. The team records a reduction in cash of $20 million and an expense of $20 million. In contrast, suppose the team pays only $15 million in cash and defers $5 million until 2011 or later. The $15 million cash payment is an explicit transaction that the team records as an expense in 2010. Because no explicit transaction for the additional $5 million occurs during 2010, the team does not routinely enter it into the accounting record. However, Pujols has earned the full $20 million as a result of playing the whole season and the team must eventually pay the remaining $5 million, so a liability exists. Further, the team incurred the entire $20 million for the benefit of the 2010 season, so the $5 million deferred payment is an expense for 2010. Thus, at the end of the period, when the team prepares the 2010 financial statements, an adjustment is necessary to record the deferred $5 million payment as an expense and to record a $5 million liability for its payment.

The principal adjustments arise from four basic types of implicit transactions:

  I. Expiration of unexpired costs
 II. Earning of revenues received in advance
III. Accrual of unrecorded expenses
IV. Accrual of unrecorded revenues

Let us now examine each of these categories in detail.

I. Expiration of Unexpired Costs

Some costs expire due to the passage of time. For example, initially a company engages in an explicit transaction that creates an asset. As the company consumes the asset, it must make an adjustment to reduce the asset and to recognize an expense. The key characteristic of unexpired costs is that an explicit transaction in the past created an asset, and subsequent implicit transactions serve to recognize the consumption of this asset.

OBJECTIVE 2

Make adjustments for the expiration or consumption of assets.

For example, refer back to page 116 of Chapter 3. Biwheels paid $6,000 in January to cover rent for the months of January, February, and March. The company initially recorded $6,000 of Prepaid Rent as an asset. As each day passed, Biwheels incurred rent expense and the asset declined in value. However, there is no benefit to recording daily adjusting entries. Rather, Biwheels made a $2,000 adjustment at the end of each month to reflect the gradual expiration of the rent costs. The adjusting entry reduced the asset, Prepaid Rent, and increased Rent Expense. Another example of adjusting for asset expiration is the expensing of Office Supplies Inventory. Suppose a company purchases $10,000 of Office Supplies Inventory on March 1, 2010. At the time of the purchase an explicit transaction has occurred and the company records an increase (debit) to Office Supplies Inventory and a decrease (credit) to Cash. The journal entry to record this purchase is as follows:

Office supplies inventory	$10,000	
Cash		$10,000

At the end of March, the company determines that it has used $1,500 of the Office Supplies Inventory. This requires the following adjusting entry to increase Office Supplies Expense (debit) and reduce Office Supplies Inventory (credit):

Office supplies expense	$1,500	
Office supplies inventory		$1,500

After recording this adjusting entry, the balance sheet will show only $8,500 ($10,000 − $1,500) in Office Supplies Inventory, and the income statement will show an expense of $1,500. Will failure to record an adjusting entry cause the balance sheet and income statement to be incorrect? Yes. Even though the balance sheet will balance, both the income statement and the balance sheet will be in error. If the company fails to make the preceding adjusting entry, Office Supplies Inventory is overstated by $1,500 and expenses are understated by $1,500. Understated expenses result in overstated net income and overstated Retained Earnings, a stockholders' equity account.

Another example of the expiration of unexpired costs is the recording of Depreciation Expense and Accumulated Depreciation. You can review the accounting for depreciation on page 116 of Chapter 3.

II. Earning of Revenues Received in Advance

unearned revenue (revenue received in advance, deferred revenue)
Represents cash received from customers who pay in advance for goods or services to be delivered at a future date.

Just as a company acquires assets and recognizes the related expense over time as it uses the assets, it may receive revenue in advance and then earn the revenue over time. **Unearned revenue** (also called **revenue received in advance** or **deferred revenue**) represents cash received from customers who pay in advance for goods or services that the company promises to deliver at a future date. The company receives cash before it earns the revenue. This commitment to provide goods or services is a liability, and the company must record both the receipt of cash and the liability. For instance, airlines often require advance payments for tickets. American Airlines recently showed a balance of more than $3.7 billion in an unearned revenue account labeled Air Traffic Liability. Over time, as customers take the flights they have paid for, American reduces the liability and increases revenue accordingly.

The analysis of adjusting entries for unearned revenue is easier to understand if we visualize the financial positions of both parties to a contract. For example, recall the Biwheels Company's January advance payment of $6,000 for 3 months' rent. Compare the financial impact on Biwheels Company with the impact on the company that owns the property (the landlord), who received the rental payment:

	Owner of Property (Landlord, Lessor)					Biwheels Company (Tenant, Lessee)				
	A	=	L	+	SE	A	=	L	+	SE
	Cash		Unearned Rent Revenue		Rent Revenue	Cash	Prepaid Rent			Rent Expense
(a) Explicit transaction (advance payment of 3 months' rent)	+6,000	=	+6,000			−6,000	+6,000	=		
(b) January adjustment (for 1 month rent)		=	−2,000		+2,000		−2,000	=		−2,000
(c) February adjustment (for 1 month rent)		=	−2,000		+2,000		−2,000	=		−2,000
(d) March adjustment (for 1 month rent)		=	−2,000		+2,000		−2,000	=		−2,000

The journal entries for (a) and (b) follow:

OWNER (LANDLORD)

(a) Cash	6,000	
Unearned rent revenue		6,000
(b) Unearned rent revenue	2,000	
Rent revenue		2,000

[Entries for (c) and (d) are the same as for (b).]

BIWHEELS COMPANY (TENANT)

(a) Prepaid rent	6,000	
Cash		6,000
(b) Rent expense	2,000	
Prepaid rent		2,000

[Entries for (c) and (d) are the same as for (b).]

We are already familiar with the analysis from Biwheels' point of view. The $2,000 monthly entries for Biwheels are examples of the first type of adjustment, the expiration of a prepaid asset. From the viewpoint of the landlord, transaction (a) is an explicit transaction that recognizes the receipt of cash and an increase in Unearned Rent Revenue, a liability. Why record a liability? Because the landlord is now obligated to either deliver the rental services or refund the money if the services are not delivered. This account could be called Rent Collected in Advance or Deferred Rent Revenue instead of Unearned Rent Revenue. Regardless of the title, it is a liability account representing revenue collected in advance that the landlord has not earned, and it obligates the landlord to provide services in the future.

Notice that transaction (a) does not affect the landlord's stockholders' equity because it does not recognize any revenue. Recall from Chapter 2 that companies cannot recognize revenue on

BUSINESS FIRST

In a franchise arrangement, a central organization, such as McDonald's or the National Basketball Association, sells the right to use the company name and company products to a franchisee. The franchisee also receives the benefit of advertising through the larger company, along with management assistance and product development. More than 75 different industries use franchising to distribute goods and services to consumers, and there are more than 750,000 franchise outlets of various types in the United States. Statistics suggest that franchise operations employ more than 15 million people in the United States. The global franchising industry has revenues of almost $2 trillion. Two of the largest global franchises are Subway with almost 30,000 outlets (27% outside the United States) and McDonald's with more than 25,000 outlets (52.3% outside the United States).

Franchising raises an interesting accounting problem. How does the central organization account for the franchise fees? At first glance, it might seem clear that companies should record such fees as revenue when they receive the cash. However, under accrual accounting, companies should record revenue only after two conditions have been satisfied: (1) The company has completed the "work," that is, it has earned the revenue, and (2) there is reasonable assurance the company will actually collect the fee (it is realized in cash or will be collectible).

The Rocky Mountain Chocolate Factory is a franchisor of premium chocolate shops with more than 320 stores in the United States, Canada, and the United Arab Emirates. It provides an example of a company that collects franchise fees before it performs the related work. Rocky Mountain Chocolate sells its franchisees area development rights that grant the franchisee the exclusive right to develop outlets in a specific geographic area. In return for these rights, Rocky Mountain Chocolate Factory receives an initial franchise fee. Should Rocky Mountain Chocolate record the fee as revenue when it receives the cash? It should not because Rocky Mountain Chocolate's work is not done until the franchisee actually opens and operates the franchise stores. In the interim, Rocky Mountain Chocolate must report the fees as deferred income.

McDonald's is perennially named one of *Entrepreneur Magazine*'s top franchising organizations. In 2008, McDonald's had $70.7 billion in system-wide sales, of which franchisees and affiliates generated $54.1 billion. However, when we look at the income statement, we see total revenue of only $23.5 billion—$16.5 billion from company-owned restaurants and $7.0 billion from franchisees and affiliates. Why? McDonald's recognizes as revenues only the franchise fees, not the total product sales of its franchisees.

Sources: www.entrepreneur.com/franchises; www.franchiseconsultantsinc.com/statistics. html; McDonalds 2008 Annual Report, www1.mcdonalds.com/annualreport/index.html; Rocky Mountain Chocolate Factory 2008 Annual Report, http://rmcf5.com/corp/ investor/ docs/10KANN22908.pdf.

the income statement until it is both earned and realized. While the landlord realized the $6,000 when it received the cash, it had not earned any revenue as of that date. The landlord earns and recognizes the revenue over time as the adjusting entries in transactions (b), (c), and (d) are made. The landlord simultaneously decreases (debits) Unearned Rent Revenue and increases (credits) the stockholders' equity account Rent Revenue. The net effect is an increase in stockholders' equity at the time the owner recognizes the revenue. If the landlord fails to record the adjusting entry represented in (b), liabilities are overstated by $2,000 and revenues are understated by $2,000. Understated revenues result in understatement of both net income and stockholders' equity. Similarly, if Biwheels fails to record the adjusting entry represented previously, its assets are overstated by $2,000 and its expenses are understated by $2,000. When expenses are understated, both net income and stockholders' equity are overstated.

By looking at both sides of the Biwheels rent contract, you can see that adjustment categories I and II are really mirror images of each other. Why? If a contract causes one party to record a Prepaid Expense, it will cause the other party to record Unearned Revenue. This basic relationship holds for any prepayment situation, from a 2-year fire insurance policy to a 5-year magazine subscription. In the case of the magazine subscription, the buyer initially recognizes a Prepaid Expense (asset) and uses adjustments to spread the initial cost to an expense account over the term of the subscription. In turn, the seller, the magazine publisher, initially records a liability, Unearned Subscription Revenue, on receipt of payment for the 5-year subscription and uses adjustments to recognize the revenue over the subscription term.

Another example is Starbucks, who lists Deferred Revenue of $388.7 million among its liabilities on September 27, 2009. Starbucks sells prepaid coffee cards (stored value cards) as well as gift certificates, both of which holders can redeem for a beverage or food item. Starbucks receives cash when customers purchase the card but cannot recognize revenue until the card or certificate is redeemed. Suppose Starbucks sells stored value cards and gift certificates totaling $10,000 on September 8. The explicit transaction creates a liability, Deferred Revenue, on the balance sheet and increases Cash. By the September year-end, customers have redeemed cards and certificates worth $3,000. The company will recognize $3,000 in revenue on the income statement and reduce the Deferred Revenue account by $3,000. Another example of companies that receive revenue in advance is franchisors as described in the Business First box on page 155.

III. Accrual of Unrecorded Expenses

Wages are an example of a liability that grows moment to moment as employees perform their duties. The services provided by employees represent expenses. It is unnecessary to make hourly, daily, or even weekly formal entries in the accounts for many accrued expenses, as the cost of such frequent recording would exceed the benefits. This is true, even though computers can perform these tasks effortlessly. The costs of computing are small, but in this case the benefits are even smaller. Accountants aggregate these costs only when they prepare financial statements, and this rarely needs to be done hourly or daily. Consequently, they make adjustments to bring each accrued expense (and corresponding liability) account up-to-date at the end of the accounting period, just before they prepare the formal financial statements. These adjustments are necessary to accurately match the expenses to the period in which they help generate revenues.

Accounting for Payment of Wages

Most companies pay their employees on a predetermined schedule. Assume that Anglo Platinum pays its employees each Friday for services rendered during that week. Consider the following sample calendar for January:

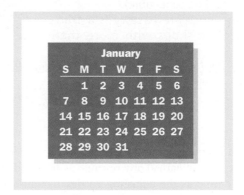

Because wage expenses accrue for an entire week before Anglo Platinum pays employees, wages paid on January 26 are compensation for work done during the week ended January 26. Assume the total wages paid on the four Fridays during January total $200,000, which is $50,000 per 5-day workweek, or $10,000 per day. Anglo Platinum makes routine entries for wage payments at the end of each week in January. As it pays wages, the company increases Wages Expense and decreases Cash. During the January shown in the preceding calendar, Anglo Platinum would pay wages on the 5th, 12th, 19th, and 26th. These events represent explicit transactions, prompted by writing payroll checks. At the end of January, the balance sheet shows the summarized amounts of these explicit transactions and their effect on the accounting equation:

	A	=	L	+	SE
	Cash				**Wages Expense**
(a) Routine entries for explicit transactions	−200,000	=			−200,000

Accounting for Accrual of Wages

Assume that Anglo Platinum prepares financial statements on a monthly basis. In addition to the $200,000 actually paid to employees during the month of January, Anglo Platinum owes $30,000 for employee services rendered during the last 3 days of the month. The company will not pay the employees for these services until Friday, February 2. To ensure an accurate accounting of Wages Expense for the month of January, Anglo Platinum must make an adjustment. Transaction (a) shows the total of the routine entries for the explicit payment of wages to employees, and transaction (b) shows the adjusting entry to accrue wages for Monday, January 29, through Wednesday, January 31. Transaction (b) recognizes both the expense and the liability.

(a) Wages expense	200,000	
Cash		200,000
(b) Wages expense	30,000	
Accrued wages payable		30,000

If Anglo Platinum does not record transaction (b), both expenses and liabilities are understated by $30,000. Understated expenses result in the overstatement of both net income and stockholders' equity.

The total effect of wages on the balance sheet equation for the month of January, including transactions (a) and (b), is as follows:

	A	=	L	+	SE
	Cash		Accrued Wages Payable		Wages Expense
(a) Routine entries for explicit transactions	−200,000	=			−200,000
(b) Adjustment for implicit transaction, the accrual of unrecorded wages		=	+30,000		−30,000
Total effects	−200,000	=	+30,000		−230,000

The adjustment in entry (b) is the first adjusting entry we have examined that shows an expense offset by an increase in a liability instead of a decrease in an asset. The accountant's problem is different for this type of accrual than it was for prepaid rent. With prepaid rent, there is a record in the accounts of an asset, and the accountant might recognize the necessity for an adjustment by asking the following question: Is the balance shown on the books correct or is an adjustment required to reduce it? With accrued wages there is no asset account to prompt such a question. However, because most end-of-period adjustments are routine, accountants know to check for adjustments such as expired rent and accrued wages because they experience these items every period.

On February 2, Anglo Platinum will pay off the liability for the work performed during the last 3 days of January, together with the wages expense for February 1 and 2:

Wages expense (February 1 and 2)	20,000	
Accrued wages payable	30,000	
Cash		50,000
(To record wages expense for February 1 and 2 and to pay wages for the week ended February 2)		

These entries clearly demonstrate the matching principle. The routine entries and the adjusting entries match the wages expense to the periods in which they help generate revenues.

Accrual of Interest

Other examples of accrued expenses include sales commissions, property taxes, income taxes, and interest paid on borrowed money. Interest is the "rent" paid for the use of money, just as rent is paid for the use of buildings. The interest accumulates (accrues) as time passes, regardless of when a company actually pays cash for interest.

Assume that Anglo Platinum borrowed $100,000 from **Standard Bank** on December 31, 2009. The terms of the loan require that Anglo Platinum repay the loan amount of $100,000 plus interest at 6% on December 31, 2010. By convention, we express interest rates on an annual basis. We can calculate interest for any part of a year as follows:

$$\text{Principal} \times \text{Interest rate} \times \text{Fraction of a year} = \text{Interest}$$

Principal is the amount borrowed ($100,000). The interest rate is expressed as an annual percentage (.06). For the full year, the interest expense is

$$\$100,000 \times .06 \times 1 = \$6,000$$

As of January 31, 2010, Anglo Platinum has had use of the $100,000 bank loan for 1 month or one-twelfth of a year. Anglo Platinum owes the bank for the use of this money, and the amount owed has accrued for the entire month of January. The amount of interest owed is ($100,000 × .06 × 1/12) = $500. The monthly cost of the loan is $500. The interest is not due to be paid until December 31, 2010. However, at the end of January, the company is liable for 1 month of accrued interest. We analyze and record the adjustment in the same way as the adjustment for accrued wages:

	A	=	L	+	SE
			Accrued Interest Payable		**Interest Expense**
Adjustment to accrue January interest not yet recorded		=	+500		−500

The adjusting journal entry is as follows:

Interest expense	500	
Accrued interest payable		500

At the end of January, Anglo Platinum owes Standard Bank $100,500, not $100,000. The adjusting entry matches the $500 interest expense with the period in which Anglo Platinum had the benefit of the bank loan. If Anglo Platinum omits the adjusting entry, liabilities and expenses will both be understated at the end of January. Would the understatement of interest expense have other financial statement implications? Yes. If interest expense is understated, both net income and stockholders' equity are overstated.

Accrual of Income Taxes

As a company generates income, it accrues income tax expense. Income taxes exist worldwide, although rates and details differ from country to country. Corporations in the United States are subject to federal income taxes and, in most states, state income taxes. For many corporations, the federal plus state income tax rates hover around 40%. Thus, for every dollar of income a company makes, it accrues $.40 of income tax expense. Of course, the company does not pay $.40 in tax as it earns each dollar. Instead, taxes accrue over the period, and the company makes an adjustment at the end of the period when it prepares financial statements.

income before income tax (pretax income, earnings before income tax)
Income before the deduction of income tax expense.

Companies use various labels to denote income taxes on their income statements: Income tax expense, provision for income taxes, and income taxes are most common. For multinational firms, income tax expense may include tax obligations in every country in which the firm operates. In preparing income statements, most companies calculate a subtotal called **income before income tax**, **earnings before income tax** or **pretax income** and then show income taxes as a separate income statement item just before net income. This arrangement is logical because income tax expense is based on pretax income. **Columbia Sportswear** is one of the largest outdoor apparel companies in the world. Its 2008 annual report contains the format adopted by the vast majority of companies.

Income before income tax	$126,243,000
Income tax expense	31,196,000
Net income	$ 95,047,000

Volkswagen, which reports under IFRS, uses a similar format for its 2008 income:

Profit before tax	€6,608,000,000
Income tax expense	1,920,000,000
Profit after tax	€4,688,000,000

IV. Accrual of Unrecorded Revenues

Just as the realization of unearned revenues is the mirror image of the expiration of prepaid expenses, the accrual of unrecorded revenues is the mirror image of the accrual of unrecorded expenses. Because the company has not received cash, there is no explicit transaction to trigger a journal entry. However, according to the revenue recognition principle, revenues affect stockholders' equity in the period a company earns them, not the period in which it receives cash. Thus, an adjustment is required to recognize revenues earned but not yet received.

Consider the $100,000 loan **Standard Bank** made to **Anglo Platinum**. As of January 31, Standard Bank has earned $500 in interest on the loan. The following tabulation shows the mirror-image effect:

	Standard Bank as a Lender					Anglo Platinum as a Borrower			
	A	= L	+	SE	A	=	L	+	SE
	Accrued Interest Receivable			Interest Revenue			Accrued Interest Payable		Interest Expense
January interest	+500	=		+500		=	+500		−500

Another example of accrued revenues and receivables is "unbilled" fees. Attorneys, public accountants, physicians, and advertising agencies may earn hourly fees during a particular month but not issue bills to their clients until the completion of an entire contract or engagement. Under the accrual basis of accounting, a company should record such revenues in the month in which it earns the revenues, not at a later time. For example, assume that a law firm renders $10,000 of services during January but does not bill for these services until March 31. Before the firm prepares financial statements for January, it makes the following adjustment for unrecorded revenues for the month:

	A	= L	+	SE
	Accrued (Unbilled) Fees Receivable			Fee Revenue
Adjustment for fees earned	+10,000	=		+10,000

The journal entry to record these unrecorded revenues is shown here:

Accrued (unbilled) fees receivable	$10,000	
Fee revenue		$10,000

What happens if the law firm does not make this adjusting entry? Assets and revenues are both understated by $10,000. Understated revenues result in understated net income and stockholders' equity.

Utility companies often recognize unbilled revenues for utility services provided but not yet billed to customers. In fact, as of January 1, 2009, **Northwest Natural**, a utility that provides

OBJECTIVE 5

Make adjustments for the accrual of unrecorded revenues.

natural gas to more than 650,000 residential and business customers throughout Oregon and Washington, included more Accrued Unbilled Revenue than Accounts Receivable among its current assets:

Accounts receivable	$ 81,288,000
Accrued unbilled revenue	$102,688,000

Ethics, Unearned Revenue, and Revenue Recognition

Deciding when unearned revenue becomes earned can pose ethical dilemmas for accountants. Suppose you are the accountant for a small company that receives a $100,000 cash payment on December 15, in exchange for a commitment to provide various consulting services at a later date. At the time the company receives the cash, you appropriately record an increase in Cash and an increase in the liability account, Unearned Revenue. As we saw earlier in this chapter, as the company provides the services, the appropriate accounting treatment is to decrease the Unearned Revenue account and recognize revenue on the income statement.

When you review the contract on December 31, you conclude that the company has performed $65,000 worth of the $100,000 in consulting services. You propose an adjusting entry to recognize $65,000 in revenue (credit) and to reduce the Unearned Revenue account (debit) by $65,000. Your boss, the CFO of the company, insists that the company has completed only $10,000 in services. He argues that recognition of only $10,000 in revenue is a more conservative estimate of the percentage of services performed. In addition, he reminds you that accountants should be conservative. In this context, **conservatism** means selecting methods of measurement that anticipate expenses and liabilities and defer recognition of revenues and assets, yielding lower net income, lower assets, and lower stockholders' equity. Your boss argues that financial statements are less likely to mislead users if balance sheets report assets at lower rather than higher amounts, report liabilities at higher rather than lower amounts, and if income statements report lower rather than higher net income. He claims that it is unethical to overstate revenue and net income and understate liabilities, and that his lower estimate of $10,000 conservatively states revenue and net income.

You have overheard a conversation at the water cooler suggesting that the company expects sales to slow in the coming year, and you wonder whether that forecast has anything to do with the CFO's estimate. Could the CFO be attempting to "save" revenue to record in the coming year? Should you prepare an income statement that recognizes $10,000 of revenue associated with the service contract or insist on recording $65,000?

The issues in this scenario are complex. It is often difficult to determine exactly when consulting services have been performed. Two people, both acting in good faith, may give different estimates of the completion of these services. The $10,000 is a more conservative estimate of revenue earned. However, by reporting lower net income in the current period, the company will report higher net income in the following period. If the CFO's $10,000 estimate is intended solely to manipulate the company's revenue and earnings trend, use of that estimate is unethical.

conservatism

Selecting methods of measurement that anticipate expenses and liabilities and defer recognition of revenues and assets, yielding lower net income, lower assets, and lower stockholders' equity.

OBJECTIVE 6

Describe the sequence of steps in the recording process and relate cash flows to adjusting entries.

The Adjusting Process in Perspective

Chapter 3 presented the various steps in the recording process as follows:

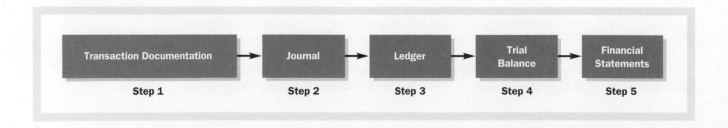

Transaction Documentation	Journal	Ledger	Trial Balance	Financial Statements
Step 1	Step 2	Step 3	Step 4	Step 5

This process has a final aim: the preparation of accurate financial statements prepared on the accrual basis. To accomplish this goal, the process must incorporate adjusting entries to record implicit transactions. When we consider the adjustments, we can further divide the final three steps in the recording process as follows:

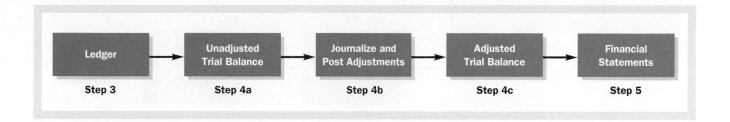

As you review these steps, remember that each adjusting entry affects at least one income statement account, a revenue or an expense, and one balance sheet account, an asset or a liability. No adjusting entry debits or credits cash. Why? If transactions affect cash, they are explicit transactions that companies record as they occur. The end-of-period adjustment process is reserved for implicit transactions that are a necessary component of the accrual basis of accounting.

Cash flows—that is, explicit transactions involving cash receipts or cash disbursements—may precede or follow the adjusting entry that recognizes the related revenue or expense. The diagrams that follow underscore the basic differences between the cash flows and the accrual accounting entries.

Entries for adjustments I and II, expiration of unexpired costs and earning of revenues received in advance, generally occur subsequent to the cash flows. For example, at the time a company receives or disburses cash for rent, only the balance sheet is affected. The subsequent adjusting entry records the later impact on the income statement.

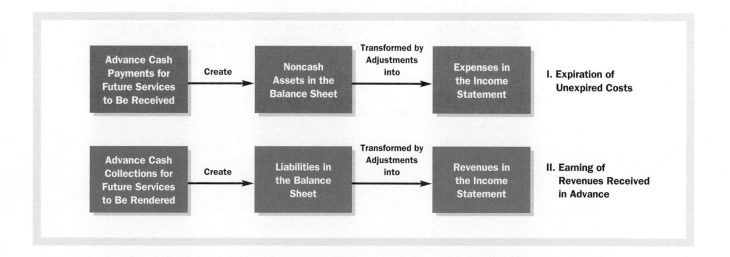

We make the entries for adjustments III and IV, accrual of unrecorded expenses and accrual of unrecorded revenues, before the related cash flows. The income statement is affected before the cash receipts and disbursements occur. The accounting entity computes the amount of goods or services provided or received prior to any cash receipt or payment. Exhibit 4-1 summarizes the major adjusting entries.

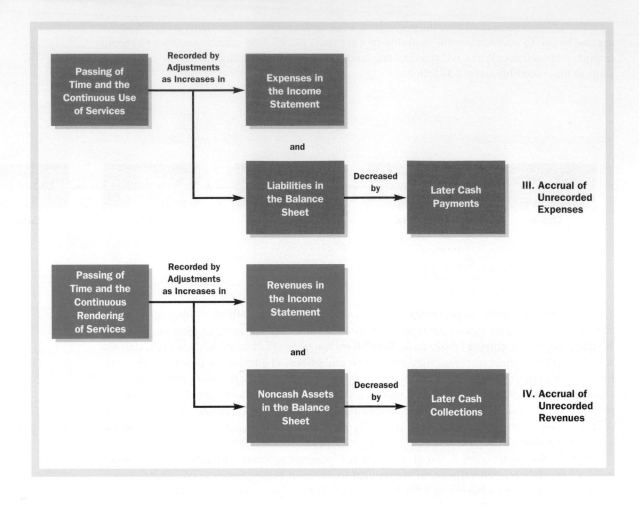

EXHIBIT 4-1

Summary of Adjusting Entries

Adjusting Entry	Type of Account Debited	Type of Account Credited
I. Expiration of unexpired costs	Expense	Prepaid expense, accumulated depreciation
II. Earning of revenues received in advance	Unearned revenue	Revenue
III. Accrual of unrecorded expenses	Expense	Payable
IV. Accrual of unrecorded revenues	Receivable	Revenue

Summary Problem for Your Review

PROBLEM

1. Chan Audio Company is a retailer of stereo equipment that began operation on January 1, 20X0. One month later, on January 31, 20X0, the company's unadjusted trial balance consists of the following accounts:

Cash	$ 71,700	
Accounts receivable	160,300	
Note receivable	40,000	
Merchandise inventory	250,200	
Prepaid rent	15,000	
Store equipment	114,900	
Note payable		$100,000
Accounts payable		117,100
Unearned rent revenue		3,000
Paid-in capital		400,000
Sales		160,000
Cost of goods sold	100,000	
Wages expense	28,000	
Total	$780,100	$780,100

Consider the following adjustments on January 31:

a. January depreciation expense, $1,000.

b. On January 2, Chan paid $15,000 of rent in advance to cover the first quarter of 20X0, as shown by the debit balance in the Prepaid Rent account. Adjust for the consumption of January rent.

c. Wages earned by employees during January but not paid as of January 31 were $3,750.

d. Chan borrowed $100,000 from the bank on January 1. The company recorded this explicit transaction when it borrowed the money, as shown by the credit balance in the Note Payable account. Chan is to pay the principal and 6% interest 1 year later (January 1, 20X1). Chan has not yet made an adjustment for the recognition of January interest expense.

e. On January 1, Chan made a cash loan of $40,000 to a local supplier, as shown by the debit balance in the Note Receivable account. The promissory note stated that the loan is to be repaid 1 year later (January 1, 20X1), together with interest at 9% per annum. On January 31, Chan needs to make an adjustment to recognize the interest earned on the note receivable.

f. On January 15, a nearby corporation paid Chan $3,000 cash as an advance rental for temporary use of Chan's excess storage space and equipment. The rental agreement covers the 3 months from January 15 to April 15. This $3,000 is the credit balance in the Unearned Rent Revenue account. On January 31, Chan needs to make an adjustment to recognize the rent revenue earned for one-half a month.

g. Chan must accrue income tax expense on January income at a rate of 40% of income before taxes.

Required

1. Enter the trial balance amounts in the general ledger. Set up the new asset account, Accrued Interest Receivable, and the new asset reduction account, the contra account, Accumulated Depreciation, Store Equipment. Set up the following new liability accounts: Accrued Wages Payable, Accrued Interest Payable, and Accrued Income Taxes Payable. Set up the following new expense and revenue accounts: Depreciation Expense, Rent Expense, Interest Expense, Interest Revenue, Rent Revenue, and Income Tax Expense.
2. Journalize adjustments (a) to (g) and post the entries to the ledger. Identify entries by transaction letter.
3. Prepare an adjusted trial balance as of January 31, 20X0.

SOLUTION

The solutions to requirements 1 through 3 are in Exhibits 4-2, 4-3, and 4-4. Accountants often refer to the final trial balance, Exhibit 4-4, as the adjusted trial balance. Why? All the necessary adjustments have been made; thus, the trial balance provides the data necessary for creating the formal financial statements.

EXHIBIT 4-2

Chan Audio Company

Journal Entries

		Debit	Credit
(a)	Depreciation expense	1,000	
	Accumulated depreciation, store equipment.		1,000
	Depreciation for January		
(b)	Rent expense.	5,000	
	Prepaid rent		5,000
	Rent expense for January		
	$15,000 \div 3 = \$5,000$		
(c)	Wages expense	3,750	
	Accrued wages payable		3,750
	Wages earned in January but not paid		
(d)	Interest expense	500	
	Accrued interest payable		500
	Interest for January		
	$100,000 \times .06 \times 1/12 = \$500$		
(e)	Accrued interest receivable.	300	
	Interest revenue		300
	Interest earned for January		
	$40,000 \times .09 \times 1/12 = \$300$		
(f)	Unearned rent revenue	500	
	Rent revenue.		500
	Rent earned for January, rent per month,		
	$3,000 \div 3 = \$1,000$; for half a month, $500		
(g)	Income tax expense	9,020	
	Accrued income taxes payable		9,020
	Income tax on January income		
	$.40 \times [160,000 + 300 + 500 - 100,000 - 28,000 - 3,750 - 1,000 - 5,000 - 500]$		
	$= \$9,020$		

Assets	=	Liabilities + Stockholders' Equity
(Increases Left, Decreases Right)		**(Decreases Left, Increases Right)**

Cash

Bal.	71,700	

Accounts Receivable

Bal.	160,300	

Note Receivable

Bal.	40,000	

Merchandise Inventory

Bal.	250,200	

Prepaid Rent

Bal.	15,000	(b) 5,000
Bal.	10,000	

Store Equipment

Bal.	114,900	

Accumulated Depreciation, Store Equipment

	(a) 1,000

Accrued Interest Receivable

(e)	300	

Note Payable

	Bal.	100,000

Accounts Payable

	Bal.	117,100

Unearned Rent Revenue

(f)	500	Bal.	3,000
		Bal.	2,500

Accrued Wages Payable

	(c)	3,750

Accrued Interest Payable

	(d)	500

Accrued Income Tax Payable

	(g)	9,020

Paid-in Capital

	Bal.	400,000

Sales

	Bal.	160,000

Cost of Goods Sold

Bal.	100,000	

Wages Expense

Bal.	28,000	
(c)	3,750	
Bal.	31,750	

Depreciation Expense

(a)	1,000	

Rent Expense

(b)	5,000	

Interest Expense

(d)	500	

Interest Revenue

	(e)	300

Rent Revenue

	(f)	500

Income Tax Expense

(g)	9,020	

EXHIBIT 4-3
Chan Audio Company
General Ledger

EXHIBIT 4-4

Chan Audio Company

Adjusted Trial Balance
January 31, 20X0

Account Title	Balance	
	Debit	Credit
Cash	$ 71,700	
Accounts receivable	160,300	
Note receivable	40,000	
Merchandise inventory	250,200	
Prepaid rent	10,000	
Store equipment	114,900	
Accumulated depreciation, store equipment		$ 1,000
Accrued interest receivable	300	
Note payable		100,000
Accounts payable		117,100
Unearned rent revenue		2,500
Accrued wages payable		3,750
Accrued interest payable		500
Accrued income taxes payable		9,020
Paid-in capital		400,000
Sales		160,000
Cost of goods sold	100,000	
Wages expense	31,750	
Depreciation expense	1,000	
Rent expense	5,000	
Interest expense	500	
Interest revenue		300
Rent revenue		500
Income tax expense	9,020	
Total	$794,670	$794,670

Balance Sheet Exhibit 4-5

Income Statement Exhibits 4-9 and 4-10

Classified Balance Sheet

Once the company has recorded all necessary adjusting entries, it is ready to prepare the financial statements. As we saw in Chapter 1, balance sheet accounts are separated into the major categories of assets, liabilities, and owners' equity. A **classified balance sheet** further groups the accounts into subcategories to help readers quickly gain a perspective on the company's financial position and to draw attention to certain accounts or groups of accounts. Assets are frequently classified into two groups: current assets and noncurrent or long-term assets. Liabilities are similarly classified into current liabilities and noncurrent or long-term liabilities.

Current Assets and Liabilities

Current assets are cash and other assets that a company expects to convert to cash, sell, or consume during the next 12 months (or within the normal operating cycle if longer than 1 year). Similarly, **current liabilities** are those liabilities that come due within the next year (or within the normal operating cycle if longer than a year). Identifying current assets and liabilities is useful in assessing the company's ability to meet obligations as they become due. For the most part, current assets give rise to the cash needed to pay current liabilities, so the relationship between these categories is important.

Assets			Liabilities and Owners' Equity		
Current assets			Current liabilities		
Cash		$ 71,700	Accounts payable		$117,100
Accounts receivable		160,300	Unearned rent revenue		2,500
Note receivable		40,000	Accrued wages payable		3,750
Accrued interest receivable		300	Accrued interest payable		500
Merchandise inventory		250,200	Accrued income taxes payable		9,020
Prepaid rent		10,000	Note payable		100,000
Total current assets		$532,500	Total current liabilities		$232,870
Long-term assets			Stockholders' equity		
Store equipment	$114,900		Paid-in capital	$400,000	
Accumulated depreciation	(1,000)	113,900	Retained earnings	13,530	413,530
Total		$646,400	Total		$646,400

EXHIBIT 4-5

Chan Audio Company

Balance Sheet
January 31, 20X0

Exhibit 4-5 shows the classified balance sheet for Chan Audio Company, which we prepared from the adjusted trial balance for the company (shown in Exhibit 4-4). In the United States a classified balance sheet generally lists the current asset accounts in the order in which the assets are likely to be converted to cash during the coming year. Therefore, Cash appears first. In the case of Chan Audio, Accounts Receivable are next because the firm should receive cash payments for these accounts within weeks or months. The Note Receivable and related Accrued Interest Receivable, the third and fourth accounts listed, are due January 1, 20X1, within the 1 year (or normal operating cycle) time frame for classification as current assets. Nonmonetary assets, such as inventories and prepaid expenses (in this case, Merchandise Inventory and Prepaid Rent), appear last in the current assets section of the balance sheet. Chan does not convert Prepaid Rent to cash, but it is a current asset in the sense that its existence reduces the obligation to pay cash within the next year.

As shown in Exhibit 4-5, we also list current liability accounts in the approximate order in which they will draw on, or decrease, cash during the coming year. Wages tend to be paid weekly or monthly, whereas interest and taxes tend to be paid monthly, quarterly, or annually.

The excess of current assets over current liabilities is **working capital** (**net working capital** or **net current assets**). In the case of Chan Audio Company, the working capital on January 31, 20X0, is ($532,500 – $232,870) = $299,630. Working capital is important because it relates current assets and current liabilities. It normally grows larger as the company grows, so it is proportional to the size of the firm.

current assets
Cash and other assets that a company expects to convert to cash, sell, or consume during the next 12 months or within the normal operating cycle if longer than 1 year.

current liabilities
Liabilities that come due within the next year or within the normal operating cycle if longer than 1 year.

working capital (net working capital, net current assets)
The excess of current assets over current liabilities.

Formats of Balance Sheets

While all balance sheets contain the same basic information, the details and formats of balance sheets and other financial statements vary across companies and accounting jurisdictions. For example, consider the balance sheets of **Columbia Sportswear** for December 31, 2007, and December 31, 2008, as shown in Exhibit 4-6. The format and classifications are those actually used by Columbia. Note the absence of a separate subtotal for noncurrent assets and noncurrent liabilities. Some companies prefer to omit these headings when there are only a few items within a specific class. Exhibit 4-6 presents a classified balance sheet in the **report format** (assets at top), which is different from the **account format** (assets at left) illustrated in Exhibit 4-5. Either format is acceptable.

Foreign companies and U.S. companies in certain industries may use formats that differ from those presented in Exhibits 4-5 and 4-6. Exhibit 4-7 shows a condensed balance sheet for **Nokia Corporation**, a Finnish company that is one of the world's largest makers of cell phones. Nokia prepares a classified balance sheet in a format that is common for companies

report format
A classified balance sheet with the assets at the top.

account format
A classified balance sheet with the assets at the left.

	December 31	
	2008	**2007**
Assets		
Current assets		
Cash and cash equivalents	$ 230,617	$ 191,950
Short-term investments	22,433	81,598
Accounts receivable, net	299,585	300,506
Inventories, net	256,312	265,874
Deferred income taxes	33,867	31,169
Prepaid expenses and other current assets	29,705	14,567
Total current assets	872,519	885,664
Property, plant, and equipment, net	229,693	210,450
Intangibles and other noncurrent assets	33,365	53,094
Goodwill	12,659	17,273
Total assets	$1,148,236	$1,166,481
Liabilities and Shareholders' Equity		
Current liabilities		
Accounts payable	$ 104,354	95,412
Accrued liabilities	58,085	62,549
Deferred income taxes	1,969	949
Income taxes payable	8,718	7,436
Other current liabilities	63	185
Total current liabilities	173,189	166,531
Income taxes payable	20,412	18,663
Deferred income taxes	—	8,968
Other long-term liabilities	10,545	2,198
Total liabilities	204,146	196,360
Shareholders' equity:		
Preferred stock; 10,000 shares authorized; none issued and outstanding	—	—
Common stock; 125,000 shares authorized; 33,865 and 35,824 issued and outstanding	1,481	17,004
Retained earnings	909,443	895,476
Accumulated other comprehensive income	33,166	57,641
Total shareholders' equity	944,090	970,121
Total liabilities and shareholders' equity	$1,148,236	$1,166,481

EXHIBIT 4-6

Columbia Sportswear Company
Consolidated Balance Sheets (in thousands)

adhering to IFRS. The amounts are presented in millions of euro. Note that Nokia lists noncurrent assets totaling €15,112 before current assets totaling €24,470. The sequencing of the liabilities and equity side of the balance sheet is reversed relative to the ordering typical in a balance sheet prepared under U.S. GAAP. Nokia first lists shareholders' equity totaling €16,510, followed by noncurrent liabilities of €2,717 and finally current liabilities of €20,355.

	December 31	
	2008	**2007**
Assets		
Noncurrent assets	15,112	8,305
Current assets	24,470	29,294
Total assets	39,582	37,599
Shareholders' Equity and Liabilities		
Total equity	16,510	17,338
Noncurrent liabilities	2,717	1,285
Current liabilities	20,355	18,976
Total shareholders' equity and liabilities	39,582	37,599

EXHIBIT 4-7

Nokia Corporation

Condensed Consolidated Balance Sheets (in millions of Euros)

Unilever Group is a dual-listed company consisting of Unilever NV in Rotterdam, Netherlands, and Unilever PLC headquartered in London, England. The company operates as a single business and is the top maker of packaged consumer goods in the world. Unilever also uses IFRS to prepare its financial statements. Exhibit 4-8 shows balance sheets for Unilever for December 31, 2008, and December 31, 2007. Unilever lists noncurrent assets before current assets and then deducts current liabilities from current assets to give a direct measure of working capital (called net current assets or net current liabilities). Unilever reports negative working capital of €2,625 million as of December 31, 2008. Recognize that, regardless of the format and modest differences in account naming conventions, balance sheets contain the same basic information.

Current Ratio

Current assets are an indicator, albeit an imperfect indicator, of how much cash a company will have on hand in the near future; current liabilities tell you how much debt the company will have to pay off with that cash in the near future. Comparing the two amounts helps financial statements users assess a business entity's **liquidity**, which is its ability to meet its near term financial obligations with cash and near-cash assets as those obligations become due.

Investors use the **current ratio** (also called the **working capital ratio**), which we calculate by dividing current assets by current liabilities, to evaluate a company's liquidity. Chan Audio's current ratio is

liquidity
An entity's ability to meet its near-term financial obligations with cash and near-cash assets as those obligations become due.

current ratio (working capital ratio)
Current assets divided by current liabilities.

$$\text{Current ratio} = \frac{\$532,500}{\$232,870} = 2.3$$

A current ratio that is too low may indicate the company will have difficulty meeting its short-term obligations. Conversely, a current ratio that is too high may indicate excessive holdings of current assets such as cash, accounts receivable, or inventories. Excessive holdings of this nature are bad for a company because they tie up money that could be more effectively used elsewhere.

How do we assess this ratio? Is a higher current ratio always better? Other things being equal, the higher a company's current ratio, the more assurance creditors have that the company will be able to pay them in full and on time. However, as with all ratios, it can be misleading to draw conclusions from the numeric value of the ratio alone. In the case of the current ratio, it is important to consider the composition of current assets and current liabilities before drawing inferences. Suppose that just prior to the end of January, Chan Audio used $70,000 of its cash to pay off part of the outstanding balance in Accounts Payable. The restated current ratio is

$$\text{Current ratio} = \frac{\$532,500 - \$70,000}{\$232,870 - \$70,000} = 2.8$$

EXHIBIT 4-8

Unilever Group Consolidated Balance Sheet

December 31, 2008, and December 31, 2007 (in millions of Euros)

	2008	2007
Goodwill	11,665	12,244
Intangible assets	4,426	4,511
Property, plant, and equipment	5,957	6,284
Pension asset for funded schemes in surplus	425	2,008
Deferred tax assets	1,068	1,003
Other noncurrent assets	1,426	1,324
Total noncurrent assets	24,967	27,374
Inventories	3,889	3,894
Trade and other current receivables	3,823	4,194
Current tax assets	234	367
Cash and cash equivalents	2,561	1,098
Other financial assets	632	216
Noncurrent assets held for sale	36	159
Total current assets	11,175	9,928
Financial liabilities	(4,842)	(4,166)
Trade payables and other current liabilities	(7,824)	(8,017)
Current tax liabilities	(377)	(395)
Provisions	(757)	(968)
Liabilities associated with noncurrent assets held for sale	—	(13)
Total current liabilities	(13,800)	(13,559)
Net current assets/(liabilities)	(2,625)	(3,631)
Total assets less current liabilities	**22,342**	**23,743**
Financial liabilities due after one year	6,363	5,483
Noncurrent tax liabilities	189	233
Pensions/post-retirement healthcare liabilities		
Funded schemes in deficit	1,820	827
Unfunded schemes	1,987	2,270
Provisions	646	694
Deferred tax liabilities	790	1,213
Other noncurrent liabilities	175	204
Total noncurrent liabilities	11,970	10,924
Share capital	484	484
Share premium	121	153
Other reserves	(6,469)	(3,412)
Retained profit	15,812	15,162
Shareholders' equity	9,948	12,387
Minority interests	424	432
Total equity	10,372	12,819
Total capital employed	**22,342**	**23,743**

Even though the restated current ratio is higher than the previous value of 2.3, it is difficult to argue that Chan is more liquid as it has only $1,700 in cash. The relative liquidity of Chan under these two different scenarios depends on the company's ability to convert its current assets such as Merchandise Inventory and Accounts Receivable to cash. This illustrates one of the difficulties in interpreting the current ratio; some current assets are less liquid than others and may take longer to convert to cash.

Variations of the current ratio attempt to distinguish among assets based on their relative level of liquidity. One common variation of the current ratio is the **quick ratio** (also known as the **acid test ratio**), which removes inventory (and potentially other less liquid assets such as prepaid expenses) from the numerator of the calculation. This provides a more restrictive view of the company's liquidity. For example, in the initial scenario depicted for Chan Audio, the quick ratio is ($532,500 − $250,200) ÷ $232,870 = 1.2. In the second scenario, the quick ratio is ($532,500 − $250,200 − $70,000) ÷ ($232,870 − $70,000) = 1.3.

An old rule of thumb was that the current ratio should be greater than 2.0. However, current ratios today are more commonly close to 1.0. In making judgments about a company's liquidity, analysts do not focus on the ratio value in isolation; rather they compare a company's current ratio with those of past years, with those of similar companies, or with an industry norm. For example, on December 31, 2008, IBM's ratio was 1.15, compared with an industry median of 1.97. Although only slightly greater than 1.0 and below the industry median, IBM's ratio is probably not a cause for concern. It is also common for firms in the utility industry to have low current ratios because of low levels of inventory and stable cash flows. For example, Portland General Electric, a regional electric power company, had a current ratio of only 0.73 on December 31, 2008. On the other hand, Google's current ratio of 8.76 on December 31, 2008, was more than seven times as large as IBM's and 12 times as large as Portland General Electric's. You will find more information on working capital and the current ratio in the Business First box on page 172.

Although some people use the current or quick ratio to measure short-term debt-paying ability, a prediction of cash receipts and disbursements is more useful. Whether a company's level of cash is too low or too high really depends on the forecasts of operating requirements over the coming months. For example, a company such as a small comic book and baseball card retailer might need very little cash on hand because upcoming debts and operating needs will be small in the next few months. Conversely, Marvel Comics, the corporation that produces the comic books sold by the small retailer, will need millions of dollars in cash to meet upcoming debt and short-term operating needs. As a rule, companies should try to keep on hand only the cash necessary to meet disbursement needs and invest any temporary excess cash to generate additional income.

> **quick ratio (acid test ratio)**
> *Variation of the current ratio that removes less liquid assets from the numerator. Perhaps the most common version of this ratio is (current assets − inventory) ÷ current liabilities.*

INTERPRETING FINANCIAL STATEMENTS

Published annual reports typically contain condensed balance sheet information. This level of detail is appropriate for external analysts and investors. Is this same level of detail sufficient for internal use?

Answer

No. Firms prepare detailed balance sheets for their internal use. Suppose that you are the person responsible for managing inventory at Columbia Sportswear's flagship store in Portland, Oregon. Rather than just knowing the total amount of inventory on hand, you would need to know what the inventory levels are for spring merchandise and for summer merchandise, for men's wear and women's wear, and for clothing and accessories. This detail and more is necessary for you to manage your operation and evaluate your performance. Outside investors are more concerned with the overall performance of Columbia Sportswear as a whole relative to competing retailers, so summarized company-wide information is sufficient.

Income Statement

We have seen that balance sheets provide decision makers with information about a company's ability to meet its short-term operating and debt needs. However, investors are also concerned about a company's ability to generate earnings and pay dividends. The income statement provides some of the information necessary to address these concerns. Income statements, like balance sheets, may include subcategories that help focus attention on certain accounts or groups of accounts. There are two commonly used income statement formats, the single-step income statement and the multiple-step income statement.

> **OBJECTIVE 8**
> Prepare single- and multiple-step income statements.

BUSINESS FIRST

MANAGING WORKING CAPITAL

Working capital refers to the portion of a company's capital that is currently invested in the "working" or day-to-day operation of the company. Under IFRS working capital consists of operating assets and liabilities, also known as short-term assets and liabilities, which will be turned around within one year. Operating assets include (1) inventory (products that will be sold or used in the manufacturing process), (2) debtors/accounts receivable (money owed to the company by customers), as well as (3) cash and bank deposits. Operating liabilities are mostly made up of creditors/accounts payable (money owed by the company to suppliers). Operating assets minus operating liabilities are referred to as net operating assets.

Every company develops their own policy relating to net operating assets. Some companies aim to minimize operating assets while maximizing operating liabilities, thereby increasing the cash available to invest in new expansion opportunities. However, most companies follow the traditional approach of ensuring that operating assets are at least double operating liabilities. This approach ensures that a company will be able to pay their creditors as they become due and stay out of the financial distress caused by cash shortage.

In uncertain or difficult financial times, such as the recession which started in 2008/2009, companies have to follow different strategies to ensure that they have enough cash—the primary operating and investment asset. The least disruptive way for a company to do this is to change its approach to managing other aspects of working capital, such as debtors, inventory, and creditors. Debtors can be collected quickly (by, for instance, decreasing the credit period from 60 to 30 days) and inventory can be kept to a minimum (using a just-in-time system). A company could also try to negotiate with their creditors to pay them later than normal, leading to indirect financing.

Under IFRS, operating assets and liabilities are usually measured at their undiscounted face value (cash amount to be paid or received). The only exception is inventory which is measured at the lowest of cost and net realisable value. In South Africa, listed companies are required to apply IFRS when drawing up their financial statements and therefore this disparity in approaches to managing working capital can be seen. Many of the differences arise due to the different industries in which the companies operate and the economic climate of South Africa and the world.

Anglo Platinum Limited reported that during the year ending December 31, 2010, strict working capital management led to an increase in cash which was used to decrease the outstanding debt—thereby improving the financial health of the company. This is seen as prudent management given the aftermath of the 2008/2009 recession and the accompanying decrease in operating cash flow. The company's net operating cash flow decreased from around $2 billion (in 2008) to just under $6 million in 2009, but recovered to approximately $1.4 billion in 2010.

Pioneer Foods Limited is a large food and beverage manufacturer in South Africa. In their annual financial statements for the year ending September 30, 2010 Pioneer Foods reported that the improvement in the company's financial ratios could be attributed partially to effective working capital management. The cash that was freed up from lowering other operating assets was also used to diminish outstanding debt.

In South Africa, a number of people do not use government health services, but go to private hospitals and doctors. The largest private hospital group is the Medi-Clinic Group. The Medi-Clinic Group operates 52 hospitals in Southern Africa, 14 in Switzerland, and two in the United Arab Emirates. During the year ending March 31, 2011, the group showed a large increase in both debtors and creditors. This is most likely due to increased turnover and does not necessarily point to any problem in the management of working capital.

Sources: Medi-Clinic Annual Report (31 March 2011), http://annualreport2011.mediclinic.com; Pioneer Foods Annual Report (30 September 2010), http://www.pioneerfoods.co.za/annual_report/ar_2010/default.asp; Anglo Platinum Annual Report (31 December 2010), http://www.investar.co.za/angloplatinumar2010; Deloitte, "Managing working capital – Cash @ Risk", Webinar, 23 October 2009.

single-step income statement
An income statement that groups all revenues and then lists and deducts all expenses without reporting any intermediate subtotals.

multiple-step income statement
An income statement that contains one or more subtotals that highlight significant relationships.

Single- and Multiple-Step Income Statements

The adjusted trial balance for Chan Audio Company (Exhibit 4-4) provides the data for the two formats of income statements shown in Exhibits 4-9 and 4-10. Exhibit 4-9 presents a **single-step income statement**. Notice that it groups all types of revenue together (e.g., Sales Revenue, Interest Revenue, and Rent Revenue) and then deducts all expenses without reporting any intermediate subtotals. Exhibit 4-10 provides an example of a **multiple-step income statement**. Rather than grouping all revenues together and then subtracting all expenses, the multiple-step income statement combines revenues and expenses to highlight significant relationships. Regardless of the presentation format, the net income number is the same. There is no theoretical or practical reason to prefer one of these formats. Experienced readers of financial statements can

Sales		$160,000
Rent revenue		500
Interest revenue		300
Total sales and other revenues		$160,800
Expenses		
Cost of goods sold	$100,000	
Wages	31,750	
Depreciation	1,000	
Rent	5,000	
Interest	500	
Income taxes	9,020	
Total expenses		$147,270
Net income		$ 13,530

EXHIBIT 4-9
Chan Audio Company
Single-Step Income Statement for the Month Ended January 31, 20X0

easily adjust from one to another. As you begin to read and evaluate actual statements, do not let the superficial differences in presentation confuse you.

The majority of U.S. companies employ the multiple-step income statement format in their external financial statements. The Columbia Sportswear income statement in Exhibit 4-11 is a multiple-step income statement. Let's take a closer look at the subtotals that commonly appear in a multiple-step statement. Most multiple-step income statements start with the separate computation and disclosure of **gross profit** (also called **gross margin**), which is the excess of sales revenue over the cost of the inventory that was sold. Chan reports a gross profit of $60,000 in Exhibit 4-10, and Columbia Sportswear's 2008 income statement shows a gross profit of $567,811,000.

The next section of a multiple-step income statement usually contains the **operating expenses**, which is a group of recurring expenses that pertain to the firm's routine, ongoing operations. Examples of such expenses are wages, rent, depreciation, and various other operation-oriented expenses, such as telephone, heat, and advertising. We deduct these operating expenses from the gross profit to obtain **operating income** (also called **operating profit** or **income from operations**). Chan reports operating income of $22,250 in Exhibit 4-10. In Exhibit 4-11, Columbia Sportswear groups all recurring operating expenses together into a category called

gross profit (gross margin)
The excess of sales revenue over the cost of the inventory that was sold.

operating expenses
A group of recurring expenses that pertain to the firm's routine, ongoing operations.

operating income (operating profit, income from operations)
Gross profit less all operating expenses.

Sales		$160,000
Cost of goods sold		100,000
Gross profit		$ 60,000
Operating expenses		
Wages	$31,750	
Depreciation	1,000	
Rent	5,000	37,750
Operating income		$ 22,250
Other revenues and expenses		
Rent revenue	$ 500	
Interest revenue	300	
Total other revenue	$ 800	
Deduct: interest expense	500	300
Income before income taxes		$ 22,550
Income taxes		9,020
Net income		$ 13,530

EXHIBIT 4-10
Chan Audio Company
Multiple-Step Income Statement for the Month Ended January 31, 20X0

EXHIBIT 4-11

Columbia Sportswear Company

Consolidated Statements of Operations (in thousands)

	Year Ended December 31	
	2008	**2007**
Net sales	$1,317,835	$1,356,039
Cost of sales	750,024	776,288
Gross profit	567,811	579,751
Selling, general, and administrative	430,350	385,769
Impairment of acquired intangible assets	24,742	—
Net licensing income	(5,987)	(5,157)
Income from operations	118,706	199,139
Interest income, net	7,537	8,888
Income before income tax	126,243	208,027
Income tax expense	31,196	63,575
Net income	$ 95,047	$ 144,452

Selling, General, and Administrative, and subtracts them from gross profit. In 2008, Columbia's income statement also reflects a nonrecurring operating expense resulting from the decline in value of intangible assets previously purchased by the company, a topic we will cover in Chapter 8. Finally, prior to computing income from operations, Columbia Sportswear also deducts from operating expenses a small amount of income from licensing activities. It reports income from operations of $118,706,000 in 2008.

The next grouping in the multiple-step income statement contains nonoperating revenues and expenses, which are revenues and expenses that are not directly related to the mainstream of a firm's operations. Nonoperating revenues are usually minor in relation to the sales revenue shown in the first section of the multiple-step statement. Nonoperating expenses are also minor, with the possible exception of interest expense. Some companies make heavy use of debt (which causes high interest expense), whereas other companies incur little debt and have low interest expense. Chan Audio Company separately itemizes Interest Expense and Interest Revenue in Exhibit 4-10. In contrast, Columbia Sportswear nets Interest Expense and Interest Revenue on the income statement. In all financial statements, accountants use the label "net" to denote that some amounts have been offset in computing the final result. Thus, if a company reports net interest, it means that interest revenue and interest expense have been combined into one number, which may result in either an expense or revenue. In the case of Columbia Sportswear, interest revenue exceeds interest expense in both years shown in Exhibit 4-11. Note that Interest Income, Net has been added to Income from Operations to arrive at Income Before Income Tax. Users of financial statements usually regard interest revenue and interest expense as "other" or "nonoperating" items because they arise from lending and borrowing money—activities that are distinct from most companies' ordinary operations of selling goods or services. Exceptions occur in companies in the business of lending and borrowing money: banks, credit unions, insurance companies, and other financial intermediaries.

If income statements keep nonoperating revenues and expenses separate from operating revenues and expenses, we can easily compare operating income over time or between companies. Comparisons of operating income focus attention on selling the product and controlling the costs of doing so. Success in this arena is an important test of a company's health.

Note where income taxes appear in both the single-step and multiple-step income statements of Chan Audio in Exhibits 4-9 and 4-10, as well as in Columbia Sportswear's income statement in Exhibit 4-11. Most companies follow the practice of showing income taxes as a separate item immediately above net income, regardless of the grouping of other items on the income statement.

IFRS and U.S. GAAP are broadly similar with respect to the presentation of the income statement. The suggested income statement format for companies reporting under IFRS includes subtotals for gross profit and pretax income. This is similar, but not identical, to the U.S. multiple-step format. However, while IFRS allows companies to display expenses either by nature or by function, U.S. GAAP requires them to show expenses by function. The income statement of

Turnover	€40,523
Operating profit	7,167
Net finance costs	(257)
Other nonoperating income (loss)	219
Profit before taxation	7,129
Taxation	(1,844)
Net profit	€ 5,285

EXHIBIT 4-12
Unilever Group
Condensed Consolidated Income Statement Year Ended December 31, 2008 (in millions of Euros)

Nokia Corporation, the Finnish cell phone company referenced earlier in the chapter, is indistinguishable in format from the multiple-step income statement of Columbia Sportswear. However, you can see a few major differences in a condensed version of the income statement of Unilever Group, the Anglo-Dutch consumer products giant, shown in Exhibit 4-12. The company reports Turnover of €40,523 (in millions) for the year ended December 31, 2008. The term **turnover**, used by some IFRS companies, is synonymous with sales or sales revenue. Unilever then reports operating profit of €7,167 million without itemizing the operating expenses. While you can deduce that operating expenses were (€40,523 – €7,167) = €33,356, the income statement does not show them directly. The remainder of the statement is similar to those shown earlier.

turnover
Sales or sales revenue.

Analysts and investors follow trends in corporate earnings. When observing earnings trends, it is important to distinguish between trends in operating versus nonoperating activities. There is a distinction between those circumstances where earnings growth is due to declining interest expense or increasing interest revenue and those circumstances where earnings growth is due to dramatic increases in sales. The first two sources of earnings growth are not directly linked to the company's routine, ongoing activities. However, when demand for the product increases, the long-term potential for continued growth is improved. The need to use caution in interpreting changes in earnings is not limited to the distinction between operating and nonoperating earnings. For example, everything else equal, a reduction in research and development expense—an operating expense—will result in an improvement in current period earnings. However, the long-term implications for the company may be negative if research and development is crucial to the development of new products.

Profitability Evaluation Ratios

For experienced managers, the income statement and balance sheet are the "language of business." These managers can compare current period income with that of the previous quarter or prior year. They have a solid understanding of their competitors' financial statements and can evaluate how their company compares with the competition. How can individuals who do not have this deep company and industry knowledge use the financial statements to gain insights into the company's performance?

OBJECTIVE 9
Use ratios to assess profitability.

Earlier in this chapter, we saw that ratios such as the current ratio help give meaning to the numbers in the balance sheet. Similarly, ratios using income statement numbers are useful in evaluating a company's **profitability**, which is the ability of a company to provide its investors with a particular rate of return on their investment. If Mary invests $100 in Columbia Sportswear and receives $10 every year as a result, $10 is her return on investment. However, absolute amounts are hard to evaluate. What if Mary had given Columbia Sportswear $200? In that case, a return of $10 would not be as attractive. Thus, it is common to express the return as a **rate of return**, a return per dollar invested. In the case of a $100 investment, a $10 return is a 10% rate of return ($10 ÷ $100). For a $200 investment, a $10 return is a 5% rate of return ($10 ÷ $200).

profitability
The ability of a company to provide investors with a particular rate of return on their investment.

rate of return
The return per dollar invested.

Profitability measures are useful decision-making tools. Investors use them to distinguish among different investment opportunities. Managers know that their company's profitability measures will affect the investment decisions of investors and that high profitability makes it easier to raise capital by selling stock or issuing debt securities. From time to time, managers may have to decide whether to buy another company, a division of a company, or a machine that will be used in manufacturing a new product. In each case, the manager will evaluate the profitability of the project as part of making the decision.

Investors use trends in profitability measures over time, and within and across industries, as a basis for predictions and decisions. We provide a very brief introduction to four profitability ratios: gross profit percentage, return on sales, return on common stockholders' equity, and return on assets. Chapter 12 expands on the interpretation of these ratios and introduces additional measures of financial performance.

Gross Profit Percentage

gross profit percentage (gross margin percentage)
Gross profit (sales revenue – cost of goods sold) divided by sales revenue.

A ratio based on gross profit (Sales Revenue minus Cost of Goods Sold) is particularly useful to a retailer or manufacturer in choosing a pricing strategy and in judging its results. This measure, the **gross profit percentage**, or **gross margin percentage**, is defined as gross profit divided by sales revenue. Chan Audio Company's gross profit percentage for January is (numbers from Exhibit 4-10)

$$\text{Gross profit percentage} = \text{Gross profit} \div \text{Sales}$$
$$= \$60{,}000 \div \$160{,}000$$
$$= 37.5\%$$

We can also present this relationship as follows:

	Amount	Percentage
Sales	$160,000	100.0%
Cost of goods sold	100,000	62.5
Gross profit	$ 60,000	37.5%

Gross profit percentages vary greatly by industry. For example, software companies have high gross profit percentages (**Microsoft**'s was almost 81% for the year ending June 30, 2008). Why? Because most costs in the software industry are in research and development and sales and marketing, not in cost of goods sold. In contrast, retail companies have lower gross margin percentages because product costs are their main expense. For example, in 2008, the gross profit percentage for **Costco** was 10.5%. Other gross margin percentages fall between the extremes, such as **Intel**'s at 55.5% and Columbia Sportswear's at 43%.

Return on Sales or Net Profit Margin

return on sales ratio (profit margin ratio)
Net income divided by sales.

Managers carefully follow the **return on sales ratio** (also known as the **profit margin ratio**), which shows the relationship of net income to sales revenue. This ratio gauges a company's ability to control the level of all its expenses relative to the level of its sales. As with the gross profit percentage, the return on sales tends to vary by industry, but the range is not as great. We can compute Chan Audio's return on sales ratio as follows using numbers from Exhibit 4-9 or 4-10:

$$\text{Return on sales} = \text{Net income} \div \text{Sales}$$
$$= \$13{,}530 \div \$160{,}000$$
$$= 8.5\%$$

Columbia Sportswear reports a return on sales ratio of 7.2% for the year ended December 31, 2008.

Return on Common Stockholders' Equity

return on common stockholders' equity ratio (ROE or ROCE)
Net income divided by invested capital (measured by average common stockholders' equity).

The **return on common stockholders' equity ratio (ROE** or **ROCE)** also uses net income, but compares it with invested capital (as measured by average common stockholders' equity) instead of sales. Many analysts regard this ratio as the ultimate measure of overall accomplishment from the perspective of the shareholder. The return on common stockholders' equity calculation for Chan Audio for the month of January is

$$\text{Return on common stockholders' equity} = \text{Net income} \div \text{Average common stockholders' equity}$$
$$= \$13{,}530 \div 1/2 \ (\text{January 1 balance, } \$400{,}000$$
$$+ \text{ January 31 balance, } \$413{,}530)$$
$$= \$13{,}530 \div \$406{,}765$$
$$= 3.3\% \ (\text{for 1 month})$$

Return on Assets

The **return on assets ratio (ROA)** compares net income with invested capital as measured by average total assets. The company invests its resources in assets, which it uses to generate revenues and ultimately, net income. The return on assets ratio measures how effectively those assets generate profits. Assuming a balance in total assets of $620,000 as of January 1, we can calculate the return on assets ratio for Chan Audio for the month of January as follows:

return on assets ratio (ROA)
Net income divided by average total assets.

$$\text{Return on assets} = \text{Net income} \div \text{Average total assets}$$

$$= \$13,530 \div 1/2 \ (\text{January 1 balance}, \$620,000$$

$$+ \ \text{January 31 balance}, \$646,400)$$

$$= \$13,530 \div \$633,200$$

$$= 2.1\% \ (\text{for 1 month})$$

Other variations of the return on assets ratio are discussed in Chapter 12.

Chan Audio's 37.5% gross profit percentage is high compared with the average of 31.1% for the retail stereo industry. Chan Audio has also maintained excellent expense control as evidenced by its 8.5% return on sales, 39.6% return on common stockholders' equity (a monthly rate of $3.3\% \times 12 = 39.6\%$ as an annual rate), and 25.2% return on assets ($2.1\% \times 12 = 25.2\%$), which are higher than the annual returns earned by the industry over the same period.

Recent examples of annual return on sales, return on common stockholders' equity, and return on assets ratios for firms in different industries are shown here:

	Return on Sales (%)	Return on Common Stockholders' Equity (%)	Return on Assets (%)
Microsoft	29.3	52.5	26.0
Costco	1.8	14.4	6.4
McDonald's	18.3	30.1	14.9
CVS Caremark	3.8	10.2	5.8
Honda (Japan)	4.2	12.2	4.5
Google	19.4	16.6	14.8
Johnson & Johnson	20.3	30.2	15.6
Starbucks	3.0	13.2	5.7

INTERPRETING FINANCIAL STATEMENTS

Which industry would you expect to have a higher gross margin percentage, the grocery industry or the pharmaceutical industry? Why?

Answer

There are many "right ways" to think about this issue. Whole Foods, a premium grocery store chain, has a gross margin of 34%. The grocery industry is a retail activity where stores buy and resell items very quickly. As a result they can accept fairly low margins because they hold the inventory briefly and face little risk of failure. In contrast, the pharmaceutical industry has to develop drugs, seek government approval to market them, and then aggressively sell them. Thus, the pharmaceutical industry has high gross margin percentages. In 2008, Pfizer had a gross margin percentage of 83.2%. It is important to remember that Cost of Goods Sold excludes Selling, General, and Administrative Costs, which are larger relative to sales in the pharmaceutical industry than in the grocery industry. In addition, the pharmaceutical industry faces huge R&D costs, which accountants treat as a period cost instead of a product cost. So R&D, which may be 15% or more of sales in the pharmaceutical industry, is not part of Cost of Goods Sold and does not affect the gross margin percentage.

Summary Problem for Your Review

PROBLEM

Johnson & Johnson (maker of Tylenol, Band-Aid products, and other health-care and personal use products) reports a statement of earnings as follows:

Johnson & Johnson
Statement of Earnings for the Year Ended December 31, 2008
($ in millions except per share figures)

Sales to customers	$63,747
Cost of products sold	18,511
Gross profit	45,236
Selling, marketing, and administrative expenses	21,490
Research expense	7,577
Purchased in-process research and development expense	181
Interest income	(361)
Interest expense	435
Other (income) expense, net	(1,015)
	28,307
Earnings before provision for taxes on income	16,929
Provision for taxes on income	3,980
Net earnings	$12,949
Basic net earnings per share	$ 4.62

1. Is this a single- or multiple-step income statement? Explain your answer.
2. What term would **Columbia Sportswear** use as a label for the line in Johnson & Johnson's statements having the $16,929 figure? (Refer to the Columbia Sportswear income statement in Exhibit 4-11 on page 174.)
3. Suggest an alternative term for Interest Income.
4. What is the amount of the famous "bottom line" that is so often referred to by managers?
5. Net earnings per share are defined as net earnings divided by the average number of common shares outstanding. Compute the average number of common shares outstanding during the year.

SOLUTION

1. As is often the case, Johnson & Johnson uses a hybrid of single- and multiple-step income statements. However, this one is closer to a multiple-step statement. A pure single-step statement would place interest income and other income with sales revenue to obtain total revenues and would not calculate a gross profit subtotal. A pure multiple-step statement would separate operating and nonoperating activities and provide a subtotal for income from operations.
2. Columbia Sportswear would use "income before income tax" to describe the $16,929 figure.
3. Interest revenue.
4. The "bottom line" is net earnings of $12,949 million. The bottom line per average common share outstanding is $4.62.
5. Companies must show net earnings per share on the face of the income statement.

Earnings per share (EPS) = Net earnings ÷ Average number of common shares outstanding
$4.62 = $12,949,000,000 ÷ Average shares
Average shares = $12,949,000,000 ÷ $4.62
Average shares = 2,802,813,853

Highlights to Remember

1 **Understand the role of adjustments in accrual accounting.** At the end of each accounting period, accountants must make adjustments so financial statements recognize revenues and expenses that do not result from explicit transactions.

2 **Make adjustments for the expiration or consumption of assets.** We record many costs initially as assets and recognize them as expenses as time passes. Examples are depreciation and the consumption of prepaid rent.

3 **Make adjustments for the earning of unearned revenues.** Some companies receive payments for revenue before they earn the revenue. They initially recognize unearned revenue as a liability. As the revenue is earned, the company must reduce the liability and recognize the revenue. Examples are rental payments received in advance or prepaid magazine subscriptions. To clarify these first two types of adjustments, you might view them as mirror images by looking at both sides of the adjustment simultaneously. For example, (a) the expiration of unexpired costs (the tenant's rent expense) is accompanied by (b) the earning of unearned revenues (the landlord's rent revenue).

4 **Make adjustments for the accrual of unrecorded expenses.** Companies may incur expenses before cash disbursements are made. Such expenses should be included in the income statement of the period when they are incurred, not in the period when they are paid. Examples are the accrual of wages or interest expense.

5 **Make adjustments for the accrual of unrecorded revenues.** Some revenues accrue before there is an explicit transaction leading to a cash flow. Interest revenue may be recorded before there is a legal obligation for receipt of payment. Similarly, utilities often provide services before a bill is issued. This results in the recognition of revenue and a receivable before the billing cycle sends out a request for payment. You can also view these final two types of adjustments as mirror images. For example, (a) the accrual of unrecorded expenses (a borrower's interest expense) is accompanied by (b) the accrual of unrecorded revenues (a lender's interest revenue).

6 **Describe the sequence of steps in the recording process and relate cash flows to adjusting entries.** The adjusting entries capture expense and revenue elements that either precede or follow the related cash flows. Entries for the expiration of unexpired costs and the earning of unearned revenues follow the cash flows, whereas entries for the accrual of unrecorded expenses and the accrual of unrecorded revenues precede the cash flows. The adjusting entries provide a mechanism for capturing implicit transactions that do not necessarily generate documents that lead to them being recorded.

7 **Prepare a classified balance sheet and use it to assess short-term liquidity.** Classified balance sheets divide various items into subcategories. Assets and liabilities are separated into current and long-term subcategories that are useful in analysis. For example, the difference between current assets and current liabilities is called working capital. The current ratio, defined as current assets divided by current liabilities, is used to help assess liquidity. The quick or acid test ratio, defined as current assets minus inventory divided by current liabilities, is also useful.

8 **Prepare single- and multiple-step income statements.** Income statements may appear in single- or multiple-step format. Single-step statements group all revenue items together and all expense items together, whereas multiple-step statements calculate various subtotals such as gross profit and operating income. Regardless of the format, published income statements are highly condensed and summarized compared with reports used within an organization.

9 **Use ratios to assess profitability.** Analysts use ratios based at least partly on the income statement to assess profitability. Among the most useful are gross margin percentage (or gross profit percentage), return on sales, return on common stockholders' equity, and return on assets.

Accounting Vocabulary

MyAccountingLab

Assignment Material

Questions

4-1 Give two examples of explicit transactions.

4-2 Give two examples of implicit transactions.

4-3 Give two synonyms for unearned revenue.

4-4 Distinguish between the accrual of wages and the payment of wages.

4-5 Give a synonym for income tax expense.

4-6 Explain why income tax expense is usually the final deduction on both single-step and multiple-step income statements.

4-7 "The accrual of previously unrecorded revenues is the mirror image of the accrual of previously unrecorded expenses." Explain by using an illustration.

4-8 What types of adjusting entries are made prior to the related cash flows? After the related cash flows?

4-9 Why are current assets and current liabilities grouped separately from long-term assets and long-term liabilities?

4-10 "Google is much more profitable than Amazon because its current ratio is nine times larger than Amazon's." Do you agree? Explain.

4-11 "Companies should always strive to avoid negative working capital." Do you agree? Explain.

4-12 Explain the difference between a single-step and a multiple-step income statement.

4-13 Why does interest expense typically appear below operating income on a multiple-step income statement?

4-14 The term "costs and expenses" is sometimes found instead of just "expenses" on the income statement. Would expenses be an adequate description? Why?

4-15 Name four popular ratios for measuring profitability, and indicate how to compute each of the four.

4-16 "Computer software companies are generally more profitable than grocery stores because their gross profit percentages are usually at least twice as large." Do you agree? Explain.

Critical Thinking Questions

4-17 Accounting Errors

You have discovered an error in which the tenant has "incorrectly" recorded as rent expense a $3,000 payment made on December 1 for rent for the months of December and January. As a young auditor you are not sure whether this must be corrected. You think it is a self-correcting error. What are the issues you should consider?

4-18 What Constitutes Revenue?

You have just started a program of selling gift certificates at your store. In the first month, you sold $6,000 worth and customers redeemed $1,750 of these certificates for merchandise. Your average gross profit percentage is 36%. What should you report as gift certificate revenue, and how much gross margin related to the gift certificates will appear in the income statement?

4-19 Operating Versus Nonoperating Expenses

You have recently begun a new job as an internal auditor for a large retail clothing chain. The company prepares a multiple-step income statement. You discover that a material amount of salaries expense was erroneously classified as a nonoperating expense. One of your co-workers argues that the error need not be corrected because the net income number is not affected by the misclassification. You disagree. Defend your position.

4-20 Accounting for Supplies

A company began business on July 1 and purchased $1,000 in supplies including paper, pens, paper clips, and so on. On December 31, as financial statements were being prepared, the accounting clerk asked how to treat the $1,000 that appeared in the Supplies Inventory account. What should the clerk do?

Exercises

4-21 True or False

Use T or F to indicate whether each of the following statements is true or false:

1. Retained Earnings should be accounted for as a noncurrent liability item.
2. Deferred Revenue will appear on the income statement.
3. Machinery used in the business should be recorded as a noncurrent asset item.
4. A company that employs cash-basis accounting cannot have a Prepaid Expense account on the balance sheet.
5. From a single balance sheet, you can find stockholders' equity for a period of time but not for a specific day.
6. It is not possible to determine changes in the financial condition of a business from a single balance sheet.

4-22 Tenant and Landlord

The Trucano Company, a retail hardware store, pays quarterly rent on its store at the beginning of each quarter. The rent per quarter is $21,000. The owner of the building in which the store is located is the Resing Corporation.

By using the balance sheet equation format, analyze the effects of the following on the tenant's and the landlord's financial position:

1. Trucano pays $21,000 rent on July 1.
2. Adjustment for July.
3. Adjustment for August.
4. Adjustment for September. Also prepare the journal entries for Trucano and Resing for September.

4-23 Customer and Airline

Kimberly Clark (KC), maker of Scott paper products, decided to hold a managers' meeting in Hawaii in February. To take advantage of special fares, KC purchased airline tickets in advance from Alaska Airlines at a total cost of $50,000. These were acquired on December 1 for cash.

By using the balance sheet equation format, analyze the impact of the December payment and the February travel on the financial position of both KC and Alaska. Also prepare journal entries for February for both companies.

4-24 Accrual of Wages

Consider the following calendar:

The Golden Rule Department Store commenced business on September 1. It is open every day except Sunday. Its total payroll for all employees is $8,000 per day. Payments are made each Tuesday for the preceding week's work through Saturday.

By using the balance sheet equation format, analyze the financial impact on the Golden Rule of the following:

1. Disbursements for wages on September 8, 15, 22, and 29.
2. Adjustment for wages on September 30. Also prepare the journal entry required on September 30.

4-25 Accrued Vacation Pay

As of December 31, 2008, **Delta Airlines** had the following account listed as a current liability on its balance sheet:

Accrued salaries and related benefits	$972,000,000

The "related benefits" include the liability for vacation pay. Under the accrual basis of accounting, vacation pay is ordinarily accrued throughout the year as workers perform service and earn vacation. For example, suppose a Delta baggage handler earns $1,250 per week for 50 weeks and also gets paid $2,500 for 2 weeks' vacation each year. Accrual accounting requires that the obligation for the $2,500 be recognized as it is earned instead of when the payment is disbursed. Thus, in each of the 50 work weeks, Delta would recognize a wage expense (or vacation pay expense) of $2,500/50 = $50.

1. Prepare Delta's weekly adjusting journal entry called for by the $50 example.
2. Prepare the entry for the $2,500 payment of vacation pay.

4-26 Placement of Interest in Income Statement

Two companies have the following balance sheets as of December 31, 20X8:

Jupiter Company

Cash	$ 50,000	Note payable*	$100,000
Other assets	150,000	Stockholders' equity	100,000
Total	$200,000	Total	$200,000
* 9% annual interest.			

Saturn Company

Cash	$ 50,000	Stockholders' equity	$200,000
Other assets	150,000		
Total	$200,000		

In 20X9, each company had sales of $700,000 and operating expenses of $600,000. Jupiter had not repaid the $100,000 Note Payable as of December 31, 20X9. Neither company incurred any new interest-bearing debt in 20X9. Ignore income taxes. Did the two companies earn the same net income and the same operating income? Explain, showing computations of operating income and net income.

4-27 Effects of Interest on Lenders and Borrowers

Bank of America lent **Miller Paint Company** $1,500,000 on April 1, 20X0. The loan plus interest of 8% is payable on April 1, 20X1.

1. By using the balance sheet equation format, prepare an analysis of the impact of the transaction on both Bank of America's and Miller's financial position on April 1, 20X0. Show the summary adjustments on December 31, 20X0, for the period April 1 to December 31. Prepare an analysis of the transaction that takes place on April 1, 20X1, when Miller repays its obligation.
2. Prepare adjusting journal entries for Bank of America and Miller on December 31, 20X0.
3. Prepare the entries that Bank of America and Miller would make on April 1, 20X1 when the loan and interest is repaid. These entries should include interest that accumulates between January 1, 20X1, and April 1, 20X1.

4-28 Identification of Transactions

Valenzuela Corporation's financial position is represented by the nine balances shown on the first line of the following schedule ($ in thousands). Assume that a single transaction took place for each of the following lines, and describe what you think happened, using one short sentence for each line.

	Cash	Accounts Receivable	Inventory	Equipment	Accounts Payable	Accrued Wages Payable	Unearned Rent Revenue	Paid-in Capital	Retained Earnings
Bal.	$19	$32	$54	$ 0	$29	$0	$0	$55	$21
(1)	29	32	54	0	29	0	0	65	21
(2)	29	32	54	20	29	0	0	85	21
(3)	29	32	66	20	41	0	0	85	21
(4A)	29	47	66	20	41	0	0	85	36
(4B)	29	47	58	20	41	0	0	85	28
(5)	34	42	58	20	41	0	0	85	28
(6)	14	42	58	20	21	0	0	85	28
(7)	19	42	58	20	21	0	5	85	28
(8)	19	42	58	20	21	2	5	85	26
(9)	19	42	58	19	21	2	5	85	25
(10)	19	42	58	19	21	2	3	85	27

4-29 Effects on Balance Sheet Equation

Following is a list of effects of accounting transactions on the balance sheet equation: Assets = Liabilities + Stockholders' equity.

a. Increase in assets, decrease in liabilities
b. Increase in assets, increase in liabilities
c. Decrease in assets, decrease in stockholders' equity
d. Decrease in assets, decrease in liabilities
e. Increase in assets, decrease in assets
f. Increase in liabilities, decrease in stockholders' equity
g. Decrease in assets, increase in liabilities
h. Decrease in liabilities, increase in stockholders' equity
i. Increase in assets, increase in stockholders' equity
j. None of these

Required
Which of the relationships previously identified by letter defines the accounting effect of each of the following transactions?

1. The adjusting entry to recognize periodic depreciation.
2. The adjusting entry to record Accrued Salaries.
3. The adjusting entry to record Accrued Interest Receivable.
4. The collection of interest previously accrued.
5. The settlement of an Account Payable by the issuance of a Note Payable.
6. The recognition of an expense that had been paid for previously. A "prepaid" account was increased on payment.
7. The earning of revenue previously collected. Unearned Revenue was increased when collection was made in advance.

4-30 Effects of Errors in Adjustments

What will be the effect—understated (u), overstated (o), or no effect (n)—on the income of the present and future periods if the following errors were made? In all cases, assume that amounts carried over into 20X1 would affect 20X1 operations via the routine accounting entries of 20X1.

	Period	
	20X0	**20X1**
1. Revenue has been collected in advance, but earned amounts have not been recognized at the end of 20X0. Instead, all revenue was recognized as earned in 20X1.	_____	_____
2. Revenue for services rendered has been earned, but the unbilled amounts have not been recognized at the end of 20X0.	_____	_____
3. Accrued wages payable have not been recognized at the end of 20X0.	_____	
4. Prepaid rent has been paid (in late 20X0), but no adjustment for rent used in 20X0 was made. The payments have been debited to prepaid rent. They were transferred to expense in mid-20X1.	_____	_____

4-31 Effects of Adjustments and Corrections

Listed here are a series of accounts that are numbered for identification.

1. Cash
2. Accounts Receivable
3. Notes Receivable
4. Inventory
5. Accrued Interest Receivable
6. Accrued Rent Receivable
7. Fuel on Hand
8. Prepaid Rent
9. Prepaid Insurance
10. Prepaid Repairs and Maintenance
11. Land
12. Buildings
13. Machinery and Equipment
14. Long-Term Debt
15. Notes Payable
16. Accrued Wages and Salaries Payable
17. Accrued Interest Payable
18. Unearned Subscription Revenue
19. Capital Stock
20. Sales
21. Fuel Expense
22. Salaries and Wages
23. Insurance Expense
24. Repairs and Maintenance Expense
25. Rent Expense
26. Rent Revenue
27. Subscription Revenue
28. Interest Revenue
29. Interest Expense

Required

All accounts needed to answer this question are listed previously. The same account may be used in several answers. Prepare any necessary adjusting or correcting entries called for by the following situations, which were discovered at the end of the calendar year. With respect to each situation, assume that no entries have been made concerning the situation other than those specifically described (i.e., no monthly adjustments have been made during the year). Consider each situation separately. These transactions were not necessarily conducted by one firm. Amounts are in thousands of dollars.

a. A $5,000 purchase of equipment on December 30 was erroneously debited to Long-Term Debt. The credit was correctly made to Cash.

b. A business made several purchases of fuel oil. Some purchases ($900) were debited to Fuel Expense, whereas others ($1,100) were charged to an asset account. An oil gauge revealed $300 of fuel on hand at the end of the year. There was no fuel on hand at the beginning of the year. What adjustment was necessary on December 31?

c. On April 1, a business took out a fire insurance policy. The policy was for 2 years, and the full premium of $2,400 was paid on April 1. The payment was debited to Insurance Expense on April 1. What adjustment was necessary on December 31?

d. On December 1, $6,000 was paid in advance to the landlord for 5 months rent. The tenant debited Prepaid Rent for $6,000 on December 1. What adjustment is necessary on December 31 on the tenant's books?

e. Machinery is repaired and maintained by an outside maintenance company on an annual fee basis, payable in advance. The $1,800 fee for the year beginning October 1 was paid on October 1 and charged to Repairs and Maintenance Expense. What adjustment is necessary on December 31?

f. On November 16, $800 of machinery was purchased, $200 cash was paid down, and a 90-day, 5% note payable was signed for the balance. The November 16 transaction was properly recorded. Prepare the adjustment for the interest.

g. A publisher sells subscriptions to magazines. Customers pay in advance. Receipts are originally credited to Unearned Subscription Revenue. On June 1, $24,000 in 1-year subscriptions (all beginning on June 1) were collected and recorded. What adjustment was necessary on December 31?

h. On December 30, certain merchandise inventory was purchased for $1,500 on open account. The bookkeeper debited Machinery and Equipment and credited Accounts Payable for $1,500. Prepare a correcting entry.

i. A 120-day, 8%, $15,000 cash loan was made to a customer on November 1. The November 1 transaction was recorded correctly. What adjustment is necessary on December 31?

4-32 Working Capital and Current Ratio

Using the **Columbia Sportswear** balance sheet in Exhibit 4-6 on page 168, compute Columbia's working capital, current ratio, and quick ratio for 2008. Compute the quick ratio as (current assets – inventories) ÷ current liabilities.

4-33 Profitability Ratios

The Nestlé Group, the Swiss chocolate company, sells many other food items in addition to various types of chocolates. Sales in 2008 were CHF 109,908 million (where CHF means Swiss francs), cost of goods sold was CHF 47,339 million, net income was CHF 18,039 million, average common stockholders' equity was CHF 54,846 million, and average total assets were CHF 110,788 million. Compute Nestlé's gross profit percentage, return on sales, return on average common stockholders' equity, and return on average total assets.

4-34 Impact of Adjusting Entries on Ratios

Exercise 4-31 asked you to write adjusting/correcting entries for transactions (a) through (i). In this problem, consider the effect on the current ratio and return on sales if the adjusting/correcting entries were not made. Indicate whether the failure to record the adjusting/correcting entry will result in these ratios being understated (u), overstated (o), or no effect (n). If additional information is necessary before you can provide the correct response, indicate with (i). Prior to the adjusting entry, the current ratio exceeds 1.0 and the company operated at a profit.

	Current Ratio	Return on Sales
(a)		
(b)		
(c)		
(d)		
(e)		
(f)		
(g)		
(h)		
(i)		

Problems

4-35 Adjusting Entries

(Alternates are 4-37 through 4-39.) Amber Marshall, certified public accountant, had the following transactions (among others) during 20X0:

a. For accurate measurement of performance and position, Marshall uses the accrual basis of accounting. On August 1, she acquired office supplies for $2,000. Office Supplies Inventory was increased, and Cash was decreased by $2,000 on Marshall's books. On December 31, her inventory of office supplies was $900.

b. On September 1, a client gave Marshall a retainer fee of $36,000 cash for monthly services to be rendered over the following 12 months. Marshall increased Cash and Unearned Fee Revenue.

c. Marshall accepted an $8,000 note receivable from a client on October 1 for tax services. The note plus interest of 6% per year was due in 6 months. Marshall increased Note Receivable and Fee Revenue by $8,000 on October 1.

d. As of December 31, Marshall had not recorded $600 of unpaid wages earned by her secretary during late December.

For the year ended December 31, 20X0, prepare all adjustments called for by the preceding transactions. Assume that appropriate entries were routinely made for the explicit transactions described earlier. However, no adjustments have been made before December 31. For each adjustment, prepare an analysis in the same format used when the adjustment process was explained in the chapter (i.e., the balance sheet equation format). Also prepare the adjusting journal entry.

4-36 Multiple-Step Income Statement

(Alternates are 4-40 and 4-51.) From the following data, prepare a multiple-step income statement for the Curran Company for the fiscal year ended May 31, 20X0 ($ in thousands except for percentage).

Sales	$1,800	Cost of goods sold	$1,000
Interest expense	138	Depreciation expense	60
Utilities expense	110	Rent revenue	20
Interest revenue	28	Wage expense	400
Income tax rate	40%		

4-37 Four Major Adjustments

(Alternates are 4-35, 4-38, and 4-39.) Leslie Baker, an attorney, had the following transactions (among others) during 20X0, her initial year in law practice:

a. On August 1, Baker leased office space for 1 year. The landlord (lessor) insisted on full payment in advance. Prepaid Rent was increased and Cash was decreased by $24,000 on Baker's books. Similarly, the landlord increased Cash and increased Unearned Rent Revenue.

b. On October 1, Baker received a retainer of $12,000 cash for services to be rendered to her client, a local trucking company, over the succeeding 12 months. Baker increased Cash and Unearned Fee Revenue. The trucking company increased Prepaid Expenses and decreased Cash.

c. As of December 31, Baker had not recorded $500 of unpaid wages earned by her secretary during late December.

d. During November and December, Baker rendered services to another client, a utility company. She had intended to bill the company for $5,400 services through December 31, but failed to do so.

Required

1. For the year ended December 31, 20X0, prepare all adjustments called for by the preceding transactions. Assume that appropriate entries were routinely made for the explicit transactions. However, no adjustments have been made before December 31. For each adjustment, prepare an analysis in the same format used when the adjustment process was explained in the chapter (i.e., the balance sheet equation format). Prepare two adjustments for each transaction, one for Baker and one for the other party to the transaction. In part c, assume that the secretary uses the accrual basis for her entity.

2. For each transaction, prepare the journal entries for Leslie Baker and the other entities involved.

4-38 Four Major Adjustments

(Alternates are 4-35, 4-37, and 4-39.) The Goodyear Tire & Rubber Company included the following items in its December 31, 2008, balance sheet ($ in millions):

Prepaid expenses (a current asset)	$295
United States and foreign taxes (a current liability)	156

1. Analyze the impact of the following transactions on the financial position of Goodyear as of January 31, 2009. Prepare your analysis in the same format used when the adjustment process was explained in the chapter. Also show adjusting journal entries.
    a. On January 31, an adjustment of $5 million was made for the rental of various retail outlets that had originally increased Prepaid Expenses but had expired.
    b. During December 2008, Goodyear sold tires for $7 million cash to U-Haul, but delivery was not made until January 28, 2009. Unearned Revenue had been increased in December. No other adjustments had been made since then. Prepare the adjustment on January 31.
    c. Goodyear had loaned cash to several of its independent retail dealers. As of January 31, the dealers owed $6 million of interest that had been unrecorded.
    d. On January 31, Goodyear increased its accrual of federal income taxes by $68 million.
2. Compute the ending balances on January 31, 2009, in Prepaid Expenses and in U.S. and Foreign Taxes Payable.

4-39 Four Major Adjustments

(Alternates are 4-35, 4-37, and 4-38.) Alaska Airlines showed the following items in its balance sheet as of December 31, 2008, the end of the fiscal year ($ in millions):

Inventories and supplies	$ 51.9
Prepaid expenses and other current assets	82.0
Air traffic liability	372.7
Accrued wages, vacation, and payroll taxes	119.5

A footnote stated, "Passenger revenue is recognized when the passenger travels. Tickets sold but not yet used are reported as air traffic liability."

The 2008 income statement included the following ($ in millions):

Passenger revenues	$3,355.8
Wages and benefits expense	943.7

1. Analyze the impact of the following assumed 2009 transactions on the financial position of Alaska. Prepare your analysis in the same format used when the adjustment process was explained in the chapter. Also show adjusting journal entries.
    a. Rented sales offices for 1 year, beginning July 1, 2009, for $8 million cash.
    b. On December 31, 2009, an adjustment was made for the rent in requirement (a).
    c. Sold 20 charter flights to Apple Computer for $100,000 each. Cash of $2 million was received in advance on November 20, 2009. The flights were for transporting marketing personnel to business conventions.
    d. As the financial statements were being prepared on December 31, 2009, accountants for both Alaska and Apple Computer independently noted that the first 10 charter flights had occurred in December. The rest will occur in early 2010. An adjustment was made on December 31.
    e. Alaska loaned $30 million to Boeing. Interest of $1.8 million was accrued on December 31.
    f. Additional wages of $35 million were accrued on December 31.
2. At year-end, in addition to liabilities for future charter flights from the transactions described in parts (c) and (d) of number 1, the company had $236 million of collections in advance for flights scheduled in 2010. Compute the proper year-end balance in the Air Traffic Liability account as of December 31, 2009.

4-40 The Gap Inc. Financial Statements

(Alternates are 4-36 and 4-51.) The Gap Inc. is a specialty retailer of clothing, accessories, and personal care products for men, women, children, and babies. Products are sold under The Gap, Old Navy, Banana Republic, Piperlime and Athleta brands. Actual financial data and nomenclature from its January 31, 2009, annual report are given next ($ in millions):

Net sales	$14,526	Earnings before income taxes	$?
Gross profit	5,447	Income taxes	617
Operating income	1,548	Retained earnings	
Operating expenses	?	Beginning of year	$9,223
Cost of goods sold	?	End of year	?
Interest expense	1	Dividends declared	243
Interest income	37	Net earnings	?

1. Compute the missing values. Prepare a multiple-step statement of income for the year ended January 31, 2009.
2. Compute the ending balance in Retained Earnings as of January 31, 2009.
3. Compute the percentage of gross profit on sales and the percentage of net earnings on sales.
4. The average common stockholders' equity for the year was $4,330.5 million. What was the return on average common stockholders' equity?

4-41 Accounting for Dues
(Alternate is 4-42.) The Stone Beach Golf Club provided the following data from its comparative balance sheets:

	December 31	
	20X1	**20X0**
Dues receivable	$90,000	$75,000
Unearned dues revenue	—	$30,000

The income statement for 20X1, which was prepared on the accrual basis, showed Dues Revenue Earned of $680,000. No dues were collected in advance during 20X1.
Prepare the 20X1 journal entries and post to T-accounts for the following:

1. Earning of dues collected in advance.
2. Billing of dues revenue during 20X1.
3. Collection of dues receivable in 20X1.

4-42 Accounting for Subscriptions
(Alternate is 4-41.) A French magazine company collects subscriptions in advance of delivery of its magazines. However, many magazines are delivered to magazine distributors (for newsstand sales), and these distributors are billed and pay later. The subscription revenue earned for the month of March on the accrual basis was €200,000 (€ refers to the Euro). Other pertinent data were as follows:

	March	
	31	**1**
Unearned subscription revenue	€190,000	€140,000
Accounts receivable	7,000	9,000

Prepare journal entries and post to T-accounts for the following:

1. Collections of Unearned Subscription Revenue of €140,000 prior to March 1.
2. Billing of Accounts Receivable (a) of €9,000 prior to March 1, and (b) of €80,000 during March (credit Revenue Earned).
3. Collections of cash during March and any other entries that are indicated by the given data.

4-43 Financial Statements and Adjustments
Rockwell Wholesalers, Inc., has just completed its fourth year of business in 20X1. A set of financial statements was prepared by the principal stockholder's eldest child, a college student who is beginning the third week of an accounting course. Following is a list (in no systematic order) of the items appearing in the student's balance sheet, income statement, and the retained earnings column of the statement of stockholders' equity:

Accounts receivable	$183,100	Advertising expense	$ 98,300
Note receivable	36,000	Cost of goods sold	590,000
Merchandise inventory	201,900	Unearned rent revenue	4,800
Cash	99,300	Insurance expense	2,500
Paid-in capital	620,000	Unexpired insurance	2,300
Building	300,000	Accounts payable	52,500
Accumulated depreciation, building	20,000	Interest expense	600
		Telephone expense	2,900
Land	169,200	Notes payable	20,000
Sales	936,800	Net income	59,598
Salary expense	124,300	Miscellaneous expense	3,400
Retained earnings,		Maintenance expense	4,300
December 31, 20X0	164,000		

Assume that the statements in which these items appear are current and complete, except for the following matters not taken into consideration by the student:

a. Salaries of $7,500 have been earned by employees for the last half of December 20X1. Payment by the company will be made on the next payday, January 2, 20X2.
b. Interest at 8% per annum on the Note Receivable has accrued for 2 months and is expected to be collected by the company when the Note is due on January 31, 20X2.
c. Part of the building owned by the company was rented to a tenant on November 1, 20X1, for 6 months, payable in advance. This rent was collected in cash and is represented by the item labeled Unearned Rent Revenue.
d. Depreciation on the building for 20X1 is $5,750.
e. Cash dividends of $60,000 were declared in December 20X1, payable in January 20X2.
f. Income tax at 40% applies to 20X1, all of which is to be paid in the early part of 20X2.

Required
Prepare the following corrected financial statements, showing appropriate support for the dollar amounts you compute:

1. Multiple-step income statement for the year ended December 31, 20X1
2. The retained earnings column of the statement of stockholders' equity for the year ended December 31, 20X1
3. Classified balance sheet at December 31, 20X1

4-44 Mirror Side of Adjustments
Problem 4-35 described some adjustments made by Amber Marshall, CPA. Prepare the necessary adjustment as it would be made by the client in transactions (b) and (c), and by the secretary in transaction (d). For our purposes, assume that the secretary keeps personal books on the accrual basis.

4-45 Mirror Side of Adjustments
Problem 4-38 described some adjustments made by Goodyear Tire & Rubber Company. Prepare the necessary adjustment as it would be made by (a) landlords, (b) U-Haul, (c) retail dealers, and (d) U.S. and foreign governments. Assume that all use accrual accounting.

4-46 Mirror Side of Adjustments
Problem 4-39 described some adjustments made by Alaska Airlines. The adjustments are lettered (a) through (f). Repeat the requirements for each adjustment as it would be made by the other party in the transaction: specifically, (a) and (b) landlord, (c) and (d) Apple Computer, (e) Boeing, and (f) employees. Assume that all use accrual accounting.

4-47 Journal Entries and Posting
The Timberland Company designs, develops, markets, and distributes premium quality footwear, apparel, and accessories. The company's balance sheet included the following ($ in thousands):

	December 31	
	2008	**2007**
Prepaid expenses	37,139	41,572
Income taxes payable	20,697	19,215

Suppose that during the fiscal year ended December 31, 2008, $36,639 thousand in cash was disbursed and charged to Prepaid Expenses. Similarly, $24,863 thousand was disbursed for income taxes and charged to Income Taxes Payable.

1. Assume that the Prepaid Expenses account relates to outlays for miscellaneous operating expenses, for example, supplies, insurance, and short-term rentals. Prepare summary journal entries for (a) the disbursements and (b) the expenses for fiscal 2008.
2. Assume that there were no other accounts related to income taxes. Prepare summary journal entries for (a) the disbursements and (b) the expenses for fiscal 2008.

4-48 Advance Service Contracts

Diebold, Incorporated, a manufacturer of automated teller machines, showed the following current liability on the balance sheet on December 31, 2008 ($ amounts in thousands):

	December 31	
	2008	**2007**
Deferred revenue	$195,164	$251,657

The footnotes to the financial statements stated the following: "Deferred revenue is recognized for any services that are billed to customers prior to revenue being realizable related to the service being provided.[…] Service contracts typically cover a 12-month period and can begin at any given month during the year. Revenue is recognized ratably over the life of the contract period."

1. Prepare summary journal entries for the creation in 2007, and subsequent earning in 2008, of the deferred revenue of $251,657. Use the following accounts: Accounts Receivable, Deferred Revenue, and Income from Advance Billings.
2. A 1-year job contract was billed to Keystone Bank on January 1, 2008, for $36,000. Work began on January 2. The full amount was collected on February 15. Prepare all pertinent journal entries through February 29, 2008. Use the following accounts: Accounts Receivable, Deferred Revenue, and Income from Service Contracts. ("Recognized ratably" means an equal amount per month.)

4-49 Journal Entries and Adjustments

Northwest Natural is a public utility in Oregon. The 2008 annual report included the following footnote:

Utility revenues, derived primarily from the sale and transportation of gas, are recognized when the gas is delivered to and received by the customer. Revenues include accruals for gas deliveries not yet billed to customers based on estimates of gas deliveries from meter reading dates to month end (accrued unbilled revenue). Accrued unbilled revenues are dependent upon a number of factors that require management's judgment, including total gas receipts and deliveries, customer use by billing cycle, and weather. Accrued unbilled revenues are reversed the following month when actual billings occur.

The income statements showed the following ($ in thousands):

For Year Ended December 31		
	2008	**2007**
Gross operating revenues	$1,037,855	$1,033,193
Income from operations	144,036	154,923

The balance sheets included the following as part of current assets ($ in thousands):

	December 31	
	2008	**2007**
Accounts receivable	$ 81,288	$69,442
Accrued unbilled revenue	102,688	78,004

Prepare the adjusting journal entry for (a) the unbilled revenues at the end of 2008 and (b) the eventual billing and collection of the unbilled revenues in 2009. Ignore income taxes.

4-50 Classified Balance Sheet, Current Ratio, and Quick Ratio
Amazon.com, Inc.'s balance sheet for December 31, 2008, (slightly modified) contained the following items ($ in millions):

Property and equipment, net	$ 854
Accrued expenses and other	1,093
Cash and cash equivalents	2,769
Other noncurrent assets	865
Other noncurrent liabilities	487
Inventories	1,399
Current portion of long-term debt	59
Other current assets	204
Accounts payable	3,594
Marketable securities, short-term	958
Accounts receivable, net	?
Intangibles, net	438
Long-term debt	409
Stockholders' equity	2,672

1. Prepare a December 31, 2008, classified balance sheet for Amazon.com. Include the correct amount for Accounts Receivable.
2. Compute the company's working capital, current ratio, and quick ratio. Compute the quick ratio as (current assets − inventory) ÷ current liabilities.
3. Comment on the company's current and quick ratios. In 2007, the current ratio was 1.39 and the quick ratio was 1.07.
4. During 2008, Amazon increased its Marketable Securities by $387. Suppose the company had not increased its Marketable Securities but had instead increased long-term investments (classified as Other Noncurrent Assets) by $387. How would this have affected Amazon's current ratio? How would it have affected the company's liquidity?

4-51 Multiple-Step Income Statement
(Alternates are 4-36 and 4-40.) Intel Corporation is one of the largest companies in the United States. Its annual report for the year ended December 27, 2008, contained the following data and actual terms ($ in millions):

Cost of sales	$16,742	Gross margin	$20,844
Research and development	5,722	Interest and other income, net	488
Marketing, general, and administrative	5,458	Provision for taxes	2,394
Restructuring and asset impairment charges	710	Gains (losses) on equity method investments, net	(1,380)
Net revenue	?	Gains (losses) on other equity investments, net	(376)

Prepare a multiple-step statement of income. Include the correct amount for Net Revenue.

4-52 Single-Step Income Statement

Harley-Davidson is the parent company of Harley-Davidson Motor, Buell Motorcycle, and Harley-Davidson Financial Services. It is most well-known for producing heavyweight, custom, and touring motorcycles as well as parts, accessories, and apparel. Harley-Davidson Financial Services provides wholesale and retail financing and insurance programs to dealers and customers. A recent Harley-Davidson annual report contained the following items ($ in thousands) for the year ending December 31, 2008:

Investment income	$ 9,495	Selling, administrative,	
Cost of goods sold	3,663,488	and engineering expense	$ 984,560
Financial services income	376,970	Interest expense	4,542
Retained earnings at end of year	6,458,778	Provision for income taxes	379,259
Financial services expense	294,205	Cash dividends declared	302,314
Adjustment to reduce retained earnings		Net sales revenue	5,594,307
for adoption of new accounting rule	11,193		

1. Prepare a combined single-step statement of income and retained earnings for the year.
2. Compute the percentage of gross profit on sales and the percentage of net income to sales.
3. The average stockholders' equity for the year was $2,245,547. What was the percentage of net income to average stockholders' equity?

4-53 Retail Company Financial Statements

The Home Depot, Incorporated, is one of the world's largest retailers. The annual report for the year ended February 1, 2009, included the data (slightly modified) shown next ($ in millions). Unless otherwise specified, the balance sheet amounts are the balances as of February 1, 2009.

Sales	$71,288	Interest expense	$ 624
Cash dividends declared	1,555	Long-term debt	9,667
Merchandise inventories	10,673	Cash	519
Paid-in capital	5,684	Accrued salaries payable	1,129
Other current assets	1,192	Short-term investments	6
Retained earnings		Provision for income taxes	1,278
Beginning of year	11,388	Property and equipment, net	26,234
End of year	12,093	Other noncurrent assets	1,568
Accounts payable	4,822	Selling, general, and administrative	
		expenses	17,846
Other expenses, net	197	Depreciation and amortization expense	1,785
Cost of sales	47,298	Other noncurrent liabilities	2,567
Other current liabilities	3,748	Income taxes payable	289
Deferred revenue	1,165	Receivables	972

1. Prepare a combined multiple-step statement of income and retained earnings.
2. Prepare a classified balance sheet.
3. The average common stockholders' equity for the year was $17,745.5 million. What was the percentage of net income to average common stockholders' equity?
4. The average total assets for the year were $42,744 million. What was the percentage of net income to average total assets?
5. Compute (a) gross profit percentage and (b) percentage of net income to sales.

4-54 Preparation of Financial Statements from Trial Balance

The Procter & Gamble Company is one of the largest consumer products companies in America. The (slightly modified) trial balance as of June 30, 2008, appears here:

The Procter & Gamble Company
Trial balance as of June 30, 2008 ($ in millions)

	Debits	Credits
Cash and cash equivalents	$ 3,313	
Investment securities	228	
Accounts receivable	6,761	
Inventories	8,416	
Deferred income taxes	2,012	
Prepaid expenses and other current assets	3,785	
Property, plant, and equipment, at cost	38,086	
Accumulated depreciation		$ 17,446
Trademarks and other intangibles, net	34,233	
Goodwill	59,767	
Other noncurrent assets	4,837	
Debt due within one year		13,084
Accounts payable		6,775
Accrued and other liabilities		10,154
Taxes payable		945
Long-term debt		23,581
Deferred income tax		11,805
Other noncurrent liabilities		8,154
Preferred stock		1,366
Common stock, stated value $1 per share		4,002
Additional paid-in capital		60,307
Retained earnings (June 30, 2007)		41,797
Accumulated other comprehensive income*		3,746
Reserve for ESOP debt retirement*	1,325	
Treasury stock*	47,588	
Net sales		83,503
Cost of products sold	40,695	
Selling, administrative, and general expense	25,725	
Interest expense	1,467	
Other nonoperating income, net		462
Income taxes	4,003	
Cash dividends declared	4,886	
	$287,127	$287,127

*Part of stockholders' equity.

1. Prepare Proctor & Gamble's income statement for the year ended June 30, 2008, using a multiple-step format.
2. Prepare Proctor & Gamble's income statement for the year ended June 30, 2008, using a single-step format. Which format for the income statement is more informative? Why?
3. Prepare Proctor & Gamble's classified balance sheet as of June 30, 2008.

4-55 Adjusting Entries and Ethics

By definition, adjusting entries are not triggered by an explicit event. Therefore, accountants must initiate adjusting entries. For each of the following adjusting entries, discuss a potential unethical behavior that an accountant or manager might undertake:

a. Recognition of expenses from the prepaid supplies account
b. Recognition of revenue from the unearned revenue account
c. Accrual of interest payable
d. Accrual of fees receivable

Collaborative Learning Exercise

4-56 Implicit Transactions

Form groups of from three to six "players." Each group should have a die and a paper (or board) with four columns labeled as follows:

1. Expiration of unexpired costs
2. Earning of unearned revenues
3. Accrual of unrecorded expenses
4. Accrual of unrecorded revenues

The players should select an order in which they want to play. Then, the first player rolls the die. If this player rolls a 5 or 6, the die passes to the next player. If the second player rolls a 1, 2, 3, or 4, this person must, within 20 seconds, name an example of a transaction that fits in the corresponding category; for example, if a 2 is rolled, the player must give an example of earning of unearned revenues. Each time a correct example is given, the player receives one point. If someone doubts the correctness of a given example, the player can challenge it. If the remaining players unanimously agree that the example is incorrect, the challenger gets a point and the player giving the example does not get a point for a correct example and is out of the game. If the remaining players do not unanimously agree that the answer is incorrect, the challenger loses a point and the player giving the example gets a point for a correct example. If a player fails to give an example within the time limit or gives an incorrect example, this person is out of the game (except for voting when an example is challenged), and the remaining players continue until everyone has failed to give a correct example within the time limit. Each correct answer should be listed under the appropriate column. The player with the most points is the group winner.

When all groups have finished a round of play, a second level of play can begin. The groups can get together and list all examples for each of the four categories by group. Discussion can establish the correctness of each entry; the faculty member or an appointed discussion leader will be the final arbitrator of the correctness of each entry. Each group gets one point for each correct example and loses one point for each incorrect entry. The group with the most points is the overall winner.

Analyzing and Interpreting Financial Statements

4-57 Financial Statement Research

Select any two companies.

1. For each company, determine the amount of working capital and the current ratio.
2. Compare the current ratios. Which company has the larger ratio, and what do the ratios tell you about the liquidity of the companies?
3. Compute the gross margin percentage, the return on sales, and the return on common stockholders' equity.
4. Compare the profitability of the two companies.

4-58 Analyzing Starbucks' Financial Statements

This problem develops skills in preparing adjusting journal entries. The balance sheet of Starbucks for the year ended September 27, 2009, included the following information (all $ amounts in millions).

	September 27, 2009	September 28, 2008
Prepaid expenses and other current assets	$147.2	$169.2
Other accrued expenses	147.3	164.4

Suppose that during the year ended September 27, 2009, $188.3 million cash was disbursed and debited to Prepaid Expenses and $143.9 million of liabilities classified as Other Accrued Expenses were paid in cash.

1. Assume that the Prepaid Expenses account relates to outlays for miscellaneous operating expenses, for example, supplies, insurance, and short-term rentals. Prepare summary journal entries for (a) the disbursements and (b) the expenses (for our purposes, debit Operating Expenses) for the year ended September 27, 2009. Post the entries to T-accounts.
2. Prepare summary journal entries for (a) the disbursements and (b) the expenses related to the Other Accrued Expenses account for the year ended September 27, 2009. (For our purposes, debit Operating Expenses.) Post the entries to T-accounts.

4-59 Analyzing Financial Statements Using the Internet

Go to www.columbiasportswear.com to find **Columbia Sportswear**'s home page. Under the About Us menu, select Investor Relations. Then select Financial Information and click on the most recent annual report. You may also select the most recent Form 10-K.
Answer the following questions:

1. Name one item on Columbia Sportswear's balance sheet that most likely represents unexpired (prepaid) costs. Name one item that most likely represents the accrual of unrecorded expenses.
2. Does Columbia Sportswear prepare a single- or multiple-step income statement? How can you tell?
3. Determine Columbia Sportswear's gross profit percentage for the past 2 years. Is the change favorable? What does Columbia Sportswear's management say about the change? (Hint: Look in Management's Discussion and Analysis.) If nothing was said, why do you think management chose not to comment? How do you think management determines the reason that gross profit changed, given the condensed nature of the income statement?
4. Calculate Columbia Sportswear's current ratio for the past 2 years. Did this ratio improve or decline? Does management offer any comment about any particular problems that could have affected this ratio? Should management be concerned about changes in the current ratio?
5. Where can you find evidence in Columbia Sportswear's annual report that the financial statements were prepared using U.S. GAAP?

5

Statement of Cash Flows

LEARNING OBJECTIVES

After studying this chapter, you should be able to:

1 Identify the purposes of the statement of cash flows.

2 Classify activities affecting cash as operating, investing, or financing activities.

3 Compute and interpret cash flows from financing activities.

4 Compute and interpret cash flows from investing activities.

5 Use the direct method to calculate cash flows from operations.

6 Use the indirect method to explain the difference between net income and net cash provided by (used for) operating activities.

7 Understand why we add depreciation to net income when using the indirect method for computing cash flow from operating activities.

8 Show how the balance sheet equation provides a conceptual framework for the statement of cash flows.

9 Identify free cash flow, and interpret information in statements of cash flow.

If you watch sporting-event commercials on television, you might think the only thing Nike spends its money on is getting athletes to endorse the company's products. Nike's first endorsement was NBA star Michael Jordan, but there have been countless others. Superstars in many sports endorse Nike products. Today's two dominant NBA stars, LeBron James and Kobe Bryant, both endorse Nike products, as do Roger Federer, winner of the most tennis grand-slam events in history, and Lance Armstrong, seven-time Tour de France winner. Paul Rodriguez Jr. is the first pro skateboarder in the Nike camp as well.

In the last decade, Nike made a major commitment to the World Cup of soccer. The company set out to create "a new generation of performance product that would take Nike to a new level of play." As part of this effort, Nike supplied shoes to Renaldo, the Brazilian superstar and Nike endorser, for the 2006 World Cup, where he was the MVP and scored his fifteenth career World-Cup goal, the most goals scored in the history of the World Cup.

In just over two decades, Nike grew from a small shoe company to a major producer of athletic footwear, apparel, and accessories, with annual

Athletes around the globe endorse Nike products—those with the famous Nike "Swoosh." Nike pays much cash for athlete endorsements and other promotional activities, in addition to paying cash to buy and sell shoes and other apparel. Tracing the flow of cash through a company is an important part of understanding its financial position and prospects. We learn about the statement of cash flows, the financial report that focuses on cash, in this chapter.

sales in fiscal 2009 of nearly $19.2 billion. The company's "Just do it!" slogan also would have been apt for early investors in Nike. A dollar invested in Nike stock in the mid-1980s would be worth nearly $100 in late 2009 (and more than $140 before the stock market decline in late 2008).

Of course, the company behind the famous Nike "Swoosh" needs cash to make the endorsements happen. A quick look at the company's balance sheet tells you Nike has plenty—nearly $2.3 billion on May 31, 2009. However, if you truly want to see where Nike spends its cash, you should pay attention to one specific financial report—the statement of cash flows.

Nike reports the cash provided or used by the company for operating, investing, and financing activities, giving you a complete picture of how Nike generated the money and where it has gone. For example, in recent years, operations such as selling merchandise have provided millions in cash for Nike ($1.7 billion in 2009). In contrast, investing and financing activities have used cash, primarily because Nike invested heavily in property, plant, and equipment and spent millions of dollars to buy back shares of its own stock. The net result of these activities in 2009 was an increase in cash of $157.2 million over the previous year's balance. ●

The primary importance of cash makes the statement of cash flows one of the central financial statements. The statement explains the changes that occur in the firm's cash balance during the year. The statement of cash flows allows both investors and managers to keep their fingers on the pulse of any company's lifeblood—cash. Attitudes toward holding cash vary. Some managers and investors like the safety of large stores of cash. For example, even after the economic downturn of 2008–2009, Microsoft held $25 billion in cash, cash equivalents, and short-term investments on March 31, 2009. Although this was down from $60 billion 5 years earlier, it still represents a large safety cushion. Other companies minimize cash holdings because cash provides only small returns to the company.

Companies that lose too much cash may need to declare bankruptcy. Bankruptcy means that a company seeks court protection from its creditors under federal law. Court protection allows a firm to delay paying certain obligations while it negotiates with its creditors to reorganize its business and settle its debts. Enron and General Motors are recent examples of large and historically successful companies that entered bankruptcy and either liquidated entirely (Enron) or reorganized large portions of their business (GM). We observed bankruptcies of many large companies in the economic downturns of 2001–2002 and 2008–2009.

Although managers and investors benefit from watching cash flows, until recently many countries did not require a statement of cash flows. For example, India began to require such a statement less than 10 years ago. Today, both the IASB and FASB require a statement of cash flows and have similar requirements for the statement. In this chapter, we examine cash flow statements and explain how managers and investors use the information in such statements.

Overview of Statement of Cash Flows

statement of cash flows (cash flow statement)
One of the basic financial statements that reports the cash receipts and cash payments of an entity during a particular period and classifies them as financing, investing, and operating cash flows.

A balance sheet shows the amount of cash a company holds at the close of business on the balance sheet date. How did the company generate this cash? Can you determine this from the balance sheet alone? No. You need a statement of cash flows. The **statement of cash flows** (or **cash flow statement**) reports the cash receipts and cash payments of an entity during a particular period and classifies them as financing, investing, and operating cash flows. Statements of cash flows, like income statements, show the performance of a company over a period of time. Both help explain why the balance sheet items have changed—the income statement shows details about how operating activities produce changes in retained earnings, while the statement of cash flows details the changes in the cash account. As the following diagram shows, these statements link the balance sheets in consecutive periods:

Purposes of Cash Flow Statement

OBJECTIVE 1

Identify the purposes of the statement of cash flows.

Why do managers and investors use a statement of cash flows?

1. It helps them understand the relationship of net income to changes in cash balances. Cash balances can decline despite positive net income and vice versa.
2. It reports past cash flows as an aid to
   a. predicting future cash flows,
   b. evaluating how management generates and uses cash, and
   c. determining a company's ability to pay interest, dividends, and debts when they are due.
3. It identifies specific increases and decreases in a firm's productive assets.

The statement of cash flows explains where cash came from during a period and where it went. Let's first be clear about what we mean by cash. Our use of the term refers not only to the currency and bank accounts that we all call cash, but also to cash equivalents. **Cash equivalents** are highly liquid short-term investments that a company can easily and quickly convert into cash, such as money market funds and Treasury bills. Hereafter, when we refer to cash, we mean both cash and cash equivalents.

Typical Activities Affecting Cash

Managers affect cash as the result of three types of decisions: operating, financing, and investing decisions. **Operating decisions** are concerned with the major day-to-day activities that generate revenues and expenses. The first major section of the statement of cash flows, **cash flows from operating activities**, summarizes the cash impact of such decisions. **Operating activities** are transactions that affect the purchase, processing, and selling of a company's products and services. For example, making sales, collecting accounts receivable, recording an expense for cost of goods sold, purchasing inventory, and paying accounts payable are all operating activities. The thing these transactions have in common is that they are an integral part of the major income-generating activities of the company.

Managers make **financing decisions** when they decide whether and how to raise or repay cash. For example, financial managers decide whether to borrow money from a bank or other lender or to repay previous borrowings. They also decide whether to issue additional capital stock or to buy back previously issued stock. To understand financing decisions, we use the section of the statement of cash flows labeled **cash flows from financing activities**. **Financing activities** are a company's transactions that obtain resources by borrowing from creditors or selling shares of stock and use resources to repay creditors or provide a return to shareholders.

After raising capital, managers must decide how to invest the capital. These **investing decisions** include the choices to (1) acquire or dispose of plant, property, equipment, and other long-term productive assets, and (2) provide or collect cash as a lender or as an owner of securities. The statement of cash flows covers the results of investing decisions in a section labeled **cash flows from investing activities**. **Investing activities** are transactions that acquire or dispose of long-lived assets or acquire or dispose of securities that are not cash equivalents. Thus, purchasing property or equipment is an investing activity, but purchasing inventory or prepaying rent are operating activities. Why? Because a company will generally use property and equipment for multiple years, whereas it will use inventory and prepaid rent within 1 year.

There is one more item you will see on the cash flow statements of companies with international operations—the effect of exchange rates on cash. Companies show this after the operating, investing, and financing activities. The effect of exchange rates is not a cash flow, but it appears on the cash flow statement because it is necessary for the reconciliation of cash balances at the beginning and end of the period. Consider a U.S. company with a bank account in London. The balance is £100,000 at the beginning of the year when the exchange rate is 2 U.S. dollars for every British pound. The company would list this as (£100,000 × $2/£) = $200,000 on a U.S. balance sheet. Suppose there were no cash flows into or out of the account during the year, but the exchange rate changed to $1.7 per £. At the end of the year a U.S. balance sheet would show this as (£100,000 × $1.7/£) = $170,000. Cash measured in dollars fell by $30,000 in the absence of any cash flow. This change in cash is what companies must show on their cash flow statements.

Exhibit 5-1 shows typical operating, investing, and financing activities reported in a statement of cash flows. The fact that these activities affect cash should be fairly obvious and straightforward. What is not always obvious is the classification of these activities as operating, investing, or financing. Take interest payments and dividend payments, for example. These both represent cash flows to those who supply capital to the firm. You might think they should be treated the same. Further, U.S. GAAP classifies interest payments as cash flows associated with operations and dividend payments as either operating or financing cash flows. This classification maintains the long-standing distinction that transactions with owners (dividends) cannot be treated as expenses, whereas interest payments to creditors are expenses. In addition, both dividends and interest received are operating activities under U.S. GAAP. Most companies reporting under IFRS use the same method as those reporting under U.S. GAAP. However, companies using IFRS have other options. They may classify dividend or interest payments as either operating or financing activities. Further, it allows companies to classify interest or dividend receipts as either operating or investing activities, as long as the classification is consistent across periods.

Margin glossary

cash equivalents
Highly liquid short-term investments that a company can easily and quickly convert into cash, such as money market funds and Treasury bills.

OBJECTIVE 2

Classify activities affecting cash as operating, investing, or financing activities.

operating decisions
Decisions that are concerned with the major day-to-day activities that generate revenues and expenses.

cash flows from operating activities
The first major section of the cash flow statement. It helps users evaluate the cash impact of management's operating decisions.

operating activities
Transactions that affect the purchase, processing, and selling of a company's products and services.

financing decisions
Decisions concerned with whether and how to raise or repay cash.

cash flows from financing activities
The section of the statement of cash flows that helps users understand management's financing decisions.

financing activities
A company's transactions that obtain resources by borrowing from creditors or selling shares of stock and use resources to repay creditors or provide a return to shareholders.

investing decisions
Decisions that include the choices to (1) acquire or dispose of plant, property, equipment, and other long-term productive assets, and (2) provide or collect cash as a lender or as an owner of securities.

cash flows from investing activities
The section of the statement of cash flows that helps users understand management's investing decisions.

investing activities
Transactions that acquire or dispose of long-lived assets or acquire or dispose of securities that are not cash equivalents.

EXHIBIT 5-1

Typical Operating, Investing, and Financing Activities

Cash Inflows	Cash Outflows
Operating activities	
Collections from customers	Cash payments to suppliers
Interest and dividends collected	Cash payments to employees
Other operating receipts	Interest and taxes paid
	Other operating cash payments
Investing activities	
Sale of property, plant, and equipment	Purchase of property, plant, and equipment
Sale of securities that are not cash equivalents	Purchase of securities that are not cash equivalents
Receipt of loan repayments	Making loans
Financing activities	
Borrowing cash from creditors	Repayment of amounts borrowed
Issuing equity securities	Repurchase of equity shares (including the purchase of treasury stock)
Issuing debt securities	Payment of dividends

The Business First box on page 204 shows how categorizing cash flows into operating, investing, and financing categories can help us understand a company's cash situation.

Preparing a Statement of Cash Flows

To see how various activities affect the statement of cash flows, consider the activities of Biwheels Company for January 20X2. We reproduce the company's transactions in balance-sheet-equation format in Exhibit 5-2 and display the resulting balance sheet and income statement in Exhibit 5-3. We use these exhibits to prepare a statement of cash flows for Biwheels for January 20X2. Notice that the cash balance for Biwheels increased from $0 at the beginning of the month to $351,000 at the end of the month. Because the statement of cash flows explains the changes in cash, the first step in developing the statement is always to compute the amount of the change, in this case an increase of $351,000. Next we examine the three sections of the statement of cash flows that combine to explain this $351,000 increase.

Cash Flows from Financing Activities

Although most companies list operating activities as the first section of the cash flow statement, we will begin our discussion with the more easily described and understood section, cash flows from financing activities. This section shows cash flows to and from providers of capital. The easiest way to determine cash flows from financing activities is to examine changes in the cash account in the balance sheet equation (or T-account) and identify those changes associated with financing activities. Exhibit 5-2 shows that Biwheels had two such transactions in January:

Transaction 1, Initial investment, $400,000

Transaction 2, Loan from bank, $100,000

Both of these transactions are cash inflows, that is, increases in cash. Therefore, Biwheels' cash flows from financing activities total $500,000:

Biwheels Company
Cash Flows from Financing Activities
for the Month of January 20X2

Proceeds from initial investment	$400,000
Proceeds from bank loan	100,000
Net cash provided by financing activities	$500,000

EXHIBIT 5-2
Biwheels Company
Analysis of Transactions for January 20X2 (in $)

Description of Transactions	Cash	+ Accounts Receivable	+ Merchandise Inventory	+ Prepaid Rent	+ Store Equipment	=	Note Payable	+ Accounts Payable	+	Paid-in Capital	+ Retained Earnings
(1) Initial investment	+400,000					=				+400,000	
(2) Loan from bank	+100,000					=	+100,000				
(3) Acquire store equipment for cash	−15,000				+15,000	=					
(4) Acquire inventory for cash	−120,000		+120,000			=					
(5) Acquire inventory on credit			+10,000			=		+10,000			
(6) Acquire inventory for cash plus credit	−10,000		+30,000			=		+20,000			
(7) Sale of equipment	+1,000				−1,000	=					
(8) Return of inventory acquired on January 6			−800			=		−800			
(9) Payment to creditor	−4,000					=		−4,000			
(10a) Sales on open account		+160,000				=					+160,000
(10b) Cost of merchandise inventory sold			−100,000			=					−100,000
(11) Collect accounts receivable	+5,000	−5,000				=					
(12) Pay rent in advance	−6,000			+6,000		=					
(13) Recognize expiration of rental services				−2,000		=					−2,000
(14) Depreciation					−100	=					−100
Balance January 31, 20X2	351,000	+155,000	+59,200	+4,000	+13,900	=	100,000	+25,200		+400,000	+57,900

583,100 = 583,100

EXHIBIT 5-3

Biwheels Company's Income Statement and Balance Sheet

Income Statement for the Month Ended January 31, 20X2

Sales revenue		$160,000
Deduct expenses		
Cost of goods sold	$100,000	
Rent	2,000	
Depreciation	100	
Total expenses		102,100
Net income		$ 57,900

Balance Sheet January 31, 20X2

Assets			Liabilities and Stockholders' Equity		
Cash	$351,000		Liabilities		
Accounts receivable	155,000		Note payable		$100,000
Merchandise			Accounts payable		25,200
inventory	59,200		Total liabilities		$125,200
Prepaid rent	4,000		Stockholders' equity		
Store equipment, net	13,900		Paid-in capital	$400,000	
			Retained earnings	57,900	
			Total stockholders' equity		457,900
			Total liabilities and		
Total assets	$583,100		stockholders' equity		$583,100

If you did not have access to the balance-sheet-equation entries, you could also look at the changes in Biwheels' balance sheet during January. Note that all balance-sheet accounts were zero at the beginning of the month. You can compute the increases in Notes Payable and Paid-in Capital as follows:

	Balance, January 1, 20X2	Balance, January 31, 20X2	Increase (Decrease)
Notes payable	$0	$100,000	$100,000
Paid-in capital	0	400,000	400,000

If Hector Lopez had invested $200,000 in 20X1 and the remaining $200,000 on January 2, 20X2, the cash inflow for January 20X2 from Lopez's investment would have been only $200,000:

	Balance, January 1, 20X2	Balance, January 31, 20X2	Increase (Decrease)
Paid-in capital	$200,000	$400,000	$200,000

Two general rules for financing activities are as follows:

- Increases in cash (cash inflows) stem from increases in liabilities or paid-in capital
- Decreases in cash (cash outflows) stem from decreases in liabilities or paid-in capital

You can see a list of some financing activities and their effect on cash in the first part of Exhibit 5-4. For example, selling common shares increases cash (+), paying dividends decreases cash (−), and converting debt into common stock has no effect on cash.

Type of Transaction	Increase (+) or Decrease (−) in Cash
Financing Activities	
Increase long- or short-term debt	+
Reduce long- or short-term debt	−
Sell common or preferred shares	+
Repurchase common shares	−
Pay dividends	−
Convert debt to common stock	No effect
Investing Activities	
Purchase fixed assets for cash	−
Purchase fixed assets by issuing debt	No effect
Sell fixed assets for cash	+
Purchase investment securities of other firms that are not cash equivalents	−
Sell investment securities in other firms that are not cash equivalents	+
Make a loan to another company or person	−
Collect a loan	+

EXHIBIT 5-4

Analysis of Effects of Financing and Investing Transactions on Cash

Cash Flows from Investing Activities

The section of the cash flow statement called cash flows from investing activities lists cash flows from the purchase or sale of plant, property, equipment, and other long-lived assets. It is usually the second section in the statement. To determine the cash flows from investing activities, look at transactions that increase or decrease long-lived assets, loans, or securities that are not considered cash equivalents. Biwheels has only one such asset, Store Equipment. There were two cash transactions relating to store equipment during January:

> Transaction 3, Acquire store equipment for cash, $15,000
>
> Transaction 7, Sale of asset [store equipment] for cash, $1,000

The first of these transactions is a use of cash, or a cash outflow. The second is a source of cash, or a cash inflow. The investing activities section of Biwheels' cash flow statement is as follows:

OBJECTIVE 4

Compute and interpret cash flows from investing activities.

Biwheels Company
Cash Flows from Investing Activities
for the Month of January 20X2

Purchase of store equipment	$(15,000)
Proceeds from sale of store equipment	1,000
Net cash used by investing activities	$(14,000)

Notice that we place the cash outflows in parentheses. Because there is a net cash outflow, investing activities used cash during January. This contrasts with financing activities, which provided cash.

The second part of Exhibit 5-4 shows types of investing activities and their effects on cash. For example, selling investment securities (except for securities that are cash equivalents) increases cash (+) and making a loan decreases cash (−). Notice that buying or selling securities that are cash equivalents does not change cash. It simply turns one type of cash into another type of cash.

BUSINESS FIRST

Cash flow is crucial for the survival of many companies. In 2008, many travel companies and airlines suffered cash flow problems due to the serious reduction of both business and leisure travelers.

Consider the following numbers from the cash flow statements of Wing On Travel (WOT) and China Travel International Investment (CT) in millions:

Fiscal year	Wing On Travel			China Travel International Investment		
	2009	2008	2007	2009	2008	2007
Cash flow from operating activities	($10,523)	($7,166)	$4,903	$80,833	$75,591	$91,065
Cash flow from investing activities	$17,483	$17,382	($47,427)	($40,242)	($72,817)	$22,230
Cash flow from financing activities	($26,968)	$27,710	($3,399)	($37,567)	($87,495)	($61,285)
	($20,008)	$37,925	($45,923)	$3,024	($84,721)	$52,010
Profit	($44,511)	($106,784)	$575	$8,411	$77,026	$92,425

WOT is a leading travel company listed on the Hong Kong Stock Exchange. Despite its reputation in long-haul travel and customer services, its losses for 2009 and 2008 were $44,511 million and $106,784 million respectively. The losses led to serious negative operating cash flows in 2009 and 2008. Although it generated $45 million from sales of subsidiaries as reflected in the positive investing activities, it also took out new bank loans worth $55.1 million and repaid bank loans worth $55.5 million in 2009.

On the contrary, its competitor, CT, reported favorable cash flows from its operating activities which contributed to its profits in 2007-2009. The negative cash flow from investing activities was mainly due to the purchase of subsidiaries for expansion.

WOT was later sold to Ctrip for $88 million for a 90% interest in the issued share capital of WOT in early 2010.

Sources: http://downloads.cathaypacific.com/cx/investor/annualreports/2008_annual-report_en.pdf
http://www.hkexnews.hk/listedco/listconews/sek
http://pages.english.ctrip.com/webhome/purehtml/en/footer/CompanyProfile.html

If you did not have access to the transactions listed in the balance sheet equation, you would need to look at changes in the long-lived assets, loans, and other investments on the balance sheet. Two general rules for investing activities are as follows:

- Increases in cash (cash inflows) stem from sale of long-lived assets, collection of loans made to others, and sale of investments
- Decreases in cash (cash outflows) stem from purchases of long-lived assets, granting of loans to others, and purchases of investments

Consider Biwheels' only long-lived asset, Store Equipment. Changes in the net amount of such assets generally result from three possible sources—(1) asset acquisitions, (2) asset disposals, and (3) depreciation expense for the period:

$$\text{Increase in assets} = \text{Acquisitions} - \text{Disposals} - \text{Depreciation expense}$$

Asset acquisitions and disposals may involve cash, but depreciation does not. Thus, it is important to identify how much of the change in the asset values resulted from the recognition of depreciation. From the balance sheet, we learn that the net amount of Biwheels' Store Equipment increased from $0 to $13,900 in January. From the income statement, we know that Depreciation Expense was $100. Thus, we know that the net acquisitions (that is, acquisitions less disposals) were $14,000:

$$\$13,900 = \text{Acquisitions} - \text{Disposals} - \$100$$

$$\text{Acquisitions} - \text{Disposals} = \$13,900 + \$100 = \$14,000$$

Only by knowing more about either the actual acquisitions or disposals can we break down net acquisitions into acquisitions and disposals. If we could determine from further analysis that

Biwheels' acquisitions were $15,000, we would know that disposals must have been ($15,000 − $14,000) = $1,000. Management has no problem examining financial records directly to determine the details, but investors have a more difficult time obtaining such details.

INTERPRETING FINANCIAL STATEMENTS

A company raises $1 million by selling common stock. The company puts $400,000 into securities that are cash equivalents and uses the other $600,000 to buy equipment. What are the effects on the cash flow statement?

Answer

The $1 million appears as cash provided by financing activities. The $600,000 appears as a use of cash in the investing section.

Because the securities are cash equivalents, the $400,000 does not appear in the investing section; instead, it is simply a rearrangement of the form in which the company holds cash. The net increase in cash from this transaction is $400,000, or $1 million from financing less $600,000 used for investing.

Noncash Investing and Financing Activities

Sometimes financing or investing activities do not affect cash, but are similar to transactions that do. Companies list such activities in a separate schedule accompanying the statement of cash flows. In our example, Biwheels Company did not have any noncash investing or financing activities. However, suppose Biwheels' purchase of the store equipment was not for cash, but was financed as follows:

A. Biwheels acquired $8,000 of the store equipment by issuing common stock.
B. Biwheels acquired the other $7,000 of store equipment by signing a note payable for $7,000.

Also consider one other possible transaction:

C. Biwheels converted $50,000 of its original note payable to common stock. That is, Biwheels issued $50,000 of common stock in exchange for a reduction of $50,000 in the note payable.

These items would affect the balance sheet equation as follows:

	Cash	+	Store Equipment	=	Note Payable	+	Paid-in Capital
A.	0		+$8,000	=			+$ 8,000
B.	0		+$7,000	=	+$ 7,000		
C.	0			=	−$50,000		+$50,000

None of these transactions affect cash; therefore, they do not belong in a statement of cash flows. However, each transaction could just as easily involve cash. For example, in the first transaction, the company might issue common stock for $8,000 cash and immediately use the cash to purchase the fixed asset. The financing cash inflow and investing cash outflow would then both appear on the statement of cash flows. Because of the importance of these noncash investing and financing decisions, readers of financial statements want to be informed of such noncash activities. Companies must report such items in a schedule of noncash investing and financing activities. Biwheels Company's schedule for hypothetical transactions A, B, and C would be as follows:

Schedule of noncash investing and financing activities	
Common stock issued to acquire store equipment	$ 8,000
Note payable for acquisition of store equipment	$ 7,000
Common stock issued on conversion of note payable	$50,000

Summary Problem for Your Review

PROBLEM

Examine the entries to Biwheels' balance sheet equation for February 20X2 in Exhibit 2-5 (p. 73) and the final February transaction, transaction 22, declaration and payment of dividends of $50,000 (p. 75).

1. Identify the items that belong in the financing and investing sections of the statement of cash flows for February.
2. Assume that Biwheels has two additional transactions during February:
   a. Bought shares of common stock of Pacific Cycle for $12,000 cash.
   b. Bought a $30,000 storage shed for $8,000 cash and signed a note payable for the remaining $22,000. The company financed the $8,000 for the cash down payment by borrowing $8,000 cash from the bank.

   How would these transactions affect the financing and investing sections of Biwheels' February statement of cash flows?
3. Prepare the financing and investing sections of Biwheels' statement of cash flows including all transactions in numbers 1 and 2. Include a schedule of noncash investing and financing activities if appropriate. Interpret the information you learn from these two sections.

SOLUTION

1. Only transaction 21, borrowing of $10,000 from the bank and using that $10,000 to buy store equipment, and transaction 22, payment of cash dividends of $50,000, involve financing or investing activities. The $10,000 loan is a financing activity, the $10,000 paid to buy the store equipment is an investing activity, and the $50,000 of dividends paid is a financing activity.
2. The $12,000 paid for Pacific Cycle shares is an investing activity. The purchase of the storage shed has three effects: (1) The $8,000 paid in cash is an investing activity, (2) the $8,000 borrowed from the bank is a financing activity, and (3) the $22,000 acquisition for a note payable is a noncash investing and financing activity.
3. The statement of cash flows would include the following. Note that we combined the two borrowings from the bank into one line: ($10,000 + $8,000) = $18,000.

Biwheels Company
Cash Flows from Financing and Investing Activities
for the Month of February 20X2

Cash Flows from Investing Activities	
Acquisition of store equipment	$(10,000)
Purchase of Pacific Cycle common shares	(12,000)
Acquisition of storage shed	(8,000)
Net cash used for investing activities	$(30,000)
Cash Flows from Financing Activities	
Borrowing from banks	$ 18,000
Payment of dividends	(50,000)
Net cash used by financing activities	$(32,000)
Noncash Investing and Financing Activities	
Note payable financing for purchase of storage shed	$ 22,000

From these sections of the cash flow statement, we learn that in February Biwheels used a total of $62,000 in cash for investing and financing activities. Either the company used cash generated by operations or it depleted its cash balance to support these activities. Of the $30,000 spent for investing activities, $18,000 increased long-lived assets and $12,000 increased Biwheels' investment in the securities of another company, Pacific Cycle. We also learn that the $18,000 in cash inflows from financing was entirely debt financing, borrowing from banks. The company did not sell or buy back any shares of its common stock. The $50,000 cash outflow for dividends was larger than the additional borrowing, resulting in a net cash outflow of $32,000 from financing activities. Finally, Biwheels also invested another $22,000 in the storage shed and financed it with debt in the form of a note payable. This transaction involved both a financing activity and an investing activity, but there was no effect on cash.

Cash Flow from Operating Activities

Analyzing the results of financing and investing activities informs investors about management's ability to make financial and investment decisions. However, users of financial statements often are more concerned with assessing management's operating decisions. They focus on the first major section of cash flow statements, cash flows from operating activities (or cash flows from operations). This section shows the cash effects of transactions that affect the income statement.

Approaches to Calculating the Cash Flow from Operating Activities

We can use either of two approaches to compute cash flows from operating activities (or cash flows from operations). The **direct method** subtracts operating cash disbursements from operating cash collections to arrive at cash flows from operations. The **indirect method** adjusts the previously calculated accrual net income from the income statement to reflect only cash receipts and cash disbursements. Both methods show the same amount of cash provided by (or used for) operating activities. The only difference is the format of the statement.

Both the IASB and FASB prefer the direct method because it is a straightforward listing of cash inflows and cash outflows and is easier for investors to understand. In fact, the Boards are likely to require the direct method in the near future. However, the vast majority of companies continue to use the indirect method. Although we will discuss the direct method first, you also need to understand the indirect method that most companies continue to use.

Before addressing the details of the direct and indirect methods, consider the types of cash flows that accountants classify as operating activities. Exhibit 5-5 lists many such activities. These cash flows are associated with revenues and expenses on the income statement. Notice that recording revenue from the sales of goods or services does not necessarily increase cash. Only sales for cash immediately increase cash. There is no cash effect of credit sales until the

direct method
A method for computing cash flows from operating activities that subtracts operating cash disbursements from cash collections to arrive at cash flows from operations.

indirect method
A method for computing cash flows from operating activities that adjusts the previously calculated accrual net income from the income statement to reflect only cash receipts and cash disbursements.

EXHIBIT 5-5

Analysis of Effects of Operating Transactions on Cash

Type of Transaction	Increase (+) or Decrease (−) in Cash
Operating Activities	
Sales of goods and services for cash	+
Sales of goods and services on credit	No effect
Collection of accounts receivable	+
Receive dividends or interest	+
Recognize cost of goods sold	No effect
Purchase inventory for cash	−
Purchase inventory on credit	No effect
Pay accounts payable	−
Accrue operating expenses	No effect
Pay operating expenses	−
Accrue taxes	No effect
Pay taxes	−
Accrue interest	No effect
Pay interest	−
Prepay expenses for cash	−
Record the use of prepaid expenses	No effect
Charge depreciation	No effect

customer actually pays. Biwheels must collect its accounts receivable to generate any cash. Similarly, cash received for services to be performed in the future is an operating cash flow even though a company may not earn the revenue until a later period.

The cash effects of expenses are similar. Sometimes the cash outflow precedes the recording of the expense on the income statement. For example, Biwheels incurred a $6,000 cash outflow for prepaid rent in January and recorded the expenditure as an asset. The entire $6,000 would appear on January's statement of cash flows. The company records rent expense later, when it uses the rented facilities. However, the entries to recognize rent expense do not affect cash. In other cases, the cash outflow follows the recording of the expense, as with payment of wages. The statement of cash flow records such transactions when the company pays the wages, not when it records the expense.

Let's examine the cost of goods sold expense. Accounting for the acquisition and selling of inventory usually requires recording three transactions: (1) purchase of inventory on credit, (2) payment of accounts payable, and (3) delivery of goods to the customer and thus the recording of an expense, where steps (2) and (3) may occur in either order. (If the purchase of inventory is for cash, steps 1 and 2 combine to form a single transaction.) Consider the following illustrative situation. Biwheels bought a bicycle seat on credit for $30 on January 7. Biwheels sold the seat on January 29 and paid the supplier on February 7. Two transactions occurred during January:

1. January 7. The balance sheet accounts Merchandise Inventory and Accounts Payable increased by $30.
2. January 29. The balance sheet account Merchandise Inventory decreased by $30, and Biwheels recorded a $30 cost of goods sold expense on the income statement. (Note that Biwheels would also record the sale on January 29, but we are focusing here on the expense part of the transaction.)

At the end of January, no cash transaction had occurred. Neither purchasing inventory on credit nor charging cost of goods sold expense affects cash. On February 7, the cash transaction occurs: Biwheels pays $30 of cash to the supplier, thereby reducing its accounts payable by $30. The end result of the three transactions is a $30 expense and a $30 payment. However, Biwheels recorded the expense in January and the cash outflow in February. January's income statement would have a $30 expense, but January's cash flow statement would have no related cash outflow. In February, the situation would be reversed. The cash flow statement would have a $30 outflow, but there would be no expense on the income statement. Notice in Exhibit 5-5 that there is no effect on cash when we recognize cost of goods sold or purchase inventory on credit, but there is a decrease in cash when we pay accounts payable or purchase inventory for cash.

Now that you know some of the operating transactions that affect cash and how the cash inflow or outflow can occur at a different time than the recording of the related revenue or expense, let's examine the two formats used for showing the cash flow effects of operations.

Cash Flow from Operations—The Direct Method

OBJECTIVE 5

Use the direct method to calculate cash flows from operations.

The direct method consists of a listing of cash receipts (inflows) and cash disbursements (outflows). The easiest way to construct the statement of cash flows from operations using the direct method is to examine the Cash column of the balance sheet equation. The following entries from Exhibit 5-2 (p. 201) affect cash:

Entry	Cash Effect
(1) Initial investment	+400,000
(2) Loan from bank	+100,000
(3) Acquire store equipment for cash	–15,000
(4) Acquire inventory for cash	*–120,000*
(6) Acquire inventory for cash plus credit	*–10,000*
(7) Sales of equipment	+1000
(9) Payments to creditors	*–4,000*
(11) Collect accounts receivable	*+5,000*
(12) Pay rent in advance	*–6,000*

We know from the previous sections that transactions 1, 2, 3, and 7 were financing or investing activities. Thus, the remaining transactions affecting cash must be operating activities. Therefore, the cash flows from operating activities include transactions 4, 6, 9, 11, and 12, which are in bold italics. The statement follows:

Biwheels Company
Cash Flows from Operating Activities
for the Month of January 20X2

Cash payments for inventory (transactions 4 and 6)	$(130,000)
Cash payments to creditors for accounts payable (transaction 9)	(4,000)
Cash collections on accounts receivable (transaction 11)	5,000
Cash payment for rent (transaction 12)	(6,000)
Net cash used by operating activities	$(135,000)

A more common format for this statement lists the cash collections first. It also combines the cash payment for inventory and cash payments to creditors for accounts payable on one line, cash payments to suppliers:

Biwheels Company
Cash Flows from Operating Activities
for the Month of January 20X2

Cash collections	$ 5,000
Cash payments to suppliers	(134,000)
Cash payments for rent	(6,000)
Net cash used by operating activities	$(135,000)

Notice the small cash inflow from operations. All sales in January were credit sales, and Biwheels collected only $5,000 during the month. Operating cash outflows that exceed cash inflows are common in young, growing companies. Companies pay for items such as rent and inventories in advance of receiving cash for the sales that result from the use of these resources.

Cash Flow from Operations—The Indirect Method

The direct method gives a straightforward picture of where a company gets cash and how it spends cash. However, it does not address the issue of how the cash flows from operating activities differ from net income. To do this, we use the indirect method, the method used by most companies. We can construct the indirect-method cash flow statement for Biwheels from January's income statement and the January 1 and January 31 balance sheets in Exhibit 5-3. (Note that all January 1 balances are zero.) Each income statement item has a parallel item or items in the statement of cash flows. Each sale eventually results in cash inflows; each expense entails cash outflows at some time. When the cash inflow from a sale or the cash outflow for an expense occurs in one accounting period and we record the sales revenue or expense in another, net income can differ from the cash flows from operations. The indirect method highlights such differences by beginning with net income and then listing all adjustments necessary to compute cash flows from operating activities. The indirect-method cash flow statement for Biwheels for the month of January is in Exhibit 5-6. Next we explain the entries in this exhibit.

If all sales were for cash and all expenses were paid in cash as incurred, cash flows from operating activities would be identical to net income. Thus, you can think of the first line of Exhibit 5-6, net income, as what the cash flow from operating activities would be if revenues equaled cash inflows and expenses equaled cash outflows. The subsequent adjustments recognize the differences in timing between revenues and cash inflows and between expenses and cash outflows. An alternative format that can help understand these adjustments is in Exhibit 5-7, where the middle column contains the adjustments shown in Exhibit 5-6. We will describe Exhibit 5-7 as we discuss each adjustment.

OBJECTIVE 6

Use the indirect method to explain the difference between net income and net cash provided by (used for) operating activities.

EXHIBIT 5-6

Biwheels Company

*Cash Flows from
Operating Activities—
Indirect Method for the
Month of January 20X2*

Net income	$ 57,900
Adjustments to reconcile net income to net cash provided (used) by operating activities	
Depreciation	100
Increase in accounts receivable	(155,000)
Increase in inventory	(59,200)
Increase in accounts payable	25,200
Increase in prepaid rent	(4,000)
Net cash provided by (used for) operating activities	$(135,000)

ADJUSTMENT FOR DEPRECIATION The first adjustment is to add the depreciation expense back to net income. We do this because we deducted depreciation of $100 when computing the net income of $57,900, but it does not represent an operating cash outflow in January. Depreciation is an expense, but the related cash flow occurred as an investing activity when Biwheels paid for the equipment. Because we deducted $100 of depreciation in computing January's net income, adding it back simply cancels the deduction. There is no cash flow effect of depreciation.

To highlight the effect of depreciation, let's for a moment assume that Biwheels received all $160,000 of revenue in cash and paid all $102,000 of nondepreciation expenses in cash. The income statement and statement of cash flows from operating activities would be as follows:

Income Statement		Cash Flows from Operating Activities	
Sales	$ 160,000	Cash inflows from sales	$ 160,000
Nondepreciation expenses	(102,000)	Cash outflows for expenses	(102,000)
Depreciation	(100)	Net cash provided by operating activities	$ 58,000
Net income	$ 57,900		

The only difference between net income and cash provided by operating activities in this example is the $100 of depreciation. To compute the net cash provided by operating activities, we simply add the $100 to the net income: ($57,900 + $100) = $58,000. The center column of line

Net Income		Adjustments		Cash Flows from Operating Activities	
A. Sales revenues	$ 160,000	Increase in accounts receivable	$(155,000)	Cash collections from customers	$ 5,000
		Increase in inventories	(59,200)		
B. Cost of goods sold	(100,000)	Increase in accounts payable	25,200	Cash payments to suppliers	(134,000)
C. Rent expense	(2,000)	Increase in prepaid rent	(4,000)	Cash payments for rent	(6,000)
D. Depreciation	(100)	Depreciation	100		0*
Net income	$ 57,900	Total adjustments	$(192,900)	Net cash provided by (used for) operating activities	$(135,000)

*Depreciation is not a cash flow.

EXHIBIT 5-7

Biwheels Company

Comparison of Net Income and Cash Provided by Operating Activities

D of Exhibit 5-7 shows depreciation is one of the adjustments to net income when computing cash provided by operating activities.

Let's examine depreciation more closely. Suppose depreciation was $500 rather than $100. Net income would be $57,500, and net cash provided by operating activities would still be $58,000, the sum of net income ($57,500) and depreciation ($500). Net cash provided by operating activities did not change. That is, the amount of depreciation has no effect on the cash provided by operating activities. To calculate cash flows, we add back to net income exactly the same amount we subtracted for depreciation, essentially canceling the earlier deduction.

Depreciation is an expense for which there is never an operating cash flow. The related cash flow was an investing outflow at the time the company paid for the underlying asset. The remaining adjustments for Biwheels represent situations where timing creates differences between net income and cash flows from operations. That is, over time the total revenue or expense will equal the total operating cash inflow or outflow, but the company may report some revenues or expenses on the income statement in one period and the related cash inflows or outflows on the statement of cash flows in another.

ADJUSTMENT FOR REVENUES Consider revenues. The sales revenue of $160,000 shown on the income statement immediately affects the Accounts Receivable account on the balance sheet and eventually will affect the Cash account. If all sales were for cash, sales would not affect accounts receivable, the associated cash flows would occur at the time of sale, and the cash inflow would equal the sales. However, Biwheels' sales are all on open account. Thus, the sale initially increases accounts receivable, and the cash inflow occurs when Biwheels collects the receivables. You can compute the amount of cash collections from income statement and balance sheet data in one of two ways. First, you can compute the total collections Biwheels could possibly collect in the month, which is the accounts receivable balance at the beginning of the month plus the sales of the month. From this you subtract the amount that Biwheels has not yet collected, the accounts receivable at the end of the month. This gives collections in January of $5,000:

Beginning accounts receivable	$ 0
+ Sales	160,000
Potential collections	$160,000
– Ending accounts receivable	155,000
Cash collections from customers	$ 5,000

Alternatively, you can start with the sales for the month. If accounts receivable had remained unchanged (that is, accounts receivable at the end of the month equaled the accounts receivable at the beginning of the month), cash collections would equal sales. If accounts receivable had increased, meaning that collections fell short of the sales, net income would be higher than cash flows from operations. If accounts receivable had decreased, meaning that collections exceeded sales, net income would be lower than cash flows from operations. In January, Biwheels' accounts receivable increased from $0 to $155,000, so cash collections were only $5,000:

Sales	$ 160,000
Decrease (increase) in accounts receivable*	(155,000)
Cash collections from customers	$ 5,000

*The format "decrease (increase)" means that decreases are positive amounts and increases are negative amounts.

Because Biwheels' accounts receivable increased in January, we need to deduct the $155,000 from net income to get cash provided by operating activities. Line A in Exhibit 5-7 shows this adjustment.

If accounts receivable had decreased, it would mean that collections exceeded sales. We would then add the decrease in accounts receivable to sales to determine the cash collections.

OBJECTIVE 7

Understand why we add depreciation to net income when using the indirect method for computing cash flow from operating activities.

INTERPRETING FINANCIAL STATEMENTS

Suppose all $160,000 of Biwheels' sales were for cash. Compute the cash collections from customers using the formula sales plus or minus the changes in accounts receivable. Explain.

Answer

If all sales were in cash, accounts receivable would have remained at $0. Because there was no increase or decrease in accounts receivable, there would be no adjustment of sales to get cash collections from customers:

Sales	$160,000
Decrease (increase) in accounts receivable	0
Cash collections from customers	$160,000

ADJUSTMENT FOR COST OF GOODS SOLD Just as we adjusted sales to compute cash collections from customers, we can adjust the cost of goods sold line in the income statement to compute cash outflow for payments to suppliers. To do this, we look at one income statement account, Cost of Goods Sold, and two balance sheet accounts, Inventory and Accounts Payable. We adjust cost of goods sold to get cash payments to suppliers in two steps:

Cost of Goods Sold	1. Adjusted to Get →	Purchases	2. Adjusted to Get →	Payments to Suppliers

These two steps yield the following:

Step 1

Ending inventory, January 31	$ 59,200
+ Cost of goods sold in January	100,000
Inventory available in January	$159,200
– Beginning inventory, January 1	0
Inventory purchased in January	$159,200

Step 2

Inventory purchased in January	$159,200
+Beginning accounts payable, January 1	0
Total amount to be paid	$159,200
– Ending accounts payable, January 31	(25,200)
Amount paid in cash during January	$134,000

In step 1, we compute the amount of inventory purchased in January, independent of whether we purchase the inventory for cash or credit. The calculation requires taking the amount of inventory used in January (that is, the cost of goods sold), plus the amount of inventory left at the end of January, less the amount that was already in inventory at the beginning of the month. If Biwheels had bought all of its inventory for cash, we could stop at this point. Its cash outflow to suppliers would equal the amount purchased, $159,200. However, because Biwheels purchased some inventory on credit, we must take step 2. If Biwheels had paid off all its accounts payable by the end of January, it would have paid an amount equal to the beginning accounts payable plus the purchases in January, a total of $159,200. Yet, $25,200 remained payable at the end of January, meaning that of the $159,200 of potential payments, Biwheels paid only ($159,200 – $25,200) = $134,000 in January.

From these two steps, we can determine the two adjustments needed to adjust cost of goods sold to a cash flow number:

Cost of goods sold in January	$100,000
Increase (decrease) in inventory during January	59,200
Decrease (increase) in accounts payable during January	(25,200)
Payments to suppliers during January	$134,000

Purchases that build up inventory require cash, but do not affect the cost of goods sold. Thus, if there had been no change in accounts payable in January, the cash outflow for payments to suppliers would have exceeded the cost of goods sold by the $59,200 increase in inventory: $100,000 cost of goods sold + $59,200 increase in inventory = $159,200 of inventory purchased. However, because accounts payable increased by $25,200, Biwheels did not pay the entire $159,200 in January. Of the $159,200 potential cash outflow, Biwheels will pay $25,200 in the future, so the company paid only ($159,200 – $25,200) = $134,000 in January.

These adjustments that convert cost of goods sold to payments to suppliers are necessary to adjust net income to cash provided by operating activities as required in an indirect method cash flow statement. Look at line B of Exhibit 5-7. Remember that we subtract cost of goods sold in computing net income just as we subtract the cash payments to suppliers in determining cash provided by operating activities. If the cash outflow is greater than the cost of goods sold, cash provided by operations will be less than net income. Because the increase in inventory caused the cash outflow to exceed the cost of goods sold by $59,200, cash provided by operations will be $59,200 less than net income. In contrast, the increase in accounts payable caused the cash outflow to fall short of cost of goods sold by $25,200, which results in cash provided by operations that is $25,200 more than net income.

ADJUSTMENTS FOR OTHER EXPENSES Before considering line C in Exhibit 5-7, let's create a general approach to adjustments. Then we can apply the approach to that line.

- Adjust for revenues and expenses not requiring cash:
    Add back depreciation.
    Other adjustments of this type are introduced in later chapters.
- Adjust for changes in noncash assets and liabilities relating to operating activities:
    Add decreases in assets.
    Deduct increases in assets.
    Add increases in liabilities.
    Deduct decreases in liabilities.

Adjustments so far have included adding back the $100 of depreciation expense (the only revenue or expense not requiring cash), deducting the $155,000 increase in accounts receivable (an asset), deducting the $59,200 increase in inventory (an asset), and adding the $25,200 increase in accounts payable (a liability). Take time now to verify that each of these adjustments is consistent with the preceding general rules.

Now let's consider the rent expense. Notice that Prepaid Rent, an asset account, increased from $0 at the beginning of the month to $4,000 at the end of the month. Thus, we need to deduct a $4,000 adjustment for rent, as shown in line C of Exhibit 5-7. This $4,000 balance is the result of paying $6,000 in cash for rent, but charging only $2,000 as an expense. This means that Biwheels' cash outflow for rent exceeded the rent expense by $4,000, as shown in the adjustment we made.

To summarize, look again at Exhibit 5-7. The comparison of net income to cash flows from operating activities in Exhibit 5-7 begins with the net income of $57,900 from the bottom of the first column, adds (deducts) the adjustments totaling $(192,900) in the middle column, and ends with the $(135,000) net cash used for operating activities in the right-hand column. The left-hand column calculates net income, the right-hand column calculates cash flows from operations, and the middle column shows line-by-line adjustments. Although Biwheels had a healthy net income of $57,900, it used $135,000 of cash to support its operations. Such a depletion of cash cannot continue indefinitely, regardless of how much income Biwheels generates. However, Biwheels is like other young, growing companies: It is using cash to build up its business in anticipation of positive cash flows being provided by operating activities in the future.

Reconciliation Statement

When a company uses the direct method for reporting cash flows from operating activities, users of the financial statements might miss information that relates net income to operating cash flows. Thus, those using direct-method statements must include a supplementary schedule reconciling net income to net cash provided by operations. Such a supplementary statement is effectively the operating section of an indirect method cash flow statement. In essence, companies that choose to use the direct method must also report using the indirect method. In contrast, those using the indirect method never explicitly report the information on a direct-method statement. The supplementary statement included with direct-method cash flow statements would be identical to the body of Exhibit 5-6, but it would be labeled "Reconciliation of Net Income to Net Cash Provided by Operating Activities."

The Statement of Cash Flows and the Balance Sheet Equation

To better understand how the cash flow statement relates to the other financial statements, let's examine the balance sheet equation. The balance sheet equation provides the conceptual basis for all financial statements, including the statement of cash flows. The equation can be rearranged as follows:

$$\text{Assets} = \text{Liabilities} + \text{Stockholders' equity}$$

$$\text{Cash} + \text{Noncash assets (NCA)} = L \quad + SE$$

$$\text{Cash} = L \quad + SE \quad - NCA$$

Any change (Δ) in cash must be accompanied by a change in one or more items on the right side to keep the equation in balance:

$$\Delta\text{Cash} = \Delta L + \Delta SE - \Delta NCA$$

Therefore:

$$\text{Change in cash} = \text{Change in all noncash accounts}$$

or

$$\text{What happened to cash} = \text{Why it happened}$$

The statement of cash flows focuses on the changes in the noncash accounts as a way of explaining how and why the level of cash has increased or decreased during a given period. Thus, the major changes in the accounts on the right side of the equation appear in the statement of cash flows as causes of the change in cash. The left side of the equation measures the net effect of the change in cash.

This same analysis can help explain the direct and indirect methods of reporting cash from operating activities. Exhibit 5-8 lists all of Biwheels' January transactions that we classify as operating activities. However, we have rearranged the columns in the format of the revised balance sheet equation presented above: $\Delta\text{Cash} = \Delta L + \Delta SE - \Delta NCA$. We list only the transactions that appear in the operating cash flows section of the statement of cash flows. Recall that operating activities are transactions that affect the purchase, processing, and selling of products or services.

Notice that the entries on the left side of the equal signs (those in the boxes) appear on the direct method statement of cash flows from operations. They are the direct cash flows and total an outflow of $135,000. The changes in each account (that is, the last line for each column) on the right side of the equation (those circled) appear on the indirect method statement. They also must total $135,000. Therefore, you can see that the direct and indirect method statements must always have the same totals. They differ only in format. The direct method statement is a listing of all changes in cash, whereas the indirect method statement shows the reasons for those changes. The following summarizes this analysis:

$$\Delta\text{Cash} = \Delta L + \Delta SE - \Delta NCA$$

$$\text{Direct method} = \text{Indirect method}$$

Cash | **=** | **Liabilities** | **+** | **Stockholders' Equity** | **–** | **Noncash Assets**

Description of Transactions	Cash	=	Cash		Accounts Payable	+	Retained Earnings	–	Accounts Receivable	–	Merchandise Inventory	–	Prepaid Rent	–	Store Equipment
(4) Acquire inventory for cash		=	−120,000								+120,000				
(5) Acquire inventory on credit		=			+10,000						+10,000				
(6) Acquire inventory for cash plus credit		=	−10,000		+20,000						+30,000				
(8) Return of inventory acquired on January 6		=			−800						−800				
(9) Payment to creditor		=	−4,000		−4,000										
(10a) Sales on open account		=					+160,000		+160,000						
(10b) Cost of merchandise inventory sold		=					−100,000				−100,000				
(11) Collect accounts receivable		=	+5,000						−5,000						
(12) Pay rent in advance		=	−6,000										+6,000		
(13) Recognize expiration of rental services		=					−2,000						−2,000		
(14) Depreciation							−100								−100
Total Changes	−135,000	=			25,200	+	57,900	–	+155,000	–	+59,200	–	+4,000	–	−100

EXHIBIT 5-8

Biwheels Company

Analysis of Operating Transactions for January 20X2 (in $)

Examples of Statements of Cash Flows

Exhibit 5-9 shows the complete January statement of cash flows for Biwheels. It shows that the total cash balance increased by $351,000, mainly due to $500,000 generated by financing activities. Of the $500,000 raised, operations used $135,000 and investing activities used $14,000, leaving the $351,000 balance.

You are now prepared to read most of the significant items on a real corporation's statement of cash flows. Consider Exhibit 5-10, Nike's statement of cash flows. We have simplified some items that were not covered in this chapter, but most of the items included should be familiar. Some terminology is slightly different from what we have used, but the meanings should be clear. Notice that Nike did almost the opposite of Biwheels. It generated substantial cash from operations and used that cash for both investing and financing activities.

EXHIBIT 5-9

Biwheels Company

Statement of Cash Flows for January 20X2

Cash Flows from Operating Activities		
Net income	$ 57,900	
Adjustments to reconcile net income to net cash provided by (used for) operating activities		
Depreciation	100	
Increase in accounts receivable	(155,000)	
Increase in inventory	(59,200)	
Increase in accounts payable	25,200	
Increase in prepaid rent	(4,000)	
Net cash provided by (used for) operating activities		$(135,000)
Cash Flows from Investing Activities		
Purchase of store equipment	$ (15,000)	
Proceeds from sale of store equipment	1,000	
Net cash provided by (used for) investing activities		$ (14,000)
Cash Flows from Financing Activities		
Proceeds from initial investment	$ 400,000	
Proceeds from bank loan	100,000	
Net cash provided by (used for) financing activities		$ 500,000
Net increase in cash		$ 351,000
Cash, January 2, 20X2		0
Cash, January 31, 20X2		$ 351,000

EXHIBIT 5-10
Nike, Inc.
Statement of Cash Flows (in millions) for the Year Ended May 31, 2009

CASH PROVIDED (USED) BY OPERATIONS		
Net income	$1,486.7	
Income charges not affecting cash		
Depreciation	335.0	
Other noncash charges	326.1	
Changes in certain working capital components and other assets and liabilities		
Increase in accounts receivable	(238.0)	
Decrease in inventories	32.2	
Decrease in prepaid expenses and other current assets	14.1	
Decrease in accounts payable, accrued liabilities, and income taxes payable	(220.0)	
Cash provided by operations		$1,736.1
CASH PROVIDED (USED) BY INVESTING ACTIVITIES		
Purchases of short-term investments	(2,908.7)	
Maturities of short-term investments	2,390.0	
Additions to property, plant, and equipment	$ (455.7)	
Disposals of property, plant, and equipment	32.0	
Other investment activities	144.3	
Cash used by investing activities		$ (798.1)
CASH PROVIDED (USED) BY FINANCING ACTIVITIES		
Reductions in long-term debt, including current portion	(6.8)	
Increase in notes payable	177.1	
Proceeds from exercise of stock options and other stock issuances	186.6	
Other investing activities	25.1	
Repurchase of common stock	(649.2)	
Dividends—common and preferred	(466.7)	
Cash used by financing activities		(733.9)
Effect of exchange rate changes		(46.9)
Net increase in cash and equivalents		157.2
Cash and equivalents, beginning of year		2,133.9
Cash and equivalents, end of year		$2,291.1

Summary Problem for Your Review

PROBLEM

Examine the entries to Biwheels' balance sheet equation for February 20X2 in Exhibit 2-5 (p. 73) and the balance sheet and income statement in Exhibits 2-6 and 2-7 (p. 74).

1. Prepare a statement of cash flows from operating activities for February using the direct method.
2. Prepare a statement of cash flows from operating activities for February using the indirect method.
3. Give a one-line explanation of the insight most readily learned from each of the two statements.

SOLUTION

1. See Exhibit 5-11. The numbers come directly from the first column of Exhibit 2-5. The cash collections are $130,000 collected on accounts receivable and the $51,000 cash sales. The payments to suppliers include $15,000 paid on accounts payable and $10,000 for cash purchases.
2. See Exhibit 5-12. The net income and add-back of depreciation come from the income statement. The other adjustments are differences between January 31 and February 28 balances on the balance sheet.
3. The direct-method statement shows the large excess of cash collections over cash payments. The indirect-method statement shows that the cash flow from operations exceeded net income by ($156,000 – $63,900) = $92,100 due primarily to the large increase in accounts payable and the depletion of inventory.

EXHIBIT 5-11

Biwheels Company

Statement of Cash Flows from Operating Activities—Direct Method February 20X2

Cash collections from customers	$181,000
Cash payments to suppliers	(25,000)
Net cash provided by operating activities	$156,000

EXHIBIT 5-12

Biwheels Company

Statement of Cash Flows from Operating Activities—Indirect Method February 20X2

Net income	$ 63,900
Adjustments to reconcile net income to net cash provided by (used for) operating activities	
Depreciation	100
Decrease in accounts receivable	5,000
Decrease in inventory	20,000
Increase in accounts payable	65,000
Decrease in prepaid rent	2,000
Net cash provided by (used for) operating activities	$156,000

The Importance of Cash Flow

Identify free cash flow, and interpret information in statements of cash flow.

Both the income statement and the statement of cash flows report on changes the company experiences during the period. Both are measures of performance over the period. You might wonder why accounting authorities require both. Why should the company not pick the better one? Because each one provides important, but different, information. The income statement shows how a company's stockholders' equity increases (or decreases) as a result of operations. It matches revenues and expenses using the accrual concepts and provides a valuable measure of economic performance. In contrast, the statement of cash flows explains changes in the cash account rather than owners' equity. The focal point of the statement of cash flows is the net cash flow from operating activities, often called simply cash flow. It measures a firm's performance in maintaining a strong cash position. In addition, users of financial statements often compare the cash flows from operating, investing, and financing activities. The Business First box describes some of these comparisons.

free cash flow

Generally defined as cash flows from operations less capital expenditures.

Many analysts focus on **free cash flow**—generally defined as cash flows from operations less capital expenditures. This is the cash flow left over after undertaking the firm's operations and making the investments necessary to ensure its continued operation. Some also subtract dividends, assuming they are necessary to keep the shareholders happy. Companies that cannot generate enough cash from operations to cover their investments need to raise more capital, either by selling assets or by issuing debt or equity. If investment is for growth, this situation may be acceptable. If the investment is merely to maintain the status quo, the company is probably in trouble. In the recession of 2008–2009, numerous companies experienced negative free cash flow, and many

BUSINESS FIRST

INTERPRETING OPERATING, INVESTING, AND FINANCING CASH FLOWS

Comparing cash flow from operations with the cash flow from investing and financing activities can tell a lot about a company. First let's consider companies with positive cash flows from operations. Those who have negative cash flows from investing activities in the same period, that is those who used funds to expand their invesments in fixed assets, tend to be healthy, growing firms. In the early years these firms often have positive cash flows from financing activities as the result of raising capital in the debt or equity markets. As they mature, the most successful of these companies begin to pay back debt and return capital to shareholders, making cash flow from financing activities negative. For example, in the last two decades Starbucks has had consistently positive cash flow from operations and negative cash flow from investing activities as it expanded its operations globally. Until 2003 Starbucks generally raised capital, creating positive cash flows from financing activities. Since 2003 Starbucks has used cash for financing activities, paying back debtholders and shareholders.

If companies with positive cash flow from operations also have positive cash flow from investing activities, analysts often question the company's future prospects. Such companies are depleting their asset bases, so they are not preparing for future growth. For example, Aquila Corporation, in the 2 years before its 2008 purchase by Great Plains Energy, reported $212 million cash provided by operations and $786 million cash provided by investing activities. Although operations were generating cash, Aquila needed to sell assets to generate additional cash to pay debts as they came due. The cash flow problems that necessitated Aquila's selling of assets were a main reason the shareholders approved the company's sale to Great Plains.

Companies with negative cash flow from operations are generally in one of two categories: 1) young companies that have not yet reached the point of generating positive operating cash flows, and 2) companies that are in trouble. In the first category are many biotechnology companies that must undertake years of R&D before having salable products. Medivir AB, a Swedish biotech company, and Pressure Biosciences, Inc., a Boston life-sciences company, are examples of companies that have not had positive operating cash flows but continue to raise capital and invest in additional fixed assets. If such companies do not have positive cash from financing activities, analysts examine whether their existing cash is likely to be enough to cover negative operating and investing cash flows long enough to reach profitability.

Companies with negative cash flow from operations and positive cash flow from investing activities are, either intentionally or unwittingly, liquidating the company. They are selling off their assets to support money-losing operating activities. Midway Games, the Chicago-based entertainment software company that published the *Mortal Kombat* series, had such as situation in 2008, just prior to its 2009 bankruptcy filing.

Sources: Medivir AB 2008 Annual Report; Pressure Biosciences, Inc. 2008 Annual Report; Starbucks 2008 Annual Report; Midway Games 2008 Annual Report; W. Wong, "Midway Games, Known for Mortal Kombat, Files for Chapter 11," *Chicago Tribune*, February 12, 2009.

resorted to selling off assets to meet their cash needs. For example, **Canadian Broadcasting Corporation** (CBC) announced planned asset sales of $125 million in March 2009 after reporting negative free cash flow of $133 million in 2008. Biwheels Company has a large negative free cash flow for January, [$(135,000) − $15,000] = $(150,000) meaning that it must improve its cash flow from operations or it will need to raise additional capital.

The Crisis of Negative Cash Flow

Although investors make important economic decisions on the basis of net income, the so-called bottom line, sometimes earnings numbers do not tell the full story of what is really happening inside a company. Take the case of **Prime Motor Inns**, once one of the world's largest hotel operators. At its peak, Prime reported earnings of $77 million on revenues of $410 million. Moreover, revenues had increased by nearly 11% from the preceding year. Despite its impressive earnings performance, Prime lacked the cash to meet its obligations and filed for Chapter 11 bankruptcy. Under bankruptcy protection, a firm's obligations to its creditors are frozen as management figures out how to pay those creditors. How can a firm with $77 million in earnings file for bankruptcy about a year later?

Although the company's business was owning and operating hotels, much of Prime's reported $77 million of earnings arose from selling hotels. When buyers found it difficult to obtain outside financing for these hotel sales, Prime financed the sales itself by accepting notes and mortgages receivable from buyers rather than receiving cash. Of course, Prime soon ran out of hotels to sell. In the year that Prime reported $77 million of net income, an astute analyst would have noted that Prime had a net cash *outflow* from operations of $15 million. Analyzing the cash flow statement focuses attention on important relationships such as this one.

Prime emerged from bankruptcy with 75 hotels—roughly one-half the 141 hotels it had prior to bankruptcy—and a new name, **Prime Hospitality Corporation**. By the time the company was bought a few years ago by **The Blackstone Group**, a private equity company, it operated more than 250 hotels, primarily in the AmeriSuites and Wellesley Inn & Suites chains. The investors who bought the new shares for about $1.50 when the reorganization occurred did well, receiving $12.25 a share from Blackstone.

INTERPRETING FINANCIAL STATEMENTS

What pattern in the cash flow statement would have helped to alert the careful analyst to a potential problem at Prime Hospitality Corporation?

Answer
Prime was reporting large profits under accrual accounting, but operating cash flow was negative. Prime was financing sales by accepting notes and mortgages from buyers. This predicament would have been evident from the significant increases in these notes and mortgages receivable as compared with prior years.

Summary Problems for Your Review

PROBLEM

The Buretta Company has prepared the data in Exhibit 5-13.

In December 20X2, Buretta paid $54 million cash for a new building acquired to accommodate an expansion of operations. The company financed this purchase partly by a new issue of long-term debt for $40 million cash. During 20X2, the company also sold fixed assets for $5 million cash. The assets were listed on Buretta's books at $5 million. All sales and purchases of merchandise were on credit.

Because the 20X2 net income of $4 million was the highest in the company's history, Alice Buretta, the chairman of the board, was perplexed by the company's extremely low cash balance.

1. Prepare a statement of cash flows from the Buretta data in Exhibit 5-13. Ignore income taxes. You may want to use Exhibit 5-9 (p. 216) as a guide. Use the direct method for reporting cash flows from operating activities.
2. Prepare a supporting schedule that reconciles net income to net cash provided by operating activities.
3. What does the statement of cash flows tell you about Buretta Company? Does it help you reduce Alice Buretta's puzzlement? Why?

EXHIBIT 5-13

Buretta Company Financial Statements (in millions)

Income Statement (Including Changes in Retained Earnings) for the Year Ended December 31, 20X2

Sales		$100
Less: Cost of goods sold		
Inventory, December 31, 20X1	$ 15	
Purchases	105	
Cost of goods available for sale	$120	
Inventory, December 31, 20X2	(47)	73
Gross profit		$ 27
Less: Other expenses		
General expenses	$ 8	
Depreciation	8	
Property taxes	4	
Interest expense	3	23
Net income		$ 4
Retained earnings, December 31, 20X1		7
Total		$ 11
Dividends declared and paid		1
Retained earnings, December 31, 20X2		$ 10

Balance Sheets for December 31

Assets	20X2	20X1	Liabilities and Stockholders' Equity	20X2	20X1
			Accounts payable	$ 39	$14
Cash	$ 1	$20	Accrued property tax payable	3	1
Accounts receivable	20	5			
Inventory	47	15	Long-term debt	40	0
Prepaid expenses	3	2	Common stock	70	70
Fixed assets, net	91	50	Retained earnings	10	7
			Total liabilities and		
Total assets	$162	$92	stockholders' equity	$162	$92

SOLUTION

1. See Exhibit 5-14. We can compute cash flows from operating activities as follows ($ in millions):

	Sales	$100
	Less increase in accounts receivable	(15)
(a)	Cash collections from customers	$ 85
	Cost of goods sold	$ 73
	Plus increase in inventory	32
	Purchases	$105
	Less: Increase in accounts payable	(25)
(b)	Cash paid to suppliers	$ 80
	General expenses	$ 8
	Plus increase in prepaid general expenses	1
(c)	Cash payment for general expenses	$ 9
(d)	Cash paid for interest	$ 3
	Property taxes	$ 4
	Less: Increase in accrued property tax payable	(2)
(e)	Cash paid for property taxes	$ 2

EXHIBIT 5-14

Buretta Company

Statement of Cash Flows for the Year Ended December 31, 20X2 (in millions)

Cash flows from operating activities		
Cash collections from customers (a)		$ 85
Cash payments		
Cash paid to suppliers (b)	$(80)	
General expenses (c)	(9)	
Interest paid (d)	(3)	
Property taxes (e)	(2)	(94)
Net cash used by operating activities		$ (9)
Cash flows from investing activities		
Purchase of fixed assets (building)	$(54)	
Proceeds from sale of fixed assets	5	
Net cash used by investing activities		(49)
Cash flows from financing activities		
Long-term debt issued	$ 40	
Dividends paid	(1)	
Net cash provided by financing activities		39
Net decrease in cash		$(19)
Cash balance, December 31, 20X1		20
Cash balance, December 31, 20X2		$ 1

2. Exhibit 5-15 reconciles net income to net cash provided by operating activities.

3. The statement of cash flows shows where cash has come from and where it has gone. Operations used $9 million of cash. Why? The statement in Exhibit 5-14, which uses the direct method, shows the result clearly: $94 million in cash paid for operating activities exceeded $85 million in cash received from customers. The reconciliation using the indirect method, in Exhibit 5-15, shows why, in a profitable year, operating cash flow could be negative. The three largest items differentiating net income from cash flow are changes in inventory, accounts receivable, and accounts payable. Sales during the period were not collected in full because accounts receivable rose sharply, by $15 million—a 300% increase. Similarly, Buretta spent cash on inventory growth, although it financed much of that growth by increased accounts payable. In summary, the items in parentheses in Exhibit 5-15, large increases in accounts receivable ($15 million) and inventory ($32 million), plus an increase in prepaid expenses ($1 million), show that Buretta used $48 million of cash. In contrast, the sum of the items not in parentheses show that Buretta generated only $39 million in cash, that is, $4 million + $8 million + $25 million + $2 million. Thus, the company used a net amount of $9 million in operations ($39 million – $48 million).

Investing activities also consumed cash because Buretta invested $54 million in a building, and it received only $5 million from sales of fixed assets, leaving a net use of $49 million. Financing activities did generate $39 million cash, but that was $19 million less than the $58 million used by operating and investing activities ($58 million = $9 million used in operations + $49 million used in investing).

Alice Buretta should no longer be puzzled. The statement of cash flows shows clearly that cash payments exceeded receipts by $19 million. However, she may still be concerned about the depletion of cash. Either the company must change operations so it does not require so much cash, it must curtail investment, or it must raise more long-term debt or ownership equity. Otherwise, Buretta Company will soon run out of cash.

PROBLEM

To understand how cash flow and net income vary during the life cycle of a business, consider the following example that portrays the 4-year life of a short-lived merchandising company, CB International. The first year the entrepreneurs bought twice as much as they sold because they were building their base inventory levels. CB International's suppliers offered payment

Net income (from income statement)	$ 4
Adjustments to reconcile net income to net cash provided by operating activities	
Add: Depreciation, which was deducted in the computation of net income but does not decrease cash	8
Deduct: Increase in accounts receivable	(15)
Deduct: Increase in inventory	(32)
Deduct: Increase in prepaid general expenses	(1)
Add: Increase in accounts payable	25
Add: Increase in accrued property tax payable	2
Net cash used by operating activities	$ (9)

EXHIBIT 5-15

Supporting Schedule to Statement of Cash Flows

Reconciliation of Net Income to Net Cash Provided by Operating Activities for the Year Ended December 31, 20X2 (in millions)

terms that resulted in CB paying 80% of each year's purchases during that year and 20% in the next year. Sales were for cash with a sales price equal to twice the cost of the item. Selling expenses were constant over the life of the business and CB International paid them in cash as incurred. At the end of the fourth year, CB International paid the suppliers in full and sold all the inventory. Use the following summary results to prepare four income statements and statements of cash flows from operations using both direct and indirect methods for CB International, one for each year of its life.

	Year 1	Year 2	Year 3	Year 4
Purchases	2,000 units	1,500 units	1,500 units	1,000 units
$1 each	$2,000	$1,500	$1,500	$1,000
Sales	1,000 units	1,500 units	2,000 units	1,500 units
$2 each	$2,000	$3,000	$4,000	$3,000
Cost of sales	$1,000	$1,500	$2,000	$1,500
Selling expense	$1,000	$1,000	$1,000	$1,000
Payments to suppliers*	$1,600	$1,600	$1,500	$1,300

*(.8 ×2,000) = 1,600; (.2 × 2,000) + (.8 × 1,500) = 1,600; (.2 × 1,500) + (.8 × 1,500) = 1,500; (.2 × 1,500) + (1.0 × 1,000) = 1,300.

SOLUTION

	Year 1	Year 2	Year 3	Year 4	Total
Income statement					
Sales	$ 2,000	$3,000	$4,000	$3,000	$12,000
Cost of sales	1,000	1,500	2,000	1,500	6,000
Selling expenses	1,000	1,000	1,000	1,000	4,000
Net income	$ 0	$ 500	1,000	$ 500	$ 2,000
Cash flows from operations: direct method					
Collections	$ 2,000	$3,000	$4,000	$3,000	$12,000
Payments on account	(1,600)	(1,600)	(1,500)	(1,300)	(6,000)
Payments for selling efforts	(1,000)	(1,000)	(1,000)	(1,000)	(4,000)
Cash flow from operations	$ (600)	$ 400	$1,500	$ 700	$ 2,000
Cash flows from operations: indirect method					
Net income	$ 0	$ 500	$1,000	$ 500	$ 2,000
− Increase in inventory	(1,000)				(1,000)
+ Decrease in inventory			500	500	1,000
+ Increase in accounts payable	400				400
− Decrease in accounts payable		(100)		(300)	(400)
Cash flow from operations	$ (600)	$ 400	$1,500	$ 700	$ 2,000

Balance Sheet Accounts at the end of	Year 1	Year 2	Year 3	Year 4
Merchandise inventory	$1,000	$1,000	$500	$0
Accounts payable	$ 400	$ 300	$300	0

This problem illustrates the difference between accrual-based earnings and cash flows. Observe that significant cash outflows occur for operations during the first year because payments to acquire inventory far exceed collections from customers. In fact, it is not until the third year that cash flow from operations exceeds net earnings for the year.

Highlights to Remember

1 **Identify the purposes of the statement of cash flows.** The statement of cash flows focuses on the changes in cash and the activities that cause those changes. Accrual-based net income is a useful number, but we also ask the following questions: How did our cash position change? How much of the change in cash was caused by operations, how much by investing activities, and how much by financing activities?

2 **Classify activities affecting cash as operating, investing, or financing activities.** Operating activities are the typical day-to-day activities of the firm in acquiring or manufacturing products, selling them to customers, and collecting the cash. Investing activities involve buying and selling plant, property, and equipment. It might include buying a whole company as well as specific assets. Financing activities involve raising or repaying capital such as borrowing from a bank, issuing bonds, or paying dividends to shareholders.

3 **Compute and interpret cash flows from financing activities.** Financing activities are transactions that obtain or repay capital. Cash flows from financing activities show whether a company borrows or repays money, issues additional securities, pays dividends, or buys back shares from stockholders.

4 **Compute and interpret cash flows from investing activities.** Investing activities are transactions that acquire or sell long-lived assets such as property or equipment and securities that are not cash equivalents. Cash flows from investing activities show where management has elected to invest any funds raised or generated.

5 **Use the direct method to calculate cash flows from operations.** The direct method, preferred by the FASB and IASB, explicitly lists all cash inflows and cash outflows from operating activities. We can find the relevant cash flows in the cash column in the balance sheet equation. The advantage of the direct method is that it is straightforward and easy to understand.

6 **Use the indirect method to explain the difference between net income and net cash provided by (used for) operating activities.** The more commonly used method for calculating the cash flow from operations is the indirect method, which starts with net income and adjusts it for the differences, typically account by account, between accrual income and operating cash flow. Both the direct and indirect method yield the same result. The advantage of the indirect method is that it explicitly addresses the differences between net income and net cash from operations.

7 **Understand why we add depreciation to net income when using the indirect method for computing cash flow from operating activities.** Under the indirect method, we add depreciation to net income because it is an expense not requiring the use of cash. Because we deduct depreciation when computing net income, adding it back simply eliminates the effect of deducting this noncash item. This adding back of depreciation sometimes causes some people to think of depreciation as a source of cash. This is not the case. Increasing depreciation does not affect cash flow.

8 **Show how the balance sheet equation provides a conceptual framework for the statement of cash flows.** The balance sheet equation is the conceptual base of all financial statements. By reconstructing the equation with cash alone on the left side of the equals sign, we can see how the right-hand entries provide an explanation for the changes in cash. Increases in liabilities or stockholders' equity or decreases in noncash assets increase cash, whereas decreases in liabilities or stockholders' equity or increases in noncash assets decrease cash.

9 **Identify free cash flow, and interpret information in statements of cash flow.** To understand how a company manages its cash, analysts often compare cash flows across operating, investing, and financing activities. Free cash flow, cash flows from operations less capital expenditures and possibly dividends, is a metric that helps such comparisons.

Accounting Vocabulary

cash equivalents, p. 199
cash flow statement, p. 198
cash flows from financing
activities, p. 199
cash flows from investing
activities, p. 199

cash flows from operating
activities, p. 199
direct method, p. 207
financing activities, p. 199
financing decisions, p. 199
free cash flow, p. 218
indirect method, p. 207

investing activities, p. 199
investing decisions, p. 199
operating activities, p. 199
operating decisions, p. 199
statement of cash flows,
p. 198

Assignment Material

MyAccountingLab

Questions

5-1 "The statement of cash flows is an optional statement included by most companies in their annual reports." Do you agree? Explain.

5-2 What are the purposes of a statement of cash flows?

5-3 Define cash equivalents.

5-4 The statement of cash flows summarizes what three types of activities?

5-5 Name four major operating activities included in a statement of cash flows.

5-6 Name three major investing activities included in a statement of cash flows.

5-7 Name three major financing activities included in a statement of cash flows.

5-8 There is one item on a cash flow statement that is not a cash flow but affects cash. What is it and why do companies include it on their statements of cash flow?

5-9 Where does interest received or paid appear on the statement of cash flows under U.S. GAAP? Under IFRS?

5-10 Which of the following financing activities increase cash: increase long-term debt, repurchase common shares, or pay dividends? Which decrease cash?

5-11 Which of the following investing activities increase cash: purchase fixed assets by issuing debt, sell fixed assets for cash, collect a loan, or purchase equipment for cash? Which decrease cash?

5-12 Explain why increases in liabilities increase cash and increases in assets decrease cash.

5-13 Why are noncash investing and financing activities listed on a separate schedule accompanying the statement of cash flows?

5-14 A company acquired a fixed asset in exchange for common stock. Explain how this transaction should be shown, if at all, in the statement of cash flows. Why is your suggested treatment appropriate?

5-15 Suppose a company paid off a $1 million short-term loan to one bank with the proceeds from an identical loan from another bank. The change in the short-term debt account would be zero. Should anything appear in the statement of cash flows? Explain.

5-16 What are the two major ways of computing net cash provided by operating activities?

5-17 Where does a company get the information included in the direct-method cash flow statement?

5-18 Why is there usually a difference between the cash collections from customers and sales revenue in a period's financial statements?

5-19 What two balance sheet accounts explain the difference between the cost of goods sold and the cash payments to suppliers?

5-20 What types of adjustments reconcile net income with net cash provided by operations?

5-21 "Net losses mean drains on cash." Do you agree? Explain.

5-22 The indirect method for reporting cash flows from operating activities can create an erroneous impression about noncash expenses (such as depreciation). What is the impression, and why is it erroneous?

5-23 An investor's newsletter had the following item: "The company expects increased cash flow in 2011 because depreciation charges will be substantially greater than they were in 2010." Comment.

5-24 "Depreciation is an integral part of a statement of cash flows." Do you agree? Explain.

5-25 Demonstrate how the fundamental balance sheet equation can be recast to focus on cash.

5-26 A company operated at a profit for the year, but cash flow from operations was negative.

Why might this occur? What industry or industries might find this a common occurrence?

5-27 A company operated at a loss for the year, but cash flow from operations was positive. Why might this occur? What industry or industries might find this a common occurrence?

Critical Thinking Questions

5-28 Cash Flow Patterns and Growth
You are considering an investment in a company that has negative cash flow from operations, negative cash flow from investing, and positive cash flow from financing. All the financing in the current year is from short-term debt. What does this pattern of cash flow tell you about the client's circumstance. How does this affect your investment decision?

5-29 Google and Cash Generation
On June 30, 2009, Google was generating increasing amounts of cash from operating activities each year and was unable to fully use it to grow the business. Hence, the levels of liquid investments were increasing so that cash, cash equivalents, and marketable securities comprised 55% of the company's assets. What would you imagine Google's management might have been considering as a means of using the cash and liquid investment assets?

5-30 Amazon and Negative Cash Flow from Operations
Between 2004 and 2008, Amazon.com, the industry leader in online sales of books and other consumer products, increased its free cash flow from $477 million to $1,364 million. Prior to 2002, Amazon had never generated positive cash flow from operations. What does this tell you about the stage of growth that Amazon is in?

5-31 Failures to Generate Cash Flow from Operations
You are discussing your investment strategies with a colleague who says, "I would never invest in a company that is not generating both positive earnings and positive cash flow from operations." How do you respond?

Exercises

5-32 Identify Operating, Investing, and Financing Activities
The following listed items were found on a recent statement of cash flows for AT&T. For each item, indicate which section of the statement should contain the item—the operating, investing, or financing section. Also, indicate whether AT&T uses the direct or indirect method for reporting cash flows from operating activities.

a. Net income (loss)
b. Dividends paid
c. Proceeds from long-term debt issuance
d. Capital expenditures net of proceeds from sale or disposal of property, plant, and equipment
e. Issuance of common shares
f. Retirements of long-term debt
g. Increase in inventories
h. Depreciation and amortization
i. Increase in short-term borrowing—net

5-33 Simple Statement of Cash Flows from Financing Activities
Bubba's Catfish, Inc., is a seafood restaurant in New Orleans. Bubba's began business in January 20X1 when investors bought common stock for $100,000 cash. Bubba's also borrowed $50,000 from Stateside Bank on January 15, on which it paid interest of $3,000 on July 15. In January the company invested $80,000 in machinery and equipment and signed a monthly rental agreement on a building with rental payments of $4,000 a month. During 20X1 Bubba's had net income of $14,000 on sales of $249,000. On December 15 the company declared and paid cash dividends

of $2,000 to its common stockholders. On December 31 the company paid $10,000 to buy common shares back from the stockholders.

Prepare a statement of cash flows from financing activities for the year 20X1.

5-34 Financing Activities, IFRS and U.S. GAAP

During 20X0, the Marseilles Shipping Company, a company reporting under IFRS, refinanced its long-term debt. It spent €160,000 to retire long-term debt due in 2 years and issued €180,000 of 15-year bonds (€ signifies euro, the European monetary unit.) It then bought and retired common shares for cash of €35,000. Interest expense for 20X0 was €23,000, of which it paid €21,000 in cash; the other €2,000 was still payable at the end of the year. Dividends declared and paid during the year were €11,000.

Prepare a statement of cash flows from financing activities. Discuss the treatment of interest expense under IFRS compared to U.S. GAAP.

5-35 Investing Activities

Brisbane Trading Company issued common stock for $320,000 on the first day of 20X0. The company bought fixed assets for $160,000 and inventory for $75,000. Late in the year, it sold fixed assets for their book value of $20,000. It sold one-half the inventory for $55,000 during the year. On December 15, the company used excess cash of $65,000 to purchase common stock of Fellski Company, which Brisbane regarded as a long-term investment.

Prepare a statement of cash flows from investing activities for Brisbane Trading Company.

5-36 Noncash Investing and Financing Activities

Jacoby Company had the following items in its statement of cash flows:

Note payable issued for acquisition of fixed assets	$122,000
Retirement of long-term debt	565,000
Common stock issued on conversion of preferred shares	340,000
Purchases of marketable securities	225,000
Mortgage assumed on acquisition of warehouse	530,000
Increase in accounts payable	42,000

Prepare a schedule of noncash investing and financing activities, selecting appropriate items from the preceding list.

5-37 Cash Received from Customers

Southwinds Publishers, Inc., had sales of $800,000 during 20X1, 80% of them on credit and 20% for cash. During the year, accounts receivable increased from $60,000 to $90,000, an increase of $30,000. What amount of cash was received from customers during 20X1?

5-38 Cash Paid to Suppliers

Cost of Goods Sold for Southwinds Publishers, Inc., during 20X1 was $500,000. Beginning inventory was $100,000, and ending inventory was $150,000. Beginning trade accounts payable were $24,000, and ending trade accounts payable were $42,000. What amount of cash did Southwinds pay to suppliers?

5-39 Cash Paid to Employees

Southwinds Publishers, Inc., reported wage and salary expenses of $205,000 on its 20X1 income statement. It reported cash paid to employees of $185,000 on its statement of cash flows. The beginning balance of Accrued Wages and Salaries Payable was $18,000. What was the ending balance in Accrued Wages and Salaries Payable? Ignore payroll taxes.

5-40 Simple Cash Flows from Operating Activities

Pegasus Strategy, Inc., provides consulting services. In 20X1, net income was $175,000 on revenues of $460,000 and expenses of $285,000. The only noncash expense was depreciation of $35,000. The company has no inventory. Accounts receivable increased by $5,000 during 20X1, and accounts payable and salaries payable were unchanged.

Prepare a statement of cash flows from operating activities. Use the direct method. Omit supporting schedules.

5-41 Net Income and Cash Flow
Refer to Problem 5-40. Prepare a schedule that reconciles net income to net cash flow from operating activities.

5-42 Simple Direct- and Indirect-Method Statements
Wytana Company saw its cash plummet by $100,000 in 20X0. The company's president wants an explanation of what caused the decrease in cash despite income of $60,000. He has asked you to prepare both direct and indirect method statements of cash flows from operations for 20X0. You have discovered the following information:

- Sales, all on credit, were $560,000.
- Accounts receivable increased by $120,000.
- Cost of goods sold was $390,000.
- Payments to suppliers were $455,000.
- Accounts payable decreased by $40,000.
- Inventory increased by $25,000.
- Operating expenses were $95,000, all paid in cash except for depreciation of $30,000.
- Income tax expense was $15,000; taxes payable decreased by $5,000.

1. Prepare a statement of cash flows from operating activities using the direct method.
2. Prepare a statement of cash flows from operating activities using the indirect method.
3. Explain why cash decreased by $100,000 when net income was a positive $60,000.

5-43 Nature of Depreciation
This continues the previous Problem, 5-42. The president looked at the indirect-method cash flow statement and suggested a way to help the cash flow problem. He suggested tripling the depreciation from $30,000 to $90,000 a year. That way the cash flow will improve by $60,000 annually. Explain why this reasoning is faulty.

5-44 Depreciation and Cash Flows
(Alternate is 5-63.) Yucatan Mexican Cafe had sales of $880,000, all received in cash. Total operating expenses were $570,000. All except depreciation were paid in cash. Depreciation of $90,000 was included in the $570,000 of operating expenses. Ignore income taxes.

1. Compute net income and net cash provided by operating activities.
2. Assume that depreciation is tripled. Compute net income and net cash provided by operating activities.

MyAccountingLab ## Problems

5-45 Statement of Cash Flows, Effect of Exchange Rates, Japan
Kansai Electric supplies power to an area of Japan that includes Osaka and Kyoto. Its operating revenues are nearly ¥2.8 trillion (about $25 billion in U.S. dollars), and its assets are nearly ¥7 trillion. The bottom of Kansai Electric's 2009 cash flow statement contained the following (in millions of Japanese yen, ¥):

Net cash used in operating, investing, and financing activities	¥ (3,378)
Effect of exchange rate changes on cash and cash equivalents	(9,783)
Net decrease in cash and cash equivalents	(13,161)
Cash and cash equivalents, beginning of year	82,914
Cash and cash equivalents, end of year	¥ 69,753

Is the effect of exchange rate changes on cash and cash equivalents a cash flow? Explain why Kansai Electric included it on the company's cash flow statement.

5-46 Cash Flows from Financing Activities

ConAgra Foods, Inc. is one of North America's leading food companies with brands such as Banquet and Healthy Choice. Its 2009 sales exceeded $12 billion. ConAgra's 2009 statement of cash flows included the following items, among others ($ in millions):

Cash dividends paid	$ (348.2)
Repurchase of ConAgra Foods common shares	(900.0)
Additions to property, plant, and equipment	(441.9)
Depreciation and amortization	318.9
Proceeds from exercise of employee stock options	6.1
Net short-term borrowings	(577.7)
Increase in inventories	(89.5)
Issuance of long-term debt	1,030.1
Net income	978.4
Repayments of long-term debt	(1,016.2)
Other financing items	(21.1)

1. Prepare the section "Cash flows from financing activities" from ConAgra's 2009 annual report. All items necessary for that section appear in the preceding list. Some items from other sections have been omitted.
2. Did ConAgra's short-term borrowings increase or decrease during 2009?

5-47 Cash Flows from Investing Activities

British Airways Plc is an international airline company that serves nearly 200 cities in most parts of the world. Its revenues in fiscal 2009 were nearly £9 billion (where £ is pounds, the monetary unit of the UK where British Airways is headquartered). The company's statement of cash flows for fiscal 2009 contained the following items (British pounds in millions):

Interest received	£ 105
Dividends received	17
Operating profit (loss)	(220)
Purchase of property, plant, and equipment	(547)
Dividends paid	(58)
Purchase of subsidiary (net of cash received)	(34)
Proceeds from long-term borrowings	377
Proceeds from sale of property, plant, and equipment	5
Purchase of intangible assets	(24)
Proceeds from sale of other investments	7
Movement in inventories, trade, and other receivables	32
Proceeds from other investing activities	214

Prepare the section "Cash flows from investing activities" for British Airways for the 2009 fiscal year. All items from that section are included in the preceding list, along with some items from other sections of the statement of cash flows. Net cash used for investing activities was £(257) million.

5-48 Noncash Investing and Financing Activities

The Gamecade Company operates a chain of video game arcades. Among Gamecade's activities in 20X0 were the following:

1. The firm traded four old video games to another amusement company for one new Ninja War game. The old games could have been sold for a total of $5,000 cash.
2. The company paid off $50,000 of long-term debt by paying $20,000 cash and signing a $30,000 6-month note payable.
3. The firm issued debt for $60,000 cash, all of which was used to purchase new games for its Northwest Arcade.

4. The company purchased the building in which one of its arcades was located by assuming the $100,000 mortgage on the structure and paying $20,000 cash.
5. Debt holders converted $85,000 of debt to common stock.
6. The firm refinanced debt by paying cash to buy back an old issue at its call price of $21,000 and issued new debt at a lower interest rate for $21,000.

Prepare a schedule of noncash investing and financing activities to accompany a statement of cash flows.

5-49 Statement of Cash Flows, Direct Method

Kansas Aerospace Company had cash and cash equivalents of $200 million on December 31, 2009. The following items are on the company's statement of cash flows ($ in millions) for the first 6 months of 2010:

Receipts from customers	$ 9,455
Interest paid, net	(140)
Capital expenditures for property and equipment	(1,710)
Purchase of treasury stock	(193)
Sales of marketable securities	191
Retirement of long-term debt	(160)
Payments to suppliers and employees	(7,499)
Issuance of common stock for employee stock plans	251
Dividend payments	(17)
Issuance of long-term debt	135
Other investing activity	(134)
Taxes paid	(167)

Prepare a statement of cash flows for the first 6 months of 2010 using the direct method. Include the balance of cash and cash equivalents at year-end 2009 and calculate the cash balance at June 30, 2010. Omit the schedule reconciling net income to net cash provided by operating activities and the schedule of noncash investing and financing activities.

5-50 Prepare a Statement of Cash Flows, Direct Method

(Alternate is 5-51.) Olympic Spas is a wholesale distributor of hot tubs. Its cash balance on December 31, 20X0, was $176,000, and net income for 20X1 was $312,000. Its 20X1 transactions affecting income or cash follow ($ in thousands):

a. Sales of $1,500 were all on credit. Cash collections from customers were $1,400.
b. The cost of items sold was $800. Purchases of inventory totaled $850; inventory and accounts payable were affected accordingly.
c. Cash payments on trade accounts payable totaled $815.
d. Accrued salaries and wages: total expense $190; cash payments, $200.
e. Depreciation was $45.
f. Interest expense, all paid in cash was $13.
g. Other expenses, all paid in cash totaled $100.
h. Income taxes accrued were $40; income taxes paid in cash were $35.
i. Plant and facilities were bought for $435 cash.
j. Long-term debt was issued for $110 cash.
k. Cash dividends of $41 were paid.

Prepare a statement of cash flows for 20X1 using the direct method for reporting cash flows from operating activities. Omit supporting schedules.

5-51 Prepare a Statement of Cash Flows, Direct Method

(Alternate is 5-50.) Yamaguchi Exports, Inc., is a wholesaler of Japanese goods. By the end of 20X0, the company's cash balance had dropped to ¥7 million, despite net income of ¥254 million in 20X0. Its transactions affecting income or cash in 20X0 were as follows (¥ in millions):

a. Sales were ¥2,510, all on credit. Cash collections from customers were ¥2,413.
b. The cost of items sold was ¥1,599.

c. Inventory increased by ¥56.

d. Cash payments on trade accounts payable were ¥1,658.

e. Payments to employees were ¥305; accrued wages payable decreased by ¥24.

f. Other operating expenses, all paid in cash, were ¥94.

g. Interest expense, all paid in cash, was ¥26.

h. Income tax expense was ¥105; cash payments for income taxes were ¥108.

i. Depreciation was ¥151.

j. A warehouse was acquired for ¥540 cash.

k. Equipment was sold for ¥47; original cost was ¥206, accumulated depreciation was ¥159.

l. The firm received ¥28 for issue of common stock.

m. Long-term debt was retired for ¥21 cash.

n. The company paid cash dividends of ¥98.

Prepare a statement of cash flows for 20X0 using the direct method for reporting cash flows from operating activities. Calculate the cash balance as of January 1, 20X0. Omit supporting schedules.

5-52 Prepare Statement of Cash Flows from Income Statement and Balance Sheet
(Alternate is 5-54.) During 20X1, Roberto Manufacturing Company (RMC) declared and paid cash dividends of $10,000. Late in the year, RMC bought new welding machinery for a cash cost of $125,000, financed partly by its first issue of long-term debt. Interest on the debt is payable annually. RMC sold several old machines for cash equal to their aggregate book value of $5,000. The company pays taxes in cash as incurred. The following data are in thousands:

Roberto Manufacturing Company
Income Statement for the
Year Ended December 31, 20X1

Sales		$470
Cost of sales		300
Gross margin		170
Salaries	$82	
Depreciation	40	
Cash operating expenses	15	
Interest	2	139
Income before taxes		31
Income taxes		8
Net income		$ 23

Roberto Manufacturing Company
Balance Sheets

	December 31 20X1	December 31 20X0	Increase (Decrease)
Assets			
Cash and cash equivalents	$105	$ 45	$ 60
Accounts receivable	45	60	(15)
Inventories	57	62	(5)
Total current assets	207	167	40
Fixed assets, net	190	110	80
Total assets	$397	$277	$120
Liabilities and Stockholders' Equity			
Accounts payable	$ 26	$ 21	$ 5
Interest payable	2	—	2
Long-term debt	100	—	100
Paid-in capital	220	220	—
Retained earnings	49	36	13
Total liabilities and stockholders' equity	$397	$277	$120

Prepare a statement of cash flows for 20X1. Use the direct method for reporting cash flows from operating activities. Omit supporting schedules. Assume that Roberto paid expense items in cash unless balance sheet changes indicate otherwise.

5-53 Statement of Cash Flows, Direct Method

The **J.M. Smucker Company** had net sales of $3,758 million from selling products such as jam (Smucker's), peanut butter (Jif), and vegetable oils (Crisco) for the year ending April 30, 2009. The income statement showed operating expenses of $3,307 million, other expenses of $55 million, and income taxes of $130 million. Assume that depreciation and amortization and other noncash expenses affect operating expenses and that other changes in current assets and liabilities affect other expenses. The company's statement of cash flows, prepared under the indirect method, contained the following items (where negative numbers represent cash outflows):

	(in millions)
Proceeds from long-term debt	$ 400
Dividends paid	(385)
Additions to property, plant, and equipment	(109)
Business acquired, net of cash acquired	(77)
Disposal of property, plant, and equipment	3
Net income	266
Depreciation and amortization	120
Other noncash expenses	57
Changes in operating assets and liabilities	
Increase in trade receivables	(79)
Decrease in inventories	35
Increase in accounts payable and accrued liabilities	68
Increase in income taxes payable	23
Other changes in current assets and liabilities, net	(45)

1. Assume that these are all the items in Smucker's cash flow statement. Prepare the statement of cash flows for J.M. Smucker using the direct method. Omit the schedule reconciling net income to net cash provided by operating activities.
2. Discuss the relation between operating cash flow and investing and financing needs.

5-54 Prepare Statement of Cash Flows from Income Statement and Balance Sheet

(Alternate is 5-52.) Jarez S.A. had the following income statement and balance sheet items (euro in millions):

Income Statement for the Year Ended December 31, 20X1	
Sales	€ 925
Cost of goods sold	(545)
Gross margin	€ 380
Operating expenses	(220)
Depreciation	(60)
Interest	(15)
Income before taxes	€ 85
Income taxes	(25)
Net income	€ 60
Cash dividends declared and paid	(30)
Total increase in retained earnings	€ 30

Balance Sheets

| | December 31 | | Increase |
	20X1	20X0	(Decrease)
Assets			
Cash	€ 30	€ 60	€ (30)
Accounts receivable	240	150	90
Inventories	450	350	100
Total current assets	720	560	160
Fixed assets, gross	890	715	175
Accumulated depreciation	(570)	(550)	(20)
Fixed assets, net	320	165	155
Total assets	€1,040	€725	€315
Liabilities and stockholders' equity			
Trade accounts payable	€ 520	€300	€220
Long-term debt	245	180	65
Stockholders' equity	275	245	30
Total liabilities and stockholders' equity	€1,040	€725	€315

During 20X1, Jarez purchased fixed assets for €315 million cash and sold fixed assets for their book value of €100 million. Operating expenses, interest, and taxes were paid in cash. No long-term debt was retired.

Prepare a statement of cash flows for 20X1. Use the direct method for reporting cash flows from operating activities. Omit supporting schedules.

5-55 Statement of Cash Flows, Direct Method, Interest Expense, Australia
CSR Limited is a leading supplier of building and construction materials headquartered in Sydney, Australia. The company's 2009 revenues were nearly A$3.5 billion, where A$ is the Australian dollar. The following items appeared in CSR's 2009 statement of cash flows (in millions), which it reports using the direct method:

Receipts from customers	A$ 3,693
Payments to suppliers and employees	(3,485)
Dividends and interest received	21
Other cash received from operating activities	49
Net cash from operating activities	214
Purchase of property, plant, and equipment	(476)
Proceeds from sale of property, plant, and equipment	169
Net repayments of borrowings	(72)
Dividends paid	(71)
Other investing activities	(11)
Income taxes paid	(64)
Net cash used in investing activities	(330)
Proceeds from issue of shares	343
Interest paid	(97)
Purchases of businesses, net of cash received	(12)
Net cash from financing activities	103
Net increase in cash	?

1. Prepare a statement of cash flows for CSR Limited using the direct method. Include the proper amount for the net increase in cash. One item, interest paid, is included in a different section of the statement than it would be on a U.S. statement of cash flows. Place it in the section that makes the cash flows in each section total to the amounts given.
2. What does the placement of interest paid tell you about the GAAP used by CSR Limited? That is, does it report under IFRS or U.S. GAAP? Where would the interest paid be shown in a statement of cash flows using the other GAAP (IFRS or U.S. GAAP)?
3. Explain why CSR places interest paid where it does. Also explain why interest paid might be placed in the alternative section you indicated in requirement 2.

5-56 Reconcile Net Income and Net Cash Provided by Operating Activities
(Alternate is 5-59.) Refer to Problem 5-50. Prepare a supporting schedule that reconciles net income to net cash provided by operating activities.

5-57 Cash Provided by Operations
Clorox Company is a leading producer of laundry additives, including Clorox liquid bleach. In the 9-month period ended March 31, 2009, net sales of $3,950 million produced net earnings of $367 million. To calculate net earnings, Clorox recorded $142 million in depreciation and amortization. Other items of revenue and expense not requiring cash decreased net earnings by $65 million. Dividends of $193 million were paid during the period. Among the changes in balance sheet accounts during the period were the following ($ in millions):

Accounts receivable	$ 21	Decrease
Inventories	42	Increase
Other current assets	20	Increase
Accounts payable and accrued liabilities	101	Decrease
Income taxes payable	9	Decrease

Compute the net cash provided by operating activities using the indirect method.

5-58 Cash Flows from Operating Activities, Indirect Method
Sumitomo Metal Industries, Ltd., is a leading diversified manufacturer of steel products. During the year ended March 31, 2008, Sumitomo earned ¥184 billion on revenues of approximately ¥1,745 billion (or almost $20 billion in the United States). The following summarized information relates to Sumitomo's statement of cash flows:

	(billions of yen)
Depreciation and amortization	¥104
Repayments of long-term debt	143
Proceeds from long-term debt	237
Other noncash revenues and expenses, net	25
Decrease in receivables	40
Increase in inventories	53
Other decreases in cash from operations due to changes in current assets and liabilities	21
Acquisition of property, plant, equipment and other assets	167
Increase in payables	1

Compute the net cash provided by operating activities using the indirect method. All the information necessary for that task is provided, together with some information related to other elements of the cash flow statement. Note that the format does not include parentheses to differentiate elements that increase cash from those that decrease cash, but the distinction should be clear from the captions (except for "Other noncash revenues and expenses, net," which is a net noncash revenue).

5-59 Reconcile Net Income and Net Cash Provided by Operating Activities
(Alternate is 5-56.) Refer to Problem 5-51. Prepare a supporting schedule to the statement of cash flows that reconciles net income to net cash provided by operating activities.

5-60 Indirect Method: Reconciliation Schedule in Body of Statement
Refer to Problem 5-52. Prepare a statement of cash flows that includes a reconciliation of net income to net cash provided by operating activities in the body of the statement.

5-61 Cash Flows, Indirect Method
The Chavez Company has the following balance sheet data ($ in millions):

	December 31				December 31		
	20X1	20X0	Change		20X1	20X0	Change
Current assets				Current liabilities			
Cash	$ 12	$ 21	$ (9)	(summarized)	$101	$ 26	$ 75
Receivables, net	53	15	38	Long-term debt	150	—	150
Inventories	94	50	44	Stockholders' equity	208	160	48
Total current assets	$159	$ 86	$ 73				
Plant assets (net of accumulated depreciation)	300	100	200	Total liabilities and			
Total assets	$459	$186	$273	stockholders' equity	$459	$186	$273

Net income for 20X1 was $60 million. Net cash inflow from operating activities was $93 million. Cash dividends paid were $12 million. Depreciation was $40 million. Fixed assets were purchased for $240 million, $150 million of which was financed via the issuance of long-term debt outright for cash.

Jorge Chavez, the president and majority stockholder of the Chavez Company, was a superb operating executive. He was imaginative and aggressive in marketing, and ingenious and creative in production. However, he had little patience with financial matters. After examining the most recent balance sheet and income statement, he muttered, "We've enjoyed 10 years of steady growth; 20X1 was our most profitable ever. Despite such profitability, we're in the worst cash position in our history. Just look at those current liabilities in relation to our available cash! This whole picture of the more you make, the poorer you get, just does not make sense. These statements must be cockeyed."

1. Prepare a statement of cash flows for 20X1 using the indirect method.
2. By using the statement of cash flows and other information, write a short memorandum to Chavez, explaining why there is such a squeeze on cash.

5-62 Prepare Statement of Cash Flows
The Goldmark Company has assembled the accompanying (a) balance sheets, and (b) statement of income and retained earnings for 20X4.

Goldmark Company
Balance Sheets as of December 31 (in millions)

	20X4	20X3	Change
Assets			
Cash	$ 4	$ 20	$(16)
Accounts receivable	52	33	19
Inventory	70	50	20
Prepaid general expenses	4	3	1
Plant assets, net	207	150	57
	$337	$256	$ 81
Liabilities and shareholders' equity			
Accounts payable for merchandise	$ 74	$ 60	$ 14
Accrued tax payable	3	2	1
Long-term debt	54	—	54
Capital stock	100	100	—
Retained earnings	106	94	12
	$337	$256	$ 81

Goldmark Company
Statement of Income and Retained Earnings for the Year Ended
December 31, 20X4 (in millions)

Sales		$280
Less: Cost of goods sold		
Inventory, December 31, 20X3	$ 50	
Purchases	185	
Cost of goods available for sale	$235	
Inventory, December 31, 20X4	70	165
Gross profit		$115
Less: Other expenses		
General expense	$ 51	
Depreciation	40	
Taxes	10	101
Net income		$ 14
Dividends declared and paid		2
Net income of the period retained		$ 12
Retained earnings, December 31, 20X3		94
Retained earnings, December 31, 20X4		$106

On December 30, 20X4, Goldmark paid $103 million in cash to acquire a new plant to expand operations. This was partly financed by an issue of long-term debt for $54 million in cash. Plant assets were sold for their book value of $6 million during 20X4. Because net income was $14 million, the highest in the company's history, Isaac Goldmark, the chief executive officer, was distressed by the company's extremely low cash balance.

1. Prepare a statement of cash flows for 20X4 using the direct method for reporting cash flows from operating activities.
2. Prepare a schedule that reconciles net income to net cash provided by operating activities.
3. What is revealed by the statement of cash flows? Does it help you reduce Mr. Goldmark's distress? Why? Briefly explain to Mr. Goldmark why cash has decreased even though net income was $14 million.

5-63 Depreciation and Cash Flows

(Alternate is 5-44.) The following condensed income statement and reconciliation schedule are from the annual report of Nguen Company ($ in millions):

Sales	$410
Expenses	350
Net income	$ 60

Reconciliation Schedule of Net Income to Net
Cash Provided by Operating Activities

Net income	$ 60
Add noncash expenses: Depreciation	25
Deduct net increase in noncash operating working capital	(17)
Net cash provided by operating activities	$ 68

A shareholder has suggested that the company switch from straight-line to accelerated depreciation on its annual report to shareholders, maintaining that this will increase the cash flow provided by operating activities. According to the stockholder's calculations, using accelerated methods would increase depreciation to $48 million, an increase of $23 million; net cash flow from operating activities would then be $91 million.

1. Suppose Nguen Company adopts the accelerated depreciation method proposed. Compute net income and net cash flow from operating activities. Ignore income taxes.
2. Use your answer to requirement 1 to prepare a response to the shareholder.

5-64 Balance Sheet Equation

(Alternate is 5-65.) Refer to Problem 5-62, requirement 1. Support the operating section of your cash flow statement by using a form of the balance sheet equation. (See Exhibit 5-8.) Use the equation Cash = Liabilities + Retained Earnings + Noncash Assets, and show how the direct method and indirect method statements arrive at the same total cash provided by operating activities.

5-65 Balance Sheet Equation

(Alternate is 5-64.) Examine the data for Olympic Spas, Inc., in Problem 5-50. Support the operating section of your cash flow statement by using a form of the balance sheet equation. (See Exhibit 5-8.) Use the equation Cash = Liabilities + Retained Earnings + Noncash Assets, and show how the direct method and indirect method statements arrive at the same total cash provided by operating activities.

5-66 Comprehensive Statement of Cash Flows

During the past 30 years, Anchorage Toys, Inc., has grown from a single-location specialty toy store into a chain of stores selling a wide range of children's products. Its activities in 20X1 included the following:

a. The company purchased 40% of the stock of Missoula Toy Company for $3,848,000 cash.
b. The organization issued $1,906,000 in long-term debt; $850,000 of the proceeds was used to retire debt that became due in 20X1 and was listed on the books at $850,000.
c. The firm purchased property, plant, and equipment for $1,986,000 cash, and sold property with a book value of $500,000 for $500,000 cash.
d. The company signed a note payable for the purchase of new equipment; the obligation was listed at $516,000.
e. Executives exercised stock options for 8,000 shares of common stock, paying cash of $170,000.
f. On December 30, 20X1, the firm bought Bellingham Musical Instruments Company by issuing common stock with a market value of $305,000.
g. The company issued common stock for $3,300,000 cash.
h. The firm withdrew $800,000 cash from a money market fund that was considered a cash equivalent.
i. The company bought $249,000 of treasury stock to hold for future exercise of stock options.
j. Long-term debt of $960,000 was converted to common stock.

k. Selected results for the year follow:

Net income	$ 798,000
Depreciation and amortization	615,000
Increase in inventory	72,000
Increase in accounts receivable	31,000
Increase in accounts and wages payable	7,000
Increase in taxes payable	35,000
Interest expense	144,000
Increase in accrued interest payable	15,000
Sales	9,839,000
Cash dividends received from investments	152,000
Cash paid to suppliers and employees	8,074,000
Cash dividends paid	240,000
Cash paid for taxes	390,000

Prepare a statement of cash flows for 20X1 using the direct method. Include a schedule that reconciles net income to net cash provided by operating activities. Also include a schedule of noncash investing and financing activities.

5-67 Statement of Cash Flows, Direct and Indirect Methods
Nordstrom, Inc., the Seattle-based fashion retailer, had the following income statement for the year ended January 31, 2009 ($ in millions):

Net sales		$8,573
Costs and expenses		
Cost of sales	$5,417	
Selling, general, and administrative	2,386	
Interest expense	131	
Less: Other income	(9)	
Total costs and expenses		$7,925
Earnings before income taxes		$ 648
Income taxes		247
Net earnings		$ 401

The company's net cash provided by operating activities, prepared using the indirect method, was as follows ($ in millions):

Net earnings	$401
Adjustments to reconcile net earnings to net cash provided by operating activities	
Depreciation, amortization, and other noncash expenses	445
Changes in	
Accounts receivable	(93)
Merchandise inventories	53
Prepaid expenses	9
Accounts payable	16
Accrued salaries, wages, and related benefits	(54)
Other accrued liabilities	147
Income taxes payable	(76)
Net cash provided by operating activities	$848

Prepare a statement showing the net cash provided by operating activities using the direct method. Assume that Nordstrom received all "other income" in cash and that prepaid expenses, accrued salaries, wages and related benefits, and other accrued liabilities relate to selling, general, and administrative expenses, as do all components of depreciation, amortization, and other noncash expenses.

5-68 Free Cash Flow

A condensed version of the Kellogg Company statement of cash flows appears in Exhibit 5-16. Use that statement to answer the following two questions.

1. What was Kellogg's free cash flow for each of the 3 years shown?
2. What does the free cash flow tell us about Kellogg's ability to generate sufficient cash flow from operations to cover ongoing investing activities and pay dividends to its shareholders?

5-69 Miscellaneous Cash Flow Questions

McDonald's Corporation is a well-known provider of food services around the world. McDonald's statements of cash flows for 2008 and 2007 are reproduced with a few slight modifications as Exhibit 5-17. Use that statement to answer the following questions:

1. In the financing activities section, all parentheses for 2008 have been removed. Which numbers should be put in parentheses?

(millions)	2008	2007	2006
Operating Activities			
Net earnings	$1,148	$ 1,103	$1,004
Items in net earnings not requiring (providing) cash			
Depreciation and amortization	375	372	353
Other noncash expenses	276	114	191
Changes in operating assets and liabilities	(81)	10	(39)
Other	(451)	(96)	(99)
Net cash provided by operating activities	1,267	1,503	1,410
Investing Activities			
Additions to properties	(461)	(472)	(453)
Acquisitions, net of cash acquired	(213)	(128)	—
Property disposals	13	3	9
Other	(20)	(4)	(1)
Net cash used in investing activities	(681)	(601)	(445)
Financing Activities			
Reductions of notes payable	(316)	(1,209)	(565)
Issuances of notes payable	190	804	1,065
Issuances of long-term debt	756	750	—
Reductions of long-term debt	(468)	(802)	(85)
Net issuances of common stock	175	163	218
Common stock repurchases	(650)	(650)	(650)
Cash dividends	(495)	(475)	(450)
Other	28	631	(322)
Net cash used in financing activities	(780)	(788)	(789)
Increase (decrease) in cash and cash equivalents	$ (194)	$ 114	$ 176

EXHIBIT 5-16

Kellogg Company and Subsidiaries

Consolidated Statement of Cash Flows, Year Ended December 31

EXHIBIT 5-17

McDonald's Corporation

Consolidated Statement of Cash Flows, Years Ended December 31

(in millions)	2008	2007
Operating Activities		
Net income	$4,313	$ 2,395
Adjustments to reconcile to cash provided by operations		
Depreciation and amortization	1,208	1,214
Other noncash expenses	150	1,303
Changes in operating working capital items		
Accounts receivable	16	(100)
Inventories, prepaid expenses and other current assets	(11)	(30)
Accounts payable	(40)	(37)
Income taxes	196	72
Other accrued liabilities	85	59
Cash provided by operations	5,917	4,876
Investing Activities		
Property and equipment expenditures	2,136	(1,947)
Purchases of restaurant businesses	147	(229)
Sales of restaurant businesses and property	479	365
Other	179	661
Cash used for investing activities	1,625	(1,150)
Financing Activities		
Net short-term borrowings (repayments)	267	101
Long-term financing issuances	3,477	2,117
Long-term financing repayments	2,698	(1,645)
Treasury stock purchases	3,919	(3,943)
Common stock dividends	1,823	(1,766)
Other	582	1,140
Cash used for financing activities	4,114	(3,996)
Effect of exchange rates on cash and cash equivalents	(96)	123
Cash and equivalents increase (decrease)	A	(147)
Cash and equivalents beginning of year	B	2,128
Cash and equivalents at end of year	$ C	$ 1,981

2. In the investing activities section, all parentheses for 2008 have been removed. Which numbers should be put in parentheses?

3. The 2008 values for the change in cash and cash equivalents and for beginning and end-of-year balances have been omitted and replaced with the letters A, B, and C. Provide the proper values for these three missing numbers.

4. Suppose the balance in Retained Earnings at December 31, 2007, was $26,464 million. Compute the Retained-Earnings balance at December 31, 2008. Assume that all dividends declared were paid in cash in 2008.

5. Comment on the relation between cash flow from operations and cash used for investing activities.

5-70 Interpretation of the Statement of Cash Flows and Ethics
Swifto, Inc., produces swim wear. The company's peak year was 2006. Since then, both sales and profits have fallen. The following information is from the company's 2009 annual report ($ in thousands):

	2009	2008	2007
Net income	$1,500	$4,500	$7,500
Accounts receivable (end of year)	900	1,800	6,000
Inventory (end of year)	1,050	2,100	2,850
Net cash provided by operations	675	1,050	2,250
Capital expenditures	900	1,050	1,350
Proceeds from sales of fixed assets	2,700	1,500	2,250

During 2010, short-term loans of $9 million became due. Swifto paid off only $2.25 million and was able to extend the terms on the other $6.75 million. Accounts payable continued at a very low level in 2010, and the company maintained a large investment in corporate equity securities, enough to generate a $3,000,000 addition to net income and $900,000 of cash dividends in 2010. Swifto neither paid dividends nor issued stock or bonds in 2010. Its 2010 statement of cash flows was as follows:

Swifto, Inc.
Statement of Cash Flows for the Year Ended
December 31, 2010 (in thousands)

Cash flows from operating activities		
Net income		$ 1,650
Adjustments to reconcile net income to net cash provided by operating activities		
Add back non-cash expenses:		
Depreciation and amortization		600
Deduct non-cash revenues:		
Investment revenue from equity investments, less $900 of dividends received*		(2,100)
Net decrease in accounts receivable		150
Net decrease in inventory		225
Net cash provided by operating activities		$ 525
Cash flows from investing activities		
Purchase of fixed assets	$ (600)	
Insurance proceeds on building fire	3,000	
Sale of plant assets	3,750	
Purchase of corporate equity securities	(2,250)	
Net cash provided by investing activities		3,900
Cash flows from financing activities		
Principal payments on short-term debt to banks	$(2,250)	
Purchase of treasury stock	(900)	
Net cash used for financing activities		(3,150)
Net increase in cash		1,275
Cash, December 31, 2009		1,800
Cash, December 31, 2010		$ 3,075

*$3,000 of revenue from equity investments was included in income. $900 of this was received in the form of dividends, so $2,100 of the income was not received in cash.

1. Interpret the statement of cash flows for Swifto.
2. Describe any ethical issues relating to the strategy and financial disclosures of Swifto.

Collaborative Learning Exercise

5-71 Items in the Statement of Cash Flows

Form groups of four to six students each. Each member of the group should select a different company, find its statement of cash flows for a recent year, and make a list of the items included in each section of the statement: operating, investing, and financing activities. Be ready to explain the nature of each item.

1. As a group, make a comprehensive list of all items the companies listed under cash flows from operating activities. Identify those that are essentially the same but simply differ in terminology, and call them a single item. For each item, explain why and how it affects cash flows from operating activities. Note whether any of the companies selected use the direct method for reporting cash flows from operating activities. (Most companies use the indirect method, despite the fact that the FASB and IASB prefer the direct method.) If any use the direct method, separate the items listed under the direct method from those listed under the indirect method.
2. Make another comprehensive list of all items listed under cash flows from investing activities. Again, combine those that are essentially identical and differ only in terminology. For each item, explain why and how it affects cash flows from investing activities.
3. Make a third comprehensive list, this time including all items listed under cash flows from financing activities. Again, combine those that are essentially identical and differ only in terminology. For each item, explain why and how it affects cash flows from financing activities.
4. Reconvene as a class. For each of the three sections on the statement of cash flows, have groups sequentially add one item to the list of items included in the statement, simultaneously explaining why it is included in that section. Then identify the items that appear on nearly all cash flow statements and those that are relatively rare.

Analyzing and Interpreting Financial Statements

5-72 Financial Statement Research

Identify an industry and select two companies within that industry.

1. Determine whether cash flow from operations is stable through time.
2. Relate cash flow from operations to investing and dividend payment needs.
3. Compare cash flow from operations to net income. Explain why they differ.

5-73 Analyzing Starbucks' Financial Statements

Find Starbucks' 2009 statement of cash flows either on Starbucks' Web site or using the SEC's Edgar database.

1. Did Starbucks' net cash provided by operating activities increase or decrease between the year ended September 28, 2008, and the year ended September 27, 2009? By how much? What two items contributed most to the change?
2. Did Starbucks' net cash used by investing activities increase or decrease between the year ended September 28, 2008, and the year ended September 27, 2009? By how much? What was the major cause of the change?
3. Explain to someone who's not an accountant what Starbucks did with the $1,389.0 million of cash generated by operating activities during the year ended September 27, 2009.
4. Suppose a friend of yours commented, "Starbucks must have poor financial management. It made more than $390 million in the year ended September 27, 2009, and it generated $1,389 million in cash from operations, yet it paid no dividends. It's shareholders got nothing." Respond to your friend's comment.

5-74 Analyzing Financial Statements Using the Internet: Nike

Go to www.nikebiz.com and select Investors to locate **Nike**'s most current financial information.

1. Take a look at Nike's Condensed Consolidated Statement of Cash Flows. Does Nike use the direct or indirect method? How can you tell?
2. Locate Management's Discussion and Analysis. Look under the section titled Liquidity and Capital Resources. What does management have to say about cash provided by operations?
3. Which is larger—cash provided (or used) by operations or net income for the period? Why is the cash provided by operations different from the amount of net income for the year?
4. Why does Nike add depreciation to net income in the operating activities section?
5. What were the primary uses of cash by investing activities in the most recent fiscal period?
6. What were the primary providers of cash or uses of cash by financing activities in the most recent fiscal period?

6

Accounting for Sales

LEARNING OBJECTIVES

After studying this chapter, you should be able to:

1 Recognize revenue items at the proper time on the income statement.

2 Account for cash and credit sales.

3 Compute and interpret sales returns and allowances, sales discounts, and bank credit card sales.

4 Manage cash and explain its importance to the company.

5 Estimate and interpret uncollectible accounts receivable balances.

6 Assess the level of accounts receivable.

7 Develop and explain internal control procedures.

8 Prepare a bank reconciliation (Appendix 6).

Not many companies seek the permission of the Central Intelligence Agency (CIA) when naming products. Yet that is precisely what System Development Laboratories did in 1977 when it created a new type of database while working on a confidential project for the U.S. government. Called the "Oracle," this new relational database structure became the world's most popular form, and for the company, now called Oracle Corporation, it was an explosive sales success story. Revenues for 2009 exceeded $23 billion for software sales and related services worldwide.

Recording and managing this sales revenue is important to Oracle's success. For every sale generated, the company must either collect cash or record an account receivable from the customer. The company must then collect the accounts receivable so it has adequate cash to continue its operations.

Managing accounts receivable and collecting cash are key activities for Oracle. The faster the company collects the cash, the less it will need to

In just over 30 years Oracle grew from a small company to one with the huge campus pictured here. Oracle is the world's largest enterprise software company. Its revenues exceeded $23 billion in 2009.

borrow (and the less interest it will pay). However, many customers need to obtain credit from their suppliers. Companies that push to collect cash too quickly may drive potential customers elsewhere. On average, it took Oracle 75 days to convert sales to cash in 2009. Oracle, like many other companies such as the major automobile firms, has a finance subsidiary that loans money to customers so that its customers can stretch payments over years. Ford Credit and General Motors Acceptance Corporation often provide low interest car loans. This is an important factor supporting auto sales, especially in a difficult market such as 2008–2009.

In a recent analysis of Oracle, a security analyst presented a prominent graph displaying the revenue growth in each part of Oracle's business. Such trends in revenue help analysts to understand what happened in the last year or the last quarter and to predict what may occur in the future. Recording sales revenue in the right time period is essential to measuring the rate of increase or decrease. For Oracle, whose company name means "source of wisdom," efficient and accurate measurement of revenues and tracking of accounts receivables is smart business. ●

Recognition of Sales Revenue

Why is the timing of revenue recognition so important? It is critical to the measurement of net income in two ways. First, it directly increases net income by the amount of the revenue. Second, it reduces net income by triggering the recognition of certain expenses—for example, companies report the cost of the items sold in the same period in which they recognize the related revenue.

Changes in revenues and net income are especially important because of the profound effects they have on stock prices. For example, the Business First box shows how growing earnings drove increases in Intel's stock price in the 1990s and stagnant earnings growth has arrested the increase in stock price in the last decade. Managers are also interested in sales and earnings growth because they often receive higher salaries or greater bonuses for increasing sales and net income. Therefore, they may prefer to recognize sales revenue as soon as possible. Owners and potential investors, however, want to be sure the economic benefits of the sale are certain before recognizing revenue. To ensure this, both IFRS and U.S. GAAP require a two-pronged test for revenue recognition: (1) A company must have delivered the goods or services to its customer, that is, it has *earned* the revenue; and (2) it must have received cash or an asset virtually assured of being converted into cash, that is, it must have *realized* the revenue.

Most companies recognize revenue at the point of sale. Suppose you buy a compact disc at a local music store. The sale meets both revenue recognition tests at the time of purchase. You receive the merchandise, and the store receives cash, a check, or a credit card slip. Because the store can readily convert both checks and credit card slips to cash, it recognizes revenue at the point of sale regardless of which of these three methods of payment you use.

However, the two revenue recognition tests are not always met at the same time. In such cases, we recognize revenue only when both tests have been met. Consider magazine subscriptions. The realization test is met when the publisher receives cash for a subscription. However, the publisher does not earn revenues until it delivers the magazines. Therefore, we delay revenue recognition until the time of delivery.

INTERPRETING FINANCIAL STATEMENTS

Consider two types of sales by Starbucks, over-the-counter sales and sales of "stored value" cards, such as gift cards. When would Starbucks recognize the revenue from each?

Answer

Starbucks recognizes revenues from over-the-counter sales at the point of sale—as it collects cash or records a credit card payment for the merchandise. In contrast, when it sells a stored value card, Starbucks initially records a liability "deferred revenue." It then recognizes revenue when customers use their cards at retail stores. Only then has Starbucks earned the revenue.

Sometimes accountants must use judgment to decide whether a sale meets the recognition criteria. A classic example is accounting for long-term contracts. Suppose Oracle signs a $40 million consulting contract with the U.S. government for designing and implementing an ERP (Enterprise Resource Planning) system for a branch of Homeland Security. Oracle signs the contract and immediately begins work on January 2, 20X0. The expected completion date is December 31, 20X1. The government will pay Oracle upon completion of the project. Oracle expects to complete one-half of the project each year. When should Oracle record the $40 million of revenue on its income statement?

The most common answer is that Oracle earns one-half of the revenue each year, so it should record $20 million of the revenue annually. Generally, companies can count on the government and major corporations to make payments on their contracts. Therefore, they can recognize revenues on such contracts as they perform the work. Because payment is virtually certain, the company realizes revenues as it earns them. Using this **percentage of completion method**, we recognize revenue on long-term contracts as production occurs, and under the matching principle we also recognize the associated expenses. When Oracle recognizes one-half of the revenue, it also recognizes one-half of the expected expenses. In the United States the percentage of completion method is appropriate only if progress measures are dependable, contract obligations are explicit, and both seller and buyer are expected to meet their obligations. If the project does not meet these criteria, especially if there is great uncertainty about whether the parties will meet the obligations of the contract, companies reporting under U.S. GAAP (but not IFRS) would delay recognition of both revenue and related expenses until completion of the contract. The IASB and FASB are currently trying to reconcile differences in revenue recognition, and it is likely that differences such as this one will disappear in the near future.

percentage of completion method

Method of recognizing revenue on long-term contracts as production occurs.

Measurement of Sales Revenue

After deciding *when to recognize* revenue, accountants must determine *how to measure* it. To measure revenue, accountants approximate the net realizable value of the asset inflow from the customer. That is, they measure revenue in terms of the cash-equivalent value of the asset received. A cash sale is simplest—it increases Sales Revenue, an income statement account, and increases Cash, a balance sheet account, by the amount of the cash payment. Consider a $100 sale:

OBJECTIVE 2

Account for cash and credit sales.

Cash	100	
Sales revenue		100

Accountants record a credit sale on open account much like a cash sale, except that it increases the balance sheet account Accounts Receivable instead of Cash:

Accounts receivable	100	
Sales revenue		100

Measuring revenue is more complex when the cash-equivalent value of the asset received is not equal to the original sales price. When might this happen? One case is when a company receives goods or services instead of cash for a sale. In such a situation, the company must estimate the cash-equivalent value of the goods or services received. Even when a sale is for cash, the cash-equivalent value may be less than the nominal amount of the sale. For example, merchants may give discounts for prompt payment or for high-volume purchases. Or sometimes the customer is unable or unwilling to pay the full amount owed.

When recognizing and measuring revenue, it is important to distinguish between gross sales and net sales. **Gross sales** is the total amount of sales before deducting returns, allowances, and discounts. **Net sales** is the result after deducting such items. We will next identify and examine returns, allowances, and discounts.

Merchandise Returns and Allowances

Suppose a store recognizes revenue for a given sale at the point of that sale, but later the customer returns the merchandise. The purchaser may be unhappy with the product's color, size, style, or quality, or he or she simply may have a change of heart. The store calls these **sales returns**; the customer calls them **purchase returns**. Such merchandise returns are minor for manufacturers and wholesalers, but they are major for retail department stores. For instance, returns of 12% of gross sales are not abnormal for stores such as Nordstrom or Macy's.

Sometimes, instead of returning merchandise, the customer demands a reduction of the original selling price. For example, a customer may complain about scratches on a household appliance or about buying a pair of shoes for $40 on Wednesday and seeing the same item on sale for $29 on Thursday. Sellers often settle such complaints by granting a **sales allowance**, which we treat as a reduction of the original selling price (the purchaser calls this a **purchase allowance**).

Companies deduct both sales returns and sales allowances from gross sales to determine net sales. Instead of reducing the revenue (or sales) account directly, managers of retail stores typically use a contra account, Sales Returns and Allowances, which combines both returns and allowances in a single account. Managers use a contra account to watch changes in the level of returns and allowances. For instance, a change in the percentage of returns in fashion merchandise may signal changes in customer tastes. Similarly, sellers of fashion or fad merchandise may find tracking of sales returns to be especially useful in assessing the quality of products and services from various suppliers. When sales figures determine commissions or bonuses, managers must know which sales personnel have especially high rates of sales returns or allowances. Because returns happen after the sales, managers separately track returns and allowances to avoid going back and changing the original entries for the sale—a messy and unreliable process.

How does a retailer adjust gross sales for sales returns and allowances? Suppose your local outlet of The Disney Store has $900,000 gross sales on credit and $80,000 sales returns and allowances. The analysis of transactions would show the following:

	A	=	L	+	SE
Credit sales on open account	+900,000 [Increase Accounts Receivable]	=			+900,000 [Increase Sales]
Returns and allowances	−80,000 [Decrease Accounts Receivable]	=			−80,000 [Increase Sales Returns and Allowances]

---

gross sales
The total amount of sales before deducting returns, allowances, and discounts.

net sales
The total amount of sales after deducting returns, allowances, and discounts.

OBJECTIVE 3

Compute and interpret sales returns and allowances, sales discounts, and bank credit card sales.

sales returns (purchase returns)
Merchandise returned by the customer.

sales allowance (purchase allowance)
Reduction of the original selling price.

The journal entries (without explanations) are as follows:

Accounts receivable	900,000	
Sales		900,000
Sales returns and allowances	80,000	
Accounts receivable		80,000

The income statement would begin as follows:

Gross sales	$900,000
Deduct: Sales returns and allowances	80,000
Net sales	$820,000
or	
Sales, net of $80,000 returns and allowances	$820,000

Managers react differently to this information than they would to knowing only that net sales were $820,000. They easily see that about 9% of the company's sales are either being returned or lost through price reductions. Then they can ask the following questions: How has this pattern changed through time? What can we do to reduce the extra service costs we incur to handle these special transactions? Should we modify our inventory selections or our inventory levels?

Cash and Trade Discounts

In addition to returns and allowances, cash and trade discounts also reduce reported sales amounts. **Trade discounts** are reductions to the gross selling price for a particular class of customers. An example is a discount for large-volume purchases. The seller might not offer a discount on the first $10,000 of merchandise purchased per year, but a 2% discount on the next $10,000 worth of purchases and a discount of 3% on all sales in excess of $20,000. The gross sales revenue recognized from a trade discount sale is the price received after deducting the discount. Thus, a trade discount is simply a reduction in the gross sales price.

trade discounts
Reductions to the gross selling price for a particular class of customers.

Companies set trade discount terms to be competitive in industries where such discounts are common or to encourage certain customer behavior. For example, manufacturers with seasonal products (gardening supplies, snow shovels, fans, Christmas gifts, and so on) might offer price discounts on early orders and deliveries to smooth out production throughout the year and to minimize the manufacturer's cost of storing the inventory. In deciding to accept early delivery, the buyer must weigh the storage costs it will incur against the reduced price the discount provides.

In contrast to trade discounts, companies deduct **cash discounts**, rewards for prompt payment, from gross sales to get net sales. Sellers quote the terms of the discount in various ways on the invoice:

cash discounts
Reductions of invoice prices awarded for prompt payment.

Credit Terms	Meaning
n/30	The full billed price (net price) is due on the thirtieth day after the invoice date.
1/5, n/30	A 1% discount can be taken for payment within 5 days of the invoice date; otherwise, the full billed price is due in 30 days.
15 E.O.M.	The full price is due within 15 days after the end of the month of sale; an invoice dated December 20 is due January 15.

For example, suppose a manufacturer sells $30,000 of computer equipment to Oracle on terms 2/10, n/60. Therefore, Oracle may remit $30,000 less a cash discount of (0.02 × $30,000), or ($30,000 − $600) = $29,400, if it makes payment within 10 days after the invoice date.

Otherwise, it must pay the full $30,000 within 60 days. The manufacturer would account for this transaction as follows, using entry 2 if Oracle pays within 10 days and entry 3 if it pays the full amount in 60 days:

	A	= L +	SE
1. Sell at terms of 2/10, n/60	+ 30,000 ⌈ Increase ⌉ ⌊ Accounts Receivable ⌋	=	+30,000 ⌈ Increase ⌉ ⌊ Sales ⌋
Followed by either 2 or 3			
2. Either collect $29,400 ($30,000 less 2%)	+ 29,400 ⌈ Increase ⌉ ⌊ Cash ⌋ −30,000 ⌈ Decrease ⌉ ⌊ Accounts Receivable ⌋	=	−600 ⌈ Increase ⌉ Cash Discounts ⌊ on Sales ⌋
or 3. Collect $30,000	+ 30,000 ⌈ Increase ⌉ ⌊ Cash ⌋ −30,000 ⌈ Decrease ⌉ ⌊ Accounts Receivable ⌋	=	(No effect)

The journal entries follow:

```
1. Accounts receivable  . . . . . . . . . . . . . . . . . . .    30,000
       Sales  . . . . . . . . . . . . . . . . . . . . . . . . .             30,000
2. Cash . . . . . . . . . . . . . . . . . . . . . . . . . . . .    29,400
       Cash discounts on sales  . . . . . . . . . . . . . . .       600
           Accounts receivable  . . . . . . . . . . . . . . .             30,000
   OR
3. Cash . . . . . . . . . . . . . . . . . . . . . . . . . . . .    30,000
       Accounts receivable  . . . . . . . . . . . . . . .                 30,000
```

Cash discounts encourage prompt payment and thus reduce the seller's need for cash. Early collection also reduces the risk of bad debts. Moreover, favorable credit terms with attractive cash discounts are a way to compete with other sellers.

Should purchasers take cash discounts? The answer is usually yes, but the decision depends on interest rates. Suppose Oracle decides to pay $30,000 in 60 days, not $29,400 in 10 days. It has the use of $29,400 for an extra 50 days (60 days − 10 days) for an "interest" payment of $600. If Oracle could borrow the $29,400 from the bank at a 10% annual interest rate, the interest cost for 50 days on $29,400 is ($29,400 × 10%) × (50 ÷ 365) = $403. It is ($600 − $403) = $197 cheaper to borrow the money from the bank. If the company does not have the cash to pay now, it should borrow the money in order to take the cash discount.

You could also calculate the annual interest rate implicit in the cash discount. The rate is ($600 ÷ $29,400) = 2.04% for the 50 days. During a year, there are (365 days ÷ 50 days) = 7.3 periods of 50 days. Thus, the annual rate is (2.04% per period × 7.3 periods per year) = 14.9%. Most well-managed companies, such as Oracle, can borrow for less than 14.9% interest per year, so they design their accounting systems to always take advantage of cash discounts. Usage of cash discounts varies through time and from one industry to another. You may be familiar with some gas stations that offer a lower price for cash payment, whereas other stations do not.

Why might a manager elect to pass up cash discounts? If a company's credit rating is poor, it may have trouble borrowing at interest rates lower than the rate implied by the cash discount. Managers in such companies should pass up the discount and pay only when the supplier requires payment.

Recording Charge Card Transactions

In a sense, companies offer cash discounts when they accept charge cards such as VISA, MasterCard, and American Express. Why? These credit card companies charge retailers a fee, and the retailers receive an amount less than the listed sales price. Why do retailers accept these cards? There are three major reasons: (1) to attract credit customers who would otherwise shop elsewhere, (2) to get cash immediately instead of waiting for customers to pay in due course, and (3) to avoid the cost of tracking, billing, and collecting customers' accounts.

Most large retailers deposit credit card charges in their bank accounts immediately via electronic transmissions, and those who still use paper charge slips generally deposit them daily (just like cash). The services of a credit card company cost money (in the form of service charges on every credit sale), and companies deduct this cost from gross sales in calculating net sales revenue. Card companies' service charges are typically from 1% to 4% of gross sales, with the large-volume retailers bearing the lowest cost as a percentage of sales. The arrangement for one large-volume retailer was 4.3 cents per transaction plus 1.08% of the gross sales using charge cards.

Suppose VISA charges a company a straight 3% of sales for its credit card services. Credit sales of $10,000 will result in cash of only [$10,000 − (0.03 × $10,000)] = $9,700. Managers usually report the $300 amount separately for control purposes:

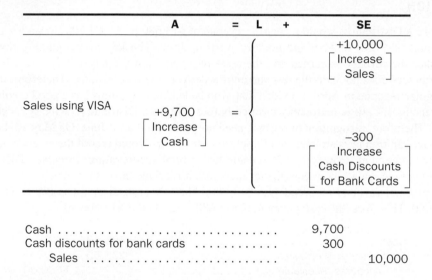

Cash		9,700	
Cash discounts for bank cards		300	
Sales			10,000

By accounting for these cash discounts separately, managers can continuously evaluate whether the costs they incur are justified.

Accounting for Net Sales Revenue

Because we record cash discounts and sales returns and allowances as deductions from Gross Sales, a detailed income statement might contain multiple elements as follows (numbers assumed):

Gross sales		$1,000
Deduct:		
Sales returns and allowances	270	
Cash discounts on sales	20	290
Net sales		$ 710

Reports to shareholders typically omit details and show only net revenues. For example, Starbucks reports "total net revenue" of $9,774.6 million on its 2009 income statement. Some companies separate revenue into categories. For example, Oracle shows software revenues separately from service revenues, and Starbucks shows revenue from company-owned retail stores separately from revenue from licensing and foodservice activities.

Summary Problem for Your Review

PROBLEM

Carlos Lopez, marketing manager for Fireplace Distributors, sold 12 wood stoves to Woodside Condominiums, Inc. The sales contract was signed on April 27, 20X1. The list price of each wood stove was $1,200, but Lopez allowed a 5% quantity discount. He also offered a cash discount of 2% of the amount owed if Woodside paid by June 10. Fireplace Distributors delivered the wood stoves on May 10 and received the proper payment on June 9.

1. How much revenue should Fireplace Distributors recognize in April, in May, and in June? Explain.
2. Suppose Fireplace Distributors has a separate account titled "Cash Discounts on Sales." What journal entries would it make on June 9 when it receives the cash payment?
3. Suppose Fireplace Distributors has another account titled "Sales Returns and Allowances." Suppose further that one of the wood stoves had a scratch and Fireplace Distributors allowed Woodside to deduct $100 from the total amount due. What journal entries would Fireplace Distributors make on June 9 when it receives the cash payment?

SOLUTION

1. Fireplace Distributors would recognize revenue of $13,680 [(12 × $1,200) less a 5% quantity discount of $720] in May and none in April or June. The key to recognizing revenue is whether the revenue is earned and the asset received from the buyer is realized. Fireplace Distributors does not earn the revenue until it delivers the merchandise. Therefore, it cannot recognize revenue in April. Provided that Woodside Condominiums has a good credit rating, the receipt of cash is reasonably ensured before Fireplace Distributors actually receives the cash. Therefore, recognition of revenue need not be delayed until June. On May 10, both revenue recognition tests are met, and Fireplace Distributors would record the revenue on May's income statement. However, if Woodside had a poor credit rating, Fireplace Distributors would not recognize and record the revenue until it received the cash in June.
2. The original revenue recorded was $13,680. The 2% cash discount is 2% × $13,680 = $273.60. Therefore, the cash payment is $13,680 − $273.60 = $13,406.40:

Cash	13,406.40	
Cash discounts on sales	273.60	
Accounts receivable		13,680.00

3. The only difference from requirement 2 is a $100 smaller cash payment and a $100 debit to Sales Returns and Allowances:

Cash	13,306.40	
Cash discounts on sales	273.60	
Sales returns and allowances	100.00	
Accounts receivable		13,680.00

Cash

OBJECTIVE 4

Manage cash and explain its importance to the company.

All revenues generate cash at some point. We next discuss the reporting and managing of cash. Many companies combine cash and cash equivalents on their balance sheets. Recall that cash equivalents are highly liquid short-term investments that can easily and quickly be converted into cash. For example, the 2009 balance sheet of Oracle begins with "Cash and cash equivalents . . . $8,995 million." Oracle describes its cash equivalents as ". . . deposits held at major banks, money market funds, Tier 1 commercial paper, corporate notes, U.S. Treasury obligations, U.S. government agency and government sponsored enterprise obligations, and other securities with original maturities of 90 days or less." Although this is a long complex list of items, they all share one characteristic: Oracle will have cash in hand when the securities mature (within no more than 90 days), or Oracle can easily sell these marketable items to other people and receive cash immediately.

Cash means the same thing to organizations that it does to individuals. It is not just paper money and coins, but it also includes other items that a bank will accept for deposit, including money orders and checks. However, banks do not treat all items accepted for deposit the same. For example, although a bank may add all deposits to the accounts of bank customers on the date received, the bank may not provide the depositor with access to the funds until the check "clears" through the banking system (until the bank receives payment from the check writer's bank). If the check fails to clear because its writer has insufficient funds, the bank deducts the amount of the check from the depositor's account.

A bank employee may talk about a deposit being "credited" to the account of a customer of the bank. A manager of the company making the deposit may be confused by the term "credited." He regarded the deposit as a debit to cash. Why would a banker say the customer's account is "credited"? Deposits in the bank are assets to the depositor but they are a liability to the bank. Suppose a company receives a check from a customer and deposits the check in its bank account. The company debits its Cash account (an asset account) to show the increase in the asset Cash-in-Bank. The offsetting credit might be to Sales if the check came from a sales transaction or to Accounts Receivable if it arose from collection of an account. In contrast, when the bank receives the check, it credits its liability account Deposits to acknowledge the increase in the amount it owes the company depositing the check.

Compensating Balances

Frequently, the entire cash balance in a bank account is not available for unrestricted use. Why? Because banks often require companies to maintain **compensating balances**, which are required minimum balances on deposit. The size of the minimum balance may depend on the amount borrowed, the amount of credit available, or both.

Compensating balances increase the effective interest rate that the borrower pays. For a loan of $100,000 at 8% per year, the annual interest will be $8,000. With a 10% compensating balance, the borrower can use only $90,000 of the loan, raising the effective interest rate on the usable funds to ($8,000 ÷ $90,000) = 8.9%.

To ensure that financial statements provide a true picture concerning cash, annual reports must disclose significant compensating balances. For example, a footnote in the annual report of Chiquita Brands International, the distributor of Chiquita and Fresh Express brand produce, disclosed the following: "The company had €11 million . . . of cash equivalents in a compensating balance arrangement. . . ." Without such disclosures, analysts and investors might think that a company has more cash available than it really does.

compensating balances
The minimum cash balances that banks require companies to maintain to partially compensate the bank for providing the loan.

Management of Cash

Cash is usually a small portion of the total assets of a company. Yet, companies manage cash especially carefully. Why? First, although the cash balance may be small at any one time, the flow of cash can be enormous. Weekly receipts and disbursements of cash may be many times as large as the cash balance. Second, because cash is the most liquid asset, it is enticing to thieves and embezzlers. If someone steals a $200 jacket, he or she may be able to get only $40 from selling stolen goods, but if the same person steals $200 cash, he or she will have $200. Third, adequate cash is essential to the smooth functioning of operations. Companies need it for everything from routine purchases to major investments, from purchasing lunch for a visiting business partner to purchasing another company. Finally, because cash itself does not earn income, it is important not to hold excess cash. The treasury department is responsible for managing the levels of cash efficiently and for ensuring that the company deposits unneeded cash in income-generating accounts.

Most organizations have detailed, well-specified procedures for receiving, recording, and disbursing cash. They immediately deposit cash in a bank account, and they periodically reconcile the company's books with the bank's records. To **reconcile a bank statement** means to verify that the bank balance and the accounting records are in agreement. The two balances are rarely identical. A company records a deposit when it sends money to the bank and records a payment when it writes a check. The bank, however, records the deposit when it receives it, possibly several days

reconcile a bank statement
To verify that the bank balance for cash is in agreement with the accounting records.

after the company recorded it. The bank typically receives and processes a check written by a company days, weeks, or even months after the company issues it. For more on bank reconciliations see Appendix 6.

The major internal control procedures set up to safeguard cash include the following:

1. Have different individuals receive cash than those who disburse cash.
2. Have different individuals handle cash than those who access accounting records.
3. Immediately record and deposit cash receipts.
4. Make disbursements using serially numbered checks and require proper authorization by someone other than the person writing the check.
5. Reconcile bank accounts monthly.

Why are such internal controls necessary? Consider a person who handles cash and makes entries into the accounting records. That person could take $200 in cash and cover it up by making the following entry in the books:

Operating expenses	200	
Cash		200

Besides guarding against dishonest actions, internal control procedures help ensure that accounting records are accurate. For example, suppose a company writes a check but does not record it in the books. The bank reconciliation will not balance. With serially numbered checks, it is possible to trace items from the checkbook to a bank statement and identify the unrecorded check.

Credit Sales and Accounts Receivable

Cash sales are important for some companies, but most sales in today's world are on credit and the trend is growing. Credit sales create challenges for measuring revenue and managing the company's assets because the company agrees to accept payment in the future for goods or services delivered today. Companies must manage these expected future payments, accounts receivable, to ensure their collection in a timely manner.

Uncollectible Accounts

OBJECTIVE 5

Estimate and interpret uncollectible accounts receivable balances.

Granting credit entails both costs and benefits. The main benefit is the boost in sales and profit that a company generates when it extends credit. Many potential customers would not buy if credit were unavailable, or they would buy from a competitor that offered credit. Among the costs of providing credit is the cost of administering and collecting the credit amount. Before a company grants credit, it reviews the customer's credit and payment history to decide whether to accept the customer. It must then track what a customer owes, send periodic bills, deposit payments, record the payment in the customer's account, and so forth. These steps require clerical time and effort. Another cost is the delay in receiving payment. The seller must finance its activities in other ways while awaiting payment. Perhaps the most significant cost is **uncollectible accounts** or **bad debts**—receivables that some credit customers are either unable or unwilling to pay. Accountants often call the loss from uncollectible accounts **bad debts expense**.

uncollectible accounts (bad debts)

Receivables determined to be uncollectible because customers are unable or unwilling to pay their debts.

bad debts expense

The loss that arises from uncollectible accounts.

The extent of nonpayment of debts varies. It often depends on the credit risks that managers are willing to accept. For instance, many smaller local establishments will accept a higher level of risk than will larger national stores such as Nordstrom. Why? Because the local stores know their customers personally. The extent of a nonpayment can also depend on the industry. For example, the problem of uncollectible accounts is especially difficult in the health care field. The Bayfront Medical Center of St. Petersburg, Florida, once reported bad debts equal to 21% of gross revenue.

Deciding When and How to Grant Credit

Competition and industry practice affect whether and how companies offer credit. The final decision is based on cost-benefit trade-offs. In other words, companies offer credit only when the additional earnings on credit sales exceed the costs of offering credit. Suppose 5% of credit sales are bad debts, administrative costs of a credit department are $5,000 per year, and $20,000 of credit sales (with earnings of $8,000 before credit costs) are achieved. Assume that the company would not receive the credit sales without granting credit. Offering credit is worthwhile because the additional earnings of $8,000 exceeds the credit costs of $[(5\% \times \$20,000) + \$5,000] = \$6,000$.

Measurement of Uncollectible Accounts

Uncollectible accounts require special accounting procedures and thus deserve special attention. Consider an example. Suppose Compuport began business on January 2, 20X1 and had credit sales of $100,000 (200 customers averaging $500 each) during 20X1. Collections during 20X1 were $60,000. The December 31, 20X1, accounts receivable of $40,000 includes the accounts of 80 different customers who have not yet paid for their 20X1 purchases. At the end of 20X1, 40% of the year's sales are still unpaid and some may never be paid. The outstanding balances are as follows:

Customer	Amount Owed
1. Jones	$ 1,400
2. Slade	125
⁓	⁓
42. Monterro	600
⁓	⁓
79. Weinberg	700
80. Porras	11
Total receivables	$40,000

How should Compuport account for these receivables? Should we assume they will all be collected? If we assume some will not be collected, how do we decide which are collectible and which are not? Of course, we would never have initially made a credit sale to someone we really believed would not pay us.

There are two basic ways to record uncollectibles: by waiting to see which customers do not pay or by making estimates today of the portion that will not be collected. The methods are called the specific write-off method and the allowance method.

Specific Write-Off Method

A company that rarely experiences a bad debt might use the **specific write-off method**, which assumes that all sales are fully collectible until proved otherwise. If uncollectibles are small and infrequent, this practice will not misstate the economic situation in a material way. When Compuport identifies a specific customer account as uncollectible, it will reduce the Account Receivable. Because Compuport deems no specific customer's account to be uncollectible at the end of 20X1, its December 31, 20X1, balance sheet would simply show Accounts Receivable of $40,000.

Now assume that during 20X2 Compuport identifies Jones and Monterro as customers who are not expected to pay. When the chances of collection from specific customers become dim, Compuport recognizes the amounts in the particular accounts as bad debts expense:

specific write-off method
A method of accounting for bad debt losses that assumes all sales are fully collectible until proved otherwise.

Specific Write-Off Method	A	= L	+	SE
20X1 Sales	+100,000	=		+100,000
	⌈ Increase Accounts Receivable ⌋			⌈ Increase Sales ⌋
20X2 Write-off	−2,000	=		−2,000
	⌈ Decrease Accounts Receivable ⌋			⌈ Increase Bad Debts Expense ⌋

The specific write-off method has been justifiably criticized because it fails to apply the matching principle of accrual accounting. The $2,000 bad debts expense recorded using the specific write-off method in 20X2 is related to (or caused by) the $100,000 of 20X1 sales. Matching requires recognition of the bad debts expense at the same time as the related revenue, that is, in 20X1, not 20X2. As a result of not matching expenses to revenues, the specific write-off method produces two errors in reported earnings. First, 20X1 income is overstated by $2,000 because

Compuport reports no bad debts expense that year. Second, 20X2 income is understated by $2,000. Why? Because Compuport charges 20X1's bad debts expense of $2,000 in 20X2. Equally important, the accounts receivable balance in 20X1 overstates the asset by $2,000. Compare the specific write-off method with a correct matching of revenue and expense:

	Specific Write-Off Method: Matching Violated		Matching Applied Correctly	
	20X1	20X2	20X1	20X2
Sales revenue	100,000	0	100,000	0
Bad debts expense	0	2,000	2,000	0

The principal arguments in favor of the specific write-off method are based on cost-benefit and materiality. Basically, the method is simple and extremely inexpensive to use. Moreover, no great error in measurement of income or accounts receivable occurs if amounts of bad debts are small and similar from one year to the next.

Allowance Method

Few companies use the specific write-off method because it violates the matching principle and most companies' bad debts are neither small nor similar from year to year. Instead, they use an alternate method that estimates the amount of uncollectible accounts to be matched to each year's revenue. This method, known as the **allowance method**, has two basic elements: (1) an estimate of the amounts that will ultimately be uncollectible, and (2) a contra account that contains the estimated uncollectible amount to be deducted from the total accounts receivable. We usually call the contra account **allowance for uncollectible accounts** (or **allowance for doubtful accounts**, **allowance for bad debts**, or **reserve for doubtful accounts**). It contains the amount of receivables estimated to be uncollectible from as-yet unidentified customers. In other words, using this contra account allows accountants to recognize bad debts in general during the proper period, before they identify uncollectible accounts from specific individuals in the following periods.

Returning to our example, suppose that Compuport knows from experience that it will not collect about 2% of sales. Therefore, the company estimates that it will not collect (2% × $100,000) = $2,000 of the 20X1 sales. However, on December 31, 20X1, we do not know which customers will fail to pay their accounts. Compuport can still acknowledge the $2,000 worth of expected bad debts in 20X1, before it identifies the specific accounts of Jones and Monterro in 20X2. The effects of the allowance method on the balance sheet equation in the Compuport example follow:

allowance method

A method of accounting for bad debt losses that uses (1) estimates of the amount of sales that will ultimately be uncollectible and (2) a contra account that contains the estimated uncollectible amount.

allowance for uncollectible accounts (allowance for doubtful accounts, allowance for bad debts, reserve for doubtful accounts)

A contra asset account that measures the amount of receivables estimated to be uncollectible.

	A	= L	+	SE
Allowance method				
20X1 Sales	+100,000	=		+100,000
	[Increase Accounts Receivable]			[Increase Sales]
20X1 Allowance	–2,000	=		–2,000
	[Increase Allowance for Uncollectible Accounts]			[Increase Bad Debts Expense]
20X2 Write-off	+2,000	=		(No effect)
	[Decrease Allowance for Uncollectible Accounts]			
	–2,000			
	[Decrease Accounts Receivable]			

The associated journal entries are as follows:

20X1 Sales	Accounts receivable	100,000	
	Sales		100,000
20X1 Allowances	Bad debts expense	2,000	
	Allowance for uncollectible accounts		2,000
20X2 Write-offs	Allowance for uncollectible accounts	2,000	
	Accounts receivable, Jones		1,400
	Accounts receivable, Monterro		600

In the 20X2 write-off journal entry, Compuport makes two credit entries to Accounts Receivable, one for $1,400 for Jones and one for $600 for Monterro. This emphasizes that companies keep accounts receivable records for each individual customer. Similarly note that the 20X1 increase of $100,000 to accounts receivable represents many (200 in this example) individual sales to specific customers.

The allowance method is superior in measuring accrual accounting income in each year and in measuring the year-end accounts receivable asset realistically. Under this method Compuport deducts from 20X1 sales the $2,000 of those sales that it believes it will never collect. This matches the bad debt expense to the sales that generated the bad debts. In addition, the year-end account receivable balance has the correct collectible amount of $38,000.

The allowance method results in the following presentation in the Compuport balance sheet, December 31, 20X1:

Accounts receivable	$40,000
Less: Allowance for uncollectible accounts	2,000
Net accounts receivable	$38,000

Oracle discloses its allowance for bad debts in the caption for Trade Receivables:

($ in millions)	2009	2008
Oracle		
Trade receivables, net of allowances of $270 and $303 as of May 31, 2009 and 2008	$4,430	$5,127

The allowance method relies on historical experience and information about economic circumstances (growth versus recession, interest rate levels, and so on) and customer composition. Of course, companies revise estimates when conditions change. For example, if a local employer closed or drastically reduced employment and many local customers were suddenly unemployed, Compuport might increase expected bad debts. Oracle discloses the following in its 2009 annual report:

We record allowances for doubtful accounts based upon a specific review of all significant outstanding invoices. For those invoices not specifically reviewed, provisions are provided at differing rates, based upon the age of the receivable, the collection history associated with the geographic region that the receivable was recorded in and current economic trends.

Applying the Allowance Method Using a Percentage of Sales

How do managers and accountants estimate the percentage of bad debts in the allowance method? In our example, Compuport managers determined a rate of 2% of credit sales, for a total of (2% × $100,000) = $2,000, based on experience. For example they might look at the last 4 years and divide the total of all bad debts by the total of all credit sales to calculate that over time 2% of credit sales are not collected. Companies that express the amount of bad debts as a percentage of total credit sales use the **percentage of sales method**, which relies on historical relationships between credit sales and uncollectible debts adjusted for current economic conditions.

percentage of sales method
An approach to estimating bad debts expense and uncollectible accounts based on the historical relationship between credit sales and uncollectible debts.

To apply the percentage of sales method, we look at the relationship between the general ledger item Accounts Receivable and its supporting detail. Details supporting Accounts Receivable are in a subsidiary ledger that lists, by customer, all sales and payments. The total of all a particular customer's sales less payments is the amount receivable from that customer. At any point in time, the sum of the balances of all customer accounts in the subsidiary ledger must equal the accounts receivable balance in the general ledger. We illustrate this process in Exhibit 6-1, panel A.

Using the allowance account, we can record bad debt expense for 20X1 without identifying specific accounts that will be uncollectible. In 20X2, after exhausting all practical means of collection, Compuport decides the Jones and Monterro accounts are uncollectible. Recording the $2,000 write-off for Jones and Monterro in 20X2 reduces their individual subsidiary accounts, reduces the general ledger Accounts Receivable account, and eliminates the Allowance for Uncollectible accounts as shown in panel B of Exhibit 6-1.

INTERPRETING FINANCIAL STATEMENTS

How does the ultimate write-off of the Monterro and Jones accounts affect total assets reported on the balance sheet?

Answer

The ultimate write-off has no effect on total assets:

	Before Write-Off	After Write-Off
Accounts receivable	$40,000	$38,000
Allowance for uncollectible accounts	2,000	—
Book value (net realizable value)	$38,000	$38,000

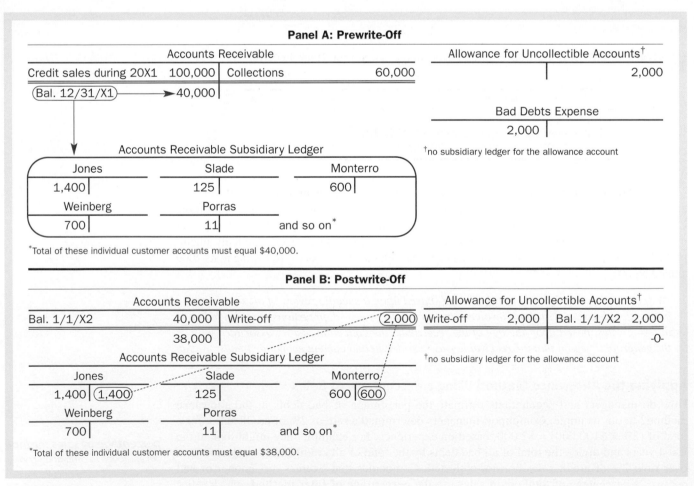

EXHIBIT 6-1

Compuport General Ledger, December 31, 20X1

Applying the Allowance Method Using a Percentage of Accounts Receivable

As with the percentage of sales method, we can use historical experience to apply the **percentage of accounts receivable method**. However, this method bases estimates of uncollectible accounts on the historical percentage of ending accounts receivable that subsequently become uncollectible, not on the percentage of credit sales that become uncollectible.

We use the Allowance for Bad Debts contra account to show the approximate amount of bad debts contained in the end-of-period accounts receivable. Under the percentage of accounts receivable method, we calculate additions to the Allowance for Bad Debts to achieve a desired ending balance in the Allowance account. Consider the historical experience in the following table:

percentage of accounts receivable method
An approach to estimating bad debts expense and uncollectible accounts that bases estimates of uncollectible accounts on the historical relations of uncollectibles to year-end gross accounts receivable.

	Accounts Receivable at End of Year	Bad Debts Deemed Uncollectible and Written Off in Subsequent Year
20X1	$100,000	$ 3,500
20X2	80,000	2,450
20X3	90,000	2,550
20X4	110,000	4,100
20X5	120,000	5,600
20X6	112,000	2,200
Six-year total	$612,000	$20,400

Average percentage not collected = 20,400 ÷ 612,000 = 3.33%

At the end of 20X7 the accounts receivable balance is $115,000. We compute the 20X7 addition to the Allowance for Bad Debts as follows:

1. Divide total bad debt losses of $20,400 by total ending accounts receivable of $612,000 to calculate the historical average uncollectible percentage of 3.33%.
2. Apply the percentage from step 1 to the ending Accounts Receivable balance for 20X7 to determine the ending balance that should be in the Allowance account at the end of the year: (3.33% × $115,000) receivables at the end of 20X7 is $3,830.
3. Prepare an adjusting entry to bring the Allowance to the appropriate amount determined in step 2. Suppose the books show a $700 credit balance in the Allowance account at the end of 20X7. Then the adjusting entry for 20X7 is ($3,830 − $700), or $3,130, to record the Bad Debts Expense. The journal entry is as follows:

```
Bad debts expense  . . . . . . . . . . . . . . . . . . . . . . .   3,130
     Allowance for bad debts  . . . . . . . . . . . . . . . .            3,130
To bring the Allowance to $3,830, the level justified
by bad debt experience during past 6 years
```

The percentage of accounts receivable method differs from the percentage of sales method in two ways: (1) The percentage is based on the ending accounts receivable balance instead of credit sales, and (2) the dollar amount calculated using the percentage is the appropriate ending balance in the allowance account, not the amount added to the account for the year.

Applying the Allowance Method Using the Aging of Accounts Receivable

We can refine the percentage of accounts receivable approach by considering the composition of the end-of-year accounts receivable based on the age of the debt. This **aging of accounts receivable method** directly incorporates the customers' payment histories. As more time elapses after the sale, collection becomes less likely. The seller may send the buyer a late notice 30 days after the sale and a second reminder after 60 days, make a phone call after 90 days, and place the account with a collection agency after 120 days. Companies that analyze the age of their accounts receivable for credit management purposes naturally incorporate this information into accounting estimates of the allowance for uncollectibles. For example, the $115,000 balance in Accounts Receivable on December 31, 20X7, for Compuport might be aged as shown in Exhibit 6-2.

aging of accounts receivable method
An analysis that considers the composition of year-end accounts receivable based on the age of the debt.

Name	Total	1–30 Days	31–60 Days	61–90 Days	More Than 90 Days
Oxwall Tools	$ 20,000	$20,000			
Chicago Castings	10,000	10,000			
Estee	20,000	15,000	$ 5,000		
Sarasota Pipe	22,000		12,000	$10,000	
Ceilcote	4,000			3,000	$1,000
Other accounts (each detailed)	39,000	27,000	8,000	2,000	2,000
Total	$115,000	$72,000	$25,000	$15,000	$3,000
Historical bad debt percentages		0.1%	1%	5%	90%
Bad debt allowance to be provided	$ 3,772 =	$ 72 +	$ 250 +	$ 750 +	$2,700

EXHIBIT 6-2

Compuport

Aging of Accounts Receivable, 20X7

This aging schedule in Exhibit 6-2 produces a different target balance for the Allowance account than the balance that resulted from the percentage of accounts receivable method: $3,772 versus $3,830. Therefore, the journal entry is slightly different. Given the same $700 credit balance in the Allowance account, the journal entry to record the Bad Debts Expense is $3,772 – $700, or $3,072:

```
Bad debts expense  . . . . . . . . . . . . . . . . . . . . . . . . . . . . . . .    $3,072
    Allowance for uncollectible accounts   . . . . . . . . . . . . . .               $3,072
To bring the Allowance to $3,772, the level justified
by prior experience using the aging method
```

Whether a company uses the percentage of sales, percentage of accounts receivable, or aging of accounts receivable method to estimate bad debts expense and the Allowance for Uncollectible Accounts, the subsequent accounting for write-offs is the same—a decrease in Accounts Receivable and a decrease in the Allowance for Uncollectible Accounts.

Bad Debt Recoveries

bad debt recoveries

Accounts receivable that were previously written off as uncollectible but then collected at a later date.

Sometimes a customer will pay an account that a company has previously written off as uncollectible. When such **bad debt recoveries** occur, we must capture the customer's true payment history. We accomplish this in two steps. First, we reverse the write-off, and then we handle the collection as a normal receipt on account. Return to the earlier Compuport example and assume that we wrote off Monterro's account for $600 in February 20X2 and then unexpectedly collected it in October 20X2. The following journal entries produce a complete record of the transactions in Monterro's individual accounts receivable account:

```
20X1       Accounts receivable  . . . . . . . . . . . . . . . . . . . .    600
               Sales  . . . . . . . . . . . . . . . . . . . . . . . . . . .          600
           To record sales of $600 to Monterro, a
               specific customer
Feb. 20X2  Allowance for uncollectible accounts  . . . . . . . .    600
               Accounts receivable   . . . . . . . . . . . . . . . .              600
           To write off uncollectible account of Monterro
Oct. 20X2  Accounts receivable  . . . . . . . . . . . . . . . . . . . .    600
               Allowance for uncollectible accounts  . . . . .                 600
           To reverse February 20X2 write-off of account
               of Monterro
           Cash . . . . . . . . . . . . . . . . . . . . . . . . . . . . . . . .    600
               Accounts receivable   . . . . . . . . . . . . . . . .              600
           To record the collection on account
```

Note that these 20X2 entries have no effect on the level of bad debt expense estimated for 20X1. At the end of 20X1, using one of the three estimation methods we just examined, Compuport estimated bad debt expense and end-of-period uncollectibles. We do not change these estimates, even if future uncollectibles are greater or less than expected. The errors in estimate affect future periods but do not produce adjustments of prior periods.

INTERPRETING FINANCIAL STATEMENTS

Examine the trade receivables balances of Oracle as of May 31, 2009 and 2008 shown on page 257. Compute the gross accounts receivable on May 31, 2009 and 2008. Did the percentage of accounts receivable deemed uncollectible increase or decrease in 2008?

Answer
Oracle's gross accounts receivable balances were as follows:

2009: $4,430 million + $270 million = $4,700 million;
2008: $5,127 million + $303 million = $5,430 million.

In 2008, Oracle deemed ($303 ÷ $5,430) = 5.58% of the accounts receivable to be uncollectible; in 2009 it was ($270 ÷ $4,700) = 5.74%. Therefore, the company expected a slightly higher default percentage in 2009 than in 2008. The change may have resulted from a change in actual experience or may have resulted from the company's belief that the recession would cause default rates to increase.

Assessing the Level of Accounts Receivable

In addition to accounting properly for bad debts, managers seek to manage bad debt levels appropriately. The more credit a company provides, the greater the sales and the greater the chances of bad debts occurring. Management and financial analysts ask questions such as the following: Can the firm increase sales without excessive growth in receivables? Do bad debt expenses rise sharply when sales grow, indicating a reduction in the credit quality of the store's customers? The secret to managing accounts receivable is to allow enough credit to facilitate sales but not allow collections to lag and receivables to build up. One way to manage accounts receivables is described in the Business First box on page 262.

One measure of the ability to control receivables is the **accounts receivable turnover**—credit sales divided by the average accounts receivable for the period during which the sales were made:

> Accounts receivable turnover = Credit sales ÷ Average accounts receivable

This ratio indicates how rapidly collections occur. Suppose you sold $100 of merchandise each day, 365 days per year, and you collected cash for every sale 10 days after the sale. In this instance, annual sales would be ($365 × $100) = $36,500, and average accounts receivable would be (10 days × $100 per day) = $1,000, giving an accounts receivable turnover of ($36,500 ÷ $1,000) = 36.5. If the turnover were 12, it would indicate that, on average, the company collects receivables after 1 month. Higher turnovers indicate that a company collects its receivables quickly—lower turnovers indicate slower collection cycles. Competitive conditions in the industry often drive the ratio. Changes in the ratio provide important guidance concerning changes in the company's policies, changes in the industry's competitive environment, and changes in general economic conditions. For example, a decline in the general level of economic activity will slow collections across the board, and this turnover measure will tend to fall for all firms.

Suppose credit sales for Compuport in 20X8 were $1 million and beginning and ending accounts receivable were $115,000 and $112,000, respectively.

> Accounts receivable turnover = $1,000,000 ÷ [0.5 × ($115,000 + $112,000)] = 8.81

We can also assess receivables levels in terms of how long it takes to collect them. This alternative to the turnover ratio has an appealing direct interpretation. How long does it take to get my

OBJECTIVE 6

Assess the level of accounts receivable.

accounts receivable turnover
Credit sales divided by average accounts receivable.

BUSINESS FIRST

MANAGING ACCOUNTS RECEIVABLE

Accounts receivables are vitally important to most companies; they are both an opportunity and a significant risk. On the one hand, granting appropriate trade credit to customers increases sales and allows for the development of a long-term relationship. However on the other hand, if a company fails to manage their accounts receivables properly, it results in undue risk of default. Even when customers pay their liabilities, the company holding the receivables may still face cash flow constraints.

So, what options do companies have for managing their accounts receivables? One option is to sell receivable; this is known as factoring. An article in Hong Kong Business reports that from 2007 to 2009, the volume of factoring by Hong Kong companies totaled around HK$87 billion. This means that rather than holding on to account receivables and collecting from customers, many Hong Kong companies sold their receivables early in order to generate cash. After factoring, the company buying the receivables will collect from the original customers when the bills are due. This company is known as the factor.

Is factoring a good idea and why do so many companies do it? Companies must balance their need for immediate cash against the cost of factoring. A factor will typically receive a discount on the amount they pay to purchase the receivables. For example, the selling company may receive 80 cents per dollar of receivables sold. As a result, the selling company has paid 20% to receive cash early. If the benefits they receive from having the cash early exceed 20%, then factoring may be a good idea. Another variable to consider is the relationship selling companies may have built up with their customers. Once a receivable is sold, the company has little control of how the factor deals with the client and this could be risky. A factor that is inflexible or overly aggressive may hurt the future business prospects of the firm. Judging by the size of the factoring business in Hong Kong, however, it appears that many firms have used factoring as a way to manage their cash flow.

Source: T. Chua, "Late and default business payment stabilising," *Hong Kong Business*, http://hongkongbusiness.hk/economy/in-focus/late-and-default-business-payment-stabilising, November 18, 2010.

---

days to collect accounts receivable (average collection period)
365 divided by accounts receivable turnover.

money after I make a sale? The **days to collect accounts receivable**, or **average collection period**, is 365 divided by the accounts receivable turnover. For our example,

$$\text{Days to collect accounts receivable} = 365 \text{ days} \div \text{Accounts receivable turnover}$$
$$= 365 \text{ days} \div 8.81$$
$$= 41.4 \text{ days}$$

There is significant variability in accounts receivable turnover levels among industries, as shown in Exhibit 6-3. The high average accounts receivable turnover for bookstores and the low turnover for jewelry stores reflect the way customers finance their purchases. Bookstore customers use primarily cash or national credit cards, such as VISA and MasterCard, so the seller receives cash quickly. Jewelry stores often directly grant credit, so receipt of cash is delayed. In other words, national credit cards tend to pay sellers quickly, but when the sellers themselves provide the credit, payments come in much more slowly. In fact, if more businesses provided their own credit to customers, as used to be the case, their accounts receivable turnover would drop sharply.

EXHIBIT 6-3

Accounts Receivable Ratios

	Median Levels	
Industry	Accounts Receivable Turnover	Days to Collect Accounts Receivable
Automobile retailer	70.3	5.2
Department stores	93.2	3.9
Furniture retailer	99.5	3.7
Jewelry retailer	60.5	6.0
Bookstores	107.2	3.4

Source: RMA, Annual Statement Studies, 2008–2009, pp. 906–907, 922–923, 986–987, 994–995, and 996–997.

Summary Problem for Your Review

PROBLEM

The balance sheet of VF Corporation, the large apparel company with brands such as JanSport, Nautica, Wrangler, Lee, and The North Face, showed accounts receivable at January 2, 2009, of $851,282,000, net of allowances of $48,163,000. Suppose a large discount chain that owed VF $8 million announced bankruptcy on January 5, 2009. VF decided that chances for collection were virtually zero and immediately wrote off the account. Show the accounts receivable and allowance account balances after the write-off, and explain the effect of the write-off on income for the year beginning January 2, 2009.

SOLUTION

The write-off does not affect the net accounts receivable. Nevertheless, both gross accounts receivable and the allowance for doubtful accounts change. Gross accounts receivable were $899,445,000 at January 2 and the allowance was $48,163,000, giving a net accounts receivable of $851,282,000. When VF takes the write-off, gross accounts receivable go down by $8 million, but the allowance does also, with the following result:

Gross receivables ($899,445,000 – $8,000,000)	$891,445,000
Less: Allowance for doubtful accounts	
($48,163,000 – $8,000,000)	40,163,000
Net receivables	$851,282,000

There would be no effect on VF Corporation's 2009 net income.

Overview of Internal Control

We previously discussed cash management processes that are examples of internal controls. **Internal controls** are checks and balances that ensure all company actions are proper and have the general approval of top management. Companies use such controls to protect their assets and to help managers maintain accurate financial records. For example, we do not want a manager to expose the company to huge speculative losses from unauthorized trading of exotic derivative securities. Here internal controls ensure that managers make decisions consistent with corporate strategy. Nor should a salesperson at a clothing store be able to walk out of the store with holiday gifts for the family without paying for them. Here internal control refers to the protection of firm assets from theft and loss. An electronic tag on a leather coat is an internal control device and so is the requirement that two people have to approve checks over $5,000.

In its broadest sense, internal controls refer to both administrative controls and accounting controls:

1. **Administrative controls** are methods and procedures that facilitate management planning and control of operations. They include the formal organizational chart that spells out responsibilities and reporting relationships, as well as departmental budgeting procedures, reports on performance, and procedures for granting credit to customers.
2. **Accounting controls** include the methods and procedures for authorizing transactions, safeguarding assets, and ensuring the accuracy of the financial records. Good accounting controls help to maximize efficiency and to minimize waste, unintentional errors, and fraud.

We focus on the following internal accounting controls, including the area over which each provides reasonable assurance:

1. Authorization. Managers execute transactions in accordance with management's general or specific intentions.
2. Recording. Accountants accurately record authorized transactions.
3. Safeguarding. There are appropriate restrictions on access to assets.
4. Reconciliation. Accountants regularly verify records against other independently kept records and/or confirm them by physical counts or examinations.

OBJECTIVE 7
Develop and explain internal control procedures.

internal controls
Checks and balances that ensure all company actions are proper and have the general approval of top management.

administrative controls
All methods and procedures that facilitate management planning and control of operations.

accounting controls
The methods and procedures for authorizing transactions, safeguarding assets, and ensuring the accuracy of the financial records.

5. Valuation. Accountants periodically review recorded amounts for impairment of values and necessary write-downs.
6. Operational Efficiency. Good internal control prevents errors and fraud while promoting efficient actions.

The first three general objectives—authorization, recording, and safeguarding—relate to a system of accountability to prevent errors and irregularities. The fourth and fifth objectives—reconciliation and valuation—aid in detecting errors and irregularities. The last objective recognizes that an internal control system's purpose is as much a positive one (promoting efficiency) as a negative one (preventing errors and fraud).

The Accounting System

accounting system

A set of records, procedures, internal controls, and equipment to collect, organize, and report the continuous flow of information about events affecting the entity's financial performance and position.

An entity's **accounting system** is a set of records, procedures, internal controls, and equipment to collect, organize, and report the continuous flow of information about the events affecting the entity's financial performance and position. Chapters 3 and 4 provided an overview of the heart of the accounting system—source documents, journal entries, postings to ledgers, trial balances, adjustments, and financial reports. The system handles repetitive, voluminous transactions, which fall primarily into four categories:

1. Cash disbursements
2. Cash receipts
3. Purchase of goods and services, including employee payroll
4. Sales and delivery of goods and services

The volume of the physical records is often staggering. For example, telephone and credit card companies process millions of transactions daily. Computers and data processing systems make it possible. Well-designed and well-run accounting systems are positive contributions to organizations and the economy. Credit card companies, for example, use sophisticated systems to evaluate transactions on your credit card and may refuse a credit transaction that seems likely to be fraudulent use of your card by an unauthorized party. Although such refusals sometimes inconvenience a legitimate card holder, they more frequently foil criminal use. Another example is FedEx Corporation, which created a dominant position in the overnight delivery market by developing an efficient system for continuously tracking items from pickup to delivery. Finally, Wal-Mart's extraordinary success as a low-price retailer is due in part to its integrated inventory control and ordering system that allows its computers to interact automatically with suppliers, whether they are companies such as Procter & Gamble in the United States or Shenzhen Zuonmens Industrial in China, to generate orders and reduce delivery times.

Checklist of Internal Control

Good systems of internal control have certain features in common. We have summarized these features in a checklist of internal control—the best practices that managers use to create or evaluate specific procedures for cash, purchases, sales, payroll, and the like.

1. **Reliable Personnel with Clear Responsibilities.** The most important control element is personnel. Incompetent or dishonest individuals undermine any system. Thus, good procedures to hire, train, motivate, and supervise employees are essential. Companies should give individuals authority, responsibility, and duties commensurate with their abilities, interests, experience, and reliability. The wrong, lowest-cost talent is expensive in the long run, not only because of fraud but also because of poor productivity.

   Clear responsibilities means having policies and procedures that specify such details as having sales clerks sign sales slips, inspectors sign initial packing slips, and workers sign time cards and requisitions. For example, grocery stores often assign each cashier a separate money tray so management can reward efficiency and easily trace shortages. It has been estimated that retailers lose more than 2% of sales to theft and mistakes—and employee theft causes much larger losses than shoplifting.

2. **Separation of Duties.** Separation of duties makes it hard for one person, acting alone, to defraud the company. This is why movie theaters have a cashier selling tickets and an usher taking them. The cashier takes in cash, the usher keeps the ticket stubs, and a third person compares the cash with the number of stubs.

   However, separation of duties is not foolproof. Suppose the ticket seller pockets the cash and issues a fake ticket. If the ticket seller and usher collude, the usher might accept the fake ticket, destroy it, and allow entry. Separation of duties alone does not prevent such collusive theft. Better supervision of the ticket seller and the usher is the primary method of preventing such collusion. Or, even in the absence of collusion, if the fake ticket is a good forgery, the usher may not be able to detect the ticket seller's theft.

Here are two examples where separation of duties would lead to better internal control:

- In a computer system, a person with custody of assets should not have access to programming or any input of records. In a classic example, a programmer in a bank rounded transactions to the next lower cent instead of the nearest cent and had the computer put the fraction of a cent into his account. For example, a customer amount of $10.057 became $10.05, and the programmer's account received $.007. With millions of transactions, the programmer's account grew very large.
- The same individual should not authorize payments and also sign the check in payment of the bill. Similarly, an individual who handles cash receipts should not have the authority to indicate which accounts receivable should be written off as uncollectible. The latter separation of powers prevents the following embezzlement: A bookkeeper opens the mail, removes a $1,000 check from a customer, and somehow cashes it. To hide the theft, the bookkeeper prepares the following journal entry to write off an amount owed by a customer:

Allowance for bad debts	1,000	
Accounts receivable		1,000

3. **Proper Authorization.** General authorizations are usually written policies, such as definite limits on what price to pay (whether to fly economy or first class), on what price to receive (whether to offer a sales discount), on what credit limits to grant to customers, and so forth. Specific authorizations require that a designated manager explicitly approve deviations from the limits set by general authorization. For example, a senior manager may need to approve overtime or the board of directors may need to approve large expenditures for capital assets.

4. **Adequate Documents.** Companies have a variety of documents and records, from source documents (such as sales invoices and purchase orders) to journals and ledgers. Immediate, complete, and tamper-proof recording of data is the goal. Companies minimize recording errors by optically scanning bar-coded data, by prenumbering and accounting for all source documents, by using devices such as cash registers, and by designing forms for ease of recording. When a merchant offers a customer a free item if a red star comes up on the cash register receipt, it is partly a way to ensure that sales clerks actually ring up the sale and charge the proper amount.

5. **Proper Procedures.** Most organizations use procedure manuals to specify the flow of documents and provide information and instructions to facilitate record keeping. Well-designed routines permit specialization of effort, division of duties, and automatic checks on each step in the routine.

6. **Physical Safeguards.** Companies minimize losses of cash, inventories, and records by using safes, locks, guards, guard dogs, and special lighting and limiting access to sensitive areas. For example, many companies require all visitors to sign a register and wear a name tag, and they may restrict access to certain places by having card scanners that grant admission only to authorized personnel.

7. **Vacations and Rotation of Duties.** Rotating employees and requiring them to take vacations ensures at least two employees know how to do each job so an absence due to illness or a sudden resignation does not create major problems. Further, employees are less likely to engage in fraudulent activities if they know that another employee periodically performs their duties and might discover the fraud. A company might accomplish rotation of duties by the common practice of having employees such as receivables and payables clerks occasionally exchange duties. In addition, a receivables clerk may handle accounts from A to C for 3 months, and then be rotated to accounts M to P for 3 months, and so forth.

8. **Independent Check.** All phases of the system should undergo periodic review by outsiders such as independent public accountants or internal auditors. By first evaluating the system of internal control and testing the extent to which employees follow the appropriate procedures, the auditor decides on the likelihood of undetected errors. When internal controls are weak, auditors will examine many transactions to provide reasonable assurance that they discover errors if any exist. If internal controls are strong, the auditor can use a smaller sample to develop confidence in the accuracy of the accounting records.

BUSINESS FIRST

LACK OF INTERNAL CONTROLS AND THE $346,770 OVERDRAFT

Banks need tight internal controls on their ATMs because they dispense cash. This is important not only to protect cash but also to maintain customer confidence. Think about how bank internal control procedures should stop potential thieves. Automated teller machines (ATMs) require the use of a customer's personal identification number (the "pin" number). As a secondary precaution, ATMs normally restrict withdrawals to a maximum amount, perhaps $300 per day, per account. To keep thieves from randomly guessing pin numbers, computers track "unauthorized" accesses. After several incorrect pin numbers, the ATM keeps the card and notifies the user to reclaim it at the bank.

Given such controls, how could someone take $346,770 from Karen Smith's bank account via ATMs? It all started when she left her bank card in her wallet, which was locked inside her van during a high school football game on a Friday night. Two thieves broke into the van, stole the bank card, and started visiting local ATMs.

Karen's big mistake was storing her pin number on her social security card, which she kept in the stolen wallet. But that alone was not enough. Oregon TelCo Credit Union happened to be updating some computer programs, and its $200 limit per account per day was inoperative—a severe lapse in controls. To access all the funds in Karen's account, the thieves put the card in and withdrew $200, time after time. When one ATM ran out of bills, the thieves visited another on a circuitous, five-county, 500-mile route.

Another internal control should have limited the thieves to the balance in Karen's account, which was much less than $346,770. Something else went wrong. Banks generally do not allow access to deposits made in an ATM until at least the next banking day so the bank can verify the deposit. Unfortunately, the TelCo system was giving immediate credit for deposits made into automated tellers. The thieves "deposited" $820,500 by inserting empty deposit envelopes and recording large deposits on the ATM keypad. They exhausted the cash in the ATMs in their five-county area by 2:30 AM and headed to Reno to buy a new truck and enjoy their wealth.

One piece of TelCo's internal control worked. Hidden cameras photographed the thieves. From the videos, the police were able to identify and arrest the perpetrators, a husband and wife team with more than 20 felony convictions between them.

Sources: "Survey: Level Four Finds ATM Security Is Top Concern for U.S. Consumers," ATMmarketplace.com (February 17, 2009); *New York Times* (February 12, 1995) p. 36.

9. **Cost-Benefit Analysis.** Highly complex systems can strangle people in red tape, impeding instead of promoting efficiency. The right investments in the accounting system can produce huge benefits. For example, the accounting firm of **KPMG** completed a study of office automation for a client. After examining the jobs of 2,600 white-collar workers, KPMG quantified a cost-benefit relationship: "A single investment of $10 million would result in a productivity savings equal to $8.4 million every year."

As many companies implement complex procedures to improve internal control, a few have taken a reverse course. They have decided that the increased costs of additional scrutiny are not worth the expected savings from catching mistakes or crooks. For example, an aerospace manufacturer routinely pays the invoice amounts without checking supporting documentation except on a random-sampling basis. An aluminum company sends out a blank check with its purchase orders, and then the supplier fills out the check and deposits it.

No internal control is perfect, but adequate internal control is essential, as illustrated in the Business First box above. The goal is not total prevention of fraud or implementation of operating perfection; instead, the goal is the design of a cost-effective tool that helps achieve efficient operations and minimizes temptation.

Reports on Internal Controls

The Sarbanes-Oxley Act requires U.S. companies to publicly report on the adequacy of their internal controls. In addition, the company's auditor must also issue a report attesting to management's assessment. **Oracle** reported the following about its internal controls in its 2009 10-K report to the SEC:

Our management is responsible for establishing and maintaining adequate internal control over financial reporting . . . [W]e conducted an evaluation of the effectiveness of our internal control over financial reporting as of May 31, 2009 . . . . Our internal control over financial reporting includes policies and procedures that provide reasonable assurance regarding the reliability of financial reporting and the preparation of financial statements for external reporting purposes in accordance with U.S. generally accepted accounting principles . . . The effectiveness of our internal control over financial reporting as of May 31, 2009 has been audited by Ernst & Young LLP, an independent registered public accounting firm.

THE AUDIT COMMITTEE   Management's responsibility for the entity's financial statements and internal controls extends upward to the board of directors. In the United States the SEC requires publicly-traded companies to have an **audit committee**, which oversees the internal accounting controls, financial statements, and financial affairs of the corporation. While audit committees are not required everywhere, their use is increasing throughout the world. Audit committees provide contact and communication among the board, the external auditors, the internal auditors, the financial executives, and the operating executives.

Audit committee members in the United States must be "outside" board members who are not managers of the company. They are considered to be more independent than the "inside" directors—employees who serve as part of the corporation's management. Oracle has a typical board composition. Of its twelve directors in 2009, four are also members of management (including founder and CEO Lawrence Ellison) and eight are "outside" directors—four executives or retired executives from other companies, two academics, a consultant, and a venture capitalist. Oracle has a combined Finance and Audit Committee that includes only outside directors. It met 17 times in 2008, more than any other board committee.

audit committee
A committee of the board of directors that oversees the internal accounting controls, financial statements, and financial affairs of the corporation.

Highlights to Remember

1 **Recognize revenue items at the proper time on the income statement.** Companies recognize revenue when two tests are met: (1) the revenue is earned, and (2) the asset received in return is realized. This is often at the point of sale, when the product is delivered to the customer. In offering products for sale, many special practices produce differences between the list price of a product and the final price that a customer pays. The term net sales represents the final proceeds to the seller—gross sales less offsetting amounts for returns, allowances, and cash discounts.

2 **Account for cash and credit sales.** At the moment a sale occurs and meets the revenue recognition requirements, a company records the full amount of the sale. This allows the sales revenue for the year to show the full level of economic activity, regardless of whether the sale is on account or for cash. The sale increases an asset account and increases the sales revenue account. For credit sales we also need to maintain detailed records about the individual customers in a subsidiary account.

3 **Compute and interpret sales returns and allowances, sales discounts, and bank credit card sales.** A company may not ultimately collect the total sales it initially recorded. It may offer various discounts or allowances, which it deducts from gross sales to arrive at net sales on the income statement. Sales returns and allowances arise when customers return merchandise or receive discounts due to damaged goods or errors in filling the order. Customers sometimes receive a cash discount as a result of prompt payment. Similarly, bank cards charge a known discount or service fee to compensate the bank for its collection services.

4 **Manage cash and explain its importance to the company.** Cash is the fuel that runs a company and must be available to meet obligations as they come due. Managing cash requires vigilance. Protecting cash from theft or loss, adequately planning for the availability of cash as needed, and reconciling the firm's accounting records with the bank's records are just some of the issues management must address.

5 **Estimate and interpret uncollectible accounts receivable balances.** Potential uncollectible accounts reduce the amount of accounts receivable reported on the balance sheet. Reporting the uncollectible portion of credit sales requires estimates that may be based on a percentage of sales, a percentage of accounts receivable, or an aging of accounts receivable. These estimates permit the financial statements to (1) properly reflect asset levels on the balance sheet and (2) properly match bad debts expense with revenue on the income statement.

6 **Assess the level of accounts receivable.** Companies and analysts use ratios to assess the level of accounts receivable. The accounts receivable turnover ratio and the days to collect

accounts receivable both relate the balance in accounts receivable to the level of credit sales during the year. Comparisons with other companies in the same industry or examination of a particular company over time draw attention to unusual circumstances and possible problems.

7 **Develop and explain internal control procedures.** It is tempting to delegate internal control decisions to accountants. However, managers at all levels have a major responsibility for the success of internal controls. To help monitor internal control, boards of directors appoint audit committees, which oversee accounting controls, the financial statements, and general financial affairs of the company. Managers and accountants should recognize that the role of an internal control system is as much a positive one (enhancing efficiency) as a negative one (reducing errors and fraud). A checklist for effective internal control includes the following: (1) reliable personnel with clear responsibilities, (2) separation of duties, (3) proper authorization, (4) adequate documents, (5) proper procedures, (6) physical safeguards, (7) vacations and rotation of duties, (8) independent check, and (9) cost-benefit analysis.

Appendix 6: Bank Reconciliations

OBJECTIVE 8

Prepare a bank reconciliation.

Exhibit 6-4 displays a bank statement for account number 96848602, one of thousands of the bank's deposits. Together, these accounts form the subsidiary ledger that supports the bank's general ledger account Deposits, a liability.

The supporting documents for the detailed checks on the statement are canceled checks, and for additional deposits they are deposit slips. Notice that the minimum balance, $33.39, is negative. This indicates an overdraft, which is a negative account balance arising from the bank's paying a check even though the depositor had insufficient funds available when the check was presented. Overdrafts may be permitted as an occasional courtesy by the bank, although most banks levy a fee for each overdraft.

Exhibit 6-5 shows selected records for another depositor in another bank. The bank balance on January 31 is an asset (Cash) of $8,000 on the depositor's books and a liability (Deposits) of $10,980 on the bank's books. The purpose of a bank reconciliation is to explain the differences between the bank's balance and the depositor's balance.

First, let's review how banks use the terms debit and credit. Banks credit the depositor's account for additional deposits because the bank has a liability to the depositor and a credit entry increases the liability. Banks debit the account for checks written by the depositor and paid by the bank because they reduce the bank's liability to the depositor. On January 8 when the bank pays the $2,000 check drawn by the depositor on January 5, the bank's journal entry would be as follows:

Jan. 8	Deposits	2,000	
	Cash		2,000
	To decrease the depositor's account		

Depositors should perform a monthly bank reconciliation to make sure the bank and depositor have recorded the same deposits and withdrawals. Reconciliations also ensure that the depositor has recorded all fees and charges and any direct deposits recorded by the bank. Bank reconciliations take many forms, but the objective is to explain all differences in the cash balances shown on the bank statement and in the depositor's general ledger at a given date. By using the data in Exhibit 6-5 we obtain the following:

Bank Reconciliation, January 31, 20X2	
Balance per books (also called *balance per check register, register balance*)	$ 8,000
Deduct: Bank service charges for January not recorded on the books (also include any other charges by the bank not yet deducted)*	20
Adjusted (corrected) balance per books	$ 7,980
Balance per bank (also called *bank statement balance, statement balance*)	$10,980
Add: Deposits not recorded by bank (also called *unrecorded deposits, deposits in transit*), deposit of 1/31	7,000
Subtotal	$17,980
Deduct: Outstanding checks, check of 1/29	10,000
Adjusted (corrected) balance per bank	$ 7,980

*Note that new entries on the depositor's books are required for all previously unrecorded additions and deductions made to achieve the adjusted balance per books.

EXHIBIT 6-4

**An Actual Bank
Statement**

Bank of America
University Branch
4701 University Way NE
Seattle, WA 98145

Richard B. Sandstrom	777	Account Number
96848602
2420 Highline Rd.		Statement Period
Redmond, WA 98110		11-21-09 to 12-20-09

SUMMARY OF YOUR ACCOUNTS
CHECKING

First Choice Minimum Balance	96848602
Beginning Balance	368.56
Deposits	5,074.00
Withdrawals	3,232.92
Service Charges/Fees	16.00
Ending Balance	2,193.64
Minimum Balance on 12-9-09	**−33.39**

CHECKING ACTIVITY

Deposits

Posted	Amount	Description
11-21	700.00	Deposit
11-25	1,810.00	Payroll Deposit
12-10	1,810.00	Payroll Deposit
12-16	754.00	Deposit

Withdrawals

Ck No.	Paid	Amount
1606	12-02	1134.00
1607	11-28	561.00
1609*	12-09	12.00
1617*	12-05	7.00
1629*	11-26	10.00
1630	11-25	16.95
1639*	12-02	96.00
1641*	12-09	1025.00
1642	12-05	50.00
1643	12-15	236.25
1644	12-17	84.72

*= Gap in check sequence.
Total number of checks = 11.

The depositor must use a journal entry to record any entries in the bank's books that also belong in the books of the depositor. The bank reconciliation indicates that the depositor must enter the bank service charge in its books:

Jan. 31	Bank service charge expense	20	
	Cash		20
	To record bank charges for printing checks		

EXHIBIT 6-5

Comparative Cash Balances, January 31, 20X2

Depositor's Records			
Cash in Bank (receivable from bank)			
1/1/X2 Bal.	11,000	1/5	2,000
1/10	4,000	1/15	3,000
1/24	6,000	1/19	5,000
1/31	7,000	1/29	10,000
	28,000		20,000
1/31/X2 Bal.	8,000		

Bank's Records			
Deposits (payable to depositor)			
1/8	2,000	1/1/X2 Bal.	11,000
1/20	3,000	1/11	4,000
1/28	5,000	1/26	6,000
1/31	20*		
	10,020		21,000
		1/31/X2 Bal.	10,980

*Service charge for printing checks.

Date	Depositor's General Journal	Debit	Credit
1/5	Accounts payable	2,000	
	Cash		2,000
	Check No. 1		
1/10	Cash	4,000	
	Accounts receivable		4,000
	Deposit slip No. 1		
1/15	Income taxes payable	3,000	
	Cash		3,000
	Check No. 2		
1/19	Accounts payable	5,000	
	Cash		5,000
	Check No. 3		
1/24	Cash	6,000	
	Accounts receivable		6,000
	Deposit No. 2		
1/29	Accounts payable	10,000	
	Cash		10,000
	Check No. 4		
1/31	Cash	7,000	
	Accounts receivable		7,000
	Deposit No. 3		

This popular reconciliation format has two major sections. The first section begins with the balance in the company's books, that is, the balance in the Cash T-account. The accountant then makes adjustments for items not entered on the books but already entered by the bank. An example is the $20 service charge. The accountant records these adjustments in the records of the company, in this case deducting the $20 service charge. The second section begins with the balance reported by the bank. Adjustments are made for items entered in the company's books but not yet entered by the bank. These items normally adjust automatically as deposits and checks reach the bank for processing. After adjustments, each section should end with identical adjusted cash balances. This is the amount that should appear as Cash in Bank on the depositor's balance sheet.

Accounting Vocabulary

accounting controls, p. 263
accounting system, p. 264
accounts receivable turnover,
    p. 261
administrative controls,
    p. 263
aging of accounts receivable
    method, p. 259
allowance for bad debts,
    p. 256
allowance for doubtful
    accounts, p. 256
allowance for uncollectible
    accounts, p. 256
allowance method, p. 256
audit committee, p. 267

average collection period,
    p. 262
bad debt recoveries, p. 260
bad debts, p. 254
bad debts expense, p. 254
cash discounts, p. 249
compensating balances,
    p. 253
days to collect accounts
    receivable, p. 262
gross sales, p. 248
internal controls, p. 263
net sales, p. 248
percentage of accounts
    receivable method, p. 259

percentage of completion
    method, p. 247
percentage of sales method,
    p. 257
purchase allowance, p. 248
purchase returns, p. 248
reconcile a bank statement,
    p. 253
reserve for doubtful accounts,
    p. 256
sales allowance, p. 248
sales returns, p. 248
specific write-off method,
    p. 255
trade discounts, p. 249
uncollectible accounts, p. 254

Assignment Material

MyAccountingLab

Questions

6-1 What is the two-pronged test for revenue recognition?

6-2 Describe the timing of revenue recognition for a defense contractor in the United States on a $50 million long-term government contract with work spread evenly over 5 years.

6-3 How do IFRS and U.S. GAAP differ in recognizing revenue on multi-year contracts?

6-4 Why is measuring revenue for a non-cash sale more complex than it is for a cash sale?

6-5 Why is the realizable value of a credit sale often less than that of a cash sale?

6-6 Distinguish between a sales return and a sales allowance.

6-7 Distinguish between a cash discount and a trade discount.

6-8 "Trade discounts should not be recorded by the accountant." Do you agree? Explain.

6-9 "Retailers who accept **VISA** or **MasterCard** are foolish because they do not receive the full price for merchandise they sell." Comment.

6-10 Describe and give two examples of cash equivalents.

6-11 "A compensating balance essentially increases the interest rate on money borrowed." Explain.

6-12 "Cash is only 3% of our total assets. Therefore, we should not waste time designing

systems to manage cash. We should use our time on matters that have a better chance of affecting our profits." Do you agree? Explain.

6-13 It is common in sub shops and pizza parlors around the Baruch College campus to find signs that say "Your purchase is free if the clerk does not give you a receipt" or "Two free lunches if your receipt has a red star." What is management trying to accomplish with these free offers?

6-14 "The cash balance on a company's books should always equal the cash balance shown by its bank." Do you agree? Explain.

6-15 List five internal control procedures used to safeguard cash.

6-16 "If everyone were honest, there would be no need for internal controls to safeguard cash." Do you agree? Explain.

6-17 What is the cost-benefit relationship in deciding whether to offer credit to customers, and whether to accept bank credit cards?

6-18 Distinguish between the allowance method and the specific write-off method for bad debts.

6-19 "The Allowance for Uncollectible Accounts account has no subsidiary ledger, but the Accounts Receivable account does." Explain.

6-20 "Under the allowance method, there are three popular ways to estimate the bad debts expense for a particular year." Name the three.

6-21 What is meant by "aging of accounts"?

6-22 Distinguish between the percentage of sales approach to applying the allowance method and the aging of accounts receivable approach.

6-23 Describe why a write-off of a bad debt should be reversed if collection occurs at a later date.

6-24 Granting credit has two major impacts on a company, one good and one bad. Describe both.

6-25 What is the relationship between the average collection period and the accounts receivable turnover?

6-26 Distinguish between internal accounting control and internal administrative control.

6-27 "The primary responsibility for internal controls rests with the outside auditors." Do you agree? Explain.

6-28 What is the primary responsibility of the audit committee?

6-29 Prepare a checklist of important factors to consider in judging an internal control system.

6-30 "The most important element of successful control is personnel." Explain.

6-31 What is the essential idea of separation of duties?

6-32 When a company makes a bank deposit, it debits its cash account. Why might a bank say your account was "credited"?

Critical Thinking Questions

6-33 Revenue Recognition

A newly created weekly free newspaper has approached your bank seeking a loan. Although the newspaper is free, it gets significant revenue from advertising. In the first 2 months of operations, it reported profits of $10,000. It has receivables of $70,000 on $200,000 of advertising revenue. Some of the revenue reported for these 2 months included special promotional pricing that gave advertisers 4 months of ads for the price of 2. All this promotional revenue was included in the income statement for 2 months. Comment on the reported profit.

6-34 Bank Credit Cards

If a company accepts bank credit cards, why might it accept specific cards instead of all of them? For example, some retailers accept **VISA** and **MasterCard**, but not **American Express** or **Diner's Club**, while the exact opposite is true for some restaurants.

6-35 Criteria for Revenue Recognition

We generally treat revenue as earned when the company delivers merchandise to the customer. At that moment, what additional uncertainty remains about the proper amount of revenue that will ultimately be realized?

6-36 Revenue Recognition and Evaluation of Sales Staff

Revenue on an accrual-accounting basis must be both earned and realized before it is recognized in the income statement. Revenue in cash-basis accounting must be received in cash. Is accrual-basis or cash-basis recognition of revenue more relevant for evaluating the performance of a company's sales staff? Why?

Exercises

6-37 Revenue Recognition

Olympic Logging Company hired Moseley Construction Company to build a new bridge across the Catfish River. The bridge would extend a logging road into a new stand of timber. The contract called for a payment of $12 million on completion of the bridge. Work was begun in 20X0 and completed in 20X2. Total costs were as follows:

20X0	$ 2 million
20X1	3 million
20X2	5 million
Total	$10 million

1. Suppose the accountant for Moseley Construction Company judged that Oympic Logging might not be able to pay the $12 million. How much revenue would you recognize each year?
2. Suppose Olympic Logging is a subsidiary of a major wood products company. Therefore, receipt of payment on the contract is reasonably certain. How much revenue would you recognize each year?

6-38 Non-cash Sales

Suppose Microsoft sold software with a retail value of $120,000 to L.A. Design, Inc. Instead of receiving cash, Microsoft received 12,000 shares of L.A. Design stock, which at the time was selling for $9 per share. What revenue should Microsoft recognize on the sale? Prepare the journal entry for this sale.

6-39 Revenue Recognition, Cash Discounts, and Returns

Kingston Bookstore ordered 1,000 copies of an introductory economics textbook from Prentice-Hall on July 17, 20X0. The books were delivered on August 12, at which time a bill was sent requesting payment of $50 per book. However, a 2% discount was allowed if Prentice-Hall received payment by September 12. Kingston Bookstore sent the proper payment, which was received by Prentice-Hall on September 10. On December 18, Kingston Bookstore returned 60 books to Prentice-Hall for a full cash refund.

1. Prepare the journal entries (if any) for Prentice-Hall on (a) July 17, (b) August 12, (c) September 10, and (d) December 18. Include appropriate explanations.
2. Suppose this was the only sales transaction in 20X0. Prepare the revenue section of Prentice-Hall's income statement.

6-40 Sales Returns and Discounts

Modesto Vegetable Wholesalers had gross sales of $900,000 on credit during the month of March. Sales returns and allowances were $50,000. Cash discounts granted were $35,000.

Prepare an analysis of the impact of these transactions on the balance sheet equation. Also show the journal entries. Prepare a detailed presentation of the revenue section of the income statement.

6-41 Gross and Net Sales

Northeast Machine Tools, Incorporated, reported the following in 20X0 ($ in thousands):

Sales	$680
Cash discounts on sales	20
Sales returns and allowances	40

1. Prepare the revenue section of the 20X0 income statement.
2. Prepare journal entries for (a) initial revenue recognition for 20X0 sales, (b) sales returns and allowances, and (c) collection of accounts receivable. Assume that all sales were on credit and all accounts receivable for 20X0 sales were collected in 20X0. Omit explanations.

6-42 Cash Discounts Transactions

G&N Electronics is a wholesaler that sells on terms of 2/10, n/30. Suppose it sold video equipment to Costco for $400,000 on open account on January 10. Payment (net of cash discount) was received on January 19. By using the balance sheet equation framework, analyze the two transactions for G&N Electronics. Also prepare journal entries.

6-43 Entries for Cash Discounts and Returns on Sales

The Yakima Wine Company, a wholesaler of Washington state wine, sells on credit terms of 2/10, n/30. Consider the following transactions:

June 9	Sales on credit to Pike Wine Mercantile, $30,000.
June 11	Sales on credit to Marty's Liquors, $15,000.
June 18	Collected from Pike Wine Mercantile.
June 26	Accepted the return of six cases from Marty's, $1,000.
July 10	Collected from Marty's.
July 12	Pike Wine Mercantile returned some defective wine that it had acquired on June 9 for $100. Yakima issued a cash refund immediately.

Prepare journal entries for these transactions. Omit explanations. Assume the full appropriate amounts were exchanged.

6-44 Credit Terms, Discounts, and Annual Interest Rates

As the struggling owner of a new Asian Fusion restaurant, you suffer from a habitual shortage of cash. Yesterday the following invoices arrived:

Vender	Face Amount	Terms
Hong Fruit & Vegetables	$ 700	n/30
Rose Exterminators	90	EOM
Nebraska Meat Supply	850	15, EOM
John's Fisheries	1,000	1/10, n/30
Garcia Equipment	2,000	2/10, n/30

1. Write out the exact meaning of each of the terms.
2. You can borrow cash from the local bank on a 10-, 20-, or 30-day note bearing an annual interest rate of 16%. Should you borrow to take advantage of the cash discounts offered by the last two vendors? Why? Show computations. For interest rate computations, assume a 360-day year.

6-45 Accounting for Credit Cards

Lebas Classic Clothing Store has extended credit to customers on open account. Its average experience for each of the past 3 years has been as follows:

	Cash	Credit	Total
Sales	$500,000	$300,000	$800,000
Bad debts expense	—	5,000	5,000
Administrative expense	—	9,000	9,000

Brigette Lebas is considering whether to accept bank cards (for example, VISA or MasterCard). She has resisted because she does not want to bear the cost of the service, which would be 4% of gross sales.

The representative of VISA claims that the availability of bank cards would have increased overall sales by at least 10%. Regardless of the level of sales, the new mix of the sales would be 50% bank card and 50% cash.

1. How would a bank card sale of $300 affect the accounting equation? Where would the discount appear on the income statement?
2. Should Lebas adopt the bank card if sales do not increase? Base your answer solely on the sparse facts given here.
3. Repeat requirement 2, but assume that total sales would increase 10%.

6-46 Trade-ins Versus Discounts

Many states base their sales tax on gross sales less any discount. Trade-in allowances are not discounts, so companies cannot deduct them from the sales price for sales tax purposes. Suppose Emilio Magid had decided to trade in his old car for a new one with a list price of $30,000. He will pay cash of $20,000 plus sales tax. If he had not traded in a car, the dealer would have offered a discount of 15% of the list price. The sales tax is 7%.

How much of the $10,000 price reduction should be called a discount? How much a trade-in? Mr. Magid wants to pay as little sales tax as legally possible.

6-47 Compensating Balances

Mauer Company borrowed $200,000 from Citibank at 8% interest. The loan agreement stated that a compensating balance of $20,000 must be kept in the Mauer checking account at Citibank. The total Mauer cash balance at the end of the year was $45,000.

1. How much usable cash did Mauer Company receive for its $200,000 loan?
2. What was the real interest rate paid by Mauer?
3. Prepare a footnote for the annual report of Mauer Company explaining the compensating balance.

6-48 Uncollectible Accounts

During 20X1, the Rainbow Paint Store had credit sales of $900,000. The store manager expects that 2% of the credit sales will never be collected, although no accounts are written off until 10 assorted steps have been taken to attain collection. The 10 steps require a minimum of 14 months.

Assume that during 20X2, specific customers are identified who are never expected to pay $14,000 that they owe from the sales of 20X1. All 10 collection steps have been completed.

1. Show the impact on the balance sheet equation of the preceding transactions in 20X1 and 20X2 under (a) the specific write-off method and (b) the allowance method. Which method do you prefer? Why?
2. Prepare journal entries for both methods. Omit explanations.

6-49 Specific Write-off Versus Allowance Methods

The **Empire District Electric Company** serves customers in the region where the states of Kansas, Missouri, Arkansas, and Oklahoma come together. Empire District uses the allowance method for recognizing uncollectible accounts. The company's January 1, 2009, balance sheet showed accounts receivable of $39,487,000, which was shown net of uncollectible accounts of $1,265,000.

1. Suppose Empire District wrote off a specific uncollectible account for $27,000 on January 2, 2009. Assume this was the only transaction affecting the accounts receivable or allowance accounts on that day. Give the journal entry to record this write-off. What would the balance sheet show for accounts receivable at the end of the day on January 2.
2. Suppose Empire District used the specific write-off method instead of the allowance method for recognizing uncollectible accounts. Compute the accounts receivable balance that would be shown on the January 1, 2009, balance sheet.

6-50 Allowance Method and Correcting Entries

The El Camino Hospital uses the allowance method in accounting for bad debts. A journal entry was made for writing off the accounts of Jane Jensen, Eunice Belmont, and Samuel Maze. Do you agree with this entry? If not, show the correct entry and the correcting entry.

Bad debts expense	14,321	
Accounts receivable		14,321

6-51 Bad Debts

Prepare all journal entries for 20X2 concerning the following data for a medical clinic that performs elective laser surgery that corrects vision. Such procedures are not covered by third-party payers such as **Blue Cross** or **Medicare**. Consider the following balances of the medical clinic on December 31, 20X1: Gross Receivables from Individual Patients, $225,000 and Allowance for Doubtful Receivables, $50,000, which makes Net Receivables $175,000. During 20X2, total billings to individual patients were $2.5 million. Past experience indicated that 10% of such individual billings would ultimately be uncollectible. Write-offs of receivables during 20X2 were $260,000.

6-52 Bad Debt Allowance

Minnesota Furniture Mart had sales of $1,100,000 during 20X1, including $600,000 of sales on credit. Balances on December 31, 20X0, were Accounts Receivable, $110,000, and Allowance for Bad Debts, $9,000. For 20X1 collections of accounts receivable were $560,000. Bad debts expense was estimated at 2% of credit sales, as in previous years. Write-offs of bad debts during 20X1 were $10,000.

1. Prepare journal entries concerning the preceding information for 20X1.
2. Show the ending balances of the balance sheet accounts, December 31, 20X1.
3. Based on the given data, would you advise Eileen French, the president of the store, that the 2% estimated bad debt rate appears adequate?

6-53 Bad Debt Recoveries

Ridgecrest Department Store has many accounts receivable. The Ridgecrest balance sheet, December 31, 20X1, showed Accounts Receivable, $950,000 and Allowance for Uncollectible Accounts, $40,000. In early 20X2, write-offs of customer accounts of $31,000 were made. In late 20X2, a customer, whose $8,000 debt had been written off earlier, won a $1 million sweepstakes cash prize. The buyer immediately remitted $8,000 to Ridgecrest. The store welcomed the purchaser's money and return to high credit standing.

Prepare the journal entries for the $31,000 write-off in early 20X2 and the $8,000 receipt in late 20X2.

6-54 Subsidiary Ledger

A lumber company made credit sales of $800,000 in 20X4 to 1,000 customers: Schultz, $5,000; Cerruti, $7,000; others, $788,000. Total collections during 20X4 were $720,000 including $5,000 from Cerruti, but nothing was collected from Schultz. At the end of 20X4, an allowance for uncollectible accounts was provided of 2.5% of credit sales.

1. Set up general ledger accounts for Accounts Receivable, Allowance for Uncollectible Accounts, and Bad Debt Expense plus a subsidiary ledger for Accounts Receivable. The subsidiary ledger should consist of two individual accounts plus a third account called Others. Post the entries for 20X4. Prepare a statement of the ending balances of the individual accounts receivable to show that they reconcile with the general ledger account.
2. On March 24, 20X5, the Schultz account was written off. Give the journal entry.

6-55 Accounts Receivable Turnover and Average Collection Period

Vulcan Materials Company, the nation's largest producer of construction aggregates, is headquartered in Birmingham, Alabama. The company had 2008 sales of $3,453 million. Beginning and ending net accounts receivable for the fiscal year were $383 million and $326 million, respectively.

Compute Vulcan's accounts receivable turnover and average collection period for the fiscal year. Assume all sales are on open account.

6-56 Accounts Receivable Ratios

Bayer AG, the German chemical and pharmaceutical company, is the third largest pharmaceutical company in the world. It had the following results in 2006–2008 (in millions of euro):

	2006	2007	2008
Sales	€28,956	€32,385	€32,918
Ending accounts receivable	€ 5,868	€ 5,830	€ 5,953

Compute the accounts receivable turnover and the average collection period for 2007 and 2008. Did Bayer's ratios improve or decline in 2008 compared to 2007? Assume all sales are on credit.

6-57 Internal Control Weaknesses

Identify the internal control weaknesses in each of the following situations, and indicate what change or changes you would recommend to eliminate the weaknesses:

a. The internal audit staff of Ventura Aerospace, Inc., reports to the controller. However, internal audits are undertaken only when a department manager requests one, and audit reports are confidential documents prepared exclusively for the manager. Internal auditors are not allowed to talk to the external auditors.
b. Beth Callo, president of Southwestern State Bank, a small-town New Mexico bank, wants to expand the size of her bank. She hired Fred Sanchez to begin a foreign loan department. Sanchez had previously worked in the international department of a London bank. The president told him to consult with her on any large loans, but she never specified exactly what was meant by "large." At the end of Sanchez's first year, the president was surprised and pleased by his results. Although he had made several loans larger than any made by other sections of the bank and had not consulted with her on any of them, the president hesitated to say anything because the financial results were so good. Callo certainly did not want to upset the person most responsible for the bank's excellent growth in earnings.
c. Isabelle Reed is in charge of purchasing and receiving watches for Import Jewelry, Inc., a chain of jewelry stores. Reed places orders, fills out receiving documents when the watches are delivered, and authorizes payment to suppliers. According to Import Jewelry's procedures manual, Reed's activities should be reviewed by a purchasing supervisor. However, to save money, the supervisor was not replaced when she resigned 3 years ago. No one seems to miss the supervisor.

6-58 Assignment of Duties

General Shoe Wholesalers is a distributor of several popular lines of shoes. It purchases merchandise from several suppliers and sells to hundreds of retail stores. Here is a partial list of the company's necessary office routines:

1. Verifying and comparing related purchase documents: purchase orders, purchase invoices, receiving reports, etc.

2. Preparing vouchers for cash disbursements and attaching supporting purchase documents
3. Signing vouchers to authorize payment (after examining vouchers with attached documents)
4. Preparing checks to pay for the purchases
5. Signing checks (after examining voucher authorization and supporting documents)
6. Mailing checks
7. Daily sorting of incoming mail into items that contain money and items that do not
8. Distributing the mail: money to cashier, reports of money received to accounting department, and remainder to various appropriate offices
9. Making daily bank deposits
10. Reconciling monthly bank statements

The company's chief financial officer has decided that no more than five people will handle all these routines, including himself as necessary.

Prepare a chart to show how these operations could be assigned to the five employees, including the chief financial officer. Use a row for each of the numbered routines and a column for each employee: Financial Officer, A, B, C, D. Place a check mark for each row in one or more of the columns. Observe the rules of the textbook checklist for internal control, especially separation of duties.

6-59 Simple Bank Reconciliation
Study Appendix 6. Belleville Hospital has a bank account. Consider the following information:

a. Balances as of July 31: per books, $48,000; per bank statement, $33,860.
b. Cash receipts of July 31 amounting to $9,000 were recorded and then deposited in the bank's night depository. The bank did not include this deposit on its July statement.
c. The bank statement included service charges of $140.
d. Patients had given the hospital some bad checks amounting to $11,000. The bank marked them NSF and returned them with the bank statement after charging the hospital for the $11,000. The hospital had made no entry for the return of these checks.
e. The hospital's outstanding checks amounted to $6,000.

Required
1. Prepare a bank reconciliation as of July 31.
2. Prepare the hospital journal entries required by the given information.

Problems

6-60 Completed-Contract Method
Post Properties, Inc., is an Atlanta-based real estate investment trust (REIT) that owns and manages upscale multi-family apartment communities and develops condominium properties. The company had 2008 revenues exceeding $280 million. The company's annual report had the following statement: "As of December 31, 2008, all newly developed condominium projects are accounted for under the Completed Contract Method." Part of the company's balance sheet showed the following (in thousands):

Real estate assets	
Land	$ 258,593
Building and improvements	1,802,496
Furniture, fixtures, and equipment	205,221
Construction in progress	189,393
Land held for future investment	81,555
	$2,537,258
Less: Accumulated depreciation	(553,814)
For-sale condominiums	14,610
Assets held for sale, net of accumulated depreciation of $42,379	85,097
Total real estate assets	$2,083,151

1. Why do you suppose Post Properties chose the completed-contract method over the percentage of completion method for its condominium projects?
2. Suppose Post Properties spent $14 million (in cash) in 2009 developing condominium properties that will be sold to the public in 2010 at a total sales price of $40 million. Prepare the journal entry in 2009 to account for the $14 million expenditure.
3. Suppose the company spent another $12 million cash to finish the condominiums in 2010 and sold half of them for $20 million cash by the end of 2010. Prepare the journal entries to recognize the completion and sale of the condominiums.
4. How would the accounting for these condominiums differ if Post Properties were reporting under IFRS?

6-61 Bank Cards

VISA and MasterCard are used to pay for a large percentage of retail purchases. The financial arrangements are similar for both bank cards. A news story said,

> If a cardholder charges a $600 briefcase, for instance, the merchant deposits the sales draft with his bank, which immediately credits $600 less a small transaction fee (usually 2% of the sale) to the merchant's account. The bank that issued the customer his card then pays the merchant's bank $600 less a 1.5% transaction fee, allowing the merchant's bank a 0.5% profit on the transaction.

1. Prepare the journal entry for the sale by the merchant.
2. Prepare the journal entries for the merchant's bank concerning (a) the merchant's deposit and (b) the collection from the customer's bank that issued the card.
3. Prepare the journal entry for the customer's bank that issued the card.
4. The national losses from bad debts for bank cards are about 1.8% of the total billings to cardholders. If so, how can the banks justify providing this service if their revenue from processing is typically 1.5%–2.0%?

6-62 Sales Returns and Allowances

Crown Crafts, Inc., produces children's products such as infant and toddler bedding, bibs, soft goods, and accessories. Major customers include Wal-Mart and Target. A footnote to the company's 2009 financial statements read, "Sales are recorded when goods are shipped to customers and are reported net of allowances for estimated returns and allowances in the consolidated statements of income." The first line of Crown Crafts' income statement was (in thousands) "Net sales . . . $87,398."

1. Suppose customer returns in 2009 were 2.5% of gross sales and sales allowances were 1.5% of gross sales. Assume that the company also gave customers cash discounts of $1,240 thousand. Compute the amount of gross sales. Round to the nearest thousand.
2. Crown Crafts had only one line for net sales on its income statement. Prepare a more detailed presentation of sales, beginning with gross sales and ending with net sales.

6-63 Managing Cash

Volvo Group, the Swedish auto company, had 2008 sales of SEK 304 billion, where SEK stands for Swedish kroner. Among its SEK 372 billion total assets on its balance sheet were cash and cash equivalents of SEK 18 billion. The company has many internal controls related to cash. A new employee in the internal audit department asked why so much effort was put into monitoring cash when it was less than 5% to total assets. Prepare an answer for the new employee.

6-64 Allowance for Credit Losses

Tompkins Financial Corporation, a multibank holding company headquartered in Ithaca, New York, included the following in the footnotes to its 2008 annual report ($ in thousands):

> Changes in the allowance for loan and lease losses at December 31 are summarized as follows:

	2008
Reserve at beginning of year	$16,092
Provisions charged to operations	5,428
Recoveries on loans and leases	442
Loans and leases charged off	(3,290)
Reserve at end of year	$18,672

1. Terminology in bank financial statements sometimes differs slightly from that in statements of industrial companies. Explain what is meant by "allowance for loan and lease losses," "provisions charged to operations," and "loans and leases charged off" in the footnote.
2. Prepare the 2008 journal entries to record the writing off of specific credit losses, the recovery of previously written off credit losses, and the charge for credit losses against 2008 income. Omit explanations.
3. Suppose the bank analyzed its loans at the end of 2008 and decided that a reserve for loan and lease losses equal to $20 million was required. Compute the provision that would be charged in 2008.
4. The bank had income before income taxes of $43,941,000 in 2008. Compute the income before income taxes if the reserve for loan and lease losses at the end of 2008 had been $20 million?

6-65 Aging of Accounts

Consider the following analysis of Accounts Receivable, February 28, 20X0:

Name of Customer	Total	Remarks
Huang Nurseries	$ 20,000	25% over 90 days, 75% 61–90 days
Michael's Landscaping	8,000	75% 31–60 days, 25% under 30 days
Shoven Garden Supply	12,000	60% 61–90 days, 40% 31–60 days
Loring Farm	20,000	All under 30 days
Hjortshoj Florists	4,000	25% 61–90 days, 75% 1–30 days
Other accounts (each detailed)	80,000	50% 1–30 days, 30% 31–60 days, 15% 61–90 days, 5% over 90 days
Total	$144,000	

Prepare an aging schedule, classifying ages into four categories: 1–30 days, 31–60 days, 61–90 days, and over 90 days. Assume that the prospective bad debt percentages for each category are 0.2%, 0.8%, 10%, and 85%, respectively. What is the ending balance in Allowance for Uncollectible Accounts?

6-66 Percentage of Ending Accounts Receivable

Consider the following data:

	Accounts Receivable at End of Year	Accounts Receivable Deemed Uncollectible and Written Off During Subsequent Years
20X1	$210,000	$ 8,000
20X2	170,000	6,000
20X3	195,000	7,000
20X4	230,000	10,300
20X5	275,000	13,000
20X6	240,000	9,820

The unadjusted credit balance in Allowance for Uncollectible Accounts at December 31, 20X7, is $600. By using the percentage of ending accounts receivable method, prepare an adjusting entry to bring Allowance for Uncollectible Accounts to the appropriate amount at December 31, 20X7, when the Accounts Receivable balance is $250,000. Base your estimate of the percentage on the actual loss experience in the prior 6 years.

6-67 Estimates of Uncollectible Accounts

Tolon Company has made an analysis of its sales and accounts receivable for the past 5 years. Assume that all accounts written off in a year related to sales of the preceding year and were part of the accounts receivable at the end of that year. That is, no account is written off before the end of the year of the sale, and all accounts remaining unpaid are written off before the end of the year following the sale. The analysis showed the following:

	Sales	Ending Accounts Receivable	Bad Debts Written Off During the Year
20X1	$680,000	$ 90,000	$12,000
20X2	750,000	97,000	12,500
20X3	750,000	103,000	14,000
20X4	850,000	114,000	16,500
20X5	840,000	110,000	17,600

The balance in Allowance for Uncollectible Accounts on December 31, 20X4, was $16,100. Use all the relevant data above in answering the following questions.

1. Determine the bad debts expense for 20X5 and the balance of the Allowance for Uncollectible Accounts for December 31, 20X5, using the percentage of sales method.
2. Repeat requirement 1 using the percentage of ending accounts receivable method.

6-68 Percentage of Sales and Percentage of Ending Accounts Receivable

Flagstaff Equipment Company had credit sales of $7 million during 20X0. Most customers paid promptly (within 30 days), but a few took longer; an average of 1.2% of credit sales were never paid. On December 31, 20X0, accounts receivable were $480,000. The Allowance for Bad Debts account, before any recognition of 20X0 bad debts, had a $1,200 debit balance.

Flagstaff produces and sells mountaineering equipment and other outdoor gear. Most of the sales (about 80%) come in the period of March through August; the other 20% is spread almost evenly over the other 6 months. Over the last 6 years, an average of 18% of the December 31 balance in accounts receivable has not been collected.

1. Suppose Flagstaff Equipment uses the percentage of sales method to calculate an allowance for bad debts. Present the accounts receivable and allowance accounts as they should appear on the December 31, 20X0, balance sheet. Give the journal entry required to recognize the bad debts expense for 20X0.
2. Repeat requirement 1, except assume that Flagstaff Equipment uses the percentage of ending accounts receivable method.
3. Which method do you prefer? Why?

6-69 Student Loans

The 2008 annual report of the University of Washington includes information about its receivables from student loans in a footnote to the financial statements ($ in thousands):

	2008	2007
Student loans	$75,387	$72,802
Less: Allowances	(8,861)	(8,402)
Total, net	$66,526	$64,400

1. Compare the quality of the loans outstanding at the end of 2008 with the quality of those outstanding at the end of 2007.

2. Suppose the university had granted $500,000 of additional loans before the end of 2008. Using the allowance method, which accounts would be affected by the additional loans and by how much? Use the bad-debt percentage for loans outstanding at the end of 2008.

6-70 Discounts and Doubtful Items

Eli Lilly, a major pharmaceutical company, includes the following in its June 30, 2009, balance sheet ($ amounts in millions):

Accounts receivable, net of allowances of $99.4	$2,841.3

1. Compute the ratio of the allowance for doubtful items to gross accounts receivable for June 30, 2009. In 2005, this ratio was 2.8%. What are some possible reasons for the changes in this ratio?
2. Independent of the actual balances, prepare a journal entry to write off an uncollectible account of $150,000 on July 2, 2009.

6-71 Uncollectible Accounts

Nike, Inc., is a worldwide supplier of athletic products. Its balance sheet on May 31, 2009, included the following data ($ in millions):

Accounts receivable, less allowance for doubtful accounts of $110.8	$2,883.9

1. The company uses the allowance method for accounting for bad debts. The company added $50.7 million to the allowance during the year ending May 31, 2009. Write-offs of uncollectible accounts were $18.3 million. Show (a) the impact on the balance sheet equation of these transactions and (b) the journal entries.
2. Calculate the allowance balance on May 31, 2008.
3. Suppose Nike had used the specific write-off method for accounting for bad debts. By using the same information as in requirement 1, show (a) the impact on the balance sheet equation and (b) the journal entry.
4. How would these Nike balance sheet amounts on May 31, 2009, have been affected if the specific write-off method had been used up to that date? Be specific.

6-72 Uncollectible Accounts

Oracle is the world's largest supplier of database software. Its balance sheet included the following presentation:

	May 31	
	2009	**2008**
	($ in millions)	
Trade receivables, net of allowance for doubtful accounts of $270 as of May 31, 2009, and $303 as of May 31, 2008	$4,430	$5,127

During 2009, Oracle added $95 million to its allowance for estimated doubtful accounts. (a) Calculate the write-offs of uncollectible accounts, and show (b) the impact on the balance sheet equation of these transactions and (c) the journal entries.

6-73 Allowance for Doubtful Accounts

Daimler AG is a German automobile and truck manufacturer. Its brands include Mercedes, smart, and a variety of truck and bus brands. Like many automobile companies, Daimler not only sells cars and trucks, it finances many of the sales. On its annual report, the company separates trade receivables from the receivables from financial services. Its 2008 annual report contained the information in Exhibit 6-6.

EXHIBIT 6-6

Daimler AG

Receivables Information from Financial Statement Notes (amounts are in millions of euro)

Receivables from financial services:

	December 31, 2008	December 31, 2007
Gross carrying amount	€43,321	€39,807
Allowance for doubtful accounts	(934)	(594)
Carrying amount, net	€42,387	€39,213

Changes in the allowance account for receivables from financial services:

	2008
Balance at January 1	€ 594
Charged to costs and expenses	712
Amounts written off	(237)
Reversals	(131)
Currency translation and other changes	(4)
Balance at December 31	€ 934

Trade receivables:

	December 31, 2008	December 31, 2007
Gross carrying amount	€ 7,619	€ 6,738
Allowance for doubtful accounts	(620)	(377)
Carrying amount, net	€ 6,999	€ 6,361

Changes in the allowance account for trade receivables:

	2008
Balance at January 1	€ 377
Charged to costs and expenses	280
Amounts written off	(42)
Currency translation and other changes	5
Balance at December 31	€ 620

1. Use the information in Exhibit 6-6 to reproduce the journal entries affecting the allowance for doubtful accounts for both trade receivables and receivables from financial services during the year ending December 31, 2008. Treat "Reversals" as reductions in bad debt expense and in the allowance for doubtful accounts.
2. Compare the allowance for credit losses as a percentage of end-of-period gross receivables for trade receivables compared to receivables from financial services for December 31, 2008. Which receivables are riskier? Explain.
3. Compare the allowance for credit losses as a percentage of end-of-period gross receivables at December 31, 2008, with that at December 31, 2007, for both trade receivables and receivables from financial services. Are receivables more risky in 2007 or 2008? Explain.

6-74 Negative Balance in Allowance for Bad Debts Account

This problem is an extension of exercise 6-52. Only the amount of write-off of bad debts is different.

Minnesota Furniture Mart had sales of $1,100,000 during 20X1, including $600,000 of sales on credit. Balances on December 31, 20X0, were Accounts Receivable, $110,000, and Allowance for Bad Debts, $9,000. For 20X1 collections of accounts receivable were $560,000. Bad debts expense was estimated at 2% of credit sales, as in previous years. Suppose a recession hit during 20X1 and the write-off of bad debts was $25,000, which is much higher than expected.

1. What is the balance in the Allowance for Bad Debts account at the end of 20X1? If left unadjusted, how would this affect the Net Accounts Receivable? Does this seem reasonable?
2. What should Minnesota Furniture Mart do to rectify this situation?

6-75 Average Collection Period

Consider the following:

	20X3	20X2	20X1
Sales	$2,000,000	$2,500,000	$2,400,000

	December 31		
	20X3	20X2	20X1
Accounts receivable	$ 170,000	$ 190,000	$ 180,000

Of the total sales, 80% are on account.

Compute the days to collect accounts receivable for the years 20X2 and 20X3. Comment on the results.

6-76 Classic Case of Sales, Accounts Receivable, and Ethics

Writing in *Corporate Cashflow*, Howard Schillit described how the market value of Comptronix fell from $238 million to $67 million in a few hours when it was revealed that management had "cooked the books." Comptronix provided contract manufacturing services to makers of electronic equipment. Its 1991 financial results looked strong.

	1991	1990	Change
Sales	$102.0 million	$70.2 million	+45%
Accounts receivable	12.6 million	12.0 million	+ 5%
Accounts receivable turnover	8.1	5.9	

However, the relationship between sales and accounts receivable sent signals to knowledgeable analysts.

1. Discuss the relationship that you would expect between sales and accounts receivable in a normal situation.
2. What unethical actions might cause sales to grow so much faster than accounts receivable? What unethical actions might cause the opposite, that is, for accounts receivable to grow faster than sales?
3. What is the most likely type of "cooking the books" that occurred at Comptronix?

6-77 Audit Committee Role

In a recent court decision, a U.S. corporation was required to delegate certain responsibilities to its audit committee. The audit committee was required to do the following:

1. Consult with its independent auditors before deciding any significant or material accounting question or policy.
2. Retain independent auditors to perform quarterly reviews of all financial statements prior to public issuance.
3. Conduct internal audits, with personnel reporting directly to the audit committee (internal auditors must report quarterly to the audit committee).
4. Retain or dismiss independent and internal auditors.
5. Consult with the independent auditors on their quarterly reviews of financial statements.
6. Review all monthly corporate and division financial statements and the auditor's management letter.
7. Receive quarterly reports from independent auditors on internal control deficiencies.
8. Review and approve all reports to shareholders and the SEC before dissemination.

The court also ruled that the audit committee must be composed of at least three outside directors who have no business dealings with the firm other than directors' fees and expense reimbursements.

a. Prepare a partial corporation organization chart to depict these requirements. Use boxes only for Audit Committee, Independent Auditors, Internal Auditing, Finance Vice-President, and

Board of Directors. Connect the appropriate boxes with lines: solid lines for direct responsibility, and dashed lines for information and communications. Place numbers on these lines to correspond to the eight items specified by the court decision.

b. Identify the main elements of the chapter checklist of internal control that seem most relevant to this system design.

6-78 Embezzlement of Cash Receipts

Fix-A-Dent Company is a small auto body shop. It has only a few employees.

The owner of Fix-A-Dent, who is also its president and general manager, makes daily deposits of customer checks in the company bank account and writes all checks issued by the company. The president also reconciles the monthly bank statement with the books when the bank statement is received in the mail.

The assistant to Fix-A-Dent's president renders secretarial services, which include taking dictation, typing letters, and processing all mail, both incoming and outgoing. Each day the assistant opens the incoming mail and gives the president the checks received from customers. The vouchers attached to the checks are separated by the assistant and sent to the bookkeeper, along with any other remittance advices that have been enclosed with the checks.

The bookkeeper makes prompt entries to credit customers' accounts for their remittances. From these accounts, the bookkeeper prepares monthly statements for mailing to customers.

Other employees include mechanics and other auto-repair personnel.

For the thefts described next, explain briefly how each could have been concealed and what precautions you would recommend for forestalling the theft and its concealment:

1. The president's assistant takes some customers' checks, forges the company's endorsements, deposits the checks in a personal bank account, and destroys the check vouchers and any other remittance advices that have accompanied these checks.
2. The same action is taken as in requirement 1, except that the vouchers and other remittance advices are sent intact to the bookkeeper.

6-79 Film Processing

Write no more than one page about the possible areas where internal controls should be instituted in the following business described briefly. Keep in mind the size of the business, and do not suggest controls of a type impossible to set up in a firm of this sort. Make any reasonable assumptions about management duties and policies not expressly described.

You have a film-developing service in Boston, with 10 employees driving their own cars 6 days a week to contact about 40 places each, where film is left to be picked up and developed. Drivers bring film in one day and return the processed film the second or third day. Stores pay the driver for his or her charges made on film picked up at their stores, less a percentage for their work as agents. The driver then turns this cash in to the Boston office, where all film is developed and books are kept. Between 6 and 10 employees work at the office in Boston, depending on the volume of work. You run the office and have one full-time accounting-clerical employee. Route drivers are paid monthly by miles of route covered.

6-80 Appraisal of Internal Control System

The following is from the *San Francisco Chronicle*:

> The flap over missing ferry fares was peacefully—and openly—resolved at a meeting of the Golden Gate Bridge District finance committee yesterday.
>
> Only a week ago, the subject was a matter of furious dispute in which bridge manager Dale W. Luehring was twice called a liar and there were prospects of a closed meeting on personnel matters.
>
> But yesterday, after a week of investigation, the meeting turned out to be public after all, and attorney Thomas M. Jenkins revealed the full total of stolen ferry tickets equaled $26.20.
>
> The controversy began when auditor Gordon Dahlgren complained that there was an auditing "problem" and that he had not been informed when four children swiped $13.75 worth of tickets February 28. Committee chairman Ben K. Lerer, of San Francisco, ordered a full investigation.

Jenkins said the situation was complicated because children under 5 have been allowed to ride the ferry without a ticket, but after May 1 everyone will have to have a ticket, allowing for a closer audit.

Secondly, Jenkins explained, the "vault" in which tickets are deposited was proved insecure (resulting in two thefts totaling $26.20 worth of tickets) but has been replaced.

In the future, it was decided, all thefts of cash or tickets must be reported immediately to the California Highway Patrol or the local police, the bridge lieutenant on duty, the general manager, the security officer, the auditor-controller, and the transit manager.

In addition, employees must make a full written report within 24 hours to the president of the district board, the chairman of the finance-auditing committee, the auditor-controller, the attorney, the bus transit manager, the water transit manager, the toll captain, and the chief of administration and security.

What is your reaction to the new system? Explain, giving particular attention to applicable criteria for appraising an internal control system.

6-81 Casino Skimming

An article in the *Wall Street Journal* reported that about $7 million in quarters disappeared from the slot machines of four casinos of **Argent Corporation** in an 18-month period. The coins weighed nearly 150 tons, and the odds against such a payout to players of the slot machines is 1 in 3,875,000,000,000,000,000,000,000,000,000,000,000,000,000,000,000,000—an extremely unlikely event, to say the least. The disappearance was part of the biggest known skim operation ever. Skimming is taking a portion of gambling revenues before they can be counted for tax purposes.

Internal control is especially important in casinos. Meters in the slot machines record the winnings paid to customers. Coins are taken immediately to the slot counting room when machines are emptied. In the counting rooms, coins are weighed, and a portion is returned to the change booths.

What items in the chapter checklist of internal control seem especially important concerning slot machine operations? How could the money from slot machine operations have been stolen in such large amounts?

6-82 Employee Dishonesty

Consider the following true newspaper reports of dishonesty:

a. At a small manufacturer, supervisors had access to time cards and handed out W-2 forms each year. The supervisors pocketed $80,000 a year in the paychecks for phantom workers.
b. A manager at a busy branch office of a copying service had a receipt book of his own. Jobs of $200 and $300 were common. The manager stole cash by simply giving customers a receipt from his book instead of one of the company's numbered forms.
c. A purchasing agent received tiny kickbacks on buttons, zippers, and other trims used at a successful dress company. The agent got rich, and the company was overcharged $10 million.

Specify what control or controls would have helped avoid each of the listed situations.

6-83 Internal Control Weaknesses

Identify the internal control weaknesses in each of the following situations.

a. Josh Robey, a football star at the local university, was hired by football supporter R.D. Case to work in the accounting department of Case Machining during summer vacation. Providing summer jobs is one way Case supports the team. After a week of training, Robey opened the mail containing checks from customers, recorded the payment in the books, and prepared the bank deposit slip.
b. Juan Sanchez manages a local franchise of a major 24-hour convenience store. Sanchez brags that he keeps labor costs well below the average for such stores by operating with only one clerk. He has not granted a pay increase in 4 years. He loses a lot of clerks, but he can find replacements.
c. Bronko Underhill operates an **Exxon** service station. Because it takes much extra time for attendants to walk from the gas pumps to the inside cash register, Underhill placed a locked

cash box next to the pumps and gave each attendant a key. Cash and credit card slips are placed in the cash box. Each day the amounts are counted and entered in total into the cash register.

d. Lazlo Perconte trusts his employees. The former manager purchased fidelity bonds on employees who handle cash. Perconte decided that such bonds showed a lack of trust, so he ceased purchasing them. Besides, the money saved helped Perconte meet his budget for the year.

6-84 Cooking the Books

In *The Accounting Wars,* author Mark Stevens presents a chapter on "Book Cooking, Number Juggling, and Other Tricks of the Trade." He quotes Glen Perry, a former chief accountant of the SEC's Enforcement Division: "Companies play games with their financial reports for any number of reasons, the most common being the intense pressure on corporate management to produce an unbroken stream of increasing earnings reports." Stevens then lists Perry's "terrible 10 of accounting frauds—ploys used to misrepresent corporate financial statements":

1. Recognition of revenues before they are realized
2. Recognition of rentals to customers as sales
3. Inclusion of fictitious amounts in inventories
4. Improper cutoffs at year-end
5. Improper application of last-in, first-out (LIFO)
6. Creation of fraudulent year-end transactions to boost earnings
7. Failure to recognize losses through write-offs and allowances
8. Inconsistent accounting practices without disclosures
9. Capitalization or improper deferral of expenses
10. Inclusion of unusual gains in operating income

Suppose you were a division manager in a major corporation. Give a brief specific example of each of the 10 methods.

6-85 Straightforward Bank Reconciliation

Study Appendix 6. The City of Blooming Prairie has a checking account with Security Bank. The city's cash balance on February 28, 20X1, was $30,000. The deposit balance on the bank's books on February 28, 20X1, was also $30,000. The following transactions occurred during March.

Date	Check Number	Amount	Explanation
3/1	261	$11,500	
3/6	262	9,000	Payment of accounts payable
3/10		12,000	Collection of taxes receivable
3/14	263	15,000	Acquisition of equipment for cash
3/17		16,000	Collection of license fees receivable
3/28	264	8,000	Payment of accounts payable
3/30	265	21,000	Payment of interest on municipal bonds
3/31		25,000	Collection of taxes receivable

All cash receipts are deposited via a night depository system after the close of the municipal business day. Therefore, the receipts are not recorded by the bank until the succeeding day.

On March 31, the bank charged the City of Blooming Prairie $100 for miscellaneous bank services.

1. Prepare the journal entries on the bank's books for check 262 and the deposit of March 10.
2. Prepare the journal entries for all March transactions on the books of the City of Blooming Prairie.
3. Post all transactions for March to T-accounts for the City's Cash in Bank account and the bank's Deposit account. Assume only checks 261 to 263 have been presented to the bank in March, each taking 4 days to clear the bank's records.
4. Prepare a bank reconciliation for the City of Blooming Prairie, March 31, 20X1. The final three City of Blooming Prairie transactions of March had not affected the bank's records as of March 31. What adjusting entry in the books of the City of Blooming Prairie is required on March 31?
5. What would be the cash balance shown on the balance sheet of the City of Blooming Prairie on March 31, 20X1?

6-86 Semicomplex Bank Reconciliation

Study Appendix 6. An employee, Omar Larson, has a personal bank account. His employer deposits his weekly paycheck automatically each Friday. Larson's check register (checkbook) for October is summarized as follows:

Reconciled cash balance, September 30, 20X1				$ 100
Additions				
Weekly payroll deposits	October			
	3			800
	10			800
	17			800
	24			800
Deposit of check received for sale on eBay	25			475
Deposit of check received as winner of cereal contest	31			400
Subtotal				$4,175
Deductions				
Checks written No. 325–339	1–23	$3,200		
Check No. 340	26	120		
Check No. 341	30	90		
Check No. 342	31	340	3,750	
Cash in bank, October 31, 20X1				$ 425

The bank statement is summarized in Exhibit 6-7. Note that NSF means "not sufficient funds." The check deposited on October 25 bounced (that is, was not honored by the payer's bank). By prearrangement with Larson, the bank automatically lends sufficient amounts (in multiples of $100) to ensure that his balance is never negative.

1. Prepare Larson's bank reconciliation, October 31, 20X1.
2. Assume Larson keeps a personal set of books on the accrual basis. Prepare the compound journal entry called for by the bank reconciliation.

6-87 Ethics and Bank Reconciliations

Study Appendix 6. The Oakfield Chamber of Commerce recently hired you as an accounting assistant. On assuming your position on September 15, one of your first tasks was to reconcile the August bank statement. Your immediate supervisor, Ms. Santelli, had been in charge of nearly all accounting tasks, including paying bills, preparing the payroll, and recording all transactions in the books. She has been very helpful to you, providing assistance on all the tasks she has asked you to do. The reconciliation was no different. Without assistance, you were able to locate the following information from the bank statement and the Chamber's books:

Balance per books	$16,510
Balance per bank statement	16,500
Bank service charges	30
NSF check returned	3,000
Deposit in transit	4,600
Outstanding checks	9,850

You also found a deposit on the bank statement of $3,300 that was incorrectly recorded as $3,030 on the Chamber's books.

When you could not reconcile the book and bank balances, you asked Ms. Santelli for help. She responded that an additional $2,500 deposit was in transit.

1. Assume the information you obtained without Ms. Santelli's help is accurate and complete. Prepare the August bank reconciliation with the original information, showing that the book and the bank balances do not reconcile.

EXHIBIT 6-7

**Bank Statement of
Omar Larson**

SUMMARY OF YOUR CHECKING ACCOUNTS	
Beginning balance	$ 100.00
Deposits	4,575.00
Withdrawals	3,795.00
Service charges/fees	25.00*
Ending balance	855.00
Minimum balance on 10-28	**−80.00**

*$10.00 for returned check; $15.00 monthly service charge.

CHECKING ACTIVITY

Deposits

Posted	Amount	Description
10-03	800.00	Payroll deposit
10-10	800.00	Payroll deposit
10-17	800.00	Payroll deposit
10-24	800.00	Payroll deposit
10-25	475.00	Deposit
10-28	100.00	Automatic loan
10-31	800.00	Payroll deposit

Withdrawals

Ck. No.	Paid	Amount
325–339 Various dates in October. These would be shown by specific amounts, but are shown here as a total.		$3,200.00
340	10–27	120.00
NSF	10–28	475.00

Total number of checks = 16

2. Prepare a reconciliation using the new number, $7,100, for deposits in transit.
3. Why might Ms. Santelli have instructed you to add $2,500 to the deposits in transit? What might she be trying to hide? If there were deceit, when might it be discovered?
4. What actions would you take if you were the accounting assistant?
5. By coincidence, you noticed a $2,500 cancelled check, signed by Ms. Santelli, to an individual whose name you did not recognize. How would this change your answer to number 4?

Collaborative Learning Exercise

6-88 Revenue Recognition

Form groups of three to six students. Each student should pick one of the six industries listed at the top of the next page. The Standard Industrial Classification (SIC) number is provided for each industry. This number may be helpful in locating companies in that industry, especially if using search routines in electronic media.

Members of each group should learn as much as possible about the revenue recognition issues in their industry. Select at least two companies in the industry, and examine the description of each company's revenue recognition policies in the footnotes (usually in footnote 1 or 2) to the financial statements. Two possible companies are listed for each industry, but do not feel restricted to using the companies listed.

After the individual research on a particular industry, get together as a team and report on what each member has learned. Compare and contrast the issues relating to when revenue is earned and realized in each industry. Discuss why issues that are important in one industry are unimportant in another.

- 2721—Periodicals Publishing and Printing
  Marvel Entertainment Group
  Readers Digest Association

- 4512—Air Transportation, Scheduled
  Alaska Air Group
  Southwest Airlines Company

- 4911—Electric Services
  Duke Power
  Puget Sound Energy

- 6311—Life Insurance
  Allstate Corporation
  USLIFE, Incorporated

- 7811—Motion Picture, Videotape Production
  Dick Clark Productions
  Walt Disney Company

- 8062—General Medical and Surgical Hospitals
  Columbia/HCA Healthcare
  Regency Health Services

Analyzing and Interpreting Financial Statements

6-89 Financial Statement Research

Select an industry and choose two companies within that industry.

Calculate the accounts receivable turnover and days to collect accounts receivable for the two companies for 2 years and comment on the results.

6-90 Analyzing Starbucks' Financial Statements

Find **Starbucks'** 2009 financial statements either through the SEC Edgar database or on Starbucks' Web site.

1. Starbucks combines cash and cash equivalents on the balance sheet. Examine the first footnote to the financial statement and determine how Starbucks defines cash equivalents.
2. The first line of Starbucks' income statement is "Net revenues." From the Revenue Recognition section of footnote 1 to the financial statements, determine what items are deducted from gross revenue to yield net revenue.
3. Calculate the days to collect accounts receivable for the year ended September 28, 2009, assuming all sales were on account.

6-91 Analyzing Financial Statements Using the Internet: Oracle

Go to www.sec.gov to search for **Oracle Corporation** in the EDGAR database or go to the Oracle Web site. Find Oracle Corporation's latest 10K filing (annual report).

Answer the following questions about the company:

1. Under Part I, Item 1, how does Oracle categorize its products and services? What are its operating segments?
2. Examine the Revenue Recognition accounting policy in the Notes to Consolidated Financial Statements. When does Oracle recognize revenue from new software licenses? For software license updates and product support contracts?
3. From the Notes to Consolidated Financial Statements, determine whether Oracle finances sales to its customers on a long-term basis.
4. Examine Oracle's balance sheet. Which method of accounting for uncollectible accounts does the company use? How can you tell?

7

Inventories and Cost of Goods Sold

LEARNING OBJECTIVES

After studying this chapter, you should be able to:

1 Link inventory valuation to gross profit.

2 Use both perpetual and periodic inventory systems.

3 Calculate the cost of merchandise acquired.

4 Compute income and inventory values using the three principal inventory valuation methods allowed under both U.S. GAAP and IFRS and the one method allowed only by U.S. GAAP.

5 Use the lower-of-cost-or-market method to value inventories under both U.S. GAAP and IFRS.

6 Show the effects of inventory errors on financial statements.

7 Evaluate the gross profit percentage and inventory turnover.

8 Describe characteristics of LIFO and how they affect the measurement of income (Appendix 7A).

9 Determine inventory costs for a manufacturing company (Appendix 7B).

Have you ever gone to your local hardware store and been frustrated because it did not have what you wanted? A goal of **The Home Depot** is to help you avoid this frustration. The company does it by keeping a large inventory—30,000 to 40,000 different items, more than three times the number at a typical hardware store. As former CEO and Chairman Bernie Marcus said, one of the three main values at The Home Depot is assortment: "everything a do-it-yourselfer needs to complete a project."

Inventory requires a large investment by retail companies—$10.7 billion at The Home Depot, about 26% of the company's total assets—and accounting for this inventory is important. By carefully monitoring inventory levels, The Home Depot makes sure it does not

The aisles of The Home Depot are stacked high with products so customers can find what they need. These products are the company's inventories, and managing its inventories is essential to The Home Depot. Recording this inventory on its balance sheet and recognizing cost of goods sold when a customer buys an item are important steps in measuring the company's assets and income. We learn about inventory accounting in this chapter.

lose sales by having too little inventory and does not lose money by investing in too much inventory. Sales have grown 9% per year over the last 10 years and gross margins have improved, but management was able to reduce inventories from 32% of sales to 26%.●

In Chapter 6, we learned how to account for sales revenues. Of course, when a company sells a product, it also incurs costs. For example, The Home Depot must buy the tools it sells. Similarly, a Toyota dealership has to pay for every car it sells. The company must recognize the cost of tools or Toyotas sold along with the related revenues.

Determining the cost of the Toyota sold is easy enough—you look up the cost on the invoice for the specific car you sold. Unfortunately, the calculations are not always that simple. Because The Home Depot purchases products such as tools in quantity and holds them in inventory, it is often difficult to trace the precise cost of a single product. As a result, companies must develop procedures to determine the value of their inventories and the cost of goods sold. The Home Depot had sales of $71.3 billion in the year ended February 1, 2009, with cost of goods sold of $47.3 billion. This provides a gross margin of $24.0 billion or 34% of sales, up from 30% in 1999.

This chapter examines various methods for valuing and accounting for inventories that companies such as Toyota or The Home Depot use to calculate cost of sales, inventory, and gross margin measures. You will find different inventory accounting practices around the globe, and multiple methods exist even in the same country or in the same industry. By understanding these differences, you are able to distinguish differences between companies that arise solely from different accounting practices and real economic differences that distinguish two firms based on their profitability.

Gross Profit and Cost of Goods Sold

OBJECTIVE 1

Link inventory valuation to gross profit.

For merchandising firms, an initial step in assessing profitability is determining gross profit (also called profit margin or gross margin), which you learned in Chapter 4 is the difference between sales revenues and cost of the goods sold. Sales revenues must cover the cost of goods sold and provide a gross profit sufficient to cover all other costs including R&D, selling and marketing, administration, and so on. As illustrated in Exhibit 7-1, companies report products being held prior to sale as inventory, a current asset in the balance sheet. When they sell the goods, the cost of the inventory becomes an expense, Cost of Goods Sold or Cost of Sales, in the income statement. We deduct this expense from Net Sales to determine Gross Profit, and we deduct additional expenses from Gross Profit to determine Operating Income. The Business First box provides additional information about The Home Depot and other retailers.

EXHIBIT 7-1

Merchandising Company (Retailer or Wholesaler)

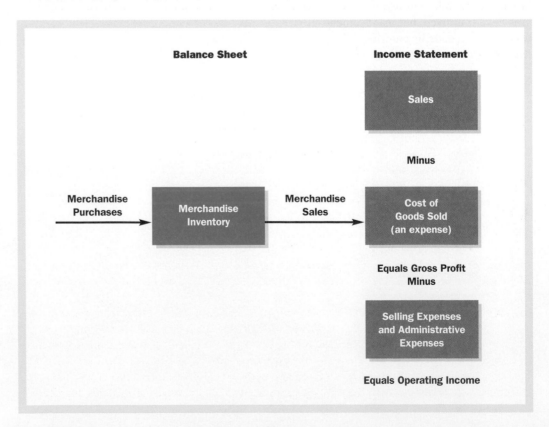

BUSINESS FIRST

INVENTORY MANAGEMENT AND MERCHANDISING

The Home Depot is on a roll. Following its founding in Atlanta in 1978, its growth has been phenomenal. It is the nation's second-largest retailer (behind Wal-Mart) and is a component of the Dow Jones Industrial Average. The company has stores worldwide and generated revenue growth of 9% per year for the 10 years ending February 1, 2009. However, earnings grew only 4% per year. The last 5 years have not been as strong. The following data presents some comparisons:

5-Year Average Annual Growth Rates

	Revenue	EPS
The Home Depot	3%	–11%
Wal-Mart	9	9
JCPenney	0.5	–4
Lowe's	7	3

The Home Depot attends to details. Of its 40,000 items, including precut Venetian blinds, tool rentals, Christmas trees, and even pretzels, most are responses to customer suggestions.

When General Electric (GE) experienced shortages in light bulb inventories, Bernie Marcus, The Home Depot founder and CEO, immediately cut a deal with Phillips, the Dutch electronics company, to replace GE as light bulb supplier. The Home Depot also seeks new opportunities. In surveys of customers, they found GE was named the third best brand for water heaters, despite the fact that GE did not make water heaters. What's the solution? Pay GE a royalty for use of the name, pay Rheem to manufacture water heaters with the GE name, and become the exclusive distributor for a great product.

The Home Depot uses advanced technology. Inventory tracking and order placement occurs through wireless pen-based PCs that staff wheel up and down aisles to transmit current inventory counts and to execute orders based on a database of sales history and forecasts. The Home Depot's credit approvals take less than a second, an industry standard. The company pioneered self-checkout in its industry.

Of course, today no one is safe from competition. Lowe's is running hard as the second player in this market. Although it is only 70% the size of The Home Depot, its growth rates are impressive with revenue growth of 7% and EPS growth of 3%. Stay tuned.

Sources: The Home Depot 2008 Annual Report; Wal-Mart 2009 Annual Report; JCPenney 2008 Annual Report; Lowe's Companies, Inc 2009 Annual Report; "Profit in a Big Orange," *Forbes*, January 24, 2000, pp. 122–128.

The Basic Concept of Inventory Accounting

In theory, accounting for inventory and cost of goods sold is very simple. Suppose Christina sells T-shirts. Periodically, she orders many shirts of various sizes and colors. They sell, she orders more, and her business operating cycle continues on in this way. After a year, Christina prepares financial statements to evaluate her success. To calculate the value of inventory on hand, she counts all the inventory items remaining at year-end. She then develops a **cost valuation** by assigning a specific value from the historical-cost records to each item in ending inventory. If the shirts cost $5.00 each and there are 100 shirts remaining in inventory, Christina's total ending inventory is $500. Suppose she had no shirts at the beginning of the year, and total purchases for the year were $26,000. Her cost of goods sold would thus be $25,500 ($26,000 of available shirts minus $500 of unsold shirts). Notice that the key to calculating the cost of goods sold is accounting for the remaining inventory.

Unfortunately, determining the cost of goods sold and accounting for inventory are not this simple in practice. In the following sections, we show you the major techniques companies use for measuring inventories and examine problems that arise in using these techniques. As a manager or investor, you want to know how inventory accounting methods can affect reported earnings and how events such as inflation or changing inventory levels affect inventory values and thereby affect earnings. Let's begin by examining two major types of systems for keeping inventory records.

cost valuation

Process of assigning a specific value from the historical-cost records to each item in ending inventory.

Perpetual and Periodic Inventory Systems

OBJECTIVE 2

Use both perpetual and periodic inventory systems.

perpetual inventory system

An inventory system that keeps a continuous record of inventories and the cost of goods sold that helps managers control inventory levels and prepare interim financial statements.

physical count

The process of identifying, counting, and assigning a specific cost to all items in inventory.

inventory shrinkage

Losses of inventory from theft, breakage, or loss.

There are two main systems for keeping merchandise inventory records: perpetual and periodic. A **perpetual inventory system** keeps a continuous record of inventories and cost of goods sold that helps managers control inventory levels and prepare interim financial statements. To verify this continuous record-keeping process, companies periodically physically count and value the inventory. A **physical count** is the process of identifying, counting, and assigning a specific cost to all items in inventory. Physical counts at least annually verify the accuracy of the perpetual records. Home Depot discusses these issues in the notes to the financial statements: "Independent physical inventory counts or cycle counts are taken on a regular basis in each store and distribution center to ensure that amounts reflected in the accompanying Consolidated Financial Statements for Merchandise Inventories are properly stated."

The physical count helps management remove damaged or obsolete goods from inventory. It also helps reveal **inventory shrinkage**, which refers to losses of inventory from theft, breakage, and loss. Inventory shrinkage can be quite large in some businesses. The perpetual system also provides managers with information to aid in pricing and ordering because inventory records are always up-to-date. Once cumbersome and expensive, perpetual inventory systems are inexpensive today due to new technology such as computerized inventory systems and optical scanning equipment at checkout counters.

Previous chapters have used the perpetual system to record inventory transactions without referring to it by name. It works as follows:

		A	=	L	+	SE
a. Purchase	+	Increase Merchandise inventory	=	+ Increase Accounts payable		
b. Sale	+	Increase Accounts receivable	=		+	Increase Sales revenue
Cost of goods (inventory) sold	−	Decrease Inventory	=		−	Increase Cost of goods sold

In the perpetual inventory system, the journal entries are as follows:

```
a. When inventory is purchased:
     Merchandise inventory. . . . . . . . . . . . . . . .   xxx
          Accounts payable (or cash) . . . . . . . . . .          xxx
b. When inventory is sold:
     Accounts receivable (or cash). . . . . . . . . . . .   xxx
          Sales revenue . . . . . . . . . . . . . . . . . .          xxx
     Cost of goods sold . . . . . . . . . . . . . . . . . .   xxx
          Inventory . . . . . . . . . . . . . . . . . . . . .          xxx
```

Thus, in the perpetual inventory system, we record the sale of an item and the accompanying inventory reduction simultaneously.

In contrast, the **periodic inventory system** does not involve a day-to-day record of inventories or of the cost of goods sold. Instead we compute the cost of goods sold and an updated inventory balance only at the end of an accounting period, when we take a physical count of inventory. We used this periodic inventory system in the example of Christina's T-shirt business.

Under the periodic system, calculations for the cost of goods sold start by combining the opening inventory for the period plus purchases during the period. This sum is called the **cost of goods available for sale**. We then subtract the ending inventory from the cost of goods available for sale to compute the cost of goods sold. In the periodic system the cost of goods sold is a residual amount. The logic is that if we had inventory available and it is no longer here, then we sold it. Of course, practically speaking, if someone stole the item, its cost will also be included in cost of sales.

periodic inventory system

An inventory system that computes the cost of goods sold and an updated inventory balance only at the end of an accounting period when the company takes a physical count of inventory.

cost of goods available for sale

Sum of opening inventory for the period plus purchases during the period.

$$\underbrace{\text{Beginning inventory} + \text{Purchases}} - \underbrace{\text{Ending inventory}} = \underbrace{\text{Cost of goods sold}}$$

Goods available for sale − Inventory leftover = Cost of goods sold

Exhibit 7-2 compares the perpetual and periodic inventory systems. The two methods produce the same cost of goods sold figure for annual financial statements. However, the perpetual system also provides continuous assessments of inventory levels and helps managers restock with the right merchandise in a timely and effective manner. As implementation costs have fallen with the use of computerized systems, more companies find that these benefits justify the slightly higher cost of the perpetual system.

Physical Inventory

Good inventory control procedures require a physical count of items held in inventory at least annually in both periodic and perpetual inventory systems. The physical count is an imposing, time-consuming, and expensive process. You may have seen "Closed for Inventory" signs. To simplify counting and valuation, firms often choose fiscal accounting periods so the year ends when inventories are low and physical counts easier. For example, The Home Depot, Sears, JCPenney, and Lowe's all have late January or early February year-ends, which follow the holiday season.

The physical inventory is so important to income determination that external auditors usually observe the client's physical count and confirm the accuracy of the subsequent valuation. Often audit firms hire outside experts to assist them. For example, assessing a jeweler's inventory might require an expert to test the color, size, clarity, and imperfections in the diamonds on hand. Similarly, the client and auditor might rely on an engineer to measure the physical dimensions of an electric utility's coal pile so they can accurately estimate the volume and weight without actually weighing the coal itself.

A classic case of inventory fraud is the Salad Oil Swindle of 1963. Late that year an obscure company named Allied Crude Vegetable Oil and Refining was unable to repay its loans. Collateral for the loans had been $175 million worth of vegetable oil supposedly stored in 40 converted gasoline storage tanks in Bayonne, New Jersey. Investigation revealed that, instead of vegetable oil, the tanks contained seawater, soap stock, and "sludge."

Allied used ingenious techniques to hide its shortfall from the watchful auditors. Because the 40 storage tanks were connected by pipes, Allied pumped a small quantity of vegetable oil from tank to tank during the week required to complete the inventory count. The auditors counted the same vegetable oil over and over. Moreover, the company never completely filled any tank with oil. Each tank had one opening, and Allied welded a closed pipe beneath each opening. Each pipe held a few hundred pounds of real oil. When the auditors took samples, they were actually testing what was in this pipe, not what was in the tank. The tanks held mainly seawater. After authorities discovered the fraud, they opened a faucet on one tank, and water poured out for 12 days.

EXHIBIT 7-2

Inventory Systems

Periodic System		Perpetual System
Beginning inventories (by physical count)	xxx	Cost of goods sold (kept on a day-to-day basis instead of determined periodically)[*]
Add: Purchases	xxx	
Cost of goods available for sale	xxx	
Less: Ending inventories (by physical count)	xxx	
Cost of goods sold	xxx	

[*]Such a condensed figure does not preclude the presentation of a supplementary schedule similar to that on the left.

Cost of Merchandise Acquired

OBJECTIVE 3

Calculate the cost of merchandise acquired.

Regardless of whether you use the periodic or perpetual system, the basis of inventory accounting is the cost of the merchandise a company purchases or produces for resale. What makes up that cost? To be more specific, does that cost include all or part of the following: invoice price, transportation charges, trade and cash discounts, cost of handling and placing in stock, storage, purchasing department, receiving department, and other indirect charges? Companies generally include the invoice price plus the directly identifiable inbound transportation charges less any offsetting discounts in the cost of merchandise. Many companies treat the costs of the purchasing and receiving departments as period costs and charge them on the income statement as they occur. However, some companies, including The Home Depot, include these costs in the cost of merchandise. The Home Depot's notes to its financial statements describe this as follows: "Costs of Sales includes the actual cost of merchandise sold and services performed, the cost of transportation of merchandise from vendors to the Company's stores, locations or customers, the operating cost of the Company's sourcing and distribution network. . . . The cost of handling and shipping merchandise from the Company's stores, locations or distribution centers to the customer is classified as SG&A [Selling, General and Administrative expense]."

Transportation Charges

The major cost of transporting merchandise is typically the freight charges from the shipping point of the seller to the receiving point of the buyer. When the seller bears this cost, the sales invoice reads free onboard or **F.O.B. destination**. When the buyer bears this cost, it reads **F.O.B. shipping point**.

F.O.B. destination

Seller pays freight costs from the shipping point of the seller to the receiving point of the buyer.

F.O.B. shipping point

Buyer pays freight costs from the shipping point of the seller to the receiving point of the buyer.

freight in (inward transportation)

An additional cost of the goods acquired during the period, which is often shown in the purchases section of an income statement.

In theory, we should add any transportation costs borne by the buyer to the cost of the inventory acquired. In practice, though, it is not always easy to identify the transportation costs associated with specific inventory items. Companies tend to order several different items and have them shipped at the same time.

Sometimes managers want to keep freight costs separate from other inventory costs. For example, management may want to see how freight costs change over time and to compare costs using rail service to costs using trucks. Consequently, accountants frequently use a separate transportation cost account, calling it Freight In, Transportation In, Inbound Transportation, or Inward Transportation. **Freight in** (or **inward transportation**) appears in the purchases section of an income statement as an additional cost of the goods acquired during the period. It becomes part of the cost of goods available for sale, and because it increases cost of goods sold, Freight In affects the gross profit section of an income statement for the buyer.

INTERPRETING FINANCIAL STATEMENTS

Suppose that Huang Company bought several items of inventory that were shipped in a single load. Should total freight costs be assigned to each of the components of the shipment based on weight, value, number of items, volume of the item, or some other process?

Answer

Each of these bases of assignment might be correct in certain cases. For example, if you thought of coal as the product, weight would be a very good basis for assigning delivery costs. If you thought of jewelry, you might have thought of assigning costs based on the number of items and their value because outbound transportation costs would depend on packing and handling of the item and insurance for its value in case it were lost or damaged. Thus, assigning inbound transportation costs would require extensive analysis to pick the best approach, followed by a lot of clerical work to apply the technique. Because of these difficulties and the modest benefit to the company from all this work, most companies do not assign freight costs to inventories. Instead, they charge them to expense when incurred.

Returns, Allowances, and Discounts

In Chapter 6, you learned about sales returns, allowances, and discounts. The accounting for purchase returns, purchase allowances, and cash discounts on purchases is just the opposite of their sales counterparts. Using the periodic inventory system, suppose a company's gross purchases

EXHIBIT 7-3

Detailed Gross Profit Calculation

($ in thousands)

Gross sales			$1,740
Deduct: Sales returns and allowances		$ 70	
Cash discounts on sales		100	170
Net sales			$1,570
Deduct: Cost of goods sold			
Merchandise inventory, December 31, 20X1		$ 100	
Purchases (gross)	$960		
Deduct: Purchase returns and allowances	$75		
Cash discounts on purchases	5 80		
Net purchases	$880		
Add: Freight in	30		
Total cost of merchandise acquired		910	
Cost of goods available for sale		$1,010	
Deduct: Merchandise inventory, December 31, 20X2		140	
Cost of goods sold			870
Gross profit			$ 700

are $960,000 and purchase returns and allowances are $75,000. The summary journal entries are as follows:

Purchases	960,000	
Accounts payable................		960,000
Accounts payable	75,000	
Purchase returns and allowances		75,000

Suppose also that the company takes cash discounts of $5,000 on payment of the remaining $960,000 – $75,000 = $885,000 of payables. The summary journal entry is as follows:

Accounts payable	885,000	
Cash discounts on purchases.......		5,000
Cash........................		880,000

To calculate cost of goods sold, we deduct Cash Discounts on Purchases and Purchase Returns and Allowances from Purchases.

Car dealers sometimes sell cars "below cost" or "$100 below invoice." Do dealers lose money on such sales? Probably not, because gross invoice cost to the dealer and final cost of goods sold may differ. Dealers receive incentives from the manufacturers such as volume discounts or special discounts to push particular models. The dealer's invoice shows the list price before discounts and allowances, not the final net dealer cost.

A detailed gross profit section in the income statement is often arranged as in Exhibit 7-3. Although management may find such detail valuable, summary information is much more common in the annual report to shareholders:

Net sales	$1,570
Cost of goods sold	870
Gross profit	$ 700

Comparing Accounting Procedures for Periodic and Perpetual Inventory Systems

Suppose GoodEarth Products, Incorporated, has a balance of $100,000 in merchandise inventory at the beginning of 20X2 (December 31, 20X1). A summary of transactions for 20X2 follows:

a. Purchases	$990,000
b. Purchase returns and allowances	80,000

Net purchases were therefore $990,000 less $80,000, or $910,000. The physical count of the ending inventory for 20X2 led to a cost valuation of $140,000. Note how we use these figures to compute the $870,000 cost of goods sold:

Beginning + Net purchases inventory	–	Ending inventory	=	Cost of goods sold
$100,000 + $910,000	–	$140,000	=	$870,000

Cost of goods available for sale	–	Cost of goods leftover	=	Cost of goods sold
$1,010,000	–	$140,000	=	$870,000

The periodic and perpetual procedures would record these transactions differently. As the left side of Exhibit 7-4 shows, in the perpetual system we directly increase the Inventory account by the $990,000 in purchases (entry a) and decrease it by the $80,000 in returns and allowances (entry b) and the $870,000 cost of goods sold (entry c). We would increase the Cost of Goods Sold account daily as sales occur. The following T-accounts reflect how these items would appear in the general ledger (dollar amounts in thousands):

Inventory				Cost of Goods Sold		
Balance 12/31/X1	100	(b)	80	(c)	870	
(a)	990	(c)	870			
Balance 12/31/X2	140			Balance 12/31/X2	870	

These summary amounts of $990,000 in purchases and $80,000 in returns and allowances represent many smaller transactions. GoodEarth Products would record each transaction as it occurs. Similarly, GoodEarth would make similar daily entries as each sale occurs. Although the method seems to create the correct $140,000 final inventory balance, recall that the company will also conduct a physical count to verify the number. Often there are minor differences between the valuation determined by the physical count and the value shown in the perpetual record. Such differences, often due to clerical error or shrinkage, result in appropriate adjustments to increase or decrease inventory and cost of sales. If the

	Perpetual Records			Periodic Records		
a. Gross purchases:	Inventory	990		Purchases	990	
	Accounts payable		990	Accounts payable		990
b. Returns and	Accounts payable	80		Accounts payable	80	
allowances:	Inventory		80	Purchase returns and allowances . . .		80
c. As goods are sold:	Cost of goods sold	870		No entry		
	Inventory		870			
d. At the end of the accounting period:	d1. d2. } No entry			d1. Cost of goods sold	1,010	
				Purchase returns and allowances . . .	80	
				Purchases		990
				Inventory		100
				d2. Inventory	140	
				Cost of goods sold		140

EXHIBIT 7-4

GoodEarth Products, Incorporated

Comparison of Journal Entries for Perpetual and Periodic Inventory Systems ($ amounts in thousands)

physical count had yielded a value of $135,000, we would make the following journal entry (in thousands):

Inventory shrinkage expense	5	
Inventory		5

Under the periodic system on the right side of Exhibit 7-4, we record purchases and purchase returns and allowances in separate accounts, as entries a and b indicate. We call the system "periodic" because we do not compute the cost of goods sold or the inventory amount on a daily basis. Entries d1 and d2 at the bottom of Exhibit 7-4 show how we update these accounts during the eventual periodic calculation of cost of goods sold.

Entry d1 transfers the beginning inventory balance, purchases, and purchase returns and allowances, totaling $1,010,000, to cost of goods sold. This is the cost of goods available for sale. Next, we physically count the ending inventory and compute its cost. Entry d2 recognizes the $140,000 ending inventory and reduces the $1,010,000 cost of goods available for sale by $140,000 to obtain a final cost of goods sold of $870,000. The following T-accounts show how these journal entries affect the general ledger accounts (dollar amounts in thousands):

Inventory				Cost of Goods Sold			
Balance 12/31/X1	100	(d1)	100	(d1)	1,010	(d2)	140
(d2)	140						
Balance 12/31/X2	140			Balance 12/31/X2	870		

Notice that both systems reach the same result, Inventory of $140,000 and Cost of Goods Sold of $870,000.

Principal Inventory Valuation Methods

Each period, accountants must divide the cost of beginning inventory and merchandise acquired between cost of goods sold and cost of items remaining in ending inventory. Under a perpetual system, we must determine a cost for each item sold. Under a periodic system, we instead must only determine the specific costs of the items remaining in ending inventory. In both systems, we must determine the costs of individual items by some inventory valuation method. Four principal inventory valuation methods are generally accepted in the United States: specific identification; first-in, first-out (FIFO); last-in, first-out (LIFO); and weighted average. Companies reporting under IFRS cannot use LIFO. The most popular method worldwide is the weighted-average method, and the next most common choice is FIFO. In this section, we explain and compare these methods.

If unit prices and costs did not fluctuate, all four inventory methods would show identical results. However, prices change, and these changes raise central issues concerning cost of goods sold (income measurement) and inventories (asset measurement). As a simple example of the valuation method choices facing management, consider Emilio, a new vendor of a cola drink at the fairgrounds, who begins the week with no inventory. He buys one can of cola on Monday for 30¢, a second can on Tuesday for 40¢, and a third can on Wednesday for 56¢. He then sells one can on Thursday for 90¢.

As Exhibit 7-5 shows, Emilio's choice of an inventory method can significantly affect the amount reported as cost of goods sold (and hence gross profit and net income) and ending inventory. The gross profit for Monday through Thursday ranges from 34¢ to 60¢, depending on the method chosen. By using Exhibit 7-5 as a guide, we now examine each of the four methods in detail.

Specific Identification

The **specific identification method** concentrates on physically linking the particular items sold with the cost of goods sold that a company reports. Emilio could mark each can with its cost and record that cost as cost of goods sold when he hands the can to a customer. If he reached for the Monday can instead of the Wednesday can, the specific identification method would show different results. Thus, Exhibit 7-5 indicates that gross profit for operations of Monday through Thursday could be 60¢, 50¢, or 34¢, depending on the particular can Emilio hands to the customer. He could

specific identification method
This inventory method concentrates on the physical linking of the particular items sold with the cost of goods sold that a company reports.

		(1) Specific Identification			(2) FIFO	(3) LIFO	(4) Weighted Average
		(1A)	(1B)	(1C)			
Income Statement for the Period **Monday Through Thursday**							
Sales		90	90	90	90	90	90
Deduct cost of goods sold							
1 30¢ (Monday) unit		30			30		
1 40¢ (Tuesday) unit			40				
1 56¢ (Wednesday) unit				56		56	
1 weighted-average unit							
[(30 + 40 + 56) ÷ 3 = 42]		—	—	—	—	—	42
Gross profit for Monday through Thursday		60	50	34	60	34	48
Thursday's Ending Inventory, Two Units							
Monday unit @ 30¢			30	30		30	
Tuesday unit @ 40¢		40		40	40	40	
Wednesday unit @ 56¢		56	56		56		
Weighted-average units @ 42¢		—	—	—	—	—	84
Total ending inventory on Thursday		96	86	70	96	70	84

EXHIBIT 7-5

Emilio's Cola Sales

Comparison of Inventory Methods (all monetary amounts are in cents)

choose which can to sell and affect reported results by doing so. Because the specific item handed to the customer determines the cost of goods sold, the specific identification method may permit managers to manipulate income and inventory values by filling a sales order from a number of physically equivalent items with different historical costs. This would be true for Emilio. Each can is identical. It would not be true for a car dealer for whom each car has a unique identification number indicating its features such as color, style, engine, sound system, and so forth.

Specific identification is relatively easy to use for expensive low-volume merchandise, such as custom artwork, diamond jewelry, and automobiles. However, many organizations have many inventory items that are insufficiently valuable to warrant such individualized attention. However, the use of bar codes and scanning equipment is making specific identification economically feasible for more and more companies.

FIFO

first-in, first-out (FIFO)

This method of accounting for inventory assigns the cost of the earliest acquired units to cost of goods sold.

FIFO refers to **first-in, first-out**. The FIFO method is a cost assignment method and does not track the actual physical flow of individual items, except by coincidence. For identical units, it assigns the cost of the earliest acquired units to cost of goods sold. Picture Emilio putting each new can of cola at the back of the cooler to chill and selling the oldest, coldest can first. Thus, under FIFO, we assume that Emilio sells the Monday can of cola first—regardless of the actual can he delivers. As a result, we assign the costs of the newer cans to the units in ending inventory.

By using the more recent costs to measure the ending inventory, FIFO provides inventory valuations that closely approximate the actual market value of the inventory at the balance sheet date. In addition, in periods of rising prices, FIFO leads to higher net income. Note that gross profit is 60¢ in Exhibit 7-5 under FIFO because we charge the oldest, cheapest unit as cost of goods sold. Higher reported incomes may favorably affect investor attitudes toward the company. Similarly, higher reported incomes may lead to higher salaries, higher bonuses, or higher status for the management of the company. Unlike specific identification, FIFO specifies the order in which acquisition costs become cost of goods sold, so management cannot affect income by choosing to sell one identical item instead of another.

LIFO

LIFO refers to **last-in, first-out**. Whereas FIFO associates the most recent costs with ending inventories, LIFO assigns the most recent costs to cost of goods sold. The LIFO method assumes that a company sells the stock acquired most recently before it sells older stock. Picture Emilio putting each newly-acquired can into the front of a cooler. At each customer purchase, he sells the newest can in the front. This is the physical flow that corresponds to the LIFO cost system. Thus, under LIFO, we assume that Emilio sells the Wednesday can of cola—regardless of the actual can he delivers from the cooler.

last-in, first-out (LIFO)
This inventory method assigns the most recent costs to cost of goods sold.

LIFO provides an income statement perspective in the sense that net income measured using LIFO combines current sales prices and current acquisition costs. In contrast, the balance sheet includes older costs, which often are far below current prices. In a period of rising prices and constant or growing inventories, LIFO yields lower net income as shown by the 34¢ gross margin in Exhibit 7-5. Why is lower net income such an important feature of LIFO? In the United States, LIFO is an acceptable inventory accounting method for income tax purposes. When a company reports lower income to the tax authorities, it pays lower taxes, so it is not surprising that almost two-thirds of U.S. corporations use LIFO for at least some of their inventories. However, the U.S. Internal Revenue Code requires companies that use LIFO for tax purposes to also use it for financial reporting purposes.

You might think of LIFO as the good news/bad news method. Lower income taxes provide the good news, but the accompanying bad news is lower reported profits. During a period of higher inflation some years ago, the *Wall Street Journal* reported that many small firms changed from FIFO to LIFO. As an example, when Becton, Dickinson and Company changed to LIFO its annual report stated that its "change to the LIFO method . . . for both financial reporting and income tax purposes resulted in improved cash flow due to lower income taxes paid." Indeed, some observers maintain that executives of U.S. companies are guilty of serious mismanagement by not adopting LIFO when FIFO produces significantly higher taxable income.

One reason that IFRS prohibits LIFO is that it permits management to influence reported income by the timing of purchases of inventory items. Consider Emilio's case as described in Exhibit 7-5 on page 300. Suppose that acquisition prices increase from 56¢ on Wednesday to 68¢ on Thursday, the day of the sale of the one unit. How does the acquisition of one more unit on Thursday affect net income? Under LIFO, cost of goods sold would change to 68¢, and profit would fall by 12¢. In contrast, under FIFO, cost of goods sold and gross profit would be unchanged.

	LIFO		FIFO	
	As in Exhibit 7-5	If One More Unit Acquired	As in Exhibit 7-5	If One More Unit Acquired
Sales	90¢	90¢	90¢	90¢
Cost of goods sold	56¢	68¢	30¢	30¢
Gross profit	34¢	22¢	60¢	60¢
Ending inventory				
First purchase, Monday	30¢	30¢		
Second purchase, Tuesday	40¢	40¢	40¢	40¢
Third purchase, Wednesday		56¢	56¢	56¢
Fourth purchase, Thursday				68¢
	70¢	126¢	96¢	164¢

To learn more about LIFO and its effects on companies' financial statements see Appendix 7A.

Weighted Average

The **weighted-average method** computes a unit cost by dividing the total acquisition cost of all items available for sale by the number of units available for sale. Picture Emilio dropping his cooler and not knowing which can was in front. Exhibit 7-5 shows the calculations Emilio would make to average the costs of these units. The average cost is 42¢ [(30 + 40 + 56) ÷ 3].

To better understand the weighted-average method, assume that Emilio bought two cans instead of one on Monday at 30¢ each. To get the weighted average, we must consider not only the price paid, but also the number of units purchased as follows:

$$\text{Weighted average} = \text{Cost of goods available for sale} \div \text{Units available for sale}$$
$$\text{Weighted average} = [(2 \times 30¢) + (1 \times 40¢) + (1 \times 56¢)] \div 4$$
$$= 156¢ \div 4$$
$$= 39¢$$

The weighted-average method produces a gross profit somewhere between that obtained under FIFO and that under LIFO (48¢ as compared with 60¢ and 34¢ in Exhibit 7-5). During fiscal 2008, **The Home Depot** adopted the weighted-average method for its Canadian operations. It described this change in accounting principle in note 3 to its annual report, which included discussion of the new accounting system that was required to support the change: "During fiscal 2008, the Company implemented a new enterprise resource planning ("ERP") system, including a new inventory system, for its retail operations in Canada......The new ERP system allows the Company to utilize the weighted-average cost method, which the Company believes will result in greater precision in the costing of inventories and a better matching of cost of sales with revenue generated."

Cost Flow Assumptions

Because the actual physical flow of identical products is less important to the financial success of most businesses than is the flow of the units' costs, the accounting profession has concluded that companies may choose any of the allowable methods to record cost of goods sold. Basically, the units are all the same, but their costs differ, so managing the assignment of these differing costs is more important than is tracing where each specific unit goes. Because only the specific identification method is linked to the physical flow of merchandise, accountants often refer to the other inventory methods as cost flow assumptions. For example, when we decide to match the cost of the first inventory item purchased with the sales revenue from the first item sold to calculate the gross profit from the sale, we are adopting the FIFO cost flow assumption.

Notice that the cost flow assumptions do not affect the cumulative gross profit over the life of a company. Suppose Emilio sells his remaining inventory for 90¢ per can on Friday and enters a more attractive business. Exhibit 7-6 shows Friday's gross profit and the cumulative gross profit for the entire week. As you can see, the gross profit for Friday varies with the cost flow assumption used. However, the last line of the exhibit shows that the cumulative gross profit over the life of Emilio's business would be the same $1.44 under any of the inventory methods. What makes the choice of method important is the need to match particular costs to particular periods during the life of the business in order to prepare periodic financial statements and evaluate performance.

Inventory Cost Relationships

Note that all inventory methods work with the same basic numbers. Nothing in our choice of methods affects accounts payable. We record inventory purchases at cost and recognize a liability in the same way under all these methods. All that changes is how we allocate those costs between inventory and cost of sales.

Recall that during a period of rising prices, FIFO yields higher inventory and higher gross profit than does LIFO or weighted average. This result is consistent with the balance sheet equation that requires that A = L + SE. If inventory is higher under FIFO (higher assets) and the equation is to balance, either liabilities or stockholders' equity must also be higher. Higher gross profit under FIFO implies higher net income and higher stockholders' equity (SE in the equation).

EXHIBIT 7-6

Income Statements for Friday Only and for Monday Through Friday for Emilio's Cola Sales (all monetary amounts are in cents)

	(1) Specific Identification			(2) FIFO	(3) LIFO	(4) Weighted Average
	(1A)	(1B)	(1C)			
Sales, 2 units @ 90 on Friday	180	180	180	180	180	180
Cost of goods sold						
(Thursday ending inventory from Exhibit 7-5)	96	86	70	96	70	84
Gross profit, Friday only	84	94	110	84	110	96
Gross profit, Monday through Thursday (from Exhibit 7-5)	60	50	34	60	34	48
Gross profit, Monday through Friday (3 cans sold)	144	144	144	144	144	144

There are, of course, relationships other than those of the accounting equation that come into play in the various inventory methods. Consider also the link between cost of goods sold and the valuation of ending inventory. Emilio's three cola cans had a total cost of goods available for sale of $1.26. At the end of the period, Emilio must allocate this $1.26 either to cans sold or to cans in ending inventory. The higher the cost of goods sold, the lower the ending inventory. Exhibit 7-7 illustrates that interdependence. At one extreme, FIFO treats the 30¢ cost of the first can acquired as cost of goods sold and 96¢ as ending inventory. At the other extreme, LIFO treats the 56¢ cost of the last can acquired as cost of goods sold and 70¢ as ending inventory.

EXHIBIT 7-7

Emilio's Cola Sales, Monday Through Thursday

Diagram of Inventory Methods (all monetary amounts are in cents)

The Consistency Convention

consistency

Conformity from period to period with unchanging policies and procedures.

Although companies can choose any allowable inventory cost flow assumption they want, they have to be consistent over time and stick with whatever they choose. The FASB refers to **consistency** as "conformity from period to period with unchanging policies and procedures." Interpreting financial performance over time involves comparing the results of different periods. If accounting methods for inventory were changed often, meaningful comparisons over time would be impossible.

Occasionally, a change in market conditions or other circumstances may justify a change in inventory method. As noted earlier, a significant increase in inflation motivated more than 40 companies to switch to LIFO in the 1970s to capture tax benefits. With its auditor's approval, a firm may change method. However, the firm has to note the change in its financial statements as The Home Depot did when adopting the weighted-average method in Canada. The auditor must also refer to the change in its audit opinion. This alerts financial statement readers to the possible effects of the change on their analysis.

Summary Problem for Your Review

PROBLEM

Examine Exhibit 7-8. The company uses the periodic inventory system. By using these facts, prepare a columnar comparison of income statements for the year ended December 31, 20X2. Compare the FIFO, LIFO, and weighted-average inventory methods. Assume that other expenses are $1,000. The income tax rate is 40%.

EXHIBIT 7-8

Facts for Summary Problem

	Purchases		Sales	Inventory
December 31, 20X1				200 @ $5 = $1,000
January 25	170 @ $6 =	$1,020		
January 29			150*	
May 28	190 @ $7 =	$1,330		
June 7			230*	
November 20	150 @ $8 =	$1,200		
December 15	___	_____	100*	
Total	510	$3,550	480*	
December 31, 20X2				230 @ ?

*Selling prices were $9, $11, and $13, respectively, providing total sales of:

	150 @ $ 9 = $1,350	
	230 @ $11 = $2,530	
	100 @ $13 = $1,300	
Total sales	480 $5,180	

Summary of costs:

Beginning inventory	$1,000
Purchases	$3,550
Cost of goods available for sale	$4,550

SOLUTION

See Exhibit 7-9.

	FIFO		LIFO		Weighted Average
Sales, 480 units		$5,180		$5,180	$5,180
Deduct cost of goods sold					
Beginning inventory, 200 @ $5	$1,000		$1,000		$1,000
Purchases, 510 units (from Exhibit 7-8)*	3,550		3,550		3,550
Available for sale, 710 units†	$4,550		$4,550		$4,550
Ending inventory, 230 units‡					
150 @ $8	$1,200				
80 @ $7	560	1,760			
or					
200 @ $5			$1,000		
30 @ $6			180	1,180	
or					
230 @ $6.408					1,474
Cost of goods sold, 480 units		2,790		3,370	3,076
Gross profit		$2,390		$1,810	$2,104
Other expenses		1,000		1,000	1,000
Income before income taxes		$1,390		$ 810	$1,104
Income taxes at 40%		556		324	442
Net income		$ 834		$ 486	$ 662

*Always equal across all three methods.

†These amounts will not be equal in general across the three methods because beginning inventories will generally be different. They are equal here only because beginning inventories were assumed to be equal.

‡Under FIFO, the ending inventory is composed of the last purchases plus the second-last purchases, and so forth, until the costs of 230 units are compiled. Under LIFO, the ending inventory is composed of the beginning inventory plus the earliest purchases of the current year until the costs of 230 units are compiled. Under weighted average, the ending inventory and cost of goods sold are accumulations based on an average unit cost. The latter is the cost of goods available for sale divided by the number of units available for sale: $4,550 ÷ 710 = $6.408.

EXHIBIT 7-9

Comparison of Inventory Methods for the Year Ended December 31, 20X2

Summary Problem for Your Review

PROBLEM

"When prices are rising, FIFO produces profits that confuse economic profit and holding gains because more resources are needed to maintain operations than previously." Do you agree? Explain.

SOLUTION

FIFO profits certainly combine economic profits and holding gains, but well-trained analysts and managers know that. LIFO often gives a better measure of "distributable" income than FIFO. Recall Emilio's Cola Sales example in Exhibit 7-5. The gross profit under FIFO was 60¢, and under LIFO it was 34¢. The 60¢ − 34¢ = 26¢ difference is a fool's profit because it must be reinvested to maintain the same inventory level as previously. It arises from a profit on holding inventory as prices change instead of buying at wholesale and selling at retail. Therefore, the 26¢ cannot be distributed as a cash dividend without reducing the current level of operations.

Lower-of-Cost-or-Market Method

lower-of-cost-or-market method (LCM)

A comparison of the current market price of inventory with historical cost derived under whatever inventory method is used and reporting the lower of the two as the inventory value.

net realizable value

The net amount the company expects to receive when it sells its inventory.

current replacement cost

What it would cost a company to buy an inventory item today.

write-down

A reduction in the recorded historical cost of an item in response to a decline in value.

Sometimes companies cannot easily sell obsolete or damaged inventory items at amounts equal to or above their historical cost. In such a case, the historical cost overstates the value of the inventory. To avoid overstating the inventory, we use the **lower-of-cost-or-market method (LCM)**. LCM requires companies to compare the current market price of inventory with historical cost derived under whichever inventory method they are using and then report the lower of the two as the inventory value.

How companies measure current market price depends on whether they use IFRS or U.S. GAAP. Under IFRS the market price is **net realizable value**—the net amount the company expects to receive for the inventory. Under U.S. GAAP it is usually **current replacement cost**—what it would cost to buy the inventory item today.

Consider the following example of a U.S. company. The Ripley Company has 100 units in its ending FIFO inventory on December 31, 20X1. Ripley tentatively computed its gross profit for 20X1 as follows:

Sales		$2,180
Cost of goods available for sale	$1,980	
Ending inventory of 100 units, at cost	790	
Cost of goods sold		1,190
Gross profit		$ 990

Assume a sudden decline in replacement costs of our inventory during the final week of December from $7.90 per unit to $4 per unit while net realizable value fell to $5 per unit. Under U.S. GAAP, an inventory write-down of ($7.90 – $4.00) × 100 units, or $390, is in order. A **write-down** reduces the recorded historical cost of an item in response to a decline in value. When a write-down occurs, the new $4 per unit replacement cost becomes, for accounting purposes, the unexpired cost of the inventory. Thus, if replacement prices subsequently rise to $8 per unit in January 20X2, the assigned cost of each unit will remain $4. In short, the lower-of-cost-or-market method would regard the $4 replacement cost of December 31 as the "new historical cost" of the inventory. The required journal entry is as follows:

```
Loss on write-down of inventory (or cost of goods sold). . . . . . . . . 390
        Inventory . . . . . . . . . . . . . . . . . . . . . . . . . . . . . . . . . . . . . . .        390
    To write down inventory from $790 cost to $400 market value
```

The write-down of inventories increases cost of goods sold in 20X1 by $390. Therefore, reported income for 20X1 would be lowered by $390:

	Before $390 Write-Down	After $390 Write-Down	Difference
Sales	$2,180	$2,180	
Cost of goods available	$1,980	$1,980	
Ending inventory	790	400	–$390
Cost of goods sold	$1,190	$1,580	+$390
Gross profit	$ 990	$ 600	–$390

Why is $390 written down? LCM holds that of the $790 historical cost, $390 is considered to have expired during 20X1 because Ripley cannot justifiably carry forward the entire $790 cost to the future as an asset. However, if the market replacement cost falls but selling prices remain the same, the items still have their original earnings power. No loss has occurred, and no reduction in the book value of the inventory is necessary.

How would LCM differ if Ripley Company used IFRS? Because the net realizable value is $5 per unit, the write down would be only ($7.90 – $5.00) × 100 units, or $290. Except for the amount, the accounting for the decline in inventory value would be the same as under U.S. GAAP. However, if the net realizable value subsequently increases, IFRS allows companies to reverse the write down, that is to increase the inventory value up to the amount of the original cost.

EXHIBIT 7-10

The Ripley Company

Effects of Lower-of-Cost-or-Market

	Cost Method		Lower-of-Cost-or-Market Method	
	20X1	**20X2**	**20X1**	**20X2**
Sales	$2,180	$ 800	$2,180	$ 800
Cost of goods available	$1,980	$ 790	$1,980	$ 400
Ending inventory	790	—	400*	—
Cost of goods sold	$1,190	$ 790	$1,580	$ 400
Gross profit	$ 990	$ 10	$ 600	$ 400
Combined gross profit for 2 years				
Cost method: $990 + $10 =		$1,000		
Lower-of-cost-or-market method: $600 + $400 =			$1,000	

*The inventory is shown here after being written down by $390, from $790 to $400. For internal purposes, many accountants prefer to show the write-down separately, presenting a gross profit before write-down of inventory, the write-down, and a gross profit after write-down.

Conservatism in Action

LCM is an example of conservatism. **Conservatism** means selecting methods of measurement that yield lower net income, lower assets, and lower stockholders' equity. We illustrated conservatism in accounts receivable with the use of an allowance for bad debts. We estimated and recorded losses on uncollectible accounts before they were certain. With inventories, conservatism dictates that we use the LCM method.

Accountants believe that erring in the direction of conservatism is better than erring in the direction of overstating assets and net income. The accountant's conservatism balances management's optimism. Management prepares the financial statements, but the conservatism principle moderates management's human tendency to hope for, and expect, the best.

Compared with a pure cost method, the lower-of-cost-or-market method reports less net income in the period of decline in the market value of the inventory and more net income in the period of sale. The lower-of-cost-or-market method affects how much income the Ripley Company reports in each year, but not the total income over the company's life. Exhibit 7-10 underscores this point, using the U.S. GAAP method. Suppose Ripley goes out of business in early 20X2. That is, it acquires no more units. There are no sales in 20X2 except for the disposal of the inventory at $8 per unit (100 × $8 = $800). The LCM method will affect neither combined gross profit nor combined net income for the two periods, as the bottom of Exhibit 7-10 reveals. The LCM method simply transfers $390 of profit from 20X1 to 20X2. The only difference under IFRS is that $290 of profit would move from 20X1 to 20X2.

A full-blown lower-of-cost-or-market method is rarely encountered in practice. Why? Because it is expensive to get the correct replacement costs of hundreds or thousands of different products in inventory. Further, the benefit from doing so does not justify the cost. Auditors do watch for price trends in the industry that might indicate a serious concern. In particular, they watch for subclasses of inventory that are obsolete, shopworn, or otherwise of only nominal value and apply LCM selectively to such inventory.

conservatism
Selecting the methods of measurement that yield lower net income, lower assets, and lower stockholders' equity.

Effects of Inventory Errors

Inventory errors can arise from many sources. For example, incorrect physical counts might arise because accountants missed goods that were in receiving or shipping areas instead of in the inventory stockroom. Or a clerk might hit a 5 on the keyboard instead of a 6.

An undiscovered inventory error usually affects two reporting periods. The error will cause misstated amounts in the period in which the error occurred, but the effects will then be counterbalanced by identical offsetting amounts in the following period. Consider the income statements in Exhibit 7-11, which assume the physical count of ending 20X7 inventory is in error. The counters reported inventory to be $60,000, but it is really $70,000. That means that 20X7 pretax income will be $10,000 too low, and net income will be $6,000 too low.

OBJECTIVE 6

Show the effects of inventory errors on financial statements.

PANEL A

20X7	Correct Reporting	Incorrect Reporting*	Effects of Errors
Sales		$980	$980	
Deduct: Cost of goods sold				
Beginning inventory	$100		$100		
Purchases	500		500		
Cost of goods available for sale	$600		$600		
Deduct: Ending inventory	70		60		Understated by $10
Cost of goods sold		530		540	Overstated by $10
Gross profit		$450		$440	Understated by $10
Other expenses		250		250	
Income before income taxes		$200		$190	Understated by $10
Income tax expense at 40%		80		76	Understated by $4
Net income		$120		$114	**Understated by $6**
Ending balance sheet items				
Inventory		$ 70		$ 60	Understated by $10
Retained earnings includes current net income		120		114	Understated by $6
Income tax liability[†]		80		76	Understated by $4

*Because of error in ending inventory.
[†]For simplicity, assume that the entire income tax expense for the year will not be paid until the succeeding year. Therefore, the ending liability will equal the income tax expense.

PANEL B

20X8	Correct Reporting	Incorrect Reporting*	Effects of Errors
Sales		$980	$980	
Deduct: Cost of goods sold				
Beginning inventory	$ 70		$ 60		Understated by $10
Purchases	500		500		
Cost of goods available for sale	$570		$560		Understated by $10
Deduct: Ending inventory	40		40		
Cost of goods sold		530		520	Understated by $10
Gross profit		$450		$460	Overstated by $10
Other expenses		250		250	
Income before income taxes		$200		$210	Overstated by $10
Income tax expense at 40%		80		84	Overstated by $4
Net income		$120		$126	**Overstated by $6**
Ending balance sheet items				
Inventory		$ 40		$ 40	**Correct**
Retained earnings includes				
Net income of previous year		120		114	Counterbalanced and thus now correct in total
Net income of current year		120		126	
Two-year total		$240		$240	
Income tax liability				
End of previous year		80		76	Counterbalanced and thus now correct in total[†]
End of current year		80		84	
Two-year total		$160		$160	

*Because of error in beginning inventory.
[†]The $84 really consists of the $4 that pertains to income of the previous year plus $80 that pertains to income of the current year.

EXHIBIT 7-11

Effects of Inventory Errors (in thousands)

Think about the effects of the uncorrected error on the following year, 20X8, shown in Panel B. We assume that the operations during 20X8 are a duplication of those of 20X7, except that the ending inventory is correctly counted as $40,000. The beginning inventory will be $60,000 instead of the correct $70,000. Therefore, counterbalancing errors in 20X8 will exactly offset the errors in 20X7. Thus, the retained earnings at the end of 20X8 shows a cumulative effect of zero. Why? Because the net income in 20X7 is understated by $6,000, but the net income in 20X8 is overstated by $6,000.

The complete analyses for 20X7 and 20X8 show the full detail of the inventory error, and they provide us with a handy rule of thumb. If ending inventory is understated, retained earnings is understated. If ending inventory is overstated, retained earnings is overstated. These relations are clear from the balance sheet equation.

Summary Problem for Your Review

PROBLEM

At the end of 20X1, an error was made in the count of physical inventory that understated the ending inventory value by $1,000. The error went undetected. The subsequent inventory at the end of 20X2 was done correctly. Assess the effect of this error on income before tax, taxes, net income, and retained earnings for 20X1 and 20X2, assuming a 40% tax rate.

SOLUTION

	20X1	20X2
Beginning inventory	OK	$1,000 too low
Purchases	OK	OK
Goods available for sale	OK	$1,000 too low
Ending inventory	$1,000 too low	OK
Cost of goods sold	$1,000 too high	$1,000 too low

Note that 20X1 Ending Inventory becomes 20X2 Beginning Inventory, reversing the effects on Cost of Goods Sold. The 20X1 Cost of Goods Sold being too high causes 20X1 income before tax to be too low by $1,000. Therefore, taxes will be too low by .40 × $1,000 = $400, and net income will be too low by $600, causing retained earnings to be too low by $600 also. In 20X2, the effects reverse and by year-end retained earnings is correctly stated.

Cutoff Errors and Inventory Valuation

The accrual basis of accounting should include the physical counting and careful valuation of inventory at least once yearly. Auditors routinely search for **cutoff errors**, which are failures to record transactions in the correct time period. For example, suppose a company with a periodic inventory system conducts a physical inventory on December 31. Inventory purchases of $100,000 arrive in the receiving room during the afternoon of December 31. Accountants include the acquisition in Purchases and Accounts Payable, but the people counting the inventory exclude it from the ending inventory valuation. Such an error would understate ending inventory, thereby overstating cost of goods sold and understating gross profit. However, if accountants did not record the acquisition (and thus add it to Purchases) until January 2, the errors in both inventory count and purchases would understate Purchases, the Ending Inventory, and Accounts Payable as of December 31. However, cost of goods sold and gross profit would be correct because the errors would understate purchases and the ending inventory by the same amount. On the balance sheet the understated Inventory would be offset by the understated Accounts Payable.

The general approach to recording purchases and sales is keyed to the legal transfer of ownership. Auditors are especially careful about cutoff tests because the pressure for profits sometimes causes managers to postpone the recording of bona fide purchases of goods and services.

cutoff error
Failure to record transactions in the correct time period.

Similarly, the same managers may deliberately include sales orders near year-end (instead of bona fide completed sales) in revenues. For example, a news story about **McCormick & Company**, a firm known for its spices, reported, "The investigation also found that improprieties included the company's accounting for sales. In a longstanding practice, the company recorded as sales, goods that had been selected and prepared for shipment rather than waiting until after they had been shipped as is the customary accounting practice." Sometimes managers will accelerate the recognition of revenues in order to meet a sales- or profit-based target and therefore earn a bonus. This is an obvious ethical lapse.

The Importance of Gross Profits

OBJECTIVE 7

Evaluate the gross profit percentage and inventory turnover.

We began this chapter by discussing gross profits, which are the result of sales revenue less the cost of goods sold. Management and investors closely watch gross profit and how it changes over time. In comparing the gross profits of two firms, it is sometimes important to examine which inventory method each has used to calculate its gross profit.

Gross Profit Percentage

Analysts often express gross profit as a percentage of sales. Consider the following information on a past year for a hypothetical **Safeway** grocery store:

	Amount	Percentage
Sales	$10,000,000	100%
Net cost of goods sold	7,500,000	75%
Gross profit	$ 2,500,000	25%

gross profit percentage
Gross profit divided by sales.

The **gross profit percentage**—gross profit divided by sales—here is 25%. The following table illustrates the extent to which gross profit percentages vary among industries.

Company	Gross Profit Percentage
Ford Motor Company; Automobiles	2%
The Home Depot; Building supplies	34
Merck; Pharmaceuticals	84
Whole Foods; Specialty grocery retailer	37
Safeway; Grocery retailer	32
Sysco; Grocery wholesaler	20

Sources: Fidelity.com company analysis features, 2009 and Ford Motor Company annual report 2008.

wholesaler
A company that sells in large quantities to retail companies instead of individuals.

retailer
A company that sells items directly to the public—to individual buyers.

What accounts for this wide variation in gross profit percentage? The nature of the business has a lot to do with it. **Wholesalers** sell in larger quantities and incur fewer selling costs because they sell to retail companies instead of individuals. As a result of competition and high volumes, they have smaller gross profit percentages than do retailers. **Retailers** sell directly to the public—to individual buyers. Drug manufacturers earn high gross profits because of high drug prices, caused by the need for substantial R&D outlays (sometimes more than 15% of sales) and allowed by patent protection on specific drugs. The Business First box discusses some of the reasons a pharmaceutical company such as **Eli Lilly** has high gross margins. In contrast, auto manufacturers face more direct competition and earn lower gross profit percentages. In Ford's case, the recession in 2008 drove the percentage very close to zero.

Consider a pharmaceutical company that must incur large R&D costs to generate any sales from a drug. Accounting practice treats the R&D costs as a period cost when incurred instead of a product cost to be matched to future sales of the drug. Why? Because it is impossible to know, as a company incurs R&D costs, whether it will ultimately produce a viable drug whose therapeutic value will allow recovery of the costs of developing it. But the pharmaceutical company still must generate enough revenue to cover the costs of R&D, so it needs high gross margin percentages.

BUSINESS FIRST

PHARMACEUTICALS—PRICING AND AVAILABILITY

Nothing is more important than your health, and nothing is more contentious than how much drugs cost, who should pay for them, and where in the world they will be available. Eli Lilly, a major pharmaceutical company with worldwide sales of $20.4 billion, has addressed the question "Are Drug Prices Fair?" in several of its annual reports and other publications. For example, in 2009 the company's Web site presented a 48-page document entitled, "Medicines and Miracles, Improving Health..... Improving Life." Lilly argues that many widely held beliefs about the high cost of drugs are based on incomplete or misunderstood data.

Lilly stresses that today's medicines are more expensive than in the past, but they do more than ever before. Modern medicines are more cost effective than other treatments. A year's treatment with new anti-psychotic drugs costs about the same as 1 week of hospitalization for a patient with schizophrenia and improves the patient's quality of life. Much of the public outcry over pharmaceutical costs is not about the specific cost of a specific drug, but about the total cost of all drugs. Lilly indicates that medicines account for about 10% of health care spending in the United States and this has been remarkably stable since 1960. Indeed, Lilly indicates that the average American spends more on tobacco and alcohol than he or she spends on over-the-counter and prescription medicines combined.

Lilly's analyses are careful to separate "drug spending" patterns from drug price patterns. For example, when pharmaceutical companies introduce new drugs to manage a disease or attack previously untreatable medical conditions, the drugs result in an increase in spending but produce significant increases in the quality of life. In fact, changes in prescription medicine prices in 2007 rose more slowly than general inflation rates.

Pharmaceuticals have the same patent life as other innovations, but it often takes almost a decade to identify a new drug and adequately test it for both safety and effectiveness. Developing new treatments is very expensive. The industry spent $58.8 billion in research and development in 2007, and the National Institutes of Health added another $28.9 billion to research efforts. Lilly spends 19% of sales on R&D.

Lilly's answer to the debate is that pharmaceuticals are a good value in the fight against disease and preserving the quality of life. Today we are learning a great deal about genetics, gene mapping, and how genetic makeup causes treatments to succeed for one patient and fail for another. All of these have the potential to alter the costs of finding successful treatments and using them effectively for the right patients.

Pharmaceutical companies in the developed world are for-profit companies and have been criticized for ignoring solutions to important diseases in lesser-developed countries because the affected populations could not pay. Merck's expensive decision some years ago to pursue successfully a cure for a major disease prevalent almost exclusively in Africa is one of several exceptions. Both humanitarian groups and political pressure have helped encourage compromises that extend the availability of drugs to poor populations. For example, the Gates Foundation has invested more than $1.6 billion to speed vaccine development and provide immunization to the world's poor. When the Gates Foundation absorbs some of the risk of failure by funding research, more R&D can and will occur.

Sources: 1999, 2003, and 2008 Lilly Annual Reports; *BusinessWeek*, April 26, 2004, p. 65.

Estimating Intraperiod Gross Profit and Inventory

To avoid costly physical counts of inventory, some companies use the gross profit percentage to estimate ending inventory balances for monthly or quarterly reports. For example, suppose past sales of a particular Home Depot store have usually resulted in a gross profit percentage of 30%. The accountant assumes that gross profit continues to be 30% of sales and estimates the cost of goods sold for quarterly sales of $10 million as follows (in millions):

$$\text{Sales} - \text{Cost of goods sold} = \text{Gross profit}$$
$$S - CGS = GP$$
$$\$10.0 - CGS = .30 \times \$10.0 = \$3.0$$
$$CGS = \$7.0$$

If we know the store's beginning inventory is $5 million and purchases are $7.1 million, we can then estimate ending inventory to be $5.1 million as follows (in millions):

$$\text{Beginning inventory} + \text{Purchases} - \text{Ending inventory} = \text{CGS}$$
$$\text{BI} + \text{P} - \text{EI} = \text{CGS}$$
$$\$5.0 + \$7.1 - \text{EI} = \$7.0$$
$$\text{EI} = \$5.1$$

Gross Profit Percentage and Turnover

Retailers often attempt to increase total profits by increasing sales levels. They may lower prices and hope to increase their total gross profits by selling their inventories more quickly, replenishing, selling again, and so forth. In essence, they are accepting a lower gross profit per unit, but are expecting to increase total sales more than enough to compensate. With a high volume of sales activity, a smaller gross margin per unit sold provides high total profits. This is one of the reasons that stores such as **Costco**, **Wal-Mart**, and **The Home Depot** do well.

inventory turnover

The cost of goods sold divided by the average inventory held during a given period.

To relate sales levels to inventory levels we measure **inventory turnover**—cost of goods sold divided by the average inventory held during a given period. Average inventory is usually the sum of beginning inventory and ending inventory divided by 2. For The Home Depot store in the previous example, the average inventory is ($5.0 million + $5.1 million)/2 = $5.05 million. The quarterly inventory turnover is computed as follows:

$$\text{Inventory turnover} = \text{Cost of goods sold} \div \text{Average inventory}$$
$$= \$7.0 \text{ million} \div \$5.05 \text{ million} = 1.4$$

Suppose sales double if The Home Depot lowers its prices by 5%. Sales revenue on the current level of business drops from $10 million to 0.95 × $10 million, or $9.5 million. But the store sells twice as many units, so total revenue becomes 2 × $9.5 million, or $19 million. How profitable is this store? Cost of goods sold doubles from $7 million to $14 million. Total gross profit is $19 million – $14 million = $5 million. So gross profit during the quarter is $2 million higher as a result of the lower price. The inventory turnover doubles: $14 million divided by $5.05 million (the unchanged average inventory) is 2.8. However, the gross profit percentage falls from 30% to 26% ($5 million divided by $19 million).

Is the company better off? Maybe. Certainly, the current month's gross profit is larger. However, long-term strategic concerns raise the question "Is this new sales level sustainable?" For some products, when prices fall, consumers sharply increase purchases and stockpile the extras for later consumption. There is little increase in underlying demand, just a shift of future purchases to the present. Therefore, the current good sales could result in terrible future sales.

Another strategic question is "What will the competition do?" If The Home Depot's increased sales came at a competitor's expense, the competitor's response may be a similar decrease in prices. The competition might recover most of its old customers, with each buying a little more at the new price than they did at the old. Assuming all competitors decrease prices similarly, the whole market would see perhaps a 20% sales growth, not a doubling of sales. In that case, The Home Depot store would be no better off overall because the 20% sales growth would just cover the 5% price reduction.

Exhibit 7-12 illustrates two principles. Panel A shows that if a firm can increase inventory turnover while maintaining a constant gross profit percentage, it should do so. To increase inventory turnover means that a firm supports sales levels with less inventory. It can do this by more frequently restocking, for example. However, as Panel B shows, if the increased inventory turnover results from sales growth driven by a decrease in sales price, the gross margin percentage may fall. The desirability of the change depends on whether the sales gain could offset the decreased margin.

In The Home Depot store example, when a 5% price reduction produces only a 20% increase in units sold, the new gross margin of $3 million is just equal to the initial gross margin. Any sales increase less than 20% would result in a decreased gross margin. However, at any sales increase greater than 20%, the new gross margin would exceed the original $3 million. For example, at a 50% increase in sales volume, the new gross margin of $3.75 million exceeds the original by $3.75 million – $3 million = $.75 million. Basically, the lesson of Exhibit 7-12 is that you cannot focus on only one number or measure of company performance. Paying too much attention to one measure could cause you to miss the fact that another was falling fast.

	Unit Sales Increase			
	Original	20%	50%	100%
PANEL A				
No change in sales price				
Sales	$10.00	$12.00	$15.00	$20.00
Cost of goods sold (70%)	7.00	8.40	10.50	14.00
Gross margin (30%)	$ 3.00	$ 3.60	$ 4.50	$ 6.00
Inventory turnover	1.4	1.7	2.1	2.8
PANEL B				
5% reduction in sales price				
Sales (95% of above)	$ 9.50	$11.40	$14.25	$19.00
Cost of goods sold (as above)	7.00	8.40	10.50	14.00
Gross margin (26% of sales)	$ 2.50	$ 3.00	$ 3.75	$ 5.00
Inventory turnover (as above)	1.4	1.7	2.1	2.8

Earlier you saw the industry variability in gross margin percentages. The same variability applies to inventory turnover percentages, as the following table illustrates:

Company	Gross Profit Percentage	Inventory Turnover
Ford Motor	2%	14
The Home Depot	34	4
Merck	84	2
Whole Foods	37	18
Safeway	32	9
Sysco	20	16

Source: Fidelity.com company analysis features, 2009

As you can see, the companies with the higher gross profit percentages tend to have lower inventory turnover. Compare Ford and Sysco with Home Depot and Merck. But there is substantial variation around this pattern

The inventory turnover measure is especially effective for assessing companies in the same industry. If one industry member has a higher turnover than another, it is probably more efficient. That is, the higher turnover indicates an ability to use smaller inventory levels to attain high sales levels. This is good because it reduces the investment in inventory. Such a company has fewer products sitting on display shelves or in warehouses and uses less capital in maintaining, moving, and displaying inventory items.

Gross Profit Percentages and Accuracy of Records

Auditors, including those from the IRS, use the gross profit percentage to help satisfy themselves about the accuracy of records. For example, the IRS compiles gross profit percentages by types of retail establishment. If a company shows an unusually low percentage compared with similar companies, IRS auditors may suspect that the company has tried to avoid taxes by failing to record all cash sales. Similarly, managers watch changes in gross profit percentages to judge operating profitability and to monitor how well a company is controlling employee theft and shoplifting.

Internal Control of Inventories

In many organizations, inventories are more easily accessible than cash. Therefore, they can become a favorite target for thieves. Retail merchants must contend with inventory shrinkage, a polite term for shoplifting by customers and embezzling by employees. The importance of shrinkage is clear from **The Home Depot** annual report that says, "Our second priority is to increase gross profit through shrink reduction, distribution efficiencies, an improved pricing model, the expansion of private brand offerings and increased foreign sourcing. In 2008, inventory shrink decreased as a result of several focused initiatives."

A University of Florida study sponsored by the National Retail Foundation estimates that U.S. retailers lose $37 billion annually to inventory shrinkage, the largest percentage of it due to employee theft. Average inventory shrinkage for retailers is 1%–3% of sales depending on the category. The study is discussed at Multichannelmerchant.com, which presents a number of possible interventions that retailers can use to reduce theft. These interventions include cameras to monitor customer and employee behavior, analysis of data to identify fraudulent returned merchandise and who is doing it, merchandise sensors to identify merchandise that has not been paid for, and perhaps most importantly improved hiring and training practices for employees. Experts on controlling inventory shrinkage generally agree that the best deterrent is an alert employee at the point of sale.

Shrinkage in Perpetual and Periodic Inventory Systems

Measuring inventory shrinkage is straightforward for companies that use a perpetual inventory system. Shrinkage is simply the difference between the cost of inventory identified by a physical count and the inventory balance in the company's general ledger. A periodic inventory system has no continuing balance of the inventory account. Cost of goods sold automatically includes inventory shrinkage. Why? Beginning inventory plus purchases less ending inventory measures all inventory that has flowed out, whether it went to customers, shoplifters, or embezzlers, or was simply lost or broken.

Summary Problem for Your Review

PROBLEM

Hewlett-Packard (HP) designs, manufactures, and services a broad array of products including perhaps your calculator or printer. Some results of product sales for the year ended October 31, 2008, were as follows ($ in millions):

Sales of products	$91,697
Cost of merchandise sold	69,342
Beginning merchandise inventory	8,033
Ending merchandise inventory	7,879

1. Calculate the 2008 gross profit and gross profit percentage for HP.
2. Calculate the inventory turnover ratio.
3. What gross profit would have been reported if inventory turnover in 2008 had been 9, the gross profit percentage remained the same as that calculated in requirement 1, and the level of inventory was unchanged?

SOLUTION

(Monetary amounts are in millions.)

1. Gross profit = Sales − Cost of merchandise sold

    = $91,697 − $69,342

    = $22,355

    Gross profit percentage = Gross profit ÷ Sales

    = $22,355 ÷ $91,697

    = 24%

2. Inventory turnover = Cost of merchandise sold ÷ Average merchandise inventory
   = $69,342 ÷ [($8,033 + $7,879) ÷ 2]
   = $69,342 ÷ $7,956
   = 8.7

3. To respond to this question you must first see that a higher inventory turnover given a constant average inventory implies an increase in sales. Increased sales with a constant gross profit percentage implies increased total gross profit. With these relationships in mind, answering the question is a process of working backward based on the ratios and relationships.

   Cost of merchandise sold = Inventory turnover × Average merchandise inventory
   = 9 × $7,956
   = $71,604

   Gross profit percentage = (Sales − Cost of merchandise sold) ÷ Sales
   24% = (S − $71,604) ÷ S
   .24 × S = S − $71,604
   S − (.24 × S) = $71,604
   S × (1 − .24) = $71,604
   S = $71,604 ÷ (1 − .24)
   S = $94,216

   Gross profit = Sales − Cost of merchandise sold
   = $94,216 − $71,604
   = $22,612

As you would expect given our calculations, the gross profit percentage remains at 24% ($22,612 ÷ 94,216).

Highlights to Remember

1 Link inventory valuation to gross profit. We link inventory valuation to gross profit because the inventory valuation involves allocating the cost of goods available for sale between cost of goods sold (used in computing gross profit—sales less cost of goods sold—on the income statement) and ending inventory (a current asset on the balance sheet).

2 Use both perpetual and periodic inventory systems. Under the perpetual inventory system, we continuously track inventories and cost of goods sold by recording cost of goods sold at the time of each sale. Under the periodic inventory system, we compute cost of goods sold using an adjusting entry at year-end. Accountants conduct a physical inventory at the end of each period under either system. They count the goods on hand and calculate a cost for each item from purchase records. Under the periodic system, the physical inventory is the basis for the year-end adjusting entry to recognize cost of goods sold. Under the perpetual system, the physical inventory is used to confirm the accounting records. Differences, if any, lead to adjustments to cost of goods sold and ending inventory.

3 Calculate the cost of merchandise acquired. The cost of merchandise acquired is the invoice price of the goods plus directly identifiable inbound transportation costs less any cash or quantity discounts and less any returns or allowances.

4 Compute income and inventory values using the three principal inventory valuation methods allowed under both U.S. GAAP and IFRS and the one method allowed only by U.S. GAAP. Valuation of inventories involves the assignment of specific historical costs of acquisition either to units sold or to units remaining in ending inventory. Four major inventory valuation methods are in use in the United States: specific identification, weighted average, FIFO, and LIFO. IFRS does now allow LIFO. Specific identification is most common for low-volume, high-value products such as automobiles, boats, or jewelry. FIFO attributes the most recent, current prices to inventory items. LIFO attributes the most recent, current prices to cost of sales. When prices are rising and inventories are constant or growing, LIFO net income is less than FIFO net income. LIFO is popular in the United States among companies who face rising prices, for whom lower profits under LIFO mean lower taxes. The U.S. tax law allows companies to use LIFO for tax purposes only if they use it also for financial reporting purposes. LIFO also allows management to affect its income by the timing of purchases of inventory. Weighted average provides results between LIFO and FIFO for both the income statement cost of sales and the balance sheet inventory number.

5 **Use the lower-of-cost-or-market method to value inventories under both U.S. GAAP and IFRS.** Conservatism leads to the lower-of-cost-or-market (LCM) method, which treats cost as the maximum value of inventory. United States companies must reduce inventory carrying amounts to replacement cost (with a corresponding increase in cost of goods sold) when inventory replacement prices fall below historical cost levels. IFRS uses net realizable value instead of replacement cost in applying LCM.

6 **Show the effects of inventory errors on financial statements.** The nature of accrual accounting for inventories creates a self-correcting quality about errors in counting or valuing the ending inventory. This occurs because the ending inventory in one period becomes the beginning inventory of the subsequent period.

7 **Evaluate the gross profit percentage and inventory turnover.** Financial analysts and managers use gross profit percentages as a measure of profitability and inventory turnover as a measure of efficient asset use. They compare these measures with prior levels to examine trends and with current levels of other industry members to assess relative performance.

Appendix 7A: Characteristics and Consequences of LIFO

OBJECTIVE **8**

Describe characteristics of LIFO and how they affect the measurement of income.

Although LIFO is prohibited under IFRS, it is very widely used in the United States, has strong tax benefits for certain companies, and has some unusual features in application. Because of its dominant role in inventory accounting in the United States, we give LIFO a little extra attention in this appendix.

LIFO and Inflation

Inflation is a key factor driving companies to use LIFO. When inflation is low, as it has been for most of the last three decades, the tax and income differences are also small. The inventory method chosen matters little. Low inflation has been the norm in the United States during most of the last hundred years, but in the 1970s, the inflation rate in the United States reached double digits for the first time. In response, more than 40 U.S. corporations switched from FIFO to LIFO, deciding the benefit of lower income taxes exceeded the cost of reporting lower profits. These tax savings were not trivial. For example, by switching from FIFO to LIFO, **DuPont** saved more than $200 million in taxes in 1974, and it anticipated greater savings in the future.

Why did some firms remain on FIFO? Some firms should choose FIFO because for them it lowers taxes. Even when prices were rising in general, some industries, such as computers, faced declining costs and prices, so FIFO minimized reported income and taxes. For those who could have lowered taxes by using LIFO, possible reasons to remain on FIFO include the high bookkeeping costs of implementing the switch, reluctance by management to make an accounting switch that reduces reported income and possibly reduces management bonuses, fear that banks would view the reduction in income unfavorably in loan negotiations, and belief that lower reported income would result in a lower stock price.

Holding Gains and Inventory Profits

LIFO's income-statement orientation provides a particular economic interpretation of operating performance in inflationary periods, based on replacement of inventory. A merchant such as Emilio in the example beginning on page 299 is in the business of buying and selling on a daily basis. To continue in business, he must be able to maintain his stock of cola and must make sufficient profit on each transaction to make it worth his while to run his soda stand. So, before he can feel he has really made a profit, he will need to restock his inventory and be ready for the next day. If he must spend 56¢ to replace the can he sold, this 56¢ cost of acquiring the item today is the current replacement cost of the inventory. Under LIFO, we calculate his profit to be 34¢ because we use that recent inventory acquisition cost of 56¢ to measure cost of goods sold. So LIFO approximates a replacement cost view of the transaction.

holding gain (inventory profit)

Increase in the replacement cost of the inventory held during the current period.

In contrast, FIFO measures profit using the 30¢ can acquired on Monday as cost of goods sold and reports a profit of 60¢. The difference between the 60¢ FIFO profit and the 34¢ LIFO profit is 26¢, which is also the difference between the historical cost of 30¢ under FIFO and the replacement cost of 56¢ under LIFO. This 26¢ difference occurs because prices are rising. We call it a **holding gain** or an **inventory profit**—the increase in the replacement cost of the inventory held during the current period. The idea is that between Monday and Thursday, Emilio's first can of cola acquired for 30¢ became more valuable as prices rose, and because he held it as inventory during those days he experienced a 26¢ gain.

Because LIFO matches the most recent acquisition costs with sales revenue, LIFO cost of goods sold typically offers a close approximation to replacement cost, and reported net income rarely contains significant holding gains. In contrast, FIFO reports a profit of 60¢ including the economic profit of 34¢ calculated as sales price less replacement costs, plus the inventory profit or holding gain of 26¢ that arose because the value of the inventory item rose with the passage of time.

LIFO Layers

The ending inventory under LIFO will have one total value, but it may contain prices from many different periods. For example, Emilio's ending inventory contained two cans, one acquired on Monday at 30¢ and one acquired on Tuesday at 40¢. We call each distinct cost element of inventory a **LIFO layer** or a **LIFO increment**—an addition to inventory at an identifiable cost level. As a company grows, the LIFO layers pile on top of one another over the years. Suppose Emilio's business grew for years, ending each year with two more cans in inventory than were there the year before. Each year would have an identifiable LIFO layer, much like the annual rings on a tree. After 4 years of inventory growth and rising prices, his ending inventory might be structured as follows:

LIFO layer (LIFO increment)
A separately identifiable addition to LIFO inventory at an identifiable cost level.

Year 1	Layer 1—1 can @ .30	
	Layer 2—1 can @ .40	.70
Year 2	Layer 3—2 cans @ .45	.90
Year 3	Layer 4—2 cans @ .50	1.00
Year 4	Layer 5—2 cans @ .55	1.10
Total inventory—8 cans		$3.70

Many LIFO companies show inventories that have ancient layers going back as far as 1940, when companies first used LIFO. Reported LIFO inventory values may therefore be far below the market value or current replacement value of the inventory. This means that the book values reported on the balance sheet will have little relevance to investors interested in assessing the value of the assets of the company. Although LIFO better presents the economic reality on the income statement, FIFO provides more up-to-date valuations of inventory on the balance sheet.

LIFO Inventory Liquidations

The existence of old LIFO layers can cause problems in income measurement when inventories decrease after a period of rising prices. Examine Exhibit 7-13. Suppose Harbor Electronics bought 100 units of inventory at $10 per unit on December 31, 20X0, to begin its business operations. The company bought and sold 100 units each year, 20X1–20X4, at the purchase and selling prices

	Purchase Price Per Unit	Selling Price Per Unit	Revenue	FIFO			LIFO		
Year				Cost of Goods Sold	Gross Profit	Ending Inventory	Cost of Goods Sold	Gross Profit	Ending Inventory
20X0	$10	—	—	—	—	$1,000	—	—	$1,000
20X1	12	$15	$1,500	$1,000	$ 500	1,200	$1,200	$ 300	1,000
20X2	14	17	1,700	1,200	500	1,400	1,400	300	1,000
20X3	16	19	1,900	1,400	500	1,600	1,600	300	1,000
20X4	18	21	2,100	1,600	500	1,800	1,800	300	1,000
20X5		23	2,300	1,800	500	0	1,000	1,300	0
Total			$9,500	$7,000	$2,500		$7,000	$2,500	

EXHIBIT 7-13

Harbor Electronics

Effect of Inventory Liquidations Under LIFO (Purchases and Sales of 100 Units 20X1–20X4, Purchases but No Sales in 20X0; Sales but No Purchases in 20X5)

shown. The example assumes replacement costs and sales prices rise by the same amount, with a difference between the two of $3 per unit. In 20X5, Harbor sold 100 units, but purchased none.

Compare the gross profit each year under LIFO with that under FIFO in Exhibit 7-13. LIFO gross profit was consistently less than FIFO gross profit because prices were rising, and the LIFO cost of goods sold reflected the latest prices, whereas the FIFO did not. What happened in 20X5? The old 20X0 inventory became the cost of goods sold under LIFO because Harbor depleted its inventory. As a result, gross profit under LIFO soared to $1,300, well above the FIFO gross profit, which was stable at $500. In general, when the physical amount of inventory decreases, under LIFO the cost of goods sold consists of old, low inventory acquisition costs associated with old LIFO layers. This is called a **LIFO liquidation**. This treatment can create a very low cost of goods sold and high gross profit.

For example, LIFO inventory liquidations by Ford Motor Company decreased its 2008 cost of sales by $209 million. In a sense, a LIFO liquidation means that the current year's income includes the cumulative inventory profit from years of increasing prices. An analyst tracking Ford's profitability would want to know that its profits in 2008 were not due solely to producing and selling automobiles that year. It was partly due to the company's inventory accounting process.

The effect of LIFO liquidations is potentially large, and security analysts estimate the effect of the choice between LIFO and FIFO on net income. The difference between a company's LIFO inventory level and what it would be under FIFO, its **LIFO reserve**, is helpful in making these estimates. Most companies that use LIFO explicitly measure and report their LIFO reserve on the balance sheet itself or in the footnotes.

Refer to Exhibit 7-13. What is the Harbor Electronics' LIFO reserve at the end of 20X1? It is $1,200 – $1,000 = $200, the difference in the LIFO and FIFO ending inventories. Note that it is the same as the difference in gross profit of $200 in 20X1. What about year 20X2? The LIFO reserve is $400 (FIFO ending inventory of $1,400 less LIFO ending inventory of $1,000). This difference represents the cumulative effect on earnings (or gross profit) during the first 2 years the company was in business. The specific effect on earnings during 20X2 is the change in the LIFO reserve, or $200. Exhibit 7-14 summarizes these effects.

From Exhibit 7-14, note that the annual difference between gross profit using FIFO and that using LIFO is the yearly change in the LIFO reserve. Finally, when Harbor sells all the inventory in 20X5, the liquidation of the LIFO inventory leads to recognition of higher earnings under LIFO than under FIFO by the entire amount of the LIFO reserve. LIFO recognizes inventory profits when a company reduces its inventory levels. The balance of the LIFO reserve at any point in time indicates the cumulative difference between FIFO and LIFO gross profit over all prior years.

How significant are the effects of LIFO? Ford Motor Company reported 2008 inventory of $8.6 billion. Ford used LIFO for some of its inventories. If it had used FIFO for all inventories, the total inventory would have been $891 million higher (a 10% difference). This means that over time, Ford has reported lower income on its tax returns by $891 million and paid lower taxes of approximately $356 million ($891 million times the approximate tax rate of 40%) as a result of its decision to use LIFO instead of FIFO.

This savings amounts to an interest-free loan from the government. If Ford were to go out of business, the sale of old inventory items would create a large LIFO liquidation, and all these delayed taxes would become due. In the meantime, Ford has the use of some $356 million it has not yet had to pay in taxes.

LIFO liquidation

A decrease in the physical amount in inventory causing old, low LIFO inventory acquisition costs to become the cost of goods sold, resulting in a high gross profit.

LIFO reserve

The difference between a company's inventory valued at LIFO and what it would be under FIFO.

EXHIBIT 7-14

Harbor Electronics

Annual and Cumulative Effects of LIFO Reserve

Year	Ending Inventory		LIFO Reserve	Change in Reserve	Gross Profit Effect	
	FIFO	**LIFO**			**Current**	**Cumulative**
X0	$1,000	$1,000	$ 0	$ 0	$ 0	$ 0
X1	1,200	1,000	200	200	200	200
X2	1,400	1,000	400	200	200	400
X3	1,600	1,000	600	200	200	600
X4	1,800	1,000	800	200	200	800
X5	0	0	0	(800)	(800)	0

Adjusting from LIFO to FIFO

Typically, disclosures in the annual report are sufficient to permit detailed analysis of LIFO effects. Ford Motor Company's 2008 report allows us to compare results under LIFO to what Ford would have reported under FIFO:

Ford Motor Company ($ in millions)

	2008 Inventory		Cost of Goods Sold
	Beginning	Ending	
LIFO	$10,121	$8,618	$127,103
LIFO reserve	1,100	891	209*
FIFO	$11,221	$9,509	$127,312

*Change in LIFO reserve is a decrease of $1,100 – $891 = $209. Therefore, cost of goods sold is $209 more under FIFO then under LIFO.

Note that Ford's LIFO reserve decreased from $1,100 million to $891 million during 2008. This decrease of $209 million in the LIFO reserve is exactly the amount by which the cost of goods sold for the year under LIFO is less than the cost of goods sold under FIFO.

INTERPRETING FINANCIAL STATEMENTS

In contrast to the effect on cost of goods sold in a specific year, we can examine the cumulative effect of the inventory accounting choice over time. The end-of-year level of the LIFO reserve allows us to answer the question, "During the years that Ford has used LIFO, what has been the total, cumulative effect on cost of goods sold over all those years?" To see this, do the mental experiment of having Ford sell all its 2008 year-end inventory for $12,000 million in early 2009. How would profit from this liquidation differ between LIFO and FIFO given inventory levels that would exist at year-end 2008 under each method?

Answer

This complete liquidation would produce higher profits under LIFO. These higher profits in the final liquidation year are equal to the cumulative amount by which gross profits were lower under LIFO in past years. The hypothetical liquidation of Ford inventories would show the following (in millions):

	LIFO	FIFO	Difference
Sales	$12,000	$12,000	—
Cost of goods sold	8,618	9,509	891
Gross profit	$ 3,382	$ 2,491	($891)

Appendix 7B: Inventory in a Manufacturing Environment

In this chapter, we examined inventory accounting from the viewpoint of a merchandiser. When a company manufactures products, the cost of inventory is a combination of the acquisition cost of raw material; the wages paid to workers who combine the raw materials into finished products; and an allocation of the costs of space, energy, and equipment used by the workers as they transform the various elements into a finished product.

OBJECTIVE 9

Determine inventory costs for a manufacturing company.

Consider how we accumulate costs in a manufacturing environment for Packit, a company that makes backpacks. The raw materials are heavy fabric, glue, and thread. The transformation occurs when workers use cutters to make the panels that other workers sew and glue together. The costs of manufacture include depreciation on the manufacturing building; depreciation on the sewing machines and cutters; and utilities to support the effort in the form of heat, power, and light. The finished goods are backpacks.

The accounting process is easiest to understand when calculating the cost of a complete year of production using the periodic approach. In the following example, Packit produced 10,000 backpacks during its first year in business at a total cost of $800,000, providing a cost per backpack of $80.00 ($800,000 ÷ 10,000 units). At year-end, if Packit has sold all 10,000 backpacks, the financial statements would include $800,000 in cost of goods sold.

Packit Company—Year 1	
Beginning inventory	—
Fabric purchased and used	$200,000
Wages paid to workers	300,000
Thread and glue used	50,000
Depreciation on building and equipment	220,000
Utilities	30,000
Total costs to manufacture	$800,000
Cost per backpack ($800,000 ÷ 10,000)	$ 80.00

In the preceding example, Packit transformed all materials acquired during the year into fin-ished products and sold all those products before year-end. In reality, if we take a snapshot of the typical backpack manufacturer at year-end, we would observe bolts of fabric, spools of thread, and gallons of glue waiting to be put into production. We call these items that are held for use in the manufacturing of a product **raw material inventory**. In addition, we would also observe fabric already cut but not assembled and some partially completed backpacks. We refer to the material,

raw material inventory

Includes the cost of materials held for use in the manufacturing of a product.

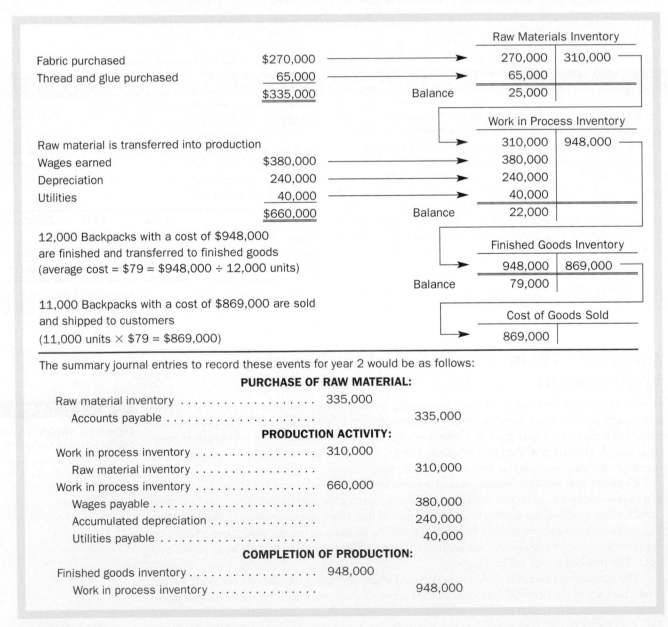

The summary journal entries to record these events for year 2 would be as follows:

PURCHASE OF RAW MATERIAL:

Raw material inventory	335,000	
Accounts payable		335,000

PRODUCTION ACTIVITY:

Work in process inventory	310,000	
Raw material inventory		310,000
Work in process inventory	660,000	
Wages payable		380,000
Accumulated depreciation		240,000
Utilities payable		40,000

COMPLETION OF PRODUCTION:

Finished goods inventory	948,000	
Work in process inventory		948,000

EXHIBIT 7-15

Packit Company Accounting for Manufacturing Costs—Year 2

labor, and other costs accumulated for partially completed items as **work in process inventory**. When manufacture is complete and the goods are ready to deliver to customers, we call the inventory **finished goods inventory**. Exhibit 7-15 shows the accounting system for managing these costs for Packit's second year of production. During this second year, Packit completed 12,000 backpacks and sold 11,000. Some remain in the assembly process at year-end, and Packit holds unused fabric, thread, and glue in preparation for future production.

The schematic in Exhibit 7-15 captures the production process. You might think of each of the accounts as corresponding to a physical reality. The raw material is stored in a locked room, ready for use. The work in process is located in the production room, and as it is finished it is physically transferred to a storage site. When Packit sells goods, it removes the items sold from that storage site and gives them to the customer in exchange for cash or an account receivable. Raw materials, work in process, and finished goods are all forms of inventory and appear on the balance sheet as current assets. They are simply in different stages of completion. The act of sale converts the asset into an expense that Packit will report on its income statement. At the end of year 2, Packit will show total inventory on its balance sheet of $126,000, as follows:

Raw materials inventory	$ 25,000
Work in process inventory	22,000
Finished goods inventory	79,000
Total inventory	$126,000

work in process inventory
Includes the cost incurred for partially completed items, including raw materials, labor, and other costs.

finished goods inventory
The accumulated costs of manufacture for goods that are complete and ready for sale.

Accounting Vocabulary

conservatism, p. 307

consistency, p. 304

cost of goods available for sale, p. 294

cost valuation, p. 293

current replacement cost, p. 306

cutoff error, p. 309

finished goods inventory, p. 321

first-in, first-out (FIFO), p. 300

F.O.B. destination, p. 296

F.O.B. shipping point, p. 296

freight in, p. 296

gross profit percentage, p. 310

holding gain, p. 316

inventory profit, p. 316

inventory shrinkage, p. 294

inventory turnover, p. 312

inward transportation, p. 296

last-in, first-out (LIFO), p. 301

LIFO increment, p. 317

LIFO layer, p. 317

LIFO liquidation, p. 318

LIFO reserve, p. 318

lower-of-cost-or-market method (LCM), p. 306

net realizable value, p. 306

periodic inventory system, p. 294

perpetual inventory system, p. 294

physical count, p. 294

raw material inventory, p. 320

retailer, p. 310

specific identification method, p. 299

weighted-average method, p. 302

wholesaler, p. 310

work in process inventory, p. 321

write-down, p. 306

Assignment Material

MyAccountingLab

Questions

7-1 When a company records a sales transaction, it also records another related transaction. Explain the related transaction.

7-2 "There are two steps in conducting a physical count of inventories." What are they?

7-3 Distinguish between the perpetual and periodic inventory systems.

7-4 "An advantage of the perpetual inventory system is that a physical count of inventory is unnecessary. The periodic method requires a physical count to compute cost of goods sold." Do you agree? Explain.

7-5 Distinguish between F.O.B. destination and F.O.B. shipping point.

7-6 "Freight out should be classified as a direct offset to sales, not as an expense." Do you agree? Explain.

7-7 Name the four inventory cost flow assumptions or valuation methods that are generally accepted in the United States. Give a brief phrase describing each.

7-8 For which of the following items would a company be likely to use the specific identification inventory method?

a. Corporate jet aircraft

b. Large sailboats

c. Pencils

d. Diamond rings

e. Timex watches

f. Automobiles

g. Books

h. Compact discs

7-9 If a company uses a FIFO cost flow assumption, will it report the same cost of goods sold using the periodic inventory method that it reports using the perpetual method? Why or why not?

7-10 Why is LIFO a good news/bad news inventory method?

7-11 "Purchases of inventory at the end of a fiscal period can have a direct effect on income under LIFO." Do you agree? Explain.

7-12 "Gamma Company has five units of inventory, two purchased for $4 each and three purchased for $5 each. Thus, the weighted-average cost of the inventory is ($4 + $5) ÷ 2 = $4.50 per unit." Do you agree? Explain.

7-13 Assume that the physical level of inventory is constant at the beginning and end of the year and that the cost of inventory items is rising. Which will produce a higher ending inventory value, LIFO or FIFO?

7-14 Will LIFO or FIFO produce higher cost of goods sold during a period of falling prices? Explain.

7-15 What is consistency, and why is it an important accounting principle?

7-16 "There is a single dominant reason why more and more U.S. companies have adopted LIFO." What is the reason?

7-17 "An inventory profit is a fictitious profit." Do you agree? Explain.

7-18 LIFO can produce absurd inventory valuations. Why?

7-19 "Conservatism always results in lower reported profits." Do you agree? Explain.

7-20 "Accountants have traditionally favored taking some losses but no gains before an asset is exchanged." What is this tradition or convention called?

7-21 What does market mean in inventory accounting?

7-22 "The lower-of-cost-or-market method is inherently inconsistent." Do you agree? Explain.

7-23 "Inventory errors are counterbalancing." Explain.

7-24 Express the cost of goods sold section of the income statement as an equation.

7-25 "Gross profit percentages help in the preparation of interim financial statements." Explain.

7-26 The branch manager of a national retail grocery chain has stated, "My managers are judged more heavily on the basis of their merchandise-shrinkage control than on their overall sales volume." Why? Explain.

7-27 Study Appendix 7A. What is an inventory holding gain (or inventory profit)?

7-28 Study Appendix 7A. What generally happens to income when a company liquidates old LIFO inventory layers?

7-29 Study Appendix 7B. What are the three types of inventory in a manufacturing company? Which of the three is usually the largest?

Critical Thinking Questions

7-30 Deciding on a Discount Policy

You are debating with your boss about whether to give customers a 2% discount for quantity purchases. You favor the idea, but your boss says, "Why give money away? If the customer buys more, we are out 2%." How do you reply?

7-31 Effect of Overstating Inventories

Phar Mor was a large, rapidly growing pharmacy chain that proved to have overstated assets by more than $400 million. Top executives accomplished the overstatement by inflating the company's inventories at numerous store locations. How would this affect the income statements of Phar Mor?

7-32 Purchasing Operations and LIFO Versus FIFO

Suppose a company bases its evaluation of the purchasing officer for a refinery on the gross margin on the oil products produced and sold during the year. During the year, the price of a barrel of oil increased from $20 to $30. The value of the inventory of oil at the beginning of the year is $20 or less per barrel. On the last day of the year, the purchasing agent is contemplating the purchase of additional oil at $30 per barrel. Is the agent more likely to purchase additional oil if the company uses the FIFO or LIFO method for its inventories? Explain.

7-33 Periodic Versus Perpetual Inventory Systems

The Zen Bootist manufactures sheepskin slippers, mittens, gloves, jackets, and leather sandals to sell at craft fairs and similar events. The majority of the company's transactions occur over the winter gift-giving season. As the business has grown, the owner has become concerned about how to account for certain items and has asked your advice about whether to use the periodic or perpetual inventory system. What do you say?

Exercises

7-34 Gross Profit Section

Given the following, prepare a detailed gross profit section for Goodman's Jewelry Wholesalers for the year ended December 31, 20X8 ($ in thousands), computing the amount for Gross Sales.

Cash discounts on purchases	$ 6	Cash discounts on sales	$ 5
Sales returns and allowances	50	Purchase returns and allowances	27
Gross purchases	650	Freight in	50
Merchandise inventory, December 31, 20X7	103	Merchandise inventory, December 31, 20X8	185
Gross profit	355		

7-35 Gross Margin Computations and Inventory Costs

On January 15, 20X4, Isabelle Muir valued her inventory at cost, $41,000. Her statements are based on the calendar year, so you find it necessary to establish an inventory figure as of January 1, 20X4. You find that from January 2 to January 15, sales were $71,200; sales returns, $2,300; goods purchased and placed in stock, $54,000; goods removed from stock and returned to suppliers, $1,000; and freight in, $500. Calculate the inventory cost as of January 1, assuming that goods are priced to provide a 24% gross profit.

7-36 Journal Entries

Coppola Company had sales of $19 million during the year. The goods cost Coppola $16 million. Give the journal entry or entries at the time of sale under the perpetual and periodic inventory systems.

7-37 Valuing Inventory and Cost of Goods Sold

Aberdeen Metals, Ltd., had the following inventory transactions during the month of March:

3/1 beginning inventory	3,000 units @ £2.00	£6,000
Week 1, purchases	2,000 units @ £2.10	4,200
Week 2, purchases	2,000 units @ £2.20	4,400
Week 3, purchases	1,000 units @ £2.30	2,300
Week 4, purchases	1,000 units @ £2.50	2,500

On March 31, a count of the ending inventory was completed, and 4,500 units were on hand. By using the periodic inventory system, calculate the cost of goods sold and ending inventory using LIFO, FIFO, and weighted-average inventory methods.

7-38 Entries for Purchase Transactions

The Schubert Company is a Swiss wholesaler of office supplies. Its unit of currency is the Swiss franc (CHF). Schubert uses a periodic inventory system. Prepare journal entries for the following summarized transactions (omit explanations):

Aug. 2	Purchased merchandise on account, CHF 350,000, terms 2/10, n/45.
Aug. 3	Paid cash for freight in, CHF 16,000.
Aug. 7	Schubert complained about some defects in the merchandise acquired on August 2. The supplier hand-delivered a credit memo granting an allowance of CHF 32,000.
Aug. 11	Cash disbursement to settle purchase of August 2.

7-39 Cost of Inventory Acquired

On July 5, Feltham Company purchased on account a shipment of sheet steel from Northwest Steel, Co. The invoice price was $195,000, F.O.B. shipping point. Shipping cost from the steel mill to Feltham's plant was $10,000. When inspecting the shipment, the Feltham receiving clerk found several flaws in the steel. The clerk informed Northwest's sales representative of the flaws, and after some negotiation, Northwest granted an allowance of $10,000.

To encourage prompt payment, Northwest grants a 2% cash discount to customers who pay their accounts within 30 days of billing. Feltham paid the proper amount on August 1.

1. Compute the total cost of the sheet steel acquired.
2. Prepare the journal entries for the transaction assuming a periodic inventory system. Omit explanations.

7-40 Entries for Periodic and Perpetual Systems

Rajiv, Co., had an inventory of $110,000, December 31, 20X7. Data for 20X8 follow:

Gross purchases on account	$950,000
Cost of goods sold	890,000
Inventory, December 31, 20X8	100,000
Purchase returns and allowances	70,000

By using the data, prepare comparative journal entries, including closing entries, for both a perpetual and a periodic inventory system.

7-41 Entries for Purchase Transactions

Equatorial Imports uses a periodic inventory system. Prepare journal entries for the following summarized transactions for 20X1 (omit explanations). For simplicity, assume the beginning and ending balances in accounts payable were zero.

1. Purchases (all using trade credit), $900,000
2. Purchase returns and allowances, $50,000
3. Freight in, $74,000 paid in cash
4. Payment for all credit purchases, less returns and allowances and cash discounts on purchases of $18,000

7-42 Journal Entries, Periodic Inventory System

Refer to the data in the preceding problem. Inventories were $71,000 on December 31, 20X0, and $120,000 on December 31, 20X1. Sales were $1,250,000. Prepare summary journal entries for 20X1 for sales and cost of goods sold (omit explanations).

7-43 Journal Entries, Periodic Inventory System

Consider the following data taken from the adjusted trial balance of the Vancouver Boat Company, December 31, 20X3 ($ in millions):

Purchases (on account)	$140	Sales (on account)	239
Sales returns and allowances	5	Purchase returns and allowances	6
Freight in (paid in cash)	14	Cash discounts on sales	8
Cash discounts on purchases	1	Other expenses	80
Inventory (beginning of year)	15		

Prepare summary journal entries. The ending inventory was $45 million.

7-44 Reconstruction of Transaction

Apple Computer, Inc., produces the well-known iMacs, iPhones, and iPads. Consider the following account balances ($ in millions):

	September 27, 2008	September 29, 2007
Inventories	$509	$346

The cost of the inventories purchased (or produced) during the 12 months between September 29, 2007, and September 27, 2008, was $21,497,000,000. The income statement for the 2008 fiscal year had an item "cost of sales." Compute its amount.

7-45 Reconstruction of Records

An earthquake caused heavy damage to the Eurasia Antique Store on May 3, 20X8. All merchandise was destroyed. Some accounting data are missing. In conjunction with an insurance investigation, you have been asked to estimate the cost of the inventory destroyed. The following data for 20X8 (recorded before the earthquake) are available:

Cash discounts on purchases	$ 2,000	Inventory, December 31, 20X7	$38,000
Gross sales	280,000	Purchase returns and allowances	7,000
Sales returns and allowances	24,000	Inward transportation	4,000
Gross purchases	159,000	Gross profit percentage on net sales	46%

7-46 Cost of Inventory Destroyed by Fire

Lin Company's insurance agent requires an estimate of the cost of merchandise lost by fire on March 9. Merchandise inventory on January 1 was $65,000. Purchases since January 1 were $190,000; freight in, $15,000; and purchase returns and allowances, $10,000. Sales are made at a gross margin of 20% of sales and totaled $200,000 up to March 9. What was the cost of the merchandise destroyed?

7-47 Inventory Shortage

An accounting clerk of the Plumlee Company absconded with cash and a truck full of electronic merchandise on May 14, 20X4. The following data have been compiled for 20X4:

Beginning inventory, January 1	$ 55,000
Sales to May 14, 20X4	300,000
Average gross profit rate	25%
Purchases to May 14, 20X4	200,000

Compute the estimated cost of the missing merchandise.

7-48 Inventory Errors

At the end of his first business year, Clifford Reyna counted and priced the inventory. A few very high-value items were hidden in a dark corner of the storage shelves and Clifford understated his 20X5 ending inventory by $10,000. His business financial statements and his tax return were affected. Assume a 40% tax rate.

1. Calculate the effect on taxable income, taxes, net income, and retained earnings for 20X5.
2. Repeat requirement 1 for 20X6, assuming the 20X6 ending inventory is correctly calculated.

7-49 Decision About Pricing

Custom Gems, Inc., a retail jewelry store, had gross profits of $1,320,000 on sales of $2,400,000 in 20X3. Average inventory was $1,000,000.

1. Compute inventory turnover.
2. Jerry Siegl, owner of Custom Gems, is considering whether to become a "discount" jeweler. For example, Jerry believes that a cut of 10% in average selling prices would increase inventory turnover in 20X4 to 1.5 times per year. Beginning and ending inventory would be unchanged. Suppose Jerry's beliefs are valid. What would his new gross profit percentage be? Would the total gross profit in 20X4 have improved? Show computations.

7-50 LIFO and FIFO

The inventory of the Shenandoah Gravel Company on June 30 shows 1,000 tons at $9 per ton. A physical inventory on July 31 shows a total of 1,100 tons on hand. Revenue from sales of gravel for July totals $102,000. The following purchases were made during July:

July 8	5,000 tons @ $10 per ton
July 13	1,000 tons @ $11 per ton
July 22	800 tons @ $12 per ton

1. Compute the inventory cost as of July 31 using (a) LIFO and (b) FIFO.
2. Compute the gross profit using each method.

7-51 Lower-of-Cost-or-Market

(Alternate is 7-77.) Fujita Company uses the inventory method "cost or market, whichever is lower." There were no sales or purchases during the periods indicated, although selling prices generally fluctuated in the same directions as replacement costs. Fujita makes adjustments for LCM each quarter. At what amount would you value merchandise on the dates that follow using U.S. GAAP? Using IFRS?

	Invoice Cost	Replacement Cost	Realizable Value
December 31, 20X1	$200,000	$185,000	$195,000
April 30, 20X2	200,000	190,000	210,000
August 31, 20X2	200,000	220,000	225,000
December 31, 20X2	200,000	175,000	190,000

7-52 Reconstruction of Transactions

Consider the following account balances of Costco Wholesale Corporation, the Seattle-based warehouse store operator ($ in millions):

	August 31 2008	September 2 2007
Merchandise inventories	$5,039	$4,879

On Costco's income statement for the fiscal year 2008, the cost of the merchandise sold was $63,503 million. Compute the net cost of the acquisition of inventory for the fiscal year ending August 31, 2008.

7-53 Gross Profit Percentage

Toys "R" Us operates more than 1,500 stores in the United States and abroad. Like most retailers, the managers of Toys "R" Us monitor the company's gross margin percentage. The following information is from the company's income statement (in millions):

	For the Year Ended		
	January 31, 2009	February 2, 2008	February 3, 2007
Sales	$13,724	$13,794	$13,050
Cost of sales	8,976	8,987	8,638

Compute the gross profit percentage for each of the 3 years. Comment on the changes in gross profit percentage.

7-54 Profitability and Turnover

Island Building Supply began 20X9 with inventory of $240,000. Island's 20X9 sales were $1,200,000, purchases of inventory totaled $1,035,000, and ending inventory was $300,000.

1. Prepare a statement of gross profit for 20X9.
2. What was Island Building Supply's inventory turnover?

Problems

7-55 Detailed Income Statement

(Alternate is 7-58.) Following are accounts taken from the adjusted trial balance of the Backbay Bathroom Supply Company, December 31, 20X5. The company uses the periodic inventory system.

Sales salaries and commissions	$160	Freight in	$ 55
Inventory, December 31, 20X4	200	Miscellaneous expenses	13
Allowance for bad debts	14	Sales	1,091
Rent expense, office space	10	Bad debts expense	8
Gross purchases	600	Cash discounts on purchases	15
Depreciation expense, office equipment	3	Inventory, December 31, 20X5	300
		Office salaries	46
Cash discounts on sales	16	Rent expense, selling space	90
Advertising expense	45	Income tax expense	42
Purchase returns and allowances	40	Sales returns and allowances	50
Delivery expense	20	Office supplies used	6
		Depreciation expenses, trucks, and store fixtures	29

Prepare a detailed multi-step income statement for 20X5. All amounts are in thousands.

7-56 Perpetual Inventory Calculations

Kennedy Electric is a wholesaler for commercial builders. The company uses a perpetual inventory system and a FIFO cost-flow assumption. The data concerning a particular product for the year 20X8 follows:

	Purchased		Sold	Balance
December 31, 20X7				110 @ $5 = $550
February 10, 20X8	80 @ $6 =	$ 480		
April 14			60	
May 9	110 @ $7 =	$ 770		
July 14			120	
October 21	100 @ $8 =	$ 800		
November 12			75	
Total	290	$2,050	255	

Calculate the ending inventory balance in units and dollars.

7-57 Gross Profit and Turnover

Retailers closely watch a number of financial ratios, including the gross profit (gross margin) percentage and inventory turnover. Suppose the results for the furniture department in a large store in a given year were as follows:

Sales	$6,000,000
Cost of goods sold	3,600,000
Gross profit	$2,400,000
Beginning inventory	$1,300,000
Ending inventory	1,100,000

1. Compute the gross profit percentage and the inventory turnover.
2. Suppose the retailer is able to maintain a reduced inventory of $900,000 throughout the succeeding year. What inventory turnover would have to be obtained to achieve the same $2,400,000 gross profit? Assume that the gross profit percentage is unchanged.
3. Suppose the retailer maintains inventory at the $900,000 level throughout the succeeding year, but cannot increase the inventory turnover from the level in requirement 1. What gross profit percentage would have to be obtained to achieve the same total gross profit?
4. Suppose the average inventory of $1,200,000 is maintained. Compute the total gross profit in the succeeding year if there is
   a. a 10% increase of the gross profit percentage (that is, 10% of the percentage, not an additional 10 percentage points) and a 10% decrease of the inventory turnover.
   b. a 10% decrease of the gross profit percentage and a 10% increase of the inventory turnover.
5. Why do retailers find the preceding types of ratios helpful?

7-58 Detailed Income Statement

(Alternate is 7-55.) Sears Holdings Corporation is a major retailer. The company's annual report contained the following actual data, which has been somewhat summarized, for the year ended January 31, 2009 ($ in millions):

Net revenues	$46,770
Purchases of inventory	32,950
Selling and administrative	11,060
Depreciation and amortization	981
Other operating expenses	309
Interest expense (net)	272
Other income	108
Income taxes	85

The balance sheets included the following actual data ($ in millions of dollars):

	January 31	
	2009	**2008**
Inventories	8,795	9,963

Prepare a detailed multistep income statement that includes the calculation of Cost of Goods Sold and ends with Net Earnings.

7-59 Comparison of Inventory Methods

(Alternates are 7-70 and 7-72.) Contractor Supply Company is a wholesaler for commercial builders. The company uses a periodic inventory system. The data concerning Kemtone cooktops for the year 20X8 follow:

	Purchases		Sold	Balance
December 31, 20X7				110 @ $50 = $5,500
February 10, 20X8	80 @ $60 =	$ 4,800		
April 14			60	
May 9	120 @ $70 =	$ 8,400		
July 14			120	
October 21	100 @ $80 =	$ 8,000		
November 12			70	
Total	300	$21,200	250	
December 31, 20X8				160 @ ?

The sales during 20X8 were made at the following selling prices:

60	@ $ 90 =	$ 5,400
120	@ 100 =	12,000
70	@ 110 =	7,700
250		$25,100

1. Prepare a comparative statement of gross profit for the year ended December 31, 20X8, using FIFO, LIFO, and weighted-average inventory methods.
2. By how much would income taxes differ if Contractor Supply Company had used LIFO instead of FIFO for Kemtone cooktops? Assume a 40% income tax rate.

7-60 Effects of Late Purchases

(Alternates are 7-71 and 7-73.) Refer to the preceding problem. Suppose 100 extra units had been acquired on December 30, 20X8, for $80 each, a total of $8,000. How would net income and income taxes have been affected under FIFO and under LIFO? Show a tabulated comparison.

7-61 LIFO, FIFO, and Lower-of-Cost-or-Market

Altobelli Company began business in Chicago on March 15, 20X0. The following are Altobelli's purchases of inventory:

March 17	100 units @ $10	$1,000
April 19	50 units @ $12	600
May 14	100 units @ $13	1,300
Total		$2,900

On May 25, the company sold 140 units, leaving inventory of 110 units. Altobelli Company's accountant was preparing a balance sheet for June 1, at which time the replacement cost of the inventory was $12 per unit.

1. Suppose Altobelli Company uses LIFO without applying lower-of-cost-or-market. Compute the June 1 inventory amount.
2. Suppose Altobelli Company uses lower-of-LIFO-cost-or-market. Compute the June 1 inventory amount.
3. Suppose Altobelli Company uses FIFO without applying lower-of-cost-or-market. Compute the June 1 inventory amount.
4. Suppose Altobelli Company uses lower-of-FIFO-cost-or-market. Compute the June 1 inventory amount.

7-62 Inventory Errors

(Alternate is 7-69.) The following data are from the 20X1 income statement of the Persian Rug Emporium ($ in thousands):

Sales		$1,650
Deduct cost of goods sold		
Beginning inventory	$ 390	
Purchases	820	
Cost of goods available for sale	$1,210	
Deduct: Ending inventory	370	
Cost of goods sold		840
Gross profit		$ 810
Other expenses		610
Income before income taxes		$ 200
Income tax expense at 40%		80
Net income		$ 120

The ending inventory was overstated by $10,000 because of errors in the physical count. The income tax rate was 40% in 20X1 and 20X2.

1. Which items in the income statement are incorrect and by how much? Use O for overstated, U for understated, and N for not affected. Complete the following tabulation (amounts in thousands):

	20X1	20X2
Beginning inventory	N	O $10
Ending inventory	?	?
Cost of goods sold	?	?
Gross margin	?	?
Income before income taxes	?	?
Income tax expense	?	?
Net income	?	?

2. What is the dollar effect of the inventory error on retained earnings at the end of 20X1 and at the end of 20X2?

7-63 LIFO, FIFO, and Prices Rising and Falling

The Steinberg Company has a periodic inventory system. Inventory on December 31, 20X1, consisted of 10,000 units @ $10 = $100,000. Purchases during 20X2 were 13,000 units. Sales were 12,000 units for sales revenue of $20 per unit.

1. Prepare a four-column comparative statement of gross margin for 20X2:
   a. Assume purchases were at $12 per unit. Assume FIFO and then LIFO.
   b. Assume purchases were at $8 per unit. Assume FIFO and then LIFO.
2. Explain the differences between LIFO and FIFO gross margin in both a and b in requirement 1.
3. Assume an income tax rate of 40%. Suppose all transactions were for cash. Which inventory method in question 1a would result in more cash for Steinberg Company and by how much?
4. Assume an income tax rate of 40%. Suppose all transactions were for cash. Which inventory method in question 1b would result in more cash for Steinberg Company and by how much?

7-64 LIFO, FIFO, and Cash Effects

In 20X8, McFarland Company had sales revenue of £440,000 for a line of woolen scarves. The company uses a periodic inventory system. Pertinent data for 20X8 included the following:

Inventory, December 31, 20X7	14,000 units @ £6	£ 84,000
January purchases	22,000 units @ £7	154,000
July purchases	30,000 units @ £8	240,000
Sales for the year	40,000 units	

1. Prepare a statement of gross margin for 20X8. Use two columns, one assuming LIFO and one assuming FIFO.
2. Assume a 40% income tax rate. Suppose all transactions were for cash. Which inventory method would result in more cash for McFarland Company, and by how much?

7-65 FIFO and LIFO

Two companies, the Lastin Company and the Firstin Company, are in the scrap metal warehousing business as arch competitors. They are about the same size, and in 20X1 coincidentally encountered seemingly identical operating situations. Only their inventory accounting systems differed. Lastin uses LIFO, and Firstin uses FIFO.

Their beginning inventory was 10,000 tons; it cost $50 per ton. During the year, each company purchased 50,000 tons at the following prices:

- 30,000 @ $60 on March 17
- 20,000 @ $70 on October 5

Each company sold 45,000 tons at average prices of $100 per ton. Other expenses in addition to cost of goods sold, but excluding income taxes, were $600,000. The income tax rate is 35%.

1. Compute net income for the year for both companies. Show your calculations.
2. As a manager, which method would you prefer? Why? Explain fully. Include your estimate of the overall effect of these events on the cash balances of each company, assuming all transactions during 20X1 were direct receipts or disbursements of cash.

7-66 Effects of LIFO and FIFO

The Delhomme Company is starting in business on December 31, 20X0. In each half year, from 20X1 through 20X4, it expects to purchase 1,000 units and sell 500 units for the amounts listed below. In 20X5, it expects to purchase no units and sell 4,000 units for the amount indicated in the following table:

	20X1	20X2	20X3	20X4	20X5
Purchases					
First 6 months	$1,000	$2,000	$3,000	$3,000	0
Second 6 months	2,000	2,500	3,000	4,000	0
Total	$3,000	$4,500	$6,000	$7,000	0
Sales (at selling price)	$5,000	$5,000	$5,000	$5,000	$20,000

Assume that there are no costs or expenses other than those shown above. The tax rate is 40%, and taxes for each year are payable on December 31 of each year. Delhomme Company is trying to decide whether to use periodic FIFO or LIFO throughout the 5-year period.

1. What was net income under FIFO for each of the 5 years? Under LIFO? Show calculations.
2. Explain briefly which method, LIFO or FIFO, seems more advantageous, and why.

7-67 Effects of LIFO on Purchase Decisions

The M. J. Chan Corporation is nearing the end of its first year in business. The following purchases of its single product have been made:

	Units	Unit Price	Total Cost
January	1,000	$ 9	$ 9,000
March	1,000	10	10,000
May	1,000	11	11,000
July	1,000	13	13,000
September	1,000	14	14,000
December	4,000	15	60,000
	9,000		$117,000

Sales for the year will be 5,000 units for $120,000. Expenses other than cost of goods sold will be $31,000.

The president is undecided about whether to adopt FIFO or LIFO for income tax purposes. The company has ample storage space for up to 7,000 units of inventory. Inventory prices are expected to stay at $15 per unit for the next few months.

1. What would be the net income before taxes, the income taxes, and the net income after taxes for the year under (a) FIFO or (b) LIFO? Income tax rates are 40%.
2. If the company sells its year-1 year-end inventory in year 2 @ $24 per unit and goes out of business, what would be the net income before taxes, the income taxes, and the net income after taxes under (a) FIFO and (b) LIFO? Assume that other expenses in year 2 are $30,000.
3. Repeat requirements 1 and 2, assuming that the 4,000 units @ $15 purchased in December were not purchased until January of the second year and were then sold in year 2. Generalize on the effect on net income of the timing of purchases under FIFO and LIFO.

7-68 Changing Quantities and LIFO Reserve
Study Appendix 7A. Consider the following data for the year 20X8:

	Units	Unit Cost
Beginning inventory	2	*
Purchases	3	24
	3	28
Ending inventory	2	†

*FIFO, $20; LIFO, $16.

†To be computed.

1. Prepare a comparative table computing the cost of goods sold using columns for FIFO and LIFO. In a final column, show (a) the difference between FIFO and LIFO inventories (the LIFO reserve) at the beginning of the year and at the end of the year, and (b) how the change in this amount explains the difference in cost of goods sold.
2. Repeat requirement 1, except assume that the ending inventory consisted of zero units.
3. In your own words, explain why, for a given year, the increase in the LIFO reserve measures the amount by which cost of goods sold is higher under LIFO than FIFO.

7-69 Inventory Errors, 3 Years
(Alternate is 7-62.) In early 20X4 at the Collins Company, a team of internal auditors discovered that the ending inventory for 20X1 had been overstated by $10 million. Furthermore, the ending inventory for 20X3 had been understated by $15 million. The ending inventory for December 31, 20X2, was correct. The income tax rate is 40%.

1. Prepare a tabulation covering each of the 3 years that indicates which of the following items in the income statement are incorrect and by how much.
   Beginning inventory
   Cost of goods available
   Ending inventory
   Cost of goods sold
   Gross margin
   Income before income taxes
   Income tax expense
   Net income
2. Is the amount of retained earnings correct at the end of 20X1, 20X2, and 20X3? If it is erroneous, indicate the amount and whether it is overstated (O) or understated (U).

7-70 Comparison of Inventory Methods
(Alternates are 7-59 and 7-72.) **Dell Computer Company** produces computers. The following data and descriptions are from the company's annual report ($ in millions):

	January 30 2009	February 1 2008
Inventories	$867	$1,180

Assume that Dell uses the periodic inventory system. Suppose a division of Dell had the accompanying data concerning the purchase and resale of computers ($ are not in millions):

	Units	Total
Inventory (February 1, 2008)	100	$ 40,000
Purchase (February 20, 2008)	200	100,000
Sales, March 17, 2008 (at $900 per unit)	150	
Purchase (June 25, 2008)	160	96,000
Sales, November 7, 2008 (at $1,000 per unit)	160	

1. For these computers only, prepare a tabulation of the cost of goods sold section of the income statement for the year ended January 30, 2009. Support your computations. Show your tabulation for four different inventory methods: (a) FIFO, (b) LIFO, (c) weighted average, and (d) specific identification. For requirement (d), assume that the purchase of February 20 was identified with the sale of March 17. Also assume that the purchase of June 25 was identified with the sale of November 7.
2. By how much would income taxes differ if Dell used (a) LIFO instead of FIFO for this inventory item and (b) LIFO instead of weighted average? Assume a 35% tax rate.

7-71 Effects of Late Purchases

(Alternates are 7-60 and 7-73.) Refer to the preceding problem. Suppose the **Dell** division acquired 60 extra computers at $700 each on January 30, 2009, a total of $42,000. How would gross profit and income taxes be affected under FIFO (that is, compare FIFO results before and after the purchase of 60 extra computers) and under LIFO (that is, compare LIFO results before and after the purchase of 60 extra computers)? Show computations and explain.

7-72 Comparison of Inventory Methods

(Alternates are 7-59 and 7-70.) **Texas Instruments** is a major producer of semiconductors and other electrical and electronic products. Semiconductors are especially vulnerable to price fluctuations. The following are from the company's annual report ($ in millions):

	December 31	
	2008	**2007**
Inventories	$1,375	$1,418

Texas Instruments uses a variety of inventory methods, but for this problem assume it uses only FIFO.

Net revenues for the fiscal year ended December 31, 2008, were $12,501 million. Cost of revenues was $6,256 million.

Assume Texas Instruments had the accompanying data concerning one of its semiconductors. Assume a periodic inventory system.

	In		Out	Balance
December 31, 2007				80 @ $5 = 400
February 25, 2008	50 @ $6 =	$ 300		
March 29			60[*]	
May 28	80 @ $7 =	$ 560		
June 7			90[*]	
November 20	90 @ $8 =	$ 720		
December 15			50[*]	
Total	220	$1,580	200	
December 31, 2008				100 @ ?

[*]Selling prices were $11, $12, and $13, respectively.

	60	@ $11 =	$ 660
	90	@ 12 =	1,080
	50	@ 13 =	650
Total sales	200		$2,390

Summary of costs to account for is as follows:

Beginning inventory	$ 400
Purchases	1,580
Cost of goods available for sale	$1,980
Other expenses for this product	$ 600
Income tax rate, 40%	

1. Prepare a comparative income statement for the 2008 fiscal year for the product in question. Use the FIFO, LIFO, and weighted-average inventory methods.
2. By how much would income taxes have differed if Texas Instruments had used LIFO instead of FIFO for this product?
3. Suppose Texas Instruments had used the specific identification method. Compute the gross margin (or gross profit) if the ending inventory had consisted of (a) 90 units @ $8 and 10 units @ $7, and (b) 60 units @ $5 and 40 units @ $8.

7-73 Effects of Late Purchases

(Alternates are 7-60 and 7-71.) Refer to the preceding problem. Suppose Texas Instruments had acquired 50 extra units @ $8 each on December 30, 2008, a total of $400. How would income before income taxes have been affected under FIFO? That is, compare FIFO results before and after the purchase of 50 extra units. Under LIFO? That is, compare LIFO results before and after the purchase of 50 extra units. Show computations and explain.

7-74 Classic Switch from LIFO to FIFO

Effective January 1, 1970, **Chrysler Corporation** adopted the FIFO method for inventories previously valued by the LIFO method. The 1970 annual report stated, "This . . . makes the financial statements with respect to inventory valuation comparable with those of the other United States automobile manufacturers."

The *Wall Street Journal* reported the following:

> *The change improved Chrysler's 1970 financial results several ways. Besides narrowing the 1970 loss by $20 million it improved Chrysler's working capital. The change also made the comparison with 1969 earnings look somewhat more favorable because, upon restatement, Chrysler's 1969 profit was raised by only $10.2 million from the original figures.*
>
> *Finally, the change helped Chrysler's balance sheet by boosting inventories, and thus current assets, by $150 million at the end of 1970 over what they would have been under LIFO. As Chrysler's profit has collapsed over the last two years and its financial position tightened, auto analysts have eyed warily Chrysler's shrinking ratio of current assets to current liabilities.*
>
> *To get the improvements in its balance sheet and results, however, Chrysler paid a price. Roger Helder, vice president and comptroller, said Chrysler owed the government $53 million in tax savings it accumulated by using the LIFO method since it switched from FIFO in 1957. The major advantage of LIFO is that it holds down profit and thus tax liabilities. The other three major auto makers stayed on the FIFO method. Mr. Helder said Chrysler now has to pay back that $53 million to the government over 20 years, which will boost Chrysler's tax bills about $3 million a year.*

Given the content of this chapter, do you think the Chrysler decision to switch from LIFO to FIFO was beneficial to its stockholders? Explain, being as specific as you can.

7-75 LIFO, FIFO, Purchase Decisions, and Earnings per Share

Iowa Seed Corn Supplies, a company with 100,000 shares of common stock outstanding, had the following transactions during 20X1, its first year in business:

Sales	1,100,000 pounds @ $5
Purchases	900,000 pounds @ $2
	300,000 pounds @ $3

The current income tax rate is a flat 40%; the rate next year is expected to be 35%.

It is December 20 and Lane Braxton, the president, is trying to decide whether to buy the 400,000 pounds he needs for inventory now or early next year. The current price is $4 per unit. Prices on inventory are expected to remain stable; in any event, no decline in prices is anticipated.

Braxton has not chosen an inventory method as of yet, but will pick either LIFO or FIFO. Other expenses for the year will be $1.4 million.

1. By using LIFO, prepare a comparative income statement assuming the 400,000 pounds (a) are not purchased and (b) are purchased. The statement should end with reported earnings per share.
2. Repeat requirement 1, using FIFO.
3. Comment on the preceding results. Which method should Braxton choose? Why? Be specific.
4. Suppose that in year two the tax rate drops to 35%, prices remain stable, 1.1 million pounds are sold @ $5, enough pounds are purchased at $4 so the ending inventory will be 700,000 pounds, and other expenses are reduced to $800,000.
   a. Prepare a comparative income statement for the second year showing the impact of each of the four alternatives on net income and earnings per share for the second year.
   b. Explain any differences in net income that you encounter among the four alternatives.
   c. Why is there a difference in ending inventory values under LIFO, even though the same amount of physical inventory is in stock?
   d. What is the total cash outflow for income taxes for the 2 years together under the four alternatives?
   e. Would you change your answer in requirement 3 now that you have completed requirement 4? Why?

7-76 Eroding the LIFO Base

Study Appendix 7A. Many companies on LIFO are occasionally faced with strikes or material shortages that necessitate a reduction in their normal inventory levels to satisfy current sales demands. A few years ago, several large steel companies requested special legislative relief from the additional taxes that ensued from such events.

A news story stated the following:

> As steelworkers slowly streamed back to the mills this week, most steel companies began adding up the tremendous losses imposed by the longest strike in history. At a significant number of plants across the country, however, the worry wasn't losses but profits—"windfall" bookkeeping profits that for some companies may mean painful increases in corporate income taxes.
>
> These outfits have been caught in the backfire of a special mechanism for figuring up inventory costs on tax returns. It's known to accountants as LIFO, or last in, first out. Ironically, it's designed to slice the corporate tax bill in a time of rising prices.
>
> Biggest Bite—Most of the big steel companies—16 out of the top 20—as well as 40 percent of all steel warehousers, use LIFO accounting in figuring their taxes. But the tax squeeze from paper LIFO profits won't affect them all equally. It will put the biggest bite on warehousers that kept going during the strike—and as a result, the American Steel Warehouse Assn. may ask Congress for a special tax exemption on these paper profits....
>
> Companies such as Ryerson and Castle have been caught because they have had to strip their shelves bare in order to satisfy customer demands during the strike. And they probably won't be able to rebuild their stocks by the time they close their books for tax purposes.

To see how this situation can happen, consider the following example. Suppose a company adopted LIFO in 1976. At December 31, 2008, its LIFO inventory consisted of three "layers":

From 1976	110,000	units @	$1.00	$110,000
From 1977	50,000	units @	1.10	55,000
From 1978	30,000	units @	1.20	36,000
				$201,000

In 2009, prices rose enormously. Data follow:

Sales	500,000	units @ $3.00 =	$1,500,000
Purchases	340,000	units @ $2.00 =	$ 680,000
Operating expenses			$ 500,000

A prolonged strike near the end of the year resulted in a severe depletion of the normal inventory stock of 190,000 units. The strike was settled on December 28, 2009. The company intended to replenish the inventory as soon as possible. The applicable income tax rate is 60%.

1. Compute the income taxes for 2009.
2. Suppose the company had been able to meet the 500,000-unit demand out of current purchases. Compute the income taxes for 2009 under those circumstances.

7-77 Lower-of-Cost-or-Market

(Alternate is 7-51.) A U.S. camera company's annual report stated, "Inventories are stated at the lower of cost or market. The cost of most inventories in the U.S. is determined by the last-in, first-out (LIFO) method." Assume severe price competition in 20X8 necessitated a write-down on December 31 for a class of camera inventories with a LIFO cost of $13 million. The appropriate valuation at market was deemed to be $8 million.

1. Assume sales of this line of camera for 20X8 were $20 million, and cost of goods sold was $14 million, and that the product line was terminated in early 20X9 and the remaining inventory was sold for $8 million. Prepare a statement of gross margin for 20X8 and 20X9. Show the results under a strict LIFO cost method in the first two columns and under a lower-of-LIFO-cost-or-market method in the next two columns.
2. Assume the company did not discontinue the product line. Instead, a new marketing campaign spurred market demand. Replacement cost of the cameras in the December 31 inventory was $9 million on January 31, 20X9. What inventory valuation would be appropriate on January 31, 20X9, if the company still holds the inventory?

7-78 LIFO Reserve

Study Appendix 7A. Whirlpool Corporation reported 2008 pretax operating income of $549 million. Footnotes to Whirlpool's financial statements read, "Inventories are stated at first-in, first-out ("FIFO") cost, except U.S. production inventories, which are stated at last-in, first-out ("LIFO") cost." The footnote showed that if the FIFO method of inventory accounting had been used for all inventories, they would have been $186 and $144 million higher than reported at December 31, 2008 and 2007, respectively.

1. Calculate the 2008 pretax income that Whirlpool would have reported if the FIFO inventory method had been used for all inventories.
2. Suppose Whirlpool's income tax rate is 34%. What were Whirlpool's income taxes using LIFO? What would they have been if Whirlpool had used FIFO?
3. Was Whirlpool's use of LIFO a good choice from a tax perspective? What is the cumulative financial effect of the choice?

7-79 LIFO Reserve

Study Appendix 7A. Brunswick Corporation reported total inventories of $911.7 million on January 1, 2009. Some inventories were valued using FIFO and some using LIFO. A footnote to the financial statements indicated the following: "Inventories valued at the last-in, first-out method (LIFO) . . . were $121.0 million and $116.2 million lower than the FIFO cost of inventories at December 31, 2008 and 2007, respectively."

1. Has the cost of Brunswick's LIFO inventories generally been increasing or decreasing? Explain.
2. Suppose Brunswick sold its entire inventory for $1,100 million the subsequent year and did not replace it. Compute the gross profit from the sale of this inventory (a) as Brunswick would report it using its current inventory methods and (b) as it would have been reported if Brunswick had always used FIFO instead of LIFO. Which inventory method creates higher gross profit? Explain.

7-80 Inventory Errors

IBM had inventories of $2.6 billion at December 31, 2008, and $2.7 billion a year earlier.

1. Suppose the beginning inventory for fiscal 2008 had been overstated by $10 million because of errors in physical counts. There were no other inventory errors. Which items in the financial statements would be incorrect and by how much? Use O for overstated, U for understated, and N for not affected. Assume a 40% tax rate and state dollar amounts in millions.

	Effect on Fiscal Year	
	2008	**2007**
Beginning inventory	O by $10	N
Ending inventory	?	?
Cost of sales	?	?
Gross profit	?	?
Income before taxes on income	?	?
Taxes on income	?	?
Net income	?	?

2. What is the dollar effect of the inventory error on retained earnings at the end of fiscal 2008 and 2007?

7-81 LIFO Liquidation

Study Appendix 7A. Lancaster Colony Corporation produces specialty foods under the Marzetti label, candles labeled Candle-lite, and glass called Indiana Glass, as well as other products. In a recent year the company's pretax income was $180.8 million. It reported the following inventories:

	Inventories	
(in millions)	**Current Year**	**Previous Year**
Finished goods and work in process	$116.4	$104.6
Raw materials and supplies	43.0	43.7
Inventories, at LIFO cost	159.4	148.3
Excess of FIFO over LIFO cost	7.4	14.5
Total inventories at FIFO	$166.8	$162.8

During the current year LIFO inventory quantities were reduced, resulting in liquidations of LIFO inventory carried at the lower costs prevailing in prior years. The effects of these liquidations increased pretax income by $7.1 million.

1. What would Lancaster Colony's pretax income have been in the current year if it had purchased enough inventory to avoid liquidating any LIFO inventory layers?
2. What would Lancaster Colony have reported as pretax income in the current year had it used FIFO to account for all its inventories?
3. How does the change in the LIFO reserve relate to the effect of the LIFO liquidation?

7-82 Year-End Purchases and LIFO

A company engaged in the manufacture and sale of dental supplies maintained an inventory of gold for use in its business. The company used LIFO for the gold content of its products.

On the final day of its fiscal year, the company bought 10,000 ounces of gold at $980 per ounce. Had the purchase not been made, the company would have penetrated its LIFO layers for 8,000 ounces of gold acquired at $750 per ounce.

The applicable income tax rate is 40%.

1. Compute the effect of the year-end purchase on the income taxes of the fiscal year.
2. On the second day of the next fiscal year, the company resold the 10,000 ounces of gold to its suppliers. What do you think the IRS should do if it discovers this resale? Explain.

7-83 Comparison of Gross Profit Percentages and Inventory Turnover

JCPenney and **Kmart** (since a 2005 merger it is **Sears/Kmart**) are long-time competitors in the retail business, although they target slightly different markets. The gross margin for each company and average inventory follow for the indicated years (both have January year-ends; 2009 refers to the year ending in January of 2009):

JCPenney

	2009	2003	2000	1995
	(in millions)			
Retail sales	$18,486	$32,347	$32,510	$20,380
Cost of goods sold*	11,571	22,573	23,374	13,970
Gross profit	6,915	9,774	9,136	6,410
Average inventory	3,450	4,938	6,004	3,711

Sears/Kmart

	2009	2003	2000	1995
	(in millions)			
Retail sales	$46,770	$30,762	$35,925	$34,025
Cost of goods sold*	34,118	26,258	28,102	25,992
Gross profit	12,652	4,504	7,823	8,033
Average inventory	9,379	5,311	6,819	7,317

*Both companies classify costs of occupancy, buying, and warehousing with cost of goods sold.

Calculate gross profit percentages and inventory turnovers for 2009, 2003, 2000, and 1995 for each company and compare them. What trends do you observe? Which company appears to perform better? To what extent do their different performances seem to relate to their relative positions in the retail market?

7-84 LIFO and Ethical Issues

Yokohama Company is a wholesaler of musical instruments in San Francisco. Yokohama has used the LIFO inventory method since 1971. Near the end of 2009, before computing cost of goods sold, the company's inventory of a particular instrument listed three LIFO layers, two of which were from earlier years and one from 2009 purchases:

	No. of Units	Unit Cost
Layer one	4,000	$40
Layer two	2,500	50
2009 Purchases	30,000	60
Total available	36,500	

In 2009, Yokohama sold 32,500 units, leaving 4,000 units in inventory.

On December 27, 2009, Yokohama had a chance to buy a minimum of 15,000 units of the instrument at a unit cost of $70. The offer was good for 10 days, and delivery would be immediate on placing the order.

Helen Yamaguchi, chief purchasing manager of Yokohama, was trying to decide whether to make the purchase and, if it is made, whether to make it in 2009 or 2010. The controller had told her that she should buy immediately because the company would save almost $80,000 in taxes. The combined federal and state income tax rate is 45%.

1. Explain why nearly $80,000 of taxes would be saved.
2. Are there any ethical considerations that would influence this decision? Explain.

7-85 Inventory Shrinkage

Lola, owner of Park Hardware Company, was concerned about her control of inventory. In December 20X7, she installed a computerized perpetual inventory system. In April, her accountant brought her the following information for the first 3 months of 20X8:

Sales	$700,000
Cost of goods sold	590,000
Beginning inventory (per physical count)	135,000
Merchandise purchases	630,000

Lola had asked her public accounting firm to conduct a physical count of inventory on April 1. The CPAs reported inventory of $150,000.

1. Compute the ending inventory shown in the books by the new perpetual inventory system.
2. Provide the journal entry to reconcile the book inventory with the physical count. What is the corrected cost of goods sold for the first 3 months of 20X8?
3. Do your calculations point out areas about which Lola should be concerned? Why?

7-86 Cheating on Inventories

The *Wall Street Journal* reported, "Cheating on inventories is a common way for small businesses to chisel on their income taxes....A New York garment maker, for example, evades a sizable amount of income tax by undervaluing his firm's inventory by 20% on his tax return. He hides about $500,000 out of a $2.5 million inventory."

The news story concluded, "When it's time to borrow, business owners generally want profits and assets to look fat." The garment maker uses a different fiscal period for financial statements to his bank: "After writing down the inventory as of Dec. 31, he writes it up six months later when the fiscal year ends. In this way, he underpays the IRS and impresses his banker. Some describe that kind of inventory accounting as WIFL—Whatever I Feel Like."

1. At a 40% income tax rate, what amount of federal income taxes would the owner evade according to the news story?
2. Consider the next year. By how much would the ending inventory have to be understated to evade the same amount of income taxes?

Use the following table and fill in the blanks:

	Honest Reporting		Dishonest Reporting	
	First Year	**Second Year**	**First Year**	**Second Year**
Beginning inventory	$ 3,000,000	$?	$ 3,000,000	$?
Purchases	10,000,000	$10,000,000	10,000,000	10,000,000
Available for sale	13,000,000	?	13,000,000	?
Ending inventory	2,500,000	2,500,000	2,000,000	?
Cost of goods sold	$10,500,000	$?	$11,000,000	$?
Income tax savings @ 40%*	$ 4,200,000	$?	$?	$?
Income tax savings for 2 years together	$?		$?	

*This is the income tax effect of only the cost of goods sold. To shorten and simplify the analysis, sales and operating expenses are assumed to be the same each year.

7-87 Manufacturing Costs

Study Appendix 7B. Sam Teasdale made custom T-shirts for himself and his friends for years before trying to treat it seriously as a business. On January 1, 20X1, he decided to become more serious. He bought some screening equipment for $5,000 that he figured was good for 10,000 screenings. He decided to use units of production depreciation. He acquired 2,000 shirts for $6,000 and rented a studio for $500 per month. During the month, he paid an assistant $1,600 and together they created three designs, screened 1,500 shirts, and sold 1,200 at $9 each. At month-end, there were 500 shirts unused, 300 finished shirts ready for sale, and Sam was trying to figure out how he was doing.

1. Calculate the cost of goods sold and the value of ending inventory (including raw material and finished goods).
2. Prepare an income statement for Sam's first month of operations. Assume a 35% tax rate.

Collaborative Learning Exercise

7-88 Understanding Inventory Errors

Form groups of three students each. (If there are more than three students in a group, extras can be paired up.) Each student should select or be assigned one of these three inventory methods:

1. Specific identification
2. FIFO
3. LIFO

Consider the following information from the annual report of Simpson Corporation. Simpson uses the LIFO method to account for its inventories ($ amounts are in millions).

For the year ended March 31, 2009 (fiscal year 2009)	
Sales	$967
Cost of goods sold (using LIFO)	534
Other operating expenses	417
Operating income	$ 16
Purchases of inventory in fiscal 2009	$562
At March 31, 2009	
Inventories @ LIFO	$169
Inventories @ FIFO	181
At March 31, 2008	
Inventories @ LIFO	$141
Inventories @ FIFO	152

Assume that Simpson had exactly the same physical sales in fiscal 2010 as in fiscal 2009, but prices were 5% higher. Thus, fiscal 2010 sales were 1.05 × $967 = $1,015. Assume that other operating expenses in fiscal 2010 were exactly the same as in fiscal 2009. Further assume Simpson bought just enough inventory in fiscal 2010 to replace what the company sold, but because of a 5% price increase on April 1, purchases of inventories in fiscal 2010 were $561. (Note that if there had been no price increase, the purchases of inventories would have equaled last year's cost of goods sold, $534.) FIFO inventory on March 31, 2010, was $190.

1. Compute operating income for Simpson for the year ended March 31, 2010, using the inventory method to which you were assigned. Those using the LIFO and FIFO methods have all the information needed for the calculations. Those using specific identification must make some assumptions, and their operating income numbers will depend on the assumptions made.
2. Explain to the other members of the group how you computed the operating income, including an explanation of how you chose the assumptions you made.

Analyzing and Interpreting Financial Statement

7-89 Financial Reporting Research

Select an industry and identify two firms within that industry.

1. Identify the inventory accounting method used by each.
2. Calculate gross profit percentages and inventory turnovers for 2 years for each firm. Comment on the comparison and any trends.

7-90 Analyzing Starbucks' Financial Statements
Refer to the fiscal 2009 financial statements for Starbucks either at http://investor.starbucks.com or on the SEC's Edgar Web site. Assume that Starbucks uses the periodic inventory method.

1. Compute the amount of merchandise inventory purchased during the year ended September 27, 2009. (Hint: Use the inventory T-account.) Assume that 80% of the costs listed under "Cost of sales including occupancy costs" are cost of sales. The other 20% are occupancy costs.
2. Compute the inventory turnover for Starbucks for the year ended September 27, 2009.
3. Calculate the gross margin percentage for each of the last 3 years. Use total net revenues and cost of sales including occupancy costs to compute the gross margin. Comment on any changes.

7-91 Analyzing Financial Statements Using the Internet: Deckers Outdoor Corporation
Go to Deckers Outdoor Corporation's latest annual report information on its Web site. Deckers Outdoor Corporation is the exclusive licensee for the manufacture of Teva footwear. Use the latest 10K filing to find financial report data.
    Answer the following questions about Deckers:

1. What percentage of revenues does Teva represent? Have revenues related to Teva products increased or decreased over the past few years?
2. Read the Summary of Significant Accounting Policies section of the Notes to Consolidated Financial Statements. How are inventories valued and accounted for? Why do you think the company uses this particular costing method?
3. Locate the income statement. How much gross profit is reported for the most recent year? Has this amount increased or decreased compared with the previous year? What explanation does management give for the changes? (Hint: Look in the Management's Discussion and Analysis section.)

8

Long-Lived Assets

LEARNING OBJECTIVES

After studying this chapter, you should be able to:

1 Distinguish a company's expenses from expenditures that it should capitalize.

2 Measure the acquisition cost of tangible assets such as land, buildings, and equipment.

3 Compute depreciation for buildings and equipment using various depreciation methods.

4 Recalculate depreciation in response to a change in estimated useful life or residual value.

5 Differentiate financial statement depreciation from income tax depreciation.

6 Explain the effect of depreciation on cash flow.

7 Account for expenditures after acquisition.

8 Compute gains and losses on the disposal of fixed assets and consider the impact of these gains and losses on the statement of cash flows.

9 Determine the balance sheet valuation of tangible assets for companies who use the revaluation method allowed under IFRS.

10 Account for the impairment of tangible assets.

11 Account for intangible assets, including impairment.

12 Explain the reporting for goodwill.

13 Interpret the depletion of natural resources.

The name NM Electronics is probably not familiar to you. NM Electronics is the name that Gordon E. Moore and Robert Noyce gave their fledging company at the time of its founding in 1968. In 1969, Moore and Noyce changed the name of their company to Integrated Electronics or Intel for short. Intel Corporation pioneered the microprocessor and is now the largest semiconductor manufacturer in the world, operating plants 24/7 in many countries around the globe.

In the early years, Intel's manufacturing processes were relatively primitive. Former Intel Chairman Andy Grove, quoted on Intel's Web site, said, "The fab area looked like Willy Wonka's factory, with hoses and wires and contraptions chugging along – the semiconductor equivalent of the Wright Brothers' jury-rigged airplane. It was state-of-the-art manufacturing at the time, but by today's standards, it was unbelievably crude." Most of the assembly work was done by hand in non-sterile

Intel is the world's largest semiconductor chip maker, based on revenue. With greater than 80% market share in the global microprocessor market, the Intel logo is familiar to consumers worldwide. Semiconductor manufacturing requires huge investments in facilities and equipment. We learn about the accounting for physical assets used in manufacturing and intangible assets, such as the Intel logo, in this chapter.

manufacturing facilities. Today, Intel has a huge investment in its manufacturing facilities. As noted on the Intel Web site, microprocessor-controlled robots transport the silicon wafers through the manufacturing process, and work is performed in cleanrooms that are atmospherically isolated from the external environment and 10,000 times cleaner than a hospital operating room. It requires an incredible investment in appropriate ventilation and air filter equipment to maintain the required temperature, humidity, pressurization, and cleanliness. Huge air filtration systems completely change the air in cleanrooms about 10 times per minute. Intel's 2008 financial statements show gross investment in Machinery and Equipment in excess of $28.8 billion and in Land and Buildings of over $16.5 billion. In 2008 alone, Intel spent almost $5.2 billion to purchase new property, plant, and equipment. ●

By now, you should understand how to account for short-lived assets, such as inventory. We match their costs to the single period in which we recognize the associated revenues. What about assets that a company does not use quickly? Many long-lived assets, such as buildings and heavy machinery, help generate revenues in multiple periods, and companies must spread the costs of such assets across those periods. To qualify for the treatment discussed in this chapter, companies must actually use the assets in their day-to-day operations and not hold them for purposes of resale or investment. For example, a company should classify an unused building or land that it holds for speculative purposes as an investment rather than as property, plant, and equipment.

How important are long-lived assets? Depending on the industry, they can be the most important assets a company owns. For example, consider the net plant and equipment accounts as presented on the balance sheets of the following companies ($ in millions) for fiscal year 2008:

Company	Total Assets	Plant and Equipment	
		Plant and Equipment, net	Percentage of Total Assets
Bank of America	$1,817,943	$13,161	0.7
Deckers	370	11	3.0
Microsoft	72,793	6,242	8.6
Time Warner	113,896	18,433	16.2
Intel	50,715	17,544	34.6
Starbucks	5,673	2,956	52.1
Chevron	161,165	91,780	56.9
Duke Energy	53,077	34,036	64.1

Why do these numbers vary so greatly? Because different types of businesses require different types of assets. **Bank of America** (B of A) is one of the largest banks in the world, providing a range of banking and nonbanking financial services. At the end of 2008, it had $1.8 trillion in assets, less than 1% in the form of property and equipment. Almost 50% of B of A's assets were in the form of loans. **Deckers** "designs, manufactures, and markets innovative function-oriented footwear and apparel" under such brand names as Teva, Simple, Ugg, and Tsubo. The company outsources most of the manufacturing to Asian and Costa Rican subcontractors and has little need for fixed assets. **Time Warner** and **Microsoft** are high-tech companies that rely heavily on intellectual property. Microsoft's balance sheet shows significant current and long-term investments, but little property, plant, and equipment (frequently referred to as PP&E). Almost 62% of Time Warner's assets are in the form of intangible noncurrent assets, whereas only 16.2% is in the form of property, plant, and equipment. As noted previously, Intel's manufacturing process requires a significant investment in buildings and equipment, which comprise 34.6% of its assets. **Starbucks** leases most of its locations, but it has made substantial investments in leasehold improvements, which are long-term investments to improve leased facilities. **Chevron** has extensive property, plant, and equipment, including oil wells, drilling rigs, buildings, and gas pumps. **Duke Energy** is a utility company with a significant percentage of its assets in the form of electric generation plants, electric and natural gas distribution and transmission facilities, and equipment.

Accounting for long-lived assets presents some interesting and unique concerns. One important consideration is when to charge the cost of a long-lived asset as an expense on the income statement. For example, if an asset helps generate revenue for 10 years, how much of its cost should we assign to each of the 10 years the company uses the asset? The answer to this question depends on the method chosen for recording depreciation. This chapter explores depreciation—both understanding the nature of depreciation and learning about various depreciation methods, each of which is a systematic and rational system for allocating the cost of the asset over its useful life. We start off, though, with a look at long-lived assets in general.

Overview of Long-Lived Assets

Most business entities hold major assets such as land, buildings, equipment, and patents. These long-lived assets help produce revenues over multiple periods by facilitating the production of goods or services and their sale to customers. Because these assets are necessary in day-to-day operations, companies do not sell them in the ordinary course of business. However, replacement of these assets is an essential part of the successful operation of a business. Keep in mind that one company's long-lived asset might be another company's short-lived asset. For example, a delivery truck is a long-lived asset for most companies, but a truck dealer would regard a delivery truck as short-lived merchandise inventory.

Long-lived assets can be either tangible or intangible. **Tangible assets** (also called **fixed assets** or **plant assets**) are physical items that you can see and touch. Examples are land, buildings, and equipment. In contrast, **intangible assets** lack physical substance. They generally consist of contractual rights, legal rights, or economic benefits. Examples are patents, trademarks, and copyrights. Intangible assets are becoming increasingly important in today's economy and they are important when companies are being valued. To find out more about the valuation of companies see the Business First box on p. 346.

There are differences in the way we account for different types of long-lived assets. Land is unique—it does not wear out or become obsolete. Therefore, we report land in the financial records at historical cost and do not depreciate it. Most other long-lived assets wear out, become inadequate for a given company's use, or become obsolete. As a company uses these assets over time, accountants convert their historical cost to expense.

In practice, accountants use various words to describe the allocation of costs over time. For tangible assets such as buildings, machinery, and equipment, they call it depreciation. They use **amortization** to refer to the allocation of the costs of intangible assets to the periods that benefit from these assets. Finally, for natural resources, they call it **depletion**.

Contrasting Long-Lived Asset Expenditures with Expenses

When a company purchases an asset, management must decide whether the asset will be used only within the current accounting year or whether it will be used over a number of years. We call all purchases of goods or services, whether for cash or on credit, **expenditures**. As explained in Chapter 2, companies make expenditures to purchase assets. For those assets to remain on the balance sheet they must continue to provide future economic benefits to the company and be reliably measured. Companies use the benefits of some assets, such as advertising services, almost immediately, so they record such expenditures directly as expenses. Companies use the benefits of other assets, such as prepaid rent, within a year, so the expenditures are classified as current assets for a short period before companies recognize them as expenses. Finally, companies **capitalize** assets that benefit more than the current accounting year; that is, they add the purchase price to a long-term asset account and recognize part of the purchase price as an expense each period as they use the asset. Capital expenditures result in new long-lived assets, or they increase the capacity, efficiency, or useful life of existing long-lived assets.

The Decision to Capitalize

Sometimes it is difficult to decide whether to capitalize or expense a particular expenditure. Consider the expenditure for work done on an engine. The company should capitalize this expenditure only if it increases the capacity, efficiency, or useful life of the engine. If it merely keeps the engine running as expected, it is an expense. In the absence of contradictory evidence, most accountants would call it an expense. Why? Because accountants and auditors watch for tendencies to understate current expenses, thereby overstating income, through the unjustified capitalization of what should be expensed.

Wherever doubt exists, accountants tend to charge an expense instead of an asset account for repairs, parts, and similar items. Conservatism leads us to guard against earnings patterns that are unusually high and increasing, which can mislead investors. Furthermore, many such expenditures are minor in magnitude, so the cost-benefit test of record keeping and the concept of materiality justify this choice. For instance, many companies charge to expense all expenditures that are less than a specified minimum such as $100, $1,000, or $5,000.

Ethics: Capitalization Versus Expense

Because decisions about whether to expense or capitalize expenditures require judgment, this is an area that management may inappropriately try to influence in order to increase reported net income. Suppose that you run the internal audit department of a large U.S. corporation. As part

---

tangible assets (fixed assets, plant assets)
Physical items that can be seen and touched, such as land, buildings, and equipment.

intangible assets
Assets that lack physical substance. They consist of contractual rights, legal rights, or economic benefits. Examples are patents, trademarks, and copyrights.

amortization
When referring to long-lived assets, it usually means the allocation of the costs of intangible assets to the periods that benefit from these assets.

depletion
The process of allocating the cost of natural resources to the periods that benefit from their use.

OBJECTIVE 1
Distinguish a company's expenses from expenditures that it should capitalize.

expenditures
Purchases of goods or services, whether for cash or credit.

capitalize
To add the purchase price of an asset to a long-term asset account, recognizing that it will benefit more than the current accounting year.

BUSINESS FIRST

VALUING COMPANIES AND THEIR ASSETS IN EMERGING MARKETS

Over the past couple of decades, the financial markets in Asia have grown at unprecedented rates. This has resulted in opportunities for both domestic and foreign companies in countries such as China, India, and Vietnam to invest and grow their businesses. Significant risks and challenges also exist, however. One of the biggest challenges, especially from an accounting perspective, is the valuation of companies and their assets.

Companies must decide whether to value assets at their historical cost or at their fair market value. Historical cost is the price that companies paid to acquire their assets. Historical cost is often desirable because it is easy to verify and the value does not change over time. Fair market value, also known as "replacement cost" or "market cost", is the amount that the assets are worth today. There is debate over the reliability of historical cost versus the relevance of market value. Beyond the two models of accounting, however, is the fundamental uncertainty of what assets are worth and how they should be valued.

A recent report by the Economist Intelligence Unit and Ernst & Young highlights some of the difficulties in valuing assets. They found, for instance, that 90% of executives surveyed considered it harder to make valuations in China than in developed economies.

Why this difficulty? Firstly, firms in emerging markets often disclose significantly less information than is required by stock exchanges and government agencies in more developed markets. In developed markets, investors are able to examine the wealth of information and as a result can make a reasonable estimate of the value of a firm and its assets. In emerging markets, much of this information is not available. Secondly, in emerging economies values are often tied to unknown growth rates. Consider a business that generates $1 million this year. Projecting future sales to grow by 5% will yield a significantly different value for the business than projecting future sales to grow by 20%. A third reason why businesses in emerging markets are extremely difficult to value is because there are many differences between these businesses and similar companies in developed countries. For example, customer preferences, level of infrastructure, and managerial skills often differ between emerging and developed economies. Another factor that makes valuing businesses difficult is the presence of intangible assets. Intangible assets are assets that are not physical in nature. They are difficult to value because they are often not included on a companies' balance sheet and because the future benefit that intangible assets bring to firms is usually immeasurable.

So, what can companies do to overcome these difficulties? Companies must perform due diligence and gather necessary information themselves if it is not provided by other firms. Firms must engage the services of auditors and other experts to evaluate the financial performance of businesses. Companies should also develop reasonable estimates of growth rates. When sufficient uncertainty exists which makes estimating risk difficult, companies can estimate over a range. Finally, companies must study the local economy to develop a better sense of the variables necessary to accurately value assets and businesses. In situations where the necessary knowledge of local market characteristics is not attainable by foreign businesses, companies can form a joint venture with a local partner or perhaps acquire a local subsidiary.

The world is becoming more global and many firms are expanding into emerging markets. While emerging markets offer exciting opportunities, businesses must also be aware of the risks.

Sources: "Guessing Game? Valuation Challenges in Asia", http://www.eiu.com/report_dl.asp?mode=fi&fi=1382768323.PDF&rf=0.

of the routine internal audit work, one of your staff members uncovers $2 billion in expenditures that the company has capitalized, although no one in the department is able to find authorization for capital spending in that amount. You begin to suspect that the $2 billion really represents operating costs that accountants have shifted to capital expenditure accounts, making the company appear more profitable. The choice of whether to capitalize or expense the $2 billion has a material effect on the company's financial performance. When you question the person in charge of capital spending about the transaction, he states that the expenditure represents "prepaid capacity," a term that is not familiar to you in spite of your extensive background in accounting. Accountants at various levels within the organization repeatedly stonewall your efforts to obtain clarification of these expenditures. Ultimately, you decide to undertake a detailed investigation. When you reveal your intentions to your company's CFO, he asks you to delay the investigation until after the current quarter, indicating that he intends to take care of the problem in the subsequent quarter.

Now you are faced with a difficult decision. Should you pursue the investigation despite the CFO's request to delay? After all, the CFO is your boss, and he and others higher up in the organization have suggested that you postpone or abandon your investigation. You have no hard evidence of wrongdoing, and if the CFO does in fact correct the problem prior to year-end, the annual financial results will be correctly stated. However, the evasiveness of company executives when questioned about these capital expenditures and the lack of documentation for them suggests that the $2 billion disbursement is just the tip of the iceberg. If you and your staff pursue this investigation and find inappropriate accounting for capital expenditures, the findings could be very detrimental to the company and your fellow employees.

This is a situation similar to the one that confronted Cynthia Cooper and her audit staff at WorldCom. We know what decision Ms. Cooper made. She and her audit team contacted the head of WorldCom's audit committee and KPMG, WorldCom's new outside auditor. Further investigation revealed one of the biggest accounting scandals in U.S. history. On June 25, 2002, WorldCom disclosed that it had wrongly treated $3.8 billion in operating costs, primarily access fees that WorldCom paid to other phone companies for the use of their lines, as capital expenditures. Rather than immediately expensing these costs, WorldCom capitalized the $3.8 billion as an asset. This allowed WorldCom to expense the $3.8 billion as depreciation on the income statement over time rather than expensing it immediately. The decision to capitalize rather than expense these costs enhanced the company's net income in the period in which it capitalized the costs, but it would decrease future periods' income as WorldCom depreciated the capitalized costs. As a result of this and other accounting manipulations, several WorldCom executives, including the CEO and CFO, were convicted of conspiracy, securities fraud, and making false financial filings and were sentenced to time in prison.

Acquisition Cost of Tangible Assets

Accounting for a long-lived asset begins with its purchase. The acquisition cost of a long-lived asset is the cash-equivalent purchase price, including incidental costs to complete the purchase, to transport the asset, and to prepare it for its intended use. Consider the following categories of tangible assets.

OBJECTIVE 2

Measure the acquisition cost of tangible assets such as land, buildings, and equipment.

Land

The acquisition cost of land includes charges to the purchaser for the cost of land surveys, legal fees, title fees, transfer taxes, and even the demolition costs of old structures that must be torn down to get the land ready for its intended use. Consider the following example for the acquisition of a piece of land to be used as the site of a new building to house company headquarters. There is an existing building on the land that must be torn down. All of the following items become part of the capitalized value of the land:

Purchase price	$500,000
Closing costs, including attorney's fees	9,500
Title search and transfer taxes	1,000
Costs of demolition of old building	6,000
Costs of clearing, grading, and filling in preparation for new building	19,000
Assumption of unpaid property taxes	10,000
Proceeds from the sale of materials salvaged from the old building	(2,500)
Total acquisition cost	$543,000

Under historical-cost accounting, companies report land in the balance sheet at its original cost. After years of rising real estate values and inflation, the carrying amount of land is often far below its current market value. Should land acquired and held since 1940 still appear at its 1940 cost on balance sheets prepared nearly 70 years later? Yes. U.S. GAAP requires companies to be conservative and carry land at its original historical cost, unless the fair value of the land has fallen below that original cost.

Buildings and Equipment

The cost of buildings, plant, and equipment should include all costs of acquisition and preparation for use. Consider the following example for used packaging equipment:

Invoice price, gross	$100,000
Deduct 2% cash discount for payment within 30 days	(2,000)
Invoice price, net	$ 98,000
State sales tax at 8% of $98,000	7,840
Transportation costs	3,000
Installation costs	8,000
Repair costs prior to use	7,000
Total acquisition cost	$123,840

As you can see, several individual costs make up the total acquisition cost. We capitalize the total of $123,840 and add it to the Equipment account. Why do we include repair costs in the amount that we capitalize as the acquisition cost of the asset? Normally, we would expense repair costs in the income statement as the costs are incurred. The difference is that repair costs incurred prior to the first use of an asset are part of getting the asset ready to use and, therefore, we include them in the acquisition cost on the balance sheet. In contrast, after the equipment is in use, we should charge ordinary repair costs as expenses on the income statement.

monetary assets

Assets such as cash or receivables that are fixed in terms of units of currency.

nonmonetary assets

Assets whose price in terms of units of currency could change over time.

Companies usually pay for capital expenditures with cash or other **monetary assets**—assets that are fixed in terms of the units of currency. However, a company may elect to pay for fixed assets with **nonmonetary assets**—items whose price in terms of units of currency could change over time. The practice of exchanging nonmonetary assets is particularly common for start-up companies. If they do not have sufficient cash but have stock that is highly valued, frequently they will pay for assets using their own stock. For example, the owner of a piece of land might sell it to a company in exchange for stock because the owner could either sell the stock immediately or hold the stock in hopes that it would increase in value. We generally record a nonmonetary exchange at the fair value of the asset surrendered, land in this example, or the fair value of the consideration received, stock in this example, whichever is the more determinable.

fair value

The value of an asset based on the price for which a company could sell the asset to an independent third party.

The **fair value** of an asset is the price for which a company could sell the asset to an independent third party. When a stock trades actively, we typically assume that the fair value of the stock is the best indicator of the value of the transaction. After all, if we asked four different appraisers to appraise the land, they would probably arrive at four different values, while the stock exchange determines a value for shares of stock at any given point in time. Suppose that Woodside Corporation sold land to Tryon Company in exchange for shares of Tryon stock. Tryon is a publicly traded stock whose share price is observable each day. An appraiser valued the land at $100,000, whereas the stock had a market value at the time of the sale of $108,000. Tryon would record the following entry, ignoring the $100,000 appraised value in favor of the market value of the stock:

Land	$108,000	
Paid-in capital		$108,000
Purchase of land in exchange for $108,000 of common stock		

Basket Purchases

basket purchase (lump-sum purchase)

The acquisition of two or more assets for a lump-sum cost.

Frequently, companies acquire more than one long-lived asset for a single overall purchase price. The acquisition of two or more assets for a lump-sum cost is sometimes called a **basket purchase** or **lump-sum purchase**. The acquisition cost of a basket purchase is split among the assets purchased according to some estimate of the relative fair values of the assets. For instance, suppose Intel acquires land and a building for $1 million. How much of the $1 million should Intel allocate to land and how much to the building? If an independent appraiser indicates that the fair values of the land and the building are $480,000 and $720,000, respectively, the $1 million cost would be allocated as follows:

	(1)	(2)	(3)	(2) × (3)
	Appraised Value	**Weighting**	**Total Cost to Allocate**	**Allocated costs**
Land	$ 480,000	480 ÷ 1,200 (or 40%)	$1,000,000	$ 400,000
Building	720,000	720 ÷ 1,200 (or 60%)	1,000,000	600,000
Total	$1,200,000			$1,000,000

Allocating a basket purchase cost to the individual assets can significantly affect future reported income if the useful lives of the various assets differ. In our example, if Intel allocates less cost to the land, it allocates more cost to the building, which is depreciable. In turn, depreciation expenses are higher, and operating income is lower.

Accounting Alternatives Subsequent to Acquisition

All companies throughout the world initially record long-lived assets at their cost. However, subsequent to acquisition there are two possible accounting methods. The most popular is the cost method. U.S. GAAP requires the cost method, IFRS allows it, and most companies worldwide use it. Under the cost method, companies carry assets at their cost less depreciation. Under certain circumstances they may write down the asset value, but they can never increase it. Most of this chapter focuses on the cost method. The alternative method, allowed only by IFRS, is the revaluation method. It is used mostly in Europe, especially in the Netherlands, Denmark, and the United Kingdom. Under this method, companies carry long-lived assets at their fair value. We discuss the revaluation method on page 362. Here we discuss depreciation as employed in the cost method and demonstrate several depreciation methods.

Depreciation of Buildings and Equipment

After purchasing tangible long-lived assets other than land, a company must depreciate the assets. Those new to accounting frequently misunderstand depreciation. It is not a process of valuation. In everyday use, we might say that an auto depreciates in value, meaning that its current market value declines. However, to an accountant, depreciation is not a technique for approximating current values such as replacement costs or resale values. It is simply a system for cost allocation. For purposes of financial reporting, both U.S. GAAP and IFRS allow companies to freely select the depreciation method they believe best portrays their economic circumstance as long as it is systematic and rational.

Depreciation is one of the key factors distinguishing accrual accounting from cash-basis accounting. If a company purchases a long-lived asset for cash, strict cash-basis accounting would treat the entire cost of the asset as an expense in the period of acquisition. In contrast, accrual accounting initially capitalizes the cost and then allocates it in the form of depreciation over the periods the company uses the asset. This more effectively matches expenses with the revenues produced.

The cost a company allocates as depreciation over the total useful life of the asset is the **depreciable value**. It is the difference between the total acquisition cost and the estimated residual value. The **residual value**, also known as **terminal value**, **disposal value**, **salvage value**, and **scrap value**, is the amount a company expects to receive from sale or disposal of a long-lived asset at the end of its useful life. The **useful life** of an asset is the shorter of the physical life of the asset (before it wears out) or the economic life of the asset. The economic life of an asset and its physical life need not be the same. The physical life of an asset depends on the wear and tear it takes while in use. At some point, a company can no longer use a piece of equipment in the production process due to deterioration. However, a company may decide to replace equipment prior to the end of its physical life. Such replacement depends on economic factors rather than physical ones. For example, given the rapidly increasing speed and decreasing cost of computers, most companies replace them long before they physically wear out. That is, their economic life is shorter than their physical life. Both the residual value and useful life are estimates a company

OBJECTIVE 3

Compute depreciation for buildings and equipment using various depreciation methods.

depreciable value
The cost a company allocates as depreciation over the total useful life of an asset. It is the difference between the total acquisition cost and the estimated residual value.

residual value (terminal value, disposal value, salvage value, scrap value)
The amount a company expects to receive from sale or disposal of a long-lived asset at the end of its useful life.

useful life
The shorter of the physical life or the economic life of an asset.

must make at the time it acquires the asset, and the estimates management makes can greatly effect a company's net income.

Depreciation methods differ primarily in the amount of cost allocated to each accounting period. A list of depreciation amounts for each period of an asset's useful life is a **depreciation schedule**. We use the following symbols and amounts to compare various annual depreciation schedules for a $41,000 delivery truck purchased by Chang Company on January 1, 20X9:

Symbols	Amounts for Illustration
Let	
C = total acquisition cost on January 1, 20X9	$41,000
R = estimated residual value	$ 1,000
n = estimated useful life (in years or miles)	4 years
	200,000 miles
D = amount of annual depreciation expense	Various

Straight-Line Depreciation

Straight-line depreciation spreads the depreciable value evenly over the useful life of an asset. It is by far the most popular method for financial reporting purposes. In fact, a recent survey showed that more than 98% of major companies use straight-line depreciation for at least some of their fixed assets. While straight-line depreciation may not be the best representation of the actual use rate of an asset, its popularity stems from its simplicity in both theory and application.

Exhibit 8-1 shows the balance sheet values for Chang Company's truck using straight-line depreciation. At the end of the fourth year, the truck has a remaining net book value of $1,000, which is the estimated residual value. The annual depreciation expense charged to Chang's income statement is as follows:

$$\text{Depreciation expense} = \frac{(\text{Acquisition cost} - \text{Estimated residual value})}{\text{Years of estimated useful life}}$$

$$D = \frac{(C - R)}{n}$$

$$D = \frac{(\$41,000 - \$1,000)}{4}$$

$$D = \$10,000 \text{ per year}$$

Depreciation Based on Units

In some cases, time is not the determining factor of the useful life of an asset. When physical wear and tear determines the useful life of the asset, accountants may base depreciation on units of service or units of production instead of units of time (years). Depreciation based on

EXHIBIT 8-1

Straight-Line Depreciation Schedule

	Balances at End of Year			
	1	**2**	**3**	**4**
Equipment (at original acquisition cost)	$41,000	$41,000	$41,000	$41,000
Less: Accumulated depreciation (the portion of original cost that has already been charged to operations as an expense)	10,000	20,000	30,000	40,000
Net book value (the portion of original cost that has not yet been charged to operations)	$31,000	$21,000	$11,000	$ 1,000

units of service is known as **units-of-production depreciation** or the **activity method** and, in some circumstances, results in a better matching of costs and revenues. In our example, Chang's truck has a useful life of 200,000 miles, so depreciation computed on a per mile basis is as follows:

$$\text{Depreciation expense per unit of service} = \frac{(\text{Acquisition cost} - \text{Estimated residual value})}{\text{Estimated units of service}}$$

$$D = \frac{(C - R)}{n}$$

$$D = \frac{(\$41,0000 - \$1,000)}{200,000 \text{ miles}}$$

$$D = \$.20 \text{ per mile}$$

If employees drive the truck 65,000 miles in the first year of use, depreciation expense for that year will be $(65,000 \times \$.20) = \$13,000$.

For some assets, such as transportation equipment, units-of-production depreciation may be more logical than the straight-line method. However, the units-of-production depreciation method is not widely used, probably for several reasons:

1. When the usage of an asset is fairly constant across time, unit-based depreciation produces approximately the same yearly depreciation amounts as does straight-line depreciation.
2. Straight-line depreciation is easier. Under straight-line, we can determine the entire depreciation schedule at the time of acquisition; however, under units-of-production depreciation, we must keep detailed records of units of service to determine the amount depreciated each year.

Declining-Balance Depreciation

Any pattern of depreciation that writes off depreciable value more quickly than does the straight-line method is considered **accelerated depreciation**. Companies use a number of accelerated depreciation methods, but we will illustrate only the **double-declining-balance (DDB) method**, also known as 200% declining-balance method. We compute DDB depreciation as follows:

1. Compute the straight-line rate by dividing 100% by the useful life stated in years. Then double the straight-line rate. In our example, the straight-line rate is $(100\% \div 4) = 25\%$. The DDB rate is $(2 \times 25\%)$, or 50%.
2. To compute the depreciation on an asset for any year, ignore the estimated residual value and multiply the asset's net book value at the beginning of the year by the DDB rate.

We can apply the DDB method to Chang Company's truck as follows:

$$\text{DDB rate} = 2 \times (100\% \div n)$$

$$\text{DDB rate, 4-year life} = 2 \times (100\% \div 4) = 50\%$$

$$\text{DDB depreciation} = \text{DDB rate} \times \text{Beginning net book value}$$

For year 1: $D = .50 \,(\$41,000)$
$\qquad = \$20,500$
For year 2: $D = .50 \,(\$41,000 - \$20,500)$
$\qquad = \$10,250$
For year 3: $D = .50 \,(\$41,000 - \$20,500 - \$10,250)$
$\qquad = \$5,125$
For year 4: $D = .50 \,(\$41,000 - \$20,500 - \$10,250 - \$5,125)$
$\qquad = \$2,563$

In this example, the depreciation amount for each year is one-half the preceding year's depreciation. However, this halving is a special case that happens only with a 4-year life asset. Remember, the basic approach of DDB is to apply the depreciation rate to the beginning net book value. Because the net book value declines each period, applying the constant

DDB rate to the net book value results in lower depreciation in each successive year. Although we illustrated the declining-balance method with DDB, other versions use different multiples. For example, the 150% declining-balance method multiples the straight-line rate by 1.5 instead of doubling it. In the case of the asset with a 4-year life, the 150% declining-balance rate is $(1.5 \times 25\%) = 37.5\%$.

Comparing and Choosing Depreciation Methods

Exhibit 8-2 compares the results of straight-line and DDB depreciation for Chang Company's truck. Note that the DDB method provides $38,438 of total depreciation and does not allocate the full $40,000 depreciable value to expense. Some companies compensate for this by switching to a straight-line schedule part way through the asset's depreciable life—a refinement that is illustrated in the last two columns of Exhibit 8-2. In addition, if the residual value is large enough, application of DDB may result in fully depreciating an asset prior to the end of its useful life. Because you cannot depreciate an asset below its estimated residual value, companies compensate for this by modifying the depreciation schedule. This modification is beyond the scope of this text.

Companies do not necessarily use the same depreciation method for all types of depreciable assets. Although Intel uses straight-line depreciation for all assets, a recent Boeing annual report states, "The principal methods of depreciation are as follows: buildings and land improvements, 150% declining balance; and machinery and equipment, sum-of-the-years' digits."

How does a company choose among the alternatives? In some cases, tradition leads a company to select the method used by other companies in its industry to enhance comparability. Sometimes one method provides superior matching of expense and revenue, as units-of-production depreciation does for certain types of equipment and manufacturing processes. Sometimes companies choose the method most consistent with the life cycle cost of the asset. Suppose a type of equipment requires little maintenance in the first years of its life, but increasing maintenance later. Accelerated depreciation with decreasing depreciation charges each year, plus rising maintenance costs each year, may provide a more constant cost per year. Thus, the choice depends on the nature of the industry, as well as the equipment and the goals of management.

	Straight-Line*		Declining-Balance at Twice the Straight-Line Rate (DDB)†		Modified DDB—Switch to Straight-Line in Year 4‡	
	Annual Depreciation	Book Value	Annual Depreciation	Book Value	Annual Depreciation	Book Value
At acquisition		$41,000		$41,000		$41,000
Year 1	$10,000	31,000	$20,500	20,500	$20,500	20,500
Year 2	10,000	21,000	10,250	10,250	10,250	10,250
Year 3	10,000	11,000	5,125	5,125	5,125	5,125
Year 4	10,000	1,000	2,563	2,562	4,125	1,000
Total	$40,000		$38,438		$40,000	

*Depreciation is the same each year, 25% of ($41,000 – $1,000).

†100% ÷ 4 = 25%. The DDB rate is 50%. Then 50% of $41,000; 50% of ($41,000 – $20,500); 50% of [$41,000 – ($20,500 + $10,250)]; etc. Unmodified, this method will not fully depreciate the existing book value.

‡The switch to straight-line occurs in year 4, and the depreciation amount is the amount needed to reduce the book value to the final salvage value.

EXHIBIT 8-2
Depreciation: Two Popular Methods
(assume equipment costs $41,000, 4-year life, and estimated residual value of $1,000)

Summary Problem for Your Review

PROBLEM

"The net book value of plant assets that appears on the balance sheet is the amount that would be spent today for their replacement." Do you agree? Explain.

SOLUTION

No. Net book value of plant assets on the balance sheet is the result of deducting accumulated depreciation from original historical cost. It is a result of cost allocation, not valuation. The depreciation process does not attempt to reflect all the technological and economic events that may affect replacement value. Consequently, there is no assurance that net book value will approximate replacement cost.

Changes in Estimated Useful Life or Residual Value

A company estimates the useful life and residual value of an asset at the time of its acquisition. The information on which it bases these estimates may change with time. If new information becomes available and the use of the revised estimate would result in a material change in depreciation expense, the company must adopt the new estimate and revise the depreciation schedule. Accounting for changes in estimated useful life or residual value is prospective in nature. In other words, the company does not go back and revise the depreciation expense taken in prior periods. Rather, it recomputes depreciation expense for the period in which it revises the estimate and for all future periods.

OBJECTIVE 4

Recalculate depreciation in response to a change in estimated useful life or residual value.

Refer to the straight-line depreciation schedule for Chang Company's truck as shown in Exhibit 8-2. Chang originally estimated a residual value of $1,000 and a useful life of 4 years for the truck. Suppose that at the beginning of year 4, Chang determines that it will continue to use the truck for 2 more years rather than 1 more year. As of the beginning of year 4, Chang has recorded a total of $30,000 in depreciation expense, $10,000 in year 1, $10,000 in year 2, and $10,000 in year 3. The net book value of the truck at the beginning of year 4 is $11,000 as shown in Exhibit 8-2. Chang still expects the residual value to be $1,000. Chang must allocate the remaining $10,000 in allowable depreciation expense over a total of 2 years: ($10,000 ÷ 2) = $5,000. The revised depreciation schedule for Chang is as follows:

	Annual Depreciation	Book Value
At acquisition		$41,000
Year 1	$10,000	31,000
Year 2	10,000	21,000
Year 3	10,000	11,000
Year 4	5,000	6,000
Year 5	5,000	1,000
Total	$40,000	

Contrasting Income Tax and Shareholder Reporting

In accounting for long-lived assets, reporting to stockholders and reporting to the income tax authorities often differ. Reports to stockholders and filings with the SEC must abide by GAAP. In contrast, reports to income tax authorities must abide by the income tax rules and regulations. Frequently GAAP rules and tax rules differ. Therefore, keeping two sets of records is necessary.

OBJECTIVE 5

Differentiate financial statement depreciation from income tax depreciation.

Depreciation for Tax Reporting Purposes

Modified Accelerated Cost Recovery System (MACRS)
The underlying basis for computing depreciation for tax purposes.

While Congress makes some changes to the U.S. tax code almost every year, since 1986 the underlying basis for computing depreciation for tax purposes has been the **Modified Accelerated Cost Recovery System (MACRS)**. The MACRS depreciation schedule is based on the declining-balance depreciation method discussed previously. However, tax depreciation and financial reporting depreciation differ. One important difference is that MACRS classifies depreciable assets into property classes. These property classes provide guidance on useful lives to be used for tax depreciation purposes. Frequently, useful lives for tax purposes are shorter than the useful lives used for financial reporting purposes. Remember that the shorter the life, the earlier a company can recognize depreciation expense. Higher expenses reported for tax purposes mean lower taxable net income, which means lower income taxes payable. MACRS allows for higher depreciation and lower taxes in the early years of an asset's service life than does the straight-line method commonly used for financial reporting. This is reversed in the later years of an asset's life. However, because of the time value of money, the company benefits from the delay in paying taxes.

Another important difference relates to residual values. Remember that the residual value reduces the depreciable value of an asset. For financial reporting purposes companies cannot depreciate an asset below its residual value. However, MACRS assumes that all assets have a zero residual value. This allows a company to depreciate the entire historical cost for tax purposes, potentially increasing the total amount of depreciation expense.

Shareholder Reporting

Although companies typically use MACRS for tax purposes, most use straight-line depreciation for shareholder reporting. Tax authorities use special rates, short lives, or immediate write-offs to achieve the goal of motivating investment in long-lived assets. In contrast, the depreciation method for shareholder reporting has a goal of matching the cost of an asset to the periods in which that asset generates revenues.

There are several practical reasons for adopting straight-line depreciation for financial reporting, namely, simplicity, convenience, and reporting of higher earnings in early years than would be reported under accelerated depreciation. Managers tend not to choose accounting methods that reduce reported earnings in the early years of long-lived assets.

Depreciation and Cash Flow

OBJECTIVE 6

Explain the effect of depreciation on cash flow.

Too often, nonaccountants confuse the relationships among depreciation expense, income tax expense, cash, and accumulated depreciation. For example, the business press contains misleading quotations such as ". . . we're looking for financing of $3.75 billion. Of that, about 60% will be recovered in depreciation and amortization." As another example, consider a *BusinessWeek* news report concerning an airline company: "And with a hefty boost from depreciation and the sale of $6 million worth of property, its cash balance rose by $10 million in the year's first quarter."

These statements imply that depreciation somehow generates cash. It does not. Depreciation simply allocates the original cost of an asset to the periods in which the company uses the asset—nothing more and nothing less. Furthermore, accumulated depreciation is merely the portion of an asset's original cost that has been written off to depreciation expense in prior periods—not a pile of cash waiting to be used.

Effects of Depreciation on Cash

To illustrate depreciation's relationship to cash, consider Acme Service Company, which began business with cash and common stockholders' equity of $100,000. Acme immediately acquired equipment for $40,000 cash. The equipment had an expected 4-year life and an estimated residual value of zero. The first year's operations generated cash sales of $103,000 and cash operating expenses of $53,000.

Assume straight-line depreciation of $10,000 and accelerated depreciation of $20,000 in the first year. Note from the first two columns of Exhibit 8-3 that the reported pretax income differs as a result of the depreciation method chosen, but cash flow from operations is the same. Comparing the pretax amounts stresses the role of depreciation expense most vividly. Why? Because before taxes, the only balance sheet accounts affected by changes in the depreciation

EXHIBIT 8-3

Acme Service Company

Income Statement and Statement of Cash Flows ($ in thousands)

	Before Taxes		After Taxes	
	Straight-Line Depreciation	Accelerated Depreciation	Straight-Line Depreciation	Accelerated Depreciation
Income Statement				
Sales	$103	$103	$103	$103
Operating expenses	53	53	53	53
Depreciation expense	10	20	10	20
Pretax income	40	30	40	30
Income tax expense (40%)	—	—	16	12
Net income	$ 40	$ 30	$ 24	$ 18
Statement of Cash Flows				
Cash collections	$103	$103	$103	$103
Cash operating expenses	53	53	53	53
Cash tax payments	—	—	16	12
Cash provided by operations*	$ 50	$ 50	$ 34	$ 38

*Sometimes called *cash flow from operations, net cash provided by operations,* or just *cash flow.* It is simply cash collected on sales less all operating expenses requiring cash and less cash paid for income taxes.

method are Accumulated Depreciation and Retained Earnings. Depreciation does not affect the before-tax ending cash balances.

Now suppose that for financial reporting purposes, GAAP allowed Acme to write off the entire $40,000 in the first year but still treat it as an investing activity. What are the company's pretax income and the cash provided by operations? Pretax income is only ($103,000 – $53,000 – $40,000) = $10,000. However, the increase in cash remains at $50,000. Why? Because cash received from sales of $103,000 and cash expenses of $53,000 do not change, leaving the $50,000 cash provided by operations unchanged.

Effects of Depreciation on Income Taxes

Now consider the after-tax portions of Exhibit 8-3 in the two rightmost columns. Depreciation is a deductible noncash expense for income tax purposes. Thus, the higher the depreciation a company deducts on its tax return in any given year, the lower the taxable income, and the lower the cash paid for income taxes. In short, if tax depreciation expense is higher, taxes are lower and the company keeps more cash for use in the business.

To emphasize the relationship between depreciation and cash and to simplify the comparison, we assume the depreciation method used for financial reporting is the same as for tax purposes. From the last two columns of Exhibit 8-3, you can see that Acme would pay $16,000 of income taxes in the first year using straight-line depreciation, but only $12,000 using accelerated depreciation. Therefore, compared with the straight-line depreciation method, the accelerated method conserves $4,000 in cash. Depreciation does not generate cash, but it does have a cash benefit if it results in lower taxes.

Summary Problems for Your Review

PROBLEM

"Accumulated depreciation provides cash for the replacement of fixed assets." Do you agree with this quotation from a business magazine? Explain.

SOLUTION

Accumulated depreciation does not generate cash. It is the sum of all the noncash depreciation expense recognized since the date a company acquired an asset. It in no way represents a stockpile of cash for replacement.

PROBLEM

Review the important chapter illustration in the section, "Depreciation and Cash Flow," on page 354. Suppose Acme Service had acquired the equipment for $80,000 instead of $40,000. The estimated residual value remains zero and the useful life remains 4 years, and sales and operating expenses are unchanged.

1. Prepare a revised Exhibit 8-3. As in Exhibit 8-3, assume the same depreciation method is used for financial reporting and tax reporting. Assume an income tax rate of 40% and round all income tax computations to the nearest thousand.
2. Indicate the major items affected by the change. Also tabulate all differences between the final two columns in your revised exhibit as compared with Exhibit 8-3.

SOLUTION

1. The revised income statements and statement of cash flows information are in Exhibit 8-4. Examine Exhibit 8-4 before attempting part 2.
2. The following comparisons of Exhibits 8-4 and 8-3 are noteworthy. The change in depreciation does not affect sales, cash operating expenses, or cash provided by operations before income taxes. Because of higher depreciation, net income is lower in all four columns of Exhibit 8-4 than it was in Exhibit 8-3. Comparison of the final two columns of the exhibits follows:

	As Shown in		
	Exhibit 8-4	**Exhibit 8-3**	**Difference**
Straight-line depreciation	20	10	10 Higher
Accelerated depreciation	40	20	20 Higher
Income tax expense based on			
Straight-line depreciation	12	16	4 Lower
Accelerated depreciation	4	12	8 Lower
Net income based on			
Straight-line depreciation	18	24	6 Lower
Accelerated depreciation	6	18	12 Lower
Cash provided by operations based on			
Straight-line depreciation	38	34	4 Higher
Accelerated depreciation	46	38	8 Higher

Especially noteworthy is the phenomenon that higher tax depreciation not only decreases net income, but also decreases cash outflows for income taxes. As a result, cash provided by operations increases.

EXHIBIT 8-4

Acme Service Company

Income Statement and Statement of Cash Flows ($ in thousands)

	Before Taxes		After Taxes	
	Straight-Line Depreciation	Accelerated Depreciation	Straight-Line Depreciation	Accelerated Depreciation
Income Statement				
Sales	$103	$103	$103	$103
Operating expenses	53	53	53	53
Depreciation expense	20	40	20	40
Pretax income	30	10	30	10
Income tax expense (40%)	—	—	12	4
Net income	$ 30	$ 10	$ 18	$ 6
Statement of Cash Flows				
Cash collections	$103	$103	$103	$103
Cash operating expenses	53	53	53	53
Cash tax payments	—	—	12	4
Cash provided by operations	$ 50	$ 50	$ 38	$ 46

Expenditures After Acquisition

In addition to the initial investment at acquisition, companies incur ongoing expenditures associated with the operation of long-lived assets. For example, repairs and maintenance costs are necessary to maintain a fixed asset in operating condition. **Repairs** include the occasional costs of restoring a fixed asset to its ordinary operating condition after breakdowns, accidents, or damage. **Maintenance** includes the routine recurring costs of activities such as oiling, polishing, painting, and adjusting that are necessary to keep a fixed asset in operating condition. Accountants generally compile these costs in a single account and regard them as expenses of the current period.

In contrast, an **improvement** (sometimes called a **betterment** or a **capital improvement**) is an expenditure that increases the future benefits provided by an existing fixed asset by decreasing its operating cost, increasing its rate of output, improving its safety, reducing its rate of pollution, or prolonging its useful life. Repairs and maintenance maintain the level of an asset's future benefits, whereas improvements increase those benefits. We generally capitalize improvements. Examples of capital improvements or betterments include the rehabilitation of an apartment house that will allow increased rents and the rebuilding of a machine that increases its speed or extends its useful life.

Suppose Chang Company's $41,000 delivery truck with a 4-year life and $1,000 residual value, presented earlier in the chapter, experiences a major overhaul costing $7,000 at the start of year 3. Chang depreciated the truck using straight-line depreciation during the first 2 years of use. If this overhaul extends the useful life of the truck from 4 to 5 years, the accounting is as follows:

1. Increase the book value of the truck ($41,000 − $20,000 = $21,000 at the end of year 2) by $7,000. Thus, we add $7,000 to Equipment.
2. Revise the depreciation schedule to spread the revised book value of the truck over the remaining 3 years, as follows (assume Chang continues to use straight-line depreciation):

	Original Depreciation Schedule		Revised Depreciation Schedule	
	Year	Amount	Year	Amount
	1	$10,000	1	$10,000
	2	10,000	2	10,000
	3	10,000	3	9,000*
	4	10,000	4	9,000
			5	9,000
Accumulated depreciation		$40,000		$47,000†

*New depreciable amount is [($41,000 − $20,000 + $7,000) − $1,000 residual value] = $27,000. New depreciation expense is $27,000 divided by the remaining useful life of 3 years, or $9,000 per year.

†Recapitulation: Original cost $41,000
Major overhaul 7,000
48,000
Less: Residual 1,000
Depreciable amount $47,000

Gains and Losses on Sales of Tangible Assets

Earlier in this chapter you learned how to account for property, plant, and equipment assets at the date of acquisition, how to account for expenditures related to the assets during their useful lives, and how to compute depreciation. However, companies sometimes sell an asset before the end of its useful life. When they sell assets, gains or losses are inevitable. We measure these gains or losses by the difference between the proceeds received and the net book value (net carrying amount) of the asset being sold.

Recording Gains and Losses

Consider Chang Company's delivery truck from our earlier example. Suppose Chang sells the truck for $21,000 in cash at the very beginning of year 3. Chang depreciated the asset using straight-line depreciation during the first 2 years of its life. Because its net book value is also $21,000, there would be no gain or loss on the transaction. Chang simply exchanges one asset, equipment, carried on the books at $21,000 for another asset, cash, of $21,000. Chang would eliminate the equipment asset and its accumulated depreciation from the records and record the cash received. The sale would have the following effects:

A				=	L	+	SE
+$21,000	−	$41,000	+ $20,000	=	$0	+	$0
Increase Cash		Decrease Equipment	Decrease Accumulated Depreciation				

Note that the disposal of the truck requires the removal of its book value, which appears in two accounts, Equipment and Accumulated Depreciation. We remove the original acquisition cost of $41,000 from the Equipment account and the $20,000 in accumulated depreciation on the truck from the Accumulated Depreciation account. Remember that a reduction in the balance in Accumulated Depreciation increases assets, hence the + sign associated with Accumulated Depreciation in the illustration.

Suppose the selling price was $27,000 instead of $21,000. The sale would result in a gain of $6,000, the difference between the sale proceeds and the net book value of the asset being sold:

Sale proceeds		$27,000
Less: Book value		
Cost	$ 41,000	
Accumulated depreciation	(20,000)	21,000
Gain		$ 6,000

This sale would have the following effects on the accounting equation:

A				=	L	+	SE
+$27,000	−	$41,000	+ $20,000	=	$0	+	$6,000
Increase Cash		Decrease Equipment	Decrease Accumulated Depreciation				Increase SE Gain on Sale of Equipment

Now suppose the selling price was $17,000 instead of $21,000. The sale would result in a $4,000 loss with the following effects:

A				=	L	+	SE
+$17,000	−	$41,000	+ $20,000	=	$0	−	$4,000
Increase Cash		Decrease Equipment	Decrease Accumulated Depreciation				Decrease SE Loss on Sale of Equipment

Exhibit 8-5 shows the T-account presentations and journal entries for these transactions. Note again that we must eliminate both the original cost of the equipment and the accompanying accumulated depreciation when we sell the asset. The net effect is to eliminate the $21,000 carrying amount of the equipment (cost of $41,000 less accumulated depreciation of $20,000).

Income Statement Presentation

In most instances, gains or losses on the disposition of plant assets are not significant enough to appear as separate line items on the income statement. In such cases, companies include these gains and losses as part of "Other Income" or "Other Expense" on the income statement and do

Sale at $27,000:

		Cash	Equipment		Gain on Sale of Equipment
		27	* 41	41	6
Cash	27				
Accumulated depreciation	20		Accumulated Depreciation, Equipment		
Equipment		41			
Gain on sale of equipment		6	20	* 20	

Sale at $17,000:

		Cash	Equipment		Loss on Sale of Equipment
		17	* 41	41	4
Cash	17				
Accumulated depreciation	20		Accumulated Depreciation, Equipment		
Loss on sale of equipment	4				
Equipment		41	20	* 20	

*Beginning balance.

EXHIBIT 8-5

Journal and Ledger Entries

Gain or Loss on Sale of Equipment ($ in thousands)

not separately identify them. The following three lines from a recent **DuPont** income statement illustrate this treatment ($ amounts in millions):

Sales	$30,529
Other income, net	1,307
Total	$31,836

Footnote 3 to DuPont's financial statements reveals that the item Other Income, net includes a net gain of $40 million arising from the sale of assets. The use of the term "net" gain suggests that DuPont sold some assets at a gain and other assets at a loss, with the gains exceeding the losses by $40 million. The $40 million is not a material transaction for analysts to understand in evaluating the company, so DuPont does not include a separate income statement line for it. To put things in perspective, the $40 million is small relative to the more than $36 billion in assets on DuPont's December 31, 2008, balance sheet.

Some companies follow DuPont's example and list other income, including gains from the sale of assets, with sales revenue at the very top of the income statement. Others exclude such gains (or losses) from the computation of major profit categories such as gross profit or operating profit. **The Coca-Cola Company** took the latter approach in its 2008 financial statements. On its income statement Coca-Cola subtracted $28 million of Other Income, net after calculating gross profit and operating income. The Management Discussion and Analysis reveals that Other Income, net includes "dividend income, rental income, gains and losses related to the disposal of property, plant and equipment. . . ." as well as other income and expense items. When interpreting a company's income statement, it is important to know which approach a company has taken with regard to other income and other expense categories.

Asset Sales and the Statement of Cash Flows

The sale of fixed assets has implications for the statement of cash flows. Sales of fixed assets are investing activities. The previous examples demonstrate three different scenarios. In the first case (case A), Chang's truck sells for exactly its net book value of $21,000. In the second case (case B), it sells for $27,000 in cash resulting in a gain of $6,000. In the final case (case C), it sells for $17,000 in cash creating a loss of $4,000. In each case, the investing section of the statement of cash flows shows the actual cash received, labeled as "Proceeds from the sale of fixed assets." This is the only impact on the body of the cash flow statement if Chang Company uses the direct method for presenting cash flows from operating activities. If it uses the indirect method, the cash flows from operating activities section starts with net income. Because gains or losses from the sale of fixed assets affect net income but have their cash effect shown in the investing section, Chang must remove these gains or losses from net income to calculate operating cash flows.

Suppose Chang Company uses the indirect method and has net income of $50,000 before accounting for the sale of the truck. To simplify the illustration, we assume no tax effects. The following table depicts the effects of the sale of the truck on net income:

	Income Before Sale	Gain (Loss)	Income After Sale
Case A: Sale at $21,000	$50,000	0	$50,000
Case B: Sale at $27,000	$50,000	$6,000	$56,000
Case C: Sale at $17,000	$50,000	($4,000)	$46,000

Net income includes the gain or loss on the sale of the truck. Therefore, the reconciliation of net income and cash flows from operating activities must remove the noncash gain or loss from net income. In case A, the $50,000 in reported net income does not include any gain or loss on the sale of the truck. Therefore, in arriving at cash flows from operating activities, we do not adjust net income. In case B, net income of $56,000 includes a $6,000 noncash gain, which we must deduct from net income to arrive at net cash provided by operating activities. Subtracting the $6,000 gain does not imply a use of cash. It simply offsets the effect of the $6,000 gain included in net income. In case C, net income of $46,000 includes the $4,000 loss. Like depreciation expense, this loss does not represent a cash disbursement. The company did not pay someone $4,000 in cash to take possession of the truck! Therefore, we must add back to net income the loss on the sale of the truck to offset its earlier deduction. The net cash provided by operating activities is the same in each case. The sale of the truck did not affect operating cash flows.

INTERPRETING FINANCIAL STATEMENTS

In January 2010, Olsson Company sells a building that had an original historical cost of $850,000 and accumulated depreciation of $575,000 at the time of sale. It sells the building for cash and records a pretax gain of $75,000. Indicate how these facts affect the statement of cash flows, prepared on an indirect method basis, for the year ended December 31, 2010. Ignore any tax consequences.

Answer

Olsson Company must deduct the gain of $75,000 from net income in the operating section of its statement of cash flows. This is necessary because the gain was included in net income, but it does not represent additional cash received from the sale. All of the cash received is classified as investing. Therefore, Olsson Company shows cash proceeds of $350,000 from the sale of the building in the investing section. The $350,000 is derived as follows:

$$\text{Net book value of building at the date of the sale} = \$850,000 - \$575,000 = \$275,000$$
$$\text{Gain on sale} = \text{Selling price} - \text{net book value}$$
$$\$75,000 = \text{Selling price} - \$275,000$$
$$\$350,000 = \text{Selling price}$$

Summary Problem for Your Review

PROBLEM

Refer to Exhibit 8-2 on page 352. Suppose the estimated residual value had been $5,000 instead of $1,000.

1. Compute depreciation for each of the first 2 years using straight-line and double-declining-balance (DDB) methods.
2. Assume that the company uses DDB depreciation and sells the equipment for $20,000 cash at the end of the second year. Compute the gain or loss on the sale. Show the effects of the sale in Equipment and Accumulated Depreciation T-accounts. Where and how would the sale appear in the income statement? Where and how would the sale appear in the statement of cash flows?
3. Assume that the company uses straight-line depreciation and sells the equipment for $20,000 cash at the end of the second year. Compute the gain or loss on the sale. Compare this amount to the gain or loss computed in the previous question.

SOLUTION

1.

	Straight-Line Depreciation = (C – R) ÷ n	DDB Depreciation = Rate* × (Beg. Book Value)
Year 1	$36,000 ÷ 4 = $9,000	.50 × $41,000 = $20,500
Year 2	$36,000 ÷ 4 = $9,000	.50 × ($41,000 – $20,500) = $10,250

*Rate = 2 × (100% ÷ n) = 2 × (100% ÷ 4) = 50%.

2.

Selling price	$20,000
Net book value of equipment sold is	10,250
$41,000 – ($20,500 + $10,250), or	
$41,000 – $30,750 =	
Gain on sale of equipment	$ 9,750

The effect of removing the book value is a $10,250 decrease in assets. Note that the effect of a decrease in Accumulated Depreciation (by itself) is an increase in assets.

Equipment			
Acquisition cost	41,000	Cost of equipment sold	41,000

Accumulated Depreciation, Equipment			
Accumulated depreciation on equipment sold	30,750	Depreciation for	
		Year 1	20,500
		Year 2	10,250
			30,750

The company may show the $9,750 gain as a separate item on the income statement labeled Gain on Sale of Equipment or Gain on Disposal of Equipment. Alternatively, it may combine the gain with similar transactions in the account Other Gains and Losses. On the statement of cash flows, the company will show the $20,000 cash received as an inflow from investing activities. If it uses the direct method for reporting cash flows from operating activities, there is no further entry. If it uses the indirect method, it must deduct the $9,750 gain from net income in computing cash flows from operating activities.

3.

Selling price	$20,000
Net book value of equipment sold is	
$41,000 – ($9,000 + $9,000) =	23,000
Loss on sale of equipment	$ 3,000

Even though the sales price is the same as in number 2, there is a loss of $3,000 instead of a gain of $9,750 because the book value is $12,750 higher. The amount of the gain or loss on equipment being disposed of depends on the depreciation method used.

Revaluation of Tangible Assets

The market value of tangible assets can either increase or decrease over time. Do the accounting rules allow companies to revalue the assets upward if the value increases or downward if the value decreases? Upward revaluations are infrequent and exist only for companies reporting under IFRS and who elect the revaluation method for long-lived assets. Downward revaluations are mandated under both IFRS and U.S. GAAP and occur when events or circumstances result in the impairment of property, plant, and equipment. An asset is considered to be **impaired** when it ceases to have economic value to the company at least as large as the carrying value (book value) of the asset.

Revaluation Method Under IFRS

Companies reporting under IFRS and electing the revaluation method carry their fixed assets at fair value regardless of whether this results in an increase or decrease in carrying value. Fair value, which is the amount for which the asset could be exchanged between knowledgeable, willing parties in an arm's length transaction, is usually determined by hiring an appraiser who uses market-based evidence. Under the revaluation method, companies can revalue plant assets up to fair value, resulting in a revaluation gain, or down to fair value, resulting in a revaluation loss. Companies typically do not include revaluation gains in net income; rather they add them directly to stockholders' equity as part of other comprehensive income. However, a company would credit the revaluation gain to income if it reverses a revaluation loss that was previously recognized as a reduction of income. Revaluation losses first offset previous revaluation gains on the same asset, and the remainder is a loss on the income statement.

Once a company begins to make revaluation adjustments, it must continue to make them regularly so that the carrying amounts of the assets are current. Also, if a company revalues any assets, it must revalue all other assets in the same asset category. Assets that are accounted for using the revaluation method are not depreciated. While IFRS allows the revaluation method, it is seldom used in practice.

Impairment of Assets

Downward revaluations due to impairment occur under both U.S. GAAP and IFRS. Both U.S. GAAP and IFRS require companies to review assets for impairment whenever circumstances suggest that impairment is possible. Indicators that may lead to a review for impairment include, but are not limited to, a significant decline in the market price of an asset, a significant change in the manner in which an asset is being used, an adverse change in legal or business environment, evidence of obsolescence or physical damage, or a forecast indicating that the company will experience continuing losses associated with the use of the asset.

Suppose that Intel, a company reporting under U.S. GAAP, owns equipment with a net book value of $150,000. Due to a change in technology and product demand, Intel determines that it must review the asset for impairment. U.S. GAAP requires a two-step process. The first step in the impairment review is a **recoverability test** that compares the undiscounted total expected future net cash flows from the use of the asset plus its eventual disposal value with the current carrying value of the asset. If the sum of the cash flows plus disposal value is greater than the carrying value, the asset is not impaired. If the sum of the cash flows plus disposal value is less than the carrying value, Intel must consider the asset to be impaired. Intel estimates the total expected

---

impaired
When an asset ceases to have economic value to the company at least as large as the book value of the asset.

OBJECTIVE 9

Determine the balance sheet valuation of tangible assets for companies who use the revaluation method allowed under IFRS.

OBJECTIVE 10

Account for the impairment of tangible assets.

---

recoverability test
The first step in the asset impairment review process under U.S. GAAP. The test compares the undiscounted total expected future net cash flows from the use of the asset plus its eventual disposal value with the current carrying value of the asset.

future net cash flows to be $127,000. Because this is less than the carrying value of $150,000, there is evidence of impairment. Thus Intel proceeds to the second step, computation of the dollar amount of the impairment loss.

The impairment loss is the amount by which the carrying value of the asset exceeds its fair value. If there is an active market for the asset being evaluated, the fair value is the market price. In the absence of an active market, Intel must estimate the fair value using appropriate valuation techniques. For example, one such valuation technique estimates the fair value of an asset as the present value of the expected future net cash flows generated by the asset. Notice that Intel used the undiscounted total of all expected future net cash flows to determine whether impairment occurred. However, it would use the present value of those expected future net cash flows to calculate the magnitude of the loss. Assume that the market price (fair value) of the equipment is $105,000. Therefore, Intel must record an impairment loss of $45,000:

Net book value of the equipment	$150,000
Minus: Fair value of the equipment	105,000
Impairment loss	$ 45,000

The entry to record the impairment loss is as follows:

Loss on impairment	$45,000	
Accumulated depreciation.		$45,000

Intel reports this loss as part of continuing operations. If the dollar amount is large enough, the loss may appear as a separate line item on the income statement. Otherwise, Intel is likely to combine it with other expenses. In this example, the new carrying value of the asset is $105,000. Even if the fair value of the equipment increases above $105,000, Intel cannot write the asset back up above $105,000. Once an impairment loss is recorded, it cannot be restored.

Footnote 1 in Intel's 2008 annual report explains its impairment review process: "We regularly perform reviews if facts and circumstances indicate that the carrying amount of assets may not be recoverable or that the useful life is shorter than we had originally estimated. We assess the recoverability of our assets held for use by comparing the projected undiscounted net cash flows associated with the related asset or group of assets over their remaining estimated useful lives against their respective carrying amounts. Impairment, if any, is based on the excess of the carrying amount over the fair value of those assets." Footnote 15 of Intel's 2008 annual report goes on to indicate that the company took $888 million in asset impairment charges from the third quarter of 2006 through the fourth quarter of 2008.

How would Intel's impairment accounting change if it reported under IFRS? The company would use a single-step process that compares the net book value of the asset to its **recoverable amount**, defined as the higher of (1) fair value minus the cost to sell and (2) the value in use, calculated as the present value of expected future net cash flows. If the net book value is greater than the recoverable amount, Intel would recognize an impairment loss for the difference. Suppose that the present value of the $127,000 in expected future net cash flows is $100,000 and that Intel would incur a cost of $7,500 to sell the asset. Its recoverable amount would be $100,000, the higher of the following:

recoverable amount
Under IFRS, the higher of (1) fair value minus the cost to sell and (2) the value in use, calculated as the present value of expected future net cash flows.

1. Fair value less cost to sell: ($105,000 – $7,500) = $97,500
2. Present value of expected future net cash flows, $100,000

Therefore, the impairment loss would be ($150,000 – $100,000) = $50,000. Unless Intel used the revaluation method and had recognized previous revaluation write-ups on this asset, the $50,000 would be a loss on its income statement.

Under U.S. GAAP, the impairment test for long-lived assets that a company is holding for resale differs slightly from that described earlier for assets in use. The recoverability test is still the first step. However, the impairment loss, if any, is the excess of the carrying value of the asset over the fair value less the cost to sell or $97,500 given the preceding information. If Intel were intending to sell the previously described asset, the impairment loss would be ($150,000 – $97,500) = $52,500. Further, if the asset's fair value less cost to sell subsequently increased from $97,500 to $110,000, Intel would write the asset back up to $110,000. Following an impairment loss, companies can write up assets held for resale as long as the write-up never results in a value in excess of the net book value of the asset at the time of the original impairment.

Intangible Assets

We now turn our attention to another group of long-lived assets—intangibles. These assets are not physical items, but instead are rights or claims to expected benefits that are often contractual in nature.

Under U.S. GAAP, the accounting for intangible assets depends on two factors: (1) whether a company acquires the intangible from an external party or develops it internally, and (2) whether the intangible asset has a finite or indefinite life. Consider the first of these factors. A company's balance sheet lists an intangible asset only if the company purchased the rights to the asset from an external party. It does not list equally valuable assets created by internal expenditures. For example, footnote 14 of Intel's 2008 annual report indicates that it paid $68 million to other companies for intellectual property assets (IP) developed by those companies. Intel recorded the $68 million as intangible assets. In contrast, suppose Intel spent $68 million to internally develop similar IP assets. Intel would charge this $68 million to expense, and it would not recognize assets.

Why is there a discrepancy between the accounting treatment for externally acquired and internally developed items? One of the criteria for recognition of an asset is that the future benefits provided by that asset can be quantified with a reasonable degree of precision. The FASB believes that it is difficult for management to value the results of its internal research and development efforts honestly and objectively. As a result, U.S. GAAP requires companies to immediately expense the costs of internal research and development, despite the fact that the company surely expects future benefits. However, when one company purchases the results of another company's efforts, the negotiated purchase price represents a verifiable historical cost from the perspective of the purchaser.

This discrepancy has generated significant debate. In recent years we have seen an increase in the number of firms in the economy that are "knowledge-based" businesses. The value of these firms lies in intangibles such as internal research and development activities and intellectual capital. However, under existing U.S. GAAP, if a company does not acquire these resources externally, it cannot record them as assets. Some analysts believe that R&D and perhaps other expenditures for intellectual capital should be capitalized and they adjust the financial statements accordingly, as shown in the Business First box.

U.S. GAAP allows an exception to the automatic expensing of internal research and development costs for computer software companies. These companies can capitalize some of the costs of developing and producing software that they intend to sell or lease. They then amortize these capitalized amounts over the estimated product life. Companies in this industry expense R&D costs up to the time when the company considers the software product to be technologically feasible. After that point, and until the product goes into production, they capitalize R&D costs. This exception can have a significant impact on the financial statements of companies in the software development industry.

IFRS takes a different approach to accounting for R&D, separating research from development costs. The IFRS standards define research costs as costs incurred for current or planned investigations undertaken with the prospect of gaining new scientific or technical knowledge and understanding. Companies cannot capitalize research costs. The standards define development costs as costs incurred for the application of research findings or specialist knowledge to production, production methods, services or goods prior to the commencement of commercial product or use. Companies must capitalize development costs when it is sufficiently certain that the future economic benefits to the company will cover the related development costs. Bayer AG, a large German pharmaceutical company that prepares its financial statements under IFRS, has over 300 operating companies worldwide and engages in significant research and development activity. In its 2008 annual report, the company makes the following observation with regard to the capitalization of development expenditures whose benefits are not certain enough to warrant capitalization: "Since development projects are often subject to regulatory approval procedures and other uncertainties, the conditions for the capitalization of costs incurred before receipt of approvals are not normally satisfied."

BUSINESS FIRST

RESTATING FINANCIAL STATEMENTS TO SHOW RESEARCH AND DEVELOPMENT

Under U.S. GAAP, most companies must immediately expense internal R&D expenditures. Why? The FASB decided that it is hard to determine whether R&D will be valuable, and, if it is valuable, it is hard to estimate the value and predict the period of time over which a company will realize this value. Some analysts believe it is important to treat R&D as an asset to fully understand the total commitment of resources a company has made. They assume a useful life and develop a hypothetical value for R&D.

To illustrate, consider the following data for Eli Lilly. R&D spending in the 5-year period 2004–2008 rose 42.7% from $2,691.1 million in 2004 to $3,840.9 million in 2008 and totaled more than $16,173 million. Suppose Lilly capitalized these amounts each year as incurred and then amortized them over the subsequent 4 years on a straight-line basis (25% per year). Under this procedure, the $2,691.1 million spent in 2004 would appear as an asset of $2,691.1 million at year-end and would give rise to amortization of $672.78 million in each of the next 4 years. By the end of 2008, it would be fully amortized and would not appear as an asset.

Consider Lilly's financial statements for 2008. If Lilly was allowed to capitalize R&D, we can calculate the 2008 R&D expense of $3,083.17 million and the R&D asset of $8,776.96 million as shown in the table below.

Under capitalization, how would the financial statements differ from what Eli Lilly reported under U.S. GAAP? Net earnings for 2008 would be higher because R&D expense on the income statement would be $3,083.17 million, instead of the $3,840.9 million actually recorded in 2008. This lowers the R&D expense by about $757.73 million. On the balance sheet, assets would be higher by $8,776.96 million or about 30% greater than the actual reported total assets of $29,212.6 million. Of course, if assets are higher, there needs to be an offsetting effect on the other side of the balance sheet equation, and retained earnings and some liabilities for taxes would also be higher.

Lilly and other pharmaceutical companies are extreme cases because R&D typically represents more than 15% of sales (about 18.8% for Lilly in 2008). Some young, biotech start-ups have even more substantial R&D spending on a proportional basis. Indeed, some of these start-ups have no sales, and if they expense R&D immediately for accounting purposes, they sometimes have essentially no assets. Yet these companies may have very high market values because the ideas they have generated have great potential. Research-intensive firms and young start-up firms are two examples where adjustments to the data from the historical-cost accounting model are often useful for analyzing the firm. The 4-year amortization period in this example is arbitrary and was chosen in part to simplify the example. In various industries, different assumptions might be appropriate depending on the rate of technological change.

(all dollar amounts in millions)

Year of R&D Expenditure	R&D Expenditure	2008 Income Statement R&D Expense	% of Annual R&D Spending Unamortized at End of 2008	Balance Sheet Asset—12/31/08
2004	$2,691.1	$ 672.78	0	$ 0.00
2005	3,025.5	756.38	25	756.38
2006	3,129.3	782.33	50	1,564.65
2007	3,486.7	871.68	75	2,615.03
2008	3,840.9	—	100	3,840.90
Total 2008 Value		$3,083.17		$8,776.96

Source: http://investor.lilly.com/secfiling.cfm?filingID=950152-09-1897.

Once a company has capitalized a purchased intangible asset, the remaining question is how to account for that asset going forward. Under U.S. GAAP the accounting treatment depends on whether the asset has a finite life or an indefinite life. Companies do not routinely amortize intangible assets deemed to have indefinite lives. Instead, they evaluate these assets periodically for impairment. In contrast, companies amortize finite-lived intangible assets over their estimated useful lives. The useful life of an intangible asset is the shorter of its economic useful life or its legal life, if any. Because of obsolescence, the economic lives of intangible assets are often

INTERPRETING FINANCIAL STATEMENTS

Suppose a major pharmaceutical company acquires a biotechnology company that is heavily involved in research and development activities. The research and development of the biotech firm has resulted in only one patented process. However, it has an extensive research pipeline. It is this pipeline that is of most interest to the pharmaceutical company. The total purchase price is $100 million. An independent valuation of the fair value of the one patent acquired in the transaction set the value at $15 million. The remainder of the purchase price is attributable to the pipeline, which is commonly called "Purchased In-Process Research and Development (IPRD)." How should the pharmaceutical company account for this acquisition?

Answer

The company would record the patent as an intangible asset valued at $15 million. It is evident that the pharmaceutical company believes the research pipeline has future benefit or it would not have been willing to pay $100 million. The accounting treatment of in-process R&D acquired in an acquisition has been a matter of considerable disagreement in recent years. Some argue that these costs, or a portion of these costs, should be treated as an asset. After all, one of the criteria for recognition of an asset is the provision of future benefits. Others argue that the benefits to be derived from the purchased IPRD are too uncertain to meet asset-recognition criteria. However, under current GAAP, the pharmaceutical company would capitalize the $85 million of purchased in-process R&D.

---

shorter than their legal lives. To gain a better understanding of this process, we now examine some specific intangible assets that have finite lives and hence are subject to amortization.

Examples of Intangible Assets

patents

Grants made by the federal government to an inventor, bestowing (in the United States) the exclusive right to produce and sell a given product, or to use a process, for up to 20 years.

Patents are grants made by the federal government to the inventor of a product or process, bestowing (in the United States) the exclusive right to produce and sell a given product, or use a process, for up to 20 years. After that time, others can manufacture the product or use the process. Suppose a company acquires a newly patented product from an inventor for $170,000. Although the remaining legal life of this patent is 20 years, because of fast-changing technology, the economic life of the patent is only 5 years. The company would amortize the asset over 5 years, the shorter of the economic or legal life, making the annual amortization expense ($170,000 ÷ 5) = $34,000.

copyrights

Exclusive rights to reproduce and sell a book, musical composition, film, or similar creative item.

Copyrights are exclusive rights to reproduce and sell a book, musical composition, film, or similar creative item. In the United States, the federal government issues these rights and provides protection to a company or individual for the life of the creator plus 70 years. The initial costs of obtaining copyrights from the government are nominal; however, a company may pay a large sum to purchase an existing copyright from the owner. For example, a publisher of paperback books will sometimes pay the author of a popular novel in excess of $1 million for the writer's copyright. Although copyrights have a long legal life, their economic lives are frequently significantly shorter.

trademarks

Distinctive identifications of a manufactured product or of a service, taking the form of a name, a sign, a slogan, a logo, or an emblem.

Trademarks are distinctive identifications of a manufactured product or of a service, taking the form of a name, a sign, a slogan, a logo, or an emblem. An example is an emblem for Coca-Cola or the "Intel Inside" logo on many computers. Trademarks, trade names, trade brands, secret formulas, and similar items are property rights with economic lives depending on their estimated length of use. If you look at Coca-Cola's balance sheet you see no accounting recognition of its secret formula. The company did not purchase the formula, rather it was developed internally. As a result, Coca-Cola did not record an asset. In fact, the story is that Coca-Cola chose to keep the formula a secret instead of patenting it because it did not want the patent protection to expire, leaving others free to produce the product. The Coca-Cola balance sheet also does not report an intangible asset for the Coca-Cola trademark, although Coke has spent millions of advertising dollars creating public awareness of the brand and millions more dollars protecting it from infringement. Coca-Cola's balance sheet does show an account entitled Trademarks. What does this account represent? Coca-Cola acquired the trademarks of such companies as *Fanta* and *Minute-Maid*, so it lists them as intangible assets. Similarly, PepsiCo includes a trademark value for *Gatorade* among its intangible assets because it purchased the trademark rights when it bought Quaker Oats Company.

franchises (licenses)

Legal contracts that allow the buyer the right to sell a product or service in accordance with specified conditions.

Franchises and **licenses** are legal contracts that grant the buyer the right to sell a product or service in accordance with specified conditions. An example is a local McDonald's franchise.

The buyer obtains the right to use the McDonald's name, to acquire branded products such as cups and bags, and to share in advertising and special promotions. In exchange, the franchisee promises to follow McDonald's procedures and maintain standards of quality, cleanliness, and pricing. Other private sector companies may award franchises for car dealerships, hotel operations, or gasoline stations. These types of franchise agreements typically have a finite life. While the terms of franchise agreements can differ significantly, most often franchisees capitalize the up-front franchise fee and amortize that fee over its useful life.

Government agencies may grant franchises or operating licenses to a company, awarding it the right to use publicly held property in the operation of its business. Examples include the use of public property for the placement of telephone or electric utility lines, or the use of the airwaves for broadcasting purposes. The lengths of the franchises vary from 1 year to perpetuity. As mentioned previously, one of the factors that determine the accounting for externally acquired intangible assets is whether the asset has a finite or an indefinite life. The FASB used a broadcast license as an explicit example of an intangible asset that might have an indefinite life. Broadcast licenses have a specified legal life but may be renewed indefinitely at a nominal cost to the broadcaster.

A **leasehold** is the right to use a fixed asset (such as a building or some portion thereof) for a specified period of time beyond 1 year. Companies often classify leaseholds with plant assets on the balance sheet, although they are technically intangible assets. A company that owns its own plant clearly counts that plant as a tangible asset. However, if a company leases the plant, then it owns only the right to use the leased plant, not the plant itself. Because the leasehold provides future benefits (in this case, the use of the plant) but does not give the company ownership of the plant, it is an intangible asset. We discuss leases of this type in Chapter 9.

leasehold
The right to use a fixed asset for a specified period of time beyond 1 year.

Related to a leasehold is a **leasehold improvement**, which occurs when a lessee (tenant) spends money to add new materials or improvements to a leased property. These improvements become part of the leased property and revert to the lessor at the end of the lease. A leasehold improvement can take various forms. Examples are the installation of new fixtures, panels, walls, and air-conditioning equipment that the lessee must leave on the premises when a lease expires. Companies generally amortize the costs of leasehold improvements over the life of the lease, even if the physical life of the leasehold improvement is longer. For example, Costco amortizes its leasehold improvements over "the shorter of the useful life or lease term."

leasehold improvement
Investments by a lessee to add new materials or improvements to a leased property that become part of the leased property and revert to the lessor at the end of the lease.

Impairment of Intangible Assets

The U.S. GAAP and IFRS rules governing impairment of finite-life intangible assets are the same as those for long-lived tangible assets discussed on pages 362–364. However, the rules for impairment of indefinite-life intangibles differ slightly from those for tangible assets. U.S. GAAP does not require a recoverability test for indefinite-life intangibles. Rather, a company compares the carrying value of the intangible asset with its fair value. If the carrying value is less than the fair value, no impairment has occurred. If the carrying value is greater than the fair value, the company must recognize an impairment loss equal to the carrying amount less the fair value. Under IFRS, the only difference in impairment accounting for tangible assets and indefinite-life intangibles is that companies must apply the impairment test annually to indefinite-life intangibles, not just when there is an indication that an asset may be impaired.

Goodwill

All of the intangible assets discussed so far are separately identifiable. In other words, they are assets that one company could sell to another. Goodwill is an intangible asset that cannot be separated from the company that owns it and therefore it cannot be sold or transferred. A company can recognize **goodwill** only when it buys another company. Goodwill is the excess of the amount paid for the acquired company over the fair value of its identifiable net assets. We discuss goodwill in more detail in Chapter 11.

Assume that Millard Corporation purchases Tigner Company for a total of $10 million in cash. At the time of the acquisition, Tigner has total assets with a fair value of $19 million and total liabilities with a fair value of $13 million. Therefore, the fair value of the assets less the liabilities of Tigner is $6 million. Nevertheless, Millard has agreed to pay $10 million for Tigner.

OBJECTIVE 12
Explain the reporting for goodwill.

goodwill
The excess of the amount paid for an acquired company over the fair value of its identifiable net assets.

Chapter 11 discusses the reasons why one company might pay a premium for another and how it would allocate the purchase price to various assets and liabilities. In our example, Millard accounts for the business combination with a summary journal entry that looks like this (in millions of dollars):

Goodwill	4	
Total assets of Tigner	19	
Total liabilities of Tigner		13
Cash		10

Millard records goodwill as a noncurrent asset on its books.

Companies do not amortize goodwill. However, they must review goodwill for impairment annually or whenever events or circumstances suggest the possibility of impairment. As an example, the credit crisis of 2008–2009 certainly qualifies as an event suggesting the need for impairment review by many companies. The details of the goodwill impairment test are beyond the scope of this textbook. However, if a company determines that the goodwill is not worth its carrying value, the company must write down the goodwill to its current fair value, which in some cases might be zero. The Business First box gives an example of goodwill and other long-lived asset impairments.

Depletion of Natural Resources

OBJECTIVE 13

Interpret the depletion of natural resources.

Our final group of long-lived assets is natural resources, such as minerals, oil, and timber (sometimes called wasting assets). Depletion is the accounting mechanism used to allocate the acquisition cost of natural resources over time. Depletion differs from depreciation because depletion focuses specifically on the physical use and exhaustion of the natural resources, whereas depreciation focuses more broadly on any reduction of the economic value of a fixed asset, including physical deterioration and obsolescence.

Accountants usually classify the costs of natural resources as noncurrent assets. However, buying natural resources is actually like buying massive quantities of inventories under the ground (iron ore) or above the ground (timber). Depletion expense is the measure of the portion of this "long-term inventory" that a company uses up in a particular period. For example, a coal mine may have a total cost of $20 million and originally contain an estimated 1 million tons of usable coal. The depletion rate would be ($20 million ÷ 1 million tons) = $20 per ton. If the company mined 100,000 tons during the first year, the depletion expense would be (100,000 × $20), or $2 million for that year. Each year the company would measure the amount of coal extracted and record the amount of depletion based on that usage.

As our coal mine example shows, companies measure depletion on a units-of-production basis. They may directly reduce the asset account, or they may accumulate depletion in a separate contra account similar to accumulated depreciation. Environmental laws and ethical responsibility often lead a firm to expend substantial amounts to return the site to a safe and attractive condition after exhausting the natural resources. When calculating the depletion per unit, companies add these expected future costs when computing the total costs subject to depletion. Therefore, the depletion per unit includes not only the original cost of the resources, but also future restoration costs. The companies add the portion of depletion that represents future costs for site restoration to a Liability for Restoration account that grows as extraction continues.

BUSINESS FIRST

IMPACT OF ASSET IMPAIRMENTS

Office Max, Inc. is one of the largest office products retailers in North America. Office Max retail stores offer name-brand and private-label products from paper and pens to office furniture and computer equipment. Office Max also has a contract division that sells directly to business and government customers. The economic downturn hurt sales in both the retail and contract segments, with 2008 sales down almost 9% from 2007, and the company expected sales to continue to drop in 2009. U.S. GAAP requires that companies test the carrying value of goodwill, intangible assets, and other long-lived assets for impairment whenever circumstances indicate that impairment may exist. The recession and credit crisis of 2008–2009 resulted in such circumstances for Office Max as well as companies in all sectors of the U.S. economy.

Office Max typically performs its long-lived asset impairment reviews on January 1. However, during the second quarter of 2008 and again in the fourth quarter, Office Max management concluded that circumstances warranted interim impairment reviews. The circumstances leading to this conclusion included generally weak economic conditions, increasing unemployment,

a decline in actual results and forecasted operating performance for the company, continued tightening of the credit markets, lower levels of consumer and business spending, intense competition, and a decline in the company's market capitalization relative to the book value of its equity.

When the dust settled at fiscal year-end December 27, 2008, the income statement of Office Max reflected a net loss of $1,662 million on sales of $8,267 million. The income statement included a line item for "Goodwill and other asset impairments" totaling $2,100 million or 25.4% of sales! The footnotes provided information on what comprised this large impairment charge. Office Max attributed almost $736 million of the charge to the impairment of a financial asset, Timber Notes Receivable, as the result of the bankruptcy of Lehman Brothers. The company attributed the remaining $1,364 million impairment to intangible and fixed assets, primarily goodwill. The following table ($ in millions) details the composition of the intangible and fixed asset impairment loss and reflects the magnitude of the impairment loss relative to the underlying asset account.

Asset Account	Balance at 12/29/07	Balance at 12/27/08	Impairment Loss	Impairment Loss as a % of Beginning Asset Balance
Goodwill	$1,217	$ 0	$1,201	98.7%*
Trade names	$ 173	$ 66	$ 107	61.9%
Fixed assets, net	$ 581	$ 491	$ 56	9.6%
Total assets	$6,284	$4,174	$1,364	21.7%

*Not equal to 100% due to a reduction in goodwill associated with the effects of foreign currency translation adjustments.

Office Max was not alone in recording large impairment charges in 2008. The companies in the table below experienced significant pretax goodwill and intangible asset impairment charges in 2008.

U.S. companies reporting under U.S. GAAP were not the only companies facing impairment losses in 2008. Consider the following companies who report

under IFRS. Royal Philips Electronics recorded goodwill impairment of €301 million. Ciba, the Swiss chemical company acquired by BASF in 2009, recognized goodwill impairment of 590 million Swiss francs. And Alcatel-Lucent, headquartered in France, reported impairment equal to almost $5 billion in U.S. dollars.

Company	Goodwill and Intangible Asset Impairment Loss	Impairment Loss as a Percentage of Beginning Balance in Goodwill and Intangible Assets
Citigroup	$10.773 billion	16.9%
Time Warner	$24.168 billion	25.7%
CBS	$14.182 billion	49.7%
Macy's	$ 5.6 billion	56.0%

Sources: http://investor.officemax.com/phoenix.zhtml?c=85171&p=irol-sec; http://files.shareholder.com/downloads/TWX/643500380x0xS950144-09-1481/1105705/filing.pdf; www.macysinc.com/Investors/vote/2009_ar.pdf; www.citigroup.com/citi/fin/data/ar08c_en.pdf; www.cbscorporation.com/investors/form_10k/index.php; www.philips.com/shared/assets/Downloadablefile/Investor/Philips2008_AnnualReport.pdf; www.ciba.com/2008-ciba-annualreport.pdf; www.alcatellucent.com/wps/portal/!ut/p/kcxml/ 04_Sj9SPykssy0xPLMnMz0vM0Y_QjzKLd4x3MQ3VL8h2VAQAgjIFVg!!; SFAS 142, "Goodwill and Other Intangible Assets"; SFAS 144, "Accounting for the Impairment or Disposal of Long-Lived Assets."

Highlights to Remember

1 Distinguish a company's expenses from expenditures that it should capitalize. Accountants must choose between capitalizing or expensing each expenditure. They should capitalize expenditures that meet the criteria for asset recognition and should expense the others. Capitalized items that provide benefits for multiple periods are considered long-lived assets.

2 Measure the acquisition cost of tangible assets such as land, buildings, and equipment. The acquisition cost includes both an asset's purchase price and all incidental costs necessary to get it ready for its intended use.

3 Compute depreciation for buildings and equipment using various depreciation methods. Depreciation is a systematic allocation of historical cost over the useful life of the asset. Three common depreciation methods discussed in the text are straight-line, DDB, and units-of-production depreciation. The straight-line method results in a constant amount of depreciation expense per year of use. We calculate it by dividing depreciable value (original historical cost less residual value) by the shorter of the physical life or the economic life. DDB is a declining-balance method that records the largest annual depreciation expense in the first full year of use and declining amounts thereafter. The annual depreciation charge is a percentage of the book value at the beginning of the year. For DDB the percentage is twice the percentage used for straight-line, that is, $2 \times (100\% \div \text{years of life})$. Units-of-production depreciation is based on the physical use of the asset, for example miles driven for a vehicle. The cost per unit is the depreciable value divided by the estimated units of use from the asset. We multiply this cost per unit by the actual units of use to determine the annual depreciation.

4 Recalculate depreciation in response to a change in estimated useful life or residual value. New information may cause the initial estimate of useful life or residual value to be revised. If the use of the new estimate would result in a significant change in depreciation expense, the new estimate must be adopted and the depreciation schedule revised. A change in estimate is treated as a prospective adjustment. The company does not go back and revise the depreciation expense taken in prior periods. Rather, the company recomputes depreciation expense for the period in which it revises the estimate and all future periods.

5 Differentiate financial statement depreciation from income tax depreciation. Financial reports to shareholders and filings with the SEC often differ from the reports filed with the tax authorities. Rules governing financial statement presentation produce information useful to investors and managers. Tax rules governing determination of tax obligations achieve political and economic goals and give taxpayers the right to make certain choices with an eye for maximizing expenses and therefore minimizing the tax obligation. Therefore, companies keep two sets of records to satisfy these two purposes.

6 Explain the effect of depreciation on cash flow. By itself, depreciation does not provide cash. However, companies deduct depreciation for income tax purposes. Therefore, the larger the depreciation reported on the tax return in any given year, the lower the annual pretax income and the lower the amount of taxes a company pays the taxing authorities. By paying less in taxes a company retains a greater amount of cash.

7 Account for expenditures after acquisition. Companies should immediately expense any expenditures that represent routine repairs or maintenance of fixed assets. In contrast, they should capitalize improvements that increase the future benefits provided by a fixed asset, adding the amount to the value of the asset.

8 Compute gains and losses on the disposal of fixed assets and consider the impact of these gains and losses on the statement of cash flows. Gains and losses on disposal of fixed assets arise because the proceeds of the sale are not identical to the book value of the asset sold (original historical cost less accumulated depreciation). If the proceeds exceed the book value, the company realizes a gain on its income statement. If the proceeds are less, it records a loss. On the statement of cash flows, the cash proceeds from sales of fixed assets constitute cash provided by investing activities. Under the direct method, the sale of fixed assets has no effect on the calculation of cash flows from operations. When calculating cash flow from operations using the indirect method, the starting point is net income, which includes any gains or losses from asset sales. To adjust net income in calculating net cash provided by operating activities, we subtract gains from, or add losses to, net income.

9 **Determine the balance sheet valuation of tangible assets for companies who use the revaluation method allowed under IFRS.** IFRS permits the revaluation of fixed assets to fair value. Under IFRS, companies can revalue fixed assets to fair value regardless of whether fair value is higher or lower than the carrying value of the assets. Assets accounted for under the revaluation method do not depreciate.

10 **Account for the impairment of tangible assets.** Events or circumstances may arise that cause an asset to have an economic value to the company that is smaller than the carrying value of that asset. The FASB has implemented a two-step process to test for the impairment of tangible assets. The first step is a recoverability test, which compares the total expected future net cash flows from the asset and its eventual disposition to the carrying value of the asset. If the carrying value is greater than the future cash flows, the asset is considered to be impaired. If the assets are held for use, the impairment loss is the amount by which the carrying value of the asset exceeds its fair value. If the assets are held for resale purposes, the impairment loss is the amount by which the carrying value of the asset exceeds its fair value less the cost to sell. IFRS employs an impairment test that requires an asset to be recognized at the lower of its net book value or its recoverable amount.

11 **Account for intangible assets, including impairment.** Intangible assets are not physical in nature. Instead, they are legal or contractual rights. Examples include patents, trademarks, and copyrights. Companies capitalize such assets when purchased from external parties. Some purchased intangibles have finite lives. Companies amortize these intangibles over their useful lives. The unamortized book value appears on the balance sheet as an asset. Other purchased intangible assets have indefinite lives. Companies do not amortize indefinite-life intangibles. However, companies review all recorded intangibles for impairment and must write them down if their fair value is less than their book value. Companies do not capitalize internally created intangible assets. Instead, they expense such outlays as incurred.

12 **Explain the reporting for goodwill.** Goodwill is an intangible asset measured as the excess of the purchase price of an acquired company over the fair value of its identifiable net assets. Companies do not amortize goodwill but must write it down when they deem its value to be impaired.

13 **Interpret the depletion of natural resources.** Depletion refers to the accounting process for allocating the cost of natural resources over the periods of extraction. Companies typically use the units-of-production method to allocate the cost of acquiring natural resources. In some cases, companies expect to incur future costs to mitigate environmental damage and return the site to an acceptable condition. Accountants estimate these future costs and include them in the annual depletion charges to appropriately match the full cost to the revenues generated over time.

Accounting Vocabulary

accelerated depreciation, p. 351
activity method, p. 351
amortization, p. 345
basket purchase, p. 348
betterment, p. 357
capital improvement, p. 357
capitalize, p. 345
copyrights, p. 366
depletion, p. 345
depreciable value, p. 349
depreciation schedule, p. 350
disposal value, p. 349
double-declining-balance (DDB) method, p. 351
expenditures, p. 345
fair value, p. 348

fixed assets, p. 345
franchises, p. 366
goodwill, p. 367
impaired, p. 362
improvement, p. 357
intangible assets, p. 345
leasehold, p. 367
leasehold improvement, p. 367
licenses, p. 366
lump-sum purchase, p. 348
maintenance, p. 357
Modified Accelerated Cost Recovery System (MACRS), p. 354
monetary assets, p. 348
nonmonetary assets, p. 348

patents, p. 366
plant assets, p. 345
recoverability test, p. 362
recoverable amount, p. 363
repairs, p. 357
residual value, p. 349
salvage value, p. 349
scrap value, p. 349
straight-line depreciation, p. 350
tangible assets, p. 345
terminal value, p. 349
trademarks, p. 366
units-of-production depreciation, p. 351
useful life, p. 349

MyAccountingLab

Assignment Material

Questions

8-1 Distinguish between *tangible* and *intangible assets*.

8-2 Distinguish among *amortization*, *depreciation*, and *depletion*.

8-3 "The cash discount on the purchase of equipment is income to the buyer during the year of acquisition." Do you agree? Explain.

8-4 Many companies expense all expenditures that are less than a predetermined dollar amount. What is the justification for this policy?

8-5 "When an expenditure is capitalized, we credit the stockholders' equity account." Do you agree? Explain.

8-6 "Accumulated depreciation is a sum of cash being accumulated for the replacement of fixed assets." Do you agree? Explain.

8-7 "The accounting process of depreciation is allocation, not valuation." Explain.

8-8 Criticize the following statement: "Depreciation is the loss in value of a fixed asset over a given span of time."

8-9 "Keeping two sets of books is immoral and unnecessary." Do you agree? Explain.

8-10 "Accelerated depreciation saves cash but shows lower net income." Explain.

8-11 "A change in the estimated useful life of a fixed asset requires restatement of depreciation expense in prior periods." Do you agree? Explain.

8-12 Contrast repairs and maintenance expenditures with expenditures for capital improvements or betterments.

8-13 The manager of a division reported to the president of the company, "Now that our major capital improvements are finished, the division's expenses will be much lower." Is this really what this manager means to say? Explain.

8-14 What determines the gain or loss on the sale of fixed assets?

8-15 Name and describe four kinds of intangible assets.

8-16 "We account for internally acquired patents differently than we account for externally acquired patents." Explain the difference.

8-17 "Accountants cannot capitalize improvements made to leased property by a tenant because the improvements become part of the leased property and therefore belong to the lessor." Do you agree? Explain.

8-18 XYZ Company's only transaction in 20X1 was the sale of a fixed asset for $20,000 cash. The income statement included only "Gain on sale of fixed asset, $5,000." Correct the following statement of cash flows.

Cash flows from operating activities	
Gain on sale of fixed assets	$ 5,000
Cash flows from investing activities	
Proceeds from sale of fixed assets	20,000
Total increase in cash	$25,000

8-19 The Lawrence Company sold fixed assets with a book value of $8,000 and recorded a gain of $6,000. How should the company report this on the statement of cash flows prepared using the indirect method?

8-20 "In a basket purchase, all assets that are part of the purchase must be depreciated over the same useful lives." Do you agree? Explain.

8-21 "The recoverability test determines the magnitude of the impairment loss on a piece of equipment used in the manufacturing process." Do you agree? Explain.

8-22 Under IFRS, how would a company record the revaluation of fixed assets to reflect an increase in fair value?

8-23 How do U.S. GAAP and IFRS differ with regard to accounting for the impairment of fixed assets held for use?

Critical Thinking Questions

8-24 Production Facilities and Depreciation

A manager in a company reporting under U.S. GAAP complained about the amount of depreciation charged on the plant for which she was responsible: "The market value of my plant just continues to increase, yet I am hit with large depreciation charges on my income statement and the value of my plant and equipment on the balance sheet goes down each year. This doesn't seem fair." Comment on this statement, focusing on the relation of asset values on the balance sheet to market values of the assets.

8-25 Research and Development and the Recognition of Intangible Assets
In the United States, expenditures for most R&D are charged directly to expense. Under IFRS, companies recognize development costs as assets when it is likely that the resultant future economic benefits will cover the development costs. Suppose you are manager of an R&D department. Which method of accounting for R&D would be most consistent with the information you use for decision making? Explain.

8-26 Capital Investment and the Statement of Cash Flows
Growing companies often need capital to purchase or build additional facilities. There are many potential sources of such capital. Describe how an investor might use the statement of cash flows to learn how a company financed its capital expansion.

8-27 Accounting Valuation of Fixed Assets
Consider two types of assets held by IBM: land purchased in 1912 when the company was known as the Computing-Tabulating-Recording Company, and machinery purchased and installed at its manufacturing plant in 2009. How close do you suppose the December 31, 2010, balance sheet value of each asset is to the fair value of the asset at that date, assuming the company uses U.S. GAAP? What if IBM uses IFRS?

Exercises

8-28 Computing Acquisition Costs
On January 1, 20X2, Edmonton University acquired a 20-acre parcel of land immediately adjacent to its existing facilities. The land included a warehouse, parking lots, and driveways. The university paid $600,000 cash and also gave a note for $3 million, payable at $300,000 per year plus interest of 10% on the outstanding balance.

The university demolished the warehouse at a cash cost of $150,000 so it could be replaced with a new classroom building. For construction of the building, the university made a cash down payment of $3 million and gave a mortgage note of $7 million. The mortgage was payable at $250,000 per year plus interest of 10% on the outstanding balance.

1. Calculate the cost that Edmonton University should add to its Land account and its Building account.
2. Prepare journal entries (without explanations) to record the preceding transactions.

8-29 Government Equipment: Computing Acquisition Costs
An office of the IRS acquired some used computer equipment. Installation costs were $10,000. Repair costs prior to use were $11,000. The purchasing manager, with a salary of $56,000 per annum, spent 1 month evaluating equipment and completing the transaction. The invoice price was $400,000. The seller paid its salesman a commission of 5% and offered the buyer a cash discount of 2% if the invoice was paid within 60 days. Freight costs were $6,400, paid by the purchaser. Repairs during the first year of use were $12,000.

Compute the total capitalized cost to be added to the Equipment account. The seller was paid within 60 days.

8-30 Basket Purchase
On February 21, 20X2, Speed-Tune, an auto service chain, acquired an existing building and land for $920,000 from a local gas station that had failed. The tax assessor had placed an assessed valuation of $200,000 on the land and $600,000 on the building as of January 1, 20X2.

Land	$200,000
Building	600,000
Total	$800,000

How much of the $920,000 purchase price should be attributed to the building? Why?

8-31 Journal Entries for Depreciation

(Alternates are 8-32 and 8-33.) On January 1, 20X1, the Dayton Auto Parts Company acquired nine identical assembly robots for a total of $594,000 cash. The robots had an expected useful life of 10 years and an expected residual value of $54,000 in total. Dayton uses straight-line depreciation.

1. Set up T-accounts and prepare the journal entries for the acquisition and for the first annual depreciation charge. Post to T-accounts.
2. On December 31, 20X3, Dayton sold one of the robots for $38,000 in cash. The robot had an original cost of $66,000 and an expected residual value of $6,000. Prepare the journal entry for the sale.
3. Refer to requirement 2. Suppose Dayton had sold the robot for $60,000 cash instead of $38,000. Prepare the journal entry for the sale.

8-32 Journal Entries for Depreciation

(Alternates are 8-31 and 8-33.) The **Alaska Airlines** balance sheet dated June 30, 2008, included the following ($ in millions):

Property and equipment	
Aircraft and other flight equipment	$3,431.0
Other property and equipment	608.6
Deposits for future flight equipment	309.8
Less: Accumulated depreciation and amortization	1,181.7
Net property and equipment	$3,167.7

Assume that on July 1, 2008, Alaska acquired some new maintenance equipment for $880,000 cash. The equipment had an expected useful life of 5 years and an expected residual value of $80,000. Alaska uses straight-line depreciation.

1. Prepare the journal entry that would be made annually for depreciation on the new equipment.
2. Suppose Alaska sold some of the equipment it originally purchased on July 1, 2008. The equipment being sold had an original cost of $330,000 and an expected residual value of $30,000. Alaska sold the equipment for $230,000 cash 2 years after the purchase date. Prepare the journal entry for the sale.
3. Refer to requirement 2. Suppose Alaska had sold the equipment for $200,000 cash, instead of $230,000. Prepare the journal entry for the sale.

8-33 Journal Entries for Depreciation

(Alternates are 8-31 and 8-32.) **The Coca-Cola Company**'s balance sheet of December 31, 2008, included the following ($ in millions):

Property, plant, and equipment	$14,400
Less: Accumulated depreciation	6,074
	$ 8,326

Assume that on January 1, 2009, Coca-Cola acquired some new bottling equipment for $1.6 million cash. The equipment had an expected useful life of 4 years and an expected residual value of $400,000. Coca-Cola uses straight-line depreciation.

1. Prepare the journal entry that Coca-Cola would make annually for depreciation on the new equipment.
2. Suppose Coca-Cola sold some of the equipment it had purchased on January 1, 2009. The equipment being sold had an original cost of $60,000 and an expected residual value of $15,000. Coca-Cola sold the equipment for $32,000 cash 2 years after the purchase date. Prepare the journal entry for the sale

3. Refer to requirement 2. Suppose Coca-Cola had sold the equipment for $41,000 cash, instead of $32,000. Prepare the journal entry for the sale.

8-34 Simple Depreciation Computations

A company acquired the following assets:

a. Conveyor, 5-year useful life, $38,000 cost, straight-line method, $5,000 expected residual value
b. Truck, 3-year useful life, $18,000 cost, DDB method, $1,500 expected residual value

Compute the first 3 years of depreciation for each asset.

8-35 Units-of-Production Depreciation Method

The Rockland Transport Company has many trucks that have an estimated useful life of 200,000 miles. The company computes depreciation on a mileage basis. Suppose Rockland purchases a new truck for $80,000 cash. Its expected residual value is $8,000. Its mileage during year 1 is 60,000 and during year 2 is 90,000.

1. What is the depreciation expense for each of the 2 years?
2. Compute the gain or loss if Rockland sells the truck for $30,000 at the end of year two.

8-36 Fundamental Depreciation Approaches

(Alternates are 8-37 through 8-39.) U-Haul acquired new trucks for $1.2 million. Their estimated useful life is 4 years, and estimated residual value is $200,000.

Prepare a depreciation schedule similar to Exhibit 8-2, p. 352 comparing straight-line and DDB depreciation.

8-37 Units-of-Production, Straight-Line, and DDB

(Alternatives are 8-36, 8-38, and 8-39.) Yukon Mining Company buys special drills for $640,000 each. Each drill can extract about 125,000 tons of ore, after which it has a $40,000 residual value. Yukon bought one such drill in early January 20X1. Projected tonnage figures for the drill are 60,000 tons in 20X1, 45,000 tons in 20X2, and 20,000 tons in 20X3. The drill is scheduled for sale at the end of the third year at the $40,000 residual value. Yukon is considering units-of-production, straight-line, or DDB depreciation for the drill.

Compute depreciation for each year under each of the three methods.

8-38 Comparison of Popular Depreciation Methods

(Alternates are 8-36, 8-37, and 8-39.) Port Angeles Cedar Company acquired a saw for $32,000 with an expected useful life of 5 years and a $2,000 expected residual value. Prepare a tabular comparison (similar to Exhibit 8-2, p. 352) of the annual depreciation and book value for each year under straight-line and DDB depreciation. If these two methods were available for tax reporting purposes, which would a company prefer to use?

8-39 Fundamental Depreciation Policies

(Alternates are 8-36 through 8-38.) Suppose the printing department of Safeco Insurance acquired a new press for $280,000. The equipment's estimated useful life is 8 years and estimated residual value is $40,000.

Prepare a depreciation schedule similar to Exhibit 8-2, p. 352, comparing straight-line and DDB depreciation. Show all amounts in thousands of dollars (rounded to the nearest tenth). Limit the schedule to the first 3 years of useful life. Show the depreciation for each year and the book value at the end of each year.

8-40 Accumulated Depreciation

Ceradyne, Inc., reported the following items on its December 31, 2008, balance sheet ($ in thousands):

Property, plant, and equipment, net	$251,928
Accumulated depreciation	113,227

1. Compute Ceradyne's historical cost of property, plant, and equipment on December 31, 2008.
2. If Ceradyne uses a 12-year economic life for computing straight-line depreciation on most of its assets, are most of its assets more than or less than 5 years old? Explain how you can determine this.

8-41 Revision of Useful Life and Residual Value Estimates

Nowling Company buys a machine for $75,000 on January 1, 2010. A residual value of $5,000 and a useful life of 10 years are estimated at the acquisition date. Nowling uses straight-line depreciation. Early in 2014, Nowling discovers that a competitor has come out with a new product that will reduce demand for Nowling's product. As a result, it estimates that the machine will no longer be of use after 2016. Nowling believes it will be able to sell the machine to a scrap dealer for $2,000 at that time.

Prepare a depreciation schedule similar to Exhibit 8-2, p. 352 comparing the original depreciation schedule (for 2010–2019) with the depreciation schedule based on the revised estimates of useful life and residual value (for 2010–2016). Show all amounts in thousands of dollars (rounded to the nearest tenth).

8-42 Depreciation, Income Taxes, and Cash Flow

Fleck Company began business with cash and common stockholders' equity of $150,000. The same day, December 31, 20X1, the company acquired equipment for $50,000 cash. The equipment had an expected useful life of 5 years and an expected residual value of $5,000. The first year's operations generated cash sales of $180,000 and cash operating expenses of $100,000.

1. Prepare an analysis of income and cash flow for the year 20X2, using the format illustrated in Exhibit 8-3 (p. 355). Assume (a) straight-line depreciation and (b) DDB depreciation. Assume an income tax rate of 40%. Fleck pays income taxes in cash. The company uses the same depreciation method for reporting to shareholders and to income tax authorities.
2. Examine your answer to requirement 1. Does depreciation provide cash? Explain as precisely as possible.
3. Suppose Fleck doubled its 20X2 depreciation under straight-line and DDB methods. How would this affect the before-tax cash flow? Be specific.

8-43 MACRS Versus Straight-Line Depreciation

Chicago Machinery bought special tooling equipment for $2.6 million. The useful life is 5 years, with no residual value. For tax purposes, assume MACRS specifies a 3-year, DDB depreciation schedule. Chicago Machinery uses the straight-line depreciation method for reporting to shareholders.

1. Explain the two factors that account for the acceleration of depreciation for tax purposes.
2. Compute the first year's depreciation (a) for shareholder reporting and (b) for tax purposes. (Ignore complications in the tax law that are not introduced in this chapter.)

8-44 Leasehold Improvements

Pizza Hut has a 10-year lease on space in a suburban shopping center. Near the end of the sixth year of the lease, Pizza Hut exercised its rights under the lease, removing walls and replacing floor coverings and lighting fixtures. Pizza Hut would not be able to remove these improvements at the end of the lease term. The cost was $120,000. The useful life of the redesigned facilities was predicted to be 12 years.

What accounts would be affected by the $120,000 expenditure? What would be the annual amortization?

8-45 Capital Expenditures

Consider the following transactions:

a. Acquired building for a down payment plus a mortgage payable
b. Paid delinquent real estate taxes on building acquired
c. Acquired new air-conditioning system for the building
d. Paid interest on building mortgage
e. Paid principal on building mortgage

f. Paid cash dividends
g. Paid travel expenses of sales personnel
h. Paid janitorial wages
i. Paid security guard's wages

Required
Answer the following by letter:

1. Indicate which transactions are capital expenditures.
2. Indicate which transactions are expenses in the current year.

8-46 Capital Expenditures

Consider each of the following transactions. For each one, indicate whether it is a capital expenditure (C) or an expense in the current year (E).

a. Paid a consultant to advise on marketing strategy
b. Installed new lighting fixtures in a leased building
c. Paid for routine maintenance on equipment
d. Developed a patent that cost $50,000 in R&D
e. Paid for overhaul of machinery that extends its useful life
f. Acquired a patent from General Electric for $40,000
g. Paid for a tune-up on one of the autos in the company's fleet

8-47 Repairs and Improvements

Yakima Wheat Company acquired harvesting equipment for $90,000 with an expected useful life of 5 years and a $10,000 expected residual value. Yakima Wheat used straight-line depreciation. During its fourth year of service, expenditures related to the equipment were as follows:

1. Oiling and greasing, $200.
2. Replacing belts and hoses, $450.
3. Major overhaul during the final week of the year, including the replacement of an engine. The useful life of the equipment was extended from 5 to 8 years. The cost was $31,000. The residual value is now expected to be $11,000, instead of $10,000.

Indicate in words how each of the three items would affect the income statement and the balance sheet in the fourth year. Prepare a tabulation that compares the original depreciation schedule with the revised depreciation schedule.

8-48 Disposal of Equipment

The Outpatient Clinic of Eastside Hospital acquired X-ray equipment for $29,000 with an expected useful life of 5 years and a $4,000 expected residual value. The hospital uses straight-line depreciation. The clinic sold the equipment at the end of the fourth year for $12,000 cash.

1. Compute the gain or loss on the sale. Show the effects of the sale on the balance sheet equation, identifying all specific accounts by name. Where and how would the sale appear on the income statement?
2. (a) Show the journal entry for the transaction in requirement 1. (b) Repeat 2a, assuming that the cash sales price was $8,000 instead of $12,000.

8-49 Gain or Loss on Sale of Fixed Assets

Luigi's Pizza Company purchased a delivery van in early 20X1 for $45,000 and depreciated it on a straight-line basis over its useful life of 5 years. Estimated residual value was $5,000. The company sold the van in early 20X4 after recognizing 3 years of depreciation.

1. Suppose Luigi's Pizza received $27,000 cash for the van. Compute the gain or loss on the sale. Prepare the journal entry for the sale of the van.
2. Suppose Luigi's Pizza received $14,000 cash for the van. Compute the gain or loss on the sale. Prepare the journal entry for the sale of the van.

8-50 Gain or Loss on Disposal of Equipment—Cash Flow Implications

Icarus Software Company sold five computers. It had purchased the computers 5 years ago for $120,000, and accumulated depreciation at the time of sale was $90,000.

1. Suppose Icarus received $30,000 cash for the computers. How would the company show the sale on its statement of cash flows?
2. Suppose Icarus received $40,000 cash for the computers. How would the company show the sale on its statement of cash flows (including the schedule reconciling net income and net cash provided by operating activities).
3. Redo requirement 2 assuming cash received was $20,000.

8-51 Various Intangible Assets and Impairment

(Alternative is 8-52.) Consider the following:

1. On December 29, 20X1, a publisher acquires the paperback copyright for a book by Steven King for $3 million. Most sales of this book are expected to take place uniformly during 20X2 and 20X3. What is the amortization for 20X2?
2. In 20X1, Company C spent $6 million in its research department, which resulted in new valuable patents. In late December 20X1, Company D paid $6 million to an outside inventor for some valuable new patents. Under U.S. GAAP, how would the income statements for the year ended December 31, 20X1, for each company be affected? How would the balance sheets as of December 31, 20X1, be affected?
3. On December 28, 20X8, Black Electronics Company purchased a patent for a piece of equipment for $500,000. The patent has 10 years of its legal life remaining. Technology changes fast, so Black Electronics expects the patent to be worthless in 5 years. What is the amortization for 20X9?
4. (a) During the fiscal year ending December 31, 20X3, Samela Corporation paid $12 million in cash for Haddock Company. At the time of the acquisition, the total assets of Haddock had a fair value of $22 million and the total liabilities had a fair market value of $15 million. What journal entry would Samela Corporation make to record the acquisition of Haddock? (b) On December 31, 20X4, Samela Corporation performed a review to determine if the goodwill recorded in the initial transaction had become impaired. The review indicated that the fair value of the goodwill was $3 million. Does Samela need to make a journal entry to recognize the impairment of goodwill? If so, prepare the entry.

8-52 Various Intangible Assets

(Alternative is 8-51.) Consider the following:

1. On December 31, 2010, Sony Corporation purchased a patent on some broadcasting equipment for $800,000. The patent has 16 years of its legal life remaining. Because technology moves rapidly, Sony expects the patent to be worthless at the end of 8 years. What is the amortization for 2011?
2. Consider alternative scenarios (a) and (b).
   a. Genentech, a biotech firm with over $13 billion in revenues, spent $2,800 million in its research departments in 2008. These expenditures resulted in valuable new patents.
   b. Suppose that in late December 2008, Genentech had paid $2,800 million to various outside companies for the same new patents.
   How would alternatives (a) and (b) affect Genentech's income statement for the year ended December 31, 2008? How would they affect Genentech's balance sheet on December 31, 2008?
3. Analogic Corporation included $2.319 million of software as an asset on its 2008 balance sheet. The notes indicated that "Software development costs incurred subsequent to establishing technological feasibility through general release of the software products are capitalized. Technological feasibility is demonstrated by the completion of a detailed program design. Capitalized costs are amortized on a straight-line basis over the economic lives of the related products, generally three years." Suppose that Analogic spends the same amount on this activity every year. How would the income statement and balance sheet change if Analogic

changed the estimated economic life from 3 years to 4 years and then amortized every dollar of capitalized software over 4 years?

8-53 IFRS Revaluation of Fixed Assets

Bauer Corporation prepares financial statements using IFRS and has elected the revaluation method of accounting for its fixed assets. Bauer has a December 31 fiscal year end and revalues its fixed assets at the end of each fiscal year. On January 1, 2008, the company purchased land at a cost of €200,000. Consider the two alternative scenarios that follow:

1. The fair value of the land at December 31, 2008, was €185,000. By December 31, 2009, the fair value of the land had increased to €230,000. What is the financial statement impact of revaluation for the year ended December 31, 2008? December 31, 2009?
2. The fair value of the land at December 31, 2008 was €250,000. By December 31, 2009, the fair value of the land had decreased to €175,000. What is the financial statement impact of revaluation for the year ended December 31, 2008? December 31, 2009?

8-54 Computation of Impairment on Long-Lived Assets

Vincent Corporation acquired an office building that it rents to a variety of small businesses. The building had an original cost of $15 million, and at the end of 20X5 it had a net book value of $11 million. Due to a change in zoning regulations effective January 20X6, Vincent believes the building has become less desirable and expects rental rates to decline. The company estimates that the fair market value of the building has decreased from $19 million to $7.5 million as a result of the zoning change. Vincent deems it necessary to review the building for possible impairment.

1. Suppose that the undiscounted expected future net cash flows from the use of the building plus its eventual disposal value are estimated to be $9 million. Compute the amount of the impairment loss, if any, that Vincent should recognize on the building, assuming that Vincent prepares its financial statements using U.S. GAAP.
2. Now assume that Vincent uses IFRS. Vincent has elected historical cost as the basis of valuing its fixed assets and carries the building at a net book value of $11 million. The undiscounted expected future net cash flows are estimated to be $9 million and the present value of these cash flows is $7.4 million. Vincent estimates that if it were to sell the building, it would incur a selling cost of $0.1 million. Compute the impairment loss, if any, that Vincent should recognize on the building.

8-55 Depletion

A zinc mine contains an estimated 1,000,000 tons of zinc ore. The mine cost $14.4 million. The tonnage mined during 20X1, the first year of operations, was 150,000 tons.

1. What was the depletion for 20X1?
2. Suppose that in 20X2 a total of 120,000 tons were mined. What depletion expense would be charged for 20X2?

Problems

8-56 Popular Depreciation Methods

The annual report of Alaska Airlines contained the following footnote:

> *PROPERTY, EQUIPMENT, AND DEPRECIATION—Property and equipment are recorded at cost and depreciated using the straight-line method over the estimated useful lives, which are as follows:*

Aircraft and other flight equipment	15–20 years
Buildings	25–30 years
Minor building and land improvements	Shorter of lease term or estimated useful life
Computer hardware and software	3–5 years
Other furniture and equipment	5–10 years

Consider a Boeing 737-100 airplane that Alaska acquired for $30 million. Its useful life is 20 years, and its expected residual value is $6 million. Prepare a tabular comparison of the annual depreciation and book value for each of the first 3 years of service life under straight-line and DDB depreciation. Show all amounts in thousands of dollars (rounded to the nearest thousand). (Note that this is a comparison of methods used for reporting to shareholders. Such methods may differ from those used for reporting to the income tax authorities.) *Hint*: See Exhibit 8-2 on page 352.

8-57 Depreciation Practices

The annual report of General Mills, maker of *Wheaties, Cheerios,* and *Betty Crocker* baking products, for the year ended May 25, 2008, contained the following ($ in millions):

	May 25, 2008	May 27, 2007
Total land, buildings, and equipment	$6,471.3	$6,095.7
Less: Accumulated depreciation	3,363.2	3,081.8
Net land, buildings, and equipment	$3,108.1	$3,013.9

During fiscal 2008, depreciation expense was $459.2 million, and General Mills acquired land, buildings, and equipment worth $622 million. Assume that no gain or loss arose from the disposition of land, buildings, and equipment and that General Mills received cash of $68.6 million from such disposals.

Compute (1) the gross amount of assets written off (sold or retired), (2) the amount of accumulated depreciation associated with the assets sold or retired, and (3) the book value of the assets sold or retired. *Hint*: The use of T-accounts may help your analysis.

8-58 Depreciation

Asahi Kasei Corporation has sales nearly the equivalent of $10 billion U.S. dollars. The company included the following in its balance sheet (¥ in millions):

Property, plant, and equipment, net of accumulated depreciation	
Buildings	¥159,951
Machinery and equipment	165,220
Land	54,096
Construction in progress	29,339
Other	15,588
Total property, plant, and equipment	¥424,194

Footnote 8 contains the following:

Accumulated depreciation comprises the following (¥ in millions):	
Buildings	¥ 217,434
Machinery and equipment	958,159
Other	88,320
Total accumulated depreciation	¥1,263,913

Footnote 2 says, "Depreciation is provided under the declining-balance method for property, plant, and equipment, except for buildings which arc depreciated using the straight-line method, at rates based on estimated useful lives of the assets, principally, ranging from five years to sixty years for buildings and from four years to twenty-two years for machinery and equipment."

1. Compute the original acquisition cost of each of the five categories of assets listed under Property, Plant, and Equipment.

2. Explain why Asahi Kasei shows no accumulated depreciation for land or construction in progress.
3. Suppose Asahi Kasei had used straight-line instead of declining-balance depreciation for all asset categories. How would this affect the preceding values shown for Property, Plant, and Equipment?

8-59 Reconstruction of Plant Asset Transactions

The Ford Motor Company's footnotes included the following ($ in millions):

Ford Motor Company

	December 31	
	2008	**2007**
Property		
Land, plant, and equipment	$58,127	$62,500
Less: Accumulated depreciation	38,237	36,561
Net land, plant, and equipment	19,890	25,939
Special tools, net	8,462	10,040
Net automotive sector property	$28,352	$35,979

The notes to the income statement for 2008 revealed depreciation and amortization expense of $11,121 million. The account Special Tools, net is increased by new investments in tools, dies, jigs, and fixtures necessary for new models and production processes. Ford then amortizes these investments over various periods and reduces the account directly. When special tools are disposed of, the account is reduced by the net book value.

Hint: Analyze with the help of T-accounts.

1. Assume that Ford spent $2,000 million on special tools in 2008. The company disposed of special tools with a net book value of $2,530 million. How much amortization did Ford record on special tools in 2008?
2. Given your answer to requirement 1, estimate the cost of the new acquisitions of land, plant, and equipment. Assume all disposals of plant and equipment involved fully depreciated assets with zero book value.

8-60 Average Age of Assets

Walgreens is a drugstore chain operating more than 6,850 stores in 49 states, the District of Columbia, Guam, Puerto Rico, and two mail-order facilities. Walgreens typically builds rather than buys stores, so it can pick prime locations. Net property, plant, and equipment comprised almost 44% of Walgreens assets as of August 31, 2008. The company had the following on its August 31, 2008, balance sheet ($ in millions):

Total property, plant, and equipment	$12,918
Less: Accumulated depreciation	3,143
	$ 9,775

A footnote states that "depreciation is provided on a straight-line basis over the estimated useful lives of owned assets." Annual depreciation expense is approximately $733 million.

1. Estimate the average useful life of Walgreen's depreciable assets.
2. Estimate the average age of Walgreen's depreciable assets on August 31, 2008.

8-61 Depreciation, Income Tax, and Cash Flow

(Alternates are 8-62 and 8-63.) Sanchez Metal Products Company had the following balances, among others, at the end of December 20X1: Cash, $300,000; Equipment, $400,000; Accumulated Depreciation, $100,000. Total revenues (all in cash) were $900,000. All operating expenses except depreciation were for cash and totaled $600,000. Straight-line depreciation expense was $60,000. Depreciation expense would have been $110,000 if Sanchez had used accelerated depreciation.

1. Assume zero income taxes. Fill in the first two columns of blanks in the accompanying table. Show the amounts in thousands.

Table for Problem 8-61
($ amounts in thousands)

	1. Zero Income Taxes		2. 40% Income Taxes	
	Straight-Line Depreciation	**Accelerated Depreciation**	**Straight-Line Depreciation**	**Accelerated Depreciation**
Revenues (all cash)	$	$	$	$
Cash operating expenses				
Cash provided by operations before income taxes				
Depreciation expense				
Pretax income				
Income tax expense				
Net income	$	$	$	$
Supplementary analysis Cash provided by operations before income taxes	$	$	$	$
Income tax payments				
Net cash provided by operations	$	$	$	$

2. Fill in the last two columns of blanks in the table above. Assume an income tax rate of 40%. Assume also that Sanchez uses the same depreciation method for reporting to shareholders and to income tax authorities.
3. Compare your answers to requirements 1 and 2. Does depreciation provide cash? Explain as precisely as possible.
4. Refer to requirement 2. Assume that Sanchez had used straight-line depreciation for reporting to shareholders and to income tax authorities. Indicate the change (increase or decrease and amount) in the following balances if Sanchez had used accelerated depreciation for shareholder and tax reporting instead of straight-line: Cash, Accumulated Depreciation, Pretax Income, Income Tax Expense, and Retained Earnings.
5. Refer to requirement 1 where there are zero taxes. Suppose depreciation was doubled under both straight-line and accelerated methods. How would this affect cash? Be specific.

8-62 Depreciation, Income Taxes, and Cash Flow
(Alternates are 8-61 and 8-63.) A recent annual report of **Wal-Mart**, a major retailing company, listed the following property and equipment ($ in millions):

Property and equipment, at cost	$125,820
Less: Accumulated depreciation	32,964
Property and equipment, net	$ 92,856

The cash balance was $7,275 million. Depreciation expense during the year was $6,739 million. The condensed income statement follows ($ in millions):

Revenues	$405,607
Expenses	(382,809)
Operating income	$ 22,798

For purposes of this problem, assume that all revenues and expenses, excluding depreciation, are for cash. Thus, cash operating expenses in millions of dollars were ($382,809 – $6,739) = $376,070.

Table for Problem 8-62
($ amounts in millions)

| | 1. Zero Income Taxes | | 2. 40% Income Taxes | |
	Straight-Line Depreciation	Accelerated Depreciation	Straight-Line Depreciation	Accelerated Depreciation
Revenues (all cash)	$	$	$	$
Cash operating expenses				
Cash provided by operations before income taxes				
Depreciation expense				
Pretax income				
Income tax expense				
Net income	$	$	$	$
Supplementary analysis				
Cash provided by operations before income taxes	$	$	$	$
Income tax payments				
Net cash provided by operations	$	$	$	$

1. Wal-Mart uses straight-line depreciation. If accelerated depreciation had been used, assume that depreciation would have been $8,739 million. Assume zero income taxes. Fill in the first two columns of blanks in the accompanying table ($ in millions).
2. Fill in the last two columns of blanks in the table above. Assume an income tax rate of 40%. Assume also that Wal-Mart uses the same depreciation method for reporting to shareholders and to income tax authorities
3. Compare your answers to requirements 1 and 2. Does depreciation provide cash? Explain as precisely as possible.
4. Refer to requirement 2. Assume that Wal-Mart had used straight-line depreciation for reporting to shareholders and to income tax authorities. Indicate the change (increase or decrease and amount) in the following balances if Wal-Mart had used accelerated depreciation for shareholder and tax reporting instead of straight-line during that year: Cash, Accumulated Depreciation, Pretax Income, Income Tax Expense, and Retained Earnings. What would be the new balances in Cash and Accumulated Depreciation?
5. Refer to requirement 1 where there are zero taxes. Suppose Wal-Mart increased depreciation by an extra $2,500 million under both straight-line and accelerated methods. How would cash be affected? Be specific.

8-63 Depreciation, Income Taxes, and Cash Flow
(Alternates are 8-61 and 8-62.) **Carrefour** is the world's second-largest retailer, just behind **Wal-Mart**. Carrefour operates over 15,000 stores under some two dozen names. While headquartered in France, 55% of the company's sales are made in other countries. The company's annual report showed the following balances (€ in millions):

Revenues	€ 88,225.2
Operating expenses	(84,924.9)
Operating income	€ 3,300.3

Carrefour had depreciation expense of €1,860.8 million (included in operating expenses). The company's ending cash balance was €5,317 million.

Carrefour reported its property and equipment in the following way (€ in millions):

Property, plant, and equipment, at cost	€30,402
Less: Accumulated depreciation	15,593
Net property and equipment	€14,809

For purposes of this problem, assume all revenues and expenses, excluding depreciation, are for cash.

Table for Problem 8-63
(amounts in millions of Euros)

	1. Zero Income Taxes		2. 60% Income Taxes	
	Straight-Line Depreciation	Accelerated Depreciation	Straight-Line Depreciation	Accelerated Depreciation
Revenues (all cash)	€	€	€	€
Cash operating expenses				
Cash provided by operations before income taxes				
Depreciation expense				
Pretax income				
Income tax expense				
Net income	€	€	€	€
Supplementary analysis				
Cash provided by operations before income taxes	€	€	€	€
Income tax payments				
Net cash provided by operations	€	€	€	€

1. Carrefour used straight-line depreciation. If accelerated depreciation had been used, depreciation would have been €2,360.8 million. Assume zero income taxes. Fill in the first two columns of blanks in the accompanying table (in millions of Euros).
2. Fill in the last two columns of blanks in the table above. Assume an income tax rate of 60%. Assume also that Carrefour uses the same depreciation method for reporting to shareholders and to income tax authorities.
3. Compare your answers to requirements 1 and 2. Does depreciation provide cash? Explain as precisely as possible.
4. Refer to requirement 2. Carrefour used straight-line depreciation for reporting to shareholders and to income tax authorities. Indicate the change (increase or decrease and amount) in the following balances if Carrefour had used accelerated depreciation for shareholder and tax reporting instead of straight-line: Cash, Accumulated Depreciation, Pretax Income, Income Tax Expense, and Retained Earnings. What would be the new balances in Cash and Accumulated Depreciation?
5. Refer to requirement 1 where there are zero taxes. Suppose the company had doubled its depreciation under both straight-line and accelerated methods. How would this affect cash? Be specific.

8-64 Rental Vehicles

AMERCO is the holding company for U-Haul International and its subsidiaries. The 2008 annual report included the following footnote:

> Property, plant and equipment are stated at cost. Depreciation is computed for financial reporting purposes using the straight-line or an accelerated method based on a declining balances formula over the estimated useful lives. . . . Routine maintenance costs are charged to operating expense as they are incurred. Gains and losses on dispositions of property, plant and equipment are netted against depreciation expense when realized.

1. Assume that U-Haul acquires some new trucks on October 1, 2008, for $100 million. The useful life is 1 year. Expected residual values are $82 million. Prepare a summary journal entry for depreciation for 2008. The fiscal year ends on December 31.
2. Prepare a summary journal entry for depreciation for the first 9 months of 2009.
3. Assume that U-Haul sells the trucks for $88 million cash on September 30, 2009. Prepare the journal entry for the sale. U-Haul considers the trucks to be "revenue-earning equipment."
4. What is the total depreciation expense on these trucks for 2009? If U-Haul could have exactly predicted the $88 million proceeds when it originally acquired the trucks, what would depreciation expense have been in 2008? In 2009? Explain.

8-65 Nature of Research Costs

Katherine Mori, a distinguished scientist of international repute, had developed many successful drugs for a well-established pharmaceutical company. Having an entrepreneurial spirit, Katherine persuaded the board of directors that she should resign her position as vice-president of research and launch a subsidiary company to produce and market some powerful new drugs for treating arthritis. However, she did not predict overnight success. Instead, she expected to gather a first-rate research team that might take 3–5 years to generate any marketable products. Furthermore, she admitted that the risks were so high that conceivably no commercial success might result. Nevertheless, she had little trouble obtaining an initial investment of $5 million. The Mori Pharmaceuticals Company was 80% owned by the parent and 20% by Katherine.

Katherine acquired a team of researchers and began operations. By the end of the first year of the life of the new subsidiary, it had expended $2 million on research activities, mostly for researchers' salaries, but also for related research costs.

The subsidiary had developed no marketable products, but Katherine and other top executives were extremely pleased about the overall progress and were very optimistic about developing such products within the next 3 or 4 years.

How would you account for the $2 million? Would you write it off as an expense in year one? Could it be capitalized as an intangible asset? If so, would you carry it indefinitely? Or would you write it off systematically over 3 years or some longer span? Why? Explain, giving particular attention to the idea of an asset as an unexpired cost.

8-66 Meaning of Book Value

Chavez Company purchased an office building 20 years ago for $1.3 million, $500,000 of which was attributable to land. The mortgage has been fully paid. The current balance sheet follows:

Cash		$ 300,000	Stockholders' equity	$1,000,000
Land		500,000		
Building at cost	$800,000			
Accumulated depreciation	(600,000)			
Net book value		200,000		
Total assets		$1,000,000		

The company is about to borrow $1.8 million on a first mortgage to modernize and expand the building. This amounts to 60% of the combined appraised fair value of the land and building before the modernization and expansion.

Prepare a balance sheet after the loan is made and the building is expanded and modernized. Comment on its significance.

8-67 Change in Service Life

The annual report of a major airline contained the following footnote:

> *Note 2, Change in accounting estimate. The company extended the estimated useful lives of Boeing 727-100 aircraft from principally sixteen years to principally twenty years. As a result, depreciation and amortization expense was decreased by $9,000,000.*

The company's annual report also contained the following data: Depreciation, $235,518,000; Net Income, $42,233,000.

The cost of the Boeing 727-100 aircraft subject to depreciation was $800 million. Residual values were predicted to be 10% of acquisition cost.

Assume a combined federal and state income tax rate of 46% throughout all parts of these requirements.

1. Was the effect of the change in estimated useful life a material difference? Explain, including computations.
2. Examination of the annual report of a competitor airline indicated that the competitor used a 10-year life. Suppose the company making the change in estimate had changed to a 10-year life instead of a 20-year life on its 727-100 equipment. Estimated residual value is 10%. Compute the new depreciation and net income. For purposes of this requirement, assume that the equipment cost $800 million and has been in service 1 year and that reported net income based on a 20-year life was $42,233,000.

8-68 Disposal of Equipment

(Alternate is 8-69.) Alaska Airlines acquired a new Boeing 737-100 airplane for $36 million. Its expected residual value was $16 million. The company's annual report indicated that straight-line depreciation was used based on an estimated service life of 20 years. Assume the company records gains or losses, if any, in Other Income (Expense).

Show all amounts in millions of dollars.

1. Assume that Alaska sold the equipment at the end of the sixth year for $32 million cash. Compute the gain or loss on the sale. Show the effects of the sale on the balance sheet equation, identifying all specific accounts by name. Where and how would the sale appear on the income statement?
2. (a) Show the journal entries for the transaction in requirement 1. (b) Repeat 2a, assuming that the cash sales price was $29 million instead of $32 million.

8-69 Disposal of Property and Equipment

(Alternate is 8-68.) Rockwell Automation is a leading provider of industrial automation power and controls. The company's annual report indicated that both accelerated and straight-line depreciation were used for its property and equipment. In addition, the annual report said, "Gains or losses on property transactions are recorded in income in the period of sale or retirement."

Rockwell received $4 million for property that it sold.

1. Assume that Rockwell originally acquired the total property in question for $65 million and received the $4 million in cash. There was a loss of $8.5 million on the sale. Compute the accumulated depreciation on the property and equipment sold. Show the effects of the sale on the balance sheet equation, identifying all specific accounts by name.
2. (a) Show the journal entry and postings to T-accounts for the transaction in requirement 1. (b) Repeat 2a, assuming that the cash sales price was $14 million cash instead of $4 million.

8-70 Gain on Airplane Crash

A few years ago, a Delta Air Lines 727 crashed in Dallas. The crash resulted in a gain of $.11 per share for Delta. How could this happen? Consider the accounting for airplanes. Airlines insure their craft at market value, $6.5 million for Delta's 727. However, the planes' book values are often much less because of large accumulated depreciation amounts. The book value of Delta's 727 was only $962,000.

1. Suppose Delta received the insurance payment and immediately purchased another 727 for $6.5 million. Compute the effect of the insurance payment on pretax income. Also compute the effect on Delta's total assets.
2. Do you think a casualty should generate a reported gain? Why?

8-71 Disposal of Equipment

Airline Executive reported on an airline as follows:

> *Lufthansa's highly successful policy of rolling over entire fleets in roughly ten years—before the aircrafts have outlived their usefulness—got started in a "spectacular" way when seven first-generation 747s were sold. The 747s were bought six to nine years earlier for $22–28 million each and sold for about the same price.*

1. Assume an average original cost of $25 million each, an average original expected useful life of 10 years, a $3.5 million expected residual value for each aircraft, and an average actual life of 8 years before disposal. Use straight-line depreciation. Compute the total gain or loss on the sale of the seven planes.
2. Prepare a summary journal entry for the sale.

8-72 Software Development Costs

Microsoft, Incorporated, is one of the largest producers of software for personal computers. Special rules apply to accounting for the costs of developing software for sale or lease. Companies expense such costs until the technological feasibility of the product is established. Thereafter, they should capitalize these costs and amortize them over the life of the product.

One of Microsoft's divisions began working on some special business applications software. Suppose the division had spent $900,000 on the project by the end of 20X7, but it was not yet clear whether the software was technologically feasible.

On July 1, 20X8, after spending another $400,000, management decided that the software was technologically feasible. During the second half of 20X8, the division spent another $2 million on this project. In December 20X8, the company announced the product, with deliveries to begin in March 20X9. The division incurred no R&D costs for the software after December 20X8.

1. Prepare journal entries to account for the R&D expenses for the software for 20X7 and 20X8. Assume that the division paid all expenditures in cash.
2. Would any R&D expenses affect income in 20X9?

8-73 Basket Purchase and Intangibles

A tax newsletter stated, "When a business is sold, part of the sales price may be allocated to tangible assets and part to a 'covenant not to compete.' How this allocation is made can have important tax consequences to both the buyer and seller."

A large law firm, organized as a professional services corporation, purchased a successful local firm for $100,000. The purchase included both tangible assets, which have an average remaining useful life of 10 years, and a 3-year covenant not to compete. Suppose the buyer has legally supportable latitude concerning how to allocate this amount, as follows:

	Allocation One	Allocation Two
Covenant	$ 72,000	$ 48,000
Tangible assets	28,000	52,000
Total for two assets	$100,000	$100,000

1. For income tax purposes, which allocation would the buyer favor? Why?
2. For shareholder reporting purposes, which allocation would the buyer favor? Why?

8-74 Depreciation Policies and Ethics

Some companies have depreciation policies that differ substantially from the norm of their industry. For example, **Cineplex Odeon** depreciated its theater seats, carpets, and related equipment over 27 years, much longer than most of its competitors. Another example is **Blockbuster Entertainment**, which depreciated the videos it rents over 36 months. Others depreciate them over a period as short as 9 months.

Growing companies can increase their current income by depreciating fixed assets over a longer period of time. Sometimes companies lengthen the depreciable lives of their fixed assets when a boost in income is desired. Comment on the ethical implications of choosing an economic life for depreciation purposes, with special reference to the policies of Cineplex Odeon and Blockbuster.

Collaborative Learning Exercise

8-75 Accumulated Depreciation

Form groups of at least four students (this exercise can be done as an entire class, if desired). Individual students, on their own, should select a company and find the fixed asset section of its most recent balance sheet. From the balance sheet (and possibly the footnotes) find the original acquisition cost of property, plant, and equipment (the account title varies slightly by company) and the accumulated depreciation on property, plant, and equipment. Compute the ratio of accumulated depreciation to original acquisition cost. Also note the depreciation method used and the average economic life of the assets, if given. (For an extra bonus, find a company that uses accelerated depreciation for reporting to shareholders; such companies are harder to find.)

When everyone gets together, make four columns on the board or on a piece of paper. Find the 25% of the companies with the highest ratios and list them in the first column. Then list the 25% with the next highest ratios in the second column, and so on. As a group, make a list of explanations for the rankings of the companies. What characteristics of the company, its industry, or its depreciation methods distinguish the companies with high ratios from those with low ratios?

Analyzing and Interpreting Financial Statements

8-76 Financial Statement Research

Select two distinct industries and identify two companies in each industry.

1. Identify the depreciation methods used by each company.
2. Calculate gross and net plant, property, and equipment as a percentage of total assets for each company. What differences do you observe between industries? Within industries?
3. Do the notes disclose any unusual practices with regard to long-lived assets?

8-77 Analyzing Starbucks' Financial Statements

Find the financial statements of **Starbucks** for the year ended September 27, 2009, and look at footnote 1. Depreciation and amortization expense was $534.7 million for the year ended September 27, 2009, according to the Consolidated Statement of Earnings.

1. What lives does Starbucks use for depreciating and amortizing its assets?
2. Suppose Starbucks extended the lives of all its depreciable assets by 50% so depreciation was smaller each year. Estimate the effect of this on net earnings reported in the year 2009. Assume that the average tax rate in the current income statement applied to this change in depreciation and that depreciation for financial reporting purposes was the same as that for tax purposes.

8-78 Analyzing Financial Statements Using the Internet

Go to www.intel.com to find **Intel**'s home page. Select Investor Relations from the bottom navigation menu. Then select Financials and Filings from the left navigation menu and click on Annual reports, 10-Ks and Proxy Statements. From there you can open the most recent 10-K.

Answer the following questions about Intel:

1. Read the Notes to Consolidated Financial Statements. What is the nature of Intel's operations? What type of property, plant, and equipment would you expect Intel to include in the account Property, Plant, and Equipment on its balance sheet?

2. In which section of its financial statements does Intel provide information on the method of depreciation and amortization used for property, plant, and equipment? What other disclosures concerning depreciable assets are available in this same location?

3. Does Intel have any intangible assets? Where in the footnotes does Intel provide information about the nature of any intangible assets? What type are they? Does Intel amortize the intangibles? If so, what amortization method is used? How are intangible assets categorized on the balance sheet?

4. What does the amount listed on the balance sheet for Property, Plant, and Equipment represent—cost, market, or some other amount? If Intel purchases no additional property and equipment assets, what will happen to the net book value over time?

5. How much depreciation and amortization expense did Intel report, as shown in its most recent annual report? Why is this amount not obvious from looking at the income statement? Which financial statement provides the depreciation and amortization amount?

9

Liabilities and Interest

LEARNING OBJECTIVES

After studying this chapter, you should be able to:

1 Account for current liabilities.

2 Measure and account for long-term liabilities.

3 Account for bond issues over their entire life.

4 Value and account for long-term lease obligations.

5 Evaluate pensions and other postretirement benefits.

6 Interpret deferred tax liabilities.

7 Use ratio analysis to assess a company's debt levels.

8 Compute and interpret present and future values (Appendix 9).

When you have a taste for a hamburger, you might stop by Jack in the Box. Originally just a drive-through hamburger restaurant, Jack in the Box has expanded to more than 2,100 outlets with $2.5 billion in sales. The San Diego-based company also operates more than 450 Qdoba Mexican Grill restaurants. As it expanded, Jack in the Box borrowed money to finance the opening of new locations. In 2008 the company opened 38 new restaurants, and it plans to open 40–45 more each year. By the end of fiscal 2008, its total liabilities were almost $1 billion, of which $516 million was long-term debt. The long-term debt was nearly 80% greater than it was 5 years earlier. Jack in the Box's largest loan was $415 million remaining outstanding on a $475 million term loan taken out in 2007. It's annual interest expense is $28 million. In this chapter, we learn how companies such as Jack in the Box account for the money they borrow.

Why would Jack in the Box want to acquire so much debt? Why does any company borrow money? Companies borrow because management believes that remaining competitive requires continual growth. If the company can use the borrowed funds to continue increasing sales and

This is a typical Jack in the Box restaurant. Jack in the Box must buy, build, or lease a building and acquire equipment and inventories before it can generate any sales. To expand the number of locations, Jack in the Box borrows money, creating a liability. In this chapter we see how to account for such liabilities.

earnings per share, both management and shareholders will benefit. The key to a company's successful borrowing is that it must earn more on the borrowed funds than it pays for them.

Companies are not the only ones that borrow money. For example, when individuals seek to buy a car or a house, lenders assess the buyer's financial position carefully and pay special attention to the size of the down payment the buyer will make. The larger the down payment, the more "equity" the borrower has in the purchase, and the more comfortable the lender is in making the loan. The financial crisis in 2008–2009 showed what can happen if lenders are not vigilant in assessing a borrower's ability to repay a loan. Many banks were stuck with loans that borrowers were not able to repay.

Similarly, potential investors in the common stock or bonds of a company carefully evaluate the amount of debt the company has relative to the amount of stockholders' equity to assess the potential risk of their investment. Thus, a major element of GAAP is the careful definition of what constitutes a liability and how best to disclose the liabilities to readers of financial statements. ●

Liabilities in Perspective

As we learned earlier, liabilities are a company's obligations to pay cash or to provide goods and services to other companies or individuals. Liabilities include wages due to employees, payables to suppliers, taxes owed the government, interest and principal due to lenders, obligations from losing a lawsuit, and so on. Such obligations usually arise from a transaction with an outside party such as a supplier, a lending institution, or an employee. A liability arises whenever an organization recognizes an obligation before paying it.

Investors, financial analysts, management, and creditors consider existing liabilities of the firm when valuing the firm's common stock, when evaluating a new loan to the company, and when making many other decisions. Problems arise when companies appear to have excessive debt or seem unable to meet existing obligations. For example, suppliers who normally sell on credit may evaluate a customer's debt level. If they conclude that debt is excessive, they might refuse to ship new items or may ship only collect on delivery (COD). Also, lenders may refuse to provide new loans, and customers, worried that the company will not be around long enough to honor warranties, may prefer to buy elsewhere. Of course, once creditors and customers go, a company's future is bleak. Debt problems can snowball quickly. Because poorly managed debt can cause huge problems, users of financial statements pay close attention to debt levels. Let's look at how **Jack in the Box** reports its liabilities. Exhibit 9-1 shows its balance sheet presentation of liabilities.

As is common practice, Jack in the Box classifies its liabilities as either current or long-term (noncurrent), which helps readers of financial statement interpret the immediacy of the company's obligations. In Chapter 4, we learned that current liabilities are obligations that fall due within the coming year or within the company's normal operating cycle (if that cycle is longer than a year). In contrast, **long-term liabilities** are those that fall due more than 1 year beyond the balance sheet date. Companies pay some long-term obligations gradually, in yearly or monthly installments. You can see from Exhibit 9-1 that Jack in the Box Company includes the portion of these long-term obligations due within the next year ($68 million on September 27, 2009) as a part of the company's current liabilities.

In the general ledger, companies keep separate accounts for different liabilities, such as wages, salaries, commissions, interest, and similar items. In the annual report, though, they often combine these liabilities and show them as a single current liability labeled "accrued liabilities" or "accrued expenses payable." Sometimes they omit the adjective accrued and call these liabilities simply "taxes payable," "wages payable," and so on. Similarly, some omit the term "payable" and simply use "accrued wages" or "accrued taxes." Jack in the Box lumps together all accrued liabilities except accounts payable.

Accountants generally measure liabilities in terms of the amount of cash needed to pay off an obligation or the cash value of products or services to be delivered. For current liabilities, which we examine next, measurement is relatively easy, and the accounting process is straightforward.

long-term liabilities

Obligations that fall due beyond 1 year from the balance sheet date.

EXHIBIT 9-1

Jack in the Box Inc.

Liabilities Section, Consolidated Balance Sheets as of September 27, 2009, and September 28, 2008 (dollars in millions)

	2009	2008
Current liabilities		
Current maturities of long-term debt	$ 68	$ 2
Accounts payable	64	100
Accrued expenses	206	214
Total current liabilities	338	316
Long-term debt, net of current maturities	357	516
Other long-term liabilities	234	161
Deferred income taxes	2	48
Total liabilities	$931	$1,041

Accounting for Current Liabilities

We record some current liabilities as a result of a transaction with an outside entity, such as a lender or supplier. We record other liabilities with an adjusting journal entry to acknowledge an obligation arising over time, such as interest or wages. Let's take a look at the accounting procedures for several different types of current liabilities.

Accounts Payable

Accounts payable are amounts owed to suppliers. Jack in the Box lists them as a separate item under current liabilities, as do more than 90% of major U.S. companies. However, a few combine accounts payable with accrued liabilities. Large sums of money flow through these accounts payable systems. Therefore, accountants carefully design data processing and internal control systems for these transactions. The key is to ensure that the company writes checks only for legitimate obligations of the company.

Internal control systems generally require managers to make all payments by check. Why? Prenumbered checks make record keeping easy, and companies can thus trace exactly where their money is going.

Good systems also require source documents, sometimes paper documents but increasingly electronic records, to support all checks. First, there must be a **purchase order**, which specifies the quantities and prices of items ordered. Second is the **receiving report**, which indicates the items received and their condition. Then accountants match the purchase order and receiving report to the **invoice**, a bill from the seller. This process permits periodic, systematic reviews to ensure that nothing goes wrong, and it leaves a trail that is easy to follow in case an error arises. Because multiple people are involved, the system often avoids errors or detects them early before their consequences are large. Many systems allow checks only to approved vendors and require a high-level employee to approve all additions to the approved-vendor list. Some corporations use computers to generate automatic payments when a supplier's computer has provided the proper source information.

Notes Payable

When companies take out loans, they generally sign promissory notes. A **promissory note**, often called a note payable, is a written promise to repay the loan principal plus interest at specific future dates. Most promissory notes are payable to banks. Jack in the Box calls its notes payable "term loans." The $415 million outstanding on this loan will be repaid with specific quarterly payments through its maturity date in 2012.

The balance sheet presentation of notes payable varies. Notes that are payable within 1 year are included with current liabilities; others are long-term liabilities. Jack in the Box has only the one term loan. It has $68 million due in the next year and $347 million after that. The payments due in fiscal 2010 are listed as current liabilities on its 2009 balance sheet; the remaining payments comprise $347 million of the $357 million of long-term debt. Many companies also have **commercial paper**, a debt contract issued by prominent companies that borrow directly from investors. The liability created by commercial paper always falls due in 9 months or less, usually in 60 days after issuance, so it is a current liability.

Companies also establish lines of credit. A **line of credit** sets up a predetermined maximum amount that a company can borrow from a given lender without significant additional credit checking or other time-consuming procedures. Lines of credit have no fixed repayment schedules. They can benefit both lenders and borrowers. The lender gets the advantage of not having to run credit checks and prepare extensive paperwork every time the borrower wants a loan. The borrower gets the advantage of having a preset amount of borrowing available. Jack in the Box calls its $150 million line of credit maturing on December 15, 2011, a "revolving credit facility." Although Jack in the Box had no borrowing on the line of credit at the end of fiscal 2009, if it did the amount would be a long-term liability because the company would not have to repay it until December of 2011. As another example, Coca-Cola explained its $6,066 million of loans and notes payable on its 2008 balance sheet as follows:

> *Loans and notes payable consist primarily of commercial paper issued in the United States. As of December 31, 2008, we had approximately $5,389 million outstanding in commercial paper borrowings. . . . In addition, we had approximately $3,462 million in lines of credit . . . available as of December 31, 2008, of which approximately $677 million was outstanding.*

OBJECTIVE 1

Account for current liabilities.

---

purchase order

A document that specifies the items ordered and the price to be paid by the ordering company.

receiving report

A document that specifies the items received by the company and the condition of the items.

invoice

A bill from the seller to a buyer indicating the number of items shipped, their price, and any additional costs (such as shipping) along with payment terms, if any.

promissory note

A written promise to repay principal plus interest at specific future dates.

commercial paper

A short-term debt contract issued by prominent companies that borrow directly from investors.

line of credit

An agreement with a bank to provide automatically short-term loans up to some predetermined maximum.

Coca-Cola borrows more in the commercial paper market than it does from banks because the interest rates are lower in the commercial paper market. However, only companies with the visibility and creditworthiness of Coca-Cola can issue commercial paper.

Accrued Employee Compensation

Accrued liabilities are expenses that a company has recognized on the income statement but not yet paid. Our first example of an accrued liability is obligations to employees for payment of wages. Many companies have a separate current liability account for such items, with a label such as salaries, wages, and commissions payable, but Jack in the Box combines this liability with the other accrued expenses.

In earlier chapters, we assumed that an employee who earned $100 per week received $100 in cash on payday each week. In reality, however, payroll accounting is never that easy. For example, employers must withhold some employee earnings and pay them instead to the government, insurance companies, labor unions, charitable organizations, and so forth.

Consider the withholding of income taxes and the employees' portion of Social Security taxes (also called Federal Insurance Contributions Act or FICA taxes). Suppose that a particular Jack in the Box restaurant has a $100,000 monthly payroll and, for simplicity, assume that the only amounts it withholds are $15,000 for income taxes and $7,000 for Social Security taxes. The withholdings are not additional employer costs. They are simply part of the employee wages and salaries that the company pays to third parties, instead of directly to the employees. The journal entry for this $100,000 payroll is as follows:

Compensation expense	100,000	
Salaries and wages payable		78,000
Income tax withholding payable		15,000
Social Security withholding payable ...		7,000

Companies must also deal with payroll taxes and fringe benefits. These are employee-related costs in addition to salaries and wages. Payroll taxes are amounts paid to the government for items such as the employer's portion of Social Security, federal and state unemployment taxes, and workers' compensation taxes. Fringe benefits include employee pensions, life and health insurance, and vacation pay. At many organizations, the fringe benefits exceed 30% of salary. Thus, a person who earns $30,000 per year in salary, effectively costs the company $30,000 plus 30% of $30,000, or $39,000. A company must accrue liabilities for each of these costs. If the company has not yet paid them at the balance sheet date, it must include them among its current liabilities.

Note that there are two parts to Social Security taxes. Employers withhold one part from the employees' wages and pay a similar amount themselves. Suppose the Jack in the Box restaurant pays an employer's FICA tax equal to the $7,000 withheld from the employee and also pays 10% of gross wages into a retirement account. The following journal entry summarizes the effect on the Jack in the Box financial statements:

Employee benefit expense	17,000	
Employer Social Security payable		7,000
Pension liability payable		10,000

Income Taxes Payable

In nearly every country in the world, corporations must pay income taxes as a percentage of their earnings. Instead of paying one lump sum at tax time, corporations make periodic installment payments based on their estimated tax for the year. Therefore, the accrued liability for income taxes at year-end is generally much smaller than the annual income tax expense.

To illustrate, suppose a corporation has an estimated taxable income of $100 million for the calendar year 20X0. At a 40% tax rate, the company's estimated taxes for the year are $40 million. It would make payments as follows:

	April 15	June 15	September 15	December 15
Estimated taxes (in millions)	$10	$10	$10	$10

The company must file a final income tax return and make a final payment by March 15, 20X1. Suppose the actual taxable income for the year was $110 million instead of the estimated $100 million. Total tax would then be $44 million. On March 15, the corporation must pay the $4 million additional tax on the extra $10 million of taxable income. The accrued liability on December 31, 20X0, would appear in the current liability section of the balance sheet as follows:

Income taxes payable	$4,000,000

For simplicity, the illustration assumed equal quarterly payments. However, the estimated taxable income for a calendar year may change as the year unfolds. The corporation must change its quarterly payments accordingly. Regardless of how a company changes its estimates, there will nearly always be a tax payment or refund due on March 15, and there will be an accrual adjustment at year-end.

Current Portion of Long-Term Debt

A company's long-term debt often includes payments due within a year that should be reported as current liabilities. The journal entry for recognizing the current portion of long-term debt reclassifies a noncurrent liability as a current liability. Using the Jack in the Box illustration in Exhibit 9-1, the reclassification journal entry in 2009 for long-term debt that becomes due in fiscal 2010 would be as follows:

Long-term debt	68,000,000	
Current maturities of long-term debt		68,000,000

Sales Tax

When retailers collect sales taxes, they are collecting on behalf of the state or local government. For example, suppose customers pay a 7% sales tax on sales of $10,000. The total collected from the customers must be $10,000 + $700, or $10,700. The transaction would affect the balance sheet as follows:

A	=	L	+	SE
+ 10,700	=	+ 700		+10,000
Increase Cash or Accounts Receivable		Increase Sales Tax Payable		Increase Sales

The sales shown on the income statement would be $10,000, not $10,700. The sales tax never affects the income statement. The $700 received for taxes affects the current liability account Sales Tax Payable and appears on the balance sheet until the company pays it to the government. The journal entries for the sale and the subsequent payment to the government (without explanations) are as follows:

Cash or accounts receivable	10,700	
Sales		10,000
Sales tax payable		700
Sales tax payable	700	
Cash		700

Returnable Deposits

Occasionally, customers must make money deposits that are to be returned in full. Well-known examples of returnable deposits are those for returnable containers such as soft drink bottles, oil drums, or beer kegs. Also, many landlords require security deposits that are to be returned in full at the end of a lease, as long as the tenants do not cause any damage to the property.

Companies that receive deposits record them as a form of payable, although the word "payable" may not be a part of their specific labeling. The accounting entries by the recipients of deposits have the following basic pattern (numbers assumed in thousands of dollars):

1. Deposit received	Cash	100	
	Deposits Payable		100
2. Deposit returned	Deposits Payable	100	
	Cash		100

The account Deposits Payable is a current liability of the company receiving the deposit.

Unearned Revenue

In Chapter 4, you learned that unearned revenue arises when a company collects cash before it earns the related revenue. These unearned revenues are usually current liabilities because they require a company either to deliver the product or service or to make a full refund within a year. Examples of unearned revenues include lease rentals, magazine subscriptions, insurance premiums, airline or theater ticket sales sold in advance, and repair service contracts signed in advance. The journal entries to record $100,000 of prepayments for services and the subsequent performance of those services and appropriate revenue recognition are as follows:

Cash	100,000	
Unearned sales revenues		100,000
To record advance collections from customers		
Unearned sales revenues	100,000	
Sales		100,000
To record sales revenues when services are performed for customers who paid in advance		

Companies use a variety of labels for revenues collected in advance of their being earned. For example, Time Warner Cable lists them as "Deferred Revenue and Subscriber-related Liabilities," The New York Times Company calls them "Unexpired Subscriptions," and Monster Worldwide, Inc., operator of the largest job-search Web site, simply lists them as "Deferred Revenues."

INTERPRETING FINANCIAL STATEMENTS

Consider a basketball team that sells season tickets for $100 each, collected at the beginning of the season. The accounting period is a calendar year, but typically 40% of the games occur in November and December, whereas the other 60% occur in January and February. The team sells all of its 15,000 seats to season ticket holders for the 2010–2011 season. Indicate how these facts would affect the income statement and the balance sheet for 2010 and the income statement for 2011.

Answer

In 2010, the team would collect ($100 × 15,000) = $1,500,000. However, it would earn only 40% of it, or $600,000, in 2010, so the 2010 income statement would show only $600,000 of revenue. The 2010 balance sheet would show a current liability of (60% × $1,500,000) = $900,000, labeled Revenue Received in Advance, Unearned Revenue, or Deferred Revenue. This $900,000 is deferred, and the team will recognize it as income on the 2011 income statement when it earns the revenue by playing the remaining games.

Product Warranties

Some current liabilities are difficult to measure precisely. For example, a sales warranty creates a liability, but warranty claims will arise in the future and accountants must estimate their amount. If warranty obligations are material, a company must accrue them when it sells products because the obligation arises at the time of sale, not when the customer receives actual repair services. For example, Ford Motor Co. describes its warranty accounting as follows: "Estimated warranty costs are accrued for at the time the vehicle is sold to a dealer."

Companies usually base the estimated warranty expenses on past experience replacing or remedying defective products. Although estimates should be close, they are rarely precisely correct. Assume that a company has $20 million in sales and has found that warranty expense averages about 3% of sales. The accounting entry related to the warranties associated with the $20 million in sales is as follows:

Warranty expense	600,000	
Liability for warranties (or some similar title) . . . ,		600,000
To record the estimated liability for warranties arising		
from current sales; the provision is 3% of current		
sales of $20 million, or $600,000		

When a $1,000 warranty claim arises, we make an entry such as the following:

Liability for warranties	1,000	
Cash, accounts payable, accrued wages payable,		
and similar accounts		1,000
To record the acquisition of supplies, outside services,		
and employee services to satisfy claims for repairs		

If the estimate for warranty expense is accurate, the entries for all claims will total about $600,000. If additional information makes it clear that the claims will differ from $600,000, we adjust the liability accordingly. For example, suppose we get information that quality problems are causing excessive warranty claims so we expect total claims to be $700,000 rather than the original estimate of $600,000. We then need to add $100,000 to the Liability for Warranties account and charge an extra $100,000 to Warranty Expense.

Companies reporting under IFRS include warranty liabilities in a category called provisions. **Provisions** are liabilities of uncertain timing or amount. They are obligations arising from a past event that are likely to be honored and for which the company can make a reliable estimate of the amount. For example, the Italian auto manufacturer Fiat included the following in its "Provisions" footnote to its 2008 financial statements (in millions of euros):

provisions
Liabilities of uncertain timing or amount.

	At 31 December 2007	Charge	Utilization	Release to Income	Other Changes	At 31 December 2008
Warranties	€1,334	€1,230	€(1,166)	€(68)	€(34)	€1,296

The charge is the 2008 warranty expense, utilization is the amount paid for warranty claims in 2008, and release to income is amounts arising from changes in warranty estimates during 2008.

This concludes our discussion of current liabilities. Now let's proceed to long-term liabilities.

Long-Term Liabilities

Long-term liabilities are obligations that are not due for at least a year. How do lenders and borrowers measure the value of such obligations? They use the time value of money, which refers to the fact that a dollar you expect to pay or receive in the future is not worth as much as a dollar you have today. If you are not comfortable with the concept and computations involving the time value of money, especially present values, it is important to study Appendix 9 carefully. As you will see, accounting has embraced present value approaches in valuing bonds, leases, pensions, and other long-term liabilities. We start with an analysis of bonds and notes.

OBJECTIVE 2

Measure and account for long-term liabilities.

Corporate Bonds

Many corporations have heavy demands for borrowed capital, so they often borrow from the general public by issuing corporate bonds in the financial markets. **Bonds** are formal certificates of debt that include (1) a promise to pay interest in cash at a specified annual rate (often called

bonds
Formal certificates of debt that include (1) a promise to pay interest in cash at a specified annual rate, plus (2) a promise to pay the principal at a specific maturity date.

nominal interest rate (contractual rate, coupon rate, stated rate)
A contractual rate of interest paid on bonds.

face amount
The loan principal or the amount that a borrower promises to repay at a specific maturity date.

negotiable
Legal financial contracts that can be transferred from one lender to another.

private placement
A process whereby bonds are issued by corporations when money is borrowed from a financial institution, not from the general public.

liquidation
Converting assets to cash and paying off outside claims.

mortgage bond
A form of long-term debt that is secured by the pledge of specific property.

debenture
A debt security with a general claim against all assets, instead of a specific claim against particular assets.

subordinated debentures
Debt securities whose holders have claims against only the assets that remain after satisfying the claims of other general creditors.

the **nominal interest rate**, **contractual rate**, **coupon rate**, or **stated rate**) plus (2) a promise to pay the principal (often called the **face amount** or par value) of the bond at a specific maturity date. Bonds generally pay interest every 6 months. Fundamentally, bonds are individual promissory notes issued to many lenders.

We often call bonds **negotiable** financial instruments or securities because one lender can transfer them to another. Sometimes companies create bonds to borrow directly from a financial institution such as a pension plan or insurance company. We call bonds issued for these purposes **private placements** because the general public does not hold or trade them. Private placements provide more than half the capital borrowed by corporations in the United States. They are popular because they are generally easy to arrange and they allow the lender to evaluate the creditworthiness of the borrower very carefully and directly. Borrowers and lenders can tailor specific features of the bond to meet their special needs.

Specific Bond Characteristics

There are many ways that issuers can tailor bonds to their needs. In this section, we discuss just some of the provisions companies can put into bonds.

PREFERENCE IN LIQUIDATION—MORTGAGE BONDS AND SUBORDINATED DEBENTURES Bond provisions help determine bondholders' priority for claims when a company is in **liquidation**, which means converting assets to cash and paying off outside claims. For example, **mortgage bonds** are secured by the pledge of specific property. In case of default, these bondholders have the first right to proceeds from the sale of that property.

In contrast, debenture holders have a lower priority claim to recover their loan amount. A **debenture** is a debt security with a general claim against the company's total assets, instead of a particular asset. At liquidation, a debenture bondholder shares the available assets with other general creditors, such as trade creditors who seek to recover their accounts payable claims, with one exception. If debenture bonds are **subordinated**, the bondholders have claims against only the assets that remain after satisfying the claims of other general creditors.

To clarify these ideas, suppose a liquidated company had a single asset, a building, that it sells for $110,000 cash. The liabilities total $160,000 as follows:

Liabilities	
Accounts payable	$ 50,000
First mortgage bonds	80,000
Subordinated bonds	30,000
Total liabilities	$160,000

The mortgage bondholders, having a direct claim on the building, will receive their full $80,000. The trade creditors (the company's suppliers, to whom the company owes money) will receive the remaining $30,000 for their $50,000 claim ($.60 on the dollar). The subordinated debenture claimants will get what is left over—nothing.

Now suppose the $30,000 of bonds were not subordinated. The bondholders would have a general claim on assets equivalent to that of the company's suppliers. The company would then use the $30,000 of cash remaining after paying $80,000 to the mortgage holders to settle the remaining $80,000 claims of the suppliers and bondholders proportionally as follows:

Liabilities		Payments	
Accounts payable	$ 50,000	5/8 × 30,000 =	18,750
First mortgage bonds	80,000		80,000
Unsubordinated bonds	30,000	3/8 × 30,000 =	11,250
	$160,000		$110,000

In order of priority, we have the mortgage bond, then unsubordinated debentures and accounts payable, and finally the subordinated debenture. Because interest rates are higher for riskier bonds, you can see that mortgage bonds would have the lowest interest rate and debentures would have the next lowest. Subordinated debentures would carry the highest interest rate.

PROTECTION OF BONDHOLDERS—BOND COVENANTS Many bonds contain **protective covenants** or simply **covenants**. Covenants generally restrict the ability of the borrower to take certain actions or give the lender the ability to force early payment under certain conditions. For example, a covenant might require immediate repayment of the loan if the borrower misses an interest payment, it may restrict sales of particular properties, or it may restrict the payment of dividends unless the borrower has generated additional earnings since issuing the debt. In general, covenants protect the bondholders' interests. Based on the concept of less risky bonds paying lower interest, you can see that these covenants have the ability to make the bond safer and therefore lower the interest rate.

Covenants often give bondholders the right to demand repayment of the loan principal if the company fails to meet some requirement in the covenants. These requirements may include maintaining a sufficient level of retained earnings (which can serve to limit dividend payments), a sufficient ratio of stockholders' equity to debt, sufficient levels of cash and accounts receivable, or they may prohibit the issuance of additional debt without first repaying the existing debt.

For example, Jack in the Box indicated that its borrowings are subject to "a number of customary covenants, including limitations on additional borrowings, acquisitions, loans to franchisees, capital expenditures, lease commitments, stock repurchases and dividend payments, and requirements to maintain certain financial ratios and prepay term loans with a portion of our excess cash flows." Lenders generally tailor bond covenants to specific borrowers and situations. In general, the more covenants there are, the more restricted the borrower is, and the more attractive the arrangement is to the lender. You can find more information on bond covenants in the Business First box on page 400.

CALLABLE, SINKING FUND, AND CONVERTIBLE BONDS Additional bond provisions can make bonds more or less attractive. Some bonds are **callable**, which means that the issuer has the option to redeem them before maturity. Typically, the redemption price exceeds the face value of the bond by an amount referred to as a **call premium**. To illustrate, consider a $1,000 bond issued in 2010 with a 2034 maturity date that is callable any time after 2024 for a price of $1,050. The call premium is $50 per $1,000 bond. Callable bonds are good for the borrower because the borrower has a choice to redeem the bond early or wait to maturity. However, it creates uncertainty for the lender, who might therefore require a higher interest rate on callable bonds. The call premium also compensates the lender for the risk of unexpected early redemption.

Sinking fund bonds require the issuer to make annual payments into a sinking fund. A **sinking fund** is a pool of cash or securities set aside solely for meeting certain obligations. It is an asset generally listed under "other assets." The sinking fund helps assure the bondholders that the company will have enough cash to repay the bond's principal at maturity. These provisions increase the attractiveness of the bond to lenders and therefore lower the interest rate.

Convertible bonds are bonds that bondholders may exchange for other securities, usually for a preset number of shares of the issuing company's common stock. Because of the conversion feature, convertible bondholders are willing to accept a lower interest rate than on a similar bond without the conversion privilege. Under U.S. GAAP, companies list convertible bonds with debt. In contrast, under IFRS convertible bonds have both debt and equity components: (1) The value of the debt component is the present value of interest and principal payments at the market rate of interest at issue for bonds of a similar risk level, and (2) the equity component is the excess that investors pay above the initial value of the debt.

Bond Interest Rates, Bond Discount, and Bond Premium

The interest rate is a key factor for all bonds. Recall that the nominal interest rate or coupon rate determines the amount of each semiannual interest payment. In addition, we are concerned with the **market rate**, which is the rate available on investments in similar bonds at a moment in time. It is the amount of interest that investors require to purchase the bond. If the market rate differs from the coupon rate, the issuing company will not receive the face amount when it issues the bond. When the market rate exceeds the coupon rate, the bond sells at a discount—the **bond discount** (or **discount on bonds**) is the amount by which the face amount exceeds the proceeds from the bond. When the coupon rate exceeds the market rate, the bond sells at a premium—the **bond premium** (or **premium on bonds**) is the excess of the proceeds over the face amount. Note that premiums and discounts do not reflect the creditworthiness of the issuer. Instead, they simply reflect differences in the nominal rate and the market rate. These differences often result from changes in market interest rates between the time a company sets the terms of the bond and when it actually issues the bond.

---

protective covenant (covenant)
A provision in a bond that restricts the actions a borrower may take, usually to protect the bondholders' interests.

callable bonds
Bonds subject to redemption before maturity at the option of the issuer.

call premium
The amount by which the redemption price of a callable bond exceeds face value.

sinking fund bonds
Bonds that require the issuer to make annual payments to a sinking fund.

sinking fund
A pool of cash or securities set aside for meeting certain obligations.

convertible bonds
Bonds that may, at the holder's option, be exchanged for other securities.

market rate
The rate available on investments in similar bonds at a moment in time.

bond discount (discount on bonds)
The excess of face amount over the proceeds on issuance of a bond.

bond premium (premium on bonds)
The excess of the proceeds over the face amount of a bond.

BUSINESS FIRST

BOND COVENANTS

A bond is a promise to pay interest and to repay principal at specific times. However, investors have learned that to control the risk that a borrower will be unable to pay in the future, it is useful to limit the borrower's freedom in a number of ways by writing restrictions into the bond contract. These covenants take many forms and may limit the ability to pay dividends or to borrow additional amounts, or they may require maintenance of certain ratios, such as debt-to-equity, current ratio, and so on.

For such covenants to be powerful, they typically require the borrower to provide the lender with audited financial statements every quarter and require the auditor to provide assurance that no violations of the covenants have occurred. If a company violates a covenant, the debt typically comes due immediately. Although the lender may not require repayment in full when this happens, the default provides the opportunity for the lender to renegotiate the terms of the loan. That may involve earlier repayment, a higher interest rate, issuance of common stock, or some other remedy.

Covenants tend to evolve in response to observed risks. It is currently common for bonds to have a "change of control" feature, which means that when the ownership of the equity (common stock) of a company changes hands, the bonds become immediately due and payable. This feature might be called the RJR provision because it became common after Kohlberg, Kravis, Roberts & Co. (KKR), a leveraged buyout firm, acquired R.J. Reynolds Tobacco Company (RJR) for $31.4 billion in a hostile takeover in 1989 (the largest corporate takeover ever until the mid-1990s). RJR had various bonds outstanding when KKR acquired it. In the transaction, KKR issued many additional bonds that were equal to RJR's existing bonds in seniority. In the process, the new company became very debt heavy, and investors worried that the merged company would not be able to repay the existing bondholders. Existing bonds fell some 14% in value on the day KKR and RJR announced the takeover. Thereafter, many lenders inserted a change-of-control feature into their bonds to ensure they had the right to get their full face (maturity) value back whenever a takeover occurred.

The financial crisis of 2008–2009 caused many companies to violate or come close to violating covenants. An example is Clear Channel, which had $15.9 million of secured senior debt with covenants related to its income. As its income fell, Clear Channel approached dangerously close to violating the covenant. A violation would allow the banks two options: Either restructure the company's huge debt or amend the terms of the secured debt for a price—higher interest rates and fees. Neither was an attractive alternative for Clear Channel.

Covenants to protect bondholders have become more common as the market for junk bonds and mezzanine bonds, both issued by more risky borrowers, has grown. For example, some covenants restrict the amount of capital investment by the borrower. One lender to a retail company required growth in same-store sales before allowing investment in expanding the number of stores. In general, the more risky the debt, the more covenants the lender will require. Although covenants protect lenders, they can also severely restrict the flexibility of the borrower. Debt with covenants is certainly a double-edged sword.

Sources: Kohlberg, Kravis, Roberts & Co. Web site (www.kkr.com); Crane, Agnes, "Clear Channel's Debt Covenant Creep," Reuters Blogs (September 1, 2009); Burns, Mairin, "Lenders Raise Flags About Red-Hot Mezz: Covenants, Expense Belie 'Miracle Cure' Status," *Investment Dealers Digest*, October 27, 2003.

Consider a $1,000 2-year bond with a coupon rate of 10% that pays interest every 6 months until maturity and pays the face amount at maturity. Exhibit 9-2 shows the bond's values at three different market interest rates. It calculates the present value of the annuity of interest payments and adds that to the present value of the repayment of face value at maturity. Note the following:

1. Although we express the quoted bond interest rates as annual rates, companies generally pay bond interest semiannually. Thus, a 10% bond really pays 5% interest each semiannual period. A 2-year bond has 4 periods, a 10-year bond has 20 periods, and so on.
2. The higher the market rate of interest, the lower the present value of the bond payments.
3. When the market interest rate equals the coupon rate of 10%, the bond is worth the face value of $1,000. We say such a bond is issued at par.
4. When the market interest rate is 12%, which exceeds the 10% coupon rate, the bond sells at a *discount*. The company receives $965.35, $34.65 less than the par value of $1,000.
5. When the market interest rate is 8%, which is less than the 10% coupon rate, the bond sells at a *premium*. The company receives $1,036.30, $36.30 more than the par value of $1,000.

	Present Value Factor	Total Present Value	Sketch of Cash Flows by Period				
			0	1	2	3	4
Valuation at market rate of 10% per year, or 5% per half year							
Principal, 4-Period line, Table 9A-2 (.8227 × $1,000) = $822.70	.8227	822.70					1,000
Interest, 4-Period line, Table 9A-3 (3.5460 × $50) = $177.30	3.5460	177.30		50	50	50	50
Total		1,000.00					
Valuation at market rate of 12% per year, or 6% per half-year							
Principal	.7921	792.10					1,000
Interest	3.4651	173.25		50	50	50	50
Total		965.35					
Valuation at market rate of 8% per year, or 4% per half-year							
Principal	.8548	854.80					1,000
Interest	3.6299	181.50		50	50	50	50
Total		1,036.30					

EXHIBIT 9-2

Computation of Market Value of $1,000 Face Value, 10% Coupon, 2-Year Bond (in dollars)

The bond discount or bond premium depends on the market interest rate at the time the company issues the bond. After issuance, market rates may vary. Bondholders can sell their bonds in the marketplace, and the price they will receive depends on the current market rate for similar bonds, not the market rate in effect at the time of issue. We call the current market rate for a bond the **yield to maturity**. It is the interest rate at which all contractual cash flows for interest and principal have a present value equal to the current price of the bond.

What determines the market interest rate or the yield to maturity? Many factors, including general economic conditions, industry conditions, risks of the use of the proceeds, and specific features of the bonds. However, we can summarize these in three basic components: the real interest rate, the inflation premium, and the firm specific risk component.

1. The **real interest rate** is the return that investors demand because they are delaying their consumption. If you could have a dollar now or later, now is generally better. The real rate of interest historically has been in the 3% range.
2. The **inflation premium** is the extra interest that investors require because the general price level may increase between now and the time they receive their money. This is an expectation, and peoples' expectations vary widely. In some countries inflation rates have exceed 100% per year, whereas in the United States and most developed countries recent inflation rates have been closer to 3% per year or less.
3. Finally, there is the **firm-specific risk**, referring to the risk that the firm will not repay the loan or will not pay the interest on time. In either event, the investor could lose everything and at a minimum will have to pursue legal avenues to collect the money due. This amount ranges widely from 1% or 2% for firms with very good credit ratings to 10% or more for firms facing financial distress.

yield to maturity
The interest rate at which all contractual cash flows for interest and principal have a present value equal to the current price of the bond.

real interest rate
The return that investors demand because they are delaying their consumption.

inflation premium
The extra interest that investors require because the general price level may increase between now and the time they receive their money.

firm-specific risk
The risk that the firm will not repay the loan or will not pay the interest on time.

The first two of these reflect general economic conditions. The third is a result of company-specific conditions and creates different rates for different companies. Creditors look carefully at the riskiness of the companies in which they invest. For example, compare a $1,000 bond issued by the U.S. government with $1,000 bonds issued by Verizon and Rite Aid. In 2009, the U.S. government bond had a yield to maturity of about 3.5% per year. At the same time similar Verizon bonds paid 4.7%, and the Rite Aid bonds paid 12.0%. From this we can conclude that Verizon bonds are riskier than U.S. government bonds, and Rite Aid bonds are even more risky.

Assessing the Riskiness of Bonds

Although assessing the riskiness of bonds is essential, many creditors cannot spend the time to do an in-depth analysis of each bond offering. Thus, commercial services have developed evaluation systems to rate bonds according to their creditworthiness. Mergent, Inc. (formerly Moody's) and Standard & Poor's (S&P), a division of McGraw-Hill, are perhaps the best known.

Higher rated bonds are safer, and companies with better ratings generally pay lower interest rates. For example, examine the following average interest rates for bonds in each rating category. The rates, for June of each year, are from the Mergent Bond Record. Aaa is the highest rating and Baa is the lowest rating shown.

Rating	Aaa	Aa	A	Baa
2008	5.68	6.11	6.43	7.07
2003	4.97	5.72	5.92	6.19
1998	6.53	6.78	6.88	7.13
1993	7.33	7.51	7.74	8.07
1988	9.86	10.13	10.42	11.00

Note that rates increase from left to right as ratings decrease. Investors will accept a lower yield for debt issued by the least risky companies. In addition, rates in every category fell steadily between 1988 and 2003. However, all climbed in 2008, reflecting a market-wide increase in risk.

To assign the ratings, Mergent often interviews management in addition to analyzing financial data such as sales levels, profitability, and the debt level. In the United States, debt obligations are legally enforceable, and many examples exist where creditors have forced a company to liquidate to pay interest or to repay principal. This is what caused the collapse of Enron, WorldCom, Sharper Image, Circuit City, and many other companies in the last decade.

Financial analysts must adapt to the realities facing specific companies. In Japan, for example, debt ratios tend to be much higher than they are in the United States. This difference partly reflects banking practices. Japanese banks lend very large sums to the biggest and most creditworthy corporations. Although the transaction has the form of debt, it tends to be part of a long-term relationship between bank and customer. The banks end up with long-term rights that look somewhat like the rights of a U.S. shareholder.

Issuing and Trading Bonds

underwriters

A group of investment bankers that buys an entire bond or stock issue from a corporation and then sells the securities to the general investing public.

A syndicate (special group) of investment bankers called **underwriters** generally sells a corporation's bonds. That is, the syndicate buys the entire issue of bonds from the corporation, thus guaranteeing that the company will obtain the funds it needs. The syndicate then sells the bonds to the general investing public. The investment banker who manages the underwriting syndicate often helps the company set the terms of the bond contract—terms such as the time to maturity, interest payment dates, interest rates, and size of the bond issue. After a company initially issues bonds, the bondholders can often trade the bonds in markets or on exchanges such as the NYSE. You can find corporate bond prices in newspaper business sections. For example, on September 7, 2009, *Barron's* included the following information on Abbott Laboratories and Dow Chemical Company bonds:

	Coupon	Maturity	Last Price	Yield
Abbott Laboratories	5.125	April 01, 2019	106.310	4.312
Dow Chemical Co	8.550	May 15, 2019	110.224	7.071

Bonds typically have a face value of $1,000, but we usually express their values in terms of percentages of face value. Abbott's 5.125% coupon bonds maturing in 2019 sell for $1,063.10 (106.310% of $1,000) and have a yield to maturity of 4.312%. The Dow Chemical bonds have a higher yield, 7.071%, indicating greater risk. Both bonds have coupon rates greater than the yield, so the price of each is greater than $1,000.

Bond Accounting

Let's look next at how we account for bonds. The body of a company's balance sheet usually summarizes the various types of bonds and other long-term debt on one line. However, most companies show details about bonds in the footnotes. In Exhibit 9-1, Jack in the Box showed $357 million of long-term debt on its balance sheet, and a footnote elaborated as follows (in thousands):

	September 27, 2009
Term loan, variable interest rate based on an applicable margin plus LIBOR, 1.57% at September 27, 2009	$415,000
Capital lease obligations, 9.97% weighted average interest rate	10,247
	425,247
Less: Current portion	(67,977)
Long-term debt	$357,270

Jack in the Box's term loan has an interest rate that varies with the London Interbank Offered Rate (LIBOR), a common index of interest rates.

Some other companies show more details. For example, Coca-Cola recently listed four specific notes plus an "other" category for total long-term debt of nearly $3 billion. Many international companies borrow around the world. For example, Royal Dutch Shell divides its nearly $20 billion of total debt into six categories, European debt, dollar debt, and other debt, each separated into fixed rate and variable rate portions.

To understand what these accounts mean, we look at how a company accounts for the issuance of bonds, the periodic interest payments, and the retirement of bonds.

Bonds Issued at Par

Suppose that on December 31, 2009, Delta Company issued 10,000 2-year, 10% debentures, at par. That means the company received exactly the amount of the bond principal or face value, and the market rate is equal to the coupon rate of 10%. Because bonds typically have a principal or face value of $1,000 each, the total issue is for 10,000 × $1,000 = $10 million. (Notice that this bond is identical to those valued in Exhibit 9-2 on page 401.) The interest expense equals the amount of the interest payments, (5% × $10 million) = $500,000 each 6 months for a total of $2,000,000 over the four semi-annual periods. Exhibit 9-3 shows how the bonds affect Delta's balance sheet equation throughout their life, assuming the company does not retire them before maturity.

The journal entries for the issue, interest, and maturity of the bond are as follows:

1.	Cash	10,000,000	
	Bonds payable		10,000,000
	To record proceeds upon issuance of 10% bonds maturing on December 31, 2011		
2–5.	Interest expense	500,000	
	Cash		500,000
	To record four payments of interest, one each 6-month period		
6.	Bonds payable	10,000,000	
	Cash		10,000,000
	To record payment of maturity value of bonds and their retirement		

OBJECTIVE 3

Account for bond issues over their entire life.

	A	=	L	+	SE
	Cash		**Bonds Payable**		**Retained Earnings**
Issuer's records					
1. Issuance	+10,000	=	+10,000		
2–5. Semiannual interest (repeated twice a year for 2 years)	–500	=			–500 ⎡Increase⎤ ⎢Interest⎥ ⎣Expense⎦
6. Maturity value (final payment)	–10,000	=	–10,000		

EXHIBIT 9-3

Bond Transactions: Issued at Par

($ in thousands)

Entry 1 is at issue, entries 2–5 are the four identical interest payments, and entry 6 is the repayment of principal at maturity.

The issuer's balance sheet at June 30, 2010; December 31, 2010; and June 30, 2011 (after the respective semiannual interest payments) shows the following:

Bonds payable, 10% due December 31, 2011	$10,000,000

Bonds Issued at a Discount

Now suppose Delta issues its 10,000 bonds when annual market interest rates are 12%, which is a 6% rate for each 6-month period. From Exhibit 9-2 we can see that Delta receives $965.35 for each bond, for total proceeds of 10,000 × $965.35 = $9,653,500. Therefore, the company recognizes a discount of $10,000,000 – $9,653,500 = $346,500 at issuance. The discount results from the fact that the company has use of only $9,653,500, not $10,000,000. The journal entry at issue is as follows:

Cash	9,653,500	
Discount on bonds payable	346,500	
Bonds payable		10,000,000

The discount on bonds payable is a contra account. The bonds payable account usually shows the face amount, and we deduct the discount amount from the face amount to get the amount shown on the balance sheet, often referred to as the net carrying amount, the net liability, or simply the book value:

Issuer's Balance Sheet	**December 31, 2009**
Bonds payable, 10%, due December 31, 2011	$10,000,000
Deduct: Discount on bonds payable	346,500
Net liability (book value)	$ 9,653,500

For bonds issued at a discount, interest takes two forms—semiannual cash outlays of (5% × $10 million) = $500,000 plus an "extra" lump-sum cash payment of $346,500 at maturity (total payment of $10,000,000 at maturity when Delta actually borrowed only $9,653,500). For the issuer, the $346,500 is another cost of using the borrowed funds over

For 6 Months Ended	(1) Beginning Net Liability	(2) Interest Expense* @ 6%**	(3) Nominal Interest† @ 5%	(4) Discount Amortized (2) – (3)	(5) Ending Unamortized Discount	(6) Ending Net Liability $10,000,000–(5)
12/31/09	—	—	—	—	$346,500	$ 9,653,500
6/30/10	$9,653,500	$ 579,207	$ 500,000	$ 79,207	267,293†	9,732,707
12/31/10	9,732,707	583,959	500,000	83,959	183,334	9,816,666
6/30/11	9,816,666	588,997	500,000	88,997	94,337	9,905,663
12/31/11	9,905,663	594,337	500,000	94,337	0	$10,000,000§
		$2,346,500	$2,000,000	$346,500		

*Market interest rate when issued times beginning net liability, column (1).

**To avoid rounding errors, an unrounded actual effective rate slightly under 6% was used. The table used to calculate the proceeds of the issue has too few significant digits to calculate the exact present value of a number as large as $10 million. The more exact issue price would be $9,653,489.

†Nominal (coupon interest) rate times par value (face value) for 6 months.

†$346,500 – $79,207 = $267,293; $267,293 – $83,959 = $183,334; etc.

§This is the face amount that Delta will repay on December 31, 2011, when the bond matures.

EXHIBIT 9-4

Effective Interest Amortization of Bond Discount

the four semiannual periods. For the investor, the $346,500 represents extra interest revenue in addition to the coupon payments. The issuer should spread the extra $346,500 over all four periods, not simply charge it at maturity. We call the spreading of the discount over the life of the bonds **discount amortization**.

How much of the $346,500 should Delta amortize each semiannual period? To determine this, companies use **effective interest amortization**, also called the **compound interest method**. The key to effective interest amortization is that each period bears a total interest expense, the cash payment plus discount amortization, equal to the net liability (the face amount less unamortized discount) multiplied by the market interest rate in effect when Delta issued the bond.

Exhibit 9-4 shows the effective interest amortization schedule for our example. The interest expense each period is the market rate of interest at issue times the net liability at the beginning of the period (see column 2). Notice that interest expense increases each semiannual period as the net liability increases until it equals the maturity value. The cash payment, column 3, is a constant $500,000, and the difference between the interest expense and the cash payment is the amount of discount amortized, shown in column 4. The amortization decreases the unamortized discount, column 5, which then increases the net liability, causing the interest expense to increase each period.

The balance sheet disclosure of the bond payable is the ending net liability, calculated as the difference between the face value and the unamortized discount. The balance sheet values each 6 months, after payment of the interest payment due on that date, are as follows:

discount amortization
The spreading of bond discount over the life of the bonds as interest expense.

effective interest amortization (compound interest method)
An amortization method that uses a constant interest rate.

Delta's Balance Sheets	December 31, 2009	June 30, 2010	December 31, 2010	June 30, 2011	December 31, 2011*
Bonds payable, 10%, due 12/31/11	$10,000,000	$10,000,000	$10,000,000	$10,000,000	$10,000,000
Deduct: Unamortized discount	346,500	267,293	183,334	94,337	—
Net liability	$ 9,653,500	$ 9,732,707	$ 9,816,666	$ 9,905,663	$10,000,000

*Before payment at maturity.

Exhibit 9-5 shows the balance sheet equation for the effective interest method of amortizing the bond discount. The journal entries follow:

12/31/09 1. Cash	9,653,500	
Discount on bonds payable	346,500	
Bonds payable		10,000,000
6/30/10 2. Interest expense	579,207	
Discount on bonds payable		79,207
Cash		500,000
12/31/10 3. Interest expense	583,959	
Discount on bonds payable		83,959
Cash		500,000
6/30/11 4. Interest expense	588,997	
Discount on bonds payable		88,997
Cash		500,000
12/31/11 5. Interest expense	594,337	
Discount on bonds payable		94,337
Cash		500,000
12/31/11 6. Bonds payable	10,000,000	
Cash		10,000,000

Bonds Issued at a Premium

Accounting for bonds issued at a premium is not difficult after you have mastered bond discounts. The key idea remains that the interest expense is the market rate of interest at issue times the net liability (book value of the bond). Bond premiums differ from bond discounts in the following ways:

1. The cash proceeds *exceed* the face amount.
2. We *add* the amount of the account Premium on Bonds Payable to the face amount of the bond to determine the net liability reported in the balance sheet.
3. Amortization of the bond premium causes interest expense to be *less than* the cash payment for interest.

To illustrate, suppose Delta issued the 10,000 bonds when annual market interest rates were 8% and semiannual rates were 4%. From Exhibit 9-2 on page 401, we can see that Delta receives $1,036.30 for each bond, for total proceeds of 10,000 × $1,036.30 = $10,363,000. Exhibit 9-6 shows how to

	A	=	L	+	SE
	Cash		**Bonds Payable**	**Discount on Bonds Payable**	**Retained Earnings**
1. Issuance	+ 9,654	=	+10,000	−346 [Increase Discount]	
Semiannual interest for 6 months ended:					
2. 6/30/10	−500	=		+79	−579
3. 12/31/10	−500	=		+84 [Decrease Discount]	−584 [Increase Interest Expense]
4. 6/30/11	−500	=		+89	−589
5. 12/31/11	−500	=		+94	−594
6. Maturity value, 12/31/11 (final payment)	−10,000	=	−10,000	0	
Bond-related totals	− 2,346	=	+ 0	+ 0	+ −2,346

EXHIBIT 9-5

Delta Company

Balance Sheet Equation Effects of Effective Interest Amortization of Bond Discount (rounded to thousands of dollars)

For 6 Months Ended	(1) Beginning Net Liability	(2) Interest Expense* @ 4%**	(3) Nominal Interest† @ 5%	(4) Premium Amortized (3) – (2)	(5) Ending Unamortized Premium	(6) Ending Net Liability $10,000,000 + (5)
12/31/09	—	—	—	—	$363,000	$10,363,000
6/30/10	$10,363,000	$ 414,517	$ 500,000	$ 85,483	277,517‡	10,277,517
12/31/10	10,277,517	411,098	500,000	88,902	188,615	10,188,615
6/30/11	10,188,615	407,542	500,000	92,458	96,157	10,096,157
12/31/11	10,096,157	403,843	500,000	96,157	0	10,000,000
		$ 1,637,000	$2,000,000	$363,000		

*Market interest rate when issued times beginning net liability, column (1).

**To avoid rounding errors, an unrounded actual effective rate slightly under 4% was used.

†Nominal (coupon interest) rate times par value (face value) for 6 months.

‡$363,000 – $85,483 = $277,517; $277,517 – $88,902 = $188,615; etc.

Delta's Balance Sheets	December 31, 2009	June 30, 2010	December 31, 2010	June 30, 2011	December 31, 2011*
Bonds payable, 10% due 12/31/11	$10,000,000	$10,000,000	$10,000,000	$10,000,000	$10,000,000
Add: Premium on bonds payable	363,000	277,517	188,615	96,157	0
Net liability	$10,363,000	$10,277,517	$10,188,615	$10,096,157	$10,000,000

*Before payment at maturity.

EXHIBIT 9-6

Effective Interest Amortization of Bond Premium

apply the effective interest method to the bond premium. The key concept remains the same as that for amortization of a bond discount: The interest expense (column 2) equals the net liability each period (column 1) multiplied by the market interest rate in effect when the bond was issued. Balance sheets show the net liability calculated as the face amount plus unamortized premium.

Exhibit 9-7 shows the effects on the balance sheet equation, and the journal entries are as follows:

```
12/31/09  1. Cash .............................  10,363,000
              Premium on bonds payable ..........              363,000
              Bonds payable ....................           $10,000,000
6/30/10   2. Interest expense ..................     414,517
              Premium on bonds payable ..........      85,483
              Cash .........................                 500,000
12/31/10  3. Interest expense ..................     411,098
              Premium on bonds payable ..........      88,902
              Cash .........................                 500,000
6/30/11   4. Interest expense ..................     407,542
              Premium on bonds payable ..........      92,458
              Cash .........................                 500,000
12/31/11  5. Interest expense ..................     403,843
              Premium on bonds payable ..........      96,157
              Cash .........................                 500,000
12/31/11  6. Bonds payable ....................  10,000,000
              Cash .........................              10,000,000
```

Companies frequently issue bonds between interest payment dates. When this occurs, the company makes an adjustment to the bond price to allow for the interest between the issue date and the first interest payment date.

	A	=		L	+	SE
	Cash		**Bonds Payable**	**Premium on Bonds Payable**		**Retained Earnings**
Issuer's records						
1. Issuance	+10,363	=	+10,000	+363 [Increase Premium]		
Semiannual interest 6 months ended						
2. 6/30/10	−500	=		−85		−415
3. 12/31/10	−500	=		−89 [Decrease Premium]		−411 [Increase Interest Expense]
4. 6/30/11	−500	=		−93		−407
5. 12/31/11	−500	=		−96		−404
6. Maturity value, 12/31/11 (final payment)	−10,000	=	−10,000	0		
Bond-related totals	− 1,637	=	+ 0	+ 0	+	−1,637

EXHIBIT 9-7

Delta Company

Balance Sheet Equation Effects of Effective Interest Amortization of Bond Premium (rounded to thousands of dollars)

Cash Flow Statement Effects

The issuance of bonds is a financing activity, so companies show the cash received as a cash inflow from financing activities on the statement of cash flows. Payments at maturity are also financing cash outflows. Semiannual interest payments are operating cash outflows under U.S. GAAP, as are all interest payments. Most companies using IFRS also classify the interest payments as operating activities, although they are allowed to list them with financing activities.

The amortization of bond discounts and premiums does not affect cash. Thus, it does not appear on a direct method statement of cash flows from operations. However, suppose a company uses the indirect method. The amortization of bond discount would be like depreciation, a noncash expense. You would add the amortization of bond discount to (or deduct the amortization of bond premium from) net income to get cash flow from operating activities. Such an adjustment in the indirect method of reporting cash flows from operations is necessary to adjust interest expense as reported on the income statement to the actual cash payment for interest.

Summary Problem for Your Review

PROBLEM

Suppose that on December 31, 2009, Procter & Gamble issued $12 million of 10-year, 10% debentures. Assume that the annual market interest rate at issuance was 14%.

1. Compute the proceeds from issuing the debentures.
2. Prepare an analysis of the following items: (a) issuance of the debentures, (b) first two semiannual interest payments, and (c) payment of the maturity value. Use the balance sheet equation (similar to the presentation in Exhibit 9-5, p. 406). Round to the nearest thousand dollars. Use a bond discount account.
3. Prepare journal entries for the items in requirement 2. Use a bond discount account.

	A	=	L		+	SE
	Cash		**Bonds Payable**	**Discount on Bonds Payable**		**Retained Earnings**
Procter & Gamble's records						
1. Issuance	+9,457		+12,000	−2,543 ⌈Increase		
2. Semiannual interest				⌊Discount		
6 Months ended						
6/30/10	−600			+62 ⌈Decrease		−662* ⌈Increase
12/31/10	−600			+66 ⌊Discount		−666* ⌊Interest Expense
3. Maturity value (final payment)	−12,000		−12,000			
Bond-related totals†	−14,543		0	0		−14,543

*7% × 9,457 = 662; 7% × (9,457 + 62) = 666.

†Totals after payment at maturity and all 20 entries for discount amortization and interest payments are made.

EXHIBIT 9-8

Analysis of Procter & Gamble's Bond Transactions

(in thousands of dollars)

SOLUTION

1. Because the market interest rate exceeds the nominal rate, the proceeds will be less than the face amount. Proceeds are the present value (PV) of the 20 interest payments of $600,000 and the $12 million maturity value at 7% per semiannual period:

PV of interest payments: 10.5940 × $600,000	$6,356,400
PV of maturity value: .2584 × $12,000,000	3,100,800
Total proceeds	$9,457,200

2. See Exhibit 9-8.

3. 12/31/09: Cash 9,457,200
   Discount on bonds payable 2,542,800
      Bonds payable 12,000,000
   6/30/10: Interest expense 662,004
      Discount on bonds payable 62,004
      Cash 600,000
   12/31/10: Interest expense 666,344
      Discount on bonds payable 66,344
      Cash 600,000
   12/31/19: Bonds payable 12,000,000
      Cash 12,000,000

Early Extinguishment

You have seen how companies account for bonds they hold until maturity. However, some companies redeem or pay off their bonds earlier, either by purchases on the open market or by exercising their rights to redeem callable bonds. We call it an **early extinguishment** when a company chooses to redeem its own bonds before maturity. When a company extinguishes debt early, it recognizes the difference between the cash paid and the net liability (face value less unamortized discount or plus unamortized premium) as a gain or loss.

Consider the bonds Delta issued at a discount (see Exhibit 9-4, page 405). Suppose Delta purchases all its bonds on the open market for $960 per $1,000 of face value on December 31, 2010 (after paying all interest payments and recording amortization for 2010):

early extinguishment
When a company chooses to redeem its own bonds before maturity.

Net liability:		
Face or par value	$10,000,000	
Deduct: Unamortized discount on bonds*	183,334	$9,816,666
Cash required, 96% of $10,000,000		9,600,000
Difference, gain on early		
extinguishment of debt		$ 216,666

*See Exhibit 9-4. Of the original $346,500 discount, Delta has amortized $79,207 + $83,959 = $163,166, leaving $183,334 of the discount unamortized.

Exhibit 9-9 presents an analysis of the transaction. Delta would show the $216,666 gain on extinguishment of debt on its income statement. The journal entry on December 31, 2010, is as follows:

Bond payable	10,000,000	
Discount on bonds payable		183,334
Gain on early extinguishment of debt		216,666
Cash		9,600,000
To record open market acquisition of entire issue of 10% bonds at 96		

Noninterest-Bearing Notes and Bonds

zero coupon bond
A bond or note that pays no cash interest during its life.

Some notes and bonds do not provide semiannual interest payments. Instead, they simply pay a lump sum at a specified date. For example, consider **zero coupon bonds**. These bonds provide no cash interest payments during their life—that is, no semiannual payments of interest. The name, zero coupon, is completely descriptive. To call such bonds noninterest-bearing, however, is misleading. Investors demand interest revenue. Otherwise, why would they bother investing in the first place? Therefore, companies sell zero coupon bonds and notes for less than the face or maturity value. The investor determines a bond's market value at the issuance date by calculating the present value of its maturity value, using the market rate of interest for bonds having similar terms and risks. The issuer amortizes the discount as interest over the life of the note.

Instead of collecting semiannual or other periodic payments, banks often discount both long- and short-term notes when making loans. Consider a 2-year, "noninterest-bearing," $10,000 face value note issued by Gamma Company on December 31, 2009, when annual market interest rates were 10% (which is 5% semiannually). In exchange for a promise to pay $10,000 on December 31, 2011, the bank provides Gamma with cash equal to the present value of the $10,000 payment:

implicit interest (imputed interest)
An interest expense that is not explicitly recognized in a loan agreement.

PV of $1.00 from Table 9A-2, 5% column, 4-period row = 0.8227
PV of $10,000 note = ($10,000 × .8227) = $8,227

The note requires no specific interest payments. However, there is **implicit interest** (or **imputed interest**), which is a form of interest expense that is not explicitly recognized as such in a loan agreement. The imputed interest amount is based on an **imputed interest rate**, which is the market rate that equates the proceeds of the loan with the present value of the loan payments.

imputed interest rate
The market interest rate that equates the proceeds from a loan with the present value of the loan payments.

	A	=	L		+	SE
	Cash		Bonds Payable	Discount on Bonds Payable		Retained Earnings
Redemption, December 31, 2010	–9,600	=	–10,000	+183 [Decrease Discount]	+217	[Gain on Early Extinguishment]

EXHIBIT 9-9

Delta Company

Analysis of Early Extinguishment of Debt on Issuer's Records (rounded to thousands of dollars)

	A	=	L		+	SE
	Cash		**Notes Payable**	**Discount on Notes Payable**		**Retained Earnings**
Proceeds of loan	+ 8,227	=	+10,000	−1,773 ⎡Increase		
Semiannual amortization				⎣Discount		
6 Months ended:						
6/30/10		=		+411		−411
12/31/10		=		+432 ⎡Decrease		−432 ⎡Increase
6/30/11		=		+454 ⎣Discount		−454 Interest
12/31/11		=		+476		−476 ⎣Expense
Payment of note	−10,000	=	−10,000			
Note-related totals	− 1,773	=	+ 0	+ 0		+ −1,773

EXHIBIT 9-10

Analysis of Transactions of Borrower, Discounted Notes

In this example, the $10,000 payment on December 31, 2011, will consist of $8,227 repayment of principal and ($10,000 − $8,227) = $1,773 of imputed interest. At issue, Gamma shows the note on its balance sheet as follows:

Note payable, due December 31, 2011	$10,000
Deduct: Discount on note payable	1,773
Net liability	$ 8,227

Exhibit 9-10 shows how Gamma recognizes interest expense for each semiannual period.

Each amortization of the discount decreases the discount account and increases the net liability. The appropriate journal entries follow:

12/31/09	Cash	8,227	
	Discount on note payable	1,773	
	Note payable		$10,000
6/30/10	Interest expense	411	
	Discount on note payable		411
12/31/10	Interest expense	432	
	Discount on note payable		432
6/30/11	Interest expense	454	
	Discount on note payable		454
12/31/11	Interest expense	476	
	Discount on note payable		476
	Note payable	10,000	
	Cash		10,000

Accounting for Leases

On page 403, we saw that **Jack in the Box** has a long-term liability called Capital Lease Obligations. Why do we treat some leases as liabilities, but not others? Because sometimes a company signs a lease that gives it most of the privileges of ownership. Essentially, it uses the lease as the method of financing the asset, so its payment obligations are similar to those of debt. Other times a company signs a lease that simply gives it permission to use the asset for a specific period of time—which qualifies as a simple rental expense.

OBJECTIVE 4

Value and account for long-term lease obligations.

lease

A contract whereby an owner (lessor) grants the use of property to a second party (lessee) for rental payments.

lessor

The owner of property who grants usage rights to the lessee.

lessee

The party that has the right to use leased property and makes lease payments to the lessor.

capital lease (finance lease)

A lease that transfers most risks and benefits of ownership to the lessee.

bargain purchase option

A provision that states that the lessee can purchase the asset from the lessor at the end of the lease for substantially less than the asset's fair value.

operating lease

A lease that should be accounted for by the lessee as ordinary rent expenses.

Leasing is a big business. Companies can acquire almost any asset imaginable via a lease contract. A **lease** is a contract whereby a **lessor** (owner) grants the use of property to a **lessee** in exchange for regular payments. Legal title to the property remains with the lessor, but the lessee uses the property as it would use property it owns. Our discussion focuses on leasing from the lessee's point of view. From an accounting perspective, whether we record a lease as a liability depends on whether it is a capital (finance) lease or an operating lease.

Operating and Capital (Finance) Leases

Accountants categorize leases into two categories, capital and operating. **Capital leases** (called **finance leases** under IFRS) transfer most of the risks and benefits of ownership to the lessee. Many such leases are similar to installment sales in which the purchaser pays the price of an item over time along with interest payments. Accountants require companies to record such leased items as if the lessee had borrowed the money and purchased the leased asset. In other words, the economic substance of the transaction prevails over the legal form. The property becomes an asset, and the obligation to pay for it becomes a liability.

The lease structure determines whether a lessee treats a lease as an operating or capital lease for accounting purposes. Under U.S. GAAP, a lease is a capital lease if it meets one or more of the following conditions:

1. The lessor transfers ownership of the asset to the lessee by the end of the lease term.
2. The lease contains a **bargain purchase option**—that is, a provision that states that the lessee can purchase the asset from the lessor at the end of the lease for substantially less than the asset's fair value.
3. The lease term equals or exceeds 75% of the estimated economic life of the property.
4. At the start of the lease term, the present value of minimum lease payments is at least 90% of the property's fair value.

Leases reported under IFRS have similar but less detailed requirements to qualify as a finance (capital) lease. Essentially the lease must cover substantially all of the asset's life and the present value of the lease payments must be approximately equal to the asset's fair value.

All other leases are **operating leases**. Examples are an office rented by the month and a car rented by the day. Companies account for operating leases as ordinary rent expenses. Operating leases do not appear as liabilities on the balance sheet.

Managers cannot classify a lease however they wish—the lease either meets the requirements of a capital (finance) lease or it does not. However, some managers structure leases so they do not meet any of the criteria of a capital lease to keep them from appearing on the balance sheet.

Consider a simple example to see how the accounting differs for operating and capital leases. Suppose the Bestick Company can acquire a truck with a useful life of 4 years and no residual value under either of the following conditions:

Buy Outright	or	Capital (Finance) Lease
Borrow $50,000 cash and agree to repay it in four equal installments at 12% interest compounded annually. Use the $50,000 to purchase the truck		Rental cost of $16,462 per year, payable at the end of each of 4 years; ownership of the truck transfers to Bestick at the end of the lease.

There is no basic difference between an outright purchase financed with debt or an irrevocable (noncancellable) lease for 4 years. The Bestick Company uses the asset for its entire useful life and must pay for repairs, property taxes, and other operating costs under either plan. Thus, it is a capital (finance) lease.

Companies make most lease payments at the start of each period, but to ease our computations we assume that each payment of $16,462 will occur at the end of the year. To make the comparison between capital leasing and purchasing, we need to calculate payments on the $50,000 loan in the purchase option:

$$\text{Let } X = \text{loan payment}$$
$$\$50,000 = \text{PV of annuity of } \$X \text{ per year for 4 years at 12\%}$$
$$\$50,000 = 3.0373 \times X$$
$$X = \$50,000 \div 3.0373$$
$$X = \$16,462 \text{ per year}$$

Note that this loan payment is exactly equal to the lease payment. Thus, from Bestick's perspective, both an outright purchase and a capital lease create an obligation for four $16,462 payments that have a present value of $50,000.

Suppose GAAP allowed Bestick to treat this lease contract as an operating lease. At the end of each year the journal entry would be as follows:

Rent expense	16,462	
Cash		16,462
To record lease payment		

No leasehold asset or lease liability would appear on the balance sheet.

Now suppose Bestick accounts for the lease as a capital lease as required by both U.S. GAAP and IFRS. Then it must place both a leasehold asset and a lease liability on its balance sheet at the present value of future lease payments, initially $50,000 in this illustration. The signing of the capital lease requires the following journal entry:

Truck leasehold	50,000	
Capital lease liability, current		10,462
Capital lease liability, long-term		39,538
To record lease creation.		

Note that the $50,000 liability has two components. The current liability is the payment due in the next year less the first year's interest: [$16,462 – (12% × 50,000)] = $10,462. The remainder, $50,000 – $10,462 = $39,538, is a long-term liability.

Bestick then amortizes the asset over 4 years. Straight-line amortization, the most common method, is $50,000 ÷ 4 = $12,500 annually.

The yearly journal entries for the leasehold amortization expense are as follows:

Leasehold amortization expense	12,500	
Truck leasehold		12,500

In addition, Bestick must record the annual lease payment. Each lease payment consists of interest expense plus an amount that reduces the outstanding liability. We use the effective interest method, as Exhibit 9-11 demonstrates. The yearly journal entries for lease payments are as follows:

Interest expense	6,000		4,745		3,339		1,764
Lease liability	10,462		11,717		13,123		14,698
Cash		16,462		16,462		16,462	16,462

The January 1, 2009, balance sheet of **Delta Airlines** on the top of the next page illustrates leased assets and the associated liabilities. Note that the amount of the total assets is less than the amount of the total liabilities.

EXHIBIT 9-11

Bestick Company

Schedule of Capital Lease Payments

End of Year	(1) Capital Lease Liability at Beginning of Year	(2) Interest Expense at 12% per Year	(3) Cash for Capital Lease Payment	(4) (3)–(2) Reduction in Lease Liability	(5) (1)–(4) Capital Lease Liability at End of Year
1	50,000	$6,000	$16,462	10,462	$39,538
2	39,538	4,745	16,462	11,717	27,821
3	27,821	3,339	16,462	13,123	14,698
4	14,698	1,764	16,462	14,698	0

	January 1, 2009
Assets	
Flight and ground equipment under capital leases:	
Flight equipment	$708
Less: Accumulated amortization	152
Flight and ground equipment under capital leases, net	$556
Liabilities	
Current obligations under capital leases	$473
Long-term obligations under capital leases	92
Total obligations under capital leases	$565

INTERPRETING FINANCIAL STATEMENTS

Explain why the $556 million net asset value of capital leases for Delta Airlines on January 1, 2009, is not the same as the $565 million of obligations under capital leases.

Answer

When a company initiates a lease, the amounts of the capital-lease asset and the capital-lease obligation are identical. Their values first diverge and then converge over time because of the accounting process. Companies typically amortize assets using the straight-line basis. In contrast, they reduce the liability each period using the effective interest method. Under this method, each lease payment includes the payment of interest and the reduction of principal. Because interest is largest in the early years of the lease, reductions in the principal of the lease obligation start off small. Hence, we expect the amount of liability to exceed that of the asset in most cases.

Differences in Income Statements

Exhibit 9-12 summarizes the major differences between the accounting for operating leases and the accounting for capital (finance) leases. The cumulative expenses are the same, $65,848, but the timing differs. Capital leases recognize larger expenses than operating leases in the early years and smaller expenses in later years. Therefore, immediate reported income is lower for capital leases. The longer the lease, the more pronounced the differences.

	Operating Lease Method	**Capital Lease Method**			**Differences**	
					(e)	**(f)**
				(d)	**(a) – (d)**	**Cumulative**
	(a)	**(b)**	**(c)**	**(b) + (c)**	**Difference**	**Difference**
	Lease	**Amortization**	**Interest**	**Total**	**in Pretax**	**in Pretax**
Year	**Payment***	**of Asset†**	**Expense‡**	**Expense**	**Income**	**Income**
1	$16,462	$12,500	$ 6,000	$18,500	$(2,038)	$(2,038)
2	16,462	12,500	4,745	17,245	(783)	(2,821)
3	16,462	12,500	3,339	15,839	623	(2,198)
4	16,462	12,500	1,764	14,264	2,198	0
Cumulative expenses	$65,848	$50,000	$15,848	$65,848	$ 0	

*Rent expense for the year under the operating-lease method.

†$50,000 ÷ 4 = $12,500.

†From Exhibit 9-11.

EXHIBIT 9-12

Bestick Company

Comparison of Annual Expenses: Operating Versus Capital Leases

An operating lease affects the income statement as rent expense, which is the amount of the lease payment. A capital lease affects the income statement as amortization (of the asset) plus interest expense (on the liability).

Differences in Balance Sheets and Cash Flow Statements

The difference between operating and capital (finance) leases on the balance sheet is straightforward. At the inception of the lease, operating leases do not affect the balance sheet, whereas capital leases create both an asset and a liability.

The effects on the statement of cash flows are not as obvious. Operating leases affect only cash flows from operations. All cash payments for operating leases are operating cash outflows. In contrast, capital (finance) leases affect both operating and financing cash flows. The cash lease payment has two components: interest expense and reduction of the lease liability. For Bestick Company, the first year's lease payment of $16,462 includes an interest expense of $6,000 and a reduction in the lease liability of $10,462, as you can see in Exhibit 9-11. The $6,000 interest expense is an operating cash outflow under U.S. GAAP. The lease reduction of $10,462 is a financing cash outflow. In the second year, the operating cash outflow is $4,745, and the financing cash outflow is $11,717. Notice that the operating cash outflow systematically declines throughout the life of the lease, whereas the financing cash outflow grows. The only difference under IFRS is that the cash flow for interest payments can be a financing item.

Summary Problem for Your Review

PROBLEM

Suppose the Sanchez Company enters into a lease to use a machine for 3 years with payments at the end of each year. Lease payments for the 3-year term of the lease are as follows:

Year 1	$ 40,000
Year 2	40,000
Year 3	40,000
Total lease payments	$120,000

Sanchez treats the lease as a capital (finance) lease and uses an interest rate of 10%.

1. Calculate the amount Sanchez should record as the carrying value of the capital-lease asset and the capital-lease liability as of the beginning of the lease on 12/31/X0.
2. How will Sanchez record the first year's payment?
3. How will the lease affect the first year's income statement?
4. How will the lease affect the first year's statement of cash flows?

SOLUTION

1. The present value of a 3-year annuity of $40,000 per year at 10% will be the initial value of the asset and the liability. From Table 9A-3, the present value factor is 2.4869.

$$(2.4869 \times \$40,000) = \$99,476$$

2. The first year's payment will be $40,000, part of which is interest and part of which is principal repayment. The interest portion is $(.10 \times 99,476) = 9,948$. The journal entry is as follows:

Interest expense	9,948	
Capital lease liability	30,052	
Cash		40,000

3. The first year's income statement will show an expense of $9,948 for interest. It will also show amortization expense on the capital-lease asset, assuming straight-line amortization, of $(\$99,476 \div 3) = \$33,159$.
4. The total cash outflow for the first year is $40,000. The interest portion, $9,948, will be an operating cash outflow. The reduction of the lease obligation of $30,052 will be a financing cash outflow.

Other Long-Term Liabilities, Including Pensions and Deferred Taxes

We next explore some other long-term liabilities that commonly appear on balance sheets—pensions, other postretirement benefits, deferred taxes, restructuring liabilities, and contingent liabilities.

Pensions and Other Postretirement Benefits

<table>
<tr><td>

OBJECTIVE 5

Evaluate pensions and other postretirement benefits.

---

pensions

Payments to former employees after they retire.

other postretirement benefits

Benefits provided to retired workers in addition to a pension, such as life and health insurance.

</td><td>

Many U.S. companies provide benefits for retired employees. Accountants place these benefits into two categories: **pensions**, which are payments to former employees after they retire, and **other postretirement benefits**, which primarily consist of health insurance, but also include any other benefits. Let's first consider pensions.

PENSIONS Pensions are divided into defined contribution plans and defined benefit plans. Accounting for defined contribution pension plans, such as 401k plans, is straightforward. Employers contribute money directly into a fund that belongs to an employee. The employee's retirement pay will depend on the amount in the fund at the time he or she retires. If the fund has performed well, the employee's payments are higher than if the fund has performed poorly. The company has no obligation beyond its initial contribution. In essence, all the risks and rewards associated with fund performance rest with the employee.

</td></tr>
</table>

In contrast, defined benefit plans create a liability for the company. Why? Because such a plan guarantees employees an amount of retirement pay, normally a certain percentage of their last few years of pay, with the percentage usually depending on their years of service. The company is obligated to make these pension payments. We measure the obligation as the present value of the expected future pension payments to currently retired employees and to employees who will retire in the future. This present value depends on many assumptions, such as when current employees will retire, what their salaries will be at the time, their life expectancies, and the interest rate used to calculate present values. Companies report the total value of this pension obligation in footnotes to their financial statements. For example, Jack in the Box reported a pension obligation of $340 million in the footnotes to its financial statements on September 27, 2009. Companies could simply accrue pension liabilities without setting assets aside. However, if a company then went bankrupt, current workers and retirees would be left without pension benefits. To avoid this, U.S. tax laws provide incentives for companies to make payments into a pension fund that is separate from the company's assets and controlled by a trustee. The money in this fund is available only to pay future pensions. Footnotes to the financial statements reveal the fair value of the assets in the pension fund. If the fair value of the assets is less than the present value of a company's pension obligations, a company lists a net liability on its balance sheet. The fair value of Jack in the Box's pension fund assets on September 27, 2009, was $232 million. Because pension obligations were greater than the assets, Jack in the Box included a ($340 million − $232 million) = $108 million liability among its other long-term liabilities on its balance sheet. Similarly, the German electronics and engineering company Siemens (which reports under IFRS) reports pension obligations of €22,654 million, pension fund assets of €20,194, and therefore a net pension liability of (€22,654 − €20,194) = €2,460 million.

How do companies account for pension expenses year by year? To apply the matching principle, they must charge the pension expense to the years an employee works. Each year that an employee gets claim to additional retirement pay, the additional claim is an expense of the year the employee works, not the year the company distributes the retirement pay. Thus, a company's pension expense each year is essentially equal to the increase in the pension liability, although this is complicated slightly by some measurement issues that are beyond the scope of this text. Consider Jack in the Box's experience in the year ended September 27, 2009. Pension expense was $12 million. In addition, Jack in the Box paid $23 million cash into the pension fund. We would account for this as follows (in millions):

	A	=	L	+	SE	
	Cash		**Pension Liability**		**Retained Earnings**	
Current pension expense	−23	=	−11		−12	⌐Increase Pension Expense⌐

The journal entry would be as follows:

Pension expense	12,000,000	
Pension liability	11,000,000	
Cash		23,000,000

To record pension expense for the year. The
expense was $12 million, and $23 million
was paid in cash to the pension fund.

OTHER POSTRETIREMENT BENEFITS Accounting for the expense of health insurance and similar postretirement benefits is similar to accounting for pensions. The key difference is that most companies do not set aside specific assets on behalf of employees. Instead, they record the full present value of expected payments as a liability. Companies recognize any increase in the liability as a current expense.

Jack in the Box's liability for other postretirement benefits, included in other liabilities on the balance sheet and explained in the footnotes, was $17.0 million on September 28, 2008. During fiscal 2009, the company paid $1.1 million for health insurance and other benefits to retirees, incurred other postretirement benefit expenses of $1.7 million, and had an actuarial loss (which caused an increase in expected future payments) of $6.2 million. Thus, the liability on September 27, 2009, was $23.8 million. The summary journal entries to record the $1.7 million expense, the $1.1 million payment, and the $6.2 million loss are as follows:

Other postretirement benefits expense	$1,700,000	
Postretirement benefits liability		$1,700,000
Postretirement benefits liability	$1,100,000	
Cash		$1,100,000
Actuarial loss on postretirement benefits	6,200,000	
Postretirement benefits liability		6,200,000

Liabilities for pensions and other postretirement benefits can be huge. For example, in early 2009 Ford Motor Company had an excess of pension liabilities over funded assets of nearly $12 billion and other postretirement benefits liabilities of more than $16 billion. This was about 13% of Ford's total assets. It is important to recognize that the funding status of a pension plan can change very quickly. Because most companies invest their pension assets in the stock and bond markets, the value of the pension assets fluctuates with the market. Medtronic, the Minneapolis-based medical technology company, had net assets of more than $90 million as a "prepaid post-retirement benefits" account in 2008. However, because of the fall in stock prices in 2008–2009, its 2009 balance sheet included a $157 million liability for underfunded benefit plans.

Internationally, practice concerning pensions and other postretirement benefits varies widely. For example, many countries provide the majority of retirement income through individual savings or through tax-supported government programs akin to the U.S. Social Security Administration. In these cases, actual company pensions are rare, so there is nothing to report. In roughly one-half of the 45 countries examined in a recent survey, it was common practice for an independent outside trustee to manage pension funds, similar to U.S. practice. In the United States, the Pension Benefit Guarantee Corporation guarantees minimal retirement benefits to more than 44 million U.S. workers in more than 29,000 pension plans, even if their company goes bankrupt and leaves a severely underfunded pension liability.

Deferred Taxes

We have previously seen that delaying the payment of taxes from the time a company earns income to when it pays cash leads to short-term taxes payable. Another source of difference between income tax expense and income tax payments arises because a nation's tax rules and the GAAP requirements for financial reporting differ. Sometimes the difference between GAAP reporting and tax laws forces companies to record some income tax expense long before they pay the taxes. This creates a **deferred income tax liability**. (Some companies also have deferred tax assets, which are beyond the scope of our coverage.) For example, Jack in the Box reported income tax expense of $79.5 million in the year ending September 27, 2009. However, Jack in the Box paid $104.5 million in income taxes, including $25 million of taxes that had previously been deferred. The situation was reversed in the previous year, when Jack in the Box

OBJECTIVE 6

Interpret deferred tax liabilities.

deferred income tax liability
An obligation arising because of predictable future taxes, to be paid when a future tax return is filed.

paid $64.0 million to the government but had an income tax expense of $70.3 million, deferring $6.3 million to future years.

The differences between income tax expense and income taxes actually paid arise because accountants designed GAAP to provide useful information to investors, whereas governments write the tax code to generate revenue and provide specific incentives to companies. Revenue recognition and expense recognition rules for tax purposes can differ from GAAP rules on two dimensions: (1) whether to recognize an item (permanent differences) and (2) when to recognize it (temporary differences).

To save their companies money, good managers struggle to pay the least amount of income tax at the latest possible moment permitted within the law. As a result, they delay the reporting of taxable revenue as long as possible, while deducting tax-deductible expense items as quickly as possible. Corporations pay taxes to the government as follows:

$$\text{Taxes paid or payable} = \text{Income tax rate} \times (\text{Taxable revenue} - \text{Tax-deductible expenses})$$

tax rate

The percentage of taxable income paid to the government.

The **tax rate** is the percentage of taxable income paid to the government. U.S. corporate tax rates range from 15% on incomes of less than $50,000 to 35% on incomes of more than $335,000. Many states also levy an income tax, with tax rates varying from state to state. To simplify our illustrations, we generally assume a flat tax rate of 40%. This is a reasonable approximation of the combination of the federal 35% rate plus a state tax rate. We provide two illustrations, one permanent difference (municipal bond interest) and one temporary difference (depreciation).

permanent differences

Revenue or expense items that are recognized for tax purposes but not recognized under GAAP, or vice versa.

PERMANENT DIFFERENCES **Permanent differences** arise when a company recognizes a revenue or expense item for either tax or financial reporting purposes but not for both. For example, suppose a U.S. company owns a bond issued by the city of New York and periodically receives interest on it. For financial reporting, the company reports this interest revenue on the income statement. Under U.S. federal law, bondholders do not pay taxes on interest received from municipal bonds issued by cities, states, and towns. Therefore, the interest revenue will never appear on the company's tax return. Dealing with this permanent difference is straightforward. We include the interest revenue for financial reporting, but we never recognize an income tax expense related to this revenue on our financial statements, and we never have to pay income tax on the revenue received. Therefore, permanent differences do not create deferred taxes.

Suppose a company with a 40% tax rate reports $100 of pretax income, of which $20 is revenue from nontaxable municipal bonds. It will pay taxes on only ($100 – $20) = $80 of income, resulting in taxes of ($80 × 40%) = $32. As a percentage of pretax income, the tax rate appears to be ($32 ÷ $100) = 32%, rather than the 40% nominal tax rate.

temporary differences

Differences between net income and taxable income that arise because some revenue and expense items are recognized at different times for tax purposes than for financial reporting purposes.

TEMPORARY DIFFERENCES **Temporary differences** arise when a company recognizes some revenue or expense item at a different time for tax purposes than for financial reporting purposes. A common temporary difference arises with depreciation. Many companies use accelerated depreciation for tax purposes and straight-line depreciation for financial reporting. Suppose Webster Company earns $40,000 per year before deducting depreciation and taxes, and pays taxes at a rate of 40% of taxable income. Webster acquires a $10,000 asset with a 2-year useful life. It can deduct the $10,000 immediately for tax purposes and will depreciate it at $5,000 per year for financial reporting.

Exhibit 9-13 shows that Webster will pay taxes of $12,000 the first year and $16,000 the second, a total of $28,000 or 40% of the $70,000 total income. What should Webster report as income tax expense each year for financial reporting purposes? One approach is to report the

EXHIBIT 9-13

Webster Company

Income for Financial Reporting and Income Tax Return

	Financial Reporting		Income Tax Returns	
	Year 1	Year 2	Year 1	Year 2
Income before depreciation and taxes	$40,000	$40,000	$40,000	$40,000
Depreciation	5,000	5,000	10,000	0
Pretax income	$35,000	$35,000	$30,000	$40,000
Taxes payable at 40%			$12,000	$16,000

amount Webster actually pays to the government each year, but neither U.S. GAAP nor IFRS permits this alternative. Instead, they require Webster to report the amount that it would have paid if the pretax income used for financial reporting had also been reported to the tax authorities. If taxable income had been $35,000 each year, the tax would have been 40% × $35,000 = $14,000 annually. Therefore, the income statement for financial reporting would show the following:

	Year 1	Year 2	2-Year Totals
Pretax income	$35,000	$35,000	$70,000
Tax expense (40% of $35,000)	14,000	14,000	28,000
Net income	$21,000	$21,000	$42,000

This method matches the income tax expense with the financial reporting revenues and expenses to which it relates.

How do we account for this income tax expense? The tax payable to the government in year 1 is $12,000, but we record a tax expense of $14,000. Think of it as a current payable for the $12,000 currently owed to the government and a $2,000 liability that arises because of predictable future taxes. This $2,000 liability is a deferred tax liability because it will be paid only when a future tax return is filed. The journal entry is as follows:

Income tax expense	14,000	
Deferred tax liability		2,000
Cash (or taxes payable)		12,000

We show the deferred tax liability of $2,000 on the balance sheet. It equals the tax rate of 40% times the $5,000 temporary difference in depreciation expense ($5,000 on the books versus $10,000 on the tax return).

Remember that differences between reported income and taxable income result in deferral of taxes, not cancellation of taxes. Thus, we recognize a liability for future taxes equal to today's tax savings. In year 2, the tax payable to the government is $16,000, but the company again records a tax expense of $14,000. Therefore, the company pays the $2,000 that it treated as a deferred tax liability in year 1. The journal entry in the second year is as follows:

Income tax expense	14,000	
Deferred tax liability	2,000	
Cash (or taxes payable)		16,000

In this example, we create the deferred tax liability in year 1 and reverse it in year 2. Because Webster will pay the $2,000 in the next year, it is a current liability. However, if we depreciate an asset over 10 years, the deferred tax liability would take 10 years to reverse. Deferred taxes that become due in more than 1 year are long-term liabilities.

The balance sheet of nearly every company contains deferred tax liabilities. For example, Jack in the Box had deferred income taxes of $2 million on September 27, 2009, as shown in Exhibit 9-1 on page 392, due primarily to the timing of depreciation. If Jack in the Box had used straight-line depreciation for both financial and tax reporting, it would have already paid $2 million more to the government in taxes. As it stands, it will still pay the $2 million, but it has delayed the payment and thereby can earn interest on the money in the meantime.

Summary Problem for Your Review

PROBLEM

The Solar Kitchen Corporation began business on January 1, 20X0, to manufacture and sell energy-efficient additions to provide solar-heated eating areas next to existing kitchens. Because of good styling and marketing to an energy-conscious public, sales soared. During 20X0, the following transactions occurred:

1. On January 1, Solar Kitchen sold 1,000 new shares of common stock at $100 per share.

2. The company immediately invested one-half of the proceeds from the stock sale in tax-free municipal bonds yielding 6% per annum. It held the bonds throughout the year, resulting in interest revenue of $50,000 × .06 = $3,000.

3. Sales for the year were $450,000, with expenses of $380,000 reported under GAAP (exclusive of income tax expense).

4. Tax depreciation exceeded depreciation for financial reporting by $30,000.

Required

1. Calculate earnings before tax for financial reporting.
2. Calculate income tax payable to the tax authorities and income tax expense for financial reporting using a 40% tax rate.
3. Make the appropriate journal entry. Assume the 40% tax rate is expected to be maintained.

SOLUTION

1. Earnings before taxes for financial reporting are as follows:

Sales revenue	$450,000
Interest revenue	3,000
Less: Operating expenses	(380,000)
Pretax income	$ 73,000

2. Tax calculations follow:

	Reporting to Tax Authorities	Financial Reporting
Earnings before tax	$73,000	$73,000
Permanent differences		
Nontaxable interest revenue	(3,000)	(3,000)
Subtotal	70,000	70,000
Temporary differences		
Depreciation	(30,000)	—
Earnings on which tax is based	40,000	70,000
Tax rate	.40	.40
Income tax payable	$16,000	
Income tax expense for financial reporting		$28,000

3.				
	Income tax expense	. . . .	28,000	
	Income tax payable	. . . .		16,000
	Deferred tax liability	. . . .		12,000

Restructuring Liabilities

In the last decade, many companies recorded restructuring charges, and some recognized significant liabilities for future costs. A **restructuring** is a significant makeover of part of the company. It typically involves closing one or more plants, reducing the size of the workforce, and terminating or relocating various activities. For example, Hewlett-Packard (HP) recorded $270 million in restructuring charges in 2008 and $387 million in 2007. At year-end 2008, HP reported a liability of $1,099 million for restructuring costs. Note that the charge against the income statement is in anticipation of costs the company expects to incur as it executes the plan. The liability at year-end is for the remaining unexecuted costs. The company may classify it as current or long-term, depending on when it expects to incur the costs. HP listed all $1,099 million as a current liability, so it plans to complete its restructuring in 2009.

restructuring

A significant makeover of part of the company typically involving the closing of plants, firing of employees, and relocation of activities.

Companies reporting under IFRS include restructuring liabilities under provisions. For example, Nestlé, the Swiss-based packaged food company, reported the following restructuring transactions in its "Provisions" footnote to its 2008 financial statements (in millions of Swiss francs, CHF):

	Restructuring
At 31 December 2007	CHF 1,007
Provisions made in the period	303
Amount used	(313)
Unused amounts reversed	(51)
Currency retranslations	(88)
At 31 December 2008	CHF 858

Nestlé lists all of its provisions with long-term liabilities. In addition to restructuring, its provisions include environmental and litigation obligations. It describes the restructuring charges as follows: "Restructuring provisions are expected to result in future cash outflows when implementing the plans (usually over the following two to three years)."

Contingent Liabilities

The liabilities you have learned about so far are all concrete. We are confident about the existence of the liability, even if we have to estimate its amount. In contrast, a **contingent liability** is a potential (possible) liability that depends on a future event arising out of a past transaction. If the probability that the event will occur is high and the company can reasonably estimate the amount of the obligation, the company should list the liability and its amount on its balance sheet. More often, a contingent liability has an indefinite amount. A common example is a lawsuit. These are possible obligations of indefinite amounts. Why? Because if a judge rules against the company, it will be obligated to pay an amount that is currently unknown. However, the judge may rule in the company's favor, in which case there is no obligation.

contingent liability
A potential liability that depends on a future event arising out of a past transaction.

If the probability that the future event will occur does not meet a probability threshold, or if a company cannot estimate the dollar amount of the potential liability, it does not report a dollar amount on its balance sheet. In this situation, some companies list contingent liabilities without a dollar amount on the balance sheet after long-term liabilities but before stockholders' equity. For example, Hewlett-Packard called this "Commitments and Contingencies" on its balance sheet with no amount specified. HP includes eight pages of footnotes explaining this, one page on Commitments and seven pages on Litigation and Contingencies. Other companies discuss environmental issues, product safety, potential strikes, and any other contingent event that might affect the company. The Business First box on page 422 describes an example of the evolution of a contingent liability to a definite liability—one where the final amount of the liability remains unknown more than 20 years after Dow Corning first reported it as a contingent liability.

Debt Ratios and Interest-Coverage Ratios

We have emphasized the link between the interest rate required by lenders and the risk associated with the loan. When people take out loans to buy a car or a house, the interest rate on the loan is smaller if the down payment is larger. Lenders believe that the higher the down payment, the less risk they bear. How does this concept work for corporations? Potential creditors often use debt ratios to measure the extent to which a company has used borrowing to finance its activity. The more the borrowing and the less the stockholders' equity, the riskier it is to lend money to the firm. Investors and analysts use a variety of ratios to help assess the risk imposed by a company's borrowing:

OBJECTIVE 7

Use ratio analysis to assess a company's debt levels.

BUSINESS FIRST

CONTINGENT LIABILITIES AT DOW CORNING, INC.

A well-known product liability issue involved Dow Corning, Inc. In the 1980s, the company began facing many accusations from patients who were unhappy with silicone breast implants made by the company and surgically installed for reconstructive or cosmetic purposes. The accusations became lawsuits over time, and the company was confronted with a major product liability. Throughout the 1980s, Dow Corning regularly reported on its ongoing litigation. However, the lawsuits being heard in court were still fairly few, and no one knew how they might be resolved. So for several years the financial statements disclosed the litigation in some detail, but the balance sheet and income statement did not show specific numbers.

In 1991, the company recorded $25 million of pretax costs for the pending litigation; in 1992, it recorded another $69 million. Remember that each of these amounts was intended to be a best estimate of future costs to be incurred. The product from which the claims stemmed had been produced and delivered years before. In fact, production of all silicone implants ceased in 1992. However, the liability estimates provided through 1992 were woefully inadequate. In 1993, Dow Corning recorded another pretax charge of $640 million. Combined with expected insurance coverage exceeding $600 million, the expected total cost of litigation exceeded $1.2 billion. Dow Corning and other manufacturers joined together to structure a settlement that would properly compensate plaintiffs, minimize legal costs, and allow the companies to survive. The deal required an agreement between the plaintiffs, the companies, and the insurance carriers. In late 1994,

agreement seemed close. Dow Corning provided another pretax charge of $241 million. Combined with additional expected insurance costs, the amounts set aside for injured parties approached $2 billion from Dow Corning and another similar amount from other manufacturers. There were more than 19,000 pending lawsuits on this product.

In May 1995, Dow Corning declared bankruptcy. The company claimed that too many plaintiffs were unwilling to agree to the settlement. Bankruptcy changed the company's whole litigation situation and left the final outcome very much in doubt. In 1998, Dow Corning recorded another pretax charge of $1.1 billion as its estimate of total additional costs to be incurred on all claims in bankruptcy, including the breast implant controversy. That is the last time Dow has charged a significant amount for implant costs. Since then the liability labeled "Implant Reserve," representing the present value of expected future settlements, has gradually decreased. However, at the end of 2008 it was still $1.6 billion. In 2008, Dow Corning earned $739 million on sales of nearly $5.5 billion. Its total stockholders' equity was $2.2 billion. You can see that this liability remains a significant drag on Dow Corning. The true liability is still being played out in the courts. However, the facts to date show the difficulty of predicting the cost of litigation. Any time your initial estimate of $25 million is off by a factor of 100, you know your prediction methods have a problem or two.

Sources: Dow Corning annual reports for 1991–2008 (included since 2003 with the 10-K filings of Corning Corporation).

---

debt-to-equity ratio
Total liabilities divided by total shareholders' equity.

long-term-debt-to-total-capital ratio
Total long-term debt divided by total shareholders' equity plus total long-term debt.

debt-to-total-assets ratio
Total liabilities divided by total assets.

interest-coverage ratio
Pretax income plus interest expense divided by interest expense.

$$\text{Debt-to-equity ratio} = \frac{\text{Total liabilities}}{\text{Total shareholders' equity}}$$

$$\text{Long-term-debt-to-total-capital ratio} = \frac{\text{Total long-term debt}}{\text{Total shareholders' equity} + \text{Total long-term debt}}$$

$$\text{Debt-to-total-assets ratio} = \frac{\text{Total liabilities}}{\text{Total assets}}$$

$$\text{Interest-coverage ratio} = \frac{\text{Pretax income} + \text{Interest expense}}{\text{Interest expense}}$$

Note that the first three ratios are alternate ways of expressing the proportion of the firm's resources obtained by borrowing. The higher the proportion, the riskier the firm and the higher the interest rate it must pay. The fourth ratio, the interest-coverage ratio, more directly measures the firm's ability to meet its interest obligation. It measures the amount of income available in relation to the company's interest expense. The lower the ratio, the more likely the company will have difficulty meeting its interest obligations.

Debt burdens vary greatly from firm to firm and industry to industry. For example, retailing companies, utilities, and transportation companies tend to have debt of more than 60% of their assets, which gives a debt-to-equity ratio of 1.5. Jack in the Box has a debt-to-equity ratio of 1.8. Computer companies and drug companies generally have lower debt levels. Microsoft's debt-to-equity ratio is 1.0 and Pfizer's is 0.9. Debt-to-equity ratios that were believed to be too high a few years ago are becoming commonplace today. The average debt-to-equity ratio for major U.S. industrial companies grew from about 1.5 in 1960 to more than 2.0 today.

INTERPRETING FINANCIAL STATEMENTS

In comparing two companies, you observe that one company has little debt with a debt-to-total-assets ratio of 20%. The second company has a much higher ratio of 80%. How would you expect their interest-coverage ratios to compare?

Answer

A low debt-to-total-assets ratio is generally associated with a high interest-coverage ratio. Why? Because low relative debt means low interest costs. Interest costs are low for two reasons: (1) a small amount of debt on which to pay interest, and (2) low interest rates because a small amount of borrowing creates less risk than large borrowings. All else equal, when debt levels and interest costs are low, we expect interest coverage to be high.

Highlights to Remember

1 **Account for current liabilities.** Liabilities are obligations to pay money or to provide goods or services. An entity's liability level is important to analysts because unpaid liabilities may produce difficulties ranging from an inability to raise additional capital to forced liquidation. To help assess debt levels, financial statements typically separate liabilities requiring payment within 1 year as current liabilities. Accounting for current liabilities is a straightforward extension of procedures covered in earlier chapters. Companies record transactions as they occur, and accruals at the end of a period capture incomplete transactions such as accruing interest, wages, utilities, or taxes.

2 **Measure and account for long-term liabilities.** Long-term liabilities involve more complex contracts that convey many rights and responsibilities over long periods of time. Companies initially record bonds, a common long-term liability, at the amount received from investors at issue. During the life of the bond, a company recognizes interest expense each period.

3 **Account for bond issues over their entire life.** The value of bonds at issue is the present value of their future interest payments plus the present value of their principal payment, both at the market rate of interest appropriate to the company's risk level and the current level of expected inflation. During the life of a bond, companies recognize interest expense using the effective interest method each period. They determine the interest paid or payable by multiplying the coupon rate of interest specified in the bond contract by the face value. They determine the interest expense by multiplying the market interest rate when the bond was issued times the book value of the bond (the net liability). The difference between the interest paid and the interest expense is the amount of the bond discount or premium that the company amortizes during the period. Amortizing a bond discount increases interest expense and amortizing a bond premium decreases it.

4 **Value and account for long-term lease obligations.** Leases are contracts that grant the lessee the right to use property owned by the lessor. Because many leases involve long time periods and place many of the risks of ownership on the lessee, GAAP contains rules to classify some leases as capital (or finance) leases. Companies account for a capital lease as if they had purchased the asset. They create both an asset and a liability when they sign a capital lease. The initial asset and liability values are both equal to the present value of payments required under the lease. The companies amortize the asset over its economic life, and they divide the lease payments into interest expense and loan repayment portions using the effective interest amortization method. During the life of the lease, the book value of the liability is typically larger than the book value of the asset because of the different amortization methods used. On the statement of cash flows, the portion of the lease payment representing interest is an operating cash outflow

under U.S. GAAP, and the portion representing a reduction in the lease liability is a financing cash outflow.

5 Evaluate pensions and other postretirement benefits. Companies must recognize measurable obligations for future pension payments and other postretirement benefits. Historical precedent leads to footnote disclosure for much of the pension information. On the income statement, the matching principle leads companies to record annually the change in their liability for future obligations for pensions and other postretirement benefits. In essence, companies record the change in the liability as an expense during the current period. Pension disclosures involve footnote presentations of the present value of the obligation, as well as the value of pension assets set aside with a trustee on behalf of the employees. For life and health insurance obligations to future retirees, companies often do not set aside assets. Thus, financial statements of such companies present a significant liability equal to the present value of anticipated future payments for life and health insurance. Both pensions and insurance obligations depend on complex forecasts of future costs, retiree life expectancies, and so forth.

6 Interpret deferred tax liabilities. Deferred tax liabilities arise because tax deductions such as depreciation expense on the company's tax return often precede the charging of the related expense on the company's books. When this happens, the immediate tax payable is less than it would appear to be if one examined the financial reports. To help investors understand the long-run tax obligations of the company, companies report tax expense as if they were paying taxes on the net income reported to shareholders. The company recognizes a deferred tax liability to reflect predictable higher taxes in the future, when these temporary differences in the recording of depreciation expense will reverse.

7 Use ratio analysis to assess a company's debt levels. Debt ratios and interest coverage ratios are two measures used to evaluate the level of a company's indebtedness. The more debt a company has, the more problems it will face if cash flow is inadequate to meet liabilities as they fall due.

Appendix 9: Compound Interest, Future Value, and Present Value

principal
The amount borrowed or the amount to be repaid.

interest
The cost the borrower pays the lender to use the principal.

interest rate
A specified percentage of the principal. It is used to compute the amount of interest.

simple interest
The interest rate multiplied by an unchanging principal amount.

compound interest
The interest rate multiplied by a changing principal amount. The unpaid interest is added to the principal to become the principal for the new period.

Interest is the cost of using money. This appendix teaches you what you need to know about interest to understand the accounting for long-term liabilities. Our discussion of interest uses amounts from interest tables to solve problems; however, many of you will be using Excel, another spreadsheet, or financial calculators to make these calculations. The mechanism is not important, but the principles are paramount to understanding these liabilities.

When you borrow money, the amount borrowed is the loan **principal**. **Interest** is the cost the borrower pays the lender to use the principal. It is the rental charge for cash, just as you pay rental charges to use an automobile or an apartment. Investing money is basically the same as making a loan. The investor gives money to a company, and that company acts as a borrower. For the investor, interest is the return on investment or the fee for lending money. Contracts that bear interest have many forms, from simple short-term promissory notes to multimillion-dollar issues of bonds.

Calculating the amount of interest depends on the **interest rate** (a specified percentage of the principal) and the interest period (the time period over which the borrower uses the principal).

We calculate **simple interest** by multiplying an interest rate by an unchanging principal amount. If the borrower pays interest in cash at the end of each period, the principal amount does not change, and simple interest is appropriate. However, more common is **compound interest**, which we calculate by multiplying an interest rate by a principal amount that increases each time interest is accrued but not paid. We add the accumulated interest to the principal, and the total becomes the new principal for the next period.

Future Value

Consider an example. Suppose Christina's T-shirt business has $10,000 in cash that it does not need at this moment. Instead of holding the $10,000 in her business checking account, which does not pay interest, Christina deposits $10,000 in an account that pays 10% yearly interest, compounded annually. She plans to let the $10,000 remain in the account and earn interest for 3 years.

After 3 years, she will withdraw all the money. The amount Christina will have in the account after 3 years, including principal and interest, is the **future value** of the $10,000 investment.

future value

The amount accumulated, including principal and interest.

Let's compute the future value of Christina's investment after 3 years. Compound interest provides interest on interest. That is, we add interest earned to the principal each period, and the following period Christina earns interest on both the original principal amount and the amount of added interest. Christina earns interest in year 1 on $10,000: (10% × $10,000) = $1,000. If she does not withdraw the interest, the principal for year 2 includes the initial $10,000 deposit plus the $1,000 of interest earned in the first year, $11,000. She earns interest in year 2 on the $11,000: (10% × $11,000) = $1,100. In the third year she will earn interest on $12,100: ($12,100 × 10%) = 1,210. The future value (FV) of the $10,000 deposit at the end of 3 years with compound interest at 10% is $13,310:

	Principal	Compound Interest	Balance End of Year
Year 1	$10,000	$10,000 × .10 = $1,000	$11,000
Year 2	11,000	11,000 × .10 = 1,100	12,100
Year 3	12,100	12,100 × .10 = 1,210	13,310

More generally, suppose you invest S dollars for two periods and earn interest at an interest rate i. After one period, the investment would be increased by the interest earned, Si. You would have $S + Si = S(1 + i)$. In the second period, you would again earn interest ($i[S(1 + i)]$). After two periods, you would have the following:

$$[S(1 + i)] + (i[S(1 + i)]) = S(1 + i)(1 + i) = S(1 + i)^2$$

The general formula for computing the *FV* of S dollars in n years at interest rate i is

$$FV = S(1 + i)^n$$

In general, n refers to the number of periods the funds are invested. Periods can be years, months, days, or any other time period. However, the interest rate must be consistent with the time period. That is, if n refers to months, i must be expressed as i% per month.

The "force" of compound interest can be staggering. For example,

	Future Values of $10,000 at End of		
Compound Interest	10 Years	20 Years	40 Years
$10,000 × (1.10)^{10} = $10,000 × 2.5937 =	$25,937		
$10,000 × (1.10)^{20} = $10,000 × 6.7275 =		$67,275	
$10,000 × (1.10)^{40} = $10,000 × 45.2593 =			$452,593

Calculating future values and compound interest by hand is tedious and time consuming. Fortunately, there are tables, calculators, or software that will do much of the work for you. We use tables in this appendix. For example, Table 9A-1 shows the future values of $1 for various periods and interest rates. Each number in the table is the solution to the expression $(1 + i)^n$. Each column represents a specific interest rate, i, and each row represents a number of periods, n. Notice that the 3-year, 10% future value factor is 1.3310 (the third row, seventh column). We calculated this number as $(1 + .10)^3$. This is consistent with our preceding example where we show that $10,000 grows to $13,310 over 3 years [($10,000 × 1.3310) = $13,310].

Suppose you want to know how much $800 will grow to if left in the bank for 9 years at 8% interest. Multiply $800 by $(1 + .08)^9$. You can find the value for $(1 + .08)^9$ in the 9-year row and 8% column of Table 9A-1.

$$\$800 \times 1.9990 = \$1,599.20$$

The examples in this text use the factors from Table 9A-1 and similar tables in this appendix, which we have rounded to four decimal places. If you use tables with different rounding, or if you use a hand calculator or personal computer, your answers may differ slightly from those given because of a small rounding error.

TABLE 9A-1

Future Value of $1

$$FV = (1 + i)^n$$

Periods	3%	4%	5%	6%	7%	8%	10%	12%	14%	16%	18%	20%	22%	24%	25%
1	1.0300	1.0400	1.0500	1.0600	1.0700	1.0800	1.1000	1.1200	1.1400	1.1600	1.1800	1.2000	1.2200	1.2400	1.2500
2	1.0609	1.0816	1.1025	1.1236	1.1449	1.1664	1.2100	1.2544	1.2996	1.3456	1.3924	1.4400	1.4884	1.5376	1.5625
3	1.0927	1.1249	1.1576	1.1910	1.2250	1.2597	1.3310	1.4049	1.4815	1.5609	1.6430	1.7280	1.8158	1.9066	1.9531
4	1.1255	1.1699	1.2155	1.2625	1.3108	1.3605	1.4641	1.5735	1.6890	1.8106	1.9388	2.0736	2.2153	2.3642	2.4414
5	1.1593	1.2167	1.2763	1.3382	1.4026	1.4693	1.6105	1.7623	1.9254	2.1003	2.2878	2.4883	2.7027	2.9316	3.0518
6	1.1941	1.2653	1.3401	1.4185	1.5007	1.5869	1.7716	1.9738	2.1950	2.4364	2.6996	2.9860	3.2973	3.6352	3.8147
7	1.2299	1.3159	1.4071	1.5036	1.6058	1.7138	1.9487	2.2107	2.5023	2.8262	3.1855	3.5832	4.0227	4.5077	4.7684
8	1.2668	1.3686	1.4775	1.5938	1.7182	1.8509	2.1436	2.4760	2.8526	3.2784	3.7589	4.2998	4.9077	5.5895	5.9605
9	1.3048	1.4233	1.5513	1.6895	1.8385	1.9990	2.3579	2.7731	3.2519	3.8030	4.4355	5.1598	5.9874	6.9310	7.4506
10	1.3439	1.4802	1.6289	1.7908	1.9672	2.1589	2.5937	3.1058	3.7072	4.4114	5.2338	6.1917	7.3046	8.5944	9.3132
11	1.3842	1.5395	1.7103	1.8983	2.1049	2.3316	2.8531	3.4785	4.2262	5.1173	6.1759	7.4301	8.9117	10.6571	11.6415
12	1.4258	1.6010	1.7959	2.0122	2.2522	2.5182	3.1384	3.8960	4.8179	5.9360	7.2876	8.9161	10.8722	13.2148	14.5519
13	1.4685	1.6651	1.8856	2.1329	2.4098	2.7196	3.4523	4.3635	5.4924	6.8858	8.5994	10.6993	13.2641	16.3863	18.1899
14	1.5126	1.7317	1.9799	2.2609	2.5785	2.9372	3.7975	4.8871	6.2613	7.9875	10.1472	12.8392	16.1822	20.3191	22.7374
15	1.5580	1.8009	2.0789	2.3966	2.7590	3.1722	4.1772	5.4736	7.1379	9.2655	11.9737	15.4070	19.7423	25.1956	28.4217
16	1.6047	1.8730	2.1829	2.5404	2.9522	3.4259	4.5950	6.1304	8.1372	10.7480	14.1290	18.4884	24.0856	31.2426	35.5271
17	1.6528	1.9479	2.2920	2.6928	3.1588	3.7000	5.0545	6.8660	9.2765	12.4677	16.6722	22.1861	29.3844	38.7408	44.4089
18	1.7024	2.0258	2.4066	2.8543	3.3799	3.9960	5.5599	7.6900	10.5752	14.4625	19.6733	26.6233	35.8490	48.0386	55.5112
19	1.7535	2.1068	2.5270	3.0256	3.6165	4.3157	6.1159	8.6128	12.0557	16.7765	23.2144	31.9480	43.7358	59.5679	69.3889
20	1.8061	2.1911	2.6533	3.2071	3.8697	4.6610	6.7275	9.6463	13.7435	19.4608	27.3930	38.3376	53.3576	73.8641	86.7362
21	1.8603	2.2788	2.7860	3.3996	4.1406	5.0338	7.4002	10.8038	15.6676	22.5745	32.3238	46.0051	65.0963	91.5915	108.4202
22	1.9161	2.3699	2.9253	3.6035	4.4304	5.4365	8.1403	12.1003	17.8610	26.1864	38.1421	55.2061	79.4175	113.5735	135.5253
23	1.9736	2.4647	3.0715	3.8197	4.7405	5.8715	8.9543	13.5523	20.3616	30.3762	45.0076	66.2474	96.8894	140.8312	169.4066
24	2.0328	2.5633	3.2251	4.0489	5.0724	6.3412	9.8497	15.1786	23.2122	35.2364	53.1090	79.4968	118.2050	174.6306	211.7582
25	2.0938	2.6658	3.3864	4.2919	5.4274	6.8485	10.8347	17.0001	26.4619	40.8742	62.6686	95.3962	144.2101	216.5420	264.6978
26	2.1566	2.7725	3.5557	4.5494	5.8074	7.3964	11.9182	19.0401	30.1666	47.4141	73.9490	114.4755	175.9364	268.5121	330.8722
27	2.2213	2.8834	3.7335	4.8223	6.2139	7.9881	13.1100	21.3249	34.3899	55.0004	87.2598	137.3706	214.6424	332.9550	413.5903
28	2.2879	2.9987	3.9201	5.1117	6.6488	8.6271	14.4210	23.8839	39.2045	63.8004	102.9666	164.8447	261.8637	412.8642	516.9879
29	2.3566	3.1187	4.1161	5.4184	7.1143	9.3173	15.8631	26.7499	44.6931	74.0085	121.5005	197.8136	319.4737	511.9516	646.2349
30	2.4273	3.2434	4.3219	5.7435	7.6123	10.0627	17.4494	29.9599	50.9502	85.8499	143.3706	237.3763	389.7579	634.8199	807.7936

Present Value

Accountants generally use present values instead of future values to record long-term liabilities. The **present value (PV)** is the value today of a future cash inflow or outflow.

Suppose you invest $1.00 today. As you learned in the discussion of future values, the $1.00 will grow to $1.06 in 1 year at 6% interest—that is, $1 \times 1.06 = $1.06. At the end of the second year, its value is $[(\$1 \times 1.06) \times 1.06] = [\$1 \times (1.06)^2] = \$1.124$.

Once you know how to calculate the future value of S dollars invested at a known interest rate i for n periods, you can reverse the process to calculate the present value of a future amount. Let PV be the present value, or value today, and FV be the future value, the value at some future date. Using the equation for future value

$$FV = PV(1 + i)^n$$

we can rearrange terms to compute the present value, PV:

$$PV = \frac{FV}{(1 + i)^n}$$

If you expect to receive $1.00 in 1 year, it is worth $(\$1 \div 1.06) = \$.9434$ today. Suppose you invest $.9434 today. In 1 year, you will have $(\$.9434 \times 1.06) = \$1.00$. Thus, $0.9434 is the present value of $1.00 a year hence, at 6%. If you will receive the dollar in 2 years, its present value is $[\$1.00 \div (1.06)^2] = \$.8900$. If you invest $.89 today at 6% interest, it will grow to $1.00 at the end of 2 years. The general formula for the PV of an FV that you will receive or pay in n periods at an interest rate of i% per period is as follows:

$$PV = \frac{FV}{(1 + i)^n} = FV \times \frac{1}{(1 + i)^n}$$

Table 9A-2 gives factors for $1/(1 + i)^n$ (which is the present value of $1.00) at various interest rates over several different periods. You may hear present values called **discounted values**, interest rates called **discount rates**, and the process of finding the present value called **discounting**. You can think of present values as discounting (decreasing) the value of a future cash inflow or outflow. Why do we discount the value? Because you will receive or pay the cash in the future, not today, so it is worth less in today's dollars.

Assume a prominent city issues a 3-year noninterest-bearing note payable that promises to pay a lump sum of $1,000 exactly 3 years from now. You desire a rate of return of exactly 6%, compounded annually. We use the phrase **rate of return** to refer to the amount an investor earns expressed as a percentage of the amount invested. How much should you be willing to pay now for the 3-year note? The situation is sketched as follows:

present value
The value today of a future cash inflow or outflow.

discounted values
Another name for present values.

discount rates
Interest rates used to compute present values.

discounting
The process of finding the present value.

rate of return
The amount an investor earns expressed as a percentage of the amount invested.

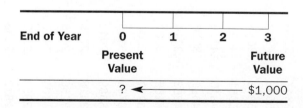

The factor in the period 3 row and 6% column of Table 9A-2 is .8396. The present value of the $1,000 payment is $(\$1,000 \times .8396) = \$839.60$. You should be willing to pay $839.60 for the $1,000 that you will receive in 3 years.

Suppose we compound interest semiannually instead of annually. How much should you be willing to pay now? Remember to pay attention to the number of periods involved, not just the number of years. The 3 years become six interest payment periods. The rate per period is one-half the annual rate, or $(6\% \div 2) = 3\%$. The factor in the period 6 row and 3% column of Table 9A-2 is .8375. You should now be willing to pay $(\$1,000 \times 0.8375)$, or only $837.50 instead of $839.60. Why do you pay less? Because with more frequent compounding the original investment will grow faster.

To see how present values work, let's return to our example. Suppose Christina's financial institution promised to pay her a lump sum of $13,310 at the end of 3 years for her investment.

TABLE 9A-2

Present Value of $1

$$PV = \frac{1}{(1 + i)^n}$$

Periods	3%	4%	5%	6%	7%	8%	10%	12%	14%	16%	18%	20%	22%	24%	25%
1	.9709	.9615	.9524	.9434	.9346	.9259	.9091	.8929	.8772	.8621	.8475	.8333	.8197	.8065	.8000
2	.9426	.9246	.9070	.8900	.8734	.8573	.8264	.7972	.7695	.7432	.7182	.6944	.6719	.6504	.6400
3	.9151	.8890	.8638	.8396	.8163	.7938	.7513	.7118	.6750	.6407	.6086	.5787	.5507	.5245	.5120
4	.8885	.8548	.8227	.7921	.7629	.7350	.6830	.6355	.5921	.5523	.5158	.4823	.4514	.4230	.4096
5	.8626	.8219	.7835	.7473	.7130	.6806	.6209	.5674	.5194	.4761	.4371	.4019	.3700	.3411	.3277
6	.8375	.7903	.7462	.7050	.6663	.6302	.5645	.5066	.4556	.4104	.3704	.3349	.3033	.2751	.2621
7	.8131	.7599	.7107	.6651	.6227	.5835	.5132	.4523	.3996	.3538	.3139	.2791	.2486	.2218	.2097
8	.7894	.7307	.6768	.6274	.5820	.5403	.4665	.4039	.3506	.3050	.2660	.2326	.2038	.1789	.1678
9	.7664	.7026	.6446	.5919	.5439	.5002	.4241	.3606	.3075	.2630	.2255	.1938	.1670	.1443	.1342
10	.7441	.6756	.6139	.5584	.5083	.4632	.3855	.3220	.2697	.2267	.1911	.1615	.1369	.1164	.1074
11	.7224	.6496	.5847	.5268	.4751	.4289	.3505	.2875	.2366	.1954	.1619	.1346	.1122	.0938	.0859
12	.7014	.6246	.5568	.4970	.4440	.3971	.3186	.2567	.2076	.1685	.1372	.1122	.0920	.0757	.0687
13	.6810	.6006	.5303	.4688	.4150	.3677	.2897	.2292	.1821	.1452	.1163	.0935	.0754	.0610	.0550
14	.6611	.5775	.5051	.4423	.3878	.3405	.2633	.2046	.1597	.1252	.0985	.0779	.0618	.0492	.0440
15	.6419	.5553	.4810	.4173	.3624	.3152	.2394	.1827	.1401	.1079	.0835	.0649	.0507	.0397	.0352
16	.6232	.5339	.4581	.3936	.3387	.2919	.2176	.1631	.1229	.0930	.0708	.0541	.0415	.0320	.0281
17	.6050	.5134	.4363	.3714	.3166	.2703	.1978	.1456	.1078	.0802	.0600	.0451	.0340	.0258	.0225
18	.5874	.4936	.4155	.3503	.2959	.2502	.1799	.1300	.0946	.0691	.0508	.0376	.0279	.0208	.0180
19	.5703	.4746	.3957	.3305	.2765	.2317	.1635	.1161	.0829	.0596	.0431	.0313	.0229	.0168	.0144
20	.5537	.4564	.3769	.3118	.2584	.2145	.1486	.1037	.0728	.0514	.0365	.0261	.0187	.0135	.0115
21	.5375	.4388	.3589	.2942	.2415	.1987	.1351	.0926	.0638	.0443	.0309	.0217	.0154	.0109	.0092
22	.5219	.4220	.3418	.2775	.2257	.1839	.1228	.0826	.0560	.0382	.0262	.0181	.0126	.0088	.0074
23	.5067	.4057	.3256	.2618	.2109	.1703	.1117	.0738	.0491	.0329	.0222	.0151	.0103	.0071	.0059
24	.4919	.3901	.3101	.2470	.1971	.1577	.1015	.0659	.0431	.0284	.0188	.0126	.0085	.0057	.0047
25	.4776	.3751	.2953	.2330	.1842	.1460	.0923	.0588	.0378	.0245	.0160	.0105	.0069	.0046	.0038
26	.4637	.3607	.2812	.2198	.1722	.1352	.0839	.0525	.0331	.0211	.0135	.0087	.0057	.0037	.0030
27	.4502	.3468	.2678	.2074	.1609	.1252	.0763	.0469	.0291	.0182	.0115	.0073	.0047	.0030	.0024
28	.4371	.3335	.2551	.1956	.1504	.1159	.0693	.0419	.0255	.0157	.0097	.0061	.0038	.0024	.0019
29	.4243	.3207	.2429	.1846	.1406	.1073	.0630	.0374	.0224	.0135	.0082	.0051	.0031	.0020	.0015
30	.4120	.3083	.2314	.1741	.1314	.0994	.0573	.0334	.0196	.0116	.0070	.0042	.0026	.0016	.0012
40	.3066	.2083	.1420	.0972	.0668	.0460	.0221	.0107	.0053	.0026	.0013	.0007	.0004	.0002	.0001

How much does she need to deposit to earn a 10% rate of return, compounded annually? Using Table 9A-2, the period 3 row and the 10% column show a factor of .7513. Multiply this factor by the future amount and round to the nearest dollar:

$$PV = .7513 \times \$13,310 = \$10,000$$

Present Value of an Ordinary Annuity

An ordinary **annuity** is a series of equal cash flows that take place at the end of successive periods of equal length. In other words, an annuity pays you the same amount at the end of each period for a set period of time. We denote its present value as PV_A. Assume that you buy a note from a municipality that promises to pay \$1,000 at the end of each of 3 years. How much should you be willing to pay for this note if you desire a rate of return of 6%, compounded annually?

annuity
Equal cash flows to take place during successive periods of equal length.

You could solve this problem using Table 9A-2. First, find the present value of each payment you will receive, and then add the present values as in Exhibit 9-14. You should be willing to pay \$943.40 for the first payment, \$890.00 for the second, and \$839.60 for the third, a total of \$2,673.00.

Table 9A-3 provides a shortcut method for calculating the present value of an annuity. We can calculate the present value in Exhibit 9-14 as follows:

$$PV_A = (\$1,000 \times .9434) + (\$1,000 \times .8900) + (\$1,000 \times .8396)$$
$$= \$1,000 \times (.9434 + .8900 + .8396)$$
$$= \$1,000 \times 2.6730$$
$$= \$2,673.00$$

The three terms in parentheses are the first three numbers from the 6% column of Table 9A-2, and their sum is in the third row of the 6% column of Table 9A-3: 9.9434 + .8900 + .83960 = 2.6730. This shortcut is especially valuable if the cash payments or receipts extend over many periods. Consider an annual cash payment of \$1,000 for 20 years at 6%. The present value, calculated from Table 9A-3, is (\$1,000 × 11.4699) = \$11,469.90. To use Table 9A-2 for this calculation, you would have to perform 20 calculations and then add up the 20 products.

You can calculate the factors in Table 9A-3 using the following general formula:

$$PV_A = \frac{1}{i}\left[1 - \frac{1}{(1+i)^n}\right]$$

Applied to our illustration we have the following:

$$PV_A = \frac{1}{.06}(1 - .83962) = \frac{.16038}{.06} = 2.6730$$

In particular, note that the higher the interest rate, the lower the present value factor in Table 9A-3. Why? Because, at a higher interest rate, you would need to invest less now to obtain the same stream of future annuity payments. For example, for a 10-year annuity the factor declines from 7.7217 for 5% to 6.1446 for 10%.

EXHIBIT 9-14

PV of Three Annual $1,000 Payments

	End of Year 6% PV Factor	Present Value	0	1	2	3
First payment	.9434	\$ 943.40 ← \$1,000				
Second payment	.8900	890.00 ← \$1,000				
Third payment	.8396	839.60 ← \$1,000				
		\$2,673.00				

TABLE 9A-3
Present Value of Ordinary Annuity of $1

$$PV_A = \frac{1}{i}\left[1 - \frac{1}{(1+i)^n}\right]$$

Periods	3%	4%	5%	6%	7%	8%	10%	12%	14%	16%	18%	20%	22%	24%	25%
1	.9709	.9615	.9524	.9434	.9346	.9259	.9091	.8929	.8772	.8621	.8475	.8333	.8197	.8065	.8000
2	1.9135	1.8861	1.8594	1.8334	1.8080	1.7833	1.7355	1.6901	1.6467	1.6052	1.5656	1.5278	1.4915	1.4568	1.4400
3	2.8286	2.7751	2.7232	2.6730	2.6243	2.5771	2.4869	2.4018	2.3216	2.2459	2.1743	2.1065	2.0422	1.9813	1.9520
4	3.7171	3.6299	3.5460	3.4651	3.3872	3.3121	3.1699	3.0373	2.9137	2.7982	2.6901	2.5887	2.4936	2.4043	2.3616
5	4.5797	4.4518	4.3295	4.2124	4.1002	3.9927	3.7908	3.6048	3.4331	3.2743	3.1272	2.9906	2.8636	2.7454	2.6893
6	5.4172	5.2421	5.0757	4.9173	4.7665	4.6229	4.3553	4.1114	3.8887	3.6847	3.4976	3.3255	3.1669	3.0205	2.9514
7	6.2303	6.0021	5.7864	5.5824	5.3893	5.2064	4.8684	4.5638	4.2883	4.0386	3.8115	3.6046	3.4155	3.2423	3.1611
8	7.0197	6.7327	6.4632	6.2098	5.9713	5.7466	5.3349	4.9676	4.6389	4.3436	4.0776	3.8372	3.6193	3.4212	3.3289
9	7.7861	7.4353	7.1078	6.8017	6.5152	6.2469	5.7590	5.3282	4.9464	4.6065	4.3030	4.0310	3.7863	3.5655	3.4631
10	8.5302	8.1109	7.7217	7.3601	7.0236	6.7101	6.1446	5.6502	5.2161	4.8332	4.4941	4.1925	3.9232	3.6819	3.5705
11	9.2526	8.7605	8.3064	7.8869	7.4987	7.1390	6.4951	5.9377	5.4527	5.0286	4.6560	4.3271	4.0354	3.7757	3.6564
12	9.9540	9.3851	8.8633	8.3838	7.9427	7.5361	6.8137	6.1944	5.6603	5.1971	4.7932	4.4392	4.1274	3.8514	3.7251
13	10.6350	9.9856	9.3936	8.8527	8.3577	7.9038	7.1034	6.4235	5.8424	5.3423	4.9095	4.5327	4.2028	3.9124	3.7801
14	11.2961	10.5631	9.8986	9.2950	8.7455	8.2442	7.3667	6.6282	6.0021	5.4675	5.0081	4.6106	4.2646	3.9616	3.8241
15	11.9379	11.1184	10.3797	9.7122	9.1079	8.5595	7.6061	6.8109	6.1422	5.5755	5.0916	4.6755	4.3152	4.0013	3.8593
16	12.5611	11.6523	10.8378	10.1059	9.4466	8.8514	7.8237	6.9740	6.2651	5.6685	5.1624	4.7296	4.3567	4.0333	3.8874
17	13.1661	12.1657	11.2741	10.4773	9.7632	9.1216	8.0216	7.1196	6.3729	5.7487	5.2223	4.7746	4.3908	4.0591	3.9099
18	13.7535	12.6593	11.6896	10.8276	10.0591	9.3719	8.2014	7.2497	6.4674	5.8178	5.2732	4.8122	4.4187	4.0799	3.9279
19	14.3238	13.1339	12.0853	11.1581	10.3356	9.6036	8.3649	7.3658	6.5504	5.8775	5.3162	4.8435	4.4415	4.0967	3.9424
20	14.8775	13.5903	12.4622	11.4699	10.5940	9.8181	8.5136	7.4694	6.6231	5.9288	5.3527	4.8696	4.4603	4.1103	3.9539
21	15.4150	14.0292	12.8212	11.7641	10.8355	10.0168	8.6487	7.5620	6.6870	5.9731	5.3837	4.8913	4.4756	4.1212	3.9631
22	15.9369	14.4511	13.1630	12.0416	11.0612	10.2007	8.7715	7.6446	6.7429	6.0113	5.4099	4.9094	4.4882	4.1300	3.9705
23	16.4436	14.8568	13.4886	12.3034	11.2722	10.3711	8.8832	7.7184	6.7921	6.0442	5.4321	4.9245	4.4985	4.1371	3.9764
24	16.9355	15.2470	13.7986	12.5504	11.4693	10.5288	8.9847	7.7843	6.8351	6.0726	5.4509	4.9371	4.5070	4.1428	3.9811
25	17.4131	15.6221	14.0939	12.7834	11.6536	10.6748	9.0770	7.8431	6.8729	6.0971	5.4669	4.9476	4.5139	4.1474	3.9849
26	17.8768	15.9828	14.3752	13.0032	11.8258	10.8100	9.1609	7.8957	6.9061	6.1182	5.4804	4.9563	4.5196	4.1511	3.9879
27	18.3270	16.3296	14.6430	13.2105	11.9867	10.9352	9.2372	7.9426	6.9352	6.1364	5.4919	4.9636	4.5243	4.1542	3.9903
28	18.7641	16.6631	14.8981	13.4062	12.1371	11.0511	9.3066	7.9844	6.9607	6.1520	5.5016	4.9697	4.5281	4.1566	3.9923
29	19.1885	16.9837	15.1411	13.5907	12.2777	11.1584	9.3696	8.0218	6.9830	6.1656	5.5098	4.9747	4.5312	4.1585	3.9938
30	19.6004	17.2920	15.3725	13.7648	12.4090	11.2578	9.4269	8.0552	7.0027	6.1772	5.5168	4.9789	4.5338	4.1601	3.9950
40	23.1148	19.7928	17.1591	15.0463	13.3317	11.9246	9.7791	8.2438	7.1050	6.2335	5.5482	4.9966	4.5439	4.1659	3.9995

Summary Problems for Your Review

PROBLEM

To make sure you understand present values, use Table 9A-2 to obtain the present values of the following:

1. $1,600, at 20%, to be received at the end of 20 years
2. $8,300, at 10%, to be received at the end of 12 years
3. $8,000, at 4%, to be received at the end of 4 years

SOLUTION

1. $1,600 (.0261) = $41.76
2. $8,300 (.3186) = $2,644.38
3. $8,000 (.8548) = $6,838.40

PROBLEM

To make sure you understand present values of annuities, use Table 9A-3 to obtain the present values of the following ordinary annuities:

1. $1,600 to be received at the end of each year for 20 years, assuming interest at 20%
2. $8,300 to be received at the end of each year for 12 years, assuming interest at 10%
3. $8,000 to be received at the end of each year for 4 years, assuming interest at 4%

SOLUTION

1. $1,600 (4.8696) = $7,791.36
2. $8,300 (6.8137) = $56,553.71
3. $8,000 (3.6299) = $29,039.20

Accounting Vocabulary

annuity, p. 429
bargain purchase option, p. 412
bond discount, p. 399
bond premium, p. 399
bonds, p. 397
call premium, p. 399
callable bonds, p. 399
capital lease, p. 412
commercial paper, p. 393
compound interest, p. 424
compound interest
   method, p. 405
contingent liability, p. 421
contractual rate, p. 398
convertible bonds, p. 399
coupon rate, p. 398
covenant, p. 399
debenture, p. 398
debt-to-equity ratio, p. 422
debt-to-total-assets
   ratio, p. 422
deferred income tax
   liability, p. 417
discount amortization, p. 405
discount on bonds, p. 399

discount rates, p. 427
discounted values, p. 427
discounting, p. 427
early extinguishment, p. 409
effective interest
   amortization, p. 405
face amount, p. 398
finance lease, p. 412
firm-specific risk, p. 401
future value, p. 425
implicit interest, p. 410
imputed interest, p. 410
imputed interest rate, p. 410
inflation premium, p. 401
interest, p. 424
interest-coverage ratio, p. 422
interest rate, p. 424
invoice, p. 393
lease, p. 412
lessee, p. 412
lessor, p. 412
line of credit, p. 393
liquidation, p. 398
long-term-debt-to-total-
   capital ratio, p. 422

long-term liabilities, p. 392
market rate, p. 399
mortgage bond, p. 398
negotiable, p. 398
nominal interest rate, p. 398
operating lease, p. 412
other postretirement
   benefits, p. 416
pensions, p. 416
permanent differences, p. 418
premium on bonds, p. 399
present value, p. 427
principal, p. 424
private placement, p. 398
promissory note, p. 393
protective covenant, p. 399
provisions, p. 397
purchase order, p. 393
rate of return, p. 427
real interest rate, p. 401
receiving report, p. 393
restructuring, p. 420
simple interest, p. 424
sinking fund, p. 399
sinking fund bonds, p. 399

MyAccountingLab ## Assignment Material

Questions

9-1 Distinguish between current liabilities and long-term liabilities.

9-2 Name and briefly describe five items that are often classified as current liabilities.

9-3 "Withholding taxes really adds to employer payroll costs." Do you agree? Explain.

9-4 "Product warranties expense should not be recognized until actual repair services are performed. Until then you don't know which products might require warranty repairs." Do you agree? Explain.

9-5 Distinguish between a mortgage bond and a debenture. Which is safer?

9-6 Distinguish between subordinated and unsubordinated debentures.

9-7 Bond covenants usually restrict the borrower's rights in various ways. An example might be a restriction that no additional long-term debt could be issued unless the debt-to-total assets ratio was below .5. Who benefits from such a covenant? How?

9-8 Many callable bonds have a call premium for "early" calls. Who does the call premium benefit—the issuer or the purchaser of the bond? How?

9-9 How does reporting for convertible bonds differ under IFRS compared to U.S. GAAP?

9-10 "When a company buys back bonds that it has issued, it always pays the book value to the bondholders. Therefore, there is never a gain or loss on extinguishing bonds." Do you agree? Explain.

9-11 "The face amount of a bond is what you can sell it for." Do you agree? Explain.

9-12 "The quoted bond interest rates imply a rate per annum, but the bond markets do not mean that rate literally." Explain.

9-13 A company plans to issue bonds with a nominal rate of 10%. At what market rates will the bonds be issued at a discount? At what market rates will they be issued at a premium?

9-14 "When a bond is issued at a discount, there are two components of interest expense." Explain.

9-15 What are the three main differences between accounting for a bond discount and accounting for a bond premium?

9-16 A company reported interest payments in the financing activities section of the statement of cash flows. Does the company report under IFRS or U. S. GAAP? Explain.

9-17 "A company that issues zero coupon bonds recognizes no interest expense until the bond matures." Do you agree? Explain.

9-18 "When accounting for a lease, it is necessary to determine whether the lease is a capital lease or a finance lease." Do you agree? Explain.

9-19 Certain leases are essentially equivalent to purchases financed with debt. A company must account for such leases as if the asset had been purchased. Explain.

9-20 "A capital (or finance) lease results in both an asset and a liability on a company's balance sheet." Explain.

9-21 "A capital (or finance) lease and operating lease are recorded differently on the balance sheet, but their effect on the income statement is the same." Do you agree? Explain.

9-22 Discuss which characteristics of a lease are evaluated in deciding whether it is a capital (or finance) lease.

9-23 "Because a company never knows how much it will have to pay for pensions, no pension liability is recognized. Pension obligations are simply explained in a footnote to the financial statements." Do you agree? Explain.

9-24 Compare and contrast permanent differences and temporary differences between GAAP and tax reporting.

9-25 "Differences in tax and GAAP rules lead to more depreciation being charged on tax statements than on financial reports to the public." Do you agree? Explain.

9-26 "It is unethical for big companies to recognize a large income tax expense on their income statements reported to the public but to pay a small amount to the government." Do you agree? Explain.

9-27 "A contingent liability is a liability having an estimated amount." Do you agree? Explain.

9-28 Name four ratios that help analysts assess a company's risk. Give a brief explanation of each.

9-29 Refer to Appendix 9. How are Table 9A-2 (p. 428) and Table 9A-3 (p. 430) related to each other?

Critical Thinking Questions

9-30 Lenders and Covenants
Why would a lender want to add a covenant specifying a maximum debt-to-total-assets ratio to a loan contract?

9-31 Refinancing Bonds
Your treasurer is new to the job and has just noticed that your bonds are trading below par (i.e., at a discount). This officer recommends that you retire the bonds by issuing new bonds because you will have a gain in the process and will reduce your interest payments. Do you believe you should accept the treasurer's recommendation?

9-32 Cash Interest Versus Interest Expense
As a lender, you are contemplating a covenant that is based on the interest-coverage ratio. A young member of your organization with a new MBA degree has suggested that you calculate the ratio using actual cash interest payments each period instead of interest expense each period. You have been asked to discuss this proposal. What do you say?

9-33 Lottery Winnings
The New York Lottery provides prizes that start at $3 million and rise each time someone fails to win the lottery. Participants in the lottery are permitted to choose to receive a lump-sum payment or 26 payments as an annuity. A recent winner of $20 million was surprised to receive a check for less than $10 million? How could you explain this to the winner?

Exercises

9-34 Accrued Employee Compensation
Giambi Company had total compensation expense for March of $37,000. The company paid $30,000 to employees during March, and it will pay the remainder in April.

1. Prepare the journal entry for recording the compensation expense for March.
2. Suppose salaries and wages payable were $5,000 at the beginning of March. Compute salaries and wages payable at the end of March.

9-35 Sales Taxes
Most of the food sold in retail stores in California is not subject to sales taxes (e.g., candy), but some items are (e.g., soft drinks). Apparently, the candy lobbyists were more effective than soft drinks lobbyists when dealing with the state legislature. Most cash registers are designed to record taxable sales and nontaxable sales and automatically add the appropriate sales tax.

The sales for the past week in the local Safeway store were $180,000 cash, of which $50,000 was taxable at a rate of 9%. By using the A = L + SE equation, show the impact on the entity, both now and when the sales taxes are paid at a later date. Also prepare corresponding journal entries.

9-36 Product Warranties
During 20X0, the LaBelle Appliance Company had cash sales of $900,000. The company estimates that the cost of servicing products under warranty will average 3% of sales.

1. Prepare journal entries for sales revenue and the related warranty expense for 20X0. Assume all sales are for cash.
2. The liability for warranties was $12,600 at the beginning of 20X0. Expenditures (all in cash) to satisfy warranty claims during 20X0 were $21,400, of which $4,500 was for products sold in 20X0. Prepare the journal entry for the warranty expenditures.
3. Compute the balance in the Liability for Warranties account at the end of 20X0.

9-37 Unearned Revenues
The Reader's Digest Association, Inc., one of the largest publishers of magazines in the world, had unearned revenues of $388 million on its March 31, 2009, balance sheet. Suppose that during April, Reader's Digest delivered magazines with a sales value of $32 million to prepaid subscribers and sold subscriptions for $35 million cash.

1. Prepare journal entries for the new subscriptions and the deliveries to prepaid subscribers.
2. Compute the amount in the unearned revenue account at the end of April 2009.

9-38 Liabilities on the Balance Sheet

Krispy Kreme Company, the doughnut company, had the following items on its February 1, 2009, balance sheet (in thousands):

Cash and cash equivalents	$35,538
Accounts payable	8,981
Deferred income tax liability	106
Total stockholders' equity	57,755
Accrued liabilities	29,222
Inventories	15,587
Current maturities of long-term debt	1,413
Long-term debt, less current maturities	73,454
Other long-term obligations	23,995

Prepare the liabilities section of Krispy Kreme's balance sheet. Include only the items that are properly included in liabilities. Separate current and long-term liabilities.

9-39 Various Liabilities

1. **Whirlpool Corporation** sells electric appliances, including automatic washing machines. Suppose that experience in recent years has indicated that warranty costs average 3.0% of sales. Sales of washing machines for April were $4.0 million. Cash disbursements and obligations for warranty service on washing machines during April totaled $104,000. Prepare the journal entries prompted by these facts.
2. **Pepsi-Cola Bottling Company of New York** gets cash deposits for its returnable bottles. In November, it received $72,000 cash and disbursed $66,000 for bottles returned. Prepare the journal entries concerning the receipts and returns of deposits.
3. **Citibank** received a $4,000 savings deposit on April 1. On June 30, it recognized interest thereon at an annual rate of 3%. On July 1, the depositor closed her account with the bank. Prepare the bank's necessary journal entries.
4. The Village Theater sold, for a total of $180,000 cash, 900 season tickets in advance of December 31 for five plays, each to be held in successive months, beginning in January.
   a. What is the effect on the balance sheet of December 31? What is the appropriate journal entry for the sale of the tickets?
   b. What is the effect on the balance sheet of January 31? What is the related journal entry for January?
5. Suppose a tabloid newspaper has lost a lawsuit. Damages were set at $550,000. The newspaper plans to appeal the decision to a higher court. The newspaper's attorneys are 90% confident of a reversal of the lower court's decision. What liability, if any, should be shown on the newspaper's balance sheet?

9-40 Priorities of Claims

Baron Real Estate Corporation is being liquidated. It has one major asset, an office building, which was converted into $16 million cash. The stockholders' equity has been wiped out by past losses. The following claims exist: Accounts Payable, $3 million; Debentures Payable, $5 million; and First Mortgage Payable, $11 million.

1. Assume that the debentures are not subordinated. How much will each class of claimants receive?
2. Suppose the debentures are subordinated.
   a. How much will each class of claimants receive?
   b. How much will each class receive if the cash proceeds from the sale of the building amount to only $12.5 million?

9-41 Discounted Present Value and Bonds

On December 31, 20X1, Kung Company issued a 3-year $1,000 bond that promises an interest rate of 12%, payable 6% semiannually. Compute the discounted present value of the principal and the interest as of December 31, 20X1, if the market rate of interest for such securities is 12%,

14%, and 10%, respectively. Show your computations, including a sketch of cash flows. Round to the nearest dollar.

9-42 Criteria for Capital Leases

Indicate which of the following leases would be a capital (financing) lease and which would be operating leases:

a. Rental of a crane for $9,000 per month on a 6-year lease, with an option to buy for $10,000 at the end of the 6 years when its fair value is $150,000.
b. Rental of an automobile on a 6-month lease for $500 per month. The auto will be returned to the dealer after the 6 months.
c. Rental of a computer for $500 per month on a 5-year lease. At the end of 5 years, the computer is expected to have a fair market value of zero.
d. Rental of 10 forklifts for $1,400 per month on an 8-year lease. The value of the forklifts at the end of 8 years is uncertain, but the total economic life is not expected to be more than 10 years.
e. Rental of a warehouse for $10,000 per month, renewable annually.

9-43 Accounting for Pensions

Mayes Company's 20X0 pension expense was $800,000, of which it paid $375,000 in cash to a trustee. By using the balance sheet equation format, show which accounts were affected by these data. Prepare the corresponding journal entry.

9-44 Deferred Taxes

Procter & Gamble Company's (P&G) net sales in 2009 exceeded $79 billion. On its income statement, P&G reported the following earnings from continuing operations ($ in millions):

Earnings before income taxes	$15,325
Income taxes	4,032
Net earnings	$11,293

Taxes due on 2009 taxable income and payments to the government for income taxes related to operations in 2009 were $3,436 million. Assume that the income tax expense and these income tax payments were the only tax-related transactions during 2009.

1. Prepare the journal entry that recognizes the $4,032 million income tax expense and the $3,436 million income tax payment.
2. Compute the change in the deferred income tax liability account for 2009.

9-45 Debt and Interest-Coverage Ratios

Great Plains Energy, Incorporated, headquartered in Kansas City, Missouri, provides electric services to customers primarily in the states of Missouri and Kansas. Its condensed income statement and balance sheet follow:

Great Plains Energy
Consolidated Statement of Income
For the Year Ended December 31, 2009
(in millions)

Net revenue	$1,965.0
Operating expenses	1,643.9
Operating income	321.1
Interest expense	180.9
Other (income) and expenses, net	(39.7)
Pretax income	179.9
Income taxes	29.5
Net income	$ 150.4

Great Plains Energy
Consolidated Balance Sheet
December 31, 2009
(in millions)

Assets		Liabilities and Shareholders' Equity	
Current assets	$ 612.5	Current liabilities	$ 958.3
Utility plant	6,651.1	Long-term liabilities	4,691.8
Investments and other assets	1,219.2	Shareholders' equity	2,832.7
Total assets	$8,482.8	Total liabilities and shareholders' equity	$8,482.8

Compute the following four ratios. In one sentence each, explain what it tells you about Great Plains Energy.

1. Debt to equity
2. Long term debt to total capital
3. Debt to total assets
4. Interest coverage

9-46 Exercises in Compound Interest
Study Appendix 9. Then answer the following questions:

1. You deposit $10,000. How much will you have in 4 years at 8%, compounded annually? At 12%?
2. A savings and loan association offers depositors a $10,000 lump-sum payment 4 years hence. How much will you be willing to deposit if you desire an interest rate of 8% compounded annually? How much at an interest rate of 12%?
3. Repeat requirement 2, but assume the interest rates are compounded semiannually.

9-47 Exercises in Compound Interest
Study Appendix 9. A reliable friend has asked you for a loan. You are pondering various proposals for repayment.

1. Repayment of a $40,000 lump sum 4 years hence. How much will you lend if your desired rate of return is (a) 10% compounded annually, (b) 20% compounded annually?
2. Repeat requirement 1, but assume the interest rates are compounded semiannually.
3. Suppose the loan is to be paid in full by equal payments of $10,000 at the end of each of the next 4 years. How much will you lend if your desired rate of return is (a) 10% compounded annually and (b) 20% compounded annually?

9-48 Compound Interest and Journal Entries
Study Appendix 9. A Berlin company has bought some equipment on a contract entailing a €200,000 cash down payment and an €800,000 lump sum to be paid at the end of 4 years. The same equipment can be bought for €788,000 cash. (€ refers to the euro, a unit of currency).

1. Prepare the journal entry for the acquisition of the equipment.
2. Prepare journal entries at the end of each of the first 2 years. Ignore entries for depreciation.

9-49 Exercises in Compound Interest
Study Appendix 9. Then answer the following questions:

1. It is your sixtieth birthday. You plan to work 5 more years before retiring. Then you want to spend $15,000 for a Mediterranean cruise. What lump sum do you have to invest now to accumulate the $15,000? Assume your minimum desired rate of return is as follows:
   a. 5%, compounded annually
   b. 10%, compounded annually
   c. 20%, compounded annually
2. You want to spend $4,000 on a vacation at the end of each of the next 5 years. What lump sum do you have to invest now to take the five vacations? Assume that your minimum desired rate of return is as follows:
   a. 5%, compounded annually

  b. 10%, compounded annually
  c. 20%, compounded annually

9-50 Exercises in Compound Interest
Study Appendix 9. Then answer the following questions:

1. At age 60, you find that your employer is moving to another location. You receive termination pay of $500,000. You have some savings and wonder whether to retire now.
   a. If you invest the $500,000 now at 8%, compounded annually, how much money can you withdraw from your account each year so at the end of 5 years there will be a zero balance?
   b. If you invest the $500,000 now at 10%, compounded annually, how much money can you withdraw from your account each year so at the end of 5 years there will be a zero balance?
2. At 16%, compounded annually, which of the following plans is more desirable in terms of present value? Show computations to support your answer.

	Annual Cash Inflows	
	Mining	Farming
1	$100,000	$ 20,000
2	80,000	40,000
3	60,000	60,000
4	40,000	80,000
5	20,000	100,000
	$300,000	$300,000

9-51 Basic Relationships in Interest Tables
Study Appendix 9. Then answer the following questions:

1. Suppose you borrow $40,000 now at 16% interest compounded annually. The borrowed amount plus interest will be repaid in a lump sum at the end of 6 years. How much must be repaid? Use Table 9A-1 and basic equation FV = Present amount $\times$ Future value factor.
2. Repeat requirement 1 using Table 9A-2 and the basic equation PV = Future amount $\times$ Present value factor.
3. Assume the same facts as in requirement 1, except that the loan will be repaid in equal installments at the end of each of 5 years. How much must be repaid each year? Use Table 9A-3 and the basic equation PV_A = Future annual amounts $\times$ Conversion factor.

9-52 Discounted Present Value and Leases
Study Appendix 9. Suppose Wal-Mart signed a 10-year lease for a new store location. The lease calls for an immediate payment of $50,000 and annual payments of $30,000 at the end of each of the next 9 years. Wal-Mart expects to earn 16% interest, compounded annually, on its investments. What is the present value of the lease payments?

Problems

MyAccountingLab

9-53 Accounting for Payroll
For the week ended January 27, the Monterrey Company had a total payroll of $100,000. The company withheld three items from employees' paychecks: (1) Social Security (FICA) tax of 7.1% of the payroll; (2) income taxes, which average 22% of the payroll; and (3) employees' savings that are deposited in their Credit Union, which are $5,000. Monterrey paid all three items together with the wages on January 30.

1. Use the balance sheet equation to analyze the transactions on January 27 and January 30.
2. Prepare journal entries for the recording of the items in requirement 1.
3. In addition to the payroll, Monterrey pays (1) payroll taxes of 9% of the payroll, (2) health insurance premiums of $6,000, and (3) contributions to the employees' pension fund of $8,000. Prepare journal entries for the recognition and payment of these additional expenses.

9-54 Liabilities on the Balance Sheet—IFRS

ArcelorMittal, headquartered in Luxembourg, is the largest steel producer in the world. It reports using IFRS. Following are items from the company's June 30, 2009, balance sheet (in millions of U.S. dollars):

Long-term debt, net of current portion	$25,667
Short-term debt and current portion of long-term debt	8,409
Long-term provisions	2,343
Property, plant, and equipment	60,755
Trade accounts payable and other	10,501
Deferred employee benefits	7,111
Total noncurrent liabilities	?
Trade accounts receivable	6,737
Short-term provisions	3,292
Other long-term obligations	1,582
Total current liabilities	30,760
Inventories	24,741
Deferred tax liabilities	6,395
Accrued expenses and other liabilities	7,783
Income tax liabilities	775
Total liabilities	73,858

Prepare the liabilities section of ArcelorMittal's balance sheet. Classify liabilities into current and noncurrent portions. Omit items that are not liabilities. Include the appropriate number for total non-current liabilities.

9-55 Convertible Bonds—IFRS and U. S. GAAP

Brockman Company issued $100,000 convertible 5-year bonds with a face value of $100,000 on January 1, 20X0. The coupon rate on the bonds was 6%, and Brockman received $100,000 cash for the bonds. Interest is paid semi-annually. The market rate for similar bonds without a conversion factor was 8%. Each $1,000 bond is convertible into 20 shares of Brockman Company common stock. At the time of issue of the bonds, Brockman common stock sold for $42 per share.

1. How would Brockman Company report the issuance of the bonds using U.S. GAAP?
2. How would Brockman Company report the issuance of the bonds using IFRS?

9-56 Convertible Bonds

Sometimes companies find it desirable to include a convertibility option to sell bonds at a reasonable interest rate. **Siemens AG**, the huge German electronics company, issued €2.5 billion of convertible bonds with a coupon rate of 1.375%, which is less interest than Siemens would have paid if the bonds were not convertible. Each €1,000 bond can be converted into 17.8 common shares of Siemens stock.

In 2008, Siemens had revenues of more than €77 billion and a net income of nearly €3.5 billion. The company pays dividends of €1.60 per share.

1. Compute the annual interest received by the holders of the convertible bonds.
2. The current price of one share of Siemens common stock is €62. If you held some of the Siemens convertible bonds, would you immediately convert your bonds to common stock? Why or why not?
3. Suppose the maturity date of the convertible bonds was rapidly approaching. Would you convert your holdings of the convertible bonds if the price of Siemens stock were €62 per share? If the price were €50 per share? Explain.

9-57 Bonds Issued at Par

On December 31, 2009, Southeast Financial, Corp., issued $20 million of 5-year, 10% debentures at par. Interest is paid semi-annually.

1. Compute the proceeds from issuing the debentures.
2. Using the balance sheet equation format, prepare an analysis of this bond transaction. Show entries for the issuer concerning (a) issuance, (b) first semiannual interest payment, and (c) payment of maturity value.
3. Show all the corresponding journal entries keyed as in requirement 2.
4. Show how the bond-related accounts would appear on the balance sheet as of December 31, 2009, and June 30, 2010. Assume that the semiannual interest payment due on the balance sheet date has been recorded.

9-58 Bonds Issued at Par

On December 31, 2009, Montana Mining, Inc. issued $25 million of 10-year, 6% debentures at par.

1. Compute the proceeds from issuing the debentures.
2. By using the balance sheet equation format, prepare an analysis of this bond transaction. Show entries for the issuer concerning (a) issuance, (b) first semiannual interest payment, and (c) payment of maturity value.
3. Show the corresponding journal entries for (a), (b), and (c) in requirement 2.
4. Show how the bond-related accounts would appear on the balance sheet as of December 31, 2009, and June 30, 2010. Assume that the semiannual interest payment due on the balance sheet date has been recorded.

9-59 Bond Discount Transactions

(Alternates are 9-60 and 9-62.) On March 1, 2009, Oregon Gas & Electric issued $200 million of 20-year, 9% debentures. Proceeds were $182,840,000, implying a market interest rate of 10%. Show all amounts in thousands of dollars.

1. By using the balance sheet equation format, prepare an analysis of bond transactions. Assume effective interest amortization. Show entries for the issuer concerning (a) issuance, (b) first semiannual interest payment, and (c) payment of maturity value.
2. Show all the corresponding journal entries for (a), (b), and (c) in requirement 1.
3. Show how the bond-related accounts would appear on the balance sheets as of March 1, 2009, and March 1, 2010. Assume the March 1 interest payment and amortization of bond discount have been made.

9-60 Bonds Issued at a Discount

(Alternates are 9-59 and 9-62.) On January 1, 2010, Lincoln Park District issued $10 million of 5-year, 6% debentures. Interest is paid semi-annually. The market interest rate at issuance was 10%.

1. Compute the proceeds from issuing the debentures.
2. By using the balance sheet equation format, prepare an analysis of this bond transaction. Show entries for the issuer concerning (a) issuance, (b) first semiannual interest payment, and (c) payment of maturity value.
3. Show the corresponding journal entries for (a), (b), and (c) in requirement 2.
4. Show how the bond-related accounts would appear on the balance sheets as of January 1, 2010, and July 1, 2010. Assume Lincoln Park District has already recorded the semiannual interest payment and amortization due on the balance sheet dates.

9-61 Bond Amortization Schedule

Consider the bond in problem 9-60: a $10 million issue of 5-year, 6% debentures when the market interest rate was 10%. It was issued on January 1, 2010.

1. Prepare a table showing the interest expense and the unamortized discount and ending liability balance for each semiannual period. Use Exhibit 9-4 on page 405 as an example. (*Hint*: Use a spreadsheet.)
2. Prepare the journal entry for recording interest for the 6-month period ended June 30, 2013.

9-62 Bond Discount Transactions

(Alternates are 9-59 and 9-60.) Assume that on December 31, 2009, Oslo Fiske issued NKR 20 million of 10-year, 10% debentures. Proceeds were NKR 15,762,000; therefore, the market rate of interest was 14%. (NKR is the Norwegian kroner.)

1. By using the balance sheet equation format, prepare an analysis of transactions for Oslo Fiske. Key your transactions as follows: (a) issuance, (b) first semiannual interest using effective interest amortization of bond discount, and (c) payment of maturity value. Round all amounts to the nearest thousand.
2. Prepare corresponding journal entries for (a), (b), and (c) in requirement 1.
3. Show how the bond-related accounts would appear on Oslo Fiske's balance sheets as of December 31, 2009, and June 30, 2010. Assume that Oslo Fiske has already recorded the semiannual interest payments and amortization.

9-63 Bonds Issued at a Premium

(Alternate is 9-64.) On January 1, 2010, Sydney Travel issued $6 million of 5-year, 10% debentures. The market interest rate at issuance was 8%. Interest is paid semi-annually.

1. Compute the proceeds from issuing the debentures.
2. By using the balance sheet equation format, prepare an analysis of this bond transaction. Show entries for the issuer concerning (a) issuance, (b) first semiannual interest payment, and (c) payment of maturity value.
3. Show the corresponding journal entries for (a), (b), and (c) in requirement 2.
4. Show how the bond-related accounts would appear on the balance sheets as of January 1, 2010, and July 1, 2010. Assume the semiannual interest payments and amortization due on the balance sheet date have been recorded.

9-64 Bond Premium Transactions

(Alternate is 9-63.) Assume that on December 31, 20X0, Michigan Woolens issued $10 million of 10-year, 10% debentures. Proceeds were $11,359,000; therefore, the market rate of interest was 8%.

1. By using the balance sheet equation format, prepare an analysis of transactions for Michigan Woolens. Key your transactions as follows: (a) issuance, (b) first semiannual interest using effective interest amortization of bond premium, and (c) payment of maturity value. Round all amounts to the nearest thousand.
2. Prepare corresponding journal entries for (a), (b), and (c) in requirement 1.
3. Show how the bond-related accounts would appear on Michigan Woolens' balance sheets as of December 31, 20X0, and June 30, 20X1. Assume that the semiannual interest payment and amortization have been recorded.

9-65 Interest Expense on the Cash Flow Statement—IFRS and U. S. GAAP

Siemens AG is Europe's largest conglomerate. It is headquartered in Berlin and Munich. The company's statement of cash flows is shown in Exhibit 9-15. Some items have been combined to simplify the presentation. Siemens reports under IFRS. What item(s) in this statement would be shown differently if Siemens reported using U.S. GAAP?

9-66 Early Extinguishment of Debt

On December 31, 2009, Greystone Charters issued $20 million of 10-year, 12% debentures. Interest is paid semi-annually. The market interest rate at issuance was 14%. On December 31, 2010 (after all interest payments and amortization had been recorded for 2010), the company purchased all the debentures for $20 million. Throughout their life, the debentures had been held by a large insurance company.

Show all amounts in thousands of dollars. Round to the nearest thousand.

1. Compute the gain or loss on early extinguishment.
2. By using the balance sheet equation, present an analysis of the December 31, 2010, transaction on the issuer's books.
3. Show the appropriate journal entry.
4. At what price on December 31, 2010, could Greystone Charters redeem the bonds and realize a $1,000,000 gain?

9-67 Early Extinguishment of Debt

On December 31, 2010, a Zurich real estate holding company issued CHF 10 million of 10-year, 8% debentures. The market interest rate at issuance was 8%. Suppose that on December 31, 2011 (after all interest payments had been recorded for 2011), the company purchased all the debentures for CHF 9.5 million. The debentures had been held by a large insurance company throughout their life. (CHF represents Swiss francs.)

EXHIBIT 9-15

Siemens Statement of Cash Flows

Siemens
Statement of Cash Flows
For the Year ended September 30, 2008
(in millions of euro)

Cash flows from operating activities	
Net income	€ 5,886
Adjustments to reconcile net income to cash provided:	
Amortization, depreciation, and impairments	3,213
Interest (income) expense, net	(75)
Other noncash (income) expenses	(4,246)
Change in current assets and liabilities	4,198
Income taxes paid	(1,564)
Dividends received	337
Interest received	875
Net cash provided by (used in) operating activities	8,624
Cash flows from investing activities	
Additions to intangible assets and property, plant, and equipment	(3,721)
Acquisitions	(5,407)
Proceeds from disposals of businesses	10,481
Other	(1,760)
Net cash provided by (used in) investing activities	(407)
Cash flows from financing activities	
Purchase of common stock	(4,350)
Proceeds from issuance of long-term debt	5,728
Change in short-term debt	(4,635)
Interest paid	(829)
Dividends paid	(1,600)
Other	(443)
Net cash provided by (used in) financing activities	(6,129)
Effect of exchange rates on cash and cash equivalents	(99)
Net increase (decrease) in cash and cash equivalents	1,989
Cash and cash equivalents at beginning of period	4,940
Cash and cash equivalents at end of period	€ 6,929

Show all amounts in thousands of Swiss francs.

1. Compute the gain or loss on early extinguishment.
2. By using the balance sheet equation, present an analysis of the December 31, 2011, transaction on the holding company's books.
3. Show the appropriate journal entry.

9-68 Noninterest-Bearing Notes
On January 2 a local bookstore borrowed from a bank on a 1-year note. The face value of the note was $80,000. However, the bank deducted its interest "in advance" at 10% of the face value.
    Show the effects on the borrower's records at inception and at the end of the year:

1. Using the balance sheet equation, prepare an analysis of transactions.
2. Prepare journal entries.
3. What was the real rate of interest?

9-69 Zero Coupon Bonds

Issuers of "deep-discount" or "zero coupon" debt securities must use an effective interest approach to amortization of discount for both tax reporting and reporting to the public. Similarly, buyers of such securities must record interest income under the effective interest rate method.

1. Assume that, in order to develop improvements for the Kindle, Amazon.com issues a 10-year zero coupon bond having a face amount of $25,000,000 to yield 10%. For simplicity, assume that the 10% yield is compounded annually. Prepare the journal entry for Amazon.com (the issuer).
2. Prepare the journal entry for interest expense for the first full year and the second full year using (a) straight-line and (b) effective interest amortization.
3. Assume an income tax rate of 40%. How much more income tax for the first year would the issuer have to pay because of applying effective interest instead of straight-line amortization?
4. What kinds of borrowers might prefer these investments over bonds that pay interest immediately?

9-70 Zero Coupon Bonds

The state of Illinois issues zero coupon bonds as part of its Illinois College Savings Bonds series. Suppose that in late 2009, the state issued 9,000 such bonds with a total $90 million maturity value. Each bond had a maturity value of $10,000, and bonds ranged in price from $9,500 for a 3-year bond to $3,600 for a 22-year bond. Consider one of the 22-year zero coupon bonds issued on December 31, 2009, for $3,600.

1. Compute the market interest rates for the 22-year zero coupon bond. How does this compare with the rate on the 3-year bonds? Assume annual compounding.
2. Prepare the state's journal entry for one 22-year bond at issuance. Do not use a discount account.
3. Prepare the state's journal entry for recording interest expense on the 22-year bonds for 2010. Round to the nearest dollar.
4. Compute the liability that Illinois would show on its balance sheet for this bond on December 31, 2010.

9-71 Capital (Financing) Lease

On December 31, 20X0, the Jackson Building Maintenance Services acquired cleaning equipment on a capital lease for three annual lease payments of $30,000 each on December 31, 20X1, 20X2, and 20X3. The implicit interest rate was 12% compounded annually.

1. Compute the present value of the capital lease.
2. Prepare journal entries at the inception of the lease on December 31, 20X0, and for each of the 3 years. Distinguish between the short and long-term classifications of the lease liability.

9-72 Comparison of Operating and Capital (Financing) Lease

Refer to the preceding problem. Compare income statement and balance sheet effects of treating the lease as a capital lease rather than an operating lease. Ignore income taxes. You can do this by filling in the blanks in the following table.

	Operating Lease	Capital Lease	Difference
Total expenses			
20X1	?	?	?
20X2	?	?	?
Two years together	?	?	?
End of 20X1			
Total assets	?	?	?
Total liabilities	?	?	?
Retained earnings	?	?	?
End of 20X2			
Total assets	?	?	?
Total liabilities	?	?	?
Retained earnings	?	?	?

9-73 Finance Leases

Air France-KLM is one of the world's largest airlines with headquarters at Paris-Charles de Gaulle Airport. It prepares its financial statements under "International Financial Reporting Standards ("IFRS") as adopted by the European Commission ("EU"). . . . [which] differ in certain respects from IFRS as published by the International Accounting Standards Board ("IASB"). . . . [However,] the financial information for the periods presented would not differ substantially had the Group applied IFRS as published by the IASB."

In accounting for its leases, Air France-KLM states that "leases are classified as finance leases when the lease arrangement transfers substantially all the risks and rewards of ownership to the lessee. . . . The assets held under a finance lease are recognized as assets at the lower of the following two values: the present value of the minimum lease payments under the lease arrangement or their fair value determined at inception of the lease. The corresponding obligation to the lessor is accounted for as long-term debt. These assets are depreciated over the shorter of the useful life of the assets and the lease term."

On March 31, 2009, Air France-KLM listed finance lease assets of €3,093 million and finance lease obligations of €3,893 million on its balance sheet. Suppose that the average life of the assets under lease is 10 years, the average implicit interest rate in the leases is 4%, and the average annual lease payment is €500 million. Compute the depreciation on the leased assets, the interest expense on the lease obligations and the ending balances in finance lease assets and finance lease obligations for the fiscal years ended March 31, 2010, and March 31, 2011. Assume that Air France-KLM uses straight-line depreciation and neither terminates nor enters into new lease contracts during either year.

9-74. Capital or Operating Lease

On December 31, 20X0, the law firm of Preston, Gomez, and Bergman is offered 30 laptop computers for the firm's partners. It can either (a) buy them outright for $100,000 cash or (b) lease them on a noncancelable lease whereby rental payments would be made at the end of each year for 3 years. The computers will become obsolete and worthless at the end of 3 years. The company can borrow $100,000 cash on a 3-year loan payable at maturity at 10% compounded annually.

1. Compute the annual rental payment, assuming that the lessor desires a 10% rate of return per year.
2. Suppose the lease could be accounted for as an operating lease. What annual journal entry would the company make?
3. The lease is a capital lease. Prepare an analytical schedule of each lease payment. Show the lease liability at the beginning of the year, and interest expense, lease payment, and lease liability at the end of the year.
4. Prepare an analysis of transactions for the capital lease, using the balance sheet equation format.
5. Prepare yearly journal entries for the capital lease.

9-75 Leases

The following information appeared in a footnote to the 2008 annual report of Delta Air Lines, Incorporated:

> *The following table summarizes, as of December 31, 2008, our minimum rental commitments under capital leases . . . with initial or remaining terms of more than 1 year:*

Years Ending December 31 (in millions)	
2009	$135
2010	134
2011	129
2012	98
2013	64
After 2013	264
Total minimum lease payments	$824
Less: Lease payments that represent interest	323
Present value of future minimum capital lease payments	$501

1. Suppose the minimum capital lease payments are made in equal amounts on March 31, June 30, September 30, and December 31 of each year. Compute the interest and principal to be paid on capital leases during the first half of fiscal 2009. Perform calculations in millions with two decimal places. Assume an interest rate of 8% per annum, compounded quarterly.
2. Prepare the journal entries for the lease payments in requirement 1 on March 31 and June 30, 2009.
3. Delta has well over $1,000 million per year in operating leases. Suppose an analyst thought it appropriate to treat some of Delta's operating leases as if they were capital leases. Assume that the payments on these operating leases were $1,000 million per year for 15 years made annually at year-end. If these operating leases were treated as capital leases and capitalized at 8%, how much would long-term debt increase? Do calculations to the closest million. Delta's long-term debt and capital leases is $15,411 million. What percentage increase in long-term debt would result from capitalizing these operating leases?

9-76 Leases

Consider footnote 7 from the 2009 annual report of FedEx:

> We utilize certain aircraft, land, facilities, retail locations, and equipment
> under capital and operating leases that expire at various dates through 2040. . . .
> A summary of future minimum lease payments under capital leases and
> noncancellable operating leases with an initial or remaining term in excess
> of one year at May 31, 2009 is as follows (in millions):

	Capital Leases	Operating Leases
2010	$164	$ 1,759
2011	20	1,612
2012	8	1,451
2013	119	1,316
2014	2	1,166
Thereafter	15	7,352
Total	$328	$14,656

1. Compute the net present value of the operating lease payments as of May 31, 2009. Use a 10% implicit interest rate. For ease of computation, assume each payment is made on May 31 of the designated year (i.e., the first $1,759 million payment is made on May 31, 2010) and that the final payment, labeled "Thereafter," is made on May 31, 2015.
2. Suppose FedEx were to capitalize the operating leases examined in requirement 1. Show the journal entries necessary to do the following:
   a. Capitalize the leases on June 1, 2009. Ignore any prior period adjustments, and do not break the lease obligation into current and long-term portions.
   b. Record the first payment on May 31, 2010.
3. FedEx's total liabilities on May 31, 2009, were $10,618 million, and its total stockholders' equity was $13,626 million. Compute its total debt-to-equity ratio. Then, suppose FedEx capitalized its operating leases using the present value calculated in requirement 1. Recompute the debt-to-equity ratio. What difference does capitalizing the operating leases make to the debt-to-equity ratio? Explain.

9-77 Capital Leases

The Home Depot is the leading retailer in the home improvement industry and one of the 10 largest retailers in the United States. The company included the following on its February 1, 2009, balance sheet and footnotes ($ in millions):

Capital lease assets	$490
Capital lease obligations (long term)	$401
Capital lease obligations (current)	16
Total capital lease obligations	$417

Total capital lease payments scheduled for the fiscal year ended February 1, 2010, are $88,000,000.

1. Prepare the journal entry for the $88,000,000 lease payments. Remember that the lease payments will include the principal payments due for the year plus interest expense accrued for the year.
2. Suppose that the capital lease assets have an average remaining life of 20 years and that no new leases are signed in the fiscal year ending February 1, 2010. Compute the balance in the capital lease asset account and the total in the capital lease obligations account (long-term and current combined) at February 1, 2010.
3. Explain why the amount in the capital lease assets account is not equal to the amount in the lease obligations accounts.

9-78 Pension Liabilities

Boeing Company, the aircraft and aerospace manufacturer, had pension obligations of $49,017 million and obligations for postretirement benefits other than pensions of $7,859 million at the beginning of 2009. The fair value of plan assets in the pension plan was $40,597 million, and the fair value of plan assets for postretirement benefits other than pensions was $79 million. Total retained earnings was $22,675 million. The total market value of Boeing common stock is approximately $36 billion.

1. Comment on the confidence that employees might have about receiving the benefits due to them.
2. Recognizing pensions and other postretirement benefits as liabilities on the balance sheet has been a controversial topic. Do you think this is important information to disclose to shareholders? Why or why not?

9-79 Pensions

Alcoa, Inc., is the world's leader in the production and fabrication of aluminum and aluminum products. The company has had a defined benefit pension plan for many years. On December 31, 2009, it pension obligation stood at $11,638 million. On the same date its pension assets totaled $8,529 million.

1. What is the impact of this defined benefit pension plan on Alcoa's balance sheet on December 31, 2009? Comment on how comfortable employees should be that they will receive their full pension benefits.
2. During 2009 Alcoa's pension expense was $143 million and it contributed $136 million cash to the pension assets. Prepare journal entries for these two summary transactions.
3. Optional question: What factors affect the balances in the Pension Assets and Pension Obligations accounts other than pension expense and pension funding?

9-80 Deferred Taxes

Cadbury plc is a major global company based in London. It is the second largest confectionary company in the world. Recent sales were nearly £6 billion (where £ is the British pound). The company's 2008 income statement included the following, using Cadbury's terminology (£ in millions):

Profit before taxation	£400
Taxation	(30)
Profit for the period from continuing operations	£370

As a result of operations, the deferred tax liability account decreased by £213 million. Assume there was no change in taxes payable.

1. Compute the income taxes paid to the government.
2. Prepare the journal entry to record taxes on ordinary activities.
3. Explain why the amount of income taxes paid to the government was not the same as the amount of income taxes recorded on the income statement.

9-81 Deferral of Taxes and Reversal of Temporary Differences

Assad Company bought an asset for $400,000 on January 1, 20X0. The asset has a 10-year life and zero salvage value. Assad uses straight-line depreciation for financial reporting purposes and

DDB depreciation for tax purposes. The DDB schedule switches to straight-line depreciation for the remaining book value when the resulting straight-line depreciation exceeds the amount of depreciation on the original DDB schedule. This results in the following depreciation charges:

Year	Straight-line Depreciation	DDB Depreciation
20X0	$40,000	$80,000
20X1	40,000	64,000
20X2	40,000	51,200
20X3	40,000	40,960
20X4	40,000	32,768
20X5	40,000	26,214
20X6	40,000	26,214
20X7	40,000	26,214
20X8	40,000	26,214
20X9	40,000	26,214

The company's tax rate is 40%.

1. Compute the amount in the deferred tax account at the end of each year.
2. Is the deferred tax account an asset or a liability? Explain.
3. What is the amount in the deferred tax account at the end of the life of the asset? Explain what caused the deferred tax account to reach this value at the end of the asset's life.

9-82 The Income Tax Footnote

Yum! Brands Inc. operates many franchised food outlets, including Pizza Hut, Taco Bell, A&W, and KFC. The company had 2008 operating revenues of more than $11 billion and income before income taxes of $1,280 million. Footnote 22 to the financial statements provided the following:

The details of our income tax provision (benefit) are set forth below:

	2008	2007
	($ in millions)	
Current		
Federal	$168	$175
Foreign	148	151
State	(1)	(3)
	315	323
Deferred		
Federal	(12)	(71)
Foreign	3	27
State	10	3
	1	(41)
Net tax expense	$316	$282

1. Provide the journal entries to record income tax expense for 2008.
2. Compute net income for 2008.

9-83 Debt-to-Equity Ratios

The total debt and stockholders' equity for three companies follows. The companies are described as follows:

- General Electric is a multinational technology and services company and is a large, well-established company.

- **Google** is a fast-growing company focusing on Internet search.
- **Amgen** is a biotechnology company pioneering the development of products based on advances in recombinant DNA.

	Total Debt		Stockholders' Equity	
(in millions)	**2008**	**2004**	**2008**	**2004**
General Electric	$684,157	$623,303	$104,665	$110,821
Google	2,646	285	22,690	589
Amgen	16,057	9,516	20,386	19,705

1. Compute debt-to-equity ratios for each company for 2004 and 2008.
2. Discuss the differences in the ratios across firms.
3. Discuss the changes in individual company ratios from 2004 to 2008.

9-84 Review of Chapters 8 and 9

The Kroger Company, a Cincinnati-based supermarket chain, operates nearly 2,500 stores throughout the United States. The company's annual report for the fiscal year ended January 31, 2009, contained the following ($ in millions):

The Kroger Company

	January 31	February 2
	2009	**2008**
Property, plant, and equipment, at cost	$23,900	$22,436
Less: Accumulated depreciation and amortization	10,739	9,938
Net property, plant, and equipment	$13,161	$12,498
Current portion of long-term debt	$ 558	$ 1,592
Long-term debt less current portion	7,505	6,529

Kroger's statement of cash flows listed capital investments of $2,149 million and depreciation and amortization of $1,442 million for the fiscal year ended January 31, 2009. Assume that all capital investments and all depreciation and amortizations were for property, plant, and equipment. (The use of T-accounts should help your analysis.)

1. Compute the dollar amounts of the following:
    a. Accumulated depreciation relating to properties and plants disposed of during the fiscal year ended January 31, 2009.
    b. Original acquisition cost of properties and plants disposed of during the fiscal year ended January 31, 2009.
2. Compute the dollar amount of the net increase or decrease in total long-term debt during the fiscal year ended January 31, 2009.

9-85 Liabilities for Frequent Flier Miles and Ethics

Most airlines in the United States have frequent flier programs that grant free flights if a customer accumulates enough flight miles on the airline. For example, United Airlines offers a free domestic flight for every 25,000 miles flown on United. United describes its program as follows in a footnote to the financial statements:

> *The deferred revenue measurement method used to record fair value of the frequent flyer obligation . . . is to allocate an equivalent weighted-average ticket value to each outstanding mile, based upon projected redemption patterns for available award choices when such miles are consumed.*

In its 2008 annual report, American Airlines reported a liability of $1.7 billion for 607 billion awarded frequent flyer miles. At 25,000 miles per round-trip, this represents approximately 24 million domestic flights owed to customers, an average of $70 per flight. However, some airlines maintain that the true liability is closer to $10 per flight, including only the cost of food, insurance, and other miscellaneous expenses. They argue that all other costs would be incurred even in the absence of the person traveling free.

Suppose airlines use one estimate of the cost of these "free" flights for their internal decision making and another for computing the liability for their publicly reported balance sheet. Comment on the ethical issues.

9-86 Present Value and Sports Salaries
Study Appendix 9. On December 13, 2007, Alex Rodriguez signed a 10-year, $275 million contract with the New York Yankees. Assume that all payments in the contract are paid on January 2 of the respective years, beginning on January 2, 2008. The contract includes a $10 million signing bonus paid at out as follows: $2 million on January 2, 2008, $1 million paid January 2 of each year 2009–2013, and $3 million on January 2, 2014. The salary is as follows (in millions):

2008	$27	2013	$28
2009	$32	2014	$25
2010	$32	2015	$21
2011	$31	2016	$20
2012	$29	2017	$20

Assume that the appropriate discount rate is 10%.

1. What was the present value of the contract on January 2, 2008?
2. How much present value (as of January 2, 2008) did Rodriguez lose by receiving the $10 million signing bonus over 7 years instead of immediately?
3. Do you agree that the contract was worth $275 million? Explain.

Collaborative Learning Exercises

9-87 Characteristics of Bonds
Form groups of three to six persons each. Each person should select a company that has long-term debt in the form of bonds (or debentures). Pick one of the company's bonds, and note the interest rate on the bond. If the company does not list bonds individually, you may need to select one of the groups of bonds that it presents.

Find out as much as you can about the factors that might explain the bond's interest rate. Among the items to look for are characteristics of the bond (such as the size of the issue, the length of the term, and any special features such as subordination, convertibility, and covenants) and characteristics of the company (such as its industry, its debt-to-equity ratio, and its interest-coverage ratio). Also, try to find out when the bond was issued and the level of prevailing interest rates at the time of issue. (Companies do not usually show the issue date in the footnotes to their financial statements. You might try looking at past annual reports to see when the bonds first appeared on the financial statement.) Prevailing interest rates may be represented by the rates on U.S. Treasury securities. Note the amount by which the interest rate of the bond exceeds the rate of a U.S. Treasury security of the same duration.

After students have performed their independent research, they should get together and compare results. Do the factors identified explain the differences in rates across the companies? How do the factors relate to the riskiness of the bonds? Is the amount by which the bond interest rate exceeds the U.S. Treasury rate related to the bond's riskiness?

9-88 Accounting for Pensions
Form groups of two or more students. Divide each group into two debate teams. Each team should be assigned one of the two following positions:

1. Pensions and other postretirement benefits are legitimate liabilities of a company and should be recognized as such on their balance sheets. They are expenses of the periods in which the benefiting employees work, so the obligation to pay them should be accrued at that time.
2. Pensions and other postretirement benefits are not legal liabilities of a company and should not be included among their liabilities on the balance sheet. They are essentially expenses in the period when the benefits are paid.

Each team can be given 5–10 minutes to defend its positon, followed by approximately 2 minutes each for rebuttals. Then a general class discussion of the issues can follow. The class might take a vote on which group made the most convincing argument.

Analyzing and Interpreting Financial Statements

9-89 Financial Statement Research

Select any two companies from the airline industry, and find each company's footnote describing its leases. (Possible companies include **Alaska Airlines**, **American Airlines**, **Continental Airlines**, **Delta Airlines**, **United**, and **US Airways**, but do not feel restricted to these.) Compute each company's debt-to-equity ratio under each of three assumptions:

1. With leases as reported
2. With all leases treated as operating leases
3. With all leases treated as capital leases

For this calculation assume all operating lease payments due after the fifth year are spread evenly over years 6–15. That is, one-tenth of the remaining lease payments will be made each of the next 10 years. Use a 10% interest rate for computing the present value of the operating leases. Comment on the differences made by the three treatments of leases. Also, comment on the differences in ratios between the two companies.

9-90 Analyzing Starbucks' Financial Statements

Find **Starbucks'** financial statements for the fiscal year ended September 27, 2009, either via the Starbucks Web site or on the SEC's Edgar database. Focus on the liabilities section of the balance sheet and footnote 10.

1. Compute the following three ratios at September 27, 2009, and September 28, 2008. Assess the changes in these ratios:
   a. Debt-to-equity ratio
   b. Debt-to-total-assets ratio
2. Comment on Starbucks' amount of long-term liabilities compared to its amount of current liabilities.

9-91 Analyzing Financial Statements Using the Internet: Macy's, Inc.

Go to www.macysinc.com to find financial information for **Macy's**. Select For Investors, and click on the most recent annual report or 10-K.

Answer the following questions about Macy's and its long-term debt:

1. Locate the discussion of Lease Obligations in the Notes to Consolidated Financial Statements. Macy's has both capital leases and operating leases. What percentage of its future lease commitments are for capital leases?
2. How do the operating lease payments affect Macy's financial statements? Explain how these operating leases are considered "invisible debt."
3. What items comprise Macy's long-term debt? Is any portion of that debt considered "current"? Where is the current portion reported on the financial statements? Was any long-term debt issued in the most recent year? Was any long-term debt retired in the most recent year?
4. Describe who is eligible for Macy's pension and other postretirement benefits. How are these items reported on the financial statements? What discount rate is used for determining the present value of these items? Does this rate differ from the rate used a year ago? If so, what difference does that make on the present value of the obligations?

10

Stockholders' Equity

LEARNING OBJECTIVES

After studying this chapter, you should be able to:

1 Describe the rights of shareholders.

2 Account for common stock, including payment of dividends.

3 Contrast bonds, preferred stock, and common stock.

4 Identify the economic characteristics of and account for stock splits.

5 Account for both large- and small-percentage stock dividends.

6 Explain and report stock repurchases and other treasury stock transactions.

7 Record conversions of debt for equity or of preferred stock into common stock.

8 Use the rate of return on common equity and book value per share.

United Parcel Service (UPS) has a distinctive brown fleet of trucks and a distinguished position as the world's largest package delivery company. The company's 426,000 employees deliver more than 12 million packages each business day in more than 200 countries from 1.8 million shippers to 6.1 million recipients. To do this requires about 100,000 delivery vehicles including more than 570 aircraft worldwide. Some 2,200 of the delivery vehicles use alternative fuels, either hybrid electric or compressed natural gas. As its annual report notes, "Small package shipment is the bond that joins retailer and buyer in this direct-to-consumer business model."

UPS has been one of the key beneficiaries of the shift to Web-based businesses. The firm continues to serve old-line, bricks-and-mortar companies, but the nature of the business is being transformed to a "time-definite" service. Companies once shipped items without knowing their precise arrival day or time. Today, UPS assures a package's time of arrival and provides the ability to monitor its progress constantly. The company offers a choice of three time-specific delivery periods each day. Customers have efficient electronic access to the information that allows them to request a pickup, track an order, and serve a customer. They rely on UPS for full logistics support for ordering, scheduling, shipping, and receiving.

UPS employees like the man pictured here control UPS through their voting rights as shareholders. The public has relied on UPS for delivery services for almost a century but has only had access to UPS stock since it became public in 1999.

In addition to its package delivery service and logistical support, UPS has a company called UPS Capital that lends businesses money, finances inventory, and even buys accounts receivable. UPS also offers warehousing and order fulfillment services for small- to medium-size firms through UPS e-Logistics.

Supporting this worldwide service requires very modern, high-tech processing. UPS Worldport is a 4 million square foot automated facility near the company's air hub in Louisville, Kentucky. Overhead cameras read smart labels and have the capacity to guide sorting of 304,000 packages per hour. To do this requires 122 miles of conveyor belts, 4,500 miles of fiber-optic cable, and databases able to process 59 million transactions per hour. Similar high tech facilities were created in 2006 at the Cologne/Bonn airport in Germany and in 2008 in Tamworth, England. Also in 2008 the company opened a major air hub in Shanghai China, serving all of China and providing direct service to the Americas, Europe, and the rest of Asia.

UPS has been a public company since November 10, 1999. When UPS chose to "go public," it found a receptive audience, raising some $5.5 billion by selling more than 109 million shares at approximately $50 per share. In the U.S., the SEC regulates public companies, as described in the Business First box on p. 452. UPS used the proceeds of the sale not only to fund its aggressive growth and development plans, but also to purchase shares from employee shareholders. The company had been employee owned for years, and the public offering allowed employees

BUSINESS FIRST

The U.S. Securities Acts of 1933 and 1934 created the SEC in response to economic and political pressure associated with the stock market crash of 1929 and the Great Depression. The SEC regulates accounting practices and ensures that companies with publicly traded securities provide information to shareholders on a timely basis. It has delegated its authority for setting accounting standards to the FASB. On rare occasions, the SEC overrules the FASB. In most cases the SEC is one of many contributors to the public discussions that the FASB facilitates as it debates future accounting practice. Public companies that have many shareholders who buy and sell shares in public markets such as the NYSE must file quarterly and annual reports with the SEC (forms 10-Q and 10-K, respectively) and also file special reports (form 8-K) whenever something material happens to the company. The SEC Web site (www.sec.gov) indicates that "Companies with more than $10 million in assets whose securities are held by more than 500 owners must file annual and other periodic reports." These reports are accessible from the SEC Web site, and Web sites of individual companies often link to SEC filings, usually in a section called "Investor Relations."

Security analysts closely monitor the quarterly results of public companies. We often observe large changes in market value and significant selling or buying of shares based on the results of one quarter of business. Some investors and managers believe this motivates an excessively short-term view in management decision making. They think a "closely held" private company has much more freedom to take the long view. Private companies can make investments that will take years to bear fruit and can accept short-term negative results in search of longer-term successes.

When a company such as UPS chooses to have an initial public offering (IPO) and allow its shares to trade widely, it is agreeing to comply with costly and complicated SEC rules in exchange for access to a large pool of capital. UPS raised $5.5 billion of capital when it went through its IPO.

The majority of companies that most of us know are well-established companies that issued their common stock years ago. However, entrepreneurs are continually forming corporations. Silicon Valley in California, Silicon Alley in New York City, and other high-tech locations originated thousands of new ventures in the last two decades. Most of these firms failed, but a few are thriving, including Amazon, eBay, Yahoo, and Google.

A complicated marketplace exists for funding of new ventures. New corporations often start with a few investors and then seek additional funding as their original ideas prove to be doable, exciting, and profitable. Groups of investors called venture capitalists support exciting ideas early in the process. If a company successfully implements these ideas, it may issue additional shares to the public through an IPO. An underwriting firm generally manages the IPO, and it sells shares to individual investors and to institutional investors such as pension funds, insurance companies, and mutual funds. Regardless of who owns the firm and whether it is public or private, the accounting procedures are very similar.

Since 1990 there have been about 280 IPOs per year in U.S. markets, but there is great variability from year to year. There were between 63 and 80 in 2001, 2002, and 2003, and in 2008 there were only 21. When three IPOs occurred in the week of May 18, 2009, the *New York Times* reminded investors that "The creation of risk capital, of which IPO demands is a leading indicator, is crucial to getting the economy back on its feet." One of the offerings was OpenTable, an online restaurant reservation service. Initially offered at $20 per share, it ended its first day of trading at $31.89 per share, up 59%. It is common for IPOs to rise sharply on the first day—over the last 18 years the average first day gain has been 22%.

Sources: www.sec.gov; *NY Times*, pB2, May 21, 2009 and pC2, May 22, 2009; "Some Factoids about the 2008 IPO Market," Jay Ritter, May 11, 2009 @ http://bearcba.ufl.edu/ritter.

to realize the value of their long-term investment in the company. Even now, employees and retirees own most of the outstanding shares.

In the first half of 2009, the UPS share price fluctuated between $39.01 on March 4 and $56.62 on May 11. The investor with perfect foresight could have earned a return of 45% during this two month period in the spring of 2009. But no one has perfect foresight and this wild swing in share prices for UPS reflects the extreme volatility in share prices during the recession of 2008 and the recovery starting in 2009. ●

Background on Stockholders' Equity

Thus far, we have focused on transactions affecting assets and liabilities. Now we examine stockholders' equity in more detail. After all, stockholders such as those of UPS want to know details about their interests. Moreover, stockholders supply a significant portion of the capital that corporations employ, so knowing the rights and responsibilities of stockholders is important to understanding how companies raise capital.

The accounting equation must balance. If we know the amounts of assets and liabilities, the stockholders' equity is the residual, the difference between the assets and liabilities. This is why we call the stockholders the residual claimants to the corporation. When a company goes out of business, sells its assets, and pays creditors out of the proceeds, the stockholders receive whatever is left. It is now time to address issues relating to how we classify and report transactions between a company and its shareholders and how analysts use this information to evaluate the company.

We show the owners' equity section of the UPS annual report in Exhibit 10-1. Some of what appears there is no surprise because common stock and retained earnings are old friends at this point. However, UPS has two classes of common stock and in addition has preferred stock that is authorized but unissued, additional paid-in-capital, accumulated other comprehensive loss, deferred compensation arrangements, and treasury stock. Most of the items in stockholders' equity arise from explicit transactions between the company and its shareholders.

The retained earnings are a result of the historic profitability of UPS that has enabled it to finance much of its exceptional growth by retaining earnings in the business. Assets of the company reported in the balance sheet total $32 billion and total stockholders' equity of $6.8 billion represents 21% of that. Note that these accounting values do not correspond to the market value of UPS. It was selling for about $50 per share in mid-2009, which means the total market value of equity was $49.8 billion ($50 per share times 996 million shares held by investors). This is more than 7 times greater than its book value.

A number of the accounting practices for shareholders' equity are based on legal characteristics of corporations, so we make frequent reference to the rights and privileges of shareholders and the consequences of various financing decisions on the firm and its owners. UPS is unusual in having two classes of common stock. Employees hold the class A common stock, and it is not publicly traded. The class A shares have 10 votes each, while class B shares have 1 vote each. Thus the employees control votes for electing the board of directors, authorizing shares of stock, and approving mergers and other significant corporate decisions. Class A shares are directly convertible into class B shares. During 2008, employees converted 33 million shares of class A stock to class B stock, probably so the employee could sell the shares

EXHIBIT 10-1

UPS Shareowners' Equity

(in millions except per share amounts)

	December 31	
	2008	**2007**
Preferred stock, no par value; authorized—200 shares, none issued	$ —	$ —
Class A common stock; shares issued 314 and 349 in 2008 and 2007	3	3
Class B common stock; shares issued 684 and 694 in 2008 and 2007	7	7
Additional paid-in capital	—	—
Retained earnings	12,412	14,186
Accumulated other comprehensive loss	(5,642)	(2,013)
Deferred compensation arrangements	121	137
	6,901	12,320
Less: Treasury stock (2 shares in 2008 and 2007)	(121)	(137)
	$ 6,780	$12,183

and receive cash. At $50 per share, this represents a sale of $1.7 billion in ownership by long-term employees to new investors.

Internationally, there are substantial differences in the structure of corporate/business activity. For example, in many countries large corporations are primarily privately owned by a few individuals, instead of having broad public ownership and public financial reporting as in the United States. In many countries banks provide the majority of financing, so large public issuances of shares are rare. Many formerly planned economies have been transitioning from state-owned-and-operated business entities into private ones. In many countries the government remains the largest employer because it owns many economic entities such as power producers, phone providers, and airlines, not to mention the mail system, which remains a government monopoly even in the United States. However, from an accounting perspective, worldwide movement toward IFRS and convergence of IFRS with U.S. GAAP has significantly reduced the international variation in accounting for stockholders' equity.

Accounting for Common Stock in Publicly Held Corporations

OBJECTIVE 1

Describe the rights of shareholders.

In the United States, a company incorporates in accordance with state law, while in most of the world the national government determines corporate law. Despite state-level registration of corporations in the United States, since the 1930s there has been significant federal regulation of corporations. Regulation increased with the 2002 Sarbanes-Oxley Act. Corporate governance differs around the world. To find out how it operates in Malaysia, turn to the Business First box.

Corporate charters specify the rights of stockholders (or shareholders) that generally include the right to (1) vote, (2) share in corporate profits, (3) share in any assets left at liquidation, and (4) possibly acquire more shares of subsequent issues of stock. The extent of an individual stockholder's power is determined by the number and type of shares held.

Corporations hold annual meetings of shareholders, where they take votes on important matters. For example, the shareholders elect the board of directors. They may also vote on changing employee bonus plans, choosing outside auditors, making decisions to merge, and handling similar matters. Large corporations make heavy use of the proxy system. A **corporate proxy** is a written authority granted by individual shareholders to others (usually members of corporate management) to cast the shareholders' votes. By using a proxy, shareholders may express (vote) their preference without traveling to the site of the annual meeting.

corporate proxy
A written authority granted by individual shareholders to others to cast the shareholders' votes.

The ultimate power to manage a corporation almost always resides with the common shareholders, but shareholders of publicly owned corporations usually delegate that power to the company's top managers. The modern large corporation frequently has a team of professional managers including a chief executive officer (CEO), a chief operating officer (COO), a chief financial officer (CFO), and perhaps a chief information or technology officer. Collectively these leaders are sometimes referred to as the "C-suite," named after the use of chief in their titles.

Increasingly, companies are requiring top managers to own a significant number of shares in the firm. When managers own shares directly or hold stock options to acquire shares, they are more likely to share a common economic interest with shareholders. When the company's stock rises in value, the managers benefit personally.

preemptive rights
The rights to acquire a proportional amount of any new issues of capital stock.

Stockholders also may have **preemptive rights**, which are the rights to acquire a proportional amount of any new issues of capital stock. Whenever a company issues new shares of stock, more people can become owners, in which case each existing shareholder's percentage of ownership decreases. The preemptive privilege allows present shareholders to purchase additional shares directly from the corporation before it can sell new shares to the general public. In this way, the shareholders are able to maintain their percentage of ownership. Such rights are much more common in Europe than in the United States.

Perhaps the most important right of common shareholders is limited liability. Recall from Chapter 1 that this means that creditors of the corporation have claims only on the assets owned by the corporation, not on the assets of the owners of the corporation. In contrast, the creditors of a partnership have potential rights against the savings, homes, and automobiles of the individual partners.

Issuing Common Stock

Regardless of where in the world a company is located, to incorporate it creates articles of incorporation that detail the number and types of capital stock that it can issue. We call these **authorized shares**. When the company receives cash in exchange for stock certificates, the shares become **issued shares**. We call shares that are issued and held by the stockholders **outstanding shares**.

To account for a stock issuance, we record the receipt of cash and create a common stock account to represent the ownership interest. In 2009, UPS stock was selling for around $50 per share, so it would record a stock issuance of 1 million additional shares as follows:

Cash	50,000,000	
Common Stock		50,000,000

Many U.S. companies, however, separate their common stock recognition into two categories—par value and additional paid-in capital. Legally, par value was originally a measure of protection for creditors because it established the minimum legal liability of a stockholder. In this way, the creditors would be assured the corporation would have at least a minimum amount of ownership capital—for example, $10 for each share issued. A corporation could not issue stock for less than its par value. In practice, corporations usually set the par values far below the full market price of the shares when issued. Although neither U.S. GAAP nor IFRS have specific requirements for reporting capital raised from

OBJECTIVE 2

Account for common stock, including payment of dividends.

authorized shares
The total number of shares that a company may legally issue under the articles of incorporation.

issued shares
The aggregate number of shares sold to the public.

outstanding shares
Shares in the hands of shareholders.

stockholders, most U.S. companies separate par value from additional paid-in capital, while most companies using IFRS have a single capital account—for example, **Volkswagen**, the German Auto maker, calls it Subscribed Capital and **Carrefour**, the French supermarket chain, calls it simply Capital.

Consider UPS shares that have a par value of $.01 each. The entry to record issuance of 1 million additional shares would separate out par value as follows:

Cash	50,000,000	
Common stock at par		10,000
Additional paid-in capital		49,990,000

Some companies use the term "stated value" rather than "par value." Similarly, the language used to describe additional paid-in capital varies widely. For economic purposes, most of these distinctions are of little importance. However, you encounter them in annual reports and should understand their meaning. The following illustrates the diversity of practice:

Company	Par Value per Share	Name for Additional Paid-in Capital
AT&T	$1.00	Capital in excess of par value
McDonald's	.01	Additional paid-in capital
Home Depot	.05	Paid-in capital
Exxon-Mobil	No par value	No separate account
Royal Dutch Shell	Nominal value €.07	Balances combined in Ordinary share capital

Sometimes a company buys back shares of stock from its own shareholders. It might buy them to reduce shareholder claims permanently, a procedure we discuss later in the chapter. More often, companies plan to hold the shares for later use, usually to grant them as part of employee bonuses or stock purchase plans. We call such temporarily held shares **treasury stock**. They are issued, but because the company holds them, they are no longer outstanding. For example, as of December 31, 2008, UPS had authorized 10.2 billion shares in total for class A and class B. Issued shares totaled 998 million, of which UPS had reacquired 2 million shares that it lists as treasury stock.

treasury stock

A company's own stock that it has purchased and holds for later use.

Number of Shares (in millions)	
Authorized	10,200
Deduct: Unissued	9,202
Issued	998
Deduct: Shares held in treasury	2
Total shares outstanding	996

Cash Dividends

Dividends are proportional distributions of income to shareholders in a company, usually in the form of cash. In the United States, companies tend to pay dividends in equal amounts each quarter, although the board may declare, change, or eliminate a dividend at any time. Some firms tend to pay a special, larger dividend once per year.

declaration date

The date the board of directors formally announces that it will pay a dividend.

Companies do not automatically pay dividends. A company's board of directors votes to approve each dividend. We call the date on which the board formally announces that it will pay a dividend the **declaration date**. On this date, the dividend becomes a liability. The board specifies a future date as the **date of record**. All stockholders owning stock on that date will receive the dividend. A person who holds the stock on the declaration date, but sells before the date of record, will not receive the dividend. The actual **payment date** is the day the company mails the checks; it usually follows the date of record by a few days or weeks.

date of record

The date that determines which shareholders will receive a dividend.

payment date

The date a company pays dividends.

A company records entries for dividends at two times, when it creates the liability and when it pays the dividend:

Date of Declaration

Sept. 26	Retained earnings	20,000	
	Dividends payable.		20,000
	To record the declaration of dividends to be paid on November 15 to shareholders of record as of October 25		

Date of Payment

Nov. 15	Dividends payable	20,000	
	Cash		20,000
	To pay dividends declared on September 26 to shareholders of record as of October 25		

If a company prepares a balance sheet between declaration and payment, the dividend payable will appear as a liability. The amount of cash dividends declared by a board of directors depends on many factors, primarily the market expectations, the current and predicted earnings, and the corporation's current cash position and financial plans concerning spending on plant assets and repayments of debts. Remember that payment of cash dividends requires cash. Thus, the single biggest factor affecting the size of dividends is the availability of cash that the company has not otherwise committed.

Investors expect companies that have historically paid regular dividends to continue to do so. General Electric is an example of a company that had paid dividends every quarter for more than 100 years. Its dividend increased each year recently, from quarterly payments of $.08 per share in 1995 to $.31 per share in 2008, until the financial crises caused it to fall to $.10 in June of 2009. Investors also expect that companies that have not paid dividends because cash was better used to finance expansion will continue to identify growth opportunities requiring additional investment. eBay is an example of a growing company that does not pay cash dividends.

What other factors might affect the company's decision to pay a dividend? In some states and some countries, the dividend decision depends on the amount of retained earnings because the law forbids dividend payments exceeding the company's accumulated net income. A similar limitation may occur because of bond covenants that restrict dividend payments. Ultimately, investors carefully watch changes in dividend patterns. If a company has maintained a series of uninterrupted dividends over a span of years, it will make an effort to continue such payments, even in the face of net losses. In fact, companies occasionally borrow money for the sole purpose of maintaining dividend payments.

Elimination and initiation of dividend payments are big events that cause investors to pause and consider carefully what the company's decision means about the future. This careful consideration is necessary because the meaning of dividend changes can be confusing. Consider a company that initiates or increases a dividend. The good news is that it has resources to distribute to shareholders while continuing to grow and do business. The bad news is that it does not have hugely profitable investments to make in its ongoing business that require all the cash it can generate.

Preferred Stock

The two most common types of stock are common stock and preferred stock. Common stock, as the name implies, is the most basic type. All corporations have it, and the shareholders who own it have the rights discussed earlier. **Preferred stock** offers owners different rights and preferential treatment. Usually preferred shareholders have a right to receive a cash dividend each year and their right to dividends takes precedent over any dividend claims of common shareholders. Often the amount of the preferred dividend is expressed as the product of the dividend rate times the par value. A $100 par, 5% preferred stock would pay a $5 dividend.

Stock represents a contract between the company and its owners, and the terms of preferred stock can include almost any arrangement the parties select. For example, preferred stock owners do not usually have voting rights, but they do have a preferred claim on assets. Therefore, at liquidation, preferred stockholders receive any available company assets, up to the amount of a specified liquidation value, before common stockholders receive anything.

OBJECTIVE 3

Contrast bonds, preferred stock, and common stock.

preferred stock
Stock that offers owners different rights and preferential treatment.

Preferred stock is like common stock in that dividends are not a legal obligation until the board of directors declares them. Unlike common stock, the amount of the preferred stock dividend is generally specified and does not change over time. Although UPS has authorized preferred shares, none are currently outstanding.

Cumulative Dividends

What happens when the board votes to skip a preferred stock dividend? Just because a company can decide not to pay the dividend now may not mean that the company has completely avoided the obligation. Preferred stock dividends are often **cumulative**. Cumulative preferred stock requires that undeclared dividends accumulate and the company must pay them in the future before it can pay any common dividends. From the standpoint of a common shareholder, accumulated unpaid dividends, called **dividend arrearages**, are somewhat like debt obligations. Why? Because a company must pay them before the common shareholders can receive dividends. Moreover, in the event of liquidation, a company must pay cumulative unpaid preferred dividends before common stockholders receive any cash.

To illustrate the operation of cumulative preferred stock, consider Exhibit 10-2. Panel A contains the stockholders' equity of Acumulado Corporation on December 31, 20X0, and panel B shows the consequences of subsequent years of net income and dividends.

Acumulado's board of directors elected not to declare and pay preferred dividends in 20X1 and 20X2. This decision makes economic sense, given that Acumulado Corporation posted losses both years. You may be thinking that the company had more than enough in retained earnings to be able to pay the dividends despite the losses, but retained earnings is not the same as cash. The large retained earnings balance resulted from many prior years of profitable operations, but in those prior years the company reinvested the cash generated by operations into productive business assets. When a firm encounters losses such as Acumulado experienced in 20X1 and 20X2, cash flow may be reduced, and there is often insufficient cash available to pay dividends.

Even though the company skipped making the $5 million annual preferred dividend payments, its obligation to make those payments remained and accumulated, becoming $10 million by the end of 20X2. When operating results improved in 20X3, the board declared and paid a partial dividend of $3 million, leaving $2 million additional arrearages, which raised the

---

cumulative

A characteristic of preferred stock that requires that undeclared dividends accumulate and the company must pay them before it can pay any common dividends.

dividend arrearages

Accumulated unpaid dividends on preferred stock.

EXHIBIT 10-2

Acumulado Corporation Preferred Dividends

PANEL A

Stockholders' Equity, December 31, 20X0:	
Preferred stock, no par, cumulative, $5 annual dividend per share	
Issued and outstanding, 1,000,000 shares	$ 50,000,000
Common stock, no par, 5,000,000 shares	100,000,000
Retained earnings	400,000,000
Total stockholders' equity	$550,000,000

PANEL B

	Net Income	Preferred Dividends Declared	Preferred Dividends In Arrears	Common Dividends Declared	Ending Balance, Retained Earnings
20X0					$400,000,000
20X1	$ (4,000,000)	—	$ 5,000,000	—	396,000,000
20X2	(4,000,000)	—	10,000,000	—	392,000,000
20X3	21,000,000	$ 3,000,000	12,000,000	—	410,000,000
20X4	49,000,000	17,000,000	—	$ 2,000,000	440,000,000
20X5	32,000,000	5,000,000	—	17,000,000	450,000,000

total arrearage to $12 million. In 20X4, Acumulado had a banner year and improved profitability and cash flow enough to pay a full dividend and more. Dividends to preferred shareholders of $17 million cover not only the 20X4 dividend, but also all accumulated dividends in arrears. With accumulated preferred dividends now completely paid, the firm may pay a dividend to the common shareholders for the first time in 4 years. Note that the ending balance in retained earnings in each year is equal to the beginning balance, plus net income (or minus a net loss) minus dividends declared.

Would you rather own cumulative or noncumulative preferred stock? In the preceding example, a holder of noncumulative preferred stock would receive nothing in 20X1 or 20X2, $3 million in 20X3, and $5 million in 20X4. In contrast, the owner of cumulative shares received $3 million in 20X3 and $17 million in 20X4. The cumulative feature is certainly preferred, but as with most choices, it is not free. Because cumulative preferred shares are more secure, they typically pay a lower dividend than noncumulative shares. The cumulative feature must be explicit in the contract. It is not automatic.

Preference in Liquidation

In addition to the cumulative dividend feature, preferred stock usually has a specific **liquidating value**—the amount a company needs to pay to all preferred stockholders, in addition to any dividends in arrears, before it distributes any assets to common stockholders when the company is liquidated. The stock certificate generally states the exact liquidating value, which is often the same as par value. Because par value often defines the liquidating value and may define the amount of the dividend, it is economically important for preferred stock. Of course, before preferred shareholders receive any assets, the company must also pay off all debt obligations.

liquidating value
The amount a company needs to pay to all preferred stockholders, in addition to any dividends in arrears, before it distributes any assets to common stockholders when liquidating a company.

Consider an illustration of the liquidation of assets when short- and long-term debt, preferred stock, and common stock are all present. Exhibit 10-3 shows how to distribute cash to different claimants. The priority of the claims generally decreases as you move down the chart. The first column presents the book values. The next seven columns show the distributions to each class of claimant under different circumstances.

As you can see, when there is not enough cash to go around, common stockholders are always the last to get paid and often wind up getting nothing. However, in those instances when there is excess cash left over, common stockholders get that excess. This illustrates the risks and rewards of stock ownership. When things go well, common shareholders do very well. When things go badly, common shareholders are the first to suffer. Keep in mind, though, that both common and preferred stockholders are protected by limited liability. They do not have to add additional personal assets to the company when it cannot pay off its debts.

(in thousands)	Account Balances	Assumed Total Cash Proceeds to Be Distributed						
		$1,500	$1,000	$500	$450	$350	$200	$100
Accounts payable	$ 100	$ 100	$ 100	$100	$100	$100	$100	$ 50*
Unsubordinated debentures	100	100	100	100	100	100	100	50*
Subordinated debentures	200	200	200	200	200	150		
Preferred stock ($100 par value and $120 liquidating value per share)	100	120	120	100	50			
Common stock and retained earnings	500	980	480					
Total liabilities and shareholders' equity	$1,000							
Total cash proceeds distributed		$1,500	$1,000	$500	$450	$350	$200	$100

*Ratio of 50:50 because each has a $100,000 claim.

EXHIBIT 10-3

Liquidation of Claims Under Various Alternatives *(in thousands)*

Other Features of Preferred Stock

In addition to being cumulative and having liquidation value, preferred stock may have other features. As with our discussion of debt, each feature affects the attractiveness of the stock issue. If you add the cumulative feature to a 5% preferred, investors will pay more for a share of preferred stock. Another way to express the same idea is to say that if you add the cumulative feature to a preferred share, you reduce the size of the fixed dividend that investors require to be willing to invest in the preferred stock.

Each of the following features can also affect the attractiveness of the preferred stock. For example, a participating preferred stock ordinarily receives a fixed dividend, but it can receive higher dividends when the company has a very good year—one in which common stockholders receive especially large dividends. **Participating** means that holders of these shares participate in the growth of the company because they share in the growing dividends. A **callable** preferred stock gives the issuing company the right to purchase the stock back from the owner on payment of the **call price**, or **redemption price**. This call price is typically set 5%–10% above the par value or issuance price of the stock to compensate investors for the fact that the stock can be bought back at the issuer's choice.

A **convertible** preferred stock gives the owner the option to exchange the preferred share for shares of common stock. Because the ability to convert the stock can be quite valuable in future years if common stock prices grow significantly, convertible securities typically carry a lower dividend rate. For example, a regular preferred stock with an 8% dividend might sell for the same price as a 6% convertible preferred stock.

It is not possible to describe every imaginable kind of preferred stock because individual investors and issuers have the opportunity to develop a unique security that exactly meets their needs, and they can adapt that security to the particular market conditions they face at the time. In fact, the investment banking community works hard to develop new types of preferred stock that exactly fit the particular needs of certain investors and therefore provide less expensive capital for the issuing company.

Comparing Bonds and Preferred Stock

Preferred stocks are quite similar to bonds. Both are contracts between an investor and an issuer that spell out each party's rights and responsibilities. Preferred stocks and bonds each pay a specific return to the investor. However, they differ greatly as to the size and nature of those returns. We call the return to bondholders "interest," and it appears on the earnings statement of the company issuing the bond as an expense. In the United States, interest income is taxable to the recipient and tax deductible to the issuing company. In contrast, the specific return to preferred shareholders is a "dividend" and represents a distribution of profits. Dividends do not reduce net earnings and are not tax deductible to the issuer. Dividends reduce the Retained Earnings account directly. For the recipient, dividends may be fully taxed, partly taxed, or untaxed, depending on whether the stockholder is an individual, a corporation, or a special entity such as a pension plan or an insurance company. The tax rate on most dividends received by individuals is now 15%, but this tax rate is subject to frequent change over time. Some preferred dividends are not eligible for this low tax rate, especially those issued by real estate investment trusts and others that are backed by securities held in a trust. This tax rate is a U.S. tax rate, and dividends issued by non-US companies are subject to a higher tax rate in the U.S.

Preferred stocks and bonds also differ in that bonds have specific maturity dates, at which time the company must repay the principal amount, but most preferred stock has an unlimited life. From the investor's perspective, such preferred stock is riskier than bonds because it never matures and the company is not required to declare dividends. It is not always easy to determine whether a security is a debt or an equity instrument. Some preferred stock, for example, does have a mandatory redemption date. This makes it so similar to a bond that both U.S. GAAP and IFRS require companies to classify such a preferred stock as if it were debt.

participating
A characteristic of preferred stock that allows holders of shares to participate in the growth of the company because they share in the growing dividends.

callable
A characteristic of bonds or preferred stock that gives the issuer the right to purchase the stock back from the owner at a fixed price.

call price (redemption price)
The price at which an issuer can buy back a callable preferred stock or bond, which is typically 5%–10% above the par value.

convertible
A characteristic of bonds or preferred stock that gives the owner the option to exchange the bonds or shares of preferred stock for shares of common stock.

Summary Problem for Your Review

PROBLEM

From the following data, prepare a detailed statement of stockholders' equity for Sample Corporation, December 31, 20X1:

Additional paid-in capital, preferred stock	$ 50,000
Additional paid-in capital, common stock	1,000,000
9% preferred stock, $50 par value, callable at $55, authorized 20,000 shares, issued and outstanding 12,000 shares	
Common stock, stated value $2 per share, authorized 500,000 shares, issued 400,000 shares	
Dividends payable	90,000
Retained earnings	2,000,000

SOLUTION

Dividends payable is a liability. Therefore, it does not appear on a statement of stockholders' equity:

Sample Corporation Statement of Stockholders' Equity, December 31, 20X1

9% preferred stock, $50 par value, callable at $55, authorized 20,000 shares, issued and outstanding 12,000 shares		$ 600,000
Common stock, stated value $2 per share, authorized 500,000 shares, issued 400,000 shares		800,000
Additional paid-in capital		
Preferred	$ 50,000	
Common	1,000,000	1,050,000*
Retained earnings		2,000,000
Total stockholders' equity		$4,450,000

*Many presentations would not show the detailed breakdown of additional paid-in capital into preferred and common portions.

Additional Stock Issuance

Existing companies occasionally issue additional shares to investors, executives, or current shareholders. There are several motivations and several procedures for additional stock issues. When a firm simply wants to raise additional equity capital, the process is much like the original stock issue described earlier. Investors provide cash and receive additional new shares in exchange. We next examine other procedures for increasing the number of shares held by investors—stock options, restricted stock, stock splits, and stock dividends.

Stock Options

Stock options are rights to purchase a specific number of shares of a corporation's capital stock at a specific price for a specific time period. Companies often give them to employees as part of their compensation. The idea is that employees who hold options make money only if they stay with the company and the value of the stock increases, in which case the shareholders also make money. Shareholders can benefit from stock options because they motivate employees to work hard and to make decisions that increase the value of their shares. In addition, stock options are especially valuable to executives and other employees because they can gain the benefits of stock price increases without bearing the risks of price declines. The company typically gives (or grants) the option to an employee with the provision that the employee must remain with the company for a period of time before being allowed to exercise the options, at which point the options become

stock options
Rights to purchase a specific number of shares of a corporation's capital stock at a specific price for a specific time period.

vested options

Options that the holders have the power to exercise.

vested options—options that the holders have the power to exercise. Once vested, the employee may exercise the options anytime before they expire, usually for another 5 years or so.

Stock options are a form of employee compensation like salaries and wages. Although it is logical to treat them as an expense, neither U.S. GAAP nor IFRS required expensing of options until 2005. Now companies must recognize the fair value of options, measured at the date the options are granted, as an expense spread over the period between the grant date and the date the options vest. Measurement of the fair value of options should be based on market price, if available, or on option-pricing models if there is no appropriate market price. Options pricing models generally calculate the fair value of options based on the exercise price, life, share price, volatility of share prices, dividends, and the risk-free interest rate. Footnotes in the financial statements must detail the number and characteristics of options outstanding.

Accounting for options was one of the most contentious accounting issues ever. Both the FASB and IASB faced immense political pressure from large companies and some of their supporters in government to prevent the expensing of stock options. In the United States, Congress considered several bills that would prohibit the FASB from requiring companies to expense stock options. Nevertheless, in 2004 the IASB issued a standard that required expensing the fair value of options, and the FASB followed suit in 2005 with a nearly identical standard. The European Union endorsed the IASB standard, and the U.S. Congress never passed blocking legislation.

UPS has an incentive compensation plan that includes the granting of stock options. During 2008, it granted 199,000 options. Suppose 30,000 options to buy shares at $50 per share became vested in 2008 and had a fair value of $7 per share. The 2008 journal entry would be as follows:

Compensation expense, stock options	$210,000	
Additional paid-in capital		$210,000

Now, suppose executives exercise all 30,000 options 5 years later. The journal entry in 2013 would be as follows:

Cash	1,500,000	
Common stock.		300
Additional paid-in capital		1,499,700
To record issue of 30,000 shares, par value $.01, upon exercise of options to acquire them @ $50 per share		

Note that the journal entry is indistinguishable from the issuance of new shares at the exercise price, which may differ significantly from the market price. Suppose the market price in 2013 were $44. An executive would simply buy shares in the open market instead of exercising the option and paying $50. UPS would record no transaction. However, if the market price were $60, the executive would exercise the option to buy at $50 and have the opportunity to either sell immediately and capture the $10 per share gain or hold the shares in hopes of further appreciation.

Restricted Stock

restricted stock

Stock paid to employees that generally has constraints such as not being able to sell it until it vests and then generally being able to sell it only back to the company at the current market price.

Many companies are beginning to use restricted stock instead of options to motivate their employees. Granting **restricted stock** is like paying employees with common stock instead of cash. Restricted stock generally has constraints such as not being able to sell it until it vests and thereafter some firms require that it be sold back to the issuing company. When a company issues restricted stock, it records a salary and wage expense equal to the value of the stock and adds an equal amount to paid-in-capital. Employees get an asset that will increase and decrease in value exactly in proportion to the shareholders' increases and decreases in value. In addition, employees holding restricted stock receive the same dividends that common stockholders receive.

A major benefit of restricted stock over stock options is that it is still worth something, even when stock prices fall sharply. A major problem for many high-tech companies that lost 90% of their value in the early 2000s is that their stock options became worthless and often remained so. The cycle repeated itself in 2007–2009, although in that period it was financial services shares that dropped the most. When the stock market was rising annually, the recipient of stock options got something that turned out to be very valuable. As the stock market fell from 2000 to 2002 and from 2007 to 2009, it became evident that stock options did not always pay off. Proponents of restricted stock believe it is better than options because it truly aligns managerial benefits with shareholder benefits. In contrast, stock options pay off for managers the most when the company earns very large returns. Therefore managers receiving stock options may have incentives to undertake riskier projects than shareholders prefer.

In addition to granting stock options, UPS issued 6.2 million shares of restricted stock to employees in 2008. That year the company recognized compensation expense related to stock-based items such as options and restricted stock of $516 million.

INTERPRETING FINANCIAL STATEMENTS

UPS had 2008 operating income of $5,382 million. This included a deduction of $516 million for stock-based payments. If UPS had not recognized any of this stock-based compensation as an expense, what income would the company have reported? Would you regard this as a material item in UPS's income statement? Why or why not?

Answer

Operating income would have been higher by $516 million: $5,382 million + $516 million = $5,898 million. This is 9.6% higher than the reported amount. This could definitely make a difference to users of the information, so it is clearly a material item.

Stock Splits and Stock Dividends

Stock options and restricted stock put additional shares in the hands of employees. Companies can also issue new shares to current shareholders in several other ways. We examine two of these ways: the stock split and the stock dividend.

Accounting for Stock Splits

A **stock split** refers to the issuance of additional shares to existing shareholders without any additional cash payment to the firm. Issuance of one additional share for each share currently owned is a "two-for-one" split. For example, suppose the Allstar Equipment Company has 100,000 shares outstanding with a market value of $150 per share and par value of $10 per share. The total market value of the stock is thus $15 million. Suppose Allstar Equipment gives each shareholder an additional share for each share owned. The total number of shares would increase to 200,000. If nothing else about the company changes (assets, liabilities, and equity all stay the same), the total market value of the outstanding stock should still be $15 million. With 200,000 shares outstanding, though, the market value per share should drop to $75. Shareholders are as well-off as they were before because they have paid no additional money and they still have the same proportional ownership interest in the company.

So why bother? Good question—there is no perfect answer. Many companies do split their stock. A common result is that stock price falls 50% in a two-for-one split. Thus, one good explanation for issuing a split is that it causes the stock price to fall on a per share basis. If investors like to invest $1,000–$20,000 at a time, and stocks trade in units of 100 shares, you can see that investors would prefer stocks trading in a range between $10 and $200 per share. Most stocks do trade in that range, and companies that split are often at the high end of that range. However, there is no rule about share prices. Berkshire Hathaway is an example of a company whose common stock trades at about $122,000 per share at this writing. For more about Berkshire Hathaway, see the Business First Box on page 464.

Some people argue that the stock split is a way to communicate with shareholders and remind them that their company is growing. It is true that after two two-for-one stock splits, investors realize that they have four times as many shares as they originally bought. However, we would expect a similar pleased reaction from an investor who still had the same original 100 shares that were now valued at four times their purchase price.

Would the accountant need to do anything to acknowledge Allstar's stock issuance of 100,000 additional shares? Yes. There are now twice as many shares outstanding. If the company retains a par value of $10 per share, we would need to add $1 million to the common stock account. Typically we transfer this from additional paid-in capital. This transfer does not change total owner's equity. It merely rearranges it. Sometimes the company decides to adjust par value

OBJECTIVE 4

Identify the economic characteristics of and account for stock splits.

stock split
Issuance of additional shares to existing stockholders for no payments by the stockholders.

by exchanging existing shares for twice as many new shares that carry a reduced par value. Assume that Allstar does not just issue an additional share for each current share. Instead, investors return the 100,000 shares of common stock at $10 par value to Allstar in exchange for 200,000 shares of common stock at $5 par value. Nothing changes in the stockholders' equity section, except the description of shares authorized, issued, and outstanding. The aggregate par value is unchanged, no cash has changed hands, each owner has the same proportionate interest as before, and each has the same relative voting power.

Panel A of Exhibit 10-4 shows the journal entries for the two approaches to stock splits. Panel B shows the effect on shareholders' equity. As noted in panel C, in both cases, total shareholders' equity is unchanged and the total market value of the firm should also be unchanged, which implies that the market price of an individual share should be one-half of its prior value.

Accounting for Stock Dividends

Stock dividends are also issuances of additional shares to existing shareholders without additional cash payment, but the number of new shares issued is usually smaller than it is in a split, and there is no change in par value. For example, a 10% stock dividend is the issuance of 1 new share for every 10 shares currently owned.

OBJECTIVE 5

Account for both large- and small-percentage stock dividends.

---

stock dividends
Distribution to stockholders of a small number of additional shares for every share owned without any payment to the company by the stockholders.

PANEL A: ALTERNATE JOURNAL ENTRIES

Option 1. Issue 100,000 new $10.00 par value shares	Additional paid-in capital Common stock	1,000,000	1,000,000
Option 2. Exchange 200,000 new $5.00 par value shares for the old ones	No entry		

PANEL B: ALTERNATE OUTCOMES

	Common Stock	Additional Paid-in Capital	Retained Earnings	Owners' Equity
Option 1	$1,000,000	$4,000,000	$6,000,000	$11,000,000
Split, retain par	1,000,000	(1,000,000)		
Result	2,000,000	$3,000,000	$6,000,000	$11,000,000
Option 2	$1,000,000	$4,000,000	$6,000,000	$11,000,000
No change				

PANEL C: COMMON OUTCOMES

For both treatments, total owners' equity is the same at $11,000,000

For both treatments, the total market value of the firm should remain constant and the two-for-one stock split should cut price per share in half

EXHIBIT 10-4

Comparing Two Approaches to Stock Splits

Allstar Equipment

LARGE-PERCENTAGE STOCK DIVIDENDS Companies issuing large-percentage stock dividends issue new shares and increase the common stock account for the par value of the newly issued shares. Companies account for large-percentage stock dividends (typically those 20% or higher) at par or stated value. That means that an accounting entry simply transfers the par or stated value of the new shares from the retained earnings account to the common stock account.

As in the case of stock splits, the market value of the outstanding shares tends to adjust completely when a firm issues a stock dividend, provided that the firm lowers the per share dividend proportionately. Consider the Allstar Equipment Company and the effect of possible stock dividends on share price. The original $150 share price would fall to $125 with a 20% stock dividend [$15,000,000 ÷ (100,000 shares + 20,000 shares)] and to $75 with a 100% dividend. The total market value of the company stays at $15 million in all cases.

Suppose the Allstar Equipment Company chose to double the number of outstanding shares by issuing a 100% stock dividend. The total amount of stockholders' equity would be unaffected. However, its composition would change as shown in panel A of Exhibit 10-5. From a shareholder's perspective, this is essentially identical to a two-for-one stock split. Thus, accountants often refer to this as a two-for-one stock split "accounted for as a stock dividend." There is no economic difference between the 100% stock dividend and the two-for-one stock split. The accounting differs only with regard to where the amount added to common stock at par value comes from—from additional paid-in capital for a stock split and from retained earnings for a stock dividend. Firms often prefer to account for a stock split as a stock dividend because it saves clerical costs. The company does not need to receive permission for a change in par value, and it does not have to exchange stock certificates. It simply sends out certificates for the additional shares.

However, the company does have an economic decision to make. What happens to the cash dividend? One possibility is to adjust the cash dividend proportionately. For a 100% stock dividend or a two-for-one stock split, this means that the cash dividend per share is cut in half and total cash dividends remain unchanged. It is at least as common for the company to increase the

EXHIBIT 10-5

Stock Dividends

Allstar Example:
Originally 100,000 Shares;
$10 Par Value and $150
Market Value per Share

PANEL A: LARGE STOCK DIVIDEND (100%)

Issue 100,000 new $10 Par Value Shares Accounted for at Par

Retained earnings $1,000,000

Common stock $1,000,000

	Common Stock	Additional Paid-in Capital	Retained Earnings	Owners' Equity
Original	$1,000,000	$4,000,000	$ 6,000,000	$11,000,000
100% Dividend	1,000,000		(1,000,000)	
Result	$2,000,000	$4,000,000	$ 5,000,000	$11,000,000

PANEL B: SMALL STOCK DIVIDEND (2%)

Issue 2,000 new $10 Par Value Shares Accounted for at Market Price of $150

Retained earnings $300,000

Common stock 20,000

Additional paid-in capital 280,000

	Common Stock	Additional Paid-in Capital	Retained Earnings	Owners Equity
Original	$1,000,000	$4,000,000	$6,000,000	$11,000,000
2% Dividend	20,000	280,000	(300,000)	
Result	$1,020,000	$4,280,000	$5,700,000	$11,000,000

total cash dividend being paid. Investors watch this issue carefully to assess the company's belief about future cash flow and future investment opportunity.

SMALL-PERCENTAGE STOCK DIVIDENDS Companies account for stock dividend of less than 20% at market value, not at par value. This rule is partly the result of tradition and partly due to the fact that small-percentage stock dividends are more likely to accompany increases in the total dividend payments or other changes in the company's financial policies. Security analysts argue that the decision to increase total dividends communicates management's conviction that future cash flows will rise to support these increased distributions. This is a positive statement about the firm's prospects.

Panel B of Exhibit 10-5 illustrates the effects of a 2% stock dividend. As before, the individual shareholder receives no assets from the corporation, and the corporation receives no cash from the shareholder. The major possible economic effect of a stock dividend is to signal increased cash dividends. Suppose the board of the company in our example consistently voted to pay cash dividends of $1 per share. Often companies maintain this cash dividend per share after a small stock dividend. After a 2% stock dividend, the owner of 1,000 shares can now expect a future annual cash dividend of $1 × 1,020 = $1,020 instead of $1 × 1,000 = $1,000. In this case, when a company maintains its dividend rate per share, announcing a stock dividend of 2% has the same economic effect as announcing an increase of 2% in the cash dividend.

The company records small-percentage stock dividends (under 20%) by transferring the market value of the additional shares from retained earnings to common stock and additional paid-in capital. We refer to this transfer as a "capitalization of retained earnings." It is an accounting signal to the shareholders that the company is investing $300,000 for the long term in productive assets such as plant, property, and equipment. U.S. practice concerning the use of market values in accounting for small-percentage stock dividends is arbitrary and is not consistently adopted worldwide.

Summary Problem for Your Review

PROBLEM

Charlie Company distributes a 2% stock dividend on its 1 million outstanding $5 par common shares. The stockholders' equity section before the dividend was as follows:

Common stock, 1,000,000 shares @ $5 par	$ 5,000,000
Additional paid-in capital in excess of par	20,000,000
Retained earnings	75,000,000
Total stockholders' equity	$100,000,000

The common stock was selling on the open market for $150 per share when Charlie Company distributed the dividend. How will the stock dividend affect the stockholders' equity section? If net income were $10.2 million next year, what would be the earnings per share before considering the effects of the stock dividend and after considering the effects of the stock dividend?

SOLUTION

	Before 2% Stock Dividend	Changes	After 2% Stock Dividend
Common stock, 1,000,000 shares @ $5 par	$ 5,000,000	+(20,000 @ $5)	$ 5,100,000
Additional paid-in capital	20,000,000	+[20,000 @ ($150 − $5)]	22,900,000
Retained earnings	75,000,000	−(20,000 @ $150)	72,000,000
Total	$100,000,000		$100,000,000

Earnings per share before considering the effects of the stock dividend would be $10,200,000 ÷ 1,000,000, or $10.20. After the dividend earnings per share would be $10,200,000 ÷ 1,020,000, or $10.

Note that the dividend has no effect on net income, the numerator of the earnings-per-share computation. However, it does affect the denominator and causes a mild decrease in EPS that, in theory, should cause a slight decline in the market price of a share of stock.

Why Use Stock Splits and Dividends?

Experts debate the importance of stock splits and stock dividends even as companies continue to use them. We have reviewed the arguments surrounding the use of stock splits and stock dividends to control the price per share. Wal-Mart, for example, split two-for-one on 11 occasions since its public offering on October 1, 1970. In the spring of 2010, it was selling at $55 per share. An initial investment of $1,650 in 100 shares in 1970 would have grown to 204,800 shares worth $11,264,000. This represents a return of nearly 25% per year.

Often a stock split or stock dividend accompanies other announcements, such as new corporate investment strategies or changes in cash dividend levels. Suppose the firm has traditionally paid a special cash dividend at year-end, but plans to expand production substantially, which absorbs available cash and makes the payment of this special dividend difficult. The firm might combine the announcement of the planned expansion with an announcement of a small stock dividend. The small-percentage stock dividend does not draw on cash immediately, but provides stockholders with an increase in future cash dividends in proportion to the percentage of new shares issued.

Fractional Shares

Corporations ordinarily issue shares in whole units. When shareholders are entitled to stock dividends in amounts equal to fractional units, corporations issue additional shares for whole units plus cash equal to the market value of the fractional amount.

For example, suppose a corporation issues a 3% stock dividend. A shareholder has 160 shares. The market value per share on the date of issuance is $40. Par value is $2. The shareholder would be entitled to .03 × 160 = 4.8 shares. The company would issue four shares plus .8 × $40 = $32 cash. The journal entry is as follows:

Retained earnings (4.8 × $40)	192	
Common stock, at par (4 × $2)		8
Additional paid-in capital (4 × $38)		152
Cash (.8 × $40)		32
To issue a stock dividend of 3% to a holder of 160 shares		

The Investor's Accounting for Dividends and Splits

So far, we have focused on how the corporation deals with stock splits and dividends. What about the stockholder? Consider the investor's recording of the transactions described so far. Suppose Jesse bought 1,000 shares of the original issue of Allstar Equipment Company stock for $50 per share:

Investment in Allstar common stock	50,000	
Cash		50,000
To record investment in 1,000 shares of an original issue of Allstar Equipment Company common stock at $50 per share		

If Jesse sold the shares to Katrina at a price other than $50, Jesse would record a gain or loss and Katrina would carry the shares at the amount she paid Jesse. Meanwhile, this sale would not affect the stockholders' equity of Allstar Equipment Company. The company would simply change its underlying shareholder records to delete Jesse and add Katrina as a shareholder.

The following examples show how Jesse would record the stock split, cash dividends, and stock dividends—treating each as an independent event, not as sequential events. Note that several events that produced journal entries for Allstar do not cause entries for Jesse:

a. Stock split at two-for-one:	No journal entry, but Jesse would make a memorandum in the investment account to show that he now owns 2,000 shares at a cost of $25 each, instead of 1,000 shares at a cost of $50 each.		
b. Cash dividends of $2 per share:	Cash	2,000	
	Dividend income		2,000
	To record cash dividends on Allstar Equipment Company stock		
Or:	Alternatively, Jesse might use the following two entries:		
Date of declaration:	Dividends receivable	2,000	
	Dividend income		2,000
	To record dividends declared by Allstar Equipment Company		
Date of receipt:	Cash.	2,000	
	Dividends receivable.		2,000
	To record the receipt of cash dividends		
c. Stock dividends of 2%	No journal entry, but Jesse would make a memorandum in the investment account to show that [assuming the stock split in (a) had not occurred] he now owns 1,020 shares at an average cost of $50,000 ÷ 1,020, or $49.02 per share.		
d. Stock split in form of a 100% dividend:	No journal entry, but Jesse would make a memorandum in the investment account to show that [assuming the stock splits and stock dividends in (a) and (c) had not occurred] he now owns 2,000 shares at an average cost of $25 instead of 1,000 shares @ $50. Note that this memorandum has the same effect as the memorandum in (a).		

Summary Problems for Your Review

PROBLEM

A few years ago Metro-Goldwyn-Mayer (MGM) declared and distributed a 3% stock dividend. The applicable market value per share was $7.75. The par value of the 966,000 additional shares issued was $1.00 each. In addition, the total cash paid to shareholders in lieu of issuing fractional shares was $70,000. Prepare the appropriate journal entry.

SOLUTION

Retained earnings	7,556,500	
Common stock, $1.00 par value		966,000
Capital in excess of par value		6,520,500
Cash		70,000

To record 3% stock dividend, total shares issued, 966,000 at $7.75, a total market value of $7,486,500. In addition, cash of $70,000 was paid in lieu of issuing fractional shares, so the total charge to retained earnings was $70,000 + (966,000 × $7.75) = $7,556,500.

PROBLEM

Baker Company has 2,000 shares of $10 par common stock outstanding and splits its stock five-for-one. How will the split affect its balance sheet and its earnings per share? How would your answer change if the company said that it "accounted for" the split as a stock dividend?

SOLUTION

The total amount of stockholders' equity would not change, but there would be 10,000 outstanding shares at $2 par, instead of 2,000 shares at $10 par. Earnings per share would be one fifth of that previously reported, assuming no change in total net income applicable to the common stock.

If the question were framed as "the company recently issued a five-for-one stock split accounted for as a stock dividend," then Baker Company would maintain the original par value per share, and a journal entry would increase the par value account for common stock by $80,000 (8,000 additional shares times $10 par value per share) and reduce retained earnings by $80,000, leaving total stockholders' equity unchanged and EPS at one fifth its original value.

Retained earnings	80,000	
Common stock at par		80,000

Repurchase of Shares

So far, we have seen how companies sell shares and how they sometimes issue additional shares to current shareholders. You should not think, though, that stock always flows out of a company. Sometimes companies repurchase shares, usually for one of two purposes: (1) to reduce shareholder claims permanently, called retiring stock, and (2) to hold shares temporarily for later use, most often to be granted as part of employee option, bonus, or stock purchase plans. As we learned earlier in this chapter, we call temporarily held shares treasury stock or treasury shares.

Why do companies repurchase their own stock? The two most common reasons are 1) management's belief that the stock is undervalued by the market, and 2) a company may need shares to distribute to employees as part of a stock option or employee stock purchase plan. Or the company may simply have more cash than it requires for ongoing investment in new projects, and the board of directors may decide to return some capital to its shareholders. It could pay higher dividends, but often the board prefers repurchasing shares. Why? For one thing, buybacks allow the company to return cash to shareholders without creating expectations of permanent increases in dividends. Further, buybacks put the cash in the hands of shareholders who want it, because shareholders decide whether to sell or hold their shares.

OBJECTIVE 6

Explain and report stock repurchases and other treasury stock transactions.

By repurchasing shares, a company liquidates some shareholders' claims, and total stockholders' equity decreases by the amount of the repurchase. The purpose of the repurchase determines which stockholders' equity accounts are affected. We next discuss accounting for permanent and temporary repurchases using the illustration of the Allstar Equipment Company. Recall that Allstar shares have a market value of $150 per share. We also need to know Allstar's book value per share—total common shareholders' equity divided by number of outstanding shares. Allstar's total stockholders' equity of $11 million combines the original purchase price of shares in the past (par value plus additional paid-in capital) with the periodic earnings of the firm that have remained in the business (retained earnings). Allstar's book value per share is $11,000,000 ÷ 100,000 shares = $110 per share.

Retirement of Shares

Once a company has repurchased shares, it may retire them or hold them for reissue. Suppose the board of Allstar Company purchases and retires 5% of its outstanding shares at $150 per share for a total of 5,000 shares × $150, or $750,000 cash. Allstar originally issued these shares at $50 per share. The repurchase reduces total stockholders' equity by $750,000. How much of this do we charge against the common stock, additional paid-in capital, and retained earnings accounts? We reduce the common stock and additional paid-in capital accounts by the amount of capital contributed by the original purchasers of the shares that Allstar retired. In addition, the company cancels the stock certificates and no longer considers the shares either outstanding or issued. We illustrate this in panel A of Exhibit 10-6.

The following journal entry reverses the original paid-in capital and charges the additional amount to retained earnings:

Common stock	50,000	
Additional paid-in capital	200,000	
Retained earnings	500,000	
Cash		750,000

To record retirement of 5,000 shares of stock for $150 cash per share. The paid-in capital is $50 per share ($10 par value + $40 additional paid-in capital), so we reduce retained earnings by the additional $100 per share.

dilution

Reduction in stockholders' equity per share or EPS that arises from some changes among shareholders' proportional interests.

Note how the book value per share of the outstanding shares has declined from $110.00 to $107.89. We call this phenomenon **dilution**—a reduction in shareholders' equity per share or EPS that arises from changes among shareholders' proportionate interests. As a rule, boards of directors avoid dilution unless expected future profits will more than compensate for a temporary undesirable reduction in book value per share.

Treasury Stock

Now suppose Allstar's board of directors decides not to retire the 5,000 repurchased shares but to hold them temporarily as treasury stock. Perhaps the company needs the shares for an employee stock purchase plan or for executive stock options. The repurchase still decreases stockholders' equity. It is NOT an asset. Why? Because a company cannot own part of itself.

If treasury stock is not an asset, then what is it? The Treasury Stock account is a contra account to Owners' Equity, just as Accumulated Depreciation is a contra account to related fixed-asset accounts. Like retiring shares, purchasing treasury stock decreases stockholders' equity by $750,000 (5,000 shares purchased at $150 per share). Unlike the accounting for retirements, common stock at par value, additional paid-in capital, and retained earnings do not change with treasury stock purchases. Instead, we deduct the separate treasury stock account from total stockholders' equity. Panel B of Exhibit 10-6 shows Allstar's stockholders' equity section before and after the purchase of the treasury shares. Companies do not pay dividends on treasury stock because shares held in the treasury are not outstanding shares:

Shares issued	100,000
Less: Treasury stock	5,000
Total shares outstanding	95,000

PANEL A: REPURCHASED SHARES RETIRED

	Before Repurchase of 5% of Outstanding Shares	Changes Because of Retirement	After Repurchase of 5% of Outstanding Shares
Common stock, 100,000 shares @ $10 par	$ 1,000,000	–(5,000 shares @ $10 par) = –$50,000	$ 950,000
Additional paid-in capital	4,000,000	–(5,000 shares @ $40) = –$200,000	3,800,000
Total paid-in capital	5,000,000		4,750,000
Retained earnings	6,000,000	–(5,000 @ $100*) = –$500,000	5,500,000
Stockholders' equity	$11,000,000		$10,250,000
Book value per common share:			
$11,000,000 ÷ 100,000	$ 110.00		
$10,250,000 ÷ 95,000			$ 107.89

*$150 acquisition price less the $50 (or $10 + $40) originally paid in.

PANEL B: REPURCHASED SHARES HELD AS TREASURY STOCK

	Before Repurchase of 5% of Outstanding Shares	Changes Because of Treasury Stock	After Repurchase of 5% of Outstanding Shares
Common stock, 100,000 shares @ $10 par	$ 1,000,000		$ 1,000,000
Additional paid-in capital	4,000,000		4,000,000
Total paid-in capital	$ 5,000,000		$ 5,000,000
Retained earnings	6,000,000		6,000,000
Total	$11,000,000		$11,000,000
Deduct:			
Cost of treasury stock		$750,000	(750,000)
Stockholders' equity			$10,250,000

Book value per common share is calculated on shares outstanding and is identical to the values in panel A.

EXHIBIT 10-6

Stock Repurchase

Allstar Example

Companies usually resell treasury shares at a later date, perhaps through an employee stock purchase plan. Exhibit 10-7 shows the outcomes when Allstar reissues these treasury shares above or below the acquisition cost. We show in panel A journal entries for reissue at $180 (above the $150 acquisition cost) and in panel B the result for reissue at $120 (below the $150 acquisition cost). In panel C, we present the different shareholder equity sections for each outcome.

The specific accounting practices for repeated purchases and sales of the company's own stock vary from company to company. However, one rule remains constant: Treasury stock transactions never produce expenses, losses, revenues, or gains in the income statement. Why? A corporation's own capital stock is part of its capital structure. It is not an asset of the corporation. A company cannot make profits or losses by buying or selling its own common stock.

There is no important difference between unissued shares and treasury shares. In our example, Allstar could accomplish the same objective by (1) acquiring 5,000 shares, retiring them, and issuing 5,000 "new" shares; or (2) acquiring 5,000 shares and reselling them. Although some account balances within stockholders' equity would differ under these alternatives, neither the number of shares outstanding nor the total stockholders' equity would change. **Starbucks** was an active repurchaser of stock in 2008, spending $311 billion to repurchase 12.2 million shares. It then issued more than 6 million shares for the exercise of stock options, and another 2.8 million shares for other reasons.

EXHIBIT 10-7

Reissuance of Treasury Shares

Allstar Repurchased 5,000 Shares for $150 per Share Creating a Treasury Stock Balance of $750,000

PANEL A: REISSUE AT $180 PER SHARE		
Cash	900,000	
Treasury stock.		750,000
Additional paid-in capital.		150,000

PANEL B: REISSUE AT $120 PER SHARE		
Cash	600,000	
Additional paid-in capital	150,000	
Treasury stock.		750,000

PANEL C: COMPARATIVE BALANCES

	With 5,000 Shares in Treasury @ $150	Reissued @ $180	Reissued @ $120
Common stock	$ 1,000,000	$ 1,000,000	$ 1,000,000
Additional paid-in capital	4,000,000	4,150,000	3,850,000
	5,000,000	5,150,000	4,850,000
Retained earnings	6,000,000	6,000,000	6,000,000
Deduct treasury stock	(750,000)		
	$10,250,000	$11,150,000	$10,850,000

Effects of Repurchases on Earnings Per Share (EPS)

Repurchasing shares, whether they are retired or put in treasury, reduces the number of shares outstanding. This tends to increase EPS. For example, suppose that Allstar generates net income of $950,000 each year and that using $750,000 to repurchase shares would not reduce future net income. Under these circumstances, repurchasing 5,000 shares increases EPS by $.50:

EPS = net income ÷ average number of shares outstanding				
Before repurchase	$950,000	÷	100,000 shares	= $ 9.50
After repurchase	$950,000	÷	95,000 shares	= $10.00

In contrast, using $750,000 to pay dividends leaves the number of shares unchanged at 100,000 and the EPS at $9.50. See the Business First box for a comparison of how companies use dividends, splits, and repurchases.

INTERPRETING FINANCIAL STATEMENTS

As a manager, would you choose to distribute cash to your investors as a dividend or via share repurchase? How does this decision affect the financial statements?

Answer

The text raises several issues. One question pertains to the future. If you begin paying dividends, investors will expect you to continue to do so. Thus, you would want to assess future cash flow and your ability and desire to continue dividend payments before initiating dividends. A one-time distribution is probably better as a share repurchase, as are distributions that are likely to be highly variable over time. Shareholders often prefer repurchases because they can choose to participate or not, and if they do participate they pay taxes only on their gains. The tax benefit to repurchases is even greater in countries where the tax on capital gains is less than that on dividends, as once was the case in the United States.

As a manager, you would note that neither dividends nor repurchases affect the income statement, and they have the same effect on total financing cash flows. You might also note that dividends reduce only retained earnings, whereas the effect of share repurchases depends on the book value of the shares, the market value of the shares, and whether they are retired or held in treasury. Ultimately, the financial statement effects of this choice are minor.

Other Issuances of Common Stock

Companies do not always receive cash when they issue common stock. A company may issue shares for other assets or in exchange for its own corporate security—a bond or preferred stock.

Noncash Exchanges

Often a company issues its stock to acquire land, a building, or common stock of another company, or to compensate a person or company for services received. The buyer and seller should both record the transaction at the "fair value" of either the securities or the exchanged assets or services, whichever is easier to determine objectively.

Conversion of Securities

Some companies issue bonds or preferred stock that allow the owner to convert them into common stock. The conversion feature makes the securities more attractive to investors and increases the price the issuer receives (or, equivalently, reduces the interest or dividend it must pay). If the owner of convertible securities exercises the conversion privilege, the issuer simply adjusts the accounts as if it had issued the common stock initially. This may have significant effects on the company's proportion of debt and equity, and it may eliminate some substantial cash commitments previously associated with interest or dividend payments.

For example, suppose Purchaser Company paid $160,000 for an investment in 5,000 shares of the $1 par value convertible preferred stock of Issuer Company in 20X1. In 20X8, Purchaser Company converted the preferred stock into 10,000 shares of Issuer Company common stock ($1 par value). Exhibit 10-8 shows the effect on the accounts of Issuer Company.

Purchaser Company also experiences a change in form of the investment, with no change in historical cost. The carrying value, or book value, of the investment remains $160,000. To show that the investment is now common stock instead of preferred stock, Purchaser Company might transfer the $160,000 from one investment account to another. Alternatively, it might change subsidiary records that document the composition of a single general ledger account called Investments.

OBJECTIVE 7

Record conversions of debt for equity or of preferred stock into common stock.

	Assets	=	Liabilities	+		Stockholders' Equity		
	Cash			Preferred Stock	Additional Paid-in Capital, Preferred	Common Stock	Additional Paid-in Capital Common
Issuance of preferred (20X1)	+160,000	=		+5,000	+155,000		
Conversion of preferred (20X8)		=		−5,000	−155,000	+10,000	+150,000

The journal entries would be as follows:

On Issuer's Books

20X1 Cash	160,000	
Preferred stock, convertible		5,000
Additional paid-in capital, preferred		155,000

To record issuance of 5,000 shares of $1 par preferred stock convertible into two common shares for one preferred share

20X8 Preferred stock, convertible	5,000	
Additional paid-in capital, preferred	155,000	
Common stock		10,000
Additional paid-in capital, common		150,000

To record the conversion of 5,000 preferred shares to 10,000 common shares ($1 par)

EXHIBIT 10-8
Analysis of Convertible Preferred Stock

Retained Earnings Restrictions

The most closely watched part of stockholders' equity, both by shareholders and creditors, is retained earnings. Boards of directors can make decisions that benefit shareholders but hurt creditors. For example, directors might pay excessive dividends that jeopardize payments of creditors' claims. To protect creditors, state laws or contractual obligations often restrict dividend-declaring power. Many lenders require debt covenants that restrict certain uses of cash, such as dividend payments.

Authorities typically do not permit boards to declare dividends if those dividends would cause stockholders' equity to be less than total paid-in capital. Therefore, retained earnings must exceed the cost of treasury stock. If there is no treasury stock, retained earnings must be positive. This restriction limits dividend payments and thus protects the position of the creditors. For example, consider the following ($ in millions):

		After Dividend Payments of	
	Before Dividends	$10	$4
Paid-in capital	$25	$25	$25
Retained earnings	10	—	6
Total	$35	$25	$31
Deduct:			
Cost of treasury stock	6	6	6
Stockholders' equity	$29	$19	$25

Without restricting dividends to the amount of retained earnings in excess of the cost of treasury stock, the corporation could pay a dividend of $10 million. This would reduce the stockholders' equity below the paid-in capital of $25 million. With the restriction, unrestricted retained earnings (and maximum legal payment of dividends) is $10 million – $6 million, or

$4 million. In this case, the existence of treasury stock creates a restriction on the company's ability to declare dividends.

Most companies with restrictions of retained earnings disclose them by footnotes. Occasionally, restrictions appear as a line item on the balance sheet called **restricted retained earnings** or **appropriated retained earnings**—a part of retained earnings that companies cannot reduce by dividend declarations. In Europe, companies often call them reserves. Accountants have used the term **reserve** in many ways, but we will use it to mean only one thing: restrictions of dividend declarations. In the United States, reserves are not common. When they exist, they generally represent a statement by the board of directors of its intent to restrict dividend payments to retain cash for a particular purpose such as a plant expansion. In many countries, laws further restrict the payment of dividends, resulting in a shareholders' equity line called legal reserves. For example, in France and Germany companies must restrict 5% of each year's net income until their legal reserves reach a specified level.

An acknowledgment of a restriction on dividend payments is contained in the following reference in an annual report of **Coherent, Inc.**, the world's leading manufacturer of lasers:

> *The Company's domestic lines of credit are generally subject to standard covenants related to financial ratios, profitability and dividend payments.*

restricted retained earnings (appropriated retained earnings)
Any part of retained earnings that companies may not reduce by dividend declarations.

reserve
A restriction of dividend-declaring power as denoted by a specific subdivision of retained earnings.

Other Components of Stockholders' Equity

Two other elements commonly appear in stockholders' equity and deserve brief mention here. The UPS shareholders' equity in Exhibit 10-1 included a deduction of $5,642 million labeled Accumulated Other Comprehensive Loss. The major portion of this item relates to unrecognized pension and postretirement benefit costs. Companies must recognize the funded status of defined benefit pension and other post retirement plans as an asset or liability in the balance sheet. Changes in the funded status arise when contracts change, interest rates change, or the market value of securities held by the pension plan change. During 2008 the fair value of UPS pension plan assets declined by more than $5 billion from $17.9 billion to $12.8 billion. Companies initially record such losses in other comprehensive income (loss), and such losses reduce shareholders' equity. Companies then amortize them against income over time if asset values do not recover.

The other element of UPS shareholders' equity that we have not discussed explicitly is the Deferred Compensation Arrangements. UPS is one of many companies that enhance the commitment of its employees to work hard and provide good service by rewarding them with shares of stock. Here, employees have delayed their right to receive shares for purposes of estate planning and tax management. UPS recognizes the obligation to deliver shares in the future in a Deferred Compensation Arrangements account and includes the number of shares it expects to issue in the denominator when calculating EPS.

Financial Ratios Related to Stockholders' Equity

Analysts answer many questions pertaining to stockholders' equity by using ratios. One important question is "How effectively does the company use resources provided by the shareholders?" To assess this, analysts relate the net income generated by the firm to the historic investment by its shareholders. We define the **rate of return on common equity (ROE)** as

$$\text{Rate of return on common equity} = \frac{(\text{Net income} - \text{Preferred dividends})}{\text{Average common equity}}$$

The rate of return on common equity is of great interest to common stockholders because it focuses on the company's profitability in relation to the book value of the common equity. The denominator is the average of the beginning and ending common equity balances. Note that the common equity balance is the total stockholders' equity less the preferred stock at book value (or at liquidating value if it exceeds the book value). The calculations for Calvin Company are in Exhibit 10-9, with panel A presenting comparative stockholders' equity for 2 years together with earnings information and panel B using that information to calculate ROE.

OBJECTIVE 8
Use the rate of return on common equity and book value per share.

rate of return on common equity (ROE)
Net income less preferred dividends divided by average common equity.

PANEL A

	December 31	
	20X2	**20X1**
Stockholders' equity		
10% preferred stock, 100,000 shares, $100 par	$ 10,000,000	$ 10,000,000
Common stock, 5,000,000 shares, $1 par	5,000,000	5,000,000
Additional paid-in capital	35,000,000	35,000,000
Retained earnings	87,000,000	83,000,000
Total stockholders' equity	$137,000,000	$133,000,000
Net income for the year ended December 31, 20X2	$11,000,000	
Preferred dividends @ $10 per share	1,000,000	
Net income available for common stock	$10,000,000	

PANEL B: ROE

$$\text{Rate of return on common equity} = \frac{\text{Net income} - \text{Preferred dividends}}{\text{Average common equity}}$$

$$= \frac{\$11,000,000 - \$1,000,000}{\frac{1}{2}[(\$133,000,000 - \$10,000,000) + (\$137,000,000 - \$10,000,000)]}$$

$$= \frac{\$10,000,000}{\frac{1}{2}(\$123,000,000 + \$127,000,000)}$$

$$= \frac{\$10,000,000}{\$125,00,000} = 8.0\%$$

EXHIBIT 10-9
Calvin Company Owners' Equity

ROE varies considerably among companies and industries and from year to year, as follows:

	2008	**2002**	**1996**
UPS	31.7	28.0	n/a
McDonald's	30.1	10.1	19.5
IBM	59.0	15.4	24.8
PepsiCo	34.8	36.9	16
ExxonMobil[†]	38.5	15.5	16.0
Royal Dutch Shell	20.6	n/a	n/a
Daimler[*]	4.2	12.8	n/a

*Daimler was Daimler/Chrysler in 2002

[†]ExxonMobil values in 2008 and 2002, premerger values for Mobil for 1996

ROE patterns often spark questions that increase your understanding of the company. McDonald's ROE fell sharply in 2002. Why? Because the company reported significant reductions in profit margins. IBM has highly variable ROE. This variability might arise from difficult business activity, but it may also relate to changes in accounting practice. For example, the changes in accounting practice for postretirement benefits in 2005 have caused many companies to record losses in Accumulated Other Comprehensive Income, which reduced Owners' Equity significantly. Many companies also had significant share repurchase programs during this period, which also reduced owners' equity.

A second ratio is book value per share. When preferred stock is present, the calculation of the **book value per share of common stock** adjusts for the preferred. The calculation for Calvin Company using 20X2 data from panel A of Exhibit 10-9 follows:

$$\text{Book value per share of common stock} = \frac{\text{Total stockholders' equity} - \text{Book value of preferred stock}}{\text{Number of common shares outstanding}}$$

$$= \frac{\$137,000,000 - \$10,000,000}{5,000,000} = \$25.40$$

The market value of a stock is usually more than its book value, but not always. This relationship is often captured by calculating a **market-to-book ratio**—market price per share divided by book value per share. Consider UPS. It had a market value of $55.32 and a book value of $6.80 at the beginning of 2009. This gives a market-to-book ratio of 8.1 to 1. Other comparisons are shown below (taken from Yahoo!'s financial site in May 2009) with each company's ratios compared to its value in 2003:

	Market to Book Ratios	
	2009	**2003**
UPS	8.1	5.7
McDonald's	4.8	2.5
IBM	10.0	5.3
PepsiCo	6.8	7.3
ExxonMobil	3.1	3.0

Shareholders value a stock based on what they believe the future earning power will be, not based on the historical cost of assets. Book values are balance sheet values that show a mix of the historical cost and the market values of assets. Comparing market values with book values often helps highlight the causes behind the difference in values. Given the very steep declines in market values in 2008, it is somewhat surprising that the market to book ratios were stable or rising. One explanation is that the book value declined more sharply than the market values because of losses in other comprehensive income due to pension valuations or due to impairments of goodwill.

What do these differences in values mean in the real world? A market value well above the book value may be appropriate if the company has many unrecorded assets (as in high R&D industries) or appreciated assets (such as real estate).

Highlights to Remember

1 Describe the rights of shareholders. On the balance sheet, stockholders' equity is the book value of the residual interests of a corporation's owners. By incorporating, the company provides limited liability for its owners and provides them with various rights, including the right to vote for the board of directors. Among equity holders, preferred shareholders have more senior claims to dividends and may have other special rights, including cumulative dividends, participating dividends, conversion privileges, and preference in liquidation. Preferred stocks are similar to bonds in many ways.

2 Account for common stock, including payment of dividends. When shares of common stock are issued, the company will typically record the receipt of an asset and show an increase in common stock at par or stated value with the remainder of the value received shown as additional paid-in capital. When a dividend is paid it represents a reduction of an asset and an offsetting reduction of retained earnings. Issuances of common stock increase shareholders' equity and payments of dividends decrease shareholders' equity but different accounts are affected by the two transactions.

3 **Contrast bonds, preferred stock, and common stock.** Bonds, preferred stock, and common stock are all claims on the assets of the corporation. Bonds are the senior claim and are specific legal obligations with required dates for payment of interest and repayment of principal. Preferred stock may have many specific rights attached to it, but dividends become obligations only when the board of directors declares them, and preferred stock typically has no maturity date. Preferred shareholders typically receive dividends and repayment of principal before common shareholders. We often call common stock the residual claim because common shareholders typically receive what is left after paying all other obligations. In liquidation of a failed company, common shareholders may receive little or nothing. However, when a company grows rapidly and prospers, the value of the common stock will increase much more than the value of either bonds or preferred stock.

4 **Identify the economic characteristics of and account for stock splits.** Stock splits alter the number of shares held by the owners, without altering the economic claims of the shareholders. As a result, no change typically occurs in the total market value of the company, but the value of individual shares changes in proportion to the size of the split or dividend. A two-for-one split would typically cause the market price per share to decline by 50%. Stock splits require either a transfer from additional paid-in capital to common stock or a change in par value of the common stock and no journal entry.

5 **Account for both large- and small-percentage stock dividends.** Accounting for stock dividends involves rearranging the owners' equity account balances. We can rearrange par value accounts, paid-in capital accounts, and retained earnings without changing the total owners' equity. The exact procedure depends on the size of the stock dividend.

6 **Explain and report stock repurchases and other treasury stock transactions.** Companies sometimes acquire treasury stock, which are shares of their own stock purchased in the open market. These shares may later be retired, resold, or used to meet obligations under option agreements. Transactions in the company's own stock never give rise to gains and losses and do not affect the income statement. Such transactions with the shareholders give rise only to changes in the equity accounts.

7 **Record conversions of debt for equity or of preferred stock into common stock.** Generally, when investors convert debt or preferred stock into common stock, we transfer the book values of the debt or preferred stock into owners' equity. Part is shown as par or stated value and the remainder as additional paid-in capital.

8 **Use the rate of return on common equity and book value per share.** Security analysts use the return on common stockholders' equity as a primary ratio to assess the effectiveness of management and the profitability of the firm. Higher is better. Analysts often compare the market value per share with the book value per share. A high ratio of market value to book value generally means good growth prospects and possibly unrecorded assets, such as internally developed patents.

Accounting Vocabulary

appropriated retained earnings, p. 475
authorized shares, p. 455
book value per share of common stock, p. 477
call price, p. 460
callable, p. 460
convertible, p. 460
corporate proxy, p. 454
cumulative, p. 458
date of record, p. 456
declaration date, p. 456

dilution, p. 470
dividend arrearages, p. 458
issued shares, p. 455
liquidating value, p. 459
market-to-book ratio, p. 477
outstanding shares, p. 455
participating, p. 460
payment date, p. 456
preemptive rights, p. 454
preferred stock, p. 457
rate of return on common equity (ROE), p. 475

redemption price, p. 460
reserve, p. 475
restricted retained earnings, p. 475
restricted stock, p. 462
stock dividends, p. 464
stock options, p. 461
stock split, p. 463
treasury stock, p. 456
vested options, p. 462

Assignment Material

Questions

10-1 What is the purpose of preemptive rights?

10-2 "Common shareholders have limited liability." Explain.

10-3 Can a share of common stock be outstanding but not authorized or issued? Why?

10-4 "Treasury stock is unissued stock." Do you agree? Explain.

10-5 "Cumulative dividends are liabilities that must be paid to preferred shareholders before any dividends are paid to common shareholders." Do you agree? Explain.

10-6 "The liquidating value of preferred stock is the amount of cash for which it can currently be exchanged." Do you agree? Explain.

10-7 What are convertible securities?

10-8 In what way is preferred stock similar to debt and to common stock?

10-9 Which are riskier—bonds or preferred stock? Why? Whose perspective are you taking—the issuer's or the investor's?

10-10 Why do U.S. GAAP and IFRS record an expense when a company grants stock options to its employees?

10-11 Why do you suppose companies offer their employees stock options instead of simply paying higher salaries?

10-12 "The only real dividends are cash dividends." Do you agree? Explain.

10-13 "A 2% stock dividend increases every shareholder's fractional portion of the company by 2%." Do you agree? Explain.

10-14 "A stock split can be achieved by means of a stock dividend." Do you agree? Explain.

10-15 "When companies repurchase their own shares, the accounting depends on the purpose for which the shares are purchased." Explain.

10-16 "When a company retires shares, it must pay the stockholders an amount equal to the original par value and additional capital contributed for those shares plus the stockholders' fractional portion of retained earnings." Do you agree? Explain.

10-17 Why might a company decide to buy back its own shares instead of paying additional cash dividends?

10-18 "Treasury stock is not an asset." Explain.

10-19 "Gains and losses are not possible from a corporation acquiring or selling its own stock." Do you agree? Explain.

10-20 What is the proper measure for an asset newly acquired through an exchange (e.g., an exchange of land for securities)? Explain.

10-21 Why does a conversion option make bonds or preferred stock more attractive to investors?

10-22 Restrictions on dividend-declaring power may be voluntary or involuntary. Give an example of each.

10-23 Why might a board of directors voluntarily restrict its dividend-declaring power?

10-24 "A company's ROE indicates how much return an investor makes on the investment in the company's shares." Do you agree? Explain.

10-25 "A common stock selling on the market far below its book value is an attractive buy." Do you agree? Explain.

Critical Thinking Questions

10-26 Company Share Prices and Intentions to Repurchase Shares

Your friend has thought about repurchases of common stock by the issuing company and has concluded that this is unethical. Specifically, this friend says that the company knows more than you do and if the company decides to repurchase shares, it is taking advantage of shareholders. How do you respond?

10-27 The Prohibition on Income Recognition from Trading in the Company's Shares

Your friend has considered stock repurchases and thinks that it is proper for the company to buy its own shares and subsequently reissue them, recognizing a profit in doing so that should be reported on the income statement. How do you respond?

10-28 The Meaning of Par Value

Your friend has decided that par value is a meaningless notion and complicates accounting practice without adding value to the financial statements. How do you respond?

10-29 Changes in Stock Prices When the Shares Are Split

Your friend has developed a stock investing strategy that suggests you should always buy the shares of companies when they split their stock or issue large stock dividends. How do you respond?

Exercises

10-30 Distinctions Between Terms

Disposal Services, Inc., a waste management company, had 3 million shares of common stock authorized on August 31, 20X2. Shares issued were 2 million. There were 250,000 shares held in the treasury. How many shares were issued and outstanding? How many shares were unissued? Label your computations.

10-31 Distinctions Between Terms

On December 31, 2008, **IBM Corporation** had 4,688 million shares of common stock authorized. There were 2,097 million shares issued, and 758 million shares held as treasury stock. How many shares were issued and outstanding? How many shares were unissued? Label your computations.

10-32 Preferences as to Assets

The following are account balances of Reliable Autos, Inc., ($ in thousands): Common Stock and Retained Earnings, $300; Accounts Payable, $300; Preferred Stock (5,000 shares; $20 par and $24 liquidating value per share), $100; Subordinated Debentures, $300; and Unsubordinated Debentures, $200. Prepare a table showing the distribution of the cash proceeds on liquidation and dissolution of the corporation. Assume cash proceeds of the following ($ in thousands): $1,400, $1,100, $800, $600, $400, and $200, respectively.

10-33 Issuance of Common Shares

Kawasaki Heavy Industries is a large Japanese company that makes ships, aircraft engines, and many other products in addition to motorcycles. Its 2009 sales of ¥1,339 billion were equivalent to $13,623 million. Kawasaki's balance sheet includes (yen in millions):

Common stock, 1,669,629,122 shares issued in 2009	
Total paid-in-capital from the 2009 issue	¥158,611

1. Assume all 1,669,629,122 shares had been issued at the same time at a ¥62 par value. Prepare the journal entry.
2. Is the relationship between the size of the common stock and the size of the capital surplus different from what one might expect to find for a U.S. company? Explain.

10-34 Cumulative Dividends

The Ute Data Services Corporation was founded on January 1, 20X1.

Preferred stock, no par, cumulative $5 annual dividend per share	
Issued and outstanding, 1,000,000 shares	$ 40,000,000
Capital stock, no par, 6,000,000 shares	90,000,000
Total stockholders' equity	$130,000,000

The corporation's subsequent net incomes (losses) were as follows:

20X1	$ (5,000,000)
20X2	(4,000,000)
20X3	15,000,000
20X4	20,000,000
20X5	14,000,000

Assume the board of directors declared dividends to the maximum extent permissible by law. The state prohibits dividend declarations that cause negative retained earnings.

1. Tabulate the annual dividend declarations on preferred and common shares. There is no treasury stock.
2. How would the total distribution to common shareholders change if the preferred stock were not cumulative?

10-35 Cumulative Dividends

In recent years, the Winslow Company had severe cash flow problems. In 20X0, the company suspended payment of cash dividends on common stock. In 20X1, it ceased payment on its $3 million par value 7% cumulative preferred stock. No common or preferred dividends were paid in 20X1 or 20X2. In 20X3, Winslow's board of directors decided that $1.0 million was available for cash dividends.

Compute the preferred stock dividend and the common stock dividend for 20X3.

10-36 Cash Dividends

Honda, the Japanese automobile company, paid dividends in fiscal 2009 of ¥77 per share on 1,814.6 million shares.

Prepare the journal entries relating to the declaration and payment of fiscal 2009 dividends by Honda.

10-37 Exercise of Stock Options

Lyndon Systems granted its top executives options to purchase 4,000 shares of common stock (par $2) at $20 per share, the market price today. The options may be exercised over a 4-year span, starting 3 years hence. Suppose all options are exercised 3 years hence, when the market value of the stock is $40 per share.

Prepare the appropriate journal entry on the books of Lyndon Systems. Discuss the economic benefits to managers and the benefits to the company from these options.

10-38 Stock Split

An annual report of Dean Foods Company included the following in the statement of consolidated retained earnings:

Charge for stock split	$4,401,000

The balance sheets before and after the split showed the following:

	After	Before
Common stock $1 par value	$13,203,000	$8,802,000

Define stock split. What did Dean Foods do to achieve its stock split? Does this conflict with your definition? Explain fully.

10-39 Reverse Stock Split

According to a news story, "The shareholders of QED approved a 1-for-10 reverse split of QED's common stock." Accounting for a reverse stock split applies the same principles as accounting for a regular stock split. QED Exploration, Incorporated, is an oil development company operating in Texas and Louisiana. QED's stockholders' equity section before the reverse split included the following:

Common stock, authorized 30,000,000 shares, issued 23,530,000 shares	$ 287,637
Additional paid-in capital	3,437,547
Retained income	2,220,895
Less: Treasury stock, at cost, 1,017,550 shares	(305,250)
Total stockholders' equity	$5,640,829

1. Prepare QED's stockholders' equity section after the reverse stock split.
2. Comment on possible reasons for a reverse split.

10-40 Stock Dividends

Company Release-10/28/2009 09:00
Tompkins Financial Corporation Declares Cash Dividend.
Ithaca, New York (Business Wire)

Tompkins Financial Corporation (TMP- NYSE AMEX) announced today that its Board of Directors approved payment of a regular quarterly cash dividend of $0.34 per share, payable on November 16, 2009, to common shareholders of record on November 6, 2009.

Company Release- 07/23/2003 10:27
Tompkins Trustco, Inc. Announces Cash and Stock Dividends
Ithaca, New York July 23, 2003 (Business Wire)

Tompkins Trustco, Inc. (TMP- American Stock Exchange) announced today that its Board of Directors approved payment of a regular quarterly cash dividend of $0.30 per share, payable on August 15, 2003, to common shareholders of record on August 5, 2003. The Board also approved the payment of a 10% stock dividend payable on August 15, 2003, to common shareholders of record on August 5, 2003.

1. At September 30, 2009, there were 9,755,480 shares issued with a par value of $.10 per share. There were 79,310 shares in the treasury. Assume no shares were acquired or sold by/from the company after September 30. Give the journal entry to record the declaration of the cash dividend.
2. At June 30, 2003, Tompkins reported 7,397,133 shares issued with a par value of $.10 per share. At June 30, 24,529 shares were in the treasury. The share price was $45 when the stock dividend was issued. Assume no treasury shares were acquired or sold after June 30. Prepare the journal entry to record TMP's stock dividend.
3. Tompkins issued 10% stock dividends in 1995, 2003, 2005, and 2006. In 1998 Tompkins issued a three-for-two split. If an investor purchased 100 shares in 1994, how many shares would the investor have in 2009?

10-41 Treasury Stock

During 2008, Tompkins Financial Corporation repurchased 1,500 of its own shares at an average price of $38.67 per share. Par value was $.01 per share. Assume the shares were originally issued for $25.

1. Prepare the journal entry for the 2008 purchase of shares assuming that they were treated as treasury shares.
2. In fact, Tompkins did not add the repurchased shares to treasury stock. Instead, it canceled the shares and returned them to unissued status. This is accounted for with a debit to Capital Stock at Par Value, a debit to Paid-in Surplus for the surplus created by the initial issuance, and a debit to Retained Earnings for the remainder. Give the actual entry Tompkins made.

10-42 Book Value and Return on Equity

Reach Company had net income of $12 million in 20X8. The stockholders' equity section of its 20X8 annual report follows ($ in millions):

	20X8	20X7
Stockholders' equity		
8% Preferred stock, $50 par value, 400,000 shares authorized, 300,000 shares issued	$ 15.0	$ 15.0
Common stock, $1 par, 5 million authorized, 2 million and 1.8 million issued	2.0	1.8
Additional paid-in capital	32.0	30.0
Retained earnings	69.0	65.2
Total stockholders' equity	$118.0	$112.0

1. Compute the book value per share of common stock at the end of 20X8.
2. Compute the rate of return on common equity for 20X8.
3. Compute the amount of cash dividends on common stock declared during 20X8. (*Hint:* Examine the retained earnings T-account.)

10-43 Financial Ratios and Stockholders' Equity

Consider the following data for New York Bankcorp:

	December 31	
	20X2	**20X1**
Stockholders' equity		
Preferred stock, 200,000 shares, $20 par, liquidation value $22	$ 4,000,000	$ 4,000,000
Common stock, 4,000,000 shares, $2 par	8,000,000	8,000,000
Additional paid-in capital	5,000,000	5,000,000
Retained income	3,000,000	1,400,000
Total stockholders' equity	$20,000,000	$18,400,000

Net income was $2.4 million for 20X2. The preferred stock is 10%, cumulative. The regular annual dividend was declared on the preferred stock, and the common shareholders received dividends of $.20 per share. The market price of the common stock on December 31, 20X2, was $11.00 per share.

Compute the following statistics for 20X2: rate of return on common equity, earnings per share of common stock, price-earnings ratio, dividend-payout ratio, dividend-yield ratio, and book value per share of common stock.

10-44 Stockholders' Equity Section

The following are data for the Roselli Corporation on December 31, 20X8:

6% cumulative preferred stock, $40 par value, callable at $42, authorized 100,000 shares, issued and outstanding 100,000 shares	$ 4,000,000
Treasury stock, common (at cost)	4,000,000
Additional paid-in capital, common stock	9,000,000
Dividends payable	100,000
Retained earnings	12,000,000
Additional paid-in capital, preferred stock	1,000,000
Common stock, $2.50 par value per share, authorized 1.8 million shares, issued 1.2 million shares of which 60,000 are held in the treasury	3,000,000

Prepare a detailed stockholders' equity section as it would appear in the balance sheet at December 31, 20X8.

10-45 Effects on Stockholders' Equity

Indicate the effect (+, –, or 0) on total stockholders' equity of General Services Corporation for each of the following:

1. Declaration of a stock dividend on common stock
2. Sale of 100 shares of General Services by Jay Smith to Tom Jones
3. Net earnings for the period of $600,000
4. Issuance of a stock dividend on common stock
5. Failing to declare a regular dividend on cumulative preferred stock
6. Declaration of a cash dividend of $50,000 in total
7. Payment of item 6
8. Purchase of 10 shares of treasury stock for $1,000 cash
9. Sale of treasury stock, purchased in item 8, for $1,200
10. Sale of treasury stock, purchased in item 8, for $800

MyAccountingLab   ## Problems

10-46 Dividends and Cumulative Preferred Stock

Renton Interiors, Inc., maker of seats and other interior equipment for Boeing aircraft, started 20X8 with the following balance sheet:

6% Cumulative convertible preferred stock, par value $10 a share, authorized 150,000 shares; issued 52,136 shares	$ 521,360
Common stock, par value $.20 a share, authorized 2,000,000 shares, issued 1,322,850 shares	264,570
Additional paid-in capital	2,063,351
Retained earnings	2,463,951
Less: Treasury stock, at cost	
Preferred stock, 11,528 shares	(80,249)
Common stock, 93,091 shares	(167,549)
Total stockholders' equity	$5,065,434

1. Suppose Renton Interiors had paid no dividends, preferred or common, in the prior year, 20X7. All preferred dividends had been paid through 20X6. Management decided at the end of 20X8 to pay $.04 per share common dividends. Calculate the preferred dividends that would be paid during 20X8. Prepare journal entries for recording the declaration and payment of preferred and common dividends. Assume no preferred or common shares were issued or purchased during 20X7 or 20X8.
2. Suppose 20X8 net income was $400,000. Compute the 20X8 ending balance in the Retained Earnings account.

10-47 Dividend Reinvestment Plans

Many corporations have automatic dividend reinvestment plans. Individual shareholders may elect not to receive their cash dividends. Instead, an equivalent amount of cash is invested in additional stock (at the current market value) that is issued to the shareholder.

Royal Dutch Shell had total assets of $282 billion at December 31, 2008, and declared a quarterly cash dividend of $.40 per share in the fourth quarter of 2008.

1. Suppose holders of 10% of the company's 6.2 billion outstanding shares decided to reinvest in the company under an automatic dividend reinvestment plan instead of accepting the cash. The market price of the shares on issuance was $50 per share. Prepare the journal entry or entries for these transactions. For purposes of this problem assume Shell shares have no par and no stated value.
2. A letter to the editor of *BusinessWeek* commented,

> *Stockholders participating in dividend reinvestment programs pay taxes on dividends not really received. If a company would refrain from paying dividends only to take them back as reinvestments, it would save paperwork, and the stockholder would save income tax.*

Do you agree with the writer's remarks? Explain in detail.

10-48 Multiple Classes of Common Stock

In 2009 *Fortune* magazine listed Royal Dutch Shell as the world's largest corporation and *Forbes* listed it as the second largest. Shell has multiple forms of common stock. It offers class A and class B shares. Class A shares pay cash dividends in Euros, unless the shareholder elects otherwise. Class B shares pay dividends in pounds sterling (UK currency) unless the shareholder elects otherwise. In addition, for U.S. shareholders, Shell provides ADRs (American Depository Receipts), which pay dividends in U.S. dollars.

1. Consider why a company would choose to create multiple classes of common stock.
2. Why would a European-based integrated petroleum company present its IFRS financial statements in U.S. dollars as the reporting currency.

10-49 Dividends

(Alternate is 10-50.)

1. The Minneapolis Company issued 400,000 shares of common stock, $4 par, for $25 cash per share on March 31, 20X1. Prepare the journal entry.
2. Minneapolis Company declared and paid a cash dividend of $1 per share on March 31, 20X2. Prepare the journal entry.
3. Minneapolis Company had retained earnings of $9 million by March 31, 20X5. The market value of the common shares was $50 each. A common stock dividend of 5% was declared and shares were issued on March 31, 20X5. Prepare the journal entry. Also present a tabulation that compares the stockholders' equity section before and after the declaration and issuance of the stock dividend. Also include at the bottom of the tabulation the effects on the overall market value of the stock, the total shares outstanding, and the number of shares and percentage of ownership of an individual owner who originally bought 5,000 shares.
4. What journal entries would be made by the investor who bought 5,000 shares of the Minneapolis common stock and held this investment throughout the time covered in requirements 1, 2, and 3?
5. Refer to requirement 4. Suppose the investor sold 200 shares for $58 each the day after receiving the stock dividend. Prepare the investor's journal entry for the sale of the shares.

10-50 Dividends

(Alternate is 10-49.)

1. Garcia Company issued 600,000 shares of common stock, $1 par, for $9 cash per share on December 31, 20X5. Prepare the journal entry.
2. Garcia Company declared and paid a cash dividend of $.50 per share on December 31, 20X6. Prepare the journal entry. Assume only the 600,000 shares from part 1 are outstanding.
3. Garcia Company had retained earnings of $7 million by December 31, 20X9. The market value of the common shares was $30 each. A common stock dividend of 2% was declared and shares were issued on December 31, 20X9. Prepare the journal entry. Also present a tabulation that compares the stockholders' equity section before and after the declaration and issuance of the stock dividend. Also include at the bottom of the tabulation the effects on the overall market value of the stock, the total shares outstanding, and the number of shares and percentage of ownership of an individual owner who originally bought 5,000 shares.
4. What journal entries would be made by the investor who bought 5,000 original-issue shares of Garcia Company common stock and held this investment throughout the time covered in requirements 1, 2, and 3?
5. Refer to requirement 4. Suppose the investor sold 200 shares for $33 each the day after receiving the stock dividend. Prepare the investor's journal entry for the sale of the shares.

10-51 Meaning of Stock Splits

A letter of January 31 to shareholders of United Financial, a California savings and loan company, said

> Once again, I want to take the opportunity of sending you some good news about recent developments at United Financial. Last week the board raised United's quarterly cash dividend 12 percent and then declared a 5-for-4 stock split in the form of a 25 percent stock dividend. The additional shares will be distributed on March 15 to shareholders of record February 15.

On March 16, the board approved a merger between National Steel Corporation and United Financial. The agreement called for a cash payment of $33.60 on each outstanding United Financial share. The original National Steel offer (in early February) was $42 per share for the 5.8 million shares outstanding.

1. As a recipient of the letter of January 31, you were annoyed by the five-for-four stock split. Prepare a letter to the chairman indicating the reasons for your displeasure.
2. Prepare a response to the unhappy shareholder in requirement 1.
3. A shareholder of United Financial wrote to the chairman in early March: "I'm confused about the change in the agreed upon price per share. I owned 100 shares and thought I'd receive $4,200. Now the price has dropped from $42.00 to $33.60." Prepare a response to the shareholder.

10-52 Stock Dividend and Fractional Shares

The Soderstrom Company declared and distributed a 5% stock dividend. The stockholders' equity before the dividend was as follows:

Common stock, 10,000,000 shares, $1 par	$ 10,000,000
Additional paid-in capital	40,000,000
Retained earnings	50,000,000
Total stockholders' equity	$100,000,000

The market price of Soderstrom's shares was $10 when the stock dividend was distributed. Soderstrom paid cash of $30,000 in lieu of issuing fractional shares.

1. Prepare the journal entry for the declaration and distribution of the stock dividend.
2. Show the stockholders' equity section after the stock dividend.
3. How did the stock dividend affect total stockholders' equity? How did it affect the proportion of the company owned by each shareholder?

10-53 Issuance and Retirement of Shares, Cash Dividends

On January 2, 20X1, Chippewa Investment Company began business by issuing 20,000 shares at $1 par value for $200,000 cash. The cash was invested, and on December 26, 20X1, all investments were sold for $214,000 cash. Operating expenses for 20X1 were $4,000, all paid in cash. Therefore, net income for 20X1 was $10,000. On December 27, the board of directors declared a $.10 per share cash dividend, payable on January 15, 20X2, to owners of record on December 31, 20X1. On January 30, 20X2, the company bought and retired 1,000 of its own shares on the open market for $8.00 each.

1. Prepare journal entries for issuance of shares, declaration and payment of cash dividends, and retirement of shares.
2. Prepare a balance sheet as of December 31, 20X1.

10-54 Issuance, Splits, and Dividends

(Alternate is 10-55.)

1. Lopez Company issued 100,000 shares of common stock, $5 par, for $35 cash per share on December 31, 20X1. Prepare the journal entry.
2. Lopez Company had retained earnings of $4 million by December 31, 20X5. The board of directors declared a two-for-one stock split and immediately exchanged two $2.50 par shares for each share outstanding. Prepare the journal entry, if any. Present the stockholders' equity section of the balance sheet before and after the split.
3. Repeat requirement 2, but assume that instead of exchanging two $2.50 par shares for each share outstanding, one additional $5 par share was issued for each share outstanding. Lopez said it issued a two-for-one stock split "accounted for as a stock dividend."
4. What journal entries would be made by the investor who bought 2,000 shares of Lopez Company common stock and held this investment throughout the time covered in requirements 1, 2, and 3?

10-55 Issuance, Splits, and Dividends

(Alternate is 10-54.) **AT&T**'s December 31, 2008, balance sheet showed total shareowners' equity of $96,347 million and indicated the following detail:

Common stock, par value $1.00 per share	$6,495,000,000

1. Suppose AT&T had originally issued 200 million shares of common stock, $1 par, for $14 cash per share many years ago, for instance, on December 31, 19X1. Prepare the journal entry.
2. Suppose AT&T had retained earnings of $5 billion by December 31, 19X5. The board of directors declared a two-for-one stock split and immediately exchanged two $.50 par shares for each share outstanding. Prepare the journal entry, if any. Present the stockholders' equity section of the balance sheet before and after the split.

3. Repeat requirement 2, but assume that one additional $1 par share was issued by AT&T for each share outstanding (instead of exchanging shares) and accounted for as a stock dividend.

4. What journal entries would be made by the investor who bought 1,000 shares of AT&T common stock and held this investment throughout the time covered in requirements 1, 2, and 3?

10-56 Stock Split and 100% Stock Dividend

The Rubin Company wants to double its number of shares outstanding. The company president asks the controller how a two-for-one stock split differs from a 100% stock dividend. Rubin has 300,000 shares ($1 par) outstanding at a market price of $20 per share.

The current stockholders' equity section is as follows:

Common shares, 300,000 issued and outstanding	$ 300,000
Additional paid-in capital	2,300,000
Retained income	4,500,000

1. Prepare the journal entry for a two-for-one stock split.
2. Prepare the journal entry for a 100% stock dividend.
3. Explain the difference between a two-for-one stock split and a 100% stock dividend.

10-57 Treasury Stock

(Alternate is 10-63.) **Minnesota Mining and Manufacturing Company (3M)** presented the following data in its 2008 annual report:

	December 31	
	2008	**2007**
	(in millions)	
Stockholders' equity		
Common stock $.01 per share	$ 9	$ 9
Additional paid-in capital	3,001	2,785
Retained earnings	22,248	20,316
Treasury stock	(11,676)	(10,520)
Unearned compensation	(57)	(96)
Other comprehensive income	(3,646)	(747)
Stockholders' equity, net	$ 9,879	$ 11,747

1. During 2008, 3M reacquired 21.4 million treasury shares for $1,603 million. Give the journal entry to record this transaction.

2. 3M also issued some treasury shares as part of its employee stock option and investment plans. What was the cost of treasury shares issued in 2008?

3. Suppose that on January 2, 2009, 3M used cash to reacquire 100,000 shares for $76 each and held them in the treasury. What is the new stockholders' equity after the acquisition of treasury stock? Also prepare the journal entry.

4. Suppose the 100,000 shares of treasury stock are sold for $90 per share. Prepare the journal entry.

5. Suppose the 100,000 shares of treasury stock are sold for $50 per share. Prepare the journal entry.

10-58 Treasury Shares

During 2008 outstanding common shares of **General Electric** (GE) increased from 9,987,599,000 to 10,536,897,000. GE declared dividends of $12,649,000,000. The treasury stock account had a beginning balance of $36,896,000,000 and an ending balance of $36,697,000,000. The total cost of purchases of treasury shares in 2008 was $3,508,000,000. During 2008 GE stock fell consistently from about $37 per share in January to $13 per share at year end. Assume that the average price of treasury stock purchased in 2008 was $20 per share and the average carrying value of treasury stock disposals was $25 per share.

1. Compute the carrying value of the treasury shares sold during 2008.
2. What was the net increase (or decrease) in number of treasury shares in 2008?
3. Comment on the decision to buy/sell treasury stock during the year.

10-59 Repurchase of Shares and Book Value per Share

ExxonMobil repurchased common shares during 2008 and, as a result, the Treasury Stock account increased by $34,420 million. The market price of ExxonMobil shares averaged $81.00 per share during the year. There were 8,019 million shares issued and 3,043 million shares in the treasury at year end. The condensed 2008 shareholders' equity section of the balance sheet showed the following (dollars in millions):

Common stock, no par	$ 5,314
Earnings reinvested	265,680
Treasury stock	(148,098)
Other	(9,931)
Total stockholders' equity	$ 112,965

1. Estimate the number of shares repurchased for the treasury.
2. Compute the book value per share at December 31, 2008.

10-60 Retirement of Shares

Houston Financial Systems, Inc., has the following:

Common stock, 6,000,000 shares @ $2 par	$ 12,000,000
Paid-in capital in excess of par	48,000,000
Total paid-in capital	$ 60,000,000
Retained earnings	10,000,000
Stockholders' equity	$ 70,000,000
Overall market value of stock @ assumed $30	$180,000,000
Book value per share = $70,000,000 ÷ 6,000,000 = $11.67	

The company used cash to reacquire and retire 200,000 shares for $30 each. Prepare the stockholders' equity section before and after this retirement of shares. Also prepare the journal entry.

10-61 Disposition of Treasury Stock

Chirac Company bought 10,000 of its own shares for $10 per share. The shares were held as treasury stock. This was the only time Chirac had ever purchased treasury stock.

1. Chirac sold 5,000 of the shares for $11 per share. Prepare the journal entry.
2. Chirac sold the remaining 5,000 shares later for $9 per share. Prepare the journal entry.
3. Repeat requirement 2, assuming the shares were sold for $7 instead of $9 per share.
4. Did you record gains or losses in requirements 1, 2, and 3? Explain.

10-62 Effects of Treasury Stock on Retained Earnings

Assume that Ming Company has retained earnings of $8 million, paid-in capital of $24 million, and cost of treasury stock of $6 million.

1. Tabulate the effects of dividend payments of (a) $4 million and (b) $1 million on retained earnings and total stockholders' equity.
2. Why do states forbid the payment of dividends if retained earnings do not exceed the cost of any treasury stock on hand? Explain, using the numbers from your answer to requirement 1.

10-63 Treasury Stock

(Alternate is 10-57.) Capetown Company has the following [in rands (R), the South African unit of currency]:

Common stock, 2,000,000 shares @ R3 par	R 6,000,000
Paid-in capital in excess of par	34,000,000
Total paid-in capital	R40,000,000
Retained income	18,000,000
Stockholders' equity	R58,000,000
Overall market value of stock @ assumed R40	R80,000,000

Book value per share = R58,000,000
    ÷ 2,000,000 = R29

1. The company used cash to reacquire 100,000 shares for R40 each and held them in the treasury. Prepare the stockholders' equity section after the acquisition of treasury stock. Also prepare the journal entry.
2. Suppose all the treasury stock is sold for R50 per share. Prepare the journal entry.
3. Suppose all the treasury stock is sold for R30 per share. Prepare the journal entry.
4. Recalculate book value after each preceding transaction.

10-64 IFRS

Fortis is an insurance company with a complex ownership structure in which a Belgium company and a Netherland company each own 50% of Fortis. Investors buying a Fortis share essentially buy one share each of the two parents. Under IFRS accounting the interest of the two parents are combined and one consolidated financial statement is issued. Shareholders may choose to receive their dividend payments from either the Belgium or the Netherlands parent. Speculate on why the source of the payment might matter to the shareholder.

10-65 Convertible Securities

Suppose Boston Company had paid $150,000 to Hartford Company for an investment in 10,000 shares of the $5 par value preferred stock of Hartford Company. The preferred stock was later converted into 10,000 shares of Hartford Company common stock ($1 par value).

1. Using the balance sheet equation, prepare an analysis of transactions of Boston Company and Hartford Company.
2. Prepare the journal entries to accompany your analysis in requirement 1.

10-66 Issue of Common Shares

Intermec Corporation, a leader in the field of bar code data collection, had the following stockholders' equity on December 31, 2008 ($ in thousands):

Common stock: authorized 250,000,000 shares with $.01 par value, issued and outstanding 61,766,000 shares	$ 618
Additional paid-in capital	694,296
Accumulated deficit	(162,402)
Accumulated other comprehensive (loss)	(50,756)
Total stockholders' equity	$ 481,756

a. In 2006, Intermec repurchased $100 million, or approximately 3.18 million shares, of common stock under a share repurchase program.
b. In 2008 the company approved an employee stock purchase plan that allows employees to purchase stock at 85% of the fair market value. When employees participate in this plan, Intermec recognizes compensation expense in the amount of the 15% discount. Compensation expense recognized in 2008 was $516,000. Assume an average market price of $20 per share.
c. In 2008 Intermec received $4,362,000 for the exercise of stock options. Assume that new shares were issued and that the average exercise price of the options was $15.00 per share.

Net income for the year was $35,686,000. No dividends were paid.

1. Prepare journal entries for the transactions in a, b, and c. Omit explanations.
2. At the end of 2008 Intermec had an accumulated deficit of ($162,402,000). At the current rate of earnings, how many years will it be before Intermec could pay a dividend of $1 per share without exhausting retained earnings?

10-67 IFRS Company – Forms of Ownership

Carrefour is a French company with extensive retail activity in over 25 countries but not yet in the United States. Its Web site reminds us of how extensive share ownership has become and how different countries and customs structure the costs and benefits of share ownership. The following information is extracted from the company's Web site about share ownership:

TO BE [A] SHAREHOLDER

The ways in which Carrefour shares are held

Shareholders may hold Carrefour shares in two different ways: as "registered" shares or as "bearer" shares.

Bearer shares

Bearer share accounts are held by your financial intermediary (lending establishment or investment company) and are therefore not known to Carrefour.

Registered shares

There are 2 ways in which shareholders may hold registered shares:

Intermediary registered shares

Your portfolio of shares is held by your financial intermediary, which is responsible for managing the portfolio.

Your shares are however registered in Carrefour's accounts, which enables us to identify you and make direct contact with you.

Directly registered shares

Your shares are registered directly and solely in Carrefour's accounts, which enables us to provide you with a bespoke service.

Your shares are registered in a shareholding account opened with CACEIS Corporate Trust, which manages the Carrefour shareholding service.

The benefits of registered shares

When you hold directly or intermediary registered shares, you benefit from the following advantages:

Guaranteed personalised information service

Prior to General Meetings, we will send the following directly to your home:
- the meeting convening notice;
- a postal voting form;
- an application form for an entrance pass.

Our shareholders' newsletters will also be sent to you automatically.

Finally, you will have access to a telephone helpline at CACEIS Corporate Trust, which manages the Carrefour shareholding service. A team of advisers will be at your disposal to inform you about the management of your shares, the tax rules applicable to securities and the organisation of General Meetings.

Double voting right

Each share that has been held in registered form for at least 2 years benefits from a double voting right.

Preferential access to the company's General Meetings

The holders of registered shares are automatically invited to attend General Meetings and need not accomplish any prior formality.

*If you opt for **directly registered shares**, you will furthermore benefit from:*
Free management of your shares.

The holders of registered shares do not pay any custody fees or any of the fees inherent in the day-to-day management of their securities, namely fees for:

- conversion of their shares into bearer shares, security transfers;
- swaps, donations, estates;
- share transactions;
- payment of dividends.

Legal and tax implications

The tax treatment for bearer and registered shares is the same.

1. Given the information provided, how would you choose to hold your shares, as bearer or registered shares? If you chose registered, would you choose directly or intermediary registered shares? Explain.

10-68 Noncash Exchanges

Suppose Cartier Company acquires some equipment from Marseilles Company in exchange for issuance of 10,000 shares of Cartier's common stock. The equipment was carried on Marseilles's books at the €530,000 original cost less accumulated depreciation of €100,000. Cartier's stock is listed on the Paris Stock Exchange; its current market value is €50 per share. Its par value is €1 per share.

1. By using the balance sheet equation, show the effects of the transaction on the accounts of Cartier Company and Marseilles Company.
2. Show the journal entries on the books of Cartier Company and Marseilles Company.

10-69 Covenants and Leases and Buying and Selling Stock

Mitchell Energy and Development Corporation was one of the country's largest oil and gas producers before it was purchased by **Devon Energy**. Some years ago, the notes to its financial statements revealed the existence of certain debt agreement restrictions on the level of consolidated stockholders' equity as well as on various asset-to-debt ratios:

> *The bank credit agreements contain certain restrictions which, among other things, require consolidated stockholders' equity to be equal to at least $300,000,000 and require the maintenance of specified financial and oil and gas reserve and/or asset value to debt ratios.*

1. Given the existence of the asset-to-debt covenants, was Mitchell more likely to be able to enter into operating leases or capital leases without violating the covenants?
2. If Mitchell Energy and Development had refused to agree to these conditions at the time of the debt issues, how would it have affected the market price of the debt it issued?
3. Before being acquired, Mitchell issued 4.68 million additional shares at $53 per share. Give the journal entry to record the issue, assuming no par stock.
4. Devon Energy subsequently agreed to buy Mitchell Energy by giving each shareholder in Mitchell Energy $31 in cash and .585 shares of Devon Energy for each share of Mitchell Energy. Devon's shares were valued at $50.76. How much profit would an investor who bought 1,000 shares of Mitchell Energy at $53 per share just before the acquisition make when the merger was complete?

10-70 Financial Ratios

Consider the following data from two companies in very different industries. **Adobe Systems** is a software company. **Empire District** is an electric utility serving the Midwest. (Amounts except earnings per share and market price are in millions.)

	Total Assets	Total Liabilities	Net Income	Earnings per Share	Market Price per Share
Adobe Systems	$5,821	$1,411	$871	$1.59	$37
Empire District	1,714	1,185	39	1.17	19

1. Compute the market-to-book ratio, the price to earning ratio, and the rate of return on stockholders' equity for both Adobe Systems and Empire District.
2. Explain what might cause the differences in these ratios between the two companies.

10-71 Classis Case of Shareholders' Equity Section

Enron Corporation was a worldwide energy company with annual revenues in excess of $40 billion in 1999. Its main activities were in natural gas and electricity. Enron's collapse was one of the most spectacular elements of the recent past. Enron filed for bankruptcy protection on December 2, 2001, and 2 years later its common stock shares were trading at $.04 per share. Events surrounding Enron led to the failure of its audit firm, **Arthur Andersen**. The data here are from the company's 1999 annual report ($ in millions).

For the Year Ended December 31	1999	1998
Other stockholders' equity	895	70
Common stock held in treasury, 1,337,714 shares and 9,333,322 shares, respectively	(49)	(195)
Common stock, no par value, 1,200,000,000 shares authorized, 716,865,081 shares and 671,094,552 shares issued, respectively	6,637	5,117
Retained earnings	2,698	2,226
Preferred stock, cumulative, no par value, 1,370,000 shares authorized, 1,296,184 shares and 1,319,848 shares issued, respectively	130	132
Accumulated other comprehensive income	(741)	(162)

1. Prepare Enron's shareholders' equity section of the 1999 balance sheet. Include the amount for total stockholders' equity.
2. Enron paid $355 million of cash dividends on common stock and $66 million of cash dividends on preferred stock in 1999. Compute Enron's net income for 1999.
3. Explain Enron's net acquisition or disposition of treasury shares during 1999. Include the increase or decrease in total number of shares and the average cost per share of those acquired or sold. What is the average purchase price (cost) of the shares remaining in the treasury at the end of 1999?
4. Calculate book value per share at December 31, 1999, and the market-to-book ratio on that date, given a market price per share of about $45.
5. The price per share peaked in 2000 at about $91. Estimate the loss in total market value for Enron from its peak until December 2003. Assume 716 million shares outstanding.

10-72 Stock Options and Ethics

Bristol-Myers Squibb is one of the largest pharmaceutical companies in the world. In 2002, the company granted executives options to purchase 40,112,732 shares of common stock. Suppose all shares were granted with an exercise price of $37.55 per share, which was the market price of the stock on the date the options were granted, and all options could be exercised anytime between 3 and 5 years from the grant date, provided that the executive still works for Bristol-Myers Squibb.

Assume at the same time the stock options were issued Bristol-Myers Squibb also issued warrants with the same $37.55 exercise price that are exercisable any time in the next 5 years. The company received $12 for each such warrant.

1. How much expense was recorded at the issue of each stock option? How would this answer differ in 2009?
2. How much value was there to the executive for each stock option issued in 2002? Given the vesting and exercise provisions, how much might executives have realized from these options by 2009? Use one of the Web-based financial sites to review the price performance of Bristol-Myers over these 7 years.
3. How much did it cost the firm for each stock option that was issued?
4. Might the fact that individual executives hold stock options affect their decisions about declaring dividends? Comment on the ethics of this influence.

Collaborative Learning

10-73 Price to Book and ROE

Form groups of three to six students each. Each student should pick two companies, preferably from different industries. Find the appropriate data and compute the market-to-book ratio and the ROE for each company.

Assemble the group and list the companies selected, together with their market-to-book ratio and ROE. Rank the companies from highest to lowest on price to book ratio. Then rank them on ROE.

Explain why companies rank as they do in each list. Are the rankings similar; that is, is the ranking based on market-to-book similar to the rankings on ROE? Explain why you would or would not expect similarity in the rankings.

Analyzing and Interpreting Financial Statements

10-74 Financial Statement Research

Select a company and use its financial statements to answer the following questions:

1. Identify each transaction that affected stockholders' equity during the most recent 2 years.
2. Indicate which accounts were affected and by how much.
3. List any transactions that appear unusual. For example, many companies have a change in shareholders' equity that arises from tax benefits related to stock options. This and a few other common transactions are beyond our scope in this introductory course.

10-75 Starbucks' Annual Report

Find **Starbucks'** financial statements for the fiscal year ended September 27, 2009, either via the Starbucks Web site or on the SEC's Edgar database.

1. Prepare the journal entries to record any dividends declared in the year ended September 28, 2009.
2. How much cash did Starbucks generate from the issuance of common stock in the year ended September 28, 2009?
3. Compute Starbucks' return on common equity and book value per share in fiscal 2008 and 2009. Comment on the changes in the two ratios between 2008 and 2009.

10-76 Analyzing Financial Statements Using the Internet: United Parcel Service

Go to www.ups.com to find the home page of **United Parcel Service** (UPS). Select UPS Investor Relations near the bottom of the page. Click on Financials to locate UPS's latest annual report.

Answer the following questions about UPS:

1. Identify the classes of stock that UPS has authorized as of the end of its most recent fiscal period, with their par values. Have all the shares in each category been issued? Can you tell if the shares were issued above par? How?
2. How many additional shares of common stock is UPS able to issue as of its most recent balance sheet date? If these shares were all issued and outstanding, how would the values reported on the balance sheet change? Does UPS have any treasury stock?
3. What is the cause of any changes in the Common Stock accounts during the period?
4. Did UPS declare any stock splits or stock dividends during its most recent 2-year comparative reporting period? If so, what effect did these have on the number of shares of stock outstanding? Why do you think UPS would want to declare a stock split or stock dividend?
5. Does UPS have a stock option plan?

11

Intercorporate Investments and Consolidations

LEARNING OBJECTIVES

After studying this chapter, you should be able to:

1 Explain why corporations invest in one another.

2 Account for short-term investments in debt securities and equity securities.

3 Report long-term investments in bonds.

4 Contrast the equity and market methods of accounting for investments.

5 Prepare consolidated financial statements.

6 Incorporate noncontrolling interests into consolidated financial statements.

7 Explain the economic meaning and financial reporting of goodwill.

Deciding to buy and finance a new car is one of the most important decisions you can make as a consumer. If you have gone through this process, you realize that automakers sell financing (auto loans) as well as automobiles. Wherever you buy a Ford car, you can also "buy" your financing through a fully owned subsidiary, Ford Credit. Just what is the relationship between Ford Motor Company and Ford Credit? They are separate entities, each with its own financial records. However, they are so closely related that authorities require them to combine financial records when preparing financial statements for the public.

On June 16, 2009, Ford Motor Company celebrated the 106th anniversary of its founding by Henry Ford and 11 other investors. Twelve years after the founding, Henry Ford gave a one-line speech to celebrate the company's successful mass production of automobiles. He said simply "A million of anything is a great many." At that time the company's production lines could produce one Model T every 10 seconds. By the time Ford celebrated its 100th anniversary in 2003, it had produced more than 300 million vehicles.

Exhibit 11-1 provides a brief timeline of Ford's 106-year history through 2009, and Exhibit 11-2 provides a global overview of the breadth of the Ford Motor Company's activities and brands. Acquisitions have been a consistent pattern in the life of the company, beginning with the acquisition of

This Ford Focus RS is manufactured by Ford Motor Company and is easily financed for the buyer by Ford Credit. Ford Motor prepares consolidated financial statements that include the financial results for all of the brands it produces and for Ford Credit and other subsidiaries.

Lincoln as an entry into the luxury car market in 1922. This pattern of acquiring prestige brands continued in 1989 with the purchase of Jaguar and in 1999 with the purchase of Volvo. Ford also created some significant businesses internally, forming Ford Credit in 1959 and Motorcraft, its parts supplier, in 1961. All of these companies have been wholly owned subsidiaries that Ford consolidated into one set of financial statements. Ford has also sold subsidiaries, including Hertz, Aston Martin, Jaguar, and Land Rover between 2005 and 2008.

Not all of Ford's companies are wholly owned. In 1979, Ford acquired 25% of Mazda, a Japanese manufacturer. It later increased its ownership interest to 33%, and then in 2008 reduced it to 14%. As we see in this chapter, the accounting for a 25% or 33% interest in an affiliate is different than the accounting for a wholly owned or even majority-owned subsidiary and the accounting for a 14% interest differs yet again.

Pick up the annual report of most major or even middle-sized companies and you find **consolidated** financial statements. This term means that the financial records of two or more separate legal entitles have been combined into the statements presented. Ford describes its statements as follows: "Our financial statements include consolidated majority-owned subsidiaries . . . . The equity method of accounting is used for our investments in entities in which we do not have control . . . but over whose operating and financial policies we have the ability to exercise significant influence."

EXHIBIT 11-1

Ford Motor Company Throughout the 100 Years

1903	Henry Ford and 11 investors found the company
1914	Production capacity reached one Model T every 10 seconds; wages of $5 per day were paid, twice the prevailing wage
1915	Henry Ford acknowledged production of millionth car in one line speech: "A million of anything is a great many"
1922	Acquired Lincoln to enter luxury auto market
1956	Sold first shares to the public
1959	Formed Ford Credit
1961	Formed Motorcraft
1979	Acquired 25% of Mazda
1987	Acquired control of Aston Martin
1989	Acquired Jaguar
1994	Hertz becomes wholly owned subsidiary
1999	Acquired Volvo
2000	Acquired Land Rover
2001	Spun-off Visteon
2002	Sold approximately $1 billion of noncore businesses
2003	Manufactured 300 millionth vehicle
2003	Celebrated 100th anniversary
2005	Sold Hertz to three private equity companies
2007	Sold Aston Martin
2008	Sold Jaguar and Land Rover
	Reduced Mazda share to 14%

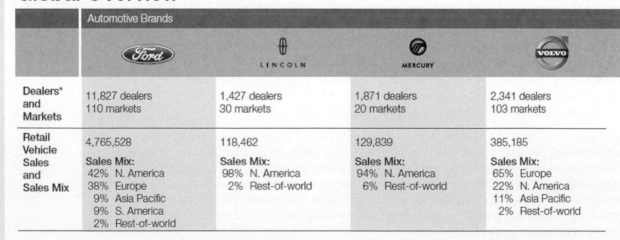

Global Overview

	Automotive Brands			
	Ford	**LINCOLN**	**MERCURY**	**VOLVO**
Dealers* and Markets	11,827 dealers 110 markets	1,427 dealers 30 markets	1,871 dealers 20 markets	2,341 dealers 103 markets
Retail Vehicle Sales and Sales Mix	4,765,528 Sales Mix: 42% N. America 38% Europe 9% Asia Pacific 9% S. America 2% Rest-of-world	118,462 Sales Mix: 98% N. America 2% Rest-of-world	129,839 Sales Mix: 94% N. America 6% Rest-of-world	385,185 Sales Mix: 65% Europe 22% N. America 11% Asia Pacific 2% Rest-of-world

EXHIBIT 11-2

Overview from 2008, Ford Motor Company Annual Report

The process of consolidating financial statements used to be an accountant's nightmare. It took days and sometimes nights for many accountants. The consolidation process filled pages of 13-column paper worksheets. Today, thanks to computers and sophisticated software packages, some very complex companies consolidate statements in hours.

Why did Ford buy Jaguar and then sell it? Why buy a large part of Mazda and then sell some but not all? How is the accounting different for 100% ownership than for 33% or 14%? In this chapter we address some of the strategic questions and explain how and why the accounting differs depending on the ownership percentage. ●

consolidated statements
This term means that the financial records of two or more separate legal entities have been combined into the statements presented.

An Overview of Corporate Investments

When a firm has excess cash, smart managers invest the cash rather than holding it in the company's checking account. While some bank accounts pay interest, companies seek enhanced returns from both short- and long-term debt securities issued by governments, banks, or other corporations. They also invest in marketable corporate equities. For example, Ford classified $17.9 billion of marketable securities as current assets on its 2008 consolidated balance sheet.

OBJECTIVE   1

Explain why corporations invest in one another.

Corporate Marriage and Divorce

Corporate mergers can be a little like marriages. The challenge is to combine and retain the right combination of people and products to succeed over the long haul. Cisco, Microsoft, Intel, Oracle, and other technology companies often buy smaller, innovative young companies to capture their new ideas and, often, their talented employees.

In other cases, firms combine large similar companies hoping to integrate the firms and create cost savings from eliminating duplications. For example, British Petroleum acquired AMOCO and then ARCO to form BP, one of the largest companies in the world. Three companies with very similar operations created the opportunity for major savings when BP eliminated many redundant, repetitive activities and applied best practices throughout the combined entity.

Just as not all marriages work, not all business combinations work. This outcome is disturbingly common. A 2004 study by Bain and Company found 70% of mergers failed to increase

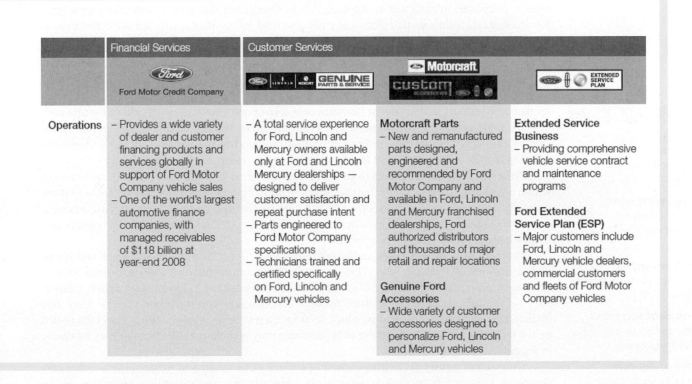

shareholder value, and a 2007 study found that over 90% failed to reach financial goals. The bankruptcy of **General Motors**, **Fiat**'s merger with **Chrysler**, and the negotiations between **Porsche** and **Volkswagen** were all much in the news in mid-2009. Kevin Voigt, in a 2009 article in CNN.com, reported that a group of analysts trying to identify a successful automobile merger could only think of two: the formation of General Motors in 1908 as a union of **Buick**, **Oldsmobile**, **Cadillac**, and other independents; and Volkswagen's combination with **Skoda** and **SEAT** in 1990. See the Business First box for insights from a *Forbes* article on creating successful acquisitions.

Sometimes companies sell parts of themselves when they purchase another company. In some cases the sale is for strategic reasons, and in others regulators demand it. For example, when BP bought ARCO its plan included the sale of $3 billion in assets. The U.S. government challenged BP's acquisition of ARCO. BP agreed to sell ARCO's Alaskan assets and some of its own assets in the North Sea in order to obtain regulatory approval.

When combinations fail, one solution is to sell the subsidiary to another company as Ford did when it sold **Jaguar** and **Land Rover** to the Indian automotive group **Tata** in June, 2008. By June 2009, sales for Jaguar and Land Rover had fallen 32% and Tata posted its first loss in 7 years.

Not all disposals of parts of a company involve sales. **Merck**, a prominent pharmaceutical company, spun off its **Medco** unit when their merger failed to deliver the expected benefits. This means that Merck distributed its shares in Medco directly to Merck shareholders so they became the owners of Medco. Merck, a high-margin company that develops and then manufactures branded, patent-protected drugs, earned no benefits from owning Medco, a low-margin company that distributed drugs to patients.

Spin-offs often separate dissimilar business segments to create opportunities for more creative and innovative growth. Managers of the spin-off company can be compensated more directly based on the performance of the new, often smaller, company. A study of 146 spin-offs over 30 years concluded that investments in shares of spin-off firms outperformed the stock market by an average of 35% in their first 3 years as separate companies.

After companies create intercorporate linkages, their accountants must report on the financial results of these complicated entities. Current accounting procedures for intercorporate linkages use three approaches based on the percentage of ownership: up to 20%, between 20% and 50%, and above 50%. After choosing an accounting procedure, there is a question about *where* to report the asset on the balance sheet, among current or long-term assets. This classification is based on purpose or intent. An investment is a current asset if it is a short-term investment, one the owner expects to convert to cash within one year. All debt securities that mature within one year meet this standard. Investments that a company plans to hold longer than a year are noncurrent assets and usually appear as either a separate investments category or as a part of other assets.

Short-Term Investments

OBJECTIVE 2

Account for short-term investments in debt securities and equity securities.

short-term investment
A temporary investment in marketable securities of otherwise idle cash.

marketable securities
Any notes, bonds, or stocks that can readily be sold.

short-term debt securities
Largely notes and bonds with maturities of 1 year or less.

certificates of deposit
Short-term obligations of banks.

As its name implies, a **short-term investment** is a temporary investment of otherwise idle cash in marketable securities. **Marketable securities** are notes, bonds, or stocks that can be easily sold. A company's short-term investment portfolio of short-term debt securities and short-term equity securities are highly liquid (easily convertible into cash) and have stable prices.

Ordinarily, companies expect to convert items classified as short-term investments into cash within a year after the date on the balance sheet. While a company may not convert some of these securities into cash within 12-months, we still classify them as current assets because management intends to convert them into cash as needed. The key point is that conversion to cash is easily available at the option of management.

Short-term debt securities are largely government- and business-issued notes and bonds with maturities of 1 year or less. They pay a fixed amount of interest. Debt securities include short-term obligations of banks, called **certificates of deposit**, and **commercial paper**, consisting of short-term notes payable issued by large corporations with top credit ratings. They also include **U.S. Treasury obligations**, which refer to interest-bearing notes, bonds, and bills issued by the federal government. All these debt securities may be held until maturity or may be resold in securities markets.

Short-term equity securities consist of capital stock (shares of ownership) in other corporations. Companies, as well as individuals, regularly buy and sell equity securities on the NYSE or other stock exchanges. If the investing firm intends to sell the equity securities it

How does a company increase the odds that its business combination will be one of the successful ones? A KPMG study cited shoddy due diligence, a lack of synergy between the two companies, too little planning, and lousy execution as common reasons for failure. A successful acquisition avoids these pitfalls. More specifically, *Forbes* recommends the following:

1. Do not wait for a deal to come to you. Investment bankers and company brokers seek buyers for companies that want to be acquired. However, *Forbes* advises acquirers to take an active approach. Find the right partner and convince them to be acquired instead of choosing among companies that are for sale.

2. Stick to your knitting. Expansion should be aimed at increasing what you already do. Periodically, conglomerate mergers have been popular. These combinations of very diverse businesses on the grounds that good managers can manage anything and larger companies are better have failed at an even higher rate than usual.

3. Know what you are buying. "Due diligence" is the phrase for carefully investigating the target company. It is the corporate equivalent of kicking the tires or having a mechanic examine a potential used-car purchase. Important questions to ask follow: What is the order backlog? Will critical employees stay? Is debt subject to a change of ownership clause? Are there unrecorded liabilities such as environmental pollution or deferred maintenance that leave plant, property, and equipment in need of repair? The list is long.

4. Learn their tribal customs. Companies have different work cultures. Consider a U.S. company headed by a rapid decision maker. The U.S. buyer might be willing to sign a merger agreement immediately, but a Swiss seller might want to think about it. Although a U.S. buyer might be able to act alone, a Chinese seller might seek a consensus among many managers. Processes for sealing the deal differ.

5. Start integration well before the deal is closed. The most difficult task is the merger of workforces and overcoming cultural differences. It must start early and receive total attention.

Notice that the accounting issues do not make the list of do's and don'ts. There are important steps in bringing the financial accounting for the combining companies together, but they are rarely critical to their success.

Source: "The Race to Embrace," *Forbes*, October 30, 2000, pp. 184–191.

---

holds within a year or within its normal operating cycle, then we classify the securities as short-term investments.

At acquisition, companies record these securities at cost. How they are reported after acquisition depends on whether they are classified as trading securities, available-for-sale securities, or held-to-maturity securities. **Trading securities** are short-term investments, including both debt and equity securities, that the company buys with the intent to resell them shortly. Companies list such securities among current assets on their balance sheets and measure them at fair value (basically market value). **Held-to-maturity securities** are debt securities that the company purchases with the intent to hold them until they mature. They are shown on the balance sheet at amortized cost, not market value. In Chapter 9, we examined the amortization of premiums and discounts on bonds payable by the issuer of the debt. Corporations that invest in bonds use the same approach, as illustrated later in this chapter. Unlike trading securities, which are always classified as short term because of the owner's intention, held-to-maturity securities are classified according to the time remaining until they mature. If the time to maturity is less than a year, they are short-term investments and thus current assets. Otherwise, they are long-term investments and thus noncurrent assets.

Available-for-sale securities include all debt and equity securities that are neither trading securities nor held-to-maturity securities. They include equity securities that the company does not intend to sell in the near future and debt securities that the company neither plans to sell shortly nor to hold to maturity.

Both IFRS and U.S. GAAP allow companies to account for most held-to-maturity securities and available-for-sale securities as if they were trading securities if a company opts for this method at acquisition. According to IFRS, this is "fair value through profit and loss" accounting. So far, few companies have chosen this option.

commercial paper
Short-term notes payable issued by large corporations with top credit ratings.

U.S. Treasury obligations
Interest-bearing notes, bonds, and bills issued by the U.S. government.

short-term equity securities
Capital stock in other corporations held with the intention to liquidate within 1 year as needed.

trading securities
Current investments in equity or debt securities held for short-term profit.

held-to-maturity securities
Debt securities that the investor expects to hold until maturity.

available-for-sale securities
Investments in equity or debt securities that are not held for active trading but may be sold before maturity.

Changes in Market Prices of Securities

You now know how companies show short-term investments on the balance sheet. How do we show the returns (interest, dividends, and market price changes) on these investments?

Held-to-maturity investments are easy because interest revenue is the only return reported on such securities. Changes in market value are ignored. Interest revenue appears directly on the income statement, increasing income and therefore increasing stockholders' equity.

Returns on trading securities and available-for-sale securities come in two forms: (1) dividend or interest revenue, and (2) changes in market value. Companies always record the former on the income statement when earned. However, they treat changes in market value differently for trading securities than for available-for-sale securities. As the market value of *trading* securities changes, companies report gains from increases in price and losses from decreases in price in the income statement. In contrast, gains and losses that arise as market values of *available-for-sale* securities rise and fall do not affect the income statement. Instead, we add such unrealized gains and losses to other comprehensive income. Recall from chapter 2 that other comprehensive income is a summary of all changes in equity except those arising from net income or from transactions with stockholders.

Companies reporting under IFRS will show other comprehensive income in a separate statement of comprehensive income, while those using U.S. GAAP generally report this in the statement of stockholders' equity in a separate column. Notice that increases in prices of both trading securities and available-for-sale securities increase stockholders' equity, and decreases in prices decrease stockholders' equity. For trading securities, the increase or decrease is included in retained earnings because the gains and losses are included in net income. For available-for-sale securities, the increase or decrease is in accumulated other comprehensive income.

We call this method of accounting for trading securities and available-for-sale securities the market method. Under the **market method**, the reported asset values in the balance sheet are the market values of the publicly traded securities. Suppose two companies acquire identical assets at the same price on the same day, but one company reported them as trading securities and the other reported them as available-for-sale securities. The two companies would report identical asset values on their balance sheets, but they would differ in how they report changes in those market values. Assume the portfolio of assets purchased by the two companies cost $50 million and had the market values at the end of four subsequent periods shown in Exhibit 11-3.

Exhibit 11-3 shows the results for the four periods, ignoring income tax effects. Most companies present the market value directly as a single line on the balance sheet. The notes provide the linkage to cost and the amount of unrealized gain or (loss).

The unrealized gain (loss) for trading securities affects net income and therefore also increases (decreases) retained earnings. Over the four periods, the loss of $5 million and

market method

Method of accounting that reports market values of publicly traded securities in the balance sheet; for trading securities changes in market value affect the income statement; for available-for-sale securities changes affect owners' equity directly.

EXHIBIT 11-3

Financial Statement Presentation

Trading Securities and Available-for-Sale Securities ($ in millions)

	End of Period			
	1	**2**	**3**	**4**
Assumed market value	50	45	47	54
Asset presentation—both methods				
Short-term investment at cost	50	50	50	50
Unrealized gain (loss)	0	(5)	(3)	4
Carrying value/fair value	50	45	47	54
Income statement—Trading securities only				
Unrealized gain (loss) on changes in market value	0	(5)	2	7
Other comprehensive income—Available-for-sale securities only				
Unrealized gain (loss) on changes in market value	0	(5)	2	7
Stockholders' equity—Trading securities only				
Retained earnings	0	(5)	(3)	4
Stockholders' equity—Available-for-sale securities only				
Accumulated other comprehensive income	0	(5)	(3)	4

subsequent gains of $2 million and $7 million provide a cumulative net increase in retained earnings of $4 million by the end of period 4 ($9 million of gains less $5 million of losses).

Notice that we use the term unrealized gain (loss) to describe three different items: (1) the adjustment to historical cost to arrive at fair value on the balance sheet, (2) the effect on net earnings for trading securities, and (3) the effect on other comprehensive income for available-for-sale securities. This is common, and you will need to determine the precise meaning of the term from its context.

The journal entries for the two classes of securities for periods 2, 3, and 4 would appear as follows, without explanations:

Period	Trading securities			Available-for-sale-securities		
2	Unrealized loss*.	5		Unrealized gain or loss**.	5	
	Marketable securities		5	Marketable securities		5
3	Marketable securities	2		Marketable securities	2	
	Unrealized gain*		2	Unrealized gain or loss**		2
4	Marketable securities	7		Marketable securities	7	
	Unrealized gain*		7	Unrealized gain or loss**		7

*Shown on the income statement.
**Shown on a statement of comprehensive income under IFRS or directly to accumulated other comprehensive income under U.S. GAAP.

The details in Exhibits 11-4 and 11-5 are taken from Note 3 of Ford's annual report that also notes the following: "On November 18, 2008 we sold a portion of our investment in Mazda and reclassified our remaining investment to Marketable Securities. The fair value of our investment in Mazda at December 31, 2008 was $322 million." As we will see shortly, when Ford owned 33% of Mazda, it was accounted for using the equity method and now, with only 14% ownership the appropriate accounting has changed to the market method for trading securities.

All marketable securities held at January 1, 2008, or subsequently acquired are reported as trading securities. Where available, we use quoted market prices to measure fair value. If quoted market prices are not available, such as for federal agency securities, asset-backed securities, and corporate obligations, prices for similar assets and matrix pricing models are used. In certain cases, where there is limited transparency to valuation inputs, we may contact securities dealers and obtain dealer quotes.

Investments in marketable and loaned securities at December 31 were as follows (in millions):

	2008		2007	
	Fair Value	Unrealized Gains/(Losses)(a)	Fair Value	Unrealized Gains/(Losses)(a)
Automotive Sector				
Trading(b)	$ 9,296	$(1,443)	$10,901	$(55)
Available-for-sale	—	—	1,458	9
Total Automotive sector	9,296	(1,443)	12,359	(46)
Financial Services Sector				
Trading	8,607	(32)	1	—
Available-for-sale	—	—	3,147	9
Held-to-maturity	—	—	8	—
Total Financial Services sector	8,607	(32)	3,156	9
Intersector elimination(b).	(492)	—	—	—
Total Company.	$17,411	$(1,475)	$15,515	$(37)

(a) Unrealized gains/(losses) are reflected in fair value data provided in this table; unrealized gains/(losses) on trading securities are recorded in income on a current period basis.
(b) The Fair Value column reflects an investment in Ford Credit debt securities shown at a carrying value of $492 million (estimated fair value of which is $437 million) at December 31, 2008.

EXHIBIT 11-4

Ford Motor Company

Note 3. Marketable, Loaned, and Other Securities

	Amortized Cost	Unrealized Gains	Unrealized Losses	Fair Value
Automotive Sector				
Available-for-sale				
U.S. government	$ 214	$ 1	$—	$ 215
Mortgage-backed	575	6	1	580
Other debt securities	660	3	—	663
Total Automotive sector	$1,449	$10	$ 1	$1,458
Financial Services Sector				
Available-for-sale				
U.S. government	$ 632	$ 1	$—	$ 633
Government-sponsored enterprises	1,944	4	—	1,948
Mortgage-backed securities	324	2	1	325
Other debt securities	139	2	1	140
Equity securities.	99	2	—	101
Subtotal	3,138	11	2	3,147
Held-to-maturity	8	—	—	8
Total Financial Services sector	$3,146	$11	$ 2	$3,155

EXHIBIT 11-5

Ford's Available-for-Sale and Held-to-Maturity Securities at December 31, 2007

($ in millions)

INTERPRETING FINANCIAL STATEMENTS

Suppose Chavez Company had $100,000 of marketable securities on its balance sheet at the beginning of 20X0 and the market value of these securities increased to $108,000 during 20X0. Regardless of whether these are trading securities or available-for-sale securities, when the market value of the securities increases by $8,000, the marketable securities asset increases by $8,000. What other change in the balance sheet is necessary to keep the balance sheet equation in balance if these are trading securities? If they are available-for-sale securities?

Answer

Gains and losses on trading securities, the annual *change* in market value each period, appear in the income statement. Therefore,

if Chavez Company's securities are trading securities, its net income will include the $8,000 gain, and the retained earnings component of stockholders' equity will increase by $8,000, balancing the $8,000 increase in assets.

Because gains and losses on available-for-sale securities are not part of net income, they do not affect retained earnings. Rather, if Chavez Company's securities are available-for-sale securities, the $8,000 gain will increase other comprehensive income, which increases a separate part of stockholders' equity, accumulated other comprehensive income. As explained in Chapter 2, other comprehensive income includes all changes in equity that are not part of net income and are not the result of transactions with stockholders.

comprehensive income

Net income plus other comprehensive income and includes all changes in equity except those arising from transactions with stockholders.

Comprehensive Income

Net income and other comprehensive income combine to form **comprehensive income**—a summary of all changes in equity except those arising from transactions with stockholders. Two similar firms, one with trading securities and one with available-for-sale securities would not report comparable net income but would have comparable comprehensive income. There are a few items of other comprehensive income besides net income and changes in the value of available-for-sale securities, but they are beyond the scope of this text.

In the balance sheet, included in owners' equity, Ford reports Accumulated Other Comprehensive Income (Loss) of $(10,085) million in 2008 and $(558) million in 2007. These are cumulative amounts. The accumulated other comprehensive loss increased by $9,527 million during 2008. Included with other items of other comprehensive income (loss) are Ford's gains and losses on its available-for-sale securities.

Long-Term Investments in Bonds

Chapter 9 explained how firms account for bonds payable. The issuer amortizes bond discounts and premiums as periodic adjustments of interest expense using the effective-interest method. Investing firms use a similar method to account for investments in bonds held to maturity.

OBJECTIVE 3

Report long-term investments in bonds.

Bonds Held to Maturity

Exhibit 11-6 should look familiar. It is like Exhibit 9-4 on page 405, but it takes the perspective of the investor rather than the issuer. Therefore, we use the phrase *book value* to refer to the first column instead of the label net liability used in Exhibit 9-4. Recall that book value is a general term for the amounts reported in the financial statements.

Exhibit 11-6 shows the values for 10,000, 2-year bonds paying interest semiannually with a face value of $1,000 each and a 10% coupon rate (5% interest every 6 months). The bonds were issued to yield 12%. Because they pay only a 10% coupon interest rate, they are sold at a discount. Therefore an investor acquiring the whole issue would pay only $9,653,500. Interest (rental payment for the $9,653,500) takes two forms—four semiannual cash receipts of $500,000 (5% × $10 million), plus an extra lump-sum receipt of $346,500 ($10 million face value less amount paid at issue) at maturity.

The extra $346,500 to be paid at maturity (the discount) relates to using the proceeds over the 2 years. Therefore, like the issuer, the investor amortizes the discount:

	6/30/10	12/31/10	6/30/11	12/31/11
Semiannual interest revenue:				
Cash interest payments, .05 × $10 million	$500,000	$500,000	$500,000	$500,000
Amortization of $346,500 discount*	79,207	83,959	88,997	94,337
Semiannual interest revenue	$579,207	$583,959	$588,997	$594,337

*For the amortization schedule, see column 4 of Exhibit 11-6. Note that $79,207 + $83,959 + $88,997 + $94,337 = $346,500.

As Exhibit 11-6 shows, the discount makes up the difference between the coupon interest rate of 10% and the market interest rate of 12%. Amortization of a discount increases the interest revenue. Investor accounting for bonds issued at a premium is similar, except that amortization of premium decreases the interest revenue of investors.

Exhibit 11-7 shows how the investor and the issuer account for the bonds throughout the bonds' lives. Note that interest revenue for the investor and interest expense for the issuer are identical in each period.

For 6 Months Ended	(1) Beginning Book Value	(2) Effective Interest @ 6%*	(3) Nominal Interest @ 5%	(4) Discount Amortized (2)–(3)	Period End Values Face Amount	Period End Values Unamortized Discount	Period End Values Ending Book Value
12/31/09	—	—	—	—	$10,000,000	$346,500	$ 9,653,500
6/30/10	$9,653,500	$579,207	$500,000	$79,207	10,000,000	267,293†	9,732,707
12/31/10	9,732,707	583,959	500,000	83,959	10,000,000	183,334†	9,816,666
6/30/11	9,816,666	588,997	500,000	88,997	10,000,000	94,337	9,905,663
12/31/11	9,905,663	594,337	500,000	94,337	10,000,000	0	10,000,000

*To avoid rounding errors, an unrounded actual effective rate slightly under 6% was used.
†$346,500 – $79,207 = $267,293; $267,293 – $83,959 = $183,334; etc.

EXHIBIT 11-6

Effective Interest Amortization of Bond Discount

		Investor's Records				Issuer's Records		
12/31/09	1.	Investment in bonds	9,653,500		1.	Cash	9,653,500	
		Cash		9,653,500		Discount on bonds payable	346,500	
						Bonds payable		10,000,000
6/30/10	2.	Cash	500,000		2.	Interest expense	579,207	
		Investment in bonds	79,207			Discount on bonds payable		79,207
		Interest revenue		579,207		Cash		500,000
12/31/10		Cash	500,000			Interest expense	583,959	
		Investment in bonds	83,959			Discount on bonds payable		83,959
		Interest revenue		583,959		Cash		500,000
6/30/11		Cash	500,000			Interest expense	588,997	
		Investment in bonds	88,997			Discount on bonds payable		88,997
		Interest revenue		588,997		Cash		500,000
12/31/11		Cash	500,000			Interest expense	594,337	
		Investment in bonds	94,337			Discount on bonds payable		94,337
		Interest revenue		594,337		Cash		500,000
12/31/11	3.	Cash	10,000,000		3.	Bonds payable	10,000,000	
		Investment in bonds		10,000,000		Cash		10,000,000

EXHIBIT 11-7

Accounting for Bonds

PANEL A: INVESTOR'S LOSS

Carrying amount		
Face or par value	$10,000,000	
Deduct: Unamortized discount on bonds*	183,334	$9,816,666
Cash received		9,600,000
Difference, loss on sale		$ 216,666

*The remaining discount is $88,997 + $94,337 = $183,334, or $346,500 − $79,207 − $83,959 = $183,334.

PANEL B: JOURNAL ENTRIES AT DECEMBER 31, 2010

Investor's Records		Issuer's Records	
Cash	9,600,000	Bonds payable	10,000,000
Loss on disposal of bonds	216,666	Discount on bonds payable	183,334
Investment in bonds	9,816,666	Gain on early extinguishment	216,666
To record the sale of bonds on the open market		Cash	9,600,000
		To record the repurchase of bonds on the open market.	

EXHIBIT 11-8

Early Extinguishment

Early Extinguishment of Investment

Suppose in our example that the issuer buys back all its bonds on the open market for $9.6 million on December 31, 2010 (after all interest payments and amortization were recorded for 2010). The investor's loss is calculated in panel A of Exhibit 11-8. The journal entries for the investor and the issuer are shown in panel B.

Recall that this same extinguishment of debt was initially analyzed from the issuer's viewpoint in Chapter 9 on page 409. For the issuer to extinguish the bonds early, either the bond must grant the issuer the right to repay the debt early or the investor must choose to sell the bonds back to the issuer.

The Market and Equity Methods for Intercorporate Investments

Many companies invest in the equity securities of another company. The accounting for equity securities from the issuer's point of view was discussed in Chapter 10. The investor's accounting depends on the relationship between the "investor" and the "investee." The question is: How much can the investor influence the operations of the investee? For example, the holder of a small number of shares in a company's stock cannot affect how the company invests its money, conducts its business, or declares and pays its dividends. We call this type of investor a passive investor. Such investors use the market method described earlier, and report the investment at market value and record dividends as income when received.

As investors acquire more substantial holdings of a company's stock, they have increased influence. A stockholder with 2% or 3% ownership of a company has little difficulty making appointments to speak with company management. At 5% ownership, U.S. law requires the investor to report the ownership publicly in a filing with the SEC. As ownership interest rises to 20% and beyond, the investor begins to affect decisions, to appoint directors, and so on.

Once the investor has "significant influence," a term that both IFRS and U.S. GAAP define as 20%–50% ownership unless a company can clearly demonstrate otherwise, the market method no longer reflects the economic relationship between the influential investor and the investee (or **affiliated company**). Such an investor must use the **equity method**, which records the investment at acquisition cost and makes adjustments for the investor's share of dividends and earnings or losses experienced by the investee after the date of investment. As a result, the investor's share of the investee's earnings increases the book value at which the investment is carried and reported. Likewise, dividends received from the investee and the investor's share of the investee's losses reduce this carrying amount.

How do companies apply the market and equity methods? Suppose Buyit Corporation invests $80 million in each of two companies, Passiveco and Influential. Influential has a total market value of $200 million, generates earnings of $30 million, and pays dividends of $10 million. Because of its $80 million investment, Buyit owns 40% ($80 million ÷ $200 million) of Influential and must account for that investment using the equity method. Passiveco, however, is four times larger. It has a total market value of $800 million, generates earnings of $120 million, and pays dividends of $40 million. Buyit thus owns only 10% ($80 million ÷ $800 million) of Passiveco and uses the market method to account for this investment.

We compare the methods in Exhibit 11-9. Panel A shows the effects on the balance sheet equation, and panel B shows the different journal entries for the two cases. The example assumes that the market values of Passiveco and Influential do not change during the period.

Under the market method, Buyit recognizes income from Passiveco when dividends are received. Although the income statement and retained earnings are affected, Buyit's investment account is unaffected by the event. It remains at $80 million. In contrast, under the equity method, Buyit recognizes income as Influential earns it instead of when Influential pays dividends. Cash dividends from Influential do not affect net income; they increase cash and decrease the investment balance. Buyit's claim on Influential grows by its share of Influential's net income and the dividend is a partial liquidation of Buyit's "claim." It would be double-counting to include the $4 million of dividends as income after the $12 million of income is already recognized in Buyit's income statement as it is earned. Thus the investment

OBJECTIVE 4

Contrast the equity and market methods of accounting for investments.

affiliated company
A company that has 20%–50% of its voting shares owned by another company.

equity method
Accounting for an investment at acquisition cost, adjusted for the investor's share of dividends and earnings or losses of the investee subsequent to the date of investment.

PANEL A: EFFECTS ON THE BALANCE SHEET EQUATION

| | Market Method—Passiveco* | | | | Equity Method—Influential** | | | |
| | A | | = | L + SE | | A | | = | L + SE |
	Cash	Investments		Liab.	SE	Cash	Investment		Liab.	SE
1. Acquisition	−80	+80	=			−80	+80	=		
2. a. Net income of Passiveco	No entry and no effect									
b. Net income of Influential							+12	=		+12
3. a. Dividends from Passiveco	+4		=		+4					
b. Dividends from Influential						+4	−4	=		
Effect for year	−76	+80	=		+4	−76	+88	=		+12

*Passiveco: Under the market method, the investment account is unaffected. The dividend increases the cash amount by $4 million. Dividend revenue increases stockholders' equity by $4 million.

**Influential: Under the equity method, the investment account has a net increase of $8 million for the year. The dividend increases the cash account by $4 million and reduces investments. Investment revenue increases stockholders' equity by $12 million.

PANEL B: JOURNAL ENTRIES

Cost Method—Passiveco			Equity Method—Influential		
1. Investment in Passiveco	80		1. Investment in Influential.	80	
Cash		80	Cash		80
2. No entry.			2. Investment in Influential.	12	
			Investment revenue[†]		12
3. Cash	4		3. Cash	4	
Dividend revenue[‡]		4	Investment in Influential		4

[†]Frequently called "equity in earnings of affiliated companies."
[‡]Frequently called "dividend income."

EXHIBIT 11-9

Comparing Market and Equity Methods

(in million of dollars)

account grows by $8 million during the year ($12 million of income less $4 million of dividends received).

The major reason for using the equity method instead of the market method is that the equity method does a better job of recognizing increases or decreases in the economic resources that the investor can influence. The reported net income of an "equity" investor (an investor who owns more than 20% of a company and thus uses the equity method) is increased by its share of net income or decreased by its share of net loss recognized by the investee.

Why does GAAP not permit shares accounted for under the equity method to be carried as an asset valued at market price? One explanation is that market prices are only good estimates of sales prices when small transactions occur. For example, 55 million of the 2.2 billion outstanding shares of Ford changed hands on August 22, 2009. August is a month of relatively low trading volumes and Ford usually trades 114 million shares per day. An investor who wanted to sell 100, 1,000, or even 100,000 shares could do so at about the $7.74 per share market price observed that day. However, if an investor owned 30% of Ford and wanted to sell those 600 million shares, it could have a huge effect on the market price, potentially driving it down sharply. Thus, quoted market prices are not good measures of the value of large ownership interests. In addition, observed market prices may not be good estimates of the value of larger equity interests because the investor and investee have significant business relationships. For example, they may be customer and supplier or have joint R&D enterprises, or they may have overlapping boards of directors. In such cases, sale of a large investment interest might also mean significant changes to future business relationships and therefore changes in the value of the investee.

Summary Problem for Your Review

PROBLEM

The following is a summary of material from a Dow Chemical annual report ($ in millions):

	$:
Marketable securities and interest-bearing deposits	706
	:
Total current assets	8,847
Investments:	
Investment in nonconsolidated affiliates	1,359
Other investments	2,872
Noncurrent receivables	390
Total investments	4,621
Properties	24,276
Less: Accumulated depreciation	15,786
Net property	8,490
Goodwill	1,834
Deferred charges and other assets	1,707
Total	$25,499

Note that the statements are somewhat compressed and no detail for current assets is shown.

1. Suppose Marketable Securities included a $24 million portfolio of equity securities. Their market values on the following March 31, June 30, and September 30 were $20, $23, and $28 million, respectively. Compute the following:
   a. Carrying amount of the portfolio on each of the three dates
   b. Gain (loss) on the portfolio for each of the three quarters
2. Suppose the $2,872 million of Other Investments included a $9 million investment in the debentures of an affiliate that was being held to maturity. The debentures had a par value of $10 million and a 10% nominal rate of interest, payable June 30 and December 31. Their market rate of interest when the investment was made was 12%. Prepare the Dow journal entry for the semiannual receipt of interest on June 30.
3. Suppose Dow's 20%–50% owned companies had net income of $200 million. Dow received cash dividends of $70 million from these companies. No other transactions occurred. Prepare the pertinent journal entries. Assume that on average Dow owns 40% of the companies.

SOLUTION

1. Amounts are in millions.
   a. Market: $20, $23, and $28.
   b. $20 − $24 = $4 loss; $23 − $20 = $3 gain; $28 − $23 = $5 gain. Gain or loss would be reported in the income statement for trading securities or in other comprehensive income for securities available for sale.

2.
Cash	500,000	
Other investments (in bonds)	40,000	
Interest revenue		540,000

Six months' interest earned
is .5 × .12 × $9,000,000 = $540,000
Amortization is $540,000 − (cash received of
.5 × .10 × $10,000,000) = $540,000 − $500,000

3.
Investments in 20%–50% owned companies	80,000,000	
Investment revenue		80,000,000

To record 40% share of $200 million income

Cash	70,000,000	
Investments in 20%–50% owned companies		70,000,000

To record dividends received from 20% to 50% owned companies

Consolidated Financial Statements

parent company

A company owning more than 50% of the voting shares of another company, called the subsidiary company.

subsidiary

A corporation owned or controlled by a parent company through the ownership of more than 50% of the voting stock.

So far we have dealt with partial ownership of one company by another. Sometimes, though, one company owns enough of another to essentially have control over its decisions. This may be a case where, as in the historical case of Ford and Jaguar, one company buys 100% of another company. In other cases, one company buys a majority (more than 50%) share of a second company and effectively takes control of that second company. In cases where one company has control over another, a parent–subsidiary relationship exists. The **parent company** is the owner, and the **subsidiary** is the "owned" company that is fully controlled by the parent. Parent and subsidiary companies must prepare *consolidated financial statements*.

Both IFRS and U.S. GAAP require consolidated statements when one company has control over another, but they define "control" slightly differently. IFRS places greater reliance on unusual facts and circumstance. Both generally require consolidation if ownership is greater than 50%. However, under IFRS if a single large shareholder held 49% and controlled board seats the 51% shareholder would typically use the equity method. Similarly, under IFRS, a parent company might own less than 50% of a subsidiary company but consolidate it because of its ability to control the actions of the subsidiary. Under GAAP consolidation is generally restricted to situations where a parent has financial control of over 50% of the voting rights. Thus there will be cases where under IFRS a subsidiary company must be consolidated while it is treated as an equity investment under U.S. GAAP.

Why have subsidiaries? Why not integrate the smaller companies into the larger parent to create a single legal entity? The reasons include limiting the liabilities in a risky venture, saving income taxes, conforming with government regulations with respect to a part of the business, doing business in a foreign country, and expanding in an orderly way while retaining the ability to subsequently sell or spin off the separate corporate subsidiary. For example, there are often tax advantages for the sellers when an acquisition involves selling the capital stock of a going concern instead of its individual assets. Sometimes foreign subsidiaries face more favorable treatment from their country of residence than a foreign parent corporation would experience. Or, as when Merck spun off Medco, the transaction was easier and less costly because Medco was an existing separate subsidiary corporation.

Subsidiaries are not folded into the parent company, but instead remain separate legal entities from their parents. One parent can have numerous subsidiaries. Ford Motor Company has some 60 different subsidiaries just in the United States. So how do we account for subsidiaries if they are separate legal entities? We start by keeping records for the subsidiary that are independent of the parent's, then we combine the financial statements of the parent company with those of its subsidiaries to create consolidated statements.

The Acquisition

To illustrate consolidated financial statements, consider two companies: the parent (P) and a subsidiary (S). Initially, they are separate companies with assets of $650 million and $400 million, respectively. P acquires all the stock of S by purchasing the shares from the company's current owners for $213 million paid in cash. We illustrate this transaction in panel A of Exhibit 11-10. Panel B shows the balance sheets of the two companies before and after this transaction. Panel C shows the journal entries for the acquisition. Figures in this and subsequent tables and discussion are in millions.

This purchase transaction is a simple exchange of one asset for another, from P's perspective. In terms of the balance sheet equation, cash declines by $213, and the asset account, Investment in S, increases by the same amount (remember that amounts are in millions). The subsidiary S is entirely unaffected from an accounting standpoint, although it now has one centralized owner with unquestionable control over economic decisions S may make in the future. In this example, the purchase price and the "Investment in S" equal the stockholders' equity of the acquired company. Note that the $213 purchase price is paid to the former owners of S as private investors. The $213 is not an addition to the existing assets and stockholders' equity of S. That is, the books of S are unaffected by P's investment and by P's subsequent accounting thereof. S still exists as a separate legal entity, but with a new owner, P.

Each legal entity keeps its own set of books. Interestingly, the consolidated entity does not keep it own set of books. Instead, accountants use working papers to prepare the consolidated statements as shown schematically in Exhibit 11-11.

How do we consolidate the financial statements? Basically, we add up the individual financial statement values of the parent and the subsidiary. Consider a consolidated balance sheet prepared immediately after P's acquisition of S. The consolidated statement shows the details of all assets and

EXHIBIT 11-10

Before and After the Acquisition, Parent (P) Buys Subsidiary (S) for $213

($ in millions)

PANEL A: THE EVENTS

100% Purchase of S by P

Before Purchase

Purchase

Cash

S Shares

P Pays Cash to Shareholders in S

After Purchase

Dashed line defines consolidated corporation

PANEL B: THE BALANCE SHEETS

	Before Purchase		After Purchase	
	S	**P**	**S**	**P**
Cash	$100	$300	$100	$ 87
Net plant	300	350	300	350
Investment in S				213
Total assets	$400	$650	$400	$650
Accounts payable	$187	$100	$187	$100
Bonds payable	—	100	—	100
Stockholders' equity	213	450	213	450
Total liabilities and SE	$400	$650	$400	$650

PANEL C: THE JOURNAL ENTRIES

P Books

Investment in S.   213

  Cash.   213

S Books

No entry

EXHIBIT 11-11

Preparing Consolidated Statements

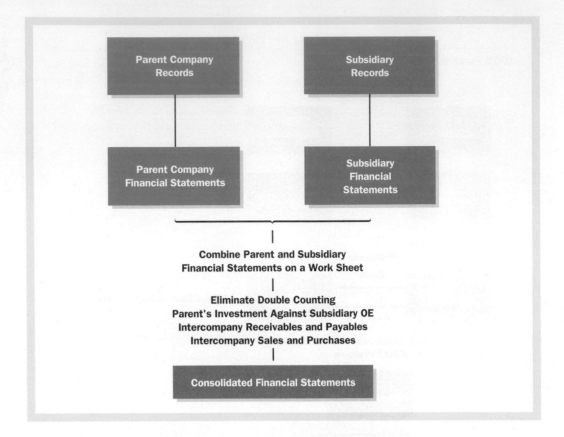

liabilities of both the parent and the subsidiary. The Investment in S account on P's books represents P's investment in S, which is really composed of all the assets and liabilities of S. This same amount is represented in S's books by stockholders' equity. If the consolidated statements simply add the individual balance sheet values of S and P, the $213 amount is represented twice, once as P's Investment in S account, and again in S's stockholders' equity. The consolidated statements should not count this amount twice because the result would misstate the true assets and liabilities. We avoid this double-counting by eliminating the investment in S on P's books, and the stockholders' equity on S's books.

On the work sheet for consolidating the balance sheets, the entry to eliminate the double-counting of ownership interest in journal format is as follows:

| Stockholders' equity (on S books). . . . . | 213 | |
| Investment in S (on P books). . . . . | | 213 |

Separately, after the purchase, P has assets of $650 and S has assets of $400, so you might think the consolidated company would have assets totaling $1,050. However, when we consolidate and eliminate the double-counting of the investment amount in S, the consolidated assets are $1,050 − $213, or $837. The consolidated result, expressed in terms of the accounting equation, shows consolidated liabilities of $387 and stockholders' equity of $450 as follows:

100% Ownership

	Assets			=	Liabilities	+	Stockholders' Equity
	Investment in S	+	Cash and Other Assets	=	Accounts Payable, etc.	+	Stockholders' Equity
P's accounts, Jan. 1							
Before acquisition			650	=	200	+	450
Acquisition of S	+213		−213	=			
S's accounts, Jan. 1			400	=	187	+	213
Intercompany eliminations	−213			=			−213
Consolidated, Jan. 1	0	+	837	=	387	+	450

After Acquisition

After the initial acquisition, P accounts for its long-term investment in S by the same equity method used to account for an unconsolidated ownership interest of 20%–50%. Suppose S has a net income of $50 million for the subsequent year (year one). The parent company P using the equity method accounts for the net income of its subsidiary by increasing its Investment in S account and its Stockholders' Equity account (in the form of retained earnings) by 100% of $50 million.

The income statements for the year are as follows (numbers in millions assumed):

	P	S	Consolidated
Sales	$900	$300	$1,200
Expenses	800	250	1,050
Operating income	$100	$ 50	$150
Investment revenue*	50	—	
Net income	$150	$ 50	

*Pro rata share (100%) of subsidiary net income, often called equity in earnings of affiliate or subsidiary.

P's parent-company-only income statement would show its own sales and expenses plus its proportional share of S's net income (as the equity method requires). This is the leftmost column of the preceding table. The income statement for P shows the same $150 million net income as the consolidated income statement. The difference is that P's "parent-only" income statement shows its 100% share of S as a single $50 million item, whereas the consolidated income statement combines the detailed revenue and expense items for P and S. The journal entry on P's books is as follows:

```
Investment in S . . . . . . . . . . . . . . . . . . . . . . .    50
     Investment revenue* . . . . . . . . . . . . . . . . .         50
*Or "equity in net income of subsidiary."
```

To avoid counting the $50 million net income twice—once as S's net income and again as P's investment revenue—P must eliminate it in consolidation. Thus, after P records this year's net income, the amount that will eliminate the investment in S on the work sheet used for consolidating the balance sheets is $213 + $50 = $263, which is P's new Investment in S balance and S's new Stockholders' Equity.

Exhibit 11-12 reflects the changes in P's accounts, S's accounts, and the consolidated accounts ($ in millions). Consolidated statements sum the individual accounts of two or more separate legal entities. We prepare them periodically via work sheets.

Intercompany Eliminations

When accountants consolidate the financial records of two companies, they must avoid double counting any items. Exhibit 11-12 emphasizes elimination of the parent's investment account and the subsidiary's owners' equity. In many cases, the parent and subsidiary do business together, which leads to another type of double-counting. For example, suppose S charges P $12 for products that cost S $10, and the sale is made on credit. The two firms make the following journal entries on their separate books:

P's Records			**S's Records**		
Merchandise inventory	12		Accounts receivable	12	
Accounts payable		12	Sales revenue		12
			Cost of goods sold	10	
			Merchandise Inventory		10

However, has anything happened economically? No—as far as the consolidated entity is concerned, the product is just moved from one location to another. If P paid cash to S, the cash just shifts from "one pocket to another." So this transaction is not an important one from the perspective of the consolidated company, and it should be eliminated. It is important that each separate legal entity keeps track of its own transactions for its own records. When we consolidate, we eliminate the intercompany receivable and payable, eliminate the costs and revenues, and ensure

	Assets			=	Liabilities	+	Stockholders' Equity
	Investment in S	+	Cash and Other Assets	=	Accounts Payable, etc.	+	Stockholders' Equity
P's account							
Beginning of year	+213	+	437	=	200	+	450
Operating income			+100	=			+100*
Share of S income	+50			=			+50*
End of year	263	+	537	=	200	+	600
S's accounts							
Beginning of year			400	=	187	+	+213
Net income			+50	=			+50*
End of year			450	=	187	+	263
Intercompany eliminations	−263			=			−263
Consolidated, end of year	0	+	987	=	387	+	600

*Changes in the retained earnings portion of stockholders' equity.

EXHIBIT 11-12

Consolidation Work Sheet

that the consolidated entity carries the inventory at its original cost, $10. We eliminate these items with the following consolidation journal entries on the consolidation work sheet:

Accounts payable (P)	12	
Accounts receivable (S)		12
Sales revenue (S)	12	
Cost of goods sold (S)		10
Merchandise Inventory (P)		2

The parenthetical letters show whose records contain the underlying account balances. Remember, neither company records these entries on its individual records. They exist only in the consolidation work sheet.

Noncontrolling Interests

OBJECTIVE 6

Incorporate noncontrolling interests into consolidated financial statements.

---

noncontrolling interests
The outside shareholders' interests, as opposed to the parent's interests, in a subsidiary corporation.

Our example of the consolidation of P and S assumes P purchased 100% of S. However, companies often purchase less than 100% of a subsidiary. One company can control another with just 51% of the shares. For example, Corning owns more than 50% but less than 100% of many companies. Corning consolidates each company into its consolidated financial statements, but recognizes the claim on some of the consolidated assets held by other owners. These claims are called noncontrolling interests. **Noncontrolling interests** represent the claims of nonmajority shareholders in the assets and earnings of a company whose accounts are consolidated into the accounts of the major shareholder. Prior to 2009, these partial interests were called minority interest, and that is the wording you will frequently see in older financial statements. On its consolidated 2008 earnings statement, Ford shows a reduction of net income of $214 million due to noncontrolling interests. On the consolidated balance sheet, Ford shows a $1,195 million of noncontrolling interests. Note that the labels are identical: noncontrolling interests. Thus, it is up to you, the reader, to know that the $214 million on the income statement is the current year increase, whereas the $1,195 million on the balance sheet is the cumulative effect.

To apply this concept to our example, assume that our parent company (P) bought only 90% of S. Exhibit 11-13, using the basic figures of the previous example, shows the overall approach to a consolidated balance sheet immediately after the acquisition. In panel A, the graphic shows that some shareholders of S continue to have a noncontrolling interest in the consolidated entity. P pays $192 million for 90% of S (0.90 × $213 million). The noncontrolling

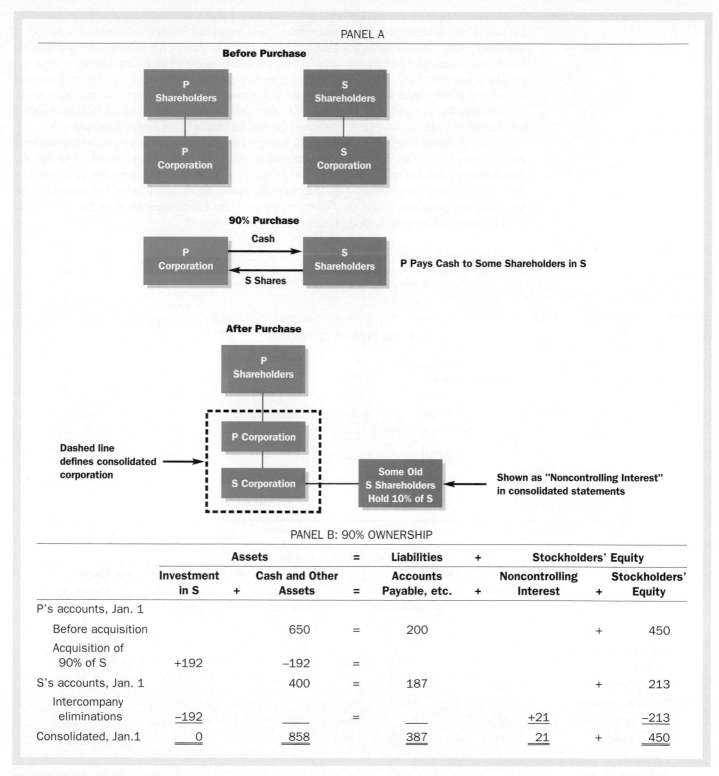

PANEL A

Before Purchase

P Shareholders

S Shareholders

P Corporation

S Corporation

90% Purchase

Cash

P Corporation → S Shareholders

S Shares

P Pays Cash to Some Shareholders in S

After Purchase

P Shareholders

P Corporation

S Corporation

Dashed line defines consolidated corporation →

Some Old S Shareholders Hold 10% of S

← Shown as "Noncontrolling Interest" in consolidated statements

PANEL B: 90% OWNERSHIP

	Assets		=	Liabilities	+	Stockholders' Equity		
	Investment in S	+ Cash and Other Assets	=	Accounts Payable, etc.	+	Noncontrolling Interest	+	Stockholders' Equity
P's accounts, Jan. 1								
Before acquisition		650	=	200			+	450
Acquisition of 90% of S	+192	−192	=					
S's accounts, Jan. 1		400	=	187			+	213
Intercompany eliminations	−192		=			+21		−213
Consolidated, Jan.1	0	858	=	387		21	+	450

EXHIBIT 11-13

90% Purchase of S: P Pays Cash to Some S Shareholders; Some S Shareholders Retain Noncontrolling Interest

interest is 10%, or $21 million. (All dollar amounts are rounded to the nearest million.) Panel B illustrates that P's balance sheet shows the $192 million investment, and in consolidation we show the noncontrolling interest at $21 million, the amount by which the $213 million of net assets added in consolidation exceeds P's investment of $192 million. You can think of the noncontrolling interest as representing the interests of those shareholders who own the 10% of the subsidiary stockholders' equity that is not owned by the parent company.

Suppose the 90% acquisition occurred on January 1 and S has net income of $50 million for the year. P and S follow the same procedures in their individual income statements, regardless of whether P owns 100% or 90% of S. P reports either 100% or 90% of S's earnings as a line item on P's income statement labeled something like Equity in Earnings of Subsidiary. However, the presence of a noncontrolling interest changes the consolidated income statement. In consolidation, all the income is combined, and then the 10% share due to noncontrolling shareholders is subtracted. We illustrate this in panel A of Exhibit 11-14. Note that the parent-only income statement shows net income of $145, as does the consolidated income statement in the far right column.

Panel B shows how the noncontrolling interest from the income statement during the year increases the level of the noncontrolling interest on the balance sheet at year-end. Note that the noncontrolling interest of $21 that existed on January 1 increased by $5 during the year to reflect the noncontrolling shareholders' 10% interest in the year's net income of $50. As indicated in the intercompany elimination near the bottom of panel B, the eliminating entry on the work sheet used for consolidating the balance sheets is as follows:

Stockholders' equity (on S books).....................	263	
Investment in S (on P books)......................		237
Noncontrolling interest (on consolidated statements)......		26

PANEL A: THE INCOME STATEMENT

	P	S	Consolidated
Sales	$900	$300	$1,200
Expenses	800	250	1,050
Operating income	$100	$ 50	$ 150
Investment revenue*	45	—	
Net income	$145	$ 50	
Noncontrolling interest (10%) in subsidiary's net income			5
Net income to consolidated entity			$ 145

*Pro rata share (90%) of subsidiary net income, often called equity in earnings of affiliate or subsidiary.

PANEL B: THE BALANCE SHEET

	Assets			=	Liabilities	+	Stockholders' Equity		
	Investment in S	+	Cash and Other Assets	=	Accounts Payable, etc.	+	Noncontrolling Interest	+	Stockholders' Equity
P's accounts									
Beginning of year, before acquisition			650	=	200			+	450
Acquisition	+192		−192	=					
Operating income			+100	=					+100
Share of S income	+45			=					+45
End of year	237	+	558	=	200			+	595
S's accounts									
Beginning of year			400	=	187			+	213
Net income			+50	=					+50
End of year		+	450	=	187				+263
Intercompany eliminations	−237			=			+26**		−263
Consolidated, end of year	0	+	1,008	=	387	+	26**	+	595

**Beginning noncontrolling interest plus noncontrolling interest in net income: 21 + (.10 × 50) = 21 + 5 = 26.

EXHIBIT 11-14

Effect of 90% Ownership During the Year

Summary Problem for Your Review

PROBLEM

1. Review the section on noncontrolling interests on pages 512–514. Suppose P buys 60% of the stock of S for a cost of .60 × $213, or $128 million. The total assets of P consist of this $128 million plus $522 million of other assets, a total of $650 million. P's Liabilities and Stockholders' Equity can be found in Exhibit 11-10. The S assets and equities are unchanged from the amount given in Exhibit 11-10 on page 509. Prepare an analysis showing what amounts would appear in a consolidated balance sheet immediately after the acquisition.

2. Suppose S has a net income of $50 million for the year, and P has an operating income of $100 million. Other details of their income statements are as described in the example on page 514. Prepare an analysis showing what amounts would appear in a consolidated income statement and year-end consolidated balance sheet.

SOLUTION

1.

	Assets			=	Liabilities	+	Stockholders' Equity		
	Investment in S	+	Cash and Other Assets	=	Accounts Payable, etc.	+	Noncontrolling Interest	+	Stockholders' Equity
P's accounts, January 1:									
Before acquisition			650	=	200			+	450
Acquisition of 60% of S	+128		−128	=					
S's accounts, January 1			400	=	187			+	213
Intercompany eliminations	−128			=			+85		−213
Consolidated, January 1	0	+	922	=	387	+	85	+	450

2.

	P	S	Consolidated
Sales	$900	$300	$1,200
Expenses	800	250	1,050
Operating income	$100	$ 50	$ 150
Pro rata share (60%) of unconsolidated subsidiary net income	30	—	
Net income	$130	$ 50	
Outside interest (40%) in consolidated subsidiary net income (noncontrolling interest in income)			20
Net income to consolidated entity			$ 130

The balance sheet equation that shows the details of this analysis is at the top of the next page.

	Assets			=	Liabilities	+	Stockholders' Equity		
	Investment in S	+	Cash and Other Assets	=	Accounts Payable, etc.	+	Noncontrolling Interest	+	Stockholders' Equity
P's accounts									
Beginning of year	128	+	522*	=	200			+	450
Operating income			+100	=				+	+100
Share of S income	+30			=					+30
End of year	158	+	622	=	200			+	580
S's accounts									
Beginning of year			400	=	187			+	213
Net income			+50	=					+50
End of year			450	=	187			+	263
Intercompany eliminations	−158			=			+105†		−263
Consolidated, end of year	0	+	1,072	=	387	+	105	+	580

*650 beginning of year − 128 for acquisition = 522.
†85 beginning of year + .40 × (50) = 85 + 20 = 105.

Purchase Price Not Equal to Book Value

OBJECTIVE 7

Explain the economic meaning and financial reporting of goodwill.

When one company acquires another, the amount paid is usually higher and sometimes lower than either the net book value or the net fair value of the assets owned by the acquired company. So far, we have assumed that the total amount paid, the net book value, and the net fair value were all the same. When these amounts differ, the acquiring company uses the actual amount paid as the basis for accounting for the acquisition.

In a typical case, the acquiring company pays more than the fair value of the net assets acquired, which in turn is greater than the book value of the net assets. In such a case, consolidation requires a two-step adjustment. First, the initial consolidated statement must show all acquired assets and liabilities at their fair market value. Second, if the purchase price exceeds even the fair market value of the acquired net assets, the consolidated statement must show an asset called goodwill. **Goodwill** is the excess of the cost of an acquired company over the sum of the fair market value of its identifiable individual assets less the liabilities.

goodwill
The excess of the cost of an acquired company over the sum of the fair market value of its identifiable individual assets less the liabilities.

Why do companies pay more than the fair value of the net assets when acquiring a company? Imagine a newspaper. It has simple assets—a building, desks and computers, a printing press, and some paper and ink. Yet newspapers are often purchased for more than the value of these physical assets. The reason is that they have existing contracts, subscribers, advertising customers, and name recognition—so the going concern, the familiar newspaper, is worth more than the collection of physical assets. If the existing newspaper continued and you bought similar assets and created a new competing newspaper, profits would be a long-time coming.

Goodwill can be a significant portion of consolidated assets. **Ford** reported $1.6 billion of goodwill at December 31, 2008. This is 1% of the total consolidated assets of Ford. However, goodwill is a much more significant asset for **Walt Disney Company**, where its $22 billion in goodwill is 35% of its total assets of $62 billion.

Accounting for Goodwill

To see the impact of goodwill on the consolidated statements, refer to our example in Exhibit 11-10 where P acquired a 100% interest in S. Suppose P paid $253 million rather than $213 million. Upon examining S's assets, accountants found that a building with a book value of $20 million had a fair market value of $35 million. Fair market values of all other assets equaled their book values. This means that, of the $40 million excess of purchase price over book value of net assets, we can attribute $15 million to identifiable assets (the building), and the remaining $25 million is goodwill. The eliminating entry on the work sheet for consolidating the balance sheet, illustrated in Exhibit 11-15, is as follows (in millions of dollars):

Stockholders' equity (on S books).	213	
Goodwill (on consolidated balance sheet)	25	
Building (added to S's book value only on		
consolidated balance sheet).	15	
Investment in S (on P's books)		253

Subsequent to the acquisition, under both IFRS and U.S. GAAP, the goodwill will decrease only if the acquiring company does not maintain the value of the goodwill. If the value of the goodwill decreases—called **impairment of goodwill**—the consolidated company must reduce the goodwill account by the amount of the decrease in value and charge that amount as an expense. In contrast, the consolidated company will depreciate any amount of purchase price assigned to an identifiable asset over the remaining life of that asset. Thus, a company that plans to maintain the value of the goodwill and wants to report high net income prefers to assign the excess of the purchase price over the book value to goodwill rather than to identifiable assets.

impairment of goodwill
Reductions of the goodwill account because the value of the goodwill falls below its current carrying amount.

Goodwill and Noncontrolling Interests—IFRS Versus U.S. GAAP

Accounting for goodwill under IFRS can differ slightly from that under U.S. GAAP when there are noncontrolling interests. Under U.S. GAAP, consolidated balance sheets include 100% of the goodwill even if a parent acquires less than 100% of the subsidiary. As a result, the amount of the noncontrolling interest includes the proportion of the goodwill belonging to the noncontrolling shareholders in addition to their claim on other assets and liabilities.

Companies reporting under IFRS can use the same method as those reporting under U.S. GAAP. However, they also have an option to measure the noncontrolling interest at the proportionate fair value of acquired assets without regard to goodwill. Therefore, there will be cases where both goodwill and the noncontrolling interest in a consolidated enterprise will be measured at a much higher number under U.S. GAAP than under IFRS. Why? Because under IFRS a parent company excluded the noncontrolling shareholders' portion of goodwill both from the assets (goodwill) of the consolidated entity and from the value assigned to the noncontrolling interests.

	Assets					=	Liabilities	+	Stockholders' Equity
	Investment in S	+	Cash and Other Assets	+	Goodwill	=	Accounts Payable, etc.	+	Stockholders' Equity
P's accounts									
Before acquisition			650			=	200	+	450
Acquisition of S	+253		−253			=			
S's accounts			400			=	187	+	213
Intercompany eliminations	−253		+15**		+25*	=	___		−213
Consolidated	0	+	812		25*	=	387	+	450

*The 25 million "goodwill" would appear in the consolidated balance sheet as a separate intangible asset account. It is often shown as the final item in a listing of assets.

**The $15 million increase to cash and other assets shows the increase due to the market value of the building exceeding its book value.

EXHIBIT 11-15

Creating Goodwill as of January 1

Goodwill and Abnormal Earnings

As you might suspect, the final price paid by the purchaser of an ongoing business is the culmination of a bargaining process. Therefore, the exact amount paid for goodwill is subject to the negotiations concerning the total purchase price. A popular logic for determining the maximum price follows.

Goodwill is the price paid for "excess" or "abnormal" earning power. The steps to value the abnormal earning power are summarized in panel A of Exhibit 11-16. Essentially we determine the market value of the net identifiable assets of an ordinary company (M in this case) and treat that as the reasonable cost of acquiring the ordinary earnings the company generates ($80,000 in this case). The market value is 10 times earnings. Company N has identical net assets worth $800,000, but also has location, human resource, or reputation advantages that allow it to earn an extra $20,000 more than Company M. We calculate a price for these abnormal earnings using a multiple of six. The multiples of 10 times earnings and 6 times abnormal earnings are arbitrary. Actual values differ from year to year and from company to company. But the multiple for abnormal earnings will always be smaller because these earnings are not worth as much per dollar as ordinary earnings. Why? Because abnormal earnings are likely to be harder to maintain. The total value of Company N is $920,000, as shown in panel B of Exhibit 11-16.

Equity Affiliates, Noncontrolling Interest, and the Statement of Cash Flows

Consider the cash flow statement for a company with equity affiliates (firms for which the investor uses the equity method). If it uses the direct method to report cash flows from operating activities, no special problem arises because only the cash received from the affiliate as a dividend appears as an operating cash flow. However, suppose the company uses the indirect

EXHIBIT 11-16

Valuation of Goodwill

PANEL A: COMPUTATION OF VALUES

	Ordinary Company M	Extraordinary Company N
1. Fair market value of identifiable assets, less liabilities	$800,000	$800,000
2. Normal annual earnings on net assets at 10%	80,000	80,000
3. Actual average annual earnings for past 5 years (including for Company N an excess or abnormal return of $20,000)	80,000	100,000
4. Maximum price paid for normal annual earnings is 10 times line 2	800,000	800,000
5. Maximum price paid for abnormal annual earnings (which are riskier and thus less valuable per dollar of expected earnings) is six times $20,000	—	120,000*
6. Maximum price a purchaser is willing to pay for the company (line 1 plus line 5)	800,000	920,000

*This is the most the purchaser is willing to pay for goodwill.

PANEL B: VALUE OF COMPANY

$20,000	**Abnormal layer × 6 = $120,000**
$80,000	**Normal layer × 10 =** 800,000
	Total purchase price $920,000

method. Because net earnings are increased by the investor's share of its affiliates' earnings or are decreased by its share of the affiliates' loss, we must adjust reported income for the non-cash portion of the income or loss from affiliates. Suppose the investor had net income of $7.6 million, including equity in earnings of an affiliate of $2.5 million, and received $1.3 million in dividends from the affiliate. Cash flow from the affiliate is $1.3 million. Because net earnings include $2.5 million, the indirect method must adjust net earnings by $2.5 million – $1.3 million = $1.2 million, the amount of the equity in earnings that was not received in cash.

Summary of Accounting for Equity Securities

Exhibit 11-17 summarizes the basic relationships in intercorporate investments. As we have seen, the accounting for investments in common stock depends on the nature of the investment:

1. Investments that represent more than a 50% ownership interest are usually consolidated. A subsidiary is a corporation controlled by another corporation. The usual condition for control is ownership of a majority (more than 50%) of the outstanding voting stock.
2. The equity method is generally used for a 20%–50% interest because such a level of ownership creates a presumption that the owner has the ability to exert significant influence. Under the equity method, the cost at date of acquisition and the income statement are adjusted for the investor's share of the earnings or losses of the investee subsequent to the date of investment. Dividends received from the investee reduce the carrying amount of the investment.

Percentage of Ownership	Type of Accounting	Balance Sheet Effects	Income Statement Effects	Major Journal Entries
100%	Consolidation	Individual assets, individual liabilities added together. For subsidiaries purchased for more than the fair value of identifiable net assets, goodwill is shown	Individual revenues, individual expenses added together. If goodwill exists, it must be checked for impairment	In work sheets for preparing consolidated statements, to eliminate reciprocal accounts, to avoid double-counting, and to recognize any goodwill
Greater than 50% and less than 100%	Consolidation	Same as 100% ownership, but recognition given to noncontrolling interest	Same as 100% ownership, but recognition given to noncontrolling interest near bottom of statement when consolidated net income is computed	Same as 100% ownership, but recognition of noncontrolling interests is included in work sheet entries
20% to and including 50%	Equity method	Investment carried at cost plus pro rata share of subsidiary earnings less dividends received	Equity in earnings (losses) of *affiliated* or *associated* companies shown on one line as addition to (deduction from) income	Investment............ xx Equity in earnings..... xx To record earnings Cash................. xx Investment.......... xx To record dividends received
Less than 20%	Market method	Investment carried at market value	For trading securities, annual changes affect the income statement. For available-for-sale securities, cumulative unrealized gains and losses appear in other comprehensive income	Marketable securities..... xx Income statement gain or loss......... xx To record appreciation.... Marketable securities..... xx Other comprehensive income.......... xx To record appreciation

EXHIBIT 11-17

Summary of Accounting for Equity Securities

3. Marketable equity securities are generally carried at market value when ownership is below 20%. These investments are passive in the sense that the investor exerts no significant influence on the investee. Unrealized gains and losses appear in the income statement for trading securities and in a statement of comprehensive income (for IFRS companies) or the other comprehensive income column of the statement of stockholders' equity (for U.S. GAAP companies) for available-for-sale securities.

Highlights to Remember

1 Explain why corporations invest in one another. Corporate investments arise for many reasons. Smaller investments may create a relationship that leads to communication and sharing of information. As investments rise in size, the investor obtains more influence over the investee, leading to changes in the behavior of both parties. When investments exceed 50% ownership of the investee, the investor obtains control sufficient to dictate behavior. The owner totally controls decision making and dictates what is made, to whom it is sold, from whom parts are purchased, how activity is financed, whether dividends are paid, what new assets are purchased, and so on.

2 Account for short-term investments in debt securities and equity securities. The accounting for intercorporate investments depends on the purpose of the investment, on whether it is an equity or debt security, and on the level of control the investor has over the issuer of the security. For short-term debt securities and short-term equity securities, accounting is at market. Trading securities are held to be resold, and the gains and losses from changes in market value go directly to the income statement. Marketable securities that are available-for-sale are reported at market in the balance sheet, but gains and losses are part of other comprehensive income until the securities are sold.

3 Report long-term investments in bonds. When the investor's intention is to hold debt securities to maturity, the investor's accounting uses the effective interest rate method in the same manner that the issuer does. That is, the investor amortizes discount and premium to affect interest revenue.

4 Contrast the equity and market methods of accounting for investments. For equity securities held for the long term, the accounting is linked to the investor's level of control of the issuer of the equity security. For ownership interests of less than 20%, accounting for equity securities requires classification as either available for sale or trading. The accounting is based on fair value. As the ownership interest ranges from 20% to 50%, the increasing control the investor can exert over the issuer leads to earnings recognition in the income statement, proportional to the percentage of ownership. Under the equity method, the investment account is increased by the share of the issuer's earnings (or decreased by a proportionate share of losses). When dividends are received, the investment account is decreased with no effect on earnings.

5 Prepare consolidated financial statements. As the ownership interest exceeds 50%, the investor controls the subsidiary. Consolidation, which involves combining all the assets and liabilities of the related corporate entities, is appropriate. For 100% owned subsidiaries, the main concern is the elimination of intercompany transactions: sales, receivables, and payables.

6 Incorporate noncontrolling interests into consolidated financial statements. Noncontrolling interests are the rights of other shareholders in consolidated subsidiaries that are more than 50% owned and therefore consolidated, but are not 100% owned. Noncontrolling interests are treated much like the equity interests of an investor. On the income statement, net income available to common shareholders of the consolidated entity is reduced by the proportional interests of the noncontrolling shareholders. On the balance sheet, the noncontrolling interests are a measure of the equity claims of noncontrolling shareholders on the assets of consolidated subsidiaries.

7 Explain the economic meaning and financial reporting of goodwill. Goodwill refers to the excess of the purchase price of an acquired company over the fair value of its identifiable net assets. Economically, it arises because the acquired firm has created the ability to earn extraordinary returns by creating market power. The market power might take the form of an exceptional brand name, such as what Coca-Cola has developed. Because of the brand recognition, Coca-Cola can sell soft drinks at higher prices and earn higher returns than unbranded colas. From an accounting perspective, companies record goodwill only when it is acquired by purchasing a controlling interest in another company. Companies do not amortize goodwill; they write it off (reduce it) only when management concludes that the value of the goodwill has declined (is impaired).

Accounting Vocabulary

affiliated company, p. 505
available-for-sale securities, p. 499
certificates of deposit, p. 498
commercial paper, p. 499
comprehensive income, p. 502
consolidated statements, p. 497
equity method, p. 505

goodwill, p. 516
held-to-maturity securities, p. 499
impairment of goodwill p. 517
market method, p. 500
marketable securities, p. 498
noncontrolling interests, p. 512
parent company, p. 508

short-term debt securities, p. 498
short-term equity securities, p. 499
short-term investment, p. 498
subsidiary, p. 508
trading securities, p. 499
U.S. Treasury obligations, p. 499

Assignment Material

MyAccountingLab

Questions

11-1 Why is *marketable securities* an ill-chosen term to describe short-term investments?

11-2 Distinguish among trading securities, available-for-sale securities, and held-to-maturity securities.

11-3 "The cost method is applied to investments in short-term securities." Do you agree? Explain.

11-4 "Increases in the market price of short-term investments become gains on the income statement; decreases become losses." Do you agree? Explain.

11-5 Suppose an investor buys a $1,000 face value bond for $950, a discount of $50. Will amortization of the discount increase or decrease the investor's interest income? Explain.

11-6 What is the equity method?

11-7 "The equity method is usually used for long-term investments." Do you think this is appropriate? Explain.

11-8 Contrast the *market* method with the *equity* method.

11-9 What criterion is used to determine whether a parent–subsidiary relationship exists? Are U.S. GAAP and IFRS the same or different? Explain.

11-10 Why have subsidiaries? Why not have the corporation take the form of a single legal entity?

11-11 Suppose Company A buys 100% of the common shares of Company B for cash. How does Company B record the receipt of this cash on its books?

11-12 Why does consolidating a balance sheet require "eliminating entries"?

11-13 "A consolidated income statement will show more income than a parent-company-only statement when both the parent and subsidiary have positive net income." Do you agree? Explain.

11-14 What is a noncontrolling interest?

11-15 Distinguish between *control of* a company and *significant influence over* a company.

11-16 "Goodwill is the excess of purchase price over the book values of the individual assets acquired." Do you agree? Explain.

11-17 Does GAAP require amortization of goodwill against net income? If not, when does goodwill decrease?

11-18 Why might a company prefer to own 19.9% interest in an affiliate instead of a 20.1% interest?

11-19 When is there justification for not consolidating majority-owned subsidiaries?

11-20 Suppose P company received $20,000 in cash dividends from Y company, a 40% owned affiliated company. Y company's net income was $80,000. How will P's statement of cash flows show these items using the direct method?

11-21 Why do noncontrolling interests arise in connection with consolidated statements, but not with investments in affiliated companies?

11-22 Would you expect the consolidated income statement to report higher net income than shown in the parent's separate financial statements? Explain.

Critical Thinking Questions

11-23 Consequences of Marking to Market

As president of a young technology company, you and your chief financial officer are discussing your great success in investing in other high-growth companies in your industry. When you raised $20 million in capital, you actually needed $10 million immediately so you invested the other $10 million in a portfolio of dynamic companies that you accounted for as available-for-sale securities. Over the last year, the value of these companies doubled. You are trying to figure out how next year's reported income will compare with this year's if you liquidate that portfolio and invest it in the core business.

11-24 Scoping Out an Acquisition Strategy

You recently hired a young MBA who is advising you that you should grow more aggressively and who is suggesting that you should do so by acquiring other small companies. Your cookware and tableware importing business has been quite successful, but you are not sure that this new employee's plan to acquire a series of retail cooking/kitchenware stores makes sense. What issues would you raise in discussing this proposal?

11-25 Accounting Consequences of Changing Ownership Interest

You own 19% of a company that you do business with and are considering buying another 5% of the company. The company provides a great product and great service. The company's share price has been rising because of its potential. However, it is currently not profitable from an accounting perspective because the company is doing a great deal of research and development. You have asked your CFO to advise you about the consequences of this increase in your ownership position. What would you expect the CFO to say?

11-26 Transactions Between Companies

Your company has sales of $100 million and profits of $10 million. A similar, smaller company with sales of $25 million and profits of $5 million appears to be an attractive merger candidate. You currently buy 50% of the smaller company's production. The CEO has indicated that this would be a great acquisition because it would increase sales by 25% and profits by 50%. As CFO what issues do you raise concerning this proposed purchase and the CEO's analysis.

Exercises

11-27 Trading Securities

The McMillan Company has a portfolio of trading securities consisting of common and preferred stocks. The portfolio cost $160 million on January 1. The market values of the portfolio were as follows ($ in millions): March 31, $155; June 30, $140; September 30, $152; and December 31, $160.

1. Prepare a tabulation showing the balance sheet presentations and income statement presentations for interim reporting purposes.
2. Show the journal entries for quarters 1, 2, 3, and 4.

11-28 Available-for-Sale Securities

The MacGregor Company has a portfolio of securities identical to that of the McMillan Company (see Exercise 11-27). However, MacGregor classified the portfolio as available-for-sale securities. The portfolio cost $160 million on January 1. The market values of the portfolio were as follows ($ in millions): March 31, $155; June 30, $140; September 30, $152; and December 31, $160.

1. Prepare a tabulation showing the balance sheet presentations and income statement presentations for interim reporting purposes.
2. Show the journal entries for quarters 1, 2, 3, and 4.

11-29 Bond Discount Transactions

On December 31, 20X1, a company purchased $1 million of 10-year, 10% debentures for $885,300. The market interest rate was 12%.

1. Using the balance sheet equation format, prepare an analysis of bond transactions for the investor. Assume effective interest amortization. Show entries for the investor concerning (a) purchase, (b) first semiannual interest payment, and (c) payment of maturity value.
2. Show the corresponding journal entries for the preceding (a), (b), and (c).

3. Show how the bond investment would appear on the balance sheets as of December 31, 20X1, and June 30, 20X2.

11-30 Bond Premium Transactions

On December 31, 20X1, the Guzman Company purchased $2 million of 5-year, 10% debentures for $2,162,220. The market interest rate was 8%.

1. Using the balance sheet equation format, prepare an analysis of transactions for the investor's records. Key your transactions as follows: (a) purchase, (b) first semiannual interest payment using effective interest amortization of bond premium, and (c) payment of maturity value.
2. Prepare sample journal entries for the preceding (a), (b), and (c).
3. Show how the bond-related accounts would appear on the balance sheets as of December 31, 20X1, and June 30, 20X2.

11-31 Market Method or Equity Method

Yukon Outdoor Equipment acquired 25% of the voting stock of Bearpaw Snowshoes for $60 million cash. In year 1, Bearpaw had a net income of $28 million and paid a cash dividend of $16 million.

1. Using the equity and the market methods, show the effects of the three transactions on the accounts of Yukon Outdoor Equipment. Use the balance sheet equation format. Also show the accompanying journal entries. Assume constant market value for Bearpaw.
2. Which method, equity or market, would Yukon use to account for its investment in Bearpaw? Explain.

11-32 Equity Method

Company X acquired 40% of the voting stock of Company Y for $90 million cash. In year 1, Y had a net income of $50 million and paid cash dividends of $30 million.

Prepare a tabulation that uses the equity method of accounting for X's investment in Y. Show the effects on the balance sheet equation. What is the year-end balance in the Investment in Y account under the equity method?

11-33 Consolidated Statements

Able and Baker companies had the following balance sheets at December 31, 20X8 ($ in thousands):

	Able	Baker
Assets		
Cash	$ 600	$100
Net plant	1,700	400
Total assets	$2,300	$500
Liabilities and stockholders' equity		
Accounts payable	275	$ 80
Long-term debt	425	220
Stockholders' equity	1,600	200
Total liabilities and stockholders' equity	$2,300	$500

On January 1, 20X9, Able purchased 100% of the common stock of Baker for $200,000.

1. Prepare a balance sheet for Able Company immediately after its purchase of Baker Company.
2. Prepare a balance sheet for the consolidated entity immediately after the purchase of Baker Company.
3. Suppose Able Company had net income of $250,000 in 20X9 (before recognizing its share of Baker's income) and Baker Company had net income of $40,000 in 20X9. Neither company sold items to the other. What was the 20X9 consolidated net income?

11-34 Noncontrolling Interest

Suppose P company owns 90% of S company and S company earns $200,000. What is the amount of the noncontrolling interest shown in P company's consolidated income statement? What is the amount of the noncontrolling interest shown in S company's individual income statement?

11-35 Goodwill

Megasoft, Inc., purchased 100% of the common shares of Zenatel for $270,000 on January 1, 20X7. Zenatel's balance sheet just before the acquisition was as follows ($ in thousands):

Cash	$ 90
Net fixed assets	220
Total assets	$310
Liabilities	$240
Stockholders' equity	70
Total liabilities and stockholders' equity	$310

The fair market value of Zenatel's assets and liabilities was equal to its book values.

1. Compute the amount of goodwill Megasoft would recognize on this purchase. Where would this goodwill appear on Megasoft's financial statements?
2. Megasoft's 20X7 net income from all operations excluding those of Zenatel were $100,000. Zenatel had a net loss of $10,000. Compute consolidated net income for 20X7.
3. Repeat requirement 2 assuming Megasoft concluded goodwill was impaired by $20,000.
4. How much goodwill appears on the consolidated balance sheet after requirement 3?

11-36 Affiliated Companies

Suppose P company owns 30% of S company. S company earns $200,000 and pays total dividends of $40,000 to its shareholders. What appears in the consolidated income statement of P company as a result of S company's activity? What would be the change in the account titled Investment in Equity Affiliates on P company's balance sheet?

11-37 Consolidations in Japan

A few years ago, Japan's finance ministry issued a directive requiring the 600 largest Japanese companies to produce consolidated financial statements. The previous practice had been to use parent-company-only statements. A story in *BusinessWeek* said,

> *Financial observers hope that the move will help end the tradition-honored Japanese practice of "window dressing" the parent company financial results by shoving losses onto hapless subsidiaries, whose red ink was seldom revealed.... When companies needed to show a bigger profit, they would sell their product to subsidiaries at an inflated price....Or the parent company charged a higher rent to a subsidiary company using its building.*

Could a parent company follow the quoted practices and achieve window dressing in its parent-only financial statements if it used the equity method of accounting for its intercorporate investments? Explain.

Problems

11-38 Trading Securities

Before its acquisition by **Royal Dutch Shell**, **Pennzoil Company** held a portfolio of trading equity securities that cost $660,100,000 and had a market value of $955,182,000 on January 1. Assume that the same portfolio was held until the end of the first quarter of the subsequent year. The market value of the portfolio was $980,160,000 at January 31, $940,000,000 at February 29, and $960,000,000 at March 31.

1. Prepare a tabulation showing the balance sheet presentation and income statement presentation for monthly reporting purposes.
2. Show the journal entries for January, February, and March.
3. How would your answer to requirement 1 change if the securities were classified as available for sale?

11-39 Short-Term Investments

The VanDankan Company has the following footnote to its financial statements:

Note 4: Short-Term Investments
The company holds the following short-term investments at December 31 (in thousands):

	Cost	Market Value
Trading securities		
U.S. government bonds	$670,000	$660,000
Held-to-maturity securities		
Bonds issued by Beta, Corp.	540,000	560,000
Available-for-sale securities		
Common shares of Gamma, Corp.	300,000	770,000

1. Compute the amount that VanDankan would show on its balance sheet for short-term investments.
2. Suppose the market values of the three securities at the beginning of the year had been as follows (in thousands):

U.S. government bonds	$680,000
Bonds issued by Beta, Corp.	550,000
Common shares of Gamma, Corp.	710,000

Prepare journal entries to recognize the changes in market values that would be recorded in VanDankan's books at the end of the year.

11-40 Early Extinguishment of an Investment

On December 31, 20X2, an insurance company purchased $10 million of 10-year, 10% debentures for $8,852,950. On December 31, 20X3 (after all interest payments and amortization had been recorded for 20X3), the insurance company sold all the debentures for $9 million. The market interest rate at purchase when the bonds were issued was 12%. Interest payments are semi-annual.

1. Compute the gain or loss on the sale for the insurance company (i.e., the investor).
2. Prepare the appropriate journal entries for the insurance company (i.e., the investor).

11-41 Consolidated Statements, Noncontrolling Interests

Consider the following for Chow Company (the parent) as of December 31, 20X8:

	Chow	Subsidiary*
Assets	$800,000	$200,000
Liabilities to creditors	$300,000	$ 80,000
Stockholders' equity	500,000	120,000
Total	$800,000	$200,000

*70% owned by Chow.

The $800,000 of assets of Chow includes an $84,000 investment in the 70% owned subsidiary. The $84,000 includes Chow's pro rata share of the subsidiary's net income for 20X8. Chow's sales were $870,000 and operating expenses were $802,000. These figures exclude any pro rata share of the subsidiary's net income. The subsidiary's sales were $550,000 and operating expenses were $500,000. Prepare a consolidated income statement and a consolidated balance sheet. Assume neither Chow nor its subsidiary sold items to the other.

11-42 Consolidated Financial Statements and Noncontrolling Interest

The parent company owns 70% of the common stock of Company S-1 and 60% of the common stock of Company S-2. The balances as of December 31, 20X4, in the condensed accounts follow:

	($ in thousands)		
	Parent	**S-1**	**S-2**
Sales in 20X4	300,000	80,000	100,000
Investment in subsidiaries*	58,000	—	—
Other assets	142,000	90,000	20,000
Liabilities to creditors	100,000	20,000	5,000
Expenses in 20X4	280,000	90,000	90,000
Stockholders' equity, including current net income	100,000	70,000	15,000

*Carried at equity in subsidiaries.

Prepare a consolidated balance sheet as of December 31, 20X4, and a consolidated income statement for 20X4 ($ in millions of dollars). Assume none of the companies sold items to each other.

11-43 Consolidated Financial Statements

Company P acquired a 100% voting interest in Company S for $120 million cash at the start of the year. Immediately before the business combination, each company had the following condensed balance sheet accounts ($ in millions):

	P	**S**
Cash and other assets	$600	$160
Accounts payable, etc.	$200	$ 40
Stockholders' equity	400	120
Total liab. and stk. eq.	$600	$160

1. Prepare a tabulation of the consolidated balance sheet accounts immediately after acquisition. Use the balance sheet equation format.
2. Suppose P and S have the following results for the year:

	P	**S**
Sales	$600	$180
Expenses	450	170

Prepare income statements for the year for P, S, and the consolidated entity. Assume neither P nor S sold items to the other.
3. Present the effects of the operations for the year on P's accounts and on S's accounts, using the balance sheet equation. Also tabulate the consolidated balance sheet accounts at the end of the year. Assume that liabilities are unchanged.
4. Suppose S paid a cash dividend of $5 million. What accounts in requirement 3 would be affected and by how much?

11-44 Noncontrolling Interests

This alters the preceding problem. However, this problem is self-contained because all the facts are reproduced as follows: Company P acquired a 70% voting interest in Company S for $84 million cash at the start of the year. Immediately before the business combination, each company had the following condensed balance sheet accounts ($ in millions):

	P	**S**
Cash and other assets	$600	$160
Accounts payable, etc.	$200	$ 40
Stockholders' equity	400	120
Total liab. and stk. eq.	$600	$160

1. Prepare a tabulation of the consolidated balance sheet accounts immediately after acquisition. Use the balance sheet equation format.

2. Suppose P and S have the following results for the year:

	P	S
Sales	$600	$180
Expenses	450	170

Prepare income statements for the year for P, S, and the consolidated entity. Assume neither P nor S sold items to the other.

3. Using the balance sheet equation format, present the effects of the operations for the year on P's accounts and on S's accounts. Also tabulate consolidated balance sheet accounts at the end of the year. Assume that liabilities are unchanged.

4. Suppose S paid a cash dividend of $10 million. What accounts in requirement 3 would be affected and by how much?

11-45 Goodwill and Consolidations

This alters problem 11-44. However, this problem is self-contained because all the facts are reproduced as follows: Company P acquired a 100% voting interest in Company S for $150 million cash at the start of the year. Immediately before the business combination, each company had the following condensed balance sheet accounts ($ in millions):

	P	S
Cash and other assets	$600	160
Accounts payable, etc.	$200	$ 40
Stockholders' equity	400	120
Total liab. and stk. equity	$600	$160

Assume the fair values of the individual assets and liabilities of S were equal to their book values.

1. Prepare a tabulation of the consolidated balance sheet accounts immediately after the acquisition. Use the balance sheet equation format.
2. Suppose the book values of the S individual assets are equal to their fair market values except for equipment. The net book value of equipment is $40 million and its fair market value is $50 million. The equipment has a remaining useful life of 5 years. Straight-line depreciation is used.
   a. Describe how the consolidated balance sheet accounts immediately after the acquisition would differ from those in requirement 1. Be specific as to accounts and amounts.
   b. By how much will consolidated income differ in comparison with the consolidated income that would be reported if all equipment had fair value equal to its book value on S's books as in requirement 1?

11-46 Purchased Goodwill

Consider the following balance sheets ($ in millions):

	Company A	Company B
Cash	150	15
Inventories	60	25
Plant assets, net	60	30
Total assets	270	70
Common stock and paid-in surplus	70	30
Retained earnings	200	40
Total liab. and stk. equity	270	70

Company A paid $90 million to Company B stockholders for all their stock. The "fair value" of the plant assets of Company B is $40 million. The fair value of cash and inventories is equal to their carrying amounts. Companies A and B continued to keep separate books.

1. Prepare a tabulation showing the balance sheets of companies A and B, intercompany eliminations, and the consolidated balance sheet immediately after the acquisition.
2. Suppose that $50 million instead of $40 million of the total purchase price of $90 million could logically be assigned to the plant assets. How would the consolidated accounts be affected?
3. Refer to the facts in requirement 2. Suppose Company A had paid $100 million instead of $90 million. State how your tabulation in requirement 2 would change.

11-47 Change from Amortization of Goodwill to Impairment

1. Philip Morris purchased General Foods for $5.6 billion, merging it into Kraft Foods. Only $1.7 billion of the purchase price could be assigned to identifiable individual assets and liabilities. How much goodwill was created in the purchase?
2. Philip Morris changed its name to Altria in 2002 to emphasize that it was no longer primarily a tobacco company. It owned Miller Brewing Company and Kraft Foods, as well as operated a financing subsidiary. As a result of numerous acquisitions through time, its 2002 balance sheet showed $37,871 million in goodwill. On its income statement in 2001 goodwill amortization was $1,104 million, while in 2002 only $7 million of goodwill impairment was recorded. In 2002, net earnings were $11,102 million versus $8,500 million in 2001 for a 31% increase. How much of the increase was due to the change in accounting practice that eliminated goodwill amortization? Ignore taxes.
3. During 2002, Altria sold its wholly owned and consolidated Miller Brewing subsidiary to the South African Brewing Company (SAB) in exchange for SAB stock. Altria is now an owner of more than a 20% equity interest in SAB and will account for this equity interest in the future by recognizing its proportional share of SAB earnings as equity in earnings of an affiliate in its income statement. In 2002, this transaction gave rise to a gain of $2,631 million before income taxes of approximately $900 million. Estimate 2002 net earnings for Altria if neither the change in goodwill amortization nor the sale of Miller had occurred, and contrast the percentage change to the original 31% increase.

11-48 Allocating Total Purchase Price to Assets

Two Hollywood companies had the following balance sheet accounts as of December 31, 20X7 ($ in millions):

	Cinemon	Bradley Productions		Cinemon	Bradley Productions
Cash and receivables	$ 30	$ 22	Current liabilities	$ 50	$ 20
Inventories	120	3	Common stock	100	10
Plant assets, net	150	95	Retained earnings	150	90
Total assets	$300	$120	Total liab. and stk. eq.	$300	$120
Net income for 20X7	$ 19	$ 4			

On January 4, 20X8, these entities combined. Cinemon issued $180 million of its shares (at market value) in exchange for all the shares of Bradley, a motion picture division of a large company. The inventory of films acquired through the combination had been fully amortized on Bradley's books.

During 20X8, Bradley received revenue of $21 million from the rental of films from its inventory. Cinemon earned $20 million on its other operations (i.e., excluding Bradley) during 20X8. Bradley broke even on its other operations (i.e., excluding the film rental contracts) during 20X8.

1. Prepare a consolidated balance sheet for the combined company immediately after the combination. Assume $80 million of the purchase price was assigned to the inventory of films.
2. Prepare a comparison of Cinemon's consolidated net income between 20X7 and 20X8, where the cost of the film inventories would be amortized on a straight-line basis over 4 years. What would be the net income for 20X8 if the $80 million were assigned to goodwill instead of the inventory of films and goodwill was not amortized?

11-49 Prepare Consolidated Financial Statements

From the following data, prepare a consolidated balance sheet and a multiple-step income statement for Midlands Data Corporation. All data are in millions and pertain to operations for 20X2 or to balances on December 31, 20X2:

Short-term investments at current market value	$ 35
Income tax expense	90
Accounts receivable, net	110
Noncontrolling interest in subsidiaries	90
Inventories at average cost	390
Dividends declared and paid on preferred stock	10
Equity in earnings of affiliated companies	20
Paid-in capital in excess of par	82
Interest expense	25
Retained earnings	218
Investments in affiliated companies	100
Common stock, 10 million shares, $1 par	10
Depreciation and amortization	20
Accounts payable	200
Cash	55
First mortgage bonds, 10% interest, due December 31, 20X8	80
Property, plant, and equipment, net	120
Preferred stock, 2 million shares, $50 par, dividend rate is $5 per share, each share is convertible into one share of common stock	100
Accrued income taxes payable	30
Cost of goods sold and operating expenses, exclusive of depreciation and amortization	710
Subordinated debentures, 11% interest, due December 31, 20X9	100
Noncontrolling interest in subsidiaries' net income	20
Goodwill	100
Net sales and other operating revenue	960

11-50 IFRS Consolidations

Royal Dutch Shell prepares its financial statements "in accordance with the provisions of the Companies Act 1985, Article 4 of the International Accounting Standards (IAS) Regulation and with International Financial Reporting Standards (IFRS) as adopted by the European Union" according to its 2008 Annual Report, footnote 1.

1. Footnote 1 goes on to state that there are not material differences from IFRS as issued by the IASB, and "therefore the Consolidated Financial Statements have been prepared in accordance with IFRS as issued by the IASB." Speculate as to why this extra language would be appropriate or necessary in Shell's financial statements.
2. Footnote 12 explains that although Shell has a 52% interest in Aera, an exploration and production company in the United States, it does not consolidate Aera. Speculate as to why accounting for Aera using the equity method might be appropriate under IFRS.

11-51 Complex Intercorporate Investments, IFRS

Daimler, a German automobile company, acquired Chrysler, a U.S. company, in 1998. On January 1, 2005, Daimler adopted IFRS. The Chrysler merger was not successful, and in 2007 Daimler sold 80.1% of Chrysler to Cerebus Capital Management.

1. In 2008 Daimler held 19.9% of Chrysler. Speculate as to how that interest was accounted for by Daimler—consolidation, the equity method, or the market method.
2. Transactions often have contingent assets and liabilities. Daimler made loans to Chrysler in 2008, Chrysler did not perform well, and the loans had little value. Worse, Daimler wanted to end its relationship completely, but it had a significant contingent liability to Chrysler's underfunded

pension plan. On April 27, 2009, Daimler entered into an agreement with Chrysler, Cerebus, and the U. S. government agency, the Pension Benefit Guarantee Corporation (PBGC), to pay $200 million into the pension plan in 2009, 2010, and 2011. The PBGC pays retired employees a minimal pension even if their former employer is bankrupt and their pension plan has insufficient resources. Moreover, if Chrysler declared bankruptcy before 2012, Daimler would pay an additional $200 million to the PBGC. The agreement ends Daimler's 19.9% stake in Chrysler and waives repayment on Daimler's outstanding loans to Chrysler. Discuss how these obligations to the pension plan and elimination of the ownership interest and loans would affect Daimler's financial statements in 2009.

11-52 Equity Method and Cash Flows

Moscow Resources Company owns a 40% interest in Siberia Mining Company. Moscow uses the equity method to account for the investment. During 20X6, Siberia had net income of 100 million rubles and paid cash dividends of 40 million rubles. Moscow's net income, including the effect of its investment in Siberia, was 486 million rubles.

1. In reconciling Moscow's net income with its net cash provided by operating activities, the net income must be adjusted for Moscow's pro rata share of the net income of Siberia. Compute the amount of the adjustment. Will it be added to or deducted from net income?
2. Under the direct method, will the dividends paid by Siberia affect the amounts Moscow lists under operating, investing, or financing activities? By how much? Will the amount(s) be cash inflows or cash outflows?

11-53 Effect of Transactions Under the Equity Method

Coca-Cola's 2008 financial statements revealed that it has extensive equity method investments including Coca-Cola Hellenic Bottling Company, Coca-Cola Amatil Limited, and Coca-Cola Enterprises. In total, the balance sheet showed equity investments of $7,777 million at December 31, 2007, and $5,779 million at December 31, 2008. During 2008 Coca-Cola included an equity loss of $874 million in its income statement, and its cash flow statement indicates that approximately $254 million in dividends was received from equity investees.

1. Compute the approximate reduction in Coca-Cola's equity investment asset that cannot be explained by either increases (decreases) due to its share in earnings (losses) or decreases due to dividends received. You may find a T-account will help your analysis.
2. Coca-Cola uses the indirect method to construct its cash flow statement. Indicate how these transactions with equity investees would be shown in the statement of cash flows.

11-54 Equity Method, Consolidation, and Minority Interest

On January 2, 20X6, Jordan Shoe Company purchased 40% of Sports Clothing Company (SCC) for $2.0 million cash. Before the acquisition, Jordan had assets of $10 million and stockholders' equity of $8 million. SCC had stockholders' equity of $5 million and liabilities of $1 million, and the fair values of its assets and liabilities were equal to their book values.

SCC reported 20X6 net income of $500,000 and declared and paid dividends of $100,000. Assume that Jordan and SCC had no sales to one another. Separate income statements for Jordan and SCC were as follows:

	Jordan Shoe Company	Sports Clothing Company
Sales	$12,500,000	$4,500,000
Expenses	11,100,000	4,000,000
Operating income	$ 1,400,000	$ 500,000

1. Prepare the journal entries for Jordan Shoe (a) to record the acquisition of SCC and (b) to record its share of SCC net income and dividends for 20X6.
2. Prepare Jordan Shoe's income statement for 20X6 and calculate the balance in its investments in SCC as of December 31, 20X6.
3. Suppose Jordan had purchased 80% of SCC for $4 million. Using the balance sheet equation format, prepare a tabulation of the consolidated balance sheet immediately after acquisition. Prepare the journal entries for both Jordan and SCC to record the acquisition. Omit explanations.
4. Prepare a consolidated income statement for 20X6, using the facts of requirement 3.

11-55 Equity Investments and Noncontrolling Interests

Corning has significant equity investments, and several of its consolidated subsidiaries have noncontrolling interests (called minority interests by Corning) outstanding. Corning's consolidated income statement for 2008 shows the following (dollars in millions):

Income before minority interest and equity earnings	$3,928
Minority interests	1
Equity in earnings of associated companies	1,328
Net income	$5,257

1. Assuming each of the equity companies is 40% owned by Corning, estimate the 2008 earnings for these companies.
2. Assuming each of the noncontrolling interests is a 20% interest, estimate the 2008 earnings of these companies.
3. Corning prepares a cash flow statement using the indirect method. On it, net income is adjusted by $752 million for undistributed earnings of associated companies. Estimate dividends received from equity investees.

11-56 Goodwill and Intangibles

Gannett Co. owns many media companies, including numerous small-town papers and the national newspaper, USA Today. In 2007, revenues totaled $7.4 billion with net income of $1,056 million. In 2008, revenues fell slightly to $6.8 billion, but Gannett had a net loss of $6,647 million, due primarily to an impairment of goodwill of $7.5 billion.

1. Gannett's 2008 balance sheet showed goodwill of $2.9 billion out of total assets of $7.8 billion and its 2007 balance sheet showed goodwill of $10.0 billion out of total assets of $15.9 billion. Express goodwill as a percentage of total assets for each year, and indicate what that suggests about Gannett's growth. Did Gannett grow by starting new newspapers or by acquiring them?
2. What happened to the excess earnings capacity of Gannett specifically and of newspapers more generally during 2008? How is this reflected in Gannett's income statement and balance sheet?
3. Back in 2002, Gannett complied with new FASB rules and ended the amortization of goodwill, which had contributed to a $234 million charge for amortization of goodwill in 2001. Net incomes in 2001 and 2002 were $831 million and 1,160 million, respectively. Calculate the increase in net earnings from 2001 to 2002 as reported by Gannett. Compute the increase in net earnings if there had been no change in accounting rules and amortization of goodwill, and other intangibles in 2002 was the same as in 2001. There was no goodwill impairment. Comment.

11-57 The Value of a Stock for Stock Exchange

On October 27, 2003, the following appeared in a news release:

> Bank of America Corporation and FleetBoston Financial Corporation today announced a definitive agreement to merge, creating the nation's premier financial services company. The company will bring unmatched convenience, innovation and resources to customers and clients throughout the nation and around the world.
>
> The merger, to be accomplished through a stock-for-stock transaction, establishes a new Bank of America that will serve approximately 33 million consumer relationships, with leading market shares throughout the Northeast, Southeast, Midwest, Southwest and West regions of the United States...
>
> Under terms of the agreement, FleetBoston Financial stockholders will receive .5553 shares of Bank of America common stock for each of their shares. The exchange ratio was derived from the share price of Bank of America at the close of business on October 22, 2003, to establish the transaction's value at almost $47 billion, or $45 per FleetBoston Financial share.

Following this announcement, FleetBoston shares rose sharply and Bank of America shares dropped approximately 10%.

Discuss these events. How is this different than Bank of America agreeing to pay $45 per share in cash?

11-58 Intercorporate Investments and Statements of Cash Flow

The 20X6 balance sheet of Global Resources, Corp., contained the following three assets:

	20X6	20X5
Long-term debt investments held to maturity	$ 166,000	$ 166,000
Investment in Alberta Mining Company, 43% owned	$ 941,000	$ 861,000
Investment in Sutter Gold Company, 25% owned	$1,154,000	$1,054,000

The long-term-debt investments were shown at cost, which equaled maturity value. Interest income was $14,000 for these debt investments, which had been owned for several years. The equity method was used to account for both Alberta Mining and Sutter Gold. Results for 20X6 included the following:

	Alberta Mining Company	Sutter Gold Company
Global Resources, Corp., pro rata share of net income	$120,000	$100,000

Global Resources received some dividends from affiliates. Estimate the dividend amounts using the pro rata share of net income and the changes in the investment accounts.

A schedule that reconciles net income to net cash provided by operating activities contained the following:

Net income	$696,000
Depreciation	130,000
Increase in noncash working capital	(15,000)

Note: The increase in noncash working capital is the net change in current assets and liabilities other than cash.

Given the available data, complete the reconciliation of net income to cash from operations.

11-59 Intercorporate Investments and Ethics

Hans Rasmussen and Alex Renalda were best friends at a small undergraduate college and they fought side by side in the jungles of Vietnam. On returning to the United States, they went their separate ways to pursue MBA degrees, Hans to a prestigious East Coast business school and Alex to an equally prestigious West Coast school. However, 30 years later, their paths crossed again.

By 1999, Alex had become president and CEO of Medusa Electronics after 15 years with the firm. Hans had started working for **American Airlines**, but had left after 9 years to start his own firm, Rasmussen Transport. In April 2004, Rasmussen Transport was near bankruptcy when Hans approached his old friend for help. Alex Renalda answered his friend's call, and Medusa Electronics bought 19% of the stock of Rasmussen Transport.

In 2009, Rasmussen was financially stable and Medusa was struggling. In fact, Alex Renalda thought his job as CEO might be in jeopardy if Medusa did not report income up to expectations. Late in 2009, Alex approached Hans with a request—quadruple Rasmussen's dividends so Medusa could recognize $760,000 of investment income. Medusa had listed its investment in Rasmussen as an available-for-sale security. Although Rasmussen had never paid dividends of more than 25% of net income, and it had plenty of use for excess cash, Hans felt a deep obligation to Alex. Thus, he agreed to a $4 million dividend on net income of $4.5 million.

1. Why does the dividend policy of Rasmussen Transport affect the income of Medusa Electronics? Is this consistent with the intent of the accounting principles relating to the market and equity methods for intercorporate investments? Explain.
2. Comment on the ethical issues in the arrangements between Hans Rasmussen and Alex Renalda.

Collaborative Learning Exercise

11-60 International Perspective on Consolidation
Form groups of four to six students. Each student should pick a country from the following list:

Australia	Japan
United Kingdom	Sweden

Find out the policy on consolidating financial statements in the country you select. If possible, find out when consolidated statements were first required and what criteria are used to determine what subsidiaries should be consolidated. If the country has adopted IFRS, see if you can determine how IFRS differs from prior, local GAAP.

Meet as a group and share your information. What generalizations can you draw from the policies you found? Propose explanations for the differences you find among countries. Discuss the effect of consolidation policies on comparisons of financial statements across countries.

Analyzing and Interpreting Financial Statements

11-61 Financial Statement Research
Select five companies in any industry. Review each company's financial statements to determine whether an acquisition occurred during the most recent year. For each acquisition, identify as much as possible concerning each of the following:

1. Did the company use cash or stock?
2. What percentage of the target was purchased?
3. Can you determine whether the acquired company was previously either a customer or a supplier of the acquiring company? If so, which one?

11-62 Starbucks' Annual Report
Starbucks includes the following items on its balance sheet for the year ended September 27, 2009, and September 28, 2008 (amounts in millions):

	2009	2008
Short-term investments—Available-for-sale securities	21.5	3.0
Short-term investments—Trading securities	44.8	49.5
Long-term investments—Available-for-sale securities	71.2	71.4
Equity and cost investments	352.3	302.6

The investments are carried at fair value, except for the equity and cost investments.

1. Estimate the effect on 2009 earnings before tax from changes in value of the investments that are accounted for as Long-Term Available-for-Sale Securities. Their cost was $72.5 million and the cost of this category of investments at the end of the prior year was $77.9 million.
2. Estimate the effect on 2009 earnings before tax from changes in value of the investments that are accounted for as Trading Securities. Assume that no such securities were sold or acquired in 2009.
3. Starbucks' goodwill decreased from $266.5 million at the beginning of fiscal 2009 to $259.1 million at the end of the year. Starbucks did not recognize any goodwill from purchases of companies during fiscal 2009. What is the most likely cause of the $7.4 million decrease in goodwill?

11-63 Analyzing Financial Statements Using the Internet
Go to www.ford.com to locate the Ford home page. Click on Investors near the top of the page. Then, select the most recent annual report under the category Company Reports.

Answer these questions about Ford.

1. How does Ford determine the companies it consolidates and those that it reports on the equity method?
2. What information does Ford provide about its marketable securities shown on the consolidated balance sheets? Can you tell which ones are classified as trading securities?
3. Did Ford report any goodwill? Why would Ford want to pay more than the value of the net assets of a company it acquired?

12

Financial Statement Analysis

LEARNING OBJECTIVES

After studying this chapter, you should be able to:

1 Locate and use sources of information about company performance.

2 Analyze the performance of a company using trend analysis, common-size financial statements, and segment disclosures.

3 Use basic financial ratios to guide your thinking.

4 Evaluate corporate performance using various metrics, including ROA, ROE, and EVA.

5 Calculate EPS when a company has preferred stock or dilutive securities.

6 Understand the nature of irregular items and how to adjust for them.

7 Use financial information to help assess a company's value.

No doubt you have seen the Nike trademark Swoosh on a wide range of products, from running shoes to swimwear to golf accessories. Nike is the world's #1 shoemaker, designing and selling shoes for a variety of sports, including football, basketball, baseball, soccer, golf, tennis, and running. Footwear sales comprised almost 54% of Nike's 2009 revenue, up from 52% in 2008. The remaining 46% of Nike's 2009 revenue came from the sale of athletic apparel and equipment.

Nike operates on a May 31 fiscal year end. During the 12 months ending May 31, 2009, Nike shares traded at a low of $38.24 and at a high of $70.28. The *Wall Street Journal* reported a closing price of $57.05 on May 29, 2009 (the last trading day of the fiscal year). This was up 49.2% from the low of $38.24, which occurred just a few months earlier on March 9, 2009. While up from the low, the stock price at May 29, 2009, was down 16.6% from the $68.37 price a year earlier, on May 30, 2008. What caused this fluctuation in stock price? Can the fluctuation be explained by changes in Nike's sales or earnings? Or are other factors at work? Did Nike's competitors experience similar fluctuations in stock price? Or is the variance unique to Nike?

In prior chapters, we concentrated on how to collect financial data and how to prepare and evaluate financial statements. In financial statement analysis, we interpret these financial data to more fully understand the story they tell about the company. However, understanding Nike requires more than just understanding its financial statements. You must be attuned to economy-wide forces such as the rate of inflation, demographic shifts, interest rate changes, and unemployment, as well as industry and firm-specific factors.

Let's look at the performance of the stock market during the 12 months from May 30, 2008, to May 29, 2009, to help evaluate the fluctuations in

Nike's stock price. The S&P 500 stood at 1,400 at May 30, 2008, and had declined to 919 by May 29, 2009. Similarly, the Dow Jones Industrial Average was at 12,638 at May 30, 2008, and by May 29, 2009, it had declined by almost 33% to 8,500. Both the S&P 500 and the Dow Jones Industrial Average experienced 12 month lows on March 9, 2009, the same day that Nike's stock was at its low point. This suggests that the fluctuation in Nike's stock price was not entirely the result of industry or firm-specific factors.

At the firm-specific level, Nike's sales revenue was up almost 3% in fiscal year 2009 relative to 2008. However, earnings declined slightly more than 21% in that same time period. Why did Nike earn less per dollar of sales in 2009 than in 2008? The financial statements and related disclosures reveal several factors that contributed to the decline in earnings. In response to the deterioration in overall economic conditions, Nike took steps to keep the company in a position to be successful in the long term. These actions had an impact on the company's profitability. According to discussion in the annual report, the company engaged in restructuring to "stream-line the management structure, enhance consumer focus, drive innovation more quickly to market, and establish a more scalable cost structure." These actions resulted in a one-time restructuring expense of $195 million. In addition, Nike took impairment charges for goodwill and other intangible assets that reduced pretax income by more than $400 million. As discussed in Chapter 8, due to the economic downturn, many companies experienced similar impairment losses during the same time period. In fact, Timberland, one of Nike's primary competitors, also took restructuring and impairment charges against income.

The economic recovery may not occur at the same rate worldwide. How geographically diversi-fied is Nike? If foreign markets rebound faster, will Nike be in a position to benefit? Slightly more than 58% of Nike's sales in 2009 came from overseas business, up from 53.5% in 2007. Although sales in the United States increased by 5.6%, sales outside the United States increased

27.8%. In predicting Nike's future performance, separate forecasts of domestic and international growth and profitability will improve the accuracy of forecasts for the whole company.

People perform financial analysis for different reasons. Suppliers want to see if a customer is likely to be able to pay for items bought on credit or if it can afford a price increase. Customers want to know if a company will still be operating in a year to honor a warranty. Managers, creditors, investors, and the CEO's mother all have their reasons for reading the statements.

financial statement analysis
Using financial data to assess some aspect of a company's performance.

Regardless of your interest in the company, **financial statement analysis** involves using financial data to assess some aspect of a company's performance. Our focus is on the investor. Investors read financial statements either to check on their current investments or to plan future investments. They analyze these statements and other material to determine whether their beliefs about the company have been borne out and to develop expectations about the future.

How do we use financial statements to forecast the future? We begin with a solid understanding of the company's past performance. Throughout the book we have shown you various ratios and other tools of analysis, so you should have some understanding of how to assess performance. This chapter integrates the tools you have already seen and teaches you several new ones as we focus on the techniques investors use to improve their investment decisions. ●

Sources of Information About Companies

Publicly available information takes many forms. The now familiar annual report is one form, known for its completeness and its reliability, given the attestation of an independent registered public accounting firm or auditor. In addition to the financial statements we have already seen (income statement, balance sheet, statement of cash flows, and statement of stockholders' equity), annual reports usually contain the following:

1. Footnotes to the financial statements
2. A summary of significant accounting policies used
3. Management's discussion and analysis (MD&A) of the financial results
4. The report of the Independent Registered Public Accounting Firm
5. Management's statement of its responsibility for the financial statements
6. Management's report on internal controls
7. Selected comparative financial data for a series of years
8. Narrative information about the company

These sections of the annual report are important to financial analysis. Footnotes are so important that at the bottom of each financial statement there is language that directs the reader to the footnotes. Some analysts and other financial statement users read the footnotes and the MD&A before examining the financial statements themselves. These two sections of the annual report provide a context for interpreting the numbers reported in the financial statements.

In addition to the annual reports distributed to shareholders, companies must also submit reports to the SEC. While there are many different types of SEC filings, some of the most important are the 10-K, 10-Q, and 8-K. Form 10-K often contains information not included in the annual report, although many companies now provide the full 10-K to shareholders. Form 10-Q includes unaudited quarterly financial statements, so it provides more timely, although less complete, information than does the annual report. Companies use Form 8-K to notify investors of any unscheduled material event of importance. Examples include a change in the board of directors or management, a change in auditors, significant asset sales, or bankruptcy. In addition, companies issue proxy statements in connection with shareholder meetings. These statements contain useful information such as the qualifications of board members, executive compensation and stock option awards, and audit fee disclosures. The SEC requires other reports for specific events, such as the issuance of common shares or debt. All SEC filings are available to investors. See the SEC Web site (www.sec.gov) for easy access to EDGAR (**E**lectronic **D**ata **G**athering, **A**nalysis and **R**etrieval **S**ystem), the SEC electronic information source. Also, many companies include links to their SEC filings from their own Web sites.

Companies issue annual reports and SEC Form 10-K and 10-Q filings well after the events being reported have occurred. For example, a company classified by the SEC as a large accelerated filer must file its 10-K within 60 days after the end of the fiscal year and its 10-Q within 40 days after the quarter end. In addition to 8-Ks, you can find more timely information in periodic company press releases, which provide the public with news about company developments. The Internet has made it possible for the general public to gain almost immediate access to company press releases, which are often available on company Web sites. In addition, many companies routinely hold conference calls with security analysts to discuss new developments, and they make these calls accessible to investors via Webcasts.

Numerous online services compile and sell databases of press releases and other corporate information. Investors also rely on articles in the general financial press such as the *Wall Street Journal*, *BusinessWeek*, *Forbes*, *Fortune*, and *Barron's*. Trade and industry-specific publications and Web sites are other useful information sources. For example, the *Industry Standard* (www. thestandard.com) and *Red Herring* (www.redherring.com) concentrate on news about young dynamic companies and high-tech industries. Services such as **Value Line**, **Moody's**, and **Standard and Poor's** (S&P) provide investors with useful information, as do credit agencies such as **Dun & Bradstreet**. In addition, stockbrokers prepare company analyses for their clients, and private investment services and newsletters supply analysts' reports and stock recommendations to their subscribers.

The Internet has changed the way investing is done. Investors can purchase and sell securities electronically without ever talking to a broker. Many Internet sites provide continuous information about security prices and access to analysts' reports on various industries and securities. Much of this information is free, but some sources require the investor to have a brokerage account with the firm or to subscribe to a fee-based service. While the rapid dissemination of information made possible by the Internet can help investors make investment decisions, it can also quickly spread false rumors as illustrated in the Business First box on page 538.

Investors should always get information before they invest, and the sources we have described provide a wealth of information. Of course, some investors may request even more information. Banks or other creditors making multimillion-dollar loans may ask for a set of projected financial statements or other estimates of predicted results, known as **pro forma statements**. Not every investor needs this level of detail. There is so much information available to the public that wading through it all is frequently overwhelming. Although we can gain much information from other sources, our discussion focuses on analyzing the information contained in the financial statements themselves.

pro forma statements
A set of projected financial statements or other estimates of predicted results.

Objectives of Financial Statement Analysis

Different types of investors expect different types of returns. If you are a stockholder, you expect an increase in the value of the stock you hold. If you have invested in a company with a history of paying dividends, you also expect a dividend. If you have loaned the firm money, you expect to receive interest and the return of the loan amount. Although the types of returns they expect are different, equity investors and creditors both risk not receiving those returns. Therefore, both stockholders and creditors use financial statement analysis to help (1) predict their expected returns and (2) assess the risks associated with those returns.

The primary concerns of creditors are short-term liquidity and long-term solvency. **Short-term liquidity** refers to an organization's ability to meet current payments, such as interest, wages, and taxes, as they become due. **Long-term solvency** refers to a company's ability to generate enough cash to repay long-term debts as they mature.

In contrast, equity investors, while concerned about liquidity and solvency, are more typically concerned with profitability and future security prices. Why? Because dividend payments depend, in part, on how profitable operations are, and stock prices depend on the market's assessment of the company's future prospects. Investors gain when they receive dividends and when the value of their securities rises. Rising profits spur both events, and declining profits may have negative implications for both dividend policy and stock price. A struggling company may elect to reduce or even terminate its dividend. The 2008–2009 downturn in the economy, which led to falling profits and declining share prices, caused many companies, even some of the largest and best-known companies, to reduce or suspend dividends. For example, after 71 years of steady or increasing dividends, **General Electric** reduced its dividend by 68% in 2009 as its price fell from nearly $42 in late 2007 to a low of $7.06 the week of March 2, 2009. At about the same time, investors in **Dow Chemical**, a company that had never decreased its dividend in its 114-year

short-term liquidity
An organization's ability to meet current payments, such as interest, wages, and taxes, as they become due.

long-term solvency
An organization's ability to generate enough cash to repay long-term debts as they mature.

BUSINESS FIRST

TRUTH AND LIES IN THE DIGITAL AGE

"A lie can travel halfway around the world while the truth is still putting on its shoes." –attributed to Mark Twain

Web sites and focused business newscasts have increased the speed with which information reaches the markets. In addition, the widespread use of the Blackberry and similar devices allow investors access to such information anytime and anyplace, enabling them to act more quickly. However, the availability and widespread dissemination of information does not make it trustworthy. For example, Apple shares opened at a price of $104.00 on October 3, 2008. That day the CNN citizen journalism Web site, iReport.com, reported that Apple CEO Steve Jobs had been rushed to the hospital after suffering a major heart attack. The rumor, which was false, caused Apple's shares to drop to an 18-month low of $94.65. While the market partially recovered, closing at $97.07, many investors took losses as they sold on the downslide. Similarly, the Thai stock market fell dramatically over a two day window in October 2009 following Internet rumors about the health of the King. In one day alone, the Thai bourse plunged by 8.22%. Subsequently, several people were charged with intentionally disseminating incorrect information over the Internet.

Some erroneous information releases are perpetrated by people who hope to benefit. Mark Jakob fabricated a news release about Emulex, a designer, developer, and supplier of networking products. As a result, Mr. Jakob netted $241,000 in profit by trading on Emulex stock. However, he ultimately had to pay $455,652 to settle an SEC lawsuit against him and was sentenced to 44 months in prison.

Other situations result from a series of human and computer errors. One of the most bizarre tales of dissemination of erroneous information involves United Airlines. An old *Chicago Tribune* article on the 2002 United Airlines bankruptcy filing resurfaced on the Internet on September 8, 2008. Traders reacted to this old bankruptcy announcement as though it were new information, triggering a sell-off of shares. United shares opened at $12.17 on September 8, 2008, and fell to a low of $3.00 within moments of the article being posted to the Bloomberg News service. NASDAQ officials briefly halted trading on the stock. Trading resumed after United issued a statement denying the rumor and the shares closed at $10.92. See the stock price graph.

How could this happen? In an editorial posted on *PR Week*, just a few days after the United incident, the author comments, "Anyone who has ever worked on the back end of a Web page knows how easily and quickly errors can occur . . . . one mouse click can send out false information, which is then aggregated by news services, e-mailed, copied into blogs and spat out by RSS feeds."

An article in the *New York Times* gives the following account. The problem began shortly after midnight on Sunday, September 7, 2008. A link to an article originally published in the *Chicago Tribune* in 2002, appeared in the "Most Viewed" section of the business page of a south Florida newspaper owned by the Tribune Company. A spokesperson for the *Chicago Tribune* claimed that a single click on the archived article in the middle of the night on a Sunday could have positioned it on the "Most Viewed" list. Within a minute, the automated scanning system of Google News located the link and followed it to the article,

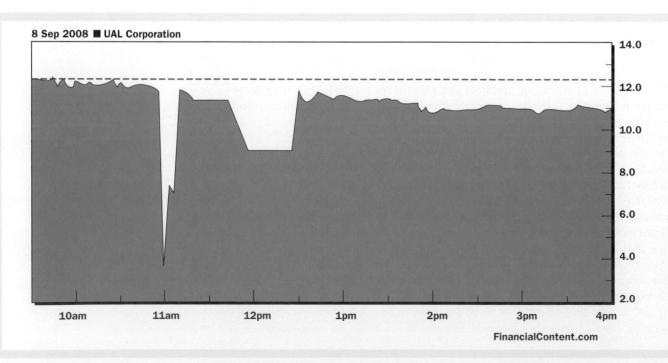

8 Sep 2008 ■ UAL Corporation

FinancialContent.com

entitled "United Airlines Files for Bankruptcy," in the *South Florida Sun-Sentinel*'s archives. Google's system treated the article as though it was new. Google did not put a link to the article on its main news page, but it was added to the news index along with the date it was found.

On Monday morning, September 8, a researcher at an investment newsletter, *Income Securities Advisors, Inc. (ISA)*, did a Google search using the words "bankruptcy" and "2008." The search brought up the article from the *South Florida Sun-Sentinel* Web site that referenced United Airlines bankruptcy filing. According to a spokesperson for *ISA*, neither the specific date of the article nor the actual date of the United bankruptcy filing appeared in the *Sun-Sentinel* article, and the Web page carried the date, September 7, 2008, at the top. A summary of the article was posted by the *ISA* researcher to the Bloomberg News service, a real-time news service that provides coverage of companies, markets, industries, economies, and governments. While Bloomberg has its own news group, it also distributes stories from select third-party providers. Upon receipt of the information from the *ISA* researcher, Bloomberg distributed a news headline, citing the *South Florida Sun-Sentinel* article, and the share sell-off began.

This sequence of events demonstrates how quickly information, both factual and false, can be transmitted in the digital age.

Sources: "United Incident Reinforces the Need for Web Strategy," September 15, 2008, *PR Week*, p. 8; Cohen, Noam, "Spinning a Web of Lies at Digital Speed," *New York Times*, October 13, 2008, Section B, p. 3; Helft, Miguel, "How Series of Mistakes Hurt Shares of United," *New York Times*, September 15, 2008, Section C, p. 1; WSJ Staff Reporter, "Emulex Stock Saboteur Agrees to Pay $455,642 to Settle SEC Civil Suit," *Wall Street Journal*, July 25, 2001, p. B4; Snyder, Brett, "United Stock Tanks on False Bankruptcy Rumors," (http://industry.bnet.com/travel/1000193/united-stock-tanks-on-false-bankruptcy-rumors/); © FinancialContent Services, Inc.

history, saw its dividends fall by 64%. This contributed to a 17% drop in Dow's share price in the week of the dividend announcement. **Carnival Corporation**, the large cruise ship operator, completely suspended its dividend in October of 2008 to preserve cash and help fund new ships without taking on additional debt. Upon the suspension announcement, Carnival shares fell 11.5%. Dividend cuts were also common in Europe. For example, in May 2009 **BT Group Plc**, the UK's largest phone company, cut its dividend by 89%.

Research from **Standard and Poor's** indicates that 288 of the roughly 7,000 U.S. public companies that report dividend information decreased their dividends during the last 3 months of 2008. That made the fourth quarter of 2008 the worst quarter for dividends since S&P began collecting data in 1956.

Not all companies that experience a downturn in earnings cut dividends. **Nike**'s stock price declined as income fell in fiscal year 2009. However, Nike actually increased the per share dividend to $0.98 in 2009 from $0.875 in 2008. Also, note that not all successful companies pay dividends. For example, despite its enormous profitability, **Microsoft** did not pay a dividend until 2002 and **Google** has yet to pay a dividend.

Profitability is important not only to equity investors, but also to creditors. Why? Because the profitable operations that allow for dividends and drive stock prices to higher levels also provide the cash to repay loans and finance growth. Therefore, both creditors and equity investors are interested in a company's future profitability. If their concern is with the future, what is the value of analyzing financial statements, which deal solely with past events? Trends in past sales, operating expenses, and net income often continue, so financial statement analysis of past performance is often a good indicator of future performance.

Evaluating Trends and Components of the Business

Thorough analysis of financial statement information requires the use of a variety of different tools. The next two sections discuss two of the most popular techniques—trend analysis and common-size financial statements. A third technique, ratio analysis, should already be familiar because you have encountered ratios in earlier chapters. Nevertheless, a later section of this chapter consolidates and adds to your knowledge of ratio analysis. We apply each technique to the same company, **Nike**, as we demonstrate the application of these analysis techniques.

OBJECTIVE 2

Analyze the performance of a company using trend analysis, common-size financial statements, and segment disclosures.

Trend Analysis

Annual reports contain balance sheets for the current and previous year and the other financial statements for the current and previous 2 years. In addition, they include key financial data for at least the last 5 years and often for 10. In evaluating trends, we may or may not find these numbers to be adequate. Supplemental sources provide much longer and richer access to information by archiving and adjusting older data. For example, Compustat PC is a CD-ROM database that provides 20 years of financial information extracted from the financial statements. Mergent Online is a subscriber database that provides Internet access to complete company financial data, along with other information. Many free online databases such as Reuters and Yahoo! offer historical records of select financial performance measures, and it is possible to access prior year's SEC filings at www.sec.gov.

trend analysis

An analysis technique that compares financial trends and changes from one year to the next and identifies patterns that have occurred in the past.

The essence of **trend analysis** is to compare financial trends and changes from one year to the next and identify patterns that have occurred in the past. You then ask why that trend exists and whether you expect it to continue. If sales have been growing steadily but inventories have not, can this continue? Or will future inventory growth require substantial additional investment? If inventories have been growing steadily but sales have not, why is the company holding so much inventory?

Trend analysis also prompts investors to ask what could cause the trends to end. The housing and credit crisis of the mid- to late 2000s saw an unprecedented decline in interest rates as the Federal Reserve Bank attempted to jump-start the slumping economy. As the economy recovers, the Federal Reserve Bank is likely to raise interest rates. Rising interest rates hurt many industries. Banks are hurt because they must pay more for the money that they lend. Automobile manufacturers are hurt because car buyers face higher car payments when interest rates rise and therefore buy fewer cars. The same analysis follows for builders of new houses. In contrast, rising interest rates often help companies such as The Home Depot, which serves the homeowners' needs for home improvement materials. Why? Because people who would like to move to a nicer home but conclude that interest rates are too high often decide to remodel their existing home. These examples illustrate how you might think about trends in sales and profits in particular industries.

To see how trend analysis works, let's examine the income statements and balance sheets of Nike as shown in Exhibits 12-1 and 12-2. The income statement in Exhibit 12-1 has been slightly modified from that presented in the annual report to highlight key figures and relationships. The first two columns show Nike's information for 2009 and 2008. The third column shows the dollar amount of the change in each item from 2008 to 2009. Finally, the fourth column shows the percentage change, computed as follows:

$$\text{Percentage change 2008 to 2009} = \frac{2009 \text{ amount} - 2008 \text{ amount}}{2008 \text{ amount}} \times 100$$

For example, Nike's Revenues increased by $549.1 million or almost 3.0%:

$$\text{Percentage change} = \frac{\$19,176.1 - \$18,627.0}{\$18,627.0} \times 100 = 2.9\%$$

At the same time, Nike's Cost of Sales increased $332.1 million or 3.2%:

$$\text{Percentage change} = \frac{\$10,571.7 - \$10,239.6}{\$10,239.6} \times 100 = 3.2\%$$

You can add or subtract the dollar change amounts in the third column to obtain meaningful subtotals. However, you must use care when considering the effect of increases or decreases on revenue and expense accounts. Increases in revenues and increases in expenses have offsetting effects on net income. In Exhibit 12-1, the increase of $549.1 million in Revenues is offset by the increase in Cost of Sales of $332.1 million. While the sign of the change in Revenues and the sign of the change in Cost of Sales are both positive, they have opposite effects on gross margin and net income. The increase in Revenues increases the gross margin. The increase in Cost of Sales decreases the gross margin. In dollar terms, the increase in Revenues of $549.1 million exceeds the increase in Cost of Sales of $332.1 million, resulting in a $217.0 million increase in gross margin. However, the percentage increase in gross margin is only 2.6% compared to the

	For the Year Ended May 31, 2009	For the Year Ended May 31, 2008	Increase (Decrease)	
			Amount	Percentage*
Revenues	$19,176.1	$18,627.0	$ 549.1	2.9%
Cost of sales	10,571.7	10,239.6	332.1	3.2%
Gross margin	8,604.4	8,387.4	217.0	2.6%
Selling and administrative expense	6,149.6	5,953.7	195.9	3.3%
Restructuring charges	195.0	—	195.0	
Goodwill impairment	199.3	—	199.3	
Intangible and other asset impairment	202.0	—	202.0	
Operating expenses	6,745.9	5,953.7	792.2	13.3%
Operating income	1,858.5	2,433.7	(575.2)	(23.6%)
Interest expense	(40.2)	(38.7)	1.5	3.9%
Interest income	49.7	115.8	(66.1)	(57.1%)
Other income (expense), net	88.5	(7.9)	96.4	
Nonoperating income	98.0	69.2	28.8	41.6%
Income before income taxes	1,956.5	2,502.9	(546.4)	(21.8%)
Income taxes	469.8	619.5	(149.7)	(24.2%)
Net income	$ 1,486.7	$ 1,883.4	$(396.7)	(21.1%)
Basic earnings per share	$ 3.07	$ 3.80	$ (0.73)	(19.2%)
Diluted earnings per share	$ 3.03	$ 3.74	$ (0.71)	(19.0%)
Dividends declared per common share	$ 0.98	$ 0.875	$ 0.105	12.0%

*Percentage column numbers cannot be added.

EXHIBIT 12-1

Nike, Inc.

Consolidated Statements of Income ($ in millions, except per share data and percentages)

revenue growth of 2.9%. Similarly, total operating expenses increased by $792.2 million or 13.3%. This increase in operating expenses caused operating income to decline by $575.2 million or 23.6%. Note that although you can add the changes in dollars as you move down the column, you cannot add the changes in percentage terms.

Finally, nonoperating activities generated income of $98.0 million in 2009 and income of $69.2 million in 2008. This $28.8 million increase in nonoperating income helps offset the $575.2 million decline in operating income. Do not be fooled by the change amounts in the nonoperating section of the income statement. Interest Expense increased from $38.7 million to $40.2 million, resulting in an increase of $1.5 million in column 3 of Exhibit 12-1. This $1.5 million increase in expense decreases nonoperating income year-over-year. Other Income (Expense), net increased from an expense of $7.9 million to income of $88.5 million, resulting in a $96.4 million increase reported in the third column. This $96.4 million increase in the Other Income (Expense), net line item increases nonoperating income year-over-year. The decline in operating income offset by the increase in nonoperating income results in a net decrease in income before taxes of ($1,956.5 million – $2,502.9 million) = $546.4 million.

In its income statement, Nike does not distinguish between operating and nonoperating revenues and expenses. We made the distinction in Exhibit 12-1 to enhance discussion. Some analysts might take exception to the classification in Exhibit 12-1 and prefer to treat the Intangible and Other Asset Impairment line item as a nonoperating item. There is not universal agreement on the distinction between operating and nonoperating activities. When you are comparing companies, it is important to recognize differences in classification.

We need both dollar and percentage changes to identify trends and understand their true meaning. For example, the revenue increase of $549.1 million is approximately the same in absolute dollar magnitude as the $546.4 million decrease in income before income taxes.

	May 31, 2009	May 31, 2008	Increase (Decrease) Amount	Percentage*
Assets:				
Cash and equivalents	$ 2,291.1	$ 2,133.9	$157.2	7.4%
Short-term investments	1,164.0	642.2	521.8	81.3%
Accounts receivable, net	2,883.9	2,795.3	88.6	3.2%
Inventories	2,357.0	2,438.4	(81.4)	(3.3%)
Deferred income taxes	272.4	227.2	45.2	19.9%
Prepaid expenses and other current assets	765.6	602.3	163.3	27.1%
Total current assets	9,734.0	8,839.3	894.7	10.1%
Property, plant, and equipment, net	1,957.7	1,891.1	66.6	3.5%
Identifiable intangible assets	467.4	743.1	(275.7)	(37.1%)
Goodwill	193.5	448.8	(255.3)	(56.9%)
Deferred income taxes and other assets	897.0	520.4	376.6	72.4%
Total assets	$13,249.6	$12,442.7	$806.9	6.5%
Liabilities and Shareholders' Equity:				
Current portion of long-term debt	$ 32.0	$ 6.3	$ 25.7	407.9%
Notes payable	342.9	177.7	165.2	93.0%
Accounts payable	1,031.9	1,287.6	(255.7)	(19.9%)
Accrued liabilities	1,783.9	1,761.9	22.0	1.2%
Income taxes payable	86.3	88.0	(1.7)	(1.9%)
Total current liabilities	3,277.0	3,321.5	(44.5)	(1.3%)
Long-term debt	437.2	441.1	(3.9)	(0.9%)
Deferred income taxes and other liabilities	842.0	854.5	(12.5)	(1.5%)
Redeemable preferred stock	0.3	0.3	0.0	0.0%
Shareholders' Equity:				
Common stock at stated value				
Class A convertible	0.1	0.1	0.0	0.0%
Class B	2.7	2.7	0.0	0.0%
Capital in excess of stated value	2,871.4	2,497.8	373.6	15.0%
Accumulated other comprehensive income	367.5	251.4	116.1	46.2%
Retained earnings	5,451.4	5,073.3	378.1	7.5%
Total shareholders' equity	8,693.1	7,825.3	867.8	11.1%
Total liabilities and shareholders' equity	$13,249.6	$12,442.7	$806.9	6.5%

*Percentage column numbers cannot be added.

EXHIBIT 12-2

Nike, Inc.

Consolidated Balance Sheets (in millions, except percentages)

However, the $549.1 million represents a 2.9% increase in Revenues while the $546.4 million represents a 21.8% decrease in income before income taxes. Similarly, in Exhibit 12-2, the 407.9% increase in the Current Portion of Long-Term Debt seems large, but the dollar increase of $25.7 million is much smaller than the change in many other accounts.

Although it is always possible to compute and interpret dollar changes, some percentage changes are not meaningful. Look at Exhibit 12-1. Nike includes three items on the 2009 income statement that do not appear on the 2008 income statement: Restructuring Charges of $195.0 million, Goodwill Impairment of $199.3 million and Intangible and Other Asset Impairment of $202.0 million. If you try to compute the percentage increase between 2008 and 2009, the denominator of the percentage change calculation is zero and the percentage is undefined. Another problem arises when a company reports a negative dollar amount in one time period and a positive amount in the comparison period. For example, Nike nets other income and expense on the income statement. The net amount was an expense of $7.9 million in 2008 and an income of $88.5 million in 2009. It is not meaningful to compute a percentage change in this case.

From Exhibit 12-1, we observe that Nike experienced a 2.9% increase in revenue in 2009 relative to 2008. Increased sales activity frequently results in increased levels of accounts receivable if the company sells on account and increased levels of inventory if management wants to be sure it has sufficient product to deliver to the customer. This suggests that the observed increase in revenue on the income statement may be accompanied by an increase in accounts receivable and inventory. Analysis of Nike's balance sheets in Exhibit 12-2 reveals that Accounts Receivable increased 3.2% but Inventories actually declined 3.3%.

Changes in dollar amounts and percentages such as those referenced in the previous paragraph help analysts see patterns. Although recognizing patterns is key, understanding what caused those patterns is even more important. What possible explanations exist for the changes in various financial statement accounts, such as sales revenue, inventory, and receivables? Where would we look for answers? One source used by analysts is the section of the company's annual report and 10-K called the **management discussion and analysis** (or **MD&A**). In the United States, the SEC dictates the content of the MD&A. It concentrates on explaining the major changes in the company's operating results, liquidity, and capital resources. The MD&A includes, but is not limited to, disclosures about a company's capital resources and liquidity, including off-balance sheet arrangements and capital expenditures; the results of operations, including discussion of trends in sales and expenses and an explanation of any unusual or infrequent events; disclosures about contractual obligations and commitments and trading activities; discussion of critical accounting policies and estimates; and the impact of adoption of new accounting policies.

Let's return to the relationship of revenues, inventory, and receivables and see if we can explain the trends in these financial statement items. Nike is in a seasonal business where sales are typically highest in the fourth quarter of the fiscal year, which ends in May. An unexpected surge in sales activity near year end could result in an increase in accounts receivable and depleted inventories. Is this the only possible explanation for the observed relationships? No. The worldwide economy was in a downturn during 2008 and 2009. This downturn became more pronounced during the last half of Nike's fiscal year ended May 31, 2009. Nike's MD&A indicates that the company experienced reduced sales activity as consumers cut back on discretionary spending. Sales revenue in the first half of the year was up 11.4% from $8,994.6 million in 2008 to $10,022.3 million. Sales activity in the second half of the year was down from $9,632.4 million in 2008 to $9,153.8 million in 2009, a decline of almost 5%. This suggests a different explanation for the observed changes in Accounts Receivable and Inventories. As demand dropped in the latter part of fiscal 2009, Nike cut back on inventory; hence, the 3.3% decrease in Inventories on the balance sheet. With regard to the increase in Accounts Receivable, the MD&A indicates that the higher receivables balance was the result of slower collection cycles, reflecting the challenging retail environment experienced by Nike's customers.

What additional questions arise from analyzing trends in Nike's financial statements? Let's start by considering the income statement in Exhibit 12-1. As you already know, Nike's Revenues and Cost of Sales both increased in 2009. The $549.1 million increase in Revenues outpaced the $332.1 million increase in Cost of Sales. So the company's gross margin, as measured in dollars, was $217.0 million greater in 2009 than in 2008. At this point, it appears that Nike is on track to report higher net income in 2009. However, closer scrutiny of the income statement reveals that net income in 2009 was actually less than in 2008 by $396.7 million. How do we explain this? Examination of the balance sheet in Exhibit 12-2 also raises some interesting questions. Why did Short-Term Investments increase by 81.3%? Does this represent a change in investment strategy? Why did the Current Portion of Long-Term Debt increase by 407.9% while Notes Payable increased 93%? Has there been a change in financing strategy? Why did current assets increase by 10.1% while current liabilities decreased by 1.3%? Has there been a change in working capital management? Why did Identifiable Intangible Assets decrease by 37.1% and Goodwill decrease by 56.9%? The answers to these questions say a lot about how management runs a company, how it will perform in the future, and whether it would be a good investment.

As indicated earlier, an analyst might note that Nike's Revenues increased by 2.9% while net income decreased by 21.1%. A declining net income is generally not good news. When relationships

management discussion and analysis (MD&A)
A section of the annual report and 10-K, the content of which is dictated by the SEC, that concentrates on explaining the major changes in operating results, liquidity, and capital resources.

do not look as good as expected, the question is whether a crisis exists. When relationships look better than expected, the question is whether the company can sustain this situation. To see how trends develop over time, analysts often look at more than 2 years of financial information. Exhibit 12-3 shows a 5-year summary of key items for Nike, which enables you to compute a longer trend. For example, percentage changes in revenue are as follows:

$$\frac{\$19,176.1 - \$18,627.0}{\$18,627.0} \times 100 = 2.9\% \qquad \frac{\$18,627.0 - \$16,325.9}{\$16,325.9} \times 100 = 14.1\%$$

2009   **2008**

$$\frac{\$16,325.9 - \$14,954.9}{\$14,954.9} \times 100 = 9.2\% \qquad \frac{\$14,954.9 - \$13,739.7}{\$13,739.7} \times 100 = 8.8\%$$

2007   **2006**

The 2.9% increase in sales in 2009 is lower than the sales growth experienced in prior years.

compound annual growth rate (CAGR)
Year-over-year growth rate over a specified period of time.

By applying the present value techniques of Chapter 9, we can compute the **compound annual growth rate (CAGR)** in sales for the 4-year period. The CAGR is the year-over-year growth rate over a specified period of time and can be computed using the following formula:

$$CAGR = \left[\frac{\text{Ending sales value}}{\text{Beginning sales value}} \right]^{(1/\# \text{ of years})} - 1$$

In this case, a 4-year annual growth rate for sales of 8.69% will increase revenue from the initial 2005 level of $13,739.7 to that at the end of the period, $19,176.1. We obtained this

	For the Year Ended May 31				
	2009	**2008**	**2007**	**2006**	**2005**
Income statement data					
Revenues	$19,176.1	$18,627.0	$16,325.9	$14,954.9	$13,739.7
Cost of sales	10,571.7	10,239.6	9,165.4	8,367.9	7,624.3
Gross margin	8,604.4	8,387.4	7,160.5	6,587.0	6,115.4
Selling and administrative expense	6,149.6	5,953.7	5,028.7	4,477.8	4,221.7
Restructuring charges	195.0	0.0	0.0	0.0	0.0
Impairments	401.3	0.0	0.0	0.0	0.0
Nonoperating (income) expense, net	(98.0)	(69.2)	(68.1)	(32.4)	33.9
Income before taxes	1,956.5	2,502.9	2,199.9	2,141.6	1,859.8
Income taxes	469.8	619.5	708.4	749.6	648.2
Net income	$ 1,486.7	$ 1,883.4	$ 1,491.5	$ 1,392.0	$ 1,211.6
Earnings per share, basic	$ 3.07	$ 3.80	$ 2.96	$ 2.69	$ 2.31
Earnings per share, diluted	$ 3.03	$ 3.74	2.93	$ 2.64	$ 2.24
Dividends per share	$ 0.98	$ 0.875	$ 0.71	$ 0.59	$ 0.4753
Selected balance sheet data (as of May 31)					
Current assets	$ 9,734.0	$ 8,839.3	$ 8,076.5	$ 7,346.0	$ 6,351.1
Current liabilities	3,277.0	3,321.5	2,584.0	2,612.4	1,999.2
Property, plant, and equipment, net	1,957.7	1,891.1	1,678.3	1,657.7	1,605.8
Total assets	13,249.6	12,442.7	10,688.3	9,869.6	8,793.6
Long-term debt	437.2	441.1	409.9	410.7	687.3
Shareholders' equity	8,693.1	7,825.3	7,025.4	6,285.2	5,644.2

EXHIBIT 12-3

Nike, Inc.

Five-Year Financial Summary ($ in millions, except per share data)

precise growth rate with a calculator. However, you can use the tables in Chapter 9 to approximate this value. The future value multiple is 2009 sales divided by 2005 sales, or ($19,176.1 ÷ $13,739.7) = 1.395671. In Table 9A-1, p. 426, the future value factor for 4 years for 8% is 1.3605 and for 10% is 1.4641. The observed value of 1.395671 falls about one third of the way between these two values, so the CAGR must be close to 8.7%. The 8.69% value we computed qualifies. While this may seem like a reasonable growth rate for Nike, given the short time period analyzed here, the impact of a single observation can have significant impact on the CAGR. If you use the CAGR for purposes of forecasting a company's future performance, you must exercise caution.

Common-Size Statements

To make it easier to evaluate a company's performance over time or to compare companies that differ in size, we often analyze income statements and balance sheets using **common-size statements** in which we express the components as relative percentages. Nike's common-size statements appear in Exhibit 12-4, side by side with the income statements from Exhibit 12-1 and balance sheets from Exhibit 12-2.

common-size statements
Financial statements in which components are expressed as relative percentages.

The income statement percentages are based on sales revenue equal to 100%. We express each element of the income statement as a percentage of revenues. In 2008, Nike's gross margin was 45.0%, falling slightly to 44.9% in 2009. To better understand this gross margin, we might compare it with a specific competitor's values or with industry averages. For example, Under Armour reported a gross margin of 48.9% and Timberland reported a gross margin of 45.5% for the year ended December 31, 2008. Both Under Armour and Timberland outperform Nike on gross margin. The small year-over-year decline in Nike's gross margin may not be alarming, but it would be interesting to determine if the margins of other firms in the industry are following a similar trend or if Nike's decline is unusual. In fact, both Under Armour and Timberland experienced greater declines in gross margin year-over-year than did Nike. Although the use of common-size financial statements facilitates the comparison of different sized firms, remember that differences other than size may need to be considered. For example, a manufacturing company's choice of depreciation method affects the reported gross margin, because it impacts cost of sales.

The behavior of each expense in relation to changes in total revenue is often revealing. That is, which expenses go up or down as sales fluctuate? For example, between 2008 and 2009 Nike's

| | For the Year Ended May 31 | | | |
	2009		2008	
Statements of Income				
Revenues	$19,176.1	100.0%	$18,627.0	100.0%
Cost of sales	10,571.7	55.1%	10,239.6	55.0%
Gross margin	8,604.4	44.9%	8,387.4	45.0%
Selling and administrative expense	6,149.6	32.1%	5,953.7	32.0%
Restructuring charges	195.0	1.0%	—	0.0%
Goodwill impairment	199.3	1.0%	—	0.0%
Intangible and other asset impairment	202.0	1.1%	—	0.0%
Operating expenses	6,745.9	35.2%	5,953.7	32.0%
Operating income	1,858.5	9.7%	2,433.7	13.0%
Interest expense	(40.2)	(0.2%)	(38.7)	(0.2%)
Interest income	49.7	0.3%	115.8	0.6%
Other income (expense), net	88.5	0.5%	(7.9)	0.0%
Nonoperating income	98.0	0.6%	69.2	0.4%
Income before income taxes	1,956.5	10.3%	2,502.9	13.4%
Income taxes	469.8	2.5%	619.5	3.3%
Net income	$ 1,486.7	7.8%	$ 1,883.4	10.1%

EXHIBIT 12-4
Nike, Inc.
Common-Size Statements (in millions, except percentages)

	May 31			
	2009		**2008**	
Balance Sheets				
Assets:				
Cash and equivalents	$ 2,291.1	17.3%	$ 2,133.9	17.1%
Short-term investments	1,164.0	8.8%	642.2	5.2%
Accounts receivable, net	2,883.9	21.8%	2,795.3	22.5%
Inventories	2,357.0	17.8%	2,438.4	19.6%
Deferred income taxes	272.4	2.0%	227.2	1.8%
Prepaid expenses and other current assets	765.6	5.8%	602.3	4.8%
Total current assets	9,734.0	73.5%	8,839.3	71.0%
Property, plant, and equipment, net	1,957.7	14.8%	1,891.1	15.2%
Identifiable intangible assets	467.4	3.5%	743.1	6.0%
Goodwill	193.5	1.5%	448.8	3.6%
Deferred income taxes and other assets	897.0	6.8%	520.4	4.2%
Total assets	$13,249.6	100.0%	$12,442.7	100.0%
Liabilities and Shareholders' Equity:				
Current portion of long-term debt	$ 32.0	0.2%	$ 6.3	0.1%
Notes payable	342.9	2.6%	177.7	1.4%
Accounts payable	1,031.9	7.8%	1,287.6	10.3%
Accrued liabilities	1,783.9	13.5%	1,761.9	14.2%
Income taxes payable	86.3	0.6%	88.0	0.7%
Total current liabilities	3,277.0	24.7%	3,321.5	26.7%
Long-term debt	437.2	3.3%	441.1	3.5%
Deferred income taxes and other liabilities	842.0	6.4%	854.5	6.9%
Redeemable preferred stock*	0.3	0.0%	0.3	0.0%
Shareholders' Equity:				
Common stock at stated value				
Class A convertible	0.1	0.0%	0.1	0.0%
Class B	2.7	0.0%	2.7	0.0%
Capital in excess of stated value	2,871.4	21.7%	2,497.8	20.1%
Accumulated other comprehensive income	367.5	2.8%	251.4	2.0%
Retained earnings	5,451.4	41.1%	5,073.3	40.8%
Total shareholders' equity	8,693.1	65.6%	7,825.3	62.9%
Total liabilities and shareholders' equity	$13,249.6	100.0%	$12,442.7	100.0%

Note: Some percentages are off by 0.1% due to rounding.
*Nike treats Redeemable Preferred Stock as a long-term liability.

EXHIBIT 12-4 (Continued)
Nike, Inc.
Common-Size Statements (in millions, except percentages)

Cost of Sales and Selling and Administrative Expense increased, both in absolute dollar terms and as a percentage of sales. Why? In the MD&A, Nike explains that the primary factors contributing to the decrease in gross margin "were lower gross pricing margins and increased discounts. Gross pricing margins were lower, primarily driven by higher product input costs, most notably for footwear products. Higher levels of discounts were provided across all businesses in fiscal 2009 to manage inventory levels." The increase in Selling and Administrative Expense is attributed to an increase in operating overhead due to "investments in growth drivers such as Nike-owned retail . . . . infrastructure for emerging markets . . . and non-Nike brand businesses." While the company took actions to reduce operating costs by implementing a hiring freeze and reducing travel expenses, these reductions were not sufficient to offset the aforementioned increases.

While Cost of Sales and Selling and Administrative Expense increased in both absolute dollars and as a percent of revenues in 2009 relative to 2008, the increases are relatively small and do not explain the significant drop in net income as a percent of sales from 10.1% in 2008 to 7.8% in 2009. Look closely at the income statements in Exhibit 12-4. Notice that, in 2009, Nike deducted Restructuring Charges, Goodwill Impairment, and Intangible and Other Asset Impairment. Exhibit 12-4 shows that these expenses were not present on the income statement in 2008. They are what we sometimes refer to as nonrecurring or unusual items. A **nonrecurring (unusual) item** is an income statement item that is either unusual in nature or infrequent in occurrence, but not both. We do not expect nonrecurring items to happen often for a given firm. Accounting guidance requires separate disclosure of material nonrecurring items.

As we covered in Chapters 8 and 11, a company must evaluate fixed assets, intangible assets and goodwill for impairment. If the impairment tests indicate that the assets have become impaired in value, an impairment loss is recorded on the income statement. That is exactly what happened to Nike in 2009. In 2008, Nike purchased Umbro, a leading United Kingdom-based global soccer company. However, in 2009 the decline in consumer demand and weakness in the worldwide economy suggested that goodwill and the Umbro trademark recorded in the acquisition should be tested for impairment. Impairment tests resulted in goodwill impairment of $199.3 million and other asset (trademark) impairment of $202 million.

Restructuring costs result from a significant makeover of part of a company that typically involves closing one or more plants, reducing the size of the workforce and terminating or relocating activities. As a result of restructuring, Nike reduced its workforce by 5% and incurred "pre-tax restructuring charges of $195 million, primarily consisting of severance costs related to the workforce reduction." Combined, the restructuring and impairments increased expenses by $596.3 million, accounting for over 75% of the increase in operating expenses in 2009.

The balance sheet percentages in Exhibit 12-4 are based on total assets equal to 100%. We refer to them as **component percentages** because they measure each component of the financial statements as a percentage of the total. As with the income statement, you must look for changes in balance sheet relationships. The composition of Nike's assets is relatively stable. Short-Term Investments increased from $642.2 million or 5.2% of total assets in 2008 to $1,164.0 million or 8.8% of total assets in 2009. Why? Perhaps with the general economic downturn, Nike decided to retain excess cash in the form of short-term investments as a safety cushion against continued weakness in consumer demand. Inventories decreased from 19.6% of total assets in 2008 to 17.8% in 2009. Why? As noted earlier, a reduction in inventory may be appropriate in the face of lower product demand. Identifiable Intangible Assets decreased from 6.0% of total assets in 2008 to 3.5% in 2009 and Goodwill decreased from 3.6% to 1.5% of total assets. Why did these asset categories decline? The decrease in both categories is due to the impairment charges previously discussed. On the liability side of the balance sheet, total current liabilities decreased as a percentage of total assets. What is the cause of this decrease? It is due primarily to the decrease in Accounts Payable. Nike's MD&A attributes the decline in Accounts Payable to lower purchases of inventory, consistent with the previously-mentioned decrease in Inventories on the asset side of the balance sheet.

nonrecurring items (unusual items)
An income statement item that is either unusual in nature or infrequent in occurrence but not both. These items are not expected to happen often for a given firm.

component percentages
Elements of financial statements that express each component as a percentage of the total.

INTERPRETING FINANCIAL STATEMENTS

Common-size financial statements are useful in comparing companies that are significantly different in size. However, when you engage in comparisons across companies, you must consider the accounting choices made by the companies in arriving at the numbers presented on the financial statements. Name two accounting choices that impact the comparability of financial statements. You may need to think back to previous chapters to respond to this question.

Answer

1. Depreciation method. The use of straight-line versus accelerated depreciation methods can have a significant effect on the income statement and on property, plant, and equipment values on the balance sheet.
2. Lease classification. A lease agreement structured as a capital lease will increase both assets and liabilities relative to a lease structured as an operating lease. Income statement values also vary because an operating lease results in rent expense, whereas a capital lease results in depreciation expense and interest expense.

Segment Reporting

Our analysis of trends and common-size statements has focused on the company as a whole. However, it is often useful to analyze individual segments of the business. A required footnote to financial statements provides information on the sales revenue, profits, and assets of each operating segment.

When employing financial analysis techniques, analysts often consider the different business and geographic segments of a company's activities. In its 2009 annual report Nike divides its business in two ways, by product line and by geographic segments. It identifies four major product lines: footwear, apparel, equipment, and other. The footwear, apparel, and equipment categories include all the Nike-brand sales activity except Nike Golf and Nike Bauer Hockey. Nike classifies these two product lines with non-Nike brand products such as those manufactured under the Cole Haan, Converse, Hurley, and Umbro brands in the "other" category. Nike reports sales revenue by product line, with the following 2009 results: footwear 53.7% of revenue, apparel 27.4%, equipment 5.8%, and "other" 13.1%.

For segment reporting purposes, Nike reports five operating segments that reflect its internal organization as of the year ended May 31, 2009. Nike categorizes its Nike-brand footwear, apparel, and equipment sales activity into four geographic regions: the United States, EMEA (Europe, Middle East, and Africa), Asia Pacific, and the Americas. Nike's non-Nike brand products (along with Nike Golf and Nike Bauer Hockey) comprise the fifth segment. Therefore, Nike reports five operating segments: the United States, EMEA, Asia Pacific, Americas, and Other.

Panel A of Exhibit 12-5 displays revenues, income before income taxes, and net income after taxes for the company as a whole as reported in Nike's 2009 annual report. The pretax and after-tax return on sales ratios in panel A are computed from these figures. Without further information about operating segment results, these aggregate figures cannot answer questions such as the following: What contribution did each segment make to Nike's total revenue? What contribution did each segment make to Nike's net income? Are sales of one segment driving the decline in return on sales or is the company experiencing reduced profitability in all segments?

Panel B of Exhibit 12-5 helps answer these questions by showing Nike's operating segment disclosures taken from footnote 19 of its 2009 annual report. Nike reports revenues and pretax income for five segments: United States, EMEA, Asia Pacific, Americas, and Other. One of the first things you may notice is that total segment pretax profits do not agree with the total before-tax income figures in panel A. The income statement reports 2009 before-tax income of $1,956.5 million, whereas the operating segment disclosures reflect total pretax profits of $3,585.6 million. Why? For internal reporting, Nike does not allocate expenses attributable to the corporate office and operation to the segments. This makes aggregate segment profits higher than corporate profits. Nike provides reconciliations (not shown here) of its segment numbers to the income statement numbers to clarify the differences. Even without the reconciliation, you can compute the corporate expenses for each year by subtracting total consolidated before-tax income from the segment total. For example, in 2009, corporate expenses were ($3,585.6 − $1,956.5) = $1,629.1.

Nike's 2009 sales revenue as reported on the income statement was up 2.9% relative to 2008. However, aggregate segment pretax income was down 10% from $3,985.3 million to $3,585.6 million. As a result, the pretax return on sales ratio for the combined segments fell from 21.4% to 18.7%. The segment revenue and profit information shown in panel B of Exhibit 12-5 reveals that not all segments are equally responsible for the decline in return on sales. The pretax return on sales ratios for the EMEA, Asia Pacific, and Americas segments range from 21.3% to 25.7% in 2009, and all three of the segments experienced an increase in return on sales in 2009 relative to 2008. While the pretax return on sales ratio for the United States segment decreased in 2009, it remained above 20%. However, look at the data for the Other segment. The pretax return on sales ratio for the Other segment is consistently lower than the returns reported by the United States, EMEA, Asia Pacific, and Americas segments. While 2009 sales revenue in the Other segment was less than 1.0% below 2008 levels, income before taxes decreased from a profit of $364.9 million to a loss of $196.7 million. This resulted in a decline in the pretax return on sales ratio from 14.4% in 2008 to −7.8% in 2009. What caused this significant decrease in profitability? Further exploration of the footnotes reveals that a large part of the decline is attributable to the impairment of goodwill, intangible assets, and other assets of Umbro, which is included in the Other segment.

Panel A: Consolidated Income Statement Data and Return on Sales Information

	For the Year Ended May 31		
	2009	2008	2007
Revenues	$19,176.1	$18,627.0	$16,325.9
Income before income taxes	$ 1,956.5	$ 2,502.9	$ 2,199.9
Net income (after taxes)	$ 1,486.7	$ 1,883.4	$ 1,491.5
Pretax return on sales	10.2%	13.4%	13.5%
After-tax return on sales	7.8%	10.1%	9.1%

Panel B: Segment Disclosures (all figures shown before taxes)

	Revenues	Pretax Income	Pretax Return on Sales Ratio
Year Ended May 31, 2009			
United States	$ 6,542.9	$ 1,337.9	20.4%
EMEA	5,512.2	1,316.9	23.9%
Asia Pacific	3,322.0	853.4	25.7%
Americas	1,284.7	274.1	21.3%
Other	2,514.3	(196.7)	(7.8%)
Total	$19,176.1	$ 3,585.6	18.7%
Year Ended May 31, 2008			
United States	$ 6,414.5	$ 1,402.0	21.9%
EMEA	5,629.2	1,281.9	22.8%
Asia Pacific	2,887.6	694.2	24.0%
Americas	1,164.7	242.3	20.8%
Other	2,531.0	364.9	14.4%
Total	$18,627.0	$ 3,985.3	21.4%
Year Ended May 31, 2007			
United States	$ 6,131.7	$ 1,386.1	22.6%
EMEA	4,764.1	1,050.1	22.0%
Asia Pacific	2,295.7	515.4	22.5%
Americas	966.7	199.3	20.6%
Other	2,167.7	299.7	13.8%
Other	$16,325.9	$ 3,450.6	21.1%

The footnotes also reveal that less than half of Nike's sales are in the United States. When Nike reallocates revenues attributable to the Other segment to the four geographic regions, U.S. sales constituted 41.8%, 42.6%, and 46.5% of total sales in 2009, 2008, and 2007 respectively. Clearly, if you want to forecast Nike's future performance, you must understand not only economic and demographic trends in the United States, but also trends around the globe.

INTERPRETING FINANCIAL STATEMENTS

In 2009, 41.8% of Nike's $19,176.1 million in sales were domestic sales and 58.2% were foreign sales. Suppose you predicted domestic sales to decline 2% and foreign sales to grow 4%. What would be your prediction of domestic, foreign, and total sales for the year 2010?

Answer

1. Domestic sales (.418 × $19,176.1 × .98) = $7,855.3 million.
2. Foreign sales (.582 × $19,176.1 × 1.04) = $11,606.9 million.
3. Projected total sales would be $19,462.2 for a growth rate of about 1.5%.

The preceding discussion of Nike's operating segment performance is based on 10-K disclosures for the year ending May 31, 2009. Review of Nike's 10-Q filing for the 3 months ended August 31, 2009, reveals a different operating segment structure. Why? The division of a company's overall results into operating segments should reflect how management chooses to segment the company for purposes of making operating decisions. When a company changes its internal organization, it may be necessary to realign the operating segments. This is what occurred at Nike.

Effective June 1, 2009, Nike initiated a reorganization of its Nike-brand products, excluding Nike Golf, into a new model consisting of six reportable geographic operating segments: North America, Western Europe, Central and Eastern Europe, Greater China, Japan, and Emerging Markets. These six geographic segments replace the four geographic segments (i.e., United States, EMEA, Asia Pacific, and Americas) previously used for Nike-brand products. Under the old structure, Nike also reported a segment called "Other," which included Nike Golf, Nike Bauer Hockey, and non-Nike brand products. Under the new structure, the "Other" segment is broken into two categories: the "Global Brand Divisions" category, which represents Nike-brand licensing businesses that are not part of a specific geographic operating segment, and the "Other Businesses" category, which consists of Nike Golf and non-Nike brand products.

Financial Ratios

OBJECTIVE 3

Use basic financial ratios to guide your thinking.

Although many analysis methods exist, the cornerstone of financial statement analysis is the use of ratios. Exhibit 12-6 on pp. 552–553 groups some of the most popular ratios into four categories. You have encountered most of these ratios in earlier chapters, as indicated in the second column (a dash in the column means that the ratio is being introduced in this chapter for the first time). We provide this summary to avoid the need to search for definitions in prior material.

We focus on the use of ratios by investors. However, managers also use ratios to guide, measure, and reward workers. If managers compensate workers for actions that make the company more profitable, workers are likely to do the right thing. Thus, some companies give workers a bonus if the company generates a return on equity (ROE) in excess of a predetermined benchmark or if earnings per share (EPS) exceed a specific number.

Given recent corporate scandals where companies manipulated accounting records to inflate earnings, many companies are broadening their incentive programs to include nonaccounting measures as well as accounting numbers. For example, **Duke Energy** decided that profit may not be the right measure for rewarding employees. Suppose profit increases because you raise more capital and expand the company. Should the workers necessarily earn more? Duke Energy elected to reward workers based on two factors: success in meeting goals and ROE. For one worker, the goal might be reduced injuries, and for another, improved customer service. However, everyone earns more for meeting ROE targets. ROE is a good measure of efficiency because it can be improved by increasing profitability and also by increasing the efficiency with which assets are employed.

Evaluating Financial Ratios

time-series comparisons
Comparisons of a company's financial ratios with its own historical ratios.

benchmark comparisons
Comparisons of a company's financial ratios with general rules of thumb or "best practices."

cross-sectional comparisons
Comparisons of a company's financial ratios with the ratios of other companies or with industry averages.

No single ratio by itself provides a valid basis for assessing a company's financial performance. Rather, it is important to examine a set of ratios, to perform other types of analyses, and to seek out nonfinancial information describing the firm's activities. That said, the focus of this section is the use of financial ratios. The easy part of ratio analysis is the computation of the numerical values. Once you have computed a set of ratios, you must decide what the ratios tell you about performance. There are three main types of comparisons for evaluating financial ratios: (1) **time-series comparisons** with a company's own historical ratios, (2) **benchmark comparisons** with general rules of thumb or "best practices," and (3) **cross-sectional comparisons** with ratios of other companies or with industry averages.

A few words of caution about these three types of comparisons are in order. When comparing a company's ratios in a time-series analysis, you must be aware of structural shifts in the company. For example, major acquisitions or divestitures cause the financial statements of a company to be difficult to compare across time. Consider the merger of **AOL** and **Time Warner** in early 2000. Time Warner was a media conglomerate whose activities included a cable television system servicing a significant percentage of U.S. households, publishing, music and entertainment, and film libraries. At the time of the merger, AOL was the nation's largest Internet service provider. The financial statements of the combined enterprise bore little resemblance to the financials of either of the original companies.

The use of benchmarks has the advantage of being easy to implement. However, rules of thumb vary from industry to industry and are susceptible to change over time. For example, the traditional rule of thumb for the current ratio was 2 to 1 or higher. Improvements in working capital management have made it possible for many companies to operate with a much lower current ratio. A current ratio of 1 to 1 is generally considered sufficient for a company with strong and stable cash flows, whereas a company with weak cash flows should maintain a higher current ratio. Another example is the total liabilities to total shareholders' equity ratio. In its publication, *Key Business Ratios*, Dun & Bradstreet, a financial services firm, observes that the total liabilities to total shareholders' equity ratio should not exceed 100%. However, it is not uncommon for companies in some industries to have substantially higher ratios. For example, Duke Energy, Consolidated Edison, and Spectra Energy have ratios of 153%, 237%, and 296%, respectively.

Cross-sectional comparisons require the identification of comparable companies or a set of norms for a specific industry. On the surface, this may appear straightforward. However, identification of similar companies or the appropriate industry is often difficult. Consider Berkshire Hathaway, Inc., which is a holding company comprised of many subsidiaries engaged in diverse business activities. One of Berkshire Hathaway's largest business segments is property and casualty insurance. Its holdings in this area include GEICO, one of the largest auto insurers in the United States, and General Re, one of the largest reinsurers in the world. Therefore, it might seem reasonable to compare Berkshire Hathaway to other insurance companies. However, further investigation of Berkshire Hathaway's business holdings reveals that it also owns three jewelry companies, four furniture retailers, several finance and financial products companies, a newspaper publisher, multiple apparel and footwear companies, a candy manufacturer, and numerous other companies in diverse industries. Although many companies operate in multiple industries, Berkshire Hathaway is an extreme example. Segment disclosure of the type discussed previously provides some information about the performance of different segments, but the information is limited in scope. (For more on Berkshire Hathaway see the Business First box on page 554.)

How can we find comparable companies? Historically, companies were classified according to the Standard Industry Classification (SIC) system. In 1997, the government introduced the North American Industry Classification System (NAICS). Both of these systems assign industry codes to companies based on their business activities. Several financial information services use these classification systems to provide average values for selected financial ratios and representative financial statements. Risk Management Association (formerly Robert Morris Associates), Dun & Bradstreet (D&B), and Standard and Poor's have provided these averages for many years. In addition, numerous online financial service providers compile industry information. Yahoo! Finance, Hoover's Online, and Reuters are examples. Regardless of the service you use to gather industry data, be alert to differences in computing ratios. Because there are no universally agreed upon formulas for most financial ratios except for EPS, you must know the computational formula employed before using such ratios.

Let's examine some specific ratios by comparing those for Nike from Exhibit 12-6 with both industry norms and the performance of specific competitors. The ratios shown in the following table have all been discussed in previous chapters. D&B provides the following industry ratios based on 84 companies in the sporting and recreational goods industry:

	Current Ratio (times)	Average Collection Period (days)	Total Liabilities to Stockholders' Equity (%)	Return on Sales (%)	Return on Stockholders' Equity (%)
84 Companies					
Upper quartile	3.9	20.0	40.6	3.6	22.1
Median	2.2	32.0	66.8	1.4	7.6
Lower quartile	1.4	43.0	266.1	0.0	0.4
Nike*	3.0	54.1	52.4	7.8	18.0

*Ratios are from Exhibit 12-6. Consult Exhibit 12-6 for an explanation of the components of each ratio.

Typical Name of Ratio	Introduced in Chapter	Numerator	Denominator	Using Appropriate Nike Numbers Applied to May 31 of Year	
				2009	2008
Short-term liquidity ratios					
Current ratio	4	Current assets	Current liabilities	$9,734.0 \div 3,277.0 = 2.97$	$8,839.3 \div 3,321.5 = 2.66$
Quick ratio	4	Current assets minus inventories	Current liabilities	$(9,734.0 - 2,357.0) \div 3,277.0 = 2.25$	$(8,839.3 - 2,438.4) \div 3,321.5 = 1.93$
Accounts receivable turnover	6	Credit sales	Average accounts receivable	$19,176.1 \div [\frac{1}{2}(2,883.9 + 2,795.3)] = 6.75$	$18,627.0 \div [\frac{1}{2}(2,795.3 + 2,494.7)] = 7.04$
Average collection period (in days)	6	365	Accounts receivable turnover	$365.0 \div 6.75 = 54.1$	$365.0 \div 7.04 = 51.8$
Inventory turnover	7	Cost of sales	Average inventory at cost	$10,571.7 \div [\frac{1}{2}(2,357.0 + 2,438.4)] = 4.41$	$10,239.6 \div [\frac{1}{2}(2,438.4 + 2,121.9)] = 4.49$
Long-term solvency ratios					
Total-debt-to-total-assets	9	Total liabilities[1]	Total assets	$(13,249.6 - 8,693.1) \div 13,249.6 = 34.4\%$	$(12,442.7 - 7,825.3) \div 12,442.7 = 37.1\%$
Total-debt-to-total-equity	9	Total liabilities[1]	Stockholders' equity	$(13,249.6 - 8,693.1) \div 8,693.1 = 52.4\%$	$(12,442.7 - 7,825.3) \div 7,825.3 = 59.0\%$
Interest coverage	9	Earnings before interest and taxes	Interest expense	$(1,956.5 + 40.2) \div 40.2 = 49.7$	$(2,502.9 + 38.7) \div 38.7 = 65.7$
Profitability ratios					
Return on common stockholders' equity (ROE)	4,10	Net income minus preferred dividends	Average common stockholders' equity	$1,486.7 \div [\frac{1}{2}(8,693.1 + 7,825.3)] = 18.0\%$	$1,883.4 \div [\frac{1}{2}(7,825.3 + 7,025.4)] = 25.4\%$
Gross profit rate or percentage	4	Gross profit or gross margin	Sales	$(19,176.1 - 10,571.7) \div 19,176.1 = 44.9\%$	$(18,627.0 - 10,239.6) \div 18,627.0 = 45.0\%$
Return on sales or profit margin	4	Net income	Sales	$1,486.7 \div 19,176.1 = 7.8\%$	$1,883.4 \div 18,627.0 = 10.1\%$

EXHIBIT 12-6

Some Typical Financial Ratios Applied to Nike, Inc. ($ in millions, except per share data)

(see Exhibits 12-1 and 12-2 on pages 541 and 542 for data)

Total asset turnover	—	Sales / Average total assets	$19,176.1 \div [\frac{1}{2}(13,249.6 + 12,442.7)] = 1.493$	$18,627.0 \div [\frac{1}{2}(12,442.7 + 10,688.3)] = 1.611$
EBIT to sales	—	Earnings before interest and taxes / Sales	$(1,956.5 + 40.2) \div 19,176.1 = 10.4\%$	$(2,502.9 + 38.7) \div 18,627.0 = 13.6\%$
Return on assets (ROA)	—	Earnings before interest and taxes / Average total assets	$(1,956.5 + 40.2) \div [\frac{1}{2}(13,249.6 + 12,442.7)] = 15.5\%$	$(2,502.9 + 38.7) \div [\frac{1}{2}(12,442.7 + 10,688.3)] = 22.0\%$
Earnings per share, basic (EPS)	2	Net income minus preferred dividends, if any / Average common shares outstanding	$1,486.7 \div 484.9 = \$3.07$	$1,883.4 \div 495.6 = \$3.80$
Market price and dividend ratios				
Price-earnings (P-E)	2	Market price of common share (assume $57.05 and $68.37) / Earnings per share	$57.05 \div 3.07 = 18.6$	$68.37 \div 3.80 = 18.0$
Book value per common share	10	Common stockholders' equity / Number of common shares outstanding	$8,693.1 \div 485.5 = \$17.91$	$7,825.3 \div 491.1 = \$15.93$
Market-to-book	10	Market price of common share / Book value per common share	$57.05 \div 17.91 = 3.19$	$68.37 \div 15.93 = 4.29$
Dividend-yield	2	Dividends per common share / Market price of common share	$0.98 \div 57.05 = 1.7\%$	$0.875 \div 68.37 = 1.3\%$
Dividend-payout	2	Dividends per common share / Earnings per share (EPS)	$0.98 \div 3.07 = 31.9\%$	$0.875 \div 3.80 = 23.0\%$

(1) Total liabilities computed as (Total assets − Total shareholders' equity).

Note: Year 2007 data required (in millions): Accounts receivable, $2,494.7; Inventory, $2,121.9; Stockholders' equity, $7,025.4; and Total assets, $10,688.3.
Number of common shares outstanding required (in millions) at May 31, 2009, and May 31, 2008, were 485.5 and 491.1, respectively.
Average common shares outstanding (in millions) in 2009 and 2008 were 484.9 and 495.6, respectively.

EXHIBIT 12-6 (Continued)

Some Typical Financial Ratios Applied to Nike, Inc. ($ in millions, except per share data)

(see Exhibits 12-1 and 12-2 on pages 541 and 542 for data)

BUSINESS FIRST

WARREN BUFFETT: NOTHING TO HIDE

Warren Buffett, Chairman of Berkshire Hathaway, is one of the most successful and well-known investors in the world. He is #2 on *Forbes Magazine*'s 2009 list of the 400 richest people, and his wealth derives from his skill as a manager and investor. In the early 1990s, Mr. Buffett wrote one of only three letters supporting mandatory expensing of stock options received by the congressional committee investigating the accounting treatment. His view did not carry the day then, but in 2004 the FASB issued a standard requiring that stock options be expensed. Once again, Mr. Buffett was ahead of his time in understanding the need for financial transparency.

In addition to information provided in the financial statements, footnotes, and MD&A of the Berkshire Hathaway annual report, followers of the company rely on Mr. Buffett's annual letter to his shareholders. This annual letter has become one of the best reads for accountants and investors anywhere. Mr. Buffett not only discusses the financial condition of Berkshire Hathaway, he also provides commentary on broader economic and financial issues. The full text of his letters written since 1977 is available on the company Web site at www.berkshirehathaway.com/letters/letters.html.

One of Berkshire Hathaway's businesses is Clayton Homes, the largest company in the manufactured home industry. Clayton constructs manufactured homes and also serves as lender to some home buyers. Clayton, unlike many of its peers, experienced relatively few loan failures in 2008 due to its conservative lending practices. In his 2008 letter, Mr. Buffett offered these comments on the mortgage-crisis:

Lenders happily made loans that borrowers couldn't repay out of their incomes, and borrowers just as happily signed up to meet those payments. Both parties counted on 'house-price appreciation' to make this otherwise impossible arrangement work. It was Scarlett O'Hara all over again: "I'll think about it tomorrow." The consequences of this behavior are now reverberating through every corner of our economy.

The present housing debacle should teach home buyers, lenders, brokers and government some simple lessons that will ensure stability in the future. Home purchases should involve an honest-to-God down payment of at least 10% and monthly payments that can be comfortably handled by the borrower's income. That income should be carefully verified.

Putting people into homes, though a desirable goal, shouldn't be our country's primary objective. Keeping them in their homes should be the ambition.

Berkshire Hathaway is heavily involved in the insurance industry. In this industry it is necessary to project future losses. There are numerous techniques used in this estimation process, all of which involve the analysis of historical data. However, reliance on these models without considering the effect of current events is dangerous. With regard to the tendency of some in the business world to blindly rely on historical models as guides to the future, Mr. Buffett offered the following advice in his 2008 letter:

Investors should be skeptical of history-based models. Constructed by a nerdy-sounding priesthood using esoteric terms such as beta, gamma, sigma and the like, these models tend to look impressive. Too often, though, investors forget to examine the assumptions behind the symbols. Our advice: Beware of geeks bearing formulas. If merely looking up past financial data would tell you what the future holds, the Forbes 400 would consist of librarians.

At the time Mr. Buffett wrote his 2008 annual letter, Berkshire Hathaway was a party to more than 250 derivatives contracts. Mr. Buffett believed that each of the derivative contracts held by the company had been carefully scrutinized and that the risk of loss was small. However, with respect to derivative instruments in general, and the related financial disclosures, Mr. Buffett expressed the following views:

Derivatives are dangerous. They have dramatically increased the leverage and risks in our financial system. They have made it impossible for investors to understand and analyze our largest commercial banks and investment banks. They allowed Fannie Mae and Freddie Mac to engage in massive misstatements of earnings for years. So indecipherable were Freddie and Fannie that their federal regulator, OFHEO, whose more than 100 employees had no job except oversight of these two institutions, totally missed their cooking of the books.

Improved "transparency"—a favorite remedy of politicians, commentators and financial regulators for averting future train wrecks—won't cure the problems that derivatives pose. I know of no reporting mechanism that would come close to describing and measuring the risks in a huge and complex portfolio of derivatives. Auditors can't audit these contracts, and regulators can't regulate them. When I read the pages of "disclosure" in 10-Ks of companies that are entangled with these instruments, all I end up knowing is that I don't know what is going on in their portfolios (and then I reach for some aspirin).

Source: Berkshire Hathaway Web site, www.berkshirehathaway.com.

D&B calculates the ratios for each firm in the industry sample and ranks the individual ratios from best to worst. The median is the ratio ranked in the middle. The ratio ranked halfway between the median and the best value is the upper quartile. The lower quartile is the ratio ranked halfway between the median and the worst value. The concept of best and worst must be viewed with caution. Analysts may differ in their opinions about what is good and what is bad. For example, a short-term creditor might consider a very high current ratio to be good because it suggests the assets are there to repay the debt. From an investor's perspective, however, a very high current ratio may indicate that the company is maintaining higher levels of inventory and receivables than it should. Both the creditor and the investor should consider the composition and liquidity of current assets when assessing the current ratio. A high current ratio with current assets comprised primarily of slow-moving inventory may not indicate strong short-term liquidity. Let us take a look at how analysts would interpret some of the main types of ratios.

When compared with the D&B ratios, Nike is between the median and the upper quartile of the current ratio, which measures short-term liquidity. Nike's 54-day collection period places it in the lower quartile. Suppose, like Nike, your company has an average receivables collection period that is much longer than the industry median of 32 days. One explanation might be that the company offers longer credit terms than those of its peers as a way to attract customers. An alternative explanation is that many firms in the industry give large discounts for cash purchases, whereas your company does not. A company with many cash sales may have a short average collection period for total sales, even though there are long delays in receiving payments for items sold on credit. Unfortunately, it is frequently difficult for an investor to obtain information on credit terms or the percentage of sales that were made on credit. An additional ratio that would be useful in assessing Nike's short-term liquidity is the inventory turnover ratio. D&B does not provide industry norms for this ratio.

Nike's total liabilities are 52.4% of stockholders' equity, placing it between the industry median and upper quartile. Typically, companies with lower levels of debt in relation to ownership capital are in a stronger position when business conditions deteriorate. Why? Because even when revenues decline, interest expenses and maturity dates do not change. Nike's ratio reflects a comparatively low level of risk or uncertainty with regard to its ability to meet outstanding debt obligations.

Investors are particularly interested in profitability ratios. Nike is in the upper quartile of the return on sales ratio, suggesting that it is able to generate greater income per dollar of sales than more than 75% of the comparator firms. Nike's common-size income statements can help you understand how it achieves a higher level of return on sales than the average firm in the industry. Nike's ROE of 18.0% is more than twice the industry median of 7.6% but below the upper quartile. We explore Nike's ROE in more depth later in the chapter.

Overall, Nike does not perform like the median firm in the industry. What could cause Nike's ratios to differ from the norms reported by D&B? D&B includes 84 companies in this industry classification, including companies that manufacture all types of sporting equipment from marine pleasure craft to bowling balls. Nike does manufacture sporting equipment. However, it mainly manufactures footwear and apparel. Perhaps we should compare Nike with the apparel industry or the leather products industry or the rubber and plastics footwear industry. Many companies, including Nike, fall into more than one SIC or NAICS category, making it difficult to select the appropriate industry for comparison. Perhaps we should compare Nike to individual companies that are more similar.

Hoover's Online identifies Nike's top three competitors as **adidas**, **Fila Korea**, and **New Balance**. Adidas prepares its financial statements in accordance with IFRS, making direct comparisons complex without a thorough understanding of the differences between U.S. GAAP and IFRS. Fila Korea and New Balance are private companies that do not disclose financial data to the public. Hoover's also lists **Under Armour** (UA), **Timberland** (TBL), and **K-Swiss** (KSWS) as competitors for Nike. While none of these three firms is a perfect match for Nike, each shares product lines with Nike, and all four companies compete for consumer dollars. Under Armour operates primarily in the athletic apparel market; Timberland is best known for its outdoor footwear but also manufactures apparel; and K-Swiss competes with Nike on apparel, footwear, and accessories. All four companies sell primarily through third party retailers, and all place heavy emphasis on brand management. In addition, Timberland and Nike have some dedicated retail stores.

From the chart below, you can see that the choice of comparable firms can alter your perception of a company's relative performance. The use of these specific competitors also allows us to compute inventory turnover ratios for comparison purposes.

Specific Competitor Ratio Comparisons

	Current Ratio (times)	Average Collection Period (days)	Inventory Turnover (times)	Total Liabilities to Stockholders' Equity (%)	Return on Sales* (%)	Return on Stockholders' Equity* (%)
UA	3.0	44.0	2.1	47.3	5.3	12.5
TBL	2.8	47.7	18.9	47.3	3.1	7.4
KSWS	6.3	37.4	3.0	21.7	6.1	5.9
Nike	3.0	54.1	4.4	52.4	7.8	18.0

*Income is after-tax income before extraordinary items, discontinued operations, and cumulative effect of changes in accounting method.

Does the comparison of ratios across companies provide easy answers for the investor? Generally not. While Nike's average collection period of 54 days is closer to UA and TBL than it is to the industry median of 32 days or to KSWS, we still don't know why there is a difference across this peer group. Nike's total liabilities to stockholders' equity ratio is also more in line with UA and TBL than it is to the higher industry median of 66.8% or to KSWS's lower ratio of 21.7%. And the inventory turnover ratio for the four companies ranges from 2.1 times per year to 18.9 times per year!

In addition to comparing ratios at a single point in time, changes in a company's ratios over time alert investors and creditors to problems. For example, a decrease in inventory turnover may suggest that a company's sales staff is no longer doing a very good job or that the company's products have fallen out of favor with the buying public. An alternative to the "sales are falling" explanation is the "inventory is rising" explanation. Manufacturing may be producing inventory at a pace beyond what current buyers want. Alternatively, a company may stockpile inventory in anticipation of price increases or inventory shortages. In both cases, inventory builds faster than sales and turnover falls. However, one explanation for rising inventory (over-manufacturing) is cause for concern, whereas the other may represent good inventory planning.

In this section, we focused primarily on liquidity and solvency ratios. Now we turn our attention to ratios used to assess the role of operating performance and financing decisions in the overall success of the company.

Operating Performance and Financing Decisions

OBJECTIVE 4

Evaluate corporate performance using various metrics, including ROA, ROE, and EVA.

___

financial management

Decisions concerned with where the company gets cash and how it uses that cash to its benefit.

operating management

Decisions concerned with the day-to-day activities that generate revenues and expenses.

On pages 175–177 of Chapter 4, you learned about several ratios used to measure profitability: return on sales (also called the profit margin ratio), return on common stockholders' equity (ROE or ROCE), and return on assets (ROA). Both operating performance and financing decisions affect these measures of profitability. **Financial management** is concerned with where the company gets cash and how it uses that cash to its benefit. **Operating management** is concerned with the day-to-day activities that generate revenues and expenses. In many scenarios, it is useful to focus on operating efficiency and financing decisions separately. We begin with a discussion of a version of ROA that measures a company's operating performance independent of how the company finances those operations. We then consider the impact of debt versus equity financing on the return to investors, using ROE. We expand on the traditional ROE calculation with a discussion of Economic Value Added (EVA), introduced by **Stern Stewart & Company**. Finally, no discussion of financing alternatives is complete without consideration of income tax effects and alternative measures of financing risk.

Operating Performance

In general, we evaluate the overall success of an investment by comparing investment returns with the amount of investment initially made:

$$\text{Rate of return on investment} = \frac{\text{Income}}{\text{Invested capital}}$$

However, there are several possible definitions of income and invested capital. The appropriate definition of these terms depends on how we intend to use the resulting rate of return measure. For example, depending on the setting, we may define income as net income, income from operations, earnings before interest and taxes (**EBIT**), or some other variation. We may also use different definitions of invested capital. Sometimes we define invested capital as stockholders' equity and other times as total capital provided by both debt and equity sources. The purpose of the analysis drives these choices. For example, a stockholder might be more concerned about ROE (Net income ÷ Average common stockholders' equity), whereas a lender (who has first claim on the resources generated by the company) would be more concerned with how effectively the company uses its total assets to generate returns for all suppliers of capital (EBIT ÷ Average total assets).

Suppose we are interested in assessing a firm's use of assets independently of how it financed those assets. In this case, neither return calculation introduced in Chapter 4 is appropriate. If we are interested in assessing this on a pretax basis, we should use pretax ROA, calculated as follows:

$$\text{Pretax ROA} = \frac{\text{EBIT}}{\text{Average total assets}} \qquad (1)$$

EBIT
Earnings before interest and taxes.

Alternatively, an analyst might be interested in measuring ROA after taxes but independent of financing. In this case, the ROA calculation would be as follows:

$$\text{After-tax ROA} = \frac{\{\text{After-tax net income} + [\text{Interest expense} \times (1 - \text{tax rate})]\}}{\text{Average total assets}}$$

The denominator of both ROA calculations is average total assets, those claimed by all providers of capital (stockholders and debt holders). To be consistent, the numerators also include income available to all providers of capital. Because net income measures only income available to equity holders after paying interest to debt holders, we adjust net income by adding back interest expense, either before or after taxes.

As you can see, ROA has multiple definitions in practice, depending on the numerator and denominator used in its calculation. Our discussion focuses on the version of ROA defined in equation 1 above. We could use the more precise term **pretax and pre-interest return on total assets** to identify the version of ROA defined as earnings before interest and taxes divided by average total assets, but the terminology would be cumbersome. Thus, for the remainder of this chapter, we use ROA to mean only the formula in equation 1.

pretax and pre-interest return on total assets
A version of ROA defined as earnings before interest and taxes divided by average total assets.

To further explore ROA, we can decompose the right side of equation 1 into two important ratios:

$$\frac{\text{EBIT}}{\text{Average total assets}} = \frac{\text{EBIT}}{\text{Sales}} \times \frac{\text{Sales}}{\text{Average total assets}} \qquad (2)$$

The first term on the right side of equation 2, computed as earnings before interest and taxes divided by sales, is a variation of return on sales, which we refer to as **EBIT-to-sales**. This ratio measures how much profit before deducting taxes and the cost of financing, a company generates for each dollar of sales. The second term is the **total asset turnover** ratio, computed as sales divided by average total assets. This ratio measures the sales a company is able to generate for each dollar invested in assets. Thus, for Nike in 2009 we can express the equation as follows:

EBIT-to-sales
A variation of return on sales computed as earnings before interest and taxes divided by sales.

total asset turnover
Sales divided by average total assets.

Return on total assets	=	EBIT-to-sales	×	Total asset turnover
15.5%	=	10.4%	×	1.493 times

Exhibit 12-7 displays these relationships for Nike for 2009.

This equation highlights that the EBIT-to-sales and total asset turnover ratios each contribute to the rate of return on total assets. Firms can achieve the same ROA with different combinations of EBIT-to-sales and total asset turnover. Understanding the industry provides insights. Companies in some industries have heavy fixed-capacity constraints, lengthy time to add new manufacturing capacity, and barriers that prevent new firms from entering the industry, allowing existing firms to charge high prices. Utilities and communications firms are traditional examples.

EXHIBIT 12-7

Major Ingredients of Return on Total Assets for Nike, Inc.

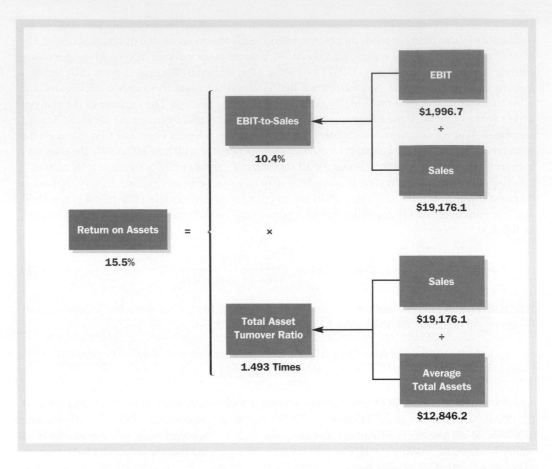

These industries are likely to display high EBIT-to-sales and relatively low total asset turnover. Companies in other industries have few barriers to entry, intense competition, and commodity-like products. Firms in these industries generally have low EBIT-to-sales and high total asset turnover. Grocery stores are a good example.

Just as decomposing ROA helps us understand what drives the operating performance of a company, we can apply a similar decomposition to ROE. In this case, the numerator is after-tax net income and the invested capital is average common stockholders' equity. Why use income after deducting taxes and interest expense in this computation? Because the numerator should represent the income that is available to common stockholders. The company must pay both interest and taxes before there is any return remaining for stockholders. In addition to the return on sales (here with after-tax net income in the numerator) and total asset turnover, the decomposition has a third component called leverage, which emphasizes the impact of financing decisions on ROE. Some analysts call this decomposition the DuPont analysis because a talented group of financial analysts working at DuPont developed it many years ago. The decomposition is as follows:

$$\text{ROE} = \text{Return on sales} \times \text{Total asset turnover} \times \text{Financial leverage}$$

$$= \frac{\text{Net income}}{\text{Sales}} \times \frac{\text{Sales}}{\text{Average total assets}} \times \frac{\text{Average total assets}}{\text{Average stockholders' equity}}$$

For Nike, in 2009 the ROE decomposes as follows:

$$\text{ROE} = \text{Return on sales} \times \text{Total asset turnover} \times \text{Financial leverage}$$

$$18.0\% = \quad 7.8\% \quad \times \quad 1.493 \quad \times \quad 1.55$$

The introduction of financial leverage in the computation of ROE leads us to a discussion of financing decisions.

Financing Decisions

Good financial performance requires an appropriate balance of debt and equity financing. In addition to deciding how much debt is appropriate, a firm must decide how much to borrow short term and how much to borrow by issuing bonds or other long-term debt. Companies must repay or refinance short-term debt quickly. When a borrower encounters trouble and cannot repay, it becomes difficult to refinance. Lenders prefer healthy, profitable borrowers, not troubled ones. Such problems are especially severe during periods when interest rates are rising because each new refinancing occurs at a higher interest rate, and the cash flow needed to cover interest payments increases.

In most cases, companies should finance long-term investments with long-term capital: long-term debt or stock. Debt is often a more attractive vehicle to companies than is common stock because (1) a company can deduct interest payments but not dividends for income tax purposes, and (2) the existing shareholders retain the same ownership rights to voting and profits. Most companies have a combination of long-term debt and stockholders' equity. We call the total long-term financing the **capitalization**, or simply the **capital structure**, of a corporation. Suppose a company's capital structure consists of long-term debt (bonds payable) and common stock. The common shareholders enjoy the benefits of all income in excess of interest expense and taxes.

Trading on the equity (also referred to as using **financial leverage**, **leveraging**, or, in the United Kingdom, **gearing**) means using interest-bearing debt to try to enhance the rate of return on common stockholders' equity. There are costs and benefits to shareholders from trading on the equity. The costs are interest payments and increased risk, and the benefit is the larger potential return to the common shareholders—as long as overall income is large enough.

To illustrate, imagine companies A, B, and C shown in Exhibit 12-8. The three companies are in the same industry, each has $80,000 in assets and each has the same ROA in a given year. However, the annual ROA varies from 20% in year 1, to 10% in year 2, and 5% in year 3. The three companies have chosen very different capital structures. Company A has no debt, Company B has $30,000 in debt, and Company C has $60,000 in debt. Company B pays 10% interest, whereas the more heavily indebted Company C must pay 12%. How do the shareholders fare in these three companies in different years?

capitalization (capital structure)
The total long-term financing of a company, consisting of long-term debt and stockholders' equity.

trading on the equity (financial leverage, leveraging, gearing)
Using interest-bearing debt to enhance the rate of return on common stockholders' equity.

	(1) Income Before Interest Expense (ROA × Assets)*	(2) Interest Expense (Debt × Interest Rate)[†]	(3) Net Income (1) – (2)	(4) Stockholders' Equity	(5) Return on Equity (3) ÷ (4)
Year 1: 20% ROA					
Company A	$16,000	$ 0	$16,000	$80,000	20%
Company B	16,000	3,000	13,000	50,000	26%
Company C	16,000	7,200	8,800	20,000	44%
Year 2: 10% ROA					
Company A	$ 8,000	$ 0	$ 8,000	$80,000	10%
Company B	8,000	3,000	5,000	50,000	10%
Company C	8,000	7,200	800	20,000	4%
Year 3: 5% ROA					
Company A	$ 4,000	$ 0	$ 4,000	$80,000	5%
Company B	4,000	3,000	1,000	50,000	2%
Company C	4,000	7,200	(3,200)	20,000	(16%)

*All three companies have $80,000 in assets.
[†]Company A, no debt; Company B, $30,000 in debt at 10%; Company C, $60,000 in debt at 12%.

EXHIBIT 12-8

Trading on the Equity Effects of Debt on Rates of Return

Exhibit 12-8 summarizes the results. The first column gives EBIT (income before interest expense and taxes). To examine financial leverage, this example focuses on interest and ignores taxes. Recall from equation 1 that we calculate the return on assets as follows:

$$\text{ROA} = \frac{\text{EBIT}}{\text{Average total assets}}$$

Therefore, EBIT equals ROA times average total assets. In this example, we assume the same ROA, and therefore the same EBIT, for each firm in a given year, but we vary the ROA from one year to the next. We can calculate EBIT each year by multiplying ROA for the year times the constant asset level of $80,000. The interest expense differs by company because each has a different level of debt, but for a given company it does not change from year to year. Our primary concern is the effect of financial leverage on the ROE.

What do we learn from Exhibit 12-8? First, a debt-free, or unlevered, company has identical ROA and ROE. Note that equity-financed, unlevered Company A's ROE and ROA are identical in years 1, 2, and 3: 20%, 10%, and 5%, respectively. Second, when a company with debt has an ROA greater than its interest rate, ROE exceeds ROA. This situation is called *favorable financial leverage* and describes both Company B and Company C in year 1. They earn 20% on their assets and pay either 10% or 12% on their debt. The earnings in excess of the interest cost increase earnings available to shareholders and increase ROE.

Year 2 is interesting because Company B has an ROA of 10%, which equals its interest rate. Thus, like Company A, Company B has ROE of 10%. In contrast, Company C experiences *unfavorable financial leverage*. Because its 10% ROA is less than its 12% interest cost, its ROE falls sharply to 4%. Year 3 further stresses the effects of financial leverage in years when the company performs poorly. When ROA falls noticeably below the firm's interest cost, ROE also falls sharply. Company B's ROE falls to 2%, whereas the more highly leveraged Company C faces a loss year and negative ROE.

When a company is unable to earn at least the interest rate on the money borrowed, the ROE is lower than it would be for a debt-free company. If earnings are low enough that the company cannot pay the interest and principal payments on debt, it may be forced into bankruptcy. The possibility of bankruptcy increases the risk to the common stockholders even more than it does to debt holders. Remember, debt holders collect their claims before stockholders do.

The more stable a company's income, the less dangerous it is to trade on the equity. Therefore, industries that have traditionally been regulated, such as electric, gas, and telephone companies, tend to have a much heavier proportion of debt than do manufacturers of computers or high-tech companies. Historically, these regulated companies have had a stable customer base and were somewhat protected from competition. Government regulations helped ensure that prices would be sufficiently high to ensure a profit. The breakup of AT&T as the dominant national phone company and recent efforts to deregulate electric utilities have produced changes in these historical patterns of financial leverage. Many utilities still have debt levels left over from their stable, regulated past. However, deregulation has made their returns much less stable and, therefore, their stock a more risky investment. The prudent use of debt is part of intelligent financial management.

Economic Value Added

Economic Value Added (EVA)

Measure of the residual wealth of a company after deducting its cost of capital from operating profit.

We calculate ROA and ROE directly from financial statement information. These ratios measure performance by relating an income statement number to investment levels reported on the balance sheet. **Economic Value Added (EVA)** is a related performance measure, developed and trademarked by Stern Stewart & Company, that measures the residual wealth of a company after deducting its cost of capital from operating profit. The idea is that a firm must earn more than it pays for capital if it is to increase in value. This is like saying that a firm must earn more than the interest expense on borrowing for borrowing to be favorable. When we refer to capital in EVA, we are referring to all capital, both debt and equity. The cost of that capital is a weighted average of interest cost and the returns required by equity investors.

Assume that a company has a weighted-average cost of capital of 10% and $1 million in capital. The company is adding value if its net operating profit after tax exceeds 10% of $1 million, or $100,000. If the net operating profit after tax is $120,000, for example, we would calculate the EVA as ($120,000 − $100,000) = $20,000. If this firm generates only $70,000 of net operating profit after tax, we would say that EVA is ($70,000 − $100,000) = negative $30,000. In the latter case, the company is losing value. If such losses are expected to continue, it would be preferable to dissolve the company and return the capital to the creditors and owners.

In applying EVA, managers often make adjustments to the accounting results reported under GAAP because they believe GAAP does not always reflect true economic value. Without exploring all such adjustments, we consider one: research and development (R&D) expenditures. Although U.S. GAAP requires most companies to expense R&D immediately, all agree that it has some economic value and that expensing R&D is a conservative approach. EVA proponents argue that it is better to arbitrarily assume a 5-year life than no life, and they restate the financial statements accordingly. You saw an example of this type of restatement on page 365 in Chapter 8. As a reminder, suppose a company capitalized the $50,000 it spent each year on R&D and assigned a 5-year life to the resulting asset. After the first 4 years, annual amortization of R&D on the income statement would equal the amount spent, $50,000. Whether the $50,000 is expensed each year as R&D expense or as amortization expense, net income is the same after the first 4 years. However, both assets and stockholders' equity will be higher if the expenditure is capitalized and amortized.

Many companies have adopted EVA as an internal management tool, including Coca-Cola, Whole Foods, Herman Miller, and K-Swiss. They believe that this procedure helps them allocate, manage, and redeploy scarce capital resources such as heavy equipment, working capital, and real estate.

Income Tax Effects of Financing Decisions

Because interest payments, but not dividends, are deductible by the company for income tax purposes, if everything else is equal, the use of debt can be less costly to the corporation than is the use of equity. Consider raising additional capital of $10 million either through long-term debt or through preferred stock. Typically preferred stock is part of shareholders' equity, and any dividends paid to preferred stockholders are not deductible for income tax purposes. Furthermore, the rate of preferred dividends is usually higher than the rate of interest on long-term debt because the preferred stockholders have greater risk due to their lower priority claim on the total assets of a company. Assume an interest rate of 6% for debt, a preferred dividend rate of 7%, and an income tax rate of 40%. Exhibit 12-9 shows the effects on net income of electing to raise capital through long-term debt versus preferred stock.

EXHIBIT 12-9

Income Tax Effects of Financing Decisions

	$10 Million Long-Term Debt	$10 Million Preferred Stock
Income before interest expense (assumed)	$5,000,000	$5,000,000
Interest expense at 6% of long-term debt	$ 600,000	—
Income before income taxes	$4,400,000	$5,000,000
Income tax expense at 40%	1,760,000	2,000,000
Net income	$2,640,000	$3,000,000
Dividends to preferred shareholders at 7%	—	700,000
Net income available to common stockholders	$2,640,000	$2,300,000
Pretax cost of capital raised	6%	7%
After-tax cost of capital raised		
($360,000* ÷ $10,000,000)	3.6%	
($700,000 ÷ $10,000,000)		7%

*Interest expense	$600,000
Less income tax savings because of interest deduction:	
(.40 × $600,000)	240,000
Interest expense after tax savings	$360,000

When you examine Exhibit 12-9, you should note three points:

1. Interest is tax deductible, so its after-tax cost can be considerably less than that of dividends on preferred stock (3.6% versus 7%). In other words, using debt makes net income attributable to common shareholders substantially higher.

2. Interest is an expense, whereas preferred dividends are not. Therefore, using preferred shares makes net income higher ($3 million versus $2.64 million). Note that trading on the equity can benefit the common stockholders by the issuance of either long-term debt securities or preferred stock, provided that the additional assets generate sufficient earnings.

3. Failure to pay interest can lead to bankruptcy, which gives creditors rights to control or liquidate the company. The consequences of failure to pay dividends are less severe.

Measuring Safety

Investors in debt securities want to be sure that the company's future operations will provide enough cash to cover scheduled payments of interest and principal. Debt securities often have provisions aimed at reducing debt holder risk, such as the right to repossess assets or the right to receive payment before common stockholders. However, because such provisions take effect only when the company is in danger of defaulting on the loans, they are nowhere near as valuable as a pattern of earnings growth. Debtholders prefer to avoid the trouble and costs of foreclosure or bankruptcy litigation. They would much rather have a steady stream of interest and repayments of principal provided by a company with good, steady earnings. They do not want to be in the position of Enron's bondholders, waiting several years after the company declared bankruptcy and then receiving only a fraction of each dollar owed them.

Debt-to-equity ratios, discussed in Chapter 9, are popular measures of risk. However, they do not focus directly on the major concern of the holders of long-term debt: the ability of the company to make interest payments and repay debt on schedule. The interest coverage-ratio, calculated as EBIT divided by interest expense, focuses on interest-paying ability. In Exhibit 12-6, interest coverage for Nike is 49.7 times in 2009.

A rule of thumb or benchmark for debt investors is that the interest coverage should be at least five times, even in the poorest year in a span of 7 to 10 years. The numerator in this ratio is computed on a before tax basis because interest expense is deductible for income tax purposes. In effect, all EBIT is available to pay interest; companies pay taxes only on the amount remaining after paying interest. This tax-deductibility feature is a major reason companies use long-term debt much more widely than they use preferred stock.

Prominence of Earnings per Share

Throughout this text, we regard earnings as a basic reporting element in the financial statements. We often express earnings on a per share basis (EPS), and EPS is itself a component in other ratios. Up to this point, we have kept EPS simple by assuming the company has only common stock. In reality, EPS can be more complicated. We now turn to several issues that complicate the computation of EPS: changes in the number of common shares outstanding during the year, the presence of preferred stock, and the existence of convertible securities.

Weighted-Average Shares and Preferred Stock

When a company has only common stock outstanding, the primary complication is calculation of the weighted-average number of common shares outstanding in the following equation (numbers assumed):

$$\frac{\text{Earnings per share}}{\text{of common stock}} = \frac{\text{Net income}}{\text{Weighted-average number of common shares outstanding during the period}}$$

$$= \frac{\$1,000,000}{800,000} = \$1.25$$

How would we calculate the 800,000 weighted-average shares in the denominator? Suppose 750,000 shares were outstanding at the beginning of a fiscal year, and the company issued

200,000 additional shares 3 months before the end of the fiscal year. The weighted average is based on the number of months that the shares were outstanding during the year. We can do the basic computation in two different ways:

750,000 × Weighting of 12/12	=	750,000		750,000 × 9/12	=	562,500
200,000 × Weighting of 3/12	=	50,000	or	950,000 × 3/12	=	237,500
Weighted-average shares		800,000				800,000

In this example, the number of shares outstanding rose because the company issued additional shares during the year. This might have occurred because executives exercised stock options and acquired more shares. Alternatively, the company might have issued a block of additional shares to outside investors at the current market price. The number of shares outstanding could also decline during the year if the company purchases shares for the treasury or retires shares.

A second complication arises if shares of nonconvertible preferred stock are outstanding. To compute the earnings applicable to common stock, we deduct the dividends on preferred stock for the current period, even if the company does not pay the dividends (figures assumed):

$$\frac{\text{Earnings per share}}{\text{of common stock}} = \frac{\text{Net income} - \text{Preferred dividends}}{\text{Weighted-average number of common shares outstanding during the period}}$$

$$= \frac{\$1,000,000 - \$200,000}{800,000} = \$1.00$$

Further, to ensure comparability of historical summaries of EPS, we must adjust for changes in capitalization structure, for example, stock splits and stock dividends. As an example, Nike's Web site indicates that Nike's common stock has split five times since 1983, with the most recent two-for-one stock split occurring in April 2007. In the 2007 annual report, Nike reports 2006 EPS of $2.69. If you look at the 2006 annual report, the EPS reported is $5.37. Why did Nike adjust the 2006 EPS when it published the 2007 annual report? Because the investor wants to be able to compare the year-to-year performance in terms of the current number of shares. Because each 2006 share outstanding counts as two 2007 shares, Nike adjusted the 2006 EPS to allow meaningful comparisons.

Basic and Diluted EPS

EPS calculations become a bit more complex when companies have convertible securities, stock options, or other financial instruments that holders can exchange for, or convert into, common shares. For example, suppose that a firm has outstanding preferred stock that is convertible into common stock.

Convertible preferred stock at 5%, $100 par, each share convertible into two common shares	100,000 shares
Common stock	1,000,000 shares

The basic EPS computation follows (numbers assumed):

Computation of earnings per share	
Net income	$10,500,000
Less: Preferred dividends	
(0.05 × $100 × 100,000 shares)	500,000
Net income available to common stockholders	$10,000,000
Earnings per share of common stock	
($10,000,000 ÷ 1,000,000 shares)	$ 10.00

However, note the effect on EPS if the preferred shareholders converted, that is, exchanged their preferred shares for shares of common stock. EPS will be "diluted," or reduced. We can calculate EPS as if conversion had occurred at the beginning of the period. No preferred dividends would be paid, but there would be 200,000 more common shares outstanding:

Net income	$10,500,000
Less: Preferred dividends	0
Net income available to common stockholders	$10,500,000
Earnings per share of common stock—assuming conversion ($10,500,000 ÷ 1,200,000 shares)	$ 8.75

The dilution of EPS caused by the conversion of the preferred stock is ($10.00 – $8.75) = $1.25 per share. Diluted EPS assumes the conversion of all potentially dilutive securities. In 2009, Nike reported basic EPS of $3.07 and diluted EPS of $3.03. The small difference in the two EPS measures indicates that Nike had few potentially dilutive securities.

INTERPRETING FINANCIAL STATEMENTS

You are considering an investment in a company, and as part of your analysis you decide to compute P-E and dividend-yield ratios. When you examine the company's income statement you find that it reports both basic and diluted earnings per share figures, and they are significantly different. Which earnings per share figure should you use in your ratio computations and why?

Answer

You should use basic earnings per share in the dividend-yield ratio. The market price represents the value of a share of stock currently outstanding and dividends are paid on outstanding shares. So the earnings per share used should reflect the shares actually outstanding, not the number of shares that would be outstanding if potentially dilutive securities were converted to common stock. The answer is not so obvious for the P-E ratio. If you think conversion is likely and will therefore reduce your claims to future net income, you might want to use diluted EPS.

Disclosure of Irregular Items

OBJECTIVE   6

Understand the nature of irregular items and how to adjust for them.

One of the goals of financial statement analysis is to evaluate or estimate a firm's future prospects. When forecasting the future, we need to distinguish the elements of the current financial statements that reflect ordinary recurring activity of the firm from those that represent one-time events or items that are not likely to be repeated. These irregular items fall into four major categories: unusual or nonrecurring items, extraordinary items, discontinued operations, and changes in accounting principle. A condensed income statement for Duke Energy in Exhibit 12-10 illustrates three of the four categories, with related account titles and numbers in bold italic type.

Unusual or Nonrecurring Items

Unusual or nonrecurring items were introduced earlier in the chapter. They are revenues or expenses that are large enough and unusual enough to warrant separate disclosure on the income statement. These items typically appear among operating expenses, with any necessary discussion or explanation in the footnotes. Examples include the impairment of property, plant, and equipment; impairment of goodwill; and restructuring charges. Unusual items represent the most frequent of the four categories of irregular items.

Companies have considerable flexibility in deciding when to treat something as an unusual item. Recently, numerous companies, including Nike, have recognized restructuring charges and goodwill impairments. We discussed restructuring activities in Chapter 9 and goodwill impairment in Chapters 8 and 11. The flexibility in timing of these expenses has raised questions of earnings management over the years.

As shown in Exhibit 12-10, Duke Energy reported impairment charges of $85 million as a separate line item on its income statement for 2008. How would an analyst use this information to project future income from continuing operations? If the analyst believes the impairment

EXHIBIT 12-10

Duke Energy Corporation

Condensed Consolidated Statements of Operations ($ in millions, except per share data)

	For the Year Ended December 31	
	2008	**2007**
Total operating revenues	$13,207	$12,720
Fuel used in electric generation and purchased power	4,407	3,946
Cost of natural gas and coal sold	613	557
Operations, depreciation, maintenance, etc.	5,660	5,719
Impairment charges	*85*	*0*
Losses (gains) on sales of other assets, net	(69)	5
Operating income	2,511	2,493
Other income, net	121	428
Interest expense	(737)	(687)
Income from continuing operations before income taxes	1,895	2,234
Income taxes from continuing operations	616	712
Income from continuing operations	1,279	1,522
Income (loss) from discontinued operations, net of tax	*16*	*(22)*
Income before extraordinary items	1,295	1,500
Extraordinary items, net of tax	*67*	*0*
Net income	$ 1,362	$ 1,500
Basic earnings (loss) per share of common stock		
Income from continuing operations	$ 1.01	$ 1.21
Earnings (loss) from discontinued operations	0.02	(0.02)
Earnings from extraordinary items	0.05	0.00
Net income	$ 1.08	$ 1.19
Diluted earnings (loss) per share of common stock		
Income from continuing operations	$ 1. 01	$ 1.20
Earnings (loss) from discontinued operations	0.01	(0.02)
Earnings from extraordinary items	0.05	0.00
Net income	$ 1.07	$ 1.18

charge is truly unusual and is unlikely to recur in future years, he or she might ignore the expense of $85 million in projecting the future. The analyst would base projections on pretax income from continuing operations before deducting impairment charges or ($1,895 million + $85 million) = $1,980 million in 2008.

Notice that because companies report unusual items with other expenses, they report such items on a before-tax basis. These items reduce pretax income and income tax expense. If we assume a 40% tax rate, the unusual item reported in 2008 reduced pretax income by $85 million and therefore reduced the tax provision by 40% of $85 million, or $34 million. The unusual item's after-tax effect would be [$85 million − (.40 × $85 million)] = $51 million. If the analyst elects to ignore the effect of the impairment charge in estimating future net income, she would add back $51 million to reported after-tax net income.

Exhibit 12-10 shows that Duke Energy did not report impairment charges in 2007. There were no impairment charges recognized in 2006, either. This suggests that the impairment truly was a nonrecurring item. Life would not be quite as easy for the equity analyst trying to assess the future earnings of Timberland. The Timberland income statements are not provided, but Timberland reported restructuring costs in 2008, 2007, and 2006 in amounts ranging from $0.925 million to $24.7 million. Although it is important to highlight these costs, it is not obvious

While metrics based on GAAP financial statement data provide valuable information to financial statement users, some companies attempt to extend the use of metrics to include aspects of performance that seem to defy traditional measurement techniques. For example, Wells Fargo computes a "happy-to-grumpy" ratio in an effort to assess whether its goal of developing a more engaged workforce is meeting with success. Other companies attempt to measure attributes such as customer satisfaction, innovation, brand loyalty, and service quality. Presumably, an increase in these attributes leads to increased sales. But the establishment of a link between these metrics and financial performance has proven to be a challenge.

You won't see Wells Fargo's "happy-to-grumpy" ratio in an SEC filing. However, some metrics based on nonfinancial information are reported because they complement traditional financial statement measures. Consider Southwest Airlines. In its 2008 10-K filing, Southwest reported a number of nonfinancial metrics that offer insight into Southwest's performance. Examples include the average passenger fare, number of trips flown, revenue passenger miles (RPMs) computed as the number of fare-paying passengers multiplied by the number of miles they travel, available seat miles (ASMs) computed as the number of available seats (whether occupied or not) multiplied by the number of miles traveled, and the load factor computed as RPM divided by ASM. The load factor shows how many available seats an airline actually sold relative to its total capacity. These metrics are considered valuable enough that the Air Transport Association provides industry-wide figures to be used for comparison purposes. In 2008, Southwest reported a load factor of 71.2% compared to the industry average of 79.5%. Other industries also report nonfinancial measures such as number of subscribers, number of advertisers, unit sales, or rate of occupancy.

Metrics that employ financial statement numbers in combination with nonfinancial data are frequently cited as indicators of performance. In the retail sector, sales revenue is used to compute valuable metrics such as same store sales, sales per square foot, and sales per employee. For example, in its 2007 10-K, Target Corporation reported revenues per square foot of $318 for 2007 and same store sales growth of 3% over 2006.

Companies may also report non-GAAP financial measures. The SEC defines a non-GAAP financial measure as a numerical measure of a company's historical or future financial performance, financial position, or cash flows that excludes or includes amounts that are included or excluded, respectively, in a GAAP measure. An example of a non-GAAP financial measure is a measure of operating income that excludes one or more expense or revenue items that are identified as "nonrecurring." An example of a non-GAAP financial ratio is a measure of operating margin that is calculated by dividing revenues into operating income, where either revenue or operating income, or both, are not calculated in accordance with GAAP.

The release of non-GAAP financial measures, particularly variations of earnings, became so prevalent in the late 1990s and early 2000s that the SEC now requires specific disclosures. If a company publicly releases any material information in earnings announcements, press releases, or SEC filings that includes a non-GAAP financial measure, the SEC requires the company to also present the most directly comparable financial measure calculated in accordance with GAAP and a reconciliation of the differences between the non-GAAP measure and the comparable GAAP measure. Companies presenting non-GAAP financial measures must also provide a statement disclosing why management believes that presentation of the non-GAAP metric provides useful information to investors regarding the company's financial condition and results of operations.

The magnitude of the difference in GAAP and non-GAAP financial measures can be significant. Hewlett Packard (HP) reported non-GAAP operating profit of $3.1 billion and non-GAAP diluted EPS of $0.93 in its first quarter 2009 earnings announcement. The comparable GAAP figures were operating profit of $2.5 billion and GAAP diluted EPS of $0.75. HP attributed the difference to amortization of purchased intangible assets, restructuring charges, and acquisition-related charges. Similarly, in its announcement of fourth quarter and fiscal year 2008 results, Google, Inc., reported non-GAAP financial measures that included operating income, operating margin, net income before taxes, net income after taxes, the effective tax rate, and EPS. For the 12 months ended December 31, 2008, Google's non-GAAP pretax income was 39.5% higher than its reported GAAP pretax income. Google attributed this difference to stock-based compensation charges, impairment charges related to equity investments, and expenses related to a settlement agreement with the Authors Guild and the Association of American Publishers.

While the difference in non-GAAP and GAAP financial measures for Hewlett Packard and Google may seem significant, they don't compare to the adjustments made by Boston Scientific Corporation for the 9 months ended September 30, 2009. Boston Scientific reported GAAP net income of $51 million and diluted EPS of $0.03 and non-GAAP net income of $878 million and diluted EPS of $0.58! A summary of the adjustments appear below.

In millions, except per share data	Net Income	Impact per Diluted Share
GAAP results	$ 51	$ 0.03
Non-GAAP adjustments:		
Intangible asset impairment charges	8	0.01
Acquisition-related charges	17	0.01
Divestiture-related gains	(2)	(0.00)
Restructuring-related charges	69	0.05
Litigation-related net charges	497	0.33
Discrete tax items	(74)	(0.05)
Amortization expense	312	0.20
Adjusted results	$878	$ 0.58

Boston Scientific explains the inclusion of the non-GAAP measures in its SEC filing on the basis that the company uses these measures internally to "evaluate performance period over period, to analyze the underlying trends in the Company's business, to assess its performance relative to its competitors and to establish operational goals and forecasts that are used in allocating resources."

Sources: Leibs, Scott, "Measuring Up," *CFO*, June 1, 2007, (www.cfo.com/article.cfm/9214066); Southwest Airlines 2008 annual report (www.southwest.com/investor_relations/swaar08.pdf); Conditions for Use of Non-GAAP Financial Measures, Securities and Exchange Commission (www.sec.gov/rules/final/33-8176.htm); Hewlett Packard, EDGAR Online, EXHIBIT 99 – Additional Exhibits, Filing Date: February 18, 2009; Google, Inc., EDGAR Online, EXHIBIT 99 – Additional Exhibits, Filing Date: January 23, 2009; Boston Scientific Corp., EDGAR Online, EXHIBIT 99 – Additional Exhibits, Filing Date: November 6, 2009.

that they are truly unusual or nonrecurring. In fact, the ongoing appearance of these costs on the income statement suggests the opposite. The footnote in Timberland's 2008 annual report describes these costs as related to severance, store closures, lease termination costs, and impairment of property, plant, and equipment.

An analyst might conclude that costs of this type will continue in future years and therefore base predictions on the pretax income from continuing operations without adding back these unusual items. Adjustment would be more appropriate for a company that had not experienced such costs in prior years, but is making what appears to be a one-time reduction in workforce levels and asset values. For decision making and forecasting purposes, companies may also adjust their income for the effects of nonrecurring or unusual items. See the Business First Box for discussion of additional means of measuring performance.

Extraordinary Items

Extraordinary items result from events that are both unusual in nature and infrequent in occurrence. Write-downs of receivables, inventories, and intangibles are not extraordinary items. Neither are gains or losses on the sale or impairment of fixed assets. Why? Because they represent ordinary business risk. The effects of a strike and many foreign currency revaluations are also ordinary items. However, the financial effects of an earthquake or government expropriation are generally extraordinary items. Interestingly enough, we do not consider the effects of most floods as extraordinary. Why not? Because most floods occur in areas that are prone to certain amounts of flooding; thus, a flood in such locations is not an unusual occurrence. Accountants treat an event or transaction as ordinary unless the evidence clearly supports its classification as extraordinary.

We exclude extraordinary items from regular operating income calculations and present each event or item that is considered extraordinary on a separate line on the income statement. Companies report these items net of tax, which means that the figure presented includes any tax effect attributable to the item. Duke Energy reports an extraordinary item of $67 million after tax on its 2008 income statement. This was a one-time gain resulting from a ruling of the Public Utilities Commission of Ohio.

Surprisingly, U.S. authorities did not allow companies to account for the terrorist attacks of September 11, 2001, as an extraordinary item. The FASB's Emerging Issues Task Force (EITF) decided that, although the events of September 11 were definitely extraordinary, treating the financial effects of those events as extraordinary items would not be an effective means of communicating with stockholders. In a news release on October 1, 2001, the EITF observed "that the

extraordinary items
Items that are both unusual in nature and infrequent in occurrence that are shown separately, net of tax, on the income statement.

economic effects of the events were so extensive and pervasive that it would be impossible to capture them in any one financial statement line item."

Discontinued Operations

discontinued operations

A component of the business that is distinguishable from the rest of the entity, both operationally and for financial reporting purposes, that a company disposes of or makes plans to dispose of. The results are reported separately, net of tax, on the income statement.

Discontinued operations occur when a company disposes of (i.e., closes or sells), or makes plans to dispose of, a component of the business that is distinguishable from the rest of the entity, both operationally and for financial reporting. If a company discontinues such a component, it should report the results of continuing operations separately from the operating results of the discontinued operations, although it must still report both on the income statement. This separation distinguishes the operations that are expected to continue from those that will not continue, enhancing the analyst's ability to forecast future performance. Companies must also separately report any gain or loss from the disposal of a discontinued operation. Like extraordinary items, discontinued operations are shown on the income statement net of tax.

In comparative income statements over multiple years, the statements must show the income or loss of the discontinued operations separately for all years in which that discontinued component operated. Otherwise, the company's current financial status, which no longer includes the discontinued component, would not be comparable to its past financial status. Because income statements reflect 3 years of comparative data, in the year a company makes the decision to discontinue an operation, it reports the effect separately for the current year and restates the prior 2 years to isolate the operations of the discontinued portion of the business. When evaluating a firm's income patterns through time, an analyst may need to estimate the amount of income attributable to discontinued operations in years prior to those restated by the company.

In Exhibit 12-10, Duke Energy discloses the income statement effects of its discontinued operations. The discontinued operations footnote is more than four pages long and complex. To simplify, the $16 million in after-tax income from discontinued operations reported in 2008 and the $22 million in after-tax net loss reported in 2007 are a combination of several different events, including the sale of two hydroelectric power plants in Bolivia. As a result of this sale, the company no longer has any assets in Bolivia. Also, the company ceased all synthetic fuel operations and exited that line of business.

Changes in Accounting Principle

Changes in accounting principles occur under two circumstances: (1) when a company voluntarily changes from one acceptable accounting method to another, and (2) when a standard setting authority issues a new accounting standard. In the year of the change in accounting principle, the company uses the newly-adopted method to prepare the financial statements. Then, in most cases, the company makes a retrospective adjustment to the financial statements of all prior periods that are presented. This restates prior period financial statements to reflect the newly-adopted accounting principle and makes prior periods consistent with the year of the change. The company also makes a cumulative adjustment to the beginning balance in Retained Earnings for the earliest year presented.

International Issues

Internationally, a variety of factors complicate financial statement analysis. Throughout the text, we consider differences in accounting methods used under U.S. GAAP and IFRS. When companies use different methods to generate the numbers in the financial statements, ratios based on those numbers may not be comparable. This is one of the reasons that comparison of Nike to adidas was not included in this chapter. In addition, we should stress the obvious but easily forgotten differences in the language of reporting and the currency of measurement. For example, most U.S. analysts cannot read financial statements in Japanese and do not readily "have a feel for" the value of yen versus dollars. Last, but not least, is the fact that different structures for security markets, different tax laws, and different preferences among citizens of different countries all affect the relative value of financial assets.

Valuation Issues

OBJECTIVE 7

Use financial information to help assess a company's value.

Accounting data are critically important to determining the value of a company. We have already examined a number of ratios that help in this effort. Exhibit 12-11 presents fundamental price and valuation information for Nike (NKE), Under Armour (UA), Timberland (TBL), and

PRICE AND VALUATION

Ticker Symbol	Current Price September 19, 2009	52-Week Range	Beta	Latest Annual EPS	Price-Earnings
NKE	$58.59	38.24–68.00	0.84	$3.07	19.36
UA	$29.60	11.94–43.52	1.72	$0.79	37.62
TBL	$14.08	7.19–19.41	1.25	$0.73	20.55
KSWS	$ 9.56	6.44–20.76	0.91	$0.60	n/a

Ticker Symbol	Price/Sales	Price/Book	Price/Cash Flow	Analyst Rating
NKE	1.48	3.27	15.53	2.22
UA	1.91	4.25	23.00	3.36
TBL	0.61	1.43	11.12	3.33
KSWS	1.19	1.06	n/a	3.75

GROWTH RATES AND DIVIDENDS

Ticker Symbol	Latest Annual Revenue (mil)	1-yr Revenue Growth	5-yr Revenue Growth	Latest Annual EPS	1-yr EPS Growth	5-yr EPS Growth
NKE	$19,176.1	2.95%	9.37%	$3.07	–19.0%	11.56%
UA	$ 725.2	14.82%	44.42%	$0.79	–4.15%	37.76%
TBL	$ 1,364.5	–9.52%	0.33%	$0.73	–13.66%	–14.70%
KSWS	$ 340.2	–23.60%	–4.54%	$0.60	–153.17%	–16.10%

Ticker Symbol	Latest Annual Dividend/Share	Dividend Yield	5-yr Dividend Growth Rate
NKE	$0.98	1.71	21.51%
UA	$0.0	0.00	0.00%
TBL	$0.0	0.00	0.00%
KSWS	$2.20	2.09	122.88%

FINANCIAL STRENGTH

Ticker Symbol	Total Debt/Equity	Long-term Debt/Equity	Current Ratio	Quick Ratio
NKE	10.13%	5.03%	2.97	2.25
UA	5.85%	3.47%	3.57	1.89
TBL	0.82%	0.00%	3.56	2.38
KSWS	1.64%	0.25%	8.57	6.75

EFFICIENCY

Ticker Symbol	Current Inventory Turnover	Current Receivable Turnover	Total Asset Turnover	Revenue/Employee (000s)	Income/Employee (000s)
NKE	4.41	6.75	1.49	$559.1	$43.3
UA	2.20	8.25	1.73	$352.7	$17.9
TBL	3.77	11.65	1.71	$215.1	$ 6.7
KSWS	2.90	6.18	0.67	$483.1	–$43.7

PROFITABILITY

Ticker Symbol	Gross Margin	Operating Margin	Pretax Margin	After-tax Profit Margin
NKE	44.87%	10.20%	10.20%	7.75%
UA	48.21%	10.39%	9.29%	5.08%
TBL	45.18%	4.51%	4.66%	3.13%
KSWS	34.02%	–12.44%	–11.35%	–9.04%

MANAGEMENT EFFECTIVENESS

Ticker Symbol	Return on Assets	5-yr Avg. Return on Assets	Return on Equity	5-yr Avg. Return on Equity
NKE	11.57%	14.25%	18.00%	22.27%
UA	8.76%	13.10%	12.32%	18.91%
TBL	5.35%	12.77%	7.25%	19.00%
KSWS	–6.07%	15.77%	–6.92%	19.09%

Data as of September 19, 2009.
Source: Reuters (www.reuters.com).

EXHIBIT 12-11

Industry Fundamentals
Nike (NKE), Under Armour (UA), Timberland (TBL), and K-SWISS (KSWS)

K-Swiss (KSWS) gathered from Reuters (www.reuters.com) as of September 19, 2009, as well as a few figures drawn from each company's most recent annual report. Information provided by Reuters is similar to that provided by many financial services. When using information gathered from outside sources, be sure you thoroughly understand the items reported. For example, the price/book, total-debt-to-equity, current, and quick ratios in Exhibit 12-11 are based on figures from the most recent quarterly financial statements. Many of the other reported values, such as the P-E ratio, ROA, ROE, and the 1-year growth rates are based on the most recent 12 months. As a result, the values for Nike presented in Exhibit 12-11 do not correspond to those values reported in Exhibit 12-6, which used data from the fiscal year ended May 31, 2009.

Valuation techniques are beyond the scope of this textbook, and we do not attempt to reach conclusions regarding the appropriateness of the reported stock prices. Rather, our intent is to demonstrate that some of the information needed for valuation is readily available and related to the outputs of financial statement analysis. Reviewing this information gives us an opportunity to emphasize the importance of financial information in valuation and to explain a few common ratios and values to which we have not given significant attention. We next describe and compare key information shown in Exhibit 12-11 and then elaborate briefly on the P-E ratio.

Some Basic Comparisons

The four stocks traded at very different prices on September 19, 2009, and all have shown significant share price variation during the period from September 2008 to September 2009. NKE, UA, and TBL are trading slightly above the middle of their respective 52-week price ranges. KSWS is trading near the low end of its range. Beta is a measure of how closely the price of the company's stock follows general market conditions. A value of 1.0 indicates the stock price moves proportionally to the market. NKE and KSWS have betas below 1.0 suggesting that they move slightly less than the market. For example, on a typical day, if the market moved up 10%, NKE would be expected to move up only 8.4%, whereas KSWS would move 9.1%. UA and TBL, on the other hand, have betas in excess of 1.0. If the market moved up 10%, UA and TBL would be expected to move 17.2% and 12.5%, respectively.

The latest annual EPS of the four companies are also widely divergent. The two companies with the most similar EPS are UA at $0.79 and TBL at $0.73. However, the market priced these stocks very differently on September 19, 2009. UA has a P-E ratio of 37.62, compared to TBL's P-E of 20.55. Note that the P-E ratio shown by Reuters is not the result of dividing the current price by the prior year's EPS. Rather, the reported P-E ratio uses the most recent 12-months' earnings in the denominator. Also note that Reuters provides no P-E ratio for KSWS, which has operated at a net loss during the last 12 months, because a negative P-E ratio is not meaningful. Exhibit 12-11 also includes items that relate stock price to sales, to book value, and to cash flow.

The Growth Rates and Dividends portion of Exhibit 12-11 displays the most recent annual revenue, EPS, and dividends per share to provide a sense of size differences among the companies. Nike is by far the largest of the four with respect to revenues. This section of the exhibit gives growth rates for 1 and 5 years for revenue and EPS, and a 5-year growth rate for dividends. While NKE and UA have experienced positive growth in revenues over the last 12 months, TBL and KSWS have seen decreased revenues and negative growth rates. All four companies have a negative 1-year growth rate in EPS. This is not surprising given the general economic downturn and market weakness during this time period. Neither TBL nor UA declare a dividend. Historically, KSWS paid a dividend of $0.20 per share. The unusually high dividend, dividend yield, and 5-year dividend growth for KSWS in Exhibit 12-11 is the result of a $2.00 per share special dividend.

The data in the Financial Strength section of the exhibit are outputs of ratio analysis. You should be familiar with the four ratios in this section. Reuters defines total debt as both short- and long-term debt but does not include operating liabilities such as accounts payable and accrued expenses. Note the differences in capital structure. NKE has a total-debt-to-equity ratio of 10.13% whereas TBL's ratio is less than 1%. None of the four firms carry much interest-bearing debt.

The Efficiency section of Exhibit 12-11 displays both standard ratios and information about performance per employee. We can see that the companies vary widely with regard to inventory, receivable, and total asset turnovers. There is also variation in the revenue-per-employee and income-per-employee metrics. While each NKE employee has generated an average of $559,100 in revenue in the last 12 months, each TBL employee has generated only $215,100.

The Profitability section of the exhibit displays four measures of profitability per dollar of sales: gross margin, operating margin, pretax margin, and after-tax profit margin. Note that NKE, UA, and TBL have fairly similar gross margins ranging from 48.21% for UA to 44.87% for NKE. However, after accounting for all operating expenses and nonoperating activity, the resultant after-tax profit margins are much more divergent. NKE reports an after-tax profit margin of 7.75%, more than twice that reported for TBL. KSWS reports the lowest values for all four metrics. In fact, the operating, pretax, and after-tax margins for KSWS are all negative!

The Management Effectiveness portion of Exhibit 12-11 reveals significant differences in the return on assets and return on equity for the four firms. For example, the ROE for the most recent 12 months ranges from 18.0% for NKE to a negative return for KSWS. After NKE, UA has the next highest ROE at 12.32%, but the difference of 5.68 percentage points is significant. As expected, when you look at the 5-year average ROE, the spread is reduced, with all four companies in the 19%–22% range. This highlights the importance of considering more than 1 year's performance.

So what might an analyst conclude? There are always more questions. What is the company planning? How many new products are in the pipeline? How are competitors changing the industry dynamics? Analysts would pursue answers to these and other questions before reaching a conclusion. Reuters does provide some information about analysts' views on these stocks. See the Analyst Rating column in the Price and Valuation section of Exhibit 12-11. A rating of 1 indicates a buy recommendation, 2 indicates that analysts expect the stock to outperform the market, 3 is a hold recommendation, 4 suggests the stock will underperform the market, and 5 is a sell recommendation. From the analysts' perspectives, NKE is viewed most favorably with a rating of 2.2. The other three stocks have ratings above 3.

Price-Earnings Ratios and Growth

Some consider the P-E ratio a useful valuation tool. The ratio relates the price of a company's stock to the earnings it is generating. Some argue that low P-E stocks might be undervalued and high P-E stocks might be overvalued. This is the view of analysts called "value investors." These investors seek securities that the market is currently undervaluing. They would not blindly buy low P-E stocks, but would use a low P-E ratio as a screen to identify securities that are likely candidates for purchase. They would then consider many other factors in determining the best investments.

The opposite view is that the best investments are growth stocks. "Growth investors" believe that high P-E stocks are likely to be high-growth stocks. The price is "high" because investors see strong growth prospects ahead. Again, the growth investor would use high P-Es to identify a group of stocks to evaluate more carefully.

Who is right? How do we relate P-E ratios to growth? When are we paying too much for future growth? As of September 2009, the average P-E on stocks of large U.S. companies was about 19. Although this was above long-term norms of around 15, it was down from recent levels, which peaked at more than 45. The P-E ratios for the four firms in our sample range from 19.36 to 37.62.

One metric that relates P-E ratios directly to earnings growth rates is the **price-earnings growth (PEG) ratio**. To compute the PEG ratio, we divide the P-E ratio by the earnings growth rate. We can calculate the P-E ratio and the earnings growth rate based on historical earnings, current earnings, or forecasted earnings. Many analysts prefer a current P-E ratio and a forecasted 5-year earnings growth rate. Due to the variation in computational methods, information sources report widely different numbers.

How do we interpret the PEG ratio? A PEG ratio greater than 1.0 indicates that the stock may be overvalued or that the market expects future EPS growth to be greater than that currently reflected in the analysts' consensus forecast EPS. Growth stocks typically have a PEG ratio greater than 1.0 because investors are willing to pay more for a stock that they expect to grow rapidly. Stocks with a PEG ratio less than 1.0 may be undervalued, or the market may believe the earnings growth estimate reflected in the consensus forecast is too high.

price-earnings growth (PEG) ratio
Price-earnings ratio divided by the earnings growth rate.

Relating Cash Flow and Net Income

Although this chapter focuses on evaluating a company's performance based on various earnings metrics (e.g., EPS, P-E, PEG), we would be remiss if we did not mention the important role of cash flow. In fact, valuation models frequently use estimated cash flows, not forecasted earnings. Both net income and cash flow from operations are positive for the healthiest of firms. However, there are four possible combinations of positive and negative net income and cash flow from operations, and it is useful to think about what they might mean.

Relationship	1	2	3	4
Cash flow from operations	+	+	−	−
Net income	+	−	+	−

In relationship 1, the two positive values confirm the profitability of the company. In the fourth case, the uniform negative values are again in agreement. When either of these patterns appears and continues for multiple periods, the implications are straightforward.

What about relationship 2? This is common in some industries. Consider high capital investment industries with large depreciation charges or rapidly growing companies in capital-intensive industries. If a company uses a declining-balance depreciation method, large depreciation charges may create losses even though operating cash flow is positive. One should examine several years to assess the pattern. Another example is real estate, where the economic returns to the company include both current operating performance and appreciation of the underlying property. The accounting model does not record appreciation in real estate, so it does not appear in the income statement. Thus, you could have negative net income even though cash flow was sufficient to cover all expenses and the investment was appreciating consistently.

Relationship 3 is often a red flag for trouble, but may also represent the case of a rapidly growing firm. The difference between cash flow from operations and net income is depreciation and accruals of current operating assets and liabilities. A very rapidly growing firm may be investing heavily in inventory for new stores and granting credit to new customers with the result that inventories and accounts receivable are growing very quickly. This may be a good situation as long as the sales demand does not outpace the company's ability to meet customer demand and pay its current obligations. We also observe this pattern in cases where sales revenue is not growing quickly, but inventory and accounts receivable are increasing. This situation tends to indicate bad management, slow-moving merchandise, and failure to manage credit. This pattern often precedes bankruptcy. In order to interpret relationship 3 for a given firm, you need to understand the firm and the industry in which it operates.

Analysts often use the relationship between cash flow from operations and net income as one of a set of indicators that address the issue of earnings quality. Earnings quality is not a well-defined or well-understood concept. However, one of the attributes of high-quality earnings that many analysts agree on is that companies should not recognize revenues prematurely and not defer expenses inappropriately. In some cases, companies may, intentionally or unintentionally, engage in accounting choices that lower the quality of earnings numbers. For example, by capitalizing costs that it should have expensed, WorldCom reported higher earnings than it should have. As a result, although earnings were higher in dollar magnitude, the quality of those earnings was lower. There is no single means to assess earnings quality. However, one ratio that some analysts use is a comparison of cash flow from operations to net income. We would expect this ratio to be consistently greater than one. Why? Because net income includes an expense for depreciation, but cash flow from operations does not contain the related cash outflow. (The cash outflow is an investing activity at the time the asset is paid for.) If the ratio is significantly less than one, this may be an indication of low-quality earnings and a pending cash flow crisis.

Summary Problem for Your Review

PROBLEM

Exhibit 12-12 contains balance sheets and income statements for Kellogg Company. Kellogg is the world's leading producer of cereal, as well as convenience foods such as cookies, crackers, toaster pastries, cereal bars, and assorted other products. For more than a century, Kellogg has been producing great-tasting, high-quality, nutritious foods.

1. Compute the following ratios for 2008: (a) current ratio, (b) quick ratio, (c) average collection period, (d) inventory turnover, (e) total asset turnover, (f) return on sales, (g) financial leverage ratio, and (h) ROE. Define the quick ratio as current assets minus inventories divided by current liabilities.

2. Compare your computed values with the values for General Mills reported below.

General Mills 2008	
Current ratio	0.98
Quick ratio	0.61
Average collection period (days)	25.3
Inventory turnover (times)	6.97
Total asset turnover (times)	0.8
Return on sales	8.88%
Financial leverage ratio	3.24
ROE	22.8%

EXHIBIT 12-12

Kellogg Company and Subsidiaries

Consolidated Balance Sheets and Statements of Earnings ($ in millions, except per share data)

Consolidated Balance Sheets	December 31, 2008	December 31, 2007
Assets		
Current assets		
Cash and cash equivalents	$ 255	$ 524
Accounts receivable, net	1,143	1,011
Inventories	897	924
Other current assets	226	243
Total current assets	2,521	2,702
Property, net	2,933	2,990
Goodwill	3,637	3,515
Other intangible assets, net	1,461	1,450
Other assets	394	740
Total assets	$10,946	$11,397
Liabilities and stockholders' equity		
Current liabilities		
Current maturities of long-term debt	$ 1	$ 466
Notes payable	1,387	1,489
Accounts payable	1,135	1,081
Other current liabilities	1,029	1,008
Total current liabilities	3,552	4,044
Long-term debt	4,068	3,270
Deferred income taxes	300	647
Pension liability	631	171
Other liabilities	947	739
Shareholders' equity		
Common stock—par value $0.25; 1,000,000,000 shares authorized; issued, 418,842,707 shares in 2008 and 418,669,193 shares in 2007	105	105
Capital in excess of par	438	388
Retained earnings	4,836	4,217
Accumulated other comprehensive income (loss)	(2,141)	(827)
Treasury stock at cost; 36,981,580 shares in 2008 and 28,618,052 shares in 2007	(1,790)	(1,357)
Total shareholders' equity	1,448	2,526
Total liabilities and stockholders' equity	$10,946	$11,397

**EXHIBIT 12-12
(Continued)**

**Kellogg Company and
Subsidiaries**

*Consolidated Balance Sheets
and Statements of Earnings
($ in millions, except per
share data)*

Consolidated Statements of Earnings

	Year Ended December 31, 2008	Year Ended December 31, 2007	Year Ended December 31, 2006
Net sales	$12,822	$11,776	$10,907
Cost of goods sold	7,455	6,597	6,082
Selling, general, and administrative expenses	3,414	3,311	3,059
Operating profit	1,953	1,868	1,766
Interest expense	308	319	307
Other expense (income), net	12	2	(13)
Earnings before income taxes	1,633	1,547	1,472
Income taxes	485	444	468
Net earnings	$ 1,148	$ 1,103	$ 1,004
Earnings per share—basic	$ 3.01	$ 2.79	$ 2.53
Earnings per share—diluted	$ 2.99	$ 2.76	$ 2.51

SOLUTION

1. Amounts are in millions of dollars.
   a. Current ratio = Current assets ÷ Current liabilities
      = $2,521 ÷ $3,552 = 0.71

   b. Quick ratio = (Current assets − Inventories) ÷ Current liabilities
      = ($2,521 − $897) ÷ $3,552 = 0.46

   c. Average collection period = (Average accounts receivable × 365) ÷ Sales
      = [(($1,143 + $1,011) ÷ 2) × 365] ÷ $12,822 = 30.7 days

   d. Inventory turnover = Cost of goods sold ÷ Average inventory
      = $7,455 ÷ [($897 + $924) ÷ 2] = 8.19 times per year

   e. Total asset turnover = Sales ÷ Average total assets
      = $12,822 ÷ [($10,946 + $11,397) ÷ 2] = 1.15

   f. Return on sales = Net income ÷ Sales
      = $1,148 ÷ $12,822 = 8.95%

   g. Financial leverage ratio = Average total assets ÷ Average stockholders' equity
      = [($10,946 + $11,397) ÷ 2] ÷ [($1,448 + $2,526) ÷ 2] = 5.62

   h. ROE = Net income ÷ Average stockholders' equity
      = $1,148 ÷ [($1,448 + $2,526) ÷ 2] = 57.8%

2. Kellogg has a return on equity ratio (57.8%) that is more than double the value reported by General Mills (22.8%). The return on sales, total asset turnover, and financial leverage ratios give some insight into what is driving the difference in ROE. The companies have very similar return on sales ratios suggesting similar performance in controlling expenses relative to sales levels. Without the ability to compare common-size income statements, it is difficult to say why Kellogg has a slightly higher ratio (8.95% for Kellogg versus 8.88% for General Mills). Kellogg also has a higher asset turnover ratio (1.15) indicating that it is able to generate more sales per dollar of assets than General Mills (0.8). Again, without more information it is difficult to know why Kellogg's total asset turnover ratio is higher. The inventory turnover ratio does suggest that Kellogg turns its inventory at a faster rate (8.19 times per year compared to General Mills 6.97), but it is slower to collect cash than General Mills as evidenced by the longer average collection period (Kellogg 30.7 days versus General Mills 25.3 days). The big driver of Kellogg's higher ROE is the successful use of financial leverage. Kellogg reports a leverage ratio of 5.62 compared to General Mills' 3.24. With regard to short-term liquidity ratios, General Mills reports higher current and quick ratios than Kellogg. Without access to the General Mills balance sheet, it is impossible to compare the composition of the current assets of the two companies. However, on the surface, General Mills' ratios suggest greater short-term liquidity.

Highlights to Remember

1 **Locate and use sources of information about company performance.** Financial and operating information is available from many sources, including company Web sites, the financial business press, analyst reports, and financial services companies. Various regulations in the United States require the issuance of annual reports and govern their content. In addition, publicly traded companies must disclose particular information by filing a 10-K, an 8-K, and other forms with the SEC on a periodic basis.

2 **Analyze the performance of a company using trend analysis, common-size financial statements, and segment disclosures.** Companies provide financial information to aid investors in assessing the risk and return of a potential investment. Creditors are particularly concerned about the solvency and liquidity of the issuer, whereas equity investors are more interested in profitability. Numerous tools are available to assist both creditors and equity investors. Trend analysis is a form of financial statement analysis that concentrates on changes in the financial statements through time. It involves comparing relationships for a period of years or quarters. We construct common-size financial statements by expressing the elements of the balance sheet as a percentage of total assets and the elements of the income statement as a percentage of total revenue. Common-size statements enhance the ability to compare one company with another or to conduct a trend analysis over time. Segment disclosures allow analysis of separate business units.

3 **Use basic financial ratios to guide your thinking.** Basic financial ratios allow us to put numbers in perspective. By relating one part of the financial statements to another, ratios facilitate questions such as "Given the change in revenues, was the change in accounts receivable reasonable?" and "Is the company's inventory level, given its size, comparable to industry norms?" The chapter reviews the ratios presented throughout the text and adds some new ratios. Liquidity ratios deal with the immediate ability to make payments. Solvency ratios deal with the longer-term ability to meet obligations. Creditors often incorporate such ratios into debt covenants to protect lenders' rights. Investors use profitability ratios to assess operating efficiency and performance.

4 **Evaluate corporate performance using various metrics, including ROA, ROE, and EVA.** Return on assets (ROA) is a type of return on investment that relates earnings before interest and taxes (EBIT) to total assets. We can subdivide ROA into EBIT-to-sales times total asset turnover. Return on equity (ROE) is the most fundamental profitability ratio for equity investors because it relates income to the shareholders' investment. We can subdivide ROE into the after-tax return on sales, total asset turnover, and financial leverage. EVA refers to Economic Value Added. It compares a company's adjusted earnings number with the minimum amount that it should have earned given the total capital in use. If the adjusted earnings exceed the required return, calculated as the weighted-average cost of capital times the capital in use, then the company has added economic value during the period.

5 **Calculate EPS when a company has preferred stock or dilutive securities.** Earnings per share (EPS) is a fundamental measure of performance. This chapter introduces some complexities in calculating EPS. Because preferred shares receive preference as to dividends, we deduct preferred dividends from earnings in the numerator. Because shares outstanding may change during the year, the denominator is the weighted-average number of shares outstanding over the year. The presence of options and convertible securities creates a potential to issue new shares that dilute current shareholders' interests. Therefore, companies report both basic and diluted EPS when significant potentially dilutive securities exist.

6 **Understand the nature of irregular items and how to adjust for them.** Unusual items, extraordinary items, discontinued operations, and changes in accounting principle are categories of irregular items. Separate disclosure of these items allows analysts to refine forecasts of future performance based on current operations. Income statements include unusual items with other expenses on a before-tax basis, but identify them separately. In contrast, income statements show extraordinary items and discontinued items separately, below earnings from operations and net of their individual tax effects. Changes in accounting principle are usually accounted for retrospectively.

7 **Use financial information to help assess a company's value.** To assess a company's valuation, you can use actual performance information reported by one of the readily available data providers. These sources report ratio values along with additional performance measures, including price-to-sales, price-to-book, and price-to-earnings. Analysts may see an investment opportunity when a company stands out on financial metrics including ROA and ROE and is growing quite rapidly but is not the highest priced based on P-E, price-to-sales, and price-to-book ratios.

Accounting Vocabulary

MyAccountingLab

Assignment Material

Questions

12-1 In addition to the basic financial statements, what information is usually presented in a company's annual report?

12-2 Give at least three sources of information for investors besides a company's annual report.

12-3 "Financial statements report on history. Therefore, they are not useful to creditors and investors who want to predict future returns and risk." Do you agree? Explain.

12-4 How do information demands of creditors differ from those of equity investors?

12-5 "It's always a bad sign when revenues increase at a faster percentage rate than does net income." Do you agree? Explain.

12-6 Suppose you want to evaluate the financial performance of a company over the last 5 years. What factors might affect the comparability of a firm's financial ratios over such a long period of time?

12-7 How do common-size statements aid comparisons across companies?

12-8 What information is presented in the MD&A section of annual reports?

12-9 Suppose you compared the financial statements of an airline and a grocery store. Which would you expect to have the higher values for the following ratios: debt-to-equity ratio, current ratio, inventory turnover ratio, average accounts receivable collection period, and ROE? Explain.

12-10 Whole Foods is a high-end grocery store specializing in natural and organic foods, as well as gourmet take-out foods. Whole Food stores are frequently located in up-scale neighborhoods. WinCo Foods is a warehouse-style food store chain with a large selection of non-brand name food products, as well as fresh meat, produce, bakery items, and bulk foods. WinCo stores are typically located in outlying areas where real estate is less costly. Which of the two companies would you expect to have the higher gross profit margin? The higher total asset turnover? Explain.

12-11 Name three types of comparisons that are useful in evaluating financial ratios.

12-12 Suppose you work for a small manufacturing company and the president said that you must improve your current ratio. Would you interpret this to mean that you should increase it or decrease it?

12-13 Suppose the current ratio for your company changed from 2 to 1 to become 1.8 to 1. Would you expect the level of working capital to increase or to decrease? Why?

12-14 Suppose you work for a small local department store that manages its own accounts receivable with a private charge card. Your boss has told you to improve the average collection period from 30 to 20 days. How would you go about this? What are the risks in your proposal that might affect the company negatively?

12-15 Distinguish between operating management and financial management.

12-16 What two measures of operating performance are combined to give return on total assets as defined in this chapter?

12-17 "Trading on the equity means exchanging bonds for stock." Do you agree? Explain.

12-18 "Borrowing is a double-edged sword." Do you agree? Explain.

12-19 Why are companies with heavy debt in relation to ownership capital in greater danger when business conditions deteriorate?

12-20 "The tax law discriminates against pre-ferred stock and in favor of debt." Explain.

12-21 "Any company that has income before interest and taxes greater than its interest expense is a relatively safe investment for creditors." Do you agree? Explain.

12-22 What causes the "dilution" in diluted EPS?

12-23 How does the accounting for unusual or nonrecurring items differ from the accounting for extraordinary items?

12-24 "Separate reporting of the results of dis-continued operations aids predicting future net income." Do you agree? Explain.

12-25 Suppose you want to compare the financial statements of Colgate-Palmolive and Procter & Gamble. What concerns might you have in comparing ratios for the two companies?

12-26 "A company with a high dividend pay-out ratio is a better investment than a company with a low dividend payout ratio." Do you agree? Explain.

Critical Thinking Questions

12-27 EVA

Your CEO has heard a lot about EVA as a management tool. This officer understands that the basic concept is to calculate an estimate of true economic profit by subtracting an appropriate charge for the firm's cost of capital from its operating profit. However, the CEO wonders why focusing on EVA is any better than focusing on ROE. Can you help explain the concept?

12-28 Assessing Value

Your accounting teacher has been talking about how important accounting numbers are in valu-ing a firm, and yet many of the people you know who invest are always talking about growth as the important measure. Who is right?

12-29 Investment Advice on the Internet

You belong to a stock investment club that is evaluating new stock acquisitions. One of the club members arrives at the meeting and suggests that the group should consider investing in a com-pany she read about on an investment blog that she follows on the Internet. She says that the blog has examples of investments recommended there that have doubled in value in just a few months. What do you think?

12-30 Which P-E

Your investment advisor called to suggest buying ABC Company and noted that its P-E was only 20 and the rest of the companies in its industry had P-Es of around 28. You looked in the *Wall Street Journal* and found it reported a P-E of 32 for ABC Company and an average P-E of around 30. How can you make sense of this?

Exercises

12-31 Common-Size Statements

Following are income statements for Lowe's and The Home Depot for the year ended January 30, 2009, and February 1, 2009, respectively:

	Lowe's (in millions)
Net sales	$48,230
Cost of sales	31,729
Gross profit	16,501
Selling, general, and administrative	11,074
Store opening costs	102
Depreciation	1,539
Interest, net	280
Total operating expenses	12,995
Pretax earnings	3,506
Income tax provision	1,311
Net earnings	$ 2,195

	The Home Depot (in millions)
Net sales	$71,288
Cost of sales	47,298
Gross profit	23,990
Selling, general, and administrative	17,846
Depreciation and amortization	1,785
Total operating expenses	19,631
Operating income	4,359
Interest and investment income	(18)
Interest expense	624
Other	163
Interest and other, net	769
Earnings from continuing operations before provision for income taxes	3,590
Provision for income taxes	1,278
Earnings from continuing operations	2,312
Earnings (loss) from discontinued operations, net	(52)
Net earnings	$ 2,260

1. The companies do not use exactly the same account titles. Align the accounts across the two companies in the manner you believe to be most appropriate. Then prepare common-size income statements for Lowe's and The Home Depot.
2. Compare the two companies by using the common-size statements.

12-32 Computation of Ratios

Merck & Co., Inc., the global pharmaceutical company, included the income statements and balance sheets in Exhibit 12-13 in its 2008 annual report. Additional information includes the following:

- Average common shares outstanding of 2,135.8 million in 2008
- Market price per share of $31.00 at its fiscal year end of December 31, 2008
- Dividends of $1.52 per share were paid on common stock during 2008
- Interest expense in 2008 was $251.3 million

Compute the following ratios for 2008:

1. Current ratio
2. Quick ratio (use current assets – inventories as the numerator)
3. Average collection period (assume all sales are on credit)
4. Total-debt-to-total-assets (define total debt as total liabilities)
5. Total-debt-to-equity (define total debt as total liabilities)
6. Return on common stockholders' equity
7. Gross profit rate
8. Return on sales
9. Total asset turnover
10. Return on assets (defined as EBIT divided by average total assets)
11. EPS (basic)
12. P-E ratio
13. Dividend-yield ratio (for common stock)
14. Dividend-payout ratio (for common stock)
15. Market-to-book value

12-33 Common Stock Ratios and Book Value

The Ebert Corporation has outstanding 550,000 shares of 9% preferred stock with a $100 par value and has issued 12 million shares of $1 par value common stock. The current market price of the common stock is $28 per share, and the latest annual dividend rate per common share is

CONSOLIDATED BALANCE SHEETS

	December 31	
	2008	**2007**
Assets		
Current assets		
Cash and cash equivalents	$ 4,368.3	$ 5,336.1
Short-term investments	1,118.1	2,894.7
Accounts receivable, net	3,778.9	3,636.2
Inventories	2,283.3	1,881.0
Deferred income taxes and other current assets	7,756.3	1,297.4
Total current assets	19,304.9	15,045.4
Investments	6,491.3	7,159.2
Property, plant, and equipment (at cost)		
Land	386.1	405.8
Buildings	9,767.4	10,048.0
Machinery, equipment, and office furnishings	13,103.7	13,553.7
Construction in progress	871.0	795.6
	24,128.2	24,803.1
Allowance for depreciation	(12,128.6)	(12,457.1)
Net property, plant, and equipment	11,999.6	12,346.0
Goodwill	1,438.7	1,454.8
Other Intangibles, net	525.4	713.2
Other assets	7,435.8	11,632.1
Total assets	$ 47,195.7	$ 48,350.7
Liabilities and shareholders' equity		
Current liabilities		
Loans payable and current portion of long-term debt	$ 2,297.1	$ 1,823.6
Trade accounts payable	617.6	624.5
Accrued and other current liabilities	9,174.1	8,534.9
Income taxes payable	1,426.4	444.1
Dividends payable	803.5	831.1
Total current liabilities	14,318.7	12,258.2
Long-term debt	3,943.3	3,915.8
Deferred income taxes and noncurrent liabilities	7,766.6	11,585.3
Stockholders' equity		
Common stock, one cent par value		
Authorized – 5,400,000,000 shares		
Issued – 2,983,508,675 – 2008 and 2007	29.8	29.8
Other paid-in capital	10,727.9	10,421.6
Accumulated other comprehensive loss	(2,553.9)	(826.1)
Retained earnings	43,698.8	39,140.8
Treasury stock, at cost		
875,818,333 shares – 2008		
811,005,791 shares – 2007	(30,735.5)	(28,174.7)
Total stockholders' equity	21,167.1	20,591.4
Total liabilities and stockholders' equity	$ 47,195.7	$ 48,350.7

**EXHIBIT 12-13
(Continued)**

**Merck & Co., Inc., and
Subsidiaries**

*($ in millions, except per
share data)*

CONSOLIDATED STATEMENTS OF EARNINGS		
	For the Years Ended December 31	
	2008	**2007**
Sales	$23,850.3	$24,197.7
Costs, expenses, and other		
Materials and production	5,582.5	6,140.7
Marketing and administrative	7,377.0	7,556.7
Research and development	4,805.3	4,882.8
Restructuring costs	1,032.5	327.1
Equity income from affiliates	(2,560.6)	(2,976.5)
U.S. Vioxx Settlement Agreement charge	—	4,850.0
Other (income) expense, net	(2,194.2)	46.2
	14,042.5	20,827.0
Income before income taxes	9,807.8	3,370.7
Taxes on income	1,999.4	95.3
Net income	$ 7,808.4	$ 3,275.4

$2.10 per share. Common treasury stock consists of 500,000 shares costing $9 million. The company has $150 million of additional paid-in capital, $20 million of retained earnings, and $12 million of investments in affiliated companies at the end of the year. Net income for the current year is $25 million.

Compute the following:

1. Total stockholders' equity
2. Common stock P-E ratio
3. Common stock dividend-yield percentage
4. Common stock dividend-payout percentage
5. Book value per share of common stock

12-34 Rate-of-Return Computations

1. Sapporo Company reported a 5% EBIT-to-sales ratio, a 9% rate of return on total assets, and ¥2 billion in average total assets. Compute (a) EBIT, (b) total sales, and (c) total asset turnover.
2. Dublin Corporation reported €1,000 million of sales, €56 million of EBIT, and a total asset turnover of four times. Compute (a) average total assets, (b) the EBIT-to-sales ratio, and (c) the rate of return on total assets.
3. Compare the two companies based on the ratios computed.

12-35 Return on Assets

The Home Depot, Inc., is the leading retailer in the home improvement industry and ranks among the largest retailers in the United States. Some data from the company's financial statements for the years ended February 1, 2009, and February 3, 2008, follow ($ in millions):

	2009	**2008**
Sales	$71,288	$77,349
Earnings before interest and taxes	4,214	7,316
Interest expense	624	696
Provision for taxes	1,278	2,410
Net income	2,260	4,395
Property, plant, and equipment, net	26,234	27,476
Total assets	41,164	44,324
Stockholders' equity	17,777	17,714

1. Compute The Home Depot's rate of return on total assets for the year ended February 1, 2009.
2. Compute the EBIT-to-sales ratio and total asset turnover for the year ended February 1, 2009. Show how these two ratios determine the return on total assets.

12-36 Trading on the Equity

In all years under consideration Bayol Company has assets of $600 million, bonds payable of $300 million, and stockholders' equity of $300 million. The bonds bear interest at 10% per annum. Carmody Company, which is in the same industry, has assets of $600 million and stockholders' equity of $600 million in each year. Prepare a comparative tabulation of Carmody Company and Bayol Company for each of the 3 years. Show income before interest, interest, net income, ROA, and ROE. The income before interest for both companies was as follows: year 1, $60 million; year 2, $30 million; and year 3, $90 million. Ignore income taxes. Show all monetary amounts in millions of dollars. Comment on the results.

12-37 Using Debt or Equity

The O'Hare Corporation is trying to decide whether to raise additional capital of $100 million through a new issue of 9% long-term debt or of 7% preferred stock. The income tax rate is 40%. Compute net income less preferred dividends for these alternatives. Assume income before interest expense and taxes is $20 million. Show all dollar amounts in thousands. What is the after-tax cost of capital for debt and for preferred stock expressed in percentages? Comment on the comparison. Compute the interest-coverage ratio for the first year.

12-38 Debt Versus Preferred Stock

In 2008, Hamilton Corporation had earnings before taxes and interest of $4,247 million. Long-term debt was $12,309 million. The company had no preferred stock outstanding, although 10 million shares were authorized.

Suppose $6,000 million of preferred stock with a dividend rate of 10% had been issued instead of $6,000 million of the long-term debt. The debt had an effective interest rate of 6%. Assume the income tax rate is 40%.

Compute net income and net income attributable to common shareholders under (a) the current situation with $12,309 million of long-term debt and no preferred stock, and (b) the assumed situation with $6,000 million of preferred stock and $6,309 million of long-term debt.

12-39 Earnings per Share

As of December 31, 2008, **JPMorgan Chase & Co.** was one of the largest banking institutions in the United States with $2.2 trillion in assets, $166.9 billion in stockholders' equity, and operations in more than 60 countries. For the year ended December 31, 2008, JPMorgan Chase had net income of $5,605 million and paid preferred dividends of $674 million. An average of 3,501 million common shares were outstanding during the year.

1. Compute JPMorgan Chase's earnings per common share in 2008.
2. Suppose all preferred stock was convertible into 600 million shares of common stock. Compute diluted earnings per common share.

12-40 EPS and Interest-Coverage Ratio Computations

Baltimore Shipping Company has outstanding 500,000 shares of common stock, $5 million of 8% preferred stock, and $8 million of 10% bonds payable. Its income tax rate is 40%.

1. Assume the company has $6 million of income before interest and taxes. Compute (a) EPS and (b) number of times bond interest has been earned.
2. Assume $3 million of income before interest and taxes, and make the same computations.

12-41 Nonrecurring Items

La-Z-Boy Incorporated is a manufacturer, marketer, and retailer of upholstery products and a marketer of imported and manufactured wood furniture products. The following excerpt is taken from the income statement included in La-Z-Boy's 2009 annual report. All dollar amounts are in thousands.

	Fiscal Year Ended		
	4/25/2009	4/26/2008	4/28/2007
Sales	$1,226,674	$1,450,941	$1,621,460
Cost of sales			
Cost of goods sold	878,089	1,051,656	1,189,734
Restructuring	9,818	5,057	3,371
Total cost of sales	887,907	1,056,713	1,193,105
Gross profit	338,767	394,228	428,355
Selling, general, and administrative	375,011	399,470	388,738
Restructuring	2,642	3,078	7,662
Write-down of long-lived assets	7,503	—	—
Write-down of intangibles	47,677	8,426	—
Operating income (loss)	(94,066)	(16,746)	31,955

1. What line items shown in the excerpts from La-Z-Boy's income statement do you consider to be unusual or nonrecurring items? Defend your response.
2. Adjust operating income (loss) as reported to "recurring operating income" in each of the three years represented.

12-42 Interpretation of Changes in Ratios
Consider each of the following as an independent case:

a. Increase in cash dividends
b. Decrease in interest coverage
c. Increase in return on sales
d. Increase in the P-E ratio
e. Increase in receivables collection period
f. Increase in current ratio

Required
1. From the point of view of a manager of the company, indicate which of these items indicates good news and which indicates bad news. Explain your reasoning for each.
2. Would any of these items be viewed differently by an investor than by a manager? If so, which ones? Why?

MyAccountingLab **Problems**

12-43 Common-Size Statements
(Alternate is 12-51.) Price-Break and Low-Cost are both discount store chains. Condensed income statements and balance sheets for the two companies are shown in Exhibit 12-14. Amounts are in thousands.

Required
1. Prepare common-size statements for Price-Break and Low-Cost for 20X9.
2. Compare the financial performance for 20X9 and financial position at the end of 20X9 for Price-Break with the performance and position of Low-Cost. Use only the statements prepared in requirement 1.
3. Calculate and compare ROE for the two firms.

12-44 Financial Ratios
(Alternate is 12-46.) This problem uses the same data as problem 12-43, but it can be solved independently. Price-Break and Low-Cost are both discount store chains. Condensed income statements and balance sheets for the two companies are shown in Exhibit 12-14. Amounts are in thousands.
  Additional information follows:

• Cash dividends per share: Price-Break, $2.00; Low-Cost, $1.50
• Market price per share: Price-Break, $30; Low-Cost, $40
• Average shares outstanding for 20X9: Price-Break, 15 million; Low-Cost, 7 million

INCOME STATEMENTS

	Price-Break	Low-Cost
	Year Ended December 31, 20X9	
Sales	$905,600	$491,750
Cost of sales	602,360	301,910
Gross profit	303,240	189,840
Operating expenses	184,130	147,160
Operating income	119,110	42,680
Other revenue (expense)	(21,930)	6,270
Pretax income	97,180	48,950
Income tax expense	38,870	19,580
Net income	$ 58,310	$ 29,370

BALANCE SHEETS

	Price-Break December 31		Low-Cost December 31	
	20X9	20X8	20X9	20X8
Assets				
Current assets				
Cash	$ 9,100	$ 10,700	$ 8,200	$ 6,900
Marketable securities	8,300	8,300	4,100	3,800
Accounts receivable	36,700	37,100	21,300	20,500
Inventories	155,600	149,400	105,100	106,600
Prepaid expenses	17,100	16,900	8,800	8,400
Total current assets	226,800	222,400	147,500	146,200
Property and equipment, net	461,800	452,300	287,600	273,500
Other assets	14,700	13,900	28,600	27,100
Total assets	$703,300	$688,600	$463,700	$446,800
Liabilities and stockholders' equity				
Liabilities				
Current liabilities (summarized)	$ 91,600	$ 93,700	$ 61,300	$ 58,800
Long-term debt	156,700	156,700	21,000	21,000
Total liabilities	248,300	250,400	82,300	79,800
Stockholders' equity	455,000	438,200	381,400	367,000
Total liabilities and stockholders' equity	$703,300	$688,600	$463,700	$446,800

1. Compute the following ratios for both companies for 20X9: (a) current, (b) quick, (c) accounts receivable turnover, (d) inventory turnover, (e) total-debt-to-total-assets, (f) total-debt-to-total-equity, (g) ROE, (h) gross profit rate, (i) return on sales, (j) total asset turnover, (k) pretax return on assets, (l) EPS, (m) P-E, (n) dividend-yield, and (o) dividend-payout. Total debt includes all liabilities. Assume all sales are on credit.
2. Compare the liquidity, solvency, profitability, market price, and dividend ratios of Price-Break with those of Low-Cost.

12-45 Trend Analysis

Reuters describes **Minnesota Mining and Manufacturing Company (3M)** as a diversified technology company with a global presence in the following industries: industrial and transportation; health care; safety, security, and protection services; consumer and office; display and graphics; and electro and communications. The income statements and balance sheets (slightly modified) for the years ended December 31, 2008, and December 31, 2007, are in Exhibit 12-15.

1. Prepare an income statement and balance sheet for 3M that has two columns, one showing the dollar amount of change between 2007 and 2008 and the other showing the percentage of change.
2. Identify and discuss the most significant changes between 2007 and 2008.

12-46 Financial Ratios

(Alternate is 12-44.) This problem uses the same data as 12-45, but it can be solved independently. **3M** was incorporated in 1929 and has grown to be one of the largest companies in the industrial conglomerates industry. The income statements and balance sheets (slightly modified) for the years ended December 31, 2008, and December 31, 2007, are in Exhibit 12-15. 3M paid a dividend of $2.00 per share in 2008. The market price per share on December 31, 2008 was $57.54.

Compute the following ratios for 3M for the year ending December 31, 2008: (a) current, (b) quick, (c) average collection period, (d) total-debt-to-total-assets, (e) total-debt-to-total-equity, (f) ROE, (g) return on sales, (h) total asset turnover, (i) return on total assets (computed as earnings before interest expense, taxes, and minority interest divided by average total assets), (j) Basic EPS (this number is given in Exhibit 12-15 but show how it was derived), (k) P-E, (l) dividend yield, (m) dividend payout, and (n) market-to-book. Total debt includes all liabilities. Assume all sales are on credit.

12-47 Time-Series Analysis

The **3M** balance sheets in Exhibit 12-15 show intangible assets of $5,390 million in 2007 and $7,151 million in 2008. Additional disclosures reveal the following detail about intangible assets, in millions:

	2008	2007
Goodwill	$5,753	$4,589
Other intangible assets	1,398	801
Intangible assets	$7,151	$5,390

EXHIBIT 12-15

Minnesota Mining and Manufacturing Company (3M) and Subsidiaries

(*$ in millions, except per share data*)

CONSOLIDATED STATEMENT OF INCOME

	Years Ended December 31	
	2008	**2007**
Net sales	$25,269	$24,462
Operating expenses		
Cost of goods sold	13,379	12,735
Selling, general, and administrative expenses	5,245	5,015
Research, development, and related expenses	1,404	1,368
(Gain) loss on sale of businesses	23	(849)
Total	20,051	18,269
Operating income	5,218	6,193
Other income and expense		
Interest expense	215	210
Interest income	(105)	(132)
Total	110	78
Income before income taxes and minority interest	5,108	6,115
Provision for income taxes	1,588	1,964
Minority interest	60	55
Net income	$ 3,460	$ 4,096
Weighted-average common shares outstanding—basic	699.2	718.3
EPS—basic	$ 4.95	$ 5.70
Weighted-average common shares outstanding—diluted	707.2	732.0
EPS—diluted	$ 4.89	$ 5.60

EXHIBIT 12-15 (Continued)

Minnesota Mining and Manufacturing Company (3M) and Subsidiaries

($ in millions, except per share data)

CONSOLIDATED BALANCE SHEET

At December 31	2008	2007
Assets		
Current assets		
Cash and cash equivalents	$ 1,849	$ 1,896
Marketable securities—current	373	579
Accounts receivable—net	3,195	3,362
Inventories	3,013	2,852
Other current assets	1,168	1,149
Total current assets	9,598	9,838
Marketable securities—noncurrent	352	480
Investments	286	298
Property, plant, and equipment—net	6,886	6,582
Intangible assets	7,151	5,390
Other assets	1,274	2,106
Total assets	$ 25,547	$ 24,694
Liabilities and Stockholders' Equity		
Current liabilities		
Short-term borrowings and current portion of long-term debt	$ 1,552	$ 901
Accounts payable	1,301	1,505
Accrued payroll	644	580
Accrued income taxes	350	543
Other current liabilities	1,992	1,833
Total current liabilities	5,839	5,362
Long-term debt	5,166	4,019
Pension and postretirement benefits	2,847	1,348
Other liabilities	1,816	2,218
Total liabilities	15,668	12,947
Stockholders' equity		
Common stock, par value $.01 per share		
Shares outstanding—2008: 693,543,287		
2007: 709,156,031	9	9
Additional paid-in-capital	3,001	2,785
Retained earnings	22,248	20,316
Treasury stock	(11,676)	(10,520)
Unearned compensation	(57)	(96)
Accumulated other comprehensive income (loss)	(3,646)	(747)
Stockholders' equity	9,879	11,747
Total liabilities and stockholders' equity	$ 25,547	$ 24,694

1. Goodwill increased $1,164 million or 25.4% from 2007 to 2008. What does this increase tell you about the activities of 3M during the year ended December 31, 2008?
2. Suppose you calculated various ratios for 3M for the year ended December 31, 2008. If you worked problem 12-46 you actually calculated many ratios. This problem does not require use of specific computations. However, you might review problem 12-46 as a reminder of the ratios that might be impacted. Assume you have been asked to compute these same ratios for 2007. Would the increase in goodwill and the activities implied by that increase complicate the comparison of ratios over the 2 years in question? If so, why?

12-48 Trend Analysis and Common-Size Statements
Ryan Company furnished the condensed data shown in Exhibit 12-16.

1. Prepare a trend analysis for Ryan's income statements and balance sheets that compares 20X9 with 20X8. Your analysis should show both the dollar amount and the percentage change between 20X8 and 20X9.
2. Prepare common-size income statements for 20X9 and 20X8 and common-size balance sheets for December 31, 20X9, and December 31, 20X8, for Ryan Company.
3. Comment on Ryan Company's financial performance and position for 20X9 compared with 20X8.

12-49 Financial Ratios
Consider the data for Ryan Company in Exhibit 12-16.

1. Compute the following ratios for the years 20X8 and 20X9:
   a. Percentage of net income to stockholders' equity (ROE)
   b. Gross profit rate
   c. Percent of net income to sales
   d. Ratio of total debt to stockholders' equity (define total debt as total liabilities)
   e. Inventory turnover
   f. Current ratio
   g. Average collection period for accounts receivable
2. For each of the following items, indicate whether the change from 20X8 to 20X9 for Ryan Company seems to be favorable or unfavorable, and identify the ratios you computed previously that most directly support your answer. The first two items that follow are given as an example.
   a. Return to owners, favorable, a
   b. Gross profit rate, unchanged, b (declined from 45.3% to 45%, could answer unfavorable)

EXHIBIT 12-16

Ryan Company

Balance Sheets and Income Statements ($ in thousands)

	December 31		
	20X9	**20X8**	**20X7**
Cash	$ 30	$ 25	$ 20
Accounts receivable	90	70	50
Merchandise inventory	80	70	60
Prepaid expenses	10	10	10
Land	30	30	30
Building	70	75	80
Equipment	60	50	40
Total assets	$370	$330	$290
Accounts payable	$ 50	$ 40	$ 30
Taxes payable	20	15	10
Accrued expenses payable	15	10	5
Long-term debt	45	45	45
Paid-in capital	150	150	150
Retained earnings	90	70	50
Total liabilities and stockholders' equity	$370	$330	$290

	Year Ended December 31	
	20X9	**20X8**
Sales (all on credit)	$800	$750
Cost of goods sold	440	410
Operating expenses	300	295
Pretax income	60	45
Income taxes	20	15
Net income	$ 40	$ 30

c. Ability to pay current debts on time
d. Collectibility of receivables
e. Risks of insolvency
f. Salability of merchandise
g. Return on sales
h. Overall accomplishment
i. Coordination of buying and selling functions
j. Screening of risks in granting credit to customers

12-50 Computation of Financial Ratios
The financial statements of the Ito Company are shown in Exhibit 12-17.
    Compute the following for the 20X8 financial statements.

1. Pretax return on total assets.
2. Divide your answer to number 1 into two components: EBIT-to-sales and total asset turnover.
3. After-tax rate of return on total assets. Be sure to add the after-tax interest expense to net income.
4. Rate of return on total stockholders' equity including returns to both common and preferred stockholders. Did the preferred and common stockholders benefit from the existence of debt? Explain fully.

EXHIBIT 12-17
The Ito Company
(¥ in millions)

BALANCE SHEETS		
	December 31	
	20X8	**20X7**
Assets		
Current assets		
Cash	¥ 2,000	¥ 2,000
Short-term investments	—	1,000
Receivables, net	5,000	4,000
Inventories at cost	11,000	8,000
Prepayments	1,000	1,000
Total current assets	¥19,000	¥16,000
Plant and equipment, net	22,000	23,000
Total assets	¥41,000	¥39,000
Liabilities and Stockholders' Equity		
Current liabilities		
Accounts payable	¥10,000	¥ 6,000
Accrued expenses payable	500	500
Income taxes payable	1,500	1,500
Total current liabilities	¥12,000	¥ 8,000
8% bonds payable	¥10,000	¥10,000
Stockholders' equity		
Preferred stock, 12%, par value $100 per share	¥ 5,000	¥ 5,000
Common stock, $5 par value	4,000	4,000
Premium on common stock	8,000	8,000
Unappropriated retained earnings	1,000	3,000
Reserve for plant expansion	1,000	1,000
Total stockholders' equity	¥19,000	¥21,000
Total liabilities and stockholders' equity	¥41,000	¥39,000

**EXHIBIT 12-17
(Continued)**

The Ito Company

(¥ in millions)

STATEMENT OF INCOME AND RECONCILIATION OF RETAINED EARNINGS		
		Year Ended December 31, 20X8
Sales (all on credit)		¥44,000
Cost of goods sold		32,000
Gross profit on sales		¥12,000
Other operating expenses		
Selling expenses	¥5,000	
Administrative expenses	2,000	
Depreciation	1,000	8,000
Operating income		¥ 4,000
Interest expense		800
Income before income taxes		¥ 3,200
Income taxes at 40%		¥ 1,280
Net income		¥ 1,920
Dividends on preferred stock		600
Net income for common stockholders		¥ 1,320
Dividends on common stock		3,320
Net income retained		¥ (2,000)
Unappropriated retained earnings, December 31, 20X7		3,000
Unappropriated retained earnings, December 31, 20X8		¥ 1,000

5. Rate of return on common stockholders' equity. This ratio is the amount of net income available for the common stockholders, divided by total stockholders' equity less the par value of preferred stock. Did the common stockholders benefit from the existence of preferred stock? Explain fully.

6. Calculate inventory turnover. How would Ito have been helped if it had been able to maintain the level of inventory from 20X7?

12-51 Common-Size Statements

(Alternate is 12-43.) Exhibit 12-18 contains the income statements and balance sheets of **The Hershey Company** for the years ended December 31, 2008, and December 31, 2007. Hershey is a manufacturer of chocolate and sugar confectionery products. The company's principal product groups include chocolate and confectionery products; food and beverage enhancers, such as baking ingredients, toppings, and beverages; and gum and mint refreshment products.

1. Prepare common-size statements for Hershey for 2007 and 2008.
2. Comment on the changes in component percentages from 2007 to 2008.

12-52 Liquidity Ratios

Exhibit 12-18 contains the income statements and balance sheets of **The Hershey Company**, manufacturer of such well-known products as Hershey's chocolate bars, Reese's peanut butter cups, Almond Joy candy bars, and York peppermint patties.

1. Compute the following ratios for 2008: (a) current, (b) average collection period, and (c) inventory turnover. Assume all sales are on credit.
2. Assess Hershey's liquidity compared with the following averages for the food processing industry as provided by **Reuters** and with ratios computed for **Tootsie Roll**, a competitor in the candy manufacturing, marketing, sales, and distribution industry. Reuters provides the following overview of the food processing industry. The industry consists of "companies engaged in processing and packaging produce, meats, fish, animal feeds, fruit juices and dairy products. The industry includes, grain milling, crop cleaning, grading and packaging, animal slaughtering and packaging operations, seafood processing,

freezing, canning operations, juice, coffee, tea, dairy and all other food manufacturers, including pet foods."

	Reuters (as of December 17, 2009)	Tootsie Roll (year ended December 31, 2008)
Current ratio	1.63 times	3.17 times
Average collection period	158.0 days*	23.4 days
Inventory turnover	1.17 times	5.90 times

*Reuters reports Receivable Turnover as 2.31 times per year. (365÷2.31) = 158.0 days.

EXHIBIT 12-18

The Hershey Company

Years Ended December 31, 2008 and December 31, 2007 ($ in thousands, except per share data)

CONSOLIDATED BALANCE SHEETS

	2008	2007
Assets		
Current assets		
Cash and cash equivalents	$ 37,103	$ 129,198
Accounts receivable—trade	455,153	487,285
Inventories	592,530	600,185
Deferred income taxes	70,903	83,668
Prepaid expenses and other	189,256	126,238
Total current assets	1,344,945	1,426,574
Property, plant, and equipment, net	1,458,949	1,539,715
Goodwill	554,677	584,713
Other intangibles	110,772	155,862
Deferred Income Taxes	13,815	—
Other assets	151,561	540,249
Total assets	$ 3,634,719	$ 4,247,113
Liabilities and Stockholders' Equity		
Current liabilities		
Accounts payable	$ 249,454	$ 223,019
Accrued liabilities	504,065	538,986
Accrued income taxes	15,189	373
Short-term debt	483,120	850,288
Current portion of long-term debt	18,384	6,104
Total current liabilities	1,270,212	1,618,770
Long-term debt	1,505,954	1,279,965
Other long-term liabilities	504,963	544,016
Deferred income taxes	3,646	180,842
Minority interests	31,745	30,598
Stockholders' equity		
Common stock, shares issued: 299,190,836 in 2008 and 299,095,417 in 2007	299,190	299,095
Class B Common stock, shares issued: 60,710,908 in 2008 and 60,806,327 in 2007	60,711	60,806
Additional paid-in-capital	352,375	335,256
Retained earnings	3,975,762	3,927,306
Treasury—Common stock shares, at cost: 132,866,673 in 2008 and 132,851,893 in 2007	(4,009,931)	(4,001,562)
Accumulated other comprehensive loss	(359,908)	(27,979)
Total stockholders' equity	318,199	592,922
Total liabilities and stockholders' equity	$ 3,634,719	$ 4,247,113

CONSOLIDATED STATEMENT OF OPERATIONS		
	For Years Ended	
	December 31, 2008	December 31, 2007
Net sales	$5,132,768	$4,946,716
Costs and expenses:		
Cost of sales	3,375,050	3,315,147
Selling, marketing, and administrative	1,073,019	895,874
Business realignment and impairment charges, net	94,801	276,868
Total costs and expenses	4,542,870	4,487,889
Income before interest and income taxes	589,898	458,827
Interest expense, net	97,876	118,585
Income before income taxes	492,022	340,242
Provision for income taxes	180,617	126,088
Net income	$ 311,405	$ 214,154
Net income per common share—Basic— Class B Common stock	$ 1.27	$ 0.87
Net income per common share—Diluted— Class B Common stock	$ 1.27	$ 0.87
Net income per common share—Basic— Common stock	$ 1.41	$ 0.96
Net income per common share—Diluted— Common stock	$ 1.36	$ 0.93

12-53 Solvency Ratios

Exhibit 12-18 contains the income statements and balance sheets of **The Hershey Company** for the years ended December 31, 2008, and December 31, 2007. Hershey manufactures and sells products under more than 80 brand names.

1. Compute the following ratios for 2008: (a) total-debt-to-total-assets and (b) total-debt-to-total-equity. To be consistent with the source of industry data, define total debt as short-term debt and long-term debt (including the current portion) only.
2. Assess Hershey's solvency compared with the following industry averages for the food processing industry as provided by **Reuters** and with ratios computed for **Tootsie Roll**, a competitor in the candy manufacturing, marketing, sales, and distribution industry. See a description of the food processing industry in problem 12-52.

	Reuters (as of December 17, 2009)	Tootsie Roll (year ended December 31, 2008)
Total-debt-to-total-assets	Not available	0.0%*
Total-debt-to-total-shareholders' equity	48.8%	0.0%*

*Tootsie Roll has no debt in its capital structure! In fact, total liabilities are only 21.8% of total assets.

12-54 Profitability Ratios

Exhibit 12-18 contains income statements and balance sheets of **The Hershey Company**. For more than 100 years, The Hershey Company has enjoyed a position as one of North America's largest manufacturers of quality chocolate and confectionery products. Today, The Hershey Company and its subsidiaries export to approximately 90 countries worldwide.

1. Compute the following ratios for 2008: (a) ROE, (b) gross profit rate, (c) return on sales, (d) total asset turnover, (e) ROA (with after-tax net income in the numerator), and (f) financial leverage. Note that to be consistent with the industry averages, return on sales and ROA are computed with after-tax net income, not EBIT in the numerator.

2. Assess Hershey's profitability in 2008 compared with the following industry averages for the food processing industry as provided by Reuters and with ratios computed for Tootsie Roll, a competitor in the candy manufacturing, marketing, sales, and distribution industry. See a description of the food processing industry in problem 12-52.

	Reuters (as of December 17, 2009)	Tootsie Roll (year ended December 31, 2008)
Return on stockholders' equity	3.46%	6.09%
Gross profit rate	5.48%	32.3%
Return on sales (Net income ÷ Sales)	1.41%	7.8%
Total asset turnover	0.23 times	0.61
Return on assets (Net income ÷ Assets)	1.21%	4.8%
Financial leverage	Not available	1.27

12-55 Market Price and Dividend Ratios

Exhibit 12-18 contains income statements and balance sheets of The Hershey Company. The following information applies to Hershey's common stock, excluding the Class B shares, which are not publicly traded. In 2008, Hershey paid common stock dividends of $1.19 per common share, the market price at December 31, 2008, was $34.74 per share, and basic EPS was $1.41.

1. Compute the following ratios for 2008: (a) P-E, (b) dividend-yield, (c) dividend-payout, and (d) market-to-book value.
2. Assess Hershey's market price and dividend ratios 2008 compared with the following industry averages for the food processing industry as provided by Reuters and with ratios computed for Tootsie Roll, a competitor in the candy manufacturing, marketing, sales, and distribution industry. See a description of the food processing industry in problem 12-52.

	Reuters (as of December 17, 2009)	Tootsie Roll (for year ended December 31, 2008)
Price-earnings	470.25	36.59
Dividend-yield	0.11%	1.26%
Dividend-payout	378.73%	45.71%
Market-to-book value	1.65	1.42

12-56 Income Ratios and Asset Turnover

The following data are derived from the 2008, 2007, and 2006 annual reports of The Coca-Cola Corporation. Dollar amounts are in millions.

	2008	2007	2006
Rate of return on stockholders' equity	27.5%	30.9%	30.5%
EBIT-to-sales ratio	24.7%	28.9%	28.2%
Total asset turnover (Sales ÷ Average assets)	.76	.79	.81
Average total assets	$41,894	$36,616	$29,695
Interest expense	$ 438	$ 456	$ 220
Income tax expense	$ 1,632	$ 1,892	$ 1,498

1. Complete the following condensed income statements for 2008 and 2006. Round to the nearest million.

	2008	2006
Sales	$?	$?
Expenses other than interest and taxes	?	?
EBIT	$?	$?
Interest expense	?	?
Pretax income	$?	$?
Income tax expense	?	?
Net income	$?	$?

2. Compute the following for 2008 and 2006:
    a. Return on total assets (computed as EBIT to average total assets)
    b. Net income-to-sales ratio
    c. Average stockholders' equity
3. Compare the ratios for 2008 with those for 2006.

12-57 Segment Disclosures

According to its 2008 annual report, **CVS Caremark** is the largest provider of prescriptions in the United States, filling or managing more than one billion prescriptions annually. The company achieves this volume of prescriptions through a combination of its pharmacy benefit management, mail order, and specialty pharmacy division, Caremark Pharmacy Services; its more than 6,900 CVS/pharmacy and Longs Drug retail stores; its retail-based health clinic subsidiary, MinuteClinic; and its online pharmacy, CVS.com. It organizes its business into two operating segments, the Pharmacy Services segment and the Retail Pharmacy segment. The following information is from the 2008 annual report. Intersegment eliminations relate to intersegment revenues that occur when a Pharmacy Services segment customer uses a Retail Pharmacy segment store to purchase covered products. When this occurs, both segments record the revenue on a stand-alone basis.

	Pharmacy Services Segment	Retail Pharmacy Segment	Intersegment Eliminations	Consolidated Totals CVS Caremark
2008				
Net revenues	$43,769.2	$48,989.9	$(5,287.2)	$87,471.9
Gross profit	3,550.0	14,740.4		18,290.4
Operating profit	2,562.5	3,483.7		6,046.2

1. Compute the gross profit rate for (a) the Pharmacy Services segment, (b) the Retail Pharmacy segment, and (c) CVS Caremark.
2. Compute the operating profit rate for (a) the Pharmacy Services segment, (b) the Retail Pharmacy segment, and (c) CVS Caremark.
3. Do both segments contribute equally to the profitability of CVS Caremark? Explain.

12-58 Income Ratios and Asset Turnover

Nicoletti Company included the following data in its 2008 annual report to stockholders (amounts in millions except for percentages):

Net income	$ 2,960
Total assets	
Beginning of year	$11,872
End of year	$17,596
Net income as a percentage of	
Total revenue	46%
Average stockholders' equity	51%

Using this data, compute the following values for 2008:

1. Net income as a percentage of average total assets
2. Total revenues
3. Average stockholders' equity
4. Total asset turnover, using two different approaches

12-59 Industry Identification

Exhibit 12-19 presents common-size financial statements and selected ratio values for seven companies from the following industries:

1. Petroleum (exploration, refining, and distribution)
2. Grocery

	A	B	C	D	E	F	G
	%	%	%	%	%	%	%
Balance sheet							
Cash and marketable securities	21.35	5.93	23.35	2.19	2.33	1.95	12.60
Current receivables	8.07	9.84	3.38	2.95	10.45	3.11	1.46
Inventories	3.94	4.25	7.38	14.82	8.19	2.14	1.42
Other current assets	5.40	2.61	5.07	2.78	2.06	2.73	4.74
Total current assets	38.76	22.63	39.18	22.74	23.03	9.93	20.22
Net property, plant, and equipment	11.95	56.95	34.59	60.87	26.80	64.13	77.16
Other noncurrent assets	49.29	20.42	26.23	16.39	50.17	25.94	2.62
Total assets	100.00	100.00	100.00	100.00	100.00	100.00	100.00
Current liabilities	24.30	19.87	15.42	25.73	32.45	8.19	19.61
Long-term liabilities	23.75	26.37	7.51	35.46	54.32	52.27	45.77
Stockholders' equity	51.95	53.76	77.07	38.81	13.23	39.54	34.62
Total liabilities and stockholders' equity	100.00	100.00	100.00	100.00	100.00	100.00	100.00
Income statement							
Revenue	100.00	100.00	100.00	100.00	100.00	100.00	100.00
Cost of sales	16.80	70.40	44.54	71.62	58.14	63.38	77.93
Gross profit	83.20	29.60	55.46	28.38	41.86	36.62	22.07
Selling, general, and administrative	30.10	2.10	14.52	24.16	26.63	17.60	17.99
R & D	16.45	0.00	15.22	0.00	0.00	0.00	0.00
Interest expense	0.00	0.00	0.00	0.81	2.41	5.61	0.95
Other expenses (income)	16.46	11.76	5.27	0.00	0.09	(1.57)	0.59
Income taxes	3.41	6.97	6.37	1.22	3.78	4.66	0.91
Net income	16.78	8.77	14.08	2.19	8.95	10.32	1.63
Ratios							
Current ratio	1.59	1.14	2.54	0.88	0.71	1.21	1.03
Long-term debt as % of equity*	13.84	7.02	4.83	81.04	81.0	63.13	73.92
ROA** (%)	7.16	15.44	9.95	5.49	10.27	2.65	4.00
ROE (%)	13.22	29.23	12.93	14.3	57.78	6.46	7.94
Inventory turnover (times per year)	1.68	31.60	4.71	11.72	8.19	7.80	nm

*Note that this is the ratio of long-term-debt-to-equity, not long-term-liabilities-to-equity.
**Computed as (After-tax net income ÷ Average total assets).
nm = not meaningful.

EXHIBIT 12-19

Common-Size Statements in Seven Industries

(Columns May Not Add Due to Rounding)

3. Airline
4. Pharmaceutical
5. Semi-conductor manufacturing
6. Utility
7. Packaged food products manufacturing

Use your knowledge of general business practices to match the industries to the company data.

12-60 Choosing Potential Investments in the Oil Industry
Exhibit 12-20 on page 595 presents some financial information for Chevron (CVX.N) and ExxonMobile (XOM.N). Which do you believe is the preferred investment based on this information gathered in December 2009? Be prepared to defend your answer.

12-61 Choosing Potential Investments in the Retail Industry
Exhibit 12-21 on pages 596–597 presents some financial information for Wal-Mart (WMT), Target (TGT), JCPenney (JCP), and Kohl's (KSS). Which do you believe is the preferred investment based on this information gathered in December 2009? Be prepared to defend your answer.

12-62 EVA at Briggs & Stratton
Briggs & Stratton Corporation is the world's largest maker of air-cooled gasoline engines for outdoor power equipment. The company's engines are used by the lawn and garden equipment industry. According to a recent annual report, "management subscribes to the premise that the value of Briggs & Stratton is enhanced if the capital invested in the company's operations yields a cash return that is greater than that expected by the providers of capital."

The following data are from Briggs & Stratton's 2009 annual report (thousands of dollars):

	2009	2008
Adjusted operating profit	$ 54,092	$ 71,460
Cash taxes	12,494	10,853
Invested capital	1,624,551	1,687,082
Cost of capital	8.5%	9.4%

1. Compute the EVA for Briggs & Stratton for 2008 and 2009.
2. Did Briggs & Stratton's overall performance improve from 2008 to 2009? Explain.

12-63 Comparing EVA for Two Companies
In November 20X9, the following relationships held for two companies in the medical devices industry. Which would you expect to have the larger EVA? Why?

	Company A	Company B
Share price	$87.75	$88.00
EPS	$ 2.45	$ 2.46
P-E	35.82	35.77
PEG ratio	2.5	2.4
Book value per share	$ 5.69	$ 4.60
Shares outstanding (billions)	2.3	1.1

12-64 MD&A and Ethics
If certain conditions are met, the SEC requires companies to disclose information about future events that are reasonably likely to materially affect the firms' operations. Many companies are understandably reluctant to disclose such information. After all, positive predictions may not materialize and negative predictions may unduly alarm investors. What ethical considerations should a company's managers consider when deciding what prospective information to disclose in the MD&A section of the annual report?

PRICE AND VALUATION

Ticker Symbol	Current Price December 17, 2009	52-Week Range	Beta	Latest Annual EPS	Price-Earnings
CVX.N	$76.78	$56.12–$79.82	0.66	$11.74	12.67
XOM.N	$68.22	$61.86–$83.24	0.45	$ 8.78	16.05

Ticker Symbol	Price/Sales	Price/Book	Price/Cash Flow	Analyst Rating
CVX.N	0.93	1.72	6.54	2.05
XOM.N	1.06	3.03	9.77	2.44

GROWTH RATES AND DIVIDENDS

Ticker Symbol	Latest Annual Revenue (mil)	1-yr Revenue Growth	5-yr Revenue Growth	Latest Annual EPS	1-yr EPS Growth	5-yr EPS Growth
CVX.N	$273,005	–41.85%	17.62%	$11.74	–46.82%	22.53%
XOM.N	$459,579	–40.03%	14.11%	$ 8.78	–53.85%	26.86%

Ticker Symbol	Latest Annual Dividend/Share	Dividend Yield	5-yr Dividend Growth Rate
CVX.N	$2.53	3.49%	12.09%
XOM.N	$1.55	2.45%	9.60%

FINANCIAL STRENGTH

Ticker Symbol	Total Debt/Equity	Long-term Debt/Equity	Current Ratio	Quick Ratio
CVX.N	11.63%	11.37%	1.40	1.15
XOM.N	8.95%	6.70%	1.08	0.85

EFFICIENCY

Ticker Symbol	Current Inventory Turnover	Current Receivable Turnover	Total Asset Turnover	Revenue/Employee (000s)	Income/Employee (000s)
CVX.N	17.79	7.76	1.02	$2,509.9	$184.4
XOM.N	14.32	9.82	1.26	$3,822.8	$267.1

PROFITABILITY

Ticker Symbol	Gross Margin	Operating Margin	Pretax Margin	After-tax Profit Margin
CVX.N	31.16%	11.86%	11.86%	7.35%
XOM.N	30.76%	12.36%	12.36%	6.99%

MANAGEMENT EFFECTIVENESS

Ticker Symbol	Return on Assets	5-yr Avg. Return on Assets	Return on Equity	5-yr Avg. Return on Equity
CVX.N	7.53%	13.97%	13.86%	27.55%
XOM.N	8.79%	17.52%	18.10%	33.96%

Data as of December 17, 2009.
Source: Reuters (www.reuters.com)

EXHIBIT 12-20

Comparison of Investments in Oil Companies

Chevron (CVX.N) and ExxonMobile (XOM.N)

PRICE AND VALUATION

Ticker Symbol	Current Price December 16, 2009	52-Week Range	Beta	Latest Annual EPS	Price-Earnings
WMT	$53.32	$46.25–$57.51	0.24	$3.40	15.60
KSS	$54.41	$32.46–$60.89	0.99	$2.89	18.77
JCP	$27.49	$13.71–$37.21	1.62	$2.58	23.96
TGT	$47.48	$25.00–$51.77	1.13	$2.87	16.63

Ticker Symbol	Price/Sales	Price/Book	Price/Cash Flow	Analyst Rating
WMT	0.51	3.04	9.83	1.63
KSS	1.01	2.28	11.42	1.75
JCP	0.37	1.42	8.72	2.20
TGT	0.55	2.39	8.70	1.95

GROWTH RATES AND DIVIDENDS

Ticker Symbol	Latest Annual Revenue (mil)	1-yr Revenue Growth	5-yr Revenue Growth	Latest Annual EPS	1-yr EPS Growth	5-yr EPS Growth
WMT	$405,607	0.18%	9.41%	$3.40	1.16%	10.61%
KSS	$ 16,389	0.54%	9.71%	$2.89	–5.68%	12.66%
JCP	$ 18,486	–7.07%	1.09%	$2.58	–67.39%	17.65%
TGT	$ 62,884	–0.80%	9.10%	$2.87	–12.72%	10.20%

Ticker Symbol	Latest Annual Dividend/Share	Dividend Yield	5-yr Dividend Growth Rate
WMT	$0.95	2.02	21.42%
KSS	n/a	n/a	n/a
JCP	$0.80	2.77	9.86%
TGT	$0.62	1.42	18.09%

FINANCIAL STRENGTH

Ticker Symbol	Total Debt/Equity	Long-term Debt/Equity	Current Ratio	Quick Ratio
WMT	69.96%	55.55%	0.88	0.22
KSS	28.01%	27.78%	1.85	0.59
JCP	73.93%	65.37%	1.88	0.79
TGT	117.13%	06.17%	1.58	0.82

EFFICIENCY

Ticker Symbol	Current Inventory Turnover	Current Receivable Turnover	Total Asset Turnover	Revenue/Employee (000s)	Income/Employee (000s)
WMT	7.63	113.92	2.37	$192.2	$ 6.6
KSS	2.79	not provided	2.79	$597.5	$32.0
JCP	2.59	40.06	1.32	$120.8	$ 1.8
TGT	4.95	8.62	1.39	$184.4	$ 6.2

EXHIBIT 12-21
Comparison of Retailers
Wal-Mart (WMT), Kohl's (KSS), JCPenney (JCP), and Target (TGT)

| | PROFITABILITY | | | |
Ticker Symbol	Gross Margin	Operating Margin	Pretax Margin	After-tax Profit Margin
WMT	24.55%	5.71%	5.24%	3.47%
KSS	37.35%	9.33%	8.60%	5.35%
JCP	38.19%	3.77%	2.32%	1.46%
TGT	29.50%	5.26%	5.26%	3.34%

| | MANAGEMENT EFFECTIVENESS | | | |
Ticker Symbol	Return on Assets	5-yr Avg. Return on Assets	Return on Equity	5-yr Avg. Return on Equity
WMT	8.21%	8.77%	20.29%	21.26%
KSS	7.10%	10.11%	12.98%	16.43%
JCP	1.93%	6.46%	5.29%	19.17%
TGT	4.65%	6.50%	15.14%	17.20%

Data as of December 16, 2009.
Source: Reuters (www.reuters.com)

EXHIBIT 12-21 (Continued)
Comparison of Retailers
Wal-Mart (WMT), Kohl's (KSS), JCPenney (JCP), and Target (TGT)

Collaborative Learning Exercise

12-65 Operating Return on Total Assets
Form groups of four to six students. Each student should choose an industry (a different industry for each student in the group) and pick two companies in that industry. Compute the following for each of the companies:

1. EBIT-to-sales
2. Total asset turnover
3. Return on total assets

Get together as a group and list the industries and the three ratios for each company in the industry. Examine how the ratios differ between the two companies within each industry compared with the differences between industries. As a group, prepare two lists of possible explanations for the differences in ratios. The first list should explain why ratios of two companies within the same industry might differ. The second list should explain why ratios differ by industry.

Analyzing and Interpreting Financial Statements

12-66 Financial Statement Research
Choose two companies in each of two industries.
Calculate the ROA, ROE, and return on sales for each of the companies. Compare and contrast the two companies in each industry and the averages for each industry.

12-67 Analyzing Starbucks' Annual Report
Use the financial statements and notes of Starbucks for the year ended September 27, 2009, and respond to the questions that follow. The financial statements are accessible through the Starbucks Web site at www.starbucks.com or on the SEC's EDGAR database at www.sec.gov.

1. Calculate ROE for the year ended September 27, 2009. Compare it with the value for the year ended September 28, 2008.

London
School of Business
& Finance

LIBRARY

2. Calculate the current ratio for the year ended September 27, 2009, and compare it with the value for the year ended September 28, 2008.
3. Calculate total-debt-to-total-assets for the year ended September 27, 2009. Compare it with the value for the year ended September 28, 2008. Define total debt as total liabilities for purposes of this problem.

12-68 Analyzing Financial Statements Using the Internet

Go to www.amazon.com to locate **Amazon.com**'s home page. Select Investor Relations. Click on SEC Filings in the left navigation menu and locate the most recent 10-K. Answer the following questions about Amazon:

1. What is Amazon's dividend policy?
2. Where does Amazon report geographic segment information? What segments exist? What information does Amazon provide on a segment basis? Which segment is the largest? Do the segments contribute equally to Amazon's operating income?
3. Calculate Amazon's total-debt-to-total-assets, total-debt-to-equity, and long-term-debt-to-equity ratios for the last 2 fiscal years. For purposes of the first two ratios, define total debt as total liabilities. What is the trend? What does this suggest about Amazon's financing policy?

Glossary

Accelerated depreciation. Any depreciation method that writes off depreciable value more quickly than the straight-line method.

Account. A summary record of the changes in a particular asset, liability, or owners' equity.

Account format. A classified balance sheet with the assets at the left.

Account payable. A liability that results from a purchase of goods or services on open account.

Accounting. The process of identifying, recording, and summarizing economic information and reporting it to decision makers.

Accounting controls. The methods and procedures for authorizing transactions, safeguarding assets, and ensuring the accuracy of the financial records.

Accounting system. A set of records, procedures, internal controls, and equipment to collect, organize, and report the continuous flow of information about events affecting the entity's financial performance and position.

Accounts receivable (trade receivables, receivables). Amount owed to a company by customers as a result of the company's delivering goods or services and extending credit in the ordinary course of business.

Accounts receivable turnover. Credit sales divided by average accounts receivable.

Accrual basis. Accounting method in which accountants record revenue as a company earns it and expenses as the company incurs them—not necessarily when cash changes hands.

Accrue. To accumulate a receivable (asset) or payable (liability) during a given period, even though no explicit transaction occurs, and to record a corresponding revenue or expense.

Accumulated deficit. A more descriptive term for retained earnings when the accumulated losses plus dividends exceed accumulated income.

Accumulated depreciation (allowance for depreciation). The cumulative sum of all depreciation recognized since the date of acquisition of an asset.

Adjustments (adjusting entries). End-of-period entries that assign the financial effects of implicit transactions to the appropriate time periods.

Administrative controls. All methods and procedures that facilitate management planning and control of operations.

Affiliated company. A company that has 20%–50% of its voting shares owned by another company.

Aging of accounts receivable method. An analysis that considers the composition of year-end accounts receivable based on the age of the debt.

Allowance for uncollectible accounts (allowance for doubtful accounts, allowance for bad debts, reserve for doubtful accounts). A contra asset account that measures the amount of receivables estimated to be uncollectible.

Allowance method. A method of accounting for bad debt losses that uses (1) estimates of the amount of sales that will ultimately be uncollectible and (2) a contra account that contains the estimated uncollectible amount.

American Institute of Certified Public Accountants (AICPA). The principal professional association in the private sector that regulates the quality of the public accounting profession.

Amortization. When referring to long-lived assets, it usually means the allocation of the costs of intangible assets to the periods that benefit from these assets.

Annual report. A document prepared by management and distributed to current and potential investors to inform them about the company's past performance and future prospects.

Annuity. Equal cash flows to take place during successive periods of equal length.

Assets. Economic resources that a company expects to help generate future cash inflows or help reduce future cash outflows.

Audit. An examination of a company's transactions and the resulting financial statements.

Audit committee. A committee of the board of directors that oversees the internal accounting controls, financial statements, and financial affairs of the corporation.

Auditor. A person who examines the information used by managers to prepare the financial statements and attests to the credibility of those statements.

Auditor's opinion (independent opinion). A report describing the scope and results of an audit. Companies include the opinion with the financial statements in their annual reports.

Authorized shares. The total number of shares that a company may legally issue under the articles of incorporation.

Available-for-sale securities. Investments in equity or debt securities that are not held for active trading but may be sold before maturity.

Bad debt recoveries. Accounts receivable that were previously written off as uncollectible but then collected at a later date.

Bad debts expense. The loss that arises from uncollectible accounts.

Balance. The difference between the total left-side and right-side amounts in an account at any particular time.

Balance sheet (statement of financial position). A financial statement that shows the financial status of a business entity at a particular instant in time.

Balance sheet equation. Assets = Liabilities + Owners' equity

Bargain purchase option. A provision that states that the lessee can purchase the asset from the lessor at the end of the lease for substantially less than the asset's fair value.

Basket purchase (lump-sum purchase). The acquisition of two or more assets for a lump-sum cost.

Benchmark comparisons. Comparisons of a company's financial ratios with general rules of thumb or "best practices."

Board of directors. A body elected by the shareholders to represent them. It is responsible for appointing and monitoring the managers.

Bond discount (discount on bonds). The excess of face amount over the proceeds on issuance of a bond.

Bond premium (premium on bonds). The excess of the proceeds over the face amount of a bond.

Bonds. Formal certificates of debt that include (1) a promise to pay interest in cash at a specified annual rate, plus (2) a promise to pay the principal at a specific maturity date.

Book of original entry. Another name for the general journal.

Book value (net book value, carrying amount, carrying value). The balance of an account shown on the books, minus the value of any contra accounts. For example, the book value of equipment is its acquisition cost minus accumulated depreciation.

Book value per share of common stock. Stockholders' equity attributable to common stock divided by the number of common shares outstanding.

Call premium. The amount by which the redemption price of a callable bond exceeds face value.

Call price (redemption price). The price at which an issuer can buy back a callable preferred stock or bond, which is typically 5%–10% above the par value.

Callable. A characteristic of bonds or preferred stock that gives the issuer the right to purchase the stock back from the owner at a fixed price.

Callable bonds. Bonds subject to redemption before maturity at the option of the issuer.

Capital lease (finance lease). A lease that transfers most risks and benefits of ownership to the lessee.

Capitalization (capital structure). The total long-term financing of a company, consisting of long-term debt and stockholders' equity.

Capitalize. To add the purchase price of an asset to a long-term asset account, recognizing that it will benefit more than the current accounting year.

Cash basis. Accounting method that recognizes revenue when a company receives cash and recognizes expenses when it pays cash.

Cash discounts. Reductions of invoice prices awarded for prompt payment.

Cash dividends. Distributions of cash to stockholders that reduce retained earnings.

Cash equivalents. Highly liquid short-term investments that a company can easily and quickly convert into cash, such as money market funds and Treasury bills.

Cash flows from financing activities. The section of the statement of cash flows that helps users understand management's financing decisions.

Cash flows from investing activities. The section of the statement of cash flows that helps users understand management's investing decisions.

Cash flows from operating activities. The first major section of the cash flow statement. It helps users evaluate the cash impact of management's operating decisions.

Certificates of deposit. Short-term obligations of banks.

Certified public accountant (CPA). In the United States, a person earns this designation by meeting standards of both knowledge and integrity set by a State Board of Accountancy. Only CPAs can issue official opinions on financial statements in the United States.

Charge. A word often used instead of debit.

Chart of accounts. A numbered or coded list of all account titles.

Chief executive officer (CEO). The top manager in an organization.

Classified balance sheet. A balance sheet that groups the accounts into subcategories to help readers quickly gain a perspective on the company's financial position and to draw attention to certain accounts or groups of accounts.

Close the books. To transfer the balances in all revenue and expense accounts to retained earnings, which resets the revenue and expense accounts to zero so that they are ready to record the next period's transactions.

Commercial paper. A short-term debt contract issued by prominent companies that borrow directly from investors.

Common stock. Par value of the stock purchased by common shareholders of a corporation.

Common stockholders. The owners who have a "residual" ownership in the corporation.

Common-size statements. Financial statements in which components are expressed as relative percentages.

Comparability. A characteristic of information produced when all companies use similar concepts and measurements and use them consistently.

Compensating balances. The minimum cash balances that banks require companies to maintain to partially compensate the bank for providing the loan.

Component percentages. Elements of financial statements that express each component as a percentage of the total.

Compound annual growth rate (CAGR). Year-over-year growth rate over a specified period of time.

Compound entry. A transaction that affects more than two accounts.

Compound interest. The interest rate multiplied by a changing principal amount. The unpaid interest is added to the principal to become the principal for the new period.

Comprehensive income. Net income plus other comprehensive income and includes all changes in equity except those arising from transactions with stockholders.

Confirmatory value. A quality of information that allows it to confirm or contradict existing expectations.

Conservatism. Selecting methods of measurement that anticipate expenses and liabilities and defer recognition of revenues and assets, yielding lower net income, lower assets, and lower stockholders' equity.

Consistency. Using the same accounting policies and procedures from period to period.

Consolidated statements. This term means that the financial records of two or more separate legal entities have been combined into the statements presented.

Contingent liability. A potential liability that depends on a future event arising out of a past transaction.

Contra account. A separate but related account that offsets or is a deduction from a companion account. An example is accumulated depreciation.

Contra asset. A contra account that offsets an asset.

Convertible bonds. Bonds that may, at the holder's option, be exchanged for other securities.

Convertible. A characteristic of bonds or preferred stock that gives the owner the option to exchange the bonds or shares of preferred stock for shares of common stock.

Copyrights. Exclusive rights to reproduce and sell a book, musical composition, film, or similar creative item.

Corporate proxy. A written authority granted by individual shareholders to others to cast the shareholders' votes.

Corporation. A business organization that is created by individual state laws.

Correcting entry. A journal entry that cancels a previous erroneous entry and adds the correct amounts to the correct accounts.

Cost of goods available for sale. Sum of opening inventory for the period plus purchases during the period.

Cost of goods sold (cost of sales, cost of revenue). The original acquisition cost of the inventory that a company sells to customers during the reporting period.

Cost valuation. Process of assigning a specific value from the historical-cost records to each item in ending inventory.

Cost-benefit. A criterion that states that an organization should change its accounting system when the expected additional benefits of the change exceed its expected additional costs.

Credit. An entry or balance on the right side of an account.

Creditor. A person or entity to whom a company owes money.

Cross-referencing. The process of numbering, dating, and/or some other form of identification to relate each general ledger posting to the appropriate journal entry.

Cross-sectional comparisons. Comparisons of a company's financial ratios with the ratios of other companies or with industry averages.

Cumulative. A characteristic of preferred stock that requires that undeclared dividends accumulate and the company must pay them before it can pay any common dividends.

Current assets. Cash and other assets that a company expects to convert to cash, sell, or consume during the next 12 months or within the normal operating cycle if longer than 1 year.

Current liabilities. Liabilities that come due within the next year or within the normal operating cycle if longer than 1 year.

Current ratio (working capital ratio). Current assets divided by current liabilities.

Current replacement cost. What it would cost a company to buy an inventory item today.

Cutoff error. Failure to record transactions in the correct time period.

Data processing. The procedures used to record, analyze, store, and report on chosen activities.

Date of record. The date that determines which shareholders will receive a dividend.

Days to collect accounts receivable (average collection period). 365 divided by accounts receivable turnover.

Debenture. A debt security with a general claim against all assets, instead of a specific claim against particular assets.

Debit. An entry or balance on the left side of an account.

Debt-to-equity ratio. Total liabilities divided by total shareholders' equity.

Debt-to-total-assets ratio. Total liabilities divided by total assets.

Declaration date. The date the board of directors formally announces that it will pay a dividend.

Deferred income tax liability. An obligation arising because of predictable future taxes, to be paid when a future tax return is filed.

Depletion. The process of allocating the cost of natural resources to the periods that benefit from their use.

Depreciable value. The cost a company allocates as depreciation over the total useful life of an asset. It is the difference between the total acquisition cost and the estimated residual value.

Depreciation. The systematic allocation of the acquisition cost of long-lived assets to the expense accounts of particular periods that benefit from the use of the assets.

Depreciation schedule. The list of depreciation amounts for each period of an asset's useful life.

Dilution. Reduction in stockholders' equity per share or EPS that arises from some changes among shareholders' proportional interests.

Direct method. A method for computing cash flows from operating activities that subtracts operating cash disbursements from cash collections to arrive at cash flows from operations.

Discontinued operations. A component of the business that is distinguishable from the rest of the entity, both operationally and for financial reporting purposes, that a company disposes of or makes plans to dispose of. The results are reported separately, net of tax, on the income statement.

Discount amortization. The spreading of bond discount over the life of the bonds as interest expense.

Discount rates. Interest rates used to compute present values.

Discounted values. Another name for present values.

Discounting. The process of finding the present value.

Dividend arrearages. Accumulated unpaid dividends on preferred stock.

Dividend-payout ratio. Common dividends per share divided by earnings per share.

Dividend-yield ratio. Common dividends per share divided by market price per share.

Double-declining-balance (DDB) method. A common form of accelerated depreciation. It is computed by doubling the straight-line rate and multiplying the resulting DDB rate by the asset's beginning net book value.

Double-entry system. The method usually followed for recording transactions, whereby every transaction affects at least two accounts.

Early extinguishment. When a company chooses to redeem its own bonds before maturity.

Earnings multiple. Another name for the P-E ratio.

Earnings per share (EPS). Net income divided by weighted-average number of common shares outstanding during the period.

EBIT-to-sales. A variation of return on sales computed as earnings before interest and taxes divided by sales.

EBIT. Earnings before interest and taxes.

Economic Value Added (EVA). Measure of the residual wealth of a company after deducting its cost of capital from operating profit.

Effective interest amortization (compound interest method). An amortization method that uses a constant interest rate.

Entity. An organization or a section of an organization that stands apart from other organizations and individuals as a separate economic unit.

Equity method. Accounting for an investment at acquisition cost, adjusted for the investor's share of dividends and earnings or losses of the investee subsequent to the date of investment.

Expenditures. Purchases of goods or services, whether for cash or credit.

Expenses. Decreases in net assets as a result of consuming or giving up resources in the process of providing products or services to a customer. Expenses decrease the owners' equity.

Explicit transactions. Observable events such as cash receipts and disbursements, credit purchases, and credit sales that trigger the majority of day-to-day routine journal entries.

Extraordinary items. Items that are both unusual in nature and infrequent in occurrence that are shown separately, net of tax, on the income statement.

F.O.B. destination. Seller pays freight costs from the shipping point of the seller to the receiving point of the buyer.

F.O.B. shipping point. Buyer pays freight costs from the shipping point of the seller to the receiving point of the buyer.

Face amount. The loan principal or the amount that a borrower promises to repay at a specific maturity date.

Fair value. The value of an asset based on the price for which a company could sell the asset to an independent third party.

Faithful representation. A quality of information that ensures that it captures the economic substance of the transactions, events, or circumstances it describes. It requires information to be complete, neutral, and free from material errors.

FASB Financial Standards Codification. A compilation of all standards and other elements of U.S. GAAP into a single searchable database that is organized by topic to make it easy to research financial reporting issues.

Financial accounting. The field of accounting that serves external decision makers, such as stockholders, suppliers, banks, and government agencies.

Financial Accounting Standards (U.S. GAAP). The set of GAAP that applies to financial reporting in the United States.

Financial Accounting Standards Board (FASB). The private sector body that is responsible for establishing GAAP in the United States.

Financial management. Decisions concerned with where the company gets cash and how it uses that cash to its benefit.

Financial statement analysis. Using financial data to assess some aspect of a company's performance.

Financing activities. A company's transactions that obtain resources by borrowing from creditors or selling shares of stock and use resources to repay creditors or provide a return to shareholders.

Financing decisions. Decisions concerned with whether and how to raise or repay cash.

Finished goods inventory. The accumulated costs of manufacture for goods that are complete and ready for sale.

Firm-specific risk. The risk that the firm will not repay the loan or will not pay the interest on time.

First-in, first-out (FIFO). This method of accounting for inventory assigns the cost of the earliest acquired units to cost of goods sold.

Fiscal year. The year established for accounting purposes, which may differ from a calendar year.

Form 10-K. A document that U.S. companies file annually with the Securities and Exchange Commission. It contains the companies' financial statements.

Franchises (licenses). Legal contracts that allow the buyer the right to sell a product or service in accordance with specified conditions.

Free cash flow. Generally defined as cash flows from operations less capital expenditures.

Freight in (inward transportation). An additional cost of the goods acquired during the period, which is often shown in the purchases section of an income statement.

Future value. The amount accumulated, including principal and interest.

General journal. A complete chronological record of an organization's transactions and how each affects the balances in particular accounts.

General ledger. The collection of all ledger accounts that support an organization's financial statements.

Generally accepted accounting principles (GAAP). The term that applies to all the broad concepts and detailed practices to be followed in preparing and distributing financial statements. It includes all the conventions, rules, and procedures that together comprise accepted accounting practice.

Going concern (continuity). A convention that assumes that an entity will persist indefinitely.

Goodwill. The excess of the amount paid for an acquired company over the fair value of its identifiable net assets.

Gross profit (gross margin). The excess of sales revenue over the cost of the inventory that was sold.

Gross profit percentage (gross margin percentage). Gross profit (sales revenue – cost of goods sold) divided by sales revenue.

Gross sales. The total amount of sales before deducting returns, allowances, and discounts.

Held-to-maturity securities. Debt securities that the investor expects to hold until maturity.

Holding gain (inventory profit). Increase in the replacement cost of the inventory held during the current period.

Impaired. When an asset ceases to have economic value to the company at least as large as the book value of the asset.

Impairment of goodwill. Reductions of the goodwill account because the value of the goodwill falls below its current carrying amount.

Implicit interest (imputed interest). An interest expense that is not explicitly recognized in a loan agreement.

Implicit transactions. Events (such as the passage of time) that do not generate source documents or any visible evidence that the event actually occurred. We do not recognize such events in the accounting records until the end of an accounting period.

Improvement (betterment, capital improvement). An expenditure that increases the future benefits provided by an existing fixed asset by decreasing its operating cost, increasing its rate of output, improving its safety, reducing its rate of pollution, or prolonging its useful life.

Imputed interest rate. The market interest rate that equates the proceeds from a loan with the present value of the loan payments.

Income (profits, earnings). The excess of revenues over expenses.

Income before income tax (pretax income, earnings before income tax). Income before the deduction of income tax expense.

Income statement (statement of earnings, statement of operations). A report of all revenues and expenses pertaining to a specific time period.

Indirect method. A method for computing cash flows from operating activities that adjusts the previously calculated accrual net income from the income statement to reflect only cash receipts and cash disbursements.

Inflation premium. The extra interest that investors require because the general price level may increase between now and the time they receive their money.

Intangible assets. Assets that lack physical substance. They consist of contractual rights, legal rights, or economic benefits. Examples are patents, trademarks, and copyrights.

Interest rate. A specified percentage of the principal. It is used to compute the amount of interest.

Interest-coverage ratio. Pretax income plus interest expense divided by interest expense.

Interest. The cost the borrower pays the lender to use the principal.

Interim periods. The time spans established for accounting purposes that are less than a year.

Internal controls. Checks and balances that ensure all company actions are proper and have the general approval of top management.

International Accounting Standards Board (IASB). An international body established to develop, in the public interest, a single set of high-quality, understandable, and enforceable global accounting standards.

International Financial Reporting Standards (IFRS). The set of GAAP that applies to companies reporting in more than 100 countries around the world.

Inventory. Goods held by a company for the purpose of sale to customers.

Inventory shrinkage. Losses of inventory from theft, breakage, or loss.

Inventory turnover. The cost of goods sold divided by the average inventory held during a given period.

Investing activities. Transactions that acquire or dispose of long-lived assets or acquire or dispose of securities that are not cash equivalents.

Investing decisions. Decisions that include the choices to (1) acquire or dispose of plant, property, equipment, and other long-term productive assets, and (2) provide or collect cash as a lender or as an owner of securities.

Invoice. A bill from the seller to a buyer indicating the number of items shipped, their price, and any additional costs (such as shipping) along with payment terms, if any.

Issued shares. The aggregate number of shares sold to the public.

Journal entry. An analysis of the effects of a transaction on the various accounts, usually accompanied by an explanation.

Journalizing. The process of entering transactions into the general journal.

Last-in, first-out (LIFO). This inventory method assigns the most recent costs to cost of goods sold.

Lease. A contract whereby an owner (lessor) grants the use of property to a second party (lessee) for rental payments.

Leasehold. The right to use a fixed asset for a specified period of time beyond 1 year.

Leasehold improvement. Investments by a lessee to add new materials or improvements to a leased property that become part of the leased property and revert to the lessor at the end of the lease.

Ledger account. A listing of all the increases and decreases in a particular account.

Lessee. The party that has the right to use leased property and makes lease payments to the lessor.

Lessor. The owner of property who grants usage rights to the lessee.

Liabilities. Economic obligations of the organization to outsiders, or claims against its assets by outsiders.

LIFO layer (LIFO increment). A separately identifiable addition to LIFO inventory at an identifiable cost level.

LIFO liquidation. A decrease in the physical amount in inventory causing old, low LIFO inventory acquisition costs to become the cost of goods sold, resulting in a high gross profit.

LIFO reserve. The difference between a company's inventory valued at LIFO and what it would be under FIFO.

Limited liability. A feature of the corporate form of organization whereby corporate creditors (such as banks or suppliers) ordinarily have claims against the corporate assets only, not against the personal assets of the owners.

Line of credit. An agreement with a bank to provide automatically short-term loans up to some predetermined maximum.

Liquidating value. The amount a company needs to pay to all preferred stockholders, in addition to any dividends in arrears, before it distributes any assets to common stockholders when liquidating a company.

Liquidation. Converting assets to cash and paying off outside claims.

Liquidity. An entity's ability to meet its near-term financial obligations with cash and near-cash assets as those obligations become due.

Long-lived asset. An asset that a company expects to use for more than 1 year.

Long-term liabilities. Obligations that fall due beyond 1 year from the balance sheet date.

Long-term solvency. An organization's ability to generate enough cash to repay long-term debts as they mature.

Long-term-debt-to-total-capital ratio. Total long-term debt divided by total shareholders' equity plus total long-term debt.

Lower-of-cost-or-market method (LCM). A comparison of the current market price of inventory with historical cost derived under whatever inventory method is used and reporting the lower of the two as the inventory value.

Maintenance. The routine recurring costs of activities such as oiling, polishing, painting, and adjusting that are necessary to keep a fixed asset in operating condition.

Management accounting. The field of accounting that serves internal decision makers, such as top executives, department heads, college deans, hospital administrators, and people at other management levels within an organization.

Management discussion and analysis (MD&A). A section of the annual report and 10-K, the content of which is dictated by the SEC, that concentrates on explaining the major changes in operating results, liquidity, and capital resources.

Market method. Method of accounting that reports market values of publicly traded securities in the balance sheet; for trading securities changes in market value affect the income statement; for available-for-sale securities changes affect owners' equity directly.

Market rate. The rate available on investments in similar bonds at a moment in time.

Market-to-book ratio. Market value per share divided by book value per share.

Marketable securities. Any notes, bonds, or stocks that can readily be sold.

Matching. The recording of expenses in the same time period that we recognize the related revenues.

Materiality. A convention that asserts that an item should be included in a financial statement if its omission or misstatement would tend to mislead the reader of the financial statements under consideration.

Modified Accelerated Cost Recovery System (MACRS). The underlying basis for computing depreciation for tax purposes.

Monetary assets. Assets such as cash or receivables that are fixed in terms of units of currency.

Mortgage bond. A form of long-term debt that is secured by the pledge of specific property.

Multiple-step income statement. An income statement that contains one or more subtotals that highlight significant relationships.

Negotiable. Legal financial contracts that can be transferred from one lender to another.

Net assets. Assets less liabilities.

Net income (net earnings). The remainder after deducting all expenses from revenues.

Net loss. The difference between revenues and expenses when expenses exceed revenues.

Net realizable value. The net amount the company expects to receive when it sells its inventory.

Net sales. The total amount of sales after deducting returns, allowances, and discounts.

Nominal interest rate (contractual rate, coupon rate, stated rate). A contractual rate of interest paid on bonds.

Noncontrolling interests. The outside shareholders' interests, as opposed to the parent's interests, in a subsidiary corporation.

Nonmonetary assets. Assets whose price in terms of units of currency could change over time.

Nonrecurring items (unusual items). An income statement item that is either unusual in nature or infrequent in occurrence but not both. These items are not expected to happen often for a given firm.

Notes payable. Promissory notes that are evidence of a debt and state the terms of payment.

Open account. Buying or selling on credit, usually by just an "authorized signature" of the buyer.

Operating activities. Transactions that affect the purchase, processing, and selling of a company's products and services.

Operating cycle. The time span during which a company uses cash to acquire goods and services, which in turn it sells to customers, who in turn pay for their purchases with cash.

Operating decisions. Decisions that are concerned with the major day-to-day activities that generate revenues and expenses.

Operating expenses. A group of recurring expenses that pertain to the firm's routine, ongoing operations.

Operating income (operating profit, income from operations). Gross profit less all operating expenses.

Operating lease. A lease that should be accounted for by the lessee as ordinary rent expenses.

Operating management. Decisions concerned with the day-to-day activities that generate revenues and expenses.

Other comprehensive income. Changes in stockholders' equity that do not result from net income (net loss) or transactions with shareholders.

Other postretirement benefits. Benefits provided to retired workers in addition to a pension, such as life and health insurance.

Outstanding shares. Shares in the hands of shareholders.

Owners' equity. The owners' claims on an organization's assets, or total assets less total liabilities.

Paid-in capital in excess of par value (additional paid-in capital). When issuing stock, the difference between the total amount the company receives for the stock and the par value.

Paid-in capital. The total capital investment in a corporation by its owners both at and subsequent to the inception of business.

Par value (stated value). The nominal dollar amount printed on stock certificates.

Parent company. A company owning more than 50% of the voting shares of another company, called the subsidiary company.

Participating. A characteristic of preferred stock that allows holders of shares to participate in the growth of the company because they share in the growing dividends.

Partnership. A form of organization that joins two or more individuals together as co-owners.

Patents. Grants made by the federal government to an inventor, bestowing (in the United States) the exclusive right to produce and sell a given product, or to use a process, for up to 20 years.

Payment date. The date a company pays dividends.

Pensions. Payments to former employees after they retire.

Percentage of accounts receivable method. An approach to estimating bad debts expense and uncollectible accounts that bases estimates of uncollectible accounts on the historical relations of uncollectibles to year-end gross accounts receivable.

Percentage of completion method. Method of recognizing revenue on long-term contracts as production occurs.

Percentage of sales method. An approach to estimating bad debts expense and uncollectible accounts based on the historical relationship between credit sales and uncollectible debts.

Period costs. Items supporting a company's operations for a given period. We record the expenses in the time period in which the company incurs them.

Periodic inventory system. An inventory system that computes the cost of goods sold and an updated inventory balance only at the end of an accounting period when the company takes a physical count of inventory.

Permanent differences. Revenue or expense items that are recognized for tax purposes but not recognized under GAAP, or vice versa.

Perpetual inventory system. An inventory system that keeps a continuous record of inventories and the cost of goods sold that helps managers control inventory levels and prepare interim financial statements.

Physical count. The process of identifying, counting, and assigning a specific cost to all items in inventory.

Posting. The transferring of amounts from the general journal to the appropriate accounts in the general ledger.

Predictive value. A quality of information that allows it to help users form their expectations about the future.

Preemptive rights. The rights to acquire a proportional amount of any new issues of capital stock.

Preferred stock. Stock that offers owners different rights and preferential treatment.

Present value. The value today of a future cash inflow or outflow.

Pretax and pre-interest return on total assets. A version of ROA defined as earnings before interest and taxes divided by average total assets.

Price-earnings (P-E) ratio. Market price per share of common stock divided by earnings per share of common stock.

Price-earnings growth (PEG) ratio. Price-earnings ratio divided by the earnings growth rate.

Principal. The amount borrowed or the amount to be repaid.

Private accountants. Accountants who work for businesses, government agencies, and other nonprofit organizations.

Private placement. A process whereby bonds are issued by corporations when money is borrowed from a financial institution, not from the general public.

Privately owned. A corporation owned by a family, a small group of shareholders, or a single individual, in which shares of ownership are not publicly sold.

Pro forma statements. A set of projected financial statements or other estimates of predicted results.

Product costs. Costs that are linked with revenues and are charged as expenses when the related revenue is recognized.

Profitability. The ability of a company to provide investors with a particular rate of return on their investment.

Promissory note. A written promise to repay principal plus interest at specific future dates.

Protective covenant (covenant). A provision in a bond that restricts the actions a borrower may take, usually to protect the bondholders' interests.

Provisions. Liabilities of uncertain timing or amount.

Public accountants. Accountants who offer services to the general public on a fee basis.

Public Company Accounting Oversight Board (PCAOB). An agency that regulates many aspects of public accounting and sets standards for audit procedures.

Publicly owned. A corporation that sells shares in its ownership to the public.

Purchase order. A document that specifies the items ordered and the price to be paid by the ordering company.

Quick ratio (acid test ratio). Variation of the current ratio that removes less liquid assets from the numerator. Perhaps the most common version of this ratio is (current assets − inventory) ÷ current liabilities.

Rate of return on common equity (ROE). Net income less preferred dividends divided by average common equity.

Rate of return. The return per dollar invested.

Raw material inventory. Includes the cost of materials held for use in the manufacturing of a product.

Real interest rate. The return that investors demand because they are delaying their consumption.

Receiving report. A document that specifies the items received by the company and the condition of the items.

Reconcile a bank statement. To verify that the bank balance for cash is in agreement with the accounting records.

Recoverability test. The first step in the asset impairment review process under U.S. GAAP. The test compares the undiscounted total expected future net cash flows from the use of the asset plus its eventual disposal value with the current carrying value of the asset.

Recoverable amount. Under IFRS, the higher of (1) fair value minus the cost to sell and (2) the value in use, calculated as the present value of expected future net cash flows.

Registered public accounting firm. An accounting firm that registers with the PCAOB and therefore is allowed to audit companies with publicly-traded stock in the United States.

Relevance. The capability of information to make a difference to the decision maker.

Reliability. A quality of information that assures decision makers that the information captures the conditions or events it purports to represent.

Repairs. The occasional costs of restoring a fixed asset to its ordinary operating condition after breakdowns, accidents, or damage.

Report format. A classified balance sheet with the assets at the top.

Reserve. A restriction of dividend-declaring power as denoted by a specific subdivision of retained earnings.

Residual value (terminal value, disposal value, salvage value, scrap value). The amount a company expects to receive from sale or disposal of a long-lived asset at the end of its useful life.

Restricted retained earnings (appropriated retained earnings). Any part of retained earnings that companies may not reduce by dividend declarations.

Restricted stock. Stock paid to employees that generally has constraints such as not being able to sell it until it vests and then generally being able to sell it only back to the company at the current market price.

Restructuring. A significant makeover of part of the company typically involving the closing of plants, firing of employees, and relocation of activities.

Retailer. A company that sells items directly to the public—to individual buyers.

Retained earnings (retained income). Total cumulative owners' equity generated by income or profits.

Return on assets ratio (ROA). Net income divided by average total assets.

Return on common stockholders' equity ratio (ROE or ROCE). Net income divided by invested capital (measured by average common stockholders' equity).

Return on sales ratio (profit margin ratio). Net income divided by sales.

Revenue (sales, sales revenue). The increase in net assets resulting from selling products or services. Revenues increase owners' equity.

Revenue recognition. Criteria for determining whether to record revenue in the financial statements of a given period. To be recognized, revenues must be earned and realized or realizable.

Sales allowance (purchase allowance). Reduction of the original selling price.

Sales returns (purchase returns). Merchandise returned by the customer.

Sarbanes-Oxley Act. The source of most government regulation of the accounting profession in the United States.

Securities and Exchange Commission (SEC). The government agency responsible for regulating capital markets in the United States.

Short-term debt securities. Largely notes and bonds with maturities of 1 year or less.

Short-term equity securities. Capital stock in other corporations held with the intention to liquidate within 1 year as needed.

Short-term investment. A temporary investment in marketable securities of otherwise idle cash.

Short-term liquidity. An organization's ability to meet current payments, such as interest, wages, and taxes, as they become due.

Simple entry. An entry for a transaction that affects only two accounts.

Simple interest. The interest rate multiplied by an unchanging principal amount.

Single-step income statement. An income statement that groups all revenues and then lists and deducts all expenses without reporting any intermediate subtotals.

Sinking fund. A pool of cash or securities set aside for meeting certain obligations.

Sinking fund bonds. Bonds that require the issuer to make annual payments to a sinking fund.

Sole proprietorship. A business with a single owner.

Source documents. The original records supporting any transaction.

Specific identification method. This inventory method concentrates on the physical linking of the particular items sold with the cost of goods sold that a company reports.

Specific write-off method. A method of accounting for bad debt losses that assumes all sales are fully collectible until proved otherwise.

Statement of cash flows (cash flow statement). One of the basic financial statements that reports the cash receipts and cash payments of an entity during a particular period and classifies them as financing, investing, and operating cash flows.

Statement of stockholders' equity (statement of shareholders' equity). A statement that shows all changes during the year in each stockholders' equity account.

Stock certificate. Formal evidence of ownership shares in a corporation.

Stock dividends. Distribution to stockholders of a small number of additional shares for every share owned without any payment to the company by the stockholders.

Stock options. Rights to purchase a specific number of shares of a corporation's capital stock at a specific price for a specific time period.

Stock split. Issuance of additional shares to existing stockholders for no payments by the stockholders.

Stockholders' equity (shareholders' equity). Owners' equity of a corporation. The excess of assets over liabilities of a corporation.

Straight-line depreciation. A method that spreads the depreciable value evenly over the useful life of an asset.

Subordinated debentures. Debt securities whose holders have claims against only the assets that remain after satisfying the claims of other general creditors.

Subsidiary. A corporation owned or controlled by a parent company through the ownership of more than 50% of the voting stock.

T-account. Simplified version of ledger accounts that takes the form of the capital letter T.

Tangible assets (fixed assets, plant assets). Physical items that can be seen and touched, such as land, buildings, and equipment.

Tax rate. The percentage of taxable income paid to the government.

Temporary differences. Differences between net income and taxable income that arise because some revenue and expense items are recognized at different times for tax purposes than for financial reporting purposes.

Time-series comparisons. Comparisons of a company's financial ratios with its own historical ratios.

Timeliness. A characteristic of information that reaches decision makers while it can still influence their decisions.

Total asset turnover. Sales divided by average total assets.

Trade discounts. Reductions to the gross selling price for a particular class of customers.

Trademarks. Distinctive identifications of a manufactured product or of a service, taking the form of a name, a sign, a slogan, a logo, or an emblem.

Trading on the equity (financial leverage, leveraging, gearing). Using interest-bearing debt to enhance the rate of return on common stockholders' equity.

Trading securities. Current investments in equity or debt securities held for short-term profit.

Transaction. Any event that affects the financial position of an entity and that an accountant can reliably record in money terms.

Treasury stock. A company's own stock that it has purchased and holds for later use.

Trend analysis. An analysis technique that compares financial trends and changes from one year to the next and identifies patterns that have occurred in the past.

Trial balance. A list of all accounts in the general ledger with their balances.

Turnover. Sales or sales revenue.

U.S. Treasury obligations. Interest-bearing notes, bonds, and bills issued by the U.S. government.

Uncollectible accounts (bad debts). Receivables determined to be uncollectible because customers are unable or unwilling to pay their debts.

Understandability. A characteristic of information that is presented clearly and concisely.

Underwriters. A group of investment bankers that buys an entire bond or stock issue from a corporation and then sells the securities to the general investing public.

Unearned revenue (revenue received in advance, deferred revenue). Represents cash received from customers who pay in advance for goods or services to be delivered at a future date.

Units-of-production depreciation (activity method). A depreciation method based on units of service or units of production when physical wear and tear is the dominating influence on the useful life of the asset.

Useful life. The shorter of the physical life or the economic life of an asset.

Verifiability. A characteristic of information that can be checked to ensure it is correct.

Vested options. Options that the holders have the power to exercise.

Weighted-average method. This inventory method computes a unit cost by dividing the total acquisition cost of all items available for sale by the number of units available for sale.

Wholesaler. A company that sells in large quantities to retail companies instead of individuals.

Work in process inventory. Includes the cost incurred for partially completed items, including raw materials, labor, and other costs.

Working capital (net working capital, net current assets). The excess of current assets over current liabilities.

Write-down. A reduction in the recorded historical cost of an item in response to a decline in value.

XBRL. Extensible business reporting language, an XML-based computer language that allows easy comparisons across companies.

Yield to maturity. The interest rate at which all contractual cash flows for interest and principal have a present value equal to the current price of the bond.

Zero coupon bond. A bond or note that pays no cash interest during its life.

INDEX

Photo Credits